West's Law School Advisory Board

JESSE H. CHOPER
Professor of Law,
University of California, Berkeley

DAVID P. CURRIE
Professor of Law, University of Chicago

YALE KAMISAR
Professor of Law, University of Michigan
Professor of Law, University of San Diego

MARY KAY KANE
Chancellor, Dean and Distinguished Professor of Law,
University of California,
Hastings College of the Law

LARRY D. KRAMER
Dean and Professor of Law, Stanford Law School

WAYNE R. LaFAVE
Professor of Law, University of Illinois

ARTHUR R. MILLER
Professor of Law, Harvard University

GRANT S. NELSON
Professor of Law,
University of California, Los Angeles

JAMES J. WHITE
Professor of Law, University of Michigan

WEALTH TRANSFER PLANNING AND DRAFTING

By

Jeffrey N. Pennell
Richard H. Clark Professor of Law
Emory University

AMERICAN CASEBOOK SERIES®

Mat #14625844

West, a Thomson business, has created this publication to provide you with accurate and authoritative information concerning the subject matter covered. However, this publication was not necessarily prepared by persons licensed to practice law in a particular jurisdiction. West is not engaged in rendering legal or other professional advice, and this publication is not a substitute for the advice of an attorney. If you require legal or other expert advice, you should seek the services of a competent attorney or other professional.

American Casebook Series and West Group are trademarks registered in the U.S. Patent and Trademark Office.

© 2005 West, a Thomson business
      610 Opperman Drive
      P.O. Box 64526
      St. Paul, MN 55164–0526
      1–800–328–9352

Printed in the United States of America

ISBN 0–314–22671–0

Summary of Contents

Preface
Glossary
Chapter 1. Introduction
Chapter 2. Getting Started
Chapter 3. Ethics
Chapter 4. Use of Trusts in Estate Planning
Chapter 5. Family Trust Planning
Chapter 6. Trustee Selection and Succession
Chapter 7. Planning for Couples
Chapter 8. Planning for Charity
Chapter 9. Life Insurance
Chapter 10. Retirement Benefits
Chapter 11. Paying Estate Obligations
Chapter 12. Inter Vivos Transfers
Chapter 13. Postmortem Planning and Estate Administration
Chapter 14. Planning for Incapacity
Chapter 15. Death and Dying
Chapter 16. The Big Picture
Chapter 17. A Brief Introduction to the Income Taxation of Estates, Trusts, Grantors and Beneficiaries
Chapter 18. A Brief Introduction to Wealth Transfer Taxation
Chapter 19. Forms
Tables
Index

Table of Contents

PREFACE
GLOSSARY

Chapter 1. Introduction — 1-1
Estate Planning as a Profession — 3
Education and Practice Concerns — 5
    Direction of the Profession — 5
    Inheritance Has Changed — 5
    Tax Law Changes — 6
    Demographics — 7
    Shrinking Talent Pool — 7
    Litigation and Malpractice — 8
    Personal Counseling — 11
    One Stop Shopping — 14
    Fiduciary Services — 15
The Intangible Element — 15
    Interpersonal Aspect of Personal Counseling — 16

Chapter 2. Getting Started — 2-1
Gathering Information — 1
    Family and Personal Data — 3
    Family and Personal Objectives — 4
    Financial Data — 5
    Tax Information — 7
Consultations — 7
The Engagement Letter — 7
Conflicts of Interest — 9
Confidentiality — 9

Chapter 3. Ethics — 3-1
Conflicts of Interest — 3
    Representing Spouses — 6
    Dynastic Family Planning — 12
    Which Rule Applies? — 15
    Other Common Conflicts — 16
    Obligations Imposed — 18
    Who Is the Client? — 19
Independent Judgment — 22
    Ancillary Activities — 24
    Uncertain Scope — 27
Preservation of Client Confidences — 29

Confidences in Representing Spouses	30
Other Situations	36
Adequate Representation	40
Fees	42
Fiduciary Administration Concerns	44
Confusion in Existing Authority	46
Your Duty to the "System"	50
Solicitation and Advertising	54
Your Dilemma	57
The Malpractice Aspects of All This	57
Selected Provisions from the Restatement (Second) of Agency	62

Chapter 4. Use of Trusts in Estate Planning — 4-1

Trust Uses	1
Flexibility and Dead Hand Control	2
Bifurcated Enjoyment	6
Property Management	7
Asset Protection	9
Avoiding Will Contests	14
Probate Avoidance	16
Statutory Entitlements	19
Pour Over from Wills to Trusts	19
Receptacle Trusts	21
Tax Minimization	21
Reasons to Favor Probate	23
Subchapter S Election Concerns	25
Joint Settlor Trusts	26
Declarations of Trust	27
Sample Declaration of Trust	30
Oshins, Megatrusts: Representation Without Taxation	32

Chapter 5. Family Trust Planning — 5-1

"Typical" Family Plan	1
Group Trusts for Children	16
Group Trust With "Peel-Off" Provision	18
Family Planning Considerations	20
Powers of Appointment	21
General or Nongeneral Power?	22
Scope of Nongeneral Powers	24
Unexpected Sources of Power of Appointment Tax Liability	25
Drafting Powers of Appointment	29
Inadvertent Exercise	32

Chapter 6. Trustee Selection and Succession — 6-1

Assume a Testamentary Trust	3
Powers Over Corpus	3
Powers Over Income	5
Administrative Powers	7

While The Settlor Is Alive	8
Use and Definition of Standards	10
Deemed Trustees	12
Final Thoughts	17

Chapter 7. Planning for Couples — 7-1

Introduction	1
Importance of the Marital Deduction in Estate Planning	3
Basic Marital Deduction Planning	8
Basic Structure of Estate Planning for Spouses	9
Tax Sensitive Outright Gift to S	11
A Note About Community Property	16
Drafting in Contemplation of Disclaimer	16
Planning and Drafting for Larger Estates	20
The Time-Value of Money Rationale for Deferral	23
Analysis of "Six Month Equalizer" Plan	28
Basis Concerns	32
Using the Previously Taxed Property Credit	32
A Note About Formula Clauses and Computations	34
Generation-Skipping Transfer Tax Exemption	36
Administration Expenses and the "Swing Item" Election	38
Marital Deduction Qualification	40
Survivorship	41
The Interest Must Be "Deductible"	43
Exceptions to the Nondeductible Terminable Interest Rule	48
Marital Deduction Transfers: Forms of Disposition	49
Marital Deduction Power of Appointment Trust	50
Estate Trusts	59
Qualified Terminable Interest Property	60
Qualified Domestic Trusts	77
Selecting and Drafting Marital Deduction Trusts	79
Selecting the Type of Marital Trust	79
A Combined Trust Plan	87
Drafting Considerations	87
Marital Deduction "Savings Clauses"	94
Funding Marital Deduction Transfers	95
Types of Marital Deduction Formula Clauses	96
True Worth Pecuniary	102
Fairly Representative Pecuniary	111
Minimum Worth Pecuniary	114
Funding the Reverse Pecuniary Marital	117
Funding the Formula Fractional Share	123
Pick-and-Choose Fractional Share Funding	131
Single Fund Marital	135
Generation-Skipping Transfer Tax Aspects of Marital Funding	138
Conclusions Regarding Marital Deduction Funding	139
Planning in Contemplation of Divorce	141

Planning in Contemplation of Marriage	142
Planning for Unmarried Cohabitants	142

Chapter 8. Planning for Charity — 8-1

The Various Deductions	2
Transfers to Public Charities	5
Other Transfers	7
Donees: Entities That Qualify	11
Transfers That Qualify	16
Undivided Portion of Entire Interest Not in Trust	17
Charitable Remainder Trusts	19
Conservation Easements	31
Charitable Lead Trusts	33
Reformation, Disclaimer, and Settlement	37
Strategies: Choosing Among Alternatives	38

Chapter 9. Life Insurance — 9-1

Understanding the Product	1
Annuities	2
Endowments	3
Term Insurance	4
Permanent Insurance	6
Combination and Specialty Products	10
Premium Payment and Split Dollar Insurance	11
Standard Contract Provisions	16
Comparing Policies	22
Is It Insurance?	25
Policy Ownership	26
Beneficiary Designation	32
Income Tax Exclusion	39
Transfer-For-Value Exception	41
Policy Exchanges	43
Estate Taxation	44
Incidents Held in a Fiduciary Capacity	45
Incidents Held by Controlled Corporation	46
Estate Taxation If Owner Is Not the Insured	47
Transfers Within Three Years of Insured's Death	47
Policy Facts Versus Intent	49
Gift Taxation	49
Crummey Clause Power of Withdrawal	51

Chapter 10. Retirement Benefits — 10-1

Gift Taxation	2
Estate Taxation	3
Income Taxation	6
Nonqualified Plans	10
Rules Governing Distributions	10
Income Tax Consequences of Distributions	17

Spousal Rollover	18
Spousal Annuity Rules	20
Planning Issues Relating to Designating Beneficiaries	22

Chapter 11. Paying Estate Obligations — 11-1

Tax Payment Burden on the Residue	1
Procedure	8
Time of Payment	8
Transferee Liability	8
Extension of Time to File or Make Payment	9
Apportionment Options	11
Inside Apportionment	11
Outside Apportionment	12
Equitable Apportionment	12
Apportionment of Rate Differentials	13
Apportionment of Credits	13
Apportionment to Temporal Interests	14
Apportionment Among Multiple Entities	14
Federal Rules Applicable to Tax Apportionment	16
Estate Tax	16
Generation-Skipping Transfer Tax	19
Summary of State Law: Silence Generates What Result?	20
Equitable Apportionment	22
Apportionment of State Inheritance and Foreign Taxes	23
Apportionment of Fees and Expenses	23
Apportionment of Interest and Penalties	23
Computing Various Entitlements	23
Apportionment to Nonprobate Assets	24
Apportionment to Temporal Interests	24
Conflict of Laws and Enforcement Jurisdiction	25
Planning Aspects of the Apportionment Rules	27
Retirement Benefits	27
Administrative Uncertainties	28
Spousal Planning Choices	29
Benefit of Rates	31
Generation-Skipping Transfer Taxes	32
Principal and Income Rules	32
Drafting Considerations	33
Items to Consider	34
Clearly Specify Intent	37
In re Estate of Ogburn	38
Sample Tax Clause	43

Chapter 12. Inter Vivos Transfers — 12-1

Basis	1
The Economics of Prepaying Wealth Transfer Tax	2
The Tax Exclusive Gift Tax Computation Outweighs New Basis at Death	3

The Time-Value-of-Money Myth	5
Other Reasons to Favor Inter Vivos Transfers	8
Transfers That Avoid Gift Tax	10
Exclusions and Exceptions	12
Annual Exclusion	13
Qualified Minor's Trusts	23
Ed/Med Exclusion	26
Unified Credit	28
Gift Splitting	28
Inter Vivos Marital Deduction	30
Inter Vivos Charitable Deduction	32
Conservation Easements	33
Charitable Gift Annuities	34
Inter Vivos Charitable Remainder Trusts	35
Gifts of Insurance to Charity	37
Economics of Charitable Transfers	38
Comparisons of Alternate Charitable Plans	40
Disclaimers	41
Incomplete Gifts	45
Taxation of Completed Gifts	47
Blockage Discounts	48
Fractional Interests	49
Nonmarketability and Minority Interest Discounts	50
Statute of Limitation for Revaluation	51
Income Shifting	53
Evaluating Alternative Income Shifting Devices	54
Additional Income Tax Considerations	60
Selected Inter Vivos Transfer Approaches	65
Cancellation of Indebtedness	66

Chapter 13. Postmortem Planning and Estate Administration   **13-1**

Personal Representative Defined	1
Jurisdiction for Administration	2
Personal Representative's Primary Duties	3
Fees	6
Postmortem Estate Planning	10

Chapter 14. Planning for Incapacity   **14-1**

Planning for Property Management	2
Planning for Health Care	3
Spend Down Planning	5

Chapter 15. Death and Dying   **15-1**

Death	1
Stages of Dying	4
Stage One: Denial	4
Stage Two: Anger	4

Stage Three: Bargaining	6
Stage Four: Depression	7
Stage Five: Acceptance	8
Fear	8
Grief and Bereavement	9
Skills	11
Additional Sources	13
Conclusion	14

Chapter 16. The Big Picture — 16-1

Objectives	1
Negatives to Avoid	1
Affirmatives	3
Taxes	4
Maxims	4
Estate Planning Top Ten List	5
Estate Planning Judgment	8

Chapter 17. A Brief Introduction to the Income Taxation of Estates, Trusts, Grantors and Beneficiaries — 17-1

Taxable Income	2
Distributable Net Income	3
Determining DNI	3
Simple Trusts	5
Estates and Complex Trusts	8
In-Kind Distributions and Specific Bequests	9
The Tier Rules	10
Income and Deductions in Respect of a Decedent	11
Grantor Trust Rules	14
Summary	17

Chapter 18. A Brief Introduction to Wealth Transfer Taxation — 18-1

The Federal Gift Tax	3
Gift Defined	3
Annual Exclusion and Exclusion for Education and Medical Care Expenses	5
Charitable Deduction	6
Marital Deduction	6
Gift Splitting by Spouses	6
Concurrent Interests	7
Preventing Valuation Freezes	7
The Unified Estate and Gift Taxes	7
The Federal Estate Tax	8
The Gross Estate	8
The Taxable Estate	13
Valuation	14
Alternate Valuation	20

Special Use Valuation	21
Computing the Estate Tax	23
The Federal Generation-Skipping Transfer Tax	25
Skip Persons	27
Taxable Transfers	29
Amount and Payment of the Tax	31
Exceptions to the Tax	34
State Wealth Transfer Taxes	37

Chapter 19. Forms — 19-1

Engagement Letter [Long Form]	4
Engagement Letter [Short Form]	11
Estate Inventory	13
Will	15
Selected Trustee and Advisor Provisions	36
Trust Agreement	39
Durable Powers	47
Unlimited Power of Attorney	49
Durable Power of Attorney for Health Care	58
Living Will	70

TABLES

INDEX

Preface

This book began with a notion to create a text for a course that exposes students to estate planning techniques in a tax driven endeavor. Too many tax acts later, it now is the reality that over 99% of all decedents' estates in America are nontaxable. This has made tax conscious estate planning relevant to a shrinking and exceptionally small slice of the population.

You can't always predict, however, which clients will fall below the taxable estate line. That depends in part on Congress, which keeps changing the limits. It also varies with the client's age and health, employment, expectancies, and how they likely will die (natural causes after a long and expensive illness, or a wrongful or accident death that may produce a huge damage recovery or double indemnity life insurance payment). Thus, often it is not possible to simply ignore the wealth transfer taxes, even if they seem unlikely ever to be an issue. Nevertheless, it is important not to lose sight of the fact that the vast majority of individuals who need estate plans (not just wills and trusts either) do not need or care to be concerned about tax minimization.

Here at Emory Law School the wealth transfer tax course no longer is a prerequisite for the course on estate planning. We reversed the order in which students historically took these courses to reflect the desire of many students to represent clients who need planning that does not focus primarily on taxes. A student may study Trusts and Estates, then learn how to put together an estate plan, and only later study the wealth transfer taxes, to hone their skills in representing the most wealthy clients.

This change in the prior order of things necessitated a different focus for materials used in our estate planning course. That change is reflected in this book. Students in this course need to know some things about tax (particularly the income tax). Often this is because tax realities influenced the forms of planning that remain popular or useful, even though the original impetus for the particular form of planning has waned. The tax origins of many plans have morphed but have not disappeared, making it necessary to straddle the fence between planning devoted primarily to tax minimization and planning that is hardly influenced by taxes.

By way of simple example, the irrevocable life insurance trust originally was designed for individuals who wanted to prevent inclusion of the proceeds of insurance on their life from being subjected to estate tax when they died. An important part of that planning was to pay premiums inter vivos without incurring gift tax. That led to the form of planning known as the ILIT and, in that trust, a device known as a Crummey power, sometimes of the hanging power variety. Those forms of planning are still commonplace, and much can be learned about trust planning and drafting in general by studying this particular variety of trust, even though many clients no longer need to worry about exclusion of life insurance from their taxable estates at death. A sample of such a trust is included in Chapter 19, which is an annotated collection of sample forms.

In our tax conscious estate planning course, students need not have studied wealth transfer tax as a prerequisite, but they still need to be able to talk about Crummey powers and the factors that influenced their design. Preparation for that study requires some exposure to and background in the tax laws, which this book provides. Tax background is not assumed. It is provided, but in a far less intense or dedicated manner than if this was the separate course on wealth transfer taxation. With that understanding, this book is meant to be useful both to students who have the tax background already and to those who have not yet needed to acquire it. The necessary learning is presented here in a manner designed not to overwhelm and, in many cases, in a way that just helps students understand why estate planners do certain things in the ways that have developed.

So this book is designed for a course in which tax is not the primary focus, yet tax is seldom ignored. There is an introduction to the wealth transfer taxes in Chapter 18 for the benefit of those who want an overview of that tax system but have not taken that course as a prerequisite. Even students who previously studied the wealth transfer taxes as a stand alone course may find it useful to read that chapter as a refresher, perhaps as a way to put into perspective the learning they acquired in a specialized course with a much finer focus. Chapter 17 is an introduction to the income taxation of estates, trusts, grantors, and beneficiaries. This is a seldom studied but integral aspect of the estate planning art and today probably is the more important of these two overview chapters.

This book eschews problems but provides a variety of sample forms, some in Chapter 19 and others sprinkled throughout. In the main, however, forms and especially hypotheticals are left for individual instructors to provide to their students. Frankly, this is a reflection of a number of realities, the most important of which being three. First, every instructor has a different view of the demographics of the target population for students in their course. The culture of estate planning varies with a number of factors, such as the job market into which students in that school and course will likely move. Second, the types of problems or exercises that are appropriate to a given course will vary based on the instructor's experience, also reflecting factors such as locale (for example, a course in Manhattan, Kansas, may need to focus more on real estate holdings, family corporations, and water rights, whereas a course in Manhattan, New York, may need to focus more on portfolio investments, retirement benefits, foreign nationals, and literary or artistic rights and royalties). And third, sample documents harvested from local drafters vary a good bit, simply because planners do things differently in different parts of the country, based on laws and cultural differences that are appropriate to the local community (the most obvious example being the difference between community and noncommunity property states).

One final note relates to the scope of coverage in this book. Everyday planning for individuals whose estates may or may not be taxable does not routinely entail the use of "gimmicks" that no rational individual would ever request upon entering uninitiated into the estate planning process. It is a fair guess that no one would think on their own to ask for a grantor retained annuity trust, or a sale of a remainder interest in their principal personal residence to an intentionally defective grantor trust. This book does not focus on forms of planning of this variety, largely because the expected client base of the students using the book is not likely to generate the need (at least not early in a new planner's practice) and partly because these are the types of planning that change with the next tax reform endeavor. Because a book of this variety is not a full fledged treatise, this effort tries to focus on planning that has the relative estate planning shelf life of diamonds and gold, not bread or milk. Some instructors may choose to illustrate some of that planning, especially to show the diversity of the practice and because it is interesting (some might even say "sexy"). But it is not a staple of normal practice and it is left for another day.

It has been tremendously beneficial for me to work and study with practicing lawyers in seminars and at professional meetings nation wide. In addition, the early formulation of these materials involved an immensely valuable collaboration with Professor Stanley Johanson at the University of Texas Law School. Over the years too many students to mention have studied a variety of these materials and provided useful insight and comments. And my colleague Anne Rector provided a much needed and appreciated style edit. All of these contributed to the value of these materials. Many thanks to all.

First and last, however, and ever present in both the best and the worst aspects of a project like this, the most enduring and important in all things is my bride, Michelle.

Dedication

In bits and pieces we all reflect the influences of
so many people and experiences. In loving
memory and grateful appreciation.

John S. Pennell
(1916-2004)

GLOSSARY

Accrued But Undistributed Income: In normal fiduciary administration income is paid on a periodic basis, such as monthly or quarterly. Income received by the trust but not yet distributed is accrued but undistributed income. So is income that has been earned by the trust but not yet received, such as dividends declared by the payor but not yet distributed to shareholders of record.

Advance Directive: See Living Will below.

Ancillary Administration: Primary estate administration normally is conducted in the state of a decedent's domicile. It applies to personal property (moveables) located anywhere, including intangibles (which are deemed to have a situs where the decedent was domiciled), and realty (immoveables) in the domiciliary state. Ancillary administration occurs in nondomiciliary jurisdictions where realty is located.

Applicable Exclusion Amount: The amount of property that may be transferred free of wealth transfer tax by virtue of the unified credit. For estate tax purposes in 2004 this was $1.5 million but for gift tax purposes it was $1.0 million. The estate tax exclusion amount will rise under changes enacted in 2001 but the gift tax exclusion is frozen.

Attorney-in-Fact: The agent who is charged with the responsibility, and who is given authorization, to act on behalf of the principal under a power of attorney.

Bargain Sale to Charity: The same transaction as a part-sale, part-gift transfer involving private individuals, only in this case involving a sale for less than full and adequate consideration to a charity. See part-sale, part-gift below.

Basis: In an income tax context adjusted basis (most folks just say "basis" alone) is the amount used to determine gain or loss on any asset. The difference between amount realized on a transaction and basis is the gain or loss. In this respect adjusted basis is essentially the cost of an item, subject to a slew of adjustments. For example, if you paid $250,000 for a house, upgraded the kitchen for another $50,000, and then sold for $325,000, your basis would be $300,000 (total investment) and gain would $25,000. Under §1014 the basis of most assets included in a decedent's gross estate for federal estate tax purposes becomes their fair market value. So, if that residence had been held until death and was worth $450,000 for federal estate tax purposes the basis in the property would be $450,000 in the hands of the beneficiary who receives it. Similarly, if the home went down in value to $200,000 at death the basis would become $200,000.

Bracket Run: In a progressive tax system subjecting wealth (or income) to tax in the highest marginal bracket will produce more tax than if some tax can be generated at the lower rates in the progression. Intentionally causing wealth (or income) to be taxable in the less than highest marginal brackets to avoid it being taxed in a later year at the highest rate is a "bracket run," designed to take advantage of this principle.

Buy-Sell Agreement: Typically in a closely held business context, co-owners agree that on specified events (such as disability, retirement, or death) one will sell and another will buy the interest of the other at a contractually determined (often by a formula) price. A cross-purchase agreement involves purchase by the other co-owners. An entity-purchase plan entails the business itself making the purchase, rather than the other owners.

Bypass Trust: See Nonmarital Trust below.

Closing Letter: The government will issue a closing letter to a personal representative when it has completed its review of an estate tax return and all matters regarding the tax liability of the estate have been resolved.

Community Property: In ten American jurisdictions property acquired by onerous activity by either spouse while married is deemed to be owned half by each spouse. This is not a right to half upon termination of the marriage (by dissolution or death) but rather a true 50% ownership by each, from origination of the entitlement. Community property does not change if the spouses change domicile to a noncommunity property state. Instead, "once community, always community," which means that a married couple that lived in a community property jurisdiction at any time during their marriage is likely to have at least some community property (unless they affirmatively converted it into separate property). The current community property jurisdictions are: Alaska (by election, a "voluntary" community property by statute), Arizona, California, Idaho, Louisiana, Nevada, New Mexico, Texas, Washington, and Wisconsin (by statute, the Uniform Marital Property Act).

Commutation: The process by which temporal interests (such as a life estate and the following remainder or reversion, typically in a trust) are valued and then paid off by distributing the fair market value of the respective interests (in cash or in kind), effectively accelerating termination of the lead interest and allowing the respective beneficiaries to separate and go free.

Concurrent Interests: Co-owners may hold title to property as tenants-in-common or community property, as joint tenant or as tenants-by-the-entireties. All are generally referred to as concurrent ownership interests.

Conduit Taxation: Also known as passthrough taxation, items of income, deduction, credit, and loss in an entity such as a partnership or a trust (or an estate) pass through to the owners or beneficiaries for taxation as if the entity did not exist. Most trusts (and all estates) are only modified conduits for taxation, as explained in Chapter 19.

Court Trust: A trust, typically created by a will, that is subject to court supervision. Trusts created during life (not testamentarily) typically are not subject to court oversight, although court involvement may be invoked when necessary.

Credit Shelter Trust: See Nonmarital Trust below.

Crummey Power: *Crummey v. Commissioner* confirmed that gift tax annual exclusion present interest treatment was established by granting trust beneficiaries lapsing powers to withdraw contributions made to the trust. The Crummey power of withdrawal technique is common in irrevocable life insurance and other inter vivos gift trust vehicles, and typically is limited to the amount that can lapse tax free under §2514(e) (the "five or five" exception). Sometimes a withdrawal power is used in conjunction with larger contributions and will lapse to the extent the lapse is tax free under §2514(e) and "hang" with respect to the balance of the withdrawal amount. That hanging power remains available for exercise until a future year when it too can lapse tax free. See Chapters 9 and 12.

Death Tax: The pejorative term used to describe estate and inheritance taxes, whether imposed at the state or federal level.

Decouple: When Congress altered the §2011 state death tax credit in 2001 the revenue impact on state governments caused many to amend their laws. Many states only imposed a tax that was equal to the amount allowed as a credit against the federal estate tax. By now increasing the state tax those states are said to have "decoupled" their taxes from the federal regime. Often they did this by granting a different applicable exclusion amount exemption amount than the federal entitlement.

Deductions in Respect of a Decedent (DRD): Like IRD (see below) that was earned by a decedent before death but is received and taxed to the beneficiary who inherits it postmortem, deductions in respect of a decedent are expenses that were incurred by the decedent inter vivos but the deductions therefor were not properly allowed premortem. The recipient of IRD is entitled to offset that income with DRD items that relate to it.

Defective Grantor Trust: Many grantor trusts (see below) *intentionally* are made so, and are referred to as "defective," which is regarded as desirable. Sometimes known as an IDGT or Intentionally Defective Grantor Trust.

Delaware Tax Trap: Congress adopted §2041(a)(3) to prevent a form of tax free perpetual trust planning that was made possible by a special rule in Delaware dealing with the Rule Against Perpetuities and nongeneral (nontaxable) powers of appointment. That Code section has come to be known as the Delaware tax trap and now is used on occasion as a method to intentionally incur estate tax as a cheaper alternative to the generation-skipping transfer tax. See Chapter 18.

Dependent Administration: A supervised estate administration in probate court, as compared to independent or unsupervised administration that may be available for small estates or by election permitted by the decedent's will.

Designated Beneficiary: The individual or entity (such as a trust) selected by the owner of a life insurance policy or a retirement benefit account.

Direct Skip: A form of generation-skipping taxable transfer made to a beneficiary more than one generation below the transferor (e.g., to a grandchild). See Chapter 18.

Disability Insurance: Insurance coverage that pays on events tied to the insured's ability to function, typically in gainful employment. The critical element in a D.I. plan is the definition of disability, which may be stated in terms of the inability to perform the specific duties of a particular job or profession (an "own-occupation" policy) but it could be the inability to perform the duties of any income producing activity for which the insured is in any way qualified (which is less useful but more common because it is less expensive).

Disclaimer: A beneficiary's renunciation of entitlements under an estate plan. If qualified under §§2046 and 2518 there are no wealth transfer tax consequences to rejection of the wealth. If not qualified, the rejection can be regarded as an acceptance followed by a taxable transfer. See Chapter 18.

Distributable Net Income (DNI): A pivotal concept in the income taxation of trusts and estates, this constitutes the items of a fiduciary entity's income and deductions that can be "carried out" by distributions during the year for taxation to the beneficiaries. See Chapter 17.

Dividend Option: Life insurance dividends are a return of excess premiums paid. The insurer makes them available to the owner of the policy in several alternative ways. For example, the dividend may be returned in cash. Or used to buy additional coverage on the insured's life with no proof of insurability. Or applied to reduce future premiums. Unlike dividends on stock, the return of premium is a rebate and not taxable as income to the owner. Instead the dividend reduces the owner's basis in the policy. See Chapter 9.

Domicile: As distinguished from citizenship, domicile is more akin to residency of a fixed or permanent nature and establishes the jurisdiction to which an individual is subject for such purposes as determining intestate succession for owned assets (other than realty), and taxation on the individual's estate at death. A change of residence that is temporary will not alter the state of domicile; a change of domicile requires change that is intended to be permanent in nature.

Durable Power of Attorney: Those granted for health care are discussed under Health Care Proxy. A durable power for financial management authorizes the attorney in fact as agent to make decisions relating to property management and transfer. "Durable" means that the power survives the principal's incapacity. No power of attorney survives the principal's death.

Dynasty Trust: The term applied to a trust that takes advantage of the GST (see below) exemption for multiple generations of beneficiaries, often lasting in perpetuity.

Elective Share: See Statutory Forced Heir Share below.

Entitlement Program: Any of a vast variety of governmental benefit programs, such as Social Security, Medicare, or Medicaid.

Estate Freeze: Taxpayers seek to prevent growth in the value of an asset from being subjected to wealth transfer tax in the future. Chapter 14 of the Internal Revenue Code was enacted in large part to combat estate freezing transactions.

Estate Stacking: If one spouse leaves wealth to the other, the aggregate wealth is taxed all in the donee spouse's hands and, in a progressive tax system, stacking the wealth together like this may cause the aggregate to be taxed in a higher marginal bracket than if no marital transfers had been made.

Exclusive Power: A power of appointment that permits the powerholder to favor one or more of the permissible appointees but to exclude others. Compare Nonexclusive Powers below.

Family Trust: See Nonmarital Trust below.

Financial Planning: The process of evaluating a client's investment, insurance, cash flow, and related economic or financial needs. Many financial planners are certified by one or more of a variety of organizations. Some "sell product" (such as insurance, annuities, or general investments) and are compensated by the commissions earned on the products they sell. Others earn fees for services only, usually at a fixed or hourly rate.

General Power: Typically used in the context of a power of appointment but the term is applied under the wealth transfer taxes to other indirect powers that permit the powerholder to benefit the powerholder personally, the powerholder's estate, or creditors of either.

Gift Splitting: Federal gift tax §2513 permits either spouse in a married couple to make gifts that are treated for all gift tax purposes as if made half by each. An election is required, on an "all-or-nothing" annual basis that regards all gifts made in a given tax year as split.

Grantor Trust: Trusts normally are separate tax paying entities for income tax purposes, but the income, deductions, credits, and losses of a grantor trust may be attributed to the settlor (or in some cases to a third party, under "pseudo" grantor trust rules) as if the trust did not exist. In that case these tax attributes flow through and are reported by the grantor (or pseudo grantor). A variety of interests or powers retained by the settlor or, in some cases, bestowed on the settlor's spouse or even a nonadverse third party may trigger this treatment, which in many cases is regarded as favorable, all as discussed in Chapter 17.

Gross Up Rule: Effected by Internal Revenue Code §2035(b), gift tax paid on gifts made within three years of a decedent's death is added into the decedent's gross estate. This generates estate tax on the dollars used to pay the gift tax and in that manner negates the tax exclusive effect of the gift tax discussed in Chapter 12.

GST (Generation-Skipping Transfer) Exemption: Linked in amount to the estate tax applicable exclusion amount and made operational by an "inclusion ratio" determined by an "applicable fraction," this is the amount of property that may be protected from the generation-skipping transfer tax, often in perpetuity. See Chapter 18.

Hanging Power: See Crummey Power above.

Health Care Proxy/Power of Attorney: As distinguished from a living will, which has a very narrow application, this document is a durable power of attorney (see above) that permits the attorney in fact as agent to make health care decisions authorized by the principal who grants the power.

Homestead: Defined by state law, usually as a principal personal residence used as a dwelling or home, often limited in terms of the acreage or surrounding buildings that are included. Homestead often is subject to restrictions on disposition (to guarantee residence to a surviving spouse or children) and usually is protected against attachment by creditors. It also may enjoy special treatment for state and local property taxation.

ILIT: Irrevocable life insurance trust. See Chapter 9.

Incidents of Ownership: Internal Revenue Code §2042 requires gross estate inclusion of insurance on the life of a decedent even if the decedent did not own the policy, *if* the insured decedent held any incidents of ownership over the policy. These are powers granted under the policy to affect enjoyment of the policy or the proceeds paid at the insured's death, such as the power to designate the beneficiary or change the settlement option, or the right during the insured's life to borrow against the policy or pledge it as collateral for a third party loan. See Chapter 9.

Income in Respect of a Decedent (IRD): Income earned premortem but paid postmortem retains its character and taxability in the hands of the taxpayer who inherits the right to receive that income. Acceleration of IRD means that all the income tax liability is compressed into the year in which an acceleration event occurs, even if the income itself has not yet been received. See Chapter 17.

Incremental Tax: The added tax incurred on the next dollar of inclusion, computed at the highest applicable marginal rate, rather than the average rate of tax computed on a total estate.

Independent Administration: The antithesis of Dependent Administration. See above.

Insurance Trust: An inter vivos trust created to receive the proceeds of life insurance, typically on the life of the settlor. Sometimes this trust is an ILIT (irrevocable life insurance trust) but most are revocable.

Inter Vivos Transfer: Any form of property transfer during life, typically irrevocable and therefore a completed gift for federal gift tax purposes.

Inter Vivos Trust: See living trust below.

Intestate: A testamentary (at death) transfer passing by virtue of the rules of descent and distribution to heirs at law.

Individual Retirement Account (IRA): Created as a trust or a custodial account. Subject to Internal Revenue Code §408, with special rules for administration and distributions. This is not a qualified retirement plan subject to §401 or the myriad rules applicable to qualified plans.

Joint and Survivor Annuity: An annuity payable to two persons jointly, often in equal shares while they both are alive and then to the survivor (often in a reduced amount, such as 50%). See also Sole and Survivor Annuity below.

Keogh Plan or H R. 10 Plan. This is an Internal Revenue Code §401(c) qualified retirement plan applicable to self employed individuals, partners in a partnership, or sole unincorporated proprietors.

Living Trust: The name sometimes given to a trust created and funded for administration during the settlor's life. Also known as an inter vivos trust, as distinguished from a testamentary trust (created at death by the settlor's will).

Living Will: A document authorized by state statute by which the maker declares an intent regarding application or withdrawal of life support measures. Often subject to restrictions relating to time for execution and scope of coverage. See Durable Power of Attorney for Health Care or Health Care Proxy above.

Medicaid Qualifying Trust: A misnomer because such a trust is a countable asset for purposes of determining Medicaid *dis*qualification. See Chapter 14.

Movable: In a conflict of laws analysis the determination of applicable law often turns on whether the assets involved are movable or immovable, meaning personalty or realty. Frequently the law of the situs of realty governs, while personal property (both tangible and intangible) is governed by other factors — often the law of the donor's domicile or the place of a trust's administration.

Net Gift: If a donor imposes on the donee the obligation to pay the gift tax liability on the transfer itself the amount of the gift is regarded as the fair market value of the transfer, reduced by the obligation imposed on the donee, the net amount being the taxable value of the gift. This requires a circular, interrelated calculation because the tax on the net gift is lower due to the reduced value of the gift, which is a function of the tax imposed.

Nonclaim Statute: As part of the probate process most jurisdictions provide by statute that proper notice to creditors (actual notice typically is required to known or reasonably ascertainable creditors; published notice usually is sufficient with respect to all others) generates an accelerated statute of limitation that precludes creditor claims against the estate after a shortened claim period.

Nonexclusive Power: A power of appointment that requires the powerholder to appoint a more than insignificant amount to every permissible appointee. Compare Exclusive Power above.

Nongeneral Power: Typically used in the context of a power of appointment but a term applied under the wealth transfer taxes to other indirect powers that permit the powerholder to alter the disposition of property but not to benefit the powerholder personally, the powerholder's estate, or creditors of either. "Limited" powers may permit the powerholder to benefit only a very narrow class of beneficiaries. A "statutory" power permits the powerholder to benefit anyone in the world *except* the powerholder, the powerholder's estate, or creditors of either (that is, the broadest power permitted by the wealth transfer tax without being general).

Nonmarital Trust: Planning that shelters a decedent's unified credit (see below) typically places the amount subjected to tax in the estate of the decedent into a trust, typically for the overlife benefit of the decedent's surviving spouse. (Often the spouse is not the exclusive beneficiary, and sometimes individuals other than the spouse are the exclusive beneficiaries.) Such a trust may be known as the family, credit shelter, bypass, or B trust. All reference planning that subjects the applicable exclusion amount to tax in the decedent's estate to use the decedent's unified credit and precludes inclusion again in the estate of the surviving spouse. Thus, this trust, drafted to provide enjoyment (generous benefits are allowed) without subsequent inclusion, "bypasses" the estate of the trust beneficiaries. See Chapter 7.

Nonparticipant: In a qualified retirement benefit plan the covered employee is the participant and that employee's spouse commonly is referred to as the nonparticipant spouse.

Nonqualified Plan: See Qualified Plan below.

Participant: The employee covered under a qualified retirement benefit plan.

Part-Sale, Part-Gift: For income tax purposes a sale for less than full and adequate consideration may be regarded as two transactions, one a sale of a portion of the property for fair market value and the other a gift of the difference between the value of the entire property and the amount paid. The same transaction involving a charity as the purchaser is known as a bargain sale to charity. The difference between the two otherwise identical transactions is how basis is allocated between the sale portion and the gift portion for gain or loss realization purposes.

Per Stirpes, Per Capita, or Per Capita at Each Generation: The three most common forms of intestate entitlement among descendants of a designated ancestor (such as the decedent). Each form of division differs in terms of how representatives stand in the shoes of their deceased ancestor, such as grandchildren taking the share that a child (their parent) would have received if living. Each state statute of descent and distribution (intestate distribution) will specify which of these methods may apply under certain circumstances, and some statutes employ combinations in a variety of situations.

Pick Up Tax: See Sponge Tax below.

Power to Appoint: Also referred to as a power of appointment. Authority granted under a trust that permits the holder of the power to alter the disposition of property subject to the power. These may be general or nongeneral, inter vivos or testamentary, exclusive or nonexclusive, or subject to other restrictions.

Pretermitted Heir: Usually a child, often limited to one born or adopted after execution of a will. Sometimes any descendant or even a surviving spouse. In each case the person is protected by a statute that requires disinheritance of that person by will to be express and intentional. Failure to mention the individual by will creates an entitlement to the share that person would have received if the decedent had died intestate.

Pseudo Grantor Trust: See Grantor Trust above.

Qualified Plan: Federal law provides tax benefits to certain employee retirement benefit plans that comply with statutory requirements. These are qualified plans, which permit the employer to deduct payments made to the plan on behalf of employees who will not include those amounts in income until plan benefits are distributed to them (or to their designated beneficiaries). Nonqualified plans provide the same income tax deferral to the employee but do not permit accelerated deduction for the plan sponsor.

QTIP: Qualified terminable interest property, which is a form of disposition that qualifies for the federal estate or gift tax marital deductions under §§2056(b)(7) and 2523(f).

Reciprocal Trust Doctrine: A tax result addressed to a form of planning in which two individuals, often spouses, create virtually identical trusts for each other, giving interests or powers to the other that would create undesirable tax consequences if retained by the settlor. For example, H may create a trust for W with W as trustee and W may create a trust for H with H as trustee. The doctrine allows the government to "uncross" the trusts, by treating them as if each settlor created the trust that grants that settlor the interests or powers, with the appropriate tax result as if the crossing of the trusts did not occur.

Reciprocal Wills: Often prepared for spouses, with mirror image dispositions that provide for the survivor and then in an agreed upon manner for beneficiaries common to both after the second death. These may (but need not) be contractual wills with consequences for breach if the survivor deviates from the agreed plan after the first testator dies.

Reverse QTIP Election: Taking advantage of a generation-skipping transfer tax rule it is possible for a decedent's estate to designate any part of a QTIP trust (see above) as the settlor's property, notwithstanding subsequent inclusion of that trust in the estate of the settlor's surviving spouse, the life beneficiary of that trust. In this manner the settlor's generation-skipping transfer tax exemption may be used to make the reverse elected portion exempt from generation-skipping transfer tax, notwithstanding the ordinary rule that would regard the spouse as the transferor and would require the spouse's exemption to be used to make the trust exempt.

Revolving Door Power: This power usually is granted to a trust beneficiary or is retained by the trust's settlor, to remove and replace trustees, either at will or for cause. See Chapters 5 and 6, particularly their discussions of *Estate of Wall* and Rev. Ruls. 79-353 and 95-58.

Rollover Election: See Spousal Rollover below.

S Corporation: Under Subchapter S of the Internal Revenue Code certain small closely-held corporations are taxed under conduit or passthrough principles that essentially treat the corporation as not existing. Instead, the shareholders must report all the income and are entitled to all the deductions, losses, and credits of the entity.

Separate Property: The antithesis of community property, this is property that either spouse in a community property jurisdiction owns in their sole right and includes property that was brought to the marriage, property acquired by either during the marriage but not by onerous activity (e.g., by gift or bequest), and (in most community property states) income earned on separate property.

Settlement Option: Typically under a life insurance contract the owner may select the beneficiary *and* the method of payment of the proceeds. The method for payment might be a life estate with remainder to another party, an annuity for the life of the designated beneficiary, interest only with a refund, or other alternatives. If the owner does not select the settlement option the beneficiary may be able to select a settlement option before the proceeds are paid as a lump sum.

Shelter the Unified Credit: The term used for intentionally incurring estate tax in the estate of the first to die of a married couple, rather than taking advantage of the unlimited marital deduction. The wealth thus taxed takes advantage of that decedent's unified credit and the property thus taxed is placed in a credit shelter, bypass, family, or nonmarital (all synonyms) trust that will not be includible in the estate of the surviving spouse, even though generous benefits may be provided to the spouse during his or her overlife. See Nonmarital Trust above, and Chapter 7.

Sole and Survivor Annuity: An annuity payable to one person for life, and then (sometimes in a lesser amount) to another if living. See also Joint and Survivor Annuity above.

Spend Down Planning: Steps undertaken to qualify an individual for needs-based governmental entitlements, typically Medicaid.

Split Interest Trust: Trusts that provide for a private beneficiary and a charity, one after the other, as in a charitable lead trust or a charitable remainder trust. These must satisfy extensive and complex qualification rules under §664 to entitle the donor to a charitable deduction for the charitable component. See Chapter 8.

Sponge Tax: State estate taxes that merely "soak up" the Internal Revenue Code §2011 credit for state death tax. Also known as state "pick up" taxes. The §2011 credit was repealed in stages, fully effective at the end of 2004, and many states have enacted or revised their laws to impose a more substantial wealth transfer tax. See Decouple above.

Spousal Annuity: A qualified retirement benefit plan must comply with a federal requirement that the plan provide a survivor annuity for the plan participant's surviving spouse. This mandatory entitlement differs based on whether the participant dies before or after retirement and may be waived only with the nonparticipant spouse's consent. See Chapter 10.

Spousal Rollover: As discussed in Chapter 10, an IRA owner's surviving spouse as the IRA beneficiary may elect to roll over distributions to a new IRA of the spouse's creation and thereby defer income taxation until the spouse is required to take down distributions from that spousal rollover IRA.

Spousal Waiver: The consent permitted from a nonparticipant spouse to relinquish or waive the spousal annuity entitlement under a qualified plan.

Springing Power: A power of attorney that withholds authority from the attorney-in-fact until a determination is made, typically that the principal granting the power is incompetent, when it "springs" into existence.

Statutory Forced Heir Share: A surviving spouse's elective share entitlement in the estate of a decedent whose estate plan is rejected in favor of this mandatory alternative. This right is available in every noncommunity property jurisdiction except Georgia.

Statutory Power: See Nongeneral Power above.

Stub Income: See Accrued But Undistributed Income above. Income that has not yet been distributed when the current income beneficiary dies must be disposed of in some manner. Typically it is paid to the next beneficiary, rather than to the deceased beneficiary's estate or subject to a power of appointment in the deceased beneficiary. This generates a marital deduction qualification issue discussed in Chapter 7.

Subchapter J: This short hand reference is to Internal Revenue Code §§641-692, which comprise the income taxation of trusts, estates, grantors, and beneficiaries, and IRD. See Chapter 17.

Supplemental/Special Needs Trust: Drafted to provide items in excess of basic support and not be a countable asset or resource for purposes of determining the beneficiary's qualification for Medicaid.

Swing Items: Certain items that qualify for deduction by an estate or trust for income tax purposes also may be allowed as estate tax deductions. Pursuant to §642(g) most of these items must be deducted either on Form 1041 for income tax purposes or on Form 706 for estate tax purposes and may not do double duty. Thus, they are said to "swing" between the two returns.

Taxable Distribution: A nonexempt distribution of income or principal from a generation-skipping trust to a skip person beneficiary, such as a grandchild of the transferor. See Chapter 18.

Taxable Termination: Any nonexempt termination of the present interest of any beneficiary in a generation-skipping trust. See Chapter 18.

Testamentary: By will (as in a testamentary power to appoint — one that is exercisable by the powerholder's will) or having the same effect as a transfer at death (as in an inter vivos transfer with retained enjoyment such that the true effect is as if the transferor retained the entire property until death and transferred it by will).

Tier Rules: The income taxation of complex trusts distinguishes between mandatory income distributions (Tier 1) that carry out distributable net income in first priority during a year, and all other distributions (Tier 2) that carry out DNI only to the extent any remains after Tier 1 distributions during the year. See Chapter 17.

Transmutation: A term normally applied to any conversion of community property into separate property of either or both spouses, such as by turning it into tenancy in common rather than community property.

Trust Mill: An operation, often itinerant, usually involving a single licensed professional assisted by a bevy of nonprofessionals who conduct seminars (often advertised in the Sunday newspaper supplement) on estate planning or probate avoidance, at or following which cookie-cutter trusts are churned out for large numbers of "clients" with little information gathering or tailoring to the specific situation of the consumer and quite often with significant errors. Some Attorneys General or consumer protection officials at the state level are attempting to crack down on this activity under unauthorized practice of law or consumer fraud statutes.

Trust Protector: Some modern trusts (particularly asset protection trusts) provide that a trusted third party has powers over the trust that could defeat the planning involved if retained by the settlor. Examples are a power to remove and replace trustees, to change the situs of the trust for administration, to dictate investments or even to alter, amend, or terminate the trust. Powers of appointment can be just as useful in some circumstances.

Unitrust: Historically found only in charitable split interest trusts, now made popular by government acceptance that a properly constructed unitrust interest will be regarded as the functional equivalent of an income interest. Useful in cases in which a straight income interest is too unpredictable as an entitlement, a unitrust directs distribution of an amount that is a percentage of the fair market value of the trust, determined annually. So, as inflation increases the market value of a trust, the annual annuity also increases and better protects the buying power of the entitlement. Some trusts use a "smoothing" provision that creates a unitrust entitlement that is a percentage of the *average* value of the trust for a three or five year period, so as to moderate the impact of wide swings in value over a short time.

Upjohn Clause: A provision that prohibits a powerholder (such as a trustee) from making any distribution that would have the effect of discharging the powerholder's legal obligation to support the distributee (such as a dependent).

Valuation Freeze: See Estate Freeze above.

Wasting Asset: An asset that is losing value over time (such as a life estate, leasehold, patent, or other temporal interest) or that is subject to depreciation or depletion (such as mineral interests subject to extraction) or even diminution due to income taxation (such as a right to receive IRD).

Wealth Transfer Taxation: The collection of Internal Revenue Code Chapters 11, 12, 13, and 14 used to be referred to as just the "Estate and Gift Tax" (Chapters 11 and 12, respectively). Because of the generation-skipping transfer tax in Chapter 13 and the Special Valuation Rules in Chapter 14 it is more appropriate today to refer to the entire package of excise taxes on wealth transfers in general.

Young Spouse: For purposes of the minimum distribution rules discussed in Chapter 10, life expectancy of a participant's spouse is deemed to be the same as the life expectancy of the participant, *unless* the spouse is over 10 years younger than the participant. Such a spouse is referred to as a "young" spouse for this purpose.

WEALTH TRANSFER PLANNING AND DRAFTING

Chapter 1

INTRODUCTION

Any arrangement governing the transfer of property is an estate plan, and the process by which these arrangements are formulated is estate planning. Despite high income taxes, costs of living (and sometimes the health care costs of dying), expenditures for dependents, and other expenses or extractions, many people possess or control sufficient wealth to make careful estate planning important. This text introduces some of the myriad issues that must be addressed to transfer property in ways that preserve its maximum utility and the benefits it may bestow.

Statutes of descent and distribution determine to whom property passes, to the extent a person dies intestate (without a valid will). Thus, we each have the default estate plan provided by state law unless we create different plans by will or other device, including inter vivos transfers. Wills are ambulatory (they do nothing during the testator's life). In contrast, outright gifts transfer complete ownership and control of property immediately. Between these two extremes are various devices such as concurrent ownership (e.g., tenancy by the entirety, joint tenancy with right of survivorship, joint bank accounts, and jointly owned government bonds), revocable or irrevocable inter vivos trusts, and retirement benefit or life insurance beneficiary designations.

It is difficult to dispose of an entire estate solely by effective inter vivos arrangements. So no matter what else is done, wills are essential to most estate plans. For example, joint tenancy with right of survivorship avoids the need for a will only until the last tenant dies. Each concurrent owner needs a will because the survivor of them may not have time (or the requisite capacity) to make a will when the need becomes clear.

Comprehensive estate plans deal with many forms of wealth, including tangible and intangible property, cash, or real estate owned individually or jointly; business interests owned individually, in partnership form, or incorporated and represented by closely held stock; property held in trust, sometimes subject to a power to revoke or appoint; life insurance; and social security or other deferred compensation or retirement benefits. An estate plan also should anticipate expectancies that may accrue under trusts or wills of other people.

Many factors determine the most intelligent plan for a particular estate. Over 99% of all decedent estates are not subject to federal wealth transfer taxation because they fall below the federal estate tax "applicable exclusion amount" ($1.5 million in the year this book was published, potentially rising to $2.0 million and then $3.5 million if certain changes adopted by Congress in 2001 actually occur). Even if an estate is subject to federal, state, or foreign taxation, the best estate plan may not be the one that minimizes taxes. Irrespective of taxation, estate planning may be more important for individuals with smaller estates because poor planning wastes money that beneficiaries of small estates can ill afford. In addition, nontax considerations often should influence the plan. These might include the business or financial acumen of intended beneficiaries; whether minor, disabled, or otherwise incapacitated beneficiaries are involved; the nature and location of property subject to the estate plan; the need for asset protection and flexibility to meet changing conditions; the significance of probate costs and delay; and expected costs of operating a trust or other property management or dispositive devices.

Also regardless of taxation, planning relative to small and large estates basically is the same. In both instances we seek to accomplish the most effective disposition with the least possible diminution in value. Although large estates may present a greater variety of problems, almost any problem arising in a large estate may be encountered in a smaller one. Indeed, smaller estates often present more challenges because the range of available solutions may be more limited. Thus, accomplished estate planners should be equipped to work effectively with large and small estates alike.

No artificial distinction or division between small and large estates is sensible for estate planning purposes. Any particular estate may be too small to employ certain arrangements, while the same estate may be regarded as large for other purposes. Moreover, some techniques may not be appropriate in *large* estates. Nevertheless, the asset value of an estate is significant. For example, inter vivos gifts usually are sensible only if adequate funds remain for the donor's own needs. Thus, inter vivos gifts typically are not relevant in planning a small estate, unless there is a practical assurance that the assets will be available to meet the donor's needs. So, whether gifts should be made depends on such factors as the donor's age and foreseeable needs, the nature of the property involved, and the donees.

A person whose estate is too small to make inter vivos gifts to place property in a revocable inter vivos trust still might avoid probate delays and expenses. The value of property subject to disposition may be significant in deciding which types of interests to create in various intended beneficiaries. Often other factors (such as the beneficiary's age, net worth, inexperience in managing property, or the beneficiary's own estate planning goals) may justify placing even very small dollar amounts in trust. Normally, however, long-range trusts will not be employed for smaller estates, although for a short duration almost any type of trust might be appropriate without regard for the amount involved. Trustee fees and the requisite level of expertise may affect the decision to employ a trust. A professional trustee's fees may be too costly but individual trustees (who may be available for less) may not be qualified or appropriate.

In smaller estates life insurance frequently is a principal asset, making it important to choose between leaving the proceeds with the insurance company under a beneficiary settlement option and paying them outright to a designated beneficiary or to an insurance trust. Whether the insured should continue to own the policy becomes an increasingly important issue in estates that are large enough to be subject to federal estate tax.

Finally, even a person with little other wealth may possess a power to appoint substantial assets held in a trust created by someone else (e.g., a surviving spouse who may appoint property in a trust created by a predeceased spouse). The same problems may be involved in determining whether to exercise the power, and the types of interests to create, as arise in a large estate of owned assets to be disposed of by an estate plan. Already you can see that this can get complicated in a hurry, and not just in big or taxable estates.

Estate Planning As A Profession

Before undertaking a course in estate planning you may ask what this specialty is about, who concentrates in it (and why), and where it is heading.

Estate planning constantly undergoes change, perhaps more than any other specialty within the legal profession. At one time it involved predominantly drafting wills and trusts and probating estates; its practitioners were scriveners with fiduciary skills. In the 1950s and 1960s it went through a transition into a much more intensely tax-oriented practice. Many property-based lawyers acquired the skills of a new breed of practitioner to keep abreast of the tax factors that drove much of the estate planning practice for nearly the past half century.

Through the last quarter of the 20th century Congress enacted significant legislation aimed at minimizing tax gaming. Estate planners learned to cope with a tax environment that became much more hostile. The profession also became much more stratified because Congress took more and more people out of the wealth transfer tax system by steadily increasing the base exemption level. Today the tiny portion of the decedent population in America that is subject to wealth transfer taxation will shrink further if phased-in changes in exemption levels occur as legislated by Congress in 2001. Whether the tax is repealed, restored, or reformed, for 99% of the population federal wealth transfer taxation need not be the defining catalyst or concern for most estate planning. However, as the federal wealth transfer tax wanes, *state* taxes and federal *income* taxes are revitalized and remain relevant.

Along with all this tax change, and perhaps a reason for the tax climate, has been a major change in American demographics. The population has gotten older as individual life expectancies have increased. As a result, the estate planning practice changed to reflect the needs of an aging population. Indeed, a new elderlaw specialty arose, related to estate planning enough that parallel concerns and expertise sometimes apply to certain clients.

Although we lack a better term, traditional "estate planning" does not fully encompass what specialists in these areas do for clients today. The historical trusts and estates practice became the estate planning practice of the mid-to-late 20th century by embracing tax as well as more historical wealth transmission problems. The latest transition is from the tax-driven estate planning practice to an even more diverse endeavor. Today the practice encompasses a broad range of services that touch on every aspect of a family's financial life and may entail working with several generations of family clients. Invariably the practice includes state and federal income tax, state or federal wealth transfer taxation, state and local property taxation, and even international taxation in some cases. It also involves traditional will and trust drafting, probate, and other forms of fiduciary administration.

These lawyers still draft and revise dispositive documents and assist in the administration of estates and trusts. But some also engage in investment and financial counseling and most cannot avoid broader issues involving insurance, retirement benefits, closely held businesses (particularly succession planning), traditional portfolio investments, property management, health care and governmental benefits law, matrimonial and family law, planning in anticipation of incapacity (that is, planning for people who are going to *live* as well as for those who are going to die), and a range of other related activities.

These lawyers structure gifting programs, prepare business agreements, and plan dispositions that minimize tax and administrative costs or that qualify (or preserve qualification) of donors *or* donees for entitlement programs. These advisors may represent or serve as fiduciaries, and frequently fill the role of counselor, arbitrator, psychologist, and friend in addition to being a client's "lawyer." This latest transition represents a challenge and an opportunity to the practicing bar and provides fulfillment on both intellectual and personal levels. As compared to many of the controversy aspects of the legal profession, there is more heart-food and "everyone wins" potential in this endeavor.

Unfortunately, the future of the traditional estate planning profession is a bit uncertain because the personal counseling needs of the general public are not being served adequately by many traditional estate planners. Starting some time ago, far-sighted commentators identified changes in the desires and needs of the public and the necessary redirection of the profession that serves them. Although not written so long ago, these authors proved to be way ahead of their time. See Langbein, *The Twentieth-Century Revolution in Family Wealth Transmission*, 86 MICH. L. REV. 722 (1988) (hereafter cited as *Langbein*); Eubank, *The Future for Estate Lawyers*, 10 REAL PROP., PROB. & TRUST J. 223 (1975); Cantwell, *The Probate and Trust Lawyer in 2000 A.D.*, 10 REAL PROP., PROB. & TRUST J. 233 (1975). Traditional estate planning as a practice specialty is expanding to serve clients who need a total plan that considers their lifetime and testamentary goals. This largely explains the recent explosive growth in "financial planning" and other ancillary services.

Education and Practice Concerns

It is important to recognize that developments in the law and practice have not occurred suddenly (indeed, at the highest and very low ends of the client spectrum they are not relevant at all). Moreover, although there has been a significant change in the nature and scope of the practice, the dimensions and reasons for that change only now are becoming clear and some uncertainty remains, particularly as Congress waffles about wealth transfer tax repeal.

Direction of the Profession

At some law firms the traditional estate planning practice has produced a decreasing percentage of the firm's total billings. Some firms are reluctant to make new partners in this department. This especially was true during the "go-go" decades at the end of the 20th century. Moreover, the *perception* in some quarters is that traditional estate planning is not intellectually demanding because it involves mainly the production of documents that "a trained monkey at a word processor" could mass-produce. If that were true, how would the monkey decide which document to churn out?[1]

All of these *perceptions* are inaccurate. In addition to handsome compensation that tends to be much more steady than other "on-again, off-again" specialties (such as investment capital markets and bankruptcy), estate planners enjoy the psychic benefits of doing good on an intimate basis, working for real people with truly human needs, responses, and emotions. Moreover, the latest transitions have improved both the nature and scope of the practice and the perception by outsiders of the challenges and values involved. Still, it is easy to understand why misperceptions exist.

Inheritance Has Changed

Some misunderstanding of the role and function of estate planners is attributable to two fundamental changes in the nature of modern

---

1. Some pundits also would say that the once highly revered mergers and acquisitions practice resembled "a bunch of monkeys trading bananas." Let's not fling these charges around.

inheritance. First, educating children is the principal form of wealth transfer in many families. Parents (and often grandparents) often do not (get to) wait until death to transfer their wealth. Second, wealth accumulated before retirement often is held in a pension payable as an annuity that will terminate at death; no pool of capital remains after the annuitant dies. Add a third reality, the high cost of end-of-life health care, and these lifetime uses of property mean that "[t]ransfer on death, the fundamental pattern of former times, is . . . ceasing to characterize the dominant wealth holding and wealth transmission practices of the broad middle class." *Langbein* at 745-746.

These changes have influenced how many middle-class clients view the estate planning profession. In addition, the legal needs of the public with respect to inheritance today, and the perceived role and function of estate planning lawyers, are affected by the fact that property ownership often favors nonprobate assets and probate simplification. This means that legal services are less often required in the transfer of wealth that passes at death. Says Langbein, "one of the worst consequences of the nonprobate system is that it tempts people into the mistake of thinking that avoiding probate is the equivalent of estate planning." *Id.* at 749. Thus, both the actual and the perceived nature of wealth transfer planning has changed.

Tax Law Changes

A second (and perhaps more obvious) reason for change in the perception of traditional estate planning relates to tax laws. In large measure the futurists were right when they predicted that adoption of the unified credit (sheltering $1.5 million from tax at death after 2003, and slated to rise even further) would greatly diminish the number of clients for whom *tax* planning is necessary. Today, planning for the most significant percentage of clients involves less wealth than the applicable exclusion amount of the unified credit. For all but the richest 1% planning is not a tax-oriented endeavor.

On the other hand, the futurists could not have anticipated the astounding number of tax law changes that have made it necessary to review existing plans for clients with substantial wealth, often on an annual or biannual cycle. With this need to do renewed planning comes the need to do on-going, nearly continuous research and development to devise responses to tax and other law changes. All of this has significantly affected the traditional estate planning practice, increasing the intellectual challenge for lawyers with clients of both modest and substantial wealth.

The need for research and development poses a significant cost, and many lawyers who traditionally did estate planning work cannot afford to devise the necessary responses. Many now choose to limit their practice to the nontaxable 99% of the population and, in the process, limit their malpractice liability by eliminating those plans with the greatest risk of disruption caused by tax law changes. These estate planners have simply chosen not to serve clients who have more sophisticated tax-related needs. Thus, attorneys who serve estate planning needs have become stratified and the costs of change have decreased the profitability of those who have remained in the taxable side of the profession. In a word, the specialty has become more demanding for high end planning.

Demographics

Furthermore, many law firms that have confronted the changing demographics of clients with moderate to substantial wealth have done so in a nonintuitive way. Surprising about their perception of the estate planning specialty is that the number of clients with traditional estate planning and personal counseling needs is expanding even as the tax laws reduce the need for tax driven planning. For example, the baby boomers of the post-War years are now at that stage in their lives when, for the first time, they are seriously considering their need for quality professional estate planning services. They have families, realize that mortality is a reality, and they have financial commitments that must be guaranteed even as they finally are becoming financially established. When their parents ultimately die they may inherit far more wealth than any prior generation. Meanwhile the elderly are living longer, meaning that added generations of older clients are still alive today and their heirs wait longer to inherit.

For the lack of anyone else to adequately service their needs, older-elderly clients bring to estate planners a raft of problems that seldom were considered not so long ago. These include planning for retirement and (later) for the possibility of incompetence, planning for health care or the termination of life support systems, and planning involving government entitlements (benefits such as social security and Medicaid). The perception of the estate planning profession has improved as more lawyers have expanded their practice to serve these needs. Moreover, some other professionals who have attempted to service these needs are unable to do as complete a job as estate planning and elderlaw attorneys. Thus, significant opportunities await counselors who are able to satisfy these demands.

Shrinking Talent Pool

All that being said, the number of clients with unmet needs is increasing faster than the number of professionals who are positioned to serve them. Today the profession is lean and a great need exists for advisors who are positioned to assist this burgeoning cadre of clients, virtually all with nontaxable estates. Unfortunately, there may be no other practice area that takes as long to master.

The need for full-service counselors in this area cannot be met overnight. Lawyers with vision who perceive these trends and develop their skills have a significant competitive edge. Those lawyers are eager to hire bright, talented young attorneys who recognize the evolution of traditional estate planning and the significant demand for it. These practitioners likely are the best prospects as mentors for those who are new to this area of practice, and the mentor relation is especially important given the length of the learning process and the steep pitch of the learning curve.

Litigation and Malpractice

In addition to directing their services to previously unmet client needs, some traditional estate planners are being thrust into negotiation and litigation (controversy) work more than ever before. In fact, some traditional estate planners report that they now serve two markets. They provide estate planning and estate administration services in the first. In the second, they help to cure mistakes by assisting clients who received inadequate assistance from others, whether in the form of improper drafting, inadequate tax planning, imprudent investment advice, or otherwise deficient fiduciary services.

Given all that goes into the estate planning endeavor, it is predictable that mistakes occur, That risk raises questions about the extent of malpractice liability. One popular misconception is that this area of practice is so complex that certain mistakes are prima facie nonactionable. Thus, there is a notion that some elements of the art are beyond mastery, and this notion is augmented by a community standard defense (which is made unreliable by the inability to define the proper "community" in which to measure the average or minimum competence of estate planners in general).

The most commonly miscited example of this is the malpractice liability of the attorney who prepared the testamentary trust that violated the Rule Against Perpetuities in Lucas v. Hamm, 364 P.2d 685 (Cal. 1961). Involved was the so-called administrative infinality or administrative contingency rule (which presumes that any ministerial act could last forever). The trust was distributable five years after probate administration of the settlor's estate terminated, which might occur after expiration of the permissible period of the Rule. The court held that failure to anticipate this special aspect of the Rule Against Perpetuities was not negligence, explaining that the trust actually would violate the Rule only if estate administration might not be completed within the period of lives in being plus 16 years, and that the likelihood of such a delay was so remote that an attorney exercising ordinary skill in the same circumstance might make the same mistake.

Contrary to many popular misconceptions and statements about the case, the court did *not* accept the attorney defendant's blanket assertion that the Rule Against Perpetuities is so difficult that any violation is excusable. Indeed, the intermediate court specifically noted that general practitioners who are faced with a difficult aspect of a specialized subject must seek an expert's aid. Although that court's imposition of liability on the attorney was reversed, the California Supreme Court also rejected the argument that no perpetuities violation can be malpractice.

Far more interesting about *Lucas* was the high court's treatment of the attorney defendant's argument that the plaintiff, who was a disappointed beneficiary under the trust, had no standing to sue because the plaintiff was not the client and therefore was not in privity of contract with the attorney defendant.[2] The personal representative of an estate (or the trustee of a negligently drafted trust) may have no standing to sue to recover damages suffered by intended beneficiaries because the fiduciary entity often is unaffected by an attorney's negligence. For example, unless additional taxes or administration expenses are incurred, the estate may be unreduced by a mistake that alters the relative interests of the estate's beneficiaries. So the *Lucas* plaintiff relied on an earlier landmark case, Biakanja v. Irving, 320 P.2d 16 (Cal. 1958), which rejected the privity defense in a negligent will drafting situation and created instead an exception to the privity defense in the estate planning context as a matter of public policy.

According to *Biakanja*, liability will be imposed if (1) the estate planning engagement was intended to benefit the plaintiff, (2) the plaintiff's harm attributable to the attorney's mistake was foreseeable, (3) it is certain that the plaintiff suffered injury, (4) the connection between the defendant's conduct and the injury was immediate, (5) there is a strong public policy of preventing future harm that is fostered by imposing liability on the attorney notwithstanding the plaintiff's lack of privity, and (6) the imposition of attorney liability to beneficiaries of negligently

---

2. Although some courts are still insulating attorneys from liability, based on the notion that beneficiaries of an estate plan cannot sue the drafter without privity of contract, many more courts are holding that an attorney who fails to properly craft an estate plan to qualify for certain common benefits or to effect the desires of the contracting client will be held liable to disappointed beneficiaries. There is abundant authority supporting a strict privity requirement, but most of it is not current. Indeed, one report found only six states in which relatively recent cases specifically respect the privity defense in an estate planning context. Beglieter, *First Let's Sue All the Lawyers — What Will We Get: Damages for Estate Planning Malpractice*, 51 HASTINGS L.J. 325, 327 n.19 (2000) (Maryland, Nebraska, New York, Ohio, Texas, and Virginia). See, e.g., Noble v. Bruce, 709 A.2d 1264 (Md. 1998); Lilyhorn v. Dier, 335 N.W.2d 554 (Neb. 1983); Deeb v. Johnson, 566 N.Y.S.2d 688 (App. Div. 1991); Weingarten v. Warren, 753 F. Supp. 491 (S.D. N.Y. 1990) (applying New York law to preclude a malpractice case lacking privity between a trust remainder beneficiary and an attorney for the trustee); Simon v. Zipperstein, 512 N.E.2d 636 (Ohio 1987); Dickey v. Jansen, 731 S.W.2d 581 (Tex. App. 1987); Copenhauer v. Rogers, 384 S.E.2d 543 (Va. 1989). Cf. Estate of Arlitt v. Paterson, 995 S.W.2d 713 (Tex. Ct. App. 1999) (an action against attorneys that would be barred by the lack of privity may survive if the plaintiffs establish a breach of duty not to commit "negligent misrepresentation," which the court stated differs from malpractice (although the court did not articulate in what sense); in addition, the decedent's surviving spouse may survive the privity defense if the attorney represented both spouses jointly, as is the practice of virtually all estate planners who represent married couples). Subsequently, Robinson v. Benton, 842 So. 2d 631 (Ala. 2002) (the client died before the attorney complied with the client's request to destroy an existing will and draft a new one), concluded that privity is a requisite in Alabama as well. See also Nevin v. Union Trust Co., 726 A.2d 694 (Me. 1999) (denying a beneficiary's action against a drafting attorney on privity grounds, but only because the decedent's personal representative could assert the cause of action).

drafted estate plans does not impose an undue burden on the legal profession.

This result favors a disappointed beneficiary's tort or third party contract action to redress an attorney's estate planning mistakes. Today the privity defense is a minority rule in the estate planning context. Among the factors noted, the two common sticking points in proving a malpractice case are whether it is certain that the plaintiff suffered an injury and whether imposition of liability imposes an undue burden on the attorney.

To illustrate, consider an allegation that the decedent intended to benefit the plaintiff in an amount greater than the will bequeaths. Typically the issue is (1) whether the plaintiff may introduce extrinsic evidence of the decedent's alleged intent and (2) whether the burden on the drafting attorney to disprove this alleged intent to avoid liability many years after the estate planning representation ended is too great. Some cases (such as mistakes in execution or the proper application of state law relating to the rights of a pretermitted heir) present much easier facts to address in this connection.[3] On the other hand, a case alleging that an attorney failed to follow a testator's instructions about the inclusion or amount of a bequest would pose a far more difficult situation.

Perhaps the most daunting aspect of malpractice exposure for estate planners is that the statute of limitation may not *begin* to run until the plaintiff should have discovered the error, which in many cases is not until the estate planning client has died. See, e.g., Heyer v. Flaig, 449 P.2d 161 (Cal. 1969) (the continuing nature of the attorney's malpractice and the fact that there were no beneficiaries who could allege a loss until the testator's death prevented the running of the statute of limitation before the testator's death). In a few jurisdictions the statute of limitation is said to begin running when the attorney ceases to represent the client. In estate planning, this typically produces the same result because the representation normally ends only when the client dies. And it has been held that a claim for malpractice may survive even the attorney's death notwithstanding the common assertion that some issues are not worth worrying about because,

---

3. See, e.g., Guy v. Liederbach, 459 A.2d 744 (Pa. 1983) (plaintiff, as a named beneficiary and the designated personal representative was directed by the defendant attorney to sign the will as a witness, which invalidated both the bequest and the appointment); Heyer v. Flaig, 449 P.2d 161 (Cal. 1969) (will that intended to benefit testator's two children negligently failed to preclude testator's postexecution spouse from claiming a statutory share); Stowe v. Smith, 441 A.2d 81 (Conn. 1981) (alleging that the decedent intended to provide for distribution of a trust to the plaintiff when the plaintiff reached the age of 50 and distribution to the plaintiff's descendants only if the plaintiff died prior thereto; the will called for distribution to those descendants on the earlier to occur of plaintiff's death or reaching the age of 50); Licata v. Spector, 225 A.2d 28 (Conn. 1966) (failure to procure the proper number of witnesses to the will); Needham v. Hamilton, 459 A.2d 1060 (D.C. 1983) (omission of residuary clause from will that attorney redrafted to insert an additional bequest); Auric v. Continental Casualty Co., 331 N.W.2d 325 (Wis. 1983) (attorney restated decedent's will and in the process failed to have the new will properly executed).

if they arise, it will be long after the *attorney* has died. McStowe v. Borenstein, 388 N.E.2d 674 (Mass. 1979).

Finally, it bears noting that ethics and malpractice are not the same, and that theoretically a violation of the ethics rules is not tantamount to malpractice. Model Rules of Professional Conduct Scope Comment [6] states:

> Violation of a Rule should not give rise to a cause of action nor should it create any presumption that a legal duty has been breached. The Rules are designed to provide guidance to lawyers and to provide a structure for regulating conduct through disciplinary agencies. They are not designed to be a basis for civil liability. Furthermore, the purpose of the Rules can be subverted when they are invoked by opposing parties as procedural weapons. The fact that a Rule is a just basis for a lawyer's self-assessment, or for sanctioning a lawyer under the administration of a disciplinary authority, does not imply that an antagonist in a collateral proceeding or transaction has standing to seek enforcement of the Rule. Accordingly, nothing in the Rules should be deemed to augment any substantive legal duty of lawyers or the extra-disciplinary consequences of violating such a duty.[4]

Nevertheless, the same activity that constitutes an ethics violation also may constitute malpractice, and some cases support attorney liability on the basis of an ethics violation.

Fiduciaries, investment advisors, financial advisors, and other professionals are facing increasing scrutiny and potential litigation. Indeed, with some de facto deregulation of the practice of law (nonlawyers performing tasks once regarded as the sole province of attorneys), there is a growing need for attorneys to help rectify problems or settle disputes. Some lawyers who harbor a desire to resolve disputes select estate planning to obtain the best of both worlds: a challenging office practice and a varied and sophisticated controversy specialty. The first requisite to that switch-hitting approach is knowing how things *should* be done, so as to know when they were done improperly.

Personal Counseling

Many traditional estate planners are meeting their clients' greater needs by becoming full service personal counselors who advise generations of family members about their myriad legal and related needs. Some attorneys report that their practice has evolved so that they are the primary provider of legal and other services relating to their clients'

---

4. See also RESTATEMENT (THIRD) OF THE LAW GOVERNING LAWYERS §74(2) (1999), stating that an ethics violation does not create a cause of action but may be considered on the question of lack of proper care.

wealth. They resolve legal questions of traditional estate planning dimensions, issues related to the operation of a closely held business, health care or retirement planning problems, conflict of interest and ethics concerns, and nonlegal questions such as how to make money work more profitably for the family. These lawyers are a new generation of specialist. In a sense, they are more generalized specialists who encompass more areas in their practice, rather than fewer.

As an indication of this generalized practice, consider a client whose child was arrested for driving under the influence or who is subject to domestic abuse. For several reasons that client is more likely to seek help from the lawyer who drafted the estate plan than from a lawyer who reorganized the family business or did a real estate deal or fixed an employment problem. A law school curriculum designed to encompass all the areas touched by an estate planner likely would include courses in property law (including joint ownership, encumbrances, gifts, and future interests); trusts and estates (including intestacy, powers of appointment, future interests, and fiduciary administration); income, corporate, partnership, and wealth transfer taxation; income taxation of trusts, estates, grantors, and beneficiaries; state, local, and foreign tax; business associations and business planning; estate planning; accounting theory; social security and retirement benefits law; elderlaw; and domestic relations or family law. This book presumes that only the first two courses are prerequisites. It assumes that you have no knowledge of taxation, because it is designed to be accessible to the greatest number of readers who can assist the greatest number of clients. The specialized knowledge you need is provided as we go along.

To comprehend the nature of such a practice, imagine to whom an instantly wealthy winner of the state lottery would turn for help in dealing with all that money. An estate planner is the specialist in the legal profession who is able to provide that guidance, along with more sophisticated assistance to clients with far more complicated needs. Some attorneys decide that they cannot afford the learning-curve expense involved in keeping up-to-date in this ever changing environment. They leave their clients without the services they need. Because these clients are not served adequately elsewhere, the new breed of estate planning attorney is called upon to represent the client as the specialist the client consults first. Moreover, many estate planners accept so many referrals from other lawyers that "boutique" firms doing only estate planning and counseling are commonplace. As boutique lawyers, they don't represent the risk of piracy (diverting the client's other work from the referring lawyer), and therefore are more popular as a referral object than the mega firms that may have separate departments staffed with multiple lawyers who collectively could accomplish the same tasks.

Networking

Attorneys provide personal counseling often wisely conclude that they are unable or unwilling to handle every type of issue or problem, legal or otherwise, that arises in the context of a client engagement. These lawyers become a direct service-provider and a "clearinghouse" of legal and other services for their clients. Sometimes they identify and engage other specialists who can perform necessary services while overseeing the total representation and ascertaining that the product of these referred services is properly integrated into the client's overall situation. There also are a growing number of miniature "family offices" headed by the former estate planner. In either role the attorney replicates a law firm by locating independent service-providers to whom various tasks could be referred, much like a medical profession general practice "family doctor" or internist who refers patients to other specialists when appropriate.

Yet another practice format is for the attorney (or perhaps a group of attorneys) to form a captive organization (perhaps a subsidiary of the attorney's own firm or an entity owned by a number of otherwise unrelated attorneys, akin to a lawyers' title co-operative). Referrals are made to this entity because it allows the attorneys to maintain better control over the cost to the client. It also allows a better form of oversight in terms of hiring personnel in the service-providing organization. And it affords a better review of all the different pieces that go into the final product. There is some debate whether this third form of ancillary business activity by lawyers is appropriate, as discussed in Chapter 3 at pages 22 through 27 on ethics involving conflicts of interest and lack of independent professional judgment.

Although the most promising or appropriate of these formats is something on which most attorneys will not agree, two things are clear. First, although there may be substantial similarities or overlap, this practice and its networking or referral aspects is not the same as "financial planning." Financial planning is one of numerous functions that could be performed by an attorney or referred to a third party, but the term "financial planning" does not do justice to the scope and complexity of the services that an estate planner directly or indirectly might provide. Furthermore, unlike some financial planners, the estate planner avoids the ethical concerns that flow from deriving commissions on the sale of financial products. Second, the most important aspect of this form of practice is that the estate planner remains in control of the planning and services provided to the client, and can oversee and ensure that each element of the planning is properly performed and integrated. The client need not worry about missing pieces to the puzzle presented by the client's situation.

Perhaps the most difficult aspect of the attorney's relationship with clients is how to refer aspects of the planning to other professionals. For a lawyer in a large law firm, this aspect may involve referral of certain tasks to other lawyers in the firm, or to non-lawyers, but typically not to lawyers outside the firm. Lawyers who are not in a large firm may delegate aspects to outside lawyers and non-lawyers alike. In this respect, the legal profession is light-years behind the medical profession, with many lawyer referral arrangements being poorly analyzed, structured, or supervised. Lawyers who practice in a setting that makes such referrals relevant should consider establishing a referral network and procedure.

To address this problem, the Real Property, Probate and Trust Law Section of the American Bar Association developed a comprehensive manual on how to engage in referral arrangements, LAW OFFICE WITHOUT WALLS, A HANDBOOK FOR THE CORRESPONDENT RELATIONSHIP AMONG ATTORNEYS (1987) covers such important questions as what type of referral relationships are available; how to identify consultants; how to structure the financial arrangement between the client and the two advisors; maintaining malpractice liability insurance and drafting hold harmless provisions; and the ethical aspects of referrals. The manual originally was designed to assist rural lawyers. Typically they are the primary source of legal services available to their clients, but in many cases they find the law has become so sophisticated that they must rely on specialists to supply expertise. These American Bar Association materials are equally relevant, however, to lawyers who are highly skilled in some aspects of a representation (in most cases being business or estate planning) but are responsible for other aspects of the client's affairs and must secure expert assistance to avoid committing malpractice.

One-Stop-Shopping

As the foregoing illustrates, many clients want "one-stop-shopping" for their financial and related needs.

Many clients who come to a lawyer for a will or estate planning . . . want someone to tackle virtually every aspect of their present and future financial life. They want someone to visualize the big picture and to paint it for them in detail, present and future, after having analyzed it and formulated recommendations.

Eubank, *The Future for Estate Lawyers*, 10 REAL PROP., PROB. & TRUST J. 223, 224 (1975). The financial planning and multiple disciplinary practice concepts are, in large part, responses to clients who want a single advisor to help them deal with all their financial and related problems, whether those problems involve estate planning, retirement planning, family or health law, investment advice, business counseling, property management, or other matters.

For these clients, probably the most important single element they hope to find in an advisor is someone they trust. In most cases their relationship with an estate planner provides exactly this element, often to a degree that cannot be duplicated by other professionals. Thus, from the attorney's perspective, it is essential to learn how to provide all the services needed by a client, either directly or through referrals, in a manner that justifies the client's trust. The client is better served with such arrangements, and the attorney better manages the personal counseling engagement and ensures better overall results for the client.

Fiduciary Services

Similar to one-stop-shopping for personal counseling, many clients need an individual to perform fiduciary services for themselves and their beneficiaries. Especially on the East coast, private trust operations conducted by law firms satisfy a desperate need of many clients who, for whatever reason, have no other satisfactory candidate to serve as their fiduciary. In addition, some attorneys provide fiduciary services because they are better able to satisfy individual client needs than traditional fiduciaries. And some attorneys serve as fiduciaries simply because it pays well.

Attorneys who wish to serve their clients' fiduciary needs must consider the costs involved, the personnel required, the standard of care to which they will be held, the potential for malpractice liability (and whether their existing insurance coverage protects them), and whether any investment advice will be incident to the practice of law or will make it necessary or desirable to register as an investment adviser.[5] Perhaps most important, they will need to avoid even the appearance of impropriety, in the form of conflicts of interest, overreaching, or self-dealing, all as discussed in Chapter 3 at pages 24, 28, and 55-56 on ethics. There is danger in being an inept fiduciary: don't consider this as a casual sidelight to your practice, no matter how lucrative or tempting it appears.

The Intangible Element

Estate planners have numerous career opportunities. The psychic benefits that attorneys derive from this practice come from the people with whom they deal, the close client contact and clients' strong reliance on their counsel, the interpersonal and counseling skills that are involved and, for some, lifestyle differences between this practice and that experienced by other attorneys. Estate planning and personal counseling are services that most individuals need (regardless of wealth), they reach into the lives of virtually every person, and the work is challenging, gratifying, and remunerative. It is not, however, for everyone. Consider the following

---

5. See Investment Advisers Act of 1940, 15 U.S.C. §80b-2(a)(11)(B): "'Investment adviser' . . . does not include . . . any lawyer . . . whose performance of [investment advisory] services is solely incident to the practice of his profession . . . ." And see id. §80b-3(b)(3), providing an exception from the registration requirements if fewer than 15 clients are represented and the adviser does not hold out as providing such services.

testimonial (from a transcript of a professional estate planners' association meeting):

> The reality is that, in a large firm, the trusts and estates department is not the driving force in terms of numbers of people and the perception of the community. If I were starting practice anew and if my principal purpose was to try to be a major force in a large law firm, I would not select trusts and estates as an area of practice. That's not my objective in life, however. I've seen enough of the driving forces in major firms and the style of practice and the kinds of people with whom I would deal and I would rather be a trusts and estates practitioner or a personal lawyer. There is much that gives us a greater satisfaction and worth. The practice is different but I think in the major firms the lawyers involved in personal law are the heart and soul of the institution. They tend to be the ones who relate to the outside world and are involved more likely than not in professional activity and have a far more well-rounded and diversified practice.
>
> We have a different kind of existence, we play a different role in the profession. We are serving a major piece of society and we have the satisfaction of knowing that we have a highly varied practice.

As expressed by another commentator:

> The trust-and-estate field is the one branch of the legal profession that specializes in [helping] . . . people build, maintain, and protect families. . . . You help clients provide for spouses, children, parents, friends, [to] . . . channel the noblest human aspirations into workable means. . . . The trust-and-estate lawyer can make a boast that comes honestly to the lips of too few lawyers. It is that virtually every human being you touch in the course of your work is better off for your having been there.

Langbein, *The Twentieth-Century Revolution in Family Wealth Transmission and the Future of the Probate Bar*, 14 THE PROBATE LAWYER 1, 46-47 (1988). With these thoughts in mind, we turn to an aspect of estate planning and personal counseling that often gets lost in a tax-oriented shuffle. We address it now at the beginning of this course, and come back to it periodically all the way through. It is worth remembering at all times, in all circumstances.

Interpersonal Aspects of Personal Counseling

Mastery of technical legal skills is a challenge but it is not the most difficult aspect of successful client representation. Instead, especially for lawyers not yet experienced in interpersonal relations, it is the need to keep the human equation of the relationship in focus and avoid being lured to other aspects of the chore that are less important to the client. In a word, psychological or interpersonal aspects of the counselor's role must be kept in mind when representing the *people* who are your clients.

For example, estate planning interviews are a critical component of the engagement. It is essential that you discover or develop your personal "style" and hone your counseling techniques, because the way you begin the representation may set the tone for your entire relation. You know the expression about not getting a second chance to set a first impression. It is hard to cause someone who formed a first impression to realize that they pegged you wrong and should relate to you differently. The tone you set from the first meeting or telephone conversation likely will either create or imperil the trust that clients need to feel in you before allowing you to truly "represent" them.

As you can well imagine, every estate planner has a slightly different style, all their own, and it either "works" for them or it stands in their way. I could no more mimic your personal style than you could emulate mine, although we both could learn something useful from each other about how to put clients at ease, how to make the most of the limited time spent with a client, and how best to establish the rapport that is critical to effective client representation. The important aspect here is that you *think* about who *you* are, how you relate to people, how people respond to you, and ways that you can improve on that critical aspect of your client representation. Truly, it isn't just "what" you know that counts in estate planning. A large chunk of your success will be a function of whether you can relate to the people you serve, and they to you.

If you could be better at your people skills (and few of us could not improve), now is a great time to begin thinking about how to make that happen. Focus on how others interact, how they make strangers feel comfortable with them, how they command or earn respect or trust. Try to look in the mirror and think about how these things work for you. If you are less successful than you would like to be at these critical elements (and who is not?), start asking the hard, embarrassing questions from people you love and trust: what must you do to be more effective in relating to people? Putting yourself in their shoes always works an improvement, as does being nice, friendly, and polite: all the things you learned (or should have) as a child. A heartfelt smile still goes a long way toward making someone feel welcome.

Some aspects of the interrelation can be learned easily. For example, imagine being your client, in terms of the message you send by your demeanor, your dress, the staff you employ, their attitude and grace, and the office atmosphere you create and control. Can you remember a job interview, perhaps a doctor visit, or some other situation in which you were quite ill at ease, uncertain about your place in another person's environment and what to expect, anxious about what would be expected of you or how you would be perceived? What could your host have done differently to put you more at ease? Your client may feel the same way coming to your office, meeting with you for the first time. Does your office décor, your staff, and your style say the right things to visitors? How do clients perceive your work space, and what message do you intend to send? Are you intimidating, with a massive desk set between you and your guests, imposing books on the shelves, imponderable journals on the side table or in the reception room, diplomas, trophies, and honorifics on the wall? Is that how you want to be perceived, first or lasting?

What about the placement of your furniture: is the desk a barrier or did you arrange your space to foster conversation? Perhaps you would do well to sit around a small table or even in an upholstered chair setting such that you are removed from your computer, the phone, the piles and mess on your desk, and other reminders that your client is infringing on your principal work space and time. Think about "seeing" with your client's eyes. Literally! Does the glare from a window prevent you from seeing your client's eyes because of the reflection in their eyeglasses, which may prevent you from reading their visual reactions? Much more important for many older clients, does that glare hurt their eyes such that they are in pain when facing you and the window behind, and literally cannot wait to leave your office? In a word, have you sought to put your clients at ease, or do you intimidate them (or worse)?

You might do well to cruise the hallway in an office environment, making a mental note of your visceral reaction when observing the work spaces and the furniture layouts of various people. Try to put your personal feelings in touch with what you experience in those places, even if you don't understand *why* you react positively or otherwise. Attempt to catalog the kinds of things that seem to make a place feel inviting or off putting. After a while you will discover that people and the places they occupy have an impact on their client relations. There are ways to arrange your space and even forms of decoration if you want formality, rigidity, or sharp dividing lines in your representation. But if you want to place clients at ease, there are things and arrangements that are better suited to that purpose. Experiment, judge reactions, get a feel for it from the client's side of the environment you create, until you generate the kind of atmosphere that works to your client's best interest in the representation you want to foster.

There are other, more substantive things to focus upon. For example, are you prone to be judgmental about your client's wishes, family, foibles and flaws? Shaffer, *Some Thoughts on the Psychology of Estate Planning*, 113 TRUSTS & ESTATES 568 (1974), wrote about an attorney who opined that it was wrong (not "the proper way") for a client to want division of an estate per capita among a child and two grandchildren, in equal thirds. Shaffer wrote that he was appalled that the attorney actually said so to the client, and suggested that the client's "psychological satisfaction" through disposition of an accumulated estate is "not to be scoffed at." Yet clients need to know whether a desired plan is likely to create problems, and whether the solution crafted to address those problems is likely to be worse than the original objective sought by the client.

The point is that there is a line between being sensitive to the client's feelings about such an important endeavor as the disposition of an inheritance and doing a disservice by not advising the client about alternatives and the experience of doing things one way or another. You need not opine that distribution of an estate at the age of 18 or 81 is "too darn early" or "way too late" to point out the dangers of an inheritance before the age of maturity or after the greatest need for wealth is long past. Note also that each of these things may betray your personal prejudice: what *is* the "right" age to receive an inheritance? We all harbor a notion in that regard, but nothing makes one person's prejudice more compelling than another.

An important exercise for you during this course of study is to identify your personal opinions and quirks about various topics relevant to the estate planning engagement. Do you, for example, have preconceived ideas about the better pattern for wealth transmission, the use of dead hand controls, the role of women, or of children in a family business? Do you instinctively favor per stirpes division of an estate over per capita, or per capita at each generation? And do you think like a beneficiary or like a donor when you conjure the "right" age for an inheritance? You may not be surprised to learn that you still think like a beneficiary, notwithstanding that your client wants you to think like a donor. As this course unfolds, consider your approach to various problems revealed in these kinds of quirks and whether the personal prejudices we all possess are appropriate to your role as counselor.

Author Shaffer recommended that an attorney not be reluctant to state to a client that "I don't like that" about an aspect of the plan that seems inappropriate to the attorney. But he also admonished that the attorney must avoid passing judgment by saying that a proposal is "wrong" or "bad." Is there a better way to deal with such an issue without being judgmental at all, and is there a reason to be as forthright as Shaffer suggests?

Shaffer also suggested that clients can tell the sometimes subtle difference between an attorney's sharing feelings about a client's desires and being judgmental. Clients can detect other subtle prejudices as well. One of the most prevalent of these is sexism, manifested in numerous ways but often revealed by an attorney's assumption that the man in a husband-wife representation is the "lead" or primary client. You may discover some glaring will or trust drafting errors made because the attorney wrote a man's document with care and then carelessly tried to "flip" it to serve as the woman's plan as well — in the process failing to make all the appropriate gender specific or gender related changes.

Sometimes prejudice is revealed in such a benign manner as use of the masculine gender in speech that could refer to either spouse as the client. You will notice in reading this book that it is gender neutral to the fullest possible extent, mainly to persuade you that it is easy enough to write and speak without gender bias. Hopefully it also will help you get in the habit of being aware of sexist assumptions. This can be important in both interpersonal and economic currency and can be illustrated by a simple, rhetorical question. Assume that you represent a husband and wife; he has been the breadwinner and most of their wealth is in his name. In your dealings with them you assumed that he would die first and you treated him with more deference than his wife. If she *is* the surviving spouse and has the choice, and if she perceives your subtle (and maybe not so subtle) clues that you regard her as an appendage to "the real" representation, do you think she will hire you as attorney for the estate after his death?

The following excerpts also indicate of the type of attitudes you might expect to develop as you become experienced in estate planning. Knecht, *The Human Equation in Estate Planning*, 114 TRUSTS & ESTATES 854 (1975), reported that his main focus as a rookie estate planner "was on the technique of the business — new ways that you could utilize trusts, wills, . . . and all the rest. Part of the fun was in being able to move property around as you wished, and part was in the excitement of saving taxes in the process." He reports that "wishes of the individual clients were always paramount" but admits that the client's "deep inner needs and feelings did not too much enter into my field of awareness." At some point, all that changed:

It seems that the primary matter of concern is first to find out what the clients are thinking about — where their main feeling lines run. This encompasses not only the material things with which we are dealing, but also how [they] regard the personalities in the total framework. One of the great insights that has come to me is that the *beliefs* people profess are many, many times almost the opposite of their real *value* structures, that is, the way they *act out* situations when they have to apply those beliefs. And I'm far more concerned with that final action . . . .

In a less than direct way, Knecht says something that is stressed throughout this book. Many newly minted attorneys can't resist the urge to "try out" all the tools of their trade by seeking opportunities to employ all the wonderful tax or related planning techniques of the moment. As Knecht admits, over time most counselors learn to resist that urge and to avoid creating a twenty thousand dollar masterpiece if a two thousand dollar plan is really all the client wants or needs. In the context of estate planning with an eye on the tax laws, this sometimes is referred to as not letting the "tax tail wag the family-planning dog." In addition, he surely is right in saying that "if you want to save taxes, there will be some price that will have to be paid in some part of the picture. Most commonly, this is in the form of surrendering a freedom."

A significant percentage of the fancy planning techniques recommended to clients are rejected. Clients shun those recommendations in most cases simply because they are not what the client wants or perceives to be necessary. Sometimes the price to be paid, or the risk of the plan failing, is too great. To guard against the tendency to over plan, it makes sense to ask, often in the initial interview, what the client would do with his or her property if there were no tax or other laws. Only then can you present suggestions that work the desirable goal of minimizing taxes or other intrusions without corrupting the desired family plan. This is not to say that you should not learn techniques or that you should be reluctant to use them when appropriate. It is natural and essential for new lawyers to master that aspect of the craft first. Rather, use caution until experience can be your guide in judging whether good technical planning should bow to more important personal goals of the client.

A wise estate planner wrote the following list of professional skills required by successful estate planners:

Some of the characteristics I have seen in the best practitioners are that they are people-oriented and caring, sensitive and thoughtful about relationships, nonjudgmental and kind, they listen well and summarize or interpret accurately, they are perceptive (attuned to verbal and nonverbal signals) and communicate effectively (most especially without legalese). They like challenges, want to be involved, exhibit leadership and accept responsibility. They have learned to organize, define objectives, build confidence, facilitate, and cooperate.

What other skills or characteristics would you add to such a list? You might reflect on which of these you have (or are likely to develop), and consider how different you think other types of lawyers are from those who select estate planning for a professional specialty. In that regard, surveys of estate planners reveal that they *are* different individuals by personality than your "typical" lawyer, be it a litigator or otherwise. See Moore & Pennell, *Survey of the Profession II*, 30 U. MIAMI INST. EST. PLAN. ¶1502 (1996). You can "test" your personality profile and compare it to survey results by going online and searching for "Myers-Briggs" or the "Keirsey Temperament Sorter." All kinds of folks are excellent estate planners, but some square pegs don't conform so well to a round hole. The question to ask yourself as we turn to more substantive issues is: are you cut out to be an estate planner? This is a good time to begin that introspection.

Chapter 2

GETTING STARTED

Some clients' reasons for initiating estate planning are straightforward and pleasant, such as the birth of a child, a planned trip, or an impending marriage. Other clients may be motivated by a desire to keep property out of the hands of an expectant heir, fear of adverse tax results, an impending divorce, knowledge of a fatal illness, or other equally disturbing factors. Most importantly, estate planning disturbs many people because it is a tacit recognition of their mortality.

You must earn your clients' confidence as quickly as possible, because you will gather relevant information and inquire into personal details of their lives. You also must be sensitive to client reasons for planning their estates, their feelings about the process, and problems that the estate planning process may create or exacerbate, as you discuss personal circumstances, tax matters, dispositive devices, assets, fees, and other substantive matters.

Gathering Information

Now and again you will be asked to prepare estate planning documents without being told all the relevant facts. Be extraordinarily careful with such a situation, because it is a prescription for error. Almost without exception you must know the facts about the client's situation before performing any estate planning representation. Many clients are unwilling to reveal information about themselves, especially to someone they don't really know. To succeed as an estate planner you must become both a counselor to your client and in many respects a confidant. You must acquire basic and sometimes very private information without appearing either too curious or too impersonal.

Does it seem odd to you that some clients refuse to admit their need for estate planning services, or that you may need to educate them about the need for expert specialized estate planning guidance before they will even consider the value of full disclosure to make that planning feasible? Don't be surprised, for example, if a client comes to see you only because a spouse or trusted professional advisor has insisted that their estate plan be done. Don't be reluctant to discuss the value of undertaking the task and explaining what the process will involve, all to put the client at ease with the notion of revealing necessary information to you. Even a client referred to you by another professional advisor may not be fully aware of the need for estate planning and what it may entail. Beware, for example, of a client who is thinking in terms of "just a simple will" and assumes that you don't need to know specific asset information to accomplish that "routine" drafting chore.

After your client understands the scope of normal estate planning, you must discuss the potential costs involved and establish a fee agreement, preferably reduced to writing. You should inform the client about the potential tax and other costs of administering and transferring the estate, because eventually you should consider ways to minimize those costs. Although attorneys are notoriously reluctant to discuss fees and costs, a frank discussion early in the process often is the best way to avoid later problems. Not surprisingly, frequently cost is foremost in the minds of clients, and an early discussion tends to put them at ease. Notice, however, that you must understand the client's situation before any of this can be done. Thus, as you gather information pertinent to the estate planning you are about to provide, recognize that the extent of this fact gathering may differ, consistent with the extent of the engagement and any limitations imposed by the client.

Usually you (or someone under your supervision) will gather the facts before establishing an appropriate plan and drafting necessary documents. This is true regardless of the origin of the representation (whether you were the initial contact or became involved by referral). Obtaining information that is pertinent to the circumstance is subject to limitations imposed by the amount of time available to perform the estate planning process, the relative costs involved, the client's willingness to reveal or produce needed information, and the extent of the particular estate planning task that you have agreed to perform. For example, you need not obtain detailed information about every investment or asset the client owns if you are not responsible for the client's overall financial plan. Knowing asset classes (e.g., stocks, bonds, realty) and general value usually will suffice. Nor is it normally your responsibility independently to verify facts or other representations made by the client in a typical engagement. It may be wise to establish a procedure by which the client confirms the accuracy of information reported to you and to create a record that this was done, but usually you need not go beyond an inquiry or request for information if the client is unwilling to respond or unable to comply.

Estate planners differ, sometimes greatly, on how best to solicit necessary information. Some prefer that the client complete a questionnaire, sometimes even before the first office visit. This requires the client to sift through relevant information (files, drawers, and boxes) and allows you, during that first meeting, to clarify or correct the information provided, to obtain additional information as suggested by answers on the initial questionnaire, and then to concentrate on the client's needs as revealed in the questionnaire. This approach is not feasible if the client is infirm or marginally incompetent. Some clients will respond better to a request for information only after a conference in which you have developed some rapport, discussed the nature of the process, and explained the need for all this disclosure.

Some estate planners prefer the client to complete a questionnaire *after* the first interview because it is easier to determine whether to use a long or short form (or to forego the questionnaire approach entirely and interview the client directly). Attorneys also differ on how to conduct the client interview. Some attorneys believe an effective interview can be conducted by an associate, paralegal, or other nonlawyer member of the estate planner's staff. Others insist the lead attorney should interview the client. Moreover, estate planners disagree about whether it is best to use a less than comprehensive questionnaire; some argue that many (most?) clients are overwhelmed by this task so they opt for a shorter form that elicits only basic information about the client's assets, philosophy, and dispositive wishes. The detailed approach may trigger additional thought by the client about these matters, but a long form questionnaire may overwhelm, give offense, or discourage further action by clients of more modest means, needs, or capacity.

The most obvious function served by a client questionnaire is to help identify assets and the amount of wealth involved. This should not be overestimated, however, because some clients will refuse to reveal relevant information or will forget to mention assets, especially those that have little or no tangible value to them during life (a common example is employment related benefits like group term life or disability insurance and a retirement fund). Often a questionnaire is designed to allow you to conduct a follow up interview that reveals other less obvious facts. The questionnaire also may educate your client by focusing attention on the nature and extent of various assets and the potential recipients involved.

A final difference in approach relates to the perceived need to inspect or review various client documents. At a minimum the client needs to produce any existing power of attorney, will or trust, and any document granting a power of appointment or other benefits that could cause inclusion of nonprobate property in the client's estate. Additional useful documents are insurance policies, beneficiary designations for insurance and retirement benefits, and agreements that impose obligations on the estate (such as prenuptial or property settlement agreements). In many cases you will not know enough about the client to ask for copies of these documents until after the initial client interview.

Sample client questionnaires are reproduced in Chapter 19. No matter how basic or detailed you choose to be, the following information is likely to be important to most estate planning engagements.

Family and Personal Data

The correct names of the client and all family members, their dates of birth, marriage(s), divorce(s), occupation, employment (to verify employee benefit information), and the dependency status of various family members (or others) are basic. It may seem silly to ask the client to provide all names in writing, but few things are as embarrassing (and as easily avoidable) as producing documents that misspell the name of the client or a beneficiary. For all of these individuals, it may be appropriate to inquire about obligations arising from marriages or divorce, about special health problems (either physical or mental), adoptions, nonmarital children, children of the "new biology," and domicile. Discussions about some of these items may require that you meet privately with each spouse if you are representing a married couple, because they may need to reveal information that they never have told their spouse; this raises significant ethical and conflict of interest questions addressed in Chapter 3.

You also may need to ask questions to determine domicile for state law purposes: employment, residence(s), location of moveable assets, drivers licenses, and automobile or voter registrations. It is wise to inquire of married clients about prior residences, particularly if they may have lived in a (non)community property state (whichever differs from your own state property law) at any time during the marriage. Also ask about military service; National Service Life Insurance or other government benefits may be available. Because the estate tax marital deduction is denied if a surviving spouse is not a citizen of the United States (unless special planning is applied), you also *must* inquire in every situation about the spouses' citizenship.

Family and Personal Objectives

The questionnaire or client interview must ascertain the client's desires about beneficiaries, including provisions for a surviving spouse, descendants, parents or other relatives, friends, employees, dependents, and charities. Often it is instructive to get a sense of the client's feelings about the use and protection of wealth before you suggest ways to structure various gifts. This may entail asking whether disposition should be by outright bequest or only in trust, inquiring about the exercise of life insurance or retirement plan options, or about exercising powers of appointment. The issue may arise whether lifetime gifts are desirable. Other important factors are the client's attitude about fiduciaries (corporate, professional individuals, family members, and others), and the client's desires concerning guardians for any minors or incapacitated beneficiaries. The client should note other dispositive matters of particular concern, and you may need to prompt the client regarding any special needs of various family members or beneficiaries. Recognizing that the client's desires regarding all of the foregoing choices are paramount, you should be prepared to discuss their relative advantages and disadvantages.

Financial Data

You need to determine the client's assets and their value largely to ascertain the effect of state, federal, or foreign wealth transfer taxes that may apply, and to evaluate whether administrative problems relating to the form or location of assets are likely. For example, a valuable collection of tangible art objects will generate insurance, storage, shipping, and valuation problems after a client's death or incapacity, and realty located in another jurisdiction may pose ancillary administration issues that easily could be avoided with proper planning.

Although most estate planners are not competent — and many are not willing — to render general investment advice, a basic asset evaluation will reveal whether the client has serious diversification problems, opportunities involving basis[1] or other income tax attributes, shared ownership issues, and liquidity problems. Because asset mix and values are likely to change (perhaps significantly) over a client's lifetime, a precise listing of assets by type, fair market value, and basis may not be worth the effort required to produce it. Instead, a net worth statement that provides general financial information may be the easiest single item to obtain.

Although you should obtain information about all major assets or asset groups that the client owns, a client may fail to complete a questionnaire that is too burdensome or imposing. Thus, the questionnaire should compromise between an inquiry that provides essential information and educates the client about the need to consider certain basic investment and portfolio issues, and one that is merely a make-work turn-off. Be sure to obtain information about liabilities as well as assets, particularly if debts may be accelerated by death or a transfer of encumbered property.

A substantial amount of additional information will be required if you agree to prepare a complete financial plan for the client (in addition to preparing an estate plan). You may need to know income tax basis, investment reviews, property insurance, disability or medical insurance, information regarding cash flow, and so forth. Otherwise, keeping in mind the scope of the engagement and any limitations imposed by the client, and assuming the circumstances are favorable, you should:

- Determine how assets, such as bank accounts, real estate, stocks, and bonds are titled (for example, in the client's name, in a spouse's name, as joint tenants or tenants by the entireties, or as tenants in common, and whether any is community property).

- Establish the status of existing business interests, such as stock in closely held corporations, partnership interests, sole proprietorships, real estate, oil and gas interests, or other joint ventures. If real estate is involved, you probably will not need to

---

1. Basis is an income tax concept that is used to calculate gain or loss and that informs a variety of other concepts (such as the depreciation deduction). For our purposes it essentially means the taxpayer's cost or investment in the asset. See §1011 et seq.

examine the legal description, but it may help to inspect the deed or title and any title insurance policies and perhaps to glance at a survey. It will be helpful to ascertain that homestead has been elected if the property could qualify. If a business is involved, you may want to review the corporate records, partnership or operating agreements, and any existing redemption, buy-sell, shareholders, option, or similar agreement. In these cases, a meeting with the client's accountant or other business advisors also may be wise.

- Special care is required with respect to insurance and it is wise not to take the client's or the insurance agent's word for any information that you can verify (unless the policy is insubstantial), because the risk and attendant cost of an error at any of several levels is significant. Ascertain the amount of insurance on the client's life, the type of policy involved, and the options selected or available. Be particularly careful to review the exercise of any policy options and other incidents of ownership (such as applicable beneficiary designations) and confirm who possesses all available incidents of ownership. Often it will be impossible to deal with life insurance effectively without complete and accurate information about the insured and owner of the policy, the face amount of the coverage, date of issue, carrier, policy number, primary and contingent beneficiary designations, accidental death benefit, policy loan interest rate, outstanding loans, basis, premium (and how it is being paid), and the current dividend option. In addition, you must ascertain whether the policy is community property and whether prior planning has attempted to remove the proceeds of the policy from the client's gross estate for wealth transfer tax purposes. Also inquire about disability insurance, especially if provided in the workplace.

- Investigate retirement benefits available to the client and question the client regarding any nonqualified deferred compensation, stock option, or other benefits. You may need to review the summary plan description provided by the client's employer if substantial benefits are involved. In all cases you should verify beneficiary designations, income tax consequences of the plan and any of its options, and (in extraordinary circumstances) you may need to study copies of the applicable plan documents.

- Obtain information regarding unusual assets, such as patents, copyrights, intellectual property and other unusual intangibles, collections, valuable works of art, or other valuable items of tangible personal property. Also inquire about vested or contingent remainder interests, expectancies, intrafamily loans or advancements, powers of appointment, and trusts of which the client is a beneficiary or trustee or over which the client may be deemed to have a power of appointment.

Tax Information

Be sure to ascertain whether the client made gifts in prior years and whether they eroded the unified credit and generation-skipping transfer tax exemption that otherwise is available. Although you often will not like the answer, you need to inquire whether gift tax returns were filed as required by law and you may want to obtain copies of both income and gift tax returns for prior years. Determine the approximate income of the client, the client's spouse, and any children who are being considered as part of a dynastic plan. This will give some indication about future growth potential and the opportunity for income shifting. It also may allow a double check on information solicited previously about gifts, employment, and assets, and may confirm dependency status and indicate whether disability insurance planning is relevant.

Consultations

You should consider whether other professional advisers should be involved in the planning process at an early stage if a useful relationship exists between the client and accountants, financial or investment advisors, insurance counselors, fiduciaries, or other legal counsel. Coordination with them (with the client's consent) is advisable and proper if their input may be valuable in preparing a proper estate plan. Indeed, in many cases these individuals will have done much of the investigation into facts that you need and can save you valuable time and protect you from errors or blind spots that otherwise might cause your planning to be flawed. Also be sensitive to the dynamics involved if the client has selected fiduciaries, especially if the fiduciary was the source of the recommendation that you be retained. As discussed in Chapter 3, serious ethical issues can arise if a fiduciary is involved in the early stages of a representation but you later determine that it might be better if that particular fiduciary not be used.

The Engagement Letter

Estate planners do not focus exclusively on postmortem aspects of an estate plan to the exclusion of lifetime needs and objectives. Instead, often they are employed to advise clients on comprehensive lifetime planning as well as disposition of the client's estate after death, in each case in a manner that effects the client's wishes with minimum expense, taxation, disruption, and anxiety.

Many clients will experience some form of disability during life that will present a need for assistance in physical care, asset management, or both. Pay attention to providing for the cost of medical care, including insurance or other protection against catastrophic or extended medical costs. In addition, the planning process should provide an appropriate mechanism to deal with disability. Otherwise it may be necessary to conduct the client's affairs in a judicially supervised proceeding, which frequently can be cumbersome and expensive. Even absent a disability, some clients will want help in managing their affairs. Before beginning the representation, therefore, the attorney and client should reach some understanding about the scope of the representation and, in some states, this understanding must be reduced to a written agreement. Even if not mandated, an engagement letter usually is a good idea.

The engagement may entail any or all of the following:

- Living wills that express a preference about medical procedures in terminal illness situations, and powers of attorney for health care that permit substituted judgment in other, less dramatic medical care situations.

- Durable powers of attorney for financial matters that provide a simple alternative to a guardianship, conservatorship, or living trust, and permit the agent to accomplish the client's needs and objectives after the client becomes disabled.

- Inter vivos trusts that combine in one instrument the potential for lifetime management of property, succession of management upon disability, and disposition following death.

- Buy-sell agreements that make appropriate provision for disposition of stock upon retirement, disability, and death.

- Arrangements to defer payment of taxes under §6166 with respect to any qualifying business interest.

- Income tax related transactions that have favorable inter vivos tax implications (such as sale of a principal personal residence), and use of the annual exclusion and the unified transfer tax credit to make gifts. An estate often can effectively be reduced by transfers that qualify for the gift tax marital deduction or gifts of property that shift future income or appreciation.

- An irrevocable life insurance trust that creates wealth and, if necessary, liquidity in a format that avoids inclusion in the estates of either the client or the client's surviving spouse.

- Taking steps to insure that the client's estate is sufficient to adequately support surviving dependents. You may appropriately play a role in instituting and encouraging the process of estate enhancement. Some of the more readily available estate augmentation devices include life insurance, qualified retirement benefit plans, Keogh accounts, IRAs, and various education saving and investment programs.

The text of an engagement letter might look similar to those found in Chapter 19. As you read them, consider such things as whether they set the interest rate you would choose on late payments, the proper retainer you would feel comfortable collecting, and the right tone you want to set at the outset of an engagement.

Conflicts of Interest

A conflict of interest may be discovered early in the investigatory phases of an estate planning interview, but often it will not be revealed until the client discloses assets and liabilities. You cannot merely continue to represent the client once a conflict is discovered, at any stage of the estate planning process. Instead, you will need to advise the client that you must withdraw from the representation unless an appropriate resolution can be reached. (See, e.g., Rule 1.7 of the Model Rules of Professional Conduct, stating the proposition that mutual consent, based on full disclosure, will permit continued representation notwithstanding the conflict). For example, as discussed in more detail in Chapter 3, conflicts may develop in drawing estate plans for parents and their children, or for spouses. In addition, a conflict of interest also may require that you withdraw if a client wishes to benefit you or a member of your immediate family. (See, e.g., Rule 1.8(c) of the Model Rules of Professional Conduct, also discussed in Chapter 3.)

Confidentiality

You must preserve the confidentiality of all information revealed in the estate planning process, including information concerning or identifying the client and the client's assets, liabilities, family, and beneficiaries. As noted in the sample engagement letters, you should make it a point to assure a client that facts and documents disclosed during the estate planning process will be kept confidential to the extent the client has not consented to disclosure to others. Otherwise, the client may withhold essential information, and full disclosure usually is essential to proper estate planning.

For example, the client may have a disabled child for whom special provision should be made, or an adopted or nonmarital child who might make an otherwise unexpected claim against the estate. Facts may disclose that it would be unwise for a particular individual to serve as a fiduciary or to receive a substantial amount of property outright. Potential beneficiaries may be inexperienced in investments or may suffer from profligacy, improvidence, substance abuse, or addiction. There may be antagonism between siblings, between children and parents or stepparents. There also may be embarrassing or confidential relationships or histories. Each of these matters could be confronted in the estate plan, but only if fully disclosed.

The point here, as we turn to a more directed study of ethics for estate planners and then to more substantive matters, is that none of these facts is likely to be revealed to you unless you have the client's confidence. To gain that will require that you be conscious about it, work affirmatively to make the client comfortable with the process, and garner the client's trust and respect.

Chapter 3

ETHICS ISSUES

"You Can't Teach Ethics"

The notion seems doubtful that lawyers either have ethics or they don't, and that you cannot improve on that condition. But even if it was true, many attorneys appear to have a strong sense of what is ethical (maybe "proper" or "right" is a better term). More importantly, the vast majority of estate planners[1] are of a personality type that makes them more sensitive than most attorneys to concerns about ethics, conflicts, and propriety. It is part of what drives them to specialize in this area of legal service. What some attorneys (including estate planners) seem to lack, however, is a sense of the issues and problems that can arise in the ethics arena. Moreover, the rules governing the legal profession are not about morality as much as they are guidelines and prohibitions that regulate the practice of law and, as such, are as susceptible to learning as the Internal Revenue Code or a local probate code.

This Chapter seeks to raise your level of consciousness about certain "predictable" ethical dilemmas in estate planning and fiduciary administration in situations that often generate problems or issues. In some situations the ethics issue is clear and the appropriate action is identifiable. In many other cases there is no "correct" response to the problems that are identified. In these circumstances, a good result is recognition of the problem, which must be considered in the context in which it arises. Often, conscious recognition and a sensitivity to these concerns is the best that can be expected.

This Chapter also illustrates this area lacks clear answers and direction because the ethics rules weren't written by or for estate planners. Many of the existing rules don't apply or, if they do apply (which is arguable), they apply woodenly. Many ethics rules that were written from a conflict resolution perspective impose obligations and restrictions that are inappropriate in the planning context. Indeed, if applied literally, some of these rules threaten the very existence of the family counseling that many

---

1. Other professional disciplines have ethics rules but none are as extensive as those affecting lawyers. Most relations involved in this arena fall under the law of Agency, from which most of the obligations and prohibitions found in the ethical rules applicable to lawyers are derived. When the disciplinary rules seem lacking in scope, the default source for guidance always is the law of Agency and, much to the surprise of many readers, that law often is more rigid and demanding than the rules lawyers have articulated in their specialized set of mandates and guidelines. See, e.g., the selected Agency principles reproduced at page 62 of this chapter.

estate planners provide, at a time when that focus is what many clients need and want.

Many of these issues were addressed in the RESTATEMENT (THIRD) OF THE LAW GOVERNING LAWYERS, and improvements are developing all the time. Noted in place are changes in the Model Rules as proposed by the American Bar Association Commission on Evaluation of the Rules of Professional Conduct, commonly known as the ETHICS 2000 COMMISSION, REPORT WITH RECOMMENDATION TO THE HOUSE OF DELEGATES (August 2001). Although these changes are not specifically relevant except as individual states ultimately adopt them, they spotlight issues of interest and concern.

Throughout this Chapter a healthy dose of hesitation seems appropriate, given the subjective and none too precise nature of many of the principles and rules discussed. Studies like that in Moore & Pennell, *Practicing What We Preach: Esoteric or Essential*, 27 U. MIAMI INST. EST. PLAN. ¶1200 (1993), and Moore & Pennell, *Survey of the Profession II*, 30 U. MIAMI INST. EST. PLAN. ¶1500 (1996), are interesting because they show how many estate planners (do not) address these rules, but beware. Minimal compliance or adherence to a "community standard" regarding various situations is not adequate. There is no reasonable level of compliance in the ethics arena that looks to what everyone else is doing, the way there is with respect to some aspects of malpractice liability. There is no acceptable level of compliance short of full compliance with these rules.

Also note: This Chapter makes primary reference to the Model Rules of Professional Conduct promulgated by the American Bar Association. Although a small handful of states have not adopted those standards, they have been embraced in whole or in substantial part in virtually every state, replacing the Disciplinary Rules and Ethical Considerations of the American Bar Association's prior Model Code of Professional Conduct. A practitioner in a state that still imposes the Model Code standards will benefit from a consideration of the more recently developed Model Rules, which establish minimum standards rather than the "aspirational" goals of the Model Code.[2] In this respect, the Model Rules should be regarded as a *lesser* obligation than the Model Code. Moreover, because these are ethics rules, the professional is subject to being judged in the harshest possible light consistent with preserving the profession's responsibility (and opportunity) to govern itself. And no responsible attorney will split hairs on which set of rules is applicable any more than someone knowingly would violate the spirit or the letter of a rule in reliance on the "audit lottery" ("maybe you won't get caught") of ethics enforcement.

In that regard, let's consider an often overlooked aspect of these rules. When there is a violation the appropriate punishment is not a damage award.

---

2. A cross reference table to the old Disciplinary Rules and Ethical Considerations of the Model Code is included among the materials promulgated with the Model Rules.

Rather, it is a sanction (such as a "simple" reprimand, a suspension, or disbarment), for which there is no insurance! Instead, you and your dependents (including your employees and their dependents) pay a hefty price, usually in terms of lost income, which could result in foreclosure or other creditor action if you are unable to service debt obligations as a result. Frankly, you deserve to protect yourself (and all these others who depend on you) from being put in the line of fire under an ethics allegation.

So one way to think about these rules is as *your* protection against the consequences of an ethics complaint (the same way that your professor looks upon the anonymous grading system as a protection against any allegation of impropriety in grading). These rules are designed to protect *you* as much as they protect your clients from you. As you consider the information in this Chapter, it pays to remember how hard you are working to become a lawyer, and to make a commitment not to risk your livelihood over silly aspects of noncompliance if the safe approach is easy to perform. Save your risk taking for challenges that are hard to address, because everyone who depends on you suffers if you can't prove that you did the right thing. Your family, your employees and their families, and your other clients need for you to be able to defend yourself against groundless attack (assuming you did everything right). So you should protect all of them by doing all of this by the numbers, the way a good attorney does anything that is important.

Although compliance with every ethics rule is important, this Chapter does not address several obvious obligations (Model Rule 1.3 to serve clients diligently and Model Rule 1.4 to communicate with the client) that more than a few attorneys violate. These rules involve no real conceptual difficulty for estate planners, and can be addressed simply by paying attention. Instead, this material focuses on ethical issues confronting estate planners that usually fall under the following general categories: (1) conflicts of interest; (2) failure to exercise independent judgment; (3) violation of client confidences; (4) incompetent or inadequate representation; (5) excessive fees; (6) special estate administration concerns; (7) a general sense of duty to the "system"; and (8) misconduct involving solicitation and advertising.

Conflicts of Interest

Easily the most important (and perhaps the most common, enduring, and troubling) ethical dilemmas facing estate planners are conflicts of interest.

[T]he probate, trust and estate planning practitioner is frequently found in a thicket of multiple representations where the conflicts between the various parties' interests are subtle, pervasive, indirect, continuously shifting and, in many instances, even difficult to recognize. . . . The solutions prescribed by the Model Rules —

withdrawal by the attorney or disclosure and consent — . . . frequently will be impractical, expensive and ineffective for the probate and trust attorney and clients.

Link et al., *Developments Regarding the Professional Responsibility of the Estate Planning Lawyer: The Effect of the Model Rules of Professional Conduct*, 22 REAL PROP., PROB. & TR. J. 1, 2 (1987). Compounding the difficulty of this issue is the fact that three separate provisions in the Model Rules speak to conflicts of interest, with differing standards or levels of conflict and different consent requisites.

For example, Model Rule 1.7(a)(1)[3] deals with the representation of multiple clients whose interests are *directly adverse* to each other. This rule applies if an attorney is asked to bring suit against another active client of the attorney. The attorney's duty is to obtain the informed consent, confirmed in writing, of *each* client before undertaking the representation. Seldom is this rule applicable in a normal estate planning practice (except, perhaps, when a disappointed heir seeks to contest a will under which the attorney is acting as advisor to the personal representative).

Model Rule 1.7(a)(2) involves a similar conflict but applies if a client's interests are only *materially limited* by the attorney's representation of another client, a former client, a third person, or the lawyer's own personal interest. This rule *often* applies in a general estate planning practice. Under it, the attorney still must first obtain the informed consent, confirmed in writing, of each client whose representation may be affected. Usually this means that every mutually represented client must be consulted and must consent. In addition, both Rules 1.7(a)(1) and 1.7(a)(2) require the attorney to determine that the attorney will be able to provide competent and diligent representation to each affected client.

According to Comment 18 to Rule 1.7, regarding consent:

An informed consent requires that each affected client be aware of the relevant circumstances and of the material and reasonably foreseeable ways that the conflict could have adverse effects on the interests of that client. See Rule 1.0(e) (informed consent). The information required depends on the nature of the conflict and the nature of the risks involved. When representation of multiple clients

---

3. (a) Except as provided in paragraph (b), a lawyer shall not represent a client if the representation involves a concurrent conflict of interest. A concurrent conflict of interest exists if:

    (1) the representation of one client will be directly adverse to another client;

    (2) there is a significant risk that the representation of one or more clients will be materially limited by the lawyer's responsibilities to another client, a former client or a third person or by a personal interest of the lawyer.

RESTATEMENT (THIRD) OF THE LAW GOVERNING LAWYERS §§209 and 211 (hereafter RESTATEMENT) are the analogous provisions to Model Rules 1.7(a)(1) and (a)(2). Note also that the Ethics 2000 recommendations would alter Rule 1.7 but that these changes must be adopted by each state that relies on the Model Rules as their template, which will take some time.

in a single matter is undertaken, the information must include the implications of the common representation, including possible effects on loyalty, confidentiality and the attorney-client privilege and the advantages and risks involved.

According to Comment 20 to Rule 1.7, consent must be confirmed in writing, so as

to afford the client a reasonable opportunity to consider the risks and alternatives and to raise questions and concerns. . . . [T]he writing is required in order to impress upon clients the seriousness of the decision the client is being asked to make and to avoid disputes or ambiguities that might later occur in the absence of a writing.

Notice that neither Comment requires that the consent itself be in writing. It can be the product of an oral discussion and understanding. But a written follow up (confirmation) is required. Most estate planners commit the understanding or consent to writing just because the attorney ought to be able to prove the bona fides of the representation if the question arises (especially after a client's death). And again, let's make no mistake: when these issues come up, your professional reputation (and maybe career) are on the line. It would be just plain stupid to have done the right thing in dealing with clients and not be able to prove it.

A third rule deals with a new client whose interests are *materially* adverse to those of a former client. Model Rule 1.9[4] requires the *former* client's consent before undertaking such a representation. The difficult aspect of this rule for most estate planners is determining whether a representation is complete so that the conflict is with a former client and Rule 1.7 is not applicable. Nevertheless, making a determination between

---

4. (a) A lawyer who has formerly represented a client in a matter shall not thereafter represent another person in the same or a substantially related matter in which that person's interests are materially adverse to the interests of the former client unless the former client gives informed consent, confirmed in writing.

(b) A lawyer shall not knowingly represent a person in the same or a substantially related matter in which a firm with which the lawyer was associated had previously represented a client:

(1) whose interests are materially adverse to that person; and

(2) about whom the lawyer had acquired information protected by Rules 1.6 and 1.9(c) that is material to the matter;

unless the former client gives informed consent, confirmed in writing.

(c) A lawyer who has formerly represented a client in a matter or whose present or former firm has formerly represented a client in a matter shall not thereafter:

(1) use information relating to the representation to the disadvantage of the former client except as Rule 1.6 or Rule 3.3 would permit or require with respect to a client, or when the information has become generally known; or

(2) reveal information relating to the representation except as these Rules would permit or require with respect to a client.

RESTATEMENT §213 is the analogous provision.

these rules will not be very important because the obligations are so similar. Knowing that consents all around are required is the critical necessity.[5]

Representing Spouses

Under Ethics 2000 it no longer seems to matter which of these varied standards and consent requirements applies in a given situation. To illustrate, consider the following hypothetical:

Client has been represented for years by one of Attorney's partners; the firm has handled Client's substantial commercial and general corporate matters. Client is persuaded that it is time to have a new estate plan. Client makes an appointment to see Attorney and, at the initial meeting, appears with Spouse for their preliminary interview.

The fundamental issue confronting Attorney at the outset of this representation is whether to represent both Client and Spouse and, if so, whether consents are required (and from whom). For our purposes the single most important realization is that the interests of Client and Spouse may not be identical, or even compatible, for a number of reasons. For example, the risk of conflict is significant if they may have:

- Separate assets (not uncommon even in community property jurisdictions), problems in characterizing property as separate or community property, or the need to create separate estates for both spouses to shelter tax benefits such as their unified credits and generation-skipping transfer tax exemptions.
- The right (in noncommunity property jurisdictions) to take a statutory forced heir share (an issue that becomes more severe under traditional marital deduction planning as the applicable exclusion amount rises, and if Congress makes good on repeal of the estate tax in 2010, as illustrated in Chapter 7).
- ERISA-governed retirement benefit spousal annuity entitlements.
- An interest in using mirror image documents but an attraction to trusts that deny control to the surviving spouse.
- Children by another relation (now or potentially in the future).
- The risk of creditors of one spouse acquiring access to assets of the other spouse.
- The potential use of gift splitting.

And so on. Client and Spouse may be happy and harmonious in their objectives and plans, but either spouse may want planning that is not

---

5. A fourth provision, Model Rule 2.2, was deleted by Ethics 2000 because it was confused and, for our purposes, it is reasonably clear that this rule (dealing with Intermediation) did not apply to consultative situations involving multiple potentially conflicting parties in business and similar transactions, including estate planning.

necessarily in the best interests of the other of them. There always is the *potential* for conflicts of interest in a representation of both spouses.

To illustrate, Attorney might advise Client to use a trust in lieu of a 100% outright disposition to Spouse if Client wants Spouse to leave it entirely to their common children at Spouse's later death. Spouse might feel abused if Attorney talked Client out of leaving everything outright to Spouse. Alternatively, Attorney might feel obliged to advise Spouse on how to challenge Client's estate plan, whereas Attorney might at the same time be advising Client on how to move or settle assets in a form that precludes an effective spousal forced share election.[6]

Based on the facts as they are revealed, there may be more or less reason to be concerned about the wisdom of Client's plan and the need to engage in certain forms of planning to guarantee its success. For example, Spouse may have a paramour (the soap opera type of illustration), children by a former marriage (the real life example), or charitable objectives that are not shared by Client (something most folks never would worry about). But Attorney won't know any of this until after the representation has begun. Thus, the fundamental issue to be considered — theoretically even before Attorney hears one word from either Client or Spouse — is whether Attorney can even *begin* to represent both. Indeed, Attorney will not really know whether it is proper to represent both until Attorney has interviewed each, perhaps giving both the opportunity to speak with Attorney in private (which is something that many attorneys refuse to do because they might actually discover a conflict. Does "don't ask, don't tell" make sense here?).

RESTATEMENT §201 describes a conflict of interest as "a substantial risk that the lawyer's representation of the client would be materially and adversely affected by . . . the lawyer's duties to another current client, a former client, or a third person." RESTATEMENT §211 uses essentially the same standard. Presumably the Restatement allows for the law of averages when it speaks of a "substantial risk." Neither the Model Code nor the Model Rules refer to such a "substantial risk," but Rule 1.7(a) employs the seemingly synonymous "significant" risk. Under each of these standards our question is whether a conflict waiver is needed. As you think about this issue, ask yourself why you would not just get one in all events.

Comment c(iii) to RESTATEMENT §201 defines "substantial" to mean that, "in the circumstances, the risk is significant and plausible, even if it is not certain or even probable that it will occur." More to the point, RESTATEMENT §211 comment c presents the following illustrations:

---

6. Before you prejudge the efficacy, ethics, or extent of this kind of advice, please see Pennell, *Minimizing the Surviving Spouse's Elective Share*, 32 U. MIAMI INST. EST. PLAN. ¶900 (1998). For example, *she* might be disinheriting *him*, and for all the right reasons!

1. Husband and Wife consult Lawyer for estate-planning advice about a will for each of them. Lawyer has had professional dealings with the spouses, both separately and together, on several prior occasions. Lawyer knows them to be knowledgeable about their respective rights and interests, competent to make independent decisions if called for, and in accord on their common and individual objectives. Lawyer may represent both clients in the matter without obtaining consent (see §201). While each spouse theoretically could make a distribution different from the other's, including a less generous bequest to each other, those possibilities do not create a conflict of interest, and none reasonably appears to exist in the circumstances.

2. The same facts as in Illustration 1 except that lawyer has not previously met the spouses. Spouse A does most of the talking in the initial discussions with Lawyer. Spouse B, who owns significantly more property than Spouse A, appears to disagree with important positions of Spouse A but to be uncomfortable in expressing that disagreement and does not pursue them when Spouse A appears impatient and peremptory. Representation of both spouses would involve a conflict of interest. Lawyer may proceed to provide the requested legal assistance only with consent given under the limitations and conditions provided in §202.

3. The same facts as in Illustration 1 except that Lawyer has not previously met the spouses. But in this instance, unlike in Illustration 2, in discussions with the spouses, Lawyer asks questions and suggests options that reveal both Spouse A and Spouse B to be knowledgeable about their respective rights and interests, competent to make independent decisions if called for, and in accord on their common and individual objectives. Lawyer has adequately verified the absence of a conflict of interest and thus may represent both clients in the matter without obtaining consent (see §202).

Implicit in these illustrations is the assumption that conflicts do not necessarily exist between all spouses but that consent (presumably from both spouses) may be required under certain circumstances. If the spouses are in reasonable agreement about the terms of their respective wills, the Restatement suggests that no conflict exists that would create an ethics problem from the outset and that no mutual representation consent is yet required.

Illustration 2 suggests that not much needs to change before a sufficient conflict may be deemed to be a real potential between these spouses, requiring a mutual representation informed consent. How likely is it that you will be able to obtain such a consent when it becomes apparent that one is needed? As illustrated at page 30 with respect to confidences, mutual representations (and changes requested by one client without the knowledge of another) easily could create an ethics issue involving conflicts of interest long after the representation has begun.

In the context of the Model Rules, the potential for a conflict between spouses *presupposes* that Rule 1.7 is applicable. As a practical matter, at the outset of this representation the proper result is to obtain an informed consent from both Client and Spouse. The Restatement is merely creating cover for those lawyers who do not do so. Don't be the lawyer skittering around seeking cover when it hits the fan! You will be wise to take the precaution of obtaining their consent early, because doing so then will not be a problem (assuming there is no real conflict). If either spouse is unwilling to consent you may smoke out the fact that a conflict *does* exist, in which case you may be well advised not to even begin the representation. Indeed, in a case in which immediate facts suggest a real conflict, you might be well advised to *encourage* Spouse, as a new client, to seek independent representation (and in some cases Spouse might agree). If Spouse nevertheless remains comfortable with a mutual representation, you should obtain a written consent to that effect, as insurance against a future challenge.

In most cases both spouses will prefer to use one attorney, especially in single marriage situations or those in which only one of the spouses has any wealth. After all, hiring just one attorney is going to be expensive enough in terms of time, money, and aggravation, and Client and Spouse may not be all that eager to do estate planning in the first place. The Model Rules permit this mutual representation, provided the requisite inquiries and cautions are considered and consents are obtained. Sample joint representation letters are available in ENGAGEMENT LETTERS: A GUIDE FOR PRACTITIONERS, a June 1999 monograph published by the Professional Standards Committee of the American College of Trust and Estate Counsel. Several examples appear in Chapter 19 at pages 4 and 11.

In addition to consent, the attorney should obtain an agreement regarding confidentiality of communications. The need for this can be illustrated by a simple modification of the hypothetical in which Client arrives alone for the initial interview. Client states that, although Client wants Attorney to draft estate plans for both Client and Spouse, today was not a good day for Spouse to be interviewed. Instead, Client proposes to tell Attorney what Spouse owns and what Spouse wants in Spouse's documents. In such a case, no responsible attorney should be willing to take Client's word for what Spouse would want. Independent verification of the facts is appropriate, perhaps by separately interviewing Spouse. If this works out such that Attorney is going to consult privately with each of Client and Spouse, then the possibility exists that secrets of each may be revealed to Attorney but not to the other spouse. If relevant to the plan of the other spouse, the issue then is whether Attorney may (or *must*) share those secrets with the ignorant spouse. A detailed discussion of this more knotty issue appears, beginning at page 30.

Now, let's consider a variation:

Sometime long after another attorney drafted their estate plans, Client and Spouse were informed by their respective employers that the Retirement Equity Act of 1984 "requires some sort of spousal annuity" and, on consultation with their respective plan advisors, they learned that the beneficiary designations that their attorney originally arranged with them as part of their estate planning do not comply. They were, however, informed that a spousal waiver and consent will allow them to proceed with the planning that Attorney now recommends.

Retirement benefits are important parts of a client's total wealth. Attorney may represent Client and Spouse in the preparation of these documents, if Attorney recognizes the conflicts between what may be best for each as a surviving spouse and what each wants as their estate plan. Note, however, that waiver and consent may be desirable to the participant but likely are not in the nonparticipant spouse's best interests. See Chapter 10.

As a third example, consider:

Client has children by a prior marriage, to whom Client makes gifts that Spouse splits for gift tax purposes. Each spouse uses the gift tax annual exclusion and (for larger gifts) consumes a portion of their unified credits to cover the gift tax cost of these transfers.

Should Attorney in this case explain to Spouse that Spouse's unified credit is being used by Client and that Spouse may incur an estate tax at death, or a gift tax if Spouse subsequently wants to make other gifts? Indeed, should Attorney advise Spouse to seek compensation for the use of this credit? This lawyering might not be viewed kindly by Client, and again a potential conflict of interest exists.

Finally, closely related to the foregoing examples, but not quite a part of normal estate planning, is the situation in which Client comes to Attorney with plans to marry and asks for help in preparing a premarital agreement that will cover the spouses' rights if they divorce, or when one dies. Here Attorney would have a clear conflict of interest in representing both Client and the intended spouse.

A white paper produced by a Task Force of the American Bar Association Real Property, Probate and Trust Section, *Report of the Special Study Committee on Professional Responsibility, Comments and Recommendations on the Lawyer's Duties in Representing Husband and Wife*, 28 REAL PROP., PROB. & TRUST J. 765 (1994), took a position that is reflected in the Restatement illustrations at page 7. The Task Force opined that marriage is not per se a conflict of interest and that an estate planner therefore may wait to determine whether a conflict in fact is likely to arise during the representation of spouses.

To wit: the White Paper specified that a lawyer may assume that spouses will conform to their marriage vows. According to that White Paper, to create the kind of conflict anticipated by the Model Rules, spouses must disagree over their rights (such as to property) rather than just disagree about the goals either of them may have with respect to their individual property rights. The White Paper also establishes the notion that one spouse imparting confidences to the attorney but not to the other spouse should waive a conflict flag. Nevertheless, not all confidences create conflicts. Among those that do are:

- Action related confidences that ask the lawyer to reduce or defeat the other spouse's rights or interests in the confiding spouse's property.
- Prejudicial confidences that reveal adversity between the spouses (such as a plan to file for divorce following receipt of an interspousal transfer from the unknowing donor spouse).
- Confidences indicating that one spouse's reliance on the plan of the other (or other understandings) is misplaced.

The Restatement's "wait and see" approach to determining whether an actual conflict exists raises the problem of what to do when a conflict appears to be more than hypothetical. As discussed at page 31, withdrawal may not be appropriate at that time.

The White Paper requires an attorney to act like a fiduciary, determining the harm of disclosure, measured against the harm of nondisclosure, and then acting accordingly. This position has been directly rejected by at least one state ethics board, as discussed at page 31. It also may be contrary to the gist of Comment 31 to new Rule 1.7, which appears to suggest that disclosure is a mandate, not subject to the lawyer's discretion.

The White Paper also opined that the attorney who acquires a confidence need not withdraw, although the attorney may not assist one spouse to the detriment of the other. That position was rejected by the ethics opinion discussed at page 31, and by new Rule 1.7 Comment 29, both of which articulate an absolute requirement to withdraw. The American Bar Association White Paper further articulated that any withdrawal should be such as not to disclose the confidence inadvertently, while the ethics opinion articulates that a noisy withdrawal is permissible (and may be appropriate). As you can begin to see, this is a quagmire with no clear path, unless a conflict waiver is obtained at the outset and that waiver addresses the confidentiality issue.

Finally, the White Paper suggested that in no concurrent representation of spouses may the attorney assert inconsistent rights to assets, conceal assets belonging to the other spouse, or actively deceive either spouse. If separate individual attorneys could engage in such conduct on behalf of one spouse or the other, however, it is impossible to defend the notion that concurrent but separate representation precludes such conduct (assuming that it otherwise would be lawful). But imagine trying to convince a jury of that (or an ethics review panel of your colleagues in the Bar).

Now let's consider how all these formulations would inform an ethical attorney's response in the following situation:

Attorney has not previously represented either spouse. Both are 85 years old and they have been married for 50 years. Between them they have six children: he has three by a prior marriage, she has one by a prior marriage, and they have two together. Virtually all their property is held as joint tenants with right of survivorship in a noncommunity property jurisdiction. Husband is incompetent but Wife and Attorney speculate that he would want his property to pass to his five children equally, as it will by intestacy (he has no will). Wife desires to leave all her property to one of their two common children, disinheriting her other two children and all of his children.

May Attorney represent just Wife in an action to partition the joint tenancy and then draft a will that effectuates her desires? Could Attorney also represent Husband (or Wife as his personal representative) in that partition action?

Dynastic Family Planning

The foregoing examples involved the most commonly recognized conflict of interest situation in estate planning: representing spouses. Less frequently encountered but easily more likely to present actual as opposed to only potential conflicts is the dynastic family plan illustrated by the following hypothetical:

Daddy Warbucks is Attorney's client. Daddy's daughter, Annie, works for Warbucks Enterprises and she also is a client of Attorney. Daddy and Annie have heard cocktail party chatter about various gimmicks and schemes, they have some general business succession issues, income and wealth shifting objectives, and tax minimization concerns that they would like to consider. Daddy and Annie would like Attorney to represent them in a way that ensures an effective dynastic plan that will satisfy the needs of Daddy, Annie, and Annie's children.

In this case what may be good for Annie as beneficiary of Daddy's estate may not be best in terms of minimizing the overall tax burdens or the succession of Daddy's estate.

To illustrate, income taxes could be lower if Daddy made some direct bequests to Annie's children, entirely bypassing Annie. But Annie is likely to feel abused by a recommendation that "her" inheritance be given to someone else, even a natural object of Annie's bounty. Similarly, Daddy may create a power of appointment in Annie for flexibility in dealing with yet unknown taxes or other changes in the law, but clearly may prefer that Annie never exercise it "needlessly." In drafting Annie's will, may (or must) Attorney advise Annie that the power exists? What if Daddy rejects Attorney's advice to discuss this with Annie? Annie may be no worse off for Attorney representing both Daddy and Annie than if she had retained some other attorney who might not know all (or any) of the specifics of Daddy's estate plan. However, the issue of "damages" is not relevant to the question whether a conflict between Daddy and Annie constitutes an ethical violation.

Further, if Annie was going to purchase stock from Daddy for what is thought to be full and adequate consideration but the transaction nevertheless runs the risk of part-sale, part-gift taxation, whose interests would Attorney represent in fashioning the contract of sale to avoid this result? And what if the contract imposes any gift tax incurred on Annie as a "net gift" arrangement (by which Annie would pay any gift tax incurred)? Would any of this depend on whether there are other beneficiaries of Daddy's estate? Any advice to Annie and Daddy regarding a buy-sell agreement could be troublesome. Especially tricky might be the question whether and how to purchase disability insurance to finance a disability purchase buy-sell agreement.

Under slightly different facts Attorney may realize that Daddy Warbucks might re-evaluate some of the planning that is being considered if Daddy knew some of the things about Annie's current marriage and her children that Attorney has deduced from Annie's plan. Indeed, it might come up in a different situation: what if Annie was about to be married and Daddy wanted Attorney to draft a prenuptial agreement for Annie and her intended, to protect Annie's Warbucks Enterprises stock in the case of a divorce?

The situation would pose even greater problems if Daddy, knowing that Annie otherwise would tend to procrastinate, offers to pay the fee for all the services Attorney renders for both Daddy and Annie. See page 19 dealing with Model Rule 1.8(f). Daddy might even offer to serve as an intermediary between Attorney and all the family members for purposes of gathering and relaying information that is essential, taking back and explaining all recommendations, and so forth.

Further, added issues of conflict and even the potential for a charge of undue influence might arise if Daddy has another child who is not active in the business or will be treated differently than Annie (for example, receiving different assets, or receiving a share in trust rather than outright). This would be even more troubling if Attorney represents Annie as well as Daddy. For a troubling example of this see Hotz v. Minyard, 403 S.E.2d 634 (S.C. 1991), in which the family attorney was sued on grounds of breach of fiduciary duty to the child who was treated badly by the decedent, based on the attorney-client relation of the attorney with *that* child.

A conflict of interest also can arise if an attorney attempts to represent both a corporation and some but not all shareholders, or represents all shareholders in preparing a buy-sell agreement, documents for incorporation of a business, or other general business matters. American Bar Association Standing Committee on Ethics and Professional Responsibility Informal Decision 564 (1962) involved an attorney who represented both a corporation and the executor of an estate that held stock of the corporation: the attorney was deemed to have a conflict of interest when the estate and the corporation became adversaries. But a quintessential example of dynastic representation involving conflicts of interest is *In re* Estate of Halas, Jr., 512 N.E.2d 1276 (Ill. App. Ct. 1987), in which a major Chicago law firm represented the decedent's father as executor of the decedent's estate, as trustee of the decedent's testamentary trusts, as chief executive officer of the Chicago Bears football club (the family business) and individually, represented the business as corporate counsel, and represented the decedent's sister and her family. In its role as attorney for this dynasty the law firm recommended recapitalizations that the court concluded would benefit some family members but disadvantage others, including beneficiaries of the decedent's estate, to whom the court held the attorneys owed fiduciary duties through their representation of the personal representative.[7]

Some estate planning attorneys have separately incorporated firms for consulting with family businesses because of the extent of family conflicts and some ethical dilemmas in situations such as these. In the legal or business advising involved, these attorneys strongly advocate common representation of families to minimize the extent of surprises,

---

7. The following appears in 69 Fordham L. Rev. at 1154-1155 (2000), involving an attorney describing a family representation. Notice the distance between the ethical mandates and *this* attorney's sense of an impermissible conflict of interest.

I represent family businesses and every member of the family . . . all shareholders and sometimes two or three generations. And their interest are different. They're not really technically adverse, but occasionally they get to be adverse. . . . I'm a sort of "godfather" and everybody knows that I'm representing the grandfather and the grandchildren and the business and so forth. . . . Occasionally . . . there's a conflict — and I'm totally neutral. . . . If it's ever really a conflict — in the sense of hostility — I don't serve anybody. I just say, "I'll represent the business if you want me to. You guys go get separate lawyers." . . . I represent one company where I represent every member of the family. I'm trustee of shares in a trust under a will. I'm trustee of a voting trust. . . . And, if they have a fight, then it gets resolved that I'm representing the company. . . . [W]hen you get down a generation, some of them need money, some don't need money. Some are rich, some are poor. Some want to see the company grow, some want more money out of the company. . . . The members of the family are a mother and five daughters. The husband of one of the daughters runs the business. The amount of his salary and bonus is an inherent conflict. . . . When the mother dies and the "girls" . . . become the real parties in interest, they may have a fight. Some may want to sell out. Should the corporation buy? Should other shareholders buy? . . . The husband of the one daughter who runs the business now has his son in the business and none of the cousins is in. There could be some tension. I don't know if there will be conflict.

[M]y client . . . is the business and the son-in-law who runs it . . . and his son. Cause those are the people I deal with every day . . . . [O]ne of the girls . . . happens to be a client of mine — unrelated to this. And I'm very friendly with this daughter and her husband . . . a lawyer.

disappointment, and animosity about decisions that affect various members. In an effort to avoid the ethics rules that may apply, however, these attorneys will not represent family members as clients when also consulting with them as their business advisor. This may be a more conservative approach than necessary to the question of conflicts between clients in dynastic family business situations. It also may not succeed in preventing exposure to the ethics rules. Nevertheless, it is impressive that the potential for conflict is significant and potentially impossible of resolution within the dictates of the Model Rules.

Which Rule Applies?

None of these representations is unusual, and the Ethics 2000 revision of the Model Rules more readily accommodates these mutual representations. The rules applicable to these situations make it clear that family counsel must obtain mutual informed consents, preferably at the outset of the representation, always confirmed in writing. This appears to be the only method to avoid concerns under each of the potentially applicable rules. As such, it is difficult to think of a reason not to obtain such letters if they are available. Furthermore, it seems fair to ask why a responsible attorney would run the risk of committing an ethics violation in such a situation by engaging in the mutual representation if mutual consents are *not* obtainable.

A common comment made by attorneys in response to this suggestion is that it would be irresponsible for the attorney to raise issues of possible conflict if there is no reason to believe that there is a real conflict between the parties. The notion expressed appears to be that the mere mention of the possibility of conflict could "poison" an otherwise peaceful relationship and destroy the sense of mutual trust that existed between the clients before they consulted the attorney. According to this argument, the attorney should use objective independent judgment to determine whether it is in the clients' best interests to raise the possibility of conflict and that the attorney should not discuss conflict possibilities if the attorney independently determines that a real conflict is not likely, based on the facts and circumstances of the situation.

These attorneys would embrace a rule that consent is required only if an actual conflict exists and not if there is merely a potential for conflict in the particular situation. They also would advocate that an attorney should be entitled to presume that no conflict actually exists until it is made clear from the facts that this is not true. See *Report of the Special Study Committee on Professional Responsibility, Comments and Recommendations on the Lawyer's Duties in Representing Husband and Wife*, 28 REAL PROP., PROB. & TRUST J. 765, 777-780 (1994).

Whether this *ought* to be the approach taken by the Model Rules, and the ancillary problems raised by such a proposal, is an interesting academic inquiry.[8] But for *practical* purposes it is sufficient to note that it presently is not the rule, as is reasonably clear from reading the rules. The RESTATEMENT §211 examples quoted at page 7 are meant to give some comfort in the spousal representation arena because so many attorneys do not yet obtain the requisite consents at the outset of a representation. Similarly, Ethics 2000 Rule 1.7 Comment 8 stated: "The mere possibility of subsequent harm does not itself require disclosure and consent. The critical questions are the likelihood that a difference in interest will eventuate and, if it does, whether it will materially interfere with the lawyer's independent professional judgment . . . ."

Unfortunately, the need for those Restatement examples marking out an exception (and their limitation to the spousal representation context) may simply confirm the clear need in other situations to obtain the preemptive consent, even prior to discovery of an actual (as opposed to a potential) conflict. All this makes it dangerous to adopt the wait and see approach today. And if that is true, would you rely on a different result in representing spouses? Put another way, why *not* just get the consent? The answer may lie in the reality that an informed consent to a mutual representation requires the existing attorney to make a sufficient disclosure to guarantee that the clients perceive the possible risks of a mutual representation and, on the basis of an adequate understanding, give a truly informed and voluntary consent. Should you be unwilling?

Other Common Conflicts

Two additional examples may help illustrate conflicts in estate planning that, if not already commonplace, certainly will become so:

Child is a client of Attorney's firm and comes to Attorney asking Attorney to represent Elder, Child's aged parent, in the preparation of estate planning documents. In the course of an initial meeting Child reveals that Elder is in a nursing home located some distance away, that Elder is not able to travel, and that Elder is only sometimes able to sit and discuss business or other technical matters. Child offers to provide Attorney with any necessary information regarding assets and the desired dispositive plan. Child also states that Elder wants to give Child a durable power of attorney to facilitate annual exclusion gifting and other estate, tax, and general business planning.

Parent, a longstanding client of Attorney, comes to Attorney with Trust Officer (who represents a major corporate fiduciary that also is a client of Attorney's firm). They are seeking advice about Parent's child, Minor, who is the beneficiary of a trust (drafted many years ago by some other attorney who represented Minor's grandparent) that is scheduled to terminate at Minor's age 21, which is several months from now. Trust

---

8. See Pennell, *Professional Responsibility: Reforms Are Needed to Accommodate Estate Planning and Family Counseling,* 25 U. MIAMI INST. EST. PLAN. 18-1 to 18-75 (1991).

Officer and Parent feel strongly that Minor is not mature enough to handle the amount of money that will be distributed and wonder what kinds of "protection" are available to Minor. They ask Attorney to represent and advise Minor regarding the available options, and they assure Attorney that all fees will be paid by Parent. The likely recommendation is a rollover of the trust distribution directly into an irrevocable trust (or revocable with the consent of Parent or the trustee) that will be held for the benefit of Minor until termination and distribution to Minor at a more "reasonable" age.

In the last example, imagine how the situation might differ if Minor does not yet know that the soon-to-be-distributed trust exists. That isn't uncommon.

A third example is not unique, but arises less frequently:

Attorney represents Fiduciary, which was named as personal representative and trustee under the estate plan of Decedent. Attorney drafted the documents and is asked to advise beneficiaries under that plan in the course of the representation.

A similar situation can exist if an attorney is asked to represent both the income and remainder beneficiaries of a trust, or several beneficiaries under a will. A related but more easily recognized conflicts issue arises if the drafter of an estate plan is later asked to represent a disappointed heir in a will contest.

Implicating the ethics rules *and* the government's tax shelter disclosure regulations as well, Illinois State Bar Association Advisory Opinion 00-01 on Professional Conduct responded to a request for guidance on the consequences of entering into a confidentiality agreement pursuant to which the attorney was asked to agree never to divulge the ideas contained in a package provided to the attorney's client by an accounting firm. Based on the assumption "that the package of ideas . . . includes interpretations and applications of the tax laws and regulations that would be useful . . . in performing legal services for" other clients, the Opinion states that signing the confidentiality agreement would create a prohibited conflict of interest that would violate Model Rule 1.7 as a "material limitation" on the attorney's representation of those other clients. "[A] lawyer cannot agree to keep confidential interpretations of the law."

In addition, the Opinion states that "the restrictions placed on Lawyer's ability to represent other clients . . . in the future without facing a conflict of interest may go to the spirit of Rule 5.6" (which prohibits a lawyer from entering into an agreement that restricts the rights of a lawyer to practice). Finally, the Opinion cautioned that "there is a line that can be crossed at some point at which the accountant's services may become the 'practice of law.'" Although it ducked the question (by stating that unauthorized practice of law questions are very fact specific), the opinion seems to reflect that the Illinois authorities were concerned about the appearance or reality that an attorney in league with an accounting firm in the endeavor to which the agreement relates may be engaged in the assistance of a nonlawyer in the unauthorized practice of law. That *also* is an ethics violation, as discussed at page 28.

Have you begun to notice: the tentacles of the ethics rules reach many situations, and not always in obvious ways. Because estate planning touches so many representations and issues, this is a serious concern and ethics considerations always should be on your radar screen. That is why this Chapter comes so early in this book.

Obligations Imposed

In each case discussed in this Chapter the ethics rules require the attorney to determine at the outset what course of conduct is required before engaging in any of the requested representations. The first requisite under Model Rule 1.7 is to determine, based on a reasonable belief (whatever that means), that the representation will not adversely affect the relationship with the other client with whom a conflict may exist. Then, under Model Rule 1.7(b) (not as an alternative but as an additional requirement) the attorney must consult with both potentially injured clients to inform them of the possibility for conflict. Each affected client must be informed of the implications of the common representation and the risks and advantages involved.

Based on these consultations, the attorney must obtain an informed consent to the representation, confirmed in writing. If the conflict involves a client the attorney no longer actively represents, Model Rule 1.9 requires that the former client consent after consultation, again confirmed in writing. Although Rule 1.9 assumes that the new client will receive undivided attention and loyalty, making the new client's consent unnecessary, note that Rule 1.7 *also* requires the new client's consent.

If a mutual representation is contemplated (as would appear to be common with spouses or dynastic families), the attorney must conclude that the matters involved can be resolved compatibly to each client, in their respective best interests. In addition, if the attorney is unable to resolve their problems compatibly, the attorney must be *confident* that there will be no material prejudice to their interests. Further, the attorney must be *confident* that each client will be able to make adequately informed decisions in the course of the mutual representation, and the attorney must reasonably believe that the common representation can be undertaken impartially and without improper effect on the attorney's responsibilities to each client. Because the representation necessarily will be affected, the key here is whether it will be an *improper* effect.

Finally, each client must consent, the consent must be informed, confirmed in writing, and (presumably) given by a client who is capable of giving consent. See, e.g., RESTATEMENT §202(1). Thus, for example, in a mutual representation that requires the consent of Elder or Minor, it is questionable whether either can give an adequate consent and, although a guardian or conservator normally could consent on behalf of someone under disability, here that would seem to be inappropriate if the conflict is with the same person seeking to give the consent on their behalf. See RESTATEMENT §202, comment c(ii).

Full disclosure requires more than just informing the clients that the attorney is undertaking to represent both of them. Instead, the attorney must explain "the nature of the conflict of interest in such detail so that they can understand the reasons why it may be desirable for each to have independent counsel, with undivided loyalty to the interest of each of them." *In re* Boivin, 533 P.2d 171, 174 (Or. 1975). This too may be impossible in practical application.

Another obligation is imposed if one of the clients will pay the attorney's fee for all of the collective engagements, which is pretty common in the spousal representation and may be common in dynastic and the other illustrated situations as well. Model Rule 1.8(f)[9] requires the attorney to inform the nonpaying client that someone else is paying the fee, and the attorney must conclude that this does not create divided loyalties that interfere with the attorney's independent judgment. Further, the nonpaying client must give an informed consent to this arrangement. This rule does *not* require a written confirmation, but why would you not?

Oh, by the way, there are confidentiality issues with respect to these situations that we will address in due course. See page 29. They prove to be the devil in all of this and, when you understand them, they will change the way you resolve certain issues. So, it isn't time yet to decide how you will choose to practice in these varied situations.

Who Is the Client?

The most beguiling issue in some of these cases is one the ethics rules do not address: who is the client? For example, if Child engages Attorney to represent the marginally capable Elder, or Parent asks Attorney to advise Minor, are the clients Elder and Minor (initially this seems obvious) or Child and Parent, who hire Attorney and seem to have the most interest in the representation? See, e.g., *In re* Estate of Gillespie, 903 P.2d 590 (Ariz. 1995) (Child obtained documents for Elder, who attorney never met); Indiana Ethics Opinion No. 2 (2001) (grandchild obtained documents for Elder, who attorney did not consult and who was

---

9. A lawyer shall not accept compensation for representing a client from one other than the client unless:

    (1) the client consents after consultation;

    (2) there is no interference with the lawyer's independence of professional judgment or with the client-lawyer relationship; and

    (3) information relating to representation of a client is protected as required in Rule 1.6.

See also RESTATEMENT §215(1).

represented by another attorney). And with Client and Spouse or Daddy and Annie, can the client be regarded as the spousal unit or the dynastic family, or is it each individual independently?

There appears to be no reason why Child and Parent cannot *also* be regarded as clients, but it probably cannot be claimed that Elder and Minor are *not* Attorney's clients. Thus, an informed consent must be obtained from them, reflecting their knowledge of the fact that Attorney is representing the interests of others who may not have the best interests of Elder and Minor in mind (or who may view the best interests of Elder and Minor differently than do Elder and Minor). Consequently, the ability of Elder or Minor to even give consent remains a problem. In addition, questions of undue influence may infect the planning independent of the ethics obligations involved. The bottom line: the ethics rules provide slim guidance other than to assume the informed consent of each affected individual is required and should be confirmed in writing.

As a reality check, it may be helpful to ask two questions posed by Boston attorney and tax ethics commentator, the late Fred Corneel: (1) who does the attorney think is the client, and (2) who do the clients think is their attorney? It is a pretty safe guess that a conflict exists if the attorney's vision of the role being played and the role the clients think the attorney is playing differ. Another indication of possible conflicts is if the attorney cares how a nonclient feels about a particular situation, which may indicate that there is a conflict of interest. A further danger signal is if the attorney's role has changed during the representation (for example, the attorney now represents both spouses after having represented only one, or vice versa).

Sometimes the answer to your question "who is the client" is obvious, albeit painful. For example, in the case of a premarital agreement, the client should be regarded as one or the other of the couple and the attorney probably commits malpractice by not insisting that the other obtain independent representation. See Springs & Bruce, *Marital Agreements: Uses, Techniques, and Tax Ramifications in the Estate Planning Context*, 21 U. MIAMI INST. EST. PLAN. ¶705.3 (1987). Failure to do so would be more than an ethical violation, because the surest way to ensure the effectiveness of a premarital agreement is to guarantee that both sides of the agreement have adequate *independent* representation. Thus, the spouse(s) desiring the agreement would be ill-served if the attorney did not insist on this measure as the most effective protection of the parties' best interests. Even if they are not willing to pay for two lawyers, normally the attorney should not accept no for an answer when recommending that they each employ independent counsel. And, if that recommendation is not accepted, the attorney still should regard only one of the parties as the client and should make it clear that the other was encouraged to obtain independent representation and voluntarily refused to do so. Indeed, some observers would argue that the attorney should withdraw entirely if they refuse the advised separate independent representation.

Finally, consider Model Rule 1.14, which deals with clients under disability. Comment 4 reads:

> If a legal representative has already been appointed for the client, the lawyer should ordinarily look to the representative for decisions on behalf of the client. In matters involving a minor, whether the lawyer should look to the parents as natural guardians may depend on the type of proceeding or matter in which the lawyer is representing the minor. If the lawyer represents the guardian as distinct from the ward, and is aware that the guardian is acting adversely to the ward's interest, the lawyer may have an obligation to prevent or rectify the guardian's misconduct.

Materials added to this comment by Ethics 2000 may imply that the attorney also acts on behalf of the ward or that the ward is the attorney's de facto client. American Bar Association Standing Committee on Ethics and Professional Responsibility Informal Decision C-778 (1964) specifically dealt with this situation, the guardian having told the guardian's attorney that the guardian had misappropriated funds. The Decision determined that the attorney did not represent the ward and had no duty to the ward. The attorney was obliged, however, to advise the guardian to make amends, but could not reveal the misappropriation. The discussion beginning at page 44 reveals that this vision is not shared universally and the appropriate answer may be not nearly so clear!

New Rule 1.14(b) provides

> (b) When the lawyer reasonably believes that the client has diminished capacity, is at risk of substantial physical, financial or other harm unless action is taken and cannot adequately act in the client's own interest, the lawyer may take reasonably necessary protective action, including consulting with individuals or entities that have the ability to take action to protect the client and, in appropriate cases, seeking the appointment of a guardian ad litem, conservator or guardian.

Further, Comment 5 adds that:

> If a lawyer reasonably believes that a client is at risk of substantial physical, financial or other harm unless action is taken, and that a normal client-lawyer relationship cannot be maintained as provided in paragraph (a) because the client lacks sufficient capacity to communicate or to make adequately considered decisions in connection with the representation, then paragraph (b) permits the lawyer to take protective measures deemed necessary. Such measures could include: consulting with family members, using a reconsideration period to permit clarification or improvement of circumstances, using voluntary surrogate decisionmaking tools such

as durable powers of attorney or consulting with support groups, professional services, adult-protective agencies or other individuals or entities that have the ability to protect the client. In taking any protective action, the lawyer should be guided by such factors as the wishes and values of the client to the extent known, the client's best interests and the goals of intruding into the client's decisionmaking autonomy to the least extent feasible, maximizing client capacities and respecting the client's family and social connections.

Neither authority resolves the "who do you represent" imbroglio, nor is it clear what are the lawyer's duties if the ward is not meant to be a client.

As so viewed, at a minimum this situation creates another potential conflict for the attorney in the Elder or Minor cases. Were you waiting for an answer to these difficult questions, as if a ball exists that cleverly is being hidden from you? Were it so! Estate planners quite simply are groping in the dark on these unresolved questions. And no, you would *not* be better off not knowing that these questions exist! Ignorance here truly is not bliss. It is just all the more dangerous. So, what do you do? The best advice is to shun the conflict. Don't put yourself in harm's way, and praise the client (Child or Parent) who lets you stand aside and hires a truly independent attorney.

Independent Judgment

The general ethics rules relating to an attorney's independence of judgment can create ethical problems for estate planners in some unexpected ways. Clearly subject to scrutiny is any attorney self dealing with an estate or trust under the attorney's administration. Model Rule 1.8(a) requires that all terms be fair and reasonable and fully disclosed in writing, and that the client consent in a signed writing recording the essential terms of the transaction and the lawyer's role in it. See RESTATEMENT §207. See also Florida Bar v. White, 368 So. 2d 1294 (Fla. 1979) (an attorney was suspended for buying land from a client at a price the client asked because, among other things, the attorney did not advise the client that the land might be worth more or that the client should obtain an independent appraisal or independent representation). This rule is not news to fiduciaries: avoiding self dealing is a clear responsibility under the law of fiduciary administration (although the ethical mandate here is less strict than the fiduciary prohibition).

Also well known to most estate planners is Model Rule 1.8(c), prohibiting an attorney from preparing

an instrument giving the lawyer or a person related to the lawyer any substantial gift unless the lawyer or other recipient of the gift is related to the client. For purposes of this paragraph, related persons include a spouse, child, grandchild, parent, grandparent or other relative or individual with whom the lawyer or the client maintains a close, familiar relationship.

RESTATEMENT §208 similarly precludes a lawyer from drafting an instrument effecting any gift from a client to the lawyer "unless the lawyer is a relative or other natural object of the client's generosity and the gift is not significantly disproportionate to those given other donees similarly related to the donor." The Restatement also precludes acceptance of a gift, regardless of who prepared the instrument of transfer, unless the gift is insubstantial, the attorney is a relative or other natural object of the client's bounty, or the client was encouraged to and had a reasonable opportunity to seek independent representation, which is a more lenient standard than the Model Rule (it is more akin to the older Model Code Ethical Consideration 5-5).

Although there is some room to wiggle in Rule 1.8(c), centering around the question of what is a "substantial" gift, the notion of whether a client is sufficiently "related to the donee" was addressed more clearly by Ethics 2000, and it will be clear enough what the rule prohibits in the vast majority of situations in which this issue might arise.

Any responsible estate planner ought to be able to reach a clear conclusion about whether to require separate representation if the client insists upon making a bequest to the attorney or a member of the attorney's family.[10] For example, if the attorney feels uncomfortable about the appearance of the gift, it probably is too large to slip under the "substantial gift" threshold. But consider tough cases like *In re* Boulger, 637 N.W.2d 710 (N.D. 2001), in which the drafter was a life long friend of the decedent and only later became the decedent's attorney as well, had represented the decedent's business for years, and was made a remote contingent beneficiary but did not actually receive any bequest. The court held that the Rule does not invite debate about probabilities of various contingencies and held that a bright line rule requires sanctions to protect the public, notwithstanding the absence of evidence in the particular case of overreaching or undue influence.

Model Rule 1.8(a) also prohibits entering into a business transaction with a client or knowingly acquiring an ownership, possessory, security, or other pecuniary interest adverse to the client, unless the transaction and terms are fair and reasonable to the client, the essential terms are fully disclosed in writing to the client, the client is advised in writing of the desirability of seeking independent legal counsel on the transaction, and the client consents in writing.

---

10. See, e.g., *In re* Randall, 640 F.2d 898 (8th Cir. 1981) (a former president of the American Bar Association was disbarred for drawing a will totally disinheriting the testator's only child and grandchildren and leaving the attorney the entire $2 million estate). See generally deFuria, *Testamentary Gifts From Client to the Attorney-Draftsman: From Probate Presumption to Ethical Prohibition*, 66 NEB. L. REV. 695 (1987); Johnston, *An Ethical Analysis of Common Estate Planning Practices — Is Good Business Bad Ethics*, 45 OHIO ST. L.J. 57 (1984) (hereafter cited as Johnston); and see Annot. *Attorneys at law: disciplinary proceedings for drafting instrument such as will or trust under which attorney-drafter or member of attorney's family or law firm is beneficiary, grantee, legatee, or devisee*, 80 A.L.R.5th 597 (2000).

In this regard, Comment b to RESTATEMENT §207 specifically states that "proving fraud or actual overreaching might be difficult. Hence, the law does not require such a showing on the part of a client." And Comment c gives the following illustration:

2. Lawyer represents the surviving Spouse of a long-time Client. Lawyer advises Spouse that farmland owned by the estate should be sold to pay taxes. Using the name of a business associate as purported buyer, Lawyer purchases the land from Spouse without disclosing Lawyer's involvement in the purchase. Even if the price is objectively fair, Lawyer has violated the requirement that Lawyer's identity be disclosed to the client.[11]

In addition, related enough to this to be included in Model Rule 1.8(h) is the prohibition against agreeing with the client to a limitation of the attorney's liability to the client for malpractice unless the client is advised in writing about the desirability of being independently represented.

Less clear is whether this Rule 1.8(h) also would apply to an attorney who agrees to act as a fiduciary and, in that capacity, is exonerated or granted limited liability under the terms of a document that the attorney drafted. Comment 8 states that Rule 1.8 does not prohibit the lawyer from seeking to be named as fiduciary but is silent regarding normal exoneration language. Some authorities state that such a provision in the document itself may be ineffective for the intended purpose.[12] But quite independent of that result is the issue whether the mere act of placing the provision in the trust constitutes an ethical violation for which the attorney also can be sanctioned, in addition to whatever liability would flow from the underlying violation as to which exoneration or limited liability was asserted.

Ancillary Activities

Assume that Attorney also is a financial planner or sells insurance, and makes recommendations in the estate planning engagement regarding the purchase of products that Attorney sells. Although troublesome, is this activity sufficiently different that an ethical mandate clearly applies? The obvious issues of self dealing and lack of independent professional judgment probably cannot be ameliorated even if the nonlegal or ancillary activities of the attorney are performed in separate legal entities.[13] Thus, Model Rule 5.7 appears to impose on the attorney in the nonlegal or ancillary activity the same rules of professional conduct imposed on the

---

11. See generally Annot., *Conduct of attorney in capacity of executor or administrator of decedent's estate as grounds for disciplinary action*, 92 A.L.R.3d 655 (1979).

12. See 3 Scott & Fratcher, THE LAW OF TRUSTS §222.3 (4th ed. 1988); Johnston at 105 (cited in note 10); Christie v. Dold, 524 N.W.2d 866 (S.D. 1994); Annot., *Attorney at law: disciplinary proceedings based upon attorney's naming of himself or associate as executor or attorney for executor in will drafted by him*, 57 A.L.R.3d 703 (1974).

13. See Illinois Professional Ethics Opinion 89-14, involving an attorney who ran a separate insurance business in a separate office, with separate letterhead, but still was regarded as subject to independent professional judgment concerns.

lawyer's provision of law-related services, unless the attorney takes "reasonable measures to assure that a person . . . knows that the . . . protections of the client-lawyer relationship do not exist."

In addition, Model Rule 1.8(a) presumably applies, requiring

- Disclosure of the possibility for conflict.
- That the client be advised of the desirability of seeking and be given a reasonable opportunity for independent representation.
- That the client consent in a signed writing.
- That all dealings be on absolutely fair and reasonable terms and be disclosed in a manner that can be reasonably understood by the client.

Quaere what are fair and reasonable terms and adequate disclosure. And how to make clients who are so informed and given the opportunity for independent representation feel free to go elsewhere without fear of offending the attorney or being treated as second class clients.

Even if this example seems clear, what about moving one step away:

Attorney is licensed to sell insurance; because of that certification, when Attorney refers a client to another insurance agent Attorney customarily receives a portion of the sales commission from the other agent as a referral fee.

Attorney uses the same real estate broker to market realty held in any estate that Attorney probates, and the broker rebates a portion of the sales commission to Attorney as a referral fee.

Do the same rules apply here as if Attorney sold the insurance directly to the client or acted as the real estate broker?

It is irrelevant to the ethics issue that the commission charged to the client in each case is no greater than if Attorney were not involved. An ethics violation can result even if there is no damage to the client. Yet these cases appear to be no different from receiving a referral from an insurance agent or fiduciary or being hired as a fiduciary's attorney. The fact that the attorney earns a fee for legal work as opposed to a mere referral is entirely irrelevant to the question whether the attorney's independent judgment is impaired by the relationships involved. If any of these situations involves an impropriety in the absence of disclosure and consent, then presumably they all should be regarded as improper under one or both of Rules 1.8 or 5.7.[14]

---

14. Id., holding that insurance commission referral fee arrangements also are subject to the independent judgment rules, stating that "the lawyer should disclose his interest in any life insurance commissions and obtain consent of the client . . . ;" Illinois State Bar Association Advisory Opinion No. 99-06 (1999) (attorney received a fee from a trust company to which the attorney referred business); *In re* Clark's Estate, 188 N.E.2d 128 (N.Y. 1962) (the attorney for an estate received a portion of a real estate broker's commission, which was deemed a conflict of interest, stating that the attorney and fiduciary

As a final illustration that may give pause, consider the case in which, when asked for a deserving "contingent beneficiary" (to take if all named objects of the decedent's bounty fail to survive), an attorney recommends a particular charity with which the attorney is involved or interested.[15] Presumably the attorney's independent judgment may be clouded in such a situation, and these facts should be regarded as no less problematical because a charity is involved and the attorney is not receiving a fee or otherwise being tangibly compensated. Disclosure of the personal interest should suffice, however, to absolve any possible ethics violation. To avoid prejudice to the attorney's charity, it might be appropriate to give an inquiring client a list of several deserving charities with a notation that the attorney is involved with or interested in one of them, without identifying which.

An important reminder is the law of Agency (selected aspects of which are reproduced at the end of this Chapter), which applies totally independent of the ethics provisions that might apply in each of these situations. Most notable in this respect is the rule stated in §388 of the RESTATEMENT (SECOND) that "an agent who makes a profit in connection with transactions conducted by him on behalf of the principal is under a duty to give such profit to the principal" unless the principal and agent have agreed otherwise. The comment clarifies that this rule operates even if the agent "acted with perfect fairness to the principal and violated no duty of loyalty in receiving the amount." An ethics obligation thus appears to be the least of the agent's exposure.

Model Rule 5.7 has gone through numerous iterations that reveal a true conflict within the Bar relating to what rule ought to apply. A number of states have adopted their own rules concerning ancillary business activities, with varying degrees of success and controversy, all as revealed by the comments to Rule 5.7. Perhaps the only clear thing in this context is that there are numerous ways an attorney's independent judgment may be challenged and attorneys therefore should be cautious and vigilant about

---

owe the same duty of undivided loyalty to the estate and that the lack of harm to the beneficiaries is irrelevant); cf. New York State Bar Association Ethics Opinion 667 (1994) and State Bar of Michigan Opinion RI-146 (1992) (both holding that an attorney's receipt of a referral fee from a real estate broker was a conflict of interest), and Pennsylvania Bar Association Legal Ethics & Professional Responsibility and Professional Guidance Committees Joint Opinion 2000-100 and authorities cited therein. See also American Bar Association Standing Committee on Ethics and Professional Responsibility Informal Decision C-709 (1964) (it was improper for an attorney/real estate broker to collect a legal fee and a real estate commission from a sale following a representation; there was no discussion of disclosure or whether the terms were fair and reasonable); id. Informal Decision C-682 (1963) (it is improper to conduct a real estate business and practice law if the one serves as an improper form of advertising or feeder of business to the other); Utah State Bar Ethics Advisory Committee Opinion 146A (1995) (it is improper for an attorney licensed to sell insurance to solicit legal work from insurance customers who did not seek out the attorney for legal services). Cf. Estate of Harrison, 745 A.2d 676 (Pa. 2000) (payment of a referral fee by a personal injury attorney to a guardian was a conflict of interest and prohibited self dealing for fiduciary law purposes, basically applying the same principal-agent principles).

15. Cf. RESTATEMENT §§206 (comment c Illustration 3) and 208 (comment d).

keeping track of the rules as they develop and change, in terms of their impact on the ancillary work that lawyers may perform.

Uncertain Scope

Examples of two relatively common situations confronting estate planners help to illustrate the uncertain scope of the independent judgment rule. As revealed in Illinois State Bar Association Professional Ethics Opinion 90-2, Model Rule 1.7 applies if an attorney recommends a corporate fiduciary to a client without revealing that the fiduciary is a client of the attorney's firm. In fact, in that case the attorney was found guilty of an ethics violation for his insistence that the client name the fiduciary. But what if:

Insurance Agent refers business to Attorney and Attorney reciprocates, based on a longstanding relationship. Alternatively, Attorney is contacted by Fiduciary to draft estate planning documents for Customer, who already has agreed to establish a trust arrangement with Fiduciary as trustee. As is common in the community, the unspoken policy is that Attorney will be hired to represent Fiduciary in its capacity as personal representative and trustee under Customer's estate plan.

Although the multiple representation rules are not directly on point if the insurance agent or fiduciary are not clients of Attorney, a case can be made that an attorney should inform a client that the attorney's independent judgment may be affected by reciprocal relations such as these.

To illustrate that this is sensible, consider what the typical attorney would do if it was clear that the trust or insurance recommendation made by the referent is not appropriate under the circumstances. At least on a theoretical level there is an ethics issue in cases like this because, potentially, the attorney's independent judgment may be clouded. See Model Rule 5.4(c) (an attorney may not be influenced by the fiduciary that recommends or employs the attorney to represent a client). Yet the closest authorities found on point concluded that, although there is an ethical violation in this situation, it is not because of the independent judgment rule.[16] Instead, they conclude that the attorney's participation in a matter

---

16. See *In re* Mid-America Living Trust Assoc. Inc., 927 S.W.2d 855 (Mo. 1996), and Cincinnati Bar Association v. Kathman, 748 N.E.2d 1091 (Ohio 2001), and their extensive collection of authority, both holding that trust mills are the unauthorized practice of law and that attorneys who assist in reviewing or drafting documents commit the violation of aiding the unauthorized practice, along with violation of the independent judgment rule attributable to fee sharing arrangements. A fine summary is *State and Local Action Against Trust Mills: The Unauthorized Practice of Law*, 27 ACTEC J. 162 (2001). See also The Florida Bar re: Advisory Opinion, 613 So. 2d 426 (Fla. 1992); Committee on Professional Ethics and Conduct of the Iowa State Bar Association v. Baker, 492 N.W.2d 695 (Iowa 1992); People v. Volk, 805 P.2d 1116 (Colo. 1991); People v. Macy, 789 P.2d 188 (Colo. 1990) (attorneys were sanctioned for reviewing living trusts that were sold by nonlawyers to customers, which was found to be improper assistance to nonlawyers engaged in the unauthorized practice of law); People v. Boyls, 591 P.2d 1315 (Colo. 1979) (similar, the difference being that the nonlawyers were engaged in the sale of "family equity" trusts that

involving preparation of estate planning documents constitutes aiding in the unauthorized practice of law. Given the uncertain state of the law relative to unauthorized practice, it is questionable whether such a result would be reached consistently today. Whether our hypotheticals nevertheless would run afoul of the independent judgment admonition is not clear.

A related situation was presented in Oregon Legal Ethics Opinion 457 in 1981, involving a religious organization that referred members to an attorney "together with the proposed estate plan and distribution," all clearly in anticipation of receiving a bequest from the client. Stating that the attorney must be in a position of total fidelity to the client and not to the organization making the referral, the opinion recognized that it is permissible to accept referrals from a third party but that the opportunity for undue influence is significant if the referent is expecting a benefit in return.

Also not on point but worthy of consideration is authority stating that it would be a violation of the rules against solicitation if an attorney named him or her self as attorney for a fiduciary (or named him or her self as fiduciary).[17] Although this was the case under Model Code Ethical Consideration 5-6 ("A lawyer should not consciously influence a client to name him as executor, trustee, or lawyer in an instrument"), that rule was

---

were regarded as shams designed to defraud the federal government for income tax purposes); *In re* Pearce, 806 P.2d 21 (Mont. 1990) (an attorney organized a corporation that provided "financial advice and . . . selling and preparing estate plans" under a plan by which employees would secure powers of attorney from potential clients that permitted the corporation to engage an attorney to draft the plan; the attorney-organizer usually was selected without indication of his involvement with the corporation and the court disbarred him for, among other things, preparing estate plans without a contract with the clients, which essentially amounted to finding that he improperly assisted the corporation in its representation of the clients); *In re* Morin, 878 P.2d 393 (Or. 1994) (this attorney was disbarred for conducting seminars but then leaving the attorney's paralegals to perform much of the actual client conference, information gathering, document drafting, and execution, which in many cases was faulty for lack of valid witnessing, which the attorney knew); State Bar of Michigan Standing Committee on Professional and Judicial Ethics Opinion RI-191 (1994) (the attorney proposed to establish a business that would employ nonlawyer agents to sell will and trust forms door-to-door with review by the attorney); Utah State Bar Ethics Advisory Committee Opinions 146A (1995) (an attorney may represent a financial planner but not that planner's customers) and 97-09 (an attorney may prepare legal documents for the client of a nonlawyer estate planner but must deliver them directly to the client and not to the nonlawyer for delivery to the client); American Bar Association Standing Committee on Ethics and Professional Responsibility Formal Opinion 122 (1934). And see Illinois State Bar Association Professional Ethics Opinion 90-13 (a bank whose trust officer prepares land trust agreements for customers and drafts a deed to convey property to the trust was engaged in the unauthorized practice of law; although the trust officer was not an attorney, the opinion states that a trust officer who was an attorney would not eliminate the problem and would further constitute an ethical violation by the attorney) and Advisory Committee of Nebraska State Bar Association Formal Opinions 81-10 (it was improper for an attorney to recommend that clients purchase insurance from an agent who referred the client to the attorney) and 81-11 (it was improper for an attorney employed by an insurer to represent the insured's attorney to draft documents for the insured to implement an estate plan that includes an insurance purchase). See RESTATEMENT §§4 and 5(2), and Gibbs, *The Marketing of Living Trusts by Non-Attorney Promoters*, 20 ACTEC NOTES 193 (1994).

17. American Bar Association Standing Committee on Ethics & Professional Responsibility Formal Opinion 602 (1963). For more discussion of the solicitation issue see page 56.

not specifically incorporated in the Model Rules. And again, this ruling does not speak our hypotheticals.

Although several rules come close to dealing with all of these hypotheticals, it is at least arguable that these cases do not pose an ethical violation under the Model Rules. At best they may be regarded as creating "the appearance of impropriety," which once was prohibited under the Model Code but also has been removed in the Model Rules and the Restatement, presumably because it was a catch-all rule with no definable boundaries. More would be required than just this general bromide about avoiding the appearance that something inappropriate is involved. As a practical matter, fiduciaries regularly engage the drafting attorney to represent the fiduciary as personal representative or trustee, without any formal obligation or agreement in advance. Most estate planners would be astounded by a suggestion that there is room for concern about impropriety in such a situation, even if it is not disclosed in writing to the client. Nevertheless, the rule regarding independence of judgment on its face seems relevant and therefore worthy of your respect and consideration.

Preservation of Client Confidences

Certainly one of the easiest rules to state, and usually to follow, is Model Rule 1.6(a),[18] which requires confidentiality of client communications and all confidential information acquired from or *about* the client relative to the representation. "The confidentiality rule, for example, applies not only to matters communicated in confidence *by* the client but also to all information relating to the representation, *whatever its source*." Comment 3 to Model Rule 1.6(a) (emphasis added). In the estate planning context, this obligation extends to virtually all information regarding family, assets, dispositive pattern, and so forth. It extends to information acquired during a prospective client conference under new Rule 1.18 and exists even after the client's death. See American Bar Association Standing Committee on Ethics and Professional Responsibility Informal Opinion 1293 (1974).

RESTATEMENT §112(1) prohibits use or disclosure "if . . . doing so will adversely affect a material interest of the client or if the client has instructed the lawyer not to use or disclose such information"; this is a less rigid standard than the Model Rule imposes. But Comment c(i) to §112 states that adverse effects include "material frustration of the client's objectives . . . or material misfortune, disadvantage, or other prejudices to a client . . . [including] personal embarrassment that could be caused to a person of normal susceptibility and a normal interest in privacy."

---

18. A lawyer shall not reveal information relating to representation of a client unless the client gives informed consent [or] the disclosure is impliedly authorized in order to carry out the representation . . . .

RESTATEMENT §111 defines confidential client information to exclude only information "that is generally known" and only applies the confidence rule if information was acquired during the course of or as a result of the representation, which also is less restrictive than the Model Rule. But Comment b to §111 indicates that information from any source, including nonprivileged sources and communications from a client not protected by the attorney-client privilege, are included in the confidentiality prohibition. Finally, Comment d to §111 states that "information is not generally known when a person interested in knowing the information could obtain it only by means of special knowledge or substantial difficulty or expense."

Notwithstanding these differences, at its most basic application this would appear to be a very easy rule to comprehend and apply, yet numerous attorneys share stories or trivia about clients as "cocktail chatter" in direct violation of this rule. This is not to say the rule is wrong (if it may be a bit overinclusive, surely it is better to err on that side), but it requires more thoughtful attention than some lawyers appear to give to it.

Confidences in Representing Spouses

Far more problematic is the application of Model Rule 1.6(a) in a not uncommon client situation.

Client and Spouse engaged Attorney for estate planning advice; Attorney agreed to represent them both only after informing them of potential conflicts of interest and obtaining their consent to the mutual representation. Wills were drafted for each that, contrary to Attorney's best judgment and advice, essentially leave everything to the survivor of Client and Spouse and by the survivor to their children. Several days (hours/months/years — it doesn't matter) after execution of their wills, Client calls Attorney to request a codicil making a "modest" bequest to Client's [fill in the blank: "child" (from a previously undisclosed liaison); "secretary, in recognition of long years of devoted service"; "close friend"; "personal trainer"; "paramour" (candor being the best policy)]. It is clear that Client would prefer that Spouse not know about this provision in Client's will. Indeed, Client indicates that Spouse would alter Spouse's will if Spouse knew about this deviation from their agreed plan.

Or try another variation.

Client calls to say that, quite unknown to Spouse, Client has discovered that Spouse has been unfaithful. Client is not going to seek a divorce ("because of the children" or perhaps "because of my political aspirations"), but Client wants to exclude Spouse from Client's estate plan. Again, for purposes of family harmony, Client insists that Attorney preserve the confidence.

These facts may be a bit too dramatic, but the same issue can arise in numerous contexts. What if, for example, Spouse informs Attorney that

Spouse plans to divorce Client as soon as a plan involving split gifting or credit shelter transfers from Client to Spouse is complete. Or Client calls to request a bequest to a relative who Spouse does not favor, to inform Attorney that Client has a nonmarital child of whom Spouse is unaware (roughly one in three births in America today is out of wedlock), or perhaps Client and Spouse have children by prior marriages who they agreed to treat equally but now Client wants to renege on that agreement *and does not want Spouse to know*. Now Attorney is on the horns of a dilemma.

In a vacuum, Attorney's ethical obligation to Spouse probably dictates that Attorney inform Spouse of any changes to Client's plan that would affect the wisdom or the assumptions underlying Spouse's plan. At the very least, if Spouse were to come to Attorney at a later time to ask if Attorney knows of any reason to consider a change to Spouse's will, Attorney probably would have a duty to "suggest" that Spouse reconsider the outright and absolute nature of the bequest to Client. Attorney certainly would do so if Attorney's knowledge came from a nonprotected source. But Attorney's ethical obligation to Client may preclude Attorney from revealing the change Client requests and certainly would preclude Attorney from making the kind of slightly veiled comments to Spouse that might put Spouse on notice about Client's change of heart. So what should Attorney do?

First, Attorney could refuse to represent Client in drafting the codicil (and some ethics opinions state that the attorney *must* refuse to represent Client in any change that does not preserve or protect the best interests of Spouse). Even if Attorney does not do the requested work, Attorney still has knowledge that creates a conflict in further representing Spouse. And Client probably will go elsewhere and make the change, so Attorney's refusal will not protect Spouse in any way.

Second, Attorney could withdraw from representing Spouse, although Attorney probably cannot withdraw from representing just Spouse without raising some suspicions that ultimately might tip off Spouse. Moreover, Attorney might have a duty to Spouse *prior* to resignation.

A third alternative would be to withdraw from representing both Client and Spouse (indeed, this is probably the notion that most ethical lawyers would embrace as the least problematic) but, again, resignation might come too late to satisfy Attorney's duties to Spouse. Florida Bar Ethics Department Advisory Opinion 95-4 (1996) opined that Attorney *must* withdraw and cannot disclose the secret because the duty of confidentiality supersedes the duty to communicate all information relevant to the engagement.[19] There is nothing to support the Florida conclusion that one

---

19. Cf. New York State Bar Association Committee on Professional Ethics Opinion 555 (1984), which involved partner A who informed Attorney that A was committing a breach of partnership with partner B. Attorney represented both partners but A's communication was conveyed "in confidence" and the question was whether Attorney must or may disclose the information to partner B. The

ethics obligation is more important than or superior to another, and Attorney may be conflicted by turning tail on the innocent Spouse just to protect Client, who has the secret. The point is that Attorney may do wrong no matter what Attorney does now.

The Report of the Special Study Committee on Professional Responsibility, *Comments and Recommendations on the Lawyer's Duties in Representing Husband and Wife*, 28 REAL PROP., PROB. & TRUST J. 765, 783-793 (1994), addresses this situation, spinning a series of distinctions and a theory of permitted disclosure that requires exercise of attorney discretion that actually may magnify the attorney's exposure. It has been rejected by the American Bar Association Standing Committee on Ethics and Professional Responsibility and by the Florida Bar Ethics Department, which shows that even the best talent can go wrong in seeking to resolve such a dilemma. In this respect, Comment 31 to Rule 1.7 provides:

> As to the duty of confidentiality, continued common representation will almost certainly be inadequate if one client asks the lawyer not to disclose to the other client information relevant to the common representation. This is so because the lawyer has an equal duty of loyalty to each client, and each client has the right to be informed of anything bearing on the representation that might affect that client's interest and the right to expect that the lawyer will use that information to that client's benefit. See Rule 1.4. The lawyer should, at the outset of the common representation and as part of the process of obtaining each client's informed consent, advise each client that information will be shared and that the lawyer will have to withdraw if one client decides that some matter material to the representation should be kept from the other. In limited circumstances, it may be appropriate for the lawyer to proceed with the representation when the clients have agreed, after being properly informed, that the lawyer will keep certain information confidential. . . .

Notice that this Comment assumes the mode of representation will be a joint or "common" representation rather than a concurrent separate representation. Quaere whether it also assumes that this duty cannot be altered by agreement? At a minimum the Comment seems to negate discretion in the attorney whether to reveal or hold the secret in confidence. The Comment appears to assume that either the attorney *will* disclose or *must* withdraw. Notice that Florida said that Attorney may *not* disclose and must withdraw.

Committee held that Attorney could not reveal the information to B and must withdraw from representing either partner. A vigorous dissent agreed that Attorney could not continue to represent either partner but argued that Attorney should reveal the secret to partner B.

How does an estate planner get into such a situation, and how can it be prevented? The problem posed relates directly to the fact that the attorney did not reach an understanding regarding confidences between Client and Spouse when the mutual representation began. Such an understanding might take any of at least three forms. The attorney could maintain the secrets of either client that are communicated to the attorney in confidence, notwithstanding that the ignorant spouse may not be as well represented as a result. The attorney could tell the other spouse of any secret that is revealed if the attorney, in the exercise of discretion, feels it is relevant to the other spouse, notwithstanding the otherwise improper violation of the confidences obligation. Or the attorney could in all events tell the other spouse of any secret that is revealed, notwithstanding the otherwise improper violation of the confidences obligation. Assuming such an agreement is reached with each spouse at the beginning of the representation, and that any of these approaches might be permissible,[20] the issue then is which is preferable?

The "priestly" approach of preserving all secrets ensures that either spouse will feel free to approach the attorney in confidence, to share information each feels unable to reveal in the presence of the other spouse. This ought to help ensure that the attorney's representation of each will be based on the most relevant information available.

This approach puts the attorney in a box. In representing one of the spouses the attorney must maintain an independent judgment, unaffected by what has been learned in confidence from the other spouse. Thus, the difficult practical issue is whether Attorney will be able to avoid consciously or unconsciously pushing Client to a more circumspect plan if Spouse came to Attorney and let it be known that Spouse has a paramour that Spouse would like to benefit, and Client later comes to Attorney wanting to maintain a plan that is all "kisses and hugs" (obviously totally ignorant about Spouse's philandering).

In addition, the attorney may have trouble keeping track of and keeping a lid on information learned from one that is not known by the other. This may not be so difficult if the secret is a blockbuster, but what if it seems insignificant to the attorney (which is why withdrawal did not seem necessary) notwithstanding that it was important to the client? Would *you*, for example, remember that Client's codicil leaving a vase to Spouse's hated sibling is a bone of contention?

The "discretionary" approach was regarded by the Florida Bar Ethics Department Advisory Opinion 95-4 as corrupting and absolutely improper, stating that this is not a matter that the attorney may decide in the attorney's discretion. Comment 31 to Rule 1.7 also does not appear to regard this middle of the road approach as an option. And most attorneys faced with the

---

20. See RESTATEMENT §30 regarding the ability of client and attorney to limit the attorney's duties that otherwise would apply.

issue whether to disclose will not know how to exercise that discretion.[21] Indeed, if the secret is a doozie that might imperil the marriage, most estate planners will pull the covers up over their head and hope the problem rights itself or goes away without requiring action of any kind on the attorney's part. After all, estate planners are do-good types: they hope to fashion results that are a win-win for everyone involved, and they absolutely loathe the creation of unnecessary conflict. A few might swear that they would exercise the discretion and tell the innocent spouse, notwithstanding the probable fallout consequences, but they probably are lying to themselves about their ability or willingness to jump-start a family feud.

The mandatory "show and tell" approach may be preferable. It is favored by the overwhelming majority of estate planners in practice and seems to be anticipated by the Restatement and Ethics 2000 Reporters. Under this approach, the attorney might agree with each spouse that the attorney will not meet or speak alone with either spouse, or that any information acquired from either that is relevant to the other will be shared. The presumption in this approach is that fairness requires full sharing of information unless the clients specifically agree otherwise. Unfortunately, however, this approach discourages each spouse from approaching the attorney with secrets that might be relevant to their planning, which may mean that the attorney will do a less than complete job of best representing a spouse who has a relevant secret.

To address *this*, some attorneys require clients to agree in a written engagement letter to tell the attorney all matters that may affect the plan, as a precaution against malpractice if the client does not do so and the plan is flawed as a result. Others follow a slightly different approach when representing spouses by requiring them to inform the attorney of any fact or circumstance, any dispute or conflict, that might cause the attorney to have a conflict of interest in the dual representation. Quaere whether this truly is effective, even if it puts the clients on notice of the severity of the need for all relevant information. Nevertheless, the attorney escapes being in the middle of a terrible situation and essentially puts the monkey on the back of the spouse with the secret. Presumably the holder of the secret will go to another attorney if revelation of the secret is important to adequate representation, which takes care of the mutual representation problem in the right manner: the client decides what is best.

An unfortunate problem with the show and tell approach is that it is not in the best interests of the client. This approach is for the protection of the attorney, which may make it appear less than legitimate. Yet the priestly approach is criticized by some precisely because it exposes the

---

21. See, e.g., A. v. B. v. Hill Wallack, 726 A.2d 924 (N.J. 1999) (an attorney acquired information regarding a paternity suit against one spouse from an outside source and sought instruction whether the attorney was permitted or required to reveal it to the other spouse; the court held that the attorney *must* reveal it, in part due to a joint representation agreement that anticipated that secrets would not be kept and in part because the information did not come from the one spouse and therefore no expectation of confidentiality could exist).

attorney to liability. As a practical matter, if the innocent spouse is injured because the attorney knew the secret but did not share it, a jury might find the attorney negligent notwithstanding the letter of the mutual representation agreement.

An additional problem with the show and tell approach is the passage of time. What happens if, years after the representation, Client comes to Attorney and, forgetting the rule about secrets, tells Attorney about a child born out of wedlock, a torrid affair now going on, or something else that is relevant to Client and Spouse's planning? Now that Attorney knows the secret, must it be shared with Spouse?

Quaere whether a prior consent, given in the vacuum of a then happy marriage with no known secrets, is effective at a later date when a specific conflict-revealing secret is disclosed to the attorney. See American Bar Association Standing Committee on Ethics and Professional Responsibility Formal Opinion 372 (1993) (former waiver of objection to future conflicts of interest), suggesting that the answer is no. The opinion states that "if the waiver is to be effective with respect to a future conflict, it must contemplate that particular conflict with sufficient clarity so the client's consent can reasonably be viewed as having been fully informed" and that "courts are very reluctant to conclude from a prospective waiver an agreement by the client to waive rights of confidentiality." Comment 22 to Ethics 2000. Rule 1.7 states:

Whether a lawyer may properly request a client to waive conflicts that might arise in the future is subject to the test of [whether] . . . the client reasonably understands the material risks that the waiver entails. The more comprehensive the explanation of the adverse consequences of those representations, the greater the likelihood that the client will have the requisite understanding. Thus, if the client agrees to consent to a particular type of conflict with which the client is already familiar, then the consent ordinarily will be effective with regard to that type of conflict. If the consent is general and open-ended, then the consent ordinarily will be ineffective, because it is not reasonably likely that the client will have understood the material risks involved.

Another response might be that the representation has ended and, along with it, the obligations established in the mutual representation agreement. Quaere, however, whether this really is true. This scenario underscores the potential value of an "exit" letter that makes it clear to the client that the representation has ended and that all prior deals are off. See page 41 for a further discussion of "exit" letters.

Also note Model Rule 1.9, dealing with conflicts of interest involving former clients, which might apply in cases such as this. Even if an exit letter makes it clear that the original Client and Spouse representation has ended, Attorney may be unable to avoid the prohibitions of Model Rule

1.9 with respect to former clients once Client reveals the secret that persuades Attorney that Client and Spouse may have adverse interests. Client essentially becomes a new client with a "substantially related matter" with regard to a former client (Spouse) with arguably "materially adverse" interests. Will Client permit Attorney to consult with Spouse to determine whether Spouse will consent to Attorney's representation of Client on this matter, and would Spouse's consent be valid if something less than full disclosure is made? Maybe Attorney should just assume that withdrawal is the only viable option once the secrets bell has been rung. With an effective exit letter perhaps Attorney has no duty to Spouse flowing from the secret and the worst aspect of this situation is that Attorney must reject future work from Client.

Notably, Model Rule 1.9 does not define "matter" for purposes of this rule and that the definition in Rule 1.11(d)[22] clearly does not apply outside Rule 1.11 (and would not be appropriate even if it did). Neither does Rule 1.0 define the term. As a practical matter then, it may be that either the priestly or the show-and-tell approach will put an attorney in the position of having to withdraw from representing either spouse if a relevant secret is revealed. Withdrawal may alert the ignorant spouse that some problem exists, although not with any specificity.

None of this is avoidable unless the initial representation agreement anticipates these problems and can constitute a proper informed consent (which is questionable). And notice that the mutual representation aspect was relatively easy compared to these secrets aspects. The duty of confidentiality is a far more difficult aspect of mutual representations, yet many engagement letters deal with the conflict issue but say nothing about secrets.

Similar problems could arise in representing Child after having represented Parent, and unquestionably would preclude representing a will contestant after having represented the testator. At one time it may have been questionable whether the ethics rules were meant to apply this expansively in all these common family estate planning situations. Today it seems pretty certain that the rules drafters have considered these types of situations and consciously have not provided any special exceptions. Nor is it apparent that the rules ought to differ.

Other Situations

Several other situations raise confidentiality concerns. One that is obvious and not much different from the mutual representation of spouses

---

22. (d) As used in this Rule, the term "matter" includes:

(1) any judicial or other proceeding, application, request for a ruling or other determination, contract, claim, controversy, investigation, charge, accusation, arrest or other particular matter involving a specific party or parties; and

(2) any other matter covered by the conflict of interest rules of the appropriate government agency.

is common representations among family members, such as a dynastic family situation. A second serious (and growing more common) concern relates to clients with diminished capacity.

Attorney has represented the entire Client family since before Client's spouse died. Through friends and personal observation Attorney is aware that Client is "slipping" and that Client probably needs asset management and perhaps even a personal representative. Indeed, one of Client's children may be taking advantage of the situation financially, and Client may need extended, and costly, medical and custodial services.

Model Rule 1.14(a) dictates that, if "a client's capacity to make adequately considered decisions in connection with a representation is diminished . . . the lawyer shall, as far as reasonably possible, maintain a normal client-lawyer relationship with the client." Then Model Rule 1.14(b) says that

when the lawyer reasonably believes that the client has diminished capacity, is at risk of substantial physical, financial or other harm unless action is taken and cannot adequately act in the client's own interest, the lawyer may take reasonably necessary protective action, including consulting with individuals or entities that have the ability to take action to protect the client and, in appropriate cases, seeking the appointment of a guardian ad litem, conservator or guardian.

This Rule is altered by Ethics 2000 to clarify that an attorney who reasonably believes that protective action is required does not breach the duty of loyalty or improperly violate the client's confidences by seeking appointment of a guardian or other protective action. Furthermore, Comment 8 to Rule 1.14 clarifies that "[w]hen taking protective action. . . the lawyer is impliedly authorized to make the necessary disclosures, even when the client directs the lawyer to the contrary."

Thus, for example, the court involved in the appointment may ask what caused the attorney to believe a guardian is required. The attorney may make needed disclosures if the answer is that the client wanted some weird dispositive provision, or it is clear that some less than meritorious (or even "normal") relationship is involved. Presumably the attorney may disclose even if doing so will put other family members on notice of affairs and facts that the client may reasonably have assumed would be kept confidential. Comments 2 and 8 to Rule 1.14 have been expanded, consistent with several ethics opinions that place the client's best interests (as determined by the attorney) above the absolute rule of confidentiality.[23]

---

23. American Bar Association Standing Committee on Ethics and Professional Responsibility Formal Opinion 96-404 (the attorney for an incompetent client may take the least restrictive protective action possible under the circumstance — although the attorney should *not* represent a third party who is petitioning for a guardianship of the client) and Informal Opinion 89-1530 (an attorney may discuss a client's suspected medication abuse with a physician notwithstanding the client's objection); Colorado Ethics Opinion 96/97-7

Presumably these will trump other pronouncements, such as: "[i]f suggestions of a guardianship would require the use to the disadvantage of the client or the revelation of a confidence or other secret, such use or revelation would be improper."[24]

RESTATEMENT §35(4) also allows the lawyer to seek an appointment "when doing so is practical and will advance the client's objectives or interests . . . ." This must be done consistent with §35(2), which provides that a lawyer representing a client "in a matter against the interests" of a guardian or other representative (see §35(3)), or a client for whom no guardian or other representative is available to act and whose ability to make adequately considered decisions is impaired, "must, with respect to a matter within the scope of the representation, pursue the lawyer's reasonable view of the client's objectives or interests as the client would define them if able to make adequately considered decisions on the matter, *even if the client expresses* no wishes or gives *contrary instructions*" [emphasis added].

A related situation might involve a client, perhaps elderly or suffering a terminal disease, who the attorney suspects is abusing prescription drugs or, worse, is being overprescribed (for a variety of reasons, such as to make the client more "manageable"). Alcohol dependency also might prompt an attorney's concern over the client's welfare. The attorney must consider whether it is in the client's best interests to discuss it with the client's doctor

---

(an attorney may disclose sufficient information for a diagnostician to make a determination to the extent necessary to serve the best interests of the client); Florida Ethics Opinion 85-4 (an attorney may seek appointment of a guardian over the client's objections if deemed in the client's best interests); Maine Bar Board of Overseers Professional Ethics Committee Opinion 84 (1988) (an attorney may inform a client's child about an issue of incapacity; the client neither consented to nor forbade the communication); State Bar of Michigan Committee on Professional and Judicial Ethics Opinion CI-889 (1983) (an attorney may be required to obtain a medical examination before drafting a client's estate plan that deviated from expected norms); New Jersey Advisory Committee on Professional Ethics Opinion 625 (1989) (an attorney's determination of the need for a guardianship should include consultation with appropriate medical experts and family members); New York City Bar Association Committee on Professional Ethics Formal Opinion 1987-7 (an attorney with an impaired client may seek a conservator and disclose confidential information in the process to protect the client's interests); Oregon State Bar Association Board of Governors Formal Opinion 1991-41 (notwithstanding a client's express direction "to mind Attorney's own business," the attorney may "take steps to protect what Attorney believes to be Client's best interests," subject to the admonition that the attorney "take the least restrictive form of action sufficient"); Pennsylvania Bar Association Committee on Legal and Professional Responsibility Opinion 87-214 (1988) (an attorney may seek court appointment of a physician to consider the client's competence); Virginia Ethics Opinion 570 (1984) (same).

24. Standing Committee on Professional Responsibility and Conduct of the California State Bar Formal Opinion 1989-112 ("it is unethical for an attorney to institute conservatorship proceedings contrary to the client's wishes" because doing so would breach the duties of confidentiality and to avoid conflicting interests; the opinion did allow withdrawal); Illinois Professional Ethics Opinion 89-12, arising out of a divorce representation and citing Model Code EC 7-12 for the proposition that the attorney's duty to preserve confidences is paramount; Connecticut Bar Association Informal Opinion 86-11; Nassau County, N.Y., Bar Opinion 90-17. See generally Tremblay, *On Persuasion and Paternalism: Lawyer Decisionmaking and the Questionably Competent Client*, 1987 UTAH L. REV. 515; Devine, *The Ethics of Representing the Disabled Client: Does Model Rule 1.14 Adequately Resolve the Best Interests/Advocacy Dilemma?*, 49 Mo. L. REV. 493 (1984).

(or, if necessary, with another doctor) without the client's consent if the attorney does not feel able to discuss the situation with the client directly. This issue is made all the more difficult by the fact that the client may not be competent to consent if the attorney's evaluation is correct.

Fortunately it is more clear today that Rule 1.6 (which authorizes disclosures that are reasonably necessary to conduct the representation) and Rule 1.14 (which authorizes protective action by the attorney on the client's behalf) extend to these types of situations. For example, American Bar Association Standing Committee on Ethics and Professional Responsibility Informal Opinion 1500 (1983) authorized an attorney to disclose a client's intent to commit suicide, based on policy grounds placing the sanctity of human life above the attorney's ethical obligation regarding confidentiality. And id. 1530 (1989) authorized an attorney to communicate to an attending physician that the client appeared to be abusing drugs prescribed by that doctor. Quaere whether a similar balance routinely will be drawn in less dramatic or clear-cut situations.

The comments to Model Rule 1.14 now provide better guidance in any of these cases, although they still require an attorney to be thoughtful and wise. Consider new Comments 5-7:

5. If a lawyer reasonably believes that a client is at risk of substantial physical, financial or other harm unless action is taken, and that a normal client-lawyer relationship cannot be maintained as provided in paragraph (a) because the client lacks sufficient capacity to communicate or to make adequately considered decisions in connection with the representation, then paragraph (b) permits the lawyer to take protective measures deemed necessary. Such measures could include: consulting with family members, using a reconsideration period to permit clarification or improvement of circumstances, using voluntary surrogate decisionmaking tools such as durable powers of attorney or consulting with support groups, professional services, adult-protective agencies or other individuals or entities that have the ability to protect the client. In taking any protective action, the lawyer should be guided by such factors as the wishes and values of the client to the extent known, the client's best interests and the goals of intruding into the client's decisionmaking autonomy to the least extent feasible, maximizing client capacities and respecting the client's family and social connections.

6. In determining the extent of the client's diminished capacity, the lawyer should consider and balance such factors as: the client's ability to articulate reasoning leading to a decision, variability of state of mind and ability to appreciate consequences of a decision; the substantive fairness of a decision; and the consistency of a decision with the known long-term commitments and values of the

client. In appropriate circumstances, the lawyer may seek guidance from an appropriate diagnostician.

7. If a legal representative has not been appointed, the lawyer should consider whether appointment of a guardian ad litem, conservator or guardian is necessary to protect the client's interests. Thus, if a client with diminished capacity has substantial property that should be sold for the client's benefit, effective completion of the transaction may require appointment of a legal representative. . . . In many circumstances, however, appointment of a legal representative may be more expensive or traumatic for the client than circumstances in fact require. Evaluation of such circumstances is a matter entrusted to the professional judgment of the lawyer. In considering alternatives, however, the lawyer should be aware of any law that requires the lawyer to advocate the least restrictive action on behalf of the client.

Adequate Representation

Model Rule 1.1 requires an attorney to be competent to perform the representation undertaken,[25] and the same requirement applies under Model Rule 5.3 to assistants employed by the attorney.[26] Given the increasing complexity of the legal and other aspects of estate planning and fiduciary administration, it bears noting that an act might be malpractice and it also may constitute an ethical hickey for which sanctions by the Bar may be appropriate. Nevertheless, many attorneys still believe that anyone can draft a "simple will" notwithstanding the reality, in the current estate planning environment, that there are short wills and simple lawyers but probably no simple wills. The relevant question then is what to do about a representation that is over the head of a particular practitioner?

---

25. A lawyer shall provide competent representation to a client. Competent representation requires the legal knowledge, skill, thoroughness and preparation reasonably necessary for the representation.

26. With respect to a nonlawyer employed or retained by or associated with a lawyer:

> (a) a partner, and a lawyer who individually or together with other lawyers possesses comparable managerial authority in a law firm shall make reasonable efforts to ensure that the firm has in effect measures giving reasonable assurance that the person's conduct is compatible with the professional obligations of the lawyer;
>
> (b) a lawyer having direct supervisory authority over the nonlawyer shall make reasonable efforts to ensure that the person's conduct is compatible with the professional obligations of the lawyer; and
>
> (c) a lawyer shall be responsible for conduct of such a person that would be a violation of the rules of professional conduct if engaged in by a lawyer if:
>
>> (1) the lawyer orders or, with the knowledge of the specific conduct, ratifies the conduct involved; or
>>
>> (2) the lawyer is a partner or has comparable managerial authority in the law firm in which the person is employed, or has direct supervisory authority over the person, and knows of the conduct at a time when its consequences can be avoided or mitigated but fails to take reasonable remedial action.

Probably the most important act a "general practitioner" can perform to protect against malpractice liability and the related ethical violation is to establish a good referral network to engage experts in areas in which the referring attorney is deficient. Similarly, even an "expert" may need to employ a consultant if the representation involves the law of another jurisdiction or ancillary issues about which estate planners normally are not experienced.

An attorney ought to address several ethics questions when crafting a referral agreement.[27] Issues of confidentiality of information (what may the referring attorney tell the expert without consent from the client);[28] who will communicate with the client in furtherance of the Rule 1.4 obligation to keep the client reasonably informed; how will the diligence requisite of Rule 1.3 be audited to ensure that the representation is proceeding properly; questions regarding fees, including what is reasonable, who is to determine the fee, who will do the billing, who suffers the loss if the client does not pay, and matters involving referral fees or fee splitting; the matter of piracy of the client's other business; and responsibility for mistakes, such as if the referring attorney passes along inaccurate information or the expert makes a blunder that the referring attorney is not competent to discover.

Adequate representation also involves questions regarding the scope of a representation. The ethical issue here is "when does the representation end"? Many estate planners now use engagement letters to specify the tasks that the attorney has undertaken to perform, along with a fee estimate that is addressed to those tasks. Increasingly, an "exit" letter is sent once the attorney is through with the assigned tasks, usually with the final bill, informing the client that the representation has been completed. As with the initial engagement letter, the exit letter may make it clear that the attorney assumes no responsibility to inform the client of any changes in the law or otherwise that might require a reconsideration of the plans completed (unless the client chooses to pay for this added service).[29] As

---

27. *See* American Bar Association Standing Committee on Ethics and Professional Responsibility Formal Opinion 98-411, dealing with lawyer-to-lawyer consultations and addressing such questions as the duties of confidentiality on both the referring and on the consulted lawyer, and whether the consulted lawyer is subject to any attorney-client obligations to the referring lawyer's client. The Opinion recommends anonymous or hypothetical consultations as a method of reducing the number and significance of ethical considerations in consultations.

28. Notice that the older Model Code EC 2-22 states that an attorney should not associate another lawyer outside the firm without the client's consent. See also EC 4-2, which is softer in stating that the attorney should not "seek counsel" from another attorney without consent if the client's identity, confidences, or secrets might be revealed. The Model Rules do not contain these prohibitions, except to the extent Model Rule 1.5(e) addresses fee splitting.

29. Without such a statement, American Bar Association Standing Committee on Ethics and Professional Responsibility Formal Opinion 210 (1941) suggests that it is not only the attorney's right, it may also be the attorney's *duty* to inform the client of relevant changes (unless the attorney has reason to believe the client has changed attorneys). See also id. Informal Opinion 1356 (1975) (holding that such contact is not an inappropriate form of

discussed at page 35, another advantage of the exit letter is that it potentially reduces problems regarding on-going mutual representations. For example, if Client blurts out about Client's nonmarital child or paramour, the attorney might have no obligation to convey that information to Spouse because neither Client nor Spouse is the attorney's client with respect to the now completed estate planning representation.

From a practical perspective, these letters must be written carefully and with a great deal of tact to avoid severing a relationship that otherwise may continue into the future. Client relations require that an exit letter both encourage the client to think of the attorney as available for further consultations and make it clear that all prior representations are completed, at least for the moment. Unfortunately, with some (perhaps many) clients this may not be possible, because they are on-going clients for other matters and the representation of them as a client in general will not terminate. Moreover, some attorneys will continue to represent clients to keep them apprised of law changes — for an annual retainer that the exit letter can announce. In this respect the exit letter need not be a final termination but, instead, serves to inform the client about what has been done and what might be considered for the future. But does that turn off any shared secrets agreement?

Perhaps the best result of an exit letter is its ability to inform the client what (not) to expect from the attorney in the future. Aside from its law office economics and malpractice minimization attributes, note too what the exit letter suggests about the ethics world in which estate planners operate. The situation of an estate planner's representation differs from a typical litigation matter that ultimately comes to a rather definite closure. The ethics rules generally presume that representations come to such clean, definable endings, but estate planners and their clients often regard themselves as traveling through life together, dealing with changes as they develop. This ongoing relationship may illustrate that the applicable rules sometimes fail to reflect the reality of an estate planner's relation to clients.

Fees

Model Rule 1.5 deals with fees, providing (among other things) three rules of particular relevance to estate planners.

First, the attorney's fee must be reasonable, based on a list of factors including the time and labor involved, the novelty and difficulty involved and the skill required to perform the service properly, the likelihood that this representation would preclude another representation, the amount

---

solicitation). Cf. Stangland v. Brock, 747 P.2d 464, 469 (Wash. 1987) ("the attorney has no continuing obligation to monitor the testator's management of his property to establish that the scheme originally established in the will is maintained," stating that the time and expense of monitoring would make it impossible to provide reliable and economical service to a client). Presumably a client is not obliged to pay for such a service and, absent compensation, the attorney is not obliged to provide it.

customarily charged in the locality for similar services, and so forth. Not listed (although arguably it should be) is the time when payment will be received, recognizing that a delay (sometimes a significant period) may occur in probate and in some estate planning situations.

Johnston, *Estate Planners' Accountability in the Representation of Agricultural Clients*, 34 U. KAN. L. REV. 611, 633-634 (1986), questions whether the tradition of providing estate planning documents at a loss in anticipation of receiving a windfall when representing the client's estate constitutes an ethical violation in two respects. One is because the lower fee may impel the attorney to do a less than adequate job at the front end, and the other is because the charge for representing the probate estate may be excessive, based on the factors noted. Moreover, an attorney may commit both malpractice and an ethical violation if probate avoidance otherwise might be appropriate but was not recommended because of such a fee-generation factor.

American Bar Association Standing Committee on Ethics and Professional Responsibility Informal Opinion 98 regarded it as unethical to offer to draft a will for free if the client would recommend to the personal representative that the drafter should be hired to represent the personal representative. The natural and unanswered question is at what price for drafting a will this improper form of solicitation is avoided. Moreover, a special concern with respect to fees arises if the attorney charges a flat percentage fee for assisting in probating a will and administration of an estate. Model Rule 1.5(a) requires a fee to be reasonable in relation to the work performed. Only one of many listed factors is the custom in the community for charging fees, which along with the ambiguous factor referring to the "labor" involved usually are the only objective factors supporting a percentage fee approach.

Second, if the attorney has not regularly represented the client the basis of the fee must be communicated to the client, "preferably in writing, before or within a reasonable time after commencing the representation." Ethics 2000 adds that this is not required with a regularly represented client who will be billed on the same basis or rate.

And third, fees may not be split between attorneys who are not in the same firm unless "the division is in proportion to services performed by each or each lawyer assumes joint responsibility for the representation; the client agrees to the arrangement, including the share each lawyer will receive, and the agreement is confirmed in writing; and the total fee is reasonable." This Rule addresses fee splitting and referral fee agreements between lawyers. It is not so clear, particularly in the context of Multiple Disciplinary Practices (MDPs), whether it speaks to fee splitting with nonattorneys such as financial planners, insurance agents, or accountants. Model Rules 5.4(a) and 7.2(c) clearly prohibit such arrangements and those arrangements also present conflict of interest concerns[30] that will present major controversial questions with which the Bar will wrestle for the foreseeable future in the context of MDPs. It is not appropriate to address this debate here at this time.

The requirement in Model Rule 1.5(b) regarding a statement, "preferably in writing," specifying how fees will be computed is worthy of note because many (and probably most) estate planners do not abide by this dictate. Not so directly addressed by the Model Rules are a smattering of other related questions. One is illustrated by American Bar Association Standing Committee on Ethics and Professional Responsibility Informal Opinion 1517 (1986). The question involved was charging a corporate client for work performed for an individual shareholder, employee, or officer. The opinion notes the concern that, because the firm charges the corporation, the fee will end up being deducted for income tax purposes when it is not a deductible expenditure by the shareholder, employee, or officer. Another concern is that the corporation might be unaware that the individual essentially is using corporate funds to pay for personal services. The informal opinion concluded that charging the fee to the corporation is permissible, provided the basis of the fee is noted, indicating the portion of the fee that was for personal work for the individual involved. In this way the corporation can determine whether to treat this benefit as income or as a dividend to the individual, whether to deduct any part of the fee paid from the individual's salary or dividends, and whether any part of the fee was a proper charge to the corporation or deduction from its income for tax purposes. A related question might be whether to apportion an attorney's fee for postmortem estate planning that benefited beneficiaries rather than the estate proper.

Fiduciary Administration Concerns

One significant and largely unanswered ethical issue haunts attorneys who engage in fiduciary administration, either as the fiduciary (trustee,

---

30. American Bar Association Standing Committee on Ethics and Professional Responsibility Informal Opinion 1288 (1974) and Kentucky Bar Association Ethics Opinion E-391 (1996) (it is improper for an attorney to draft a will for free if the client made a donation to a church or charitable organization that referred the attorney); American Bar Association Standing Committee on Ethics and Professional Responsibility Informal Opinion 1254 (1972) (it is improper for an attorney to draft a will and be paid by a worldwide ministry, which identifies donors and refers them to the attorney for the preparation of wills, based on aiding the unauthorized practice of law and lack of independent judgment concerns); id. Informal Opinion 970 (1966) (it is improper for a union attorney to draft wills for union members for free, as aiding the unauthorized practice of law by the union); Chicago Bar Association Committee on Professional Responsibility Opinion 82-3 (it is improper for a law firm to agree with a bank to provide a free estate analysis to bank customers); Advisory Committee of Nebraska State Bar Association Opinion 81-12 (an attorney may not draft wills for free if the client was referred by a local savings and loan as part of a promotion designed to attract depositors); id. Opinion 81-10 (it is improper for an attorney to compensate an insurance agent for client referrals by recommending that the clients purchase insurance from the agent); Texas Professional Ethics Committee Opinion 498 (1994) (a corporate attorney may not perform services for which the corporation receives a direct or an indirect fee in the form of commissions on products sold).

personal representative, or guardian) or, more commonly, as the attorney engaged to assist in the administration of a fiduciary entity. The question is to whom do the attorney's duties and loyalties run, and with what ancillary or derivative obligations? Because this topic is addressed in gagging detail in Pennell, *Representations Involving Fiduciary Entities: Who Is the Client?*, 62 FORDHAM L. REV. 1319-1356 (1994), and the *Report of the Special Study Committee on Professional Responsibility, Counseling the Fiduciary*, 28 REAL PROP., PROB. & TRUST J. 825 (1994), it is not discussed in anything more than bare bones detail here.

The unfortunate reality is that this issue is as confused and distressing as any to be found anywhere in the estate planning practice and the authorities and therefore the fundamental obligations are numerous and conflicting. The fortunate reality is that the attorney who anticipates the issue can dodge virtually all questions with a well drafted provision in an engagement letter, making it clear "who is the client" and avoiding in large part issues of spillover or ancillary duties. Doing so therefore necessarily is the first, last, and best advice on this topic.

In most situations this "who is the client" issue is of academic interest only, because the potential for a real conflict among the fiduciary, beneficiaries, and other claimants (such as creditors or disappointed heirs) never ripens into a real controversy. But in a small percentage of cases involving fiduciary administration, the real and present issue is whether an attorney who is engaged to advise the administration represents the fiduciary who hired the attorney, the beneficiaries of the fiduciary entity, or the entity itself. This issue is complicated geometrically if the attorney also acts as fiduciary and takes the position that the attorney also serves in a legal advisory role. "Who is the client" is a relevant question for a number of reasons, the most important being concerns about:

- Confidentiality and work product privilege. For example, if the fiduciary reveals to the attorney (or the attorney discovers in the course of the representation) that the fiduciary has made a mistake, or acted in a dishonest or criminal manner, may (or *must*) the attorney reveal this information to, or may it be discovered by, the beneficiaries or a court that supervises the administration? Or does the duty of confidentiality preclude such revelation? A fine summary of the law on this point is found in Wells Fargo Bank v. Superior Court, 990 P.2d 591 (Cal. 2000), and see Longan, *Middle-Class Lawyering in the Age of Alzheimer's: The Lawyer's Duties in Representing a Fiduciary*, 70 FORDHAM L. REV. 902 (2001).
- Conflicts of interest. To whom do the attorney's loyalties belong if multiple fiduciaries are involved and they disagree, or if the fiduciary and the beneficiaries disagree (an easy illustration being over fees), or if the fiduciary is a creditor of the entity or one of several beneficiaries and their interests conflict, and does the attorney have a conflict of interest in the context of such a

representation? *In re* Estate of Fogelman, 3 P.3d 1172 (Ariz. Ct. App. 2000), appears to say that representation of the fiduciary and creditors of the estate (in other matters) poses a conflict of interest. According to Kansas Bar Association Ethics Opinion 99-06, representation of a corporate fiduciary in its capacity as trustee or executor of a particular trust or estate also prevents the attorney from representing another party in an unrelated action against the same corporation in its corporate capacity. This opinion regarded as irrelevant the fact that the corporation is wearing a very different hat when acting as fiduciary than when it is engaged in the business of hiring and firing employees, engaging in commercial banking and consumer transactions of all types, dealing with its own shareholders, and the like.

- Privity and the right to sue. Although not specifically an ethics issue, the very closely related issue exists of the attorney's liability and the rights of various parties to assert a cause of action against the attorney, or to dismiss the attorney.

The identity of the client may be confused further if the attorney also represented the settlor of the trust or the decedent whose estate is being administered, or their families, any of which may justify various expectations about the attorney's role.

Confusion in Existing Authority

Comment 27 to Model Rule 1.7 states that:

> In estate [sic] administration the identity of the client may be unclear under the law of a particular jurisdiction. Under one view, the client is the fiduciary; under another view the client is the estate or trust, including its beneficiaries. In order to comply with conflict of interest rules, the lawyer should make clear the lawyer's relationship to the parties involved.

The limited authority on this issue is not consistent and virtually none comes from ethics disputes (the reported cases involve ancillary issues like fee disputes or evidentiary privilege). The comment appears to anticipate that the attorney may choose who will be the client by an indication communicated when entering into the relationship. Doing so in an engagement letter is easy and advisable, but experience suggests that few such engagement letters are used. See also RESTATEMENT §163, requiring that the attorney also make clear to others (such as beneficiaries) that they are not clients, if misunderstanding otherwise would be likely.

The "default rule," which applies absent an agreement otherwise, holds in the majority of situations that the fiduciary is the client, not the estate or trust, nor the beneficiaries or ward. However, the vast confusion in this area arises because so many cases imply duties (often akin to the fiduciary's own duties) that run from the attorney directly to the beneficiaries. See, e.g., Illinois State Bar Association Ethics Advisory

Opinion 98-07 (1999) and 91-24 (1992), in which a guardian's attorney was required to take remedial action when the guardian filed false accountings that disguised misappropriations, with reliance on Rule 3.3 (candor to a tribunal) to justify disclosure in violation of the otherwise applicable duty of confidentiality. Nevertheless, the majority position found in case law and ethics opinions is to the effect that the lawyer's duties (if indeed they rise to that level) to the beneficiaries do not create a true lawyer-client relationship.

Just to illustrate how sloppy and disconcerting this awkward and ill-defined relation can be, 1 Hazard & Hodes, THE LAW OF LAWYERING: A HANDBOOK ON THE MODEL RULES OF PROFESSIONAL CONDUCT §1.3:108 (2d ed. 1990), stated that the fiduciary *entity* was the client and that the *fiduciary* was a "primary" client while the *beneficiaries* were "derivative" clients. RESTATEMENT OF THE LAW GOVERNING LAWYERS §73(4) Comment h contains the following statement, consistent with this view:

A lawyer representing . . . a fiduciary . . . must sometimes use care to protect a beneficiary. This duty arises when the lawyer has knowledge of circumstances indicating that intervention is necessary to prevent or mitigate a violation of fiduciary duty by the lawyer's client. The duty should be recognized only when action by the lawyer would not violate the appropriate professional rules. . . . Because fiduciaries are generally obliged to pursue the interests of their beneficiaries, the duty does not subject the lawyer to conflicting or inconsistent duties. . . .

The duty recognized by Subsection (4) arises only when circumstances known to the lawyer make it clear that appropriate action by the lawyer is necessary to prevent or mitigate a breach of the client's fiduciary duty. This Subsection thus creates no duty of inquiry . . . [and] applies only to breaches constituting crime or fraud . . . and those in which the lawyer has assisted or is assisting the fiduciary.

Under Subsection (4) a lawyer is not liable for failing to take action that the lawyer reasonably believes to be forbidden by professional rules . . . . Thus, a lawyer is not liable for failing to disclose confidences when the lawyer reasonably believes that disclosure is forbidden . . . . For example, a lawyer is under no duty to disclose a prospective breach in a jurisdiction that allows disclosure only regarding a crime or fraud . . . . However, liability could result from failing to attempt to prevent the breach of fiduciary duty through means that do not entail disclosure. . . .

This formulation is unsatisfactory for a number of reasons, not the least of which being that the attorney often has an allegiance or loyalty to the beneficiaries rather than to the fiduciary. Indeed, the attorney may have a conflict of interest by virtue of having represented the decedent or settlor of an estate or trust and the surviving spouse or other family members who are beneficiaries of the entity.

Few courts have considered this alternative vision of the client representation that regards the entity (rather than the fiduciary or the beneficiaries) as the client. This probably is because of the historical notion that a decedent's estate or a trust does not have a jural existence (the civil procedure experts remind us that it is necessary to sue the personal representative or trustee, rather than the estate or trust), notwithstanding the fact that the entity exists for tax and other purposes.[31] Nevertheless, an engagement letter that identifies the entity as a separate jural personality and treats it as the client has several important advantages.

One is to make clear the attorney's responsibilities to the various parties who have an interest in the administration.[32] Rather than trying to establish the meaning and extent of fiduciary, derivative, or ancillary duties, the attorney knows that legal representation of a fiduciary entity is guided by the same focus as that which guides the fiduciary administration itself (the best interests of the entity) evaluated in an objective sense rather than with a view toward protection of some but not all of the various constituents or agents involved.

A second advantage is relevant in the very few cases in which actual fiduciary misconduct arises. The attorney avoids the question of the attorney's ability to reveal the fiduciary's breach of duty by regarding the entity as the client rather than the fiduciary. This confidentiality issue is distinct from the evidentiary privilege question[33] whether a beneficiary who has become aware of the fiduciary action may discover from the attorney information about the breach. The entity-as-client approach also clarifies somewhat to whom the attorney owes fidelity if a conflict of interest arises.

A third advantage lies in the fact that the law surrounding questions that arise in representing other entities (such as corporations) is reasonably well developed and can be relied upon to inform the analogous issues that arise in the fiduciary context. In those cases in which the issue of fiduciary wrongdoing is raised, a rule that favors the fiduciary with confidentiality as the attorney's client protects the party least entitled to protection. Often that

---

31. For a fine exegesis of this notion involving attorney fees in a bankruptcy estate context, see Hansen, Jones & Leta v. Segal, 220 Bankr. Rep. 434 (D. Utah 1998) (holding that the bankruptcy estate is not recognized as a legal person and that "evaluating an amorphous fiduciary duty to unknown obligees" by equating the duties of counsel with those of the debtor in possession is improper, confusing, unhelpful, and unnecessary).

32. See, e.g., Estate of Fitzgerald v. Linnus, 765 A.2d 251 (N.J. Super. Ct. App. Div. 2001) (an attorney for an executor limited the engagement and therefore had no duty to represent the executor personally and thus avoided malpractice liability for the executor's failure to personally disclaim a bequest).

33. See RESTATEMENT §134A. This distinction frequently is overlooked. See, e.g., Oregon State Bar Board of Governors Formal Opinion 1991-119 ("unless one of the exceptions to the attorney-client *privilege* rule applies" an executor's attorney may not reveal confidential information regarding the fiduciary's breach or intended breach of duty) (emphasis added).

rule also conflicts with the beneficiaries' expectations, and may conflict with the attorney's own sentiments and former client representations.

Assume for the sake of this discussion that the attorney has not been hired in the wake of a fiduciary breach, with the fiduciary paying that lawyer out of its own funds in defense of its wrongdoing. Instead, this case involves the attorney who has been involved in the fiduciary administration from the beginning and discovers that the fiduciary either has committed (or is about to commit) a violation of its fiduciary duties. According to Hazard, *Rectification of Client Fraud: Death and Revival of a Professional Norm*, 33 EMORY L.J. 271 (1984), the effect of the confidentiality obligation of Rule 1.6 under a regime that regards the fiduciary as the client is to force the attorney to abandon the representation to avoid being accused of participation or complicity in the fiduciary's wrongdoing. This does not serve the interests of the beneficiaries (who might rightly be regarded as the real parties in interest), it does not rectify the wrongdoing, and it leaves the attorney to draw the very difficult line of when withdrawal is required. Under the majority rule that regards the fiduciary as the client, the attorney's withdrawal may not even put the parties most entitled to protection on notice that they should seek representation of their own to investigate something that is amiss. Those individuals are not protected unless the attorney is able to signal knowledgeable beneficiaries that something is wrong by the manner in which a withdrawal is accomplished.

According to the majority approach, the attorney cannot disclose any information that reveals the wrongdoing if the fiduciary is the attorney's client. See American Bar Association Standing Committee on Ethics and Professional Responsibility Formal Opinion 94-380, which rejected a position that disclosure was impliedly authorized because of the fiduciary's obligations to the beneficiaries. That opinion stated that "[d]isclosure of client confidences is not impliedly authorized simply because the client owes duties to third parties." Thus, only the manner of withdrawal may constitute a warning that there is a problem.

Little logic supports a rule grounded in a duty of confidentiality to a wrongdoing fiduciary. The fiduciary is protected if the beneficiaries are too ignorant, impaired, or naïve to react if the attorney for a fiduciary learns of wrongdoing and can signal that a problem exists only by the manner of withdrawal. This charade would be eliminated if the attorney were permitted to notify beneficiaries (or, in appropriate cases, an appointing court) directly that a problem exists. That desirable objective can be achieved if an exception exists in Model Rule 1.6 for disclosures of fraudulent or criminal conduct, but that exception is not uniform among the states and may be of questionable application depending on the circumstances and the nature of the fiduciary action.

The better practice is to specify in the attorney's engagement letter that the fiduciary is merely a representative of the fiduciary entity and speaks on behalf of that entity to the extent the fiduciary is acting within the bounds of its duties. Under this approach, the entity proper is the client and the attorney's duties run to the entity, not to the fiduciary personally. Modeled after Model Rule 1.13 and RESTATEMENT OF THE LAW GOVERNING LAWYERS §212 (dealing with representation of entities such as corporations), this approach regards the fiduciary as an agent of the client who may direct the attorney only to the extent the fiduciary is acting within the bounds of its authority. The fiduciary as an agent could not hide behind the attorney's duty of confidentiality to protect against disclosure of wrongdoing.

A fiduciary who is in trouble always can hire its own counsel, paying that attorney from its own funds, but such a fiduciary could not dismiss the entity's attorney in an effort to cover up wrongdoing. Moreover, the attorney who was aware of that wrongdoing could advise the fiduciary to make it right or to hire separate counsel, and the attorney then would be free to make disclosure to the true parties in interest.

To illustrate how such a representation would apply:

Attorney represented Decedent (D) and D's surviving spouse (S) and drafted estate plans for both of them. D's plan named D's child (C) as executor of D's estate and as trustee of several following trusts that will be held for the primary benefit of S for life, remainder to D's descendants (C and C's siblings, and their descendants). During the course of administration Attorney discovers that C has made several decisions that work to the benefit of the remainder beneficiaries of the trusts, including C personally, and to the detriment of S. Attorney has advised C that these decisions were improper and recommended corrective action, but C has not followed Attorney's advice.

Rather than merely withdraw from this representation, Attorney may remind C that Attorney represents D's estate (and perhaps also the following trusts) and not C personally. In that capacity, Attorney may disclose information relating to C's improper decisions and their effects to S, notwithstanding C's misguided objections that Attorney is subject to the attorney-client privilege (meaning that Attorney could not be *forced* to divulge this information). Faced with this disclosure, C either will make the corrections recommended by Attorney or will hire counsel to represent C or all the remainder beneficiaries in arguing that the actions taken were proper. S also may need to hire counsel and, lacking a Rule 1.7 consent, Attorney should not represent any of these beneficiaries.

Your Duty to the "System"

Several difficult (and perhaps unanswerable) questions arise in a general context that is here labeled the attorney's obligation to the legal "system." To illustrate, consider another hypothetical:

Attorney's client is, at the very best, only periodically competent; in all likelihood if the question were raised a court would find the client to be unable to execute a will. Because everyone involved thinks it is in the best interest of the client and the client's family, however, a will has been prepared, which Attorney causes to be executed.

The issue here is whether Attorney, as an officer of the court, has committed a violation of Model Rule 3.3[34] regarding candor to a tribunal. The alleged misconduct is causing to be put into motion the local law presumption that a will complying with all the formalities of the Wills Act is valid and the testator thereof competent.[35] Use of a self-proving affidavit in a case such as this probably ensures that the question of proof never will be raised, meaning that the system may never get the opportunity to challenge the presumptions of validity and competence. In favor of allowing execution is the argument that the attorney is obliged to the client to make the best possible case, which in this situation may include giving the client the benefit of the doubt about capacity to execute and letting the system resolve the issue if ever raised. Clearly, however, there is a point at which a reasonable argument regarding capacity cannot be made and participation in an execution in that case would be improper. The issue is where to draw that line.

Although everyone involved may feel that execution is best, the attorney still has allowed the probate system to be deceived. The ethics rules regard this as improper, without room to wiggle under a theory that (like a "little white lie") no one is harmed. If there is a problem here, it may be in the probate code's unwavering prohibition of execution of a will without adequate capacity (although it is hard to conjure a flexible rule that would apply appropriately in all situations) or in the presumption of capacity that attends a formally executed will. The ethics rules merely preclude the attorney from intentionally bypassing the probate code restrictions by deceiving the court.

A far more likely and more troubling circumstance is illustrated by a second hypothetical:

In the course of doing estate and gift tax planning for Donor, Attorney discovers that gifts were made in a prior year that should have been reported on a gift tax return, but were not.

---

34. (a) A lawyer shall not knowingly:

    (1) make a false statement of fact or law to a tribunal or fail to correct a false statement of material fact or law previously made to the tribunal by the lawyer or offer evidence that the lawyer knows to be false. If a lawyer, the lawyer's client, or a witness called by the lawyer, has offered material evidence and the lawyer comes to know of its falsity, the lawyer shall take reasonable remedial measures, including, if necessary, disclosure to the tribunal . . . .

35. See, e.g., Uniform Probate Code §3-406(b).

The issue here is Attorney's obligation with respect to the Internal Revenue Service concerning the deficiency in Donor's compliance with the gift tax laws. If the government can be likened to a tribunal, then Model Rule 3.3(a)(1) might be deemed to require disclosure of this material fact to avoid assisting Donor in a criminal or fraudulent act. In that regard, Ethics 2000 amends the definition of a "tribunal" to include an "administrative agency . . . acting in an adjudicative capacity." Quaere whether that would include the Internal Revenue Service, for example at an administrative level.

Circular 230[36] is the government's own rules regulating practice

---

36. 31 C.F.R. §§10.0 to 10.93. Most significant to most estate planners is §10.34, which was amended in 1994 to more closely comply with the rules of §§6694 (understatement of income tax liability) and 6662 (accuracy related penalty). These rules impose ethical sanctions that may include disbarment or suspension from practice before the government and relate to all forms of returns, notwithstanding that the §6694 rules that inform the standards adopted relate only to income tax return preparation. Those rules used as a template for standard of practice dictates are indicated in bracketed references following each of the rules, which are reproduced in relevant part below:

(a) Standards of conduct—

(1) Realistic possibility standard. A practitioner may not sign a return as a preparer if the practitioner determines that the return contains a position that does not have a realistic possibility of being sustained on its merits (the realistic possibility standard) unless the position is not frivolous and is adequately disclosed. A practitioner may not advise a client to take a position on a return, or prepare a portion of a return on which a position is taken, unless

(i) The practitioner determines that the position satisfies the realistic possibility standard; or

(ii) The position is not frivolous and the practitioner advises the client of any opportunity to avoid the accuracy-related penalty in section 6662 . . . by adequately disclosing the position . . . . [§6694(a)(1)]

(2) Advising clients on potential penalties. A practitioner advising a client to take a position on a return, or preparing or signing a return as a preparer, must inform the client of the penalties reasonably likely to apply to the client [and] of any opportunity to avoid any such penalty by disclosure, if relevant, and of the requirements for adequate disclosure. This paragraph . . . applies even if the practitioner is not subject to a penalty with respect to the position.

(3) Relying on information furnished by clients. A practitioner . . . generally may rely in good faith without verification upon information furnished by the client. However, the practitioner may not ignore the implications of information furnished to, or actually known by, the practitioner, and must make reasonable inquiries if the information as furnished appears to be incorrect, inconsistent, or incomplete. [§6694(a)(2); Treas. Reg. §1.6694-1(e)]

(4) (i) Realistic possibility. A position is considered to have a realistic possibility of being sustained on its merits if a reasonable and well-informed analysis by a person knowledgeable in the tax law would lead such a person to conclude that the position has approximately a one in three, or greater, likelihood of being sustained on its merits. The authorities described in [Treas. Reg. §1.6662-4(d)(3)(iii)] . . . may be taken into account for purposes of this analysis. The possibility that a position will not be challenged by the Service (e.g., because the taxpayer's return may not be audited or because the issue may not be raised on audit) may not be taken into account. [§6662(d)(2)(B)(i); Treas. Reg. §1.6694-2(b)(1)]

(ii) Frivolous. A position is frivolous if it is patently improper. [Treas. Reg. §1.6694-2(c)(2)]

(b) Standard of discipline. . . . [O]nly violations of this section that are willful, reckless, or a result of gross incompetence will subject a practitioner to suspension or disbarment from practice before the Service.

before it in the tax arena. It specifies in §10.21 that "[e]ach attorney . . . who knows that the client has not complied with the revenue laws . . . or has made an error in or omission from any return . . . shall advise the client promptly of the fact . . . ." Although Attorney is required to advise Donor to amend an erroneous return or to file a missing return, Circular 230 does *not* require Attorney to blow the whistle on Donor. Moreover, the better position regarding Model Rule 3.3 is that the government is not in the position of a tribunal in this respect,[37] meaning that disclosure notwithstanding the Model Rule 1.6 obligation of confidentiality is not required.

Attorney must not, however, participate in any furtherance of that noncompliance. For example, if Donor makes another gift for which a return is required, Attorney may not simply report the latest gift as if the prior gifts had not been made. To do so would join Attorney with Donor in making a representation that no prior taxable gift was made that should be included in the adjusted taxable gifts base, which is untrue. By virtue of the Code §6701 aiding and abetting penalties, Attorney should not participate in filing a gift tax return for the latest gift if that return will be in error because the prior gifts were not reported.[38]

Under Model Rule 1.16(b),[39] Attorney may withdraw from the representation of Donor. Under Model Rule 4.1(a),[40] Attorney probably *must* withdraw from at least that portion of the representation that involves filing an improper gift tax return. It is not enough to simply sit silent while

---

Notable about these rules is that a practitioner can be sanctioned either as a return preparer or for having advised a return preparer. They specifically negate consideration of the audit lottery in determining whether or how to report an item. And they dovetail into the substantial authority rules of §6662, which include only the Code, Regulations (proposed, temporary, and final), legislative history, cases, and administrative pronouncements from the government (revenue rulings, revenue procedures, private letter rulings, technical advice memoranda, general counsel memoranda, actions on decision, notices, and announcements). No other authority, no matter how reliable it may seem or how necessary resort to it may be in the absence of other guidance, may support the determination whether there was a one in three likelihood of success on the merits.

As with any rules relating to standards of practice in a professionalism or ethics arena rather than a malpractice forum, there is no community standard defense to a violation of these rules, and the ultimate sanction could be a loss of the right to practice, as to which insurance is no protection. As a consequence, these rules have real significance.

37. See American Bar Association Committee on Ethics and Professional Responsibility Formal Opinion 314 (1965).

38. The §6694 penalties imposed on an income tax return preparer for an understatement of tax would not apply to a wealth transfer tax return. Nevertheless, the attorney also must be aware of exposure, if the attorney helps the client file income tax returns, if income from gifted property might be taxable to the client on the grounds of an improper assignment of income from property not yet effectively given away.

39. (b) . . . a lawyer may withdraw from representing a client if

    (1) withdrawal can be accomplished without material adverse effect on the interests of the client;

    (2) the client persists in a course of action involving the lawyer's services that the lawyer reasonably believes is criminal or fraudulent . . . .

40. In the course of representing a client a lawyer shall not knowingly: (a) make a false statement of material fact or law to a third person . . . .

Donor continues to mislead the government. This duty to withdraw from the representation would extend to any situation in which an attorney knows a client is committing a mistake (or, worse, a fraud) and is not willing to correct it after being advised to do so by the attorney. A good illustration would be an attorney representing a fiduciary who is improperly accounting, complying with the income tax, or making distributions, even after being advised by the attorney of the proper approach. In each of these cases it appears that the ethics rules work properly and that Circular 230 does not impose an inconsistent obligation. And, as a practical matter, do you *want* such a client?

A more intangible question is the obligation an estate planner owes to the general system of self assessment and compliance to avoid putting ideas in the mind of a client that the attorney believes to be insupportable under the tax laws, or to affirmatively counsel a client to avoid transactions that are not likely to succeed. The real issue is whether it is ethical to permit a client to play the audit lottery by taking a position or engaging in a transaction that never may be discovered by the government and that, if identified, would not produce the results the client desires. Although some authority exists in this respect in the tax shelter arena,[41] there appears to be no other authority directly on point in "normal" tax planning situations. The difficult issue is knowing where to draw the line involved in Model Rule 1.2(d), which provides that:

A lawyer shall not counsel a client to engage, or assist a client, in conduct that the lawyer knows is criminal or fraudulent, but a lawyer may discuss the legal consequences of any proposed course of conduct with a client and may counsel or assist a client to make a good faith effort to determine the validity, scope, meaning or application of the law.

It probably is fair to state that an attorney who actively participates in planning that involves legal positions that are just plain wrong, with the only justification being that the government is not likely to discover the issue, has committed an ethical violation in addition to the Circular 230 violation if, in compliance mode, the position is not adequately disclosed.[42] Short of that, however, the ethics rules provide no guidance in this darkest of gray areas, particularly if the client's activity is neither criminal nor fraudulent.

Solicitation and Advertising

The last two items of potential misconduct for an estate planner noted here are related. Overreaching, duress, or solicitation of business,

---

41. See Circular 230 §10.33.
42. See generally Model Rule 8.4(c):

It is professional misconduct for a lawyer to: . . . (c) Engage in conduct involving dishonesty, fraud, deceit or misrepresentation.

including solicitations to name the attorney as a fiduciary or as attorney for a fiduciary named in a document, is improper. Being named as the fiduciary or as the attorney for the fiduciary is permissible, provided the attorney did not instigate the designation. American Bar Association Standing Committee on Ethics and Professional Responsibility Informal Decision 602 (1963); Virginia Legal Ethics Opinion 1515 (1994). New York State Bar Association Committee on Professional Ethics Opinion 481 (1978) states that the attorney may suggest that the client name the attorney if the circumstances

> support a firm conviction that the client would request his lawyer to serve in that capacity if he were aware of the lawyer's willingness to accept the responsibility. Not only should the lawyer have enjoyed a long-standing relationship with the client, but it must also appear that the client is experiencing difficulty in selecting other persons qualified and competent to serve as executor.

Id. Opinion 610 (1990) is consistent, although it quotes a local Surrogate's Court rule that:

> In all probate proceedings, where the purported will and/or codicil of the deceased nominates an attorney as a fiduciary or a co-fiduciary, there shall be annexed to the probate petition an affidavit of the testator setting forth the following:
>
> 1. That the testator was advised that the nominated attorney may be entitled to a legal fee, as well as to the fiduciary commissions authorized by statute;
>
> 2. Where the attorney is nominated to serve as a co-fiduciary, that the testator was apprised of the fact that multiple commissions may be due and payable out of the funds of the estate; and
>
> 3. The testator's reason for nominating the attorney to serve as fiduciary.
>
> Failure to submit an affidavit of this nature may warrant the scheduling of a hearing in order to determine whether the appointment of the attorney as fiduciary was procured by the exercise of fraud and/or undue influence upon the decedent.

See generally *Report of the Special Study Committee on Professional Responsibility, Preparation of Wills and Trusts that Name Drafting Lawyer as Fiduciary*, 28 REAL PROP., PROB. & TRUST L. 803, 821-822 (1994), which opines that, under Rule 1.8(h), it also may be improper to include a provision exculpating the drafter for negligence in acting as fiduciary. This should be true only if the exculpation provision is more protective than the attorney normally provides regardless of the identity of the fiduciary.

The hard part about this situation is proving there was no impropriety in the designation, especially because any statement by the client to that effect may be every bit as suspicious as the designation itself. Moreover, regular insertion of a provision designating the attorney as fiduciary for every client would be improper[43] and may not be binding, no matter how it is worded. In addition, drafting a will for free provided that the client recommend that the drafter be hired as attorney for the personal representative also is improper.[44]

Even in less severe cases, the practical reality is that being named as a fiduciary or as attorney for a fiduciary raises eyebrows. The presumption is that impropriety resulted in the designation unless the attorney can establish otherwise. And in any case, allowable fees are likely to be scrutinized carefully. See, e.g., *In re* Estate of Weinstock, 351 N.E.2d 647 (N.Y. Ct. App. 1976); *In re* Estate of Thron, 530 N.Y.S.2d 951, 955 (Surr. Ct. 1988), both involving appointment of two lawyers from the same firm as coexecutors, the court in *Thron* stating that "[t]he appointment of two or more members from the same law firm as co-executors in double commission cases, in almost every instance, can only be the product of gratitude, greed or ignorance."

Unsolicited retention of a will for safekeeping also arguably constitutes an ethical violation because it makes it more difficult for a client to engage another attorney if changes are desired in the future. Retaining the will also makes it harder for the testator's survivors to employ another attorney to represent the personal representative. Compare American Bar Association Standing Committee on Ethics and Professional Responsibility Informal Opinion 981 (1967) (authorizing the practice if done as an accommodation to the client), and Pennsylvania Bar Association Committee on Legal Ethics and Professional Responsibility Formal Opinion 2001-300 (concluding that the practice is not unethical if the client affirmatively requests the attorney to provide custody and the attorney informs the client in writing that the client may retrieve the document at any time and that the personal representative is under no obligation to hire the attorney postmortem), with State of Texas Professional Ethics Committee Opinion 280 (1964) (holding that use of a statement that a will was executed in duplicate and that one executed original was retained by the drafting attorney constitutes unauthorized solicitation of the probate representation). Quaere whether retention imposes a greater duty on the attorney to keep the client informed about law changes. It also may generate a duty under many states' laws to produce the will when the client dies. See, e.g., Uniform Probate Code §2-

---

43. See American Bar Association Standing Committee on Ethics and Professional Responsibility Informal Opinion 602 (1963); State v. Gulbankian, 196 N.W.2d 733 (Wis. 1972).

44. No Model Rule directly addresses such solicitation, but see Model Rule 7.3, which is quite vague.

902. This duty may be more of an undertaking than the lawyer wishes to assume, as is the cost of providing fireproof security.

Your Dilemma

Admittedly the existing ethics rules were not written primarily for the estate planning and fiduciary administration practice and, understandably, many of them make less than great sense in those contexts. Even those rules that are general enough to apply in those settings may not reflect the needs of clients for family planning representation. Worse, many rules that are appropriate in a litigation setting are inappropriate in a counseling practice. Nevertheless, the most important defensive tactics to protect against alleged ethical violations are common sense, unassailable honesty, disclosure, and knowing written consents regarding all conceivable conflicts of interest (especially including mutual representations), dissemination of confidential information, deemed solicitations (including designation as a fiduciary or its attorney), and fees.

As stated by a respected attorney who speaks with wisdom about malpractice and ethics issues:

- Never enter into a business transaction with a client.
- Do not serve on the client's board of directors.
- Do not ever . . . attempt to put two clients into business together.
- Do not accept service as a fiduciary in a trust or will created by a client.
- Do not accept any engagement which might be in conflict with the interest of an existing client, no matter how lucrative the engagement might be.
- Honor the profession: avoid even the appearance of impropriety.

I did not always follow [this] advice. I . . . regret the result of each and every deviation I made. A pure professional relationship is one in which the lawyer, the accountant, the advisor, has nothing to gain from his or her relationship with the client other than a reasonable compensation for services fairly and objectively rendered.

The Malpractice Aspect of All This

Theoretically a violation of the ethics rules is not tantamount to malpractice. Model Rules Scope Comment 20 states:

Violation of a Rule should not itself give rise to a cause of action against a lawyer nor should it create any presumption in such a case that a legal duty has been breached. In addition, violation of a Rule does not necessarily warrant any other nondisciplinary remedy, such as disqualification of a lawyer in pending litigation. The Rules are designed to provide guidance to lawyers and to provide a structure for regulating conduct through disciplinary agencies. They are not designed to be a basis for civil liability. Furthermore, the purpose of the Rules can be subverted when they are invoked by opposing parties as procedural weapons. The fact that a Rule is a just basis for a lawyer's self-assessment, or for sanctioning a lawyer under the administration of a disciplinary authority, does not imply that an antagonist in a collateral proceeding or transaction has standing to seek enforcement of the Rule. Nevertheless, since the Rules do establish standards of conduct by lawyers, a lawyer's violation of a Rule may be evidence of breach of the applicable standard of conduct.

Because the ethics and malpractice concepts differ, an ethics violation is not necessarily an act of malpractice. Nevertheless, the same activity that constitutes an ethics violation also may constitute malpractice and cases may support attorney liability on the basis of an ethics violation.[45] Moreover, some commentators and courts confuse the terminology (if not the concept) so that some refer to an attorney's violation of the ethical rules as malpractice or vice versa.

To guard against malpractice, some of the more common mistakes can be prevented (or the likelihood minimized) by taking the following steps:

1. Refer to a specialist matters that are out of the attorney's area of expertise (most especially including matters that involve the law of another jurisdiction). It is curious that the legal profession lags light years behind the medical profession in the area of referrals. No jury would excuse a podiatrist for malpractice in brain surgery; why would a fact finder be any more accepting of an inexperienced attorney who messes up in drafting an estate plan?

---

45. Thomason, *How estate planners can cope with the increasing risk of malpractice claims*, 12 EST. PLAN. 130 (1985), states: "Courts frequently cite and rely on [the ethics rules] to determine whether an attorney's conduct meets an acceptable standard of care in civil damage actions." Id. at 130, citing no cases. More accurate is the assessment that most courts have declined to hold that an ethics violation establishes civil liability. See Dahlquist, *The Code of Professional Responsibility and Civil Damage Actions Against Attorneys*, 9 OHIO N.U. L. REV. 1 (1983). Nevertheless, several cases have stated that the ethics rules may define or provide evidence of the proper standard of conduct required of attorneys. See, e.g., Woodruff v. Tomlin, 616 F.2d 924 (6th Cir. 1979) (stating that, although the Code of Professional Responsibility did not undertake to define standards for civil liability, it constituted "some evidence" of the requisite standards imposed on attorneys); Beattie v. Firnschild, 394 N.W.2d 107 (Mich. Ct. App. 1986) (an ethics violation is "rebuttable evidence of malpractice"); Lipton v. Boesky, 313 N.W.2d 163 (Mich. Ct. App. 1981) (same); Sullivan v. Birmingham, 416 N.E.2d 528 (Mass. Ct. App. 1981) (violation of an ethics rule that was intended to protect persons in the plaintiff's position may be evidence of the attorney's negligence); In re Taylor, 363 N.E.2d 845 (Ill. 1977) (the ethics rules are a "safe guide" of standards required of attorneys); and cf. Jenkins v. Wheeler, 316 S.E.2d 354 (N.C. Ct. App. 1984) (relying on ethics rules regarding conflicts of interest to establish a duty that would give rise to attorney civil liability).

2. Keep current. An attorney who attempts to practice in the estate planning arena without committing the time to regular review of developments (both tax and nontax related) is asking for trouble.

3. Establish routines, procedures, and guidelines, *and follow them*. An astounding number of malpractice cases involve situations in which seemingly simple functions were overlooked (like failing to provide the requisite number of witnesses to an execution supervised by an attorney, or having the wrong spouse sign a will prepared in a reciprocal will situation). Matters that seem routine easily can be overlooked without attention to detail, and the failure to properly perform routine matters is hard to defend.

4. Proofread documents *before* they go out. Estate planners want to rely on word processing notwithstanding the proclivity of computers to stutter or burp at the wrong moment, causing a provision to be omitted or jumbled. Frequently enough, a sentence or provision is omitted accidentally; the added time is well spent verifying that every paragraph is in place and says what it is supposed to say.

5. Obtain independent reviews of all unusual drafts. Even more dangerous than failing to include all necessary provisions is the proclivity to draft a provision and immediately send it to the client, without having a colleague review it to ascertain that it truly says what the drafter intended.

There is hardly a more dangerous trap in drafting than failing to have an unbiased set of eyes review a document. Even the best drafters will admit that it is all too easy to create a provision and, because the drafter knows what it is supposed to say, upon reviewing it conclude that it is clear, only to find that another person is not able to ascertain the drafter's intent. All drafters get too close to their work to see some of the mistakes or ambiguities created.

If another opinion is not available, then a wise drafter will try to set the document aside long enough to forget what the client wanted. The point is that the drafter should let the draft get old and cold (enough so that the drafter forgets), then re-read the draft, and then check it against the drafter's notes, all to verify that the document says what the drafter and the client originally intended. Gaining enough objectivity in this manner is difficult and requires time that many planners simply cannot make available.

By all means, when asking another reviewer to read a document, don't explain what the document is meant to say: have that person read it and explain what it said to them. The draft needs refinement if that explanation is not what the drafter and the client intended. Drafters who must review their own drafting seldom get this kind of disinterested, objective input, but waiting to review the document until the drafter has forgotten what the client intended (in hopes of accomplishing the same result) is the only effective method of accomplishing anything like the same result.

6. The review factor is only one of many reasons why it is bad business to do "rush" jobs. Although the ethical obligation is to avoid delay, the malpractice risk flows from too much haste. Sometimes an accelerated project cannot be avoided, but even then the client should be informed of the risks involved. The attorney is justified in informing the client that the time constraints imposed create risks and that the client cannot expect the same quality of service that a more reasonable time commitment would permit. Limiting the attorney's duty in such a case also may be permissible. See RESTATEMENT §30, but compare §76 (limiting duties is permissible, but limiting liability for malpractice in performing the attorney's duties is not).

7. Document the file, not only when a rush job creates the risk of error, but with respect to any aspect of the planning that might generate questions in the future. If recommendations were rejected by the client, document the fact that they were made and why they were not accepted. If special circumstances led to deviations from normal procedures or caused consideration of unusual factors, document what they were and what decisions were made (and why) and what consequences were anticipated. As with valuations, with estate planning the attorney must be prepared to prove many years later that a proper job was done under the circumstances. Be sure to inform the client about dangers to anticipate in their future dealings (such as the need to revise the plan if an unmarried client with children marries again in the future or if a young client has or adopts a child).

8. In general, impose an affirmative obligation on clients to inform the attorney about their situation, about any unusual assets or relationships, and about all changes that might be relevant to the plan. Don't accept a client's refusal to provide needed information, or at the very least document that the request was made and refused and that the client was informed of the attendant risks. Moreover, don't take the client's word (or that of other advisors, such as an insurance agent or stock broker) for anything of substance that can be verified. Who owns life insurance, who is the designated beneficiary, what does a power of appointment provide, how is property titled (and the like), all can be verified and, more importantly, all can be misrepresented by individuals who don't understand the legal and practical issues involved.

9. Pay careful attention to the integration of documents and plans. For example, the tax payment provisions in a will and pour over trust, or the presumptions of survivorship in reciprocal wills, easily can be inconsistent and may defeat intent. To illustrate, one common glitch is each spouse leaving property to a third party if the other does not survive for X days, giving that person a windfall if one spouse survives but for fewer than X days. Another less common example is

conducting an asset transfer for a client and failing to review the estate plan to determine whether that conveyance negates a specific disposition to a designated beneficiary (and potential plaintiff).

10. Be wary of "mixing and matching" or "cutting and pasting" documents. Especially with documents produced by others, the risk of including something that is inappropriate or, more likely, omitting something that is essential, increases geometrically when a drafter adopts material from sources that were not tailored for the task at hand. Marginally competent planners who don't know why a provision was included or can't find a guide to what provisions need to be included should try hard not to create their own documents. Instead, look for someone who has done this work, even if it is not perfect.

11. Try not to be the first kid on the block to try any new gimmick. Estate planners (particularly those more steeped in the tax side of it than the property or "people" side) seem to have an almost irresistible desire to embrace new techniques. Like the first several articles written about any new tax bill, there are bound to be mistakes made by those who are charting new ground. As the old chestnut says: "The second mouse gets the cheese." A client who can wait a while before jumping into a new routine almost always will be better served and the attorney will have less risk of overlooking something significant.

12. Be nice. Potential plaintiffs find it harder to sue attorneys who are likeable, helpful, sympathetic, responsive, and even polite. It is impossible to overstate the number of situations involving demonstrable blunders committed by planners who were in over their head, or distracted, or otherwise not able to do the job properly, in which the family had a clear cause of action that they decided not to pursue against the attorney, often for no better reason than that the family felt charitable to an attorney who had been there for the decedent, perhaps someone the family was proud to regard as a friend. When all else fails, remember that Mama was right: "it don't cost nothin' to be nice."

Selected Provisions from
RESTATEMENT (SECOND) OF AGENCY

§387. General Principle.

Unless otherwise agreed, an agent is subject to a duty to his principal to act solely for the benefit of the principal in all matters connected with his agency.

Comment b. *Scope of duty.* The agent's duty is not only to act solely for the benefit of the principal in matters entrusted to him (see §§388-392) but also to take no unfair advantage of his position in the use of information or things acquired by him because of his position as agent or because of the opportunities which his position affords. See §§393-398. . . . His duties of loyalty to the interest of his principal are the same as those of a trustee to his beneficiaries. See the RESTATEMENT OF TRUSTS §170.

§388. Duty to Account for Profits Arising Out of Employment.

Unless otherwise agreed, an agent who makes a profit in connection with transactions conducted by him on behalf of the principal is under a duty to give such profit to the principal.

Comment a. . . . [A]n agent who, without the knowledge of the principal, receives something in connection with, or because of, a transaction conducted for the principal, has a duty to pay this to the principal even though otherwise he has acted with perfect fairness to the principal and violates no duty of loyalty in receiving the amount. See §203 of the RESTATEMENT OF TRUSTS.

Illustration 2. P authorizes A to sell land held in A's name for a fixed sum. A makes a contract to sell the land to T, who makes a deposit which is to be forfeited if the transaction is not carried out. T forfeits the amount. A sells the land to another person at the price fixed by P. A is under a duty to account to P for the amount received from T.

Comment b. *Gratuities to agent.* An agent can properly retain gratuities received on account of the principal's business if, because of custom or otherwise, an agreement to this effect is found. Except in such a case, the receipt and retention of a gratuity by an agent from a party with interests adverse to those of the principal is evidence that the agent is committing a breach of duty to the principal by not acting in his interests.

§389. Acting as Adverse Party without Principal's Consent.

Unless otherwise agreed, an agent is subject to a duty not to deal with his principal as an adverse party in a transaction connected with his agency without the principal's knowledge.

Comment c. *Where no harm to principal.* The rule stated in this Section is not based upon the existence of harm to the principal in the particular case. It exists to prevent a conflict of opposing interests in the minds of agents whose duty it is to act solely for the benefit of their principals. The rule applies, therefore, even though the transaction between the principal and the agent is beneficial to the principal.

§390. Acting as Adverse Party with Principal's Consent.

An agent who, to the knowledge of the principal, acts on his own account in a transaction in which he is employed has a duty to deal fairly with the principal and to disclose to him all facts which the agent knows or should know would reasonably affect the principal's judgment, unless the principal has manifested that he knows such facts or that he does not care to know them.

Comment a. *Facts to be disclosed.* One employed as an agent violates no duty to the principal by acting for his own benefit if he makes a full disclosure of the facts to an acquiescent principal and takes no unfair advantage of him. Before dealing with the principal on his own account, however, an agent has a duty, not only to make no misstatements of fact, but also to disclose to the principal all relevant facts fully and completely. . . .

If the principal has limited business experience, an agent cannot properly fail to give such information merely because the principal says he does not care for it; the agent's duty of fair dealing is satisfied only if he reasonably believes that the principal understands the implications of the transaction.

Comment c. *Fairness.* . . . An agent who is in a close confidential relation to the principal, such as a family attorney, has the burden of proving that a substantial gift to him was not the result of undue influence.

§391. Acting for Adverse Party without Principal's Consent.

Unless otherwise agreed, an agent is subject to a duty to his principal not to act on behalf of an adverse party in a transaction connected with his agency without the principal's knowledge.

Comment e. *Evidence.* The receipt of anything of a substantial nature from an adverse party to a transaction is evidence that the agent is acting on behalf of such person and is sufficient, without more, to sustain a judgment against the agent. Likewise, the promise of an indirect reward by the other party is sufficient evidence of improper conduct, as when a buyer tells a selling agent that if the sale to him is made, he will employ the agent to take charge of the premises for him.

Comment g. *Liability of third persons.* A person who knows that another has employed an agent to conduct a transaction with him is subject to liability to the other for secretly employing the other to act on his account in the transaction. Such an agreement is illegal and unenforceable. The defrauded principal can rescind the transaction with the other principal, or he can affirm it and recover damages from him, or damages or profits from the agent . . . .

§392. Acting for Adverse Party with Principal's Consent.

An agent who, to the knowledge of two principals, acts for both of them in a transaction between them, has a duty to act with fairness to each and to disclose to each all facts which he knows or should know would reasonably affect the judgment of each in permitting such dual agency, except as to a principal who has manifested that he knows such facts or does not care to know them.

Comment a. *Fairness.* An agent employed by both parties to a transaction, with knowledge by them of his double employment, has the same duty to act with fairness to each that an agent has in dealing with his principal on his own account. See §390. If he is employed to complete a transaction for them, he must act with consideration for the interest of each; if he is employed by each to give advice, his advice must be impartial.

§394. Acting for one with Conflicting Interests.

Unless otherwise agreed, an agent is subject to a duty not to act or to agree to act during the period of his agency for persons whose interests conflict with those of the principal in matters in which the agent is employed.

Comment a. . . . Under the rule stated in this Section, the agent commits a breach of duty to his principal by acting for another in an undertaking which has a substantial tendency to cause him to [dis]regard his duty to serve his [first] principal with only his principal's purposes in mind. . . . The danger that he will not be impartial and that he will use confidential information obtained in the business of one in the affairs of the other makes it improper for him to act for both.

Comment d. *Attorneys* . . . With full disclosure, it is proper, and frequently desirable in the interests of economy, for an attorney to represent clients whose claims are only theoretically adverse.

§395. Using or Disclosing Confidential Information.

Unless otherwise agreed, an agent is subject to a duty to the principal not to use or to communicate information confidentially given him by the principal or acquired by him during the course of or on account of his agency or in violation of his duties as agent, in competition with or to the injury of the principal, on his own account or on behalf of another, although such information does not relate to the transaction in which he is then employed, unless the information is a matter of general knowledge.

Comment b. *Scope of rule.* The rule stated in this Section applies not only to those communications which are stated to be confidential, but also to information which the agent should know his principal would not care to have revealed to others or used in competition with him. . . .

Comment d. *Before and after agency.* A person who, in view of a prospective agency, invites a confidence from or permits the prospective principal to reveal confidential information to him, is subject to the same duties with respect to such information as if, at the time the confidence is given, he were in fact an agent.

Chapter 4

USE OF TRUSTS IN ESTATE PLANNING

Introduction

Trusts are marvelous devices. The mainstay for modern estate planning, nothing serves as many functions for estate planners as trusts. With them settlors literally write their own rules, crafting trustee duties and beneficiary interests that may effect any purpose that is not illegal or against public policy.

> The purposes for which trusts can be created are as unlimited as the imagination of lawyers. There are no technical rules restricting the creation of trusts. . . . Through the trust it is possible to separate the benefits of ownership from the burdens of ownership. . . . It is possible to create successive interests that could not be effectively created by giving successive legal interests . . . [and] to protect the beneficiaries in the enjoyment of their interests by making those interests inalienable and putting them beyond the reach of creditors.

Scott & Fratcher, THE LAW OF TRUSTS §1 at 2 (4th ed. 1987). This Chapter explores the benefits of trusts employed for estate planning purposes and compares the legal consequences of trusts to those of wills or other less useful vehicles.

Because a will almost always is a necessary component in an estate plan that disposes of all of an individual's wealth, this comparison does not anticipate a selection *between* alternatives. Rather, it provides a foundation to determine to what extent trusts effectively may supplement wills for property disposition purposes, and it informs the planning process when both might be useful. Although many trusts are created by wills (testamentary trusts), any comparison should consider the advantages of trusts created during the settlor's life (inter vivos or living trusts) as a supplement to the package of estate planning documents that often includes a will, an advance directive for health care, a living will, an organ donor designation, and perhaps a durable power of attorney for property management.

Trust Uses

Although estate planners often tend to think in tax terms, the nontax oriented reasons for using inter vivos trusts probably are twice as numerous. In addition, as periodic tax reforms continue to illustrate, the nontax reasons are the ones that most likely will endure.

Historically, trusts evolved to accomplish objectives that otherwise were impossible to achieve, such as circumvention of feudal duties or restraints on alienation. They continue to be viable for related purposes today because they allow us to sidestep various wills or estates concepts. For example, as compared to the procedure that must be followed in altering a will, use of any trust format as the settlor's primary estate planning document (coupled with a pour-over will) permits easier amendment of the estate plan during the settlor's continued life. More importantly, state law restrictions on the freedom of testation that apply only to probate assets (for example, in many states the statutory entitlement of a surviving spouse) often may be circumvented by using a trust that avoids probate. In addition, to the extent those restrictions are not avoidable under *one* state's laws they may be circumvented by placing the property in a trust that is subject to more favorable laws of *another* state. Indeed, clients who want interstate or transnational mobility in their affairs find trusts to be more transportable than other forms of property ownership.

Trusts also provide for voluntary property management with more flexibility than is available with other devices, such as durable powers of attorney that preserve the agent's powers beyond the principal's incompetence. Due to their flexibility, trusts also prove to be the answer when more conventional business devices (for example, a bailment or escrow) prove to be too inflexible. The beauty of trusts is that they permit the creation of unique relations and the ability to tailor the agreement to govern the engagement.

A good example of this is tort litigation settlement trusts that allow the parties to lawsuits to settle on favorable terms to each, notwithstanding significant differences of opinion about damage recovery elements such as the plaintiff's life expectancy or expected medical care costs. In cases of disagreement a defendant may fund a trust with a certain amount of money to provide defined benefits for the balance of the plaintiff's life, with a reversion to the defendant at the plaintiff's death. If the funding proves to be excessive, as the defendant may assume, all the defendant has lost is the use of its money until the plaintiff dies. Meanwhile the plaintiff is protected by a fund that potentially is large enough to take care of all anticipated needs, with a sufficient cushion for an optimistic life expectancy or a pessimistic medical cost prognosis. How better could both parties protect their legitimate interests in such a circumstance?

Flexibility and Dead Hand Control

More to the point for estate planning purposes, trusts also permit the imposition of either attractive or reprehensible (depending on who you represent) "dead hand" controls over the future use of property. A settlor essentially may tie the hands of generations of beneficiaries to assure the accomplishment or avoidance of certain uses, or to reward or punish certain conduct. These settlor objectives can be enforced in most cases subject only to the Rule Against Perpetuities (which is being reformed or repealed in more and more states) or prohibitions against restrictions or conditions on use that violate public policy. For example, a total restriction on a beneficiary's first marriage might be invalid, but a lesser restraint or a forfeiture of benefits upon a remarriage may be respected. See RESTATEMENT (SECOND) OF PROPERTY, DONATIVE TRANSFERS §6.2 in particular and §§5.1 through 10.2 with respect to restraints in general (1983). Flexibility to adapt uses to changing conditions also is attainable if coupled with judicious use of powers of appointment, trustee discretion, and trust protector provisions. That flexibility becomes more important the longer an estate plan will last.

Sometimes a settlor's unbending desires should be mandated in a trust that may last multiple generations. In more cases, however, the key to effective estate planning is providing flexibility to adapt to changing circumstances, whether those be family, tax, property management, investment, or other law or circumstantial developments. The most direct mechanism to provide for change is a power to terminate, alter, or amend a trust, which can be reposed in almost anyone (for many tax purposes excluding the settlor, and other than the settlor's spouse if it is appropriate to avoid grantor trust income tax problems). Thus, this power could be retained by the settlor in many cases; in all events it may be given to a committee, to the fiduciary, or to a trust protector. The issues are to what extent and under what kinds of circumstances the power should be granted, what to do with the trust property on a termination, and any tax exposure to the powerholder, especially if that person is a beneficiary.

Trusts have another advantage over wills. A will (or testamentary trust) can be defeated if all the beneficiaries agree not to probate the will in the first instance. On the other hand, trusts can be made more finely adaptable with a number of surgical approaches. For example, common are "small trust" termination provisions, allowing the fiduciary to terminate a trust if the fees are excessive in relation to the income generated by the trust. Less common but more important in long term trusts are provisions permitting termination in the trustee's discretion. This authority may be based on a variety of factors, such as

- impossibility to accomplish the trust purposes (e.g., to prevent trust assets from being counted in determining a beneficiary's need for government entitlements, or creditor protection through an off-shore trust rather than spendthrift trust provisions),

- accomplishment of trust purposes (e.g., providing education, or assuring support for an incapacitated beneficiary),

- a change in the law or circumstances making the trust purpose no longer relevant (e.g., protection of assets from a since repealed wealth transfer tax).

The extent of any permissible change should be made clear. Appropriate parameters may include

- beneficiaries who may be added or affected (e.g., only the settlor's blood relatives and their spouses),
- powers of appointment that may be granted or retracted (e.g., for generation-skipping transfer tax purposes),
- changes to accomplish or preclude certain consequences (e.g., causing grantor trust income tax exposure to the settlor of an inter vivos trust, eliminating or altering a source of wealth transfer taxation to a beneficiary or fiduciary, eliminating a spendthrift clause to permit beneficiaries to transfer their interests, or tinkering with a vesting provision to avoid violation of the Rule Against Perpetuities),
- changes needed to conform to new laws (e.g., increased federal security law reporting requirements).

Moreover, the document must specify those provisions that under no circumstances may be altered (e.g., anything that would cause loss of the marital deduction or of the status of an exempt generation-skipping trust, provisions relating to the identity and accountability of fiduciaries, or the provision under which all these changes are authorized).

In addition, procedures for exercise should be established (e.g., only independent fiduciaries may act, only with the approval of a court of competent jurisdiction, and only to accomplish a reduction of taxes or a furtherance of the settlor's objectives). State statutory or judicial authority to reform a trust (particularly the nonadministrative or nonministerial aspects) may be too restrictive.[1] As a consequence, this kind of provision should be considered for inclusion in any trust that will have an extended duration or in which other forms of flexibility (e.g., powers of appointment) will not be effective or appropriate. The point is that trusts permit this kind of engineering for future adaptations.[2]

---

1. Reformation may be a growing trend, but it still is quite localized and the circumstances in which it typically is granted are somewhat monochromatic, with many cases making changes seeking only to minimize or avoid generation-skipping transfer taxation. But see Uniform Trust Code §411, which is designed to facilitate trust reformation in the future.

2. RESTATEMENT (THIRD) OF PROPERTY — DONATIVE TRANSFERS §12.2 and the Uniform Trust Code are modeled after various cases or legislative provisions that permit trust alteration. Most reformations do not run afoul of the Claflin doctrine, which precludes premature termination (prior to fulfillment of the settlor's objectives), although at the extreme edges reformation may present that issue. Not incidentally, these authorities come on the heels of the almost total abandonment of the privity defense to malpractice liability of a drafting attorney, which makes reformation a useful protection against exposure. After all, mistakes *do* happen, and disappointed beneficiaries may sue. It also follows behind the mass marketing of poorly drafted trusts by "trust mill" operators, with postmortem efforts

The document also should provide standards or criteria that guide the exercise of discretion, if qualified individuals are expected to exercise powers to terminate, alter, or amend a trust. The trust document also should include exoneration and indemnification from liability to any disgruntled beneficiary because the powerholder either did act or chose not to. And the fiduciary should be protected from liability for following the dictates of a committee or protector acting in this capacity. The document also should establish that the holder of any power to terminate, alter, or amend may relinquish the power if appropriate or necessary, and a provision should govern the appointment of successors to ensure that someone always is in a position to exercise the powers that exist.[3]

Many lesser powers also may be appropriate in a given case in addition to or instead of the dramatic power to terminate, alter, or amend an otherwise irrevocable trust. For example, authority to divide or consolidate trusts can be essential for effective, efficient, and equitable administration. Changes also may be desirable for tax purposes, such as allocation of generation-skipping transfer tax exemption, partial marital deduction qualified terminable interest property elections or reverse elections, disclaimers, income tax avoidance of the §643(f) multiple trust rule, or to permit an S Corporation election with respect to shares held in trust.

Consolidation may be relevant with respect to trusts created by different transferors for the same beneficiary and with the same trustee, as to which virtual identity of provisions might exist. In many cases consolidation is precluded because the applicable period of the Rule Against Perpetuities differs with respect to each trust. Thus, the ability to round 'em up may require authority in a trustee to distribute trust assets to another trust, created specifically for consolidation, rather than to just merge the assets from various trusts or shares. In this respect, the issue is the extent of the trustee's discretion in selecting appropriate vehicles for distribution or to create a new trust to be the recipient of a distribution from one or more other trusts. The trustee would effectively alter the terms of any of the trusts, to make terminating distributions to a newly created trust and then go out of existence.

Again, the point is that flexibility is important the longer an estate plan will last. Various mechanisms exist to provide it if a trust is the primary vehicle in the plan, including powers of appointment, flexible trust distribution provisions, and powers to terminate, alter, or amend trust provisions. It ought to be possible in any case to provide whatever degree

---

to rectify the messes left behind. See generally Dobris, *Changes in the Role and the Form of the Trust at the New Millennium, or, We don't Have to Think of England Anymore*, 62 ALBANY L. REV. 543, 565 (1998).

3. For help in drafting provisions that permit the alteration of existing document, see McBryde & Keydel, *Back to the Future for the Estate Planner: Building Flexibility in Estate Planning Documents*, 30 U. MIAMI INST. EST. PLAN. ¶1200 (1996), abridged and reprinted as *Building Flexibility in Estate Planning Documents*, 135 TRUSTS & ESTATES 56 (Jan. 1996).

of flexibility the settlor wants or feels comfortable providing, all depending on the confidence the settlor has in the beneficiaries, the fiduciary, trust committees, or protectors.

Bifurcated Enjoyment

Trusts also permit a sharing or bifurcation of enjoyment in myriad contexts. For example, a group or "pot" trust for descendants provides flexibility and fairness, reflecting the way the settlor would use money if still alive (plus important generation-skipping transfer tax minimization and deferral opportunities). In such a trust distributions are made in the trustee's discretion among the class of beneficiaries until some specified time or event (e.g., when all the settlor's children have received an education), followed by division of what remains into equal shares.

In a different setting, use of a trust to provide lifetime support of a settlor's surviving spouse while guaranteeing ultimate receipt of the remainder by children of a former marriage is especially important. In this way all or a substantial part of a settlor's property may be held for the spouse without disinheriting the ultimate natural objects of the settlor's bounty. Without the ability to control final distribution of this gift, the settlor would be forced to choose between the surviving spouse and the children. The "handcuff" feature of a §2056(b)(7) qualified terminable interest property marital deduction trust permits lifetime enjoyment by the surviving spouse while assuring that designated remainder beneficiaries ultimately will receive the property.

Bifurcation between present and future interest beneficiaries is not unique to trusts (a legal life estate and remainder disposition could be used instead). But trusts are more elegant and the remainder beneficiaries enjoy better protections while the life tenant is freed from uncertainties that surround the permissible consumption or enjoyment of property subject to a legal life estate. In addition, property held in trust (rather than commingled with the beneficiary's other assets) is more likely to generate the beneficiary's respect as wealth that is meant to pass to the next generation, even if the plan gives the beneficiary nearly unlimited control and enjoyment during life.

Other uses of trusts that involve dead hand control include

- providing support to a dependent beneficiary only until marriage, remarriage, or some other event that terminates the need for benefits;
- guaranteeing the support or education of various beneficiaries but providing for charity once those needs have been met;
- protecting a child's surviving spouse (the forgotten family members) after a child's death without diverting ultimate ownership from lineal descendants;

- permitting enjoyment by successive generations without fear of dissipation through profligacy, improvidence, or inexperience;
- creating incentives to encourage or discourage certain conduct;[4]
- providing benefits to individual beneficiaries whose financial peccadilloes or litigation exposure (such as the potential professional malpractice of a doctor or lawyer) make it likely that outright ownership would expose the wealth to the claims of predators.

Property Management

Trusts also permit expert management, assuming a competent trustee (which need not mean a corporate fiduciary) is involved. Sometimes trusts also facilitate administration of property. To illustrate, consider the hassles of several beneficiaries' concurrent ownership of a life insurance policy or income producing property. Numerous problems that could paralyze joint tenants or tenants in common are easily avoided if a sole trustee administers that property on behalf of several trust beneficiaries. Fiduciary administration is especially useful in the context of a split purchase or ownership of property that normally would not be easy to administer if held in legal life estate and remainder form by two different parties. A good example might be commercial real estate or mineral interests that should be leased over a longer period than a term of years or the present interest beneficiary's life expectancy.

Trust administration also produces better management if the beneficiary either lacks the desire, experience, or ability to manage property, or is immature or improvident and cannot (yet) be trusted to manage property. At the other end of the spectrum, as the elderly get older and live beyond their most active years, management of assets may be a relevant concern for the settlor as well as for the ultimate beneficiaries. An individual may reach a stage in life when day-to-day management of investment properties or business interests (particularly involving record keeping and management decision making) is more work or inconvenience than the individual wishes to assume. Especially if the individual currently uses some other form of asset management arrangement, such as an investment advisory or stock depository service, the same management benefits are available through the use of a durable power of attorney or a revocable living trust.

Thus, in a complex investment and economic environment, an individual with substantial assets may need management assistance available through a revocable living trust that provides proper and professional asset management and application of funds for the individual's benefit. And, although durable powers of attorney can be useful in many cases, often third parties are not as willing to deal with a

---

4. See McCue, *Planning and Drafting to Influence Behavior*, 34 U. MIAMI INST. EST. PLAN. ¶600 (2000).

powerholder as they are with a trustee, particularly if greater amounts of wealth are involved.

Individuals who need professional assistance need not relinquish control of their property. In a revocable living trust the settlor may act as trustee while able, with a seamless change of administration when the need arises for a successor trustee to take over. Indeed, with a durable power of attorney the agent's powers may not become effective until certain conditions have occurred, such as the principal's incapacity. And unlike the durable power of attorney, living trusts created for the settlor's own benefit may continue after the settlor's death.

Both living trusts and durable powers of attorney can be amended, modified, or revoked at any time, and each is way more desirable than the alternatives: conservatorships or guardianships (which require court supervision and may limit the individuals who may be appointed); or statutory arrangements (including the Uniform Transfers to Minors Act or its predecessor Uniform Gifts to Minors Act, which cannot be tailored to fit specific needs). For example, the state law ability of a guardian, conservator, or other personal representative to deal with the property of an incompetent ward usually is severely restricted, relative to the authority that may be granted to either a durable power holder or a trustee. State law will vary on questions such as the ability to exercise or relinquish powers of the ward, to alter the ward's existing estate plan, or to make gifts of the ward's property, usually determined under the state law substituted judgment doctrine. Trusts and their less powerful durable power counterparts simply have no equal in that regard.

An individual who is not yet ready to undertake the trust approach also could nominally fund a trust created currently and later transfer assets to the trust as the individual becomes more comfortable with it (or less capable of dealing with the property). Such an inter vivos trust gives the trustee a trial run, allowing the settlor to assess the trustee's performance and to advise the trustee with respect to difficult administrative questions created by unusual assets. The key to this standby trust plan is for some other person to have a durable power of attorney to transfer assets to the trust if the settlor becomes incompetent before the trust is fully funded. In this regard the trust and durable power of attorney need not be treated or viewed as alternatives. Both may be useful.

Living trusts also can be used in management of realty. For example, a property owner may be liable for the cost to clean up polluted property, even if the owner had nothing to do with the contamination and knew nothing of it when the property was acquired. See Comprehensive Environmental Response, Compensation and Liability Act of 1980 (CERCLA), 42 U.S.C. §§9601-9657. Because this liability may extend to fiduciaries, many knowledgeable professionals refuse to accept property in an estate or trust unless an environmental audit has been conducted and a clean report has been received. If a landowner dies with probate realty and a will naming a professional personal representative, the lack of adequate notice and time to conduct an audit may cause the fiduciary to reject the appointment rather than be appointed and later learn it has a contaminated asset and liability on its hands. Thus, it may be wise to create a living trust to hold property that the decedent wants to be held in a fiduciary capacity, to better guarantee that a fiduciary will accept the appointment after adequate notice and an opportunity to inspect the property. In this regard, however, it may be wise to consider whether it is possible to extinguish CERCLA claims under a nonclaim statute by allowing the property to pass through probate.[5]

In addition, CERCLA §9607(n) exempts most garden-variety fiduciaries from most sources of personal liability attributable to contaminated assets held in a fiduciary capacity. The full quantum of assets of the fiduciary entity are subject to liability, but the fiduciary's liability is limited to those assets held in the fiduciary entity unless the fiduciary negligently caused or contributed to the environmental contamination. Although the original property holder's entire estate may be liable for the costs of any remediation, it may be possible to minimize liability with proper planning, such as by placing the potential risk property in a separate trust that insulates other assets in the settlor's estate and does not expose the fiduciary to personal liability. These precautions may be the only way to guard against a knowledgeable fiduciary's cautious rejection of a needed appointment.

Asset Protection

A related but substantially more troublesome element of liability for toxic torts is the issue whether a landowner who is responsible for a CERCLA mandated clean up can insulate *other* assets from the risk of seizure to pay for that compliance. And this raises a related question: whether any property owner may insulate assets from potential future liability to any claimant, such as trade or financial creditors or judgment holders from tort recoveries (such as malpractice or hazardous business endeavors). Spendthrift trusts generally are effective to protect trust assets from the creditors of the trust beneficiaries and from other claimants.[6]

---

5. See *Witco Corp. v. Beekhuis* discussed in note 28.
6. See 2A Scott & Fratcher, THE LAW OF TRUSTS §151 et seq. (4th ed. 1987); RESTATEMENT (SECOND) OF TRUSTS §151 et seq. (1959). In §157.5 of the former and §157 Reporter's Comment (a) of the latter, Professor Scott advocated an involuntary tort creditors' exception to any spendthrift protection otherwise available. Both Sligh v. First Nat'l Bank, 704 So. 2d 1020 (Miss. 1997) (the plaintiff was severely and permanently injured by the habitually and criminally negligent beneficiary of a discretionary trust), and *In re* Estate of Nagel, 580 N.W.2d 810 (Iowa 1998) (tortfeasors were settlors of a revocable trust that became irrevocable when the settlors died during their tort that resulted in a judgment), allowed recovery of tort claim judgments against spendthrift trusts. Miss. Code Ann. §91-9-507 (1998) codified judicial spendthrift protection in Mississippi shortly after *Sligh* was decided, prompting speculation that it reverses that decision (because it does not distinguish between types of creditors), and *Nagel* is not much of an inroad: had the settlors lived until the judgment was presented the trust would not have been immune. RESTATEMENT (THIRD) OF TRUSTS §59 (2003) is the corresponding provision to §157.

However, a spendthrift clause usually cannot protect a *settlor* who is a beneficiary of the trust, at least to the extent of any retained interest or power in a domestic trust.[7]

Therefore, to protect a settlor from the settlor's creditors probably requires either that the trust be located beyond the jurisdiction of courts that would respect the creditor's claims, or that the trust be made irrevocable and the settlor retain no enjoyment that can be attached.[8] Making the trust irrevocable would entail potential gift tax on creation of the trust. Worse, it is possible for a settlor to relinquish sufficient enjoyment to incur a gift tax, and preclude creditor attachment, but still be regarded as having retained enough enjoyment or control to be regarded as the trust's owner for income tax grantor trust purposes. Furthermore, irrevocability, creditor protection, and gift taxation would not necessarily preclude inclusion of the value of the trust property in the settlor's gross estate at death.

Thus, as a practical matter, protection from improvidence probably is effective only (1) with respect to beneficiaries other than the settlor, (2) to the limited extent that the settlor wishes to put the trust property beyond the settlor's indiscreet adventures but not beyond the reach of the settlor's creditors (which is not likely the settlor's desire), (3) to the extent the settlor is willing to incur gift tax with no guaranteed protection from subsequent income or estate tax, or (4) to the extent the settlor creates an effective offshore asset protection trust.

In addition, a handful of American jurisdictions purport to provide the same asset protection benefits of a spendthrift clause for a third party or an offshore trust, to insulate a settlor's own interests in an onshore trust, provided that creation of the trust was not a fraudulent transfer or otherwise intended to hinder, delay, or defraud creditors existing at the time of creation. See Alaska Stat. §34.40.110; Del. Code Ann. tit. 12, §§3570-3576; Mo. Rev. Stat. §456.080; Nev. Rev. Stat. §166.040; R.I. Gen. Laws §18-9.2; Utah Code Ann. §25-6-14.[9] It is too early to determine whether creditors will be able to obtain judgments against a trust that a court in one of these states would respect and insulate from liability. Under the full faith and credit provisions of the United States Constitution it is questionable whether onshore asset protection trust planning will succeed to insulate the trust settlor's own property from the settlor's own creditors *if* the settlor has retained an interest in the trust.

---

7. 2A Scott & Fratcher, *id.* §156.3; RESTATEMENT (SECOND) OF TRUSTS §156 (1959). RESTATEMENT (THIRD) OF TRUSTS §§58(2), 60 (2003) are the corresponding provisions to §156.

8. 4 Scott & Fratcher, *id.* §330.12; RESTATEMENT (SECOND) OF TRUSTS §330 (1959). RESTATEMENT (THIRD) OF TRUSTS §63 (2003) is the corresponding provision to §330.

9. Allegedly Colo. Rev. Stat. §38-10-111 also affords creditor protection against any but existing creditors, but *In re* Cohen, 8 P.3d 429 (Colo. 1999) (dicta in a lawyer discipline case) casts doubt on that interpretation.

Asset protection planning is desirable to some individuals because they fear either political instability, economic uncertainty, or liability flowing from the fact that theirs is a deep pocket that may attract vexatious litigants. Individuals desiring protection own businesses that entail significant risk, such as a hazardous chemical or waste disposal operation, or who might be engaged in financially hazardous ventures that expose them to substantial future liability. This may describe professionals such as you: lawyers, doctors, accountants, engineers, architects and such who are subject to potential malpractice liability exceeding their insurance coverage and who cannot protect themselves adequately with a limited liability venture.

As a means of insulating a "nest egg" portion of their wealth (i.e., an amount that would not make the transferor insolvent, as defined under state law) without making an irrevocable transfer that is subject to gift tax, the most frequently considered asset protection device is a foreign situs (offshore) trust.[10] These almost always are created in a jurisdiction that has enacted Statute of Elizabeth override legislation, making it difficult or impossible for future creditors to reach assets that were not fraudulently transferred.[11] In this way the settlor may acquire a degree of protection

---

10. For literature dealing with this form of planning consult ASSET PROTECTION: DOMESTIC AND INTERNATIONAL LAW AND TACTICS (Osborne, ed., 1995); Boxx, *Gray's Ghost — A Conversation About the Onshore Trust*, 85 IOWA L. REV. 1195 (2000); Bruce, Gray, & Luria, *Exploring the Protection of Assets Trusts*, 130 TRUSTS & ESTATES 32, 39 (Nov. & Dec. 1991); Eason, *Home From the Islands: Domestic Asset Protection Trust Alternatives Impact Traditional Estate and Gift Tax Planning Considerations*, 52 FLA. L. REV. 41 (2000); Engle, *Using Foreign Situs Trusts for Asset Protection Planning*, 20 EST. PLAN. 212 (1993); Gingiss, *Putting a Stop to "Asset Protection" Trusts*, 51 BAYLOR L. REV. 987 (1999); Osborne, *New Age Estate Planning: Offshore Trusts*, 27 U. MIAMI INST. EST. PLAN. ¶1700 (1993); Rothschild, *Establishing and Drafting Offshore Trusts*, 23 EST. PLAN. 65 (1996); Sterk, *Asset Protection Trusts: Trust Law's Race to the Bottom?*, 85 CORNELL L. REV. 1035 (2000).

11. Statute of 13 Elizabeth ch. 5 (1571), the precursor to modern fraudulent transfer and creditor protection legislation, was enacted to void any conveyance that was not upon consideration and bona fide, if it was "contrived . . . to delay, hinder or defraud Creditors or others of their just and lawful Actions, Suits, Debts, Accounts, Damages, Penalties . . . and Reliefs." Because any fraudulent transfer is voidable, a fraudulent transfer into a trust will not prevent creditors from defeating the trust to reach the transferred assets, notwithstanding the settlor's lack of retained interests or powers. 4 Scott & Fratcher, THE LAW OF TRUSTS §330.12 (4th ed. 1989). This is true even in most Statute of Elizabeth override jurisdictions.

As against both present and future creditors, §4(a)(2) of the Uniform Fraudulent Transfers Act, 7A U.L.A. 301 (1999), specifies that conveyances made without fair consideration are deemed to be fraudulent without regard to actual intent if the transferor is or is about to be engaged in activities for which the transferor's remaining property is "unreasonably small" in relation to that activity, or if existing debts or debts that are likely to be incurred after the transfer will exceed the transferor's ability to pay. Prima facie, under §4(a)(1) of the Act a transfer is fraudulent if the transferor had actual intent to hinder, delay, or defraud any present or future creditor, and actual intent would be shown by any number of factors, such as that the transfer was concealed, the transferor was being sued or being threatened with suit, the transfer was of "substantially all" of the transferor's assets, the transfer occurred close to when a substantial debt was incurred, or the transferor was insolvent following a conveyance (meaning that the sum of the transferor's debts exceeds the sum of the transferor's assets or that the transferor cannot pay debts as they become due).

against future potential creditor claims if state law protections are inadequate (many states protect a limited amount of assets, such as homestead, insurance, annuities, retirement benefits, and tenancy by the entireties property against debts of only one spouse, but usually these protections pale in comparison to the potential liability that the settlor fears).

Because of creditors' ability to set aside transfers that are in actual or constructive fraud of their rights, this form of planning is effective only against the potential future claimant who is not yet even a cloud on the horizon. "Asset protection planning is a vaccine and not a cure .... [It is] best implemented when the client is least inclined to do so; that is, when the client's legal seas are calm." Engle, *Using Foreign Situs Trusts for Asset Protection Planning*, 20 EST. PLAN. 212, 217 (1993). One recommendation is to provide in the asset protection trust that all claims of present and currently existing future claimants be paid from the trust, making it clear that the protection sought by the trust is only with respect to those subsequent potential unknown claims as to which the present transfer is not an actual or even a constructive fraud.

Experienced practitioners in this arena report that advisors and reputable trust companies will not assist a client who is looking to dodge existing creditors, spousal or child support obligations, or tax liabilities, or to engage in any form of criminal activity. Indeed, to the extent asset protection planning removes property from the reach of a surviving spouse, the advisor may be committing an unintended breach of ethical duties to the spouse, if the spouse also is a client of the advisor for other purposes (such as for traditional estate planning).

The precise construct of such an asset protection trust arrangement will vary depending on the transferor's needs and desires and the laws of the various jurisdictions involved, but the general format of these asset protection devices is something in the order of a revocable trust with at least one non-United States trustee and a custodian of trust assets who is located in a different non-United States jurisdiction. There may be

---

Bankruptcy Code (11 U.S.C.) §548 is very similar to the Uniform Fraudulent Transfers Act in that it grants the trustee in bankruptcy power to set aside any transfer made within one year of filing a petition for bankruptcy if the transfer was made with actual intent to hinder, delay, or defraud any present or future creditor or it was made for less than fair market value consideration and the transferor was insolvent following the conveyance, the transferor was or was about to be engaged in activities for which the transferor's remaining property was "an unreasonably small capital," or the transferor intended to incur debts beyond the transferor's ability to pay as they matured. See, e.g., *In re* Brooks, 217 Bankr. 98 (D. Conn. 1998) (making none of the fraud based determinations in finding that the assets of an offshore trust were part of a bankruptcy estate). Cf. *In re* Portnoy, 201 Bankr. 685 (S.D. N.Y. 1996) (summary judgment denial to a debtor who created an offshore trust, arising in an action to deny bankruptcy discharge based on the debtor's alleged efforts to conceal assets).

See generally Alces, THE LAW OF FRAUDULENT TRANSACTIONS ¶1.02[1][b] and ch. 5 (1989); Henkel & Turner, *Asset Preservation Aspects of Domestic Estate Planning*, 29 U. MIAMI INST. EST. PLAN. ¶602 (1995).

cotrustees, who might be located in the United States (they might be relatives, friends, or advisors of the settlor), the custodian may be located in the United States so that physical transfer of trust assets is not required, and the custodian may employ nominee registrations that further the objective of keeping a low profile to the trust's existence.

The trust may contain an Emergency Trustee provision or other duress and flee clauses that operate in case trouble looms in the United States, such as a claim being filed against the settlor or the trust, allowing all connections that would support the jurisdiction of a United States court to be severed. The trust also may have protectors (which may include the settlor) whose function is to "advise but not instruct" the trustee, so that their involvement does not constitute a formal fiduciary role that might subject the trust to the jurisdiction of courts where the protectors are located. In addition, the protectors may have a power to remove the trustee and replace it with another (for legitimate reasons or merely to give a degree of leverage to their advisory role), although typically this power will not be exercisable in cases of duress. The trustee or custodian also may be instructed to employ an investment advisor who is located in the United States but who will make all investments through an offshore order desk arrangement.

In the final analysis the net result of these asset protection trust arrangements may be only a chicane rather than a total roadblock precluding a creditor's claim. This alone may be a sufficient impediment to recovery (in terms of the claimant's ability to locate assets and then the need to research foreign laws, hire local counsel, and prosecute an action overseas) that the claimant will settle early and for a reduced amount, or abandon hope altogether. On the other hand, the settlor of an offshore asset protection trust may be ordered to return the assets to the United States or stand in contempt of court. This could occur notwithstanding that the typical asset protection trust provides that any retained power of revocation is not available in the event of duress (which would include an involuntary revocation pursuant to a court order) and therefore compliance would be impossible.

Intent appears to be relevant in the asset protection trust context involving transfers that predate liability or any court orders, and the burden of proof is on the party seeking to impose a contempt order, to establish by more than a preponderance of evidence that the alleged contemnor acted in bad faith. Many cases involve actions in anticipation of particular decrees that were regarded as contumacious. The currently unanswerable question is whether the act of establishing an asset protection trust with a duress provision (in anticipation of a potential court order to return assets to the United States to satisfy a potential judgment) is itself sufficient to establish bad faith.

Regardless of how these issues ultimately are resolved, perhaps the most poignant reality is that a court may require the settlor to await the judicial determination of good faith while sitting in jail. Asset protection trust advocates often cite the fact that the device is merely a mechanism to slow down creditors; in this context, delay works to the disadvantage of the settlor. In effect this happened in Federal Trade Commission v. Affordable Media, 179 F.3d 1228 (9th Cir. 1999) (arising from fraudulent trade practice litigation involving a telemarketing Ponzi scheme in which the court ordered the wrongdoer to return several million dollars of profits from a Cook Islands trust). The lower court ordered the settlors of an irrevocable offshore trust to repatriate assets transferred to the trust, the trustee refused the request on the basis of a duress provision in the trust, and the court held the settlors in jail for civil contempt.

In a subsequent similar case the settlor of a Mauritius trust was jailed for contempt for failure to comply with an order to repatriate assets. He still was in jail over two years later when the court of appeals denied his appeal to that judgment. *In re* Lawrence, 279 F.3d 1294 (11th Cir. 2002). See also *In re* Coker, 251 B.R. 902 (Bankr. M.D. Fla. 2000), and Securities and Exchange Comm'n v. Bilzerian, 112 F. Supp. 2d 12 (D. D.C. 2000) (both finding trust settlors in contempt for failure to comply with court orders to repatriate assets in offshore asset protection trusts). Allegedly the contemnors in the *FTC* case also still are in jail. See Rothschild & Rubin, *Asset Protection After* Anderson: *Much Ado About Nothing?*, 26 EST. PLAN. 466, 474 n.32 (1999). "Bring your toothbrush" not being what the typical trust settlor wants to hear, and even "just" several days (to say nothing of a year) being longer than most estate planning clients are willing to spend in jail, these cases give new significance to the contempt possibilities of asset protection trusts.

Avoiding Will Contests

The time to win a will contest is when the will is prepared. See Jaworski, *The Will Contest*, 10 BAYLOR L. REV. 87 (1958). The most effective way to avoid a successful challenge to a decedent's estate plan is to use a living trust instead of a will as the principal estate planning document because, for reasons noted below, trust contests seldom succeed.

Will contests invariably entail a postmortem critique of the testator's habits, reputation, foibles, lifestyle, and sometimes even lack of capacity or other deficiency that constitutes a legitimate will contest ground. A trust may be called for if a will contest is likely, because one of the estate planner's duties is to insulate the testator's dispositive plan and reputation from challenge. And, fortunately, those cases in which a will contest is predictable usually are readily identifiable.

A significant percentage of all will contests arise in one of four fact settings. The most common involves a surviving spouse who is not a parent of the decedent's surviving children, and it really doesn't matter whether the will favors the surviving spouse or the children. A second likely source of potential litigation exists if children are not treated equally among themselves, whether they all have a common set of parents or they are half-siblings. A third dangerous situation exists if the decedent had no close relatives and the dispositive plan deviates from the intestate distribution among collateral relatives. In this case there may be parties with standing to contest the will who may be disappointed by the will's terms and are so distant in relation that they have no reticence about contesting the will and possibly besmirching the decedent's reputation. Finally, contest is likely in the growing number of cases involving "alternate lifestyles." If a client wants to leave property to a lover (i.e., not a spouse, whether of the same or a different sex), there are indications that juries, and courts reviewing evidence on appeal, are affected by their feelings about the morality or normalcy of the relationship. And the same may be true about other "unnatural" dispositions.

Some potential contests may be deflected with an explanation of the decedent's dispositive plan, or by inclusion of an in terrorem clause, by soliciting the opinions of a psychiatrist, or videotaping execution of the will. Nevertheless, a revocable trust is significantly less vulnerable to challenge than a will and usually is the contest avoidance technique of choice. The practical reality is that there are formidable obstacles to a trust contest challenge, notwithstanding the technical fact that a revocable trust is as subject to challenge on grounds of lack of capacity or undue influence as a will[12] (indeed, a greater capacity may be required to validly execute a trust, being the capacity to make a deed or contract).[13]

For example, potential heirs cannot challenge a revocable trust during the settlor's life, because the contestants are only heirs apparent or expectant and therefore lack standing. See, e.g., Davis v. Hunter, 323 F. Supp. 976 (D. Conn. 1970). Instead, concerned but disappointed potential heirs would need to have the settlor declared incompetent and a conservator appointed who could seek to revoke the trust, presumably requiring a showing that revocation is in the best interests of the settlor. All this presupposes that the potential heirs know that the trust has been created, which is not required. And potential heirs who know about the trust and are inclined to challenge it are unlikely to bring suit if the settlor is capable of amending the trust. It is one thing to contest a will when the testator cannot retaliate, but taking the settlor on during life presents an altogether different endeavor.

Moreover, actual heirs may not challenge a trust after the settlor's death because, as mere heirs, they have no standing to set aside a revocable trust on grounds of lack of capacity or undue influence. Only the duly appointed personal representative has standing to bring suit on behalf of the decedent or regarding the decedent's assets.[14] This obstacle might be

---

12. 4 Scott & Fratcher, THE LAW OF TRUSTS §333.
13. 1 Scott & Fratcher, *id.* §§18-19.
14. See 3 Scott & Fratcher, *id.* §220.1.

avoided if the heirs filed a contest before the will is admitted to probate and petitioned for the appointment of a Temporary Administrator who would be under an obligation to collect, marshal, and preserve all assets to which the decedent's estate may have a claim. The heirs might exert sufficient pressure to commence an investigation or an action with respect to the revocable trust, but this is not extremely likely either.

Enormous practical difficulties confront heirs who contest a trust even if they surmount the standing hurdle. A respectable trustee of a funded living trust usually is an excellent witness to establish that the settlor had capacity and was in control of his or her faculties and affairs during life. Furthermore, the settlor's continuing contacts with the trustee during life normally constitute a continuous validation of the capacity to deal with the trust assets. Thus, the heirs must persuade a court to rule that the trust was void from the outset, and that every act taken by the trustee in the intervening years was without legal authority. It is uncommon for a court to open this can of worms. Thus, experienced attorneys report that an attack on a trust after the settlor's death, when the trust already has operated during the settlor's life, is substantially less likely to succeed than an attack on a will. This is what makes trusts the will contest avoidance technique of choice.

Probate Avoidance

To many people the foremost factor recommending the use of living trusts or self-trusteed declarations of trust is avoidance of the need to probate trust assets. Probate estate assets are in suspended state until letters of administration are issued and a personal representative undertakes estate administration. And they must be transferred again (with another potential interruption) when probate administration ends, even if the same fiduciary acts as personal representative of the estate and trustee of any following trust.

Conversely, assets held in a revocable living trust remain under the trustee's continuous administration from before the settlor's death through administration, which may span the lives of successive sets of beneficiaries. A trustee will be careful regarding distributions that would leave the trust inadequately secured against obligations imposed on trust property (such as a portion of the settlor's estate tax liability). But most trust funds are available without interruption for the needs of beneficiaries, and management of the decedent's assets does not suffer from bureaucratic or administrative delays or disruptions common to some probate administrations. This continuity may be of particular import if the settlor's estate consists of a family business that would suffer from interrupted management.

Revocable trusts often are used to avoid the costs and delays of probate in jurisdictions in which estates are subject to court supervised administration (dependent administration),[15] as well as to avoid public scrutiny of the decedent's assets and dispositive plan that is permitted in the public probate court process.[16] State law also may limit the right of creditors to reach trust assets after the settlor's death.[17] In many cases, however, the absence of state nonclaim protection against creditor claims is a significant factor that dictates at least a modest probate estate and administration to generate a bar against late filing creditors.

Furthermore, many jurisdictions draw a distinction between "court" trusts and "noncourt" trusts, the former being created as a result of a court decree (for example, a testamentary trust), and the latter being created without any court action. Noncourt trusts arise solely by the settlor's execution of a trust instrument and conveyance of assets to the trustee. State law may permit the document to negate certain requirements and the drafter of the trust instrument may choose to do so. Otherwise court trusts may be subject to stringent court accounting proceedings, at which a court appointed guardian ad litem may be required to represent the interests of minor or contingent beneficiaries.[18]

The accounting rules applicable to testamentary trusts can be avoided by utilizing a revocable living trust as the principal dispositive vehicle with a pour over will, along with life insurance beneficiary designations and employee benefits made payable to the trustee of the revocable trust. Absent a provision to the contrary in the settlor's will, Uniform Probate Code §2-511(b) is representative of most pour over statutes in allowing testamentary additions to a revocable living trust. Under that rule additions do not make the trust a testamentary trust, which should preclude any argument that the pour over mandates court trust compliance.

Revocable living trusts are widely used in estate planning as the principal document in the dispositive plan in jurisdictions that lack independent administration. These trusts will contain tax payment and dispositive provisions, and the will serves an ancillary function by making a pour over gift of remaining assets into the revocable trust. On the other hand, in the growing number of states that offer independent administration (or the Uniform Probate Code unsupervised administration

---

15. See Dacey, How to Avoid Probate — Updated! (Crown 1980), R. Esperti & R. Peterson, The Living Trust Revolution: Why America Is Abandoning Wills and Probate (Viking 1992); and R. Esperti & R. Peterson, The Loving Trust: The Right Way To Provide For Yourself and Guarantee the Future of Your Loved Ones (Viking 1988). Although many attorneys are critical of the probate avoidance craze, these have been very popular and highly marketed techniques.

16. Public scrutiny of the decedent's living trust is not generated even if the probate estate pours over to the trust, unless the will makes the mistake of incorporating the trust by reference. Any required notice from the estate should be given to the trustee of the pour over trust, not its beneficiaries, thus obviating any indirect revelation of that aspect of the decedent's estate plan. See 1A Scott & Fratcher, The Law of Trusts §54.3 (4th ed. 1987).

17. See 5 American Law of Property §23.18 (Casner ed. 1952); 4 Scott & Fratcher, *id.* §330.12.

18. See 2A Scott & Fratcher, *id.* §172, and 3A Scott & Fratcher, *id.* §260.

procedures), estate planners need not be as concerned about excessive probate costs and are not nearly as ardent about avoiding probate as they once were especially if the personal representative does not compute its fee as a percentage of the probate estate.

Nevertheless, avoiding ancillary administration of out-of-state assets may be appropriate, even if the decedent's home state is not a probate avoidance state and even if other reasons exist to make probate advantageous. Seldom is it desirable to conduct probate and administration in every jurisdiction in which assets are located. Some jurisdictions offer an ancillary administration that is simple and inexpensive, but real property located in most states may generate costs to clear title through ancillary proceedings that may be substantial in relation to the value of the property. This particularly is true because often knowing the law isn't sufficient to conduct an ancillary administration; local practice may vary and require research that the estate easily could avoid. A revocable trust is just the best of several planning arrangements that can be used to avoid the delay and cost of these ancillary probate proceedings.[19]

The revocable trust also may be appropriate for a mobile client, by centralizing management while the client retains control through a power to alter, amend, or revoke the trust. For example, mid-level executives who are moved from location to location as their employers advance them up the management ladder, or the "snowbird" retired client who spends the summer up North and winters down South, both may find a trust to be useful for administration.

In addition, historically many states replaced their inheritance taxes with only a "pick-up" estate tax designed solely to absorb the §2011 credit for state death taxes. More recently many states have enacted inheritance taxes that can be substantial, and repeal of §2011 effective after 2004 caused many states to (re)enact separate estate or inheritance taxes. Use of a revocable trust can put intangible assets beyond the reach of the taxing authority of any state in which the settlor resides only temporarily. Without this planning more than one state may claim the right to impose its tax, which could be costly (either alone or in combination with other states' taxes). See, e.g., Blood v. Poindexter, 534 N.E.2d 768 (Ind. Tax Ct. 1989) (the decedent avoided Indiana inheritance tax by transferring Indiana realty to an Illinois trust, which effected a conversion of the property to intangible status for tax purposes).

Finally, for clients who are moving to a noncommunity property jurisdiction but are maintaining community property ties, settlement of

---

19. For example, joint tenancy with right of survivorship would avoid ancillary administration, but only until the last tenant's death. Or, if the client is willing, making a gift of the property also can eliminate ancillary administration. Title is cleared while the client is alive by executing, delivering, and recording a deed. Either transfer will require the filing of a gift tax return under §6019(1) if the value of the property exceeds the §2503(b) gift tax annual exclusion. And payment of some gift tax may be required if the client's unified credit is not sufficient to cover any gift tax incurred.

their community assets in a revocable trust situated in the community property state will tend to ensure that the community character of the assets will be recognized and administration will not be thwarted by ignorance regarding community property when one of the spouses dies. This may be of particular importance if the community assets have substantially appreciated in value, such that the income tax new basis at death accorded to both halves of the community under §1014(b)(6) will be important to the estate. Compare Rev. Rul. 68-80, in which community property assets, moved to another state and reinvested in another form, were denied the benefit of §1014(b)(6).

Statutory Entitlements

An additional factor that is worthy of consideration (but often it benefits from a separate discussion because of emotional baggage that it may carry) relates to the use of trusts to disinherit. Creditors of a decedent probably cannot be disfranchised by creation of a trust during the settlor's life,[20] but it may be possible to minimize or eliminate the statutory forced heir entitlement of a surviving spouse (or a descendant's civil law legitime entitlement) to a portion of a settlor's wealth. This issue is relevant with respect to a decedent's share of community property, or as to any separate property to the extent state law grants rights to a protected beneficiary, but only to the extent a living trust is immune to challenge. It is likely appropriate if, for example, spouses are estranged but for some reason will not divorce, or if one spouse needs to provide for other objects of their bounty in addition to their surviving spouse (who might be expected to object to a division of benefits). It also can be relevant for clients who want to qualify the surviving spouse for Medicaid (or other needs-based governmental entitlements). This significant but controversial topic is discussed in depth in Pennell, *Minimizing the Surviving Spouse's Elective Share*, 32 U. MIAMI INST. EST. PLAN. ¶900 (1998).

Pour Over from Wills to Trusts

Notwithstanding the utility of creating and funding revocable inter vivos trusts, seldom is a trust a total substitute for the use of a will. Usually at least a portion of the settlor's wealth is not transferred to the trust (or, having been placed in the trust, it was removed by inattention to proper accounting or other inadvertent acts during the balance of the settlor's life). Thus, a will usually is necessary to transfer assets not impressed with the trust, and often a will is desirable to glean advantages of probate administration. In these cases a will typically "pours over" to the trust. The trust serves as the primary estate planning document, but the will provides simple directions regarding disposition of a limited number of selected

---

20. See RESTATEMENT (SECOND) OF TRUSTS §156 and the asset protection trust discussion at page 2. RESTATEMENT (THIRD) OF TRUSTS §§58(2), 60 (2003) are the corresponding provisions to §156.

probate assets (such as personal effects), a tax payment provision (with directions regarding whether the will or the trust governs tax payment to the extent they create inconsistent obligations), and distribution of the inevitable residue of the testator's estate to the receptacle trust. Usually the pour over trust was created by the testator, but in some cases the pour over is by another testator (often the settlor's surviving spouse).

In an historical context it was not always clear that pour over wills were valid. Early in the development of this planning the prevailing legal concept underlying the delegation by will to a trust of dispositive control was the doctrine of incorporation by reference, by which a completely separate document like the trust was treated as if it was a part of the will. Incorporation by reference required compliance with numerous rules and respected only the trust terms as they existed when the will was executed. Subsequent amendments of the trust did not count unless they were followed by re-execution of the will.[21]

The doctrine of independent legal significance was crafted because of these and other legal impediments to a successful and complete incorporation by reference. It also avoids creating by incorporation a testamentary or court trust governed by the will. See Second Bank-State Street Trust Co. v. Pinion, 170 N.E.2d 350 (Mass. 1960) (breakthrough case recognizing the trust's independent significance and validating this approach). Under the doctrine a will may pour property over to a trust (typically a revocable living trust that was created by the testator as settlor), to be governed by the terms of the trust as amended from time to time, without the inconvenience or impossibility of re-execution of the will after each trust amendment.[22]

Because a revocable trust has its own independent legal significance, the doctrine permits the trust to be a beneficiary under a will and serve in lieu of separate dispositive provisions in the will, all without the trust being incorporated by reference as a part of the will or being subject to probate administration or court trust supervision. In addition, under the law of many states a receptacle trust need not have its own separate valid existence prior to the pour over but may be validated in the first instance by the testator's bequest to it, if all other requisites for a valid trust have been met. See Uniform Testamentary Additions to Trusts Act and §2-511 of the Uniform Probate Code; Clymer v. Mayo, 473 N.E.2d 1084, 1090 (Mass. 1985): "We agree with the [lower] court's conclusion that 'the statute is not conditioned upon the existence of a trust but upon the existence of a trust *instrument*.'" Many states also permit a pour over to a trust established after execution of the testator's will, including testamentary trusts created by the will of another person that was not

---

21. See generally 1A Scott & Fratcher, THE LAW OF TRUSTS §54.1 (4th ed. 1987).
22. See *id.* §54.2, and Uniform Probate Code §2-511, which also is the freestanding Uniform Testamentary Additions to Trusts Act that is the law in the vast majority of states, even those that have not adopted the Uniform Probate Code. 8B U.L.A. 360 (2001).

executed until after execution of the testator's will, provided that the receptacle trust is in existence when the testator dies (meaning that the other testator must have predeceased the pour over testator).[23]

Indeed, a pour over will does not fail even if the receptacle trust terminates or is revoked before the testator dies, unless the testator provides to the contrary.[24] And there is authority that, if a pour over does fail, the testator's disposition will be effected by treating the will as an incorporation of the receptacle trust by reference. Because not all state laws are as liberal as these, however, and because absence of the receptacle trust when the testator dies means that the pour over might fail for lack of a taker, the safest approach in all cases is to guarantee that the pour over is to a trust with at least a nominal trust corpus when the will is executed and that the trust will remain in existence until the testator dies.

Receptacle Trusts

Two final nontax reasons to create trusts during a settlor's life are to serve as a receptacle for benefits received in a divorce settlement or under a personal injury claim, and to receive and coordinate the disposition of the proceeds of life insurance policies and the death benefits under deferred compensation plans. The former may allow for expert management of funds the beneficiary otherwise could not administer. The latter permits more rapid collection of proceeds than if a testamentary trust was named because the inter vivos trust presents no delay in having a will admitted to probate, which is required before the testamentary trustee can be qualified to act, which also must occur before collection can be undertaken. This allows more timely payment of estate taxes and accelerated administration and investment of these funds, which represent the bulk of the decedent's wealth in some estates.

Tax Minimization

There are several tax minimization reasons for using trusts in addition to the numerous nontax advantages they provide, but they are not widely embraced. The most obvious, and easiest to implement for a settlor's transfer tax purposes, is creation of an irrevocable living trust that will not be includible in the settlor's gross estate at death. This is not common, and the value of any property held in a *revocable* living trust at the death of the settlor will be includible in the settlor's gross estate as if no transfer into trust had been made during life. See §2038(a)(1).

No gift taxable transfer is made by the settlor of a revocable living trust (except to the extent distributions are made to third parties) until the settlor releases the power to revoke the trust. On the other hand, the settlor's transfer of assets to an immediately irrevocable trust will invoke

---

23. 1A Scott & Fratcher, *id.* §54.4.
24. *Id.* §54.3.

an immediate gift tax, computed on the present value of the assets transferred. Again, this favors revocable trust planning and usually means there are no tax advantages to inter vivos trust planning.

There are advantages that may be worth pursuing of making current gifts rather than waiting to incur a subsequent gift or estate tax, but not many clients will embrace this planning during the current period of uncertainty about repeal of the estate and generation-skipping transfer taxes. See Chapter 12. In some cases, however, an intentional acceleration of the wealth transfer tax liability may reduce taxes and increase the overall net worth of the assets involved. Still, this is exceptionally rare planning, even among the super wealthy.

More sophisticated planning that couples bifurcated enjoyment with transfer tax minimization objectives yields techniques that §2702 may regulate (but does not eliminate): grantor retained annuity trusts, grantor retained unitrusts, and qualified personal residence trusts, all created during the settlor's life. This does favor use of trusts, but again it is not a predominant motive for inter vivos trust use. It is fair to note that gifts as complicated as these specialized and highly regulated techniques can be made without using a trust, but any reluctance regarding loss of control or about the donee's ability to manage the property can be minimized with appropriate use of trusts. In addition, compliance with highly complicated statutory requirements that must be met if tax objectives are to be gleaned generally is facilitated with a trust instrument rather than with some form of deed or other arrangement. Nevertheless, these concepts are not further explored here because they are not the stuff of everyday planning for middle-rich or smaller estates, and also because of the avowed nontax tenor of this book.

On the other hand, trusts present a number of income tax opportunities because they are respected as separate income tax paying entities with their own rate schedule, allowing a final bit of opportunism. Trusts have the unique advantage of allowing the settlor to control the income tax liability for trust income. By intuitive drafting it is possible to cause a trust or its beneficiary to be regarded as the owner of the trust income, making the trust or the beneficiary pay tax on its income. Alternatively, a trust may be intentionally "defective" for income tax grantor trust purposes, which allows the settlor to continue to incur income tax as if no trust were created. The choice among these options may depend on the relative income tax rates and any advantages of engineering the liability for income tax with respect to trust income.[25] The point is that trusts make the choice possible, unlike virtually any other approach.

Perhaps the best tax aspect of trusts overall is that they may provide current enjoyment of a high level of benefits without causing state or

---

25. See Chapter 17 for discussions of the many reasons why defective grantor trust planning is sensible and how to make a trust defective for grantor trust rule purposes.

federal estate or gift taxes to the beneficiary. Indeed, if properly done, a trust may even give a beneficiary full power over trust administration as trustee.[26] And trusts enjoy certain advantages over outright dispositions to younger generation beneficiaries even if the generation-skipping transfer tax is applicable. These also are beyond the intended scope of this Chapter but are addressed in the next.[27]

Reasons to Favor Probate

Notwithstanding all this gush about trusts, they are not always a panacea and seldom exist without an accompanying pour-over will. Moreover, a number of factors may diminish the utility of revocable living trusts, and a significant number of reasons explain why knowledgeable estate planners nationwide wisely embrace probate in appropriate circumstances to glean the many benefits that only probate can provide.

Often the most important benefit is that probate allows a court to determine the proper beneficiaries in "sticky" situations, such as a potential conflict among several sets of descendants of a decedent who had several spouses or consorts. Probate also provides nonclaim statutory protections against "stale" claims of creditors, which otherwise must be brought within a normal statute of limitation period that may expire long after the client's death.[28]

Integration of the total estate plan also is made easier in some cases by directing all assets back to the probate estate. One illustration of this is to control otherwise nonprobate property (such as retirement benefits or life insurance) that could overfund a marital deduction bequest if made payable directly to the decedent's surviving spouse. Another illustration is failing to coordinate the total dispositive pattern. A third might be losing the availability of liquid assets for tax payment or other purposes. All of these might be manageable without a pour back to the estate, but there could be significant complications either for the family or in the plan.

---

26. See Halbach, *Tax-Sensitive Trusteeships*, 63 OR. L. REV. 381 (1984); Horn, *Whom Do You Trust: Planning, Drafting and Administering Self and Beneficiary-Trusteed Trusts*, 20 U. MIAMI INST. EST. PLAN. ¶500 (1986); Pennell, *Estate Planning: Drafting and Tax Considerations in Employing Individual Trustees*, 60 N.C. L. REV. 799-820 (1982), abridged and reprinted in 9 EST. PLAN. 264-272 (1982).

27. See 2 Casner & Pennell, ESTATE PLANNING §11.4 (1999), for a gagging treatment of generation-skipping transfer tax planning, and Chapter 18 for a less overwhelming overview.

28. A compelling illustration of the value of this protection is Witco Corp. v. Beekhuis, 38 F.3d 682 (3d Cir. 1994), in which CERCLA environmental clean up liability was precluded by a state probate law nonclaim statute. The decedent was a potentially responsible party and the party that incurred remediation costs sued the decedent's estate for contribution, relying on the three year statute of limitation under CERCLA, 42 U.S.C. §9613(g)(3). The personal representative was granted summary judgment because the court determined that the period for filing claims under the state law nonclaim statute had expired and that the state nonclaim statute could coexist with the CERCLA statute of limitation. Essential to the decision was that the plaintiff was aware of a potential contribution claim against the decedent and, under state law, could have filed its potential claim in a timely manner in the decedent's probate proceeding.

Furthermore, for postmortem planning purposes, disclaimers may be easier and produce more certain results under state law if the disclaimed interest is a probate entitlement. And, because certain laws apply with respect to estates but not trusts, in many states the effect of divorce on various dispositions is more clear in probate than it is for nonprobate dispositions. The same may be true regarding the rights of adopted or nonmarital descendants and children of the "new biology," the treatment of a slayer, and the effect of lapse, ademption, advancements, and tax apportionment rules, just to name a few. Care is required in this domain, however, because sometimes these disparities are advantageous, in terms of avoiding certain state law restrictions that apply to estates but not to trusts. Thus, it is impossible to proclaim a best approach for all cases.

For a number of reasons, in the income tax arena estates subject to probate may be slightly more desirable than living trusts that continue after the settlor's death. For example, estates are not required by §644 to use a calendar year for tax reporting purposes, as must trusts that are recognized for income tax purposes. Estates also are entitled to a two taxable year moratorium on compliance with the estimated tax rules, which is available to a trust under §6654(l) only if the trust was entirely a grantor trust prior to the deceased settlor's death and it is the pour-over receptacle of the residue of the settlor's estate. A revocable living trust may be entitled to the same treatment as an estate if both the executor and the trustee make an election under §645(a). However, this alternative is available only if the trust was treated as a grantor trust under §676 because it was revocable by the grantor during life. And treatment as if the trust was part of the estate is available only for a limited period after the settlor's death. The timing rules for reporting income distributions make these rules important, and proper estate administration takes advantage of them to accelerate or defer a beneficiary's year for reporting that income, as appropriate.

Similarly, a number of other disparities also favor estates to the extent a §645(a) election to treat a trust as part of the settlor's estate does not provide equivalent treatment. For instance, under §6013, a decedent's surviving spouse and the decedent's personal representative may elect to file a joint income tax return for the decedent's final income tax year. This election is not available to the trustee of a probate avoidance trust, even if the trust income was taxable to the decedent during life under the grantor trust rules. And under §1361, stock of an S Corporation may be held in an estate for the duration of reasonable estate administration; it may be held in a trust for only two years after the deceased shareholder's death unless the trust qualifies as an Electing Small Business Trust (ESBT) or as a Qualified Subchapter S Trust (QSST).

A number of other important differences between living trusts and probate estates also favor estates for wealth transfer tax purposes. For example, the existence of an "executor" is important for making certain elections under the estate and generation-skipping transfer taxes, and for purposes of discharging personal liability for estate, gift, and income taxes of the decedent.

Living trusts can create additional complications that may diminish their appeal, especially if the trust has a nonprofessional trustee. For example, a nonprofessional trustee may need to open one or more bank accounts, rent a safety deposit box, and perhaps hire a custodial accounting service to replicate the safekeeping of trust property that most professional fiduciaries offer. Moreover, the settlor must transfer legal title to trust assets to the trustee, securities must be reregistered and, if land is involved, deeds must be executed and recorded. These acts may attract nondeductible state and local transfer taxes that would not apply at death, potentially could trigger a due-on-sale clause in a mortgage on nonresidential property, might violate restrictions that apply to restricted stock or stock options, could cause the loss of nonassignable title insurance coverage, and might generate the legal and other costs of making effective conveyances under state law.

Furthermore, the trustee must maintain adequate records and keep trust assets and activities separate from the trustee's own assets and activities. This particularly is important if it is contemplated that a professional fiduciary will succeed a nonprofessional trustee at some future time, because a professional fiduciary typically will be more careful about reviewing its predecessor's conduct if it does not succeed another professional fiduciary. Professional trustees' fees are avoidable if the settlor or a family member is serving as trustee. But a custodial or investment advisory service fee might be only slightly less than a professional fiduciary's total fee, especially if the fiduciary would provide services (such as tax return preparation, dividend and interest collection and investment, and automated inventory, valuation, and accounting services) for which other professional fees otherwise would be incurred.

In any event, all of these legal fees and other costs attributable to creation, funding, and administration of funded revocable living trusts are in addition to the cost to prepare a will, which remains an essential aspect of the overall plan. These costs may be regarded as just a prepayment rather than an added excise, to the extent they would be incurred at death as part of normal estate administration, but few people appreciate the opportunity to accelerate even unavoidable expenses. And if the estate plan calls for distributions immediately after the settlor's death, these costs and any trustee's fee for termination of the revocable living trust may exceed the costs that would have been incurred in a normal probate of the settlor's entire estate.

Subchapter S Election Concerns

Many of your clients will own a family business, perhaps incorporated and run as a Subchapter S entity for income tax purposes. Under §1361(c)(2)(A)(i), a revocable trust is a permissible shareholder in an S

Corporation because of grantor trust treatment (typically under §§676 and 677). But §1361(c)(2)(A)(ii) allows the Subchapter S election to continue for only two years after the settlor's death. If it is desired to have the election continue beyond the two year period, the stock must be distributed from the trust either into the settlor's estate or to a beneficiary, or the trust must qualify under §1361(d)(3) as a QSST or under §1361(e) as an ESBT. A QSST may have only one current income beneficiary (who must be a United States citizen or resident), all trust income must be distributed currently to that beneficiary, the beneficiary's income interest may terminate no sooner than the beneficiary's death or termination of the trust, and trust principal may be distributed only to that one beneficiary while that beneficiary is alive. An ESBT may have numerous individuals, estates, and certain charities as beneficiaries and there is no mandatory income distribution requirement, but all S Corporation income is taxed at the highest rates under the Code (even if it is distributed to the beneficiaries). In some contexts, a QSST may not be favorable because a separate trust for each beneficiary would be required and income could not be accumulated; an ESBT may be preferable in those cases, notwithstanding the high income tax impost. By way of comparison, however, an estate may be an S Corporation shareholder for as long as the estate properly is under administration, without compliance with any of these requirements.

Joint Settlor Trusts

Trusts created by multiple settlors can create problems that may be better avoided than cured. Seldom is there a good reason for creation of a joint settlor trust unless the property being contributed to it is concurrently owned (community property or tenants in common, joint tenancy, or tenancy by the entireties), or the joint settlors are spouses. Partition is possible with respect to community property, but it might be a mistake to do so because community property enjoys an income tax benefit under §1014(b)(6), which provides a new income tax basis in both halves of the community property on the death of the first spouse to die. This normally is a desirable result and does not apply to noncommunity property because typically only half the property is includible in the first decedent's estate. In addition, a variety of Private Letter Rulings illustrate that spouses may be able to employ a joint settlor trust to better plan to shelter their collective unified credits than through bifurcation of their assets in hopes of guessing correctly which spouse will die first. See Chapter 7 at page 68 for a full discussion of this useful planning opportunity for spouses whose aggregate wealth is more than the applicable exclusion amount but less than double that amount.

A joint settlor revocable living trust may be sensible if it is funded with community or other concurrent ownership property, particularly if other reasons support the selection of a revocable living trust for property management and disposition during the spouses' joint lives and thereafter during the surviving spouse's overlife. In community property situations a revocable living trust also may be useful to keep each spouse's separate property separate (such as separate property brought to a community property state from a noncommunity property jurisdiction, property inherited by one of the spouses, or property owned by either spouse before the marriage).

Both spouses must join in creation of a joint settlor trust if the trust is to become irrevocable with respect to any property upon the death of the first spouse to die. This is because, otherwise, the surviving spouse loses a valuable property right and might be able to defeat the trust on grounds that the trust constitutes a fraud on that spouse. In any case in which a trust becomes irrevocable during a settlor's life, further care is required to ensure that a completed gift does not occur unintentionally, in this case consisting of the surviving spouse's property interests contributed to the trust. A power of withdrawal exercisable by the surviving spouse with respect to his or her property interests would make irrevocability of the trust harmless, as would retention by the surviving spouse of any power to appoint that property, exercisable inter vivos or only at death. Alternatively, these concerns all can be avoided if the surviving spouse retains a power to revoke or amend any separate trust funded with his or her property interests.

The point never to overlook is that there are two transferors, each with respect to their respective shares of the community property and any of their separate property interests. The survivor should retain some power over his or her property but not over the decedent's property interests, to the extent the plan is to preclude estate taxation to the survivor of any part of the decedent's property in the joint trust.

Declarations of Trust

A settlor who wants to retain control or benefits in a revocable living trust often creates a self-trusteed declaration of trust, in which the settlor is trustee and beneficiary, typically with exclusive enjoyment and control until incompetence or death. Frequently the self-trusteed declaration of trust is warranted for asset management purposes because the client is unwilling to relinquish control presently but the client's health is poor, because there is concern that senility approaches, or because the trust was created for probate avoidance purposes.

The self-trusteed declaration of trust allows the mechanics for independent administration to be put into operation, with the settlor still in charge until a change in management becomes necessary. Instead of waiting for disability or incapacity to become a reality, the trust can be created and funded immediately so that, at the right time, the successor trustee simply steps forward and continues uninterrupted administration of the trust corpus. Although something akin to this might be accomplished through the use of a durable power of attorney, the transition would not be as smooth or rapid as with the declaration of trust. Similarly, many durable powers are rejected a "stale" if they are more than six months old, but established trusts seem to garner more respect from outsiders the older the trust is.

Indeed, if a corporate fiduciary is to be successor trustee, the plan might even include placing assets in the corporate fiduciary's name under a custodianship arrangement, or naming the corporate fiduciary as a cotrustee at the outset, all to minimize transition problems. The trust could be drafted to sharply limit the powers and liabilities of the corporate fiduciary while the settlor is serving as co-trustee. In effect, the corporate fiduciary would have only record keeping and custodial duties while the settlor is serving as a trustee. In this way the transition would be even quicker and the corporate fiduciary's concerns would be reduced regarding its duties to account and its responsibility for acts of the settlor as the trustee the corporate fiduciary succeeds. Many corporate fiduciaries will negotiate a reduced fee to reflect the fact that they would be serving only in a reduced custodial or investment advisory role during the settlor's trusteeship.

A final reason to use a self-trusteed declaration of trust is if the settlor is the best trustee of certain assets that are located in jurisdictions in which ancillary administration is to be avoided through the use of a living trust. In these cases the plan is useful even if no other reason for using a trust exists and is all the more appropriate if the settlor's ability to act as trustee is not in question. In either case, the primary advantage of the self-trusteed declaration of trust is that creation involves no taxable transfer for wealth transfer tax purposes, the trust is ignored for income tax purposes, and about the only tangible manifestation that anything different has happened with respect to the settlor's ownership of the trust property is transfer of trust assets from the name of the settlor individually into the name of the settlor as trustee of the trust.

This extreme form of trust with retained enjoyment and control is deemed acceptable under state law as against the charge that it is testamentary and therefore invalid for failure to comply with the statute of wills. Obviously any lesser degree of control or retained enjoyment also will survive challenge.[29] The only potential danger of any concern is that the settlor's legal interest as trustee and equitable interest as beneficiary will merge, causing termination of the trust. Merger is precluded, however, if at least one other person is given a beneficial interest (either present or future, vested or contingent), even if that interest is subject to revocation by the settlor.[30] Thus, the settlor may call for distribution of the trust at

---

29. See RESTATEMENT (SECOND) OF TRUSTS §§17(a) and 57; 1A Scott & Fratcher, THE LAW OF TRUSTS §§17.1, 57.2, 57.6 (4th ed. 1987). RESTATEMENT (THIRD) OF TRUSTS §§10, 25 (2003) are the corresponding provisions to §§17(a), 57.

30. See 2 Scott & Fratcher, id. §§99, 100; Farkas v. Williams, 125 N.E.2d 600 (Ill. 1955) (landmark self-trusteed declaration of trust validation case); Will of Sachler, 548 N.Y.S.2d

death in the same manner as would a testator who devises the residue of his or her estate. More commonly, the trust would continue after the settlor's death as it would under either an independently-trusteed living trust or a testamentary trust plan.

Excepting that the declaration of trust had the settlor as its trustee, essentially it is the same as any other trust, only no formal transfer of assets, recordation, or consideration is required. Instead, the trust is valid if four essentials exist. First, there must be a sufficiently clear expression of intent to create the fiduciary relation. Almost any unambiguous indication will suffice. Second, the trust must have enforceable terms for an ascertainable beneficiary other than the settlor. This need not be a current beneficiary, but it must be a beneficiary with an interest that supports the existence of the trust without merger. Third, there must be an identifiable trust corpus. Lacking an actual delivery or transfer of assets, a segregation or identification of trust assets is essential to avoid the appearance that the trust is dry or testamentary (because otherwise it appears that nothing really changes until death). Funding the trust through identification of trust assets is done by registering assets represented by indispensable document (such as stock certificates, deeds, certificates of deposit, and bank account passbooks), execution of a bill of sale for other assets in favor of the trustee, maintenance of books of account that show trusteed ownership, creating trust margin and brokerage accounts, and rental of a separate trust safety deposit box.

Fourth is the essential trust validity requirement of independent trust administration. This is perhaps most important and most difficult to maintain due to natural client proclivities. The settlor must begin to act like a fiduciary and avoid acts that belie trust ownership. Fiduciary principles must be followed. For example, the settlor should render periodic accountings, conform investments to the requirements established by the trust document or local law, and avoid any conduct that bespeaks self-dealing. The estate planner must make the settlor aware of the need to act like a trustee if the trust is to be respected, and should consider whether the settlor is capable of compliance with fiduciary principles (and probably should avoid using a declaration of trust if the assessment is not favorable).

There are few special considerations to be reflected in using the self-trusteed declaration of trust, but one sensitive issue that must be reflected is succession of trustees, because it involves replacement of a settlor who, due to senility or other diminished capability, may not recognize the need

---

866 (Surr. Ct. 1989); Contella v. Contella, 559 So. 2d 1217 (Fla. Dist. Ct. App. 1990).

Some jurisdictions have enacted statutes to confirm that merger will not occur if the settlor is the trustee and beneficiary, provided that there is some other future interest beneficiary of the trust. See, e.g., Cal. Prob. Code §15209 and Ohio Rev. Code Ann. §1335.01(C) (enacted to overrule Mathias v. Fantine, 1990 Ohio App. LEXIS 826, which held that a self-trusteed declaration of trust was invalid under the doctrine of merger, *notwithstanding* the existence of remainder beneficiaries).

to relinquish control. Thus, it is imperative that the designated successor be contacted and be willing to act before putting the plan into effect.

In addition, there must be a method for determining when succession is to occur. Death, resignation of the settlor as trustee, or incapacity of the settlor are normal triggering events for the successor to take over, with determination of incapacity being the touchy issue. Determination should not be made by the successor, because the successor may be seen as having a conflict of interest, the successor may not be competent to judge, or it may be too time consuming to bring sufficient facts to the successor to permit it to judge the settlor's condition. Instead, a common and effective procedure is for the settlor's spouse, adult child, a physician, or any combination of them, to make the determination. Doing so will be more effective if the settlor executed an authorization for the physician to share otherwise private information that is protected by the Health Insurance Portability and Accountability Act (HIPAA) privacy provisions.

In this last respect, because many physicians are reluctant to take on such a responsibility, a physician's opinion should be required only if there is a close and continuing relationship between the settlor and a family physician. The physician should be notified before the document incorporates this procedure and should be asked to agree to take on this responsibility. And the decision should be made conclusive on all concerned parties. Finally, the document should anticipate that the particular physician may not be available when the decision must be made, and should address that issue by naming a substitute or by allowing the remaining evaluators of the settlor's capacity to act alone. These issues are illustrated by the following skeletal example.

Sample Declaration of Trust

I, [Settlor], have transferred to myself as trustee the property listed in the attached schedule, and I declare that I hold that property and all investments and reinvestments thereof and additions thereto (herein collectively referred to as the "trust estate") upon the following trusts:

FIRST: During my life the trustee shall pay the income from the trust estate in convenient installments to me or otherwise as I may from time to time direct in writing, and also such sums from principal as I may request at any time in writing.

If at any times I am unable to manage my affairs, the trustee may use such sums from the income and principal of the trust estate as the trustee deems necessary or advisable for my care, support, comfort, or any other purpose the trustee considers to be for my best interests, and for the health and maintenance in reasonable comfort of any person dependent upon me, adding to principal any income not so used.

For purposes of this declaration, I shall be considered to be unable to manage my affairs if I am under a legal disability or by reason of illness or mental or physical disability am unable to give prompt and intelligent consideration to financial matters. The determination of my inability shall be made by _____ and my physician, or the survivor of them, and the trustee may rely upon written notice of that determination. I hereby authorize all health care providers to release to _____ any medical information needed to make a medical determination concerning my capacity for purposes of this provision.

SECOND: Upon my death the trustee shall pay from the principal of the trust estate. . . . [this would be a standard tax payment provision for use in a trust with an appropriately coordinated provision in the settlor's pour over will].

THIRD: [Specific gifts that otherwise would be made under will].

FOURTH: [Marital and Residuary Dispositive Provisions].

FIFTH: [Administrative Provisions — typical except for]:

SECTION *: I may resign at any time by written notice to the successor trustee. After my resignation, death, or inability to manage my affairs, _____, of _____, shall be successor trustee.

Every successor trustee shall have all the powers given the originally named trustee. No successor trustee shall be personally liable for any act or omission of any predecessor. With my approval if I am living, otherwise with the approval of the beneficiary or a majority in interest of the beneficiaries then entitled to receive or have the benefit of the income from the trust, a successor trustee may accept the account rendered and the property received as a full and complete discharge to the predecessor trustee without incurring any liability for so doing, *except that a successor to me as trustee shall accept the assets delivered to the successor trustee as constituting all of the property to which the successor trustee is entitled and shall not inquire into my administration or accounting as trustee.*[31]

---

31. This form is based on forms produced by The Northern Trust Company, www.northerntrust.com, which grants permission to attorneys to use any part or all of its forms in the preparation of wills and trusts for clients, all subject to a notice and disclaimer that "no form is a substitute for informed legal judgment. The attorney must make an independent determination as to whether a particular form . . . is generally appropriate for a client and, further, whether it must be modified to meet any special circumstances and objectives of the client." Typically any user of this type of form who designates a corporate successor trustee would want the trustee to take possession of the trust, and to ensure that the designated fiduciary will serve. The settlor usually will want to include the italicized language.

Note that the preparation of forms by nonattorneys may constitute the unauthorized practice of law. See, e.g., *In re* Advisory Opinion, 613 So. 2d 426, 427, 428 (Fla. 1992) ("nonlawyer companies selling living trusts are engaging in the unlicensed practice of law and . . . the public is either actually being harmed or has the potential of being harmed by this practice. . . . '[A]ttorney review . . . does not . . . remove the activity from the unlicensed practice of law.'"). By stipulation the opinion "does not apply to the activities of corporate fiduciaries associated with financial trust departments or to the practice of public

SIXTH: The law of the state in which the trust property from time to time has its situs for administration shall govern the validity and interpretation of the provisions of this declaration.

SEVENTH: [Typical provision permitting additions to trust].

EIGHTH: [Revocability].

In Witness whereof I have signed this declaration this ___ day of _____.

_____
Individually and as trustee

An excellent illustration of numerous tax and non-tax advantages to be gained from the use of trusts can be gleaned from the following excerpt. The planning discussed typically is attractive only to very wealthy people and is not likely to be adopted by the typical client. Nevertheless the concepts are sound in many situations.

Oshins, *Megatrusts: Representation Without Taxation*, 48 N.Y.U. INST. ON FED. TAX'N (1990)[32]

. . . A taxpayer places property into a trust, electing to allocate his or her [generation-skipping transfer tax (GSTT)] exemption against the transfer so that the trust is wholly exempt from the GSTT. The term of the trust will be extended as long as possible, subject only to the constraints of the rule against perpetuities. The trust will be managed with the avoidance of wealth transfer taxes a primary consideration insofar as consistent with the objective of providing comfortably for the trust beneficiaries. The trust corpus can form a "family bank" "or asset pool" for the use of the descendants (and the spouse if the transfer did not qualify for the marital deduction or gift tax exclusion) of the creator. . . . The trust beneficiaries will be expected to pay for their own consumables. Such a trust is the Megatrust™.

Special Megatrust™ Features

In order to maximize both flexibility and transfer tax savings, the Megatrust™ should be designed as a sprinkling trust whereby the

---

accountancy," but other jurisdictions are pursuing the unauthorized practice of law in the context of living trust "mills" without exception. See Cincinnati Bar Ass'n v. Kathman, 748 N.E.2d 1091 (Ohio 2001), and *In re* Mid-America Living Trust Assoc., Inc., 927 S.W.2d 855 (Mo. 1996) (involving ethics violations by attorneys assisting in this unauthorized practice), and abundant authorities cited in each; Ballsun, *Summary Chart of Responses to Trust Mills*, 21 PROB. NOTES 330 (1996), and an updated version in Comm. Rep., *State and Local Action Against Trust Mills: The Unauthorized Practice of Law*, 27 ACTEC NOTES 162 (2001); Lopata, *Can States Juggle the Unauthorized and Multidisciplinary Practices of Law?: A Look at the States' Current Grapple with the Problems in the Context of Living Trusts*, 50 CATHOLIC U.L. REV. 467 (2001).

32. Adapted from the 48th Institute on Federal Taxation, copyright 1990 by New York University, published by Matthew Bender & Co. Reprinted with permission.

trustee will have broad discretionary powers to distribute income or principal to, and provide the use of trust assets for, the trust beneficiaries subject to a set of guidelines.

Operationally, however, it is anticipated that few, if any, distributions will be made in the absence of a compelling reason to make such distributions. . . .

The trustee is expected but not mandated to follow an investment pattern designed to enable the trust to realize and optimize its goal of avoiding transfer taxes for multiple generations. The trustee is encouraged to acquire assets for the "use" of the beneficiaries rather than funding the individual's personal acquisition of the assets. In order to facilitate this result, the trust should contain specific language to permit investments in assets such as homes, artwork, jewelry, and the like, which have significant appreciation potential. For example, if a beneficiary wishes to acquire a home, the trustee could acquire the home as an asset of the Megatrust™, rather than distribute funds to the beneficiary who would utilize such funds to acquire the home personally. As a result, the beneficiary will have the use and enjoyment of the property without the transfer tax problems.

. . . The trustee should also have latitude to make loans to the beneficiaries rather than distributions and should be authorized to allow the beneficiaries the use of trust assets. The trustee should be directed to take into account all factors and all tax results prior to any transfers to beneficiaries.[33]

In drafting the document, attorneys should resist the temptation to draft too "tightly, " as flexibility is extremely important. Thus, the instrument should not preclude distributions, as the beneficiaries might need the trust assets for basic living expenses or even luxuries if the beneficiaries could not adequately provide for such items themselves.[34] Further, tax considerations might dictate that a transfer should be made. From an income tax perspective, a distribution might be desirable even at the cost of reducing the transfer tax benefits. . . .

The trustee should be authorized to retain income even though the trust income tax bracket may exceed that of the beneficiaries and such retention would be counterproductive from an income tax standpoint. Thus, precatory language providing that the trustee may

---

33. Sample language: "Consistent with the objective of reducing wealth transfer taxes, the trustee shall have broad discretion in withholding distributions and providing the beneficiaries the use of trust assets, after taking into account all factors the trustee shall deem relevant, including, but not limited to, immediate and future income and transfer taxes."

34. In some cases, the trustee might consider making loans to a beneficiary rather than making distributions.

take into account both immediate and future income and transfer taxes should be utilized . . . .

Broad use of powers of appointment should also be considered to deal with changing family circumstances and changing . . . laws. Typically, with the Megatrust™, the power holder will be the member of the oldest generation of any separate trust (representing a family branch) of the Megatrust™. Thus, adjustment can be made in the event of changes in the law or family circumstances. . . .

Surprisingly Broad Application

The visceral reaction is that the Megatrust™ will only be employed for those clients who enjoy considerable wealth and are willing and able to afford to embark on a major gift giving program. However, many Megatrust™ candidates will be persons with large life insurance policies.[35] With the proliferation of large insurance sales, many families potentially will have instant wealth and should consider the Megatrust™ as the vehicle to receive such wealth. Other candidates may come from clients who seek asset protection, particularly from malpractice suits. . . .

As a method of finessing marital discord which might occur subsequent to the funding of the trust, consideration should be given to conditioning the spouse's participation in the trust by adding a requirement that he or she be married to, and living with, the grantor at the time of distribution or death of the grantor and, further, by defining the "spouse" as the one who is married to the grantor at the time of distribution or death. This allows a new spouse to become a beneficiary of the trust in the event of a remarriage after a death or divorce. Additionally, by giving the donee spouse a [nongeneral] power of appointment broad enough to include the donor spouse (e.g., "to anyone other than the donee spouse, the spouse's estate, creditors [of the donee spouse] or creditors of the spouse's estate"), the property may be returned to the creator of the trust. Of course, to the extent it is, the tax and future creditor protection is lost. To prevent the use of the power in a manner undesirable to the trust creator, the exercise of the power might be made subject to the consent of a third party. . . .

---

35. See Brody, *Putting a Premium on Generation-Skipping Transfer Tax Planning-The Use of Life Insurance*, 23 U. MIAMI INST. ON EST. PLAN. Ch. 10 (1989). Irrevocable Life Insurance Trusts designed to last for multiple generations subject to the rule against perpetuities are commonly known as "Dynasty Trusts," which bear many of the similarities of the Megatrust™ and are considered a form of Megatrust™. The Megatrust™, however, is broader in scope. Additional distinguishing refinements include the concepts of leveraging the benefits through asset selection and trust management. . . .

The Economics

The compounding effect of the Megatrust™ coupled with the avoidance of transfer taxes for multiple generations can lead to some incredible results. The following chart illustrates the differences in result for a $1,000,000 contribution into a Megatrust™ that will last for 120 years and outright transfers subject to an estate tax of 50 percent every 30 years.[36]

Annual After Tax Growth	Value of Megatrust after 120 years	Value of Property if no trust
6.00%	$1,088,187,748	$68,011,734
7.00%	3,357,788,383	209,861,774
8.00%	10,252,992,943	640,812,059
9.00%	30,987,015,749	1,936,688,484
10.00%	92,709,068,818	5,794,316,801
11.00%	274,635,993,245	17,164,749,578
12.00%	805,680,255,013	50,355,015,938

The savings potential is often greater than illustrated since the example ignores the fact that property received outright will probably be reduced further due to (1) divorce settlements; (2) creditor problems; and (3) the fact that assets are less likely to be dissipated in a trust than if held outright even if the invasion rights in a trust are extremely broad and generous. . . .

A Beneficiary Can Receive More Rights and Benefits in a Trust Than With Outright Ownership

From the beneficiary's perspective, he or she is potentially better off receiving property in trust than receiving the property outright. . . .

In addition to rights tantamount to outright ownership, the beneficiary enjoys certain benefits that outright ownership does not allow. These rights include creditor, marital discord, and transfer tax protection. . . .

Clients will often reject multi-generational planning, feeling that their children will take care of the grandchildren. This approach fails to recognize that, by placing property in trust . . . 16 times as much as can be transferred to the fifth generation if a 50 percent estate tax can be avoided at each generation level.

---

36. It is arbitrarily assumed that the property would be taxed every 30 years as it appears to be a reasonable assumption that each successive generation would survive the preceding generation by such period.

Discretionary ("Sprinkle" or "Spray") Trust

Absent special circumstances . . . income should be retained in the trust and reinvested to increase the transfer tax savings. The discretionary ("sprinkle" or "spray") trust is the vehicle which best achieves the aims of the Megatrust™. It can be designed to provide substantially greater flexibility, affording more opportunity to take advantage of this unique concept. . . .

An additional feature which may be of some interest to the client who is concerned about the property being "tied up" in an irrevocable trust for over 100 years is to give a third person, who may be the independent trustee or the trust protector, a power of appointment to enable the trust to be restructured; a provision which makes a revocable irrevocable trust. A power might also be given to the trustee or any other third person to alter the provisions contained in the document and even terminate any separate trust or trusts if circumstances warrant a termination. Flexibility is a key ingredient in a long term arrangement, in order to make the document fit the family situation as it develops. Consideration might be given to providing that this power be exercised in a "nonfiduciary capacity" to preclude an attack if such power is exercised for the benefit of some beneficiaries and to the detriment of others. This right to amend has been referred to as a " . . . tool for obtaining unparalleled flexibility in estate planning . . . ."[37]

As shown by this extract, trusts are wonderfully useful devices that often provide more flexibility than any other device in the estate planner's arsenal. Frequently they outperform wills as the primary dispositive vehicle but seldom are they a total substitute for the use of a will. Usually at least a pour-over will is necessary and often a trust is used in conjunction with an intended probate administration rather than in lieu of it. Finally, although there are numerous tax reasons to favor the use of trusts, the estate planner should be reluctant to utilize a trust (or any other device) that is not justified by any of the many non-tax reasons for the use of such tools. As illustrated by this Chapter, those can include:

- flexibility, in terms of the discretion and powers that may be created,
- transportability, in terms of situs and the ability to avoid probate,
- durability and respectability (as compared to many "schemes" being marketed),
- self-enforcement (usually without the need for judicial intervention),

---

37. Early, *The Irrevocable Trust That Can Be Amended*, 18 U. MIAMI INST. ON EST. PLAN. Ch. 17 (1984).

- elasticity (in terms of bifurcation of interests and expandability to accept added beneficiaries),
- future looking (in terms of interests yet to be enjoyed),
- protective (as against creditors, incapacity, will contest or surviving spouse elective share claims, and potentially to create federal entitlements),
- creative (in terms of generating incentives for beneficiaries),
- efficient (in comparison to the cost and delay of probate in some jurisdictions),
- definitional (in terms of preserving the identity of assets),
- springing into existence in the future, allowing the trust to lie dormant until needed.

And trusts can be tax efficient too!

Chapter 5

FAMILY TRUST PLANNING

"Credit Shelter," "Bypass," "Nonmarital," or "Family" trusts are synonyms describing the portion of most estate plans that does not qualify for the federal estate tax marital deduction. Long ago that portion typically was all of the estate only if there was no surviving spouse. Today in the vast majority of estates (over 99% of the decedent population) even with a surviving spouse there will be no marital trust because the estate is below the tax threshold. So, this trust might be the entire estate dispositive scheme (other than any preresiduary specific bequests, which in most cases are de minimis).

These trusts offer "family planning" options that often are desired for a client's total integrated plan. The options are used only in this one trust simply because they cannot be used in marital deduction trusts (because they would disqualify the marital deduction). Thus, this is where flexibility is added to most estate plans, with provisions for beneficiaries in addition to (or sometimes other than) the settlor's surviving spouse. Options may include accumulations of income, discretionary distributions of principal, nongeneral powers of appointment, and so forth.

In addition, this is where we study what happens after both spouses are gone and the plan continues for surviving family beneficiaries such as descendants. These trusts could provide for others as well (but *not* for charity, as we will see in Chapter 8) but nonfamily beneficiaries are not very common and will not enter our focus here.

"Typical" Family Plan

Most family plans follow relatively predictable norms, the most common of which being represented by the provisions illustrated in this Chapter. For example, during a surviving spouse's overlife, the typical family trust frequently provides for the needs of the settlor's surviving spouse and descendants in the trustee's discretion, with a customary priority favoring the surviving spouse but not to the exclusion of others. If there is enough wealth or a need to include others, this trust is where the plan expands to embrace every intended object of the decedent's bounty.

This planning is subject, however, to the tax conscious recognition that preferably any marital deduction trust should be exhausted before any assets are moved from the family trust into the spouse's hands for potential inclusion in the surviving spouse's taxable estate at death. Moreover, the family trust itself must be drafted carefully to ensure that it will not be includible in the surviving spouse's taxable estate at death. This means that no taxable powers should be bestowed, either expressly or by virtue of trustee powers granted or imputed to the surviving spouse. The most important tax trap to avoid is any "general" or taxable power of appointment. This characterization may apply to any one of numerous forms of provision that may be exercised in favor of the powerholder, the powerholder's estate, or creditors of either. See Internal Revenue Code §2041, as discussed in Chapter 18. Trustee selection, especially considering the designation of beneficiaries as trustee, also is a critical component in an effective tax plan and is discussed in Chapter 6.

Following the death of the surviving spouse, the most common (but also the most inflexible) plans then divide into separate (typically equal) shares for children, with several alternative patterns for administration and distribution. Planning choices that provide flexibility are noted in the following sample provisions. They are indicated by *alphabetical* annotations (which, unlike normal footnotes, usually illustrate options that might fit into or replace portions of the plan. So don't ignore those!). Much of the form language in this material appear courtesy of The Northern Trust Company, www.northerntrust.com, and are reproduced with permission. Attorneys are specifically granted authority to reproduce these forms in their representation of clients.

5.01[a/] Residue: All the residue of my estate, wherever situated, including lapsed legacies, but expressly excluding any property over which I may have power of appointment at my death,[b/] I give to _____, as trustee. The trust shall be designated the "Family Trust" and shall be held and disposed of as follows:

[a/] Coming before the typical residuary family trust provision in a traditional estate plan would be a debts, expenses, and tax payment provision of the type discussed in Chapter 11; a paragraph defining the testator's family (for easy identification and as a verification that, for example, in referring to "children," the document means to include all the children who are listed, even if adopted, of the half-blood, nonmarital, or perhaps even posthumously conceived); a personal effects provision (making specific bequests that qualify for the income tax §663(a)(1) exception to avoid DNI carryout on distributions of personalty before termination of the estate); and any marital deduction provision. This plan illustrates a typical "up-front" marital bequest with residuary family trust provision. In a "reverse" plan the marital and family trusts would be reversed in both order and in how they are defined. The first sentence of paragraph 5.01 would be replaced with a formula provision defining the nonmarital bequest, but the substance of the plan would remain the same. All this is discussed in Chapter 7 dealing with marital deduction planning.

In an age of "blended" families a special set of considerations may be required to provide for children and more remote descendants. Consider the following provision as an alternative definition of family that highlights various issues that might be encountered in the future:

5.02 <u>Income Distributions</u>: If my spouse[c] survives me, then commencing with my death the trustee shall pay the income from the Family Trust in convenient installments, at least quarterly, to my

---

Family: My [spouse's] name is _____ and [he/she] is herein referred to as "my spouse." I have X children now living, namely:

A, born ***
B, born ***
C, born ***

In addition, my spouse has Y children now living, namely:

D, born ***
E, born ***
F, born ***

I intend to provide by this document for all of my children and I intend to provide for all of my spouse's children as if they were my own children. Accordingly, all references in this document to "my children" or to "child" (and similar terms) shall be deemed to include each of A, B, C, D, E, and F. I also intend to treat descendants of all of these children as if they were my descendants. Further, I intend to provide for adopted children as if they were natural born [excluding, however, any individual adopted as an adult unless that individual lived with the adopting parent when the individual was a minor], I make no distinction between children born in or outside of wedlock, and children conceived before but born after the death of their biological parents shall be treated as alive at the time of conception. However, children conceived after the death of their biological parent shall not be regarded as the child of that deceased parent.

[b] This "expressly excluding" provision regarding powers of appointment is discussed at page 32, relating to inadvertent or "blanket" exercise of powers of appointment.

[c] Using gender neutral language like "spouse" here is a less personal approach to drafting but it avoids the need to convert pronouns and other gender specific references, which minimizes the risk of making errors in some planning situations. For example, planners who use gender specific references typically draft one spouse's document and then "flip" it by converting items such as "him" to "her" and "he" to "she" and substituting names in appropriate places, all to create the other spouse's plan. Often that chore is avoidable by using gender neutral terminology, but this approach is less personal and it may not suit your preferred style. Some document assembly software systems "personalize" like this better than others, based on a master template with all names and pronouns that are inserted automatically by the program. Manual conversion of pronouns and names or cross references is an invitation for mistake that is better avoided either with better software or gender neutral drafting.

spouse during my spouse's lifetime;[d] but if the income so payable to my spouse shall at any time or times exceed the amount the trustee deems appropriate for my spouse's health and maintenance in reasonable comfort (considering my spouse's other income and means of support known to the trustee, including the income from the Marital Trust, the desirability of augmenting my spouse's separate estate, and any other circumstances and factors deemed pertinent), the trustee may pay any part or all of the excess income to any one or more of my descendants and their respective spouses from time to time living, in equal or unequal proportions, according to their respective needs for health, education (including postgraduate), maintenance, and support in reasonable comfort,[e] or accumulate the same and add it to principal as

---

[d] The balance of this provision would be deleted if mandatory income to the surviving spouse is desired.

The choice between mandatory and discretionary income is likely to be based on a number of factors during the overlife of the surviving spouse, or after the spouse's death and during the term of the next generation of beneficiaries. For example, flexibility is important in some cases, providing the trustee with the ability to distribute income to the beneficiaries most in need. The ability of various beneficiaries to manage income otherwise foisted upon them also is important, with the protection of a discretionary income payment provision or a spendthrift clause being useful in some cases but virtually irrelevant in others. The relative income tax rates of the beneficiaries and the trust play a role, although income taxation of accumulated income is less of a factor if the tax rate differential between the trust and its beneficiaries is not extreme. Distributed income will increase the beneficiary's net worth (which could be a problem for tax, creditor right, or even for divorce property settlement purposes), unless it is being dissipated through gifting or consumption. Finally, in some cases application of the §2013 previously taxed property credit at the beneficiary's death is a relevant factor, with a mandatory income provision producing a credit for taxes paid by the settlor on the trust property within ten years before or two years after the beneficiary's death. See the discussion of this planning in the marital deduction planning Chapter 7 at pages 32-34.

[e] In most situations the drafter relies on generally accepted conventions regarding the definition and understanding of terms such as health, education, maintenance, and support. These are the "ascertainable" standards referenced in the regulations under §2041, which deals with general powers of appointment, and may be the most commonly used standards in all American trust drafting as a result. But it may be wise to add definitions (usually someplace in the boilerplate provisions in the back of the document) to collar, give guidance to, or even protect the fiduciary or the beneficiary (depending on how you view the need for specificity). Consider:

The term "health" includes both mental and physical well being, payments for psychiatric and psychological counseling, and fitness programs designed to maintain and improve the beneficiary's general condition as well as to treat any specific illness, injury, or disorder. The term "support" means payments appropriate to permit a beneficiary to maintain the standard of living to which the beneficiary was accustomed at the time of my death. The term "education" includes expenses incurred in connection with or by reason of attendance at public or private institutions, including without limitation preschool, elementary, preparatory, college, graduate, vocational, and technical institutions, all without regard to accreditation, and may include expenses related to travel, tutoring, tuition, room, board, fees, clothing, books, laboratory or other equipment or tool costs (including computer hardware and software), or other material or activities that the trustee deems to be of reasonable educational benefit or value. Each term relates solely to the individual beneficiary's personal welfare and shall not authorize unrelated distributions, such as to permit the beneficiary to aid any cause or organization (unusual or radical or otherwise).

Every so often a client worries about beneficiaries going off the deep end, or needing special incentives or protections. Each of the following provisions is directed at a specific genre of problem and might be appropriate in a special situation, but none is likely to be appropriate in vanilla estate planning situations. Each should be used with great caution.

Prohibited Distributions: The trustee shall exercise a broad discretion to determine whether the terms of this provision may apply. If the trustee suspects that a beneficiary is a member of a "cult" (any organization involving extreme devotion or attachment to or extravagant admiration for a person, principal, or other object or fixation) or is addicted to any substance, the trustee may require the beneficiary to submit within a reasonable time after actual written or oral notice to physical or psychological testing procedures (conducted by licensed professionals determined by the trustee in the trustee's absolute and unbridled discretion as appropriate) to determine whether the beneficiary is subject to any unreasonable compulsion relating to the cult or is subject to substance addiction. The trustee may require the beneficiary to undergo an appropriate clinical assessment to determine a course of treatment or conduct prescribed by licensed professionals to overcome any such compulsion or addiction, including without limitation inpatient or outpatient treatments, individual and group counseling, and attendance at support groups. All costs associated with such determinations and treatments shall be charged without interest against the beneficiary's ultimate distributive share of the trust and notwithstanding any other provisions of this document no distributions of principal or income shall be made directly to a beneficiary while suffering from such compulsion or addiction, except to the minimum extent required by any applicable law to obtain a tax benefit.

Special Considerations: I intend that no beneficiary shall depend on this trust for support and maintenance to the extent the beneficiary is mentally, emotionally, and physically capable of earning a living, and it is my desire that trust distributions never impair a beneficiary's motivation to be productive and self sustaining. I intend that a beneficiary with financial difficulties, addictive behavior (such as substance abuse, gambling, or spendthrift habits), relationship disorders or dysfunctionality, and similar maladies should address

the trustee deems advisable.[f]

5.03 <u>Principal Distributions</u>: The trustee also may pay to my spouse such sums from the principal as the trustee deems necessary or advisable from time to time for my spouse's health and maintenance in reasonable comfort,[g] and for the health, education (including postgraduate), maintenance, and support in reasonable comfort of any child[h] of mine who may be dependent upon my spouse, considering the

---

those problems that can be resolved by the beneficiary's personal industry and dedication or changes in life style and associations, and that the trustee shall be circumspect in making trust distributions in circumstances that contravene this intent. In all matters the trustee shall consider whether a beneficiary seeking assistance is productive, mature, and responsible, and may consider whether a beneficiary appropriately is unable to earn a sufficient income because of age, mental, emotional, or physical incapacity, conditions that impair the ability to manage, invest, and conserve property, or because of other sufficient reasons such as engaging in public service or being committed to raising children or providing care to dependents.

<u>Serious Unexpected Circumstances</u>: Notwithstanding any other provision of this instrument (but subject to the requirements of any applicable law to obtain a tax benefit), the trustee may withhold or postpone all distributions of income or principal to the extent deemed appropriate due to likely diversion or dissipation of the assets because of the beneficiary's involvement in serious litigation, bankruptcy, insolvency proceedings, or the beneficiary's financial, matrimonial, or personal circumstances; or because the beneficiary is living under a form of government or other condition making it highly likely that the distribution would be subject to confiscation or appropriation (other than "normal" taxation), or if serious and avoidable disadvantageous tax consequences are likely to result.

[f] Adding income to principal avoids the need for a special income accumulation account for fiduciary accounting and fee generation purposes. Most professional trustees impose a "base" fee on each trust that they must maintain an account for, including an income accumulation fund, which speaks in favor of minimizing any proliferation of unnecessary trusts.

[g] The following modification would be substituted for the balance of this provision if principal encroachment for the spouse alone is desired: "**considering my spouse's income from all sources and other readily marketable assets known to the trustee, but shall make no invasion of the Family Trust so long as any readily marketable assets remain in the Marital Trust.**"

[h] Notice that income in paragraph 5.02 may be distributed to descendants and spouses, but corpus here only is distributable to dependent children. That is unlikely (given the age of most surviving spouses and children when the first spouse dies) and limits flexibility in a way that may not be appropriate. But it assures the surviving spouse that only excess income and not income producing corpus will be distributed away from the spouse in most cases. This easily could be changed, and paragraphs 5.02 and 5.03 could be combined. As you read other suggested language in this Chapter, look for a template for such a provision that could be the model

income of each of them from all sources known to the trustee, but shall make no invasion of the Family Trust for my spouse so long as any readily marketable assets remain in the Marital Trust.^{i/} No payment of income or principal to a child of mine shall be charged against the share hereafter^{j/} provided for the child or his or her descendants.^k

---

you would use. One skill you need to develop is to take a form such as this "off the rack" and "tailor" it to a particular situation, because you don't want forms to dictate the planning you do for your clients. Instead, you want forms to help guide your drafting much like a garment is properly fitted by taking a stitch here or letting out a hem there to fit your client's needs.

i/ Dissipation of the marital trust is dictated before invasion of the family trust because the marital trust will be includible in the surviving spouse's taxable estate at death while undistributed amounts of the family trust will not. The authority to invade corpus to permit the spouse to make inter vivos gifts should be in the marital trust to facilitate that dissipation at the spouse's cheaper gift tax rates, as discussed in Chapter 7 at pages 61, 85, 91, and 104-105.

j/ Why do so many lawyers use here*in*after? One consequence of it would be to restrict this advancement dictate to distributions under this document and not speak to related or integrated documents or dispositions. Whichever term you resonate with, in this and so many other things you need not assume that the drafting you use as a model is "good," or client friendly. You should try to develop your own voice in drafting.

k/ The following would be substituted for the last sentence if distributions are to be treated as an advancement: "**Each distribution to a child of mine shall be treated as an advancement and charged (at its date of distribution value and without interest) against the share hereafter provided for the child or his or her descendants.**" This treatment might be especially appropriate for extraordinary distributions, such as to pay for a wedding, or certain advanced higher education expenses, or to purchase a home or a business. Notice that this provision does not (but could, and in some cases should) account for income earned or appreciation in the value of the distributed property, charge interest for the early receipt of the distributed property, or reflect any difference in income, gift, estate, or generation-skipping transfer tax attributable to early distribution. Consider the following additional language to charge at values that reflect current realities without having to trace a particular distribution (which could generate significant administrative complexity):

Any shares of stock in Family Corp. (or any related or successor entity) distributed to a child of mine shall be treated as an advancement and charged at their fair market value at the time for division of this trust and not at the actual date of distribution value of that stock. The value for making an adjustment for any other distribution shall be the date of distribution value (without interest), multiplied by a fraction of which the numerator is the cost of living index as of January 1 of the year of division of this trust based on the [locale] Urban Consumer Index published by the Bureau of Labor Statistics of the United States Department of Labor (the Index) and the denominator is the corresponding Index number for January 1 of the year in which the

5.04 Disclaimer:[l/] A disclaimer by my spouse of any part or all of the Marital Trust or other property shall not preclude my spouse from receiving benefits from the disclaimed property in the Family Trust.[m/]

5.05 Division into Shares: Upon the death of my spouse, or upon my death if my spouse does not survive me,[n/] the trustee shall divide the Family Trust, including any amounts added thereto from the Marital Trust,[o/] into equal shares to create one share for each then living child

---

distribution was made. If publication of the Index is discontinued, then the trustee shall use comparable statistics for the cost of living in the city of [locale] as they are computed or published by any agency of the United States or a responsible financial periodical of recognized authority reasonably selected by the trustee.

Oh, by the way, do you see the flaw in each of the text and these alternatives? To whom may distributions be made, and against what are charges computed? If, for example, distribution is made to a grandchild (or the spouse of a grandchild) will it count against the share of a child who is the grandchild's parent? The text provision addresses the *converse* situation and does not mention the in-law distribution situation at all. Is that to say those distributions *will* be charged? If so, will interest be calculated, and at what values? Certainly this provision is not as extensive as needed to avoid litigation on the issue. See the difference in 5.06 at page 10.

l/ This provision is authorized by §2518(b)(4)(A). Without it postmortem estate planning of the variety discussed in Chapter 7 at pages 16-20 would not be embraced by many surviving spouses.

m/ If this trust might receive disclaimed property it must deny the surviving spouse any power of appointment (inter vivos or testamentary) as to that disclaimed property. This form does not grant the surviving spouse a power to appoint at all, which may be too restrictive. See page 21 regarding powers of appointment. If the trust might receive disclaimed property it also must collar any authority the spouse might have as trustee to make distributions to anyone. As drafted that would not be a problem with *this* form, but changes made to it would require careful thought if the spouse might be or become trustee.

n/ A very common drafting error is the assumption that the settlor's spouse will survive the settlor. This simple clause avoids the dispositive glitch that otherwise would exist if division were dictated only "upon the death of my spouse." Another, more terse, way to state the time for division would be "upon the death of the survivor of my spouse and me."

o/ The typical pattern would be to combine both spouses' property in this one trust following the surviving spouse's death. Even if the surviving spouse wishes to plan separately, this form combines all the wealth of the first spouse to die in this one trust after the survivor's death.

If the settlor does not wish to divide into shares *for descendants* the language following the death of the surviving spouse needs to be a little different, but the model is not that difficult. Consider the following template:

of mine and one share for the then living descendants, collectively, of each deceased child of mine.p/

> . . . divided into as many equal shares as needed to distribute * share(s) to X if (s)he survives me, * share(s) to Y if (s)he survives me, and * share(s) to Z if (s)he survives me. [The share that would have been distributed to a named individual if he or she had survived me shall be distributed to his or her descendants by right of representation or, if there are none, the bequest to that individual shall lapse.]

p/ Another common drafting error is failure to anticipate death of a child before division of the trust into shares for children, especially if the deceased child left descendants who should represent the child.

Another important issue is dealing with survivorship and "simultaneous" death (which is the term used loosely to refer to the situation in which two people die under circumstances such that the order of their deaths cannot be established by proof). State law often addresses this issue as between a testator and a beneficiary, but in this context the issue can be important as between one beneficiary (the second spouse to die, for example) and another (children), because the disposition of property could change if, for example, a child was deemed to have survived the division event and died immediately thereafter or died an instant before the time for division. One way to address this issue is to require that the child survive the division event by a period of time (such as 120 hours under the Uniform Probate Code or, probably preferable for a number of reasons, 30 days). A second approach is to include a simultaneous death provision such as the following, geared to the order of deaths between beneficiaries:

In all events notwithstanding any state law to the contrary, if the order of deaths between my spouse and me cannot be determined by sufficient evidence my spouse shall be treated as [surviving/predeceasing] me, and if the order of deaths between any other individuals cannot be determined by sufficient evidence the order of their deaths shall be treated as the younger of them having died first.

The presumption adopted in this provision is probably the exact opposite of what most folks would predict and is informed predominantly by tax motives. Consider the net result, for example, if a child and a grandchild were to die in a common disaster and the order of their deaths could not be determined. The grandchild will be presumed not to have survived, which makes the dispositive document govern disposition of the share the grandchild would have received if living rather than any estate plan of the grandchild (or state law intestacy if the grandchild had no other estate plan). That likely is what the average client would prefer if they thought about the issue. In a case like the grandchild it probably would send the grandchild's share to other grandchildren if the grandchild died without descendants, and that probably produces the same result as if the grandchild survived long enough to take and died intestate. But perhaps not (for example, if the grandchild was married it might preclude the grandchild's surviving spouse from benefiting), and drafting for those uncertainties is what this endeavor is all about! If there was only the one grandchild who was the child's descendant it likely would send the property to the child's other siblings, which would be a taxpayer preferable result because it would reduce or

5.06 <u>Distribution of Descendants' Shares</u>:[q/] Each share created for the descendants of a deceased child shall be distributed per stirpes to those descendants, subject to postponement of possession as provided below.[r] Each share created for a living child shall be held as a separate trust and disposed of as hereafter provided.

5.07 <u>Income Distributions From Child's Share</u>: The income from a child's share shall be paid in convenient installments, at least quarterly, to the child until complete distribution of the share or his or

---

eliminate the generation-skipping transfer tax that otherwise would apply if the property went to the grandchild for an instant and then passed from the grandchild's estate to potentially the same individuals. Avoiding such a tax result is the true motivation for this provision.

[q/] In this plan division into shares for the children is postponed until death of the surviving spouse, on the assumption that the typical client wants to provide first for the spouse, making the children wait until the survivor's death before being in line to take a share outright. In some circumstances this will be contrary to the client's intent, especially if the children are from a former marriage or the client wants the children to receive some property during the years of their greatest need, regardless of whether a surviving spouse still is alive. In such a case, the following provision would be substituted for paragraphs 5.02 through 5.05 and the succeeding paragraphs would be renumbered accordingly.

5.02 <u>Division into Shares</u>: **The trustee shall forthwith divide the Family Trust into equal shares to create one share for each child of mine living at my death and one share for the then living descendants, collectively, of each deceased child of mine.**

In addition, the first clause of paragraph 5.12 at page 14 would be altered to read **"If upon my death, or at . . . ,"** to account for the possibility that it might apply while the surviving spouse still was alive. Furthermore, the marital deduction pour over provision would be altered to provide for addition:

proportionately to the shares into which the Family Trust has been divided, provided that, if any share has been distributed in whole or in part, the property directed to be added thereto shall be distributed in the manner and to the extent provided with respect to the share as if it or the part or parts thereof were then being distributed.

[r/] See paragraph 5.13 at page 15. The theory behind this treatment is to vest shares in grandchildren or more remote descendants to avoid Rule Against Perpetuities and certain generation-skipping transfer tax problems and to minimize administrative problems in what are likely to be smaller shares (due to the number of descendants involved). A full-fledged trust for this level of beneficiary could be drafted along virtually the same lines as the illustrative provisions in the text, if it is likely that sufficient assets will be involved and if these other issues are addressed properly. Those multiple trusts are likely to be pretty small in most cases, which accounts for this form being less concerned about them. But the converse might be true, depending on growth in the assets and size of the family.

her prior death,^s/ except that, while the child is under the age of ** years,^t/ the trustee shall pay to or for the benefit of the child so much or all of the income from the child's share as the trustee deems necessary or advisable from time to time for the child's health, education (including postgraduate), maintenance, and support in reasonable comfort, adding to principal any income not so paid.

5.08 **Principal Distributions From Child's Share**: The trustee shall pay to the child such sums from the principal of his or her share as the trustee deems necessary or advisable from time to time for the child's health, education (including postgraduate), maintenance, and support in reasonable comfort, considering the income of the child from all sources known to the trustee.^u/

5.09 **Right of Withdrawal**:^v/ After division of the Family Trust

---

s/ Delete the balance of this provision if mandatory income is desired. Substitute the following if a unitrust distribution is desired in lieu of an income entitlement (supplemented by invasions of principal):

In each calendar year the trustee shall pay to the child an amount (the unitrust amount) equal to *% of the net fair market value of the trust assets (including all accrued and accumulated income) valued as of the first business day of each calendar year of the trust. The unitrust amount may be distributed in convenient installments, at least quarterly, it shall be paid first from income and then from principal to the extent income is not sufficient, and any income in excess of the unitrust amount shall be added to principal.

Note that unitrust drafting can become much more complex (for example, by using a "smoothing" approach that distributes a percentage of the average fair market value for a three year or longer prior period).

t/ Any age could be selected here. Usually something in the early to mid 20's is appropriate. Delete all of this provision prior to this point if discretionary income for the life of the child is desired. Note that you could then marry paragraphs 5.07 and 5.08 together and eliminate some redundancy. Conversely, if the age were increased substantially it might be appropriate to mirror paragraph 5.02 by allowing distributions to a child's spouse and descendants.

u/ Consideration of more than just income may be appropriate, such as with the following substitution for the clause following the last comma: **"considering the income and other assets available to the child and the advisability of supplementations, the child's character, habits and diligence, progress and aptitude in acquiring an education, ability to manage money prudently and usefully, and ability to assume responsibilities of adult life and self support."** Also consider whether this paragraph should permit invasions for a child's spouse, dependents, or descendants.

v/ The theory behind this right of withdrawal (rather than a mandatory distribution provision) is to avoid forcing beneficiaries to accept property that they would prefer to leave in trust. This right eliminates the need for a child to accept a distribution and then create a new trust (which would be particularly unfortunate if the child were incompetent at the time for

into shares and after a child has reached[w/] the age of ** years,[x/] the child may withdraw any part or all of the principal of his or her share at any time or times, but not to exceed in the aggregate one-half in value thereof prior to reaching the age of ** years.[y/] The value of the share

distribution, if the child could not be located, or if spendthrift protection would be lost in the process). For all tax purposes, however, to the extent the beneficiary does not exercise the withdrawal right the ongoing trust would be treated as if the share had been created by the beneficiary.

Substitute the following for paragraph 5.09 if mandatory distribution of the child's share is desired:

5.09 <u>Distribution of Shares</u>: When a child reaches the age of ** years, or upon division of the Family Trust into shares if he or she has then reached that age, the trustee shall distribute to the child half in value of the principal of his or her share then held hereunder; and when a child reaches the age of ** years, or upon division of the Family Trust into shares if he or she has then reached that age, the trustee shall distribute to the child the balance of his or her share.

Quaere whether a mandatory force out provision ever is appropriate. Yet virtually every form you will see mandates distribution.

The foregoing provisions need not use a two stage withdrawal or distribution. See comment y for an illustration of a three stage provision. Also note how this provision anticipates the issue explained in the next comment below of a child already being the specified age when the trust or share is created ("when . . . or upon . . .").

w/ Note that this does not say "*When* the child reaches" the specified age, because this provision must apply even if the child reached that age before division of the trust into shares, and this right is an on-going entitlement, not a one-time event, making an occurrence-"triggering" provision inappropriate.

x/ This could be any age, although typically it will be later than the age used in paragraph 5.07 to determine when (if ever) the beneficiary will begin receiving all income from the trust.

y/ This age typically is five to ten years older than the age when the first withdrawal right became exercisable, the expectation being that the beneficiary will learn a few lessons from any mistakes that were made with respect to earlier withdrawals, without risking his or her entire inheritance. If the child's share will be large enough to justify withdrawal in three stages, substitute the following for the provision prior to this point:

5.09: <u>Right of Withdrawal</u>: After division of the Family Trust into shares and after a child has reached any one or more of the following ages, the child may withdraw from the principal of his or her share at any time or times not to exceed in the aggregate:

One-third in value after ** years of age;

Half in value (after deducting any amount subject to withdrawal but not actually withdrawn) after ** years of age; and

The balance after ** years of age.

shall be determined as of the child's first exercise of this withdrawal right, plus the value of any additions made thereafter (determined at the time of the addition). The trustee shall make payment without question upon the child's written request. This right of withdrawal shall be a privilege that may be exercised only voluntarily and shall not include an involuntary exercise.[z]

5.10 <u>Testamentary Power of Appointment</u>:[aa] Upon the death of the child before receiving his or her share in full, the child's share shall be held in trust hereunder or distributed to or in trust for such appointee or appointees, with such powers and in such manner and proportions as the child may appoint by his or her will making specific reference to this power of appointment, except that any part of the child's share not subject to withdrawal prior to the death of the child may be appointed only to or for the benefit of any one or more of the child's surviving spouse, the child's descendants and their respective spouses, and my descendants (other than the child) and their respective spouses. For purposes of this provision, the term "spouse" shall include a widow or widower, regardless of remarriage.[bb]

Notice that allowing withdrawal of "one-third" of the share following *each* triggering date will not permit withdrawal of the entire share, making the declining denominator the necessary drafting method. If you don't believe this just run a simple illustration: the trust is $30 to begin and the child withdraws $10. When it is worth $20 how much should the child be able to draw down: $10 or one-third of $20?

[z] This provision is similar to a spendthrift clause, which otherwise might not apply to this withdrawal right. This provision may not be effective, but what is to be lost for inclusion?

[aa] This is a general testamentary power of appointment for wealth transfer tax purposes, but only to the extent the child is treated for tax purposes as the owner of the trust because of the power of withdrawal in paragraph 5.09. In some cases it will be preferable for this power to be available inter vivos as well. Furthermore, for generation-skipping transfer tax purposes some drafters make the entire trust subject to §2041 inclusion in the child's estate at death by granting a general power of appointment over the entire trust even if death occurs before the age specified for withdrawal. Another method of causing inclusion is appropriate exercise of a nongeneral power of appointment to trigger the Delaware tax trap of §2041(a)(3), as explained in Blattmachr & Pennell, *Adventures in Generation-Skipping, or How We Learned to Love the "Delaware Tax Trap,"* 24 REAL PROP., PROB. & TRUST J. 75-94 (1989), abridged in *Using "Delaware Tax Trap" to Avoid Generation-Skipping Taxes*, 68 J. TAX'N 242-248 (1988). Other drafting issues in this provision are addressed in detail beginning at page 21.

[bb] Why does this form not provide similar breadth elsewhere? For example, a child's descendants become beneficiaries after a child's death, even if the child's surviving spouse is still alive. If the child and spouse were dependent on this trust the child's death could be devastating to the spouse's well being. The standard trust does not provide for the child's

5.11 **Default Distribution**: Upon the death of a child any part of his or her share not effectively appointed[cc] shall be distributed per stirpes to his or her then living descendants, or if none, then per stirpes to my then living descendants, subject to postponement of possession as provided below,[dd] except that each portion otherwise distributable to a descendant of mine for whom a share of the Family Trust is then held hereunder shall be added to that share.[ee]

5.12 **Contingent Distribution**: If there is no living descendant of mine upon the death of the survivor of my spouse and me, or at any time thereafter but prior to complete distribution of the Family Trust, any trust property then held under this article and not vested or effectively appointed shall be distributed half to my heirs-at-law and half to my spouse's heirs-at-law, the heirs-at-law and the proportions they respectively shall take to be determined in each case according to the laws of descent of the State of ***** as if my spouse and I had both died at that time.[ff]

5.13 **Postponement of Possession:** Each share of the Family Trust that is distributable to a descendant who has not reached the age of **

---

surviving spouse unless the child does so through exercise of this power of appointment, which is just one of several reasons why powers are so important.

cc/ Notice that this provision refers to a failure to *effectively* exercise the power, not to a mere failure to exercise the power, making this default provision applicable if the beneficiary exercised in violation of the Rule Against Perpetuities or in favor of impermissible appointees or otherwise in violation of the power of appointment.

If a mandatory distribution of the child's share is dictated, substitute the following for the foregoing: **"If a child dies before receiving his or her share in full, then upon the death of the child his or her share . . . ."**

dd/ See paragraph 5.13.

ee/ This "add to shares" provision is designed to avoid a multiplicity of shares for any particular descendant.

ff/ Without this definition of the applicable law, the heirs-at-law would likely be determined as of the respective deaths of the settlor and surviving spouse, meaning that distribution could be required to individuals who no longer are alive (including either spouse as heir of the other). Consider whether the designated state law provides that a surviving spouse of the settlor's remarried surviving spouse is an heir-at-law and whether this settlor would want the surviving spouse's widow(er) to benefit. That issue could be addressed elsewhere by a definition provision in the boilerplate, or here by leaving 100% to the settlor's heirs-at-law. Also consider that use of the law when distribution occurs is easier than ascertaining the law when the settlor executed this document or when the settlor died, but introduces an element of uncertainty to the extent changes in the law prior to operation of this provision are incorporated by the adoption. Designation of the appropriate state law merely eliminates conflict of law disputes.

years[gg] shall immediately vest in the descendant but the trustee shall (a) establish with the share a custodianship for the descendant under a Uniform Gifts to Minors Act or a Uniform Transfers to Minors Act, or (b) retain possession of the share as a separate trust, paying to or for the benefit of the descendant so much or all of the income and principal of the share as the trustee deems necessary or advisable from time to time for his or her health, education (including postgraduate), maintenance, and support in reasonable comfort, adding to principal any income not so paid, and distributing the share to the descendant when he or she reaches the age of ** years[hh] or to the estate of the descendant if he or she dies before receiving the share in full.[ii]

5.14 <u>Facility of Payment</u>: Income or discretionary amounts of principal payable to a minor or to a person under legal disability or to a person not adjudicated disabled but who, by reason of illness or mental or physical disability, is in the opinion of the trustee unable properly to manage his or her affairs shall be paid or expended only in such of the following ways as the trustee deems best: (a) to the beneficiary directly if applicable law requires direct payment to obtain a tax benefit; otherwise (b) to the legally appointed guardian of the beneficiary; (c) to a custodian for the beneficiary under a Uniform Gifts to Minors Act or a Uniform Transfers to Minors Act; (d) by the trustee directly for the benefit of the beneficiary; or (e) to an adult relative or friend in

---

[gg] Because this share is vested, this could be any age without concern about violating the Rule Against Perpetuities.

[hh] Because these are vested shares, the designated age could be any number the settlor selects.

[ii] Substitute the following if a retained share might be of sufficient size to warrant distribution in two stages:

5.13 Postponement of Possession: Each share of the Family Trust that is distributable to a descendant who has not reached the age of ** years shall immediately vest in the descendant but the trustee shall retain possession of the share as a separate trust, paying to or for the benefit of the descendant so much or all of the income and principal of the share as the trustee deems necessary or advisable from time to time for his or her health, education (including postgraduate), maintenance, and support in reasonable comfort, adding to principal any income not so paid (except that, after the descendant has reached the age of ** years, the trustee shall pay to him or her all the income from the share in convenient installments, at least quarterly), and distributing half in value of the principal of the share to the descendant if he or she has then reached or at such time thereafter as he or she reaches the age of ** years and the balance to the descendant when he or she reaches the age of ** years or to the estate of the descendant if he or she dies before receiving the share in full.

reimbursement for amounts properly advanced for the benefit of the beneficiary.^jj/

Group Trust for Children

The foregoing plan anticipates a fund large enough to justify division into separate shares for children no later than the death of the surviving spouse. The following alternative anticipates that the trust will be held as a single fund until some time after the death of the surviving spouse (or after the death of the settlor, if the trust is not to be held for the benefit of a surviving spouse), at which time it will be divided into shares.^kk/

5.05 Group Trust: After the death of my spouse, or after my death if my spouse does not survive me, the Family Trust, including any amounts added thereto from the Marital Trust, shall be held and disposed of as hereafter provided.

5.06 Income and Principal Distributions: Until the time hereafter fixed for division into shares, the trustee shall pay so much or all of the income and principal of the Family Trust to any one or more of my children and descendants of a deceased child of mine from time to time living, in equal or unequal proportions and at such times as the trustee deems appropriate, for the health, education (including postgraduate), maintenance, and support in reasonable comfort of my children and those descendants, individually and as a group, considering their needs, other income and means of support, and any other circumstances and factors that the trustee deems pertinent, adding to principal any income not so paid. No payment made for a child or other descendant of mine shall be charged against the share hereafter provided for the child or descendant or his or her ancestor or descendants.

5.07 Division into Shares: If upon or whenever after the death of the survivor of my spouse and me there is no living child of mine under the age of ** years,^ll/ the trustee shall divide the Family Trust into equal

---

jj/ This "reimbursement" notion is critical to marital deduction qualification in a marital deduction trust context and is mimicked here because usually just one facility of payment provision is included in any document. Note that if desired a withdrawal right could be used here as well. But a power of appointment would not be very appropriate because these shares are vested already.

kk/ Some comments with respect to the foregoing provisions are equally relevant with respect to the next several illustrations but are not repeated.

ll/ Notice how elegantly this provision anticipates division regardless of the order of deaths of the settlor and settlor's spouse and the ages of the children at the death of the survivor. It also does not describe the "youngest living child" reaching the specified age, thus reflecting the possibility that the *youngest* child may never reach that age or (even more unlikely but still possible) that *no* child will reach that age. This provision applies when all

shares to create one share for each then living child of mine and one share for the then living descendants, collectively, of each deceased child of mine.[mm]

5.08 Distribution of Descendants' Shares: Each share created for the descendants of a deceased child shall be distributed[nn] per stirpes to those descendants, subject to postponement of possession as provided below. Each share created for a living child shall be held as a separate trust and disposed of as hereafter provided.

Here the provisions of paragraphs 5.07 through 5.14 from the former illustration would be renumbered and used for the balance of the trust provisions.

---

living children have reached the designated age *or* if all children have died. In either case, no *living* child would be *under* the specified age.

The age you select is a function of why you used a group trust. For example, consider those criteria noted beginning at page 20. If the motivation was equality of treatment in paying for education, most folks would select an age such as 25. That is not too low as to thwart graduate school education or to hamper a child on "the extended plan," but not so high as to delay everyone while a "perpetual student" continues to defer getting on with their life. If the rationale for the group trust was to provide a safety net for a disabled child, however, it may be that division or distribution should not occur until that child's death. Note that with an older age it might be wise to include descendants and surviving spouses of deceased children. Also consider how these criteria inform selection of trustee, the size for a small trust termination provision, and other elements in the draft.

mm/ If distribution is to occur immediately upon division rather than having the shares held for children until a later age, substitute the following for paragraphs 5.07 through 5.12 from the former illustration:

5.07 Distribution of Shares: If upon or whenever after the death of the survivor of my spouse and me there is no living child of mine under the age of ** years, the trustee shall distribute the Family Trust per stirpes to my then living descendants, subject to postponement of possession as provided below.

Here the provisions of paragraphs 5.12 through 5.14 from the former illustration would be renumbered and used as the balance of the Family Trust provisions. Notice again how such a plan could disfranchise the surviving spouse of a child who might become destitute as the settlor's grandchildren become independently wealthy. Also note that a per stirpes distribution need not be selected; other alternatives are available.

nn/ A predeceased child could be given a power to appoint this share, effective immediately upon division. Such a power might be a good way to finesse the surviving spouse problem, although consider the default provision to the extent the child does not effectively exercise the power.

Group Trust With "Peel-Off" Provision

In some circumstances the Family Trust will be held as a group trust, as above, but never divided into shares, either for immediate distribution or to be separately held until a child reaches an older age. A good illustration of when this might be appropriate is a family with many children or with children whose ages are quite disparate, or both. Separate shares may be uneconomical or unfair, because older children benefited from the larger trust for education and other major expenses until its division into equal shares, while the younger children must consume their separate shares for some of these items that come up after division. But a traditional group trust also may be unwise because it potentially makes older children wait too long for distribution because their younger siblings have not yet reached the age for distribution.

To address these conflicting concerns, the following format permits each child to "peel-off" a share as the child reaches a specified age. Although it would be more complex, this pattern could make a fraction of a child's share subject to a power of withdrawal and hold the balance under a plan like the more traditional group trust plan last illustrated. It even could give a child a testamentary power of appointment if death occurs before distribution. Administrative and valuation problems in identifying the relative shares of the various children probably make these approaches undesirable in most cases, however.

5.05 Group Trust: After the death of my spouse, or after my death if my spouse does not survive me, the Family Trust, including any amounts added thereto from the Marital Trust, shall be held and disposed of as hereafter provided.

5.06 Income and Principal Distributions: Until complete distribution of the Family Trust, the trustee shall pay so much or all of the income and principal of the Family Trust to any one or more of my children from time to time living (exclusive of any children to whom or to whose descendants distribution has been made pursuant to the following provisions),[oo/] in equal or unequal proportions and at such times as the trustee deems best, for their health, education (including postgraduate), maintenance, and support in reasonable comfort, considering the needs, other income and means of support, and best interests of my children, individually and as a group, and any other circumstances and factors that the trustee deems pertinent, adding to principal any income not so paid. No payment of income or principal to

---

oo/ This parenthetical is essential to preserve the pattern of this plan that a child benefits only until distribution of the child's portion of the trust. This parenthetical might be deleted if a hybrid plan were used by which a child did not receive a full share by peel-off distribution, although distributions to such a child probably should be only for extraordinary purposes and then only if other funds are not available to that child.

a child of mine shall be charged against the share hereafter provided for the child or his or her descendants.

5.07 Distribution of Shares: If upon or whenever after the death of the survivor of my spouse and me a child has reached the age of ** years,[pp] the trustee shall distribute to the child that fraction of the then principal of the Family Trust of which the numerator is one and the denominator is the number of children of mine then living and then deceased leaving one or more descendants then living, exclusive of any child or children to whom or to whose descendants a distribution previously has been made.[qq]

5.08 Share of Deceased Child: If a child dies before reaching the age of ** years, then upon the death of the last to die of my spouse, the child, and me,[rr] the share of the principal of the Family Trust that the child would have received if the child had then reached the age of ** years shall be distributed[ss] per stirpes to his or her then living descendants, or if none, then per stirpes to my then living descendants, subject to postponement of possession as provided below, except that the share otherwise distributable to a child of mine who has not then reached the age of ** years shall be retained as a part of the principal of the Family Trust[tt] and except further that any share distributable to

---

pp/ This age probably needs to be higher than in the prior group trust illustration, so as to hold more of the wealth for the younger beneficiaries, but not so high as to deny benefits while a child is most in need of the money.

qq/ To understand how this provision works, consider a trust with three children: the oldest will receive one-third of the corpus upon reaching the specified age, the next child will receive half, and the last will receive the balance. A withdrawal right could be used instead of mandatory distribution, but the accounting and valuation problems this would raise probably dictate against it in most cases.

rr/ This terse but understandable triggering provision will operate regardless of the order of the three possible deaths.

ss/ Work an example to persuade yourself that this distribution of the deceased child's peel-off share is essential and properly crafted to make certain the entire trust is distributed if the last child dies before reaching the specified age and, on the death of any other child, to preserve equality to those children to whom (or to whose descendants) a distribution previously has been made. A predeceased child could be given a power to appoint this share, effective immediately upon division.

tt/ The net effect of this provision is to give a share of the deceased child's peel-off entitlement to those children (or their descendants) who already have received distributions, while retaining the balance of the deceased child's share for those children to whom distribution has not yet occurred. Again, work an example, only now assume it was the second child of three who died, childless, after one received distribution and while the third child still is a beneficiary of the trust. Half of the second child's "share" would go to the oldest child and the other half would remain in the trust for the youngest child, awaiting final distribution when that child reaches age.

a descendant other than a child of mine for whom a share of the Family Trust then is being held hereunder shall be added to that share.

Here the provisions of paragraphs 5.12 through 5.14 from the original illustration would be renumbered and used for the balance of the trust provisions.

Family Planning Considerations

Each of the foregoing illustrations demonstrated a plan that would be appropriate based on a number of competing factors. Many questions must be resolved in balancing those factors; here are a few:

How large is the available fund, and will maintenance of separate shares for individual children produce trusts that are uneconomically small, relative to trustee fees and other costs? For example, a good benchmark regarding size would be if the trustee's base fee exceeded half the income earned, or if the threshold for computing the base fee was greater than the trust corpus.

Who will be trustee and what fees and other costs will be involved? In this respect, we will learn in Chapter 6 that anyone can be trustee if the drafter is careful in drafting the document.

How does the settlor feel about equality among the children? For example, should division into separate shares be delayed until all children have been educated out of the total pot, with only the balance being divided, or does division into shares after some have been educated but before others have finished their schooling create an inequity of no great significance, given the amount of wealth involved? Alternatively, are some of the children "perpetual" students whose failure to leave academe and enter the "real" world should not be a financial burden on all the children?

Do extraordinary needs of some children dictate that the fund be held as a group trust so that all children share in the costs to support all of the children? Indeed, should the trust be held through the lives of all children (rather than presume, as do all the foregoing provisions, that at some date during the lives of the children the fund will divide and ultimately be distributed)? Generation-skipping transfer tax planning becomes important in this respect, particularly with respect to the generation-skipping tax deferral provisions, but only if the wealth involved exceeds the generation-skipping transfer exemption amount (for example, $1.5 million in 2004). Also worthy of consideration is whether descendants of all degree should be made permissible beneficiaries of both income and principal during the life of the children, with consideration of generation-skipping and discharge of obligation problems. Further, should the trust provide for surviving spouses of deceased descendants?

Do additional tax factors dictate a particular structure in the trust? For example, because compression of the income tax rates reduces the tax benefits of maintaining separate trusts, is there any other tax motivated reason to create separate trusts for each child? Should charity play a role in any of the planning involved? And how much marital deduction is appropriate in light of the client's family planning objectives?

If taxes are the primary motivation for a disposition in trust instead of outright, should the trust include a termination provision that allows escape if the wealth transfer tax laws are repealed? If so, it should apply only if the termination provision will not cause other tax problems to the powerholder (e.g., an individual trustee who might face §678 pseudo-grantor trust income tax problems, as mentioned in Chapter 17).

How much enjoyment or control does the settlor want to bestow on the beneficiaries, notwithstanding any tax consequences of that decision? In this respect, it makes sense to ask the client to describe the preferred family plan if taxes were nonexistent, and only then try to accommodate those desires with a tax conscious plan to the extent possible, making affirmative choices to the extent necessary between the desired disposition and any negative tax ramifications.

These questions all involve uncertainty and planning for whatever the future may bring. Some provisions in this plan are designed to deal with that uncertainty, such as the contingent distribution, postponement of possession, and the facility of payment provisions. The task of planning for uncertainty can be accomplished only partially by any drafter, no matter how omniscient. Beyond a certain degree, some uncertainty about the future needs of the family must be left to be resolved in the future.

Powers of Appointment

Astute estate planners resort to powers of appointment primarily to deal with uncertainty. Powers provide the ability to exercise more flexibility, by giving someone a "second look" at the estate plan in the future. "The power of appointment is the most efficient dispositive device that the ingenuity of Anglo-American lawyers has ever worked out. . . . Lawyers . . . have discovered . . . that the power of appointment is the answer to more of the problems that face the draft[er] of wills and trusts than any other device." Leach, *Powers of Appointment*, 24 A.B.A.J. 807 (1938).

Plainly no human foresight is adequate to frame in advance dispositions which will meet the exigencies of the maximum period of control or even the comparatively small fraction thereof commonly utilized by testators and settlers. Births and deaths in varying combinations, the commercial success of some family members and the failure of others, the varying capacities of individuals as to the husbanding of resources, fluctuation in income returns and the value of the monetary unit, legislative action and constitutional amendment reflecting social and political change — all these are factors whose unpredictability indicates the folly of rigid predetermined future limitations and the desirability of gifts containing a substantial element of flexibility. The power of appointment . . . is the most efficient device yet contrived by which an owner may obtain such flexibility while still controlling the general purposes to which . . . property shall be devoted.

3 RESTATEMENT OF PROPERTY Ch. 25, Introductory Note (1940).

Powers to appoint can take many forms, including inter vivos or testamentary powers of appointment, powers of withdrawal limited by a §2041(b)(1)(A) ascertainable standard, a "five or five" provision (explained below), powers in the role of trustee or distribution director, and powers of the most extreme variety to terminate, alter, or amend. As a planning tool, all are much more useful than disclaimer, which seldom is the answer to the need for flexibility. This is because documents usually are not adequately drafted to provide that a beneficiary's rejection of property will cause its disposition in the manner desired, particularly to reflect changing circumstances or unanticipated events, such as tax law changes. Sometimes a disclaimer can avert or salvage a disaster in waiting, but seldom is disclaimer the answer to most trust flexibility problems. Disclaimers defeat rather than amend, they reallocate but do not reform, and they accelerate but seldom extend trust provisions. Powers to appoint can surmount all these limitations

Tax consequences seem to cloud the focus of many estate planners when powers to appoint are involved. The most significant rationale for creating powers of appointment is to afford the flexibility of a second look at some future date, and we can finesse the tax issues when they are important. Nevertheless, we need to be aware of the tax issues.

General or Nongeneral Power?

Powers of appointment serve several useful functions for tax purposes, but also may generate unexpected liabilities. A general power of appointment is defined in §2041 as any power permitting the powerholder to benefit the powerholder, the powerholder's estate, or creditors of either. Any other permissible appointee is acceptable but irrelevant. General powers are taxable under the tax rules and, with very few exceptions, nongeneral powers are not.

Why would a donor ever give a beneficiary a general power of appointment if property over which a beneficiary holds a general power of appointment is includible in the powerholder's gross estate and it is possible to provide flexibility in a dispositive plan with nongeneral powers of appointment and limited invasion authority? The answer is that, today, there are four legitimate reasons to grant a general power of appointment, only one of which relates to providing flexibility in an estate plan.

- The first reason relates to the marital deduction. General powers of appointment were widely used before 1982 to qualify trust property for the federal estate and gift tax marital deductions under §§2056(b)(5) and 2523(e). These marital deduction power of appointment trusts are not frequently employed today because of the §§2056(b)(7) and 2523(f) QTIP marital deduction trust, introduced in 1982, which allows the marital deduction without granting control to the spouse by means of a general power of appointment. Since 1982, old-style general power of appointment marital deduction trusts are used typically if the trust is employed for management or protection purposes rather than to deny control to the surviving spouse, and often the spouse is also named as trustee or the general power is exercisable inter vivos as well as at death.

- A second use of general powers of appointment is in drafting §2503(c) qualified minors' trusts for gift tax annual exclusion purposes. Frankly, these trusts are not used very often because, as we will learn in Chapter 12, so-called Crummey powers or five or five withdrawal rights are regarded as more useful and less problematic.

In each of these two situations, the general power of appointment is granted to the powerholder as a trade-off for some tax advantage to the donor. The marital deduction or annual exclusion benefits to the donor are bestowed at the cost of inclusion to the powerholder generated by the general power of appointment. This quid pro quo explains why a general power is required in each of these situations to qualify for a particular tax benefit.

- A third use of general powers of appointment is for generation-skipping transfer tax avoidance. This use — either pursuant to a formula grant of the power, the exercise of trustee discretion, or the Delaware tax trap — is designed to attract estate or gift tax to the extent those excises are cheaper than the generation-skipping transfer tax. See Chapter 18 at page 13. Thus, the general power of appointment is again a tool to obtain a tax benefit. The only difference here is that the powerholder is the beneficiary of the tax savings generated as well as the payor of the tax liability incurred as the price for it.

- Finally, general powers of appointment frequently are granted to beneficiaries to permit immediate withdrawal of trust principal. We learned at page 11 that family planning often appropriately makes a trust available for withdrawal after a beneficiary reaches a certain age but does not mandate distribution if the beneficiary does not wish to (or simply is unable to) assume responsibility for management of the property. In this way the beneficiary (or someone acting on their behalf) need not create a new trust to hold distributed property. Instead, the beneficiary merely allows the general power of withdrawal to go unexercised. In cases such as this, because the trust property will be fully includible in the beneficiary's taxable estate at death, typically the withdrawal power is coupled with a general testamentary power of appointment, exercisable if the beneficiary dies after the withdrawal power becomes available. The testamentary general power to appoint guarantees that the beneficiary need not withdraw just to control ultimate distribution of the property.

Aside from these four situations, general powers of appointment probably are created only by inadvertence, mistake, or malpractice.

Scope of Nongeneral Powers

Congress has been quite generous in defining the powers that can be given to a beneficiary without causing the appointive property to be includible in the powerholder's estate for wealth transfer tax purposes. A donor who wants to give a beneficiary maximum flexibility in the form of powers of appointment could give any or all of the following powers without tax consequences to the powerholder.

- An *ascertainable standard invasion power* to withdraw so much or all of the trust principal as necessary for the beneficiary's health, education, maintenance, and support (HEMS). The trust may dictate that other resources available to the beneficiary be considered in determining the amounts needed for these purposes or, to provide maximum benefits, the trust may state that any amounts needed are to be "determined without regard to other resources available" for the stated purposes. See Treas. Reg. §20.2041-1(c)(2). If the latter approach is employed, the beneficiary may reach trust corpus for all the beneficiary's basic needs (house payments or rent, food bills, clothing and transportation costs, medical bills and insurance, and taxes), all without regard to the beneficiary's other income or resources.

- A noncumulative annual *power to withdraw* $5,000 or 5% of the value of the trust, exercisable with no showing of need, freeing the beneficiary from dependence on the trustee or the need to determine whether a particular withdrawal is permitted under the HEMS ascertainable standard. The lapse of such a five or five power is specifically made nontaxable by §2514(e) but a §678 pseudo grantor trust income tax problem can exist, as discussed in Chapter 12 at pages 22-23 and Chapter 17 at pages 14-15.

- A *nongeneral power to appoint* trust principal, exercisable either during life or at death in favor of any appointee other than the powerholder, the powerholder's estate, or creditors of either.

- If drafted properly, the beneficiary may be named trustee of the trust, giving the power to manage and invest trust property. Although subject to basic fiduciary standards, the beneficiary would have broad latitude to manage the property almost as if the beneficiary owned it.

Less than all of these alternatives may be granted in any given case (this is a summary of the *most* a donor can bestow) but it is an impressive array of options. And it is in addition to enjoyment of income and principal under more defined trust circumstances.

Unexpected Sources of Power of Appointment Tax Liability

Of concern to estate planners are a number of potential sources of unintentional or inadvertent tax liability caused by possessing or exercising certain trust administration provisions that add flexibility to the document. These need not be a concern unless the situation is large enough to be subject to the wealth transfer tax (now or by likely growth, or due to future changes in the law).

Revolving Door Power

For example, discussed in greater detail in Chapter 6 at page 12 is a provision often included in a trust authorizing the removal and replacement of trustees. This "revolving door" provision may cause the government to attribute all the trustee's powers to the holder of the removal and replacement authority. This especially is true if the powerholder may appoint the powerholder personally as a successor trustee, with potential general power of appointment consequences if those trustee powers are not properly constrained.

According to Treas. Reg. §20.2041-1(b)(1), a beneficiary's power to remove the acting trustee and appoint the beneficiary as a successor trustee is sufficient to cause the trustee's powers to be imputed to the beneficiary, as if the beneficiary already acted. If those powers in the beneficiary's hands would constitute a general power of appointment, §2041 inclusion would be dictated by the existence of the removal and replacement power, even if the power was not exercised.

It is important to find ways to include a revolving door power without causing the trust corpus to be includible in the powerholder's estate. This is because the revolving door power is a valuable check on the trustee, giving the powerholder a valuable degree of control if the trustee proves to be a poor choice for administration of the trust. As such, even a revolving door power that precludes appointment of the powerholder as a successor trustee is a very strong entitlement. "If the power in a beneficiary to fill a vacancy [with someone else] is combined with an unrestricted power to remove any trustee who occupies the office . . . [t]he combination powers to fill and remove give the beneficiary a powerful weapon to put pressure on the trustee to exercise the trustee's powers the way the beneficiary wants them exercised." 3A Casner, ESTATE PLANNING §12.0 at 85 n.3 (5th ed. 1986).

The government's concern is that the powerholder will appoint and remove trustees at will until one is found that will do the beneficiary's bidding. See Private Letter Rulings 9113026, 9043052, and 8916032. Based on this the government's original position was that the power to remove and replace the trustee was sufficient to impute the trustee's powers to the powerholder, even without the power to name the powerholder as a successor. See Rev. Rul. 79-353, revoked by Rev. Rul. 95-58 in the wake of Estate of Wall v. Commissioner, 101 T.C. 300 (1993), which held that Rev. Rul. 79-353 "is supported neither by cogent argument nor by cited cases supporting the conclusion reached." The Tax Court concluded that the government was wrong in its fundamental premise that a trustee subject to removal and replacement will do the bidding of the holder of a revolving door power. The court stated that established fiduciary law principles would be violated if a trustee "acquiesced in the wishes of the [powerholder] by taking action that the trustee would not otherwise take." Thus, absent proof of some prearrangement between the powerholder and the trustee, the assumption inherent in the Ruling could not be supported and the power therefore did not generate an interest that caused estate tax inclusion.

The government's revised position, stated in Rev. Rul. 95-58, is that the power to remove and replace individual or corporate trustees at will is not adequate to regard the powerholder as possessing the trustee's control over trust distributions, *provided that* any individual or corporate successor is "not related or subordinate to the [powerholder] (within the meaning of §672(c))." If you're willing to limit the scope of potential replacement trustees the concerns of Rev. Rul. 79-353 appear to be a thing of the past. Informal comments by government officials at the 1995 American Bar Association Annual Meeting indicated that Rev. Rul. 95-58 is a safe harbor ruling and that other cases may not be litigated even if not within the "not related or subordinate" confine.

There are additional ways to protect the powerholder from revolving door power inclusion, as discussed in Chapter 6 at pages 13-14. The challenge with any alternative is in creating sufficient ability to reflect changing circumstances while making the power sufficiently strong to serve as a useful deterrent to unacceptable trustee conduct.

Discharge of Legal Obligation of Support

Let's put a second source of unexpected power of appointment tax liability into perspective. Consider the common occurrence of a grandparent making a gift to a grandchild by creating a Uniform Transfers to Minors Act account with the grandchild's parent as custodian (or by creating a trust with the parent as trustee). If the parent had created the account (or trust), Treas. Reg. §20.2036-1(b)(2) would treat the parent as having retained enjoyment that would cause estate tax treatment of the account (or trust) balance at the death of the parent as if the property was still owned by the parent. Here the parent did not create the account (or trust), so the issue is whether the parent has a power of appointment under §2041 that would require similar inclusion in the parent's estate at death (or gift taxation under §2514 if the account or trust terminates during the parent's life).

Relying on Treas. Reg. §20.2041-1(c)(1), inclusion is premised on the theory that distributions from the account may discharge the parent's legal obligation to support the grandchild. This would cause those distributions to be regarded as for the parent's indirect benefit and give the parent a general power of appointment. Fortunately, the theory of indirect benefit through the discharge of obligation is insupportable in most cases. See 2 Casner & Pennell, ESTATE PLANNING §§7.1.1.10.1 and 12.4.2 (6th ed.). State law in the vast majority of American jurisdictions does not support the government's fundamental theory that distributions from a trust serve to discharge the parent's support obligation. In fact, the exact opposite is true: distributions are ignored in determining the child's needs for support unless the trust was created for the express purposes of supplanting that obligation or the parent is financially unable to provide that support. Therefore there is no discharge of the parent's obligation and no benefit to the parent from making distributions to the child.

Nevertheless, the discharge theory is embodied throughout the regulations. See Treas. Reg. §§20.2036-1(b)(2), 20.2041-1(c)(1), 1.677(b)-1, and 1.678(c)-1. The discharge theory has not been asserted by the government recently, but nothing indicates that the government has abandoned it (or ever will). Therefore, again the question arises: how can unwanted tax consequences or disputes be avoided in planning such a transfer in which the trustee or custodian may hold property for a dependent?

Notwithstanding the fact that the parent is being treated as the indirect beneficiary of all distributions to the dependent beneficiary, the curious aspect of this problem is that use of the HEMS ascertainable standard (noted at page 24) to restrict all distributions to the beneficiary is not an effective solution. Treas. Reg. §§20.2041-1(c)(2) and 25.2514-1(c)(2) clearly dictate that an ascertainable standard will protect against general power of appointment treatment only if it relates to the health, education, maintenance, and support of the *powerholder*. Here it would relate to the needs of the powerholder's dependent beneficiary.

The solution is to prevent the theory from being applied. Rather than judicially challenging the discharge of obligation theory itself, the parent simply should be precluded from making any distribution that would have the effect under state law of discharging the parent's legal obligation to the beneficiary. This requires a so-called Upjohn clause. Such a provision is not too restrictive to be acceptable planning because the parent usually is current in satisfying the legal obligation. This means that there is no outstanding obligation to be discharged by any distribution the fiduciary chooses to make and the theory therefore falls flat.

More importantly, the parent's legal obligation cannot be discharged by distributions under the law of most states. This means that no distribution actually would be precluded by this provision (because no distribution would have the prohibited effect). Instead, all the provision does is place the burden of proof on the government. The provision requires the government to prove the impossible by showing that distributions could have been made that would discharge the parent's legal obligation. The government cannot establish this in most states in the first instance, and the clause precludes it in any event.

Oddly (and inappropriately) enough, if a client already is acting as trustee or custodian for the benefit of a minor child, existing authority suggests that the parent can merely resign to avoid unwanted tax exposure. See Rev. Rul. 59-357 (but consider the second clause of §2041(a)(2) in conjunction with Treas. Reg. §20.2036-1(b)(2)). This is a situation in which there hardly is anything to be lost for trying to avoid tax exposure by merely stepping out of harm's way. And for planning purposes the message usually is: find some other fiduciary and avoid these issues entirely.

Incidents of Ownership

Yet another source of potential unexpected tax exposure relates to incidents of ownership with respect to insurance held by an insured in a fiduciary capacity. For example, imagine X as the insured under a policy of insurance held in a trust created by S with X as trustee. The concern is that those fiduciary powers held by X over that insurance will cause taxation of the insurance proceeds to X's estate if X dies while acting as trustee. A similar concern could exist if X could control the policies of insurance through the exercise of a nongeneral power to appoint trust assets.

The issues have been partially solved by the promulgation of Rev. Rul. 84-179, as discussed in detail in Chapter 6 at pages 7-8 and Chapter 9 at pages 45-46. However, because that ruling has a number of significant caveats, prudent drafters also typically deny to the insured any control over insurance on the insured's life, either by excluding that insurance from the reach of a power of appointment or by appointing an "insurance advisor" or special trustee to exercise any incidents of ownership held in a fiduciary capacity. We will discuss this again when dealing with trustee selection in Chapter 6 as well.

Have you begun to notice how many different variables you need to consider in planning an estate? Fortunately most are tax generated and most estates will not be taxable. Still, we need to be careful, and many planning approaches developed in the tax conscious environment don't change in smaller situations.

Estate of Regester

Consider the following examples to illustrate the most important source of unexpected tax liability. These all involve a powerholder's exercise of a nongeneral power of appointment that causes gift tax liability:

D is the income beneficiary of a trust that will be held for D for life, remainder to D's descendants. D also possesses a nongeneral power to appoint trust principal among the remainder beneficiaries. When D is age 65 and doing well D exercises the power to appoint $100,000 to those descendants. To determine the government's view of the gift tax consequences of this exercise you would read Treas. Reg. §25.2514-1(b)(2), Rev. Rul. 79-327, and Estate of Regester v. Commissioner, 83 T.C. 1 (1984); to the contrary is Self v. United States, 142 F. Supp. 939 (Ct. Cl. 1956), and Commissioner v. Walston, 168 F.2d 211 (4th Cir. 1948). See Note, *Taxation: Special Powers of Appointment and Transfer Taxation — It Is the Courts' Move*, 34 OKLA. L. REV. 907 (1981). You have learned that nongeneral powers are not taxable. So, what could the gift be here? It is the value of D's income interest in the $100,000.

Assume that D also is trustee of the trust and has authority to make distributions of principal to D's descendants. As trustee D distributes an additional $50,000 to the same descendants (in a transfer that does not violate an Upjohn clause precluding distributions that would have the effect of discharging any obligation D may have to support any of those descendants). To evaluate the government's view of the gift tax consequences of this distribution you would read Treas. Reg. §25.2511-1(g)(2).

It would make a difference in either of these situations if D's descendants were entitled to receive only so much of the income as an independent trustee distributes in its unfettered discretion. See Private Letter Ruling 8535020. So would insertion of a HEMS ascertainable standard. Reread Treas. Reg. §25.2511-1(g)(2). Does that make any sense to you? The most important lesson of this learning is that ascertainable standards provide protection in a wide variety of unexpected situations, so wise drafters use them unless special circumstances clearly dictate otherwise.

Drafting Powers of Appointment

As a means of addressing additional issues that should be reflected in drafting an effective power of appointment, consider the following sample powers of appointment, taken for illustration purposes from an old-style general power of appointment marital deduction trust:

My [spouse] may at any time or times[uu] during [his/her] life by instrument in writing delivered to the trustee appoint any part or all[vv] of the principal of the trust estate to or in trust[ww] for any one or more[xx] of my descendants and their respective spouses and charitable, scientific or educational purposes, with such powers and in such manner and proportions as (s)he may appoint, and the trustee shall reimburse [him/her] from the remaining principal for the amount of any gift tax incurred thereby.

In addition, my [spouse] may withdraw at any time or times from the principal of the trust estate not to exceed in the aggregate during any calendar year the greater of $5,000 or 5% of the value of the trust estate at the time of exercise.[yy] The trustee shall make payment without

---

[uu]/ Meaning that the power is not a one-time-only opportunity.

[vv]/ Meaning that the spouse may exercise the power in one lump sum or in portions, including appointment of the entire fund.

[ww]/ The authority to appoint "to or in trust" and "with such powers and in such manner and proportions" as the powerholder appoints are designed to clarify the state law ability to appoint in further trust, with interests that are less than a fee simple absolute, and otherwise to assure the fullest flexibility in designing any alternative to the plan originally drafted by the settlor. This is critical for flexibility.

[xx]/ The permission to appoint to "any one or more" of the permissible appointees establishes that this power is an exclusive entitlement. A nonexclusive power of appointment is nearly an oxymoron. If the donor truly wants every permissible appointee to get something (nonexclusive means no one may be excluded) it would be far better to give each permissible appointee that minimum portion and then allow the powerholder to appoint any excess to whomever the powerholder selects from within the class.

[yy]/ This power of appointment allows the powerholder to obtain a modest amount of corpus in any year. This is a marital deduction trust that will be fully includible in the powerholder's estate at death. As such this power need not be limited to such a small amount. In a family trust, the five or five power might be the maximum entitlement the settlor is willing to bestow, consistent with preventing inclusion of the trust in the powerholder's estate and preservation of the trust for the benefit of the permissible appointees or the default takers.

Notice the careful definition of the amount subject to withdrawal. It is the aggregate amount defined by §2514(e) in any calendar year, with the value of the trust being determined at the time of any exercise for purposes of measuring the 5% withdrawal right. Omitted is a provision limiting exercise of the power to a given day or other abbreviated period during the year. In a family trust the drafter might attempt in this manner to avoid §2041(a)(2) inclusion of any amount available for withdrawal but not withdrawn at the time of death. There is no authority establishing whether such a power of appointment will avoid tax if death occurs on any other date, and that limitation is not needed in this marital deduction trust because the trust will be includible in all events.

question upon [his/her] written request.[zz/] This right of withdrawal is a privilege that may be exercised only voluntarily and shall not include an involuntary exercise.[aaa/]

Upon the death of my [spouse] the principal and any accrued and undistributed income of the trust estate shall be held in trust hereunder or distributed to or in trust for such appointee or appointees (including the estate of my [spouse]),[bbb/] with such powers and in such manner and proportions as [he/she] may appoint by a valid will making specific reference to this power of appointment.[ccc/]

Upon the death of my [spouse] any part of the principal and accrued and undistributed income of the trust estate not effectively appointed shall be added to or used to fund the Family Trust, except that, unless my [spouse] directs otherwise by [his/her] will, the trustee shall first pay from the principal of the trust estate, directly or to my

---

[zz/] Some drafters require trustee consent as a tool to protect the powerholder from a forced withdrawal, such as by creditors or other predators. This withdrawal privilege is meant to be free from outside interference, being exercisable solely in the discretion of the powerholder. Not even the trustee may question its exercise.

[aaa/] The last sentence seems a bit schizophrenic, given the intent of the immediately preceding sentence. It is consistent with protection of the powerholder's free exercise, however, because it seeks only to preclude an involuntary exercise (such as in response to a demand by a creditor or other predator). The trustee presumably will have sufficient information upon which to ascertain whether any exercise of the power is voluntary, and it is expected that any involuntary exercise would be difficult to disguise. Although these assumptions may not be realistic, the only objective here is to give the powerholder a provision to hide behind if exercise is coerced and not what the powerholder wants.

[bbb/] This a general testamentary power of appointment, granted in this old-style all income, general power of appointment trust to qualify for the marital deduction under §2056(b)(5). In addition to those aspects about this power noted in the presently exercisable nongeneral power, several added provisions are worthy of note. The first is the specification that the power extends to not just principal but also any accrued but undistributed income on hand at the death of the surviving spouse. This is required for §2056(b)(5) marital deduction purposes and probably is desirable because the powerholder wants to distribute the entire trust, not just part of it. Also necessary for marital deduction purposes is the parenthetical, specifying that the power is a general power for marital deduction purposes by including the estate of the spouse in the class of permissible appointees. You know from the discussion at page 22 that without the tax benefit in trade for the general power of appointment it likely would not be desirable to give a general power otherwise.

[ccc/] The important aspect is the requirement that exercise be by a will "making specific reference to this power of appointment." The rationale for this provision is to preclude an inadvertent or "blanket" exercise of the power, which is the topic discussed next below.

[spouse]'s personal representative as the trustee deems advisable, the amount by which the estate and inheritance taxes assessed by reason of the death of my [spouse] shall be increased as a result of the inclusion of the trust estate in [his/her] estate for such tax purposes. The trustee's selection of assets to be sold to pay that amount, and the tax effects thereof, shall not be subject to question by any beneficiary.[ddd/]

Inadvertent Exercise

Inadvertent exercise of a power of appointment may occur in either of two ways. In some states a "silent" residuary provision in the powerholder's will (for example, "all the residue of my estate shall be distributed . . . ") is deemed to exercise all testamentary powers available to the powerholder unless it can be proven that the powerholder specifically intended *not* to exercise the power. It would be next to impossible to prove that a powerholder formulated a positive intent not to exercise a power of appointment if the powerholder had no knowledge of the power. Even with knowledge of the power it is an uphill battle to establish the intent not to exercise. In silent exercise states the ability to prove the absence of an intent to exercise would not suffice. See, e.g., Cal. Prob. Code §641, N.Y. Est., Powers & Trusts Law §10-6.1(a)(4); 60 Okla. Stat. §299.10.

Unwitting exercise also may occur by virtue of a "blanket" exercise provision in a will (for example, "all the residue of my estate, *including any property over which I may have power of appointment*, shall be distributed . . .") that seeks to exercise all available powers, whether the powerholder knows of the power or is just shooting in the dark.

Exercise of all available powers of appointment is consistent with the intent of most powerholders and, if the power is unknown, the thought often is expressed that the powerholder's disposition through exercise is bound to be better than the default disposition. In many cases nothing could be

---

ddd/ The final provisions of this paragraph all relate to payment of taxes in the estate of the powerholder, recognizing that this general power of appointment will cause inclusion of the value of the trust corpus in the powerholder's estate. A waiver of this tax payment directive is permitted if the powerholder would prefer to use other assets for payment of the tax. Otherwise, this provision is more generous than the reimbursement entitlement created by §2207, which is a pro rata allocation of taxes caused by inclusion. This provision directs payment of the incremental taxes caused by inclusion. Any other property also subject to an incremental apportionment provision (such as a QTIP marital trust subject to the §2207A right of reimbursement) should be considered and the two provisions must be coordinated. Finally, the trustee is protected from challenge by any beneficiary who objects to the selection of assets for payment of this liability. Usually the trustee will consult with the beneficiaries to determine whether any particular assets should be preserved but, lacking unanimity, the trustee ought to be protected from a disgruntled beneficiary's challenge. All of these tax payment concerns are addressed in Chapter 11.

further from the truth, especially because the default disposition often is the same as the powerholder's appointment. That being the case, there are a number of excellent reasons not to exercise unknown powers.

For example, creditors of the holder of a general testamentary power of appointment usually may reach appointive assets only to the extent the power is exercised and the powerholder is insolvent. See RESTATEMENT (Second), DONATIVE TRANSFERS §13.4 (1982); RESTATEMENT, PROPERTY §§327, 329-331. If the powerholder is insolvent, the appointive assets (often passing by default to the powerholder's descendants) may be the only property those descendants will receive when the powerholder dies. These assets ought to be protected from creditor claims. By inadvertent exercise under state law or a blanket exercise provision the powerholder instead inappropriately opens the door to creditors.

In addition, exercise without knowing the specific terms of the power runs a good chance of invalidity due to a designation of impermissible appointees (this is less likely if the power is a general power, as in this case, but might arise even with a general power that is narrowly drafted) or because of a violation of the Rule Against Perpetuities. This is extremely likely because the period of the Rule that applies to appointive assets usually runs from creation of the power (when the instrument creating the power became irrevocable). Most planners think to measure any interest that might run afoul of the Rule under the powerholder's estate plan from the powerholder's death. Were this a presently exercisable general power the rule would be otherwise but, because it *is* a testamentary power, the likelihood of invalid appointment is significant if the powerholder's estate planner did not inspect the trust granting the power.

Fiduciary liability also may arise due to an inadvertent exercise. For example, payments might be made unintentionally in violation of the appointment if the power was exercised but the trustee of the trust granting the power did not know it (because the powerholder's will did not refer to the power and no one knew to inform the trustee). That is not likely in this case but, if the power was exercised invalidly, the powerholder's estate might have a claim to the appointive assets under the doctrine of capture, and could be obliged to act under the doctrine of marshaling, both imposing an obligation on the powerholder's personal representative. Who needs that?

Given these factors it seems reasonable for the donor to protect against unwitting exercises by requiring the powerholder to be knowledgeable about the power to effect an exercise. Presumably this will be accomplished if the powerholder must make specific reference to the power to exercise it, on the theory that the power will be inspected at the time the specific reference is crafted.

In addition, wise estate planners usually protect against inadvertent exercise by their clients who may be powerholders: they simply insert a nonexercise provision in the client's will. For example, "all the residue of my estate, *but expressly excluding any property over which I may have power of appointment.*" This express nonexercise provision recognizes the general conflict of laws rule that the law of the donor's domicile, not that of the powerholder's domicile, governs issues such as validity of an exercise of powers of appointment. This, however, is subject to a modern trend to apply the law of the powerholder's domicile. See 5A Scott & Fratcher, THE LAW OF TRUSTS §642 (4th ed. 1989). Drafting to avoid the question always is wise if it is not clear which rule may apply.

Chapter 6

TRUSTEE SELECTION AND SUCCESSION

Fiduciary selection is an ebb and flow phenomenon, particularly with respect to long term trustee relationships. Relatively short term personal representatives for estate administration or for an incapacitated person during life (either as a durable power holder or a court appointed guardian, conservator, or custodian) tend to differ and are not our focus.

For years there was a definite trend away from selection of entities (such as banks) as trustees. That was followed by a resurgence of professional (both individual and entity) fiduciaries when the economy proved that being a successful investor requires more acumen than just buying and holding technology stock. As the fiduciary winds blow, good estate planners cling to the notion that flexibility is important because change is inevitable.

Selection of the "right" trustee requires debunking the myth that individuals cannot (or should not) be selected as trustee because their use is dangerous from a tax perspective. This simply is not true, *if* the planner is a careful technician. It is safe to select an individual (including the settlor or a beneficiary) as trustee, but doing so may require certain restrictions and proper planning and drafting (the most effective illustration of which being effective use of standards to collar the trustee's discretion). This Chapter is designed to assist you in selecting and drafting for employment of whomever is most appropriate for the fiduciary role in a given trust, whether corporate or individual, professional or amateur.

Please note throughout: this discussion is not meant to advocate or denigrate the use of any particular class of fiduciary, nor to opine about the quality or capability of any potential choice. That is a supremely personal topic on which opinions rightly differ, and every situation has unique elements that impact the fiduciary selection process. Were it not for tax considerations, the trustee selection and succession decision could turn solely on factors such as the following:

- What special skills does the fiduciary possess (or lack) and which skills are necessary or desirable to administer the particular trust? For example, basic traits such as reliability, integrity, and fiscal responsibility should be a given. Fiduciary accounting, tax compliance, and investment capability, prudence, and acumen usually can be purchased. Gut level managerial and "people" skills, the ability to operate a particular business, and the sensitivity to apply family-appropriate distribution discretion usually cannot.

- What are the attitudes or philosophies and the track record of the trustee and do they portend difficulties or unsatisfactory treatment of the trust and its beneficiaries? For example, is the trustee loathe to retain the family farm or closely held business stock, is it reputed to be too conservative in investing, does it tend to go overboard in restricting expenditures by or for the benefit of beneficiaries or, alternatively, would it have trouble denying inappropriate requests by profligates?

- What unique problems or exposures does the trustee present? For example, conflicts of interest due to other activities or relationships, the special nature of the trust or its beneficiaries? Particular demands on the trustee's time may make it difficult to prioritize the difficult and demanding chore of acting as a prudent fiduciary. Some trustees create special exposure to regulations generated by the type of assets held by that trust and by the trustee personally.

- What special problems does the trust present? For example, are assets located in several jurisdictions, some restricting or prohibiting involvement of certain types of fiduciary? Is there a need for unique insight into the family to inform distributions to beneficiaries?

For a more detailed discussion of nontax aspects of trustee selection see Bromberg & Fortson, *Selection of a Trustee: Tax and Other Considerations*, 19 SW. L.J. 523 (1965). These are not new or very difficult equations.

Selection of an individual trustee often is the result of a process of elimination or of designation by default, with many potentially suitable entity fiduciaries being rejected or unwilling to serve.[1] Unfortunately, experience shows that often little thought is devoted to objective criteria that appropriately might be weighed in making the trustee designation.[2]

---

1. Among commonly expressed reasons for rejecting an entity or other professional fiduciary are: cost; a perception that corporate fiduciaries are too conservative, cautious, and parsimonious (an especially serious concern to adult beneficiaries, such as a surviving spouse, who fear becoming supplicants); a strong criticism of investment performance, including both comparative returns and an almost universal reluctance to experiment with nontraditional investments such as precious metals, gems, or collectibles (although professional fiduciaries probably are *more* likely to invest in sophisticated financial products, such as derivatives); restrictions such as alien land laws that corporate fiduciaries are more likely to honor; and a more general sense that professional fiduciaries know or understand various laws better than others and often comply (to the trust's disadvantage) when another less knowledgeable trustee would not. Obviously some (and perhaps all) of these objections are ill advised!

2. It has been suggested that many people select a fiduciary with less sophistication than they use in buying a new car. See Weiss, *The Fiduciary: Guidelines for Selection, Powers and Succession*, 33 N.Y.U. INST. FED. TAX'N 273, 274 (1975).

In most respects selection of an entity (such as a bank or other institutional trustee) is safe for tax planning purposes, but it may not be appropriate for a particular case. This Chapter focuses particularly upon tax consequences and exposure flowing from selection of beneficially interested individual trustees. Typically corporate fiduciaries have no special concerns in that regard. And tax consequences to the settlor seldom are a concern, even in an inter vivos trust. Nevertheless, on occasion the tax consequences to a settlor (or a related or subordinate party) acting as trustee can be important, and they are noted after we deal with easier and more common situations.

We will learn that naming most individuals as trustee (even those with a beneficial interest) is not difficult or dangerous. But naming the trust settlor as trustee in a tax sensitive situation is not particularly desirable. It can be done, but it tends to invite close scrutiny by the government and ultimately may result in litigation.

This Chapter also discusses a number of unexpected sources of inadvertent tax liability flowing from the selection of trustees. But most of what commands our attention in this arena is obvious, pervasive, and easy to address.

Assume A Testamentary Trust

Let's begin with an assumption that the settlor no longer is in the picture. That is both the more common case and a much easier context in which to address planning and drafting regarding trustee selection. Let's also assume that the trustee is beneficially interested (or is related to a beneficiary of the trust), such that exposure may flow from the individual trustee's powers to distribute corpus or income, or otherwise to administer the trust.

Powers Over Corpus

Potential wealth transfer tax liability may flow from any power to make distributions of corpus to (or for the benefit of) the trustee individually, to his or her estate, or to the creditors of either. The lapse or termination (due to death or resignation) of a power to make distributions to the trustee personally, as beneficiary, or to someone the trustee is obligated to support may trigger either §2041 or §2514 general (taxable) power of appointment estate or gift tax liability.[3]

A significant issue lurks if the trustee has discretion to make distributions of corpus to the trustee personally *and* to other beneficiaries.

---

3. An exception applies to this general rule for gift tax purposes only. Under the five or five limitation of §2514(e) the lapse of a power in any year is not a taxable gift to the extent the trustee's power to make withdrawals of corpus is limited to an annual maximum of $5,000 or 5% of the value of the trust. But note carefully that the termination of a five or five power at the death of an individual *is* a §2041(a)(2) estate taxable event, causing estate tax inclusion of the amount subject to the power as of the date of death. And there are §678 income tax consequences of a five or five power. This means that the five or five restriction is a solution only to gift tax exposure.

Exercise of that authority to benefit others may constitute a taxable termination of the trustee's power to make distributions to the trustee individually. In addition, distributions may be treated as made to the trustee directly if those other beneficiaries are individuals to whom the trustee owes a legal obligation of support. These also would attract gift taxation to the powerholder trustee.

Finally, the right to distribute trust corpus to a trustee individually may cause trust income to be taxed to the trustee under §678, even if no income or corpus actually is distributed (to the trustee or to anyone else). This is "pseudo grantor trust" exposure and in some cases it is regarded as *favorable*. We explore these consequences beginning at page 6.

One effective drafting mechanism for avoiding all this wealth transfer and income tax exposure is to limit the trustee's powers over corpus. This limit can be effected in either of two ways.

One is by making the trustee's powers subject to an adverse party's consent. This need not be a cofiduciary: consent will suffice regardless of the capacity in which the adverse party is acting. The difficult aspect of this alternative is finding a sufficiently adverse party who nevertheless will give consent in appropriate circumstances, permitting adequate flexibility as intended by granting the trustee discretion to make distributions in the first instance.

Treas. Reg. §20.2041-3(c)(2) Example (1) contains an illustration of a sufficiently adverse party, in that case involving the taxpayer and a remainder beneficiary as trustees, with the remainder beneficiary being adverse to exercise of the taxpayer's power to distribute corpus currently. The problem is that this remainder beneficiary would not be adverse with respect to powers over current income, which illustrates a major limitation on the use of adverse parties. Often they are not adverse with respect to enough of the trust to serve as an adequate protection. Use of the adverse party consent alternative is not common for this and a number of less obvious reasons.

The second alternatively is to use an "ascertainable standard" as defined for §§2041 and 2514 purposes is effective to avoid wealth transfer tax liability. Under a different name the use of similar standards can protect against unwanted income tax exposure too. Use of such standards is so important and common that it is discussed in more detail separately, beginning at page 10.

A third alternative is to deny the tax sensitive power altogether, lodging the desired discretion instead in another individual who has no similar exposure. Worthy of consideration is the use of a "special" trustee (in this case, a "distribution director") whose sole function is to exercise discretion otherwise denied to the individual trustee. For example, if two children were to be made trustees of their own separate trusts, child A might be named as distribution director with respect to distributions to child B, and vice versa. This approach entails less restriction than naming a full-fledged cofiduciary for all purposes (including some for which that individual is unnecessary and maybe even undesirable) while denying inappropriate distribution authority to the beneficially interested trustee.

Beware, however, several issues that might apply. One concern is the "reciprocal trust doctrine" explored at page 14. Even though there is no direct authority for this proposition in this particular context, it might apply in the example given of child A directing distributions to child B and vice versa. The doctrine basically would "uncross" the reciprocal provisions to treat child A as distribution director for child A and child B as distribution director for child B. If applicable the doctrine would defeat this form of protective planning. Another caution is that any power of a trustee to control a special trustee (such as a distribution director) may generate exposure under the "revolving door" theory elaborated upon beginning at page 12. Finally, any finding of a prearrangement or an agreement-to-agree between the trustee and the special trustee also could result in the mechanism being regarded as a sham. Appearances, bona fide planning, separation, and independence are important in this (as in all things).

In addition to the foregoing rules that relate to the individual trustee's power to enjoy distributions, a power to make distributions to a dependent of the individual trustee also could generate estate or gift tax liability. The theory, discussed in Chapter 5 at page 26, easily is avoided by using the "Upjohn" limitation that prohibits the trustee from making any distributions that would have the *effect* of discharging any person's legal obligation to support the beneficiary.

A final source of exposure to an individual trustee flowing from a power to make distributions of corpus is illustrated by Treas. Reg. §25.2514-1(b)(2), Estate of Regester v. Commissioner, 83 T.C. 1 (1984), and Rev. Rul. 79-327, all as discussed in Chapter 5 at page 29. These authorities apply if the trustee also is an income beneficiary of the trust and, as trustee, distributes corpus to a third party. These corpus distributions constitute gifts of the trustee's income interest in that corpus. The best avoidance of this exposure is under Treas. Reg. §25.2511-1(b)(2), providing that an ascertainable standard limiting the trustee's distributions of corpus prevents the distribution from constituting a gift. An alternative noted earlier also would work here: repose the power to distribute corpus in a special trustee.

Powers Over Income

The foregoing discussion addresses powers to distribute corpus. The following deals with powers to distribute income and our concerns are fewer. For example, it is not entirely free from doubt but it appears that §2041 does not apply to powers over income only. This is made somewhat questionable by loose language in Treas. Reg. §§20.2041-1(b)(1) and 20.2041-1(c)(2), in each case referring to powers to affect trust property *or its income*, notwithstanding the clear reference in §2041 itself to powers over "property" with no mention of the income from it. Maybe the foregoing discussion regarding powers over corpus should be considered in relation to income also, in which case the same forms of protection ought to suffice.

Otherwise, our focus with respect to income distributions is §678. This "pseudo grantor trust" income tax provision causes taxation of all trust income to the trustee to the extent the trustee's powers permit distributions of income to the trustee as beneficiary. Distributions of corpus to the trustee as beneficiary trigger application of §678 because the corpus carries the right to all future income from the distributed corpus. But typically §678 is a concern with respect to a naked income interest. In addition, §678(c) attributes income to a trustee to the extent that income actually is distributed for the support or maintenance of someone the trustee is obliged to support or maintain.

Four exceptions to §678 exist, but only two provide reasonably useful planning or drafting opportunities. For example, §678(b) entirely eliminates exposure to the extent income is taxable to the trust's settlor under §§671-677. This is helpful in some inter vivos trust cases but is not useful here because we assumed for this discussion that the settlor is deceased. In addition, §678 applies only to the extent the trustee's powers are exercisable alone, so joint powers protect against undesirable income tax exposure to the trustee. Better than under §2041, this exception is available even if the joint holder of the power is not an adverse party. Thus, a distribution director would work quite well here. Nevertheless, because adverse party consent is required under §2041, and because it is likely that avoidance of both sections will be desired in a given situation, this joint power exception is of limited utility if not drafted to operate under §2041 too. Thus, an adverse party likely will be necessary and, as discussed above, this restricts the utility of this exception.

More importantly, the trustee's powers will be disregarded for §678 purposes under limited but consistent authority[4] if the trustee's powers are constrained by a reasonably definite standard (of the same type that would apply for §674(b)(5)(A) and 674(d) purposes). The standards that qualify are at least as broad as the ascertainable standard that will protect against §2041, so this protection *is* useful. We will discuss it more in detail at page 10.

Finally, §678(c) provides its own limitation that applies to the extent exposure exists in the first instance because of the trustee's power to distribute income for the support or maintenance of someone the trustee is obliged to support or maintain. This limitation simply restricts the amount of income taxable to the trustee to that amount actually distributed for such support or maintenance (rather than the full amount that *could* have been distributed for those purposes). Caution is required in drafting for the

---

4. The authority is old and scant. See United States v. De Bonchamps, 278 F.2d 127 (9th Cir. 1960); Funk v. Commissioner, 185 F.2d 127 (3d Cir. 1950); Smither v. United States, 108 F. Supp. 772 (S.D. Tex. 1952).

protection of this limitation, however, because it is unlike the discharge theory under §2041. Indeed, the Upjohn clause protection recommended under §2041 will not work under §678. This is because a careful reading of §678(c) and Treas. Reg. §1.662(a)-4 reveals that *discharge* of the obligation of support or maintenance is not required. Thus, a simple prohibition against distributions that discharge those obligations is not effective. Instead of including an Upjohn clause, the document must prohibit distributions for the support or maintenance of anyone the trustee is obliged to support or maintain, and this may be an unacceptably severe restriction of the trustee's discretion. That would depend on the purposes of the trust and the intended scope of trust income distributions.

Note, however, that §678 taxation of trust income to the powerholder may be desirable, for several reasons. One is that the rate of tax in trusts or estates is the highest under the Internal Revenue Code, so taxation to *any* individual could produce a smaller income tax liability than if the income were taxed to the entity. Furthermore, some planners appreciate the notion that a beneficiary can receive income that is taxed to the trustee individually. This is the functional equivalent of the trustee making a tax free gift to the beneficiary in the amount of the income tax the beneficiary need not pay. The parties are better off because *someone* is going to pay the income tax and a savings exists if the difference in the income tax rate of the trustee and the beneficiary is not greater than the gift tax avoided on this implied transfer. It pays to consider whether §678 income tax liability is favorable if the trustee is willing to make this tax free transfer to the beneficiary. Because the income will be taxed to someone (or to the trust itself), in this corner of planning and drafting the appropriate question is to whom that income would *best* be taxed. *Avoiding* income taxation to the trustee may *not* be the intuitive choice.

Administrative Powers

In addition to issues caused by trustee powers over corpus or income, other issues may arise from control over trust administration. These tend to be more specific and less extensive concerns. For example, exposure to §2042 estate tax inclusion of life insurance proceeds may arise if the trust holds insurance on the life of the trustee and the trustee holds "incidents of ownership" over that insurance (such as the power to change beneficiaries, or to borrow against a policy). This is most likely to occur with a spouse acting as trustee of a "spouse owned insurance trust" and, fortunately, this is not very common (because the unlimited marital deduction makes spouse owned insurance a thing of the past. See Chapter 9 at pages 27-28).

Further, the law is not uniform in deciding whether possession of incidents of ownership in a fiduciary capacity will cause insurance to be includible in the estate of the trustee pursuant to §2042. Indeed, Rev. Rul. 84-179 indicates that the government no longer intends to pursue this "incidents as fiduciary" theory in the main. As illustrated in Chapter 9 at pages 45-46, however, caution is required because the protection of the

Ruling is not available in three circumstances that may swallow the rule:
- If the incidents are exercisable for the trustee's personal benefit.
- If the policy originally was owned by the trustee, who became fiduciary with respect to it as part of a prearranged, integrated transaction.
- If the trustee individually transferred any of the consideration for purchasing or maintaining the policy.

In the most common case, a trustee is the insured and is paying premiums on the policy while acting as trustee. This is not protected by Rev. Rul. 84-179. The easy solution is to deny the insured-trustee any incidents of ownership over the insurance. If it is important that someone be able to exercise those incidents, then the answer is to name a special trustee as "insurance advisor" to act with respect to the insurance.

The other common administrative power that might prove disadvantageous is a form of "small trust termination" provision that may create §2041 taxable power of appointment exposure to the trustee. Typically these provisions permit termination of a trust and distribution to the current income beneficiaries if the trust corpus drops below a specified dollar amount. Some drafters grant termination powers using trigger thresholds that give the trustee discretion, exercisable for example whenever the trustee determines that continued administration of the trust no longer is "economical." Arguably this discretion is a taxable power to appoint any portion of the trust that the trustee would receive as a corpus distributee on termination. Easy solutions to this exposure include using only a specified termination figure in trusts in which the trustee also is a beneficiary who could receive a terminating distribution, precluding the trustee from sharing in the terminating distribution under a discretionary termination provision, or placing the power to determine when termination should occur in a special trustee.

These forms of exposure to a beneficiary-trustee are not very extensive, and the planning limitations to minimize or avoid problems are reasonable and easy to implement. Which leads to the simple conclusion that anyone can be trustee if a little thought and care is put into the planning and drafting. Anyone, that is, *except* the settlor, and then only if avoiding tax treatment as if the settlor still owned the trust property is to be avoided. We now turn our attention to that more difficult chore.

While The Settlor Is Alive

A trust settlor who wishes to be trustee of a trust created inter vivos faces gift, estate, and income tax exposure as if the property still was held by the settlor individually. If the intent is to avoid these results, then a wise planner simply will not recommend that the settlor act as trustee. Thus, as a practical matter, self-trusteed trusts usually are found only when gift tax is not applicable, estate tax inclusion is expected, and income shifting is not desired.

Consider the gift tax issue first. The concern is whether transfers made to the trust will be regarded as completed (and therefore immediately taxable) gifts. The presumption is that the settlor cannot make a completed gift for gift tax purposes if the settlor retains control over the property in the capacity as trustee. The settlor probably should not act as trustee if a completed gift is intended, unless the most carefully crafted trust is involved. Only very brave planners would do this, it is not commonplace, and the need for settlor involvement as trustee should be very high before undertaking this kind of endeavor.

On the estate tax side of this equation, the settlor usually wishes to avoid subsequent estate tax inclusion if a completed inter vivos gift is intended. Although very careful drafting could permit a settlor to continue to act as trustee, as a practical matter this also very rarely would be attempted. To be successful requires that the trust not own insurance on the life of the settlor (or that any incidents of ownership over policies on the settlor's life be granted to an insurance advisor or another special trustee). In addition, the settlor as trustee must be denied any power, even in a fiduciary capacity, to vote controlled corporation stock transferred to the trust. This should avoid §2036(b) inclusion of the full value of the stock in the settlor's gross estate at death. And then, while fiduciary powers of an administrative, managerial, or ministerial nature could be retained (such as to allocate receipts between income and principal and powers to direct or veto trust investments),[5] trustee powers of a nature that affect beneficial enjoyment of trust income or corpus would need to be limited by a "definite external standard"[6] of the type discussed at page 10. Finally, although not limited to situations in which the settlor is acting as trustee, application of the discharge of obligation theory under §2036(a)(1) and Treas. Reg. §20.2036-1(b)(2) should be precluded by use of an Upjohn clause (in the same manner discussed at page 5 and in Chapter 5 at page 26 for eliminating §2041 exposure to any other trustee under the same flawed governmental theory).

Avoidance of income tax liability is a far different story. The unexpected reality is that a sizeable amount of planning seeks to cause income tax "grantor trust" exposure to the settlor, causing the trust to be disregarded for income tax purposes and all income tax consequences being applied as if the settlor never made a transfer into the trust but,

---

5. See United States v. Byrum, 408 U.S. 125 (1972); Old Colony Trust v. United States, 423 F.2d 601 (1st Cir. 1970); and Lowndes, Kramer, & McCord, FEDERAL ESTATE AND GIFT TAXES §8.9 at 158 and §9.20 at 226 (3d ed. 1974).

6. Also established only by old and sparse caselaw and not defined in any manner by the Code or Treasury Regulations. See United States v. Powell, 307 F.2d 821 (10th Cir. 1962); Estate of Ford v. Commissioner, 53 T.C. 114 (1969); Estate of Budd v. Commission, 49 T.C. 468 (1968); Estate of Pardee v. Commissioner, 49 T.C. 140 (1967), acq., 1973-2 C.B. 3; Estate of Kasch v. Commissioner, 30 T.C. 102 (1958); Estate of Weir v. Commissioner, 17 T.C. 409 (1951).

instead, still was owner of the trust assets. Known as "intentionally defective grantor trusts," this planning is done for numerous reasons (such as to avoid capital gain if the settlor engages in otherwise realization transactions with the trust) but we need not explore those here. See instead Chapter 17 at pages 14-15. Suffice it to say only that acting as trustee is not a requisite to intentionally defective grantor trust liability. It usually is generated in other ways. And the income tax grantor trust rules operate independently of the gift and estate taxes. Thus, skilled planners can create defective trusts for income tax purposes while accomplishing a completed gift with no estate tax inclusion, all dehors the trustee situation.

The topic of income tax grantor trust planning is a separate endeavor; it should be carefully considered, but it really exists quite independently of the trustee selection and succession issue. Sometimes it is encountered in the form of prohibitions on distributions for the support or maintenance of anyone the grantor is obliged to support or maintain. Similarly for anyone the grantor's spouse, if any, is obliged to support or maintain — there being an income tax "spousal unity" rule. Sometimes it is encountered in the form of denying any power (to the grantor or the grantor's spouse) to deal with or to borrow trust assets for less than adequate interest or security. Sometimes it is encountered in provisions ensuring that all administrative powers are exercisable only in a fiduciary capacity by the trustee, whomever that is. And sometimes limitations are imposed on the flexibility of the trustee, known as "reasonably definite (external) standards" (as discussed next below).

Use and Definition of Standards

Several different standards were mentioned in the foregoing discussions, including the ascertainable standard of §§2041 and 2514, the reasonably definite (external) standard for grantor trust purposes, and the definite external standard of §2036. As explored (in gagging detail) in Pennell, *Estate Planning: Drafting and Tax Considerations in Employing Individual Trustees*, 60 U. N.C. L. REV. 799, 803 et seq. (1982), these are not the same standard even though several of them are worded in almost exactly the same manner. Of them, the ascertainable standard of §§2041 and 2514 is the most commonly utilized, the most frequently litigated, and the most difficult to satisfy. This means that a standard meeting the definition of an ascertainable standard will meet all the other definitions as well.

Although the ascertainable standard definition is the most difficult to meet, in terms of precision of wording, and is the least flexible of the different standards available, it is recommended that drafters use ascertainable standards for *all* purposes in which a standard is the device used for protection. This recommendation reflects several practical realities. First, because it is the best known and most commonly used, and because it is the most extensively litigated, the ascertainable standard is the best understood standard in terms of what is known to qualify. Second, simplicity and consistency are served by using the same standard for all purposes and this requires that the most restrictive standard be used throughout. In addition, litigation involving terms that may qualify as ascertainable can be unpredictable, making it desirable to use an ascertainable standard because this alone is the standard articulated or defined in "safe harbor" terms by Treas. Reg. §20.2041-1(c)(2).

By way of example, litigation involving the term "emergency" has gone both ways on the question whether it is an ascertainable standard. Treas. Reg. §25.2511-1(g)(2) (a gift tax rule) refers to "a reasonably fixed or ascertainable standard which is set forth in the trust instrument" and gives as an example "a power to distribute corpus for the education, support, maintenance, or health of the beneficiary; for his reasonable support and comfort; to enable him to maintain his accustomed standard of living; or to meet an emergency." This language virtually parrots similar regulations under §§2041 and 2514, with the exception of the reference to "emergency," as to which the government's position elsewhere is that the term relates to the "timeliness" of a distribution rather than the need for it in terms of health, maintenance, support, or other ascertainable standards. Therefore, the government believes that "emergency" does not qualify.[7] Similar uncertainty surrounds terms like "care," "comfort" (standing alone rather than as part of the phrase "in reasonable comfort"), and even "happiness." See 3 Casner & Pennell, ESTATE PLANNING §12.3.2.4.

Although some planners worry that an ascertainable standard is not as flexible as the law might permit under one of the more liberal standards, the loss of flexibility is so slight (and the need for the difference in flexibility even smaller) that this should not concern you. For example, does anyone really know the difference between alternative terms that might be utilized such as "welfare" (not ascertainable) and "support or maintenance" (ascertainable)? Perhaps more importantly, in a friendly family situation, who would challenge the exercise of discretion under any standard used, and how common is litigation whether a certain payment was proper?

If a family situation is not friendly, however, it may be appropriate to suggest that the trustee either should not be a beneficially interested individual or that all discretion ought to be limited in such a manner as to foster the greatest degree of equanimity possible. Certainly there are circumstances in which the foregoing logic is not correct, but the starting

---

7. See Estate of Sowell v. Commissioner, 708 F.2d 1564 (10th Cir. 1983), rev'g 74 T.C. 1001 (1980). Hunter v. United States, 597 F. Supp. 1293 (W.D. Pa. 1984), held "for the comfortable support and maintenance . . . or should any emergency arise" was ascertainable because it was less liberal than the clearly ascertainable term "support in an accustomed manner of living"; Wahlfeld v. United States, 47 A.F.T.R.2d 1565 (C.D. Ill. 1980), aff'd in an unpublished opinion (9th Cir. 1980), held that "financial emergency . . . as a result of accident, illness, or other unusual circumstances" was ascertainable because it was tied to health, education, support, or maintenance. Private Letter Ruling 9012053 held "to relieve emergencies" is ascertainable but only because the government felt compelled to follow the authority of Martin v. United States, 780 F.2d 1147 (4th Cir. 1986), and made it clear that in a different Circuit it would argue for a different result, as it did in Technical Advice Memoranda 9044081, 8346008, and 8339004.

point for prudent drafting is that each standard in every document be ascertainable, and then any liberalizing changes be made based on specially considered circumstances, identity of the trustee, and the needs of the beneficiaries.

Deemed Trustees

The following discussion of "deemed trustees" informs the perceived wisdom of a conservative approach to drafting standards. Simply put, drafters today never know what theory the government may propound in the future to allege that an individual should be deemed to possess all the powers of the trustee. In that regard, in a number of circumstances the government has consistently taken the position that someone other than the actual trustee should be treated as the trustee, or as possessing the powers of the trustee, with the result that tax consequences not anticipated by the drafter were imposed.

Probably the best known of these circumstances is based on the "revolving door" power involved in Rev. Rul. 79-353, in which the government held that a settlor possessed all the powers of a trustee because the settlor had the power to remove and replace the trustee at will. Even though the settlor could not be named as successor trustee (which the drafter knew would cause the result advocated by the government, under Treas. Reg. §§20.2036-1(b)(3), 20.2038-1(a)(3), and 20.2041-1(b)(1)), the government's theory was that the mere power to install trustees and remove them at will gave the holder of the revolving door power sufficient control over the trustee that the holder of the power should be deemed to possess the trustee's powers.

The revolving door power is a very important control over trustees whose track record is unknown or whose personal interest may make it more likely that impartial administration may yield to personal prejudice. Many drafters virtually always use such a revolving door power to permit the beneficiaries to maintain a degree of control over the trustee (often thought to be critical with entity fiduciaries, but reality shows it is even more important with individuals who had no track record to predict their actual performance). According to Rev. Rul. 95-58 (the government's current position on this issue), a revolving door power to replace trustees at will does not cause the powerholder to be treated as possessing the trustee's control over trust distributions, provided that any successor trustee is "not related or subordinate to the [powerholder] (within the meaning of §672(c))."

In addition, the government has approved a definition of removal for "cause" that also will avoid the revolving door issue. In Private Letter Rulings 9303018 and 9328015[8] the revolving door powers were held by

---

8. Both Rulings involved trusts with multiple trustees but, excepting the wording of the parenthetical in item 10, this did not appear to be an essential aspect of either Ruling. Given the lack of specificity in such standards as "mismanagement," "abuse," "inattention," or "unreasonable compensation" authorized by the government, this definition ought to be

trust beneficiaries who could remove and replace any disinterested trustee. Court orders were obtained to modify the revolving door provisions to clarify the settlor's intent that they be exercisable only for any of a list of 13 permissible items. The same attorneys obtained both Rulings on behalf of the same clients, involving different trusts, and the government blessed the same verbiage to incorporate in each court order. Thus, the approach approved seems likely to be a safe way to address this issue in modifying any existing trust. In addition, the definitions of cause provided in both Rulings appear to be an appropriate way to draft either a court ordered clarification of an existing trust or any new provision inserted into documents being drafted currently.

Because the ability to remove and replace trustees is so valuable and appropriate, especially when using an individual trustee who has no fiduciary track record or experience, the government's approved definition of cause is reproduced here in its entirety. You could use any or all of the listed items.

Removal of a trustee for "cause" shall mean any one of the following:

1. The legal incapacity of a trustee.
2. The willful or negligent mismanagement by the trustee of the trust's assets.
3. The abuse or abandonment of, or inattention to, the trust by the trustee.
4. A federal or state charge against the trustee involving the commission of a felony or serious misdemeanor.
5. An act of stealing, dishonesty, fraud, embezzlement, moral turpitude, or moral degeneration by the trustee.
6. The use of narcotics or excessive use of alcohol by the trustee.
7. The poor health of the trustee such that the trustee is physically, mentally, or emotionally unable to devote sufficient time to administer the trust.
8. The failure by the trustee to comply with a written fee agreement or other written agreement in the operation of the trust.
9. The failure of a corporate trustee to appoint a senior officer with at least five years of experience in the administration of trusts to handle the trust account.
10. Changes by a corporate trustee in the account officer responsible for handling the trust account more frequently than every five years (unless such change is made at the request of or with the acquiescence of the other trustee).
11. The relocation by a trustee away from the location where the trust operates so as to interfere with the administration of the trust.

---

adequate to provide sufficient latitude in most trusts to remove a trustee whose performance or personal prejudices make continued service undesirable.

12. A demand from the trustee for unreasonable compensation for such trustee's services.
13. Any other reason for which a [state] court of competent jurisdiction would remove a trustee.

This listing of items that constitute cause illustrates that the government is being flexible in terms of the types of concerns it has about the misuse of revolving door powers to gain effective control over the administration and distribution of a trust.

Another approach to the trustee removal and replacement issue without worrying about the §672(c) (not related or subordinate) safe harbor is to make the trustee's powers harmless even if imputed to the powerholder. Administrative and ministerial powers will not cause §2041 general power of appointment includibility if the trustee may not enlarge or shift beneficial interests. Treas. Reg. §20.2041-1(b)(1). And trustee powers over income or principal are harmless if limited by the simple use of ascertainable standards throughout the document and insertion of an Upjohn clause. If §678 exposure also is to be avoided, a provision denying the ability to make distributions for the support or maintenance of beneficiaries the trustee is obliged to support or maintain could be added (but that frequently is a greater degree of limitation than is thought to be acceptable).

It also may be adequate to "bifurcate" the revolving door power, giving the power to remove to one individual and the replacement power to another. If the two powerholders do not act in concert, the argument is that neither has the requisite degree of control to cause §2041 exposure. One concern with this alternative is that the power to remove alone might be deemed sufficient to trigger imputed-trustee status, on the theory that the holder of the removal power will continue to remove trustees until the holder of the replacement power appoints a suitable successor trustee. Similarly, suggested by the facts and holding in Private Letter Ruling 9043052 (but not the basis for the government's conclusion there), a requirement that a committee exercise the power and act only by majority vote may protect against exposure if no individual commands a majority of the votes.

A final common source of litigation and unexpected exposure from trustee appointment and succession provisions is application of the so-called reciprocal trust doctrine. As traditionally formulated in cases like United States v. Estate of Grace, 395 U.S. 316 (1969), the doctrine usually has been applied in situations in which two individuals, often spouses, create trusts with each other as trustee or as beneficiary. In Technical Advice Memorandum 8029001 the government was presented with an unusual fact situation that nevertheless raised the reciprocal trust doctrine. In that case F created two trusts, one with child A as trustee for child B and the other with B as trustee for A. As in most reciprocal trust cases, presumably this "crossing" was done by F because the trustee powers were not appropriate for A to hold as trustee for A and for B to hold as trustee for B.

Under a traditional reciprocal trust application, "uncrossing" occurs at the settlor level. Thus, assume that H created a trust for W with H as trustee and W created a trust for H with W as trustee. The doctrine would regard W as the settlor of the trust with H as trustee for W as beneficiary, and vice versa for the trust created by H. This would create tax consequences relating to trusts with retained enjoyment. In the Memorandum, with F as settlor of both trusts, that kind of uncrossing would work no change. So the Memorandum deemed the trusts uncrossed at the trustee level, causing B to be deemed the trustee of the trust for B and A to be deemed the trustee of the trust for A. Under such an application of the doctrine, imputed trustee powers to A and B might then cause §2041 inclusion of trust assets at each beneficiary's death.

Similarly, Private Letter Ruling 9235025 determined that a decedent, D, possessed a general power of appointment over a trust as to which D and D's sibling were cotrustees with discretion to distribute principal for D's "support, maintenance, comfort, emergencies, and serious illness." The government urged application of the reciprocal trust doctrine despite the application of New York Est. Powers & Trusts Law §10-10.1 (1992), which precluded D from participating as trustee in any decisions to make distributions to D personally. Because D and the sibling also were trustees over an identical trust for the sibling, the government relied upon Estate of Grace and *In re* Estate of Spear, 553 N.Y.S.2d 985 (Surr. Ct. 1990) (similar reciprocal trusts involving grandchildren), to conclude that this "reciprocal" trust and trustee arrangement meant that D effectively controlled distributions to the sibling and the sibling similarly controlled distributions to D. This is an "I'll scratch your back if you'll scratch mine" application of the doctrine.

Thus, the Ruling held that "it can be objectively inferred that [D] and [the sibling] would exercise their respective distributive powers on a reciprocal basis. That is, because of the reciprocal nature of the parties' distributive powers," D could ensure receipt of desired distributions from D's trust. The nature of this ruling was not that D held the powers of D's sibling directly, which would have been harmless because, as powerholder, D already was precluded by state law from making distributions for D's own benefit. Instead, the Ruling treated D as effectively controlling the sibling and, by virtue of that control, D was deemed to hold the sibling's unrestricted power to make distributions to D.

In contrast, Estate of Green v. United States, 68 F.3d 151 (6th Cir. 1995), *aff'g* an unpublished opinion (N.D. Ohio), rejected application of the reciprocal trust doctrine. This case involved grandparents who created separate identical trusts, one for each of their two grandchildren. He named her as trustee for the benefit of one grandchild and she made him trustee for the benefit of the other. The government asserted that the reciprocal trust doctrine would uncross the trusts to cause him to be regarded as trustee of the trust he created and her as trustee of the trust she created. This would then allow §§2036(a)(2) and 2038(a)(1) to apply by virtue of their retained powers over beneficial enjoyment of trust benefits by the respective grandchildren. Because neither settlor could benefit personally, the court rejected application of the reciprocal trust doctrine, stating that it requires that the settlor be in "the same economic position" as if no crossing occurred on creation of the trusts. According to the court there can be no economic position upon which the doctrine can apply if there is no economic benefit to the settlors.

Moreover, the court held that the government cannot "extend the reciprocal trust doctrine to include retained non-economic discretionary fiduciary powers . . . until the core mandate of retained economic benefits by the settlor/trustee has been satisfied," referencing *Grace* and the fact that it involved settlors who named each other as beneficiary of reciprocal trusts. A well reasoned dissent argued that the settlors did maintain "the same economic position" as if the trusts had not been crossed because their powers constituted an economic benefit as much as would retained personal enjoyment. The dissent also concluded that the retained economic enjoyment that the majority regarded as "the core mandate" of *Grace* was merely the operative fact of that case and not an immutable requirement for application of the doctrine.

The point here is that simplistic efforts to dodge unwanted liability are likely to generate litigation and potential failure. This crude form of "crossing" has proven unsuccessful in cases in which the trusts were found to be "interrelated," meaning that the trusts had substantially identical terms, were created at approximately the same time, and to the extent of their mutual value had the same economic effect as if crossing had not occurred.[9] Estate of Levy v. Commissioner, 46 T.C.M. (CCH) 910 (1983), determined that the reciprocal trust doctrine would not apply if the terms of the two trusts differed to any significant extent. In that case the effective difference was existence of a nongeneral power of appointment in one trust that was omitted in the other. No one knows whether such a minor difference would carry the day in litigation of this issue today. The *Levy* court failed to make clear what standard it was using to determine whether differences in the terms of the trusts were "significant" for purposes of the reciprocal trust doctrine. As a result, the approach may be unreliable. Nevertheless, the expectation is that *Levy* may be an effective device in appropriate cases in which limitations on the powers of a trustee are unacceptable. Otherwise, rather than rely on obvious and often ineffective schemes to disguise reality, if the doctrine might apply at all, then the "fix" is to make the trustee powers harmless if held by each beneficiary or settlor as trustee. As illustrated by the confusion among authorities, one conclusion is clear: it presently is imprudent to merely cross trustees if avoidance of tax liability is important.

---

9. See United States v. Estate of Grace, 395 U.S. 316 (1969); Krause v. Commissioner, 57 T.C. 890 (1972); Rev. Rul. 69-505.

Final Thoughts

What would you recommend if you encountered a client who already was acting as trustee under circumstances making it appear that undesirable tax liability will attach? As it turns out, resignation as trustee may be gift tax free, depending upon the gift tax consequences that applied when the trust was created (and your client's involvement in that). See Rev. Rul. 59-357. The second clause of §2041(a)(2) might suffice to dictate estate tax inclusion notwithstanding resignation (inclusion will result if resignation is followed by the client's enjoyment of interests or powers that would cause inclusion to a trust settlor under §§2036-2038). However, it probably is safe to say that the client has nothing to lose by resigning, if no present gift tax consequences will attach. Similarly, §678(a)(2) may continue to apply notwithstanding a resignation, but again the risk flowing from resignation probably is sufficiently slight to make it worth considering.

Finally, a number of summary conclusions seem appropriate. The first, and perhaps the most effective (and least difficult to accomplish), is to use ascertainable standards whenever sensitive trustees are involved. Although a degree of flexibility may be lost, often this is a slight price to pay. The use of cofiduciaries often increases costs (because each fiduciary must consent to all actions taken by any of them), so the use of special trustees (investment or insurance advisors, and distribution directors) often makes better sense. And last, but most important, usually it is safe to use whomever is the best suited fiduciary, provided that the drafter does an adequate job of drafting around the tax liabilities that may attach. No one (not even the settlor) is precluded from being trustee if proper, careful planning is employed.

Chapter 7

PLANNING FOR COUPLES

Introduction[1]

This Chapter is predominantly about planning for married individuals and it focuses almost exclusively on qualification for and utilization of the marital deduction. But not entirely, because a growing utility is planning for clients who anticipate divorce, as well as planning for couples who are not yet married, including some who cannot or will not ever marry. See page 142. As the discussion of that topic reveals, however, planning for individuals who are not married (be they surviving widows and widowers, same sex couples, or otherwise) pretty much entails the same factors and (lack of) opportunities, but it is not nearly as exciting or helpful as marital deduction planning for married individuals. Our law clearly favors and encourages marriage, at least for estate planning purposes.

This material was prepared after Congress passed legislation that would repeal the estate and generation-skipping transfer tax in 2010 (for just one year) but leave the gift tax alone. It seems likely that any change in this arena will look different from what Congress adopted in 2001, including the possibility that the repeal never will occur (because, for example, Congress will freeze the phase in of reduced rates that makes it happen). The point is that no one knows, which makes planning in this environment uncertain. When will the surviving spouse die becomes a critical inquiry because, until repeal, the unlimited federal estate and gift tax marital deductions (for qualifying dispositions of property to or for the benefit of a taxpayer's spouse) provide the most powerful estate planning tool available for married individuals.

Efficient use of the marital deduction permits effective use of both spouses' unified credits and generation-skipping transfer tax exemptions. Regardless of the size of the estate of the first spouse to die, the marital deduction allows deferral of federal wealth transfer taxes until the surviving spouse dies. Deferral of tax is the best possible plan if the survivor will die after repeal, but other planning may be more appropriate if the survivor dies before repeal (including if repeal never occurs). And the marital deduction becomes irrelevant for other than inter vivos

---

1. This Chapter is derived in part from Pennell, *Estate Tax Marital Deduction*, 843 (Tax Mgmt. BNA) ESTATES, GIFTS, & TRUSTS PORT. (2005), with the permission of the publisher, Tax Management Inc., a subsidiary of The Bureau of National Affairs Inc., Washington, D.C. All rights reserved.

intraspousal transfers if the decedent will likely die after repeal (although carryover basis has a provision that piggybacks on the qualified terminable interest property marital deduction rules). Notwithstanding all this, some plans will disinherit the surviving spouse in favor of other objects of the decedent's bounty.

With the backdrop of this uncertainty, this Chapter explores the following questions that any estate planner must answer in formulating and funding a marital bequest: How much (if any) marital deduction is appropriate: is deferral of tax until the spouse's death the best result? Which of the many forms of qualifying disposition is preferable? How should a clause be drafted to qualify the preferred disposition for the marital deduction? Which of the eight available alternatives for funding the marital bequest should be used to segregate the marital bequest from the rest of the decedent's property and transfer it to the dispositive vehicle chosen?

Two added questions are only briefly addressed: How should the generation-skipping transfer tax "reverse QTIP election" exemption allocation be factored into effective marital deduction planning? And how must the donor comply with the special requirements for bequests to a spouse who is not a United States citizen? Also addressed in fleeting detail are planning questions aimed at couples facing divorce, those at the more positive end of the spectrum who anticipate marriage, and planning for couples who will not ever marry.

Several topics addressed herein will remain of concern to estate planners even if the federal wealth transfer taxes are repealed. One aspect of this planning relates to the carry over of basis trade for repeal of the wealth transfer tax, which contains an exception of a certain base amount of property transferred to a surviving spouse, either outright or in a qualified terminable interest property (QTIP) format. Of greater concern and uncertainty is the number of state wealth transfer taxes that have been or will be re-enacted to replace revenue previously generated by the federal §2011 state death tax credit that is phased out after 2004. Those state laws might contain concepts similar to the current federal estate tax marital deduction and some may deviate in unexpected ways.

A third aspect of marital planning that likely never will go away, regardless of the tax law treatment of transfers to spouses, is the desire of some decedents to maintain control over their property and to fragment their estates between a surviving spouse and other intended beneficiaries. Most commonly, this involves descendants of a former marriage. This division of wealth, and control from the grave, likely will remain an active ingredient in traditional estate planning for married couples. So will the quintessential tension generated in many jurisdictions by a surviving spouse's statutory forced heir share entitlement and the ability to elect against an unwanted estate plan in favor of that elective share. See page 84.

This Chapter does not provide a detailed study of the federal estate tax marital deduction qualification rules and corresponding elements of its gift tax counterpart. The special technical rules for qualification are addressed in the wealth transfer taxation course and are not hard to meet even with relatively slight detailed knowledge. Planners just need to remember several basic notions (like, don't tinker with a marital form until you've done a good bit more study). The first of three major segments in this Chapter focuses on the planning aspect of the marital deduction that will first confront you: how much marital deduction is appropriate in a given situation? Although the discussion in this segment assumes familiarity with some marital deduction concepts that are covered later in the Chapter, if you are new to this area of the law you will find that these assumptions will not slow you down. This segment is written with current law in mind, on the assumption that repeal either is too far out or is too uncertain to rely upon. Neither may be true.

The second major segment of this Chapter deals more tersely with the technical requirements to qualify for the marital deduction. After determining how much marital deduction is appropriate, the planner must consult with the client to determine which of several common forms of qualifying disposition is preferable and how to draft the preferred disposition to qualify for the marital deduction. In some cases a combination of multiple dispositions will be appropriate, and is permissible. This is not a black and white selection process.

The third major segment of this Chapter deals with the administrative aspect of marital planning known as "funding" the bequest: once the planner has determined how much marital deduction is desired and has specified how it is to be transferred to or for the benefit of the surviving spouse, then the plan must dictate how the bequest is to be segregated from the decedent's property and transferred to the dispositive vehicle chosen. There are eight alternatives available for funding the marital share, each with its own particular advantages and disadvantages, which are explored and compared in the third segment. That discussion is relevant outside a marital deduction arena because essentially it informs planning for any division of any estate among multiple beneficiaries, which often is the case regardless of the decedent's family or other beneficiary cohort.

Importance of the Marital Deduction in Estate Planning

Estate tax §2056 grants an unlimited federal estate tax marital deduction for qualifying dispositions of property to or for the benefit of a decedent's surviving spouse. Correspondingly, §2523 grants an unlimited federal gift tax marital deduction for qualifying lifetime transfers to or for the benefit of a donor's spouse.[2]

---

2. Although the gift tax marital deduction is not discussed separately throughout this Chapter, in most respects it is no different from the estate tax marital deduction and should be considered to be consistent with the estate tax marital deduction unless otherwise stated

Collectively these marital deduction provisions constitute the single most important estate planning tool available to married individuals. All federal wealth transfer taxes can be deferred until the death of the surviving spouse through optimum use of the marital deduction, usually regardless of the size of the estate of the first spouse to die. All of the spouses' aggregate assets (undiminished by estate or gift tax) thus can be made available to support the surviving spouse during his or her overlife. And deferral long enough may preclude wealth transfer tax altogether if the estate tax repeal actually occurs.

Be aware, however, that the marital deduction does not necessarily reduce wealth transfer taxes if the surviving spouse dies under the present regime (before repeal of the estate tax or after it is restored). This is because a prerequisite for obtaining the deduction is that assets must be transferred in a manner that requires inclusion in the estate of the surviving spouse. Nevertheless, although an estate tax may be due at the death of the surviving spouse, the burden of the tax, and any liquidity problems that may be encountered in paying the tax, are borne by the next takers (typically, the couple's children) when the surviving spouse dies. In the interim the spouse is protected from tax, and frequently the hope is that the tax itself may go away before the surviving spouse dies.

Throughout this Chapter the first spouse to die is referred to as D and the surviving spouse is referred to as S, without regard to their gender. Unless otherwise stated, 2004 tax rates and credits are used in the tax computations. Section 2010(a) provides a credit against estate tax of the "applicable credit amount," which §2010(c) defines as the amount of the tentative tax that would be imposed if the tentative tax were computed on the "applicable exclusion amount." Most planners continue to refer to the unified credit and to the exemption equivalent or credit shelter amount that may pass free of tax, and that familiar terminology is used here as well. The credit is no longer "unified" (since 2003) because the estate tax applicable exclusion amount is slated to increase while the gift tax exemption amount is frozen at $1.0 million. Compare §§2010(c) and 2501(a)(1). Examples throughout this Chapter use an applicable credit amount of $555,800, an applicable exclusion amount of $1.5 million, and a maximum tax rate of 48%, all because those were the applicable figures in the year (2004) of publication. Those numbers may change but the economics illustrated will not.

(for example, one major difference applies if the spouse is not a U.S. citizen). In addition, §1041 is the income tax equivalent of the wealth transfer tax marital deduction, in the sense that it makes transfers between spouses neutral events for income tax purposes. Spouses do not recognize income and there is no gain or loss realization, on transfers between them. The estate tax repeal slated for year 2010 would not be matched with an income or gift tax change. There is no need for a generation-skipping transfer tax marital deduction because spouses are assigned to the same generation by definition (notwithstanding their ages) and therefore cannot run afoul of the generation-skipping transfer tax rules.

Example 1: D dies in 2004 leaving a $2.0 million estate (net of debts and expenses). If no portion of D's estate qualifies for the marital (or any other) deduction, D's taxable estate of $2.0 million would generate an estate tax of $225,000. If, instead, D leaves the entire $2.0 million to S, the entire estate will qualify for the unlimited marital deduction and no federal estate tax will be incurred at D's death. All federal estate tax will be deferred until S's death. Thus, if S dies several years after D, leaving the $2.0 million estate (net of debts and expenses) to the couple's children, S's taxable estate would generate an estate tax of $225,000 (and potentially less if the applicable exclusion amount ratchets up to an eventual $3.5 million as enacted in 2001, with a phased effective date).[3]

The potential estate tax that may be incurred on S's death may be avoided in Example 1 if D's estate does not "overqualify" for the marital deduction. That is, if D's unified credit were utilized in conjunction with the marital deduction, D's estate would not qualify for more marital deduction than was needed to eliminate taxes in D's estate. The following example illustrates an estate plan that takes advantage of the marital deduction without overqualifying for the deduction. It is said to "shelter" D's unified credit by using the marital deduction only to the extent needed to reduce federal[4] estate taxes to zero (or as close to zero as possible).

Example 2: D died with a $2.0 million estate in 2004 but left only $500,000 to S in a manner that qualified for the marital deduction. D and S will pay no estate tax:

$2,000,000	D's estate (net of debts and expenses)
(500,000)	marital deduction
1,500,000	D's taxable estate
$555,800	tentative estate tax
(555,800)	unified credit
0	D's federal estate tax payable

---

3. Notice that this example assumed that S had no other wealth. Also note that, for simplicity, unless otherwise stated, all tax computations assume that there are no deductions other than the marital deduction and that there has been no appreciation or depreciation, additions to, deletions from, or consumption of the marital bequest during S's overlife. In addition, no attempt is made to adjust for or anticipate the scheduled increase in the unified credit or reductions in the maximum marginal estate tax rates, nor for notions regarding absolute repeal of the wealth transfer tax. Although these are not necessarily realistic assumptions, they make it easier to illustrate various concepts and make valid comparisons.

4. Note throughout all of this that *state* death tax is *not* considered and might not be minimized by the planning shown. When §2011 was repealed the state law response across the nation was so diverse that it is impossible to consider the state-by-state variations that may affect marital deduction planning. For simplicity this material does not continually refer to the *federal* tax or remind you that state tax may be incurred.

When S later dies:

$500,000	S's estate (net of debts and expenses)
155,800	tentative estate tax
(555,800)	unified credit
0	S's federal estate tax payable

In Example 2, D and S could have owned up to double the applicable exclusion amount without incurring estate tax on either death, if the property was owned in the "proper" manner (half in each estate) or the spouses died in the "right" order and properly used (but did not overuse) the marital deduction (causing the applicable exclusion amount to be taxed in D's estate and leaving only the balance to be taxed in S's estate). In this respect, the marital deduction can be employed to "split" a couple's aggregate estates for transfer tax purposes in a manner that secures the tax-sheltering effect of the unified credits available to both spouses.[5]

> Example 3: Same facts as Example 2 except that D leaves the remaining $1.5 million of D's estate in trust to pay income to S for life, remainder to the couple's descendants. No effort is made to qualify the assets settled in this trust for the marital deduction. The trust corpus is not taxable in S's estate because S was given only a life estate in the trust established by D's will. Only the $500,000 in assets bequeathed to S (and any assets owned by S in S's own right) are includible in S's gross estate. If these assets have not changed appreciably in value since D's death, S's gross estate still will be less than the $1.5 million that can be sheltered by the unified credit available to S's estate. No estate tax will be due from S's estate. Use of this "nonmarital" trust estate plan produces a tax saving of $225,000 compared with Example 1, while the nonmarital trust provides economic benefits to S. Now D and S have the best of both worlds. Enjoyment of the sheltered $1.5 million amount, without paying estate tax in either estate.

In the foregoing examples, it was assumed that D owned assets worth $2.0 million and that S owned no assets. No marital deduction would be available to reduce taxes in D's estate if D survived S and did not remarry. When the property passed to the next generation on D's death, only D's unified credit would be available to reduce taxes; the unified credit available to S's estate would have been wasted. The gift tax marital deduction might be used in such a situation to minimize taxes. D could

---

[5]. For larger estates, the marital deduction can be used to allow some property to pass to S but not to fully eliminate taxes, as with an "equalizer" provision that equalizes the estates or the marginal estate tax brackets of both spouses. This will lead to a corresponding reduction of tax at S's death under the progressive estate tax rate structure. See page 23 for a discussion of equalizer provisions.

make a gift to S, ensuring that assets will be available to "shelter" the unified credit available to S's estate if S predeceases D.[6]

The problem of estate taxes incurred when the spouses "die out of order" is of less concern in community property states because each spouse owns half of all community property. Thus, to the extent of community property, each spouse has assets to shelter their respective unified credits. In all events, however, the proper division of assets during the joint life of both spouses is a serious concern because "wasting" either spouse's unified credit can represent the loss of a significant benefit.

A note about the uncertainty of planning for spouses in today's tax world is appropriate. As noted above, Congress in 2001 adopted a planned phase out of the estate tax, to be fully effective for clients who die after 2009. That law also has a repeal of the repeal that restores the tax in 2011 if Congress does not act before then to alter either part of this equation. These provisions may have global consequences on a typical client's estate plan. For example, a formula marital bequest to a surviving spouse of the smallest amount needed to reduce estate tax as much as possible is standard planning that would produce no transfer whatsoever in a zero tax world. This means that death during 2010 would produce a very different result than most decedents may have contemplated when their formula marital deduction plans were executed.

Death prior to 2010 will require thought about whether S is likely to live beyond 2009 (in which case marital deduction qualification in D's estate and concomitant deferral of tax may eliminate all tax) or whether S is likely to die before 2009 (which might make something known as §2013 previously taxed property planning viable, as discussed at page 32), or after 2010 (when everything is slated to return to the law as it was in 2001). Thus, planning should allow postmortem flexibility (for example, with disclaimer or partial QTIP elections), provide roughly identical benefits to S with or without qualification for the marital deduction (for example, because a nonmarital trust provides the same enjoyment as the marital deduction trust), anticipate a spousal election to claim any statutory forced heir share entitlement, and anticipate the potential that Congress will accelerate or eliminate the repeal, or for that matter freeze, delay, or repeal the sunset provision that repeals the repeal. What a mess!

As hard as it may be for clients to appreciate the need for affirmative planning in anticipation of all this, the context in which all these changes are slated to apply makes this a very important time during which to adjust client plans and to draft them to be flexible.

---

6. One very desirable mechanism for lifetime interspousal transfers is use of inter vivos QTIP trusts. Alternatively, the split gift provisions of §2513 might be employed to take advantage of S's unified credit but this planning typically appeals to only *very* wealthy spouses (who could give up to $3.0 million away from themselves). A third alternative also may prove to be simple marital planning, entailing use of an inter vivos plan such as the joint settlor revocable trust discussed beginning at page 68.

Basic Marital Deduction Planning

To understand marital deduction planning, it is essential always to be mindful that usually the estate tax marital deduction does not reduce the estate tax on marital assets; it only permits deferral of tax until the death of S. If properly done, it really permits wise use of both spouses' unified credits, making many estates nontaxable because the couple has less than double the applicable exclusion amount. Otherwise, to stay focused on the benefit of the marital deduction, remember that through the estate tax marital deduction, Congress has (in effect) said: "We won't tax your property to the extent you leave it to your spouse in a form that exposes it to taxation in your spouse's estate."

Thus, as a general rule, the primary requisite to qualify for the marital deduction is that the interest passing to S must be in a form that will lead to wealth transfer taxation to S (to the extent of the value of the interest when a taxable transfer by S occurs).[7] Unfortunately, there is no symmetry in the wealth transfer tax system regarding the estate tax marital deduction. The fact that an interest left to S will be includible in S's gross estate at death does not ensure qualification for the estate tax marital deduction. Some includible interests will be nondeductible because they run afoul of the "nondeductible terminable interest" rule.[8] Fortunately, there also is no symmetry in the system in the sense that there will be no payback if S were to die after repeal of the estate tax.

Notwithstanding wealth transfer tax inclusion to S, the unlimited marital deduction allows easier planning for the many marital estates that exceed the amount of property that can be transferred tax free under the shelter of the spouses' available unified credits. That is because the deduction can eliminate the problem of estate tax payment in D's estate, regardless of the size of that estate, regardless of the "mix" of the marital assets (principally community property, principally separate property, or substantial portions of each), and without concern about the liquidity of those assets for tax payment purposes.

It always pays to remember also that hard issues like liquidity problems dodged today usually will present themselves when S dies (often in an even worse form) unless the tax (or the wealth) has disappeared before S dies. So, deferral may provide the opportunity to address these problems, but it also may lull clients into thinking the problem was solved

---

7. There are exceptions to this general principle. Certain interests can qualify for the estate tax marital deduction even though the interest may terminate and have no value of its own when S dies. Nevertheless, the value represented by the interest may be includible in S's gross estate. For example, annuity payments received by S and not consumed in a manner that has no value when S dies will be includible in S's gross estate (under §2033), although the amount included may bear only a slight resemblance to the marital deduction allowed for the value of the right to receive that annuity on D's death.

8. See page 44. This is well illustrated by the annuity situation: S's net worth will be increased by annuity payments received by S, even if the estate tax marital deduction is not allowed to D's estate, in which the value of the annuity also was includible.

or avoided when in fact it is just silently and relentlessly growing. The secret to marital deduction planning is to know when, and to what extent, to embrace deferral.

Basic Structure of Estate Planning for Spouses

The interrelation of the unified credit and the unlimited marital deduction creates a basic estate planning structure for spouses. In both community and noncommunity property states, the typical (albeit not necessarily the most intuitive) marital and nonmarital dispositions provide for any specific bequests, make an "optimum" marital deduction formula gift to S (or to the trustee of a marital deduction trust), and devise the residuary estate to the trustee of the nonmarital trust.[9]

This nonmarital trust gives S, at most, an income interest for life, a right to receive principal in the trustee's discretion, and perhaps nongeneral powers of appointment exercisable during life, at death, or both, all drafted to avoid wealth transfer tax inclusion in S's estate. Thus, D's estate effectively is "split" for wealth transfer tax purposes. Proper use of both spouses' unified credits through effective marital deduction and nonmarital trust planning permits marital estates of up to double the applicable exclusion amount[10] to pass to the next generation free of wealth transfer taxes.[11]

The key to this planning is to "shelter" (or use) D's unified credit by placing the applicable exclusion amount in the nonmarital trust, using the marital deduction only for the balance of D's otherwise taxable estate. To avoid paying an estate tax in D's estate, however, the amount of the gift to the nonmarital trust cannot exceed the applicable exclusion amount (for example, $1.5 million in 2004). Indeed, because of the concept of

---

9. Also often referred to as the bypass, family, or credit shelter trust. See Chapter 5. In large estates the marital bequest may be larger than the nonmarital portion of the estate, which leads to problems in making distributions to, and greater administrative inconvenience in funding, the marital deduction bequest. For this reason, in larger estates it may be appropriate to make the formula gift to the trustee of the nonmarital trust, and make the residuary gift in a form qualifying for the marital deduction. This "reverse" or "residuary marital" formula approach is discussed at page 117. Nevertheless, the basic planning discussed here would remain the same.

10. In 2004-2005 that §2010(c) determined amount would be $1.5 million per spouse (slated to increase to $2.0 million per spouse from 2005-2008 and $3.5 million per spouse in 2009, followed by repeal of the tax in year 2010 and resurrection of the entire system in 2011 with an applicable exclusion amount of only $1 million).

11. In considering these general statements, it is assumed for purposes of simplicity that: (1) there is no §2055 charitable deduction that will affect the computations; (2) joint tenancy and other nonprobate property is not so prevalent that it overqualifies the planning discussed; (3) no credits, such as the §2011 state death tax or §2013 previously taxed property credits, are involved; (4) there are no expenses of administration or other deductions; and (5) there is no income accumulation and no appreciation or depreciation in the respective estates between the spouses' deaths and, thus, there is no growth or potential capital gain or loss to consider and no §1014 basis adjustment is relevant. These obviously unrealistic assumptions are embraced here only to simplify the discussion of even the most basic planning approaches.

"nondeductible charges," in most cases the nonmarital trust will be less (perhaps considerably less) than this amount.[12]

Because many factors affect the size of a nonmarital trust, a specific bequest equal to the applicable exclusion amount (for example, $1.5 million in 2004) would virtually always cause taxes to be paid in D's estate. Thus, some other method of creating the proper bequest must be used. The following language is a common *formula* provision that accomplishes this planning:

> **If S survives me, I give to the trustee of the Marital Trust the smallest pecuniary amount that, if allowed as a federal estate tax marital deduction, would result in the least possible federal estate tax being payable by reason of my death. In determining this pecuniary amount, my personal representative shall consider the credit or the deduction for state death taxes only to the extent those taxes are not thereby incurred or increased, and shall assume that none of the payments and devises under the preceding articles of this will qualify for a federal estate tax deduction.[13]**

Commonly referred to as an "optimum" marital deduction (rather than an "unlimited" or "maximum") bequest, this disposition qualifies for the estate tax marital deduction only the minimum amount needed to generate a nontaxable estate for D. Depending on state law it also may eliminate all state death tax as well.

Note the effect of this plan. No property would pass pursuant to the marital deduction formula if, for example, D's estate was less than the applicable exclusion amount, because no marital deduction would be necessary to reduce taxes to zero. The same result could occur if this provision were used in an estate of up to double the applicable exclusion amount ($3.0 million in 2004) that was all community property: D might bequeath D's entire residuary estate (half of the community property) to

---

12. Nondeductible charges are items that must be charged against the nonmarital gift because otherwise they would reduce the marital deduction. Nondeductible charges may include such items as: (1) state or federal taxes; (2) bequests (including to S) that do not qualify for the marital or charitable deductions; (3) §642(g) "swing" items (usually administration expenses) for which a deduction is taken against estate income rather than as an estate tax deduction under §2053; (4) adjusted taxable gifts during life that "used up" some of the §2010 unified credit; (5) generation-skipping transfer taxes (such as on a direct skip generated by a child's disclaimer that caused a bequest to pass to a grandchild); and (6) nonprobate property includible in the gross estate that passes to someone other than S or not in a manner that qualifies for the marital deduction. In explaining an "optimum marital" plan to clients, lawyers commonly refer to the "credit shelter" amount that will be available to fund the nonmarital trust. Although this colloquial explanation may ease client understanding, it may lead to subsequent misunderstanding if the trust is funded with substantially less than the illustrated applicable exclusion amount.

13. Many provisions throughout this Chapter are adapted from forms originally copyrighted by The Northern Trust Company, www.northerntrust.com, and are reprinted with permission. Authority is expressly granted to attorneys to use those provisions in the preparation of estate planning documents for clients.

the nonmarital trust and no property would need to qualify for marital deduction purposes. And no bequest would be made to S or the marital trust under this provision if D died after repeal of the estate tax.

It should not be necessary to amend this type of formula marital provision in old or new documents to accommodate gradual increases in the applicable exclusion amount, because the formula itself creates the optimum marital bequest after full usage of the unified credit. Thus, if D's death occurs during 2009, the formula provision would create a nonmarital trust of up to $3.5 million and the couple would be able to pass up to $7.0 million to their intended beneficiaries free of wealth transfer taxes. This formula should work even if Congress further raises, reduces, or freezes the applicable exclusion amount, or phases in the increase to $3.5 million sooner than 2009. Nevertheless, cautious practitioners contact clients with older documents to ascertain that they wish to take advantage of any increases in the unified credit and perhaps amend their documents to make that intent clear. Because the increase effectively disinherits the marital bequest, the plan also might reflect the potential for S to take offense and assert a forced share election.

Tax Sensitive Outright Gifts to S

The optimum marital deduction bequest might be an effective tax plan, but it may generate a smaller marital bequest than D (or S!) wants. Consider, for example, the type of planning that may be desired by clients with "average" size estates who are sensitive to but not driven by tax minimization objectives. To illustrate, assume D's estate is valued at $800,000 and S has little property. For a variety of reasons (such as future contributions to D's qualified pension plan, payments reducing the mortgage balance on the family residence, stock market appreciation, and inflation), D's estate is likely to increase in value over the years, but at an unpredictable rate. There is no way to be sure whether D's estate will exceed the applicable exclusion amount (or whether Congress may reduce that amount before D dies).

In this case there may be no marital deduction drafting or planning concerns because each spouse may prefer to make a simple outright disposition of his or her entire estate to the surviving spouse, notwithstanding any tax consequences. Recall Example 1 at page 5. D and S may have the wisdom to realize that a nonmarital trust does not save taxes in the estate of D; any taxes saved are in S's estate, making the children the real beneficiaries of optimum marital deduction planning that shelters D's unified credit.[14]

---

14. Thus, although the spouses may have no estate planning concerns, their estate planner may be quite uncomfortable, recognizing that, after D and S are deceased, their children may inquire: "Didn't you tell the folks they could have saved taxes with a bypass trust plan?" A cautious planner will explain in writing the tax consequences of a nonmarital plan and confirm (also in writing) their joint desire to forego those savings. In addition, it might be appropriate to draft in contemplation of disclaimer, as discussed at page 16.

It also may not be desirable to allocate the full applicable exclusion amount away from S, especially in a smaller estate in which this could consume a significant portion or all of D's wealth and leave S with little or nothing in a marital bequest. Indeed, depending on the nature of the estate plan, failure to carefully consider the allocation of wealth away from S could result in S's election against D's estate plan and in favor of the statutory elective share.

Thus, despite the size of D's estate, D may eschew a nonmarital trust and leave "all my property to S," giving S the freedom and flexibility of outright ownership. Assuming this is not a subsequent marriage involving children by a former spouse, the marital planning and drafting can be very simple: outright disposition to S under a will or nontestamentary dispositions (such as life insurance or employee benefit plan proceeds paid in a lump sum, or jointly held property with the right of survivorship), all qualifying for the estate tax marital deduction. And potentially all passing tax free when S subsequently dies, because the applicable exclusion amount is adequate or the tax has been repealed.

Unfortunately, the simplicity of this plan is deceptive because it is necessary to consider the contingency of deaths in quick succession. This "all my property" plan should anticipate the not uncommon possibility that S may outlive D by only a short period, in which event there could be substantial taxes in S's estate (recall Example 1, in which $225,000 of estate taxes were unnecessary), even though S died before enjoying the property enough to justify that added tax cost. And don't forget that the wealth may increase to more than the applicable exclusion amount: what if D's death is wrongful and S recovers a tort damage award of several million dollars? Indeed, what if S was so badly injured at the same time that recoveries (or the right to recover) for both D and S are subject to tax when S dies not too long after D? There are several potential solutions to this problem.

Survivorship Requirements

One approach to S dying before loss of the tax savings is compensated with enjoyment through personal use would be for D to employ a survivorship requirement, such as: "**I leave all my property to S if S survives me by X days**." Unfortunately, this will not produce the desired result:

> Example: D and S are driving home from a New Year's Eve party when their car is struck head-on by a drunk driver. D dies immediately; S dies two days later.

Nothing passes to S under the marital deduction provision if S does not survive by the requisite period. Let's assume some numbers: D's estate tax computation would show:

$1,600,000	D's gross estate
(0)	marital deduction
1,600,000	D's taxable estate
600,800	tentative estate tax
(555,800)	unified credit
45,000	D's federal estate tax payable[†]

When S dies in this nearly simultaneous death case, there would be no added taxes (assuming S did not have independent wealth).

Under this same will, if S survived the crash and died slightly more than X days after D, the tax computation in D's estate would be:

$1,600,000	D's gross estate
(1,600,000)	marital deduction
0	D's taxable estate

When S later dies:

$1,600,000	S's taxable estate
600,800	tentative estate tax
(555,800)	unified credit
45,000	S's federal estate tax payable[†]

Contrary to the expectation that it would reduce taxes, the survivorship requirement had no effect at all: the tax is the same as if S did not live long enough to inherit D's estate. D and S will pay less tax only if a nonmarital plan is employed.[15]

Also failing to produce the right result is a straight presumption of survivorship provision. It will produce the same results as if S survived D by the requisite survivorship period. For example, assume that D's will provided: "**I leave all my property to S if S survives me**" and D and S die before anyone reaches the scene of their car accident (a so-called simultaneous death if the order of their deaths cannot be proven). Under the Uniform Simultaneous Death Act (which is the law virtually everywhere), the property of each of D and S would pass as though each survived the other. Thus, D's property would pass as though S died before D, with the same tax result as in the first computation above: $45,000 of estate tax payable by D's estate.

If, instead, D employed a presumption of survivorship for simultaneous death purposes, the results would match those in the second

---

[†] This "universal" footnote will appear in numerous places in this Chapter when reference is made to the payment of taxes, to remind you that this tax payable figure may be subject to other credits, such as the §2013 credit for taxes incurred on prior transfers.

15. Under the same will, if S died years later (and asset values did not change), the tax still would be $45,000 more (assuming the unified credit and tax rates do not change) than if a nonmarital plan had been used, but S will enjoy outright ownership of the assets for S's overlife, which was D's decision. The concern is only with S's death before sufficient enjoyment justifies the $45,000 of "unnecessary" taxes.

computation above: $45,000 of tax on S's death. Thus, D could use a provision that reverses the Uniform Simultaneous Death Act result:[16]

> **For purposes of this gift S shall be considered to have survived me if S and I die under such circumstances that there is no sufficient evidence to establish the order of our deaths.**

In this case, S would be deemed to have survived the car crash that killed both D and S immediately. S would take all of D's property under D's will, generating the marital deduction for D's estate but again not reducing the tax on S's death.

None of these results is very attractive, and they all are attributable to the fact that only one spouse's unified credit is used. Whether D relies on a survivorship requirement, on the Uniform Simultaneous Death Act presumption, or on a "reverse presumption" provision, the tax sheltering effect of the unified credit is lost in either S's estate or D's estate. Thus, an unnecessary tax is incurred on the applicable exclusion amount that could be sheltered by a traditional nonmarital plan. D may be willing to accept this increase in tax if S lives long enough to enjoy outright ownership of all of D's property, but D should be reluctant to incur any tax if S does not survive for a sufficient period to reap significant benefits from this less than tax conscious plan.

Disclaimers

The second primary alternative to this problem is to rely on a disclaimer by S's personal representative if S's death occurs within the §2518 disclaimer period (usually nine months) after D's death. There are problems with disclaimers, the most important being that it must be clear under state law that S's personal representative can disclaim for S (which is not always the case). See the discussion of disclaimer disadvantages at page 18.

The Preferable Approach

Fortunately, there may be a better solution to this survivorship planning problem:

> **Marital Deduction Gift. If S survives me, I give S the smallest pecuniary amount that, if allowed as a federal estate tax marital deduction, would result in the least possible federal estate tax being payable by reason of my death. In determining this pecuniary amount, my personal representative shall consider the credit or the deduction for state death taxes only**

---

16. This presumption of survivorship is permitted under Treas. Reg. §20.2056(c)-2(e): "If the order of deaths of the decedent and his spouse cannot be established by proof, a presumption (whether supplied by local law, *the decedent's will*, or otherwise) that the decedent was survived by his spouse will be recognized . . ." (emphasis added).

to the extent those taxes are not thereby incurred or increased, and shall assume that none of the payments and devises under the preceding articles of this will qualify for a federal estate tax deduction.

For purposes of this gift, if S and I die under such circumstances that there is no sufficient evidence to establish the order of our deaths, S shall be considered to have survived me.

Residuary Estate. I give all of the residue of my estate, including any foregoing gift that lapses ("my residuary estate"):

(a) To S if S survives me by X days;

(b) If S does not survive me by X days, per stirpes to my descendants who so survive me; and

(c) If neither my spouse nor any descendant survives me by X days, to my contingent beneficiaries defined [elsewhere in the will].

Under this plan, if D dies followed by S's death within X days, D's estate tax computation would show:

$1,600,000	D's gross estate
(100,000)	marital deduction produced by formula
1,500,000	D's taxable estate
555,800	tentative estate tax
(555,800)	unified credit
0	D's federal estate taxes payable[†]

When S later dies:

$100,000	S's taxable estate
23,800	tentative estate tax
(555,800)	unified credit
0	S's federal estate taxes payable[†]

On the postulated facts of D having a $1.6 million estate and S having no independent wealth, the illustrated will provision would save the couple's children $45,000 in taxes if the calamity of deaths in quick succession were to occur. If the deaths do not occur within the specified time, this plan would provide the disposition to S that D wants.

What period should D insert for X? It must be less than six months to come within the "limited survivorship" exception to the nondeductible terminable interest rule of §2056(b)(3), as discussed at page 48. But that rule is of no concern here because the unified credit would shelter this nonmarital amount anyway, making the marital deduction unnecessary. Therefore, the period could be shorter (for example, 30 days, 7 weeks) or longer (for example, a year or more), although a much longer period could create administrative problems because closing the estate might be delayed while waiting for S to survive the contingency period. This contingency is a concern whether S dies 60 minutes or 60 days after D, so D should select a period that is a good compromise between the planning and administration issues involved.

One question that occurs to many observers is whether S will have trouble getting along for the number (X) of days that the residuary gift is contingent. The answer is almost always that the delay aspect of the residuary gift presents no problem: because S will be entitled to a family allowance under state law, and S will enjoy all nonprobate assets that are payable to S or that belong to S (such as life insurance or employee benefit plan proceeds paid in a lump sum, and assets held jointly with the right of survivorship). In addition, S may take something under the marital deduction provision (the only question is how much), which may be partially distributed (in this case any part or all of the $100,000 marital bequest) during the X day period. And S may be D's personal representative with effective control over all of D's probate estate.

A Note About Community Property

In a noncommunity property estate the planning objective is to split the marital property if the spouses die in quick succession. By contrast, in a community property estate the marital property (everything except the respective spouses' separate property) already is split, automatically and evenly by the community property laws. Therefore, the objective is to avoid unsplitting the estate if the spouses die in quick succession.

In a community property estate splitting the wealth does not require a formula marital deduction gift (with a survivorship requirement imposed on S) unless substantial separate property is involved. Instead, the estates will stay split simply by using a survivorship requirement with respect to D's entire community property estate. Thus, the only necessary provision is a residuary gift of D's entire estate "**to S if S survives me by X days**."

Drafting in Contemplation of Disclaimer

The alternative to an "all outright" plan is an intermediate approach that permits S to take a second look after D dies, to see whether a nonmarital trust is preferable. For example, the estate may have appreciated substantially since the estate plan was written and this increase in value, together with S's age and life expectancy, may make a nonmarital trust appropriate. Indeed, a trust might be a welcome alternative to a guardianship or other fiduciary relation to provide efficient asset management if S no longer is willing or able to manage wealth.

Disclaimer planning anticipates that each spouse will make an unlimited marital deduction bequest to the other, with S disclaiming so much of D's estate as appropriate to cut back to an optimum marital deduction (or other desired amount). The documents effecting this plan would look like the will provisions under "the preferable approach" at page 14, with the addition of the following provision:

Family Trust. I give any interest under any preceding provision of this will that S disclaims to the trustee of the Family Trust.

The Family Trust would contain whatever terms D selects (for example, mandatory income or a discretionary income spray, principal invasion powers in the trustee, powers to appoint in anyone other than S), such that no benefit given to S causes trust corpus to be subject to S's wealth transfer taxation or precludes a qualified disclaimer (which explains why S cannot have a traditional power to appoint).

Note that an undivided portion or a pecuniary amount may be disclaimed. Treas. Reg. §§25.2518-3(b) and 25.2518-3(c). For example, S may make a qualified disclaimer of a fraction of the residuary estate of which the numerator is the amount exceeding the desired marital deduction and the denominator is the value of the residuary estate.

Advantages

Drafting in contemplation of disclaimer alerts the right people to consider this postmortem opportunity. Because the right to disclaim exists under state law, the possibility of a disclaimer need not be mentioned in the estate plan, but a specific provision reminds S to take a second look to decide what is best. A reference to the disclaimer possibility also serves as a red flag, which is useful because a §2518 qualified disclaimer usually must be made within nine months after D's death. Affirmative provisions also may overcome any reluctance that S might feel about making a disclaimer that otherwise might be perceived "as against D's intent."

A second major advantage of drafting in contemplation of disclaimer is that the estate plan can make suitable provision for disposition of the disclaimed interest. In some circumstances it may not be clear what happens to the disclaimed interest otherwise, notwithstanding a statute that attempts to address the problem. For example, Uniform Probate Code §2-801(c) specifies that: "[u]nless the decedent . . . has otherwise provided, the property or interest renounced devolves as though the disclaimant had predeceased the decedent." The 1990 version is virtually the same in UPC §2-801(d)(1).

To illustrate, suppose that S disclaims a portion of an outright bequest under a will that was not drafted in contemplation of disclaimer. The disclaimed interest passes into a residuary trust of which S is a permissible income distributee. Under the statute, is S precluded from receiving income from the disclaimed interest, given that the disclaimed interest is supposed to pass as if the person renouncing had predeceased the decedent? Stated another way, does the statute apply in reading the outright bequest that was disclaimed, does it apply in reading the entire will with respect to the disclaimed interest, or does the trust provision override the statute? A specific designation in the document would solve this problem with a clear statement to the effect that S shall not be disqualified as a beneficiary of the receptacle trust with respect to disclaimed (or any other) property.[17] Federal law permits S to continue to enjoy income from the disclaimed property and S may not disclaim if that enjoyment is not preserved.

Disadvantages

Numerous disadvantages or potential problems attendant to disclaimer planning also deserve attention. One is that S simply may be unwilling to lose control of the property to save taxes for future takers, despite protestations made to the contrary during both spouses' lives. That is, among the world's greatest lies are: (1) "The check is in the mail"; (2) "I'm from the government and I want to help you"; and (3) "Of course I'll disclaim if it will save taxes." Closely related is fear that the property remaining after the disclaimer will not be adequate to support S after incurring some estate tax in D's estate. The disclaimed assets can remain available to S and still be a qualified disclaimer (in the context of a §2518(b)(4)(A) nonmarital trust). So this concern really relates only to prepayment of wealth transfer tax in D's estate due to S's disclaimer, which need not be a factor if all S disclaims is amounts up to the applicable exclusion amount (so no tax payment diminishes the available wealth before S's death).

A second problem with disclaimers is that S may be legally unable to disclaim, or may die before the disclaimer is made.[18] For example, a personal representative cannot disclaim on behalf of a surviving spouse who already is deceased under the original version of UPC §2-801(a). Although the 1990 version of the Uniform Probate Code corrects this problem (allowing the deceased S's personal representative to disclaim), it

---

17. Although the 1990 version of UPC §2-801(d) addresses this issue by disposing of only the disclaimed interest as if S were deceased, it still does not specify whether S should be regarded as predeceased with respect to income payable by the bypass trust from disclaimed property, and the newer version of the UPC is not the law even in most UPC states, most of which have not yet adopted the 1990 revisions.

18. See 2 Casner & Pennell, ESTATE PLANNING §7.1.6.6 (6th ed. 1999), regarding authority of a fiduciary to disclaim on behalf of a beneficiary, such as S. For example, in Estate of Delaune v. United States, 97-1 U.S. Tax Cas. (CCH) ¶60,266 (M.D. La. 1997), rev'd, 143 F.3d 995 (5th Cir. 1998), the trial court originally concluded that purported disclaimers on behalf of a surviving spouse were invalid because they were made too late under state law (because the surviving spouse already had died). The court on appeal, however, held that the disclaimers were valid under Louisiana law, which allows the renunciation of a succession by the heirs of an heir, acting on the heir's behalf. See also Estate of Chamberlain v. Commissioner, 77 T.C.M. (CCH) 2080 (1999) (the decedent allegedly intended to disclaim but failed to sign a writing to that effect before dying, the court rejecting all sorts of extrinsic evidence and ancillary documents—including Forms 706 for both spouses that were consistent with disclaimer—indicative of the intent to disclaim, and also rejected a "close is good enough" argument for substantial compliance with the disclaimer requisites).

has not been widely adopted yet. Moreover, a personal representative who is authorized by local law to disclaim will balk if the disclaimer will affect the ultimate recipients of property from each spouse, unless the personal representative is given clear standards to guide its decision and is indemnified against any liability to disaffected beneficiaries.

Third, a qualified disclaimer under §2518 is impossible if S accepted any benefits from the interest being disclaimed. Thus, D's fiduciary must be astute enough to prevent payment to or acceptance by S of income from the disclaimed property, or use by S of those assets, and sometimes the acceptance of benefits is deemed to occur in unexpected ways. Indeed, at one time the government regarded simply being a joint tenant with a decedent as an acceptance of benefits by surviving joint tenants that might preclude an otherwise qualified disclaimer of joint tenancy property. Although the government since altered its position, the fact that it took years of litigation to resolve the issue is a good reminder that disclaimer planning is fraught with peril and probably nothing to rely upon for affirmative estate planning purposes.

A fourth problem with disclaimers is disposition of the disclaimed interest. Although §2518(b)(4)(A) regards a disclaimer as effective if the interest passes to a nonmarital trust held for the benefit of S, such a disposition might not occur automatically. Thus, the document may need to specify this disposition. For example, in the all outright plan illustrated at page 14 with a survivorship contingency, D's residuary estate passes to descendants if S does not survive by the requisite period. Because S would be treated as predeceased by virtue of a disclaimer, this alternative disposition would apply unless the document specifically provided for a different disposition on disclaimer.

A similar problem is encountered in very large estates that use a residuary marital plan making a formula gift to the nonmarital trust and leaving the residue of the estate to a marital deduction trust. Property disclaimed from the marital deduction residue normally would pass by intestacy, not into the preresiduary nonmarital trust in which D probably would want it to continue to benefit S without estate tax inclusion when S subsequently dies. A special disclaimer pour back into the preresiduary nonmarital trust would be required to accomplish D and S's objectives.

Fifth, to be a qualified disclaimer, S cannot have any power to direct disposition of the disclaimed interest. For example, if S is trustee of the nonmarital trust, the disclaimer will succeed only if the trustee's powers are limited by an ascertainable standard. Moreover, if that trust grants S a power of appointment not limited by an ascertainable standard (for example, an unrestricted nongeneral testamentary power of appointment), S also must disclaim the power.[19] It will be necessary to define that portion

---

19. Note that Treas. Reg. §25.2518-3(a)(1)(iii) permits a power of appointment to be disclaimed while retaining other interests in corpus, but a power of appointment cannot be cut down or otherwise tailored to retain the power while complying with these limitations.

of the nonmarital trust as to which the power is relinquished if S is willing to disclaim the power only to the extent necessary to qualify the disclaimer and not as to all of the nonmarital trust.

Although a fractional approach might be successful, a better approach might be to create a separate trust to which all disclaimed assets will pass by express direction in the marital provision, without affecting the normal nonmarital trust. This trust would give essentially the same benefits as the nonmarital trust (except prohibited powers), and provide for consolidation with, or addition to, the nonmarital trust for ultimate distribution after S's subsequent death. It might even be useful to give S a noncumulative right to withdraw yearly the greater of $5,000 or 5% of the aggregate value of the principal (the disclaimed property) in the nonmarital trust, as permitted under Treas. Reg. §25.2518-2(e)(5) Example 7. This (albeit limited) ability to reach disclaimed corpus might overcome any reticence that S otherwise may feel about disclaiming a portion of the outright gift.

Finally, the disclaimer must properly describe the portion being relinquished out of an unlimited marital bequest. Identifiable, severable assets held in trust may not be disclaimed unless the assets are removed from the trust and pass to other beneficiaries, but a specific dollar or formula amount may be disclaimed from a trust. Treas. Reg. §§25.2518-3(a)(2); 25.2518-3(c). Thus, for example, disclaimer of the income from a specific number of shares of stock or of an identifiable piece of realty would not qualify if the stock or realty continued to be held in trust, but disclaimer of a specific dollar amount or of a fractional or percentile portion of an entire interest is allowable. Depending on the nature of the property likely to be disclaimed, some advance thought must be devoted to the form and drafting of the type of disclaimer that will be required.

Planning and Drafting for Larger Estates

All examples in this segment use an applicable credit amount of $555,800 and an applicable exclusion amount of $1.5 million. The phase-in increase of the applicable exclusion amount will reduce the aggregate dollar savings available but does not alter the principles illustrated. A major change in focus will be required if we ever get into a flat tax environment, which is slated to occur in 2006 (if Congress does not alter the changes adopted in 2001). The tax does not remain flat, however, after those changes sunset in 2011 (again unless Congress alters the 2001 changes).

The basic truism of marital deduction planning illustrated so far is that giving all of a larger estate to S may "overqualify" the marital deduction:

> Example: D and S have a $2.0 million community property marital estate. D's will bequeaths "all my property" to S.

Because of the unlimited marital deduction there will be no tax in D's estate, but the full $2.0 million is exposed to tax in S's estate, resulting in the following tax computation at S's later death:

$2,000,000	S's taxable estate
780,800	tentative estate tax
(555,800)	unified credit
225,000	S's federal estate tax payable†

The problem with this dispositive plan is that D's estate did not benefit from the tax sheltering effect of the unified credit. It would have been possible to remove $1.5 million from taxation on S's death through D's gift to a nonmarital trust of all but an optimum marital deduction formula amount, with no increase in tax at D's death and a tax reduction at S's death of $225,000. Sheltering D's unified credit by using only an "optimum" marital bequest is a better approach for tax minimization purposes. However, another planning decision must be made in a larger estate: is it wise to take full advantage of the optimum marital deduction, or would it be better to pay some tax in D's estate to increase the amount that can be sheltered from tax at S's death?

> Example: D and S own $3.5 million of community property. They forego the marital deduction entirely, so that each of their estates will be $1,750,000 at death.

In each estate the tax computations are:

$1,750,000	taxable estate
668,300	tentative estate tax
(555,800)	unified credit
112,500	federal estate tax payable†

Total taxes for both estates would be $225,000. If you run the numbers you will discover that this represents no savings over an optimum marital deduction plan that shelters $1.5 million at D's death and taxes $2.0 million at S's death. Although a savings would be available (with tax payment at D's death) in much larger estates, for most people this isn't a hard decision to make. As a consequence, for our purposes the notion of foregoing the marital deduction has only academic appeal until you represent very large estates. And it disappears once we are in a flat tax environment, so we will not explore it further from a tax savings perspective.

There are, however, a number of noneconomic reasons that favor the payment of some tax at D's death. The most important relates to family planning concerns: the question for most clients is how long their ultimate beneficiaries (typically children) must wait for their inheritance. Most children, for example, are "orphaned" in their 40s or even later, when their surviving parent dies, which may be years or even decades later than the time of their greatest financial needs. This suggests an imbalance that may persuade some clients that deferral should not be based strictly on an economic analysis.

For example, in a $5.0 million estate, the "optimum" plan would involve a nonmarital trust of no more than the applicable exclusion amount. Even if distributed immediately to beneficiaries other than S, it may be that, considering lifestyle and expected health care costs, the marital bequest will allow S to more than "scrape along." Thus, the question for the client to consider is whether to leave less to S, notwithstanding the need to pay some tax at D's death, to provide earlier and greater benefits to the ultimate beneficiaries. This question especially should be considered if S is a subsequent spouse whose death is likely to occur even later in those ultimate beneficiaries' lives.

Indeed, consistent with this notion, some clients may wish to consider a giving program benefiting younger generation beneficiaries while both spouses are living, taking maximum tax minimization advantage of two annual exclusion gifts per donee under §2503, perhaps even exhausting each spouse's unified credit.

As an alternative, if the client's unwavering desire is optimum marital planning or holding property until D dies to generate a new basis by virtue of inclusion in D's gross estate (assuming death occurs before the estate tax is repealed, with a concomitant change from §1014 new-basis-at-death to §1022 carryover basis), it might make sense to include precatory language[20] recommending that S consider making gifts to younger generation beneficiaries after D's death. To make this work most effectively may entail providing at least a portion of the marital bequest in a manner that allows S to make inter vivos gifts.

> Example: S received $1.0 million more property from D than S needs, and is willing to part with that amount in the form of a gift to children and the gift tax thereon. Assuming the worst possible case (that S's marginal gift tax bracket already is 48%), S could give the children $675,676 from the $1.0 million that S does not need; at 48% the tax on this gift would equal the remaining $324,324 that S will pay to the government.[21] This translates into an effective tax rate on the $1.0 million of just 32.43%, which is lower than the lowest marginal rate (45%) that could be imposed on D's estate if a less than optimum marital bequest is utilized. If S is in a gift tax bracket that is lower than the maximum 48%, the differential would be even greater.

To make such planning possible it would be desirable if the trust granted S

---

20. Perhaps in a letter to S that would minimize any reluctance S might feel to make gifts (even though S has more income than S can or does spend, perhaps because S remembers the Depression).

21. The algebraic formula to make this computation is:

$$\text{transfer divided by } (1 + \text{tax rate}) = \text{taxable gift}$$

So, for a 2004 calculation: $1.0 million divided by 1.48 = $675,676. Multiply that by the rate of tax to yield $324,324 of gift tax and the two together total $1 million.

the authority to appoint property (permissible in a §2056(b)(5) trust but not in a QTIP trust, due to the prohibition in §2056(b)(7)(B)(ii)(II) against anyone having a power to appoint QTIP property to anyone other than S) or to withdraw trust principal from either form of marital trust that could be the subject of a gift.

The Time-Value of Money Rationale for Deferral

Ignore for purposes of this discussion the promised repeal of the estate tax in 2010 (or its reinstatement in 2011): it may never happen, or the spouses both may die before then. More importantly, one purpose of this discussion is to reveal the truth about a pervasive estate planning myth. This very common assumption is relevant in analyzing any marital deduction planning approach that entails payment of estate tax in D's estate. The wrong minded notion is that use of the tax dollars deferred from D's death under an optimum approach will compensate for any difference in tax saved by avoiding estate stacking, which is the term used for adding D's wealth on top of S's estate.

That "time-value-of-money" assumption is false. Two examples will illustrate this, the second assuming time-value as reflected in the aggregate wealth doubling in value during S's overlife. For purposes of this illustration the source of this growth or the amount of time that it takes to occur is irrelevant.[22] What is relevant is that this doubling represents the enjoyment or use of the wealth over S's overlife and therefore illustrates the time-value of the deferred tax payment.

Before embarking on this odyssey of economic comparisons, it bears noting that the choice whether to pay estate tax in D's estate versus in S's estate is all second best planning. As just illustrated, far better planning in an environment with estate and gift taxes intact would be qualification for the marital deduction in D's estate followed by gifts by S. This series of illustrations therefore is more valuable as a means of dispelling the common but wrong minded assumption that the time-value notion makes deferral of tax preferable to either payment of estate tax in D's estate or incurring gift tax before both spouses die. To make an illustration that is meaningful, please excuse the use of very large numbers.

> Baseline Example: First assume that D's estate is $10.0 million, that S has an estate of $1.0 million, and that D dies first, with a marital deduction bequest that equalizes their taxable estates. Compared to an optimum marital deduction approach, the tax computations at the deaths of D followed by S (assuming deaths in 2004, no §2013 previously taxed property credit, and no changes in asset values) would look like:

---

22. Although there may be income tax differences whether this is due to income accumulation or capital appreciation, that factor is not considered because it is uncertain and therefore impossible to quantify. It also does not change the analysis.

Optimum Marital		Equalizer Marital
$10,000,000	D's gross estate	$10,000,000
(8,500,000)	marital deduction	(4,500,000)
1,500,000	D's taxable estate	5,500,000
555,800	tentative estate tax	2,460,800
(555,800)	unified credit	(555,800)
0	D's federal estate tax[†]	1,905,000
$1,500,000	amount of nonmarital trust remaining after D's taxes	$3,595,000

When S later dies:

Optimum Marital		Equalizer Marital
$9,500,000	S's taxable estate	$5,500,000
4,380,800	tentative estate tax	2,460,800
(555,800)	unified credit	(555,800)
3,825,000	S's federal estate tax[†]	1,905,000
3,825,000	total tax for both estates	3,810,000

Compared to the optimum marital results, the equalizer approach generates a $15,000 tax savings over both estates. To appreciate the meaning of this it is important to realize that the saving is attributable to a "full bracket run" and it is better illustrated in the example at page 29, which produces the exact same results. The total saving is attributable to taxing another $500,000 in D's estate and not in S's estate. That is, the saving represents the tax on $500,000 at a 48% flat rate ($240,000) in the estate of S under the optimum approach, compared to the tax on $2.0 million less the tax on $1.5 million ($225,000) in the estate of D under the equalizer approach (that is, the incremental tax on the same $500,000 added on top of the "normal" shelter in 2004 of $1.5 million in D's estate). Given the bracket assumptions, this $15,000 is the maximum saving available by sheltering the full amount that can be taxed at less than 48% in D's estate. In this example we taxed even more in D's estate by equalizing the $11 million between D and S but that does not improve the results, and the important number is the $15,000 saving. This number will change as tax rates fluctuate, but the concept is valid until all taxes become flat or disappear.

> Time-Value Example: Here comes the important point. Many observers assume that if S outlives D by a sufficient period of time, the income earned in the optimum example on the estate tax that would be paid in D's estate in the equalizer example will make up for any differential in tax illustrated in this comparison. Assuming (just to pick a number) a 2% after tax return on the tax deferred under an optimum plan (that is, the income that could be earned on the $1,905,000 of tax that would be paid under this

equalizer plan on D's death), many people would predict that the increase in taxes under the optimum plan would be earned back in less than six months (if S lives that long). And that is just about the time allowed as a survivorship condition under §2056(b)(3).

Naturally the after tax rate of return is not an item that is subject to ready estimation. This is just an illustration based on one arbitrarily selected assumption. In fact, a number of factors are relevant, including S's health and overlife expectancy, the likely after tax return on the $1,905,000 of deferred taxes (which in turn depends on general rates of return and S's income tax bracket), the effect of inflation, appreciation, and income accumulations that will increase (and invasions, consumption, or depreciation that will dissipate) S's estate, and the effect of other credits that may apply in one estate or the other. To minimize the effect of guesswork, the following illustration simply makes life easy by assuming that all the variables come together during the overlife of S, so that between the deaths of D and S all property values double, which reflects the use of the money during S's overlife. The same computations when S later dies now reveal:

Optimum Marital		Equalizer Marital
$9,500,000		$5,500,000
×2		×2
19,000,000	S's taxable estate	11,000,000
8,940,800	tentative estate tax	5,190,800
(555,800)	unified credit[23]	(555,800)
8,385,000	S's federal estate tax†	4,545,000
10,615,000	amount of marital trust remaining after S's taxes	6,455,000
3,000,000	double the amount of nonmarital trust remaining after D's taxes	7,190,000
13,615,000	assets remaining for family	13,645,000

Compared to the optimum marital estate stacking results, the equalizer now generates a savings of $30,000 in tax, which is double the $15,000 saving attributable to the full bracket run in D's estate under the baseline equalizer example.

Notice that the time-value assumption is that the optimum marital approach would be more economical (if S lives long enough and income yield is great enough) by investing the $1,905,000 of tax that would be paid in the equalizer approach to earn back the tax saving. Yet here the

---

23. Again assuming deaths in 2004 now in S's estate. This would produce a §2013 previously taxed property credit that, if illustrated, would preclude an apples to apples comparison. So it is ignored. As discussed beginning at page 32, that added factor would further support the absolute advantage of being in the equalizer column instead of using the optimum approach.

saving was not recovered to yield an overall better result with the optimum marital bequest. Indeed, the saving doubled when the time-value of each approach was reflected. If the wealth involved had tripled to reflect even greater time-value, the saving still would not be earned back. It too would triple.

Put another way, the tax saving in D's estate under an equalizer approach never is earned back under the optimum approach; it increases in value as the wealth itself increases in value, illustrating that the time-value bromide regarding these alternatives is, simply stated, just wrong. This is so critical (and so contrary to many advisors' understanding) that you should stop now and run the numbers personally if you do not believe it. Please be persuaded that the time-value notion regarding deferred payment of taxes may be a viable notion for income tax purposes but it is exactly wrong for wealth transfer tax purposes.[24] Mind you, no one likely will do an equalizer for these savings in this environment. No one would pay $1,905,000 sooner than necessary to save just $15,000, so the object here is to embrace the concept and not the technique for planning in the current posture of most clients.

It absolutely *is* true that the numbers involved are not compelling (in terms of prepayment of tax as against the many reasons to defer) and they decline as the spread in tax rates declines (which occurs as the applicable exclusion amount rises and the maximum rate bracket declines). But these examples *are* persuasive evidence that the time-value concept is not correct. There *are* numerous legitimate reasons to defer the payment of estate tax in the combined estates of D and S, such as lack of liquidity or fear about too little wealth remaining for S to live on. But a decision to defer taxes through use of an optimum marital bequest cannot be supported economically by the time-value notion. That is the most important lesson of this illustration.

Selective facts may create more compelling cases for prepayment or deferral. For example, an estate with great but only select income generation or appreciation potential raises new considerations that require an analysis of D's portfolio and whether there are sufficient nonappreciating assets to pay the tax incurred at D's death in a less than optimum bequest situation. This is because use of "hot" (highly appreciating) assets to pay the tax in D's estate reduces the resulting savings, as illustrated again by two examples:

> All Hot Example: D's estate of $10.0 million consists entirely of highly appreciating assets. D's estate does not qualify for the marital deduction and pays tax of $4,065,000, leaving $5,935,000

---

24. See Pennell & Williamson, *The Economics of Prepaying Wealth Transfer Tax*, 136 TRUSTS & ESTATES 49-60 (June 1997), 40-51 (July 1997), and 52-56 (August 1997), abridged and reprinted in 52 J. FIN. SERV. PROFS. 62 (Nov. 1998) and 53 J. FIN. SERV. PROFS. 42 (Jan. 1999).

in a nonmarital trust. If that balance doubles in value during S's overlife, $11,870,000 would remain at S's death, with no more wealth transfer tax to be paid.[25] If, instead, D's estate paid no tax at D's death and the entire $10.0 million doubled in value during S's overlife, a tax of $8,865,000 would be incurred on the $20.0 million includible in S's estate at death, leaving $11,135,000 after S's death. The issue then would be whether $735,000 in value saved by paying tax at D's death is significant compared to the lost use of $4,065,000 in tax dollars paid at D's death and the loss of a basis adjustment when S dies.

Half Hot Example: The economics would be more compelling, however, if D had paid the tax with assets that would not have grown in value, to protect appreciating assets from later tax. To wit, assume D's $10.0 million estate consists of equal parts of highly appreciating and nonappreciating assets. Again, D's estate does not qualify for the marital deduction and pays the same $4,065,000 of tax, leaving $5,935,000 in a nonmarital trust. Assuming the tax was paid at D's death using nonappreciating property, the full $5.0 million of appreciating assets remaining (part of the $5,935,000 left after tax payment) would double in value, so $10,935,000 would remain after S's death, after all tax is paid. If D's estate had paid no tax at D's death and the full $10.0 million estate had grown to $15.0 million (half would double, half would remain the same value), only $8,535,000 would remain after paying the $6,465,000 tax on the $15.0 million of value that would be included in S's estate at death. This $2.47 million differential may be more attractive to D in terms of prepaying the $4,065,000 in tax at D's death rather than at S's death, especially because the assets used to pay that tax would not appreciate during S's overlife.

Thus, if D's estate has a ready source of funds (such as an insurance trust that will collect the cash proceeds of insurance on D's life or other nonappreciating liquid assets), the situation may be ripe for the payment of some tax at D's death to shelter appreciating assets during S's overlife. And oh, by the way, now you see a good reason why insurance on D's life may be preferable to survivor life insurance for a married couple! See Chapter 9 at pages 7-8.

---

25. A capital gains tax may be incurred on a subsequent realization event because, as nonmarital property that is not includible in S's gross estate at death, this property will not receive a new basis to eliminate that appreciation for future income tax purposes. The significance of this factor is uncertain because S's beneficiaries may never sell the asset or may do so when there are losses to offset against the gain, and Congress may repeal §1014 before S dies (while freezing the repeal of the estate tax, leaving both to contend with), denying the basis adjustment even in the optimum marital situation.

Analysis of "Six Month Equalizer" Plan

The prior examples show that a plan that equalizes the spouses' taxable estates or tax brackets generates greater tax savings over both estates than does deferral of tax under the optimum marital bequest approach. Although there are many legitimate noneconomic reasons to defer the tax nevertheless, they are not very compelling if S does not outlive D for at least the six months that §2056(b)(3) permits as a survivorship contingency. This leads to a "six month equalizer" variation on optimum marital bequest planning that employs the following form of provision:

> **If S survives me, I give to S the smallest pecuniary amount**[26] **that, if allowed as a federal estate tax marital deduction, would result in the least possible federal estate tax being payable by reason of my death, reduced (but only if S is not living on the 180th day after my death) by the smallest amount that will cause the estate of S and my estate to be taxed in the same marginal federal estate tax bracket, determined as if S had died immediately after my death and [his/her] estate were valued as of the date on, and in the manner in, which my estate is valued for federal estate tax purposes.**
>
> **My executor shall accept the statement of S or [his/her] legal representative as to all information required in complying with this provision, without inquiring into any such information, and my executor's administration hereunder based on such information shall not be subject to question by any beneficiary. In determining the pecuniary amount my personal representative shall consider the credit or the deduction for state death taxes only to the extent those taxes are not thereby incurred or increased and shall assume that none of the payments and devises under the preceding articles of this will qualify for a federal estate tax deduction.**
>
> **For purposes of this gift, S shall be deemed to have survived me if S and I die under such circumstances that there is no sufficient evidence to establish the order of our deaths.**

This provision gives S an equalizer marital deduction amount if S survives D (and S is presumed to survive D in the simultaneous death situation) and gives S the *additional* amount needed to increase the bequest to the optimum tax deferring marital bequest if S survives D by at least six months (the maximum condition of survival that D could impose under §2056(b)(3) without losing the deduction for that added amount). Some

---

26. Although a pecuniary marital approach is illustrated here, a fractional marital approach also could be utilized.

people would regard there to be some risk involved in this optimizing bequest because S may die more than six months after D but before use of the tax dollars deferred earns enough return to make deferral of tax worthwhile. If that is a perceived problem, the planner may rely on postmortem planning through disclaimer or a partial QTIP election to effect the right sized marital deduction (with timely action within nine months or as much as 15 months, respectively, after D's death). Partial QTIP election planning is discussed beginning at page 64.

Notice that, unlike the illustration in the Baseline Example at page 23, the provision here illustrated does not equalize the *size* of D and S's taxable *estates*. Instead, this provision equalizes the marginal estate tax *bracket* in which each estate is taxed, which represents a better compromise that generates the largest marital deduction consistent with the most deferral of tax. It is a favored result because it produces the same taxes over both estates (if no growth or income accumulation is considered) but it entails far less tax payment at D's death.[27]

> Example: D and S have estates of $10.0 million and $1.0 million, respectively. A formula bracket equalizer marital bequest taxes $2.0 million[28] at D's death and the balance of the aggregate wealth at S's later death, generating the least tax over both estates consistent with maximum deferral of tax payment, as illustrated in the following computation:
>
> | | |
> |---|---|
> | $10,000,000 | D's gross estate |
> | (8,000,000) | marital deduction |
> | 2,000,000 | D's taxable estate |
> | 780,800 | tentative estate tax |
> | (555,800) | unified credit |
> | 225,000 | D's federal estate tax payable[†] |
> | 1,775,000 | amount of nonmarital trust after D's taxes |
>
> When S later dies:
>
> | | |
> |---|---|
> | $9,000,000 | S's taxable estate |
> | 4,140,800 | tentative estate tax |
> | (555,800) | unified credit |
> | 3,585,000 | S's federal estate tax payable[†] |

Total tax over both estates is still $3,810,000, which represents the same total savings of $15,000 over an optimum marital bequest approach (as illustrated in the Baseline Example at page 23).

---

27. Another alternative may be used, causing both estates to pay the same amount of tax, in cases in which absolute equality of the tax burden is desired (for example, if the estates pass to different beneficiaries after the respective spouses' deaths).

28. This figure is chosen on the assumption that the maximum estate tax rate is 48%, beginning at $2.0 million in 2004.

This bracket equalizer is preferable to the bequest equalizing the taxable estates because, although the aggregate tax paid over both estates is the same, the timing of the payments differs: the bracket equalizer defers until S's death $1,680,000 of the tax that would have been due at D's death under the taxable estate equalizer. Moreover, it is just as desirable if all the wealth doubles during S's overlife, as illustrated by the following time-value variation showing the tax at S's subsequent death:

$9,000,000	
×2	
18,000,000	S's taxable estate
8,460,800	tentative base estate tax
(555,800)	unified credit
7,905,000	S's federal estate tax payable[†]
10,095,000	amount of marital trust remaining after S's taxes
1,775,000	
×2	
3,550,000	double the amount of nonmarital trust remaining after D's taxes
13,645,000	assets remaining for family

This approach represents a savings of $30,000 over the optimum approach illustrated at page 25, which is the same savings from the full bracket run in D's estate. There is no detriment in total tax saved and, with more inclusion in S's gross estate, more new basis at S's death probably is an overall benefit. See page 32.

Because a bracket equalizer provision produces the same taxes as a bequest that equalizes the size of the two estates, the bracket equalizer generally makes better sense because $1,680,000 less tax is paid at D's death. Stated succinctly, this bracket equalizer marital bequest benefits D's estate by combining maximum deferral with taxation at the less than maximum marginal estate tax brackets to the fullest extent possible, by sheltering $2.0 million at D's death in 2004

The saving attributable to taxing an additional $500,000 (compared to an optimum marital sheltering only $1.5 million) in D's estate is a maximum of $15,000 (using the 2004 applicable exclusion amount and tax rates), based on the assumption that this additional amount would be taxed in the 48% bracket in S's estate if an optimum marital formula bequest were used. Avoiding any further tax in D's estate is preferable after reaching this $2.0 million breakpoint, because it defers until S's death all tax at the maximum marginal tax rate and permits more property to qualify for new-basis-at-death treatment by inclusion in S's gross estate. No further rate reduction would be achieved by a marital bequest intended to equalize either the estates or the taxes paid.

All of these examples assume that each estate will reach the highest marginal estate tax rate, but the theory behind bracket equalizer marital bequest planning holds true regardless of the marginal rates that actually apply in the estates of D and S. Only the maximum tax savings involved will differ. The ability to save taxes is maximized in all cases to the extent the equalizer marital bequest causes D to be taxed in the same marginal bracket as S. That saving is unaffected by appreciation if the property would appreciate at the same rate in either a marital or nonmarital trust, if appreciating assets must be used to pay the tax, and if the marginal rates remain the same.[29]

Another potential benefit of this planning is that the use of an equalizer provision does not require an educated guess regarding which spouse will die first. To illustrate, if D had a $2.0 million estate and S had a $10.0 million estate, and D died first, the equalizer estate tax computations in D's estate would be:

Optimum Marital		Equalizer Marital
$2,000,000	D's gross estate	$2,000,000
(500,000)	marital deduction	(0)
1,500,000	D's taxable estate	2,000,000
555,800	tentative estate tax	780,800
(555,800)	unified credit	(555,800)
0	D's federal estate tax[†]	225,000
When S later dies:		
$10,500,000	S's taxable estate	$10,000,000
4,860,800	tentative estate tax	4,620,800
(555,800)	unified credit	(555,800)
4,305,000	S's federal estate tax[†]	4,065,000
4,305,000	total tax for both estates	4,290,000

Again, an optimum marital deduction provision produces more aggregate tax than if D's estate qualified for no marital deduction at all (which is the closest D and S can come to an equalizer approach here). And again, if an optimum marital plan is desirable notwithstanding the tax differential, it certainly is not if S fails to survive D by at least six months. So an optimum marital deduction with a six month equalizer is the desirable plan if an optimum marital is to be used at all.

Finally, note that, even if both spouses' estates would be taxable in the highest marginal estate tax bracket, regardless of their disparate sizes, it

---

29. For example, if D's estate is $2x and the marginal estate tax rate is 48%, with no marital bequest a tax of $.96x could be paid presently, leaving $1.04x in a nonmarital trust during S's overlife. Alternatively, the $2x could be made to qualify for the marital deduction and the $.96x of tax could be paid at S's death, leaving the same $1.04x after S's death. If the $2x triples in value during S's overlife, $6x at S's death would incur $2.88x of tax, leaving $3.12x after S's death. Had the tax been paid at D's death, the remaining $1.04x in the nonmarital trust would have tripled to the same $3.12x at S's later death.

still may make sense to forego an optimum marital bequest in D's estate. Although both estates incur tax in the highest marginal bracket, the average rate of tax is less if they are taxed separately than if one estate is added to the other and the second estate is taxed entirely in the highest marginal bracket. This will remain true until the estate tax loses its progressivity because maximum tax rates have dropped and the applicable exclusion amount has risen to produce a flat tax, as slated to occur after 2005. Thus, it may pay to push a pencil to compare tax saved by equalization (versus simple optimization), to consider whether an equalizer is preferable, and to evaluate the true value of deferring all taxes until the death of S. Indeed, the major point of all these illustrations is to highlight the need to make some calculations rather than making assumptions or, worse, employing the same approach in every situation without careful consideration of each case.

Basis Concerns

One reality is that modest transfer tax savings usually are not enough to encourage most taxpayers to prepay any tax. In addition, these transfer tax savings also must be discounted by any capital gains tax that would be incurred if a sale in the future caused a realization of appreciation that a §1014 basis adjustment would eliminate if that property was includible in S's gross estate (because it qualified for the marital deduction in D's estate). This is quite an imponderable due to guesswork regarding the timing of any potential realization event, the rate of tax that might apply at that time, and the possibility that the spouse will die after repeal of the estate tax and, with it, repeal of the new-basis-at-death rule of §1014 as well.[30] You can see that any discussion about paying tax in D's estate probably is totally academic (meaning a waste of time) in virtually all cases. So the benefit of the foregoing is (1) educational (you know what really is going on) and (2) so you don't make representations that are wrong and get you sued, for doing the right thing perhaps but for wrong reasons that are documented in your letter to D and S, found in their files by their ultimate beneficiaries after both are gone.

Using the Previously Taxed Property Credit

Notwithstanding the last reality, one circumstance that flows from our prior discussion also arises often enough that you need to understand it. Postmortem planning of the size of the marital deduction should consider the effect of a §2013 credit for previously taxed property.[31] To illustrate

---

30. Carryover of basis in §1022 takes the place of new-basis-at-death in §1014 if the estate tax repeal becomes effective (in 2010). But transfers between spouses (either outright or in a QTIP format) qualify for a $3.0 million increase in basis entitlement (not $3.0 million of property with a basis equal to fair market value but an addition to basis of $3.0 million, allocated as the personal representative chooses among qualifying properties).

31. It is more complex, but in substance §2013 provides that any tax paid by D's estate on property that is includible in S's gross estate within 10 years later becomes a credit against S's estate tax payment.

why, consider the example of Technical Advice Memorandum 8512004, in which D's will bequeathed to S an amount equal to the maximum marital deduction allowable to D's estate, and bequeathed D's residuary estate to a nonmarital trust that gave S an income interest for life. S died three months after D, from causes not foreseeable at D's death. S's personal representative disclaimed the marital deduction bequest and D's entire estate passed under D's residuary clause to the nonmarital trust. Thus, a marital deduction was not available to D's estate. Aggregate estate taxes over both estates were minimized, however, because the estate tax generated in D's estate generated a §2013 credit available in S's estate.

S's income interest in the nonmarital trust was the previously taxed property that qualified for a §2013 credit, notwithstanding that no part of the corpus of that trust was includible in S's gross estate at death.[32] Under the actuarial tables, the value of S's life income interest (and the §2013 credit based thereon) far exceeded the income S actually received during the three months S survived D. Nevertheless, S's estate was able to maximize the credit at a nominal cost because use of the §7520 valuation tables is required unless S's death is clearly imminent due to an incurable physical condition that was known at D's death,[33] *and* S's life expectancy is used rather than S's actual overlife.

Example: D had an estate of $3.0 million and S had an estate of $1.5 million. S died within nine months after D's death (both in 2004) but, because S was not terminally ill when D died, valuation of S's life estate in D's property was based on the actuarial tables, as required by §7520 and Treas. Reg. §20.7520-3(b)(3).

Optimum Marital		§2013 Maximizing Marital
$3,000,000	D's gross estate	3,000,000
(1,500,000)	marital deduction	(532,268)
1,500,000	D's taxable estate	2,467,732
0	D's federal estate tax	449,511.30
3,000,000	S's taxable estate	2,032,268
705,000	S's tax B4 §2013 credit	240,488.64
(0)	§2013 credit	(240,488.54)
705,000	S's tax after §2013 credit	.10
705,000	tax over both estates	449,511.40

---

32. In essence both the income and remainder interests in the trust were taxed in D's estate, and the income interest inflated S's net worth, so it alone is deemed to be includible in S's subsequent estate.

33. See Treas. Reg. §20.7520-3(b)(3), which mandates use of the standard tables unless the individual who is the measuring life is terminally ill (meaning that the individual is known to have an incurable illness or other deteriorating physical condition and there is at least a 50% probability of death within one year).

In this case D and S saved $255,488.60 in tax paid over both estates as compared to an optimum marital result. That is a 36% tax saving, representing almost 5.7% of the aggregate wealth of D and S.

This planning requires some balancing to ensure that S has sufficient assets to generate enough tax to consume the §2013 credit produced from the tax on D's estate, and D's taxable estate is large enough to produce enough tax to generate the necessary credit. Several computations may be needed to strike the proper balance, and more computational complexity will be encountered if a state death tax is involved.[34]

Estate planners face difficult decisions in postmortem planning that incurs an estate tax in the estate of D to produce a §2013 credit in S's estate. That particularly is true today as marital deduction planning is done with one eye on whether S may outlive repeal of the estate tax and the other eye on whether S is likely to die within the §2013 ten year window after D's death. Moreover, drafting bypass trusts requires a decision whether to provide that S will receive all income annually (thereby qualifying for the §2013 credit if death occurs within 10 years after D), or to provide for an income spray to reduce S's income and estate tax liability and to permit other family planning uses of bypass trust income during S's overlife.

With the current compressed income tax rates, the real factor to consider in deciding which approach to follow is the increase in S's gross estate attributable to payment of all income to S annually, which may be an insignificant factor if S is expected to die within the 10 year §2013 period or after the year 2010 promised repeal of the estate tax. In addition, S may be able to make gifts of excess income to prevent bloating S's gross estate, or the trustee may be able to engineer the income yield in the trust with proper investments under the prudent investor rules. Moreover, granting S a five or five withdrawal power in the trust can significantly increase the value of S's interest for §2013 purposes, in some cases by as much as an additional 10%

A Note About Formula Clauses and Computations

Estate planners have drafted prolix, convoluted formula marital bequests since 1948. In most cases, provisions calling for a bequest of a

---

34. Assuming S's life estate is worth $1,079,748 (53.5%) in the $2,018,221 nonmarital trust after paying $449,511 in tax. The assumptions underlying this computation will change monthly with the §7520 interest rate and annually with S's age. To make this hypothetical computation the assumptions made were that S is age 77, the §7520 rate is 4.2%, and S is given a five or five power of withdrawal over the nonmarital trust.

Notice that no state death tax, nor the §2011 state death tax credit or §2058 state death tax deduction, is reflected in this calculation, on the theory that — at least under a pickup tax regime — there should be no state death tax if there is no federal estate tax payable after the §2013 credit is applied. That concept is not universally accepted, but was recognized as proper by *In re* Estate of Lacks, 662 N.W.2d 54 (Mi. Ct. App. 2003); Riethmann Trust v. Director of Revenue, 62 S.W.3d 46 (Mo. 2001); Estate of Turner v. Washington State Dep't of Revenue, 724 P.2d 1013 (Washington 1986); and Dickinson v. Maurer, 229 So. 2d 247 (Fla. 1969).

specific dollar amount, specified assets, or a preordained fraction are not sufficiently precise to generate the proper-sized deduction. In some cases, it is advisable to make a few specific bequests to direct distribution of certain assets to particular beneficiaries. Otherwise, the use of a specific provision is too imprecise, given the effect of other qualifying assets, valuation changes, and elections affecting the size of the marital bequest desired, equitable apportionment that may alter the size of the probate estate, and other unpredictables (such as adoption of new tax laws).

Therefore, a formula marital bequest is the appropriate approach in virtually all situations, the real issue being which of several formulas to use. At one time some planners felt comfortable using a "laundry list" approach. They would create a formula itemizing all factors that would affect the ultimate computation of the desired marital deduction. This approach involved substantial complexity, requiring a provision that anticipated at least the following items: (1) the effect and changing valuation of all relevant credits; (2) the effect of all tax elections that may be made; (3) the possibility that S or some other beneficiary may make a qualified disclaimer; (4) the computation of offsets for other qualifying assets passing to S, including some direction as to how the determination is to be made if any part of a nonmarital trust could be elected for QTIP treatment; (5) the effect of §2032(b)(2), which prevents recognition of any changes in asset values prior to satisfaction of the marital bequest that are attributable to the lapse of time or the (non)occurrence of any contingency; (6) the effect of other deductions allowed to the estate (§2053, §2054, §2055, §2057 before its repeal, or §2058 after repeal of the §2011 state death tax credit); and (7) the effect of gifts made during life. In addition, the provision had to specify: (8) which values are to be used for all these computations (those initially reported on the federal estate tax return, those finally accepted for federal estate tax purposes, or some other values); and (9) whether §2032 alternate or §2032A special use valuations are to affect the computation.

The risk of error in creating such a list, and the possibility that changes in the law would require document modification to ensure preservation of the original intent, probably speak against the use of this approach. In the current legislative world, it is difficult to draft a formula provision (marital deduction or otherwise) that effectively anticipates all the factors that should be considered, thus making "laundry list" itemized approaches to drafting a dangerous endeavor.

Some planners are content to use a "maximum marital deduction" provision with a "cut back" clause designed to reduce the marital bequest to the optimum, equalized, or other marital deduction desired amount. This approach may require addition of a provision specifying that available elections in estate administration (for example, alternate valuation, §642(g) income or estate tax deduction, or §2032A special use valuation elections) need not be exercised so as to maximize the estate to "maximize" the marital deduction as well.

It also may be fair to suggest that a cut back provision is harder for a client to understand, even though it is a more complete description of the various steps taken to arrive at the size of the marital bequest. Further, care must be taken in using a cut back clause to state accurately the amount of reduction desired. For example, it is not appropriate to reduce the maximum amount by that amount, if any, that "will reduce taxes paid to zero" because it may not be possible to minimize taxes to that extent.

Many planners therefore use a "fudge" formula that simply describes the desired objective: usually to generate the smallest marital deduction necessary to reduce taxes (federal and sometimes state, although that is very difficult to predict) to the lowest possible amount. This may be the safest approach and it certainly is the easiest to explain to the client, and for the client to understand. It may not, however, be the most palatable psychologically to S, to whom the message is abundantly clear that D "loves you very much, dear, but as my estate plan I leave you the absolute smallest possible amount necessary to generate a tax motivated result." Hopefully, both spouses adequately understand the plan, and the nonmarital trust is sufficiently generous, to avoid any negative impressions this message otherwise might generate.

A fudge formula also assumes that the fiduciary administering the plan will have the acumen to determine the appropriate bequest, considering the myriad factors that can affect the size of the deduction, and that no conflict of interest will interfere with a proper determination of that amount. It seems appropriate to suggest that a fiduciary should not be selected if there is any legitimate doubt about these qualifications, but the reality is that D may have no (or is not willing to consider) other options.

Regardless of the economic arguments that favor payment of some tax in D's estate, most marital deduction bequests are of the optimum deduction variety, sometimes with a six month equalizer, often planned with the possibility of disclaimer or a partial QTIP election for postmortem adjustment. There are, however, at least half a dozen special situations in which the size of the appropriate deduction will be affected by other forms of tax conscious planning. The planner should keep in mind, however, that family planning considerations, rather than taxes, may dictate an entirely different result, notwithstanding the clear tax benefits otherwise available. Most of these other alternatives are way too complex to dig into here, but two deserve some consideration.

Generation-Skipping Transfer Tax Exemption

The §2631 exemption from the generation-skipping transfer tax (GST) available to all transferors is an extremely important entitlement that affects marital deduction planning.

Example: D and S collectively own property of more than $3.0 million in 2004 and wish to create typical optimum marital deduction plans. After S's death the marital trust created by D will pour over into the nonmarital trust, which is a generation-skipping trust for their children and grandchildren. They must decide how to maximize their respective exemptions.

Upon S's death, all the marital trust that is includible in S's gross estate normally is treated as S's property for GST purposes. §2652(a)(1)(A). Thus, with a traditional optimum marital deduction plan, only the property originally placed in the nonmarital trust (usually no more than the applicable exclusion amount) would be treated as D's property for purposes of allocating D's GST exemption. Therefore, any excess of D's exemption would be wasted. The GST exemption and the applicable exclusion amount became the same in 2004, but the nonmarital trust may not fully shelter D's GST exemption because of erosions to the applicable exclusion amount that did not consume any GST exemption, such as inter vivos, testamentary, or nonprobate transfers that do not skip generations, or nondeductible charges in D's estate administration.

One option to avoid wasting any of D's GST exemption is to allocate a larger amount to a nonmarital trust at D's death than just the applicable exclusion amount. The notion is to place an amount in the nonmarital trust that, after incurring federal and state estate taxes on the nonmarital trust amount, would leave a balance that could be sheltered forever (along with any appreciation thereon) by D's full GST exemption.

Congress was aware, however, that the typical client will not opt to prepay any part of the wealth transfer tax in this manner and therefore that most taxpayers will not shelter the full GST exemption in a nonmarital trust if deferral of tax is available through use of the marital deduction. Congress therefore provided an election that allows D to create a QTIP marital deduction trust, allocate any part or all of D's GST exemption to it, and overcome the §2652(a)(1)(A) rule that treats S as the transferor for GST purposes after inclusion of the QTIP trust in S's gross estate. Under §2652(a)(3), D is regarded as the transferor of marital trust property, notwithstanding its subsequent inclusion in S's estate, to the extent a "reverse QTIP" election is made. Thus, if the GST exemption amount and the applicable exclusion amount do not coincide after 2003, reverse QTIP planning is available.

Certain requirements must be met to make this election, the most important being that D must use the §2056(b)(7) QTIP form of marital deduction trust, which may not be the best (or even an acceptable) approach. The point is simply that D must choose among several perhaps unattractive alternatives or lose the benefit of some or all of the GST exemption.

Administration Expenses and the "Swing Item" Election

The other important concept relates to administration expenses that fall under the income tax deduction rules (including end of life health care costs and fees paid to personal representatives, attorneys, appraisers, etc.).[35] These can be taken as deductions against the estate tax under §2053 or against the estate's income tax, but they cannot be used for both purposes (unless they constitute §691(b) deductions in respect of a decedent. §642(g)). The income tax deduction is forfeited to the extent the expenses are allowed for §2053 purposes.

In an "optimum" marital deduction estate plan that is designed to reduce estate taxes to zero, there is a commonly accepted wisdom to use these "swing item" deductions on the estate's income tax return. This is because use as an estate tax deduction does not save estate taxes; the marital deduction eliminates all estate taxes anyway. Thus, the only perceived effect of taking these items as an estate tax deduction under §2053 is to reduce the size of the marital bequest and failure to take the swing items as income tax deductions is seen by some planners as "throwing away a deduction." With this in mind, the decision for these planners is to use the swing items as an income tax deduction, allowing the marital bequest to remain unreduced but reducing income taxes that usually are payable from the nonmarital share of the estate.

This "accepted wisdom" may backfire in many larger estates, however. Imagine a situation in which there is no nonmarital portion of the estate, because the unified credit has been consumed by gifts made during life, by nonprobate property passing to persons other than S at death, or because the nonmarital property was consumed by federal or state death taxes. Because there is no nonmarital property, actual payment of the swing items reduces the *estate* that is available for distribution, which effectively reduces the amount available for the marital deduction.

The marital deduction may equal the fund that actually remains when administration is completed, but only if the swing items are claimed as an estate tax deduction. In that case federal estate taxes will be zero. If, however, these items are claimed as an income tax deduction, the marital deduction needed to eliminate taxes may be larger than the amount of estate property that actually remains available for funding the marital bequest. As a result, the marital deduction allowed will be limited to the amount actually passing as the marital bequest (after payment of the swing items), and estate taxes will be incurred because the marital deduction will not be large enough to reduce the taxable estate to zero.

The election also should be considered carefully in less dramatic situations. Taking the swing items as an income tax deduction will produce an immediate tax benefit, but at a cost of reducing the amount of

---

35. See §§162, 163, 212, and 213.

nonmarital property and increasing the amount exposed to tax on S's death, as illustrated by a simple example that assumes a 2004 decedent (so the unified credit will shelter $1.5 million of property includible in the estate) with a $1,750,000 gross estate that paid $50,000 of swing item expenses that can be deducted on the estate's estate tax return under §2053 or on the estate's income tax return by making the §642(g) election:

Deduct Under §2053		Deduct Under §642(g)
$1,750,000	gross estate	$1,750,000
(50,000)	swing items	0
(200,000)	marital bequest	(250,000)
1,500,000	taxable estate	1,500,000
1,500,000	nonmarital property	1,450,000

As this illustration shows, the marital bequest needed to produce a taxable estate as to which no estate tax actually will be paid would differ, based on the election made by the personal representative.[36]

In many cases, the assumption is that the benefit of an immediate income tax deduction will outweigh the detriment of a larger amount being exposed to estate tax when S transfers the property, because a deferral element is involved: the estate may invest and enjoy the income tax saved for the entire overlife of S. As already illustrated, that time-value-of-money notion is not correct. Thus, if the marginal income tax rate is lower than the marginal estate tax rate that will apply when S is exposed to tax, reduction of the marital bequest by claiming the swing items for estate tax purposes will produce a larger overall tax saving than taking these items as income tax deductions.[37] The imponderable in all this is whether S will outlive repeal of the estate tax, slated to occur in 2010, or whether restoration of the tax will occur in 2011. There also is an added complexity imposed by a set of regulations that address an important but very involved bit of postmortem administration that need not concern us here but that experienced estate planners consider as part of their marital deduction planning.[38]

At bottom, this segment illustrates the importance of the marital deduction to estate planning, as well as the surprising complexities that

---

36. This is one of the effects of §642(g) that leads to the do not adjustment provision described in Chapter 11 at page 48. To avoid the need to make any kind of adjustment to compensate for the consequences of the swing item election, the fiduciary should be given authority to elect either approach and probably should be *directed* to make no compensating adjustments. See the provision at page 66 to this effect.

37. Further, it might be wise to claim all the deductions under §2053 if a portion of the deductions will be lost for income tax purposes under §67(e), because the "lost" amount alone cannot be used on the estate tax return. Cf. Rev. Rul. 77-357 (involving lost deductions under the percentage floor provisions of §213).

38. See 3 Casner & Pennell, Estate Planning §13.3.6 (6th ed. 2001), dealing with Estate of Hubert v. Commissioner, 101 T.C. 314 (1993) (a 14 to 2 reviewed opinion), aff'd, 63 F.3d 1083 (11th Cir. 1995), aff'd, 520 U.S. 93 (1997), and its progeny and attendant fallout in Treas. Reg. §20.2056(b)-4(d)(5).

enter into any determination of the appropriate amount of deduction in various situations. All of the planning noted in this segment requires some ability to model and project taxes over two estates, considering such imponderables as income yield, growth, tax rates, life expectancy, and the wisdom of various postmortem elections.

Even for a math wizard, these comparisons could not be performed economically on a hand-held calculator, which probably explains why many estate planners in the past did not do them at all. Many planners find that they need the help of computer-generated projections to consider properly all the known factors. A number of very good software programs are available to users of relatively inexpensive computer hardware,[39] allowing any computer literate estate planner to insert a limited amount of information, make selected assumptions, and produce illustrations that will permit the client to make judgments based on expectations that the client believes are realistic. The result may be that the client still opts for maximum deferral of tax notwithstanding economies that indicate prepayment would be favorable. But that conclusion ought to be an informed decision made by the client, not a default choice made by the planner without modeling and evaluating the alternatives.

Marital Deduction Qualification

Only four forms of disposition could be employed before 1982 to qualify for the federal estate or gift tax marital deduction:

(1) outright transfers;

(2) §§2056(b)(5) and 2523(e) general power of appointment trusts;

(3) §2056(b)(6) life insurance settlements; and

(4) so-called estate trusts.

All four still qualify for the marital deduction but each grants S unfettered dispositive control over the marital deduction property. This control was considered "acceptable" before 1982 but changed when Congress made it possible for D's entire estate to qualify for the marital deduction. Thus, in 1981 Congress made the tax deferral benefits of the marital deduction available for dispositions in which D does not give dispositive control over marital deduction property to S.

Congress illustrated its concern about S's control over marital deduction property with an example of a decedent with children by a former marriage. H.R. Rep. No. 201, 97th Cong., 1st Sess. 160 (1981). The

---

39. See Evans, WILLS, TRUSTS, AND TECHNOLOGY: AN ESTATE LAWYER'S GUIDE TO AUTOMATION, (2d ed. 2004). Often the best sources of information about available software are periodic software reviews that regularly appear in trade journals such as Estate Planning, Probate & Property, Trusts & Estates, CCH Journal of Practical Estate Planning, and internet web sites (which evolve or change over time). See, e.g., evans-legal.com/dan; members.iex.net/~jghodges; lawofficecomputing.com; sohoconsumer.com/legal_sw.htm; abanet.org/rppt/committees/pt/k2/ home.hmt; and sites with links to other sites, such as legaline.com/estate.htm; and taxsites.com/.

report recognized that S could disinherit D's children if the plan had to give S unfettered power to dispose of the marital bequest, which Congress envisioned could be D's entire estate. Thus, Congress adopted the §§2056(b)(7) and 2523(f) QTIP form of marital transfer to avoid this potential problem. The marital deduction now is available for a trust (or legal life estate) that gives S an income interest for life, with the remainder passing on S's death to beneficiaries D selected, free from any control by S. In essence, this was the same form of trust that §§2056(b)(5) and 2523(e) already authorized but without the requisite general power of appointment.

The QTIP form of disposition would not qualify for the marital deduction absent §§2056(b)(7) and 2523(f); it would violate the nondeductible terminable interest rules of §§2056(b) and 2523(b) because S's interest terminates at death. A number of unique planning options are available *only* to QTIP trusts (the partial QTIP election, the reverse QTIP election, a valuation discount for certain fractional interests, and the $3.0 million §1022(c) increase in carryover basis provisions). As a result, QTIP trusts have become the preferred form of disposition if a trust is desired, although there are situations in which other forms of qualifying marital transfer may be preferable. Consequently, the advantages and disadvantages of each qualifying form of transfer must be evaluated. First below, however, is a quick summary of other basic requirements to qualify for the marital deduction.

Three essential requirements must be met for an interest to qualify for the §2056 estate tax marital deduction:

(1) D must be survived by a United States citizen spouse;

(2) the interest must be includible in D's United States gross estate and pass to S; and

(3) the interest must not be a nondeductible terminable interest.

The first two of these requirements are relatively simple and have no counterpart for gift tax purposes, but the nondeductible terminable interest rule presents significant estate and gift tax complexity, to which a significant degree of attention must be devoted.

Survivorship

Actual survival for however short a period will suffice, *if* it can be proven. A presumption that the spouse survived, whether supplied by local law or by the governing instrument, will be respected if the order of the spouses' deaths cannot be established by proof.[40] This deemed survivorship result applies, however, only to the extent the deductible

---

40. Referred to by many people as "simultaneous death," even though the deaths may occur over some time but still under circumstances that preclude proof of the order of death.

property will be includible in the deemed survivor's gross estate. Treas. Reg. §20.2056(c)-2(e).

Under most states' version of the Uniform Simultaneous Death Act, if two persons die under circumstances such that the order of their deaths cannot be established by proof, each decedent's property is distributed as though that person were the survivor. Thus, neither spouse's property would pass to the other.[41] The Uniform Simultaneous Death Act creates the wrong result if it is important to secure the marital deduction in the estate of one of the spouses (usually the wealthy or "propertied" spouse). Thus, a provision that reverses the Act should be used in that spouse's estate plan, reading something like:

For purposes of [this will] [the marital deduction gift made in Article *], S shall be deemed to have survived me if the order of our deaths cannot be proved.

Some drafters, probably informed by §2056(b)(3)(A), refer to deaths "as a result of a common disaster resulting in the death" of both spouses. This is *not* good drafting, because a presumption of survivorship in this situation may not be respected.

To illustrate, assume that both D and S were injured in the same automobile accident, with D dying immediately and S lingering before dying. Here the "common disaster" provision would be met but any presumption that D survived would be ineffective for federal estate tax purposes because the actual order of their deaths could be proved. See Treas. Reg. §20.2056(c)-2(e) (first sentence) and Estate of Gordon v. Commissioner, 70 T.C. 404 (1978) (allowing the deduction but analyzing the issue fully). The document for S might leave property to D, but no marital deduction would be allowed. Further, a "common disaster" provision may raise problems of construction as to whether the deaths were the result of a common disaster or, instead, were from independent causes (for example, S died of cardiac arrest on the way to the hospital after suffering non-life-threatening injuries in the same car crash that killed D).

In addition, care must be exercised to ensure that both spouses use consistent presumptions (both should not presume the other to have survived except in unusual cases or if each employs an equalizer provision) and that the presumptions are in the proper documents (for

---

41. The object of the Uniform Simultaneous Death Act is to avoid subjecting either spouse's property to administration or taxation in more than one estate. Thus, jointly owned property is deemed to be held by the spouses in equal shares as tenants in common, with each spouse's share passing as if the other spouse were the first to die, and life insurance proceeds are paid as if the beneficiary predeceased the insured. The Uniform Simultaneous Death Act has been supplanted by a "120-hour" rule in states that have enacted the Uniform Probate Code. This newer rule requires an heir or beneficiary to survive the decedent by 120 hours, absent a will provision requiring the beneficiary to survive the testator by some other period. UPC §§2-104 and 2-601 (1998) (§§2-104 and 2-702 in the 1990 version).

example, a will provision probably would not govern a dispositive direction in an inter vivos trust, and vice versa).

The Interest Must Be "Deductible"

In addition to making certain that the taxpayer's spouse is a United States citizen (or planning with a qualified domestic trust, a topic that we will address beginning at page 77), the most important requirement to qualify for the marital deduction is that the interest passing to S must be "deductible." Any interest is deductible unless it falls into one of several categories of nondeductible interests. Treas. Reg. §20.2056(a)-2(b).[42]

Inclusion in Decedent's Gross Estate

An interest is nondeductible to the extent that it is not includible in D's gross estate. Treas. Reg. §20.2056(a)-2(b)(1). This test is a counterpart of the "passing" requirement under §2056(c) that also requires the interest to be includible in D's gross estate. An interesting way to consider the nature of this rule is illustrated by Lake Shore Nat'l Bank v. Coyle, 296 F. Supp. 412 (N.D. Ill. 1968), rev'd on other grounds, 419 F.2d 958 (7th Cir. 1969), in which an outright bequest of a specified sum was "to be paid . . . out of the income of my estate" and the marital deduction was disallowed, on the ground that estate income is not includible in D's gross estate.

On one level that's a silly statement, because inclusion of the corpus of any asset necessarily embraces (indeed the value of any asset anticipates) the right to receive income from that asset in the future. And the bequest (the value of the income earned and paid to S) will be includible in S's gross estate at death because it increases S's net worth. So there is no reason to fear that a marital deduction to D's estate will not be matched with payback liability in S's estate. In addition, a gift of an annuity interest or a note payable over time would qualify for the marital deduction, which is difficult to distinguish from a guaranteed entitlement to a specified dollar bequest that just happens to be payable as income is received.

On the other hand, if the gift of this bequest payable from income qualified for the marital deduction, then presumably a temporal interest in the corpus of other estate property (such as a life estate or term of years) also ought to qualify, and we are going to learn shortly that the nondeductible terminable interest rule would preclude this. As will become clear, the nondeductible terminable interest rule makes *no* sense, but a court will not just ignore the nondeductible terminable interest rule in a case like *Coyle*. Which makes the result stated predictable and consistent with other requirements that will be explored in more detail. It also forewarns us that there is a good bit of nonsense in these requirements.

---

42. Note that most of the following discussion applies equally for gift tax marital deduction purposes too, with comparable §2523(b) authority, but mirror image citation is avoided for the sake of simplicity.

The Nondeductible Terminable Interest Rule

The most significant (and the most troublesome) requirement to qualify for the marital deduction is that the interest passing to S must not be a "nondeductible terminable interest." As a general principle, this requirement reflects the notion that an interest passing to S must be subject to inclusion in S's gross estate to the extent not consumed or disposed of during S's overlife. This is appropriate because, in its basic operation, the marital deduction permits only deferral of the estate tax. Recall that Congress in effect has said, "We won't tax your property to the extent you leave it to S in a form that exposes it to taxation in S's estate."

The clearest example of an interest that qualifies for the deduction is an outright, fee simple gift of property to S. Care is required here, because it does not necessarily follow that an interest that will be includible in S's gross estate will qualify for the marital deduction. The §2056(b)(1) issue is whether the interest is a nondeductible terminable interest: if it terminates or fails on the lapse of time or the (non)occurrence of an event or contingency, the marital deduction will be disallowed if, after the termination, the interest passes to a third party. The fact or likelihood that the interest will be subject to inclusion in S's gross estate is not sufficient to qualify for the deduction.

> Example: D left an interest in trust for S until S's death or remarriage, remainder to D's children.

This is a nondeductible terminable interest because, on the occurrence of an event (S's remarriage or death), the interest passing to S will terminate and an interest in the property (the remainder interest) will pass from D to someone other than S (the children as remainder beneficiaries). See Treas. Reg. §§20.2056(b)-1(g) Example (1); 20.2056(b)-7(d)(3). This is true notwithstanding that a portion of this interest, income paid to S, increases S's net worth for subsequent estate taxation. To complicate matters, not all terminable interests are nondeductible. Treas. Reg. §20.2056(b)-1(d). Thus, the key to analysis is first to determine whether an interest is terminable and then to ascertain whether it is nondeductible.

"Terminable Interest" Defined

A "terminable interest" is any interest in property that will terminate or fail either on the mere lapse of time (for example, a term of years, a patent, copyright, or royalty interest) or on the occurrence or nonoccurrence of some event or contingency (such as death or remarriage of S, death or survivorship of a third party, or failure to perform certain acts). The determination whether an interest is terminable is made as of D's death, even though subsequent facts may reveal that the interest will not in fact terminate.

Similarly, postmortem conversions or elections of any kind by S cannot alter the terminable interest character of an interest. Treas. Reg. §20.2056(b)-1(e)(3). Conversely, postmortem actions will not convert a deductible interest into a nondeductible terminable interest. For example, selection by S of an insurance policy settlement option that involves a terminable interest does not make the insurance proceeds nondeductible if a lump-sum payment option could have been selected, nor will an interest be rendered nondeductible merely because S must make a purely procedural or ministerial election as a prerequisite to receiving it.

Nondeductible Terminable Interests

Not all terminable interests are not deductible. Indeed, terminable interests are deductible unless: (1) the interest was acquired by D's personal representative at D's direction; or (2) upon termination of S's interest (a) another interest in the same property will pass (b) for less than full and adequate consideration (c) from D (d) to a third person whose enjoyment or possession (e) commences upon termination of S's interest. §2056(b)(1).

To determine whether an interest in the same property passed from D both to S and to some other person, a distinction must be made between "property" and an "interest in property." Treas. Reg. §20.2056(b)-1(e)(2). The term "property" is used in a comprehensive manner and includes all objects or rights that are susceptible of ownership. The term "interest" refers to the quantum or quality of ownership of property. Thus, for example, if D devises to S an estate for life in FarmAcre, the interest passing to S is the life estate and the property in which that interest exists is FarmAcre. If, however, all D owns is a term of years that survives D's death and that D gives to S, the property for estate tax inclusion and marital deduction qualification is the term interest that D owns and this bequest would qualify for the marital deduction. If that distinction seems goofy, that's because it is! By and large these rules are senseless.

The following examples illustrate the operation of the rules governing nondeductible terminable interests.

> Example 1: D bequeaths to S an installment note that is payable over six years.

The note is a terminable interest because it will be extinguished upon the obligor's final payment in six years. It is not a nondeductible terminable interest, however, and thus it qualifies for the marital deduction, because no interest in the property will pass to any person other than S on termination. For the same reason, a patent, copyright, or royalty (which have no interest that survives termination of the underlying property interest that can pass to a third party) all are terminable interests that are deductible, because no interest passes from D to a third person for enjoyment or possession after S's enjoyment terminates.

> Example 2: D purchased a joint and survivor annuity contract providing for payments to D and S and then to the survivor of them. On the death of the survivor of D and S all payments will cease. D dies and the present value of the remaining annuity payments to which S is entitled is included in D's gross estate under §2039. It also qualifies for the marital deduction.

Notwithstanding that it is a terminable interest, the value of the annuity qualifies for the marital deduction because it was includible in D's gross estate and no interest owned by D in the annuity (the property) survives S and passes to a third party. §2056(b)(7)(C) and Treas. Reg. §20.2056(b)-1(g) Example (3).

> Example 3: D's will directed D's personal representative to use estate funds to purchase a single life, no refund annuity for S.

D's estate is not entitled to a marital deduction under §§2056(b)(1)(C) and 2056(b)(7)(C). This result is illogical; S's annuity is no different from that in Example 2, except for the manner in which it was acquired. Indeed, D's estate would be entitled to a marital deduction if D's will bequeathed cash to S, who used the money to purchase an identical single life annuity for S. Illustrated here is the first form of nondeductible terminable interest. Fortunately for most purposes its senseless application functionally is irrelevant because estate plans seldom (if ever) direct the personal representative to purchase terminable interests.

> Example 4: D and S executed a joint and mutual will that gave D's property to S and, upon S's death, left their combined assets to their children.

No marital deduction is allowable for D's estate if, under state law, the will is a binding contract that prohibits S from disposing of D's assets other than pursuant to the will. This is just one of several reasons why knowledgeable estate planers shun joint and mutual wills, especially between spouses.

> Example 5: D's father created a 50-year term in Blackacre, giving it to D outright. When D died the term had a number of years to run, which D gave to S.

This is a deductible, albeit terminable, interest because D did not convey the remainder to a third party. The interest left to S would be a nondeductible terminable interest if D had created the 50-year term by bequeathing the remainder thereafter to C. But here the marital deduction is allowable because D did not create the interest following the term. The terminable interest passing to S also would qualify for the marital deduction under §2056(b)(1)(A) if D had sold the remainder interest to C for its full fair market value at the time of the sale. There is no logical foundation to support the statute's disparate treatment of these identical interests passing to S.[43]

The Unidentified Asset Rule

To the extent the pool of assets (or proceeds of assets) available to satisfy a marital deduction gift includes particular assets that do not qualify for the marital deduction (nondeductible terminable interests or interests that are not includible in D's gross estate), §2056(b)(2) states that, in computing the allowable marital deduction, "the value of [any] interest passing to [the surviving] spouse shall . . . be reduced by the aggregate value of such particular assets." Captioned "Interest in Unidentified Assets" for reasons that never have been entirely clear, §2056(b)(2) has serious consequences if triggered: the marital deduction is reduced if a particular asset *could* be used to satisfy the marital bequest, without regard to whether the asset actually is so distributed.

> Example: D's will bequeaths half of D's residuary estate to S. The residuary estate includes the right to the rentals of an office building under a 20-year lease that D reserved under a deed of the building by way of a gift to a child several years before D's death.

The rental right is a nondeductible terminable interest: the interest will terminate on the happening of an event (cessation of the rental payments upon expiration of the lease) and an interest in the property passes to the child. Treas. Reg. §20.2056(b)-2(d). Cf. Estate of Reeves v. Commissioner, 100 T.C. 427 (1993) (apparently the only case ever to apply §2056(b)(2), even in an ancillary manner).

This is the only example in the regulations to illustrate the unidentified asset rule. As suggested by the labored facts of the example, "unidentified assets" rarely are encountered. Fortunately, the cited regulation suggests an easy way to eliminate any concern about operation of the rule: "If [D's] will provided that [S's] bequest could not be satisfied with a nondeductible interest, the entire bequest is a deductible interest." Accordingly, a boilerplate provision such as the following should be employed in any will or trust in which the marital deduction is involved:

> **No asset (or the proceeds of any asset) shall be distributed in satisfaction of the marital deduction bequest as to which the marital deduction would not be allowed if it were distributed outright to my spouse.**

In a similar manner, an estate plan that employs a reverse pecuniary or residuary marital gift (under which the residuary estate is intended to qualify for the marital deduction) should shunt away from the marital bequest any

---

43. The policy rationale underlying the nondeductible terminable interest rule is discussed and criticized in Abrams, *A Reevaluation of the Terminable Interest Rule*, 39 TAX L. REV. 1 (1983).

unidentified assets that possibly may be included in the estate, as follows:

> **In funding the bequest to the nonmarital trust, my executor shall first distribute assets (or the proceeds of assets) as to which the marital deduction would not be allowed if distributed to my spouse.**

Exceptions to the Nondeductible Terminable Interest Rule

When the marital deduction was introduced by the Revenue Act of 1948, Congress established the §2056(b)(1) nondeductible terminable interest rule as the primary test for determining whether an interest passing to S qualifies for the deduction. The 1948 Act carved out several important exceptions to the rule, however, permitting certain trust settlements to qualify for the marital deduction notwithstanding that S is given only a terminable interest. In addition, Congress provided for a "limited survivorship" exception to the nondeductible terminable interest rule, which applies to outright gifts as well as to trust dispositions.

Limited Survivorship Exception

It is a common practice to include a clause requiring a legatee to survive the testator by a stated period (for example, 120 hours, 30 days, 6 months) to take under the will. A survivorship clause tends to ensure that the property will pass to alternate beneficiaries the testator designated in the will, rather than to designated takers under an antilapse statute or to the heirs or devisees of a legatee who did survive but not long enough to really enjoy the property. An additional purpose of a survivorship condition is to avoid double administration and, for tax sensitive planning, to prevent estate stacking or double taxation (subject to the previously taxed property credit of §2013) of the same property in two estates if the testator and the legatee die in quick succession.

Absent a special exception, a survivorship condition attached to an interest bequeathed to S would trigger the nondeductible terminable interest rule: the bequest would fail and an interest in the property would pass from D to some person other than S upon the happening of an event or contingency (death of S within the contingency period). Fortunately, §2056(b)(3) provides that a bequest subject to a survivorship condition is not a nondeductible terminable interest if the condition of survival is for a period not exceeding six months[44] and the contingency of S dying within that period does not occur.

---

44. The six month survivorship period expires on the day of the sixth calendar month after the decedent's death that numerically corresponds to the day of the calendar month on which death occurred. Rev. Rul. 70-400. To avoid any questions if the sixth calendar month does not (normally) have a date that numerically corresponds to the date of the decedent's death (for example, if the date of death is March 31, August 29-31, October 31, or December 31), many drafters require survival by 180 days, which is never longer than any six calendar month period.

Thus, a survival requirement for up to six months can be attached to an interest passing to S without necessarily disqualifying it for the marital deduction. No marital deduction will be available if S does not survive for the stated period because no interest will actually pass from D to S. But the interest passes and the condition is ignored for marital deduction qualification purposes if S survives for the requisite period.

Marital Deduction Transfers: Forms of Disposition

Before investigating the complex rules that relate to sophisticated forms of disposition meeting the nondeductible terminable interest rule under the special exceptions of §§2056(b)(5) through 2056(b)(8), it is worth stating the obvious. Under §2056(c), outright dispositions to S of nonterminable assets qualify for the marital deduction whether passing, for example, by will, intestate succession, dower or curtesy (or statutory substitute therefor), right of survivorship, the exercise or nonexercise of a general power of appointment, as life insurance, or an employee benefit paid in a lump sum. The same is true for inter vivos gifts outright to a spouse. Moreover, outright transfers have the advantage of simplicity: generally they are easy to draft[45] and are easy for the client to understand.

The most important factor to consider is that clients prefer outright dispositions.[46] When asked which form of disposition clients most frequently choose (outright bequest or a transfer in one of the three most common types of trust that qualify for the marital deduction), the consistency of response is dramatic: over two-thirds of all respondents select the outright bequest as the first choice for a husband's plan and three-fourths make the same response when drafting the wife's,[47] in each case assuming

---

45. One item of potential complexity relates to the state law right to receive income on a marital bequest not in trust for the period of probate administration. Under Uniform Principal and Income Act §5(b)(2), a bequest *not in trust* that also is not a specific bequest is not entitled to income earned during administration of the estate. Unless state law or the document provides for the payment of interest instead, it is conceivable that the government would insist on a reduction in the value of that bequest for marital deduction purposes, under Treas. Reg. §20.2056(b)-4(a). Some state statutes that address these issues with respect to estate distributions will not apply if the outright marital bequest is from a funded inter vivos revocable trust that was used to avoid probate.

Also consider whether state law abatement rules would protect the marital bequest if assets of the estate are inadequate to satisfy all estate obligations. It may be wise to specify that a formula pecuniary bequest should take abatement priority over other nondeductible bequests if protection of the marital deduction is paramount.

46. See Quilliam, *How Leading Texas Probate Lawyers Are Handling Marital Deduction Problems (An Empirical Study)*, ADVANCED ESTATE PLANNING & PROBATE COURSE (State Bar of Texas) 1987 (survey of Texas estate planners); cf. Moore & Pennell, *Practicing What We Preach: Esoteric or Essential?*, 27 U. MIAMI INST. EST. PLAN. ¶1217 (1993) (survey of University of Miami Estate Planning Institute registrants revealing that, on a frequency of "sometimes" or more often, 60% of the respondents' clients give their surviving spouse inter vivos control over marital deduction assets, although this control may not be in the form of an outright bequest).

47. Because the survey was among community property lawyers whose married clients owned predominantly community property, it is not likely that this sex based disparity can be explained by asset ownership patterns. The most likely single explanation is that all the survey respondents were males, raising the question of the respondents' proper role in determining "client preferences." Quilliam noted that, although the rating criteria called for

neither spouse has children by a former marriage. These percentages drop as the size of the estate grows and with older clients, although almost 40% still opted for the outright bequest when the facts assumed the wife is over age 60 when the husband's will is drafted. More than half still selected the outright bequest when the husband is over age 60.

In addition to planned estates, in which outright dispositions are the most popular form of marital transfer, it also is notable that estate planning "by default" also "favors" outright transfers. For example, S's intestate share if D dies without a valid will qualifies for the marital deduction, as does S's statutory forced heir share if S elects against D's estate plan.[48]

Marital Deduction Power of Appointment Trust

The principal original exception to the nondeductible terminable interest rule adopted in 1948 is §2056(b)(5), which permits the use of a trust that gives S a life income interest without the remainder, provided S also is granted a distinctive form of general power of appointment. Some clients prefer not to leave property outright to S out of a concern for S's ability to manage assets, or for S's age and possible subsequent incapacity, or to resist "predators" such as greedy children, persistent charities, creditors, or hopeful suitors (the often-feared "gigolo" or "gold-digger" factor). Before the §2056(b)(7) QTIP trust was introduced in 1981, "power of appointment" trusts (sometimes referred to as "§2056(b)(5) trusts" or, more simply, as "(b)(5) trusts") were the most widely used means of securing the marital deduction by way of a trust disposition.[49]

To qualify for the marital deduction under §2056(b)(5), a trust must provide that:

(1) All trust income must be payable to S at least annually for life.

(2) The trust must grant S an "all events" general power of appointment by which S can appoint trust property to S or to S's estate.

(3) No other person can be a beneficiary of the trust during S's overlife.

A power in the trustee to distribute property to anyone other than S (for example, to descendants in case of need) would disqualify the trust,[50]

---

an indication of the client's preference, "one can hardly doubt that 'attorney preference' plays a major role in the decisions made by the client." Quilliam, however, does not criticize this attorney influence, recognizing that attorneys can apply their experience in "guiding the client . . . to an intelligent choice." It is possible that these disparities will become less pronounced as demographics in the legal profession in general, among estate planners in particular, and among the client base all change.

48. Treas. Reg. §20.2056(c)-2(c).

49. A similar but seldom used form of disposition involving insurance proceeds held in a trust like settlement is authorized under §2056(b)(6). Its requirements are similar to the §2056(b)(5) requisites.

50. See Treas. Reg. §20.2056(b)-7(h) Example 4; Technical Advice Memorandum 8508002 (a trust that gave the trustee discretion to pay taxes and administration expenses

although the trustee can be given a discretionary power to distribute trust property to S that S might thereafter transfer to third parties, and S can be given an inter vivos power to appoint the trust property to third parties. See Rev. Rul. 72-154.

> Example: The trustee of a §2056(b)(5) trust is directed to distribute trust corpus to D's children as S directs from time to time.

This provision is permissible in a §2056(b)(5) trust because distributions directed by S are treated as distributed to S first, followed by a gift by S to the children.

State law governing administration of the trust is controlling in determining whether these requirements are met. Treas. Reg. §20.2056(b)-5(e). For example, silence as to the frequency of income payment will not prevent qualification unless applicable local law permits payment to be made less frequently than annually. Thus, a qualifying §2056(b)(5) trust could be drafted as simply as:

> **The trustee shall pay the trust income to S in convenient installments, at least annually, for life. On the death of S the trustee shall distribute the trust estate, including any accrued but undistributed income, to such persons, including S's estate, as S may appoint by will. To the extent this power is not effectively exercised, on the death of S the trustee shall distribute the balance of the trust estate per stirpes to my then living descendants.**

Unlike the §2056(b)(7) QTIP trust, which requires an election by D's personal representative to qualify for the marital deduction, a §2056(b)(5) trust with the proper provisions automatically qualifies for the deduction. This is not necessarily a good thing, because the QTIP allows for postmortem planning that reduces the amount includible in S's gross estate that the automatic qualification of a §2056(b)(5) trust does not permit (short of a disclaimer by S).

The rationale behind the three essential §2056(b)(5) qualification requirements (the right to receive all trust income at least annually, general power of appointment, and restriction on the trustee's power to distribute corpus to other persons) can be explained in terms of their tax results. Except for capital gains (and rare forms of other income allocable to corpus for fiduciary accounting purposes), which may not be taxable currently to S, the income tax and estate tax consequences of a §2056(b)(5) trust are the same as if the marital deduction amount had been bequeathed outright to S: all of the trust's fiduciary accounting income

---

out of corpus did not qualify for the marital deduction); Technical Advice Memoranda 9147065 and 9139001 (a "sweetheart" price to purchase closely held stock and a requirement that a child must consent to any sale violated the sole benefit requirement).

will be taxed to S currently and, because of the general power of appointment, the trust corpus will be includible in S's gross estate at death (or subjected to §2514 gift tax if S exercises or releases the power during life).

In addition, taxation of all the trust corpus to S is guaranteed by precluding distributions to third parties. The sole benefit requirement also may be understood as an adjunct to the requirement that S be entitled to all trust income for life, because corpus distributions to third parties diminish trust corpus that generates S's income entitlement. But it may be most accurate to consider the sole benefit requirement as founded in a concern that trust corpus not avoid wealth transfer tax in S's hands, which Congress may have thought possible if trust distributions were made by the trustee directly to third parties.

General Power of Appointment

Not just any general power of appointment will suffice for §2056(b)(5) trust qualification purposes. A "general power" for §2041 purposes could be one that is exercisable in favor of S, S's estate, or creditors of either. However, the power required for §2056(b)(5) trust qualification must be exercisable in favor of either S or S's estate. The creditor-type power alone would cause §2041 estate tax inclusion but would not qualify for the deduction under §2056(b)(5). Thus, although any other permissible appointees are allowable, exercise in favor of S or S's estate must be authorized by the power. And care is required to avoid the likely disaster of causing inclusion to S producing a marital deduction for D.

The §2056(b)(5) requirement that the general power of appointment be exercisable by S "alone and in all events" means that there can be no substantive restrictions on the grant of the power or conditions on the power's exercise. An inter vivos general power exercisable only after (or until) a certain date, or only if a certain contingency does (or does not) occur, will not qualify, nor will one that requires another party's consent to exercise. Treas. Reg. §§20.2056(b)-5(g)(3) and 20.2056(b)-5(g)(4). Probably the most common form of disqualifying limitation on a general power of appointment terminates the power (or the entire trust interest in S) if S remarries. A related disqualification would occur if any one or any thing other than S could divest S's power, such as in the event of incompetence.

Although general *testamentary* powers were more common before 1982, inter vivos general powers in the form of *withdrawal* rights are more common among those choosing the §2056(b)(5) trust approach today, particularly as a permissible method to allow S to make inter vivos transfers.[51] As a drafting matter, it is less dangerous to also give S a

---

51. An inter vivos power may alter certain elements of the trust, notably §678 pseudo grantor trust income tax exposure on capital gains allocable to corpus and exposure to creditor claims. Rule Against Perpetuities differences also might be relevant, although it is

general testamentary power of appointment that is expressly exercisable in favor of "**such persons, including S's estate,**[52] **as S appoints by will,**" because reliance on an inter vivos general power alone to satisfy the "all events" requirement is risky if it may be determined that the power's exercise is subject to restrictions.

All Income Annually

S must be entitled to all trust income annually for the trust to qualify as a §2056(b)(5) trust. The same requirement applies to QTIP trusts as well.[53] As a result, this requirement is the single most significant aspect of marital deduction qualification for estate plans that do not pass the marital deduction bequest outright to S.

As with the general power of appointment requirement, qualification for this exception to the nondeductible terminable interest rule can be thwarted by unauthorized conditions or restrictions on the income interest. The most common is an income interest that terminates on remarriage. Also encountered are improper interests for a term of years (even if S's life expectancy is shorter than the specified term) and provisions in favor of third parties that might apply during S's overlife (for example, distribution of a percentage of the trust corpus when a child reaches a specified age).

Caution also must be exercised to ensure that the trust's administrative provisions do not give the trustee any power that unduly restricts S's right to income. Treasury Regulation §20.2056(b)-5(f)(1) provides:

> [S] is "entitled for life to all of the income" . . . if the effect of the trust is to give [S] substantially that degree of beneficial enjoyment of the trust property . . . which the principles of the law of trusts accord to a person who is unqualifiedly designated as the life beneficiary of a trust. Such degree of enjoyment is given only if it was [D's] intention, as manifested by the terms of the trust . . . that the trust should produce for [S] . . . such an income, or that [S] should have such use of the trust property as is consistent with the value of the trust corpus and with its preservation. The designation of [S] as sole income beneficiary for life . . . will be sufficient to qualify the trust unless the terms of the trust and the surrounding circumstances considered as a whole evidence an intention to deprive [S] of the requisite degree of enjoyment.

---

unlikely that perpetuities concerns are at the forefront of such a planning decision.

52. Adding the specificity of "including S's estate" is wise because there is case law that would regard "such person or persons" as being restricted and nongeneral. See, e.g., Estate of Allen v. Commissioner, 29 T.C. 465 (1957); Rev. Rul. 76-502.

53. Treas. Reg. §20.2056(b)-7(d)(2) provides that the "principles of §20.2056(b)-5(f), relating to whether the spouse is entitled for life to all of the income from the entire interest, apply . . ." to the income requirements for QTIP trusts.

It is immaterial whether the requisite degree of enjoyment is effected by rules specifically stated in the trust instrument or by principal and income rules supplied by state law, provided that the rules for allocation of receipts and expenses between income and principal are considered in relation to the nature and expected productivity of trust assets, the nature and frequency of expected receipts, and any provisions as to changes in the form of investments. Treas. Reg. §20.2056(b)-5(f)(3).

The regulations embrace a relaxation of the definition of fiduciary accounting income to reflect allocations between income and principal in a fiduciary's discretion in a total return trust investment environment. They also reflect the shift of beneficial interests from a traditional income interest to the more modern unitrust entitlement that anticipates a total return concept. Specific state laws or trust authority or directions that are consistent with state law may call for equitable adjustments between traditional fiduciary accounting income and principal to ensure that income and remainder beneficiaries are treated fairly. Provisions may not depart fundamentally from traditional income and principal concepts, but reasonable reallocations are permitted to the extent not prohibited by local law, if they are applied in an impartial manner. Moreover, state law may substitute a 3 to 5% of annual fair market value unitrust entitlement as the functional equivalent of an all income distribution mandate. See Chapter 8 beginning at page 20 regarding the similar nature of a charitable "unitrust" entitlement.

Example 1 of Rev. Rul. 69-56 specifies that the following powers or directions, relating to allocation or apportionment of receipts and expenditures to or between income and principal, safely may be conferred on the trustee of a marital deduction trust without reducing or losing the deduction:

(1) to apportion or not to apportion, between successive beneficial interests, interest income and expense, rental income and expense, real estate taxes, or other items of periodic income or expense;
(2) to treat ordinary cash dividends as income based on the time when received, regardless of the declaration or record date;
(3) to treat extraordinary cash dividends, stock dividends, and capital gains dividends of regulated investment companies as principal;
(4) to charge fiduciary commissions, legal and accounting fees, and similar administration expenses to income or principal; and
(5) to maintain reasonable reserves for depreciation, depletion, amortization, and obsolescence, and to amortize or not to amortize premium and discount with respect to interest-bearing bonds and similar obligations.

The ruling assumed that the exercise of powers such as these may be authorized by state law. It also recognized that there may be no state law authority in some cases, or that state law may deny authority unless the trust specifically bestows such powers. The ruling assumed, however, that the trust instrument contained no provisions directing the fiduciary to favor other trust beneficiaries over S.

The question of which items are properly allocable to fiduciary accounting income (and thus are subject to the all-income-annually requirement) cannot be answered definitively in every case. Thus, reasonable discretion usually may be exercised under state law in determining whether an item of receipt or expenditure properly is credited or charged to income. Treas. Reg. §20.2056(b)-5(f). Nevertheless, local principal and income act requirements should be regarded as the lodestar, and the trust document should not authorize unreasonable deviation from those state law principles.

In Example 2 of Rev. Rul. 69-56 the governing instrument granted the fiduciary a general power to determine the manner in which receipts and disbursements will be allocated or apportioned between income and principal. Because a fiduciary's determination must fairly balance the interests of the income beneficiary and the remainder beneficiaries under state law, that power was not deemed to evidence an intention to deprive S of the beneficial enjoyment required by the statute, nor did it result in disallowance or diminution of the marital deduction.

In Example 4 of Rev. Rul. 69-56 the governing instrument conferred administrative powers not pertaining to the allocation or apportionment of receipts and disbursements. These included powers to retain cash without investment for any period of time the fiduciary deemed advisable (for example, if it was inadvisable to invest that cash). They also included powers to make distributions in cash or in kind (or partly in each) at current values, allocating specific assets to particular distributees and, for these purposes, to make reasonable determinations of current values. These powers also were not deemed to evidence an intent to deprive S of the beneficial enjoyment required by the statute, provided that they were subject to reasonable limitations under applicable state law.

Some clients may seek to minimize the income payable to S, believing that it may exceed S's needs (as the client views that issue) or wrongly thinking that it is cheaper (for income tax purposes) to accumulate the income for ultimate payment to other beneficiaries. It could not be distributed currently without violating the all-income-annually or exclusive benefit requirements.

To avoid conflict in this respect, or efforts to accomplish indirectly what the client could not do directly, inherent in Treas. Reg. §20.2056(b)-5(f)(5) is a requirement that the trust may not invest in unproductive[54]

---

54. Unresolved is whether the trust may be invested in significantly *under*productive assets (for example, returning 1% when average investments return 7%). The regulation refers to "property which is not likely to be income producing during the life of the surviving spouse," which may mean that the likelihood of income production at a

assets without the consent of S. A provision that reflects this requirement might read something like: "**Unproductive property shall not be held as an asset of the trust for more than a reasonable time during the lifetime of S without [his/her] written consent.**" Alternatively, it would suffice to provide that "**S shall have the right by written notice to require the trustee to convert unproductive property in the trust to productive property within a reasonable time.**" Treas. Reg. §20.2056(b)-5(f)(4). A third alternative is to provide that the fiduciary must distribute sufficient corpus to compensate for inadequate income production. A fourth variation would allow S to withdraw corpus to the extent of any deficiency in income production. See the sample language for unproductive property purposes at page 88.

Also note that a personal residence and other non-income-producing but *personal use* property may be held in a marital deduction trust even though it will not produce income, because personal enjoyment is as valuable to S as the receipt of income from some other asset. Treas. Reg. §§20.2056(b)-5(f)(4); 20.2056(b)-7(h) Example 1. But many other forms of investment may trigger an unproductive property provision, including unimproved land or assets like gold bullion that are held solely for their appreciation potential (or assumed protection against loss), stock in a closely held business that has a history of reinvesting earnings instead of declaring dividends, and life insurance.

Indeed, an investment in insurance (such as a survivor life policy) that does not produce income (dividends are a return of premiums paid, not earnings or a "return" on the investment) and that also may divert other income for payment of premiums usually should be avoided in a marital deduction trust of the §2056(b)(5) or §2056(b)(7) all-income-annually variety. This is true unless S may require conversion. Furthermore, to avoid diversion of trust income from S, premium payments must be permitted only from principal.

In the usual case a marital deduction trust is not established for some time after D's death, pending administration of D's estate. An interest does not fail to satisfy the income payment requisite merely because S is not entitled to income from estate assets for the period before distribution of those assets by the personal representative, unless the delay is authorized or directed by D's will beyond a period reasonably required for administration of the estate. Treas. Reg. §20.2056(b)-5(f)(9), which does not absolve the need to pay income (or interest) during administration.

Income must be payable (or be subject to withdrawal by S) at least annually, in the year earned. Treas. Reg. §20.2056(b)-5(f)(8). See Rev. Rul. 72-283 (disqualification occurred because the trust directed payment of one year's income the following year, which the government regarded

---

reasonable rate at any time during S's overlife expectancy prevents disqualification under this regulation.

as failing the current distribution requirement). It is customary (and usually desirable) to provide that trust income shall be distributed "at least annually," or more frequently. However, no problem is presented if the trust merely states that the trustee shall distribute the trust income to S for life, without a literal statement that the payments must be made at least annually, because the frequency of payment requirement is satisfied unless applicable local law or the trust terms permit payment to be made less frequently than annually.[55] Even if state law is silent on the issue of frequency of payment, general common law principles require that income be paid in "reasonable intervals," such as quarterly or semiannually. See 2A Scott & Fratcher, THE LAW OF TRUSTS §182 (4th ed. 1987).

In addition to the frequency of payment issue, accrued but undistributed income at S's death must be paid to S's estate or be subject to a general testamentary power of appointment in a §2056(b)(5) trust. See the QTIP stub income discussion at page 60.

Specific Portion Requirement

Under §2056(b)(5) the right to all income annually and the general power of appointment must pertain to the same "specific portion" of a trust. Normally this is not a problem because the typical estate plan that uses a marital deduction trust creates (at a minimum) two trusts: a nonmarital trust and a marital deduction trust, with the full marital deduction trust granting both the requisite income interest and, if §2056(b)(5) is relied upon, the all-events general power of appointment. That §2056(b)(5) marital deduction trust typically is designed to fully qualify for the marital deduction. Partial qualification of the estate as a whole for the marital deduction is effected by making the nonmarital trust contain the portion of the estate as to which the marital deduction is not desired.

Sometimes, however, it is desirable to create only one trust (a "single fund marital" trust) of which only a portion (the "marital portion") qualifies for the deduction through an overlap of the income interest and the general power of appointment. One approach to a single fund marital is to grant S all income from the entire fund and permit appointment pursuant to a general power over that portion as to which the marital deduction is desired. As to this appointable portion, the two interests overlap and qualify for the deduction.

---

55. Treas. Reg. §§20.2056(b)-5(e) and 20.2056(b)-7(g), both providing virtually verbatim that:

> To determine whether the frequency of payment requirement . . . is satisfied where a trust instrument is silent, provisions of local law should be taken into account. Silence of a trust instrument on this issue will not be regarded as a failure to satisfy the condition that the income must be payable to the surviving spouse annually or more frequently, unless applicable local law permits payment to be made less frequently than annually.

> Example 1: A trust grants S a right to receive half the income and a power to appoint three-fourths of the corpus at death. The marital deduction will be allowed with respect to half the value of the trust, not just three-eighths (half of three-fourths).

Treas. Reg. §20.2056(b)-5(c)(5) Example 2. To qualify in this manner as a specific portion for marital deduction purposes the power must be over a fractional or percentage portion of the trust, not a specified dollar amount. §2056(b)(10) and Treas. Reg. §20.2056(b)-5(c). This precludes estate freezing of the type illustrated by the following example:

> Example 2: D created a trust of $200,000 that pays all the income from $100,000 of trust corpus to S for life and grants S a general testamentary power to appoint $100,000. Before S dies the trust corpus doubles in value.

Because the power of appointment applies only to $100,000, if this approach was permitted the remaining $300,000 would pass tax free at S's death. A trust that complied with the fractional or percentage requirement would grant the income and power of appointment with respect to half the trust and the amount of income payable to S and the amount of trust corpus includible in S's gross estate would grow proportionately as the trust appreciated (only $200,000 would pass tax free at S's death). Any identifiable portion is sufficient, such as a fraction of which the numerator is the amount of the deduction desired and the denominator is the size of the fund against which the fraction is to be applied. See page 123 regarding proper description of such a fraction.

Legal Life Estate with General Power of Appointment

The §2056(b)(5) marital deduction is allowable for the full value of property in which S is given a legal life estate not in trust, if coupled with a general power to appoint the property underlying the legal life estate. Treas. Reg. §20.2056(b)-5(a); Rev. Rul. 77-30. Many estate planners eschew this approach because of the difficulty of appending a power of appointment to a legal life estate, and because the rights of S as the holder of a legal life estate often are less clear or beneficial under state law than those of an income beneficiary of a trust. Furthermore, drafting an appropriate document enumerating the rights and powers of the life tenant may be more difficult than drafting a traditional trust, in large part because it is not very common and thus may hold more risk of error and require more time. See Casner, *Legal Life Estates and Powers of Appointment Coupled with Life Estates and Trusts*, 45 NEB. L. REV. 342 (1966); Schuyler, *Drafting Provisions for Legal Life Estates and the Marital Deduction*, 44 ILL. B.J. 452 (1956).

Because a legal life estate can be qualified terminable interest property without more, attaching a general power of appointment to a legal life estate probably is not a desirable alternative. Moreover, either a QTIP trust or a more traditional trust granting a general power of appointment will provide protection against incapacity of S, provide management of the property, and grant spendthrift protections, all lacking in the legal life estate context, while still avoiding probate in S's estate. Given that S may be designated as trustee of such a trust, if desired, and avoidance of tax inclusion to S at death is not an objective, it would seem that a very strong aversion to trusts must exist before the legal life estate alternative would be desirable.

Estate Trusts

A marital deduction "estate trust" is the only form of trust (or trust equivalent) qualifying for the federal estate tax marital deduction under §2056 that does not require annual payment of all trust income to S for life. Instead, the estate trust can provide for the discretionary payment of income to S or its total accumulation, because the remainder passes to S's estate at death. See Treas. Reg. §20.2056(c)-2(b)(1)(iii). If properly drafted, the estate trust avoids the nondeductible terminable interest rules of §2056(b) entirely, because nothing passes to a third party after S's death: all accumulated income, along with principal, is distributed to S's estate at death (hence the name of the trust).[56] As a result, this is not a nondeductible terminable interest at all, and therefore need not qualify for any exception to §2056(b)(1).

The principal characteristic of an estate trust must be considered carefully in evaluating the estate trust's advantages: like an outright marital bequest, this approach gives S control of the property at death, which makes it subject to predators as well as to S's caprice. Nevertheless, there are several reasons to employ an estate trust in lieu of an outright distribution or one of the other forms of qualified marital deduction trust. One is that the estate trust allows accumulations of income not needed during S's overlife, which can avoid the need to distribute and then manage any money that is beyond the needs or capabilities of S. Another is that S need not receive all income annually, so there is no danger in an estate trust if assets are unproductive or underproductive of income.

A perceived advantage of accumulating income in an estate trust to be taxed at the trust's rates was sharply undercut when the income tax bracket thresholds applicable to trusts were compressed and reduced to their current levels, but the relative rates may be adjusted again to favor trust accumulations. It also is possible that S's rates are no lower, which would make accumulation for other reasons harmless.

---

56. Payment to S's heirs is not the equivalent of payment to S's estate and will not qualify; those persons' receipt of an interest after termination of S's interest would constitute the trust as a nondeductible terminable interest.

Qualified Terminable Interest Property

The following disposition would not have qualified for the estate tax marital deduction before 1982:

> **The trustee shall pay the trust income to S in convenient installments, at least annually, for life. On the death of S the trustee shall distribute the trust estate, including any accrued but undistributed income, to such of my descendants as S may appoint by will. To the extent this power is not validly exercised, on the death of S the trustee shall distribute the balance of the trust estate per stirpes to my then living descendants.**

This disposition creates a terminable interest because S is granted only a naked life estate that terminates at death, and because an interest in the property (the remainder interest) passes to someone other than S or S's estate after S's death. Although S is granted a power of appointment, it is a nongeneral power that cannot be exercised in favor of S or S's estate. Therefore, this trust does not qualify as an exception to the nondeductible terminable interest rule under §2056(b)(5).

Congress enacted the §2056(b)(7) exception (and its §2523(f) gift tax counterpart) to the nondeductible terminable interest rule to permit marital deduction qualification without granting testamentary control over the deductible property to S. This exception causes the illustrated trust to qualify for the marital deduction unless D's personal representative elects to opt out of automatic QTIP treatment. Otherwise, property settled in an otherwise qualifying trust and scheduled on D's estate tax return as marital deduction property will generate a marital deduction in D's estate under §2056(b)(7). Then, by virtue of §§2044 and 2519, it will be wealth transfer taxed to S upon release or assignment of the income interest during life or its termination at death. This all occurs notwithstanding that S has been given only a naked life estate.[57]

The §2056(b)(7) exception to the nondeductible terminable interest rule applies if S is entitled to a §2056(b)(5) income interest for life, no other beneficiary has any rights in the trust during S's overlife, and an irrevocable QTIP election is made.

By Treas. Reg. §20.2056(b)-7(d)(2) all of the well-established §2056(b)(5) rules about guaranteeing the income interest are adopted by reference. One notable difference between the §2056(b)(5) and QTIP income requirements spawned some controversy, however, notwithstanding governmental efforts to be QTIP accommodating. Unlike a §2056(b)(5) qualifying trust, in which S must be given a general power to appoint any accrued but undistributed income at death ("stub" income earned before S's

---

57. Estate tax inclusion under §2044 essentially is the clone of §2041 inclusion of a §2056(b)(5) trust, and §2519 is the counterpart for gift tax purposes of §2514.

death but not yet distributed under the fiduciary's periodic distribution procedure), the QTIP regulations provide that stub income of a QTIP trust at S's death need not be subject to such a power, nor must it be paid to S's estate. Treas. Reg. §20.2056(b)-7(d)(4). Instead, although the stub income will be subject to §2044 inclusion in S's estate at death, along with the rest of the QTIP trust property, it may be distributed in the same manner as the QTIP trust corpus. Treas. Reg. §20.2044-1(d)(2). As a result, S need not be given control of its devolution, nor must an estate administration be opened for S to dispose of this item. Trusts that fail to address this issue should not fail to qualify for the QTIP marital deduction.

If a QTIP trust is silent about stub income, the state Principal and Income Act may cover the issue and mandate distribution of the stub income to S's estate, meaning this issue may exist only in documents that alter state law by specifically addressing the concept (which may be a good thing, if done right).

No General Power of Appointment Is Required

Unlike the §2056(b)(5) trust, D need not give S a general power to appoint QTIP trust corpus. Thus, the QTIP trust is attractive to many clients who want to "handcuff" S while at the same time qualifying for the marital deduction. This does not preclude D from granting S a power to appoint the property at death[58] (but not during life)[59] to or among a class of permissible appointees specified by D. Nor does it preclude giving S a power to withdraw QTIP trust corpus during life, provided that there is no restriction on withdrawal that S must make a gift and that therefore constitutes a constructive power of appointment in violation of the statute. (It probably does not even pay to provide for corpus distributions to S in an amount equal to any gifts S made previously, as a form of "reimbursement." The concern is that the government might apply a step transaction theory to treat this as a prohibited distribution through S to those distributees, with potential QTIP disqualification.)

A general power of appointment in the form of a withdrawal right during life or a testamentary power might make the trust a §2056(b)(5) marital trust, however. The marital deduction would be available, but a §2056(b)(5) trust automatically qualifies for the deduction so partial QTIP election planning (discussed next below) would be lost. In addition, the §2652(a)(3) reverse QTIP election for generation-skipping transfer tax purposes may not be available, nor would certain valuation opportunities. Thus, it would be wise to be certain that any power of appointment granted to S would fail to qualify for §2056(b)(5) purposes, such as by imposing a delay before it becomes available or by requiring a third party's consent to exercise.

---

58. Authorized under §2056(b)(7)(B)(ii) (flush language).
59. Prohibited by §2056(b)(7)(B)(ii)(II).

In addition, the second primary requisite to qualify as a QTIP trust is that, although the trustee may invade principal for S's benefit, no one (according to the legislative history, *not even S*) may have a power to divest S of any interest in the trust. This requirement is really just a subset of the all income annually requisite in §2056(b)(7)(B)(ii), in that it precludes anyone from having the ability to disfranchise S's income entitlement by distributing trust corpus and the income it produces to another person.

The limits of this no divestiture restriction are uncertain. For example, Rev. Rul. 85-35 provides that a standard facility of payment provision does not disqualify a §2056(b)(5) marital deduction trust. See page 89 for a sample. Technical Advice Memoranda 8706008 and 8503009 drew the same conclusion for QTIP trusts. Thus, if S is unable to manage normal affairs, the trustee properly may pay income for S's benefit (rather than directly to S) and even may distribute income to a next friend or guardian for use on S's behalf. According to the government, "the purpose of the . . . facility of payment clause is to make certain that the beneficiary has the beneficial ownership of the trust income and to provide protection and assistance to the beneficiary" rather than to deny or divert ownership or enjoyment of the beneficial interest.

Caution must be exercised in drafting such a provision, however, as illustrated by the clause involved in Technical Advice Memorandum 9318002, which read:

> Regardless of any other provision of this instrument . . . as often as the Trustee deems it appropriate so to do, in order to carry out the spirit and purpose of this provision, *payment* to any beneficiary herein *may be discontinued, and in lieu thereof, the Trustee may expend* for the account of such beneficiary and for his or her support, comfort, happiness and welfare, *such amounts as would otherwise be paid over directly to such beneficiary.* [Emphasis added.]

Used in a trust with a beneficiary as trustee, this provision was deemed to give the trustee a general power of appointment because the terms "comfort, happiness, and welfare" are not ascertainable standards. See Treas. Reg. §20.2041-1(c)(2) and Chapter 6 at pages 10-12. This type of provision is not meant to authorize distributions at all; usually such "facility of payment" provisions are intended only to permit a trustee to avoid making distributions directly to a beneficiary and instead to expend amounts required or authorized under other provisions directly for the beneficiary or to reimburse others for amounts they expended for the beneficiary.

For example, the trustee might choose to pay the beneficiary's rent, utility, and grocery bills rather than give the beneficiary amounts needed for those living expenses. Thus, a more carefully drafted provision might specify:

> If income or discretionary amounts of principal become payable to a minor or to a person under legal disability or to a person not adjudicated disabled but who, by reason of illness or mental or physical disability, is in the opinion of the trustee unable properly to manage his or her affairs, then that income or principal shall be paid or expended only in such of the following ways as the trustee deems best: (a) directly to the beneficiary or his or her attorney in fact; (b) to the legally appointed guardian of the beneficiary; (c) to a custodian for the beneficiary under a Uniform Transfers or Gifts to Minors Act; (d) by the trustee directly for the benefit of the beneficiary; (e) to an adult relative or friend in reimbursement for amounts properly advanced for the benefit of the beneficiary.

Particularly useful about this provision are the statements in (d) that the trustee may pay items directly for the beneficiary and in (e) that amounts paid to others are in reimbursement for amounts already expended for the beneficiary, along with the absence of any language that might imply that this provision itself is a principal distribution authority that is inappropriate for tax purposes.

Some added flexibility also is available in a QTIP trust. For example, S may be given a withdrawal right during life and anyone may have a power of appointment exercisable at or after S's death, all without violating the sole beneficiary restriction. See §2056(b)(7)(B)(ii) (flush language). Caution is appropriate if ever it could be asserted that the general power of appointment creates a §2056(b)(5) general power of appointment trust. It appears that the government is not concerned with the question whether the trust qualified under §2056(b)(5) versus §2056(b)(7), but practitioners should be cautious if automatic qualification for the marital deduction under §2056(b)(5) would be undesirable. As discussed next, the QTIP election provides desirable postmortem planning options.

The QTIP Election

The final requirement to qualify as a QTIP disposition is made necessary because, unlike the §2056(b)(5) trust, qualification for the §2056(b)(7) QTIP marital deduction simply is not meant to be automatic. For the transfer to be treated as qualified terminable interest property, an election is contemplated under §2523(f)(4) by the donor spouse on a gift tax return if the transfer is made during life, and under §2056(b)(7)(B)(v) by D's personal representative on the estate tax return if the transfer is made at death.

The requisite election to be treated as a QTIP marital deduction trust is necessary because, without it, this form of trust would not necessarily be includible in S's estate. The only other major requirement imposed on the trust for qualification is that S be entitled to receive all income annually.

Although that mandatory income entitlement is common to other forms of marital deduction disposition, it alone in a QTIP trust would not identify the trust as marital deduction property. Nor would it cause estate or gift tax inclusion to S when a subsequent transfer of the trust corpus occurs.

Because there have been so many problems with QTIP elections, however, the current position is the converse of the statutory expectation. QTIP treatment is automatic unless the donor or the personal representative elects *out* of that treatment. The government's administrative position is exactly opposite the statutory presumption. If property is scheduled on the estate tax return as deductible and if the tax is computed with that deduction reflected, the forms presume the election unless an affirmative election out of QTIP treatment is made.

Naturally all of this applies only to transfers that otherwise are "QTIPable" because they would qualify if the election were made. As to those interests, the government has gone so far as to presume at S's death that any interest that *was* QTIPable did qualify and produce a deduction in D's estate. Therefore, such an interest is presumed to be §2044 includible in S's gross estate, unless all these presumptions are proven to the contrary. See Treas. Reg. §20.2044-1(c). The gift tax comparable rule is in Treas. Reg. §25.2519-1(b). Because it is imperative that S receive an income interest in the property in all events, the only consequence of the election is to fix the tax consequences to D or D's estate and, later, to S.

Authorizing the Election

It is not wise in most cases for a decedent to direct the personal representative regarding the QTIP election, dictating whether and to what extent it should be made. Rather, to the extent any statement is thought to be appropriate, the governing document could contain precatory language suggesting factors the personal representative may consider in deciding whether to make a total, partial, or no election.

For example, it would be particularly unfortunate to direct an election if the spouses die in quick succession and equalization would be the best tax-oriented result. A fine-tuned partial election could be used to minimize the estates' taxes, especially to under-utilize the marital deduction in D's estate and thereby produce estate taxes that would permit a §2013 previously taxed property credit in S's estate. Similar results can be generated by partial disclaimer if the will directed the personal representative to make the QTIP election. But other impediments may interfere with that plan. Thus, the election ought to be left to the personal representative's judgment in most cases, because drafting documents today for operation potentially many years in the future makes it difficult (if not impossible) to know all the elements that may affect the proper postmortem planning.

Complicating this issue, however, is the notion that a fiduciary's duty to maximize D's estate by minimizing its taxes may make it imprudent for a personal representative ever to make a partial election if the effect is to cause D's estate to pay tax. Because the personal representative's duties run only to the single estate represented, it is necessary to view D's estate alone, making an election that results in payment of tax an act that arguably is against the estate's interest (even though it may be prudent when viewing both spouses' estates together). See Ascher, *The Quandary of Executors Who Are Asked to Plan the Estates of the Dead: The Qualified Terminable Interest Election*, 63 N.C. L. REV. 1, 48 (1984).

The point is that, although partial elections are contemplated by §2056(b)(7)(B)(iii) and (iv) and Treas. Reg. §20.2056(b)-7(b)(2), they might not be permissible under state fiduciary law principles unless D's document grants this authority. Thus, many well drafted documents authorize the personal representative to exercise the election in its discretion and hold the personal representative harmless for the effects of this decision on any beneficiary.[60] By way of example:

> **Qualification for Marital Deduction: To the extent my personal representative so elects, it is my intent that the marital deduction bequest and the property comprising this trust estate shall qualify for the federal estate tax marital deduction applicable to my estate. No power or discretion with respect to allocations of property to this trust or administration of the trust shall be exercised or exercisable inconsistent with this intent.[61] I expect that my personal representative will make an election to treat some part or all of this trust as qualified terminable interest property, although I recognize that circumstances could arise in which such an election would not be in the best interests of the beneficiaries of my estate. The decision whether and to what extent to make that election shall be in the sole discretion of my personal representative, whose decision shall be conclusive on all concerned and who shall have no personal liability for any**

---

60. The clause recommended by Ascher, 63 N.C. L. REV. at 48 (1984), reads:

I hereby authorize my executor, in his sole discretion, to elect that none, any part, or all of any amount passing under this trust be treated as qualified terminable interest property for purposes of qualifying for the marital deduction allowable in determining the federal estate tax and any state death tax on my estate, regardless of the fact that such taxes are thereby increased or that there is a change in the proportions in which various persons (including my executor) share in my estate. The decision of my executor shall be binding and conclusive upon all persons interested in my estate, and my executor shall have no liability as a result of such decision.

61. The general "savings clause" language regarding D's intent with respect to the marital deduction bequest makes sense, merely to resolve any doubts in favor of deductibility. On the advisability of using such a clause, see Johanson, *The Use of Tax Saving Clauses in Drafting Wills and Trusts*, 15 U. MIAMI INST. EST. PLAN. ¶2100 (1981).

> consequences of that election. The election, even if not made, shall be deemed to have been made with respect to the entire trust for purposes of determining the amount of the bequest to this trust.

It probably is advisable to put this language in the QTIP trust provisions, rather than in a clause appearing elsewhere in the document dealing with tax elections generally. This is an important matter relating to the marital deduction and, if all QTIP related provisions are in one place, there is less likelihood of using the wrong clause in the wrong form or, worse, of overlooking something because it does not appear where the personal representative might be looking.

The last sentence of the sample clause specifies that, regardless of the extent to which the personal representative makes the QTIP election, the amount of the marital deduction bequest nevertheless will be determined pursuant to the formula clause, as if the election was made with respect to the entire trust. The corresponding balance of the estate passing into the nonmarital trust will be computed accordingly. Sophisticated postmortem estate planning presents the personal representative with a bewildering array of elections, including whether to make the §642(g) swing item election, determining the best size of any partial QTIP election, and whether to allocate any part of D's GST exemption to the QTIP trust, just to name some of the most common.

Each election can affect the size of the marital deduction, the amount of income and estate taxes incurred, and ultimately the size of various entitlements. Liability to beneficiaries who feel wronged by these elections can be significant, and the personal representative's task is made all the more sensitive by the constant threat of litigation. As a consequence, many well drafted estate plans also include a provision, such as the following, that addresses the chore of making these elections.

> **Tax Elections:** In determining the wealth transfer and income tax liabilities related to my estate, my personal representative's decision as to all available tax elections shall be conclusive on all concerned and my personal representative shall have no personal liability for any consequences of any election. The marital deduction bequest shall not be construed as requiring that the personal representative exercise any tax election[, other than the election to have the marital deduction gift treated as qualified terminable interest property,][62] only in such manner as will result in a larger allowable estate tax marital deduction than would be obtained if a contrary election had been made. No adjustment shall be made between

---

62. This bracketed provision is to be used only if the will mandates that the QTIP election be made, which normally is not recommended.

principal and income or in the relative interests of the beneficiaries to compensate for the effect of any elections or allocations made by my personal representative. If my personal representative joins with S in filing income tax returns, or consents for gift tax purposes to having gifts made by either of us during my life considered as made half by each of us, any resulting liability shall be borne by my estate and S in such proportions as they may agree.

Because partial QTIP elections are anticipated by the Code and regulations, they should be authorized by the estate plan so that postmortem planning may evaluate and adjust the size of the appropriate election.

If a partial election is made, Treas. Reg. §§20.2044-1(d)(3) and 25.2519-1(c)(3) make it clear that principal invasions can be charged against the portion as to which the QTIP election was made, before invasions reduce the nonelected share. Thus, the property included in S's gross estate is reduced by invasions from the QTIP trust as though no invasions were made from the nonelected portion and no distributions were made from the nonmarital trust. See Treas. Reg. §20.2044-1(e) Example 4.

On the basis of the present state of the law, the following format is thought to qualify to accomplish this form of planning:

A portion of the Marital Trust, herein referred to as the "qualified terminable interest portion," shall qualify for the federal estate tax marital deduction. The value of the qualified terminable interest portion at any time may be determined by multiplying the value of the trust estate at that time by the fraction then in effect. Commencing with my death, and until the first distribution of principal pursuant to the provisions of §[*], the numerator of the fraction shall be equal to [the amount or formula determined deduction desired], and the denominator shall be the value as finally determined for federal estate tax purposes of all interests in property included in the Marital Trust. At the time of each payment of principal pursuant to the provisions of §[*], the fraction shall be adjusted, first by restating it so that the numerator and denominator are the values of the qualified terminable interest portion and of the trust estate, respectively, immediately prior to the payment, and then by subtracting the amount of the payment from each of the numerator and the denominator, except that the numerator shall not be reduced below zero.

As authorized by regulation, the last sentence of this provision creates a "rolling fraction," which has the effect of treating any invasions of principal for S's benefit (pursuant to §[*], permitting discretionary distributions by the trustee or withdrawals by S), as coming from the elected qualified terminable interest portion. The effect is to reduce the amount of property includible under §§2044 and 2519 on termination or disposition of S's income interest.

> Example: The initial fund consisted of $1.25 million and the initial fraction was one-fifth (which produced an optimum marital deduction at the time). A distribution of assets worth $100,000 is made to S when the trust is valued at $1.3 million. The fraction immediately before the distribution, restated to reflect current values, is 260,000/1,300,000 ($1/5$ of $1.3 million) and, immediately after the distribution, the fraction is 160,000/1,200,000 ($2/15$). The amount that would be includible in S's estate if S dies when the balance of the trust is valued at $1.8 million would be $240,000 ($2/15$ of $1.8 million). Had the fraction not been adjusted, the inclusion amount would have been $360,000 ($1/5$ of $1.8 million). Thus, the effect of the rolling fraction adjustment is to take all of the distribution to S from the marital portion rather than just 20% of it.

The practical problem in the administration of a trust with a rolling fraction is that, before the fraction can be adjusted, it first must be restated to reflect current values. Thus, every asset in the fund must be revalued, which may create a difficult, time-consuming, and potentially expensive administrative chore. Consequently, most planners direct division of the original fund into two separate shares following a partial election, which accomplishes the same result as the rolling fraction, without the need to engage in the administrative chore of adjusting the fraction. Some plans also provide that any nonelected portion of a QTIP trust pours over to the nonmarital trust to make administration easier.

Inter Vivos QTIPs and Joint Settlor Revocable Trusts

Estate planning for spouses with disparate wealth often leads to the suggestion that the more wealthy spouse make a gift to the less wealthy spouse to cover the contingency of "deaths out of order." Often a planning concern in noncommunity property states, the tax-sheltering benefit of one unified credit or that spouse's GST exemption may be lost if the nonpropertied spouse dies first and no inter vivos intraspousal gifts were made. Until the advent of the inter vivos QTIP trust, the only ways to address this concern were by outright lifetime gift to the less wealthy spouse, by an inter vivos general power of appointment marital deduction trust (which gave the donee spouse unfettered power to dispose of the transferred property), or by a §2513 inter vivos split gift to a third party (which took the property out of the marital coffers entirely).

Since its enactment in 1982, §2523(f) allows the propertied spouse to create an irrevocable inter vivos QTIP trust to pay income to the donee spouse for life with the remainder passing as the donor spouse originally designated in the trust (or as the donee may appoint pursuant to a nongeneral testamentary power of appointment, if granted by the trust). See §§2523(f)(3) and 2056(b)(7)(B)(ii) (flush language). The donor spouse may make an inter vivos QTIP election under §2523(f)(4), making the initial transfer gift-tax free and, on the donee spouse's death, corpus will be includible in the donee spouse's gross estate, thus sheltering that spouse's unified credit and taking advantage of the donee spouse's GST exemption. All without giving the donee spouse more control over the trust property than the donor chooses.

If control is not a concern and if bifurcation of the wealth between the two spouses to create a chunk for each is not viable or desirable, a different but equally effective alternative may be available in the joint settlor trust approach. This plan provides very desirable marital deduction results as illustrated by Private Letter Ruling 200101021, in which spouses created a joint settlor trust, funded with tenancy by the entirety or joint tenancy property. While both spouses were alive either could revoke the trust unilaterally, in which case the property would be partitioned and delivered to them in equal shares. D was given a general testamentary power to appoint all of the trust property and, in default of exercise, the property was allocated first to a credit shelter trust and any excess to S outright.

The government's conclusions regarding the tax consequences are entirely favorable to taxpayers. When D died all the trust property was includible in D's estate, half under §2038 due to the transfer with retained power of revocation and half under §2041 due to the general testamentary power of appointment. The property deemed gifted by S to D was regarded as qualified for the gift tax marital deduction as if it was a death bed inter vivos gift just before D died. This view of S making a completed gift to D immediately before D's death is as if D and S had figured out who would die first and placed title to their joint property entirely in D's name. Because there is no gift tax on creation of the trust and no estate tax to be paid because any property includible in D's estate is matched by a §2056 marital deduction or sheltered by the unified credit, this planning is desirable because there is no need to guess which spouse will die first. Their collective property can be placed in the trust to take advantage of D's unified credit or GST exemption, effectively accomplishing what inter vivos transfers to equalize estates would do.

The most desirable aspect of this planning relates to whether S may enjoy a life estate in all of the trust property after D's death. In such a plan, the question is whether that secondary life estate in a nonmarital trust will cause §2036(a)(1) (transfer with retained enjoyment) to apply when S subsequently dies. The government's private letter ruling position is that trust property includible in D's gross estate under §2041 is regarded as if D were the transferor and any secondary life estate in S is deemed created by D, rather than having been retained by S. Under this vision, §2036(a)(1) would not apply at S's subsequent death.

According to a variety of Private Letter Rulings, inclusion in S's gross estate is avoided, like the position taken in Treas. Reg. §25.2523(f)-1(f) Example 11 regarding the effect of §2044 inclusion of an inter vivos QTIP trust in D's estate, followed by a secondary life estate in S. That treatment avoids §2036(a)(1) inclusion when S dies because estate tax inclusion in D's estate "cleanses" S's involvement with the trust, and makes this planning effective and harmless. There are a variety of refinements to this planning (often meant to minimize the control granted to D to exercise the general power of appointment) and you would not engage in this plan if D and S do not trust each other. But the overall result is very desirable in any client situation in which spouses have more than the applicable exclusion amount but not enough to split it and shelter either unified credit regardless of the order of their deaths.

Estate and Gift Tax Attributable to QTIP Trusts

Absent a contrary provision in S's will, §2207A provides that any tax attributable to inclusion of QTIP trust corpus in S's gross estate under §2044 (and any interest and penalties attributable thereto) is recoverable from the corpus of the QTIP trust. See the discussion regarding tax payment in general in Chapter 11. The amount of tax attributable to the QTIP trust, computed under §2207A(a)(1), is the difference between the amount of the actual estate tax in S's estate and the amount of estate tax that would be due if the corpus of the QTIP trust was not includible. Thus, §2207A allows a recovery of the amount by which S's estate tax is increased by inclusion of the QTIP, sometimes referred to as the "incremental" tax attributable to the QTIP. However, no recovery is granted for any amount of S's unified credit exhausted by the inclusion (because §2207A is for tax paid, not for tax payable), nor for any state estate or inheritance taxes attributable to the QTIP trust. Treas. Reg. §§20.2207A-1(a)(1) (last two sentences) and 20.2207A-1(b).

As discussed in Chapter 11 at page 18, an unexpected inequity can result under §2207A because the QTIP property is taxed at the highest estate tax rate applicable to S's estate. In addition, failure of S's estate to exercise the right to recover the tax under §2207A is a taxable gift "from the persons who would benefit from the recovery" (usually S's residuary beneficiaries) "to the persons from whom the recovery could have been obtained" (the QTIP remainder beneficiaries). Treas. Reg. §20.2207A-1(a)(2). This gift may be negated to the extent S's beneficiaries cannot compel recovery because S waived the right or, presumably, because the QTIP remainder beneficiaries are judgment proof. Treas. Reg. §20.2207A-1(a)(3). So waiver might avoid nasty gift tax problems, but it also may be inappropriate if S's estate otherwise is unable to pay its estate taxes or does not wish to alter the relative equities of these rules.

A surviving spouse who assigns all or any part of a QTIP income interest triggers a gift of the full value of the remainder interest in the QTIP trust under §2519, in addition to a §2511 gift of the value of the assigned income interest. S is liable for the gift tax on both transfers, but is entitled under §2207A to recover only the gift tax attributable to the gift of the remainder interest from "the person receiving the property," which is the trustee if the property continues to be held in trust. Treas. Reg. §25.2207A-1(e). As illustrated only obliquely by Treas. Reg. §25.2207A-1(f), the §2207A right of reimbursement for gift taxes does not extend to any tax imposed under §2511 on the gift of the income interest.

Failure of S to exercise the §2207A right of recovery on an inter vivos assignment also may result in a taxable gift, again to the persons who are benefited thereby. The gift under §2519 is the value of the corpus less the amount of any §2207A reimbursement to which S was entitled, and S makes an *added* gift of the amount of any reimbursement not collected. See Treas. Reg. §§25.2207A-1(b), 25.2519-1(c). Some drafters preclude assignment simply to avoid the potential for all these unexpected additional gifts. That can reduce flexibility for planning by S, but caution always is in order.

Annuities, Employee Benefit Payments,
and Individual Retirement Accounts

An annuity generally will qualify for the marital deduction if there is no refund or survivor benefit payable (other than to S's estate) that would cause the annuity to be a nondeductible terminable interest. If the annuity is a terminable interest because there is an interest in a beneficiary other than S, automatic QTIP qualification will salvage the marital deduction if the annuity was includible in D's gross estate under §2039 and S is the sole beneficiary during S's overlife. See §2056(b)(7)(C), applicable unless D's personal representative affirmatively elects out of this automatic QTIP qualification. A corresponding automatic gift tax marital deduction is provided by §2523(f)(6) if joint annuity payments begin during a participant's life.

The regulations are silent on qualification of a joint and survivor annuity as commonly found in employee benefit plans that meet the §401(a)(11) spousal annuity rules. Treas. Reg. §20.2056(b)-7(h) Example 10 deems the annuity payable from an individual retirement account directly to S to qualify for the marital deduction under §2056(b)(7)(B)(ii), leaving as a major unresolved issue only individual retirement accounts in which a QTIP trust (rather than S directly) is the sole designated beneficiary during S's overlife but a remainder benefit is payable to a third party after S's death. Rev. Rul. 2000-2 establishes the requirements to qualify such an IRA for marital deduction QTIP election purposes.

The marital deduction qualification issue is easy if S possesses a lifetime power to accelerate payments by making a complete withdrawal from the IRA, because that power satisfies the all-income-annually requisite of either a (b)(5) or a QTIP trust and constitutes a general power of appointment for §2056(b)(5) purposes as well. Treas. Reg. §§20.2056(b)-5(f)(6); 20.2056(b)-7(d)(2). Qualification also is easy if whatever remains in the IRA passes to S's estate at death because the estate trust qualification for marital deduction treatment would apply and nondeductible terminable interest problems would not exist. So the discussion here is about IRA designations of a QTIP trust as beneficiary in which the power of complete withdrawal is not available.

For most purposes the real significance of Rev. Rul. 2000-2 therefore, and the reason for its issuance, is §2056(b)(7) QTIP qualification, which turns on the all-income-annually requirement. Like any typical QTIP trust, S was entitled to all income of the QTIP trust that was the designated beneficiary of the IRA in that Ruling. More critical then was that S was given a power by the QTIP trust to compel the QTIP trustee to withdraw from the IRA annually an amount equal to all the income earned by the IRA assets during that year and distribute that same amount to S as income beneficiary of the QTIP trust. The QTIP trustee would receive the annual minimum distribution amount from the IRA if S did not exercise that withdrawal right. If S *did* exercise the right, however, the Ruling states that the QTIP trust would receive the minimum distribution amount *or* the amount of the IRA income for the year, whichever is greater.

In that context, and put another way, the only issue is income earned in the IRA in excess of the minimum distribution amount: the minimum distribution amount will come out of the IRA in all events. A glance at the mortality tables reveals that the likelihood of the IRA having income in excess of the minimum distribution amount declines as the designated beneficiary (S in this case) ages. By way of example, if S is a 60-year-old surviving spouse, the minimum distribution amount is about 4.1% of the value of the IRA; if S is age 65 that percentage rises to 5%. Either way, many fiduciaries report that they do not earn that much income annually, meaning that the minimum distribution amount will exceed the income amount and all the issues here addressed disappear.

Assuming, however, that there is an excess income issue, the question is whether the IRA qualifies as QTIP elected marital deduction property. Rev. Rul. 2000-2 concluded that S was entitled to all income annually from the IRA as well as from the trust by virtue of S's power to compel the QTIP trustee to make withdrawals from the IRA of the excess income. The Ruling also states that both the IRA and the QTIP trust were subject to §§2519 and 2044; indeed, "[b]ecause the trust is a conduit for payments equal to income from the IRA to [S, the] executor needs to make the QTIP election . . . for both the IRA and the testamentary trust." In effect, this double election mandate makes it clear that the government views *the IRA itself* as qualified terminable interest property, as opposed to thinking of the IRA as just a proper asset of or payable to a QTIP trust. That is an important vision because most observers think of the IRA as merely an asset; the government instead elevates the IRA to the same status as the QTIP trust and, most importantly, requires a separate QTIP election with respect to both the trust and the IRA.

Instead of a power granted to S to demand that the QTIP trustee make withdrawals from the IRA, dicta in Rev. Rul. 2000-2 states that the same marital deduction qualification result would apply if the trust simply required the trustee to withdraw from the IRA annually an amount equal to the excess income earned by the IRA assets and distribute that amount to S.

The hard question for planners is which approach to follow, given the reality that a power in S to compel the QTIP trustee to make a withdrawal from the IRA could lapse and with that lapse may flow all sorts of issues.[63] So perhaps the better approach, all around, is to forego any perceived income tax benefits of leaving the excess income in the IRA and just ensure that the QTIP trustee is obliged to obtain from the IRA any excess income amount. Another alternative not noted by the Ruling is for the QTIP trust simply to require the trustee to distribute (or allow S to withdraw) QTIP trust corpus equal to any difference between the minimum distribution and the IRA income amount. That also will qualify under the all-income-annually requirement.

For marital deduction purposes alone, knowing that the government requires the double QTIP election (trust and IRA both) makes compliance easy and predictable. How to make qualified plan benefits satisfy the marital deduction QTIP requirements entails more difficult questions regarding how much income is earned annually by an IRA or a qualified plan held for a participant's account and payable to S. As explained in Chapter 10, the best course is simply to name S individually as beneficiary, if D is willing to give S control over the distribution amounts.

Qualified Plan Spousal Annuity Issues

Different questions surround qualified employee benefit plans, which are required by §401(a)(11) to create spousal annuities for the benefit of surviving spouses of plan participants. These annuities may be waived under §417(a) if the participant's spouse consents to a different beneficiary designation, but Congress failed to consider the tax consequences of the consent. For example, §2523(f)(6) provides that (1) any gift caused by a

---

63. For example, does S become a transferor to the QTIP trust, or to the IRA itself? There would be completed gift and annual exclusion issues, §2702 valuation possibilities, estate tax inclusion concerns (if the inclusion provision is §2036(a)(1), for example, instead of §2044, which could inform different estate tax right of reimbursement entitlements), and potential GST transferor issues if S is a transferor to the trust. There are a host of income tax qualification and ownership questions in addition to all those wealth transfer tax problems if lapse of S's power to compel withdrawal is regarded a contribution to the IRA itself.

participant's retirement, which locks in a spousal joint and survivor annuity, automatically qualifies for the marital deduction as QTIP property unless the participant affirmatively elects out of this treatment, and (2) §2044 will not apply to include the annuity in the nonparticipant spouse's gross estate if the nonparticipant spouse predeceases the participant. Similar automatic QTIP treatment is provided by §2056(b)(7)(C) if the participant dies and a qualified preretirement annuity locks in for the benefit of S.

Unresolved are the tax consequences (1) if the nonparticipant spouse dies before the participant retires, or (2) when the participant retires and the annuity locks in for the benefit of the participant for life. Does the nonparticipant spouse have any kind of property interest in the plan by virtue of the spousal annuity rule? Is there a wealth transfer from or to either spouse in either of these events? If so, does that transfer qualify for the gift or estate tax marital deduction? These unanswered questions may be exacerbated in community property jurisdictions because it seems even more likely that each spouse owns a portion of the participant's employee benefit.[64]

Technical Advice Memorandum 8943006 considered the estate tax consequences of a nonparticipant spouse's community property interest in a qualified employee benefit plan (S was the plan participant). A portion of the value of the plan was includible in D's gross estate under §2039 by virtue of D's community property interest in the plan and D's will gave all D's community property to D's children. Nevertheless, the government concluded that, under state law, no part of the qualified plan would pass to anyone other than S, who was the participant, a result confirmed by Boggs v. Boggs, 520 U.S. 833 (1997). Thus, D's interest in the plan was held to qualify for the estate tax marital deduction. The Technical Advice Memorandum noted that §2056(b)(7)(C) normally would qualify S's interest in the plan for the marital deduction if D had been the plan participant. Essentially this is the same treatment, granted in the reverse situation presented, as §2056(b)(7)(C) with respect to any portion of a plan that is includible in a nonparticipant's gross estate under §2033.

Although it is not yet clear whether a nonparticipant spouse in a *non*community property state *has* a property interest in such a plan that is includible under either §2033 or §2039, Technical Advice Memorandum 8943006 should clarify that any amount that *is* includible will qualify for the marital deduction. Unfortunately, however, neither §2056(b)(7)(C) (which applies only to §2039 interests includible in a participant's gross estate or to the community property interest of a nonparticipant that is includible under §2033) nor the final QTIP regulations specifically address these questions.

---

64. §2056(b)(7)(C) recognizes the nonparticipant spouse's interest. It provides that the nonparticipant spouse's interest in an annuity arising under state community property laws qualifies as QTIP property if it is included in the nonparticipant spouse's gross estate under §2033 and passes to the surviving participant spouse.

See Treas. Reg. §20.2056(b)-7(f). It also is unclear whether a nonparticipant spouse makes a gift to a participant spouse when the participant spouse retires and, if so, whether that gift qualifies for the gift tax marital deduction. Consistent results dictate that the answer to the second question should be yes to the full extent of any gift the nonparticipant spouse is deemed to make, but these gift tax issues also were reserved under Treas. Reg. §25.2523(f)-1(c)(4). Presumably the appropriate result is that the nonparticipant spouse in a noncommunity property jurisdiction has no property interest whatsoever for tax purposes.[65]

QTIP and Charitable Remainder Trusts

Although adopted along with §§2056(b)(7) and 2523(f) and regarded by many planners as QTIP substitutes, §§2056(b)(8) and 2523(g) are truly independent and not governed by or even surrogates for those QTIP rules. Instead, these provisions are additional distinct exceptions to the nondeductible terminable interest rule and apply if a donee or surviving spouse:

(1) is given a unitrust or annuity trust interest for life pursuant to the charitable remainder trust split interest rules of §664; and

(2) is the only beneficiary who is not a charitable beneficiary (other than the donor, if a lifetime transfer is involved).

If D creates a qualifying charitable remainder annuity trust or unitrust, S's lead interest will qualify for the marital deduction under §2056(b)(8) and the charitable remainder will qualify for the charitable deduction under §2055. Similar rules apply for inter vivos transfers. D or D's estate will incur no tax on the total value of the trust and, because no QTIP election is involved, there will be no §2044 inclusion in S's gross estate at death or §2519 exposure inter vivos. Indeed, there will be no estate tax inclusion of the trust corpus under any Code section at S's death if properly structured, and the trust property will pass unreduced by wealth transfer tax to the charitable remainder beneficiary.

Although a number of substantive differences apply, an alternative approach exists through conventional QTIP planning. As explained in the legislative history to §2056(b)(8), a charitable remainder deduction can be obtained through a normal QTIP trust:

---

65. Were this not true: (1) a participant's getting married and thereby creating potential rights in a new spouse could be regarded as a gift, which is silly, even if it were to qualify for the marital deduction; (2) the participant's receipt of benefits under the plan would constitute a gift by the nonparticipant to the participant that would need to go through the marital deduction qualification routine, which also would be silly; and (3) the fact that §2503(f) applies to a nonparticipant's waiver during the participant's life but not otherwise essentially would force spouses to waive spousal annuity entitlements during participants' lives, to avoid these consequences, which would be the wrong policy result. Forcing a nonparticipant spouse to waive the annuity to be better off is exactly the opposite of what Congress was attempting to accomplish by creating the §401(a)(11) entitlements.

The general rules applicable to qualifying income interests may provide similar treatment where a decedent provides an income interest in the spouse for her [sic] life and a remainder interest to charity. If the life estate is a qualifying [§2056(b)(7)(B)(ii)] income interest, the entire property will . . . be considered as passing to the spouse. Therefore, the entire value of the property will be eligible for the marital deduction and no transfer tax will be imposed. Upon the spouse's death, the property will be included in the spouse's estate [under §2044] but, because the spouse's life estate terminates at death, any property passing outright to charity may qualify for a charitable deduction.[66]

Thus, for example, a trust might provide that "the trustee shall pay the trust income to S at least quarterly for life. On S's death the trustee shall distribute the trust principal to [qualified charitable organization]." Being a QTIP trust interest, the §2056(b)(7)(B)(v) QTIP election automatically would apply to the extent D's estate reports the value of the trust principal on Schedule M of its estate tax return, Form 706. The entire trust corpus would qualify for a marital deduction in D's estate, it would cause §2044 inclusion in S's gross estate, and it would qualify for a §2055 charitable deduction in computing S's taxable estate. By virtue of §2044(c), the remainder in a QTIP trust qualifies for a charitable deduction in S's estate because the interest is deemed to pass to the charity from S, in whose estate it is includible. Again, there would be no tax in either estate.

An advantage of the QTIP alternative over the §2056(b)(8) qualified charitable remainder trust approach is that it is not necessary to draft within the complicated confines of the §664 charitable remainder trust rules, and corpus distributions may be made to S from the QTIP trust. Alternatively, the §2056(b)(8) split interest trust approach provides a number of advantages over the QTIP alternative.

For example, if created inter vivos, the §2523(g) inter vivos version of the §2056(b)(8) trust generates a §170 income tax deduction for D that the QTIP alternative would not generate. In addition, the tax character of the trust precludes ordinary income, capital gains, and income in respect of the decedent from being subject to income tax to the extent not carried out to S as beneficiary of the annual payment. Nor must the trust distribute all its income annually to S or worry about satisfying the qualified income interest rules.[67] Indeed, under the authority of §664(f), the trust may be drafted to distribute to the qualified charitable remainder beneficiary prior to S's death, either because S's interest is limited to a term of years or because it is made terminable on a contingency (such as remarriage).[68]

---

66. H.R. Rep. No. 201, 97th Cong.; 1st Sess. 162 n.4 (1981).

67. Because §2056(b)(8) provides that the nondeductible terminable interest rule of §2056(b)(1) does not apply at all, this trust is not an exception to that rule and need not meet the income payment requirements common to §§2056(b)(5) and 2056(b)(7) trusts.

68. Although §664(f)(2) precludes the contingent acceleration of the charitable remainder

Qualified Domestic Trusts

A final marital deduction qualifying trust concept addresses a larger concern than many individuals contemplate. A surprising number of estate planners report that an unexpected number of their clients' spouses are not United States citizens. And it is not just practitioners with an international clientele or who practice in border states or cities with an international community who are discovering this phenomenon. It occurs throughout the United States, with respect to clients from varying walks of life and with experiences as varied as: "we met while we were students," or "when I was in the Service," or "while I was on assignment overseas," or "when we both were working in New York/San Francisco/Miami/etc.," or "my in-laws immigrated when my spouse was a child." Notwithstanding the frequency of these types of situations, however, this fact might not be considered as part of the estate planning process unless your client happens to mention the spouse's citizenship to you, and failing to consider this fact will cause a serious problem.

The issue presented by a client whose spouse is not a United States citizen was created in 1988 when Congress adopted §§2056(d) and 2056A to address what it perceived to be an abuse: qualifying property for the marital deduction notwithstanding that S is not a United States citizen and, therefore, may remove the property from United States taxing jurisdiction before it is subject to United States wealth transfer taxation. Although §2056(a) always required D to be a United States citizen or resident to qualify for the estate tax marital deduction (a requirement that, ironically, was relaxed in 1988 if D complies with the marital deduction requirements), no similar requirement was imposed on S until 1988.

Citizenship Requirement

Congress apparently was persuaded that there is a significant possibility of D qualifying marital deduction property that S might remove from the United States to avoid paying estate tax as the recompense for marital deduction qualification in D's estate. So §2056(d)(1) was enacted to provide that the marital deduction under §2056(a) is not available if S is not a United States citizen unless the special qualified domestic trust (QDOT) requirements of §2056A are met. In addition, the §2040(a) consideration furnished rule for concurrent ownership property was made applicable by §2056(d)(1)(B). This causes inclusion of joint tenancy property (or tenancy by the entireties) held by D and a noncitizen S based on their respective contributions to the property instead of including half the value of qualified joint property in D's gross estate under §2040(b). By virtue of this provision, only that portion of a joint tenancy that is includible in D's gross

---

from being reflected in valuing the remainder for charitable deduction purposes, it nevertheless may be D's desire to terminate S's enjoyment on the happening of such a contingency.

estate under §2040(a) may meet the special §2056A rules to qualify for the marital deduction. Treas. Reg. §20.2056A-8(a)(3).

Also enacted in 1988, §2523(i) provides that the gift tax marital deduction is not allowable if S is not a United States citizen, with no §2056A-type exception to permit inter vivos marital deduction qualification. In its place, however, the §2503(b) gift tax annual exclusion was increased to $100,000 (indexed for inflation after 1998, it was $114,000 in 2004) per year, for gifts made to a spouse who is not a citizen, provided only that the gift otherwise would qualify for the normal gift tax marital deduction and meets the gift tax annual exclusion present interest requirements. The trade-off for this "super" inflated annual exclusion benefit is loss of the §1014 basis adjustment that otherwise would be available if D held the property until death. But inter vivos super annual exclusion treatment is advantageous if the gifted property is not suited to QDOT ownership or administration.[69]

Exceptions

Several exceptions apply to the §2056(d) disallowance of the marital deduction if S is not a United States citizen. For example, transfers governed by wealth transfer tax treaties are governed by whichever of the treaty or §2056A (but not both) is selected by the taxpayer. Treas. Reg. §20.2056A-1(c). More importantly, §2056(d)(2) permits the estate tax marital deduction if a §2056A QDOT is utilized. Under this exception, property passing from D directly to a QDOT will qualify for the estate tax marital deduction. So too will property passing to S who then transfers or irrevocably assigns it to a QDOT before D's estate tax return is filed and before the QDOT election is required.[70] It is not necessary that D create the QDOT.

Treas. Reg. §§20.2056A-2(b)(2) and 20.2056A-4(b)(1) list S, D, and D's personal representative as potential creators of a QDOT. Treas. Reg. §§20.2056A-4(b)(5) and 20.2056A-4(d) Example 5 dramatically illustrate the consequences of S receiving property outright that S contributes to a QDOT. The example concludes that S's transfer constitutes an immediate

---

69. §2523(i)(3) also restored the former §§2515 and 2515A joint tenancy rules for gift tax purposes that were repealed in 1981 when the unlimited gift tax marital deduction was adopted. In general, under these rules, creation of a joint tenancy (other than a revocable joint tenancy, such as a bank account) or tenancy by the entirety is a gift to the extent consideration furnished by each tenant is not equal. In a revocable joint tenancy the gift occurs on withdrawal by any tenants of amounts in excess of their contributions, and that gift may qualify for the super annual exclusion. On termination of a joint tenancy, a gift occurs to the extent the property is not distributed in the same proportions as the consideration furnished, with the added proviso that gift taxation on creation subsequently authorizes treatment of the donee as having provided an equal share of the consideration. For a detailed exegesis, see Plaine & Siegler, *The Federal Gift and Estate Tax Marital Deduction for Non-United States Citizen Recipient Spouses*, 25 REAL PROP., PROB. & TR. J. 385, 436-443 (1991). For a much too cursory treatment see Treas. Reg. §25.2523(i)-2(b), which may reveal that the government does not care to get into these issues.

70. Treas. Reg. §§20.2056A-2(b)(2) and 20.2056A-4(b)(1). The election is described in §2056(d) and Treas. Reg. §20.2056A-3(a) as timely if made on the last timely filed estate tax return (including extensions) or on the first return filed not more than one year late.

gift of a remainder interest that does not qualify for the gift tax annual exclusion. As revealed in Treas. Reg. §20.2056A-4(d) Example 1, however, this gift would be incomplete and no gift tax would be incurred if S retained a testamentary power of appointment over the trust. Because the property is transferred to a trust in which S enjoys an income interest for life, the full value of the transferred property will be includible in S's gross estate under §2036(a)(1) (with the appropriate §2001(b) adjustment to avoid any double tax incurred). And, because S is the transferor (rather than D), the §2652(a)(3) reverse QTIP election is not available to take advantage of D's generation-skipping transfer tax exemption.

Overall, examples illustrate that relatively poor results are produced by S's contributions to a QDOT. This places importance on ascertaining citizenship in the planning stage and crafting the estate plan to create and fully fund a QDOT without the need for action by S.

QDOT Qualification Requirements

It probably is easiest to think of a §2056A(a) QDOT created by D as a §2056(b)(5), §2056(b)(7), §2056(b)(8), or estate trust[71] that meets the §2056A(a)(1) requirements:

(1) At least one trustee must be a United States citizen or domestic corporation. An individual trustee "must have a tax home . . . in the United States" to meet the United States citizen requirement. Treas. Reg. §20.2056A-2(d)(2).

(2) The United States citizen or domestic corporation trustee must withhold tax on any corpus distribution.

(3) All income must be payable to the noncitizen spouse annually (unless an estate trust is being used). See Treas. Reg. §20.2056A-2(b)(1).

(4) An election must be made on D's last timely filed estate tax return or first late return. Treas. Reg. §20.2056A-3(a). Partial QDOT elections are not allowed, but a trust may be severed and only one of the trusts elected. Treas. Reg. §20.2056A-3(b).

(5) The QDOT also must comply with any "requirements . . . prescribe[d by regulations] to ensure the collection of any tax imposed" by §2056A(b). §2056A(a)(2).

---

71. §2056A(c)(3) grants the Treasury regulatory authority to treat as trusts for purposes of QDOT qualification any legal arrangements that have substantially the same effect as trusts. The recognition of nontrust arrangements is intended to permit qualification for estates of decedents whose nonresident spouses reside in countries in which the use of a trust is prohibited (as it is in some civil law countries). The Conference Report states that regulations, if any, would only permit a marital deduction with respect to nontrust arrangements under which the United States would retain jurisdiction and adequate security to impose United States transfer tax on transfers by S of the property transferred by D. H.R. Rep. No. 220, 105th Cong., 1st Sess. 719 (1997).

(6) And a bifurcated rule imposes the requirement that a trust either:

- employ at least one trustee that is a §581 United States bank or trust company (a domestic law firm or other citizen acting as trustee will not suffice);
- furnish a bond or letter of credit in an amount equal to 65% of the federal estate tax value of the trust corpus; or
- if the federal estate tax value is no more than $2 million, the trust instrument must prohibit investment of more than 35% of the annually determined fair market value in real estate located offshore.[72]

Taxation of QDOTs

Wealth transfer tax is imposed on QDOTs in an unusual manner. Effectively, §2056A(b) treats a QDOT as not really qualifying for a normal estate tax marital deduction in D's estate but, rather, as merely deferring D's tax from D's death until a later triggering event. That is, the tax imposed under §2056A(b)(2)(A) is computed as if D had died at the time of the later triggering event and the taxable property was then includible in D's gross estate. Like a gift tax computation, the amount by which D's taxes would have been increased by inclusion of such property is the amount of tax that is to be paid by the QDOT, with no imposition of interest for the deferral inherent in the delay between D's death and the triggering event. In addition, although the tax is paid by the QDOT trustee, it is treated under §2056A(b)(7) as paid by D's estate.

QDOT property normally will be taxable in S's estate as well (because a QDOT created by D must comply with the normal marital deduction trust rules and will be subject to United States taxation if still in existence at S's death). Double tax under the QDOT regime is meant to be precluded by §2056(d)(3), which grants a special §2013 credit to S's estate for application against any estate tax incurred in S's gross estate. This credit is based on taxes deemed paid by D's estate with respect to QDOT property — all without the §2013(a) percentage limitation, which normally reduces the available credit based on the time elapsed between deaths.

The triggering events for imposition of the §2056A(b) tax are:

1. death of S (before repeal of the estate tax);
2. any termination of the qualified status of the trust;

---

72. An entity passthrough rule is applied in Treas. Reg. §20.2056A-2(d)(1)(ii)(B) to determine the ownership of assets held by corporations or partnerships with 15 or fewer shareholders or partners, and a §267 related party attribution rule is applied to determine the number of shareholders or partners, all presumably to preclude the use of entity ownership of assets to avoid the offshore investment limitations. A similar paranoia is exhibited in Treas. Reg. §20.2056A-2(d)(1)(ii)(C), which refers generally to "other entities (such as . . . a trust)" in which a QDOT owns an interest.

3. any distribution from the QDOT during S's overlife except mandatory distributions of income required to qualify as a QDOT and distributions of corpus "on account of hardship."[73]

Lifetime distributions to S attract tax like an estate tax computation because the trustee must pay the tax on those distributions and that tax payment is regarded as another taxable distribution to S. The net result is that taxes paid by the trust by virtue of the distribution are subjected to the tax itself. Treas. Reg. §20.2056A-5(b)(1).

The tax computation rules can be avoided if S becomes a citizen. §2056A(b)(12). Only limited additional administrative requirements must be met if S was a resident at, and at all times after, D's death, or if no taxable distributions were made to S before becoming a citizen.

To be in a position to comply with all these requirements, you need a client questionnaire or interview that specifically inquires whether your client's spouse is a United States citizen. The significance of this should not be underestimated, given the number of clients whose spouses are not citizens and the unnecessary loss of deferred taxation if a QDOT is not employed.

Selecting and Drafting Marital Deduction Trusts

Selecting the Type of Marital Trust

For most estate planners, the §2056(b)(7) QTIP trust has displaced the §2056(b)(5) power of appointment trust as the favored vehicle for settling marital deduction gifts that do not pass outright. The estate trust does not enjoy much use and neither the §2056(b)(6) insurance settlement nor the §2056(b)(8) charitable remainder trust alternative is more than rarely employed.

Estate planners prefer QTIP trusts primarily because of the control the testator retains over disposition of the trust corpus after S's death, the postmortem planning opportunities provided by the partial QTIP election and the §2652(a)(3) GST reverse QTIP election, and better creditor protection than with the power to appoint.[74] For many taxpayers who

---

73. §2056A(b)(3)(B). Treas. Reg. §20.2056A-5(c)(1) adopts an expanded version of the hardship definition found in Treas. Reg. §1.401(k)-1(d)(2)(i), allowing distributions that respond to an immediate and substantial financial need relating to S's health, maintenance, education, or support, or the health, maintenance, education, or support of any person S is legally obligated to support, but only to the extent other resources (such as personally owned publicly traded stock or a certificate of deposit that could be cashed in) are not reasonably available.

74. Moreover, QTIPs are favored by §1022(c)(3)(B) and will draw even more adherents as repeal of the estate tax approaches, promised for year 2010, because with it comes the imposition of carryover basis. This provision allows D to convey property outright to, or to a QTIP trust for the benefit of, S and obtain a basis improvement of up to $3.0 million (along with another $1.3 million of basis increase available to every decedent's estate, regardless of the destination of their property).

cannot or will not leave property to a spouse outright, the QTIP is the only vehicle of choice.

The §2056(b)(5) trust remains popular only with clients who might prefer to make an outright gift to S but desire the protection and management aspects of a transfer in trust. It also may be attractive to occasional clients because the general power creates Rule Against Perpetuities second look opportunities or a new qualified disclaimer nine month window. An estate trust generates probate inclusion and consequent expenses when S subsequently dies, but it avoids the need to produce and pay a reasonable amount of income to S annually (or provide for unproductive property otherwise) and may be attractive for that reason when control over investment is an issue.

If an outright bequest is not appropriate, the choice in most cases is between the §2056(b)(5) general power of appointment trust and the §2056(b)(7) QTIP trust. Thus, the following discussion elaborates upon perceived advantages of each, outlining situations that may dictate specific trust choices.

Advantages of QTIPs

The QTIP trust has three significant current advantages over other alternatives: flexibility in postmortem planning, creditor protection, and control. There is a valuation opportunity made available by it, and an additional advantage in the form of §1022(c)(3)(B) if carryover of basis becomes the law.

Early in the life of the QTIP denying control to S was regarded as its primary attribute. D controls disposition of the property after S's death, which is particularly desirable if there are children by a former marriage (the reason cited by Congress for creating the QTIP). Even in single-marriage situations, in which D's descendants also are S's descendants, many clients are attracted by the ability to control disposition of the remainder after S's death or by giving S, at most, a narrow nongeneral testamentary power of appointment.

Eliminated with the QTIP is any concern that S will remarry and again take advantage of the marital deduction, or otherwise divert the marital deduction property from the natural objects of D's bounty. It bears noting, however, that remarriage and disinheritance are almost uniquely male traits: surviving widows remarry far less often and rarely disinherit their own children. So to the extent this rationale is sensible, it almost always should be when drafting a woman's estate plan in anticipation of her husband being the surviving spouse. In fact, however, it is most frequently employed by men in drafting for their surviving widows, probably because they assume their wives will do what they would do as the surviving spouse.[75] Good estate planning advice would question the way this plays out in many cases.

Creditor protection advantages relate to the state law treatment of general powers of appointment, which in some jurisdictions allows creditors of the powerholder to reach assets subject to the power even if the power is not exercised. The QTIP trust provides a level of protection beyond compare to the extent creditor problems may exist and appointive assets may be subject to attachment by creditors. Truth be known, however, creditor concerns rarely arise in the kind of client population you will represent.

So the primary reason to favor the QTIP in happy single-marriage situations without creditor concerns is postmortem estate planning flexibility. The QTIP election need not be made with respect to the entire trust; partial elections are permissible. This partial election ability permits postmortem planning by qualifying only the most appropriate portion of the QTIP trust for the marital deduction, thereby fine-tuning the size of each spouse's estate. There is no similar postmortem planning opportunity in a §2056(b)(5) trust (other than by the more cumbersome and much less reliable postmortem disclaimer), because qualification for the marital deduction is automatic.

Closely related to postmortem partial election planning is the §2652(a)(3) GST exemption allocation election, which also is available only for QTIP trusts. This planning opportunity is another valuable source of postmortem flexibility and again it is unique to the QTIP. And apropos the unique treatment of QTIP trusts for postmortem purposes, a similar and singularly unique valuation opportunity is available only to QTIP owned assets includible in S's estate at death. See Chapter 12 at page 9 regarding the courts' refusal to aggregate QTIP property with S's other wealth or with power of appointment property for valuation purposes.

Advantages of Power of Appointment Trusts

The §2056(b)(5) trust remains in vogue for clients who otherwise might be inclined to give S outright ownership of marital deduction property but are concerned (because of S's age or condition) about the need for management in the event of incapacity, or want to provide protection against "predators" during S's overlife. Many of these trusts are likely to be drafted with S as original trustee and grant S a power of withdrawal that permits S to obtain outright possession at any time during life but otherwise providing the trust mechanism if S is unable or unwilling to manage the property.

---

75. See Pennell, *Minimizing the Surviving Spouse's Elective Share*, 32 U. MIAMI INST. EST. PLAN. ¶903.2 (1998).

Elective Share Concerns

In states that grant an elective share to a disappointed surviving spouse (all noncommunity property states except Georgia grant some form of statutory forced heir entitlement to a disgruntled spouse), there is a greater risk under a QTIP plan than a §2056(b)(5) trust plan that S will elect against D's estate plan. Some elections will be motivated simply by the perception that D cut S out of effective control.

Although a QTIP trust life estate may be worth considerably more than the outright statutory forced heir share, S nevertheless may choose to elect a smaller outright entitlement merely to acquire the property with the ability to deal with it in ways that a naked life estate in a QTIP trust would not permit. If S is young, the life estate will be worth more, but so too is the intangible benefit of unfettered enjoyment. Thus, the risks seem more than insignificant that some surviving spouses will reject the QTIP and disrupt the estate plan by electing their statutory share outright, especially if S ultimately wants to benefit individuals other than the remainder beneficiaries of the QTIP trust.

The most immediate effect of this election is that D's estate must generate sufficient cash or other assets to satisfy the statutory share, which may cause severe disruption in the administration of D's estate. A reduction in the marital deduction may occur if the elective share is smaller in value than the corpus of the QTIP trust, in which case estate taxes may increase, which will exacerbate the need for liquidity.

A second, less obvious, consequence is that S may be permitted to continue to benefit from the balance of D's estate plan. State laws typically provide that S is treated as predeceased for all purposes under D's will by virtue of making the statutory forced heir share election. Thus, S cannot take a share outright and continue as beneficiary of what remains in any testamentary trust. But most states do not have a similar rule if D's estate plan was created by an inter vivos trust, rather than a will. See, e.g., N.Y. Est. Powers & Trusts Law §§5-1.1-A(a)(4)(A) and 5-1.1-A(b). Life insurance, deferred compensation, joint tenancy with the right of survivorship, and other nonprobate property also may pass to S, in addition to the elective share of the probate estate, all quite contrary to D's wishes.

Thus, an inter vivos trust or other nonprobate transfers that serve as will substitutes should specify that S shall be treated as predeceased if an election against D's will is made. Similar provisions have been held to be harmless for marital deduction purposes: they do not constitute a nondeductible terminable interest. See, e.g., Estate of Mackie v. Commissioner, 64 T.C. 308 (1975) (a spousal election was required to perfect a bequest under the will and did not disqualify the marital deduction); Treas. Reg. §20.2056(c)-2(c); and Rev. Rul. 82-184, which held that there is no substantive difference between a bequest that relates back to D's date of death and S's election against a will, or between S having a choice between accepting a testamentary bequest or taking a statutory forced heir share, because S has a choice between two groups of assets in either case.

A fine mechanism to consider if the elective share is a concern (especially if denial of control is not D's primary objective) is to use the QTIP alternative with S as a trustee, with powers appropriately limited to avoid their rising to the level of a general power of appointment that might cause §2056(b)(5) to apply instead of §2056(b)(7) (in which case the postmortem flexibility of the QTIP may be lost with automatic marital deduction qualification). Also consider giving S a power to withdraw some or all of the QTIP corpus, as discussed next.

Better Mechanism for Inter Vivos Gifts

A marital deduction §2056(b)(5) approach also may be more attractive than a QTIP trust because it may give S a power to appoint trust property inter vivos. No narrow inter vivos power to appoint is permissible in a QTIP. So making gifts from a §2056(b)(5) trust is both easier than from a QTIP trust and potentially more palatable to D, because D may limit the range of donees to whom inter vivos gifts may be made. The only way S may make gifts out of a QTIP trust is first by withdrawal or trustee distribution to S under a power granted by the trust, followed by a gift by S personally. §2056(b)(7)(B)(ii)(II). With this approach the ultimate donee could be anyone S chooses. Under the §2056(b)(5) alternative, however, S may be given the power to make gifts via a nongeneral inter vivos power of appointment, which is easier to exercise and permits D to limit appointment to only those beneficiaries D chose to include within the defined class of permissible appointees. Thus, using a narrowly drafted nongeneral inter vivos power of appointment, D allows S flexibility but alleviates undue concern over an "undesirable" dissemination of the family wealth.

Furthermore, the nongeneral inter vivos power of appointment, while accomplishing the same inter vivos control and predator protection objectives of a QTIP approach, may overcome any psychological resistance S might feel about the QTIP handcuff feature. Indeed, it may make it easier to persuade S to make lifetime transfers, because the power verifies to S that making lifetime transfers by exercise is consistent with D's wishes. We know that the gift tax on inter vivos transfers by S are cheaper than estate taxation in D or S's estates, and we also know that gifting is not common. So any way we can encourage these more favorable transfers likely is a good thing.

Permits Inter Vivos Assignment of Income

A §2056(b)(5) power of appointment trust also is advantageous if D wants to give S the option of assigning a portion of the marital trust income interest during life. This may be an important consideration in larger estates for spouses who are in the maximum income tax bracket (not to mention a high state income tax bracket as well), because Uncle Sam is an unwelcome cobeneficiary of the trust income (unless a tax-free municipal bond investment strategy is pursued).

Although an assignment of a QTIP income interest[76] is possible, it produces such harsh tax consequences under §§2519 and 2702 that a transfer of any portion of the income interest in a QTIP trust usually is an unmitigated disaster.[77] An assignment of a QTIP income interest results in a gift under §2511 of the portion of the income interest that is assigned, which is a result most planners would expect, and is a cost S usually is willing to bear. But the assignment also has the draconian effect of triggering a gift of the entire value of the remainder interest in the QTIP trust under §2519 and, according to Treas. Reg. §§25.2519-1(a) and 25.2519-1(g) Example 4, also may trigger application of §2702, causing the value of the gift to equal the full value of the trust proper.

> Example: S released just 10% of a QTIP trust income interest. Under §2511, S made a gift of an amount equal to 10% of the value of the total income interest in the trust. No §2207A right of reimbursement exists for the gift taxes thereon but the §2503(b) gift tax annual exclusion is available. In addition, under §2519, S is deemed to have transferred 100% of the value of the remainder interest in the trust. See Treas. Reg. §25.2519-1. No annual exclusion is allowable because this gift is of a future interest (except to the extent the remainder beneficiary is the assignee of the income interest and, under state law, a merger occurs).
>
> Although §2044 exposure at S's death is avoided due to application of §2519 during life, §2036(a)(1) is said to apply to 90% of the value of the corpus at S's death on the theory that §2519 treats S as having transferred the full trust corpus while retaining a §2036(a)(1) life estate in 90%. Double taxation is avoided because the last sentence of §2001(b) will purge the prior §2519 inclusion of that 90% interest from the adjusted taxable gifts base. The full date of death value of that 90% interest is taxed, however, and S has prepaid some tax by incurring gift tax on this same 90% that is taxable at death. Treas. Reg. §§20.2044-1(e) Example 5 and 25.2519-1(g) Example 4. If death does not occur within three years the advantage — perhaps the only advantage — of this particular transaction for wealth transfer tax purposes is exclusion of the gift tax dollars paid from S's gross estate at death.

---

76. Notice that there is an important distinction between a gift of a portion of the income from a QTIP trust, taxable under §2511, and a gift of a portion of the income *interest* itself, which triggers taxation under §2519.

77. See Treas. Reg. §25.2519-1(g) Example 4.

In addition, if the assignment is to a member of S's family (as defined in §2704(c)(2); see §2702(e)), the gift of the remainder is deemed to be a gift of the full value of the trust, also subject to adjustment at death but further exacerbating the effects of accelerating the tax. See Treas. Reg. §25.2702-6 regarding an adjustment to prevent double taxation that does not operate properly, particularly with respect to double taxation of the retained income interest in a §2702 transfer.

An assignment of any portion of the income interest would have produced only the §2511 gift if this example had involved a §2056(b)(5) trust. Although a cheaper shift of the QTIP income interest could be effected by S withdrawing principal through a drawdown power and then making a gift of the withdrawn amount, this approach gives S control over corpus, which may be inconsistent with D's intent.

Overall it seems fair to conclude that, if D wishes to permit income assignments, a §2056(b)(5) trust should be used, exempting S's income interest from any spendthrift clause or permitting an "assignment" of the income interest by giving S a narrow nongeneral inter vivos power of appointment. And perhaps the most instructive advice to give with respect to QTIPs is to preclude S from triggering §2519(a) unless S retains absolutely no interest or enjoyment in the property. Even in that case acceleration of the tax may be wise planning only if S is expected to die before estate tax repeal (if in fact that actually occurs).

A Combined Trust Plan

The foregoing considerations suggest that, for larger estates, it might be advantageous to employ several marital deduction trusts: a §2056(b)(7) QTIP trust as to a portion; a §2056(b)(5) power of appointment trust (in which S also may be given a narrow nongeneral inter vivos power) for another portion; an estate trust for assets that should not be made productive of a reasonable amount of income; and perhaps even some outright transfers as well. These multiple trust plans take advantage of various forms of marital deduction trust, although an undeniable disadvantage is the multiplicity of entities and the corresponding complexity that might exist at one time.

Drafting Considerations

Throughout this discussion of dispositions qualifying for the marital deduction, a number of issues have been mentioned for which special drafting is appropriate. This section provides examples of drafting that deals with these various issues. In reviewing these please remember that there usually are several ways to address a particular issue, and sample language should never be used without a careful determination that it is appropriate for a particular application.

Unproductive Property

Regardless of whether it is contemplated that a marital deduction trust actually may own unproductive property, prudence dictates that the boilerplate provisions of any marital trust (other than an estate trust) include language either: (1) permitting S to require that the trustee make the property productive or convert it within a reasonable time; (2) requiring the trustee to obtain S's consent to continue to retain unproductive property; (3) requiring the trustee to distribute corpus equal to any difference between reasonable income and what the trustee earned; or (4) permitting S to require the trustee to make payments to S out of other assets to compensate for such lost income. Treas. Reg. §§20.2056(b)-5(f)(4) and 20.2056(b)-5(f)(5). Language that would serve the unproductive property function applying the most popular first option might read:

> **The trustee may retain as trust investments property of any kind acquired at any time and in any manner. The trustee may hold property unproductive of income and may invest and reinvest all or any part of the trust estate in property of any description (including shares of open or closed end investment trusts or companies and wasting assets) regardless of location and without regard to any requirement to diversify either as to kind or amount. By written instrument delivered to the trustee, S may require the trustee to convert or make productive within a reasonable time after delivery of the notice any property that does not produce a reasonable income.**

The second alternative approach of requiring the trustee to dispose of assets not producing a reasonable return unless S consents to their retention precludes the government from challenging the effect of the provision set out in full above if S is unable to require disposition (for example, due to incapacity). But an inability to obtain consent to retention is a detriment of that alternative provision.

Much less common alternatives are the withdrawal right or requiring allocation of corpus to income for distribution in compensation for deficient income production, either through an equitable adjustment as authorized under state law or in the form of a unitrust interest, as authorized by Treas. Reg. §§1.643(b)-1 and 20.2056(b)-5(f)(1). Either or both may become more widely favored with more recent focus on Principal and Income Act and Prudent Investor Act changes and income definition regulations that reflect and respect both.

Spendthrift Clause

The traditional form of "disabling" spendthrift clause prohibits voluntary or involuntary transfer of a beneficial interest and presents no problem for marital deduction qualification as a §2056(b)(5) trust. Treas. Reg. §20.2056(b)-5(f)(7) provides:

An interest passing in trust will not fail to satisfy the condition that the spouse be entitled to all the income merely because its terms provide that the right of the surviving spouse to the income shall not be subject to assignment, alienation, pledge, attachment or claims of creditors.

The same result should apply with respect to the power of appointment requirement in a §2056(b)(5) trust that precludes involuntary exercise.[78] However, a "forfeiture" spendthrift clause (under which an attempted transfer terminates the beneficial interest) will disqualify any marital deduction trust. See, e.g., Miller v. United States, 267 F. Supp. 326 (M.D. Fla. 1967) (forfeiture of an income interest if S attempted to assign it or a creditor attempted to attach it).

In general, a spendthrift clause usually is thought to give desirable protection against creditors' claims and against anticipation of the income interest by assignment. In a QTIP trust, a spendthrift clause gives added protection against S inadvertently or unadvisedly triggering the draconian rule of §2519(a) on a partial or total assignment of the QTIP income interest, which would subject the entire remainder interest to gift tax.

A sample spendthrift clause that would serve the intended purpose might read:

No beneficiary of any trust shall have the power to anticipate, encumber, or transfer any interest in the trust estate in any manner. No part of any trust estate shall be liable for or charged with any debts, contracts, liabilities, or torts of a beneficiary or be subject to seizure or other process by any creditor of a beneficiary.

There are, however, circumstances in which a spendthrift provision is not advisable and spendthrift clauses should not be treated as boilerplate for mindless inclusion in every document.

Facility of Payment Clause

Instruments often authorize the trustee to make distributions in a variety of ways other than directly to the beneficiary. One version of a "facility of payment" provision appears at page 63. Another variant might specify:

During the term of a trust, the trustee may make any of the distributions authorized elsewhere herein (i) directly to the

---

78. See Wilson v. United States, 254 F. Supp. 822 (E.D. Pa. 1966), rev'd and rem'd on other grounds, 372 F.2d 232 (3d Cir. 1967); Estate of Benjamin v. Commissioner, 44 T.C. 598 (1965). Cf. Virginia Nat'l Bank v. United States, 443 F.2d 1030 (4th Cir. 1971).

beneficiary, (ii) if the beneficiary is under a legal disability or if the trustee determines that the beneficiary is unable properly to manage his or her affairs, to a person furnishing support, maintenance, or education for the beneficiary or with whom the beneficiary is residing, in reimbursement *for expenditures on the beneficiary's behalf*, or (iii) if the beneficiary is a minor, to a custodian for the beneficiary, as selected by the trustee, under the Uniform Transfers to Minors Act or Uniform Gifts to Minors Act of any state. Alternatively, the trustee may apply all or a part of the distribution directly for the beneficiary. Any distribution under this paragraph shall be a full discharge of the trustee with respect thereto.[79]

Although this facility of payment clause applies to the marital deduction trust, distribution mode (ii) does not violate the all-income-annually requirement of a §2056(b)(5) or QTIP trust because, "[a]mong the powers which if subject to reasonable limitations will not disqualify the interest passing in trust are . . . the power to apply the income or corpus *for the benefit of the spouse*. . . ." Treas. Reg. §20.2056(b)-5(f)(4) (emphasis added). And see Rev. Rul. 85-35 and Technical Advice Memorandum 9514002 (allowing facility of payment provisions in §2056(b)(5) trusts) and Technical Advice Memorandum 8706008 (QTIP trust). Not qualifying would be the type of provision involved in Estate of Walsh v. Commissioner, 110 T.C. 393 (1998), which terminated S's income interest in the event of incapacity (perhaps in a misguided effort to qualify S for governmental assistance in that event).

Delay in Funding Marital Trusts

There is no requirement that S be entitled to income from D's estate before the marital deduction trust is funded, provided D's will does not authorize or direct the executor to delay that distribution and funding beyond a reasonable period. Treas. Reg. §20.2056(b)-5(f)(9). See pages 109 and 129 regarding the separate share rule and distributable net income carryout aspects of postmortem planning in the marital deduction context. The following provision permits interim distributions for income tax or other planning purposes:

Prior to final distribution of my estate (which shall not be delayed beyond the time reasonably required for administration of my estate), my personal representative may

---

79. The emphasized language is taken verbatim from Technical Advice Memorandum 8706008. In Technical Advice Memorandum 8901008 a facility of payment clause, giving the trustee discretion to distribute income as deemed prudent if S became incapacitated, prevented the deduction under §2056(b)(5). And Estate of Tingley v. Commissioner, 22 T.C. 402 (1954), aff'd sub nom., Starrett v. Commissioner, 223 F.2d 163 (1st Cir. 1955), denied the marital deduction because a facility of payment provision terminated S's right to request income and permitted the trustee to accumulate income if S became incapacitated.

> make partial distributions to one or more beneficiaries or trusts. As a consequence, my estate and any trust created under my will may exist contemporaneously. A distribution may be made subject to any indebtedness or liability of my estate.

The parenthetical phrase is derived virtually verbatim from Treas. Reg. §20.2056(b)-5(f)(9).

Accumulated Income

Many trust instruments and a few applicable local laws provide that the trustee shall distribute the trust estate, including any accrued or accumulated but undistributed income, to the next beneficiaries upon the death of any income beneficiary. In a §2056(b)(5) trust this accrued but undistributed income creates no qualification problem if it is subject to S's required general power of appointment. Treas. Reg. §20.2056(b)-5(f)(8). Many planners had feared, however, that a QTIP trust would need to grant the power to appoint such income, or that such QTIP "stub income" must be paid to S's estate. Fortunately, Treas. Reg. §20.2056(b)-7(d)(4) allays that fear, stating:

> An income interest does not fail to constitute a qualifying income interest for life solely because income between the last distribution date and the date of the surviving spouse's death is not required to be distributed to the surviving spouse or to the estate of the surviving spouse.

> In addition, "[i]f any income from the property ... has not been distributed before the decedent-spouse's death, the undistributed income is included in the decedent-spouse's gross estate." Treas. Reg. §20.2044-1(d)(2). As a consequence the remainder provision following S's life estate can distribute the corpus and any accrued but undistributed income to the next takers without special concern.

Powers over Corpus

Although no one (including S) may be given a power to appoint QTIP trust corpus to a third party during S's overlife, invasion powers exercisable in favor of S are permissible in a QTIP, a §2056(b)(5), or an estate trust.

D probably will not want to give S an invasion power over corpus if a primary reason for using a QTIP trust is to prevent S from having a power of disposition over the property (for example, to ensure that the remainder at death passes to D's children by a former marriage). It might be advisable to give S a power to withdraw principal if the QTIP trust is used because it is regarded as superior for postmortem planning purposes, to permit S to make charitable or annual exclusion (or larger, if S is expected to die before repeal of the estate tax) gifts that will reduce S's taxable estate.

There is good reason to limit any draw down power in any of these trusts with an ascertainable standard relating to health, education, maintenance, or support, or to limit the withdrawal to the greater of $5,000 or 5% of the trust corpus, independent of any standard (or to impose both limitations). Although the corpus of each of these trusts will be taxed in S's gross estate in any event, certain tax advantages will be lost if S is given a broader (for example, "comfort and benefit") inter vivos power of withdrawal.

To illustrate, a QTIP trust will be taxed in S's gross estate only to the extent the QTIP election was made. If only a partial election was made, the QTIP trust should be in a form that will not cause the nonelected portion to be includible in S's gross estate, and restrictions that will preserve the benefit of a partial election are appropriate. Moreover, granting an unrestricted inter vivos power of withdrawal to S will cause capital gains to be taxed to S under §678 rather than to the trust, notwithstanding that there is no cash flow to S from the proceeds of any gain realized with which to pay the tax. Therefore, any invasion power given to S appropriately might be limited.

Note, however, that in neither case would failure to use the proper invasion standard be a marital deduction disaster, because even a totally unrestricted power of withdrawal would qualify an intended QTIP trust as a §2056(b)(5) entity and should not preclude estate trust qualification. Only the postmortem partial QTIP election, GST reverse QTIP election, or income tax planning opportunity would be lost.

D also may want to give the trustee discretion to distribute trust principal to S, thereby reducing the corpus that will be includible in S's gross estate. The trust could contain "request but not require" language providing that, in meeting S's needs, marital trust principal first should be distributed before distributions for these purposes are made from the nonmarital trust.[80] D also might write a letter to S, couched entirely in precatory terms, suggesting that S consider making gifts to D's descendants out of any marital trust principal that is distributed. This language should not, however, be placed in the trust. See Technical Advice Memorandum 8915004, in which the inclusion of precatory language imperiled an outright marital deduction bequest. Although the deduction was allowed, the fact that a determination was required indicates that controversy could arise from such a provision.

Moreover, careful note should be made of the fact that it is not permissible to authorize the trustee to distribute principal to S solely on

---

80. See Treas. Reg. §20.2044-1(d)(3) with respect to the use of a rolling fraction method to charge distributions to the elected portion in a QTIP trust as to which a partial election was made but the trust was not severed.

condition that S agree to give that distributed principal to designated intended donees. Distributions to S for the avowed purpose of enabling S to make gifts will not jeopardize qualified trust treatment. But distributions to S must not be *conditioned* on S making the gift. Such a provision would disqualify the trust for the marital deduction as a violation of the prohibition that no person has power to appoint any part of the property to any person other than the surviving spouse. See §2056(b)(7)(B)(ii)(II) and the nearly identical language in §2056(b)(5).

The marital trust may give S a withdrawal power over principal that terminates on remarriage, without disqualifying the trust for either §2056(b)(5) or QTIP treatment.[81] Termination in an estate trust also would be harmless.

QTIP Trust Nongeneral Testamentary Power of Appointment

The QTIP trust provision that "no person [may have a] power to appoint any part of the property to any person other than the surviving spouse" does not apply to a power exercisable only at or after S's death. §2056(b)(7)(B)(ii)(II). Thus, S may be given a testamentary power of appointment in a QTIP trust. Unless properly restricted, however, a general testamentary power of appointment in the QTIP trust might be deemed to convert the trust into a §2056(b)(5) marital deduction power of appointment trust. In that case no election would be required to secure the marital deduction. Instead, the deduction would be automatic (more so than the "automatic" deemed election, which can be undone). This means that the postmortem flexibility of the partial QTIP election and the GST §2652(a)(3) reverse QTIP election might be lost. It might not even qualify for the §1022(c)(3) QTIP benefit under carryover basis if that ever becomes the law. Thus, if D desires to give S the flexibility of testamentary disposition over the property, normally this should be secured through the use of a nongeneral testamentary power.

S might be given a narrow nongeneral testamentary power to appoint QTIP property even if a principal reason for using the QTIP trust is to prevent S from altering the devolution of the remainder interest (for example, to secure the remainder for D's children by a former marriage), provided that the testamentary power is limited to permit S only to alter the shares within the class of remainder beneficiaries.

> Example: D's current marriage is childless but D has children and grandchildren by a former spouse. D's will gives S a narrow nongeneral testamentary power to appoint "to such one or more of my descendants as S appoints by will," with a gift in default of appointment to those descendants per stirpes. This will allow S to

---

81. However, the trust would need to qualify as QTIP property if the inter vivos withdrawal power was the general power used to qualify for §2056(b)(5) treatment.

take a second look at D's family to alter the dispositive provisions in the same way D might if still alive.

QTIP trusts used for postmortem planning flexibility in cases of a single marriage in which D's descendants also are S's descendants appropriately might grant S even broader nongeneral testamentary powers (up to and including a statutory power to appoint to anyone in the world except S, S's estate, or creditors of either). For example, the power might give S the opportunity to alter an equal division to reflect the beneficiaries' economic circumstances, such as if one child has been financially successful or has "married well" and another has not. And powers of appointment tend to ensure filial devotion to S,[82] which also may be important.

Marital Deduction "Savings Clauses"

Marital deduction "savings clauses" have proven useful for salvaging a deduction that otherwise inadvertently might be lost. A typical savings clause provides:

> **It is my intent that the marital deduction gift and the property comprising the trust estate shall qualify for the federal estate tax marital deduction applicable to my estate. To this end, no power or discretion with respect to allocations of property to this trust or with respect to administration of the trust shall be exercised or exercisable except in a manner consistent with this intent.**

A number of rulings reveal the utility of savings clauses. For example, in Mazzola v. Myers, 296 N.E.2d 481, 489-490 (Mass. 1973) (trust corpus consisted approximately 95% of closely held stock that had no dividend history; the document expressed a strong desire that the stock be retained), a provision limiting the breadth of any power or authority so as not to affect marital deduction qualification was deemed to mandate trustee action that would qualify the trust for the marital deduction, stating that "even very broad discretionary powers are always subject to the control of a court of equity to assure that in the exercise of those powers the purposes of the trust are fulfilled." A similar result was reached in Rev. Rul. 75-440 in which boilerplate language authorizing the trustee to invest in life insurance (an unproductive asset) was determined to apply only to the nonmarital trust.

Although such provisions are not reliable, and may not always be effective, experienced planners recommend them because usually they cannot hurt and may be the needed salvation when unexpected qualification issues arise. See Johanson, *The Use of Tax Saving Clauses in Drafting Wills and Trusts*, 15 U. MIAMI INST. EST. PLAN. ¶2100 (1981). However, provisions of this ilk must be used with caution. For example, in

---

82. Or, to put it more simply, as Professor Ed Halbach coins the phrase, "a power to appoint is also a power to disappoint."

what probably was a benign attempt to provide flexibility in a trust to deal with unanticipated tax and other changes in the future, the revocable inter vivos trust involved in Technical Advice Memorandum 9325002 granted a power after the settlor's death to either the trustee or any beneficiary to

> apply to a court of competent jurisdiction to amend this Agreement if the purposes of this Agreement may be defeated or hindered because of change in circumstance or change in law. The court may amend the terms of this Agreement and restrict or remove any of the powers, duties, rights and privileges of the Trustee, the beneficiaries, or any other person.

The government held that the power to amend disqualified the trust for marital deduction treatment, notwithstanding a general provision that "the grantor intends that the Marital Trust . . . shall be available for the federal estate tax marital deduction" and that "[t]he Trustee's powers and discretions shall not be exercised or exercisable except in a manner consistent with such intent" and that the trust should "be construed" in accordance with that intent. Rejecting arguments that the power to amend was limited by the statement of intent to qualify for the marital deduction, the government stated that this provision literally authorized a court to restrict or even remove S's income interest if circumstances changed and, for example, S no longer needed that income or could not manage the money. In rejecting the argument that the savings clause should avoid disqualification, the Technical Advice Memorandum reinforced the message that the government thinks little of savings provisions designed to negate anything else in a document that might disqualify the marital deduction. They definitely should not be used in lieu of careful drafting that avoids all known problems.

Funding Marital Deduction Transfers

"Marital deduction funding" is one of three major aspects of planning for the marital deduction. But the questions explored and the issues that arise in dividing an estate between marital and nonmarital bequests are viable in more than just this one context. They are relevant whenever D's wealth is divided among trusts or beneficiaries, not just S and others, and many of those issues will continue to apply even if the wealth transfer tax is repealed. So this is a good place to address these kinds of questions, with an understanding that they have a global significance in estate planning and drafting.

The curious thing is that few of the issues relevant to this aspect of estate planning relate to the marital deduction in particular or to the wealth transfer taxes in general. Yet people hardly ever consider these issues in any other context. So this discussion is written in the context of current law and planning specifically in the context of marital deduction bequests, solely because that is where it most often is considered in the current environment. But you should try to remember that marital deduction funding has broader application and you might consider funding issues that affect other planning involving bifurcation of property interests among beneficiaries of an estate or trust.

Occasional comments herein refer to the possibility for changes in the law (including those adopted in 2001, but not effective until 2010, the most important of which being repeal of the estate tax and institution of carryover basis). However, constant reference is not made to the possibility of wealth transfer tax repeal, adoption of carryover basis, nor to any possible consequences thereafter, purely because those are not current realities and may never come to fruition. Certainly the division of estates, even between S and other current beneficiaries, will prevail even after any such changes. So this topic likely has the most staying power of any aspect of marital deduction planning, because of its broad application.

The funding issue viewed through a marital deduction lens must be resolved after the amount of any marital bequest has been determined and the form of disposition has been selected: outright, estate trust, §2056(b)(5) general power of appointment trust, §2056(b)(7) QTIP trust, or whatever other disposition suits D's fancy (to the extent wealth transfer tax requirements do not inform the issue). The issue now is: how is that bequest to be transferred to that distributee? A summary of your funding options appears beginning at page 139.

Types of Marital Deduction Formula Clauses

Numerous variations are available to express the nature and amount of any bequest, but there are only two basic categories of bequests for funding purposes: pecuniary and fractional.

A *pecuniary* bequest makes a gift of money, often using a formula provision like:

> **I give the smallest pecuniary amount that, if allowed as a federal estate tax marital deduction, would result in the least possible federal estate tax being payable by reason of my death.**

This form of gift is analogous to a bequest of "$10,000 to my alma mater," although this marital pecuniary bequest is determined pursuant to a formula[83] and the amount of the bequest is likely to be a tad larger. The document also likely authorizes satisfaction of the bequest with assets in kind in lieu of in cash only. The traditional common law notion is that the personal representative is obliged to convert all property in the estate (if not specifically bequeathed) to cash and to distribute that cash. This would be expected with a pecuniary gift in the more traditional form of a set

---

83. This pecuniary gift could have been produced by a fraction applied against a fixed fund, such as ½ of D's gross estate or even ½ of $50,000. The existence of a fraction in the determination of the formula pecuniary dollar amount does not convert this gift of a cash amount into a fractional gift as next described.

dollar amount (versus a formula determined bequest). See generally 4 Scott & Fratcher, THE LAW OF TRUSTS §347 (4th ed. 1989). Typically the document grants the personal representative authority to distribute assets in kind, including allocations in whole or in part that do not reflect a pro rata division of all estate assets.

A *fractional* share formula clause makes a gift of assets, using a provision like:

> **I give a fractional share of my residuary estate of which (a) the numerator is the smallest amount that, if allowed as a federal estate tax marital deduction, would result in the least possible federal estate tax being payable by reason of my death, and (b) the denominator is the value of my residuary estate as finally determined for federal estate tax purposes.**

This form of gift is analogous to a bequest of the residuary estate "to my children, A and B, in equal shares," but the marital fractional share is determined pursuant to a formula and the fraction is not likely to be as clean as ½ or ⅓. Instead, it may be something like:

$$\frac{\$245{,}663.38 \text{ (optimum marital deduction sought)}}{\$1{,}745{,}663.38 \text{ (fund after debts, expenses, \& taxes)}} = 14.07278\%$$

This gift differs from a pecuniary bequest that is determined by applying a fraction as part of a formula because the fund against which the fraction is applied is not a fixed amount. This multiplicand fluctuates in value as various activities occur, such as paying taxes, making tax elections, or incurring valuation changes or investment gains and losses. A fractional entitlement applied against a fixed dollar fund is not common and is not discussed further here. It can confuse issues because it may look something like a fractional bequest but it is treated essentially like a pecuniary bequest.

Avoiding uncertainty about the nature of the gift created is an essential planning function, because the tax and other consequences of these alternatives are severe, as this discussion will illustrate. Indeed, as this material demonstrates, administrative and mathematical problems can result under a fractional share approach. Unfortunately, as the discussion of the separate share regulations also will reveal, those administrative and mathematical problems may visit pecuniary funding alternatives as well.

Within these two basic approaches (fractional or pecuniary) there are at least five basic types of pecuniary formula clauses and two types of formula fractional bequests, all tied to different mechanisms for accomplishing the funding. As shown in the provisions above, the expression of the amount of the formula marital deduction bequest itself essentially is the same, whether determined under the fractional or pecuniary clause. The difference among them lies in the provisions governing asset allocations (funding). The funding alternative is an important aspect of marital deduction planning or any other endeavor that entails division of an estate because those differences are significant.

Available Funding Mechanisms

In resolving the issues that surround the funding question, the alternative funding mechanisms explored in detail here include:

(1) The pecuniary marital approach, which may utilize one of three funding options:

- A true worth pecuniary gift, under which assets distributed in kind are valued at their date of distribution values.

- A fairly representative pecuniary gift (also called an "FET" or "Rev. Proc. 64-19" pecuniary), under which each asset is valued for funding purposes at its basis for federal income tax purposes. Under §1014, usually basis is the federal estate tax value of assets included in D's estate.[84] The requirement currently relevant under Rev. Proc. 64-19 is that assets selected for distribution be fairly representative of the appreciation and depreciation between D's death and the date(s) of funding of all assets available for distribution.

- A minimum worth pecuniary gift, under which each asset is valued for funding purposes at the lesser of its date of distribution value or its federal estate tax value,[85] sometimes with an added requirement under a "New York" style provision that the total fair market value of all assets distributed be approximately equal to the amount of the deduction.

(2) The reverse pecuniary approach, under which the pecuniary gift is made to the trustee of the nonmarital trust and the residuary estate comprises the marital deduction gift. This form of clause is also called the "credit consuming," "front-end credit shelter," or "residuary" marital. In terms of funding, the reverse pecuniary could conceivably take any of the three forms (true worth, fairly representative, or minimum worth) indicated above for a pecuniary marital, but only the first two approaches are safe for marital deduction qualification purposes.

---

84. This would change if repeal of the wealth transfer tax in 2010 actually were to occur (and repeal is not retracted in 2011, also as slated to occur), accompanied with adoption under §1022 of carryover basis. In that case presumably marital deduction planning and funding would change, or disappear entirely. One aspect to consider is the $3.0 million basis improvement provision in §1022(c)(3) that might be satisfied with a funding or allocation regime that is informed by factors similar to those discussed in this section.

85. Again, until new basis at death is repealed and carryover basis takes its place, this is the asset's basis for federal income tax purposes.

(3) The fractional marital approach, which makes a gift of a fractional share of the residuary estate as the marital deduction bequest. A fractional marital bequest may utilize either "pro rata" allocation in funding or "pick-and-choose" funding.

(4) A single fund marital, which requires no actual funding at all, but is considered along with the rest because it is an available option to consider when selecting among funding alternatives. It essentially occurs whenever a partial QTIP election is made, if the nonelected portion is not carved off and distributed separately.

Attorney Practices in the Choice of Funding Approaches

According to a survey of experienced estate planners,[86] most lawyers have a favorite formula that they use in all their marital deduction wills and trusts unless there are unusual circumstances that dictate the use of another approach. Although no alternative will be best in all cases, the study suggests that there are a number of good reasons for sticking with a limited number of funding approaches in most situations. For example, there is much less likelihood of a drafting error if a particular, tried-and-true approach is used. In addition, both the drafter and the fiduciary likely have a greater familiarity with administration of "favored" formula clauses, making them less prone to mistake in actual operation. Moreover, the economics of estate planning and probate practice are such that marginal benefits that may be derived from a complex and seldom-used funding formula may be largely offset by increased planning and administrative costs (as well as any costs of error).

Given these realities, estate planners as a whole might be expected to agree on which of the many alternatives is preferable, and in some respects this is true. But the empirical study showed some intriguing variations in favorite funding mechanisms. For example, if the marital deduction formula bequest is likely to be smaller than the nonmarital gift, the survey respondents reported that they were likely to use a true worth pecuniary approach almost 75% of the time. Others used the minimum worth, fairly representative, and true worth reverse pecuniary approaches with almost equal regularity, but none chose the fairly representative form of reverse pecuniary bequest or either form of fractional bequest.

If the marital deduction formula gift is likely to be substantially larger than the nonmarital gift, however, and if there are no unusual factors that clearly dictate another choice, only about one-third of the respondents would likely use the true worth pecuniary approach, while an equal number would use the true worth reverse pecuniary approach. The

---

86. Quilliam, *How Leading Texas Probate Lawyers Are Handling Marital Deduction Problems (An Empirical Study)*, Advanced Estate Planning & Probate Course (State Bar of Texas) 1987 (survey of the marital deduction planning practices of Texas estate planners with strong Texas and "national" reputations); cf. Moore & Pennell, *Practicing What We Preach: Esoteric or Essential?*, 27 U. MIAMI INST. EST. PLAN. ¶1211 (1993) (survey of University of Miami Estate Planning Institute registrants).

remaining respondents chose the minimum worth, fairly representative, and fairly representative reverse pecuniary approaches with almost equal regularity, and again none chose the fractional bequest.

Asked how often they deviated from these selections in the substantial marital gift situation, over 80% said they would use their favored approach over 70% of the time, suggesting that most of these practitioners are virtually wedded to one approach in each of the two primary types of case. Of particular curiosity is that approaches not selected in one locale enjoy wide popularity in other geographic regions. This seems to suggest that familiarity in a given region — among drafters and fiduciaries — is important to the selection process.

Reliance on one or two principal funding mechanisms is the practice of many highly skilled estate planners. Different alternatives better fit particular client situations because there are major differences in the operation and consequences of the various approaches to marital deduction funding. As the following discussion reveals, it therefore is worthwhile to assess standard responses to the funding issue with some regularity.

Importance of the Funding Decision

Notwithstanding notions about prepayment of estate tax by equalizing estates or taking advantage of the §2013 credit, the most common marital and nonmarital estate plan results in a nonmarital bequest that avoids payment of tax on D's death. As a result, the nonmarital share seldom exceeds the applicable exclusion amount (and any increased exemption equivalent of the state death tax §2058 deduction).

In many instances, however, the nonmarital bequest will be considerably less than these amounts because of nondeductible charges imposed against nonmarital property (or, less often, because of inter vivos gifts that incurred tax that consumed some of the unified credit).

An estate that hovers in value just above the applicable exclusion amount raises the question whether to fund a very small marital bequest of the amount in excess of the nonmarital portion. At the other extreme, if the estate were very large and the nonmarital bequest were to be no greater than what remains of the applicable exclusion amount, it might make sense to make the credit shelter amount a pecuniary bequest and allow the residue to qualify as the marital deduction trust without the need to fund that very large amount. In either case, it might be better to maintain the full estate in a single fund, of which either a very small fraction or a very large one qualifies for the marital deduction.

Further influencing the marital deduction funding decision is the §2631(a) GST exemption. The marital funding approach selected affects the ability to leverage that exemption with appreciation or risks wasting it with depreciation. Although not the primary focus of the following discussion, potential GST exemption allocation consequences also must be kept in mind.

Factors Affecting Choice of Funding Approach

A variety of factors are relevant in evaluating the advantages and disadvantages of the available funding mechanisms. For example, which bequest (the marital, nonmarital, or neither) would be easier from an administrative perspective to fund, considering revaluation of assets, mathematical complications, and concerns about flexibility? Second, what is the likelihood that estate assets will appreciate or depreciate between the date of D's death and the date(s) of funding (which may be several years later)? Which of the marital or the nonmarital bequest ought to be funded, and in what manner, to minimize any capital gain that will be realized in funding? And if estate assets do change in value before the date(s) of funding, which bequest should bear the loss from depreciation or benefit from appreciation, and with what effects? Third, several more arcane income tax consequences must be considered, such as distributable net income (DNI) carryout, application of the separate share rule, and acceleration of income in respect of a decedent (IRD).

All of these factors are evaluated here, in light of the present state of the law and reported (if at times only intuitive or anecdotal) perceptions and practices of estate planners. Unfortunately, normally the choice of the appropriate funding mechanism is made when the will or trust instrument is drafted, because planners are wary of giving the personal representative direct authority that might disqualify the deduction under the §2056(b)(1) terminable interest principles. So part of this endeavor is about making educated guesses about which approach might be best years in the future. It is good to revisit the choice of funding mechanisms on a routine basis.

Funding the Pecuniary Marital — In General

A pecuniary marital deduction provision directs distribution (to S or to the trustee of a marital trust) of a pecuniary amount that is to be segregated from the fund available for distribution. The language used must carefully avoid reference to a fractional share, or words that might be confused therewith, such as a "part" or a "portion" equal to the desired deduction, because unclear language could be construed to cause significant differences in result under the various funding alternatives.[87] Moreover,

---

87. See, e.g., *In re* Estate of Nicolai, 373 P.2d 967 (Or. 1962) (the relevant provision referred to "a portion of my estate equal in value to" and authorized the personal representative to select and distribute assets to be distributed in satisfaction of the bequest; although it was taken from a publication that represented it to be a pecuniary bequest, the court found it to be a fractional form because that result would cause more property to pass to the surviving spouse); *In re* Will of Newell, 591 N.Y.S.2d 293 (Surr. Ct. 1992) (a bequest of "an amount equal to twenty per cent of the value of my residuary estate" was a fractional bequest, recognizing that use of the term "amount" usually indicates a pecuniary bequest but placing more importance on the fact that the gift was a part of the residue, which usually carries a portion of the appreciation or depreciation in the estate assets and is more consistent with a fractional bequest). See also cases cited in *Nicolai* and in Covey,

the chosen pecuniary funding provision should specify which pecuniary funding alternative is preferred (true worth, fairly representative, or minimum worth) for the task of laying aside the pecuniary amount.

In the unfortunately all too common event of a total failure to address the funding issue, however, a court probably would employ one of two common law principles to ascertain the intended result (or at least to ascribe an intent even if none likely ever existed). First, unless a local probate code or trustee powers act provides otherwise, a court might rule that the funding must be in cash. In that case assets likely would be sold (perhaps triggering gain or loss) to generate the necessary liquidity. Fortunately, state law in many jurisdictions and many documents avoid this problem by a provision that authorizes satisfaction of legacies in cash or in kind, even though the marital deduction provision is silent and application to the marital bequest may not have been the anticipated result of a boilerplate provision.

Second, with respect to assets distributed in kind, the common law rule is that fair market value at the date(s) of distribution is used to measure the extent to which a distribution satisfies the pecuniary amount. This second common law dictate generates the term "true worth" pecuniary that sometimes is applied to a date of distribution pecuniary marital funding provision.

True Worth Pecuniary

The true worth pecuniary (sometimes called just the true or date of distribution pecuniary) probably is the most commonly selected marital funding approach[88] in planned estates in which the funding routine is not left to implication under the vagaries of local law.

If S or the marital trust was entitled to receive $X under the pecuniary formula, assets aggregating $X in value at the date(s) of distribution would be distributed under this form of provision, regardless of their values (and thus their income tax bases under the §1014 new basis at death rule) as determined for federal estate tax purposes. S or the trust would receive cash or assets in kind worth no more nor less than $X at the date(s) of distribution, regardless of changes in asset values during the period of

---

MARITAL DEDUCTION AND CREDIT SHELTER DISPOSITIONS AND THE USE OF FORMULA PROVISIONS 57-60 (United States Trust Co. 3d ed. 1984). At one time Covey suggested that some courts, sympathetic to surviving spouses when estate assets have appreciated in value, have all but misconstrued wills to find that a fractional share gift was made. See Covey, THE MARITAL DEDUCTION AND THE USE OF FORMULA PROVISIONS at 22 (United States Trust Co. 2d ed. 1978).

88. See Moore & Pennell, *Practicing What We Preach: Esoteric or Essential?*, 27 U. MIAMI INST. EST. PLAN. ¶1211 (1993). On a scale of one to five, with five being "always" and one being "never," the three most commonly used approaches were the true worth pecuniary marital bequest (49% reported they use it "sometimes," "often," or "always," for an average score of 2.72), the true worth reverse pecuniary bequest (also 49% report using it sometimes or more often, with a slightly lower frequency in the always category and an average score of 2.67), and the pick-and-choose fractional (45% use it sometimes or more often, for an average score of 2.46).

administration. As a consequence, fluctuations in the size of the estate would not affect the entitlement or the distributing estate's obligation, unless the estate lost so much value that there were not enough assets left to satisfy fully the pecuniary amount. Traditional abatement rules would protect the preresiduary marital bequest until exhaustion of the intestate and residuary estates.

Sample true worth pecuniary language might read:

My executor shall select and distribute to the trustee the cash, securities and other property, including real estate and interests therein, that will constitute the trust, employing for the purpose values current at the time of distribution.

The true worth pecuniary form of funding is perceived to have four primary advantages.

Maximum Pick-and-Choose Flexibility

The fiduciary doing the funding under a true worth pecuniary is granted full flexibility in "picking and choosing" assets to be distributed in satisfaction of the pecuniary amount. Thus, the fiduciary specifically should be directed not to use any nonqualifying assets that are included in the fund that is available for distribution (by a provision such as "**no asset or proceeds of any asset shall be selected as to which a marital deduction is not allowable**"). Otherwise, §2056(b)(2) is likely to apply (governing unidentifiable assets), causing those nonqualifying assets to be regarded as the first assets distributed to the marital share and thereby reducing the allowable deduction correspondingly.

In addition, some assets that qualify for the marital deduction simply may be inappropriate for allocation to the marital share; alternatively, some assets ought to be allocated specifically *to* the marital deduction share. For example, HomeAcre appropriately might be allocated in its entirety to the marital share if S uses it as a personal residence. This especially is true if the residence is not likely to appreciate significantly in value, and because it is a permissible form of non-income-producing asset that may be held in a §2056(b)(5) or QTIP marital deduction trust.[89] Conversely, stock in FamilyCo might be allocated away from the marital bequest to the fullest extent possible if a child (perhaps by a former marriage) runs the business but does not get along well with S, especially if the business is expected to appreciate in value.

---

89. Normally non-income-producing property will be directed away from the marital trust unless it is clear that S will consent to its retention under a consent provision designed to preserve the deduction under Treas. Reg. §20.2056(b)-5(f)(4). According to the last sentence of this regulation, however, retention of personal use property is permitted in a §2056(b)(5) trust, notwithstanding the non-income-producing character of these assets, and this should be true in a QTIP trust as well.

Even more importantly, flexibility in funding also is desirable if control blocks of stock are available for funding. For example, allocation of all shares to one trust may prevent loss of voting control. Perhaps more useful, expeditious allocation may require distribution of fewer assets to S or to the marital trust.

> Example: D's estate included 100% of the stock in a closely held business. D's will created a pecuniary marital bequest and the personal representative, exercising its pick-and-choose discretion, allocated 51% of the stock to the trust under a true worth approach.

The estate may claim a control block premium in valuing the stock bequeathed to S or allocated to the trust for marital deduction purposes, allocating more than a pro rata 51% of the total value of the entire stock holding to those shares. See Estate of Chenoweth v. Commissioner, 88 T.C. 1577, 1588 (1987). Deeming S or the marital trust to receive more value by virtue of this allocation allows other assets that would have been allocated to remain in the estate, which effectively increases the size of the residuary nonmarital trust.

Moreover, the control premium effectively may disappear free of tax if a portion of this control block is shifted away from S or the marital trust before S dies. At D's death the marital deduction is leveraged by the control premium and during S's overlife that excess value is dissipated tax free by a gift or sale of only those shares needed to divest control — presumably at a "per share" discounted value if done properly.

> Example: Assume that D owns 75% of FamilyCo stock and is unwilling to part with any of the stock during life. An alternative that guarantees a marital deduction in the same amount as the value subjected to tax is for D to bequeath a control block of the stock to S (or a marital deduction trust), followed by S making an inter vivos gift of a minority interest that will leave a minority interest to be included in S's estate — both the gift and the amount left at death valued at a discount.

The most effective postmortem division of a control block of stock requires that S be given some control over the ultimate destination of the stock. For example, in a QTIP marital deduction trust, S would need an inter vivos power to withdraw the stock to make a gift of enough to reduce the amount retained to a minority interest. Alternatively, D could create a §2056(b)(5) marital deduction trust that grants S an inter vivos power of appointment to make the same division of the stock.

If either alternative is acceptable to D, then the value of the stock S transfers subject to gift tax would be discounted to reflect its minority status, and the remaining minority interest includible at S's death similarly would be discounted. This means that D's controlling interest would be subjected to wealth transfer tax at a net minority discount, and the difference between the control premium allowed for marital deduction purposes in D's estate and the minority discount applied in valuing S's gift and remaining estate would escape wealth transfer tax entirely.

Spouse Protected Against Depreciation

A second perceived advantage of the true worth pecuniary is that S or the marital trust is protected to the fullest possible extent from depreciation occurring in the estate between the date of D's death and the date of final funding. The full risk of depreciation falls on the nonmarital residue because S is entitled to assets worth the amount of the marital bequest as of the date(s) of distribution.

On the flip side is the reality that the residue could be entirely wiped out if it is small enough, either in absolute terms or relative to the marital share and the entire estate. This could result due to a combination of nondeductible charges, such as: (1) generation-skipping transfer taxes on a direct skip; (2) state death taxes in a jurisdiction that does not grant an unlimited marital deduction or does not recognize the QTIP trust; (3) any nonmarital specific or general bequests for which no state death tax deduction is available; (4) taxes on nonprobate property not passing to S; and (5) costs of administration claimed on the fiduciary income tax return (Form 1041) as income tax deductions, rather than on the estate tax return (Form 706) under §2053. Nondeductible charges payable from the residuary estate could eliminate the nonmarital residue entirely, but the marital bequest would abate only after the residue was totally exhausted.

It probably is fair to say that D's primary intent in most cases is to protect S to the greatest possible extent, even if the marital share (which will be taxed at S's death) is preserved against diminution. Thus, the true worth pecuniary probably is favorable to D. In other cases the will may make sufficient nonmarital specific bequests and there is a demonstrable risk that the estate may depreciate enough that insufficient assets will exist to fund the marital bequest and these others. In such a case a provision should be included to alter the common law abatement rules to specify whether the marital bequest is to abate first, last, or pro rata.

Alternatively, a provision may be added to specify that the nonmarital dispositions receive at least a guaranteed minimum amount (for example, to provide a source of funds for children of a former marriage). However, this provision could cause the marital bequest to abate and thereby generate taxes in D's estate (that themselves would cause the marital bequest to further abate).

Because the fiduciary could be criticized for a delay in funding a true worth pecuniary during a declining market, a specific provision also usually should be added to the document to remove any possible duty to act with haste under these circumstances.

Freezes Value of Marital Bequest

The true worth pecuniary marital has a third advantage: the marital bequest will receive no more than the pecuniary amount. The marital bequest is frozen in value because appreciation between death and distribution will inure to the benefit of the nonmarital residue, which typically will not be includible in S's gross estate at death (even though it may be held for S's overlife enjoyment). As a consequence of the normal nonsharing of appreciation, the marital bequest cannot be overfunded with assets that are worth more than the pecuniary amount at the time of distribution and, thus, any tax imposed at S's death will be minimized.

Relative Ease of Administration

The fourth historical advantage to using the true worth pecuniary is an offshoot of the fact that pecuniary bequests may not share in estate income received. Instead they may be entitled to interest under state law, at a state law mandated rate. Pecuniary bequests also do not participate in gain or loss realized during the course of administration. Because the pecuniary marital bequest is frozen in value, no sharing or allocation problems are raised by these items as they are under other forms of funding following interim distributions or if the amount of the marital bequest is altered because of an audit of the estate tax return. This aspect of funding is explained more fully in the context of those funding approaches that suffer most from these administrative problems. It also is impacted by the separate share rule regulation that may provide that this one form of pecuniary marital bequest is beyond even the DNI carryout rules.

Potential Realization of Gain or Loss

On the flip side, true worth pecuniary funding is perceived to have four primary disadvantages. The most significant disadvantage of the true worth pecuniary is that distribution of assets in kind, in satisfaction of the pecuniary amount, is deemed to be a sale or exchange for income tax purposes.[90]

Based on a theory that the pecuniary amount is a fixed obligation owed to S or to the marital trust, funding is treated as if the fiduciary sold the assets distributed in kind and distributed the cash proceeds of the sale, which S or the marital trust immediately used to purchase those same assets, giving them a new basis equal to fair market value. As a consequence, any appreciation or depreciation in distributed assets between their basis and their date of distribution value triggers realization of gain or loss.

---

90. See, e.g., Treas. Reg. §1.1014-4(a)(3); Kenan v. Commissioner, 114 F.2d 217 (2d Cir. 1940), aff'g 40 B.T.A. 824 (1939); Suisman v. Eaton, 15 F. Supp. 113 (D. Conn. 1935). The true worth pecuniary marital bequest frequently is referred to as a "Suisman" (pronounced Sussman) funded pecuniary after the *Suisman* case, which imposes this capital gain or loss treatment on its funding.

The experience of many estate planners has been to live with this cost, and the eventual adoption of carryover basis will not make it a more serious cost (even if it is coupled with repeal of the wealth transfer tax, because bequests to spouses or others will not disappear just because the tax does). This is because Congress amended §1040 to provide that gain recognized in satisfaction of a pecuniary bequest with appreciated property in kind is limited to the difference between fair market value at funding and at death. The practice has been to leave it to the personal representative to minimize this income tax cost. Fast funding (quickly after D's death, before assets have fluctuated much in value) is the primary means of minimizing this problem.

Requires Revaluation of Assets

A second disadvantage common to the true worth pecuniary and to most other funding alternatives is that assets distributed to S or to the marital trust must be revalued as of the date(s) of distribution. Although in many cases this may present no problem (for example, if the estate consists primarily of cash or listed securities), in some situations revaluation is an onerous and expensive administrative task. Worse, failure to determine the proper value of distributed assets could cause unexpected tax exposure to the recipient.

For example, Rev. Rul. 84-105 involved the estate and gift tax consequences when a pecuniary bequest for S was inadequately satisfied by the personal representative. This underfunding was not attributable to misvaluation but, in a true worth funding situation, it easily could be if estate assets distributed to S are overvalued. Because S did not object to or attempt to appeal the order of the court that approved the underfunding, the government ruled that a gift was made when the time for such a challenge expired. Fortunately, S's acquiescence in the underfunding was not regarded as an event that caused a loss of any part of D's marital deduction. Instead, the situation was treated as if the marital bequest was fully funded and S later made a taxable gift of the deficiency. Because the gift tax is not repealed, this kind of untoward consequence could arise in the future on a misfunded bequest of any variety.

Along the same line in Bergeron v. Commissioner, 52 T.C.M. (CCH) 1177 (1986), S was deemed to have made a gift of an underfunded amount of the marital bequest when the probate court's distribution order became unappealable, and computation of the amount of the gift reflected that S was the income beneficiary of the nonmarital trust, which was the recipient of the underfunded amount from the marital trust. As a consequence, the court determined that the value of the gift was only the value of the remainder interest in the property that fell into the nonmarital trust — which was a future interest for which no gift tax annual exclusion under §2503(b) was available.

This aspect of *Bergeron* illustrates several troublesome problems. S will be treated as the grantor to the extent the underfunded amount passes to a nonmarital trust of which S is a beneficiary. This causes a portion of the nonmarital trust corpus to be includible in S's gross estate at death under §2036(a)(1) because S made a deemed transfer with a retained interest. Because S's estate will be purged of the prior gift and will receive a credit for any gift tax previously paid, all by operation of §2001(b), inclusion is no different than if this amount had gone into the marital trust and was taxed at S's death, except that S prepaid the tax by incurring the lifetime gift tax on the value of a remainder interest in the underfunded amount.[91]

Further, because overvaluation results in a gift of a remainder with a retained life estate, §2702 potentially applies to require gift taxation of the full value of the trust property, notwithstanding S's deemed retention of a life estate. Overall, with a gift tax return required and potentially a tax to pay, S could be looking at substantial exposure (with interest and penalties in some cases), all flowing from a misvaluation (or a missed valuation) at the time of funding.

These results place a significant burden on the personal representative, and ultimately on S, to know the value of property allocated pursuant to a true worth funded marital bequest. It thus is necessary to determine both the precise amount that should be allocated under D's estate plan and the value of assets actually allocated. Although valuation at the time of distribution can be avoided under some funding alternatives, most marital funding options involve the need to revalue. As it turns out, the pick-and-choose pecuniary using true worth valuation is one of the least onerous alternatives available.

In this context, it may pay to remember that the government uses death of S in most instances as its opportunity to evaluate the funding of marital bequests in D's estate, in terms of the values used, the timing of distributions, and the sharing of postmortem income and appreciation. Funding usually occurs after a closing letter issues in D's estate, and the statute of limitation for estate tax purposes cannot be extended under §6501(c)(4) to permit the government to inspect the funding after all is done. As a result, S's death is the only opportunity reasonably available to the government to evaluate the bona fides of the marital funding. Thus, the government can be expected to continue to exercise vigilance at that time, with potentially very large liabilities for gift tax, interest, and penalties if the funding is deemed to have been improper.

---

91. If S dies after estate tax repeal the gift is a huge negative because proper funding followed eventually by death after repeal of the estate tax would result in no wealth transfer tax liability at all. Moreover, the underfunded amount in the bypass trust presumably would not qualify for the §1022(c)(3) adjustment to basis, meaning that a portion of that $3.0 million benefit may be squandered if the balance of the marital deduction trust is inadequate to soak up all of that basis improvement entitlement.

To short circuit the government's ability to raise these issues when S dies, which could be many years later, taxpayers ought to consider seeking comfort in the safe harbor of the gift tax disclosure rules. Treas. Reg. §§20.2001-1 and 25.2504-2 confirm that a federal gift tax return is effective to begin the gift tax statute of limitation even if no return is required. The regulations also now provide that this closure is effective for *all* gift tax purposes (specifically including annual exclusion qualification, and presumably also for deduction qualification) and *not* just for valuation purposes alone. Thus, disclosure that is "adequate to apprise the Internal Revenue Service of the nature of the gift and the basis for the value reported"[92] may be a very wise option to preclude expensive and difficult valuation battles conducted when S dies.

Distributions Carry Out DNI

A third and possibly negative consequence, also common to most marital bequests, is that distributions in satisfaction of the bequest usually carry out distributable net income (DNI) for income tax purposes. This potential may not apply at all for a true worth pecuniary marital bequest, however, *if* under state law S is not entitled to income earned from D's date of death. This is because the separate share rule may provide that the true worth pecuniary bequest is a separate share with income of zero. Other forms of marital funding constitute separate shares that present DNI calculation problems and permit DNI carryout with each distribution made to the marital or bypass trust, or to S. To better appreciate this would require a short diversion into a topic not otherwise addressed here. Suffice it to say that the true worth pecuniary offers a way to avoid DNI carryout that otherwise is not available to other pecuniary bequests.

This nonapplication normally would be a good thing, because application of the separate share rule to most marital bequests imposes a nasty administrative burden that cannot be waived by a provision in a will or trust.

The other important difference between marital funding approaches that are regarded as separate shares for DNI calculation and carry out purposes is in the amount of DNI carried out. In each of these cases, distributions are deemed to distribute that DNI to S or the marital trust, to be taxed there to the extent the entity making the distribution has taxable income that results in DNI. In a true worth pecuniary the amount carried out is equal to fair market value. In other cases it could be a lesser amount equal to the basis of the asset distributed.

Distributions May Accelerate IRD

The fourth potentially negative consequence of true worth pecuniary funding applies to all pecuniary bequests, marital and nonmarital alike.

---

92. Treas. Reg. §301.6501(c)-1(f)(2).

Under §691(a)(2), distribution of a right to receive income in respect of a decedent (IRD) in satisfaction of a pecuniary amount causes an acceleration of the income represented by the IRD item. All of that income is taxed in the tax year of distribution, resulting in a bunching of income and potentially higher income taxes as a result.

For example, most retirement benefits are IRD. All of the built-in income tax liability flowing with that IRD will be taxed in the year of distribution if a right to receive distribution of that benefit is distributed in funding a pecuniary marital bequest. So, if federal estate tax value of a retirement benefit is $900,000 and adjusted basis is §1014(c) carryover (usually zero), distribution in satisfaction of $900,000 of marital deduction bequest would cause the estate to realize $900,000 of income tax liability. The recipient would receive a corresponding basis increase to $900,000 that will be recovered over distribution of the benefit.

This §691 acceleration result is avoidable by making a specific bequest of the right to receive this IRD (either to or away from the marital share, as appropriate), because disposition as a specific bequest does not accelerate the income represented by the IRD. See §691(a)(2) (last sentence).

The classic wisdom suggests that it is best to seize this opportunity and allocate the right to receive items of IRD by a specific bequest to S or to the marital deduction trust, because income taxes attributable to the IRD make it a wasting asset, thus reducing the amount includible in S's gross estate. This built-in liability is preserved to be imposed on S if allocation of the right to receive the IRD is by a specific bequest, avoiding acceleration of the income that otherwise would occur by using it in satisfaction of the pecuniary gift.

Taxation to S may be most effective in reducing the amount subject to estate taxation (if indeed the tax will still exist and apply) on S's death. This is another very complex income tax topic on which a good deal more could be said, but the details are not appropriate for the level of this discussion. So, let's be aware of the need to consider IRD when choosing marital deduction funding approaches and move on. The final analysis of the true worth pecuniary bequest from a tax perspective is that it allows flexibility in funding without the risk of overfunding the bequest, but at the cost of potentially triggering capital gain and accelerating IRD when distributions occur.

The true worth pecuniary may be indicated if postmortem appreciation (and thus the potential for triggering gain on distributions) is not likely (because, for example, sufficient cash and fixed-value assets will be available for funding the marital gift). Alternatively, if substantial appreciation is anticipated, the true worth pecuniary may be appropriate if: (1) it is important to freeze the value of S's estate (especially if S owns substantial other property); (2) liquid assets are plentiful and make it unlikely that funding in kind with gain or loss realization will occur; or (3) fast-funding will make it possible to minimize the recognition of gain.

Several factors may militate against employing the true worth pecuniary. For example, a marital deduction funding format that does not require revaluation may be preferable if the estate consists largely of illiquid assets (such as a business interest or unimproved realty) whose value is debatable and difficult to determine. The true worth pecuniary also can be a source of irritation to S if not carefully explained at the beginning of the estate administration period, because S may have difficulty appreciating why a tax on gain should be paid if no assets actually have been sold and why DNI is being carried out to be taxed to S. Finally, competing camps of beneficiaries (for example, S and beneficiaries of D's residuary estate who are children by D's former marriage) may make the pick-and-choose funding discretion a liability for the personal representative.

Fairly Representative Pecuniary

The fairly representative pecuniary funding alternative (sometimes known as the Rev. Proc. 64-19 approach) is not nearly as common a form of pecuniary marital deduction funding as its true worth counterpart.[93] Typical language calls for the personal representative to

> **select and distribute to the trustee the cash, securities and other property that will constitute the trust, employing for the purpose of valuation the federal estate tax value of any asset, or the replacements of or the proceeds of any asset, included in my gross estate and the adjusted basis for federal income tax purposes of any other asset, provided that the assets distributed shall be selected in such a manner that they have an aggregate fair market value fairly representative of the appreciation or depreciation in the value to the date or dates of distribution of all assets then available for distribution.**

Under §1014(a), the basis of most assets for funding purposes under a fairly representative pecuniary clause is their federal estate tax value. Hence, this approach sometimes also is known as a Federal Estate Tax (or FET) funded pecuniary marital.

The basis of assets the estate acquires after D's death would be cost (or a substituted basis if other assets were exchanged for them, which would *not* be the same thing if carryover basis becomes the law). Historically some drafters referred to basis rather than federal estate tax value, which would produce very different results than under current law if carryover basis were to become the law and pecuniary bequests to surviving spouses remained

---

93. See Moore & Pennell, *Practicing What We Preach: Esoteric or Essential?*, 27 U. MIAMI INST. EST. PLAN. ¶1211 (1993). The fairly representative pecuniary was reported as used with an average score of 2.12 but almost 50% of the respondents reported that they "never" use it.

viable. Although §1040 might limit the amount of gain recognized, it would not alter the fact that using basis as the value for distribution purposes would be very different from what it is today. Thus, users of this approach presumably should no longer refer just to basis but instead to fair market value (for federal estate tax purposes if the tax still exists; otherwise, if planning of this variety remains viable for some reason, perhaps a reference to fair market value for state transfer tax or federal income tax basis adjustment purposes may be a viable substitute) for assets held at death, and adjusted basis for any assets acquired postmortem.

The fairly representative approach provides two fundamental advantages over true worth pecuniary funding. The primary advantage is that gain and loss, although realized on a distribution in kind, are equal to zero under current law because the amount realized through satisfaction of the pecuniary entitlement is an amount exactly equal to basis. This avoids the primary perceived disadvantage (realization of gain or loss on distribution) of the true worth pecuniary marital approach. With §1040 and allocation at date of death (federal estate tax) value the same results ought to obtain under a carryover basis regime as under current law.

Because no gain or loss is recognized under the fairly representative pecuniary approach, basis and date of distribution fair market value of distributed assets are not necessarily equal. In this context, §643(e) limits the amount of DNI carried out on distributions in kind to the lesser of basis or fair market value. This is likely to result in a smaller amount of DNI carried out than under a true worth pecuniary approach. Many estate planners regard this result as advantageous, but it likely loses its attraction under the separate share rule, which would regard the funding estate or trust as having separate accounts for DNI computation and carry out purposes. So the DNI issue largely is ignored.

Compared with the true worth pecuniary approach, the fairly representative pecuniary approach has three distinct disadvantages

Tends to Overfund or Underfund the Marital Bequest

The fairly representative approach has the potential for either overfunding or underfunding the marital bequest because asset values at the time of distribution are likely to differ from the amount — date of death (federal estate tax) value, or basis — of the pecuniary bequest that distributions in kind are deemed to satisfy.

> Example: An asset has a value on the date of distribution of $400,000 but a date of death (federal estate tax) value or basis of only $300,000. Distribution of that asset to S or to a marital trust is deemed to satisfy only $300,000 of the marital deduction bequest. It therefore may be necessary to transfer more property to S or to the marital trust (to be exposed to tax at S's death) than would be

necessary if a true worth pecuniary were used and the same asset were deemed to satisfy a full $400,000 of entitlement.

If it were possible to avoid such overfunding, an astute fiduciary would want to allocate depreciated assets to the marital share, thus reducing the amount subject to tax at S's death.

Example: If the marital share were entitled to receive $400,000, the fiduciary might allocate an asset with a date of death (federal estate tax) value or basis of $400,000 but a current fair market value of only $300,000 in hopes of totally satisfying the pecuniary bequest.

The government promulgated Rev. Proc. 64-19 to prevent this type of abuse through allocation of more depreciated than appreciated assets to S or to the marital trust. Rev. Proc. 64-19 requires that the marital bequest receive assets that are fairly representative (a ratable share) of all appreciation and depreciation in the value of all assets available for funding. The language in the "provided that" clause of the fairly representative pecuniary funding provision at page 111 addresses this requirement. Because not all drafters are aware of the need for such a provision, some states have enacted statutes that call for such ratable sharing to save the marital deduction in estate plans that fail to expressly comply with Rev. Proc. 64-19. See, e.g., N.Y. Est. Powers & Trusts Law §2-1.9(b)(2).

Requires Revaluation of All Assets

A second disadvantage of the fairly representative approach is directly attributable to the ratable sharing requirement: every asset available for funding must be revalued to determine whether all appreciation and depreciation in fact was apportioned properly. This may make administration more onerous than the true worth pecuniary, which requires revaluation of only those assets actually distributed. With the advent of the income tax separate share rule applicable to estates, however, frequent revaluations may be required in both alternatives.

Restricts Pick-and-Choose Flexibility

A third disadvantage is that pick-and-choose flexibility is restricted because the personal representative must select assets that represent a ratable sharing of the overall appreciation and depreciation of the fund available for distribution. Some observers suggest that the obligation to balance the allocation of appreciated and depreciated assets has the effect of making a fairly representative pecuniary clause operate functionally the same as a fractional share of the residue bequest. That is, some fiduciaries report that they comply by merely fractionalizing most assets to allocate a pro rata portion of each appreciated and each depreciated asset in funding to the marital and nonmarital shares. Indeed, the easy way to satisfy the fairly representative distribution requirement is to make a pro rata distribution of each asset.

On the other hand, some estate planners suggest that fairly representative funding calls not for an exactly equal allocation of appreciation and depreciation but, rather, for a rough justice. There may be more pick-and-choose flexibility than meets the eye in actual practice, especially in a harmonious family setting in which the personal representative's funding decision is not likely to be challenged (except, perhaps, by the government, which experience reveals is not common). The expected compliance method affording more flexibility is for the personal representative to determine the aggregate appreciation or depreciation in the estate between death and the date of distribution, ascertain the marital bequest's portion of it, and then pick-and-choose assets that meet two requisites: (1) their aggregate federal estate tax values equal the amount of the deduction, and (2) their aggregate fair market values at the date(s) of distribution approximate the proper portion of the total available fund to satisfy the ratable sharing requirement. Hitting these two targets will be easier to accomplish in some estates than in others.

The primary distinction between the true worth and the fairly representative pecuniary approaches is avoidance of gain and loss on funding, at a cost of arguably increased administrative difficulty in the fairly representative approach due to revaluation, the potential loss of flexibility in selecting assets, and the risk of overfunding. Because the fairly representative pecuniary has the same §691 income in respect of a decedent consequences as the true worth pecuniary, it is indistinguishable from that more common approach on these grounds.

Some fiduciaries may regard the loss of flexibility in some cases as advantageous because the fiduciary is protected from criticism by contentious beneficiaries. And difficult administration may occur in a true worth pecuniary to the extent the separate share rule is applicable, which again reduces the distinction between these approaches.

Minimum Worth Pecuniary

The third form of pecuniary marital funding provision commonly is known as the minimum worth alternative, and sometimes it is drafted with a "New York style" additional provision. Either format essentially is a hybrid combination of the true worth and fairly representative pecuniary funding provisions, using language along the following lines:

> **My personal representative shall select and distribute the cash, securities, and other property, including real estate and interests therein, that will constitute the marital bequest, employing for the purpose of valuation the lesser of (a) the federal estate tax value of any asset, or the replacements of or the proceeds of any asset, included in my gross estate and the**

adjusted basis for federal income tax purposes of any other asset for federal income tax purposes or (b) the current value of the asset at the time of distribution.

This approach is designed to avoid problems with both the true worth and the fairly representative alternatives by allocating assets in satisfaction of the pecuniary amount at the lesser of (1) basis[94] for federal income tax purposes and (2) value as of the date(s) of distribution. For the same reason as with a federal estate tax funded pecuniary, users of this approach should refer not just to basis but instead to fair market value (for federal estate tax purposes if the tax still exists; otherwise, if planning of this variety remains viable for some reason, perhaps a reference to fair market value for state transfer tax or federal income tax basis adjustment purposes may be a viable substitute) for assets held at death, and adjusted basis for any assets acquired postmortem.

The same DNI and IRD issues attendant to the fairly representative pecuniary funding provision apply to the minimum worth approach. But if allowed to work properly, there are three attractive aspects of the minimum worth approach.

No Realization of Gain on Funding

Like the fairly representative pecuniary funding approach, the possibility of incurring gain should be avoided because assets are never deemed to be worth more than their basis (or, in a carryover basis environment, no more than the §1040 date of death (federal estate tax) value in satisfaction of the pecuniary amount). Alternatively, however, the minimum worth funding approach presents the possibility to incur loss. The lesser value controls if basis is greater than fair market value at the date of distribution (and for this purposes there is no need to substitute date of death (federal estate tax) value, because §1040 does not apply for loss computation purposes), resulting in a loss transaction (as if the asset were sold for its date of distribution fair market value, which is less than its basis).

Pick-and-Choose Flexibility

Depreciation cannot be allocated to S or to the marital trust as it can be in a fairly representative pecuniary approach because no asset is deemed to be worth more than its actual fair market value in funding the marital bequest. For example, if an asset is worth $300,000 and has a date of death (federal estate tax) value or basis of $350,000, distribution satisfies only the lesser amount ($300,000) and there is no possibility of the marital trust being underfunded with overvalued assets. Thus, the ratable sharing rule of

---

94. Because allocation at basis may trigger a state's Rev. Proc. 64-19 statute, the drafter of a minimum worth funding provision must negate the application of such a statute to prevent inadvertent and unnecessary application of the "fairly representative" rule.

Rev. Proc. 64-19 is avoided, along with the accompanying inflexibility introduced by compliance with it.

Only Distributed Assets That Have Decreased In Value Must Be Revalued

Fair market value at the date of distribution is relevant only if it is lower than basis or date of death (federal estate tax) value. Thus, it is necessary to know the fair market value of only those assets actually distributed to S or to a marital trust that have decreased in value from their date of death (federal estate tax) value or basis. Sometimes it is not possible to know in what direction value has changed, but often it is clear that value has not declined, meaning those assets need not be revalued at the date of distribution. This minimizes an administrative problem attendant (albeit in differing degrees) to both the true worth and fairly representative pecuniary approaches. Unfortunately, this form of pecuniary marital is a separate share for income tax DNI calculation and carryout purposes, which means that some revaluation and administrative burdens exist today that historically were avoidable.

Disadvantages

Perhaps the most significant aspect of the minimum worth approach is the latitude it gives a fiduciary to favor S. Because assets are allocated at the lower of their date of death (federal estate tax) value or basis and value at the date(s) of distribution, however, the potential exists to overfund the marital bequest and increase S's subsequent gross estate.

> Example: An asset currently worth $400,000 has a date of death (federal estate tax) value of only $300,000 and a carryover basis of just $1. The asset would satisfy only $300,000 of the pecuniary amount (if allocated in kind), yet S or the marital trust receives an asset worth $400,000 (reduced by any future capital gain tax on the built-in appreciation). If overfunding the marital share is to be avoided, this $400,000 asset could be sold and only $300,000 of the cash proceeds distributed, at a cost of realizing $100,000 of capital gain on the sale.

Some fiduciaries may prefer the minimum worth approach because it provides an option either to overfund the marital bequest or to incur gain by a sale and distribution of the proceeds. These fiduciaries might favor the ability to avoid gain on funding if overfunding is not a serious problem (for example, because S is likely to dissipate enough of the bequest before death to avoid federal estate tax).

There is a corresponding risk of bankrupting the residuary portion of an estate if sufficient depreciated assets are allocated to the marital bequest.

Example: An asset has a date of death (federal estate tax) value or basis of $400,000 but is worth only $300,000 on the date of distribution. That asset, plus another $100,000, would be required to satisfy $400,000 of marital bequest entitlement, leaving less property for the nonmarital trust than if the fairly representative approach had been employed or if an asset with a fair market value closer to its basis had been distributed.

This risk of bankrupting the nonmarital residue in the fiduciary's exercise of discretion may jeopardize qualification of any residuary charitable bequest. See Treas. Reg. §20.2055-2(b). Moreover, as with the situation with a true worth pecuniary, here a fiduciary risks exposure to litigation by disaffected nonmarital beneficiaries if it delays funding the marital bequest in a declining market.

A specific provision could be added to the document to remove any possible duty to act with impartiality or undue haste in funding during a declining market. The New York style minimum worth provision is a response to this exposure if the fiduciary should not be placed in this position. Based on a collective asset (as opposed to a solitary asset) theory, the New York style provision requires that the aggregate value of all assets distributed to S or to the marital trust be no less than and, "to the extent practicable, no more than" the amount of the desired marital deduction, thus putting a cap on the ability to overfund the marital share, but at a cost of diminishing the overall flexibility of the minimum worth approach.

The minimum worth approach may avoid gain and also grant more pick-and-choose flexibility than in the fairly representative pecuniary, with fewer administrative problems attributable to revaluation. It is, however, a more sophisticated alternative than either the true worth or the fairly representative pecuniary approaches and may require a professional fiduciary and a friendly family situation if it is to be used safely. The minimum worth formula can be a dangerous instrumentality if there is a risk of litigation, particularly in a disharmonious family (for example, involving a subsequent spouse and children by a former marriage), and most especially if S is the fiduciary with discretion in funding. It seldom is used in practice.[95]

Funding the Reverse Pecuniary Marital — In General

The most recently developed marital deduction pecuniary funding approach is variously labeled the reverse pecuniary, credit consuming pecuniary, front end credit shelter pecuniary, or residuary marital. This type of provision addresses concerns of planners to whom flexibility in funding, minimization of administrative problems, and avoidance of

---

95. See Moore & Pennell, *Practicing What We Preach: Esoteric or Essential?*, 27 U. MIAMI INST. EST. PLAN. ¶1211 (1993). The minimum worth pecuniary was reported as used with an average score of 1.54; 65% of the respondents reported that they "never" use it and another 24% report that they use it only "seldom."

overfunding the marital bequest are important objectives. These planners traditionally favored the true worth pecuniary and usually did not select an alternative that avoids capital gain. Perhaps this was because realization of gain was deemed of lesser import, considering the maximum tax rate on most long-term capital gain was only 20% historically (and now it may be 15% or less) and, with flexibility in funding, gain could be minimized by the judicious selection of assets.

Nevertheless, the potential for realization of gain on funding is significant under a true worth pecuniary format in very large estates in which the marital bequest will be very large relative to the nonmarital residue. The reverse pecuniary approach calls for a credit shelter nonmarital bequest to be funded by a pecuniary method, to minimize the capital gain and administrative difficulties in such an estate. This leaves the larger residue to qualify for the marital deduction, all using a provision like the following:

> **My personal representative shall allocate to the Family Trust all assets available for distribution that would not qualify for the federal estate tax marital deduction if allocated to the Marital Deduction Trust, plus the largest pecuniary amount, if any, that will not thereby increase federal estate taxes payable by reason of my death. In determining the pecuniary amount my personal representative shall consider any credit or deduction for state death taxes allowable to my estate only to the extent those taxes are not thereby incurred or increased, and shall assume that (a) none of the Family Trust and (b) all of the Marital Deduction Trust hereafter established (including any part thereof disclaimed by S), qualifies for the federal estate tax marital deduction. My personal representative shall allocate the residue of my estate to the Marital Deduction Trust. It is my intent that the Marital Deduction Trust will qualify for the federal estate tax marital deduction and that it not exceed the smallest amount that would result in the least possible federal estate tax payable by reason of my death.**

The terms reverse pecuniary, credit consuming pecuniary, front end credit shelter pecuniary, and residuary marital all reflect this reversal of the traditional marital bequest.

The credit shelter bequest is segregated and funded under this approach, at the risk of incurring gain, carrying out DNI, accelerating IRD, etc. The marital portion, which is expected to be the larger amount, is not funded per se because it is the residue. The result may not completely avoid the drawbacks of traditional pecuniary funding, but it minimizes those problems by funding the smaller nonmarital bequest rather than the larger marital deduction bequest.

In some cases it will be uncertain whether the marital or the nonmarital portion will be larger. In these situations it might be acceptable to allow the personal representative to choose which to fund as a pecuniary bequest, although this may raise qualification concerns because the residue will fluctuate in value while the pecuniary bequest (whether it is the marital or nonmarital portion) may be frozen in value (if a true worth pecuniary funding approach is used). Thus, the election to choose between the marital and the nonmarital as the funded bequest effectively allows the personal representative to shift fluctuations in value between the two portions.

Under a fairly representative funded reverse pecuniary, this fluctuation in value would be shared ratably by the marital and nonmarital portions, which should raise no problems. Under a true worth approach the funded bequest will be frozen in value, and control over the amount of the marital bequest might raise the kind of questions litigated in Estate of Smith v. Commissioner, 66 T.C. 415 (1976), aff'd, 565 F.2d 455 (7th Cir. 1977), in which the government attacked an equalizer marital formula approach. Fortunately, the government lost its argument that elections made by the personal representative in *Smith* necessarily would affect the size of the marital bequest, allegedly making it nondeductible because it was unascertainable. Subsequent developments may indicate that the government's attitude has changed. Still, why beg for litigation?

Finally, note that the reverse pecuniary format is not appropriate if the nonmarital portion is meant to qualify for the charitable deduction, because the operative provisions would allocate all value in the estate to that nonmarital portion (because the full amount of D's estate could pass to it without increasing D's taxes).

Funding Options

The most appropriate reverse pecuniary funding mechanism must be considered, because this approach only minimizes but does not completely avoid funding problems. A fractional approach would not be chosen because the primary reason for using the reverse pecuniary (preserving flexibility while minimizing administrative problems and capital gain) would be defeated by the traditional fractional approach (as we will see beginning at page 123). A minimum worth reverse pecuniary also should not be used because the ability to overfund the pecuniary bequest (the nonmarital portion) means that the personal representative also has the opportunity to underfund the marital bequest. This manipulation ability generates concern about marital deduction disqualification.

Thus, the only funding approaches that are appropriate under the reverse pecuniary plan are the true worth and fairly representative alternatives.

True Worth Reverse Pecuniary

The true worth reverse pecuniary approach has become very popular[96] and is the subject of Rev. Rul. 90-3, which resolved several now academic concerns about the validity of this form of planning. In a nutshell, only two potential issues were raised by the true worth reverse pecuniary approach. The first related to the fact that, in a reverse pecuniary situation, the marital deduction portion is the residue of the estate, which can fluctuate in value between the date of death and the date when the nonmarital bequest is finally funded. Although the marital residue may receive a larger amount than the deduction claimed, due to appreciation, it also may be smaller than the deduction claimed, due to depreciation.

Viewing the reverse pecuniary bequest as analogous to the pecuniary bequest involved in Rev. Proc. 64-19, the concern was that there is: (1) no ratable sharing of appreciation or depreciation (because the marital portion receives or suffers all fluctuations); and (2) no assurance that the residuary marital will receive assets having an aggregate fair market value at the date(s) of distribution that is at least equal to the deduction claimed. These were the only two circumstances under which Rev. Proc. 64-19, based on its special facts, granted a marital deduction notwithstanding fluctuations that were possible.

Rather than as a Rev. Proc. 64-19 concern, a different and more proper way to view the depreciation issue is as a valuation question: how much is the bequest worth if the marital portion could suffer all the depreciation? The proper answer is that the depreciation risk is offset by the fact that the marital portion also benefits from all appreciation. Therefore, valuation is not affected and the deduction should not be at risk. This is not, however, how the government viewed the issue.

The second issue involved the fact that, under the reverse pecuniary approach, capital gain can be incurred on funding the pecuniary nonmarital bequest, which gain will be taxed under normal state law principles to the estate residue, which is meant to qualify for the marital deduction. Therefore, the issue is whether this potential capital gain tax should reduce the marital deduction under §2056(b)(4)(B). Because it may not be known how large that tax will be until after final funding, which almost certainly will not occur until after final audit of the estate tax return, the issue is whether inability to determine the amount of the §2056(b)(4)(B) reduction makes the marital bequest itself unascertainable and therefore nondeductible.

In Rev. Rul. 90-3 the government directly addressed and determined affirmatively that a reverse pecuniary bequest funded using values at the date(s) of distribution does qualify for the marital deduction,

---

96. See Moore & Pennell, *Practicing What We Preach: Esoteric or Essential?*, 27 U. MIAMI INST. EST. PLAN. ¶1211 (1993). 49% of the respondents reported that they use it "sometimes" or more frequently, with an average score of 2.67.

notwithstanding the possibility that postmortem fluctuations in the fair market value of estate assets may diminish the amount S received. According to the ruling, this depreciation possibility does not create a Rev. Proc. 64-19 problem or cause the residuary bequest to be a nondeductible terminable interest under §2056(b).

That conclusion was consistent with the government's prior conclusions in Rev. Rul. 81-20, which determined that the personal representative is obligated to treat all beneficiaries in an impartial manner and explained that a personal representative's obligation under applicable state law to act impartially and fairly to all beneficiaries is satisfied if a pecuniary bequest is funded with assets valued at fair market value on the distribution date(s), provided that distribution is not unreasonably postponed.

Because state law requires a personal representative to act in an impartial manner, and because the nonmarital trust must receive a fixed amount in any event, any reduction in the marital residue would be occasioned solely by reason of any decline in the market value of the residue after D's death. Consistent with the rationale of Rev. Rul. 81-20, that diminution in value will not affect deductibility of the marital bequest. Simply stated, market value fluctuations will not ordinarily cause a residuary bequest to become nondeductible.

Not mentioned in Rev. Rul. 90-3 is the added fact that the capital gain issue makes sense only if there is "phantom gain" in a case in which there is no real appreciation.

> Example: An estate appreciated $X during administration and that gain was realized on funding the nonmarital trust bequest. Because the residue benefits from all appreciation, the residue here is better off by the amount of $X, less any capital gain tax thereon. Because the capital gain tax cannot consume the full $X of appreciation, the marital residue is better off due to the real appreciation in value, even though it pays any income tax on the gain.

It is only if there is no real appreciation, but gain is generated because of a reduction in basis (for example, due to a depreciation or depletion deduction), that the residue is worse off by virtue of a realization of gain on funding. Even in a carryover basis environment, §1040 will limit gain to real appreciation generated postmortem, again unless basis actually is reduced, so this element should not change even if carryover basis becomes the law.

Fairly Representative Reverse Pecuniary

The reverse pecuniary approach can be drafted with an FET funding provision and a provision inspired by Rev. Proc. 64-19 fairly representative sharing of appreciation or depreciation, effectively avoiding both issues raised by the true worth reverse pecuniary. This is simply because: (1) no gain or loss is realized in a fairly representative funding approach (in either the present new basis at death environment or the §1040 limited gain environment with carryover basis in place), whether the marital or the nonmarital portion is funded using date of death (federal estate tax) values; and (2) the fairly representative provision automatically negates any disproportionate depreciation concern. Thus, Private Letter Ruling 9007016 ruled that a marital deduction is available under an FET funded reverse pecuniary clause if the provision complies with Rev. Proc. 64-19, and approved the following language to ensure a fairly representative allocation of appreciation and depreciation:

> Anything hereinafter to the contrary notwithstanding, any allocation of assets among the Family Trust, Qualified Terminable Interest Generation-Skipping Trust, and Marital Trust shall, with respect to each such trust, be comprised of assets having an aggregate market value at the time of such allocation fairly representative of the net appreciation or depreciation in the value of the property available for such allocation between the date of valuation for federal estate tax purposes and the date or dates of said allocation and selection. For this purpose, any installment obligations distributed outright to my surviving spouse under [Section *] shall be considered in the aggregate together with all assets in the Marital Trust.

This approach does not totally prevent appreciation in the amount of the marital bequest. Thus, it is less economically effective than the true worth pecuniary marital approach, under which the marital bequest cannot increase during the administration period. Nevertheless, the fairly representative reverse pecuniary is more economical than the true worth reverse pecuniary, under which all appreciation during the period prior to funding is allocable to the marital residue, to be taxed at S's death. As a result, this approach represents a more reasonable compromise that an increasing number of drafters have selected as their preferred funding approach in larger estates.[97]

Reverse Pecuniary Comparison

A true worth reverse pecuniary bequest operates like a true worth pecuniary marital bequest, except it freezes the nonmarital bequest and allows the value of the marital portion to fluctuate. As a result, the marital portion may be over- or underfunded compared to a true worth pecuniary marital bequest. The fairly representative reverse pecuniary bequest operates exactly like a fairly representative pecuniary marital bequest, with the same advantages and disadvantages. Both reverse pecuniary approaches minimize the administrative chore by funding the smaller nonmarital portion, and the true worth reverse pecuniary similarly minimizes gain or loss realized by the

---

97. See Moore & Pennell, *Practicing What We Preach: Esoteric or Essential?*, 27 U. MIAMI INST. EST. PLAN. ¶1211 (1993). The fairly representative reverse pecuniary was reported as used with an average score of 2.18 although 46% of the respondents reported that they "never" and another 21% that they "seldom" use it.

funded share. The fairly representative reverse pecuniary is a more equitable approach and is unlikely to be challenged by the government or by disappointed beneficiaries. Existing authority indicates that the government will permit either the true worth or the fairly representative reverse pecuniary approach.

Funding the Formula Fractional Share

A fractional share marital formula provision is fundamentally a different approach from a pecuniary marital bequest. It directs the fiduciary to divide D's estate into portions, with the deductible part described something like:

> **a fraction of the trust property of which (a) the numerator is the smallest amount that, if allowed as a federal estate tax marital deduction, would result in the least possible federal estate tax being payable by reason of my death, and (b) the denominator is the value as finally determined for federal estate tax purposes of the property that became, or the proceeds of sale, investment, or reinvestment of which became, trust property.**

This marital formula provision creates a fraction, the numerator of which is the amount of the deduction sought (which may be described in the drafter's customary manner) and the denominator of which is the value of the assets available for funding. As described next, although most drafters' attention is focused on the amount of the numerator (because it is the amount of marital deduction that is sought), the denominator is critically important as well and must be defined properly.

Preresiduary Versus True Residuary Fraction

Division into marital and nonmarital shares under a fractional marital is possible either before or after payment of debts, expenses, and taxes (provided that the ultimate debit of those items is against the nonmarital share if payment occurs before division).[98] At first glance, it might seem that the amount of the marital bequest, as finally determined, will be the same regardless of whether the approach selected is division before or after payment of those items, as long as the numerator describes the proper marital deduction amount and the denominator is the fund (whether before or after payment) that is the source of the fractional share.

For example, if the fund is $1.7 million before those payments and $1.6 million thereafter, optimum marital bequests of either:

$$\frac{\$200{,}000}{\$1{,}700{,}000} \times \$1{,}700{,}000 \text{ versus } \frac{\$200{,}000}{\$1{,}600{,}000} \times \$1{,}600{,}000$$

---

98. Other items might be distributed before division as well, but for ease of illustration only these common payments are discussed here.

should produce the same optimum marital result. Although the marital deduction will be the same under each alternative, it is not true that the marital bequest itself will be the same. Indeed, significant consequences flow from this drafting decision. Thus, thought should be devoted to the proper sequence for payment of taxes and other charges or distributions (and in rare cases the priority in which certain specified assets will be liquidated to generate the funds with which to make payment), all in relation to division of the estate into the marital and nonmarital portions.

> Example: D's estate plan called for a marital deduction (or a partial §2056(b)(7) QTIP election is made postmortem) of a certain fraction of the estate (not necessarily that amount needed to reduce taxes to zero) and, because other assets passed to S, the amount specified to be set aside for S (by fractional distribution or partial QTIP election) totals $3 million. The state law concept of equitable apportionment dictates that all taxes be paid out of nonmarital property because the marital bequest generates no taxes, and the document clearly directs that no taxes or other charges are payable from the marital share.
>
> D's estate was worth $4 million at death in 2003. Taxes and other charges imposed on the nonmarital estate total $250,000, leaving $3.75 million (valued as of the date of death), of which $3 million is to qualify for the marital deduction. Before the time for final distribution of the estate (but after payment of the taxes and other charges), the remaining $3.75 million increases in value to $6 million.
>
> The fraction to apply to the $6 million remaining in the estate to determine the marital bequest will be either 3.0/4.0 (75%) or 3.0/3.75 (80%), depending on the sequence of paying taxes and charges in relation to dividing the estate.
>
> The 80% division assumes that D's fraction was based on the true (or net) residue, after payment of all taxes and other charges, with the fraction being $3 million over $3.75 million (using date of death values) to generate the proper sized entitlement.
>
> The 75% division assumes that D was directing a division of the gross residue, before payment of all taxes and other charges, with equitable apportionment dictating that all the $250,000 of taxes and other charges be paid from the nonmarital share after division. S would be entitled to $3 million over $4 million (again using date of death values) under this analysis and the remaining nonmarital 25% would bear the taxes and other charges after division.
>
> Using date of death values under either approach, the marital entitlement would be $3 million, thus protecting qualification for a marital deduction of that amount. The issue is worthy of consideration, however, because the choice of fraction in this

example produces a difference of $300,000 to S (a 5% difference in the division of $6 million ultimately available for distribution when administration ends). A similar difference arises in allocating estate income earned before division into the marital and nonmarital portions, and will affect income tax separate share rule calculations as well.

The size of the marital deduction claimed on the federal estate tax return (Form 706) is not in question, nor is equitable apportionment challenged. The simple issue is whether taxes and other charges or distributions are to be paid first, followed by division, or whether division occurs first, followed by payment of those charges out of the nonmarital fund.

There is no right result or best approach to this issue. Depending on the circumstances, D might prefer either the net residue or the gross residue approach. For example, if D's desire is to minimize the amount subject to tax on S's death, the gross residue (preresiduary 75%) approach would be favored. Similarly, the gross residue approach would be favored to maximize any generation-skipping transfer tax exemption allocated to the nonmarital trust, because the nonmarital portion will enjoy more appreciation and, thus, better maximize the exemption.

Alternatively, if generating cash to pay estate obligations is a concern, payment of those charges first, followed by division of the net residue (80%), might provide the greatest flexibility in selecting assets for sale to generate the necessary liquidity. Division of the net residue also is dictated if D wishes to provide the greatest protection to S.

You and your client must discuss and resolve this issue with a clear dictate in the marital bequest. Obviously, the estate plan should define terms such as "the residue available for division or distribution" to reflect clearly D's decision to divide the estate either before or after the payment of taxes and other charges.

Pro Rata Division of Assets

In actually allocating assets as part of a fractional marital bequest, it is not entirely clear, but it appears to be the better supported conclusion under traditional common law principles, that the marital share is entitled to a pro rata portion of each and every asset available for funding.[99] Thus,

---

99. See Covey, THE MARITAL DEDUCTION AND THE USE OF FORMULA PROVISIONS 95 (United States Trust Co. 2d ed. 1978); Trapp, *Drafting and Funding Marital and Nonmarital Formula Bequests*, 17 U. MIAMI INST. EST. PLAN. ¶¶301.2 & 301.4 (1983); Polasky, *Marital Deduction Formula Clauses in Estate Planning—Estate and Income Tax Considerations*, 63 MICH. L. REV. 869 (1965). See also *In re* Estate of Kantner, 143 A.2d 243 (N.J. Super 1958), and *In re* Burnett's Will, 89 N.Y.S.2d 152 (Surr. Ct. 1949). Arguing that a different result ought to apply, see *Current Tax Problems of Decedents' Estates*, 3 REAL PROP., PROB. & TR. J. 361, 365, 367-368 (1968). The alternative approach would be to determine a pecuniary entitlement by multiplying the fraction against the available fund at the time of actual division, with this amount then being funded by selectively distributing assets valued at that time and collectively worth that amount. This pick-and-choose

for example, if the fraction were 500,000/2,000,000, each and every asset would be allocated 25% to S or to the marital trust and 75% to the nonmarital trust.

Selecting pro rata fractional funding has five primary advantages.

No Gain or Loss on Funding

Gain and loss are not realized on funding because each asset is simply divided between the marital and nonmarital portions under a pro rata approach. Instead, basis in each asset is apportioned ratably under Treas. Reg. §1.1014-4(a)(3) and income earned during administration (but prior to division) also is pro rated under most states' Principal and Income Act. See, e.g., Uniform Principal and Income Act (1997 Act) §202; Revised Uniform Principal and Income Act §5(b)(2). In effect, each portion is treated as owned by its respective recipient as of D's death and distributions in funding are regarded as merely an allocation of what each already owns, not a satisfaction of some unidentified pecuniary entitlement.

No Rev. Proc. 64-19 Concerns

By its terms, Rev. Proc. 64-19 does not apply to the pro rata fractional approach. Nor does it need to, because fractionalization of each asset automatically works to ratably apportion all appreciation and depreciation. The corresponding disadvantage of this approach, however, is that the marital bequest is not frozen in value: appreciation or depreciation is ratably apportioned.

Income Tax Treatment

A fractional marital bequest is a separate share for DNI calculation and carryout purposes. DNI of the separate share is carried out by distributions only to the extent dictated by §643(e) (the lesser of fair market value or basis). Treas. Reg. §§1.663(a)-1(b)(2)(iii), 1.663(a)-1(b)(3) Example 2. Because neither gain nor loss is realized by distribution, fair market value and basis will likely differ, even if carryover basis does not ever become law (unless the §643(e)(3) election is made). The difference potentially means that less DNI will be carried out during any interim year than under either true worth pecuniary approach. Moreover, the right to receive IRD is not being used to satisfy a pecuniary obligation, so IRD is not accelerated on division of the assets under §691 (because there is no sale or exchange involved).

---

fractional approach is discussed beginning at page 131 and may be authorized by a specific provision in the document.

No Revaluation of Assets Required

Assets need not be revalued to make the requisite pro rata division. It simply does not matter what assets are worth to make a pro rata division of each and every asset.

No Fractious Disputes

Absence of discretion in picking and choosing assets both removes any risk of bankrupting just the residuary credit shelter portion and minimizes the risk of litigation by contentious beneficiaries. The fiduciary has no discretion and, thus, cannot be faulted for how it exercises its role.

Tends to Overfund or Underfund the Marital Bequest

Despite these five advantages, not all aspects of the pro rata fractional approach are favorable. Four distinct disadvantages exist. For example, like a fairly representative pecuniary bequest, the fractional marital fluctuates in value as the overall estate changes in value during the period between D's death and funding, which results in overfunding or underfunding the marital bequest.

No Pick-and-Choose Flexibility

A more serious disadvantage of pro rata allocation is that the fiduciary has absolutely no discretion or flexibility in funding. Each asset must be fractionalized, even though some assets more appropriately might be allocated to the marital bequest and others to the nonmarital trust. Pro rata fractionalization of each asset can cause the loss of control and break up round lots for trading purposes, with an attendant loss of any advantages of blockage and marketability.

In addition, to avoid allocation of a portion of any nonqualifying assets to S or to the marital trust, as to which no deduction would be allowable, an added provision must be included to purify the fund ("purge the pot") against which the fraction will be applied. For example:

> **The trust property is all property that was included in my gross estate for federal estate tax purposes (or that constitutes proceeds of sale, investment, or reinvestment of property so included) and that became a part of the trust estate, but [(a) excluding property as to which a marital deduction would not be allowable by reason of the nature of the property[, and (b) including assets qualifying for the credit with respect to foreign death taxes only to the extent required to obtain a marital deduction in an amount equal to the numerator].**[100]

---

100. The first portion of this provision is designed to avoid the §2056(b)(2) issue by which nonqualifying assets available for allocation reduce the marital deduction. The bracketed portion of this provision normally would be used only if property is likely to be included in the fund against which the fraction will be applied as to which the §2014

Capital Gain if Non-Pro-Rata Distributions Are Made

Lacking document or state law *authority to do otherwise*, a fractional bequest requires a pro rata division of each asset. For example, under a devise of a residuary estate "to my children, A and B, in equal shares," A and B own undivided equal interests in each asset composing the residuary estate (under what might be characterized as an item theory), and not just a claim to half the value of the residuary estate (under an aggregate theory). Absent a provision in the document giving the personal representative authority to make non-pro-rata distributions, a taxable exchange may occur to the extent the beneficiaries request (or accede to) a non-pro-rata allocation of property between them, as if the assets were distributed pro rata and then they made cross exchanges between themselves.

This cross exchange may generate a gain or loss to each distributee and produce a new basis equal to fair market value in that portion of each property deemed to have been exchanged.

> Example: D's residuary estate consists of two types of assets: FarmAcre and securities. Each type of asset has a date of death value (and thus basis under §1014) of $500,000, and a distribution date value of $600,000. The personal representative distributes FarmAcre to A and the securities to B because A wants to live on FarmAcre and B wants the income from the securities.
>
> For income tax purposes A has exchanged a half interest in the securities for B's half interest in FarmAcre, each half deemed to be worth $300,000 and with a pro rated basis of $250,000, meaning that each of A and B realizes a gain of $50,000 on the deemed exchange. The transaction does not qualify for §1031 like-kind exchange treatment and each beneficiary has a basis of $550,000 in the asset they received ($250,000 as carryover basis in the half deemed distributed in the pro rata division, and $300,000 as the cost basis in the half deemed acquired by the taxable exchange).[101]

The income tax DNI carryout consequences resulting from non-pro-rata division in funding a formula fractional marital deduction bequest will differ from those in a pecuniary bequest (with full gain or loss realization on funding) but not from those involving a pro rata division with no

---

foreign death tax credit might be available. If a net residue approach were favored, a provision (c) also could be added to describe the fund as "that amount remaining after payment of all debts, expenses, and taxes."

101. Realization of gain on the deemed exchange generates a new basis in the hands of A and B equal to fair market value in the portion of each asset deemed acquired by purchase, but not in the portion acquired by the deemed pro rata division. If carryover basis becomes the law §1040 will not apply in this case because by its terms only pecuniary bequests are addressed. That may mean that cross exchanges with a much lower basis allocation could produce a much greater gain. All this is avoidable if non-pro-rata division is authorized. See Rev. Rul. 69-486.

realization of gain or loss on funding (which is how this approach is viewed, *followed* by the taxable cross exchange).

Difficult to Administer

At one time, unique administrative problems attended to fractional bequests if nonsimultaneous distributions of the marital and nonmarital portions were made, either for income tax planning purposes or to accommodate the beneficiaries' needs. The same was true if the value of any asset was changed on audit of the estate tax return, requiring a redetermination of the proper fraction. These problems still occur, but they no longer are unique to fractional bequests to the extent the separate share rule of Treas. Reg. §1.663(c)-4 now applies to pecuniary bequests.

> Example: D's personal representative valued D's year 2002 estate at $1.2 million, requiring an optimum marital bequest of $200,000. The relevant proration under an optimum marital deduction fractional formula clause therefore calls for 16.67% of each asset to be allocated to the marital bequest, based on federal estate tax values as determined on D's estate tax return. The marital share is entitled to 16.67% of all income and appreciation and should pay or suffer 16.67% of all expenses or losses incurred during administration. The estate tax value subsequently is increased to $1,250,000 on audit, requiring a marital bequest of $250,000 and allocation of 20% of each asset, income, appreciation, expense or loss to the marital portion for optimum marital deduction purposes. All future distributions must be changed to 20%, including proration of income earned during administration. If prior distributions already were made at 16.67% the personal representative either may adjust future distributions and allocations to compensate for the improper percentage used on distributions and allocations previously made, or must obtain repayment of amounts improperly distributed and remit an additional amount to S or the marital trust. All of this will require the personal representative to revalue the entire estate and recompute the fraction.

The same mathematical and administrative problems now attend to any pecuniary marital to the extent the separate share rule requires allocation of all income items in a similar manner. In the fractional marital context, the revaluation made necessary by the increase in value on audit demonstrates that one supposed advantage of the pro rata fractional share approach (assets need not be revalued at distribution to make the proper division) should not be taken at face value. And the numbers actually involved are not likely to be so clean or easy to use.

In short, the fractional approach (and any pecuniary subject to the separate share rule) can become administratively difficult and somewhat mathematical, and thereby cumbersome. Moreover, even if the original fraction remains unchanged after audit, for income tax purposes any distribution of income or principal that is made to only one share will skew the fraction and require an adjustment, unless a corresponding lock-step allocation is made to all other shares of the estate or trust. Otherwise, to assure ultimate pro rata division of income and corpus, the portion allocable to the other shares must be increased so that they receive larger, compensating distributions in the future. To accomplish this adjustment, the fraction must be changed, again requiring revaluation of the entire fund available for distribution.

> Example: The relevant portion is 16.67% of an available fund of $1.2 million. Just before year-end the personal representative distributes assets (by paying debts and expenses of $20,000 that are a charge against the nonmarital trust) and makes no compensating distribution to S or to the marital trust.

If the available fund had grown 5% in value during the year just prior to this distribution (to $1,260,000) the personal representative would first restate the fraction to reflect current values (210,000/1,260,000) and then subtract the distribution from the denominator alone, to produce a new fraction of the remaining fund (210,000/1,240,000 = 16.94%) to which S or the marital trust would be entitled. If the $20,000 distribution were made to S or a marital trust without making a corresponding distribution to the nonmarital trust, both the numerator and denominator would be reduced and the new marital fraction would be reduced to 15.33%. To adjust the fraction in this way, the entire fund must be revalued to restate the fraction, and a complex mathematical fraction is likely to result.

It might be suggested that audit valuation changes are unlikely if an optimum marital deduction will result in zero taxes payable, and that other postmortem planning can be engineered to utilize lock-step distributions or interim loans (in lieu of distributions) to avoid the need for constant complicated administration. Nevertheless, the effect of these administrative problems in the past often has been to quash flexibility in the timing of fractional distributions. In the future the only bright side of this is that fractional maritals are no worse than any pecuniary approach that is subject to the separate share rule. (The only alternative that escapes is a true worth pecuniary alternative that does not carry income to the legatee, as to which separate share treatment would not apply if state law or the document entitles the legatee to interest versus income. See Treas. Reg. §1.663(c)-5 *Example 4.*)

A further negative is that a fractional marital bequest fluctuates in value during administration and, thus, can be over- or underfunded relative to the true worth pecuniary approach. The advantages of this approach, however, are no gain or loss realization on funding pro rata, no IRD acceleration, and limited DNI carryout. Two added negatives are administrative: no flexibility in selecting assets for distribution, and potential administrative and mathematical complexity, but the latter no longer is unique to fractional maritals. With no discretion in funding, the fiduciary has little liability to contentious beneficiaries, making this a potentially desirable approach in unfriendly family situations.

Pick-and-Choose Fractional Share Funding

To avoid the perceived disadvantages of proration under the traditional fractional share marital approach, some estate planners instead draft pick-and-choose fractional formula marital deduction bequests.[102] The pick-and-choose fractional approach relies on the same fractional formula provision to define the marital bequest, but alters the common law dictate of pro rata fractionalization in funding by adding a provision similar to one found in a pecuniary marital format: assets distributed in kind to constitute the marital portion may be distributed in whole or in part, non pro rata.

To accomplish this funding, first the applicable fraction is applied at the date(s) of division, against the total available fund, to establish a dollar value for each portion. For example, in the illustration at page 124, if the fraction was $3.0/$3.75 (80%) the personal representative would simply determine 80% of the value of the date of distribution value ($6.0 million in that example) and then distribute assets worth $4.8 million. That amount is satisfied by distribution of assets selected from the available fund, using values on the date(s) of distribution of the selected assets and allowing allocation non-pro-rata until the full amount of each portion is satisfied.

There are three expected attractions of a pick-and-choose fractional formula approach.

Maximum Flexibility with No Gain or Loss

The principal advantage of the pick-and-choose fractional is the expectation that capital gain is avoided on funding as it is with a pro rata fractional marital. But unlike the pro rata fractional and the fairly representative funded pecuniary approaches, which also avoid gain, this pick-and-choose fractional plan also affords flexibility in the allocation of assets. At the same time, nonsimultaneous distributions are permitted under the pick-and-choose fractional, and changes may occur in asset values on audit of the estate tax return, both with fewer of the administrative problems normally associated with the pro rata fractional, because strict fractionalization of assets is not required. Instead, if several partial distributions are made (rather than a single one time funding of the marital

---

102. See Moore & Pennell, *Practicing What We Preach: Esoteric or Essential?*, 27 U. MIAMI INST. EST. PLAN. ¶1211 (1993). The pro rata fractional was reported as used with an average score of 2.0 but only 26% of the respondents reported that they use it even as frequently as "sometimes" or more often; the pick-and-choose fractional was reported as used with an average score of 2.46 and 45% of the respondents reported that they use it that often. In both cases, however, 41% and 35%, respectively, report that they "never" utilize either fractional approach at all.

bequest) the fraction is applied at the time of each distribution to determine the outstanding dollar amount to be satisfied. Each distribution of assets then simply reduces the amount outstanding and reduces the fraction to be applied to determine the amount of any needed subsequent distribution(s).

Although each application of the fraction (along with changes in estate tax values on audit) requires revaluation of the entire remaining fund and recomputation of the fraction, it does not require reallocation of assets previously distributed to compensate for prior distributions. And the administration is no different from what the separate share rule requires in every marital approach that is recognized as creating separate shares for income tax purposes. As a consequence, more administrative problems should be expected under the pick-and-choose fractional than under a true worth pecuniary that is not regarded as a separate share for income tax purposes, but there should be no noticeable difference from a pro rata fractional or other pecuniary approaches.

No Rev. Proc. 64-19 Concerns

A second attraction is that a pick-and-choose fractional should not be subject to Rev. Proc. 64-19 if date of distribution values are used to determine the dollar amount, to be funded using assets also valued on the date(s) of distribution. Indeed, even if this approach were subject to Rev. Proc. 64-19, it should be deemed to comply because ratable sharing of appreciation and depreciation occurs naturally by application of the fraction against the available fund at the date(s) of distribution, and that ratable sharing is preserved if assets are allocated using those same values.

Income Tax Treatment

Although there is only limited authority directly on point, the pick-and-choose fractional apparently is viewed like a pro rata fractional marital bequest for income tax purposes: DNI is carried out on allocation to separate shares, but IRD is not accelerated under §691(a)(2).

Revaluation of All Assets

The disadvantages associated with a pick-and-choose fractional relate to the procedure adopted to establish the amount of the marital share and to value assets allocated to it. To illustrate, in establishing the amount of the marital bequest, the document must direct application of the fraction against the available fund as of the date(s) of division, meaning that every asset in the fund must be revalued each time a distribution in satisfaction of the fractional bequest is made. This can be a difficult administrative burden that might be incurred several times if funding takes place in stages. The same chore now is imposed for income tax separate share rule purposes in many of the same circumstances involving other marital funding approaches, so some planners regard this as a neutral factor. This onerous aspect would be avoided in a pick-and-choose fractional if date of distribution values were not used in the process but, for several reasons, it appears to be imperative that the fraction be applied using date of distribution values.

The first reason to favor use of date of distribution values is that using federal estate tax values would present the same abuse found in Rev. Proc. 64-19. This results because appreciation and depreciation would not be shared in determining the amount to be funded if the fraction were applied against the federal estate tax value of the available fund. Thus, the marital bequest would be in jeopardy of disqualification without some other method to apportion subsequent appreciation and depreciation.

The other factor that speaks to using date of distribution values in applying the pick-and-choose fractional is that the limited authorities holding that no gain or loss is incurred on funding a pick-and-choose fractional all rely on that fact. The amount of the marital entitlement being satisfied and the value of the assets allocated thereto were determined in each case using date of distribution values. Any other approach potentially runs the risk of losing this no-realization result, which is a prime justification for using any fractional approach.

Uncertainties Surround the Pick-and-Choose Fractional

Notwithstanding the foregoing determinations, the proper characterization of the pick-and-choose fractional approach is not well established.

> Example: D's will makes a residuary bequest "to my children, A and B, in equal shares" and grants the personal representative authority to make non-pro-rata distributions to A and B. The residuary estate consists of two types of assets: FarmAcre and securities.

Precisely what do A and B own as of D's death? Do A and B each own a share of FarmAcre and a share of the securities? The difficulty is that A and B do not know what they own and will not know until the personal representative exercises its discretion by distributing assets.

The structure of the bequest raises additional questions. Do A and B own assets or do they have a right to take a pecuniary bequest equal to half of an amount determined by reference to the value of all assets comprising the residuary estate? Is this a gift of a fractional share of assets or is it more comparable to a gift of a pecuniary amount, differing from a true worth pecuniary bequest only because the fund of assets may fluctuate in value before the size of the gift is determined?

To borrow an issue from the world of pecuniary gift concerns, suppose instead that the residuary estate consists of securities worth $500,000 and a right to receive IRD also worth $500,000. On D's death, who owns that IRD item if, depending on the personal representative's exercise of discretion, the item may be distributed entirely to A, entirely to B, or part to A and part to B? And when the personal representative makes the distribution decision (however it is allocated), does this trigger an immediate income realization under §691(a)(2)?

If this bequest ultimately is determined to be a funded pecuniary bequest (which is analogous to a pecuniary gift, by which the personal representative is authorized to make distributions in kind), some rather devastating consequences would result (for example, realization of gain and acceleration of IRD). However, Technical Advice Memorandum 8447003 placed emphasis on fluctuations in the value of a trust corpus between D's death and the date(s) of distribution to distinguish this fractional bequest from a distribution in satisfaction of a fixed pecuniary amount. If this distinction carries the day, the avoidance of income tax gain or loss realization and IRD acceleration makes the pick-and-choose fractional extremely attractive. Planners using this approach believe and rely on that result.

Marital Bequest Is Not Frozen

Another disadvantage of the pick-and-choose fractional is the same as with a pro rata fractional: because the fraction applies at the time of distribution, the marital bequest will be either greater or less than it would be under a true worth pecuniary approach. Rather than a fixed pecuniary amount, the fractional approach generates a fluctuating amount that, depending on whether the available fund appreciates or declines in value, either may overfund or underfund the marital bequest, relative to the portion a true worth pecuniary approach would have generated. However, unlike the minimum worth pecuniary approach, in which overfunding often is guaranteed, there is as good a chance that the effect of a pick-and-choose fractional will be a reduction in the amount that ultimately will be includible in S's gross estate. And unlike a true worth reverse pecuniary, any appreciation is pro rated and not allocated entirely to S or the marital trust.

On balance, the pick-and-choose fractional may be attractive because it provides the flexibility of a true worth pecuniary, presumably without the capital gain associated with that form of funding and, therefore, with a limited DNI carryout and no IRD acceleration. Revaluation is a big concern but, due to the expansive application of the separate share rule to most pecuniary funding approaches, it is no greater than under the pro rata fractional or any pecuniary as to which the separate share rule applies. Indeed, certain administrative problems generated by the pro rata fractional are reduced. Although it is not frozen in value, it fares better on this score than some pecuniary approaches and is no worse than a pro rata fractional. Overall, the pick-and-choose fractional is a very attractive approach if it works as described here.

Single Fund Marital

The reverse pecuniary or the pick-and-choose fractional approaches are only partial solutions to traditional marital funding problems. The single fund marital is a more novel[103] and sophisticated planning device that sidesteps most problems associated with marital funding, because no actual funding is required. This approach (sometimes called the one-lung marital) only mathematically segregates the marital from the nonmarital portion. It thereby obviates the need for actual marital or nonmarital funding. Instead, through the application of a percentage or a fraction, a portion of an undivided residuary trust qualifies for the deduction, either in the form of a §2056(b)(5) all income with general power of appointment trust or in the form of a QTIP trust of which only a portion has been blessed with the requisite election under §2056(b)(7)(B)(v).

The single fund marital approach can be used to avoid splitting assets into separate trusts or outright distribution of uneconomically small amounts that should not be held in separate trusts. This may be appropriate if the marital trust would be tiny after setting aside the credit shelter amount in a nonmarital trust. Similarly, separate trusts may be undesirable if the nonmarital trust would be uneconomically small (for example, if lifetime gifts or nonprobate nondeductible transfers reduced the available unified credit) either in its own right or in comparison to the marital bequest.

Most importantly, traditional funding consequences (including realization of gain or loss, DNI carryout, and §691(a)(2) acceleration of IRD) all are avoided because funding of either the marital or the nonmarital amount is avoided. Note, however, that funding may be necessary at some time in the future, for example if S were granted a power of appointment over the trust and chose to exercise it.

The following is the operative provision making the single fund marital trust work properly:

> **Section 3: I intend by this article to create a single trust of which a portion, herein referred to as the marital portion, shall qualify for the federal estate tax marital deduction. The value of the marital portion at any time may be determined by multiplying the value of the trust estate at that time by the fraction then in effect. Commencing with my death and until the first distribution of principal pursuant to the provisions of Section 2, the numerator of the fraction shall be the smallest pecuniary amount that, if allowed as a federal estate tax**

---

103. See Moore & Pennell, *Practicing What We Preach: Esoteric or Essential?*, 27 U. MIAMI INST. EST. PLAN. ¶1211 (1993). The single fund marital was reported as used with an average score of only 1.9; 45% of the respondents reported that they "never" use it and another 30% report that they use it only "seldom." Surprisingly, given the relatively unique circumstances in which it would be appropriate, 1% reported that they "always" use it. Low as that response is, it still is higher than expected.

marital deduction, would result in the least possible federal estate tax being payable by reason of my death, considering the unified credit and any credit or deduction for state death taxes, but only to the extent those taxes are not thereby incurred or increased, and the denominator shall be the value as finally determined for federal estate tax purposes of all interests in property that were included in my gross estate and that became, or the proceeds of sale, investment, or reinvestment of which became, a part of the trust estate under this article, less the value as so determined of any distribution made pursuant to Section 1. The fraction shall be adjusted at the time of each payment of principal pursuant to the provisions of Section 2, first by restating it so that the numerator and the denominator are the value of the marital portion and of the trust estate, respectively, immediately prior to the payment, and then by subtracting the amount of the payment from each of the numerator and the denominator, except that the numerator shall not be reduced below zero. Unproductive property shall not be held as an asset of the trust estate for more than a reasonable time during the lifetime of S without [his/her] written consent.

This provision contains a so-called rolling fraction that has the effect of charging all distributions made to S against the marital portion. That generates the same result as if two trusts had been created and all invasions had been made from the marital deduction trust, thus minimizing the amount that will be includible in S's gross estate at death.

For flexibility, a single fund marital trust could be drafted with a provision permitting invasions of corpus for individuals other than S, and allowing S to make withdrawals.[104] Withdrawals by S would be reflected by adjusting the rolling fraction the same as for distributions to S. Distributions to other beneficiaries would be reflected by subtracting the amount of the distribution from only the denominator, and a provision would prohibit distributions to other beneficiaries to the extent the denominator would be less than the numerator after this adjustment. However, because the regulations neither address nor specifically permit distributions from the nonmarital portion to third parties, it may not be advisable until guidance is available.[105]

---

104. See Cantrill, *Fractional or Percentage Residuary Bequests: Allocation of Postmortem Income, Gain and Unrealized Appreciation*, 10 PROB. NOTES 322 (1985); Covey, THE MARITAL DEDUCTION AND CREDIT SHELTER DISPOSITIONS AND THE USE OF FORMULA PROVISIONS 80 (United States Trust Co. 3d ed. 1984); Pennell, *Marital Deduction Funding After ERTA '81*, 7 NOTRE DAME EST. PLAN. INST. at 339-342 (1983).

105. See Treas. Reg. §20.2056(b)-5(c)(1), which only refers to distributions from the specific portion that qualifies, but nothing anywhere in the regulations illustrates a partial election or specific portion that qualifies with invasion of the balance and an adjustment mechanism. See, e.g., Treas. Reg. §§20.2044-1(d)(3), 20.2044-1(e), and 20.2056(b)-7(h), which is where examples ought to appear.

The single fund marital format is subject to five potential disadvantages.

All Trust Income Must Be Distributed Annually

There are several potential income tax disadvantages to the single fund marital approach. For example, only one taxpaying entity is created for income tax purposes, and distribution of all income to S annually is required. Given the almost nonexistent tax advantages for accumulations of income in an estate trust or a nonmarital trust, these characteristics may not be a serious disadvantage. Indeed, this result may be advantageous to the extent a proliferation of multiple trusts could trigger either the multiple trust rule of §643(f), the separate share rule of §663(c), or the third trust rule of §667(c). It certainly reduces trustee fees computed using a base fee for each trust created.

No Full Basis Adjustment for Any Asset

A second disadvantage is that only the marital portion will be includible in S's gross estate but (until carryover basis becomes the law) the new basis adjustment under §1014(a) will be spread over the entire trust. Therefore, when S dies no single asset will receive a new basis equal to the fair market value that is includible in S's gross estate. There should be an aggregate increase in basis similar to the result in a two trust plan (in which basis in the entire marital trust is adjusted to fair market value and basis in the nonmarital trust is not changed). But the sale of any single asset to generate liquidity is likely to generate some gain or loss that would not be incurred in a sale of marital deduction trust assets following S's death.

Administrative Problems

Adjustments must be made on a periodic basis if a rolling fraction is used, requiring the entire trust to be revalued to recompute the fraction. This could be a severe administrative problem if the trust contains assets that are difficult to value. This burden is no different from the adjustment required during administration of D's estate under the separate share rules, but it would extend for S's full overlife (unless the smaller portion of the trust, marital or nonmarital, were flushed out at some point by an authorized discretionary distribution, leaving a pristine fund of only one variety remaining).

No Pick-and-Choose Flexibility

Assets that may not qualify for the marital deduction must be removed from the fund using the same "purge the pot" format employed in any fractional marital. This will avoid inclusion of a portion of those assets in S's estate but as to which no marital deduction would be allowed in D's estate due to §2056(b)(2). Moreover, the single fund marital approach does not allow for sheltering of appreciating assets. Thus, the single fund marital should not be used if the estate contains any "hot" assets that should be allocated to a nonmarital trust to shelter their expected appreciation in value during S's overlife. However, fractional interest discounts should be available by fragmenting ownership between the marital and nonmarital portions of the trust with a partial QTIP election or fractional general power of appointment. Indeed, these discounts should apply without actually dividing the assets and without the risk of a smaller deduction on funding with a fractional interest.

Allocation of Generation-Skipping Transfer Tax Exemption

Effective allocation of the §2631 GST exemption to a marital deduction trust, under a §2652(a)(3) reverse QTIP election, appears to require the existence of two marital deduction trusts. One would be made totally exempt for GST purposes by proper allocation of the GST exemption, while the other would be totally subject to the GST tax. The need for two trusts to best allocate the exemption sharply restricts the value of single fund planning for estates that exceed the amount of the exemption and that need to make use of any previously unallocated exemption. In many very large estates, however, the exemption may have been allocated in another manner, and allocation of the exemption may be of no concern in relatively small estates. Moreover, many estate plans do not include generation-skipping transfers, and the GST is slated to be repealed when the estate tax is repealed, meaning that GST issues may not be very compelling.

Notwithstanding its disadvantages, in noncomplex situations with easily valued assets the single fund marital may prove to be extremely attractive because of its simplicity and avoidance of most concerns that surround other funding alternatives.

Generation-Skipping Transfer Tax Aspects of Marital Funding

In addition to all the foregoing considerations, if the client's situation involves generation-skipping trust provisions, then you also must consider the dictates of §2642(b)(2)(A), which deals with allocation of the GST exemption:

If property is transferred as a result of the death of the transferor, the value of such property [for exemption allocation purposes] shall be its value for purposes of [the estate tax]; except that, if the requirements prescribed by the Secretary respecting allocation of post-death changes in value are not met, the value of such property shall be determined as of the time of the distribution concerned.

As explained by its terse legislative history:

It is expected that in appropriate circumstances the Secretary of the Treasury will require that property distributed from the estate be fairly representative of the appreciation or depreciation in the value of all property available for distribution. Cf. Rev. Proc. 64-19.

The apparent intent of this provision is to prevent taxpayers from intentionally "leveraging" the GST exemption by making asset allocations in a way that pushes disproportionate appreciation into a generation-skipping exempt trust. The classic example would be funding a pecuniary marital deduction bequest and allowing the residue of the transferor's estate to pass into a generation-skipping exempt nonmarital trust. If the marital bequest is funded using date of distribution values and the property available for satisfaction of the bequest appreciates in value, the bequest will be satisfied using fewer assets and all of the appreciation in value will benefit the residue.

The presumed concern underlying §2642(b)(2)(A) is whether this residuary trust may be made totally exempt by allocation of an amount equal to only its estate tax value, if all appreciation is leveraged into that exempt trust by virtue of the funding regime employed.

An additional question is whether a trust will be treated as a separate share and respected for exemption allocation purposes (such as a reverse QTIP trust) following a severance that is authorized under the terms of the document or under state law.

Reliable conclusions relating the GST exemption allocation rules to marital funding regimes are that ratable sharing of appreciation or depreciation, payment of interest on delayed distributions, and distributions that do not leverage the exemption will permit separate share treatment and allow allocation of the exemption to produce a zero inclusion ratio using federal estate tax values in the transferor's estate. Indeed, of all the marital deduction funding alternatives available, it appears that only the minimum worth pecuniary marital bequest runs afoul of the GST exemption allocation construct. This results because that bequest treats assets as worth the lesser of their fair market value or basis for marital deduction funding purposes, which effectively pushes disproportionate appreciation into a marital trust. In a nutshell, any other marital deduction funding approach is copacetic.

Conclusions Regarding Marital Deduction Funding

No funding alternative is entirely without disadvantages. Your task, therefore, is to consider numerous factors in making the most appropriate selection for a particular situation, balancing considerations such as the following:

- loss of flexibility in funding;
- risk of incurring gain or loss in funding;
- risk (or advantage) of overfunding the marital bequest;

- any need to ratably apportion appreciation or depreciation generated during the period of administration;
- administrative difficulties, such as revaluation of assets to fund, or periodic readjustments to fractions to reflect distributions made and application of the separate share rule for DNI calculation and carryout purposes; and
- factors such as carrying out DNI on distributions and accelerating IRD under §691(a)(2).

The most significant consequences of each approach that should be considered in weighing their various advantages and disadvantages are summarized below:

- The *true worth pecuniary* allows full pick-and-choose flexibility, without risk of overfunding and potentially without regard to the separate share rule, but at a cost of capital gain in funding and the need to do some revaluations in the funding process.
- The *fairly representative pecuniary* avoids gain or loss in the current new basis at death environment (and if properly drafted under §1040 if carryover basis becomes the law) at the risk of over- or underfunding the marital, with a reduction in flexibility and the need to revalue all assets to comply with Rev. Proc. 64-19 and the separate share rule.
- The *minimum worth pecuniary* avoids gain (but not loss) at the risk of overfunding the marital (unless the New York style collective asset modification is made), with a minimum of revaluation required, but with a higher degree of sophistication required, a need to comply with the separate share rule, and a greater risk of challenge by disaffected beneficiaries.
- The *true worth reverse pecuniary* allows full pick-and-choose flexibility and minimizes some administrative problems and gain or loss on funding, but allocates all appreciation and depreciation during administration to the marital residue.
- The *fairly representative reverse pecuniary* offers all the advantages of the true worth reverse pecuniary, and it avoids capital gain or loss on funding in the current new basis at death environment (and if properly drafted under §1040 if carryover basis becomes the law). It requires compliance with the separate share rule, along with Rev. Proc. 64-19 (which allows pro rata sharing of appreciation or depreciation between the marital and nonmarital portions).
- The *pro rata fractional* avoids gain or loss and might avoid revaluations, at a cost of lost flexibility, administrative and separate share rule problems, and a marital share that is not frozen in value.

Ch. 7   PLANNING FOR COUPLES   141

- The *pick-and-choose fractional* allows full flexibility without gain or loss on funding, but requires revaluation of all assets. It produces a marital share that is subject to the same administrative complexities as a pro rata fractional and that also is not frozen in value.
- The *single fund* marital essentially avoids most funding issues altogether but requires revaluation at periodic intervals if the rolling fraction is used. It also offers no flexibility in funding, cannot shelter appreciating assets, and cannot be used to segregate a fund for GST exemption allocation.

Unquestionably, no single approach is appropriate in all situations, given all asset mixes and different family situations. Most sophisticated estate planners find that they narrow their selection to several comfortable alternatives and choose among them as the circumstances dictate.

The following chart provides a quick comparison of the various factors recommending the marital funding alternatives considered in this Chapter.

	Traditional Up Front Pecuniary			Credit Shelter Pecuniary		Fractional		Single Fund
	True Worth	Fairly Rep	Minimum Worth	True Worth	Fairly Rep	Pro Rata	Pick and Choose	
Is the marital share frozen?	Yes	No	NO	NO!	No	No	No	No
Does funding incur gain or loss?	Yes	Yes, but is zero under §§1014 and 1040	Gain=0. Loss may be denied by §267	Yes	Yes, but is zero under §§1014 and 1040	No	No	No
Does funding accelerate IRD?	Yes	Yes	Yes	Yes	Yes	No	No	No
Is the marital an income tax separate share?	Yes, but DNI may be zero	Yes	Yes	Yes	Yes	Yes	Yes	Yes
How much DNI is carried out?	FMV	Lesser of FMV or Basis	Lesser of FMV or Basis	FMV	Lesser of FMV or Basis	Lesser of FMV or Basis	Lesser of FMV or Basis	None
How much revaluation is required?	Only assets distributed	All assets	Only loss assets distributed	Only assets distributed	All assets	All assets, often?	All assets, often	Rolling fraction
Administrative problems?	Only §663	§663 plus?	Only §663	Only §663	§663 plus?	Plenty	Plenty	Rolling fraction
Flexible?	Yes	Doubtful	Yes	Yes	Doubtful	No	Yes	No

Planning in Contemplation of Divorce

Not every dissolution of marriage is acrimonious: many divisions can be planned well in advance, in which case the same types of property transfer concerns that often inform marital deduction planning can be considered by you rather than their divorce specialist. By way of most simple example, intraspousal property settlement transfers prior to divorce will qualify for the unlimited marital deduction and need not pay any attention to the dictates of §2516. The §1040 income tax nonrealization rule for transfers between spouses makes the entire transaction entirely tax free and strongly encourages spouses to make their divisions before the gavel falls on their divorce.

One element relating to estate planning and divorce that is worthy of concern is the reality that state laws often regard termination of a marriage as a partial or total revocation of a will, or select provisions in the will, in favor of the former spouse and, under the better statutes, in favor also of the former spouse's family. As there is no way to generalize for disparate treatment found nationwide, it simply behooves you to ascertain the extent of the applicable rule, particularly if a property settlement incident to divorce obligates the client to maintain provisions in an estate plan for the former spouse (or step children or other relatives of their spouse). In the standard case in which provisions for the spouse or the spouse's family ought to be removed from the will, it makes sense to execute a new will when the dissolution process *begins*, such that the client has the best opportunity to eliminate unwanted benefits in case death occurs before the dissolution is final. Then be sure the plan either is not adversely affected by state law or is restored once the dissolution is complete, possibly by re-execution of the same documents.

Planning in Contemplation of Marriage

In addition to any prenuptial agreement planning that may be appropriate when a client is planning to marry, a number of other relatively simple premarital planning options might be considered. One nonromantic notion is to settle in a separate trust any property that the client wishes to insulate from the potential elective share of an intended spouse, the notion being that most elective share statutes do not reach trust property settled prior to the marriage. Conversely, with respect to any property the client intends to transfer to the spouse, often it makes better sense to wait until the nuptials have been completed, so as to qualify for the inter vivos marital deduction. Further, if both parties to the expected marriage own personal residence real property that may qualify for §121 capital gain relief and anticipate liquidation of one or both of their dwellings, it may be wise if either or both sell prior to the marriage, so as to maximize the benefits of their respective entitlements.

Planning for Unmarried Cohabitants

One final matter may be worthy of a short note. An increasingly common question is what planning can (or should) be considered for unmarried cohabitants? The proper answer relies on the reality that estate planners routinely craft dispositive plans for individuals who live together but cannot marry: planning (1) for parents who benefit their caretaker children, (2) for relatives (such as siblings or, sometimes, for the in-law surviving spouses of siblings) who live with and care for each other, (3) for heterosexual couples who don't countenance marriage, including some elderly couples "living in sin" because they cannot afford to remarry because it would cause a loss of valuable Social Security or other benefits acquired as survivors of their predeceased former spouses, and (4) sometimes for same sex couples who might wish to be married if only the law would permit it.

The point is that it doesn't really matter why these committed individuals (partners is a value-laden term in today's environment but descriptive of any of these relationships, both traditional and not yet so) are not married. The problem is that none of them qualifies for certain tax benefits that are reserved for married couples, such as the marital deduction. Planning for all these folks is relatively similar, and essentially without much in the way of gimmicks or special tools or opportunities.

But there are some blessings. One is that a relatively high applicable exclusion amount means that fewer individuals must be concerned about taxes at all. For them, more interesting challenges may entail concerns about will contests (brought by disapproving or suspicious surviving heirs) or contracts to make wills (as part of bargained for exchanges or commitments). In the very small cohort of clients with enough wealth to be concerned about saving taxes, another blessing is that transactions like zero gift grantor retained annuity trusts (GRATs) or charitable lead trusts (CLTs) that pass a remainder interest to a private individual without payment of gift tax may be more viable than for married couples. This is because so many of these relationships fall outside the definition of "family" in Chapter 14 of the Code and therefore do not raise the restrictions of provisions such as §2702 that are designed to increase the gift tax cost of split interest planning among family members.

Frequently the asset a client most wants to bestow on a beneficiary is a home in which they live together, in which case split interest planning often recommends itself. Most common would be a client who retains a term of years or even a life estate that §2702 would ignore for gift tax purposes if the donee was a family member but that, for many of these clients, is recognized and therefore reduces the gift tax value of the remainder interest transferred. Application of §2036(a)(1) may be a concern, but some transfers in this context are for full and adequate consideration that is provided by the donee in various forms (including labor in the context of caregiving) that may avoid application of that inclusion provision *if* the money or money's worth aspect of this consideration is satisfied and proper documentation supports the bona fides of the transaction.

More difficult are situations in which several individuals set up house and commingle assets, in which case cautions relating to concurrent ownership of property and the application of §2040 inclusion at death are important. Unexpected gifts may occur if one party is obligated on a mortgage and the other contributes to the installment payments, or one party owns legal title to property that the other is improving (through labor or monetary contributions, the former outside the gift tax but not the latter). Record keeping relating to commingling can be a serious practical issue, and a failure to adequately identify casual transfers that may exceed the gift tax annual exclusion on a routine basis could create gift tax headaches and potential administrative *and* estate tax problems whether the relationship terminates inter vivos or with the death of one of them.

Otherwise, the issues that affect these individuals really are not any different from what a normal estate plan might encounter with respect to any donor who is entirely unrelated to or just not married to the donee. Successful planning in this context merely demands that you remember the standard tools of the trade.

Chapter 8

PLANNING FOR CHARITY

The benefits of philanthropy are so powerful that the appropriateness of some charitable planning should be considered in many estate planning situations. A growing percentage of decedents have no children or other natural objects of their bounty, making charity a prime candidate for your client's beneficence. Indeed, even when surviving family members are involved, future interest end limitations to charity may be appropriate in the remote event that all other natural beneficiaries die before all trusts terminate.

Thus viewed, gifts to charity play a significant role in everyday estate planning and are desirable because of the charitable deduction available under state and federal income and wealth transfer tax laws. And not just in "larger" estates.[1] Moreover, even if the amount of wealth involved and family responsibilities are such that no primary diversion to charitable purposes is appropriate, and even if the charitable purpose is vague or ill defined,[2] what begins today as an afterthought in the overall estate plan ultimately may germinate into a larger charitable component as the client, the family, their wealth, and ultimately their overall plan all mature.

In this regard and for a number of reasons, estate planners need to know about more than just the wealth transfer tax charitable deduction provisions. The most important additional knowledge is the income tax charitable deduction rules, which drive most charitable planning and drafting by defining the entities and the forms of gifts that qualify. This is particularly important because inter vivos giving generates an income tax deduction while it removes the property from the donor's estate, tax free

---

1. In Brady v. Ceaty, 207 N.E.2d 49 (Mass. 1965), a residuary testamentary trust was created to make payments for the education "of one or more deserving boys or girls . . . worthy, needy and deserving of his or her education." Although a private express trust for indefinite beneficiaries is invalid, this trust was sustained as a valid charitable trust created for a charitable purpose, notwithstanding that the size (approximately $11,000) made it appear that few would benefit. It also was not prevented from being a charitable trust by the fact that the settlor's own relatives were not excluded as recipients.

2. For example, a trust that directed trustees to contribute "to such philanthropic causes as my Trustees may select, special consideration, however, to be given to charitable, educational and scientific fields . . ." was validated by Wilson v. Flowers, 277 A.2d 199 (N.J. 1971), notwithstanding the vagueness that normally would invalidate a private express trust. See, e.g., Burr v. Brooks, 416 N.E.2d 231 (Ill. 1981) (the common law doctrine of cy pres may be used to salvage a trust established in 1898 that finally terminated in 1976 and could not be used for the purposes the settlor originally envisioned; the property was applied to accomplish the general charitable purposes of the original grant).

under the gift tax charitable deduction, effectively generating two tax benefits (both income and wealth transfer tax deductions) for inter vivos charitable deduction planning. Waiting until death to engage in charitable planning produces only the one (wealth transfer tax benefit). Perhaps more importantly, a donor who gives to charity during life gets to enjoy seeing the good deed done.

A more venal reason you are wise to learn the complex rules relating to effective charitable planning and drafting is that knowledge in this arena opens a whole new market, representing charitable donors and the entities they benefit. Vast numbers of estate planners know next to nothing about this area of the practice, notwithstanding that being known among charities and their patrons is good business, even if the planner does no exempt organization qualification or compliance work for the charity itself. Furthermore, an estate planner's clients will be solicited by charities, which often are more than willing to provide their own counsel to provide assistance to the client in structuring a charitable giving program. If not sufficiently well versed in charitable planning, you may find that the charity's counsel is driving the plan and perhaps even steering the client's representation away from you.

There are ethical considerations in any such representation, and more in providing assistance, ranging from potential conflicts of interest to possible violation of the rule requiring an attorney to disclose when someone else (in this case the charity) is paying the fee for a client's representation. There also may be issues of improper solicitation and, depending on who is providing the assistance, the unauthorized practice of law. There may be even greater independent judgment and duty of loyalty breaches if a charity is engaged in "selling" certain forms of planning, such as a charitable gift annuity. That these issues are significant is revealed by the fact that the charitable fundraising community has formulated rules of conduct or ethical constructs, among which are the American Council on Gift Annuities Model Standards of Practice for the Charitable Gift Planner and the National Society of Fund Raising Executives Code of Ethical Principles and Standards of Professional Practice.

The Various Deductions

Charitable planning offers several deductions.[3] Fortunately, for most estate planning purposes the wealth transfer tax charitable deductions in §§2055 and 2522 are unlimited in amount. The entitlement is without restriction if the qualification rules are met. Even if an inter vivos transfer that qualifies for the gift tax charitable deduction is brought back into the

---

3. See generally Beckwith, *Estate & Gift Tax Charitable Deductions*, 261-3d Tax Mgmt. (BNA) ESTATES, GIFTS, & TRUSTS PORT. (1991); Kirschten & Freitag, *Charitable Contributions: Income Tax Aspects*, 863 Tax Mgmt. (BNA) ESTATES, GIFTS, & TRUSTS PORT. (1999).

decedent's estate at death,[4] the estate tax charitable deduction is likely to wash that inclusion with little ancillary fallout. So the degree of complication from the wealth transfer tax charitable deductions generally is slight.

Complexity *is* created, however, if an income tax deduction might be desirable (which almost always is the case). A charitable transfer may be made outright to a qualified recipient or to a trust. Split interest trusts generate complexity because the property is held for the benefit of private individuals and charity and must satisfy technical requirements that demand a high degree of sophisticated drafting, careful administration, and constant attention to detail. You will note that extensive footnoting in this Chapter contains highly technical citation to very detailed Internal Revenue Code provisions, which will make you crazy but must be kept in mind. With footnotes versus citation in the text hopefully we can keep them slightly out of sight so as not to let them distract us or slow us down. But please be aware that you are reading the simplified version. There is much more to this story than will meet your eye. That may beg credibility as you continue to read, but please do not underestimate the need for attention to detail in this corner of our world. Also take comfort in knowing that this Chapter gets easier after this segment, which ends at page 11.

Inter vivos charitable gifts are better than testamentary transfers to charity (notwithstanding the unlimited entitlement under both the gift and estate taxes) because both remove the property from the taxpayer's wealth transfer taxable estate but only the inter vivos transfer will generate a §170 income tax deduction. The wicked aspect of inter vivos charitable planning is that the §170 income tax deduction is riddled with restrictions and limitations that are among the most complex in the tax laws. To make sense of §170 often requires that the analyst consider at least five different potential factors: (1) the contribution base percentage limitation, which is affected by (2) the type of charitable donee and (3) the class of property transferred, and then there is (4) the form of transfer, and (for certain transfers) (5) whether to make an election.

---

4. A charitable remainder trust, charitable gift annuity, pooled income fund, or transfer of the remainder interest in a personal residence or a farm in which the decedent retained the lead interest all will be includible under the retained enjoyment rule of §2036(a)(1) (in the trust case in that amount needed to produce the retained annual payment). The government believes that an additional source for inclusion is §2039, as articulated in Field Service Advice 200036012 and Private Letter Ruling 200210009. Rev. Rul. 82-105, Rev. Rul. 76-273. A charitable trust that gives the settlor as trustee the power to select charities that will receive distributions may be includible in the settlor's gross estate under the retained control rules of §2036 or §2038, and the same could be true of contributions to a foundation or charitable corporation of which the contributor was an officer with the power to alter the ultimate beneficial enjoyment of the contribution. See Rev. Rul. 72-552; Rifkind v. United States, 84-2 U.S. Tax Cas. ¶13,577 (Ct. Cl. 1984) (the decedent resigned from the position that created inclusion generating powers but died within three years, triggering §2035 inclusion instead). See Private Letter Ruling 200108032 for a representative situation in which the taxpayer was shielded from having any involvement in a charity that would provide prohibited control.

To illustrate, assume in this Chapter that the transfer is from an individual (not a corporation, partnership, trust, estate, or other entity) to a qualified charity.[5] The most basic rule, from which all variations flow, entails a simple cash gift to a public charity, which qualifies for the §170(b)(1)(A) income tax charitable deduction up to an amount that cannot exceed 50% of the taxpayer's adjusted gross income[6] for the year of contribution.

The income tax charitable deduction year of contribution for a charitable gift made by a credit card charge or a personal check is the year in which the charge is made or the check is delivered and not a later year in which the charge or check is paid. See Rev. Rul. 78-38 (credit cards); Estate of Belcher v. Commissioner, 83 T.C. 227 (1984) (checks). Compare the rule that making a pledge is *not* tantamount to payment for charitable deduction purposes. The deduction is allowable in the year actual payment is made under the pledge. §170(a)(1); Petty v. Commissioner, 40 T.C. 521 (1964); Rev. Rul. 68-174; *Teitell*, OUTRIGHT CHARITABLE GIFTS ¶1.03[2]. According to Rev. Rul. 81-110, a pledge constitutes a gift for *gift* tax purposes when it becomes a binding obligation, but the taxpayer may not deduct for *income* tax purposes until the year of payment. You can begin to see how confusion easily can reign in this endeavor.

Like all other contributions in a given tax year that exceed the §170 percentage limitation, cash contributions that exceed the 50% limitation in the current year may be carried over for deduction in any of the five succeeding years. §170(d)(1)(A); Treas. Reg. §1.170A-10. Carryovers are consumed in any future year beginning with the oldest accumulated excess contribution first, but may be deducted only to the extent contributions in a new year do not consume that new year's contribution base limitation.

Recognize that the carryover rule for all of these contributions essentially treats the carryover amount as if it were a transfer in the carryover year, of the same variety that it was in the year from which it is carried over. See §170(d)(1)(A). Thus, a cash gift in year one that exceeds the year one contribution base percentage limitation will carry over to any of years two through six until exhausted, and will be treated as a current year cash contribution in those later carryover years. Cash transfers in a

---

5. The topic of which entities qualify as exempt from income taxation under which rules is way beyond the ken of these materials and, thankfully, typically is not the task of the estate planner (as opposed to an exempt organization specialist). A short discussion is provided beginning at page 11 and more expansive and helpful guidance for many of the planning and qualification issues is available in Teitell, PHILANTHROPY & TAXATION (updated annually) (hereafter *Teitell*), upon which many planners and charities alike rely extensively in this complex area. See, e.g., Teitell, OUTRIGHT CHARITABLE GIFTS ¶1.02 regarding the classification and requirements of qualified charities.

6. §170(b)(1)(A) (flush language) and Treas. Reg. §1.170A-8(b) describe the percentage limitation in terms of a "contribution base," which is defined in §170(b)(1)(F) to mean §62 adjusted gross income computed without regard to any net operating loss carryback under §172. For simplicity this discussion ignores that refinement and refers just to adjusted gross income.

later year will be applied against the contribution base percentage limitation first, but then the carryover cash transfers from prior years will be applied in a way that will consume the contribution base percentage limit in that carryover year (all before transfers of a lower priority in that later year or carryovers of lower priority transfers are permitted as deductions in that later year). Did you get that? Don't despair: there are lots of folks who work with charity to help you in this. We just need to gather up some of the basic rules.

This base rule is altered if the transfer is not "to" a *public* charity. Both contributions to certain private foundations and other nontraditional (but still qualified) charities,[7] and transfers "for the use of" public charities,[8] are subject to a reduced contribution limitation. §170(b)(1)(B). To simplify this explanation, however, it is better to address the income tax charitable deduction rules for transfers *to* public charities first, and then to compare the rules that apply for all other varieties of qualified charitable gifts.

Transfers to Public Charities

Only gifts of cash or property qualify for the charitable deduction. Gifts of services (the value of which is nondeductible under Treas. Reg. §1.170A-1(g)) or of the *use* of property do not count. The base rule for cash contributions to public charities is more beneficial than is the rule that applies if the property transferred is not cash, so let's concentrate on the noncash rules. For gifts of property it is important to distinguish between long term capital gain property and other properties transferred in kind. The full fair market value of appreciated long term capital gain property may be deducted in most cases,[9] with no realization of gain or loss on the initial contribution,[10] and the same five year carryforward provision applies to excess deductions.[11] However, the contribution base percentage limitation is reduced from 50% to only 30% of adjusted gross income.[12] That percentage limitation may be increased back to 50%, but only if an irrevocable, all-or-nothing election is made to limit the deduction for each

---

7. That is, entities that are not defined in §170(b)(1)(A) or §170(b)(1)(E). See §509, which defines a private foundation by cross reference to the qualification requirements of §501(c)(3). And see Hodgman, *Designing Private Foundations — Avoid the Cookie-Cutter Approach*, 25 Est. Plan. 481 (1998), for an interesting rendition of the relative advantages of private foundations and donor advised funds.

8. See Treas. Reg. §1.170A-8(b), distinguishing between gifts "to" a public charity and those "for the use of" such an entity, as those terms are described in Treas. Reg. §1.170A-8(a)(2).

9. §170(b)(1)(C)(i); Treas. Reg. §1.170A-8(d)(1). Subject to an exception in §170(e)(1)(B)(i), which limits the deduction to the basis of any contributed tangible personal property that is unrelated to the recipient's charitable purpose. See *Teitell* Outright Charitable Gifts ¶1.05.

10. See Campbell v. Prothro, 209 F.2d 331 (5th Cir. 1954); Rev. Rul. 55-531, Rev. Rul. 55-275, and Rev. Rul. 55-138.

11. §170(b)(1)(C)(ii).

12. §170(b)(1)(C)(i). A similar rule relating to transfers not to public charities reduces the percentage limitation to 20% of adjusted gross income. §170(b)(1)(D).

long term capital gain asset transferred during the year to the lower adjusted basis of the asset instead of its fair market value.[13] Get yourself grounded by viewing the chart at page 8 before you get dizzy trying to follow all these twists and turns.

Last among the rules involving transfers to public charities is the deduction for appreciated property contributed in kind that either is not *long term* or not *capital* gain property. In this situation the deduction is limited to the adjusted basis of the asset but the contribution base percentage limitation is 50%. There is no option to deduct fair market value, subject to a lower percentage limitation,[14] but again the same five year carryforward provision applies to excess contributions.[15] Notice that the limitation to basis is not relevant if the property is not appreciated. The deduction is limited to the lower fair market value if the asset is a loss investment.[16]

As an aside, understanding these rules is made easier by distinguishing between the contribution base percentage limitation and the amount of the deduction itself. The former determines how much of a transfer made in a given year may be recognized for deduction purposes in that year. Amounts transferred in excess of the percentage limitation must be carried over. The actual deduction rules themselves, however, take the amount of the transfer that is recognized in the current year (either a transfer actually made in the current year or a carryover from a transfer made in a prior year) and determine the deduction attributable to the transfer. These rules are not informed by the percentage limitation and may produce a deduction amount that is different from the amount recognized under the percentage limitation rules.

To illustrate, if the fair market value of property contributed to a public charity is $10x but the applicable percentage of the contribution base is only $7x, the excess of $3x will be available for carryover into future years. The percentage limitation $7x is the amount of the transfer that may be recognized in the current year. But it is not necessarily the amount of the *deduction* attributable to that transfer. For example, applying the rules just described, the *deduction* generated by a recognized

---

13. See §170(b)(1)(C)(iii) and Treas. Reg. §1.170A-8(d)(2), making reference to §170(e)(1). Although not expressly limited to long term capital gain property, the cross reference to property to which §170(e)(1)(B) otherwise would not apply entails only long term capital assets.

14. §170(e)(1)(A), operating under the 50% rule of §170(b)(1)(A) without reduction to 30% by §170(b)(1)(C) because the property is not a long term capital asset, as mandated by §170(b)(1)(C)(iv). Treas. Reg. §1.170A-4(a) is slightly more helpful, but could this torture be more complex?

15. But not under the same provision. For this, see §170(d)(1)(A); Treas. Reg. §1.170A-10.

16. See, e.g., Withers v. Commissioner, 69 T.C. 900 (1978) (no deduction is allowed for the taxpayer's higher basis, nor is a §165 loss deduction available; the taxpayer should have sold the property at a loss, used the tax loss to offset other gain or income, and donated the proceeds for a charitable deduction equal to the fair market value of the property).

transfer of property with $10x of fair market value might be limited to the aggregate basis in some or all of the property (if, for example, some of it is long term capital gain property).

The amount of the contribution base percentage limitation consumed by the gift is measured by the fair market value ($10x), not by the amount that is allowed as a deduction. And the deduction amount could be an amount less than $10x — approaching zero if the transferred property has a very low basis and the deduction rule (applicable to that type of property, given to that variety of recipient) limits the deduction to basis instead of fair market value.

In addition, the deduction attributable to certain transfers may be only a percentage of the property contributed and recognized. An example would be a gift to a split interest trust in which the value of the charitable interest is something less than 100%, determined by a factor that reflects the relative value of lead and remainder interests based on interest assumptions, monthly or term of years entitlements, and a handful of adjustments that relate to the frequency or timing of payments. See pages 19 and 39 dealing with split interest trusts and the determination of the factor used to establish the portion of the contribution that is deemed to benefit charity and therefore informs calculation of the allowable deduction.

Other Transfers

Returning to the basic rules, the deduction for contributions to organizations that do not meet the public charity definition (meaning most private foundations)[17] and for gifts that are "for the use of" (rather than "to") public charities is limited in several significant respects. First, the contribution base percentage limitation for cash gifts is limited to 30% of adjusted gross income,[18] although aggregate transfers that exceed the 30% limitation may be carried over to the next five future years (as may transfers to public charities).[19] The contribution base percentage limitation for transfers of long term appreciated assets is reduced to only 20% of

---

17. Excepted from the private foundation category are those organizations defined in §170(b)(1)(E), including private operating foundations, passthrough foundations, and donor advised funds, and §170(b)(1)(A)(viii) supporting organizations. Notice that §170(c) broadly defines the entities for which contributions are deductible, while §170(b)(1)(A) defines a more limited class of entities that avoid the more restrictive limitations applicable to donations to "private" foundations that are not excepted.

18. §170(b)(1)(B), reduced from the public charity base rule with a limitation of 50% of adjusted gross income. The percentage limitation actually is the lower of 30% *or* what remains of the 50% contribution base for cash gifts to public charities after application of §170(b)(1)(A). In effect this means that gifts to public charities are considered before gifts to other charities under §170(b)(1)(B), the latter of which cannot exceed the 30% limitation. The contribution base is computed under §170(b)(1)(F) as it is for public charities, as adjusted gross income without regard to any net operating loss carryback under §172.

19. §170(b)(1)(B).

adjusted gross income,[20] and only the adjusted basis of appreciated property may be claimed as a deduction.[21] Again, transfers exceeding the percentage limitation may be carried over for five years.[22] Finally, the contribution base percentage limitation for property transferred in kind that is not *long term* or not *capital* gain property is restricted to 30% (the same as the limitation applicable to cash gifts), with the same five year carryover for excess distributions,[23] but only the amount of the basis in those assets may be deducted.

This convoluted amalgam of rules is illustrated in the following chart:

		Property Transferred		
		Cash	Long term capital gain	Other
"To" Public Charities	Deduction	FMV	FMV[†*]	Basis
	Percentage Limit	50%	30%[*]	50%
All Other Transfers[¤]	Deduction	FMV	Basis[‡]	Basis
	Percentage Limit	30%	20%	30%

†   Limited to the basis of any §170(e)(1)(B)(i) tangible personal property that is unrelated to the recipient's charitable purpose.

*   With the §170(e)(1) election the aggregate amount deductible can be increased to 50% of the contribution base, but only adjusted basis may be deducted.

‡   Fair market value for §170(e)(5) qualified appreciated stock.

¤   This category includes transfers "for the use of" a public charity, plus all transfers to organizations described at note 17.

In looking over the chart it almost goes without saying that the nature of the given property is an important factor. The case law and rulings are replete with controversy relating to the proper classification of the scads of unusual assets given to charity, whether the asset is a capital asset held long or short term or just ordinary income property, along with questions relating to the basis of the property (to the extent the deduction is limited

---

20.   §170(b)(1)(D)(i), reduced from the 30% (or 50% with an election) rule for long term capital gain property given to a public charity.

21.   §§170(e)(1)(A) and 170(e)(1)(B)(ii). That is, instead of counting for deduction the full fair market value of the transferred property, the deduction normally applicable for gifts of long term capital gain property to public charities is reduced by the amount of any long term capital gain that would be generated if the property were sold at its fair market value, and the deduction normally applicable for gifts of other appreciated property to public charities similarly is reduced by the amount of other gain that would be generated if the property were sold at its fair market value. The reduction by the amount of unrealized long term capital gain does *not* apply if §170(e)(5) qualified appreciated stock is involved, meaning stock for which market quotations readily are available on an established securities market.

22.   §170(b)(1)(D)(ii).

23.   §170(b)(1)(B).

by basis), whether that basis was depreciated or otherwise was reduced prior to the transfer, and whether tangible personal property has a use that is related to the recipient's charitable purpose.[24]

The §170(b)(1)(C)(iii) election to cause §170(e)(1) to apply to contributions of long term capital gain property to a public charity is an irrevocable, all-or-nothing proposition. If made, it applies to every contribution of long term capital gain property during the same taxable year, and it also converts the current year deduction of any carryovers of long term capital asset transfers from any of the five prior years.[25] In some years a taxpayer may have both cash and long term capital gain property, such that the face amount of the cash or the fair market value of the stock could be deducted. Depending on how the election is made, it may make sense to give the appreciated stock to the charity and use the cash to buy replacement stock in the same amount, with a new basis equal to fair market value. Assuming the contribution base percentage limitation is not affected, and no ancillary consequences are disadvantageous, the overall result may be better, all other factors being equal. But there is a lot to consider, there are many things going on here, and knowing the client's total income tax and basis picture (along with prior year deductions and carryforwards) all are critical. You won't do any of this without consulting your client's tax accountant.

The election to increase the contribution base percentage limitation to 50% from the otherwise applicable 30% may be wise if the amount of gain is slight and the ability to deduct more of the fair market value in the year of donation is desirable. But it may not be wise, depending on the taxpayer's other tax attributes in the year of contribution. An alternative would be to sell the appreciated long term capital assets, pay capital gain tax on the appreciation out of the proceeds, and give the balance of the cash proceeds to charity (perhaps including a private foundation), subject to the otherwise applicable 50% contribution base percentage limitation on gifts of cash to a public charity. Yet a third option would be to contribute the appreciated property to a charitable remainder trust and take a reduced deduction for only the value of the remainder interest (which could be payable to a private foundation). Then in a later year the taxpayer would contribute the retained lead interest and deduct the value of that contribution subject to its own contribution base percentage limitation.

Careful calculation of the fallout consequences to the taxpayer of each alternative, and all the income tax ripple effects of the various options,

---

24. See Teitell, OUTRIGHT CHARITABLE GIFTS ¶1.04, which catalogs cases and rulings involving dozens of unusual assets that have been controversial. It is almost as if some clients want to "unload" their most weird assets on charity (or, more charitably, as if only special qualified organizations are interested in providing the desired sanctuary for the treasured assets some donors most want to preserve and protect). Imagine, for example, the apt recipient of Teitell's own extensive flyswatter collection, made (in)famous by many memorable lectures in which they have provided the helpful illustration of these rules.

25. See Treas. Reg. §1.170A-8(d)(2); Rev. Rul. 77-217.

must be compared to the amount that the charity would net if the appreciated property were contributed in kind and the tax exempt charity sold the asset and realized the capital gain. You can see why few planners are truly up on all this, and therefore why the few who are do very well with this subspecialty.

As if these rules were not convoluted enough, there also is a set of priority rules that determine how the contribution base percentage limitation is used in any given year. This confusing paradigm[26] considers first transfers made to public charities, counting first cash and then assets transferred in kind that are not long term capital gain property, and then the long term capital gain property. All that is followed by a second tier of gifts not to public charities, in the same order.

Carryovers are consumed in future years beginning with the oldest accumulated excess contribution first, but may be used only to the extent contributions in that future year do not consume that year's contribution base percentage limitation.[27] Further making the carryover less useful than it otherwise might be, amounts that could be used in a carryover year are deemed consumed, even if the taxpayer claimed the standard deduction in that year in lieu of itemizing deductions and actually claiming the carryover amount.[28]

In addition, no provision preserves carryover charitable deductions if the taxpayer dies before the five year carryover period ends. Thus, a personal representative (and potentially the taxpayer's surviving spouse, if any) will want to consider end of life and year end planning to attempt to preserve the deduction. Another alternative may make better sense if a likely effect is that a deduction may be lost because it may exceed the contribution base percentage limitation and therefore carry over into years after the taxpayer's death. To avoid that loss, the taxpayer could choose not to make the charitable transfer. Instead, the taxpayer could make a gift to the taxpayer's spouse, tax free under the gift tax marital deduction, and the spouse could make the charitable donation. This could preserve the entire deduction for use either in the year of donation by the spouse or in

---

26. These rules are only just barely decipherable from §§170(b)(1)(B)(ii), 170(b)(1)(D)(i), and Treas. Reg. §1.170A-8(f) (which has not been amended to reflect changes in the contribution base percentage limitations and other changes in the law). Publication 526 provides a worksheet that makes the calculation of deductions and carryovers easier, but no more understandable. The problem with all these rules and priorities is that they describe transfers in the order revealed in the chart at page 8 in text, but that is not how the priority rules operate. Looking at the chart, the cash column and then the "other" column and then the long term capital gain column is how the priority rules actually operate, notwithstanding how they are described in the Code.

27. See §170(d)(1)(A) and the descriptive provisions in Treas. Reg. §1.170A-10 (but note that these regulations have not been amended to reflect changes in the contribution base percentage limitation rules).

28. Treas. Reg. §1.170A-10(a)(2) (also not amended to reflect current percentage limitations and other changes in the law).

subsequent carryover years if the spouse lives long enough to consume the rollover deduction.

Donees: Entities That Qualify

The wealth transfer tax and income tax definitions of qualified charities are not precisely the same. Consequently, if a charitable deduction is sought under different taxes, the transfer must be made to a beneficiary that qualifies under each relevant definition. Two cautions here are appropriate.

First, the following material clearly is not designed (or adequate) to assist with the creation or maintenance of a charitable organization. Thus, it is not directed at how to qualify or how to create a qualified charitable organization or a private foundation. It also is not focused on the difference between various flavors of private foundation or entities that are entitled to §501 income tax exemption.

Second, even if a transfer is made to a recipient that qualifies under the appropriate definition, the transfer will not be deductible unless the gift is in a qualified form of transfer. A qualified recipient and a qualified transfer are two different concepts. The transfer rules are our focus.

The primary qualified transfer impediment is found in the split interest trust provisions. These relate to planning that provides for individuals and charitable beneficiaries alike. A second and much less common nonqualified transfer is anticipated by a rule in Treas. Reg. §20.2055-2(b)(1). It allows a deduction for a charitable gift subject to a condition precedent only if the possibility that the charitable transfer will not become effective is so remote as to be negligible. Numerous authorities regard 5% as the appropriate threshold for that standard.[29]

A third source of potential disqualification is if payment of a charitable bequest is discretionary. See, e.g., State Street Bank & Trust Co. v. United States, 634 F.2d 5 (1st Cir. 1980), in which the decedent's will listed

---

29. See, e.g., Rev. Rul. 77-374, Rev. Rul. 70-452, and compare Rev. Rul. 78-255 (the charitable deduction was allowed for a gift that was contingent on a 78-year-old widow surviving the testator by 30 days); Technical Advice Memoranda 9443004 (regarding a contingency of a school ceasing to exist as a state accredited institution at any time within a 30 year period as so remote as to be negligible and allowing the deduction, although the contingency had to be reflected in determining the value of the deduction allowed; quaere how to determine the value of a contingency that is so remote as to be negligible) and 9236003 (a contingency was so remote as to be negligible and did not disallow the deduction notwithstanding that it was enforced by the local attorney general and the charity relinquished the property) with Estate of Lockett v. Commissioner, 75 T.C.M. (CCH) 1731 (1998) (no charitable deduction was allowable for a bequest of the decedent's home under a mandate that it be set aside as a historical site, notwithstanding that the trustees complied with that request) and Technical Advice Memoranda 9443001 (the charitable deduction was disallowed for a bequest to any entity that would accept, maintain, and limit development of the property according to the decedent's wishes as judged by a personal representative; no charity accepted the bequest as conditioned and the government ruled that exercise of the personal representative's power was not so remote as to be negligible) and 8010011 (a charitable remainder interest contingent on a never-married 60-year-old man dying without a surviving child was nondeductible because of the ability to adopt a child).

various charitable gifts and an inter vivos trust provided the trustee with authority "in its absolute discretion" to pay any legacies included in the will. The §2055 deduction was allowed because the court determined under local law that, under the circumstances, the trustee would not be permitted to decline to pay those legacies. Rev. Rul. 69-285 granted a charitable deduction for the value of a residuary bequest to a named person who, as personal representative, was to distribute the funds "to whatever charities she may deem worthy," because a local court held that the will created a fiduciary obligation to distribute the funds to exclusively charitable organizations within the meaning of §2055. Private Letter Ruling 9322025 allowed a charitable deduction for a bequest that permitted the decedent's personal representative to choose the recipient or even to create a charitable beneficiary, because it was clear that the recipient had to be a qualified charity and because the personal representative had no discretion whether to comply with the bequest itself.

We will return to the qualified transfer requirement at page 16. But first, the easier qualified recipient rules deserve a little more elaboration. As noted earlier, there is a positive disconnect between the definitions of qualified recipients for estate, gift, and income tax charitable deduction purposes. This notion is confirmed by Rev. Rul. 71-200, in which the §2055(a) estate tax charitable deduction was denied because the gift was to organizations that qualify under the income, estate, inheritance, *or* gift taxes. The government noted that the word "or" would permit distributions to organizations that do not qualify for estate tax purposes whereas the word "and" would have prevented a gift that fell in the gaps between the various qualification provisions. This is such a concern that you must pay special attention, to verify that the intended recipient is a qualified charity for purposes of the particular tax involved. In sufficiently large situations it may be wise even to go behind the charity's representation to verify that the donation will produce the intended benefits.

At a bare minimum, however, in most cases a quick check to verify the proper name and continued qualified status of the recipient would be prudent. The Cumulative List of Organizations Described in §170(c) (the government's list of qualified charities) is updated annually in October and normally is reliable. The deductibility of contributions to an organization listed is assured until a revision is published. See Rev. Proc. 82-39 and Technical Advice Memorandum 9005001, which allowed the deduction for a transfer to a charity that was tax exempt but lost that exemption retroactively, because the charity was continuously listed in the cumulative list as qualified for all the tax years involved. The government ruled that a "good faith" rule applied, meaning that the status of contributions will not be affected once an organization is determined to be tax exempt, until subsequent revocation of its tax exemption is made public, unless the contributor had knowledge of the revocation, was aware that revocation was imminent, or was responsible for or aware of the activities or deficiencies that gave rise to the loss of qualification.

A careful comparison of §§2055(a) and 2522(a) reveals the nature of the differences in qualified recipient status. In most respects these provisions are very similar, but not identical. Important differences exist with respect to foreign charities under §§2106(a)(2) and 2522(b), but other than at these fringes it is likely that most vanilla recipients are qualified charities under all three relevant provisions.

Among qualified recipients there is the further distinction between public charities and private foundations,[30] which is relevant first for purposes of determining the contribution base percentage limitations that apply[31] and second to determine whether the potential hassles involved in private foundation status are necessary to accomplish the donor's objectives. The simple reality is that Congress intentionally makes it preferable for any organization to qualify as a public charity that receives its financial support from the general public rather than as a private foundation that generally is controlled and supported by a small group of donors.

Congress impresses this preference by imposing an excise tax on private foundation income,[32] along with a panoply of record keeping and reporting requirements, and an array of first and second tier excise taxes that punish self-dealing transactions with disqualified persons,[33] improper retention of income[34] or excess business holdings,[35] investing in ways that jeopardize the foundation's exempt purpose,[36] and making certain expenditures (such as for improper lobbying or political activities or certain grants and awards).[37] These varied aspects make the use of a public

---

30. See §170(b)(1)(E). §509(a) defines private foundations to include all §501(c)(3) organizations that are exempt from income tax because of their charitable operations *except* those that meet the definitions in §§509(a)(1) (§§170(b)(1)(A)(i) through 170(b)(1)(A)(vi) organizations), 509(a)(2) (publicly supported organizations), or 509(a)(3) ("supporting organizations" that serve in essentially a subsidiary or related role to a public charity). See generally Cesare, *Private Foundations and Public Charities — Definition and Classification*, 876 Tax Mgmt. (BNA) ESTATES, GIFTS, & TRUSTS PORT. (1999), and consult www.guidestar.org or www.fdncenter.org to determine whether an organization qualifies for the charitable contribution deduction and in what capacity.

31. Basically the issue is whether contributions will qualify for the higher 50% and 30% limitations that govern gifts to public charities, or the lower 30% and 20% limitations that apply to private foundations.

32. See §4940, imposing an excise tax on net investment income.

33. See §4941, which presumes that transactions between §4946(a) disqualified persons and the private foundation are self-dealing and which applies notwithstanding the fairness or reasonableness of the transaction terms.

34. See §4942, which imposes a minimum distribution amount normally equal to 5% of the value of the foundation's assets not used in carrying out the exempt purpose.

35. §4943 looks to whether a §4946(a) disqualified person and the foundation own more than minimum percentages (usually 20%, but sometimes 35%) of a business enterprise and did not make a timely disposition (usually five years is allowed) if it was acquired by gift or bequest.

36. The so-called "jeopardy investment" rule is found in §4944, which essentially imposes a prudence standard.

37. §4945.

charity more desirable even if the contribution base percentage limitations are not a concern to a particular donor.

Public charities are not totally immune to the restrictions and limitations imposed on private foundations, and a choice between public and private charities should not be made on the assumption that transactions prohibited to the latter are permitted for the former. By virtue of "intermediate sanctions"[38] that target certain "excess benefit transactions," some activities that are proscribed to private foundations also are policed in the public charity sector. Thus, insiders who engage in questionable transactions[39] with disqualified persons[40] are subject to a two level excise tax system similar to that applicable to a private foundation.[41]

Donors who seek to maintain a degree of control over the operation of the entity to which they make contributions may find that a donor advised fund strikes a desirable compromise, because it is a form of public charitable giving that does not implicate the private foundation restrictions. Often maintained under the umbrella of a community foundation, the donor advised fund permits a donor to make contributions in years in which it is desirable and wait until a later year to make recommendations (or permit another designated "agent" to do so) to the donee regarding the donor's objectives for ultimate use of the money. These recommendations cannot be binding on the donee but typically are respected if the advice is within parameters established by the fund.[42]

Another option that may be satisfactory to a donor is contributions to a supporting organization[43] that is not controlled by disqualified persons[44] but over which the donor (or perhaps an "independent" but amenable individual) has some sway. Such an entity that is operated, supervised, or

---

38. The §4958 tax on "excess benefit transactions" is so called because, before its adoption, the government had only two options regarding improper activities of public charities: ignore a violation or revoke the charity's tax exempt status. The ability to impose a §4958 excise tax provides an intermediate enforcement mechanism.

39. Defined in §4958(c)(1), an "excess benefit transaction" essentially entails a transfer for less than full and adequate consideration, including compensation, sweetheart purchase deals, payments for goods or services, and the like.

40. A "disqualified person" is anyone who, within a five year period, was in a position to exercise substantial influence over the organization or a §4946 family member of such an individual, and certain controlled entities. §4958(f)(1).

41. Essentially the excess benefit must be restored to the charity, and a penalty tax also must be paid, with a second level tax if the impropriety is not corrected in a timely manner.

42. These rules are not particularly well established and derive from the unexpected source of rules in Treas. Reg. §1.507-2(a)(8) that relate to termination of private foundation status. The notion informing those rules was that private foundations that regard restrictions imposed on their operations as sufficiently onerous would convert to public charity status but attempt to remain subject to the control of their original donors. To prevent that the regulation lists factors considered in determining whether a §507(c) termination tax should be imposed, and those factors define the parameters of a donor advised fund. The essential characteristic of the regulation is that there may be no direct or indirect material restriction on distribution of the funds; the factors listed speak to materiality and whether restrictions exist.

43. Defined in §509(a)(3).

44. Defined in §4946(a).

controlled by or in connection with a publicly supported organization may provide a sufficiently separate existence from the donor as to avoid the private foundation restrictions[45] while still providing enough opportunity for influence that the donor's objectives are met. At this level of planning it is likely that an exempt organization specialist will need to consult with the estate planner to guarantee that these intricate and technical requirements are met.

The following chart may help give some comparative clarity to all these various options:

	Gift to Existing Exempt Charity	Gift to Donor Advised Fund	Gift to Support Organization	Gift to Private Foundation
Donor Control	None	Limited	Limited	Yes
Donor "Presence"	None as Donor	None as Donor	Yes	Yes
Donor Costs	None	None	Management	Management
Required Payments	None	None	None	Yes
Tax on Investments	No	No	No	Yes
Percentage Limitation	50%/30%	50%/30%	50%/30%	30%/20%

In the same spirit that informs the use of "support" organizations, some donors would prefer to structure their giving so that it indirectly benefits certain individuals of the donor's choosing, such as by making a donation to a church or school that will find its way into scholarship assistance or missionary support for a designated object of the donor's bounty. These forms of indirect giving are difficult to structure in the manner desired by the donor, the notion being that "earmarking" the gift

---

45. The test most likely acceptable to the donor who wishes to maintain some semblance of control is found in Treas. Reg. §1.509(a)-4(i), operation "in connection with" one or more publicly supported organizations, which is found to exist if the supporting organization meets a "responsiveness test," an "integral part" test, and a "noncontrol" test, as defined in Treas. Reg. §§1.509(a)-4(i)(2), 1.509(a)-4(i)(3), and 1.509(a)-4(j). The responsiveness test basically requires that a publicly supported charity be a beneficiary of the supporting organization and that it have a significant voice in the supporting organization's management and grant making activities. Close and continuing relations such as cross-directorships, trusteeships, or officerships will suffice. The integral part test can be met if the supporting organization pays over substantially all (at least 85%) of its income to or for the use of those publicly supported charities or otherwise performs functions or funds operations that the publicly supported charity otherwise would perform. The noncontrol test essentially looks to whether §4946(a) disqualified persons are in direct or indirect control of the supporting organization. In addition, there are organizational and operational tests, and a further description of all this can be found in Treacy, *Supporting Organizations*, 871 Tax Mgmt. (BNA) ESTATES, GIFTS, & TRUSTS PORT. (1999), and Webel, *The Supporting Organization*, 15 PROB. & PROP. 55 (March/April 2001).

for particular individuals is inconsistent with donation to or for the use of the charitable organization used as the intermediary.

Thus, for example, Davis v. United States, 495 U.S. 472 (1992), refusing to follow both White v. United States, 725 F.2d 1269 (10th Cir. 1984), and Brinley v. Commissioner, 782 F.2d 1326 (5th Cir. 1986), involved a claimed charitable deduction for expenses paid during missionary service by the taxpayers' children. The court adopted a "control" test standard to determine whether a payment made to an individual was for the use of a charitable organization. That test ascertains whether the charity has sufficient discretion to determine how the donated funds will be used. The control test was not met in *Davis* because the funds were distributed directly to the missionaries rather than to the church they served. But Estate of Hubert v. Commissioner, 66 T.C.M. (CCH) 1064, 1066-1067 (1993), allowed a charitable deduction for a bequest in trust for the benefit of two charities, directing the use of income by each charity to establish or support missionary work of named individuals and then for their retirement. Essential to the court's decision was that the charity and not the individuals received the bequest and had control over its use. The court concluded that the charitable organizations had substantial control over the use of the funds and were not meant to be mere conduits to funnel money to the named missionaries. It also held that the decedent's direction that the organization use the funds for specific purposes need not defeat the charitable nature of a bequest. As a practical matter it also may have been important that the individual missionaries were not related to the decedent.

A related issue is whether charitable deductions are available if the taxpayer's transfer is not directly "to or for the use of"[46] any particular charity but instead authorizes or requires a third party (typically an individual, sometimes serving in an express fiduciary capacity) to make a selection or perform some other act. To wit, "To X, to be distributed to" whatever charities X deems worthy or "as X and I discussed prior to my death" or the like. Among the questions that must be addressed with such a poorly designed or executed gift are whether the nominal beneficiary (X in this case) is obligated (is some form of express or constructive trust created?) to pass the fund along to others, and if so whether those ultimate recipients must be organizations that qualify for the desired income, estate, or gift tax charitable deductions. State law may impose an added requirement that the class of permissible distributees be sufficiently ascertainable to avoid an invalid trust on the ground of indefiniteness.

Transfers That Qualify

Changes made in 1969 limit the forms of deductible charitable gift. Outright, no-strings-attached gifts qualify. But some donors want to retain

---

46. See §§170(c), 2055(a), and 2522(a).

an interest before parting with property, to provide for retirement, a surviving spouse, or other family needs. Before 1969 it was not uncommon for taxpayers to obtain the charitable deduction by splitting a fee simple interest in property between a private beneficiary and a charity, typically with a life interest or term of years in the private beneficiary and the remainder passing to charity. Given the valuation of temporal interests and remainders following them, there were various opportunities to maximize the private entitlement and minimize the charitable interest, such that sometimes the charitable deduction for that remainder was much greater than the interest the charity actually ultimately received. So Congress refined the law in 1969 to minimize strategic behavior.

Two general types of taxpayers make use of the charitable deduction: those motivated by the charity's objectives and those motivated by tax benefits. Congress's 1969 changes were designed to minimize the opportunities available to those who were solely motivated by the tax savings. As a result, charitable deduction planning is not likely to be fruitful unless a taxpayer has at least a minimal charitable intent. Indeed, today a charitable remainder trust cannot qualify for any deduction if the charity's interest is worth less than 10% of the fair market value of property transferred to the trust.[47]

With very few exceptions, the changes made in 1969 eliminated charitable deductions for split interests that do not guarantee the charitable component. Anything less than an undivided fee simple interest constitutes an improper split interest in property unless it complies with the highly technical §664 split interest charitable remainder or charitable lead trust rules.[48] Notably, under these dramatic changes, the charitable interest can be made deductible if a nonconforming instrument is amended to comply with the split interest trust requirements, and reformation of noncompliant documents may be available regardless of the effective date rules. See §2055(e)(3). These topics are addressed by the balance of this discussion.

Undivided Portion of Entire Interest Not in Trust

Outright transfers of all or an undivided fractional or percentage interest in each and every substantial interest or right extending over the entire term of a donor's fee simple or other ownership typically will qualify without more for the charitable deduction.[49] In a sense, an exception for future interests in tangible personalty also exists, because the

---

47. §§664(d)(1)(D) and 664(d)(2)(D), enacted in 1997 to combat capital gain income tax avoidance that used "accelerated" charitable remainder trusts with tiny charitable components.

48. An alternative to the sophisticated, technical, and more expensive (to create and operate) split interest trust approach is the charitable gift annuity, as to which the technical requirements addressed in this material do not apply.

49. §170(f)(3)(B)(ii) and the parenthetical references in §§2055(e)(2) and 2522(c)(2); Treas. Reg. §§1.170A-7(b)(1)(i), 20.2055-2(e)(2)(i), and 25.2522(c)-3(c)(2)(i); Rev. Proc. 72-45.

deduction is deferred until the personal use ends and the charity's interest becomes possessory.[50] At the time the deduction is allowed neither of these is a split interest and there is no need to apply the special rules designed to guarantee that the charity's interest is ascertainable and guaranteed against abuse.

The uncomfortable aspect of the undivided interest safe harbor is that it is not always entirely clear what constitutes a deductible undivided interest and what constitutes an improper split interest. For example, a pour over will may distribute to a revocable inter vivos trust that provides an outright distribution to charity. Although the regulations speak of an outright distribution from an *estate* to a charity, this distribution through the trust also may qualify. See Rev. Rul. 75-414. A trust distribution at death even without a pour over from the settlor's estate also ought to qualify because the trust distribution of a specified dollar amount or percentage is not properly regarded for charitable deduction purposes as an interest in the trust corpus, as to which the split interest rules should apply. It is more like a dollar claim against the trust that is not split with any other beneficiary and, therefore, is not subject to §2055(e)(2).

On the other hand, a bequest of an estate residue directly to charity will not qualify if distribution follows payment to the decedent's surviving spouse of a statutory support allowance from the residue. This is regarded as an improper split interest, deemed to pass from the decedent to both a charitable and noncharitable beneficiary to the extent of the spouse's maximum allowance payable. Rev. Rul. 83-20. Not surprisingly, a specific bequest of stock to a charity following estate administration, during which the executor is directed to pay dividends from that stock to an individual (contrary to the default rule under local law that would pay those dividends to the charitable legatee), also would create an impermissible split interest in the stock as to which no estate tax charitable deduction is available. Rev. Rul. 83-45.

A less intuitive application of the undivided fractional or percentage interest requirement is illustrated by Rev. Rul. 77-97, in which a trust required that income be paid in equal shares to the settlor's surviving spouse and a charity until the spouse died, when corpus was distributable in equal shares to the spouse's heirs and that same charity. The charity's half would have qualified for the charitable deduction if the settlor had created two equal trusts, one exclusively for the charity and the other for the spouse for life, remainder to the spouse's heirs. As it was, the charity's economic interest may have been comparable but no charitable deduction was allowed.

By way of further comparison, assume that all a donor owns is an income interest created by a third party. Assignment of all or a percentage interest in that temporal interest alone would qualify for the charitable

---

50. See §170(a)(3).

deduction under this undivided interest exception to the otherwise pervasive split interest trust rules. Treas. Reg. §§20.2055-2(e)(2)(i), 25.2522(c)-3(c)(2)(i).

Similarly, a charitable deduction is available if all the donor ever owned was the remainder interest in a split interest trust and the donor assigns all or a percentage portion of that future interest to charity.[51]

Charitable Remainder Trusts

The most common variety of split interest transfer provides for a private individual beneficiary,[52] typically for life (although it also can run for a term not exceeding 20 years). The discounted present value of a remainder following that lead interest then passes to charity and qualifies for the charitable deduction. A deduction is allowed of the value of the charitable remainder for income, estate, and gift tax purposes, respectively. §§170(f)(2)(A), 2055(e)(2), and 2522(c)(2). Valuation of the remainder interest follows traditional split interest valuation rules using the §7520 regime relating to interest and mortality assumptions.[53]

A frequent user of such a plan is a taxpayer with no natural object of his or her bounty. Rather than providing for charity by an outright testamentary bequest, this donor desires an income tax charitable deduction. So the trust is created inter vivos, with the life estate reserved to the donor personally.

---

51. Rev. Rul. 79-295, and Rev. Rul. 72-419. Such transfers are rare, however, because of the pervasive use of spendthrift limitations on transfers of trust future interests.

Even more rare (and therefore unpredictable) is Rev. Rul. 76-523, in which the taxpayer created a trust and retained a reversion, which four years later (after a change in fundamental circumstances) the taxpayer transferred to charity and was allowed a charitable deduction because the government found that the two stage division of the property into life estate and future interest and bifurcated transfers was not an effort to avoid the §170(f)(3)(A) split interest trust rules. See also Private Letter Rulings 200140027 (charitable remainder unitrust grantor severed and then assigned the lead interest in a portion of the trust to the charitable remainder beneficiary, with subsequent merger and termination of that part), and 9721014 (donors and lead interest holders of a charitable remainder unitrust were allowed to relinquish the balance of their retained interests to the charitable remainder beneficiary), in each case producing a charitable deduction notwithstanding the caveat in Treas. Reg. §1.170A-7(a)(2)(i) that precludes a charitable deduction if the partial interest in trust was created for the purpose of avoiding the split interest rules. In the earlier case the deduction was allowed especially because a 10 year separation between creation of the trusts and relinquishment was deemed to indicate a lack of such a purpose. See Private Letter Rulings 200152018 and 200127023 with respect to conversion of the lead interest into an annuity of equal or lesser value.

52. Payments actually may be made "to one *or more* persons (at least one of which is not an organization described in section 170(c) and, in the case of individuals, only to an individual who is living at the time of the creation of the trust)" (emphasis added). See §§664(d)(1)(A), 664(d)(2)(A).

53. See, e.g., Estate of Burchell v. United States, 146 F. Supp. 2d 382 (S.D. N.Y. 2001) (failed attempt to reduce the value of a private beneficiary's lead annuity interest in a charitable remainder trust, which would have increased the value of the charitable remainder for deduction purposes, because it was discovered after the taxpayer's death that the lead beneficiary was terminally ill, and died relatively quickly; the court refused evidence that would permit deviation from the mortality tables, holding that values must be used as determined applying the facts known at the date of death).

Another variant, more commonly created at death, involves a taxpayer who is concerned about the support of a dependent (such as an aged parent, a surviving spouse, or perhaps a disabled child) for life and then wants the property to pass to charity. In either case the dependent would be the life beneficiary in the split interest trust.

A third, albeit less common, illustration entails a married couple with no children, who are concerned only about the welfare and security of the surviving spouse, after whose death their property may pass to charity. If a marital deduction trust is appropriate for the surviving spouse, the trust corpus will be includible in the survivor's gross estate and the remainder passing to charity will qualify for the charitable deduction as if it was an outright bequest from the surviving spouse. As illustrated by a number of rulings, that might be a preferable approach to a joint life charitable remainder trust, because of the possibility of divorce.[54]

Congress makes a charitable deduction available for these forms of bifurcated enjoyment of trust property only if the trust complies with the technical §664 qualification rules.

Two basic variants of such qualified split interest charitable remainder trust are authorized: an annuity trust and a "unitrust." These are basically the same entity with one fundamental difference. The annuity trust provides for payment of a fixed annuity annually for the entire term of the noncharitable interest, whereas the unitrust provides for an annuity that will fluctuate as the value of the trust changes. That is, the annuity trust annual payment is a fixed percentage (it must be no less[55] than 5% and no greater than 50%) of the *initial* fair market value of the trust. §664(d)(1)(A). The unitrust annual payment is a fixed percentage (again between 5% and 50%) of the *annually determined* fair market value of the trust corpus. §664(d)(2)(A).

---

54. In Private Letter Rulings 200120016, 200045038, and 200035014 charitable remainder unitrusts were created for the lives of both spouses and then the survivor. In each case the government allowed the single trust to be divided incident to their divorce, so that each would benefit from one portion separately, then the survivor from both portions, with remainder to charity. Private Letter Ruling 200109006 similarly permitted the remainder in either portion to accelerate to the charity on the death of the respective spouse as beneficiary. There was no indication of an increased deduction for the accelerated remainder.

55. The *minimum* noncharitable payment requirement appears counterintuitive because it reduces the amount passing to the charitable remainder beneficiary. This correspondingly reduces the allowable charitable deduction, but that was not Congress' intent. Rather, the 5% minimum payout requirement makes sense because Congress wanted charitable remainder trusts to be no more favorable as tax exempt vehicles than private foundations, which are required by §4942 to make a minimum 5% annual distribution. See Estate of Atkinson v. Commissioner, 309 F.3d 1290 (11th Cir. 2002) (a charitable remainder annuity trust failed to pay the grantor $350,000 prior to death, apparently because the grantor didn't want the money; the entitlement *was* included in the grantor's gross estate for estate tax purposes), citing Treas. Reg. §1.664-1(a)(4) and explaining the rationale in holding that failure to make the required annuity trust distribution was adequate to disqualify the charitable deduction. Both entities (charitable remainder trusts and private foundations) are exempt for income tax purposes and the charitable remainder trust avoids the penalty taxes and restrictions on permissible activities and investments of private foundations.

An additional related requirement applies to both annuity trusts and unitrusts alike: a minimum charitable remainder threshold by which no deduction will be allowed if the charitable remainder is not worth at least 10% of the initial fair market value of the trust and (for unitrusts only, because additions cannot be made to an annuity trust) of each subsequent addition to the trust. §§664(d)(1)(D) and 664(d)(2)(D), added in 1997. Trusts that fail to meet the 10% minimum remainder distribution requirement may be reformed to comply by reducing the noncharitable beneficiary's interest (by altering the payout rate or the duration, or both), or the trust may be declared void ab initio. §2055(e)(3)(J).

There are a number of additional alternatives, available only in the unitrust. One limits the annual payment to just the income earned in the trust, if that amount is less than the unitrust amount in a given year. §664(d)(3)(A). The other allows for any "deficiency" in any prior year's payment under this income only limitation to be "made up" using income earned in any future year that exceeds the unitrust amount. §664(d)(3)(B). The deficiency is made up without interest or a present value adjustment to account for or compensate for the delay in payment. The first alone may be used, or both alternatives together, but neither is allowed in an annuity trust. In addition, the trust may "flip" from a net income with deficiency catch up provision unitrust to a trust without either provision, but only under certain conditions articulated in the context of an abuse prevention regime. Treas. Reg. §§1.664-3(a)(1)(i)(c) and 1.664-3(a)(1)(i)(d).

A number of more technical qualification requirements are common to both trusts, and a select few are limited to the unitrust. Basically, however, the structure of these two split interest trust alternatives is the same: an interest in a private individual that is susceptible of more accurate valuation than a straight income entitlement, followed by a remainder to charity.

A final alternative is available to spouses who might embrace the §2523(g) QTIP/charitable remainder trust as part of an inter vivos plan that generates a §170 income tax deduction (or its §2056(b)(8) testamentary cousin). This alternative permits the tax exempt charitable remainder trust to liquidate investments without capital gain taxation, and permits the settlor to direct termination of the spouse's interest on any event, not just death. Thus, for example, a unitrust or annuity trust interest for the spouse until the first to occur of death or remarriage is permissible in the split interest trust format under §§2056(b)(8) and 2523(g) because the interest passes to charity upon that premature termination, whereas it would not be permissible in a pure QTIP, even with the charitable remainder.

Counterbalancing these limited advantages is the fact that a QTIP with remainder to charity is much easier to administer and is more flexible, because it permits the trustee to make distributions of corpus to the spouse if needed.

Technical Qualification Requirements

Over the years the government has promulgated forms of qualified charitable remainder trust provisions (both the mandatory clauses and alternative options as appropriate) upon which taxpayers may rely in their own drafting.[56] Having promulgated that guidance, all with the assurance that a trust that substantially follows a sample form will be recognized as meeting all the requirements of §664 for income and wealth transfer tax charitable deduction purposes, the government then specified that it no longer will issue rulings with respect to qualification of trusts of the illustrated varieties.[57]

Note that, in addition to all the provisions found in those forms, it may be necessary to "turn off" any state laws that might be at odds with the requirements of federal law. To illustrate, the sample annuity trust forms provided in 2003 all specify that the requisite annuity "shall be paid . . . from income, and to the extent income is not sufficient, from principal." This provision probably is harmless in most cases but silly under state law in many jurisdictions that now makes prudent investing and distinctions between accounting income and principal irrelevant. Still, it would be imprudent in most cases to deviate from this provision by not overriding state law to this extent unless a very good reason existed to do so. See also Rev. Rul. 77-58. A statement of intent to qualify may be a wise general

---

56. See, e.g., Rev. Rul. 72-395 (this is the more elaborate explanation of provisions and alternatives and ought to be consulted in conjunction with the regulation provisions that it cites), which was modified by numerous revenue rulings before the government switched to issuing Revenue Procedures instead of Revenue Rulings. In chart form, the Revenue Procedure prototype forms are:

Inter Vivos	CRAT	StanCRUT	NimCRUT
One Life	2003-53	89-20	90-31 §4
Term of Years	2003-54		
Two Lives Consecutive	2003-55	90-30 §4	90-31 §5
Two Lives Concurrent & Consecutive	2003-56	90-30 §5	90-31 §6

Testamentary	CRAT	StanCRUT	NimCRUT
One Life	2003-57	90-30 §6	90-31 §7
Term of Years	2003-58		
Two Lives Consecutive	2003-59	90-30 §7	90-31 §8
Two Lives Concurrent & Consecutive	2003-60	90-30 §8	90-31 §9

Although a term not exceeding 20 years is a permissible alternative, only the 2003 version of these forms anticipates payments for a term of years.

57. Rev. Proc. 90-33. To illustrate, after rendering a ruling regarding reformation of a trust in Private Letter Ruling 9151022, the government was asked whether the balance of the unitrust provisions were acceptable, to which the government responded that "ordinarily [we] will not rule on the qualification of charitable remainder unitrusts" and advised the taxpayer that, "if you want to be certain that the reformed trust will qualify, we suggest that in the course of the reformation proceedings you ask the court to approve a revised trust instrument substantially similar to the sample" in Rev. Proc. 90-32.

override provision, with a general declaration to the effect that any state law to the contrary shall not apply or shall be interpreted consistently with that intent, but only in addition to inclusion of all the required provisions under the federal rules and regulations.

All this assistance is pretty unusual. There is no counterpart for marital deduction trust qualification, to take just one example. It confirms what planners in the know believe, that a legend should appear on the estate planning map that "here there be dragons." Fortunately there are sample forms and guidance from experts in the field, including the major charities themselves, and §2055(e)(3) reformation is available if a trust is timely found to be lacking. It also may be fair to judge the need for wide variations in planning in this arena is relatively slight. Still, the devil is in the details, and the government's forms are not necessarily the best available.[58]

Notwithstanding the government's posture that it no longer will rule on whether most charitable split interest trusts satisfy the requirements of §664 to qualify for a charitable deduction, the government remains willing to review provisions not addressed in their sample forms to determine whether they would disqualify an otherwise qualifying trust. And on occasion these rulings address a novel question that seems rather basic, although it does not appear to be answered by the government's prior pronouncements. For example, the issue in Private Letter Ruling 9419021 was who may be a grantor of a charitable remainder trust. Involved was a partnership that wanted to create a charitable remainder unitrust for a term of years, which the government held was acceptable "as long as all the partners are permissible donors."

No added definition was given to the term "permissible donor," which just goes to show that there remain limits to the government's willingness to be helpful! Or maybe it confirms that the government also is reluctant to go out on some limbs in this area of the law. And on occasion it goes too far, as some observers believe it did in Private Letter Ruling 9547004 when it opined that multiple grantors are inappropriate unless they are

---

58. Articles and commentary identify a number of issues and defects. Among them are the following: (1) the most recently revised and updated forms refer to both the 5% minimum and 50% maximum annuity payout, and the annotations refer to the 10% charitable deduction minimum, but no provision (not even in the testamentary trust forms) provides for reduction of the lead annuity as necessary to avoid running afoul of these important limitations; (2) trustee provisions are needed, including powers, appointment, resignation, and qualification; (3) the alternative contingent remainder provision could designate a charity that qualifies under §170(b)(1)(A) rather than just under §170(c) if it is desirable to restrict flexibility to preserve the higher contribution base percentage limitation (this is only an option provided rather than the primary form); (4) a larger deduction also could be generated if the form requires the annual annuity amount to be distributed less frequently than quarterly, which is not even mentioned; (5) by retaining a testamentary power to revoke the noncharitable beneficiary's interest the donor may avoid making a completed gift of the lead amount on creation of the trust; the documents anticipate changing the charitable remainder but not the noncharitable lead beneficiary (and be sure to exercise caution: an inter vivos power to alter the trust would invalidate the trust — see Treas. Reg. §§1.664-2(a)(4) and 1.664-3(a)(4); 25.2511-2(c)).

spouses, a position now incorporated in the annotations to the sample forms provided in 2003.

Many of the provisions provided by the government's sample forms are not unusual or special. Drafters easily could assimilate the gist of a paragraph and craft their own forms using language that is consistent with the drafter's preferred style in other standard documents. But several signals from the government suggest that deviation just for the sake of style or originality may not be wise. For example, Section 3 of Rev. Proc. 2003-53 states that, "[i]f the trust instrument makes reference to this revenue procedure and adopts a document substantially similar to the sample, the Service will recognize the trust as satisfying all of the applicable requirements of . . . the Code and the corresponding regulations." Section 5 further articulates that:

> The Service will recognize a trust as a qualified CRAT meeting all of the requirements of §664(d)(1) if the trust operates in a manner consistent with the terms of the trust instrument, if the trust is a valid trust under applicable law, and if the trust instrument (i) is substantially similar to the sample provided in section 4 of this revenue procedure; or (ii) properly integrates one or more alternate provisions from section 6 of this revenue procedure into a document substantially similar to the sample in section 4 . . . . A trust instrument that contains substantive provisions in addition to those provided . . . (other than . . . provisions necessary to establish a valid trust under applicable local law that are not inconsistent with the applicable federal tax requirements) or that omits any of the provisions . . . will not necessarily be disqualified, but neither will that trust be assured of qualification under the provisions of this revenue procedure.

Section 3 of Rev. Proc. 90-30, goes a bit further in advising drafters that

> [a] document will be considered to be substantially similar . . . even though, for example, the wording is varied to comport with local law and practice as necessary to create trusts, define legal relationships, pass property by bequest, provide for the appointment of alternative and successor trustees, or designate alternative charitable remaindermen.

On the other hand, a drafter may not just capitulate the drafting chore entirely by merely incorporating by reference the sum and substance of a sample document; the qualifying document must spell out these provisions and not just refer to another document that does (or, worse, merely state an intent to qualify).[59]

---

59. Section 3.02 of Rev. Rul. 72-395 specifies that

[i]ncorporation of a . . . requirement in the governing instrument . . . by a short, specific, and descriptive reference to the requirement and its citation in the regulations will . . . be acceptable [but] a general provision stating [an intent] to create a charitable remainder trust and incorporating by general reference all

As shown, there is no substitute for studying the various sample provisions and creating a carefully crafted document that considers the government's proposed samples and evaluates whether alternatives are warranted. In making that study, a handful of provisions offered for adoption by the sample forms identify positions that are worthy of comment. Most of the sample provisions and the elaboration about them herein apply to both unitrusts and annuity trusts alike; only the few that are specifically identified as uniquely applicable to one or the other do not have universal application.

Specific Issues

Creating the requisite annual payout in a split interest charitable remainder trust is not an easy task. A dollar amount could be specified in the document and, if the requisite valuation applies, that dollar amount could qualify as the fixed annuity of between 5% and 50% of the initial fair market value of an annuity trust. That could be tricky if valuation of the trust corpus might be uncertain, and it would not work in a unitrust unless the value of the trust is not likely to fluctuate more than a predictable amount.

Thus, it is more common to specify that the annuity in either form of charitable remainder trust would be a fixed percentage (or fraction) of the fair market value (either at inception in an annuity trust or yearly in a unitrust). Indeed, valuation may be an average of multiple valuation dates applied consistently during each year. Treas. Reg. §1.664-3(a)(1)(iv). That formula approach, however, raises the possibility that a misvaluation (or even miscalculation) could result and, because of that potential, the document must contain a provision calling for payment to the beneficiary of any underpayment or recovery from the beneficiary of any overpayment.

A related issue prohibits additions to annuity trusts. These trusts must determine qualification of the annual annuity amount at inception and, therefore, cannot later be augmented. Treas. Reg. §1.664-2(b). Federal transfer tax values may be used to determine the amount of the required annuity payment. Treas. Reg. §1.664-2(a)(1)(iii).

Additional contributions to a unitrust are permissible, because the unitrust entitlement is recomputed annually. However, the unitrust amount must be recomputed to reflect any new value added to the unitrust, along with the proportionate period of the year for which the added amount is considered. See Treas. Reg. §1.664-3(b), which contains a formula for making the requisite partial year calculation based on the additional contribution. And the 10% minimum charitable remainder requirement must be kept in mind as to the addition, valued under all the assumptions applicable at that time.

---

necessary requirements of the Internal Revenue Code and regulations will not [suffice].

The time for payment of an annual amount can slightly alter the value of the lead interest and therefore the value of the charitable remainder. Thus, in every situation you need to specify whether the required annual annuity will be paid all at once or in installments more frequent than annual, whether payments will be equal or otherwise, whether payments will be made at the beginning or end of a period, and how the short period at the end of a life estate should be managed. See Treas. Reg. §§1.664-2(a)(5)(i) (allowing the payment of an annuity to terminate with the payment preceding termination of the noncharitable interest) and 1.664-3(a)(1)(v)(b) (calculation of the unitrust amount in the last taxable year of a period); Rev. Rul. 79-428 (an otherwise adequate charitable remainder trust failed to qualify because the trust instrument did not provide how the amount of the final payment would be computed).

Sample documents make many of these decisions but are not the exclusive method for qualification. Because all of these decisions impact valuation, good software that calculates values will prompt the user to fill in those selections, and the document should address each issue (even if state law would provide a default answer).

Choices in this regard might make the difference between an annual amount being just under or just over a threshold requirement and should be remembered for fine tuning in relevant cases. In a unitrust the document must specify when valuation will be performed because fair market value must be determined annually. The deduction will be affected by the period of time between that valuation date and the time of each payment. Moreover, although the noncharitable annuity or unitrust payment must begin immediately at a decedent's death under a testamentary charitable remainder trust, the payment may be deferred with interest until the end of the taxable year in which complete funding of the trust occurs. Treas. Reg. §1.664-1(a)(5)(i).

Caution is required in a nontestamentary trust context. The requirement is that a charitable remainder trust must function *exclusively* as a charitable remainder trust from its inception. Treas. Reg. §1.664-1(a)(4). As a consequence, a garden variety inter vivos trust that continues after the settlor's death as a split interest trust cannot qualify for the charitable deduction as a qualified remainder trust. Instead, it must make distribution to a new trust that functions solely as a charitable remainder trust. Both trusts may be created under the same legal instrument and may have the same trustee, but administration of the one must end and the new one must begin as a separate entity. This effectively constitutes only a book entry distribution requirement, but failure to comply could prove to be a significant trap for the unwary.[60]

---

60. In large part this requirement explains the initially nonsensical result in Estate of Atkinson v. Commissioner, 309 F.3d 1290 (11th Cir. 2002), in which the government denied the charitable deduction because an annuity trust failed to make the annuity payments (meaning that more remained for the charitable remainder beneficiary) because

A second consequence of this exclusivity requirement is that an inter vivos grantor trust for income tax purposes cannot qualify. According to the regulations, it will be deemed created at the earliest time that the trust is no longer deemed owned by any person under the grantor trust rules. Treas. Reg. §1.664-1(a)(4) (second sentence). Excepted is grantor trust treatment attributable solely to the settlor or the settlor's spouse being a beneficiary. A savings clause indicating an intent to prevent such a result[61] ought to be respected and appropriately may be included in the trust document. In addition, that trust may be includible in the grantor's gross estate at death because of the same retained powers that cause grantor trust exposure. In such a case inclusion of a part or all of the trust corpus in the grantor's gross estate may result, and a charitable deduction may be allowable for part or all of that inclusion amount.[62]

A third consequence of the exclusivity requisite is that a charitable remainder trust is regarded by the government as unable to accept encumbered property from a donor who remains personally liable on the debt. This flows from the possibility that the trust will be required to satisfy the debt, in which case trust income could benefit that donor. See Private Letter Ruling 9015049, relying on Treas. Reg. §1.677(a)-1(d).

In terms of beneficiaries, the charitable remainder trust must be payable to one or more charitable organizations that qualify under §170(c), or to a trust for the benefit of such qualified charities, and no part of the remainder may be paid to any other beneficiary. Treas. Reg. §§1.664-2(a)(6)(i) and 1.664-3(a)(6)(i). The settlor, or anyone else as designated by the document, may possess the power to alter the charitable remainder beneficiaries, provided that any alternative or replacement beneficiary also is a qualified recipient.[63] Indeed, the instrument must contain an alternative remainder beneficiary provision, applicable if any named charitable

---

failure to abide by the terms of the trust meant that the trust had failed to operate exclusively as a charitable remainder trust. It also indirectly accepted contributions from the donor (as the annuitant who failed to object to the trustee's breach of the trust terms).

61. For example:

The settlor intends that this trust be treated as a charitable remainder trust under the provisions of §664 (or any successor provision) of the Code. No person shall take any action that would cause any person to be treated as the owner of any portion of this trust under Subpart E of Part 1 of Subchapter J of Chapter 1 (or any successor provisions) of the Code, except to the extent attributable to payment of distributions required hereunder.

62. See, e.g., Rev. Rul. 82-105 (the amount includible is that portion of the trust needed to produce the annual annuity or unitrust payment, and the portion deductible would be determined by the charitable interest in the trust following the grantor's death); Rev. Rul. 76-273 (the full trust corpus is includible if the assumed rate of return in the month of the decedent's death assumes that the full trust is required to produce the amount of the annual annuity or unitrust payment). The government believes that an additional source for inclusion is §2039, as articulated in Field Service Advice 200036012 and Private Letter Ruling 200210009.

63. See Rev. Rul. 76-8 (a power to identify a charitable remainder beneficiary was reserved by the grantor of an inter vivos trust); Rev. Rul. 76-7 (a power to identify a charitable remainder beneficiary was bestowed on the income beneficiary).

remainder beneficiary no longer is qualified under §170(c). See Treas. Reg. §§1.664-2(a)(6)(iv) and 1.664-3(a)(6)(iv). The alternative remainder beneficiary should be designated as one that also qualifies under §§2055 and 2522[64] if estate or gift tax charitable deductions are desired.

Caution must be paid to the fact that the charitable deduction on creation may be valued differently if a replacement charitable remainder beneficiary may be one as to which a different contribution base percentage limitation might apply.[65] The sample forms permit this to occur, but a modest revision would mandate that any successor organizations must qualify under the more restrictive rules if the greater contribution base percentage limitation is desired. Thus, for example, the sample form requires only that a successor charity be a §170(c) organization; the more restrictive limitation would require that it be a §170(b)(1)(A) organization to preserve the higher contribution base percentage limitation.

Unlike the rule that the remainder must be paid to a qualified charity, the converse is not true regarding the noncharitable lead interest. Any part (but not all) of it may be paid to a qualified charity, as long as some portion is payable to a noncharitable recipient. Treas. Reg. §§1.664-2(a)(3)(i) and 1.664-3(a)(3)(i). The noncharitable beneficiaries may be revoked by exercise of a testamentary power retained by the settlor. Treas. Reg. §§1.664-2(a)(4) and 1.664-3(a)(4). Moreover, the noncharitable beneficiaries may be defined as a class of individuals, including by exercise of the fiduciary's discretion as among them.[66] But the class must be closed and all natural persons who are members must be living and ascertainable when the trust is created if the trust interest is payable for the life or lives of those individuals. Treas. Reg. §§1.664-2(a)(3)(i) and 1.664-3(a)(3)(i).

The rationale for this class closing requirement is that the charitable remainder is a function of the value of the lead interest. If that is a life

---

64. See, e.g., Rev. Rul. 77-385 (three of four charitable remainder beneficiaries designated in the document were required to be both §§170(c) and 2055(a) qualified, the last just §170(c) qualified; the deduction allowed was limited to 75% of the value of the trust); Rev. Rul. 76-371 (a trustee power was properly limited to organizations that qualify under both the income and gift taxes); cf. Rev. Rul. 76-307, in which alternate charitable remainder beneficiaries were not limited to those that also qualified under §§2055 or 2522; the government held that the possibility that a §170(c) organization that might be selected would not also qualify under those provisions was so remote as to be negligible and therefore could be disregarded.

65. Compare Rev. Rul. 79-368 and Private Letter Rulings 9452026 and 9252023 (a retained or bestowed power to substitute charitable remainder beneficiaries, as an affirmative choice rather than in response to a contingency in the document that might cause the primary remainder to fail, will cause the lower limitation to apply), with Rev. Rul. 80-38, involving an alternative contingent remainder beneficiary in the event the primary beneficiary did not qualify; the likelihood of that happening was so remote as to be negligible, so the possibility was ignored for deduction purposes.

66. Caution, however, is required because the trustee power may not be such as would make the trust a grantor trust for income tax purposes. Treas. Reg. §§1.664-2(a)(3)(ii) and 1.664-3(a)(3)(ii); Rev. Rul. 77-73. Nor may it permit any delay in the time of payment, because timing is critical to proper valuation. Treas. Reg. §§1.664-2(a)(1)(i) and 1.664-3(a)(1)(i).

estate, the only way to determine the charitable deduction is if all the lives that measure the lead interest are ascertainable. This valuation is determined on a different basis if the lead interest is for a term (not to exceed 20 years), so the ascertainable lives in being requirement need not apply in that case. Treas. Reg. §§1.664-2(a)(3)(i) and 1.664-3(a)(3)(i). See Rev. Rul. 74-39 (a 20 year term unitrust interest that could be payable to afterborn "heirs at law" was permissible). Nor must the noncharitable beneficiaries necessarily be natural persons; entities also appear to qualify. Treas. Reg. §§1.664-2(a)(3)(i) and 1.664-3(a)(3)(i).

Pooled Income Funds

An alternative not unlike a charitable remainder trust is available to donors who do not choose to incur the cost of establishing and maintaining a separate charitable remainder trust. In a pooled income fund multiple donors commingle charitable contributions for investment purposes and retain (or give to one or more third parties) an income interest in the fund. See Treas. Reg. §1.642(c)-5(b)(2) regarding the income interest. A donor may retain a power, exercisable only by will, to revoke the income interest in a third party and in that manner prevent making a taxable gift upon contribution to the fund, but at a cost of estate tax inclusion under the retained power rules of §§2036(a)(2) and 2038(a)(1) (with a charitable deduction for the value of the remainder interest). Annual exclusion present interest treatment otherwise not available for a secondary income interest may be generated by waiting, along with a larger charitable deduction for the remainder interest. See Treas. Reg. §20.2055-2(e)(2)(v). But delayed completion of the gift, or estate tax inclusion at death, may produce a larger amount subject to wealth transfer taxation.

Only §§170(b)(1)(A)(i)—170(b)(1)(A)(vi) charities (that is, 50% contribution base percentage limitation organizations) may qualify to maintain a pooled income fund. §642(c)(5)(A). The public charity runs the fund and owns the contributed property, which means that it benefits from the remainder in the property after the retained interest expires. The charity establishes the fund, and all drafting is done on its behalf, meaning that most donors and their counsel need not know the technical rules for qualification of the fund. The government gives sample provisions[67] and therefore ordinarily will not issue advance rulings or determination letters as to whether a trust qualifies as a pooled income fund.[68] The charity is responsible for administration of the fund, and neither a donor nor a beneficiary may be a trustee or otherwise exercise direct or indirect responsibility with respect to the fund. Treas. Reg. §1.642(c)-5(b)(6). As a consequence, the charity can protect its interests and the pooled income

---

67. See Rev. Rul. 82-38, amplified in Rev. Rul. 85-57, and Rev. Rul. 90-103. Rev. Proc. 88-53 provides a sample form of declaration of trust and instruments of transfer that meet the requirements for a pooled income fund as described in §642(c)(5).

68. Rev. Proc. 88-54.

fund requirements are less restrictive and onerous than the charitable split interest trust rules. This simplified approach therefore appeals to some donors. The fund is invested essentially like a mutual fund, with the designated income beneficiary entitled to a pro rata share of whatever income is generated by the fund.[69]

Receipts are taxable as ordinary income and investment in tax exempt securities is prohibited by §642(c)(5)(C). As such there is no ordering or priority rule like that applicable to a charitable remainder trust. The private beneficiary's interest must be for life, and successive life estates are permitted but a term of years alternative is not allowable.[70] The donor may retain a testamentary (but not an inter vivos) power to revoke the income beneficiary's interest (but not the remainder to charity).[71]

Like a charitable remainder trust, the income, estate, and gift taxes all permit a deduction for the value of the remainder interest in the property transferred.[72] No capital gain is realized on the contribution of appreciated property to the trust,[73] and the contribution base percentage limitations normally applicable to any contribution of property to a public charity apply.

Remainder Interest in Personal Residence or Farm

Based again on a perception that there is little room for abuse of a charitable beneficiary, a split interest gift (not in trust[74]) of the remainder interest in any part or all of a personal residence[75] or farm[76] will qualify for

---

69. §642(c)(5)(F). In this respect the purchase of a charitable annuity is quite different because here the beneficiary has a fixed entitlement and the charity has more risk and reward.

70. See Treas. Reg. §§1.642(c)-5(b)(1), 1.642(c)-5(b)(2), 1.642(c)-5(b)(7), and Rev. Rul. 79-61 (which held that a life estate per autre vie also is not permitted). A life estate in a spouse will qualify for the marital deduction. See Treas. Reg.§§20.2056(b)-7(d)(5), 25.2523(f)-1(c)(1)(iii).

71. Treas. Reg. §1.642(c)-5(b)(2).

72. §§170(f)(2)(A), 2055(e)(2)(A), 2522(c)(2)(A); Treas. Reg. §1.642(c)-5(a)(4). The amount of the deduction is the value of the remainder following the lead income interest. The value of the lead interest is a function of the beneficiary's life expectancy and the assumed income yield, which is the highest rate of return earned by the fund for any of the three immediately preceding taxable years. §642(c)(5) (flush language). The higher the return, the higher the value of the lead interest and therefore the lower the charitable deduction. If the fund has been in existence less than three taxable years (a "young fund") the rate of return is computed as specified in Notice 89-60: "one percent less than the highest annual average of the monthly rates (prescribed by section 7520(a)(2) of the Code) for the 3 calendar years immediately preceding the year in which the fund is created (rounded to the nearest two-tenths of one percent)." See Treas. Reg. §1.642(c)-6(e)(3).

73. Treas. Reg. §1.642(c)-5(a)(3).

74. See Treas. Reg. §§20.2055-2(e)(2)(ii), 20.2055-2(e)(2)(iii), 25.2522(c)-3(c)(2)(ii), 25.252(c)-3(c)(2)(iii).

75. This need not be a *principal* personal residence, and may encompass a condominium or cooperative apartment, or a vacation home. See Treas. Reg. §§1.170A-7(b)(3), 20.2055-2(e)(2)(ii), 25.2522(c)-3(c)(2)(ii); Private Letter Ruling 8431007 (stock in a social club that included a right to occupy a residence). See §280A(d) for one definition of a residence.

76. This term includes land used by the donor or a tenant to produce agricultural products or to sustain livestock of all kinds, and improvements on that property. See Treas. Reg. §§1.170A-7(b)(4), 20.2055-2(e)(2)(iii), 25.2522(c)-3(c)(2)(iii); Rev. Rul. 78-303. See §§2032A(e)(3), 2032A(e)(4), and 2032A(e)(5) for related definitions.

an immediate charitable deduction.[77] That charitable remainder interest may follow a life estate for one or more lives (permitting the donor to retain enjoyment for life or grant it to another, such as a surviving dependent) or a term of years of any length.

The remainder interest in the charity must be irrevocably transferred. Indeed, the charitable remainder must not be subject to any condition that is not so remote as to be negligible (meaning that the chance of the condition occurring is not greater than 5%). See Treas. Reg. §1.170A-1(e). But the taxpayer may reserve a right to revoke or change the lead interest(s), which may be desirable if transfer of the lead interest(s) inter vivos would result in gift taxation that the donor wishes to defer (and estate tax inclusion at death is not problematic). Retention of the life enjoyment personally would cause §2036(a)(1) inclusion in the donor's gross estate, as would retention of a §2038(a)(1) power to alter or revoke some other individual's enjoyment, in each case with a charitable deduction in the donor's estate for the value of the charitable remainder.

Alternatively, if the lead interest is retained it ought to be possible for the donor to contribute it to the charitable remainder beneficiary and deduct its value as an additional charitable contribution. See Treas. Reg. §1.170A-7(a)(2)(i), specifying that an income tax charitable deduction is allowable if the taxpayer contributes a partial interest in property if that is all the taxpayer owns (and provided that the partial interest was not created in a transaction that was meant to avoid the split interest rules).

The deduction is limited by the contribution base percentage limitation applicable to property given in kind to a public or private charity and, for income tax (but not for wealth transfer tax) purposes, must reflect depletion or depreciation in the gifted property. Consider, for example, a building or other depreciable property (as opposed to the land on which it sits) that is part of a gift. The formula for valuing the income tax deduction must consider traditional mortality and income yield assumptions as well as a reduction either for depreciation that considers the useful life and estimated salvage value of the improvements (but not the raw land on which they sit) when that use ends, or for depletion.[78] In addition, a transfer of encumbered property raises Treas. Reg. §1.1011-2(a)(3) bargain sale to charity issues that will require bifurcation of the basis and further complicate calculation of the charitable deduction.

Conservation Easements

Another exception to the charitable split interest trust rules that applies to a gift of less than the taxpayer's entire interest in property is a "qualified

---

77. See §§170(f)(3)(B), 2055(e)(2), and 2522(c)(2).
78. See §170(f)(4) and Treas. Reg. §1.170A-12(a) regarding computation. Curiously, there appears to be no similar reduction of the deduction for wealth transfer tax purposes. See Rev. Rul. 76-473.

conservation contribution."[79] In addition to allowing estate, gift, and income tax *deductions* for the value of a conservation easement or other qualified contribution, Congress sought to reduce the estate tax value of certain property and thereby ease pressures to develop or sell open spaces to raise funds to pay the estate tax, in hopes of helping preserve environmentally significant land.

Congress did this in 1997 by enacting §2031(c), which provides an *exclusion* of value from the gross estate that operates much like an additional deduction in reducing the amount subject to estate tax. This provision applies to the extent a qualified conservation easement is donated to a §170(h)(3) qualified organization, irrevocably and perpetually restricting the ability of the owner to develop includible property for commercial purposes (other than farming). The underlying asset itself is includible in the gross estate, but the estate is entitled both to a deduction for the charitable gift and to the exclusion that reduces the value and therefore the estate tax liability. The §2031(c)(1)(A) definition of the exclusion reveals that it is in addition to any estate tax §2055(f) deduction for the same qualified contribution of the easement.

The interest that generates this exclusion is a "qualified conservation easement,"[80] which is tied to the income tax definition of a qualified conservation contribution,[81] meaning a perpetual restriction on use with a conservation purpose.[82] In essence, involved is preservation of land areas for outdoor recreation or education, protection of natural habitat, or preservation of open space for scenic enjoyment or pursuit of federal, state, or local conservation policies that will "yield a significant public benefit."[83]

An estate may qualify for the exclusion by making an election[84] that is authorized if the decedent or any family member[85] owned the property for at least three years before the decedent's death.[86] To the extent an estate qualifies, the exclusion itself is capped by a dollar limit and a percentage limit that is basically 40% of the net value of the underlying property *after* reflecting the effect of the easement on the fair market value of the property.

---

79. See §§170(f)(3)(B)(iii), 170(h), 2055(f), and 2522(d).
80. §2031(c)(8)(B).
81. §170(h)(1).
82. §170(h)(4), other than a §170(h)(4)(A)(iv) "preservation of an historically important land area or a certified historic structure."
83. Whatever that means. See §170(h)(4)(A) and Treas. Reg. §1.170A-14(d)(4)(iv)(A).
84. §2031(c)(6).
85. Defined by reference to §2032A(e)(2), which includes in the decedent's family any ancestor, spouse, lineal descendant of a parent or spouse, or spouse of any such lineal descendant.
86. §2031(c)(8)(A)(ii).

This 40% exclusion is subject to a reduction[87] such that de minimis easements generate no estate tax benefit. So, before spending any significant amount of time evaluating qualification for this exclusion, you will wisely get a ballpark estimate of the value of dedicating in perpetuity the development rights to the property. This value may be minimal, depending on the location of the realty, in which case the exclusion may be worthless or next to it. But §2031(c) may be a viable entitlement if the property is such that no one in the decedent's family would likely want to change its current use by development or sell it at a capital gain, and if the location of the property informs a meaningful value and qualification for the exclusion. Even better is the fact that the exclusion can be used again in the estates of the original donor's descendants if they retain the property subject to the easement until their deaths. Simply note that careful calculations and evaluation are required before reaching the conclusion that §2031(c) will pay dividends.

Charitable Lead Trusts

A charitable lead trust is the functional antithesis of a charitable remainder trust, in the sense that the charitable interest for which a deduction is sought is the first (the lead) entitlement in the split interest trust,[88] and the remainder passes to private individual beneficiaries (or anyone else the donor chooses). There are no applicable restrictions on the beneficiary selection. Indeed, the identity of the charitable lead beneficiary may be subject to change.[89] Each trust can be structured as an annuity or a unitrust paying the initial charitable beneficiary a percentage entitlement based on the initial or the annually fluctuating fair market value of the trust corpus. Lead and remainder annuity and unitrusts are functional equivalents in that respect.

Because certain valuation abuses are possible with respect to either the remainder interest or the interest that precedes it, many of the 1969 requirements applicable to charitable remainder trusts apply equally to these arrangements. The near functional equivalence may explain why the government has not released sample charitable lead trust forms like its qualifying charitable remainder trust forms (although a 2003 Notice requested suggestions and a project may produce such forms). Because certain concerns for the charitable interest are not present, none of the percentage collars applicable to charitable remainder trusts is imposed. The charitable deduction need not be at least 10% of the fair market value

---

87. §2031(c)(2).
88. The charity's interest need not be absolutely first, and Treas. Reg. §§1.170A-6(c)(2)(i)(E), 1.170A-6(c)(2)(ii)(D), 20.2055-2(e)(2)(vi)(f), 20.2055-2(e)(vii)(f), 25.2522(c)-3(c)(2)(vi)(f), and 25.2522(c)-3(c)(2)(vii)(f) now provide that an interest that precedes the qualified charitable annuity need not be a guaranteed annuity interest.
89. Regarding change in the lead beneficiary see Rev. Rul. 78-101 (selection by the trustee or a third party); Rev. Rul. 77-275 (selection by the grantor, which made the gift incomplete).

of the trust property at creation,[90] and the annual annuity or unitrust interest payable to the lead charitable beneficiary may be any amount.[91] It need not fall between 5% and 50% and it may run for any term of years,[92] for lives in being, or a combination of both.[93]

As a result, it is possible to fashion a lead annuity interest that approaches 100% of the present value of the property transferred to the trust,[94] effectively creating a possibility to transfer a remainder interest to private individuals at little or no tax cost if the implicit delay inherent in that plan is tolerable.[95] By way of example, such an approach (perhaps using a private foundation as the lead trust beneficiary) might be palatable with all or a portion of a wealthy couple's estates following the death of the second spouse to die, with the marital deduction in the estate of the first spouse to die deferring all wealth transfer tax until the spouse's death and then charitable deduction planning and use of the unified credit that reduces or eliminates all wealth transfer tax at the second death.

The estate and gift tax deductions for the value of the charity's lead income interest are easy and straightforward,[96] but the income tax situation presents the planner with an option. One alternative is for the trust paying the percentage annual entitlement to charity to be drafted as a grantor trust for income tax purposes, meaning that annual income is taxable to the settlor. In exchange, an income tax deduction is granted in the year the trust is created for the full value of the charity's lead interest.[97] In essence,

---

90. Compare §§664(d)(1)(D) and 664(d)(2)(D).

91. Compare §§664(d)(1)(A) and 664(d)(2)(A).

92. See Rev. Rul. 85-49 permitting a three life plus a term annuity that would exceed the 20 year maximum allowable in a charitable remainder trust.

93. See Treas. Reg. §1.170A-6(c)(2)(i)(A), which states this proposition directly, and §§20.2055-2(e)(2)(vi)(a), 20.2055-2(e)(2)(vii)(a), 25.2522(c)-3(c)(2)(vi)(a), and 25.2522(c)-3(c)(2)(vii)(a), in which it can be seen in the perpetuities saving clause provision.

94. See Treas. Reg. §§20.2055-2(f)(2)(iv) Example (1) and 25.2522(c)-3(d)(2)(iv) Example (1).

95. In some cases taxpayers have attempted to leverage the charitable deduction and artificially minimize the tax value of the remainder interest, typically relying on presumed mistakes in the valuation rules that relate to mortality assumptions, such as through the selection of a measuring life for a lead annuity that is not so demonstrably short as to make the mortality assumptions inapplicable under the 50% chance of dying within 12 months standard of Treas. Reg. §§1.7520-3(b)(3), 20.7520-3(b)(3)(i), and 25.7520-3(b)(3) but as to which the taxpayer is reasonably confident that the tables assume a longer than realistic life expectancy. The government amended Treas. Reg. §§1.170A-6(c)(2)(i)(A), 1.170A-6(c)(2)(ii)(A), 20.2055-2(e)(2)(vi)(a), 20.2055-2(e)(2)(vii)(a), 25.2522(c)-3(c)(2)(vi)(a), and 25.2522(c)-3(c)(2)(vii)(a) to constrain that abuse by restricting the selection of measuring lives who are not the donor, the donor's spouse, or a lineal ancestor or the spouse of a lineal ancestor of all the remainder beneficiaries (ignoring for this purpose any beneficiaries who have a less than 15% chance of receiving any trust corpus). Although this restriction precludes the selection of many measuring lives who are diagnosed with life shortening (but not too short) ailments, it does not preclude playing the mortality table lottery with certain family members who, by medical history or actual diagnosis, have a greater than 50% chance of living a year but a high probability of dying sooner than the tables predict.

96. See §§2055(e)(2)(B) and 2522(c)(2)(B).

97. §170(f)(2)(B).

the donor gleans an immediate one-time and usually relatively sizeable income tax deduction at creation and "pays" for it a little bit each year over time by incurring income tax on trust income, whether it is distributed to the charity or accumulated.[98]

Alternatively, the normal trust income tax rules are applicable if the trust is not drafted as a grantor trust. Thus, the trust is entitled to an income tax charitable contribution deduction under §642(c)(1) for income (but not principal) that is distributed to the charitable lead beneficiary. Otherwise the trust pays income tax on income not distributed and incurs capital gains tax on corpus sold to generate the cash to satisfy annual distribution requirements.

In the grantor trust case the income tax deduction is limited to the lower contribution base percentage limitations (for example, 30% of adjusted gross income for a cash gift, rather than 50%) because the gift is "for the benefit of" the charity rather than "to" it. In the nongrantor trust situation there is no §170 deduction to the grantor on creation and there is no limitation on the trust's §642(c) income tax deduction. In a sense, the nongrantor trust approach produces the better result, because excluding trust income from taxation to the donor is the functional equivalent of a deduction, in this case with no limitation under the contribution base percentage limitation rules. This alone may make the charitable lead trust a desirable planning tool for a donor who is so generous that the percentage limitations are proving to be a problem.

The charitable lead trust is an antithesis planning option to the more traditional charitable remainder trust in several respects. One respect reflects the needs of the donor's beneficiaries. In the remainder trust the desire is to protect private individuals for a life or lives or term of years and then benefit charity when their needs have been met. In the lead trust context the desire is to provide for charity (or produce a needed charitable deduction) but preserve the donor's wealth for the ultimate benefit of private individuals.

Another aspect reflects the changing economics of charitable split interest gift planning. If inflation is expected, the value of the remainder interest in a lead trust is likely to be worth more than the valuation presumptions and the donor's beneficiaries ultimately receive more than the tax laws assume. The charitable deduction for the lead interest is greater in a lead trust when interest rates are low (because the valuation tables assume that a greater percentage of the trust's annual production is being distributed to charity). Depending on the circumstances, a donor may wish to choose between the various alternatives to maximize available deductions and wealth for the private individual beneficiaries.

---

98. Indeed, there is a recapture of the deduction if grantor trust status terminates before the charitable lead term expires (as, for example, if the grantor dies). §170(f)(2)(B); Treas. Reg. §§1.170A-6(c)(4); 1.170A-6(c)(5) Example 3.

In terms of technical requirements, in most every respect the annuity and unitrust options available in charitable remainder and in charitable lead trusts are identical;[99] only a few differences not already noted are applicable. For example, (1) a charitable lead unitrust cannot adopt the option available in a remainder trust of paying the unitrust beneficiary the lesser of all income earned during a year (with or without a deficiency catch up provision).[100] Such a restriction would impose on the charitable lead beneficiary and permit investment shenanigans that would degrade the benefit provided relative to the deduction granted at creation. Curiously enough, (2) a charitable lead unitrust that pays to charity the larger of all the income or the annual percentage amount will not generate a larger charitable deduction,[101] so usually it is wise to just provide the annual annuity or unitrust amount with no reference to income earned. (3) The private foundation prohibitions are not quite the same in several respects.[102] (4) The government has ruled that the trust must prohibit commutation of the lead annuity or unitrust interest.[103] And (5), lead trusts pose a potential for estate tax inclusion to the donor if any prohibited control is retained over the charitable lead trust beneficiary, such as in the form of involvement as a director or officer of a private foundation or other charitable beneficiary.

A special aspect of charitable lead trust planning relates to the generation-skipping transfer tax, because it is possible to minimize the value of the remainder interest in such a plan and because the intervening charitable term interest may delay distribution for a long time. Consequently, special GST exemption allocation limitations are applied to preclude leveraging in charitable lead annuity trusts (but they do not apply to lead unitrusts, because annual unitrust payments increase as the value of the corpus does, whereas annuity trust required distributions are frozen in value at creation). Indeed, it is because appreciation is leveraged entirely

---

99. As of 2004, because there are no prescribed or model forms for lead trusts available, there is absolutely no authority anywhere to establish certain propositions. By informed appearances this may be subject to change.

100. See Rev. Rul. 77-300, and compare Treas. Reg. §§1.664-3(a)(1)(i)(b) with 20.2055-2(e)(2)(vii)(b) and 25.2522(c)-3(c)(2)(vii)(b).

101. See Rev. Rul. 88-82; Rev. Rul. 77-223, restated in Rev. Rul. 78-183. The rationale in a unitrust is because the tables assume that income in excess of the percentage amount will be accumulated and cause the trust to grow and produce a larger amount in the future, which is precluded if that excess income is distributed in the year earned.

102. §4947(b)(3)(A) excepts the need to comply with the excess business holding prohibition in §4943(c) or the jeopardy investments rule in §4944 only if the deductible value of the lead interest is less than 60% and no part of the corpus is devoted to a charitable purpose; §4947(b)(3)(B) and Treas. Reg. §1.664-1(b) except charitable remainder trusts from both provisions in all events. The apparent rationale for the difference is that a charitable lead trust that provides too large a benefit for charity looks enough like a private foundation that it must comply with all the private foundation prohibitions. In addition, these rules need not apply at all if the trust continues for noncharitable beneficiaries after the charitable lead interest terminates.

103. See Rev. Rul. 88-27, the rationale being that a commutation possibility makes duration and thus valuation indeterminable, in violation of Treas. Reg. §§1.170A-6(c)(2)(i), 20.2055-2(e)(2)(vi)(a), and 25.2522(c)-3(c)(2)(vi)(a).

to the private remainder beneficiary that many clients favor the lead annuity approach.

Reformation, Disclaimer, and Settlement

That the foregoing rules are complex goes almost without saying. It is easy to mess up, which makes salvage opportunities so valuable. Transfers that do not comply with the split interest trust rules when the transfer becomes irrevocable may be cured through efficient footwork, and other payments to charity may be allowed to qualify for the charitable deduction. There is one "specifically authorized" way to accomplish this (§2055(e)(3) reformation), and a second that is "universally accepted" but not a targeted form of relief (§2518 qualified disclaimers). Two more methods may salvage a situation that flow from a single source. One is litigation (often but not exclusively a will contest) that leads to either a settlement agreement (and usually outright payments to the charity, or elimination of nonqualified private interests that create a nonqualified split interest). The other is a judicial alteration of an otherwise nonqualified plan.

Because each of reformation and disclaimer have relatively rigid parameters and may not produce the desired result, litigation (particularly culminating in settlement agreements that rearrange property interests) has become the technique of choice. Over time the courts and eventually the government have come to accept approaches that in one manner or another protect the legitimate interests of the government while effecting compliance (or avoidance of the need to comply) with formal requirements that are a predicate to qualification for tax benefits.

The traditional view is that qualification for the charitable deduction is determined at death or the time of an inter vivos transfer, and that reformation as a matter of legislative grace is carefully constrained and the exclusive avenue to cure a defective disposition. But in reality courts and, more recently, the government itself have been more generous and accommodating of taxpayers seeking to qualify for the charitable deduction. Older cases and rulings reflecting the traditional view therefore must be discounted or ignored in light of this more agreeable policy. See Rev. Rul. 89-31, in which the government concluded to revoke or modify its prior restrictive pronouncements, stating that the government no longer will challenge the deductibility of immediate payments to charity in situations involving settlement of a bona fide will contest.

The Ruling noted that the government will examine these cases closely to assure that a settlement is not an attempt to circumvent §2055(e)(2) by instituting and settling a collusive contest. Thus, required is a finding that (1) it was a bona fide contest (2) of an enforceable right (3) that resulted in a settlement payment not in excess of what the charity would have received had the litigation not settled, (4) payable in a manner that resembled the form of payment under the challenged estate plan. Often required is a showing that the compromise agreement is (5) the product of arm's length negotiations and (6) within the range of reasonable outcomes under the governing instrument and applicable state law.

The analog for marital deduction planning holds that property passing to a surviving spouse in settlement of a will contest or similar litigation will qualify for the marital deduction to the extent the settlement is regarded as "a bona fide recognition of enforceable rights of the surviving spouse in the decedent's estate." Treas. Reg. §20.2056(c)-2(d)(2). Spurious suits designed for settlement to direct property to the spouse are not effective for marital deduction purposes, and the government scrutinizes settlements and court decrees to determine whether the litigation was bona fide.

Similarly, not every distribution to charity in lieu of a nonqualified dispositive provision will generate a charitable deduction. Consistent among cases in which the government still opposes postmortem reformation are those circumstances in which a decedent's plan did not comply with the split interest rules but the parties agreed to commute and immediately pay the charitable remainder without first instituting a bona fide will contest. The courts routinely agree with the government's disallowance of the charitable deduction in these cases and distinguish authorities that allow the deduction as involving good faith will contests or other bona fide litigation and settlement. For an estate to rectify a defective estate plan without bona fide litigation in such a situation still requires it to comply with the §2055(e)(3) reformation procedure.

Strategies: Choosing Among Alternatives

Like the choice among marital funding alternatives, charitable deduction planning presents a number of different opportunities and the choice among them typically boils down to an analysis of several sometimes conflicting variables. Depending on how those factors combine in a given situation, the best alternative for a given case is not a precise prediction. It entails some risk taking that requires some gambling on what might happen in the future. There definitely is no "right" approach for every case, although there are approaches that are better suited in certain situations.

For example, making an outright gift of a fee simple interest *does* qualify for the charitable deduction. A fact that sometimes seems to get lost on some planners and their clients is that simple planning often is the best. In a context of very simple planning, the cost of an inter vivos direct gift to charity can be determined by a formula that reflects any state and federal income tax deductions. It approaches the transaction from the perspective of a client who wants to know what the gift is going to cost, overall and after all taxes and deductions have been considered.

To make a particular sized contribution to charity, in which X is the amount of net worth reduction that the client will tolerate as a donor, the amount the client can donate to produce that reduction in net worth *after tax* is equal to X divided by 1 minus the applicable income tax rate. To compute the tax rate requires knowing the client's federal and state marginal income tax rates, and results in a formula that combines the federal and the state rate. So, as a formula, the net worth reduction the donor will tolerate is:

$$X \div 1 - \text{tax rate}$$

In which the tax rate figure is

$$\text{federal marginal rate} + ((1 - \text{federal marginal rate}) \times \text{state marginal rate})$$

To illustrate, if the federal marginal rate is 35% and the state marginal rate is 6%, and the client wants to be out of pocket $1,000 for a particular gift:

$$35\% + ((1 - 35\%) \times 6\%) = 35\% + 3.9\% = 38.9\%$$
$$\$1,000 \div 1 - 38.9\% = \$1,636.66$$

A deductible gift of $1,636.66 would generate $636.66 of tax saving, yielding a net, after the tax deduction, out-of-pocket cost of $1,000.

If the client prefers not to make an immediate outright gift to charity, then it pays to consider whether prevailing interest rate assumptions appear to be too high or too low, relative to historical yields of the property that will be used to fund the charitable transfer. Given that the income assumption employed in split interest trust valuations is 120% of the midterm applicable federal rate, and that few investments can hope to generate such a generous return, in most cases it is a fair gamble that the income assumption is too high. Similarly, if split interest planning is involved, mortality assumptions based on averages may appear too generous or too pessimistic, given a client's general health,[104] lifestyle, environment, and family history or genetics. Certain split interest planning options succeed when interest rate or mortality assumptions are too high, others when they are too low. And some aren't affected by interest rates or mortality at all.

For example, any term of years planning ignores mortality assumptions (although estate tax inclusion under §2036(a)(1) may occur if the client retains an interest and dies before the term ends). But any planning that involves an interest measured by the life of an individual puts mortality assumptions into play.

A lead annuity interest given to charity, with the remainder passing to private individuals, will produce a larger charitable deduction if interest rates are low, which is a counterintuitive result to many observers. This is

---

104. If the client has been diagnosed with an incurable malady that results in a greater than 50% chance of dying within 12 months the mortality assumptions do not apply, but an undiagnosed condition that appears likely to foreshorten life would not be considered in valuation of a life interest or the remainder following it.

because of the assumption that all the income and perhaps some of the principal will be needed to finance the lead charitable annuity. Were interest rates high the annuity would be presumed to carry out only a portion of the income earned and the tables assume that the balance of the annual yield will be accumulated and added to corpus, to be delivered eventually to the private individuals as remainder beneficiaries. In that case the remainder would be regarded as worth more of the overall value of the trust property and the charitable lead interest would be a smaller percentage portion, yielding a smaller deduction. The converse would apply if the lead interest is deemed to be overconsuming a smaller amount of interest being generated annually and therefore cannibalizing corpus and producing a much larger deduction.[105]

If a unitrust interest was employed instead of an annuity interest, however, the difference in the value of the deduction in either a high interest assumption or a low yield case would be de minimis, because interest yield does not affect the value of the underlying split interests. This is because annual entitlements always remain constant as between lead and remainder interests in a unitrust (fluctuations in value due to market forces or interest accumulations or shortfalls yield an adjustment to the next year's lead entitlement, meaning that no beneficiary makes out or loses relative to the other). Thus, higher or lower interest rates have no impact on their relative values and will not alter the allowable deduction. The same is true for a pooled income fund, but for an entirely different reason (because actual yield history rather than interest rate assumptions are the determinant in establishing the charitable deduction).[106]

The upshot of these two most important variables is that you must model the results produced from lead versus remainder interest planning, annuity versus unitrust interests, and term of years versus life estate entitlements. Then consider whether your client ultimately cares more about the tax consequences than whether the economic benefits favor the charity or the private individual. Rather than entering the planning mode with a preconceived idea about which approach to employ, the wise planner ascertains the client's overall objectives and then experiments with various assumptions and alternatives to see which is likely to produce the better result. More than a little crystal ball gazing may be involved, although experience teaches planners that certain situations are likely to produce more favorable results. Nevertheless, surprises always seem to arise, and there is little substitute for running the numbers to verify hunches and objectively evaluate the alternatives.

To illustrate, if the client wants to benefit charity only to produce a deduction that will reduce taxes and ultimately preserve property for

---

105. See Katzenstein, *Running the Numbers: An Economic Analysis of GRATs and QPRTs*, 32 U. MIAMI INST. EST. PLAN. ¶1407 et. seq. (1998) (employing the same math in the context of a grantor retained annuity trust but with the same illustrative consequences).

106. An exception applies in the case of young funds, in which case interest assumptions are used until the fund matures.

natural objects of the client's bounty, the usual presumption would be that a charitable lead interest with remainder to the private individual beneficiaries is appropriate. And in that charitable lead trust mode the likely preference is for an annuity format because the charitable bequest is frozen in value and will not benefit from any appreciation in value.

Alternatively, however, you might find that a robust lead annuity to the private beneficiaries, paid using the underlying corpus of the trust, would generate a larger charitable deduction and also retain more of the underlying trust property for the natural objects of your client's bounty, all after considering the term to be used, the applicable interest rate assumptions, the expected growth in value of the underlying property, capital gain costs on satisfaction of the lead annuity using trust corpus in kind, and the like. Moreover, in the context of such a charitable remainder trust, a unitrust probably would be preferable because it would share appreciation with the private lead beneficiary.

As this briefly shows, predictions are never as wise as actual number crunching because so often the intuitive result is not the one that actually obtains. Some of these factors work counterintuitively.[107] And the size of the deduction itself will vary such that, depending on the ultimate goal and the need or desire for a tax benefit, choosing an annuity approach that favors the remainder interest may be preferable in a remainder trust context to produce a larger deduction, or vice versa in a lead trust. These factors are not susceptible of ready evaluation applying firm guidelines.

It also pays to remember that very good results sometimes can be generated by having the noncharitable owner of a lead interest contribute it to charity if assumptions made early in the planning process prove to be very wrong. Contribution of it alone to charity may generate a wildly unexpected bonus that can salvage an otherwise less than desired original result flowing from a well planned original strategy. Which is to say that, in all these things, thinking about exit strategy also is wise and hedging bets in that regard may be a cheap form of charitable planning insurance.

A second factor that might be worthy of consideration is whether the client ultimately wants to preserve the trust corpus intact for ultimate distribution to natural objects of the client's bounty. Retention of the underlying corpus need not be inconsistent, for example, with charitable remainder trust planning, particularly if a redemption or purchase from the trust or the charity is a viable form of long range planning.

Yet another factor to consider is whether the client ultimately cares more about benefiting charity or merely employing charitable planning to

---

107. For example, many neophytes in this arena assume that a higher interest yield makes a lead interest more valuable. In fact, as noted at page 39, it may make for a smaller lead interest value, relative to the remainder, because the larger annual yield is more likely to produce accumulations that increase the value of the corpus rather than enlarge the lead interest entitlement. An income interest for life would be favored, but charitable split interest planning does not often admit to the use of naked life estate income interests. Furthermore, with a unitrust interest the income yield won't make more than a de minimis difference (and then only in the payout frequency factor).

minimize taxes. On the flip side of that issue is whether the client wishes to benefit a private beneficiary for a short period of time (such as by providing support for an older dependent who might outlive the client but not likely for very long) with ultimate enjoyment flowing to a charity of choice. Conversely again, some plans benefit charity short term (such as funding a family's private foundation) followed by long term protection of private individuals. The client may even want to benefit a private individual for the balance of that person's life, but not beginning right away. In that case only a charitable deferred gift annuity can be used if deferral is important before payments begin to a private beneficiary.

Other factors may influence choices. For example, does the client crave the control permitted in a private foundation context or wish to avoid the complexities of private foundation (and maybe even split interest trust) planning? In the latter case the client might favor the more simplistic alternative of outright gifts, pooled income funds, and charitable gift annuities that are appropriate for smaller amounts and that are easy to understand and inexpensive to implement. Indeed, the choice of approach will vary depending on whether the client requires the assurance of absolutely guaranteed payments to the noncharitable beneficiary, provided by a gift annuity or the lead annuity interest in a split interest trust, as opposed to whatever is generated by a pooled income fund or the annually fluctuating entitlement of a lead unitrust interest.

Finally, the §170 income tax deduction for inter vivos planning often seems to be overlooked by estate planners when thinking about the charitable planning alternatives that make sense to a client. One very important question is whether the client's income is high enough to take advantage of inter vivos charitable planning, as opposed to waiting until the client's death or, in some cases, the death of the client's surviving spouse. In some cases dying with the property, generating a new basis at death, making a bequest to a surviving spouse, and relying on the spouse to make an immediate charitable gift that generates an income tax deduction is better planning than making a testamentary bequest directly to charity that produces only an estate tax deduction.

This inter vivos gift approach also may be preferable to an inter vivos transfer that produces an income tax deduction for the client, if that deduction would be limited to basis. And inter vivos planning that spreads out the available charitable deduction may be preferable to making a lump sum distribution, because the latter generates an immediate deduction so large that it must be carried forward over as long as five years, with the risk of not being able to fully use it.

Indeed, one factor that ought to be reflected in modeling the results of various charitable planning alternatives is the delay in taking advantage of any income tax deduction. Some projections assume an immediate income tax saving that will be used, for example, to finance an asset replacement program, when in fact that deduction and therefore the income tax savings will be spread over as much as half a decade and will produce only the discounted present value of the ultimate income tax saving. In some cases the income tax saving will not materialize at all, or some of it may be lost, and some models fail to reflect what happens when the saving has run out (for example, after the five year carry forward of the income tax deduction ends) or is unavailable for some other reason (such as loss under the percentage limitation rule in §68). In such cases the actual benefit to the client may be far different from projections produced by an "advocate" of the plan. For these and other reasons, the marketing of certain charitable planning schemes raises concerns that should inform the client's careful and skeptical analysis.

Some assets beg to be considered in the context of charitable planning. For example, the most expensive assets for a beneficiary to inherit are qualified plans, individual retirement accounts, and other forms of deferred compensation that are includible in the estate under §2039 and carry an income tax liability as income in respect of a decedent. These often make the most attractive assets to leave to charity. Although there is a dearth of authority addressing the alternative,[108] it appears to be perfectly permissible to designate a charity outright or a qualified charitable trust as beneficiary of a qualified plan or individual retirement account, following distributions for life to the participant or the participant's spouse, or both.

Other forms of innovation using charitable planning may make sense. For example, assume that a charity really needs an immediate gift to finance a construction project but that the client needs to retain a lead annuity interest for life. Imagine that a charitable remainder annuity trust paying X% to the grantor is established, and the charity immediately borrows out all the corpus of that trust in exchange for the charity's note, payable at X% interest, structured for the same term as the lead annuity (or for a term of years likely to exceed the grantor's life expectancy in a lead life estate situation). In this way the charity could obtain the underlying corpus for its immediate needs at the cost of borrowing from the trust, which likely is lower than the charity would incur for a marketplace loan. If the charitable remainder becomes possessory before the term of the loan expires, the charity will receive its own note as the trust corpus, which will merge and extinguish the debt, meaning that the charity need not repay the debt. Because the trust and the charity are tax exempt, any discharge of indebtedness income from merger of the note upon distribution of the trust corpus is not a concern.

A viable alternative to that approach would be to purchase a charitable gift annuity with the underlying corpus that would have been used to fund the charitable remainder trust, the difference being that the purchase of the annuity might be a gain or loss realization event to the taxpayer whereas a transfer to a charitable remainder trust would not. Alternatively, however,

---

108. See Hoyt, *The Family Wins When IRD Is Used for Charitable Bequests — How To Do It*, 36 UNIV. MIAMI INST. EST. PLAN. ¶400 (2002), and Hoyt, *Transfers from Retirement Plans to Charities and Charitable Remainder Trusts: Laws, Issues and Opportunities*, 13 VIRGINIA TAX REV. 641 (1994).

the charitable gift annuity would return to the grantor amounts that in part are deferred capital gain payable in installments and in part tax free recovery of basis (indeed, the annuity payments themselves could be deferred), and only in part ordinary income (to the extent the annuity payment exceeds the capital gain and basis recovery amounts). A charitable remainder trust annuity would likely be all ordinary income because it was financed by interest payments from the charity to the trust. And the charitable annuity is the only approach that will permit deferred payment, which means that the tax liability from a transfer that generates gain also can be deferred. So, again, it pays to consider different alternative approaches to accomplishing a particular planning objective, and it is nearly impossible to state any guidelines or favored planning recommendations because every situation and the ancillary factors that are important will differ.

On the following page, in chart form, is a series of factors that may be important and a bare summary of how various charitable gift vehicles compare with respect to each.

	Outright Gift	CRUT	CRAT	Pooled Fund	Lead Trust	Remainder in Farm/Pers'l Residence	Gift Annuity
Simplicity	Yes	No	No	Yes	No	Yes	Yes
Gain or Loss?	Bargain Sale	None	None	None	None	Yes	On Purchase
§170 Deduction	FMV	Remainder	Remainder	Remainder	Lead Interest	Remainder	FMV less Annuity
May Make Additions	New Gift	Yes	No	Yes	Yes	New Asset	New Purchase
Return to Private Beneficiary	None	Fluctuates: 5% Minimum	Fixed: 5% Minimum	Fluctuates w/ Fund Earnings	Remainder	Personal Use	Annuity Based on Age at Start *
Income Tax to Lead Beneficiary	N/A	§664(b) Four Tiers Approach	§664(b) Four Tiers Approach	Ordinary Income†	N/A	As if Owner	Basis, Gain, then Ordinary Income
Income Beneficiary	N/A	Individual(s)	Individual(s)	Individual(s)	Charity	Individual(s)	Individual(s)
Remainder Beneficiary	N/A	Charity	Charity	Charity	Individual(s)	Charity	Charity
Duration	N/A	Life or under 20 years	Life or under 20 years	Life	Life or Any Term	Life or Any Term	Life or Lives
Mortality Assumption Generating Larger Deduction	N/A	Low	Low	Low	N/A for Term; o/w High	Low	Low
Income Assumption Generating Larger Deduction	N/A	N/A	High	N/A	Low (Annuity Trust Only)	Low	Low Payout Increases Deduction

* This is the only vehicle that permits deferral of payments, and the return is based on the start date, not the date of creation.

† No tax exempt investments are allowed, so earnings will be taxable.

Chapter 9

LIFE INSURANCE

Life insurance, especially term life insurance, can become prohibitively expensive late in life. In addition, many clients outlive their need for the estate augmentation or liquidity provided by life insurance. Nevertheless, life insurance is a constant in planning many estates, particularly in the middle range of estates large enough to justify your services but not so large as to be outside normal planning parameters or the need for an infusion of liquidity or capital. Along with a personal residence and retirement benefits, life insurance often is among the most significant assets in these estates. Consequently, an important aspect of the estate planning endeavor is the ownership of life insurance during life and the payment of the proceeds of life insurance postmortem (usually passing outside probate under a beneficiary designation pursuant to the insurance contract).

Notwithstanding the proliferation of life insurance (and, with it, no small degree of confusion regarding the product itself), it probably is fair to say that there really isn't much that is truly "new" in the insurance industry. Instead, most insurance policies can be understood in terms of four basic forms of coverage. It is relatively easy to dissect any product once these four "building blocks" are understood, because insurance marketing and design essentially is a function of finding new ways to combine, package, and pay for these four basic forms of coverage. To help analyze the product with that in mind, frequently it will be very enlightening to review the agent's product explanation guide, provided by the issuer, rather than the guide prepared for the purchaser. In addition, an advisor who is asked to evaluate a product might find it useful to ask for the plain English statement of the product, the contract provisions, and all their features.

Understanding the Product

In a sense, "life" insurance is a misnomer with respect to all but one of the four basic forms of coverage: annuities. All the others insure against death, not life. Which is to say that most "life" insurance guarantees the existence of an amount of money when the insured dies. The endowment, term, and permanent (sometimes referred to as "ordinary" or mistakenly as "whole life") forms of coverage fit this description of "death" insurance. The industry adheres to its description of these standard forms of coverage as "life" insurance for obvious marketing reasons. Nevertheless, only the annuity form of coverage truly is "life" insurance, because it alone insures against living too long (as opposed to insuring against dying too soon).

Annuities

Annuities are contracts that provide for a systematic liquidation of funds. For a specified sum, the basic annuity entitles the beneficiary (the annuitant) to receive a defined amount at specified intervals for a designated period of time. If that period is the annuitant's life, the issuer has agreed that it will pay the contractually specified periodic amount (monthly, quarterly, yearly, or whatever) until the annuitant dies. Thus, the purchase of an annuity protects against the risk that the annuitant might outlive his or her available resources. The purchase price is effectively converted into, and then liquidated by, the periodic payments. In their classic form, annuities simply insure against outliving the annuitant's wealth.

Variations on the "basic" annuity are desirable for several reasons. Under a basic policy, there is a risk that the annuitant whose life defines the payment period will die prematurely, before payments have been made that fully return the purchase price. Moreover, because of the eroding impact of inflation, contractual payments may wane in purchasing power to the point of leaving annuitants unable to meet their needs, thus defeating the primary underlying rationale for the purchase. Finally, the basic policy does not provide protection for several annuitants (for example, a married couple who wish to assure that each will be protected from outliving their collective resources). The basic annuity is a "straight life, fixed dollar, sole annuitant" policy. It pays a constant dollar amount for the life of one annuitant, and is the cheapest form of annuity generally available (per dollar of benefit paid) but it is comparatively inexpensive only because it carries the greatest risk.

Variations of the basic annuity are designed to reduce the annuitant's risks, in one way or another. For example, a common variation of the basic policy is a "guaranteed minimum" annuity, binding the issuer to pay a specified aggregate amount under the policy. This may be accomplished by contracting for payment of a fixed amount for a fixed period (an annuity certain). It also may be accomplished by requiring the issuer to remit a refund if the annuitant predeceases payment of a guaranteed minimum. Contingent beneficiaries must be designated under the annuity certain in case the primary annuitant predeceases expiration of the defined period. Similarly, a beneficiary must be specified (either the annuitant's estate or otherwise) in a refund policy, and payment of the refund may be agreed upon as a lump sum, in installments, or as another annuity.

Further variations are available, as for example by specifying that any refund will be used to purchase a life insurance policy. In each of these cases some risk of premature death is shifted to the issuer, so the cost of the annuity is higher (or the benefit per premium dollar paid is lower) than under a basic straight life annuity.

To combat the fear of inflation eroding the purchasing power of a fixed annuity, another alternative is a "variable" payout that provides for periodic payments tied to a fluctuating standard. For example, payment may be linked to a cost of living or inflation index, or to the performance of a particular investment portfolio maintained by the issuer, meaning that the periodic payments will vary over time. Often these variations work only in the annuitant's favor, because the policy also contains a minimum payment obligation. Again, the payment option selected affects risk, and thus the cost of the product.

Two common variants to provide multiple annuitant protection are "sole and survivor" and "joint and survivor" policies. Under a sole and survivor contract the same annuity is paid to two annuitants seriatim. Under the joint and survivor contract payments are made during the joint lives of two annuitants and thereafter in a reduced amount (often half or, less frequently, three-fourths of the original amount) during the overlife of the survivor. Once again, the option selected will affect cost, and other variations are available in combination. A joint and survivor policy will cost more than a straight life sole annuitant product but might cost less than a straight life annuity certain or refund policy.

Further variations offer the opportunity to defer payment of the annuity. For example, the purchase may be funded with annual premium payments remitted during employment years but the payout may be deferred until retirement, or the purchase may be based on a single premium, such as the proceeds of insurance on another person's life. Often payout is deferred until the annuitant reaches a certain age. In each case, the issuer of a deferred policy can afford to offer a higher payout for the same premium dollar because the issuer will invest the premium dollars before the periodic payments begin. Moreover, the income tax consequences under §72 of the purchase and payment of the annuity are especially important to the annuitant, because interest accrues tax free during the deferral period. See generally page 39. Finally, unlike the "old days" when annuities seldom were attractive investments, the industry now offers many competitive annuity products, which many purchasers regard as a respectable part of their overall investment portfolio.

Endowments

Endowments essentially are saving accounts with an insurance rider that guarantees the existence of a fixed sum at the end of a specified period of time. Thus, the purchaser may wish to accumulate a specific amount for a designated purpose before a definite time in the future, such as before retirement or to finance a child or grandchild's college education. Endowments essentially are forced saving accounts that grow as premiums are paid, coupled with insurance protection that pays any difference between the amount saved and the face value of the endowment.

An endowment guarantees that the money will exist because it insures against dying before the fund has been accumulated. Alternatively, endowments may be viewed as term insurance that provides coverage during the saving accumulation period, with a refund feature if the insured does not die. Either the term insurance pays off because the purchaser dies early or the refund is made at the specified time, but not both.

However they are characterized, endowments generally are regarded as an expensive form of coverage and only a very small percentage of all insurance written is of the endowment type. Because the issuer enjoys use of the premiums paid during the term of the policy, charities (often universities, frequently to finance their sports programs) market endowments as a form of tax deductible charitable giving by which purchasers justify the endowment's high cost by the charitable aspect of the issuer's use of the money. To many purchasers a more attractive alternative to a commercial endowment is the §529 qualified tuition program now offered by most states.

Term Insurance

Term products are pure insurance against death. They provide protection for a definite period (the term) for a designated price (the premium) based on an actuarially determined prediction of mortality. Unlike other forms of insurance, pure term insurance accumulates no cash or other values during the term. Thus, it is the "economy model" of insurance coverage. Per premium dollar, for a "good risk" individual (young, healthy, low risk occupation, and low risk avocations), it provides the greatest protection at the lowest possible price.

Term insurance is a pure gamble, however. And there is nothing to show for the premium dollars paid if the insured outlives the term. As the risk of mortality (due to age, health, occupation, or avocations) increases, so does the cost (and, unfortunately, the chances of "winning" the bet). Thus, it is uncommon to find term insurance that is available and viable for an individual over age 70.

At one time it was quite common to hear the advice to purchase term insurance and invest the difference in cost between pure term and more expensive forms of coverage. That advice is not nearly as compelling today, for several reasons. First, many purchasers simply don't have the diligence to invest the difference. Second, even if they do, they are more likely to liquidate the investment and spend the accumulation than they might be if it was tied up in permanent insurance. Indeed, purchasers can have the best of both worlds if they purchase permanent insurance and borrow against the cash surrender value of the insurance, giving them the use of the lion's share of the cost difference.

Third, coupled with the inability of many individuals to wisely or effectively invest small amounts of money, the §101 income-tax-free return aspect of permanent insurance makes this a very favorable investment.[1] This is made all the more desirable because many insurance companies earn a highly respectable return on premium dollars invested. Moreover, if carryover basis ever becomes the law, the cash proceeds paid by an insurance contract represent a more favorable return than a similarly appreciated investment portfolio with built in capital gain tax liability.

Finally, term insurance gets prohibitively expensive as the insured gets older (although periodic physicals to prove continued good health can moderate this increase). Permanent insurance issued when the need for coverage was first recognized and maintained over time typically does not change in cost. Nevertheless, term coverage accounts for the vast majority of all insurance written annually (although only a tiny percentage of all purchased term policies still are in effect at the insured's death). Indeed, term coverage often is the more sensible selection if the need for coverage will be of relatively limited duration. A good rule of thumb is that, if coverage will be needed for longer than ten years, then permanent insurance probably will be cheaper. Many insurance needs (such as to provide liquidity in a closely held business setting) will resolve themselves under a purchase agreement or other planning, if given enough time.

Term coverage is available in various forms that provide flexibility. The basic format is "straight term." It automatically terminates when the period of coverage (usually one year) expires. "Renewable term" is available for an added cost, guaranteeing the insured the right to renew the policy at expiration of the term without new proof of insurability. The premium cost at the time of renewal, however, usually is at least as high as for a newly issued policy at the insured's attained age, and sometimes is higher.[2]

---

1. See Christensen, *Life Insurance: The Under-appreciated Tax Shelter*, 135 TRUSTS & ESTATES 57 (Nov. 1996), suggesting that all "insurance" is term insurance to the extent of the risk element (proceeds returned in excess of premiums paid) and that permanent or cash value insurance merely constitutes payment of added amounts that represent an investment and its return. The difference is that earnings on that investment are free from income tax and therefore may be used to pay future premiums with before-tax dollars. In addition, under the basis first income tax rules of §72(e), withdrawals from the policy normally are not income until basis has been fully recovered, meaning that these earnings are available to a certain extent without losing the income-tax-free treatment of policy accumulations. Indeed, unlike qualified employee benefits, these internal earnings are not income in respect of a decedent and will never be taxed if payable at death. These desirable attributes can be lost if a policy is skewed too much toward an investment type of vehicle, as illustrated by comparing the taxpayer favorable Rev. Rul. 2003-91 with the taxpayer disfavorable result in Rev. Rul. 2003-92.

2. The explanation for this is self selection. The insurance company assumes that the insured is unable to qualify for new issue insurance if the insured does not seize the opportunity to qualify for term insurance at a lower rate than the rate guaranteed under an existing policy, or drop the coverage entirely. There may be some insureds in good health who value the convenience of continuing their existing policy rather than going through the hassle of qualifying for new coverage at a lower price, and they pay a higher premium for the convenience. Otherwise, only those in poor health will continue their existing policies, regardless of cost. See generally K. Black & H. Skipper, LIFE INSURANCE (12th ed. 1994). Consequently, the automatic renewal rates are higher for this class of insured, to protect the insurer from adverse selection by a class of insureds whose mortality experience exceeds the normal or expected rates of death.

"Convertible term" also may be purchased for an extra price, giving the insured the right to convert the policy into a permanent product, again without proof of insurability. This option is useful for a person who cannot presently afford the higher cost of permanent insurance but who wants to guarantee his or her insurance coverage without the risk of becoming uninsurable.[3] Together, the renewable and convertible options add great flexibility to term insurance for insureds with a small current budget but predictable future needs and an increasing ability to pay.

"Re-entry term" is the opposite of renewable term in that it grants the insured the right at future times to "prove insurability" at reduced rates, if health, occupation, hobbies, or other factors have changed for the better in terms of risk.

To address the constantly rising cost of straight term, a variation available for a steady premium is "decreasing term." Rather than increase the cost of coverage at each renewal, the insurer reflects its greater risk per premium dollar with reduced coverage. Decreasing term is most popular, however, not for its cost feature but, instead, to fill a very specific need. The most common form of decreasing term coverage is mortgage or "credit life" insurance, with the decrease in coverage being linked to a decline in the outstanding balance on an individual's home, business, automobile, or other loan. There also is a converse form of coverage ("increasing term") utilized in conjunction with "split dollar" insurance, as discussed at page 13.

Most insurance provided as an employment benefit is "group term" insurance. The premium cost (usually borne by the employer) is determined by special group rates that look to the mortality of the group rather than each individual insured within the group. The income tax treatment to an employee under employer funded group term is specified in §79, and the table used for determining the cost of coverage is contained in Treas. Reg. §1.79-3(d)(2).

Permanent Insurance

Permanent (also known as "ordinary" or, inaccurately, as "whole life") insurance coverage differs from term insurance in several respects. For example, permanent insurance usually provides a level protection at a constant (not increasing) annual premium cost, it does not terminate at the end of any specified period, and it develops nonforfeitable loan and cash surrender values. Premium cost commonly is pegged when the policy is purchased, based on the number of years the premium will be payable. Thus, the younger the insured is at the time of purchase, the lower the

---

3. Technically, virtually no one is "uninsurable." Instead, an insurer may assess the risk of death as being so great that premiums are charged as if the insured were much older (known as being "rated"). This high cost makes some potential insureds feel that insurance effectively is unavailable. It is only after a potential insured reaches a certain (very advanced) age that most insurers simply no longer will underwrite a policy.

premium usually will be, reflecting the fact that premiums will be paid for a longer period.

The method or duration of premium payment is the primary distinguishing factor among permanent life insurance products. In a straight life (also accurately known as "whole life" or "continuous pay") policy, the owner will pay a premium for every year the insured is alive (usually "only" up to age 100). This usually is the lowest annual cost permanent policy available because the owner pays for the balance of the insured's entire or whole life.

In a "limited pay" policy the premiums are level from year to year but higher each year than whole life coverage because the premiums terminate at a specified time when the policy becomes paid up (meaning that the actuarial "reserve" needed by the insurer to cover its obligation under the policy is fully funded). Common forms of limited pay policies are "20 year" and "65-life." Under the former, premiums are paid for 20 years. This form of coverage might be purchased, for example, by grandparents who wish to present a paid up policy to a grandchild before age 21. Premiums end at age 65 (or death prior thereto) under a 65-pay-life policy, historically so as not to extend into retirement when the owner's income and cash flow taper off. Limited pay policies develop cash value more quickly than continuous pay policies (because each premium is higher), but often they are uneconomical for a cash poor family and represent only a small portion of all permanent insurance written.

Many "survivor life" or "second to die" policies (typically insuring the life of the last to die of a married couple) contain a "vanishing" premium on the death of the first insured to die. In effect, the policy pays a small amount at the first insured's death. That payment is used to pay up the policy. A vanishing premium provision may affect the value of the policy if it is owned by and therefore is includible in the taxable estate of the first insured to die.

"Single premium life" was an industry darling that attracted significant legislative concern[4] because, in some respects, it looked more like an investment vehicle than like life insurance. As the policy name suggests, one payment constitutes the sole premium. The cost, which frequently is quite low, depends on the age of the insured and, for moderately young individuals, the one time payment, internal tax free build up, and low gift tax value make this a beguiling product. This especially is true if, for gifting purposes, the value of the policy does not exceed the gift tax annual exclusion and avoiding future premium payments is desirable for tax purposes.

One "gimmick" with single premium life is for the owner to pay the single premium, then immediately borrow against the policy's cash

---

4. Congress significantly reduced the tax benefits of single premium life insurance with enactment of §7702A in 1986. See page 25.

surrender value at an interest rate equal to the dividend rate[5] expected to be paid by the insurer on the policy. In essence, interest is charged on the loan but offset with policy dividends. Meanwhile, the owner builds value that is free from income tax, in the form of the insurance coverage on a minimum actual investment. More traditional single premium life insurance is regarded as attractive simply because of the income-tax-free build up in its value and the income-tax-free proceeds payable in cash at death.

A hybrid form of coverage that resembles survivor life insurance and single premium life is insurance with a "survivor's insurability rider." Rather than acquire one policy on the life of the survivor of two people, this insurance is on the life of either of the two insureds. It provides that, on the death of the first individual to die, the survivor as beneficiary of that policy may elect to apply a portion or all of the proceeds to the purchase of a single premium paid up policy on the survivor's life, without proof of insurability. This approach has two advantages: the survivor may elect to take the proceeds rather than roll them over into the new policy; and the policy is easier to deal with in the event of divorce if the individuals are married.

Instead of paying level premiums, in a "modified" or "graded" premium policy the owner pays the same aggregate premium but begins with lower initial payments and steadily increases the amount as the owner's earning potential increases. The idea is to make insurance more affordable for young owners. Similarly, in a "deferred life" policy, a small premium is paid initially to bind insurance coverage for an individual who is worried about future insurability but who cannot currently afford permanent insurance. Coverage is not in effect during the deferral period, no annual premiums are paid and, if the insured dies, no proceeds are paid. In such a case, however, most or all of the initial premium may be refundable. Normal premium payments begin if the insured survives the deferral period (as expected), with the initial payment being applied against the first premium. The insurer, meanwhile, has use of the initial payment with no risk to it, and premiums are pegged at the insured's attained age when annual premiums, and coverage, finally begin.

Usually found in a business context, a special form of permanent insurance that no longer appears to exist was "next death" coverage. It may be useful to describe it because it illustrates a problem with traditional coverage in some business contexts. Designed to fund the various obligations under a buy-sell agreement, a next death policy was intended to replace the need for each party to a buy-sell agreement to own separate policies of insurance on the life of each other party to the agreement.[6]

---

5. See page 18 regarding dividends.

6. Resulting in a multiplicity of policies, the requisite number being the product of [the number of owners] times [that number less one] — so three individuals would need six individual policies among them. Do the math: A would own policies on B and C. B would own policies on A and C. And C would own policies on A and B.

Instead, the single next death policy covered the life of the next member of the group to die, whomever that might be.

Based on multiple or joint life mortality tables, the premium cost was said to approximate half the cost of having separate policies on each party's life (with cost of the next death coverage approaching group rates as the number of members increased). Face value paid upon the death of any insured was used by each owner to finance the obligations imposed under the buy-sell agreement. A new policy on the surviving members automatically was issued, and a portion of the proceeds from the terminating policy was applied to premiums due on the newly issued policy. When only one member remained, the next policy issued was written as a normal permanent life policy on that individual's life.

The next death policy had two advantages. One was avoiding the need to own separate policies on the lives of every party to the buy-sell agreement. This is desirable because, if each party to the agreement owns permanent policies on the lives of every other party to the agreement, the person who dies first will own policies on the survivors that must be liquidated or transferred. Usually the only market for disposition of those policies is the other parties to the buy-sell agreement, but a transfer to them, other than by outright gift, may involve the §101(a)(2) transfer-for-value rule.[7] The next death policy neatly avoided this problem. The policy's other advantage was providing coverage at a lower aggregate premium than if each party to the buy-sell agreement owned a separate policy on the life of every other party to the agreement.

A second form of next death coverage also not common but becoming more important is first-to-die insurance for a married couple. This coverage is desirable compared to separate policies on each spouse's life because the insurer's administrative costs are lower and aggregate premiums therefore are lower on a single policy than on two separate policies. First-to-die coverage in this context may be advisable because many double income couples will find that the survivor cannot maintain their family's lifestyle on one income after the death of the first to die. Indeed, even in many *one* earner couples, loss of either spouse will have calamitous economic consequences that equally require an infusion of cash that a first-to-die policy can provide.

Have you begun to notice that life insurance is a complicated topic merely because there are so many options? With a single married couple representation the issue of insurance coverage would raise a number of

---

7. See page 41. A transfer to the insured would be excepted from the transfer-for-value rule, but the real need for the coverage would be by the other parties of the agreement, who need insurance to finance their purchase when the insured dies. An alternative is to form a partnership of the parties to the buy-sell agreement and allow transfers among the partners under the §101(a)(2)(B) exception. This entails an added layer of complexity and conceivably might be disregarded by the government if the partnership serves no other function. To date, however, the government has been quite liberal in permitting such partnerships to accomplish this purpose. See the discussion of this issue at page 42.

factors to weigh: when will proceeds be needed (and for what purposes), which life is cheaper to insure, who will own the policy, and how will premiums be paid (especially on a policy that survives the death of the first spouse to die).

Combination and Specialty Products

All of this gets geometrically more complex because most modern policies combine both term and permanent features, making the policy affordable and competitive while developing investment returns that are attractive to investors. For example, "Universal Life" insurance basically is term coverage that is designed to address concerns about the performance of insurance as an investment vehicle. Under the traditional form, premiums vary with the investment performance of the insurer. The premium quote usually is based on a maximum premium, a minimum premium, and a target premium. Other versions charge a level premium that is paid into a "side fund" and invested and then used to pay premiums. Increased investment performance by the insurer provides money (through the side fund) that is used to acquire added coverage, either term or permanent. The concern with universal life insurance is that it may not meet the §7702A definition of insurance, making it an investment vehicle with no income-tax-free internal build up in value.[8]

"Variable Life" insurance is another innovation that has a fixed minimum face value and fixed premium, but may pay more if formulas keyed to a consumer price index or to investment portfolio performance dictate a higher payout. Designed to directly confront criticism of permanent insurance that it is inflation poor (that today's $X policy won't have the purchasing power of $X in the future), this coverage is regulated by the Securities and Exchange Commission because of its investment attributes.

Other less common combination or "specialty" products exist, some well known, but none very common. Upon investigation, each consists of elements of the four basic forms of coverage, and each illustrates that virtually any unusual product can be broken down into its component parts, each of which *is* common. For example, "Family Income" policies pay a guaranteed income (such as 1% of face value) to the insured's surviving family until a specified date (such as when no living child is under 18 years of age), then pay the face value of the policy. This coverage essentially is an underlying policy (usually, but not necessarily, permanent coverage) in the face amount, with a decreasing term rider that funds the income payment (which essentially is an annuity payout of the proceeds of the term rider). See Treas. Reg. §1.101-4(h) for special rules to determine the income tax consequences of a family income policy. "Family Maintenance" is coverage like the family income product except income is payable for a specified number of months after the insured's death. This

---

8. See page 25 regarding the §7702A definition.

uses level term instead of decreasing term insurance because the insurer's income payment obligation never changes (the term income obligation does not decrease as the insured's family grows older). Consequently, the plan is likely to be more expensive than a family income policy.

A "Family Policy" typically is a combination of permanent coverage on a husband-father and convertible term coverage on a wife-mother and on each child. "Juvenile" policies are parent owned convertible term insurance with ownership shifting to the insured child at age 21. A single premium permanent life product bought at the child's young age might be a better investment.

"Key Man" insurance usually is corporate owned term insurance on a business owner or other key employee (male or female, notwithstanding the title). "Mortgage" or "Credit Life" insurance is a decreasing term policy tied to the outstanding balance of a loan. Usually a separately purchased decreasing term policy is a far more competitive product than those offered by creditors who market these policies as a package deal with consumer loans.

Finally, "Multiple Protection" is a combination of permanent insurance with term coverage payable if death occurs before a certain date. This sometimes is known as "Composite" life and may use level or decreasing term coverage. Usually these package plans are available at a lower cost than if separate policies were written. In all cases, the trick to analyzing the policy and its costs is to explode it into its component parts and then to analyze what a comparable coverage might entail as constructed in a different manner.

Premium Payment and Split Dollar Insurance

Payment of policy premiums often is the problem that hinders or precludes acquisition of needed coverage. It also has been the source of government efforts to require estate tax inclusion of insurance proceeds payable to a third party under policies as to which the decedent as insured possessed none of the incidents of ownership that normally define the reach of §2042(2) inclusion. In addition, several traditional methods of providing for the payment of premiums have been drastically disadvantaged by tax law changes.

For example, §163(h) precludes a deduction for personal interest incurred on policy loans that are taken to pay premiums.[9] In addition, even to the extent an interest expense deduction *is* available, the restrictions on that deduction imposed by §264(a)(3) must be confronted if policy loans are relied upon to pay policy premiums in more than three of the first

---

9. It probably is not possible to successfully allege that interest incurred on a policy loan is "investment" interest because insurance loses its special character as insurance if it is regarded as an investment vehicle. See §7702A, as discussed beginning at page 25. Treas. Reg. §1.264-4(c)(1)(i) presumes that policy loans against cash value are used to pay premiums. See, e.g., Rev. Rul. 95-53.

seven years the policy exists. See §264(c)(1). Finally, §264(a)(4) disallows a corporation's deduction of interest that it incurs on policy loans, except to the extent allowed by §264(e) with respect to loans that do not exceed $50,000 on policies that insure the life of a key person.

The most interesting topic involving premium payment is split dollar insurance, which is not a special form of coverage. Instead it is a special form of splitting the premium cost and sharing the proceeds[10] of any life policy that develops a cash value (such as permanent life, universal life, variable life, variable universal life, and survivor life policies of any of these varieties). Although the most common use of split dollar insurance is in the employment context (with the employer sharing in the premium payments), there are private split dollar plans between two individuals and a business/shareholder variety.

The premium for insurance on an individual's life is paid in two parts under a "basic," "standard," or "classic" split dollar insurance plan. A "financing party" pays the lesser of the annual increase in the cash surrender value of the policy or the total premium. With coverage like universal life the premium cost varies and the parties may need to specify that the financing party will pay the target premium to provide more certainty. The insured pays any balance of the premium. On death, the financing party is entitled to receive an amount equal to the greater of the premiums it has paid or the cash surrender value of the policy (determined immediately before the insured's death).[11] The balance of the proceeds are payable to the designated beneficiary, often a third party owner of the policy, such as an irrevocable life insurance trust.

In the typical classic split dollar plan, the insured's share of the premium is high in the initial years because cash surrender value and, thus, the financing party's payment is low. In later years the insured's share of the cost drops and may disappear entirely. To even out the insured's annual cost, a "level," "uniform," or "constant" payment variation of the classic plan exists under which the insured's total payments for the policy are computed and then averaged over the life of the policy. The effect on the financing party is the same as under the unmodified classic plan except the financing party pays more of its aggregate premiums early and thus loses more use of its money.

---

10. Most split dollar plans provide for a "rollout" at some point before the policy matures, often after the policy becomes self sustaining. The financing party receives its share of the policy value, perhaps by borrowing against the policy, and the owner retains the balance of the policy — the risk portion and any built up equity. Without care this transaction may constitute a transfer for value, with income tax consequences under §101(a)(2), as discussed beginning at page 41.

11. Because the financing party is a beneficiary of the policy by virtue of this split, §264 disallows a deduction for premiums paid by the financing party but proceeds received are not taxable as income. See Rev. Rul. 64-328. The loss of a deduction is no problem if the financing party is a private individual entitled to no deduction in any event.

Another modification of the classic plan reflects the fact that, over time, as cash surrender value increases in the policy, the financing party's share of the proceeds correspondingly increases and the insured's share concomitantly decreases. To maintain a constant dollar benefit to the insured, an increasing term insurance policy may be purchased using dividends on the policy (the "fifth dividend option" being used to pay premiums for added insurance),[12] with the amount of term coverage being equal to the financing party's share of the proceeds. Thus, with the term insurance, an amount equal to the face value always is payable to the insured's designated beneficiary.

Because cash surrender value is low and grows relatively slowly in the early years of most permanent policies, the financing party normally contributes little to the payment of the premium in those years and the insured must produce a large portion of the premium. Moreover, annual acquisition of any additional increasing term insurance must be structured carefully so that it is not includible in the insured's gross estate under a theory that each year a new policy was acquired and transferred by the insured.

Beyond such premium allocation issues, there are several ways to accomplish the "split" of the proceeds, depending on who owns the policy.[13] The financing party owns the policy under an "endorsement plan" and endorses the insured's share of the proceeds to the insured's designated beneficiary or assignee. This sometimes is regarded as a "golden handcuffs" approach that ties the insured to the financing party (as in an employment context) because the financing party controls the policy.

The insured (or the insured's assignee) owns the policy in a "collateral assignment" plan and the financing party's payments come out of the proceeds in the nature of a loan repayment. Because of the nature of the private split dollar arrangement, this has been the mechanism of choice because the financing party likely will be someone in whom ownership of the policy is to be avoided. For example, if the financing party is a controlled corporation, ownership by the corporation may attribute incidents and generate inclusion to the insured under Treas. Reg. §20.2042-1(c)(6), as discussed at page 46.[14]

---

12. See page 19 with respect to all of the dividend options.
13. In addition, with a policy such as variable life, it might be wise to specify who has certain policy rights, such as to designate the investment alternatives. See Gislason, *Split-Dollar Life Insurance: Updated Planning Techniques*, 20 EST. PLAN. 201 (1993).
14. Two other more modern ownership mechanisms have been developed, one being a "split ownership" approach in which the financing party is a co-owner of the policy rather than either party owning the policy alone and having obligations to the other. The other, which is far easier to manage, is an unsecured mechanism in which there is no formal designation with the insurer of any interest in the financing party, but instead just an unsecured side agreement by which the financing party is contractually entitled to a share of the proceeds. This approach sometimes is referred to as "sole ownership" (because only one party has any ownership interest in the policy), "undocumented" (because the insurer has no documented ownership, assignment, or beneficiary designation that identifies the

As will become clear shortly, under Treas. Reg. §§1.61-22(d) and 1.7872-15, collateral assignment agreements (in which the benefited party owns the policy) receive loan treatment. Endorsement agreements (in which the financing party owns the policy) generate compensation income results. The parties may structure their agreements based on the income tax treatment they desire. In a loan context, they also may choose whether to make it a fixed interest term loan or a demand loan for which interest is calculated annually.

Regardless of the approach chosen, by recouping the premiums it paid, through receipt of its portion of the proceeds at the insured's death, the financing party suffers no cost under the plan other than loss of the use of its money between the years of each premium payment and the time of the insured's death. Even this cost is minimized if cash value exceeds premiums paid, so that the financing party's return exceeds its outlay and effectively gives the financing party a return similar to having invested the premiums for growth during the interim. The following chart illustrates how premium payments and splitting of the proceeds might work with respect to a $100,000 face value permanent insurance policy with dividends being used to reduce premiums:

Year	Premium	CSV	Premium Payments by		Proceeds Payable to	
			Financing	Insured	Financing	Insured
1	$2,889	$200	$200	$2,689	$200	$99,800
2	2,659	2,015	1,815	844	2,015	97,985
∫	∫	∫	∫	∫	∫	∫
X	930		930	0		
	36,666	48,600	33,133	3,533	48,600	51,400

In Year 1, because the cash value increase is only $200, the financing party's payment is $200 and, if the insured were to die in that year, the financing party's share of the proceeds would be $200. In Year 2, because cash value increased by $1,815, the financing party pays that amount of the premium and, with aggregate cash value of $2,015, the financing party would receive that amount if the insured died in Year 2. By Year X, because cash value increases significantly in later years, the financing party pays all the premium and, because cash value exceeds total premiums paid, would receive proceeds equal to the cash surrender value if the insured then died.

An alternative that minimizes the financing party's share of the proceeds is an "equity" split dollar plan in which the financing party receives only its premium contributions, and not any greater cash value. As the policy develops additional value the financing party is seen as

---

financing party), or the "creditor beneficiary arrangement" (because the financing party basically occupies an unsecured creditor status).

providing an even greater benefit to the policy owner, and that added entitlement constitutes an added form of income to the benefited party.

A long term debate regarding the proper tax treatment of equity split dollar has been resolved with income tax regulations first anticipated by Notice 2001-10, which announced the conclusion that "all economic benefits conferred on an employee under [a split dollar] arrangement, excluding economic benefits attributable to the employee's own premium payments, constitute gross income to the employee." Stating that employee split dollar essentially is an interest free loan of the employer's funds used to finance the insurance purchase, the Notice also articulated that "Treasury and the IRS believe that Congress generally intended that §7872 would govern . . . ."

Notice 2002-8 articulated that the regulations would offer a second (mutually exclusive) regime. Either the compensation income §7872 interest free loan rules would apply, as if the premium payments were loans by the "sponsor" or financing party to the benefited party (typically an employee, although this treatment can apply outside the employment context). Or the arrangement would be treated as a series of transfers to the benefited party that, in the employment context, will attract compensation income consequences (inclusion to the employee; deduction by the employer). None of this directly impacts the wealth transfer tax consequences of dealing with life insurance.[15]

Thus, in a traditional employer-employee or corporation-shareholder split dollar plan of either the loan or compensation variety, the employer or corporation's payment of a portion of the premium is direct (§61) or indirect (§7872) compensation or dividend income to the employee or shareholder. The income tax benefit is measured by the cost to provide the "risk portion" or current pure term insurance protection that is provided by the policy. After taking out the financing party's share of the proceeds (representing its return for premiums paid), the balance of the proceeds are this risk portion. The cost of this risk portion once was known as the P.S. 58 cost. It subsequently was replaced by Table 2001. This is the amount (less any premiums paid by the insured)[16] that is treated as compensation or dividend income to the employee or shareholder.

---

15 Additional split dollar modifications reflect premium payment variations designed to accommodate the income tax consequences of split dollar insurance in the employer-employee or corporation-shareholder context. They are not considered further here because most split dollar planning is done by planners other than estate planners, usually in the corporate context.

16. If the insurer's actual standard rate for a single premium one year term policy in the amount of the risk portion is less than the Table 2001 cost, then the lower rate will be the measure of compensation or dividend income to the insured, again less any premium paid by the insured. Caution is necessary, however, to compare the insurer's (not some parent or subsidiary of the insurer) published, one year, standard rates (not any preferred rate available, for example, to nonsmokers, insureds younger than a certain age, or to policies of a certain size). Thus, for example, in Technical Advice Memorandum 199918060 the government rejected evidence of the insurer's rates for a three year annually renewable policy for nonsmokers underwriting amounts larger than $200,000.

Standard Contract Provisions

In addition to the type of insurance coverage provided by a particular product, or the method of premium payment chosen, other distinguishing characteristics of various products relate to the available settlement options for payment of the proceeds and various contract provision alternatives. Given all the policy variations and contract provisions noted here, and especially considering the stakes involved, it is no exaggeration to say that the typical client and perhaps the typical advisor has trouble keeping track of what a particular policy provides. For protection against error, therefore, prudence probably dictates that the estate planner inspect the policy and beneficiary designation if reasonably possible, as part of the planning process. Don't take the client's or the agent's word for things you can verify personally at little added cost to the client. And ask for the plain English version of the policy description while you're still a rookie trying to make sense of all this mumbo-jumbo.

Beneficiary Designation

Unless a different beneficiary has been designated, the beneficiary provision in a standard insurance contract typically specifies that the policy proceeds will be paid to the *owner* of the policy. The proceeds will be paid to the owner's estate if the owner is not alive (for example, because the owner also is the insured, which is not necessary but it is common). Payment to anyone else would generate a gift tax liability while the owner is alive, which the contract default rule avoids. Primary and secondary beneficiary designations are permitted, and most policies contain contract terms that address marital deduction qualification and the issue of a beneficiary dying simultaneously with the insured.

One common and permissible beneficiary designation is payment to an insurance trust created by the insured, the policy owner, or a third party, in each case during the insured's life and funded in most cases solely with the right to receive the policy proceeds. Sometimes the policy is transferred to the trust, and in some of these cases other assets also are contributed to the trust to produce income that may be used to pay policy premiums. But the typical insurance trust designated as the beneficiary of a policy is an unfunded inter vivos receptacle that has no real function or assets until the insured's death. Designation of such an unfunded insurance trust is regarded as generally preferable to payment to a testamentary trust created by the owner or the insured's will because the trustee of the inter vivos insurance trust may institute proceedings to collect the proceeds immediately after the insured's death. A personal representative or testamentary trustee usually must await appointment by the applicable probate court before acting to collect proceeds payable to them, which introduces an unavoidable and undesirable delay.

Settlement Options

Another aspect of insurance policy "construction" that may differentiate products is the available settlement options. The owner of a policy is entitled to select who will be the beneficiary *and* how the proceeds will be paid. There are several typical settlement options and, if the owner has selected a lump sum payment, the beneficiary also may be permitted to elect from among a number of available forms of payment. Common options include any one or combination of (1) a lump sum cash payment (the most popular alternative), (2) monthly interest paid at a contractually specified rate for a specified period and then distribution of the proceeds in a lump sum, (3) income (not interest) paid to a designated income beneficiary for a term or for life, with a distribution of the remainder in a lump sum, or (4) purchase (or issue) of an annuity of any variety available.

Policy Loans

One great benefit of permanent insurance over term coverage is that permanent insurance builds up a cash surrender value, obtainable either by surrendering the policy or by borrowing against it. Policy loans allow access to this fund of wealth while maintaining the coverage and, unlike most commercial loans, the borrower may forgo repayment of the loan during the insured's life. Instead, the owner pledges the policy proceeds as collateral for the loan. If the loan is not repaid before the insured dies, the insurer simply sets off the proceeds against the outstanding principal and any unpaid interest. As a consequence, the loan value will be comfortably below the amount of the cash surrender value, so that the insurer can be made whole by capture of amounts payable, even if the policy is abandoned by failure to pay any additional premiums.[17] Interest rates on policy loans usually are specified in the policy and many older contracts offer loans at attractively low rates.

Accelerated Death Benefits

Since the late 1980s another mechanism has existed to obtain the value of an insurance policy before the insured's death. This accelerated benefit is not limited to just the cash surrender value and is available not just in the case of a permanent cash value insurance product. The policy owner may obtain an "advance" on the policy proceeds under a "living needs," "living benefits," "life settlement," "accelerated death benefit rider," or "viatical settlement." In some cases this accelerated payout comes directly from the insurer under a provision in the contract. Absent such an option, it may be available from other private businesses. Essentially, the owner

---

17. Notice that failure to repay the loan and its subsequent forgiveness on surrender may result in taxable income. See §72(e)(5)(E), which applies on a surrender (or deemed surrender, in the case of an abandonment) to the extent cash value plus outstanding loans exceed the owner's tax basis in the policy.

sells the policy at a discount that reflects the life expectancy of the insured and the cost to carry the coverage until payout at the insured's death.

Owners who are interested in these accelerated death benefits often are insureds who need to capitalize on the proceeds during their remaining life, such as to cover the daunting end of life health care costs of an imminent but protracted death. Examples include individuals suffering from AIDS or Alzheimer's disease. Others simply may be willing to suffer a discount in the amount payable in exchange for the freedom to personally enjoy the proceeds, particularly if they have no surviving beneficiaries about whose welfare they are concerned.

The owner essentially elects to receive the discounted face amount during life rather than allowing the designated beneficiary to receive the full policy benefit after the insured's death. Adoption of §101(g) made it clear that accelerated death benefit amounts paid by either an insurer or a qualified viatical settlement provider will be treated as amounts paid by reason of the insured's death, thereby qualifying for the §101(a)(1) exclusion from income and not as a sale for income tax §101(a)(2) transfer-for-value purposes.

Under §101(g) the insured must be "terminally ill" or "chronically ill," meaning that they were certified by a physician as having an illness or physical condition that "can reasonably be expected to result in death in 24 months or less after the date of the certification" or that they meet the chronically ill definition in §7702B(c)(2), which entails the inability to perform certain listed "activities of daily living" (bathing, eating, toileting, and such).

Dividends

Traditionally policy dividends were available only on "participating" permanent life policies issued by "mutual" companies (which means the policyholders own the company, the way shareholders own most corporations). Dividends paid on a policy represent a return of excess premiums collected for the policy, based on the company's mortality experience and their ability to invest adequately to develop an excess "reserve" that funds their obligation to policyholders. These dividends are a return of basis, *not* income (even though a stock company would pay a similar amount to its shareholders as a dividend distribution of the company's profits, taxable as would be any dividend paid to shareholders of a corporation).[18]

In recent years some stock companies have paid an element of return (an "interest credit") to policyholders that is similar to a mutual company's

---

18. These returns are to be distinguished from any discount made available to an insured who prepays premiums and receives a benefit to compensate for the insurer's use of the premium dollars paid early, which *is* income to the insured. Rev. Rul. 65-199, Rev. Rul. 66-120 (illustrating how to determine the reportable income attributable to advance premiums).

dividends, to be competitive with mutual company products. Participating policies frequently are more expensive on a flat comparison, but compare favorably when dividends are factored into cost. Dividend projections, however, usually are not guaranteed, so the company's history and current economic position become important (albeit difficult) factors to consider when evaluating competing proposals.

Dividends paid by mutual companies and interest credits paid by stock companies reflect a number of factors: the company's yield on investments, their mortality costs, the cost of doing business (including income taxes), and lapse rates or persistency/renewal. Lapses leave funds that are available to cover the insurer's obligations to remaining policies. Furthermore, high lapse rates are not necessarily bad if they reflect that policyholders who are insurable tend to purchase new term insurance at lower rates while policyholders who continue to pay premiums on a guaranteed renewable term policy may have become uninsurable. But persistency in permanent products usually is preferable because these products may be more expensive to the company in their early years (principally due to the payment of commissions on sales). A dividend rate that is based on an assumption that mortality rates will improve or that depends on lapses to be profitable should be viewed with skepticism, but not necessarily rejected. And the credibility or risk of all these assumptions should be evaluated.

Typical policy dividend options permit: (1) accumulation at interest, payable at death, (2) payment in cash currently, (3) use to purchase additional identical coverage without evidence of insurability (for example, to match policy loan amounts that otherwise would reduce the payout at death and thereby provide level benefits; anticipated are policy loans used to pay premiums during life), (4) use to pay premiums or reduce outstanding policy loans, or (5) the "fifth option," which is to purchase term insurance (such as increasing term insurance purchased with respect to split dollar insurance).

Depending on the circumstances, the last three options are the most common, with the fifth dividend option being utilized most often in split dollar insurance plans and the fourth option being common in minimum purchase policies that are highly leveraged to provide maximum coverage with borrowed funds and the least cash outlay. The first option produces current income taxable interest (with no distribution of dollars with which to pay the income tax imposed on a current basis[19]), making this a relatively unpopular alternative. In addition, under split dollar insurance, income will result to an employee or shareholder who benefits directly from the dividend option, whether by distribution of cash, reduction of

---

19. Which is unlike the nontaxability of current dividends applied under one of the other dividend options. See Treas. Reg. §1.451-2; Nesbitt v. Commissioner, 43 T.C. 629 (1965); Cohen v. Commissioner, 39 T.C. 1055 (1963).

their share of the premium, or purchase of additional insurance that is subject to their control.

Additional Purchase

Additional purchase entitlements without evidence of insurability typically are available only in permanent life products. They permit the acquisition of designated added amounts of like coverage upon the occurrence of specified events, such as birth or adoption of a child or the insured's attainment of a certain age. These options usually are exercised to the fullest extent possible for an insured who has become rated but needs additional coverage, because all policy provisions (including premium rate) typically apply to the additional purchase. For an insured who is worried about becoming rated, this optional provision may be worth considering in any new policy comparison, although its availability will add to the premium cost.

Conversion

This provision typically permits conversion of a term product into permanent coverage under circumstances similar to those that would trigger additional purchase options, such as attained age or birth or adoption of a child. Because term insurance grows more expensive as the insured grows older, this is a valuable entitlement for an insured who anticipates an undiminished need for coverage and an improved ability to afford permanent coverage at a future conversion date.

Accidental Death

Many policies pay double or triple the face amount on an "accidental death" (depending on how that term is defined under the contract). This factor may be important to consider when trying to guestimate the size of a taxable estate, particularly if the client is not otherwise a high mortality risk, but it may not be worth the extra premium cost given the relative likelihood that it will not apply.

Common Disaster

Common disaster provisions specify that the insured is presumed to be the survivor if the insured and the beneficiary die under circumstances such that the order of their deaths cannot be established by proof. In this way, the proceeds are not paid to a deceased beneficiary's estate, which avoids double taxation, application of the §2013 previously taxed property credit, and added administrative costs. This provision may, however, be altered to permit qualification for the marital deduction by presuming a spouse as beneficiary to be the survivor, or alternatively may be altered to require survivorship by a certain number of days or hours to be regarded as having survived the insured.

Assignment

Assignment provisions generally parallel the state law right to assign a policy, such as to collateralize a loan.

Grace Period

Most policies provide that coverage will not terminate or lapse if the premium is paid within a certain period after due (often one month). Sometimes there is an automatic loan provision in policies with a cash surrender value that kicks in to borrow cash value and thus provide the funds to pay the premium after the grace period expires. Otherwise the policy value may be converted into a paid up product (with a lower face value).

Disability Waiver of Premium

A disability waiver of premium provision allows the policy to remain in full effect without further payments if the owner of a policy becomes disabled and, therefore, potentially is unable to pay further premiums. Policies with this entitlement essentially entail payment of a small annual premium that purchases term disability insurance that funds premium payments if disability occurs. Usually total disability is required and often the definition of what constitutes total disability proves difficult to meet.[20]

The disability waiver of premium provision is worthless in any policy that has a vanishing premium feature, once the premium is made to vanish (usually because loan values are sufficient to sustain the policy, or in a survivor life policy after the death of the first insured to die). Consequently, a premium quote that includes disability waiver of premiums should be scrutinized carefully to determine whether this feature generates a cost after it no longer is useful.

Fraud

Typically a policy will provide that, generally beginning 24 months after issue, all items in the policy become incontestable except misstatements of age (which may be corrected by adjustment of face value or premium) and fraud (which may result in cancellation). Examples of fraud would include intentional misstatements regarding medical history, lifestyle, occupation, avocations, or other facts that affect insurability (such as alcohol consumption or tobacco use).

---

20. Many clients ought to consider disability replacement of income insurance, for which the same issue exists whether disability means inability to perform any occupation, any occupation for which the insured is suitably trained (or capable), the occupation in which the insured currently is engaged, or something else. In addition, the standard by which any of these tests is determined may vary, all with an effect on the cost and utility of the coverage.

Unnatural Death

Most policies exempt payment if death is due to the insured's suicide, and all will bar payment to a beneficiary who caused the insured's death. These "slayer" provisions often are much broader and better drafted than similar state laws barring a slayer from inheriting from a victim.

Nonforfeitability

The principal feature distinguishing permanent and term insurance is that the former is nonforfeitable. That is, included among the rights that a permanent policy accrues, even if payment of premiums is suspended, are (1) the right to borrow the cash surrender value at a guaranteed rate of interest and without security or evidence of solvency (because the proceeds of the policy at the insured's death are pledged under the contract to repay any outstanding loan principal and unpaid interest), (2) the right to surrender the policy and receive its cash value, (3) the right to convert the policy into a paid up product by using the cash surrender value to purchase a single premium policy, and (4) the right to borrow against cash value for purposes of continued premium payment at the original face amount.

Comparing Policies

Given all the available policy variations and contract provisions, perhaps the most difficult task confronting most potential insurance consumers and their advisors is how to compare coverage and quotes. When several agents present quotes on competing policies, the consumer needs to determine which is preferable; unfortunately the consumer cannot compare the two policies because they are designed not to be comparable. Indeed, it probably is accurate to state that insurance companies intentionally work to prevent their products from being sufficiently homogeneous to compare, thereby precluding side-by-side comparison shopping. And, although there are some computerized price quoting services for certain aspects of the comparison process, even these are of little help if the coverage being compared is dissimilar.[21]

Industry experts explain that the only viable way to accurately compare the coverage offered by several competing policies is to request a policy quote based on factors and policy design features submitted by the applicant (rather than those offered by the insurer). Thus, the secret to a product comparison is to make the competing agents produce comparable quotes, based on a policy that reflects factors selected by the client rather than by the insurer or the agent. These might include

---

21. In addition, some of these are offered over the telephone at a toll free number or by internet web site operators, in each case because the comparison service deals in discount insurance and offers free product comparisons in anticipation of commissions on a sale. It may be that the client is not likely to use these services, but caution is in order to be certain that no hidden advantages are disguised in the comparison to make the operator's own coverage look more attractive.

(1) gender of the insured,

(2) date of birth (not just the age, because companies may vary on how they determine age),

(3) whether the insured is or ever was a smoker,

(4) known medical problems that will be revealed by any physical required for the level of coverage required,[22]

(5) face amount of the coverage and whether it will be level, increasing, or decreasing in amount (it also is good to know whether the base coverage is guaranteed and the mix between permanent and term coverage),

(6) the use of any dividends,

(7) additional purchase options and costs,

(8) age of the applicant to which the insurance is desired,

(9) the mortality, investment, and interest rate assumptions upon which projections are made, including the policy loan interest rate,[23]

(10) the premium type (whether split dollar, vanishing, minimum deposit, pay to age, or other limited pay options) and the discounted present value of the total premium obligation (using a predetermined discount rate),[24]

(11) rating of the company and its operational history for at least a decade,[25] and

---

22. Note that the form of physical will vary with the company's underwriting standards and the amount of coverage requested, making this worthy of consideration in designing a comparison (including whether to purchase several smaller policies rather than a single larger product with more intensive and detailed underwriting criteria or reinsurance limits).

23. A good indicator is known as the Internal Rate of Return figure that reveals the assumed performance of premiums paid, in terms of both the death benefit and the cash surrender value at various stages in the life of the policy. The comparison should not confuse yield assumptions based on a total portfolio versus a new money basis.

24. Depending on the time of payment of premiums, the overall cost may vary significantly and the overall cost can be difficult to predict without an appropriate time-value analysis. Note that all insurance policies assume annual premiums will be paid until death (or age 95 or 100 in some policies, if death does not occur first), but techniques are built into the policy to accelerate those payments or provide for their being made internally, from cash values, projected dividends, or interest credits. These sources may never develop, however, depending on performance of the company and the investment of premium dollars previously paid. Moreover, some policies have a guaranteed maximum premium, while others (especially interest or investment sensitive policies) may have no such stop.

25. Rating companies is a very difficult chore and may not be worth the effort if the policy limits are low and the company has a long and highly reputable history. But for large purchases or quotations from newer entrants in the market, the following items all may be relevant: (a) alpha rating, (b) size and class of the issuer, (c) earnings history, (d) insurance in effect, lapse history, and whether the amount of insurance and the number of insureds and agents in the field is increasing or shrinking, (e) premium income and trends over time, (f) reserve margin experience and trend, (g) policy loans outstanding, (h) investment practices and portfolio composition, (h) mortality experience, and (i) expense and net cost history.

(12) the agent's commission (which, unbeknownst to many, often is negotiable, especially on larger policies).

Before selecting an insurer, the applicant should know and be comfortable with the medical underwriting requirements for the various levels of coverage required and ought to know the mortality assumptions made in formulating the insurer's projections. Underwriting requirements are especially important to consider, to avoid applying for coverage that the applicant cannot actually qualify to receive and thereafter having to report on later applications that the applicant has been refused coverage.

Industry experts also advise applicants and their advisors to require the selling agent to present a year by year comparison from issue of the policy

---

The average individual cannot begin to analyze this kind of data. Fortunately, a number of institutions make it their business: A.M. Best, Fitch, Moody's, Standard & Poors, and Weiss, each using different criteria. Because their rankings all can be a bit misleading, the following table attempts to place them in context (notice all those As; grade inflation wasn't invented in higher education). It illustrates the 16 highest ranks and how the grade scales of the various services translate. Notice that Standard & Poors and Fitch are combined because they use the same grades.

Rank	Best	Weiss	Standard & Poors/Fitch	Moody's
1	A++	A+	AAA	Aaa
2	A+	A	AA+	Aa1
3	A	A-	AA	Aa2
4	A-	B+	AA-	Aa3
5	B++	B	A+	A1
6	B+	B-	A	A2
7	B	C+	A-	A3
8	B-	C	BBB+	Baa1
9	C++	C-	BBB	Baa2
10	C+	D+	BBB-	Baa3
11	C	D	BB+	Ba1
12	C-	D-	BB	Ba2
13	D	E+	BB-	Ba3
14	E	E	B+	B1
15	F	E-	B	B2
16		F	B-	B3

Someplace around rank 12 generally is regarded as "below average," and around 14 or below is considered "financially weak."

The table is shamelessly constructed from a table found in volume one of the highly acclaimed Insurance Counselor Series, published by the American Bar Association Real Property, Probate & Trust Section. See Schwartz & Turner, LIFE INSURANCE DUE CARE: CARRIERS, PRODUCTS, AND ILLUSTRATIONS ch. 3 (2d ed. 1994). See www.insurance.com. Other titles in the Insurance Counselor series include: FEDERAL INCOME TAXATION OF LIFE INSURANCE (1989); Millard, Brody & Lane, FEDERAL GIFT, ESTATE, AND GENERATION SKIPPING TRANSFER TAXATION OF LIFE INSURANCE (2d ed. 1998); Wynn, SPLIT-DOLLAR LIFE INSURANCE (1991); Klein & Bahls, S CORPORATIONS AND LIFE INSURANCE (1992); Brody, THE IRREVOCABLE LIFE INSURANCE TRUST: FORMS WITH DRAFTING NOTES (1995); Brody & Weinberg, THE INSURED STOCK PURCHASE AGREEMENT WITH SAMPLE FORMS (1997); Schiltz, COUNSELING PROFESSIONALS ON DISABILITY INSURANCE WITH SAMPLE AGREEMENTS AND DRAFTING NOTES (1997); and Drennan, Swirnoff & Goldstein, TAXATION AND FUNDING OF NONQUALIFIED DEFERRED COMPENSATION (1998).

to age 95 of the various quotes, showing guaranteed premium costs, net after tax cash flow, cash surrender values, and the guaranteed benefits (rather than just projections, which may be overstated) that will be paid if death occurs at certain times. This may be particularly revealing because typical clients will live well into their 80s or beyond, and many insurance policy illustrations highlight performance at age 65, when the policy is designed to show well notwithstanding that it is not a particularly good product at the ages to which the insured will likely live.

In addition, comparison projections should be provided based on dividends payable at the current rate, the current rate less 200 basis points, and no dividends. Weber, *Understanding Life Insurance Illustrations*, 133 TRUSTS & ESTATES 45, 47 (Feb. 1994). The cautions to look for are a decrease in death benefits or an increase in premiums (including reappearance of premiums that vanished in a prior year, especially if that reappearance is at a higher premium than originally payable). The applicant's advisor should not hesitate to demand this service from an agent (and, after learning the size of the commission that will be generated, should not regard it as an imposition).[26]

Is It Insurance?

There is a huge variety in insurance products and packaging, and a modern trend toward policies that compete favorably only because of extensive reliance on market investments. As a result, some concern surrounds the fundamental issue whether a particular product qualifies as insurance as defined under §7702 for income tax purposes. As originally defined, insurance requires risk shifting and risk distribution, typically from the individual insured to the group of insureds who pay premiums that provide a fund that will pay in the event of premature death. Helvering v. Le Gierse, 312 U.S. 531 (1941), applied in Commissioner v. Treganowan, 183 F.2d 288 (2d Cir. 1950).

The §7702 definition differs and two significant detriments are imposed if the §7702 definition is not met: the proceeds received on the insured's death will not qualify for the §101 exclusion from the beneficiary's income, and the internal build up in the policy value will be taxable immediately to the owner, in an amount equal to the excess of cash surrender value over premiums paid. §7702(g)(1).

A policy qualifies as life insurance for income tax purposes only if (1) it is considered under state law to provide a single integrated death benefit (not an annuity or investment vehicle, and not a product that can be

---

26. Also potentially helpful is an IQ (Illustration Questionnaire) developed by the Society of Financial Service Professionals (née the American Society of CLU and ChFC) that can assist in sorting out this information. Write to the Society at 270 So. Bryn Mawr Ave., Bryn Mawr, PA 19010-2195, Attn: Customer Service. They also make available an RQ (Replacement Questionnaire) relating to evaluation of proposals that older policies be replaced by newer coverage (typically with a new commission to the selling agent)

divided into several separable items), and (2) the policy meets either a §7702(a)(1) cash-value-accumulation test or both a guideline-premium and cash-value-corridor requirement. §§7702(a)(2)(A) and 7702(a)(2)(B).

Insurance products that are too heavily investment oriented run the risk of being deemed "modified endowment contracts" that meet the §7702(a) definition of insurance but fail a §7702A test. Before enactment of §7702A, some companies marketed single premium life insurance contracts that were essentially investment vehicles wrapped in a modest insurance policy, all designed to take advantage of the tax free internal build up afforded to life insurance. Under those policies the owner might borrow against or withdraw funds from the policy tax free under the basis allocation rules of §72(e). Congress quashed this gaming by specifying that loans against or withdrawals from modified endowment contracts are taxable as income to the extent of any accumulated build up in the policy, and as a recovery of basis only to the extent the amounts involved exceed that internal build up. In general a policy will fail to meet the §7702A test if amounts paid as premiums during the first seven years of the policy exceed the net amount that would be required if the insurance aspect of the contract provided for a paid up product using seven level annual premiums (the "7-pay test").

According to qualified analysts, casual players in this endeavor cannot realistically expect to determine whether a particular insurer's product complies with these definitions. See, e.g., Pike, *Reflections on the Meaning of Life: An Analysis of Section 7702 and the Taxation of Cash Value Life Insurance*, 43 TAX L. REV. 491 (1988). Instead, an advisor can only realistically expect to ask a company for verification that the policy meets these requirements and, perhaps (if the policy is sufficient in size), for indemnification against the tax costs if that proves to be wrong. So, your task is simply to be aware of the issue and to ask the right question if it appears that a proposal to your client has gotten a little carried away. With reputable insurers this is not likely to be a problem.

Policy Ownership

Life insurance historically has been regarded principally as a method to replace lost earnings after the insured's death, but its attractions are much more diverse. Equally important, for example, is its use to provide liquid funds to pay debts, expenses, and taxes at the insured's death. Moreover, in a business context it can provide working capital at the death of a key person and may be used to fund obligations under a buy-sell agreement. Furthermore, it provides a form of investment (to create wealth or for wealth shifting) with little fear of seizure by predators or dissipation by a donee. It is a leveraged form of ownership if the insured dies prior to the expiration of a normal life expectancy. And life insurance will be a tax favored investment if carryover basis ever becomes the law, because investment gains paid as cash proceeds will not incur capital gain or ordinary income tax.

With all this in mind, it is important to consider that life insurance need not be owned by the insured. State law designed to preclude strangers from acquiring an incentive for the insured to die prematurely usually requires an owner other than the insured to have an "insurable interest" in the insured, but that is a different question entirely. If done properly, life insurance owned by a third party is one of the best opportunities for generating and shifting wealth without wealth transfer taxation. Indeed, successful ownership of life insurance without estate tax inclusion of the proceeds in the insured's gross estate is a common desirable goal if the combined estates of the insured (and the insured's spouse, if any) will not be completely sheltered by their combined applicable exclusion amounts.

The two most common forms of third party ownership of life insurance in the estate planning context are spouse owned insurance and ownership by an irrevocable life insurance trust. Ownership by persons other than a spouse (such as by children, a sibling, or a business partner) is not common outside the buy-sell context, but spouse owned insurance and ownership by any other individual (other than the insured) is no different in terms of the consequences to the owner or to the insured. (Oh, it may differ to the extent the policy, or assets to be used for premium payment purposes, were transferred to the owner by the insured, in which case the gift tax marital deduction might apply to avoid gift tax with respect to spouse owned life insurance, but not otherwise.)

In either case, disposition of insurance owned by a natural person other than the insured must be considered because the owner might predecease the insured. In such a case the value of the policy (the interpolated terminal reserve value in most cases) will be includible in the owner's gross estate under §2033. Furthermore, it normally would be unwise to allow ownership of the policy to pass to the insured, with subsequent inclusion in the insured's gross estate when the insured dies.

Much more importantly, spouse owned insurance usually makes little or no sense from a tax perspective. This is because payment of the proceeds to the spouse will cause their inclusion in the spouse's gross estate at death and that result could be obtained just as easily by having the insured own the policy, with the proceeds payable to the spouse and qualified for the unlimited marital deduction.[27]

Moreover, designation of any beneficiary other than the spouse who is the owner will entail a gift by the spouse when the insured dies, so that also is not a very viable alternative. See page 50. Furthermore, spouse

---

27. The only exception to this statement is if the spouse is not a citizen of the United States, in which case §2056(d) must be considered and spouse owned insurance might make better sense than dealing with a §2056A qualified domestic trust. See Chapter 7 at page 77 regarding §2056(d) and noncitizen spouses.

owned insurance does not increase the settlement options available, because payment of the proceeds of any policy to the spouse directly, with the spouse's election of a delayed settlement, will qualify for the marital deduction just the same as allowing the spouse as owner to select a delayed payout. See Treas. Reg. §20.2056(d)-2(a). So neither approach (naming the spouse as the beneficiary who may select a settlement option, or making the spouse as owner designate the settlement option) gives the spouse any more or less control when the insured dies.

Thus, in a tax conscious situation, third party owners of policies are likely to be family members, a business entity or business partners, or a trust. In this respect usually it is an irrevocable insurance trust designed to preclude inclusion of the proceeds in the estate of the insured (or anyone else). Trust ownership also is easier than ownership by multiple parties if more than one owner is envisioned. Another alternative, advocated by few planners, is use of a partnership versus an irrevocable insurance trust, but the concepts are motivated by the same objectives. See Eastland, *The Use of Partnerships in Lieu of Irrevocable Insurance Trusts*, 16 TAX MGMT. (BNA) ESTATES, GIFTS & TRUSTS J. 123 (1991).

Third party ownership presents the opportunity to increase the total wealth generated by life insurance by avoiding wealth transfer taxation of the policy proceeds. The irrevocable life insurance trust usually is the more tax favorable approach for estate planning purposes for a number of reasons. For example, spouse owned insurance may be made subject to a trust but the insured cannot unilaterally control it or insulate the policy or its proceeds from incompetence, improvidence, or inexperience of the spouse as owner or beneficiary. But the irrevocable trust provides administration and management with all the creditor protections of a spendthrift trust.[28]

More directly, a well drafted irrevocable insurance trust is advantageous because the proceeds may bypass inclusion in the estate of both the insured and any other owner for transfer tax purposes. Thus, with a little simple insurance trust planning many otherwise taxable situations can be made nontaxable under the shelter of the applicable exclusion amount of the unified credit.

---

28. It also presents the opportunity for the insured as settlor of the trust to pay income tax on trust income used to pay insurance premiums without that additional benefit being regarded as an additional gift. Most irrevocable insurance trusts are unfunded, but if the trust owns a corpus that will produce income that may be used to pay premiums for insurance on the settlor's life, §677(a)(3) requires the settlor to report that income, which means that the trust obtains the benefit of tax free income (by virtue of taxation to the settlor) without an added gift tax cost to the settlor. Income taxation of this income to the settlor is not tantamount to its retention for wealth transfer tax purposes, so no §2036(a)(1) inclusion exposure exists. See First Nat'l Bank v. Commissioner, 36 B.T.A. 651 (1937); cf. Bennett v. United States, 185 F. Supp. 577 (N.D. Ill. 1960) (the value of securities transferred to an irrevocable trust was not includible in the settlor's gross estate notwithstanding trust principal was used to pay premiums; the implication was that the result would not differ even if trust income was used to pay premiums).

Notwithstanding the advantages of an irrevocable insurance trust, two factors often are perceived to be relevant and recommend spouse owned insurance if taxes are not a concern and if divorce is not perceived to be likely. One is that the spouse may dispose of the proceeds in a manner that is not (yet) irrevocable. Under the irrevocable insurance trust approach, disposition of the proceeds is locked in upon execution of the trust to the extent flexibility is not provided under the design of the plan (for example, through a trust protector or power of appointment provision that permits a third party to alter the trust terms to reflect changing circumstances). The issue is whether the irrevocable insurance trust is sufficiently flexible, even with built in powers to alter the trust terms.

More important among the factors that some regard as favoring spouse owned insurance are the gift tax consequences of a transfer of a policy or assets that will be used to pay premiums on it. If a spouse is the owner but the insured is providing the sums needed to pay premiums, normally the gift tax marital deduction will eliminate any gift tax exposure that would attend to premium payment using an irrevocable insurance trust. Planning to minimize these gift tax consequences of an irrevocable insurance trust is a significant element in third party ownership planning, as discussed beginning at page 49.

An additional ownership issue is relevant in community property jurisdictions, also involving ownership of insurance by spouses and again potentially avoidable with an irrevocable life insurance trust. In several community property jurisdictions[29] a proration approach specifies that ownership of a policy of life insurance purchased by either spouse is a function of the extent to which community property or separate property was used for premium payment purposes. Failure to use care in selecting the source of the premium payments could cause unintentional spousal ownership.[30] This ownership issue may differ depending on whether the policy is term or permanent coverage, because arguably the last premium

---

29. See, e.g., Biltoft v. Wootten, 157 Cal. Rptr. 581 (Ct. App. 1979); Modern Woodmen of American v. Gray, 299 P.2d 754 (Cal. Ct. App. 1931); Porter v. Porter, 726 P.2d 459 (Wash. 1986) (involving cash value coverage); Wilson v. Wilson, 212 P.2d 1022 (Wash. 1949). Cf. Peters v. Peters, 557 P.2d 713 (Nev. 1976) (not specifically adopting but referring to the California approach).

30. See, e.g., Estate of Burris v. Commissioner, 82 T.C.M. (CCH) 400 (2001) (the decedent as titular owner of a policy on the decedent's life was deemed to own only half, because premiums were paid with community property; title simply made the decedent the community manager, not the owner of incidents of ownership in both halves), in which the decedent-insured's possession of half the incidents of ownership caused §2042(2) inclusion of half the proceeds of the policy. The other half was taxed at its interpolated terminable reserve value at the predeceased spouse's death. The court rejected Catalano v. United States, 429 F.2d 1058 (5th Cir. 1969) (policy ownership/title governed inclusion), because *Catalano* involved ownership by the noninsured spouse and avoided inclusion in the insured decedent's gross estate, and because rules relating to ownership of the policy differ from those relating to ownership of the policy proceeds (*Catalano* dealing with policy ownership and *Burris* involving ownership of the proceeds). The court also recognized that state law ownership issues, usually litigated while the insured is alive, typically arise in a divorce context, which tends to corrupt the state law analysis.

paid for a term policy purchases all the coverage, making a proration approach really a last premium paid approach for term insurance. A few community property jurisdictions apply an annual or last premium paid test, looking to see whether community funds were used to pay the last premium, particularly with respect to term insurance.[31]

Other community property states (perhaps the majority) follow an inception of title rule[32] that regards ownership as a function of the source of the *first* premium payment (with a right of reimbursement to the community for premiums paid on separate property policies from community funds). This approach avoids difficult tracing rules that span the full premium payment life of the policy.

Finally, the Uniform Marital Property Act, as adopted in Wisconsin, applies a three part rule depending on a number of factors, all designed to minimize estate taxation: (1) the policy is deemed to be community property if the insured spouse is the owner, (2) if the noninsured spouse is the owner it is deemed to be that spouse's separate property, and (3) if a third party is the owner a proration approach is applied if any premium was paid using community property, with the proration based on duration of the policy during the marriage rather than premiums paid from separate or community property.[33]

Obviously this is a confusing issue and specific attention is required in each community property jurisdiction because there is no uniform position or result. Indeed, the situation may differ based on the type of insurance owned[34] as well as its ownership. The only general statement that is fair to

---

31. See Lock v. Lock, 444 P.2d 163 (Ariz. Ct. App. 1968); Gaethje v. Gaethje, 441 P.2d 579 (Ariz. Ct. App. 1968); Travelers Ins. Co. v. Johnson, 544 P.2d 294 (Id. 1975); Anderson v. Idaho Mutual Benefit Ass'n, 292 P.2d 760 (Id. 1956); Aetna Life Ins. Co. v. Bunt, 754 P.2d 993 (Wash. 1988); Aetna Life Ins. Co. v. Wadsworth, 689 P.2d 46 (Wash. 1984); Aetna Life Ins. Co. v. Boober, 784 P.2d 186 (Wash. Ct. App. 1990).

32. See, e.g., Rothman v. Rumbeck, 96 P.2d 755 (Ariz. 1939); Everson v. Everson, 537 P.2d 624 (Ariz. Ct. App. 1975); Perry v. Perry, 501 P.2d 568 (Ariz. Ct. App. 1972); Succession of Lewis, 189 So. 118 (La. 1939); Succession of Verneuille, 45 So. 520 (La. 1908); Doland v. Doland, 562 So. 2d 994 (La. Ct. App. 1990); Inzinna v. Inzinna, 456 So. 2d 691 (La. Ct. App. 1984); Succession of Jackson, 402 So. 2d 753 (La. Ct. App. 1981); Berry v. Metropolitan Life Ins. Co., 327 So. 2d 521 (La. Ct. App. 1976); Roselli v. Rio Communities Service Station, Inc., 787 P.2d 428 (N.M. 1990); In re White's Estate, 89 P.2d 36 (N.M. 1939); Parson v. United States, 460 F.2d 228 (5th Cir. 1972) (Texas law); Freedman v. United States, 382 F.2d 742 (5th Cir. 1967) (Texas law); Brown v. Lee, 371 S.W.2d 694 (Tex. 1963); Dent v. Dent, 689 S.W.2d 521 (Tex. Ct. App. 1985); McCurdy v. McCurdy, 372 S.W.2d 381 (Tex. Ct. App. 1963).

33. See Wisc. Stat. §766.61(3).

34. In addition to the foregoing, there may be a federal preemption with respect to coverage such as National Service Life Insurance, as to which community property ownership appears to be denied regardless of the source of premium payments. See Wissner v. Wissner, 338 U.S. 655 (1950); Rev. Rul. 74-312; Rev. Rul. 56-603; and cf. McCarty v. McCarty, 453 U.S. 210 (1981) (California courts were precluded by federal law from dividing the spouse's nondisability military retirement pay); Hisquierdo v. Hisquierdo, 439 U.S. 572 (1979), and In re Hillerman, 167 Cal. Rptr. 240 (1980) (social security benefits are not subject to community property laws), and Estate of Huston v. Commissioner, 49 T.C. 495, 499 (1968) (labeling National Service Life Insurance proceeds as the decedent's separate property).

make is that, unless care is exercised in each case, a community property policy will generate some estate tax inclusion in the estate of the first spouse to die regardless of who is the insured.[35] It also may generate gift taxation if the surviving spouse does not receive half the proceeds of a community property policy.[36] Each of these concerns encourages ownership by an irrevocable insurance trust and payment of premiums in such a way as to avoid community property ownership of the policy.[37]

Creation of an irrevocable life insurance trust is no mean feat and the trust itself is unusual in only a few respects. Either the insured or any third party may create the trust, and the policy on the insured's life can be transferred into the trust if it already exists or can be acquired originally by the trust after creation of the trust. Because gift and estate tax issues may affect the former approach, it almost without exception is preferable for the latter approach to be followed if possible. Although it could be the case that a third party will pay premiums for the insurance directly, virtually always it is preferable for the trust to pay policy premiums with funds contributed to the trust on an annual basis for that purpose, with each contribution made to qualify for the gift tax annual exclusion through the use of a Crummey power of withdrawal. All this is discussed beginning at page 51.

The trust will own the policy and make itself the designated beneficiary of the proceeds on the insured's death, and (unless the trust is meant to be exempt for generation-skipping transfer tax purposes) typically will mirror the nonmarital provisions in the insured's estate plan. Indeed, frequently the irrevocable life insurance trust will combine with the insured's nonmarital dispositions after the insured's death. Contingent provisions may provide for the insured's surviving spouse, if any, or for the payment of estate taxes, in either case to the extent the insurance is includible in the insured's gross estate at death (for reasons unrelated to the existence of these provisions).

The only aspect of drafting an irrevocable life insurance trust that will be unusual is likely to be a trustee succession provision that installs a professional fiduciary only after the insurance proceeds are collected. This provision avoids both professional fees while the trust is basically

---

35. Under Treas. Reg. §20.2042-1(c)(5), includible is at least half the value of the policy itself if the noninsured spouse dies first, at least half the value of the proceeds if the insured spouse dies first, and potentially all the insurance proceeds if the insured spouse became the full owner of the policy on the noninsured spouse's prior death. See, e.g., Estate of Cervin v. Commissioner, 111 F.3d 1252 (5th Cir. 1997); Estate of Cavenaugh v. Commissioner, 51 F.3d 597 (5th Cir. 1995), rev'g 100 T.C. 407 (1993) (inclusion limited to half the proceeds notwithstanding the insured spouse died after the noninsured spouse); Scott v. Commissioner, 374 F.2d 154 (9th Cir. 1967) (the community portion was determined using a premium payment proration under state law, which was not half because the insured was the survivor and paid premiums from separate funds after the noninsured spouse's prior death); United States v. Stewart, 270 F.2d 894 (9th Cir. 1959); Rev. Rul. 75-100.

36. Treas. Reg. §25.2511-1(h)(9).

37. Safety may dictate that both a policy being transferred from the community and any dollars earmarked for premium payment should be transmuted from community into separate property prior to the transfers.

unfunded and professional liability for the performance of due diligence relating to ownership of the insurance coverage before it matures. The trust will be irrevocable by the settlor (perhaps with a trust protector provision allowing a third party to make changes),[38] and various specific insurance powers may be found in the boilerplate. These might include allowing retention of any policy on the insured's life, permitting the payment of premiums but absolving any requirement to do so, allowing reliance on another party's representation that the premium has been paid, granting all incidents of ownership to the trustee (specifically including the power to borrow to pay premiums, to convert the policy into some other form of coverage or into a paid up product, and the power to change the beneficiary under the policy), exoneration for any liability attributable to acquisition or retention of a policy, and indemnification against any costs incurred in litigation to collect the policy proceeds.

Beneficiary Designation

Among the options available to the owner of a life insurance policy are designation of the beneficiary and payment of the proceeds under any of the settlement options available under the policy. Remember, however, that if the owner is not the insured, any beneficiary designation other than the owner personally will generate a taxable gift on payment of the proceeds, as to which no §2206 right of reimbursement is applicable. See page 50. Thus, the gift tax incurred easily could exceed the owner's other available assets and bankrupt the owner.

The proceeds of most policies may be paid (1) to a designated individual beneficiary free of trust, (2) to the personal representative of the insured's estate, in which case the proceeds will be added to the other probate assets of the insured and pass under the insured's will or by intestacy, (3) to the trustee of a testamentary trust created under the insured's will, (4) to the trustee of an inter vivos insurance trust created by the insured, by the owner, or by anyone else, or (5) by leaving them on deposit with the insurer, to be paid out under a settlement option selected by the owner.

The fourth alternative often is preferable even if an outright distribution free of trust is desired, because often the trustee will be more knowledgeable than an individual beneficiary and in a better position to immediately assert the right to payment and to contest any delay or objection by the insurer. In addition, a trust can provide all the traditional protections against spousal claims, creditors, and other predators if the beneficiary is unable or unwilling to manage the proceeds, or the owner desires to keep the proceeds out of the beneficiary's estate for subsequent

---

38. Care is required, however, to be certain that the trust protector does not make an inadvertent gift, as might occur if that person was a beneficiary of the trust. E.g., Private Letter Ruling 200122055 involved state law trust reformation authority and ruled that no gift tax would be incurred by virtue of proposed changes.

wealth transfer tax purposes. Incidentally, the trust also guarantees a level of control over the proceeds after the insured's death.

Payment to a trust almost certainly is more desirable than the fifth option because settlement with the insurer usually is inflexible. There may be no opportunity to tailor this approach even if none of the alternatives offered are appropriate for the situation.

Payment to a trust also usually is preferable to the second option (payment to the insured's estate) because addition of the proceeds to the probate estate may subject them to the claims of creditors and may cause the proceeds to be diminished by expenses of administration. Indeed, payment to the estate may actually increase those costs by permitting the calculation of fees of administration on a larger asset base. Payment to the estate also may subject those proceeds unnecessarily to the elective share of a surviving spouse or a pretermitted heir (assuming the proceeds otherwise would escape these claims), and potentially to wealth transfer taxes that otherwise are avoidable. See, e.g., §2042(1), assuming that §2042(2) otherwise would not apply. State transfer taxes may correspond to the federal rules, making this payment option a doubly harmful alternative.

Moreover, any delay in probate of the insured's will or appointment of a personal representative will delay any demand for payment and resolution of any potential problems with collection and ultimate distribution. The same problem infects payment to a testamentary trustee, who also cannot act to collect the proceeds until the will creating the trust is admitted to probate and the court appoints the trustee designated under that will.

Notwithstanding all these potential problems, payment to an estate is not an uncommon beneficiary designation and often constitutes the default beneficiary designation under the contract itself (if there is no other effective designation). One plausible explanation for this selection is that the owner wishes to govern disposition of the proceeds by a provision in the owner's will but the contract does not authorize beneficiary designations in that manner. Indeed, a relatively common issue involving life insurance beneficiary designations arises because the policy owner attempts to designate or change the beneficiary by a will provision. Usually that is not an approach authorized by the insurance contract, and often (but not always) it occurs subsequently to and inconsistent with a beneficiary designation that was made in a manner authorized by the contract. The nearly universal result is rejection of the attempted designation, although a few cases illustrate that such a beneficiary designation may be respected.[39]

---

39. See, e.g., Austin v. Sears, 292 F.2d 690 (9th Cir. 1961) (the *initial* beneficiary designation by a will was upheld because the policy provisions with respect to designation and change of beneficiary are for the insurer's benefit, not the owner or the insured, and may be relaxed if the controversy is between conflicting claimants and not the insurer); Connecticut General Life Ins. Co. v. Peterson, 442 F. Supp. 533 (W.D. Mo. 1978) (applying Missouri law, the insured's will was allowed to change the beneficiary because the court saw no plausible reason not to permit the owner to do so).

Another possible rationale for payment to the insured's estate relates to the fact that the law of most states does not provide that divorce revokes an insurance beneficiary designation in favor of the former spouse the way it does for will provisions designating the spouse. The 1990 version of Uniform Probate Code §2-804 provides that the designation of a policy owner's spouse as insurance beneficiary is deemed revoked if the marriage subsequently ends in divorce (unless the divorce order or another contract or agreement expressly provides otherwise). But this generally desirable rule has not been widely adopted and may not be valid even in adopting states with respect to insurance contracts or beneficiary designations predating enactment.[40]

The Uniform Testamentary Additions to Trusts Act[41] and other specialized state statutes specifically permit designation of a testamentary trust as beneficiary of life insurance proceeds, allowing those proceeds to be treated the same as proceeds payable to the trustee of an inter vivos trust. Nevertheless, designation of the trustee of an inter vivos insurance trust is even more safe from challenge (as invalid because the trust does not exist at death) and avoids various problems as discussed above.

Regarding payment to an unfunded inter vivos insurance trust, it generally is accepted that designation of an inter vivos trust as beneficiary of a life insurance policy is an adequate trust corpus to support the trust as being in existence from the moment the policy is made payable to the designated trustee. See Clymer v. Mayo, 473 N.E.2d 1084 (Mass. 1985); RESTATEMENT (THIRD) OF TRUSTS §25(1) comment *c* and §40 comment *b* (2003). Nevertheless, some drafters, out of an abundance of caution, purport to place a nominal sum (such as the $25 cost of a $50 Series EE United States Savings Bond) in an inter vivos insurance trust at the time of execution, to validate the trust with a tangible corpus. With no corpus that requires active administration, trustee fees typically are not imposed, even by professional trustees, until the proceeds are collected.

Insurance trusts also are widely used in buy-sell agreements. The trustee collects the insurance proceeds on an insured's death and applies

---

40. Retroactive application of Ohio Rev. Code Ann. §1339.63 (a virtually identical rule to the Uniform Probate Code provision with respect to insurance contracts predating the statute's effective date), was declared unconstitutional by Aetna Life Ins. Co. v. Schilling, 616 N.E.2d 893 (Ohio 1993) (the decedent died 20 days after the effective date of the statute and 13 years after a divorce from the spouse who was named before the divorce as beneficiary of employer funded group term life insurance), as a violation of §28 of Art. II of the Ohio Constitution, which prohibits the Ohio General Assembly from passing retroactive laws or laws that impair the obligations of existing contracts. To the same effect see Whirlpool Corp. v. Ritter, 929 F.2d 1318 (8th Cir. 1991) (involving Oklahoma law; the contract was issued before enactment but the divorce followed, the decedent being killed — apparently by the plaintiff ex-spouse but the case remands for a determination on that issue — without changing the beneficiary); but see In re Estate of Dobert, 963 P.2d 327 (Ariz. Ct. App. 1998) (virtually identical facts to *Ritter*, including the apparent slaying by the plaintiff and timing of enactment before the divorce but after acquisition of the policy and failure to change the beneficiary designation).

41. Uniform Probate Code §2-511, which is the freestanding Uniform Testamentary Additions to Trust Act, 8B U.L.A. 360 (2001).

them to purchase the insured's interest on behalf of the surviving parties to the agreement.

One overriding issue with respect to any of these beneficiary designations is how the proceeds will be made available to provide needed liquidity to the insured's estate. The availability of liquidity does not pose a serious concern if avoidance of wealth transfer taxation on the proceeds is not an issue, because the proceeds may be made payable to the insured's revocable inter vivos trust or to the insured's estate, in either case subject to a provision directing or authorizing payment of estate debts, expenses, and taxes using the proceeds. Estate tax inclusion of the proceeds under §2042(1) will result if the recipient of the proceeds is anyone charged with liability to pay estate settlement costs. In some states the local death tax is triggered only if the proceeds are payable to or for the benefit of the estate,[42] but in either case the wealth transfer tax liability would be an anticipated and presumably an acceptable consequence.

On the other hand, if the object is to avoid inclusion of those proceeds for estate tax purposes, ownership by a third party such as an irrevocable insurance trust will be required, and that raises a serious question in planning to make the proceeds available to provide estate liquidity. In this respect direct payment to the source of the estate settlement obligation is out of the question.[43]

The most straightforward method of providing liquidity from the proceeds without causing estate tax inclusion is to use them to purchase illiquid assets from the insured's estate, substituting liquid cash proceeds from the insurance for estate assets that are unmarketable or that the estate is unwilling to sell elsewhere (because they are an integral part of the insured's estate, such as stock in a closely held business). Bona fide purchase at an asset's fair market value should avoid any gift tax implications of the transaction. The estate will recognize gain or loss represented by any difference between fair market value and basis (which is federal estate tax value under §1014 unless or until carryover basis is adopted). But the purchaser will receive a new basis equal to cost (fair

---

42. Some states with a wealth transfer (either inheritance or estate) tax still exempt life insurance proceeds not paid to the estate. In such states some will and trust tax payment provisions specify that proceeds of life insurance may be used to pay estate administration expenses or taxes only to the extent other assets available for that purpose are insufficient. See Chapter 11 at page 47, §1.2.6.3 of the detailed tax payment provision.

43. An exception to this statement is use of a safety valve tax payment provision that applies only to the extent inclusion of the proceeds otherwise occurs (that is, it is triggered by some event or circumstance other than the existence of the tax payment provision itself; for example, because the policy was transferred within three years of the insured's death and §2035(a) requires inclusion). Such a tax payment provision typically provides for payment of the same taxes that would be subject to the §2206 pro rata right of reimbursement, the advantage of the tax payment clause being that it allows the drafter to dictate that a different amount of tax be paid and that this liability will apply even if inclusion is not under §2042 (to which §2206 is tied). If the insured is married many drafters also anticipate unexpected inclusion with a safety valve marital deduction provision as well.

market value at the time of the sale), which mitigates this consequence. Moreover, the potential gain will be minimized if sale occurs quickly after the insured's death.

One limitation of the sale approach is that it only substitutes insurance proceeds for estate assets. This approach does not increase the total estate available for estate settlement purposes, so some planners look for other techniques to provide estate liquidity. As a means of infusing tax free liquidity into the insured's estate, the most common alternative to a direct sale involves loans from the recipient of the proceeds to the insured's estate. In addition to the §7872 gift tax liability that might arise if the terms of a loan are more generous than an arm's length transaction, the down side of this planning relates to repayment or other settlement of the loan, which may generate unexpected income and gift tax exposure.

For example, if the insured's estate does not include sufficient cash, a plan to repay the loan in cash might require sale of appreciated assets, resulting in gain. Alternatively, gain still would be generated if the loan was repaid using assets in kind. This is because the transaction would be viewed as if the assets had been sold for cash, resulting in gain to the estate, followed by the cash being used to repay the loan, and the creditor using the cash to purchase the assets that were transferred. See, e.g., United States, v. Davis, 370 U.S. 65 (1962) (use of appreciated assets to satisfy a legal obligation constituted a sale or exchange). Thus, repayment of the loan, either in cash or in kind, fares no better in avoidance of gain than an outright sale of assets from the estate, and the delay merely increases the likelihood that gain will be recognized to the extent assets appreciate in value during the period the loan is outstanding.

Rather than repay the loan, the suggestion sometimes made is that the debt be discharged or extinguished by merger. For example, if the insured's estate will pour over into the trust that made the loan, then the obligation to repay the loan would pass into the trust, where it would merge with the trust's right to receive payment, resulting in extinguishment of the debt. Unfortunately, forgiveness or extinguishment might generate ordinary income to the estate in the amount of the debt discharged, because §61(a)(12) treats the discharge of any indebtedness as income to the debtor (the estate). Nevertheless, some observers suggest that extinguishment by merger involving the estate and an irrevocable trust should produce a different result. According to this argument, extinguishment by merger results in no taxable benefit because "there is no increase in the wealth of the combined entity, since any economic benefit to the debtor resulting from the extinguishment of the obligation is offset by the economic detriment to the creditor through extinguishment of his right to repayment."[44]

---

44. Stein, *Use of Insurance Proceeds in Irrevocable Trust for Payment of Death Costs*, 3 NOTRE DAME EST. PLAN. INST. 71, 107 (1979). Cases cited for the proposition that extinguishment does not generate ordinary income all involve corporate mergers. In each

Notwithstanding the merger, the tax consequences of the extinguishment ought to be viewed as involving different taxpayers, because the trust and the estate are separate tax paying entities up until and including the time of merger. If the economic reality is to be reflected properly for income tax purposes, it should be regarded as if the estate repaid the loan and then, if any assets remain, those assets poured over to the trust. Under such a view, the best result might be realization of gain or loss on the repayment in kind.

Alternatively, however, the government might argue that the proper treatment of the extinguishment by merger is for the trust to claim a bad debt deduction under §166 to reflect the economic detriment suffered by the trust, and for the estate to report income representing its economic benefit. Under that analysis a wash would not necessarily result for income tax purposes, considering the different taxpayers,[45] different tax brackets, different tax years, and the fact that the trust may not qualify for the §166 deduction (because, presumably, it could not show that the debt became "worthless." See Treas. Reg. §1.166-2). Any income tax treatment might be avoided if the discharge qualified as a gift but, under §102(a), presumably there is no disinterested generosity in the case of a trust as the creditor because of state law fiduciary obligations. Thus, by comparison, extinguishing the debt produces a result that may be worse than a sale or exchange, particularly if assets are selected carefully to minimize any realization of gain on a true repayment.

Another suggestion heard on occasion is that the estate should borrow from a conventional lender, pledging estate assets as collateral and using the loan proceeds to pay estate settlement costs. Then, instead of repaying that loan, the suggestion is that the estate transfer the encumbered estate assets to the irrevocable insurance trust, subject to the debt, with the trust thereafter repaying the loan. For income tax purposes this is no different than a sale of the assets to the trust for the amount of the outstanding loan balance.[46] Worse, the estate might find the government arguing that this transaction is no different in substance than if the trust had simply paid the estate's settlement costs directly (rather than using the conventional lender as a facilitator, through whom money was cycled), resulting in ordinary income with no available argument that payment was a gift by the trust. Again, this treatment would be worse than the simple sale approach for moving liquidity into the estate. Indeed, the government might even argue for §2042(1) inclusion of the proceeds, because the trust effectively used the proceeds to pay the estate's tax liability.

---

case extinguishment was part of the consideration given in a tax free §368 reorganization under which no gain or loss was recognized. In this respect those cases seem fundamentally dissimilar and probably would be distinguished.

45. The §645 election to treat the trust and estate as a single taxpayer is *not* available because this is planning for an *irrevocable* life insurance trust and the election is only available for revocable inter vivos trusts.

46. See Crane v. Commissioner, 331 U.S. 1 (1947).

A final alternative for infusing liquidity into an insured's estate probably is the most uncertain for tax purposes. Under this approach the trustee of the irrevocable insurance trust would exercise discretion granted under the trust to distribute proceeds to the estate, which would then pay estate settlement costs with no repayment obligation. The issue is the estate tax §2042(1) inclusion consequences of discretionary voluntary distributions to the estate.

The better reasoned analysis appears to be that the proceeds are not includible merely because the beneficiary of them might make contributions to the insured's estate in its unfettered discretion.[47] There are other tax consequences to consider even if the discretion alone will not cause inclusion of the proceeds in the insured's gross estate (upon which issue there is considerable doubt) and assuming the insured is willing to assume the risk that the trustee might not exercise the discretion and the estate will be left without the needed liquidity.

For example, the trust presumably cannot make a gift to the insured's estate, meaning that gift tax liability should not be a concern. For income tax purposes, however, if the estate ultimately pours over into the trust it seems possible for the government to argue that the substance of the transaction is a sale. And it may be equally plausible for the government to argue for an ordinary income treatment (from the trust effectively satisfying the estate's legal obligations in the form of estate settlement costs paid with trust assets), meaning that the sale result might be the best conclusion that might be reached. These consequences probably are more risky than those involving a legitimate loan, because §2042(1) might be deemed to apply, and neither result seems as certain or risk reduced as a simple sale before asset values cause significant gain or loss consequences.

If the estate and generation-skipping transfer taxes have been repealed and carryover basis has become the law, a §2042(1) consequence no longer will be of concern and minimizing income tax consequences will be the prime objective. Thus, some planners may wish to provide for several

---

47. See Horn, *Using Insurance Proceeds Not Included in Insured's Gross Estate to Provide Liquidity*, 13 C.L.U.J. 44, 49-50 (1979) (taking the position that the proceeds are not includible absent an obligation to make contributions, even to the extent the proceeds in fact are contributed to the estate), citing Huff, USE OF TRUSTS IN ESTATE PLANNING 238 (1977) (taking the position that discretion alone will not cause inclusion but that the proceeds are includible to the extent actual contributions are made to the insured's estate). Case law on point is very limited: see Estate of Wade v. Commissioner, 47 B.T.A. 21 (1942), Old Colony Trust Co. v. Commissioner, 39 B.T.A. 871 (1939), and Rev. Rul 77-157 (no inclusion if the proceeds are not used); and Hooper v. Commissioner, 41 B.T.A. 114 (1940) (dicta stating that inclusion would result to the extent used, relying on a case in which the trustee was directed to make payments). Estate of Rohnert v. Commissioner, 40 B.T.A. 1319 (1939), held that inclusion would not result to the extent the proceeds exceeded taxes payable, but inclusion did result to the extent proceeds *could* have been used, even though they were not. See also Bintliff v. United States, 462 F.2d 403 (5th Cir. 1972); Estate of Matthews v. Commissioner, 3 T.C. 525 (1944); Estate of Reinhold v. Commissioner, 3 T.C.M. (CCH) 285 (1944) (proceeds in excess of a collateral assignment were not includible).

different approaches in the alternative, hedging their bets until it is more clear what the situation is going to be after the insured's death.

Income Tax Exclusion

For estate planning purposes the primary income tax issue relating to life insurance essentially is to avoid losing the §101(a)(1) exclusion from income for amounts paid by reason of the insured's death. The increase in wealth represented by life insurance proceeds payable on the death of the insured is excluded from income, similar to the income tax exclusion under §102 for gifts, bequests, devises, or inheritance. But the §101(a)(1) exclusion does not extend to any income earned by investment of the underlying windfall. Thus, proceeds left on deposit with the insurer and paid with interest incur income tax liability to the extent of the interest element, as if the proceeds had been paid in a lump sum and the beneficiary then invested that amount in an interest bearing asset. See §§101(c) and 101(d). The interest payments are includible in the beneficiary's gross income but the proceeds retained by the insurer are excluded from income when finally paid.

As an illustration that reveals some of the complexity in this rule, assume that $296,000 of insurance proceeds are payable to beneficiary B in the form of a straight life monthly annuity. At the insured's death assume that B's life expectancy is 29.6 years, as determined under mortality tables prescribed by §101(d)(2)(B)(ii), and the monthly payment is $1,208, determined by reference to a table in the policy that considers the payment option selected. In this case assume that payments total $4.08 per month per $1,000 of insurance. Thus, B will receive $14,496 per year, some portion of which is attributable to the $296,000 face amount of the policy and the balance of which is attributable to the delayed payment over B's expected life.

Because B has an expected life of 29.6 years, the portion attributable to the face amount is $10,000 annually ($296,000 ÷ 29.6 years) and the $4,496 annual excess is income includible in B's gross income. Unlike the annuity rules under §72, this exclusion portion will not change even if B outlives the assumed 29.6 year life expectancy. See Treas. Reg. §1.101-4(c). Moreover, these rules apply whether the insured selected the annuity payment settlement option or the beneficiary elected to receive the proceeds in that form, §101 being applicable instead of the normal annuity rules under §72. See Commissioner v. Pierce, 146 F.2d 388 (2d Cir. 1944), and the implicit acceptance of this proposition revealed in the first sentence of Treas. Reg. §1.101-4(c). This part is easy.

Now assume that the settlement option contains a refund feature providing for payments after B's death before receiving a guaranteed minimum payment. In this case the discounted present value of the refund feature must be ascertained, using the insurer's interest rate assumptions and the mortality assumptions in the regulations. This amount is subtracted from the face value of the policy proceeds, the remaining sum is pro rated over B's life expectancy, and the excess of the annual payments constitutes income to B. See Treas. Reg. §§1.101-4(c), 1.101-4(e), and 1.101-4(g) Example (7). So, for illustration purposes, if the discounted present value of the refund is $59,200, the remaining face amount would be $236,800, the proration amount would be $8,000 ($236,800 ÷ 29.6 years) and, if the annual payment of $14,496 also was reduced (say, by the same 20% figure, to $11,597 per year) to reflect the refund feature, the excess (in this case $3,597) still would be income. Any payments made to the refund beneficiary also will be excludible from gross income to the extent determined under comparable procedures. See Treas. Reg. §1.101-4(d)(3).

The income tax exclusion does not carry through from one recipient of proceeds to distributees of that recipient. Thus, for example, proceeds collected by a corporation as owner of a policy may be excluded from the corporation's gross income under §101(a), but if paid to shareholders the proceeds lose their identity and are taxable as any other dividend. Rev. Rul. 71-79. The proceeds also are includible in the corporation's earnings and profits and therefore are subject to alternative minimum tax under §56(g)(4)(B)(i) and Treas. Reg. §1.312-6(b). For a comparison to the income tax treatment of proceeds payable to an LLC (which generally follows partnership tax rules) see Mittelman & Balter, *Using Life Insurance to Fund Buy-Sell Agreements for LLCs*, 29 EST. PLAN. 460 (2002).

Similarly, proceeds paid to an estate or trust may not be includible in the entity's gross income and therefore will not increase distributable net income, but may carry income out to a distributee as would any other corpus distribution. The reason for this, quite simply, is that there is no rule in the Code that preserves the character of this income the way the Code does for tax exempt income. See Ferguson, Freeland, & Ascher, FEDERAL INCOME TAXATION OF ESTATES, TRUSTS AND BENEFICIARIES §7.06[A] n.2 (3d ed. 1998).

The §101 exclusion does not apply to payments that are not attributable to death of the insured. Thus, for example, the surrender or lapse of a policy may generate taxable income to the extent amounts received (including prior loans that are repaid out of policy cash values) exceed the owner's basis in the policy (basically premiums paid for the risk portion and cash value, less dividends declared as a return of premium). Treas. Reg. §1.72-6(a)(1)(i). Premiums allocable to such enhancements as a waiver of premiums benefit, accidental death multiples, additional purchase options, or an inflation rider do not add to the basis in the underlying policy. For numerous reasons, not limited to ascertaining what premium dollars are allocable to what portions of the coverage, the only way to be certain of the basis in a policy is to inquire of the insurer.

In addition, assignment of an endowment policy or collection under it may generate income. Under §72(h) the owner of an endowment or other contract that calls for a lump sum payment may elect within 60 days after the contract matures to receive an annuity instead, in which case the §72(b) annuity exclusion ratio rules become applicable. Thus, installment payments are treated as consisting of a return of a pro rata portion of the annuitant's basis or investment in the policy and a taxable income portion. Note that the investment in the contract may not be equal to the total premiums paid, if supplementary benefits also are provided under the contract. Furthermore, the annuity installment payments are treated as entirely taxable income after the annuity has paid sufficient installments to return the annuitant's entire basis under this pro rata recovery approach. Finally, if the annuitant dies before fully recovering the investment in the contract, then the annuitant's estate is entitled to deduct the unrecovered amount on the annuitant's final income tax return. §72(b)(3).

Transfer-For-Value Exception

If a policy was sold or exchanged, income is recognized under the §101(a)(2) transfer-for-value exception to the §101(a)(1) exclusion of insurance proceeds from gross income. When this transfer-for-value rule applies the proceeds become subject to income tax inclusion to the extent they exceed any consideration given for the transfer and any premiums subsequently paid by the transferee.[48] Thus, to illustrate, consider the most common case of an inadvertent transfer for value that will cause a loss of the exclusion from income. Assume a policy is transferred subject to an outstanding policy loan. The amount of that debt is treated as an amount realized to the transferor under the classic authority of Crane v. Commissioner, 331 U.S. 1 (1947), and the transfer is treated as a sale even if no other consideration is exchanged. In this case the policy proceeds in excess of the policy debt (and any subsequently paid premiums) would be taxable as income.

Normally a policy loan is repaid from the proceeds at death. When this occurs every dollar received by the beneficiary is the excess over the policy debt (which constituted the consideration paid). This makes every dollar received includible in the beneficiary's gross income (less any amount representing premiums paid by the new owner after the transfer). Similarly, and far easier to protect against (because it is much more obvious), an outright sale or taxable exchange of a policy could cause the same disastrous result. See §1035 with respect to exchanges of policies that are ignored for income tax purposes.

Fortunately, several exceptions to the transfer-for-value rule will prevent loss of the exclusion from income. For example, the most useful exception usually is §101(a)(2)(A), which provides that a transfer for value is harmless *if* (*not* to the extent) the adjusted basis of the policy in the transferee's hands is determined in whole or in part by reference to the

---

48. See Treas. Reg. §1.101-1(b)(5) for examples of the operation of this rule relating to premiums paid after an acquisition for value.

basis in the transferor's hands. A good example of the operation of this rule is a part-sale, part-gift transaction under which basis to the transferee is the greater of cost (the amount paid or deemed paid, as in the case of a gratuitous transfer subject to a policy debt) or carryover of the transferor's adjusted basis. See Treas. Reg. §1.1015-4.

Under this exception to the transfer-for-value rule, if the amount paid (the policy debt) is lower than the transferor's basis, then basis to the transferee will be a carryover from the transferor. That means the transfer-for-value exception to the §101(a)(1) exclusion is avoided in its entirety. But missing this relation by even a little bit (for example, because the transferor's basis is just a dollar less than the amount of the policy debt) will cause loss of the entire protection of this exception to the transfer-for-value rule. Another application of this rule that ought to apply (although there appears to be no authority on point yet) is a transfer for value to the transferor's spouse, with nonrecognition and a carryover basis under §1041.

The other reliable exception to the transfer-for-value rule is §101(a)(2)(B), which precludes application of the rule to a sale (or exchange) of a policy to the insured, a partner of the insured, a partnership of which the insured is a partner, or a corporation in which the insured is an officer or shareholder. Thus, by simple example, the transfer-for-value rule would not apply if the insured is a principal in a corporation that owns a key person policy that the corporation wants to sell to the insured.

Similarly, if the policy was held by other shareholders (for example, to finance their purchase obligations under a buy-sell agreement) and they wanted to sell their policies to the corporation or to the insured, those transfers also would be immune to the transfer-for-value rule. Unfortunately, this exception would not apply if those shareholders sold to each other, not to the corporation or to the insured. Nevertheless, it could be *made* to apply if those shareholders instead were partners with the insured, a crazy distinction and one that therefore requires diligence.

Curiously, if there were disqualifying transfers followed by a transfer that is protected, it is the last in time that governs the income tax consequences. So a "bad" transfer followed by a cleansing "good" transfer can cure the problem if identified before the insurance matures. See Treas. Reg. §§1.101-1(b)(3)(ii) and 1.101-1(b)(5) Examples (5) and (7). In this respect, if a transfer for value to a spouse, generating a §1041 carryover of basis, will enable the §101(a)(2)(A) exception and if this last transfer would cleanse a prior bad transfer, it is conceivable that many disqualifying transfers can be cleansed by intraspousal transfers, if the issue is identified before the insured's death.

A very valuable application of the exception to the transfer-for-value rule applies for transfers to the insured. The treatment of a grantor trust is as if the trust was the grantor personally. This exception to the transfer-for-value rule is applicable if the insured is the grantor of a trust to which a policy is transferred for value. See Swanson v. Commissioner, 518 F.2d 59 (8th Cir. 1975). This is a potentially powerful method to cleanse the income tax hickey of the transfer-for-value rule because a grantor trust may be drafted such that estate tax inclusion is avoidable. Again, however, caution is required, because in this case the exception to the transfer-for-value rule is under "extensive study" by the government, which will not issue letter rulings if substantially all of the corpus of a trust is insurance policies on the life of the grantor or the grantor's spouse, the trustee has a power to pay premiums on that insurance using trust income, the trustee also has a power to use the insurance proceeds to purchase assets from or make loans to the estate of the insured, and any grantor trust rule makes the trust a grantor trust. See, e.g., the latest iteration in §3.01(5) of Rev. Proc. 2004-3 (updated annually).

Policy Exchanges

Sometimes it is advisable or desirable to "trade in" or exchange one insurance policy for another. An exchange is not an income tax gain or loss realization event if the contracts are comparable (for example, an insurance contract is exchanged for another insurance contract, or an annuity contract is exchanged for an annuity contract) and in some cases even if they are not so comparable (for example, an insurance contract may be swapped for an endowment life or annuity contract, but not vice versa). See the express language of §1035, providing that an exchange of an endowment policy for a life insurance contract would not be excepted.

Problems can arise, however, if the insured is altered under the policies,[49] or if a direct contract-for-contract exchange does not occur. For example, in a case of first impression involving a voluntary surrender of one annuity contract in exchange for cash that immediately was used to acquire a replacement annuity contract issued by another company, the court concluded that neither authority nor logic supported the government's position that nonrecognition should apply only if there was a binding obligation to use the cash to acquire the replacement policy. Greene v. Commissioner, 85 T.C. 1024 (1985), acq. in result. The government adhered to its original position in *Greene* to hold in Technical Advice Memorandum 9346002 that endorsement of a check representing the proceeds payable under one annuity in exchange for issuance of another annuity was not a qualified §1035 exchange that would entitle the replacement policy to the protection of

---

49. See Rev. Rul. 90-109 (the replacement policy was business related key person coverage that substituted one individual as insured for another, as permitted under a "change of insured" provision in the policy), which held that the change of the insured under an existing policy is sufficiently fundamental that the original contract was not just modified and the exchange did not qualify for §1035 nonrecognition, even though Treas. Reg. §1.1035-1(c) imposes a "same insured" requirement in the context of an exchange of annuities and Treas. Reg. §1.1035-1(a) does not contain a comparable requirement for life insurance contract exchanges.

§72(s). In addition, there may be boot on an otherwise qualified policy exchange, to the extent a policy loan is extinguished rather than matched with a loan against the replacement policy. See §1031(b); Treas. Reg. §1.1031(d)-2; cf. Private Letter Ruling 8604033. And other ancillary issues can arise that make policy exchanges risky if completely nontaxable exchange treatment is important.[50]

Estate Taxation

A citizen or resident[51] decedent's gross estate includes the value of insurance proceeds from a policy on the life of the decedent under §2042(1) "to the extent of the amount received by the [decedent's] executor," or under §2042(2) "to the extent of the amount receivable by all other beneficiaries . . . with respect to which the decedent possessed at . . . death any of the incidents of ownership" of the policy. In a planned estate large enough to be taxable it would be uncommon to find insurance proceeds payable to or for the benefit of the insured decedent's personal representative. So inclusion under §2042(1) seldom is applicable in planned situations.

Instead, it is the §2042(2) "incidents of ownership" test that causes most insurance proceeds to be includible in an insured decedent's gross estate. Under this test the possession of *any* incident of ownership will cause the *full* value of the proceeds to be includible in the estate of the insured decedent, and incidents held jointly (even with an adverse party) or the mere power to veto another person's exercise of incidents will suffice to trigger §2042(2) inclusion.

The term "incident of ownership" includes any direct or indirect interest, power, or right that gives the insured decedent any economic enjoyment, benefit, or control over the policy or its proceeds. This includes: any power to change the beneficiary or the settlement option; any right to surrender, cancel, assign, or revoke an assignment of the policy; and the ability to pledge the policy for a loan, or to borrow directly against the surrender value of the policy. See Treas. Reg. §20.2042-1(c)(2).

---

50. See, e.g., General Counsel Memorandum 39728 (notwithstanding that an exchange of one insurance policy for another was a qualified nontaxable transaction for purposes of §1035, and even though the holding period of the new policy and the old policy would tack under §1035, for purposes of the §264(a)(3) interest expense deduction limitations the new policy was regarded as a newly purchased policy that was not entitled to the chronological exemption of the exchanged policy); Technical Advice Memorandum 9346002 (the replacement contract was subject to §1014(b)(9)(A) and denied the basis adjustment that would have been available had it not been exchanged after 1979 for a chronologically exempt annuity contract).

51. Any amount received as insurance on the life of a nonresident not a citizen is regarded as property not situated within the United States and therefore not includible in that insured decedent's gross estate for federal estate tax purposes. See §§2103 (limiting includible property to that which is situated in the United States) and 2105(a) (specifying that life insurance proceeds on the life of a nonresident not a citizen is deemed to be not within the United States).

Because they are a return of excess premiums paid and not some form of economic return on an investment, dividends and the right to receive them or apply them under policy options are *not* an incident of ownership. In addition, the power to convert a noncontributory group term life insurance policy upon either voluntary or involuntary termination of employment is not an incident of ownership, nor should be a contingent power to purchase a policy (such as employer funded or buy-sell funding coverage), although the result with respect to that power is not yet clear.

Life insurance policies that constitute community property are taxed in the same manner as other community assets. Thus, if a community property policy names only one spouse as the insured, only half the proceeds will be includible in the insured decedent's gross estate, because any incident of ownership "possessed by the decedent as agent for [a spouse] with respect to one-half of the policy is not . . . an 'incident of ownership', and the decedent is, therefore, deemed to possess an incident of ownership in only one-half of the policy." Treas. Reg. §20.2042-1(c)(5). See also Rev. Rul. 2003-40.

Incidents Held in a Fiduciary Capacity

The proceeds of insurance normally will escape inclusion in an insured decedent's gross estate if the policy is issued initially to a third party owner or if incidents of ownership originally owned by the insured decedent are transferred or assigned properly to a third person. Nevertheless, care is appropriate to guarantee that the third party owner does not bequeath the incidents back to the insured if the transferee predeceases the insured. It also probably is wise to preclude the insured from acting in a fiduciary capacity as owner of the policy or any of its incidents. Although case law strongly supports the notion that incidents held as a fiduciary will not cause inclusion,[52] that proposition is not universally accepted[53] and the government's own position in Rev. Rul. 84-179 is that:

a decedent will not be deemed to have incidents of ownership over an insurance policy on the decedent's life where the decedent's powers are held in a fiduciary capacity, and are not exercisable for the decedent's personal benefit, where the decedent did not transfer the policy or any of the consideration for purchasing or maintaining the policy to the trust from personal assets, and the

---

52. See Hunter v. United States, 624 F.2d 833 (8th Cir. 1980); Estate of Margrave v. Commissioner, 618 F.2d 34 (8th Cir. 1980); Connelly v. United States, 551 F.2d 545 (3d Cir. 1977); Estate of Skifter v. Commissioner, 468 F.2d 699 (2d Cir. 1972); Estate of Fruehauf v. Commissioner, 427 F.2d 80 (6th Cir. 1970); Estate of Fuchs v. Commissioner, 47 T.C. 199 (1966).

53. See Terriberry v. United States, 517 F.2d 286 (5th Cir. 1975); Rose v. United States, 511 F.2d 259 (5th Cir. 1975).

devolution of the powers on decedent was not part of a prearranged plan involving the participation of decedent.

Care is required to ensure that none of the three conditions swallows the government's acquiescence to the majority rule.

In addition, the government might assert that incidents could be attributed to an insured decedent who could remove and replace trustees, even if the insured could not be named as a successor, due to the power that the right to remove and replace gave the decedent over the trustee. See Technical Advice Memorandum 8922003, relying on the revolving door power concept articulated by the government in Rev. Rul. 79-353, as discussed in Chapter 6 at page 12. Although the concept supporting that argument also appears to have been abandoned by the government in the most part, the government's capitulation is not complete.[54] Consequently, employing the drafting device of naming an insurance advisor with respect to policies on the fiduciary's own life and precluding the fiduciary from exercising any incidents of ownership with respect to those policies might be a wise precaution if the insured otherwise is the most appropriate choice as fiduciary.

Incidents Held by Controlled Corporation

Incidents of ownership held by an entity (such as a corporation or partnership) may be attributed under Treas. Reg. §20.2042-1(c)(6) to a controlling shareholder or partner who is the insured. This will occur only to the extent the proceeds are not payable to or for the benefit of the entity.[55] The critical notion is whether the insured decedent's ownership of the entity reflects an increase in the business net worth attributable to payment of those proceeds. See Treas. Reg. §20.2031-2(f). Required is control ownership of the entity by the decedent (with aggregation of stock held in voting trusts or a vanilla trust that is regarded as an income tax grantor trust).

The policy is treated as owned by the decedent personally to the extent inclusion is generated by the attribution of incidents of ownership from a controlled entity to the insured decedent. Presumably this should permit marital deduction qualification due to inclusion if the beneficiary is the insured decedent's surviving spouse, and it also means that the exclusion from income under either §101 or §102 should apply.

---

54. See Rev. Rul. 95-58, which abandons the revolving door theory only if a successor trustee cannot be a related or subordinate party.

55. For example, with respect to corporate split dollar insurance, the amount subject to inclusion due to attributed incidents is limited to the portion not paid to the corporation as the financing party. See, e.g., Rev. Rul. 76-274 (describing various situations illustrating whether a decedent or a controlled corporation possessed sufficient incidents of ownership under a split dollar plan to require inclusion in the decedent's gross estate).

Estate Taxation If Owner Is Not the Insured

Estate tax inclusion also is an issue if the policy owner is not the insured. If the owner dies while owning a policy that is not yet matured, the policy itself is includible (under §2033 or under one of the string provisions) like any other asset an individual may own at death. The estate tax value is determined much the same as is the gift tax value when a policy is transferred inter vivos. See Treas. Reg. §20.2031-8(a) regarding estate tax valuation. This is most common with respect to spouse owned life insurance if the insured spouse does not die first.

Transfers Within Three Years of Insured's Death

Getting rid of incidents of ownership is a critical technique to reduce the tax value of a client's estate, and life insurance planning often is among the easiest ways to eliminate tax liability. But it can't be done too close to death because a transfer of incidents of ownership to a third party may trigger the three year rule of §2035(a). This provision requires inclusion of life insurance proceeds if the insured decedent dies within three years after transferring ownership of the policy or any of its incidents.

For example, assume that the decedent owned a controlling interest in a closely held business that owned insurance on the decedent's life. The policy proceeds are includible in the decedent's gross estate at death if the beneficiary of that insurance is not the business itself. See Treas. Reg. §20.2042-1(c)(6), just discussed at page 46. More importantly, the insured decedent could not avoid this inclusion result by having the corporation transfer the insurance within three years of the insured's death. Rev. Rul. 82-141. Nor may the decedent preclude inclusion by divesting the controlling interest in the corporation within the three year period. Rev. Rul. 90-21. Either inclusion result presumably could be avoided if the transfer of either the decedent's controlling interest in the corporation or the corporation's interest in the policy was for full and adequate consideration in money or money's worth, but the proper value of the requisite consideration is the amount that would be includible if no transfer were made and not just the gift tax value of the policy.

Even if a transfer is made within three years of death, however, a number of authorities establish the proposition that the amount includible is limited to a portion of the proceeds determined by the ratio of premiums paid by the insured decedent to total premiums paid. See Estate of Silverman v. Commissioner, 521 F.2d 574 (2d Cir. 1975). Thus, it may be desirable during the first three years after a transfer (while the three year rule still applies) for the transferee or any other third party to pay all premiums, without any direct or indirect assistance from the insured. Thereafter, premium payment by the insured decedent on a policy transferred more than three years before death (or on any policy never transferred by the insured) is harmless and will not cause estate tax §2035(a) inclusion. See Rev. Rul. 71-497. Exclusion occurs because premium payment by the insured will not trigger application of §2035(a) if the policy itself is not subject to the three year rule, even if the premiums are paid within three years of the insured's death, and neither the premiums paid nor a portion of the proceeds paid at death is includible if the policy was not transferred by the insured within three years of death.

To illustrate, Private Letter Ruling 8724014 applied this rule to group term insurance, the important aspect being that premiums paid from inception of the policy were used in determining the amount includible, not just those premiums paid in the year of the insured decedent's death. This was not favorable to the taxpayer, who would have preferred to regard the final premium paid (by a third party) as purchasing the entire term insurance payable at death. Still, the Ruling is particularly significant because the decedent actually paid the annual premiums but the decedent's children reimbursed those payments, with that reimbursement regarded as if the children had been the original payors.

A different and perhaps the most controversial issue involving life insurance and the three year rule entails a third party's acquisition of a policy initially from the insurer (so there is no transfer of insurance incidents from the insured decedent) coupled with premium payment directly or indirectly by the insured decedent. Whether the owner is a trust (which often is preferable because it can accomplish wealth transfer tax minimization in the beneficiaries' estates) or an individual, the government wants to find a way to regard the transaction as if the insured decedent owned the incidents and transferred them to another, thereby triggering the §2035(a) three year rule.

In this context the government's theory has been a beamed transfer, deemed agency, constructive transfer analog, as if the decedent acquired the policy and then made a conveyance, all attributable to the fact that the insured decedent is financing the purchase of the insurance. After some initial success, the government now routinely loses these cases and it appears reasonably well settled that §2035(a) will not apply. Thus, providing the premiums will not cause estate tax inclusion if the decedent-insured never owns the policy.

Thus, the preferred planning approach is creation of an irrevocable life insurance trust followed by the trustee making application for insurance on the settlor's life. Done properly this is an easy and effective way to increase the taxpayer's wealth without tax consequence, the only essential aspect being that the insured must never touch the policy or any of its incidents of ownership. If you begin work with a client who already owns a policy, the same plan would require that the client live three years after creation of the irrevocable trust and transfer of a policy to it.

Policy Facts Versus Intent

In addition to making an effective transfer more than three years before the insured decedent's death, you must read the boilerplate provisions of an insurance contract carefully to avoid an inadvertent retention of any incident of ownership. The issue whether "policy facts" or "intent of the parties" should govern (for example, if the policy is mistakenly issued to the wrong person as owner) also is worthy of concern, because deviation from the policy based on error is litigated with little success by taxpayers.[56]

Gift Taxation

When transfer tax minimization is an objective, it usually is preferable if insurance is applied for and owned initially by a third party. Often, however, that is not an option and a transfer of an existing insurance policy owned by the insured to a third party becomes desirable to minimize the estate tax attributable to that coverage. (But for the commission paid on a new issue, or lack of insurability when the problem is uncovered, a desirable alternative would be to terminate the existing policy and start over with a new policy never owned by the insured.) Because sale of a policy may generate adverse consequences under the transfer-for-value rule, a gratuitous transfer (a gift for gift tax purposes) often will occur.

The value of that gift is the replacement cost if the policy is brand new, but normally the policy has been in force for some time before the gift. For these more common cases, value is the interpolated terminal reserve value of the policy plus the value of any unearned premiums (or, if the policy is paid up, the cost of a comparable single premium replacement policy).[57] Old case law suggests that the gift tax value may be higher if the

---

56. See, e.g., United States v. Rhode Island Hospital Trust Co., 355 F.2d 7 (1st Cir. 1966); but cf. Private Letter Ruling 8610068 (an insurance policy showed a corporation as beneficiary and the decedent as owner, notwithstanding that other policies on the decedent's life showed the corporation as both owner and beneficiary; the government concluded that the facts surrounding acquisition of these policies showed that the policy listing the decedent as owner was in error and held that §2042(2) was not applicable), citing Estate of Fuchs v. Commissioner, 47 T.C. 199 (1960), acq., and stating that: "When an insurance contract is mistakenly drawn up in a manner which does not reflect the intent of the parties, the insurance proceeds are not includible in the decedent's estate." To the same effect, holding intent facts to prevail over the policy facts, is Technical Advice Memorandum 9651004 (insurance policies assigned four years before death to an irrevocable trust were erroneously reissued in the insured's name within one year of death and then reissued to reflect the trust as owner; the insurer's error did not cause the insured to possess incidents of ownership within three years of death for §2035(a) purposes). For a comprehensive summary of the law on this issue see Haight, *Policy Facts and Incidents of Ownership Under Estate Tax Section 2042(2): The Legacy of* Rhode Island Hospital Trust, 28 DUQUESNE L. REV. 109 (1989).

57. See Treas. Reg. §25.2512-6(a). Form 938 will be provided by the insurer to verify the value of the gift, and efforts to guess the value of a policy should be avoided because often it is difficult to accurately determine the value of a policy for gift tax purposes (after reflecting policy dividends and other factors about which the lay observer may be unaware). Therefore, gift tax valuation should be confirmed with Form 938 before proceeding with any gift tax sensitive plan. In a term policy at the very end of the premium term the value may be unascertainable (zero) or close to it. Cf. Rev. Rul. 76-490.

insured is uninsurable when the gift is made and may even approach face value if the insured is in the terminal stage of a fatal illness.[58]

In all events, however, the policy value may be reduced if the owner borrows against any cash surrender value of a permanent policy, thereby reducing the value of the equity in the contract. The method for repaying the policy loan must be considered, however, and it must be ascertained that the loan balance is less than the owner's adjusted basis in the policy. Otherwise, a transfer subject to a debt (which may not be repaid until the policy matures and proceeds are set off against the unpaid balance) will constitute a transfer for value, with disastrous income tax consequences, as discussed at page 41. It also might constitute an indirect payment to the insured decedent's estate, with §2042(1) inclusion consequences.[59]

The gift of a life insurance policy and any gifts represented by future payment of any premiums on that policy all may qualify for the gift tax annual exclusion as gifts of a present interest. The requirements here are the same as for any other gift, based on the rights and ownership of the transferee.[60] For example, a present interest is created if the incidents of ownership are transferred outright, regardless of the beneficiary designation under the policy at the time of the transfer. A present interest exists because the transferee acquires complete power as owner of the acquired incidents of ownership to change the beneficiary, to borrow against the policy value, or to surrender it for its cash value. If the transfer is to or for the benefit of a minor the same options for present interest gifts to minors exist as with any other asset, including outright or in a §2503(c) qualified minor's trust.

An inadvertent gift may occur if the ownership of a policy is transferred either by endorsement or by assignment and the transferee does not thereafter receive the proceeds as beneficiary when the policy matures. For example, in Rev. Rul. 94-49, the insured decedent's surviving spouse was deemed to own 100% of a policy of insurance on the decedent's life (notwithstanding payment of all premiums with community property funds), which avoided estate tax inclusion of any of the proceeds in the insured decedent's gross estate. But payment of the proceeds to a third party beneficiary resulted in a gift of the full amount of the proceeds by the spouse to that beneficiary, because the policy was the spouse's separate property. See Treas. Reg. 25.2511-1(h)(9).

Furthermore, any gift tax liability is particularly difficult to deal with because the transferee will not have the proceeds with which to pay the tax. Worse, the §2206 estate tax reimbursement right does not apply to gift

---

58. United States v. Ryerson, 312 U.S. 260 (1941); Estate of Pritchard v. Commissioner, 4 T.C. 204 (1944).

59. See Bintliff v. United States, 462 F.2d 403 (5th Cir. 1972); Estate of Tracy v. United States, 82-2 U.S. Tax Cas. (CCH) ¶13,499 (W.D. N.C. 1982).

60. Treas. Reg. §25.2503-3(c) Examples (2) and (6); Rev. Rul. 55-408.

taxes. In addition to spouse owned insurance cases, this problem is particularly likely to occur in any community property situation to the extent a policy and its proceeds are deemed to be community property but the surviving spouse is not a beneficiary with respect to half of the policy.

Fortunately, "with most [insurance] companies, the change of ownership will automatically nullify any previous beneficiary arrangement. If nothing is done, the [new owner] will become the beneficiary of the policy proceeds.... [However, if] ownership is transferred, a new beneficiary designation should be completed and filed with the insurance company." Munch, FINANCIAL AND ESTATE PLANNING WITH LIFE INSURANCE PRODUCTS at 162 (1990). In all cases, it may be wise to avoid the possibility of an inadvertent gift by changing the beneficiary designation before any transfer occurs, naming the anticipated transferee as beneficiary.

Furthermore, careful attention should be devoted to the contract itself to determine how a transfer is permitted. For example, Commissioner v. Estate of Noel, 380 U.S. 678 (1965), concluded that the policies could not be assigned, nor could the beneficiary even be changed, without written endorsement on the policies. Because this had not occurred (notwithstanding the insured decedent's purported gift of the policies just after their purchase and prior to boarding an airplane that subsequently crashed) the insured retained the incidents of ownership and §2042(2) inclusion was warranted.

Crummey Clause Powers of Withdrawal

A problem that must be addressed for gift tax purposes if a policy is owned by a third party is how to pay the premiums. In some cases the owner is an individual who can afford to pay the premiums, but the more common third party owner is an irrevocable insurance trust. Most of those are unfunded, meaning that the insured (or someone who agrees to assist in the premium payment) must provide the funds with which to pay the annual premiums. Typically the funds are provided through annual gifts to the trust, with the gift tax cost of the transfer being minimized through qualification for the gift tax annual exclusion. See Treas. Reg. §25.2511-1(h)(8). In the context of group term insurance the employer's premium payment is an indirect gift in the amount determined by reference to Treas. Reg. §1.79-3(d)(2).

Because the benefits under such a trust are delayed until the insured dies and the proceeds of the insurance are paid, the unfunded irrevocable insurance trust will not qualify for the gift tax annual exclusion unless it is modified to give the beneficiaries a present entitlement of some sort. This is required because of the annual exclusion present interest rule. See Treas. Reg. §25.2503-3. The typical present beneficial interest that is given for this purpose is a power to withdraw trust property (either the policy originally contributed to the trust or annual contributions that are made to the trust before they are used to pay premiums). Typically the withdrawal right extends to the policy only in cases in which premiums are paid directly to the insurer by a third party, such as by an employer providing group term insurance coverage that is assigned to the trust and that names the trust as beneficiary. Existing authorities hold that these power of withdrawal rights constitute the various transfers into the trust as present interests for annual exclusion purposes.[61]

The Crummey clause power of withdrawal technique is simple to employ. Contributions are made to qualify for the gift tax annual exclusion simply by granting someone a power to withdraw the amounts contributed to the trust. Only a few significant requirements must be met to assure the government that the power is legitimate. For example, Rev. Rul. 81-7 required that the beneficiary have a reasonable time within which to exercise the withdrawal power and that the beneficiary (or the beneficiary's personal representative) be aware of the contributions that may be withdrawn. If a minor beneficiary is given the right to demand distributions, the contribution is a present interest if neither the trust instrument nor local law precludes appointment of a guardian who could exercise the withdrawal right on behalf of the minor. See Rev. Rul. 73-405.

Lapse of the withdrawal power can be a taxable event, however, because the power is a general power of appointment for transfer tax purposes. Thus, there can be a cost to the powerholder that is incurred as a trade off for annual exclusion treatment generated with respect to contributions to the trust, both under income tax §678 and wealth transfer tax §§2041 and 2514.

This latter exposure is limited, however, by §2514(e)(1), which excludes on an annual basis the greater of $5,000 or 5% of the value of trust corpus from the definition of an otherwise taxable lapse of a general power of appointment. This "five or five exception" is the source of additional complexity for planning purposes.

The irrevocable insurance trust, with all its refinements, essentially grants Crummey withdrawal powers that create present interest annual exclusion treatment for the donor's contribution of the amount needed to pay the policy premium, with lapses being protected by the five or five limitation of §2514(e). This is no mean feat if the insurance premium is significant, as it may be if the coverage involved makes this form of planning worthwhile. And the quantitative difference between the available annual exclusion and the five or five exception exacerbates the planning problem.

To illustrate, a married donor may contribute up to $22,000 (plus any additional inflation index amount) per beneficiary per year to such a trust

---

61. See Crummey v. Commissioner, 397 F.2d 82 (9th Cir. 1968), from which the name "Crummey clause power of withdrawal" is coined, and Chapter 19 at page 40 for an illustration.

with protection under the annual exclusion (if the donor's spouse splits the gift and their annual exclusions otherwise have not been used). At the same time, however, the trust has zero (or close to it) value, making the five or five exception relevant only with respect to $5,000 per beneficiary per year. For a donor who wants to take full advantage of the annual exclusion, the difficult planning chore is preventing a taxable lapse of a $22,000 Crummey withdrawal right with a $5,000 exception for general power of appointment lapse purposes.

To accomplish this many planners employ a "hanging power." The concept is to give a beneficiary a power to withdraw the full amount of the contribution in the year the contribution is made to the trust, but then allowing the power to lapse only to the extent of the greater of $5,000 or 5% of the value of the trust. The unlapsed portion of the power remains in effect (it "hangs") so that there is no gift tax liability on the contribution to the trust and none with respect to the power of withdrawal. The hanging power lapses in future years (when contributions to the trust are less than the amount that can lapse free of tax), to the extent possible without causing a gift tax. Because it is expected that the hanging portion of the power never will be exercised, the dollars contributed to the trust are used in the year of contribution to pay annual premiums on the policy. And the hope is that, with enough time, the hanging portion eventually will lapse away.

The following example illustrates how the hanging portion is allowed to lapse in future years when the powerholder otherwise would not fully utilize or exhaust the five or five exclusion under §2514(e). It assumes that the annual premium for insurance in the trust is $220,000 and that ten beneficiaries are given Crummey withdrawal rights of $22,000 per beneficiary per year. To the extent of the five or five exclusion, those withdrawal rights lapse in the year of contribution, and the balance hangs. For each beneficiary:

In year one:

Contribution	$22,000	
Lapse	(5,000)	
Hanging portion		17,000

In year two:

Contribution	$22,000	
Lapse	(5,000)	
New hanging portion		17,000
Old hanging portion		17,000
Total hanging portion		34,000

In year three, assume that the cash value of the insurance policy owned by the trust is $120,000; for the first time it exceeds $100,000, so a new limitation for five or five limitation purposes is determined under the 5% exception of §2514(e):

Contribution $22,000	
Lapse (6,000)	
New hanging portion	16,000
Old hanging portion	34,000
Total hanging portion	50,000

In year four, another increase in the cash surrender value allows an even greater lapse amount:

Contribution $22,000	
Lapse (7,200)	
New hanging portion	14,800
Old hanging portion	50,000
Total hanging portion	64,800

In year five[62] assume the policy requires only a small added premium payment because it becomes self sustaining through policy dividends or loans used to pay premiums:

Contribution $3,000	
Lapse (3,000)	
New hanging portion	0
Old hanging portion	64,800
Unused five or five amount (assumed, based on value of trust)	(9,000)
Total hanging portion	55,800

In year six even better facts may arise:

Contribution $0	
Lapse 0	
New hanging portion	0
Old hanging portion	55,800
Unused five or five amount (assume)	(14,000)
Total hanging portion	41,800

In years seven and beyond, in this example, similar facts would allow the hanging portion to be reduced and eventually eliminated.

Under different facts, if the insured dies before the hanging portion is eliminated, allowing a lapse with respect to the full value of the trust after collection of the proceeds similarly would produce a 5% figure that would quickly eliminate the hanging portion. The risk, however, is that the *beneficiary* might die before the hanging power is entirely eliminated, in which case there will be §2041 inclusion of the hanging portion. The other risk is that the beneficiary will exercise the withdrawal right at a time when the trust has funds available. This problem typically does not arise

---

62. Having gotten beyond the §264 four-of-seven problem.

until the insured has died and the insurance has matured into cash proceeds, and is a more significant concern then than it was while the insured was alive and able to impose pressure against withdrawal.

The hanging power also may be problematic for marital deduction qualification purposes if the hanging power remains at the insured's death, if the policy was transferred by the insured within three years of death, and if §2035(a) inclusion therefore triggers a contingent marital deduction provision. The trust could provide that the hanging portion lapses immediately at the insured's death, in this unusual and potentially unique situation with whatever gift tax consequences may flow from that result. It likely would be preferable to incur gift tax rather than estate tax attributable to loss of the marital deduction, although inclusion to the surviving spouse at the second death coupled with current gift tax on lapse of the hanging powers probably is unwise as well. So perhaps losing the marital deduction would be preferable, but only if the trust assets includible when the spouse dies will not include the hanging power amounts.

And, finally, there are generation-skipping transfer tax aspects to be considered with respect to Crummey powers. These include whether contributions to the trust might taint an otherwise chronologically exempt trust, whether contributions qualify for the §2642(c)(2) annual exclusion exemption from the generation-skipping transfer tax, the consequences on the identity of the transferor if a Crummey power lapse exceeds the §2514(e) five or five exception, and whether and then how to allocate exemption to the trust to produce a zero inclusion ratio and leverage that exemption. All of these issues are addressed in Chapter 12.

Chapter 10

RETIREMENT BENEFITS[1]

A very large portion of the wealth of many decedents who were gainfully employed (referred to herein collectively as "participants" rather than as employees, IRA owners, or otherwise) often consists of annuities and other employee benefits and deferred compensation held in various forms of retirement benefit accounts, such as:

- All manner of §401(a) qualified pension, profit sharing, or other retirement plans created by employers;
- §401(c) Keogh plans created by the self employed;
- §403(c) nonqualified retirement plans created by employers for a select group of senior employees;
- §408 individual retirement accounts (IRAs) and simplified employee pensions;
- Many other forms of deferred compensation and retirement arrangements (including Social Security, Railroad Retirement and other such federal or state benefits, stock option plans, death benefit only plans, and the like) that may have survivorship features or death benefits that survive the employee's demise. Most of these are not subject to inclusion in the decedent's gross estate for federal estate tax purposes[2] but they may constitute income in

---

1. One respected commentator on this area of the law has remarked that there are "several thousand rules—count them" that may be relevant. And they seem to be in constant flux. Much of the most useful explanatory material is in the form of continuing education outlines that are not generally commercially available, but a short bibliography of generally accessible resources that may be helpful in finding answers and staying current includes the most recent editions of Choate, LIFE AND DEATH PLANNING FOR RETIREMENT BENEFITS (5th ed. Rev. 2003); and Mezzullo, *Estate and Gift Tax Issues for Employee Benefit Plans*, 814 Tax Mgmt. (BNA) ESTATES, GIFTS & TRUSTS PORT. (1996).

2. There are dozens of such entitlements under various federal, state, and even foreign laws, and the traditional rationale for noninclusion is that these benefits are not payable pursuant to any contract or agreement by reason of employment, making §2039(a) inapplicable. For a sampling see Rev. Rul. 79-35 and Technical Advice Memorandum 8042006 (no inclusion of awards made to decedents whose families were entitled to annuity payments under German laws relating to injustices that occurred when the National Socialist Party took control of Germany); Rev. Rul. 76-102 (exclusion of payments under Federal Coal Mine Health and Safety Act of 1969); Rev. Rul. 76-501 (exclusion of veteran survivors' benefits); Rev. Rul. 77-274 and Rev. Rul. 66-234 (because amounts paid for funeral expenses under veterans' benefits or in a wrongful death action are not includible, no §2053(a)(1) deduction is allowable for those expenses); Rev. Rul. 81-182, Rev. Rul. 75-145, Rev. Rul. 67-277, and Rev. Rul. 55-87 (Social Security benefits payable to an employee's surviving spouse are not includible; the same is true for payments attributable to the tax on self-employment income); Rev. Rul. 56-637 (exclusion of worker compensation payment to dependents); Rev. Rul. 82-5 (survivors' loss benefits payable as an annuity under no fault automobile insurance was not includible); Rev. Rul. 75-127, Rev.

respect of the decedent for income tax purposes (meaning that the recipient will pay income tax on them, much as would the decedent had death not intervened). See Chapter 17 at pages 11-12.

These entitlements are designed principally for retirement purposes and typically only provide a death or survivorship benefit that is ancillary to the primary function of the plan. Although estate planners frequently focus on those elements that will be enjoyed by a decedent's survivors, the inter vivos enjoyment of these entitlements and the rules relevant to their taxation often drive the postmortem options and consequences of those benefits. So keeping one eye on the rules applicable to these assets during a client's life is critical to the estate planning endeavor.

In addition, it is wise to remember concepts that apply to all nonprobate assets and issues that can arise in a nontax context. One illustration concerns retirement benefits and insurance beneficiary designations following divorce. The question is whether a surviving former spouse, designated as the beneficiary prior to the divorce and not thereafter altered, is regarded as predeceased for purposes of any entitlement under that plan or policy. State laws routinely answer this question with respect to wills and probate property.[3] But most jurisdictions have no comparable statute dealing with nonprobate property, meaning the former spouse most likely will continue to benefit.

Finally, as introduction to this material, please be prepared for a very discouraging expedition. Estate planning is the tail on this dog, these benefits are not meant to be preserved, and the rules and options for postmortem enjoyment by those who survive the participant are not facile or very desirable. We do the best we can with this wealth, but it is frustrating and mostly it is not about the kinds of factors we consider elsewhere with other forms of a client's property. Please do not be surprised if you find yourself holding your head and bemoaning that this is a most dissatisfying journey. Sorry — that is just the way it is.

Gift Taxation

To illustrate the concept of retirement versus survivorship benefits, consider the fact that most employee benefit plans contemplate that the employee will live to enjoy various benefits and that there may be no residual death benefits whatsoever. Indeed, normally the lifetime

---

Rul. 75-126, Rev. Rul. 68-88, and Rev. Rul. 54-19 (all reflecting the exclusion of wrongful death recoveries except to the extent amounts received represent damages to which the decedent was entitled during life, such as for pain and suffering or medical expenses); Rev. Rul. 79-397 (public safety officer survivor benefits); Rev. Rul. 2002-39 (firefighter or police officers killed in the line of duty survivor death benefits; inclusion is required under §2033 for that portion of a postmortem payment representing a return of the decedent's own contributions to a pension fund but not for added benefits paid for which there was no entitlement, vested interest, or right to receive payments before death).

3. See the discussion of the analogous issue in life insurance planning in Chapter 9 at page 34.

enjoyment rights under such plans are nontransferable. More to the point, in a qualified plan this is a requisite of the anti-alienation rules found in §401(a)(13). As a consequence, most typical gift tax concerns are irrelevant to most retirement benefit plans.

If the plan permits assignment of benefits, however, and if the participant makes an assignment or an irrevocable beneficiary designation, the value the participant transfers by those acts may constitute a gift for federal gift tax purposes. It may have undesirable income tax consequences as well. See §72(e)(4)(C)(i), which provides that the lifetime transfer of an annuity contract for less than full and adequate consideration (a gift) causes income realization by the donor equal to the excess of the cash surrender value over the investment in the contract (which is the full accrued income element). Transfers between spouses that are excepted under §1041(a) avoid this income realization. §72(e)(4)(C)(ii). And transfers between a trust's grantor and the trust also should avoid income recognition.

Otherwise, gift tax issues abound. For example, it is not clear whether an irrevocable beneficiary designation qualifies for the gift tax annual exclusion, nor is the value of the gift easily determined. By adding §2503(f) in 1986, Congress addressed one such question by providing that a waiver by a participant's spouse before the participant's death of the spouse's federally guaranteed annuity entitlement is *not* a gift for gift tax purposes. See §§401(a)(11) and 417 (the participant may not defeat the spousal annuity and make an alternate beneficiary designation without the spouse's waiver and consent. §417(a)(2). See page 20.). One way to view the effect of §2503(f) is to consider it as tantamount to automatic marital deduction treatment with respect to any gift made by the participant's spouse to the participant of any benefits released by the spouse's waiver. That vision then leaves any gift occurring by the participant's beneficiary designation as coming wholly from the participant. This result protects the spouse but it does not speak to the gift tax consequence to a participant who makes an irrevocable beneficiary designation. Indeed, it may just confirm that a gift by the participant does occur.

Estate Taxation

As befits the gift tax confusion in this arena, the estate tax is only slightly more clear. Captioned "Annuities," the inclusion rule in §2039 is neither as limited nor as broad as its title might suggest. For example, some annuities are not taxable at all under the estate tax because they terminate with the decedent's death. The only wealth remaining to be included (under §2033) is whatever was paid to the annuitant during life and not exhausted by consumption or transfers before death.

In addition, some annuities that survive a decedent's death and continue to provide postmortem benefits to a survivor annuitant have been taxed under provisions other than §2039. This occurs most commonly under §2038 in the employment context in which a decedent was deemed to have made a transfer in exchange for the annuity and was regarded as retaining some degree of control over the transfer until death.[4] It also has occurred under §2033, as when a decedent owns a right to receive a stream of annuity payments for a term certain that exceeds the decedent's life.

More directly important to this discussion is that §2039 is not limited just to annuities. It also has been used to cause inclusion of the value of employee benefits paid postmortem in a lump sum. Indeed, notwithstanding its title, the primary thrust of §2039 is the estate taxation of all retirement benefits that survive a decedent's death.

Given the confusion in the wealth transfer taxation of these assets, it also is fitting that these issues relate to wealth that is among the most difficult to address in most estate planning engagements today. As just one indication of the difficulty posed, consider the most challenging question in any planning situation in which these assets will be includible: the tax payment obligation. There is no federal right of reimbursement for estate taxes attributable to inclusion of these assets, which frequently have a huge value relative to the cash flow they make available through installment payments over the life of a designated beneficiary.

Worse, there is little reason to anticipate tax payment relief under any federal estate tax deferral provision. Deferral in the discretion of the Secretary might be available for a reasonable period (not to exceed 10 years) under the "reasonable cause" standard in §6161. This might be adequate in some cases to generate enough cash after income tax on these payments to satisfy the outstanding estate tax and any interest. But the §6163 deferral with respect to future interests is not allowable. See Rev. Rul. 73-311. Thus, the obligation to pay estate taxes attributable to §2039 inclusion could vastly exceed the immediately available wealth, which creates significant potential problems.

Prior to their repeal for estates of decedents dying after 1984, §§2039(c) and 2039(e) excluded certain employee death benefits and individual retirement accounts from a decedent's gross estate. Through a

---

4. See, e.g., Rev. Rul. 76-304 (a decedent-employee's contract with an employer called for an annual salary and a death benefit payable to the decedent's designated beneficiary if the decedent was still employed by that employer at death, which the government deemed includible under §2038(a)(1), not §2039(a), as an indirect transfer with a retained power of revocation); cf. Estate of Siegel v. Commissioner, 74 T.C. 613 (1980) (disability payments could cause §2038(a)(1) inclusion as a transfer by the deceased employee that was subject to modification); Looney v. United States, 569 F. Supp. 1569 (M.D. Ga. 1983) (a death benefit only plan generated inclusion because the court aggregated multiple benefits provided to the participant); Estate of Levin v. Commissioner, 90 T.C. 723 (1988) (death benefit only plans generated inclusion under §2038(a)(1) based on the decedent's control of the payor corporation); but see Estate of Tully v. United States, 528 F.2d 1401 (Ct. Cl. 1976) (death benefits payable directly to the decedent's surviving spouse under a contract with the decedent's 50% owned employer were not §2038(a)(1) includible, in part because the decedent's 50% ownership interest did not control the employer); Fidelity-Philadelphia Trust Co. v. Smith, 356 U.S. 274 (1958) (the government's unsuccessful effort to cause inclusion under §2036(a)(1)).

series of changes this favored status swung to the exact polar opposite[5] and, through adoption in 1986 of the §4980A surtax on certain qualified employee benefits, retirement benefits became the most heavily taxed assets in some decedents' estates. Since the repeal of §4980A in 1997, retirement benefits that survive a decedent's death now are taxed with neither preference nor prejudice, and with very few exceptions there is little controversy or uncertainty regarding the estate taxation of annuities or other survivorship benefits. Thus, in general, benefits that are payable postmortem if an individual dies before full premortem payment of an entitlement are includible in the individual's gross estate for federal estate tax purposes, regardless of the extent to which they were funded or nonforfeitable before death.

For §2039 purposes, an annuity is a periodic payment of money for the life of a designated individual or for a term of years. In general, if annuity payments do not terminate at a decedent's death, §2039(a) may require inclusion of the remaining value of that annuity to the extent it is payable to another beneficiary who is entitled to receive payments because of surviving the decedent. As with §2036(a)(1), under §2039(a) the annuity must have been payable (even if it was not yet being paid) to the decedent for life, for a period not ascertainable without reference to the decedent's death, or for a period that did not in fact end before the decedent's death. Under §2039(b), this inclusion is limited to that portion of the annuity attributable to contributions by the decedent (or by an employer on the decedent's behalf). Usually that is 100%.

In addition, the amount includible under §2039(a) reflects the expected duration of the annuity payments (for example, the discounted present value of payments for the life of the participant's surviving spouse). It also reflects a discount to present value if the payments will be deferred until some later starting payment date.

To be includible under §2039(a) the payments that survive the decedent must be made under "any form of contract or agreement" under which the decedent was entitled to payments. By its own terms, §2039(a) cannot cause inclusion of annuities payable under insurance policies on the decedent's life. Thus, the insurance inclusion rule in §2042 must be applied or inclusion is avoided, because the government cannot use §2039 as an alternate inclusion provision. For example, assume that a decedent assigned all rights under an employer funded group term life insurance policy more than three years before death and avoided both §§2035 and 2042 inclusion of the proceeds at death. The fact that the settlement option was an annuity for the

---

5. The history of amendments to §2039 and their application and effect on prior revenue rulings and procedures is detailed in Rev. Rul. 88-85. Transition date rules also are addressed in Rev. Rul. 92-22. In general, benefits may still be excludible if the participant separated from service before 1985. With respect to IRAs the key is being in pay status with an irrevocable beneficiary election before 1985. In either case no changes to the form of benefit should be made before careful analysis of the question.

beneficiary's life would not permit inclusion under §2039(a), even though payment of this employee benefit was in annuity form.

There are some unresolved estate tax inclusion questions under §2039. For example, of particular significance to community property estate planners (but relevant throughout the nation) is whether a spouse of a participant in an employee benefit plan owns any interest in the plan by virtue of the §401(a)(11) spousal annuity rules. If so, one question involves what happens if the nonparticipant spouse predeceases the participant. Is any part of the retirement benefit includible in the nonparticipant spouse's gross estate, and does that part qualify for the estate tax marital deduction?

An amendment to §2056(b)(7)(C) in 1997 specifies that any portion of a plan that is includible in the deceased nonparticipant spouse's gross estate under §2033 (meaning that it is the deceased spouse's community property) qualifies for automatic marital deduction treatment. In addition, it seems relatively clear that Congress does not believe a nonparticipant spouse in a noncommunity property state has any property rights that would generate estate tax consequences.[6]

Income Taxation

The wealth transfer taxation of annuities and other retirement benefits has been relatively stable compared to the amount of change to the income tax rules that affect planning for these assets. Change has been significant and frequent since Congress adopted the Employee Retirement Income Security Act of 1974 (ERISA). Two additional important wealth transfer tax issues are the "fallout" of income tax changes made under the

---

6. Although this notion almost certainly is correct in a noncommunity property jurisdiction, it is questionable in a community property state. See Hyde v. United States, 93-2 U.S. Tax Cas. (CCH) ¶50,605 (D. Ariz. 1993), aff'd in an unpublished opinion (9th Cir. 1994) (the nonparticipant spouse had a sufficient community property interest in the participant's qualified plan to be subject to a §6331 tax levy, which was honored notwithstanding the §401(a)(13) anti-alienation rule, due to the exception for taxes in Treas. Reg. §1.401(a)-13(b)(2)(i)); but see Boggs v. Boggs, 520 U.S. 833 (1997) (a 5-4 decision that a participant's predeceased spouse could not transfer any entitlement under a qualified plan because ERISA pre-empts any state property law community property interest; the participant had remarried and was survived by that new spouse, and the opinion speaks in terms of the ERISA protection for the surviving spouse of the participant); Ablamis v. Roper, 937 F.2d 1450 (9th Cir. 1991) (the nonparticipant spouse in a community property jurisdiction did not have a property right subject to disposition under the nonparticipant spouse's will prior to death of the participant); cf. Hisquierdo v. Hisquierdo, 439 U.S. 572 (1979) (ERISA pre-emption also prevents a nonparticipant spouse from having a community property interest on divorce in the participant's retirement benefits), and Bunney v. Commissioner, 114 T.C. 259 (2000) (notwithstanding that state law regarded an IRA as funded with community income, the Tax Court concluded that recognition of community property interests in an IRA for federal income tax purposes would conflict with several fundamental aspects of §408 and therefore regarded the participant as the owner and sole distributee for income tax purposes). Contra, Allard v. Frech, 754 S.W.2d 111 (Tex. 1988) (half of a participant's pension passed under the will of a predeceased nonparticipant spouse). The issue is not relevant with respect to IRAs and simplified employee pensions, which are not governed by ERISA.

Retirement Equity Act of 1984 and the "spousal annuity" requirements that it added.

Before addressing those planning issues, however, a short digression is needed to study the income tax rules affecting retirement benefits, because these rules are integral to the estate planning that is available. Fortunately, these income tax issues are not likely to arise in the normal practice of estate planning professionals because frequently they relate to qualification of plans that have special income tax attributes. Indeed, the income tax issues described here are so complex that many seasoned estate planners conclude that the world of benefits planning is too specialized and simply delegate this work to benefits experts rather than attempting to acquire or retain the competence to create or maintain qualified plans. What follows is a brief general description of the key requirements of *qualified* plans. It is designed to establish the most basic understanding of the income and estate tax rules. These are of primary importance to estate planners who need to be conversant with clients who possess substantial retirement benefits that must be integrated into their estate plan.

Let's begin with a reality check. The amount of wealth controlled by private pension plans in America is staggering, and it grows exponentially annually. The principal reason for this investment of current earnings is the favorable income tax advantages granted to all parties involved with qualified plans. In exchange for these benefits, Congress imposes detailed qualification rules. For starters, a tax-favored "qualified" plan must satisfy all the qualification requirements of §401, the minimum participation standards of §410, the minimum vesting standards of §411, the minimum funding standards of §412, and the limitations on benefits and contributions of §415.

A qualified plan must exist for the exclusive benefit of employees and their beneficiaries and its sole objective must be to provide these individuals with a share of profits or an income after retirement. Death benefits can be only an "incidental" feature of a qualified plan. In addition, participation in, contributions to, and benefits provided under a qualified plan may not unduly discriminate in favor of officers, shareholders, or highly compensated employees. Because the definitions of what constitutes a discriminatory plan are among the elements that tend to vary from one Tax Reform Act or Congress to another, the most recent version of these rules should be the focus of study by those crafting a plan. Fortunately, these are rules about which the typical estate planner probably need not worry.

Another requirement is that the employer's contributions to the plan must "vest," meaning that contributions are not forfeited upon termination of employment. Again, the formulas or schedules for vesting have been subject to change and a number of alternatives are available. As a result, a given employer may maintain various plans with different rules, all explained in a summary plan description made available to the participant.

An estate planner normally would study this document only if the benefits involved are substantial enough to warrant this investment of time (and therefore fees).

A *contributory plan* either permits or requires employees to contribute after-tax dollars to the plan. These contributions will add to a participant's basis and complicate the tax consequences of distributions because these contributions are returned to the participant tax free. *Noncontributory plans* are funded only by pretax employer contributions and generally are easier to address for income tax purposes. This is deferred compensation and everything distributed is taxable as income. Noncontributory plans are the norm.

Defined contribution plans require specified contributions pursuant to a prescribed formula. These defined contributions build an identifiable (although not necessarily a separate or separable) fund on behalf of each participant, with no guarantees of investment performance or ultimate payout. There are two forms of defined contribution plan. *Money purchase plans* permit an annual contribution, not to exceed specified statutory limits. *Profit sharing plans* originally permitted contributions that were geared to actual profits of the employer; today contributions can be made even if there are no profits, again subject to maximum limits on contributions. So-called 401(k) *cash or deferred compensation plans* are a form of profit sharing, allowing the employee to either receive cash or defer compensation (up to a maximum amount) by contribution to the employer's profit sharing plan. The employer and employee contributions to a defined contribution plan may differ, but each must be made according to a specified formula.

Defined benefit plans establish a prescribed benefit, again by formula (such as [x%] times [years of service] times [the employee's average salary for a certain number of highest salary years before retirement]), subject to certain limits that prevent excess benefits. Contributions to a defined benefit plan are estimates of the amount that will be needed to provide the guaranteed benefit. Annual audits and actuarial determinations are required to ensure that the employer keeps the plan funded at a level deemed necessary to guarantee those benefits. Over time this form of plan has fallen into disfavor because employers do not want to be obligated for a guaranteed benefit and suffer the risk that investment performance may not correlate properly with contributions. Most plans today are of the defined contribution variety. As a result, investment performance is totally the participant's risk or reward.

Individual Retirement Accounts (IRAs) are available to individuals who are not otherwise covered by employer plans (and there are "spousal IRAs" with special limits for unemployed spouses, Roth IRAs,[7] and

---

7. Virtually no attention is devoted here to Roth IRAs because the §408A(c)(3) contribution and rollover restrictions are such that many potential users will be precluded from taking significant advantage of this opportunity. Roth IRAs may be desirable to

educational IRAs). Because of the §408(a)(1) contribution limitations for IRAs in general, the most important use of IRAs for most clients is as a "rollover" beneficiary of distributions from other qualified plans, with the ability to defer the income tax consequence of that distribution until the IRA is distributed in the future.[8] In addition, specialized plans, such as Employee Stock Ownership Plans (ESOPs), Incentive Stock Options (ISOs), Simplified Employee Pensions (SEPs), Supplemental Retirement Annuities (SRAs), and H.R.10 (Keogh) plans also exist but are less common and are not discussed separately here.

The income tax consequences to the employer-sponsor of a qualified plan are relatively straightforward. Under §404(a), the employer's contributions to the plan are deductible currently from its income as an immediate business expense. Nevertheless, under §402(a) the employer's contributions to the plan are not taxed currently as income to the employee-participant. Instead, taxation of this form of compensation is deferred until benefits are distributed or made available to the participant (or to designated beneficiaries). §83 does not alter this result. See §83(e)(2).

Deferring income to the participant has three tax advantages: First, it is anticipated that the participant will be in a lower income tax bracket in the years after retirement when distributions are received, so the benefits may incur a lower overall income tax liability. Second, if the participant is over the age of 65 when taxable distributions are received, an additional standard deduction will be available to offset this income (and additional deductions also may be available for the participant's spouse).

The third and perhaps the most important advantage of deferral is that income earned in the plan between the time of contribution and the time of distribution is exempt from income tax until distribution. This "tax free internal build up in value" applies to contributions by the employer and the participant alike in both qualified and nonqualified plans. The build up also allows a significant increase in the earning and growth potential of the invested wealth because dollars that otherwise would be paid in income tax instead are invested.[9]

---

individuals who will not need the wealth and do not want to be forced into taking minimum distributions (which are not required under §408A) or who want to designate a beneficiary, such as a generation-skipping trust, on which income tax liability should not be imposed.

8. Creditor protection may be lost on a rollover, the issue being state law protection of IRAs from creditor claims. With respect to creditor protection of qualified plans in general, see the anti-alienation rule in §401(a)(13) and Treas. Reg. §1.401(a)-13(b)(1); Patterson v. Shumate, 504 U.S. 753 (1992); In re Rueter, 11 F.3d 850 (9th Cir. 1993); In re Connor, 73 F.3d 258 (9th Cir. 1996). IRAs are exempt from bankruptcy claims but only "to the extent reasonably necessary for the support of the debtor and any dependent of the debtor. 11 U.S.C. §522(d)(10)(E)," quoted from In re Carmichael, 100 F.3d 375, 380 (5th Cir. 1996). Otherwise the issue for IRAs is a function of state law. Ice, What Are Creditors' Rights in Retirement Plan Benefits, 21 Est. Plan. 30 (1994).

9. Notwithstanding statements often made to the contrary, it is not a benefit that the income tax will be paid using "discounted" or "cheaper" dollars (considering their value in an inflationary economy), because the participant will receive the benefit distributions in the same devalued dollars.

Because income tax deferral normally is regarded as beneficial, seldom is the point made (but it is good to remember) that the Code establishes *minimum* distribution rules in most cases. If a qualified participant (who is not too young) wishes to receive benefits more quickly than is required, usually that is completely permissible under the law (although the plan may not be designed for premature distributions because of its investments and reserve estimates). The price to be paid by distributions in excess of the minimum distribution requirements is loss of deferral and potentially a higher rate of income tax if the amounts received push the recipient into a higher marginal income tax bracket.

Nonqualified Plans

The income tax difference between qualified and nonqualified plans is *not* to the participants. There still is deferral until distribution or availability of the funds. Instead, the primary consequence of being nonqualified is that the employer may not deduct its contributions until the year the participant includes the amount in income, meaning that there is no mismatch of the employer's deduction and the participant's inclusion as there is with a qualified plan (instead, both are deferred until distributions are made). The participant's inclusion, however, normally is not affected. See §§402(b), 403(c), 83(a)(1), and 83(c)(1). The fact that nonqualified plans typically are not funded or vested normally precludes current §83 taxation to the employee.

Even though nonqualified deferred compensation may be an attractive negotiated benefit, the participant incurs certain risks that are meant to be minimized under the federal requirements for qualified plans. Still, nonqualified plans are relatively popular for a number of reasons, notwithstanding deferral of the employer's deduction. For example, nonqualified plans need not meet the rigid funding, minimum participation, minimum vesting, nondiscrimination, and other technical rules that apply to qualified plans. Thus, an employer may target benefits to certain favored officers and employees and the plan need not be funded currently, so the employer may defer payment of the dollars to satisfy its obligations under the plan. In addition, certain incidental administrative costs of maintaining qualified plans may be reduced or avoided entirely. Further, the §401(a)(9) required beginning date and minimum distribution rules discussed next do not apply, nor do the penalties under §§4974 and 72(t) for early or late receipt of benefits apply, meaning that there is more flexibility in determining when to receive the benefit.

Rules Governing Distributions

The income tax treatment of retirement benefit distributions is a source of significant complication for estate planners. The distribution options are not elections about which the typical estate planner needs to be intimately aware, because the participant is entitled to receive guidance from the qualified plan's administrator on whether to take an annuity, a lump sum, or to roll over into an IRA or another plan. Instead, the importance of these income tax rules is two-fold.

First, elections made by the participant and the designated beneficiary will affect income tax planning and the flexibility available for distributions after their respective deaths, particularly with respect to providing liquidity for estate tax payment purposes.

Second, there are spousal annuity entitlements and waiver issues that must be considered and factored into the planning equation. The decision regarding a waiver of the spousal annuity will be affected by the income tax consequences of actions taken during the participant's life, by elections that are available to the spouse, and by the estate and gift tax issues considered beginning at page 20.

Fortunately, the income tax rules that apply during the participant's life need not be a principal concern, because most estate planners will not be involved in the client's decisions about pre-death enjoyment of retirement benefits. However, taxation during life must be studied to fully appreciate and understand the options available for postmortem distribution, especially if payout began during the participant's life.

In a nutshell, the income taxation of benefits during life can be described as following a "not too early, not too late" pattern. Congress seeks to ensure that participants and their beneficiaries receive benefits in a way that provides a retirement income during the full duration of their "retirement years," rather than receiving the amounts too early or too late in life. Indeed, Congress especially wants to ensure that, in normal cases, the benefits are paid to the participant rather than left to accumulate tax free for disposition to future generations (or left to increase through tax free investment of a fund that is unreduced by income taxes on investment gains).

The "required distribution" rules in §§401(a)(9), 408(a)(6), 408(b)(13), and Treas. Reg. §§1.401(a)(9)-1 and 1.408-8 A-1 impose conditions for qualified plan status that require distributions to begin by a certain time and to be made within certain periods. This "not too late" aspect is enforced by means of a §4974(a) penalty tax of 50% on the amount of any deficiency in meeting these minimum distribution standards. This penalty makes it too expensive for the participant or beneficiary who should receive distributions to leave amounts in a plan and avoid taking them into income as required.

Distributions must begin no later than April 1 of the calendar year in which the participant reaches 71½ years of age or retires, whichever is later.[10] Let's ignore a late retirement for now: most folks will be retired by

---

10. §401(a)(9)(C); Treas. Reg. §1.401(a)(9)-2 A-2. Technically, the rule as written is that distributions must begin no later than April 1 of the calendar year following the year in which the participant reached 70½ years of age. The "later of" retirement aspect of the rule

the age of 70 if they work for someone else. Because a payment is required for the year the participant reached the age of 70½ and another is required for the year the participant reaches the age of 71½, waiting to make the first distribution until April 1 of that latter year will result in a bunching of two installments in one year. Treas. Reg. §1.401(a)(9)-5 A-1(b). Delay also leaves a larger amount in the plan as of the end of the first year, with the result that a larger amount must be distributed for the second year than if the first year distribution was made in the first year, before calculating the second year required distribution. Thus, many individuals will elect to start receiving distributions in the calendar year in which they reach 70½ years of age.

For many participants payments will begin years before that, due to the §401(a)(14) default distribution rules that apply unless the participant affirmatively elects to defer distributions. There is no exception to the first payment date and no penalty tax as the price for missing it: it *must* be met. There are no options. The first payment date is coupled with a 10% penalty that applies if distributions begin before age 59½ (the §72(t) "not too soon" aspect, which applies unless distribution is on account of death, disability, separation from service, other hardships, or as a life annuity). Thus, the "window" of time during which distributions must begin is approximately 12 years (unless the participant is still working after age 71½).

These rules are important to estate planners because, once payments begin, the benefit must be paid in certain minimum annual amounts. The longer the delay in beginning distribution, the larger the amounts must be to avoid the minimum distribution penalty. This will have a carryover effect on distributions received after death, as noted below.

Benefits paid during a participant's life must be paid over one of the following periods: (1) the life of the participant, (2) a term certain that does not exceed the actuarial life expectancy of the participant, (3) the joint lives of the participant and a designated beneficiary, or (4) a term certain that does not exceed the actuarial life expectancy of the participant and a designated beneficiary. §401(a)(9)(A)(ii); Treas. Reg. §§1.401(a)(9)-2 A-1 and 1.401(a)(9)-5 A-4.

The life expectancy of the participant is redetermined on an annual basis. The same is true of the participant's spouse, but only if the spouse is more than 10 years younger than the participant (a "young spouse").[11]

---

does not apply if the participant is a 5% owner of the employer. In addition, the plan may not reflect the "later of" aspect to permit deferral beyond age 70½. Nor does the "later of" rule apply to IRA owners. See Treas. Reg. §1.408-8 A-3. As a result, a participant who is not a 5% owner might have different required beginning dates for IRA distributions and various qualified plans.

11. Treas. Reg. §1.401(a)(9)-5 A-4(b), using joint life tables in Treas. Reg. §1.72-9 Table VI. In this case the joint life expectancy of the participant and the young spouse is used to determine the inter vivos minimum required distribution. This is not elective (notwithstanding that the preamble to the proposed regulations described it as an option),

Otherwise, during the participant's life the life expectancy of any other designated beneficiary is irrelevant in establishing the minimum distribution amount payable during the participant's life: the minimum distribution table applicable during the participant's life is constructed using the life expectancy of the participant and a hypothetical beneficiary always deemed to be 10 years younger than the participant.[12]

Because life expectancy increases as an individual grows older (for example, your chances of reaching 100 are a lot better if you're already 99), automatic redetermination of the participant's life expectancy (and any applicable young spouse redetermination) minimizes the amount of each year's distribution and defers the payout as long as possible, thereby minimizing exposure to the regular income tax. In an age of reduced income tax brackets, this recalculation and deferral does not generate much income tax saving, and making most of these rules automatic eliminates the need to constantly recalculate and consider the benefits of redetermination.

Under these rules, the designated beneficiary alternatives if §401(a)(9)(A)(ii) present the opportunity to select a long-term payout, but typically only if the designated beneficiary is a child or a more remote descendant. This option may allow for significant reductions in the overall income tax cost of the distributions. To prevent an excessive amount of such deferral, however, distributions to a designated beneficiary must be "incidental" to payments to the participant, meaning that the present value of the benefit payable to the participant (and the participant's spouse) must be worth at least 50% of the participant's interest in the plan.[13]

The real significance of the income tax distribution rules for estate planning purposes lies in §401(a)(9)(B), which applies if the participant

---

but the minimum distribution rules always permit taking more than the minimum required amount if the participant wants a larger payout as if the otherwise standard rule applied. This one exception to the otherwise normal rule that the designated beneficiary's life expectancy does not matter is applied annually. Thus, the participant is thrown back into the default rule if the young spouse dies (or there is a divorce), and a participant who marries a young spouse during the year can change the next year's required minimum distribution.

12. See the Uniform Lifetime Table in Treas. Reg. §§1.401(a)(9)-5 A-4 and 1.401(a)(9)-9 A-2, which do not articulate this notion, but the latter reveals it upon careful inspection and comparison to traditional one life tables. Treas. Reg. §1.72-9 Table VI shows the source of the two life expectancy, in each case assuming the 10 year differential in ages as the source of the Uniform Lifetime Table. This rule explains why designating a beneficiary before the participant dies is not necessary, and the designated beneficiary may change up until the end of September of the first year following the year of the participant's death. Thus, for example, a postmortem beneficiary need not be designated by the required beginning date. Moreover, assuming the plan permits, the participant may change the designated beneficiary after the required beginning date, without altering the required minimum distribution. Indeed, the designated beneficiary might be subject to change postmortem (for example, by distribution—such as to pay out a charitable benefit that might alter the designated beneficiary minimum distribution calculation—or by disclaimer) until the end of September of the first year after the year of the participant's death. Treas. Reg. §1.401(a)(9)-4 A-4(a).

13. Rev. Rul. 74-359, Rev. Rul. 74-325, and Rev. Rul. 72-241.

dies before the entire interest is distributed.[14] If distributions had begun before death, then the stated rule is that the entire benefit must be distributed after death at least as rapidly as under the distribution program that was begun during life. §401(a)(9)(B)(i). The logic for this requirement is found in the annuity income tax rules of §72(s)(1)(A), which imposes the same requirement for any garden-variety annuity when the owner dies.

If distributions had *not* begun before the participant's death, then by statute the entire interest must be distributed before the sixth New Year after the participant's death. §401(a)(9)(B)(ii).

The first exception applies if payments begin within one year after the participant's death. In this case the participant may elect a benefit payable over the life expectancy of a designated beneficiary or a term certain that does not exceed the actuarial life expectancy of the designated beneficiary. §401(a)(9)(B)(iii). See the analogous annuity income tax rule in §72(s)(2). "Designated beneficiary" means any individual, so distribution to the participant's estate would preclude application of this exception. §401(a)(9)(E); Treas. Reg. §1.401(a)(9)-4 A-3. No definitive authority appears to exist, but knowledgeable commentators have represented privately that a trust making the §645 election to be treated as part of the decedent's estate will *not* be regarded as an estate for purposes of this rule. In that regard, a trust may be a designated beneficiary if:

- The trust is valid under state law (or would be but for the fact that it does not yet own any corpus, including a testamentary trust notwithstanding the technicality that it too cannot exist until the testator's will is probated postmortem).

- All trust beneficiaries who can conceivably enjoy plan benefits are individuals (that is, none are charities or estates, including indirect enjoyment by payment of estate debts, expenses, or taxes).

- Those beneficiaries are identifiable from the terms of the trust instrument, which is irrevocable and unamendable at the participant's death.[15]

---

14. See also §408(a)(6), which provides that IRA distributions must follow the same rules as those imposed by §401(a)(9) for qualified plans. In that regard, in some cases it will prove desirable that Private Letter Ruling 9416037, referencing Notice 88-38, held that one IRA may make total annual distributions based on the minimum distributions required of all the taxpayer's IRAs and satisfy this requirement. Treas. Reg. §1.408-8 A-9 limits this opportunity by precluding aggregation of multiple IRAs created by different grantors, but multiple IRAs created by the same person (the recipient personally or the same third party for the recipient) may benefit from aggregation and then selective distribution.

15. It is unknown whether the ability to add beneficiaries by adoption or exercise of a power of appointment will defeat designated beneficiary status. It ought to be adequate to proscribe addition of any beneficiary who would alter the identity of the oldest beneficiary because it is the shortest life expectancy among all beneficiaries that is used to compute the distributions. Uncertainty exists because Prop. Treas. Reg. §1.401(a)(9)-5 A-7(d) seemingly permitted a beneficiary to possess a testamentary power over the balance of a beneficiary's entitlement, and that example was deleted without explanation when the final regulations were adopted.

- A copy of the trust, or a list of the trust beneficiaries (and a copy of the trust instrument itself, if requested), is put on file with the plan administrator before the end of October of the first year following the participant's death.

Treas. Reg. §§1.401(a)(9)-4 A-5(b) and 1.401(a)(9)-4 A-6(b). The trust beneficiaries will be treated as the designated beneficiaries if these requirements are met and the beneficiary with the shortest life expectancy is used to determine the payout period. Treas. Reg. §1.401(a)(9)-5 A-7(a).

Applying these rules under the §401(a)(9) regulations produces the following principles that govern postmortem distributions (to the extent not otherwise precluded by the terms of the plan itself):

- If there is a designated beneficiary, payments postmortem must be made over that designated beneficiary's life expectancy, regardless of whether the participant died before or after the required beginning date (subject to special rules if the beneficiary is a spouse, an entity, or multiple individuals). The life expectancy of a designated beneficiary other than the participant's surviving spouse is determined in the year following the year of the participant's death and thereafter is reduced by one for each subsequent year (notwithstanding that true life expectancy does not decline by a full year for each added year of life). Treas. Reg. §1.401(a)(9)-5 A-5. On the other hand, if the participant's spouse is the sole beneficiary, the life expectancy of the participant's surviving spouse actually is determined annually, meaning that the benefits cannot pay out sooner than the spouse's actual death. Treas. Reg. §1.401(a)(9)-5 A-5(c)(2).

- If there are multiple individual beneficiaries after the participant's death, the life expectancy used is that of the oldest of them (creating the shortest payout period). As a result, postmortem severance into separate accounts or shares may be desirable, so that each beneficiary's share is distributed on the basis of just that one beneficiary's life expectancy (or to create opportunities that otherwise might not exist, as for example if one of several beneficiaries is the participant's surviving spouse). Treas. Reg. §§1.401(a)(9)-5 A-7(a) and 1.401(a)(9)-8 A-2(a)(2). Special care is required to consider the operation of "contingent" and "successor" beneficiary rules, including the effect of permissible appointees under powers of appointment, under the circumstances of each trust beneficiary.

- If the participant dies *after* the required beginning date and there is no designated beneficiary for postmortem distribution, then distributions will continue over the participant's remaining life expectancy, determined immediately before the participant's death. Treas. Reg. §§1.401(a)(9)-2 A-5 and 1.401(a)(9)-5 A-5(a)(2).

- The five year payout rule of §401(a)(9)(B)(ii) applies postmortem only if the participant dies *before* the required beginning date *and* there is *no* designated beneficiary before the second New Year after the participant's death. Treas. Reg. §1.401(a)(9)-3 A-1(a).

- If any beneficiary is not an individual (such as a charity or a fiduciary entity), the account is deemed to have *no* designated beneficiary and these rules apply according to whether the participant died before or after the required beginning date. Treas. Reg. §§1.401(a)(9)-3 A-4(a)(2), 1.401(a)(9)-4 A-3, and 1.401(a)(9)-8 A-11.

- Trust beneficiaries may be considered when determining the minimum required distribution, provided that documentation on the trust is provided by the end of October of the first year following the year of the participant's death. Testamentary trusts qualify the same as inter vivos trusts. Treas. Reg. §1.401(a)(9)-4 A-5.

The facts of Rev. Rul. 2000-2 may be useful in regard to all of these requirements. They state that the decedent was not yet in pay status under an IRA, making §401(a)(9)(B)(ii) and the exception to it in §401(a)(9)(B)(iii) relevant. The beneficiary designation under the IRA was the decedent's testamentary QTIP trust. The Ruling states that a copy of the trust and a list of the trust beneficiaries were delivered to the IRA Administrator within nine months after the decedent's death, and those facts alone apparently support the Ruling's conclusion that the surviving spouse (as the oldest trust beneficiary) was the designated beneficiary whose life expectancy would be used as the payment period under the IRA for minimum annual distribution purposes. Any undistributed IRA balance would be distributed to the QTIP trust after the surviving spouse's death, according to the Ruling, "over the remaining distribution period." Based on these facts, the Ruling concluded that the testamentary trust qualified the surviving spouse as a designated beneficiary under §401(a)(9)(B)(iii)(I), which is significant in its own right.

A second entirely separate exception applies if the designated beneficiary is the participant's surviving spouse. In that case payments may be deferred to begin no later than when the participant (not the spouse) would have reached 70½ years of age, and may extend for the life expectancy of the spouse or a term certain that does not exceed the life expectancy of the spouse. §401(a)(9)(B)(iv); Treas. Reg. §1.401(a)(9)-3 A-3(b)(2). See the annuity income tax analogue in §72(s)(3). Further, if the surviving spouse also dies before distributions begin, then the benefits must be paid following the spouse's death according to the foregoing rules, as if the spouse were the participant. Treas. Reg. §1.401(a)(9)-3 A-5.

As a planning matter, instead of electing such deferral, some advisors recommend that the surviving spouse accelerate distributions before death to incur any remaining income tax liability during life, thereby reducing the surviving spouse's estate for estate tax purposes. See Treas. Reg.

§20.2053-6(f) (no estate tax deduction is allowable for any built-in income tax liability that was not incurred before death and is not paid during administration of the decedent's estate).

A final alternative, often producing a better result, is for the surviving spouse to receive a lump sum (if this is available under the plan) and roll it over to an IRA of the spouse's creation. See page 18. Given the complexity of the minimum distribution and the minimum distribution incidental benefit rules with respect to trusts as beneficiaries, designation of the participant's spouse as the direct beneficiary who may take a lump sum and roll over the distribution or elect to receive the benefits in installments often is the option of choice if the participant is not intent on denying control to the spouse.

Income Tax Consequence of Distributions

The assumed or default income tax treatment of distributions to participants and their beneficiaries is as an annuity, with income tax imposed under §72. See §§402(a) and 408(d)(1). In a nutshell, §72 provides that annuities held by a natural person (or by an entity acting as agent for a natural person, or by an estate that acquired the annuities by reason of a natural person's death) qualify for deferral treatment. Annuity treatment would be unavailable by virtue of §72(u)(1) without an "agent for a natural person" status.

Without annuity taxation, income under an annuity contract is subject to annual inclusion (as ordinary income) as income accrues on the contract, not as deferred payments are made. §72(u)(1)(B). With annuity treatment income taxation is deferred until each payment is made. Every distribution is taxable as ordinary income, subject to exclusion of a portion that represents the participant's after-tax investment in the plan (including employer contributions that were taxable to the employee when made). Usually there is no excluded amount, but if there is it is recovered as a pro rata portion of each annuity payment. Under §72(b) this exclusion from income is limited to any unrecovered investment in the contract, so all payments are entirely taxable as ordinary income once the participant's total investment has been recovered in the form of these excluded pro rata portions of each annual payment.[16]

The fundamental alternative to annuity treatment is lump sum distribution of the participant's entire remaining interest in the plan, with

---

16. A deduction is available on the participant's final income tax return for any unrecovered investment if payments cease with the participant's death before recovery of the participant's entire investment. §72(b)(3). Curiously, §72(b)(3)(A) authorizes this deduction only if the participant dies after the annuity starting date, which appears to mean that death before then would not provide a deduction for any basis in the plan. That result seems counterintuitive unless there is a death benefit that pays that investment in the contract and therefore there is no loss to be deducted. See St. Laurent, *Estate Planning with Tax-Deferred Annuities—Special Problems Under Section 72*, 21 EST., GIFTS & TRUSTS J. 234, 236 (1996).

payment being made within a single taxable year of the participant or designated beneficiary. §402(d)(4)(A). Not all plans permit a lump sum distribution, and not all participants (or their designated beneficiaries) will qualify. The most important requirements are a length of service threshold of at least five years for distributions to a living participant and distributions that must be triggered by certain qualifying events (the participant's attainment of age 59½, death, separation from service, or disability). §§402(d)(4)(A) and (F). In addition, lump sum treatment must be elected with respect to all distributions in the same taxable year and is a once in a lifetime opportunity after the participant reaches the age of 59½. §402(d)(4)(B). Did you get all that? This is a tad complicated!

Spousal Rollover

The lump sum election is available as an alternative to annuity tax treatment for either the participant or the designated beneficiary. In addition, rollover elections are available to the participant during life, and to the participant's surviving spouse (but no one else) as a designated beneficiary after the participant's death. §§402(c)(1), (c)(5), and (c)(9). The rollover election permits the recipient (participant or spouse) to place a portion or all of a distribution in another eligible tax deferred plan, with the advantage of deferral of all income tax on the benefit itself and on any internal build up in the receptacle plan until distribution. Technical rules deal with partial rollover elections, the time within which rollovers must be made, the amount (both maximum and minimum) that may be rolled over, and the types of benefits that may be rolled over. See §§402(c) and 408(d)(3).

With respect to a participant's IRA, a surviving spouse may effect a rollover of that IRA merely by redesignating the IRA in the spouse's name as *owner* instead of as beneficiary. Treas. Reg. §1.408-8 A-5. Ostensibly, an IRA rollover by a surviving spouse is permitted only if the spouse is the sole beneficiary of the IRA and has an unlimited right to withdraw funds from the IRA. This requirement is not met if the spouse is the beneficiary of a *trust* that is the beneficiary of the IRA, even if the spouse is the *only* beneficiary of that trust. Treas. Reg. §1.408-8 A-5. See Choate, LIFE AND DEATH PLANNING FOR RETIREMENT BENEFITS ¶3.2.09 (5th ed. 2003), and Choate, *When a "Trust For The Spouse" Is Treated The Same As "The Spouse,"* 140 TRUSTS & ESTATES 36 (Sept. 2001). These seemingly clear rules are not crystal if the beneficiary is a marital deduction trust for the benefit of the participant's spouse. The issue turns on the meaning of "designated beneficiary" under §401(a)(9)(E), and developments regarding spousal rollover elections provide only helpful clues to the proper resolution of these rules.

A study of various ruling results leads to the conclusion that the important designated beneficiary factor is whether the spouse can unilaterally cause or control distribution of the qualified plan or IRA.

There have been dozens of such rulings; the following discussion is meant to be illustrative, not exhaustive. For example, Private Letter Ruling 9509028 allowed a §402 spousal rollover of qualified plan proceeds to a §402(c)(9) spousal rollover IRA, because the qualified plan distribution was to a marital deduction trust over which the spouse had a full withdrawal power. And Private Letter Ruling 9451059 allowed §§402(c)(9) qualified plan and 408(d)(3) IRA rollovers by the surviving spouse because both forms of benefits were payable to a §2056(b)(5) marital deduction trust over which the surviving spouse had an inter vivos power of withdrawal.[17]

A convoluted pathway to the surviving spouse was involved in Private Letter Ruling 9450041. The surviving spouse made a nonqualified disclaimer of qualified plan proceeds from a trust that was the designated beneficiary, causing the proceeds to become payable to a second trust. The beneficiaries of that second trust then made a qualified disclaimer of the proceeds (a new nine-month disclaimer period began to run when the spouse made the nonqualified disclaimer), which caused the proceeds to become payable to the decedent's estate, from which they passed by intestacy to the surviving spouse outright.

Because the second disclaimer was qualified and therefore did not attract gift taxation, the government determined that the net result was that the proceeds passed from the decedent's plan to the surviving spouse. This distribution qualified for the estate tax marital deduction and also made possible a §402(c)(9) rollover election by the surviving spouse, all as if the intermediate disclaimer steps had not been necessary. Therefore, the passage of the distribution was regarded as direct, not as if the property had passed into one trust, then another, then to the decedent's estate, and finally to the surviving spouse. Private Letter Ruling 9450042 reached the same result with respect to the decedent's IRA that went directly to the decedent's estate and then to the surviving spouse. In this case the government held a §408(d)(3) rollover was permissible by virtue of its contingent beneficiary provision.

---

17. In this case the Ruling noted that the spouse was a cotrustee of the trust, had a power to remove the other cotrustee, and was the controlling cotrustee in the case of a tie vote. Other Rulings also indicate that control as trustee may be essential. See, e.g., Private Letter Rulings 199925033 and 9820020, in which payment was to the decedent's inter vivos trust, as to which the spouse was trustee with the authority to allocate the proceeds to a community property survivor's subtrust or to a marital deduction subtrust over which the spouse had a power of withdrawal, 9633043 and 9426049, in which the spouse could remove the trustee and become the sole or the controlling trustee, 200011062, in which an IRA was payable to a trust as to which the spouse had a full withdrawal power *and* was trustee, 200208030 (same), which involved discretion in funding a fractional marital bequest to the trust and the balance of the qualified plan went to a bypass trust and was deemed to have a valid designated beneficiary with payout over the life of the spouse as the oldest beneficiary of that trust, and 9813018, in which payment to a trust and distribution to the spouse qualified for rollover because the spouse was the trustee. In Private Letter Ruling 9303031 the spouse was not in control and the rollover was denied. In each of these cases the inter vivos power of withdrawal appears to be the key.

Two other Rulings also permitted a tax free rollover. In Private Letter Ruling 9524020 the surviving spouse elected against the decedent's will in favor of a statutory share of the decedent's estate. Exercising a state law right to select the assets in the decedent's estate that would satisfy that elective share, the surviving spouse obtained a portion of qualified plan proceeds, which were payable to the decedent's estate as the designated beneficiary. In Private Letter Ruling 9626049 the surviving spouse and all descendants of the decedent disclaimed a fraction of the decedent's estate, causing an intestacy that the spouse was entitled to receive, and the decedent's personal representative funded that fractional entitlement with the decedent's IRAs. In both of these cases, the government ruled that these payments constituted distributions directly to the spouse and not to the estate and then to the spouse, thus permitting a tax free §402(c)(9) rollover to an IRA created by the spouse.

In Private Letter Ruling 9445029, however, the decedent's estate was the designated beneficiary of an IRA. The estate poured over to a marital deduction trust, over which the trustee proposed to exercise discretion to distribute the IRA to the decedent's surviving spouse, who then would roll the distribution over to an IRA of the spouse's creation. The government held that the rollover would not qualify under §408(d)(3) as a rollover distribution that would avoid income taxation. The Ruling gave three reasons for stating that "we do not believe it is appropriate to treat [the spouse] as the distributee of [the decedent's IRA] for purposes of section 408[(d)(3)(C)(ii)(II)]." First, the spouse was not the personal representative of the decedent's estate; second, the spouse was not treated as the owner of the marital deduction trust under §678 for income tax purposes; and third, the marital deduction trustee had unlimited discretion whether to distribute the distribution amount to the surviving spouse.

Spousal Annuity Rules

For estate planners, probably the single most significant development in the retirement benefits arena was adoption by the Retirement Equity Act of 1984 of the spousal annuity requirements of §401(a)(11). These requirements apply to all qualified defined benefit and defined contribution plans (but not to IRAs) if the participant was married for at least one year prior to the earlier of the annuity starting date or the participant's death. The plan must pay an annuity (which is taxable under §72) that is either a "qualified joint and survivor" annuity if the participant dies after the annuity starting date or a "qualified preretirement survivor" annuity if the participant dies before the annuity starting date.

A qualified joint and survivor annuity must be payable for the life of the participant and thereafter for the life of the participant's surviving spouse. §417(b). The survivorship annuity must be worth no less than 50% of the value of the joint annuity that was payable during the joint lives of the participant and the spouse (and no more than 100% of the value of that joint life annuity). Further, the combined joint and survivor annuities must be worth the actuarial equivalent of a single life annuity for the participant alone under the terms of the qualified plan.

A qualified preretirement survivor annuity is payable for the life of the participant's surviving spouse. §417(c). In a defined contribution plan, it must be worth at least 50% of the participant's account balance at death. In a defined benefit plan, the annuity must be the actuarial equivalent of the survivor annuity that would be payable under a qualified joint and survivor annuity if the participant had retired immediately before death or, if not then entitled to retire, on the earliest possible date when the participant could have retired. See §417(c)(1)(A).

It is notable that the qualified preretirement survivor annuity is not the actuarial equivalent of the benefit that would be available if the participant had survived to the annuity starting date and a qualified joint and survivor annuity had become payable. An unanswered question is whether the difference between the participant's account balance and the value of this qualified preretirement survivor annuity is forfeited, or whether it is subject to disposition by the participant in some other manner.

Knowledgeable pension specialists indicate that this issue is not resolved in most plans, although some major plans specify that the excess is forfeited (meaning the plan, rather than the participant's beneficiaries, picks up the excess). In any plan the normal rule is that, absent an effective beneficiary designation, the provisions of the plan will govern disposition of this amount rather than this amount passing under state intestacy laws. See MacLean v. Ford Motor Co., 831 F.2d 723 (7th Cir. 1987). So the participant's beneficiary designation should attempt to dispose of this excess, if possible.

A plan is exempt from the spousal annuity requirements if (1) the plan is not a defined benefit plan, a defined contribution plan, or a direct transferee of either (for example, the plan is an IRA,[18] a simplified employee pension, a §403(b) salary reduction agreement, an ESOP, a Keogh plan, or a profit-sharing plan during the participant's life), or (2) the participant's nonforfeitable accrued benefit is payable in full to the surviving spouse on the participant's death and the participant did not elect payments in a life annuity format. §401(a)(11)(B)(iii).

A plan also is exempt from the spousal annuity requirements if the participant's spouse waives the right to the annuity by consenting to the participant's designation of some other beneficiary. Temp. Treas. Reg. §1.401(a)-11(c) establishes how the consent must be documented, and §417(a)(6) establishes the timing requirements for an effective waiver and consent. For example, the consent may (but need not) be irrevocable (even though the plan cannot deny the right to revoke a consent). It also is

---

18. As a consequence, spousal consent is required before a participant may roll over to an IRA. Temp. Treas. Reg. §1.401(a)(31)-1 Q&A 14.

permissible for the participant to revoke a spousal consent. But under Treas. Reg. §1.401(a)-20 Q&A 28 the Internal Revenue Service will not recognize prenuptial agreements as a valid spousal consent, and there is little doubt that this is a permissible position.[19]

In addition, waiver of the qualified joint and survivor annuity must occur within 90 days before the required beginning date. §§417(a)(1)(A); 417(a)(6)(A). The spouse must be informed about the participant's beneficiary designation, and that designation cannot be altered without the further consent of the spouse unless the original spousal consent expressly gave the participant the right to make changes in the future without the spouse's consent. §417(a)(2)(A)(ii). Except with respect to a spouse's community property interest (due to gift tax complications), it probably is wise to obtain a consent that allows alterations by the participant without renewed consent from the spouse. See generally Treas. Reg. §1.401(a)-20 Q&A 30 et seq. with respect to the waiver and consent requirements.

Finally, a spousal consent does not mean that the spouse cannot be a designated beneficiary under the plan. Indeed, it is likely that many spousal consents will be made to permit elections other than annuities, with the spouse or a marital deduction trust as a lump sum beneficiary of the plan.

Planning Issues Relating to Designating Beneficiaries

Planning for retirement benefits may require the estate planner to become involved before the participant retires, at the time of retirement, or after the participant's death. Without question the latter is most common, although decisions made inter vivos in designating the beneficiary and in selecting a retirement payout will affect the income tax and other consequences after death. Whenever the planner gets involved, the first order of business should be to consult the plan documents to determine what options are available.

Invariably, retirement benefits are income in respect of a decedent, meaning that §1014(c) denies a basis adjustment and, in most cases, the basis of the benefit payout is zero. Thus, income tax must be paid on the amounts as they are received. An anticipated application of §1022 carryover basis (if the estate tax is repealed) will not alter this. Until repeal of the estate tax the question will remain whether the benefits should be

---

19. Notwithstanding Uniform Premarital Agreement Act §3, 9C U.L.A. 43 (2001), which authorizes the beneficiary of a retirement plan to relinquish any interest through a prenuptial agreement, according to Treas. Reg. §1.401(a)-20 Q&A 28 the spousal waiver and consent cannot be given until the participant is married; a prenuptial agreement is not effective to make the waiver. See Hurwitz v. Sher, 789 F. Supp. 134 (S.D. N.Y. 1992), aff'd, 982 F.2d 778 (2d Cir. 1992); Callahan v. Hutsell, Callahan & Buchino Revised Profit Sharing Plan, 1992 U.S. Dist. LEXIS 20773 and 813 F. Supp. 541 (W.D. Ky. 1992) (separate opinions); Zinn v. Donaldson Co. Salaried Employees Retirement Savings Plan, 799 F. Supp. 69 (D. Minn. 1992).

paid to a marital deduction trust or to a nonmarital trust. Relevant to this inquiry is whether it would be desirable to waste the marital fund with the income tax that will be payable on the benefits as received. Another option may be to use this wealth to fund a charitable gift, because the income tax imposed on that recipient is a better result than imposing it on any other beneficiary of the participant. Further, control issues and the availability of other assets to allocate to the nonmarital trust should inform these decisions.

Also relevant is the frequently unanswered question whether retirement benefits are allocable to income or principal for state fiduciary accounting purposes.[20] This issue in particular is too often overlooked; state law and the terms of the document must be considered before concluding that the appropriate treatment is clear.

Another serious issue is how wealth transfer taxes attributable to the benefits will be paid. In most situations liquidity is a serious issue with respect to retirement benefits, to the extent they are includible in an estate and do not qualify for the marital deduction. This concern is magnified if the benefits are not paid in a lump sum. In this case that means payable in one taxable year of the recipient on account of the participant's death. See §402(d)(4)(A). This may be a double-edged issue if community property ownership rights of the participant's spouse are involved. In addition, payment in a lump sum may generate an immediate income tax that otherwise could be deferred. This is the price to be paid for liquidity.

The most important question, however, is who should be the designated beneficiary and how should the designated beneficiary receive the distribution: in annuity form, as a lump sum distribution, or (if the participant's surviving spouse is beneficiary) as a rollover distribution. Factors to be considered in determining the form of distribution include:

- Expected income and estate tax rates;
- Expected return on the dollars received and whether a tax free build up in a rollover receptacle or in an annuity is desirable;

---

20. For example, Revised Uniform Principal and Income Act (1962 Act) §11, 7B U.L.A. 228 (2000), provides that principal consists of the "rights to receive payments on a contract for deferred compensation" and also provides that receipts not in excess of 5% of inventory value are income and the balance is principal. But §4 of the Act, applicable only to estates, also provides that periodic payments, including annuities, are allocable to principal to the extent accrued before death, with the portion accrued postmortem allocable to income. Further, §13(a)(6) charges income taxes on such receipts to income, although §13(c)(4) provides that income taxes incurred under §691 as income in respect of a decedent are a charge to principal to the extent the payments are allocable to principal. Analogous provisions in the Uniform Principal and Income Act (1997 Act), 7B U.L.A. 170, 184, 187 (2000), include §§409(c) (required periodic distributions such as under the minimum distribution rules are allocable 10% to income, the balance to principal; lump sum and other payments are allocable entirely to principal), 409(d) (allocating additional amounts to income as required for marital deduction qualification purposes), 502(a)(6) (charging transfer taxes to principal), and 505 (charging income taxes proportionately as the receipts are allocated).

- Life expectancy of a designated life annuitant as beneficiary or the term certain over which the benefit would be received as an annuity;
- *Liquidity*: will the funds be needed to pay taxes or otherwise, making a lump sum distribution essential (assuming it is allowable under the terms of the plan);
- The desired degree of control and investment flexibility (an annuity gives little, a rollover gives more, but a lump sum payment gives the most);
- Whether a rollover distribution is more important than restrictions on control over the property;
- Whether control exercised to make inter vivos gifts will produce more wealth for the objects of the participant's bounty than income tax deferral will produce (often the gift alternative is preferable notwithstanding the income tax cost of withdrawals to provide the necessary funds); and
- Whether a spousal consent to any beneficiary designation will be problematic.

Given the amount of uncertainty that can surround the selection of a beneficiary and payout option, many planners recommend that the beneficiary designation be structured so that disclaimers can be made to move the property through a succession of intended beneficiaries. For example, the beneficiary designation might be structured to pay an annuity or a lump sum first outright to the participant's surviving spouse (who, among other factors to recommend this approach, is the only beneficiary who can roll over to an IRA to further defer income tax), second to the participant's marital deduction trust (if any),[21] third to a nonmarital trust, then outright to the participant's surviving descendants and, finally, if all else fails, to the participant's estate, all by default or disclaimers at each higher beneficiary designation level. Moreover, added thought by the estate planner will be required to coordinate income tax elections and liquidity concerns if multiple beneficiaries may be selected.[22]

In any trust, a provision should specify that amounts received that are exempt from federal wealth transfer tax (either because the benefits are

---

21. Alternatively to a bypass trust that is capable of being elected as qualified terminable interest property. It is notable that wasting some unified credit may be a preferable result if it permits the surviving spouse to make an IRA rollover election to defer income taxes, especially if coupled with a gifting program conducted by the surviving spouse postmortem.

22. See Private Letter Ruling 9630034 for a road map of a cascading disclaimer beneficiary designation, and Keydel & Wallace, *The Revocable Trust—Disclaimer Method for Integrating Qualified Plan & IRA Benefits into an Estate Plan*, 13 PROB. NOTES 158 (1987), recommending a slightly different order of priorities and containing sample forms. By Private Letter Rulings 9319029, 9303027, and 9037048, the government deems §2518 qualification as a disclaimer for wealth transfer tax purposes as adequate for income tax purposes as well, to preclude the disclaimant from having to report income under §§691, 402(a), and 408(d)(1), respectively, and instead for the person taking by virtue of the disclaimer to be regarded as the proper income taxpayer.

chronologically exempt from repeal of the former estate tax exclusions for retirement benefits or because the unified credit is adequate to shelter this property) are to be allocated to the nonmarital trust to preserve the benefit of that exclusion. Another provision should specify how items of income in respect of a decedent should be allocated between marital and nonmarital trusts to prevent an acceleration of the income tax liability under §691(a)(2). And the trustees of each potential recipient should have the express authority to make disclaimers to permit the benefits to pass down the line of beneficiaries.

Marital deduction qualification of benefits payable in installments (to any trust other than an estate trust) requires that the surviving spouse be entitled to all income generated by the plan or account annually. §§2056(b)(5) and (b)(7)(B)(i)(II). If this income amount exceeds the minimum distribution amount for the year, the government requires either that the spouse have a power to demand, or that the trust itself requires, that the trustee make a withdrawal from the account or plan equal to that excess of the annual income generated by the plan or account over the minimum distribution amount. Treas. Reg. §20.2056(b)-7(h) Example 10 and Rev. Rul. 2000-2. It is too early to know whether the §643(b) income definition rules and their 3% to 5% unitrust safe harbor income equivalence rule might affect any of this. See Chapter 7 at page 72.

Alternatively, as discussed in Chapter 7 at page 88, the trustee could simply distribute corpus of the marital deduction trust equal to the amount of that income in the plan or account, which may permit a longer deferral of distributions from the plan (but also may be inconsistent with the decedent's desire to deny control over the trust to the surviving spouse). Unfortunately, marital deduction qualification requires no less. Congress granted §2056(b)(7)(C) automatic QTIP qualification to a spousal annuity payable *outright* to the participant's surviving spouse, which is just one of several reasons why outright distribution is a preferable approach.

If it is not essential that the full value of the participant's account balance qualify for the marital deduction, a partial QTIP election might be permissible for only the amount of corpus deemed necessary to produce the annuity payments guaranteed to the marital deduction trust or directly to the surviving spouse annually. Treas. Reg. §20.2056(b)-7(e)(2). See Technical Advice Memorandum 8446006. Based on the applicable valuation tables, this amount may not be as great as the amount includible in the decedent's gross estate under §2039 (but conceivably it could exceed that amount, in which case the marital deduction would be limited to the amount includible in the participant's gross estate).

As a practical matter, however, outright distribution to the participant's surviving spouse is the easiest approach and raises the fewest qualification issues. It allows the surviving spouse to select whether to receive an annuity, or a lump sum distribution, or to roll the distribution over for maximum income tax deferral. It allows annual redetermination of life expectancy, it avoids fiduciary liability relating to selecting among payout options or making disclaimers or other tax elections, and the income tax liability inherent in the distributions will reduce the amount taxable in the surviving spouse's estate at death. Most importantly, the spousal annuity consent that is needed to deviate from the annuity approach is not likely to raise objections from the surviving spouse. Considering all these factors, any other beneficiary designation should be made only after the most careful deliberation.

Chapter 11

PAYING ESTATE OBLIGATIONS

The obligation to pay debts, expenses, and taxes is a complex subject. It demands as much separate consideration as any dispositive provision in a will or trust. You may not expect to represent estates sizeable enough to require payment of federal estate tax, but there are state and even local wealth transfer taxes, plus income taxes incurred during estate administration, along with debts and expenses that can consume a significant portion of some decedents' wealth. This makes the provision directing payment of these liabilities an important provision in the estate plan. Yet many drafters regard this provision as boilerplate and give little individualized attention to it. This Chapter illustrates that this lack of attention is a prescription for error.

To assist readers who come to this study with varying degrees of knowledge, this discussion is organized to provide a few illustrations of why this topic is so important and how easy it is to mess up. Then follows a summary of federal and state rules regarding the time and source of payment, elaborating on what happens in the absence of other controlling principles, such as contrary will or trust provisions. Readers who are familiar with these fundamental principles may want to skip to the discussion of planning aspects of the apportionment rules, and readers who must prepare payment provisions will find that the final segment relates to drafting considerations.

Included at the very end is a sample payment provision. If you will look at page 43 and thereafter, ask yourself as you read whether a six page provision *really* is necessary! The secret is to delete what you don't need in appropriate cases. But that requires individuated attention to this topic in every estate, which is what most planners fail to do. If you treat this as boilerplate, which provisions could you safely delete? Those are the drafting issues at stake here.

Tax Payment Burden on the Residue

Under §2002 of the federal estate tax,[1] the initial obligation to pay the *entire* federal estate tax imposed on a decedent's gross estate (probate and nonprobate property alike) rests on the decedent's personal representative,

---

1. "The tax imposed by this chapter shall be paid by the executor." Executor is defined by §2203 to mean "the executor or administrator of the decedent, or, if there is no executor or administrator appointed, qualified, and acting within the United States, then any person in actual or constructive possession of any property of the decedent."

regardless of the fact that certain assets includible in the gross estate for federal estate tax purposes may not be in the possession or control of that fiduciary. This primary obligation is so extensive that any recipient of nonprobate property included in the gross estate who is compelled to pay a portion of the estate tax (for example, under transferee liability rules in §6324(a) or §6901(a)) is entitled under §2205[2] to reimbursement from the personal representative.

By virtue of the §2203 definition of executor, only "if there is no executor or administrator appointed, qualified, and acting [does] any [other] person in actual or constructive possession of any property of the decedent" become initially liable for payment of the tax. And even then the person paying the tax is entitled to reimbursement from the residue of the decedent's estate. This federal burden on the residue matches traditional common law.

To illustrate how problematic this can be, consider the following example, based on the actual result in Collier v. First National Bank, 417 S.E.2d 653 (Ga. 1992). The decedent created a revocable inter vivos trust and, because local probate procedure was not cumbersome, she also sought certain income tax advantages that were available to probate estates but not to will substitute living trusts. Thus, the decedent provided that the trust would pour back into her estate at death and be distributed from the estate to the intended remainder beneficiaries. The residue of the decedent's probate estate benefited children by a second marriage. The trust remainder went by preresiduary bequest to children of a first marriage because the trust corpus was monies inherited by the decedent from that first spouse. The decedent's will contained a traditional burden on the residue tax (and debts and expenses) payment provision that waived all rights of reimbursement.

The decedent was a domiciliary of Georgia, a state that applied the traditional common law burden on the residue rule. As a result, state law did not require apportionment of the estate tax liability among the recipients of the various assets includible in the decedent's gross estate. Nor did the decedent's will. The trust corpus that was includible in the estate passed to the children by the first marriage under the preresiduary bequest, leaving the residue of the decedent's probate estate to pay all taxes on the entire estate.

---

2. Stating:

If the tax or any part thereof is paid by, or collected out of, that part of the estate passing to or in the possession of any person other than the executor in his capacity as such, such person shall be entitled to reimbursement out of any part of the estate still undistributed or by a just and equitable contribution by the persons whose interest in the estate of the decedent would have been reduced if the tax had been paid before the distribution of the estate or whose interest is subject to equal or prior liability for the payment of taxes, debts or other charges against the estate, it being the purpose and intent of this chapter that so far as is practicable and unless otherwise directed by the Will of the decedent the tax shall be paid out of the estate before its distribution.

Not surprisingly, the children of the decedent's second marriage, as residuary beneficiaries of the estate, perceived the inequity of this plan and claimed they were entitled to reimbursement for the taxes attributable to the inter vivos trust, notwithstanding the tax payment provision in the decedent's will and its apparent waiver of all rights of reimbursement. They argued that a federal right of reimbursement (under §2207B, which is discussed at page 18) applied and that, by its express provisions, it could not be waived without making specific reference to it, which they claimed was lacking in this case.

The children of the first marriage rejoined that the §2207B right of reimbursement was not available because it applies only if property is includible in the decedent's gross estate under §2036, and they alleged that the inclusion provision was either §2033 or §2038, not §2036. The Georgia Supreme Court "resolved" the dispute by saying:

> [T]he [parties] argue that the trust assets are includable in the decedent's gross estate . . . under different sections of the Internal Revenue Code, each with different estate tax [payment] consequences.
>
> The question of whether the transfer of these assets from the decedent . . . casts tax liability on the estate or upon the trust must be answered under the Internal Revenue Code. As such, it is beyond the jurisdiction of this court.

Indeed, on that all-important issue there appears to be no direct authority. By the way, the children of the first marriage won in *Collier*, the residuary bequest to the children by the second marriage was wiped out, and the only recourse they had was to sue the drafting attorney.

In one sense the government does not care about the issue in *Collier*, as long as the property does not escape tax altogether. Rev. Rul. 75-553 involved similar facts to *Collier* and the government stated that "the trust corpus is payable to the decedent's estate and [therefore] is property of the decedent within the meaning of section 2033 and is includible in the gross estate only under that section." This caused the government to lose the opportunity to assert a lien against the trustee for transferee liability. Again under Private Letter Ruling 8940003 a trust was subject to §2033 inclusion instead of §2036 and the government lost the opportunity to assert application of §2035(a)(2) with respect to property distributed from the trust within three years of the decedent's death. Both authorities, which are directly adverse to the government's interest, nevertheless held that §2033 is the proper inclusion result, which is a strong indication that the proper inclusion provision in the *Collier* example was §2033 as well. Which would produce the "wrong" (at least a very unfair) tax apportionment result. But see Technical Advice Memorandum 9015001. On such an important question it really is notable that (to this day) we don't know the "right" answer.

In one respect the conclusion that §2033 is the proper inclusion provision is fitting because §2033 is the all-purpose inclusion rule for property owned by a decedent at death; §§2036 and 2038 are inclusion provisions designed to cause inclusion of property that §2033 does not reach. Thus, as a matter of statutory construction, it ought to be that application of §2033 precedes all other inclusion provisions. If it is adequate to cause inclusion, then no other provision applies. In the case illustrated this conclusion was asserted to be particularly apt because it would produce the same result as under local law. Although the result appears inequitable to the children by the second marriage, it is the result that would have applied had the decedent died without a will and, assuming that the estate plan was drafted with these rules in mind, presumably it represented the decedent's intent. Quaere, however, whether the documents indicate that the drafter considered this issue at all: a well crafted plan would have anticipated this issue and addressed it to state the decedent's particular intent either way, especially because the outcome (and maybe the inferred intent) appear to be inequitable.

In any event, the net result was that there was no definitive answer to the question whether §2207B applied in *Collier*. Indeed, to further illustrate how difficult this area of the law can be, §2207B was not even enacted when the trust and will were executed. As a result, the decedent's plan worked a significant and potentially unintended inequality, as did the traditional state law burden on the residue rule, yet nothing indicated that it was not the decedent's intent. And nothing changed it, which meant that the children by the second marriage effectively were disinherited, because the tax on the trust exhausted the residue.

Lest the former example be dismissed as unusual because of the pour back provision to the decedent's probate estate at death, consider that the exact same issue would arise even if the trust distributed directly to the children by the first marriage. That is true because the application of §2207B still would be in doubt. The §2207B reimbursement right would exist if the property was includible in the decedent's gross estate under §2036(a)(1) because of the retained life estate in the trust. But §2207B reimbursement would not exist if the property was includible in the decedent's gross estate under §2038(a)(1) because the trust was revocable until death.

There has not been an occasion in a federal estate tax case to question which of those two provisions applies in a garden-variety revocable trust case, the assumption being that the trust corpus is includible and, if it is not includible twice, it does not matter under which provision. Now that question may need to be answered, depending on what the decedent's tax payment provision provides and how the trust property and the balance of the decedent's estate are distributable.

The issue *was* addressed by *In re* Estate of Meyer, 702 N.E.2d 1078, 1081 n.3 (Ind. Ct. App. 1998), citing Treas. Reg. §20.2031-1(a)(2) for the proposition that there is overlap among inclusion provisions such as

§§2036 and 2038 and that property may be includible under more than one. *Meyer* stated that the trust beneficiaries' argument ("without citing to any authority") that the trust property was "more properly included" under §2038 than §2036 and, therefore, that the §2207B reimbursement right did not exist, "is without merit because the two sections are not mutually exclusive." So, the right of reimbursement *does* exist? That just shifts the *Collier* issue to whether the waiver of reimbursement provision was effective and what did the decedent *really* understand or intend. Do you doubt the drafter screwed up if these questions must be resolved by litigation?

A client does not need to have an elaborate or unusual dispositive plan to illustrate that the state law burden on the residue rule may be inappropriate or that payment provisions require deliberate consideration in even simple, commonplace estate plans. By way of example, picture the plan addressed by *In re* Estate of Maierhofer, 767 N.E.2d 850 (Ill. App. Ct. 2002). The testator intended to provide equal shares of the estate to two siblings, and bequeathed a specific property to one of them and then distributed the residue with an equalization provision designed to provide a larger share to the other sibling so that, in the end, each took equal value.

Unfortunately the residue was insufficient to accomplish the equalization (even if the second sibling took the entire residue) and was even more inadequate because the will called for payment of estate taxes, on both the preresiduary devise and the balance of the estate, all from the residue. The court rejected a pro rata tax apportionment scheme proposed by the second sibling because the clear language of the will directed payment of taxes from the residue, which put the burden disproportionately on the second sibling rather than on the siblings equally. Notwithstanding the other clear object of the will, that the two siblings emerge from probate with gifts of equal value, state law (it was a burden on the residue jurisdiction) and the document failed in that result in *Maierhofer*.

You could guarantee equality by substituting for the preresiduary devise a simple equal division of the residue, with the one sibling's share to be funded first with the specified realty. Because that property exceeded half the value of the estate, the one sibling could have been required to purchase the other's share or simply accept less than 100% ownership. Perhaps neither of those consequences was palatable to the testator. Or perhaps the estate planner never thought about them (and merely drafted what the client described without any real evaluation of the overall consequences). Imagine the second child's distress. And the subsequent malpractice suit!

Tax payment problems also can be generated simply because a client is married, because the unlimited marital deduction makes it possible to defer payment of all federal (and most states') wealth transfer tax until the death of the surviving spouse. The risk of deferral is bankrupting the surviving spouse's estate if the source for tax payment at that time is not properly specified or considered. Further, the increase in the number of second marriages requires a reappraisal of both the appropriate size of a bequest to a surviving spouse (if there are children by a prior marriage), and the proper allocation of tax liability at the survivor's death.

Issues can arise even in a single marriage situation if the decedent does not want to make the children wait until the surviving spouse's death to receive all of their inheritance. In that case there must be a source for payment of taxes in the estate of the first spouse to die, which inevitably will reduce the share left to either object of the client's bounty if taxes attributable to nonmarital bequests exceed the amount of the available unified credit.

Further, in conjunction with postmortem planning that involves the marital deduction, it is necessary to consider the source for payment of taxes caused by the surviving spouse's partial disclaimer of a marital deduction bequest, or a partial QTIP election.

It also pays to consider the unexpected. Imagine an asset or disposition about which the decedent never told the estate planner and that impacts the marital deduction and therefore the tax liability in totally unexpected ways. A fine illustration of this (albeit one that isn't likely to be encountered in just every estate plan) highlights the consequences of placing the burden of tax payment on the residue of an estate without knowing all the facts. (Indeed, is it *ever* possible to know *all* the facts?) The case involves a decedent's shadow estate plan, disposing of unknown assets to unknown beneficiaries. It was *In re* Estate of Kuralt, 981 P.2d 771 (Mont. 1999), which ultimately determined that a handwritten letter was a valid holographic will. This was not the decedent's well-crafted and fully executed document that disposed of the bulk of the decedent's wealth to the decedent's family. Instead, this was the one the decedent penned from a hospital room while dying, leaving property in Montana that the estate planner (indeed, the family) didn't know existed, to a beneficiary that neither the family nor the estate planner knew about.

In other cases the unknown asset might be an insurance policy payable to comply with some unrevealed promise or obligation (such as to support a nonmarital child, or as part of a business deal), property discovered in a safety deposit box with a handwritten note constituting a valid disposition to (or confirming a joint tenancy with) a third party, or an asset transferred inter vivos and includible in the taxable estate. All of these surprises could pass in ways that increase the gross estate for tax purposes but, because of the beneficiary, cannot qualify for the marital deduction. Disaster awaits if these items exceed the applicable exclusion amount, resulting in taxes that the estate plan unexpectedly imposes on the residue that otherwise needs to qualify for the marital deduction. Because the deduction is not available, these assets generate a tax that further eats into the property that *does* qualify for the marital deduction, which further increases the tax liability, which again consumes marital deduction property and further increases the tax, and so on. See page 16 for an illustration.

Recall that §2056(d) disallows the marital deduction if the decedent's surviving spouse is not a United States citizen (unless a qualified domestic trust is used). Unexpected discovery that the surviving spouse is not a citizen is yet another of those wake up moments that sometimes even the most careful estate planner cannot always avoid. For inexplicable reasons clients don't always reveal all the facts (even when they are asked) or they do things on the eve of dying without seeking counsel. Go figure! All of which speaks to the idiocy of placing an unknown tax burden on the residue of the estate rather than apportioning the tax to each beneficiary or asset, unless the taker or the property is specifically identified and exonerated from that liability. This is the approach followed in the sample tax payment provision at page 43.

Yet another major area of concern in the tax payment arena relates to "phantom" assets that are includible in a decedent's gross estate but not available for payment of the tax attributable to them. With respect to these, the burden on the residue rule easily can result in the probate estate being bankrupted and the decedent's estate planning objectives being totally frustrated. Imagine that your client with a nontaxable estate wins the lottery (or a very large tort judgment for injuries that eventually result in death), pushing the estate into tax trouble but with an entitlement that may not yield cash for many years.

A second source of tax on phantom assets is a §529(c)(4)(C) college saving plan "recapture" tax that is attributable to assets no longer owned. Of the limited sources for payment of the §529(c)(4)(C) estate tax, it is equitable that the donees who received the gifted assets should pay the tax generated by the property they received, as presumably they would if the decedent had died with that property includible in the gross estate and left it to the donees at death. But the funds may not exist (having been gifted to pay for college tuition). It might be necessary under state law to condition the §529 gift itself with an agreement to pay any tax incurred at death, to be certain that the estate will not be facing the phantom asset tax liability problem. Yet this may be the wrong way to resolve the problem if the gift is to fund college expenses. At a minimum it seems fair to say that, without planning at the time of the gift, the situation after death could be impossible for a personal representative to resolve as a matter of state law or practical application.

Probably the greatest concern about phantom assets and the taxes attributable to them involves retirement benefits that are includible in a decedent's gross estate under §2039 but not accessible for payment of the tax attributable to them. More severe yet is the unresolved question whether a participant's spouse has an ownership interest in a plan, either by virtue of qualified plan provisions guaranteeing a §401(a)(11) spousal annuity to the nonparticipant spouse or under community property laws that deem the account to be owned by each spouse equally.

If either source of inclusion exists and the nonparticipant spouse dies first, it is extremely unlikely that the plan would permit the nonparticipant spouse to apportion estate taxes against the plan while the participant still is alive. Indeed, it might be impossible to reach plan assets to contribute to the payment of tax even if it was the participant who died first. Potentially the marital deduction will avoid tax payment in most cases, but not always.[3] Here are real assets that are not available to pay any tax that may be attributable to them, creating the need to carefully consider the tax payment obligation of the participant and nonparticipant spouses. At the very least, a burden on the residue result may create problems and inequities. Unfortunately it may be unavoidable in this particular situation.

These issues are ignored so often by estate planners, maybe because they pose no clear answers. Please do not be the planner who included a boilerplate provision because you just didn't think about these issues. This is the single most common source of messed up plans (and probably of drafter liability), and not just with respect to taxes, although those tend to be the cases that do not settle (probably because the numbers are too large).

Procedure

Time of Payment

The time allowed to raise the necessary capital must be considered in addition to evaluating the source and liquidity of funds needed to pay debts, expenses, federal estate tax, and any state death taxes. In this respect, the date the federal estate tax return is due and the tax must be paid is most important, although it may be possible to defer payment of the tax. Under §6151(a), the tax must be paid when the return is required to be filed, which is nine months after the decedent's death,[4] unless an extension of the time for payment is secured.[5] Notice that an extension of the time for filing the return does not constitute an extension of the time for payment of the tax. A separate extension for each is required. Treas. Reg. §§20.6081-1(d); 20.6151-1(a).

Transferee Liability

The time for payment is important to more than the question of liquidity, however, because liability for payment of the tax may extend to each transferee or holder of property included in the gross estate if the tax is not paid when due. Personal transferee liability attaches to the extent of the lesser of the total tax that is due or the value of any property received or held by a transferee. In addition, if the tax is not paid when due,

---

3. Technical Advice Memorandum 8943006 held what §2056(b)(7)(C) now expressly confirms in most cases: a nonparticipant spouse's community property interest in a qualified plan is deemed to pass to the surviving participant spouse and to qualify for the marital deduction, but that result is not guaranteed if the nonparticipant's interest is not a function of community property laws.

4. See §6075(a). A nearly automatic six month extension to file the return is available upon request. Treas. Reg. §20.6081-1(b).

5. See §§6161 (extension for reasonable cause), 6163 (extension with respect to future interests), and 6166 (extension of the tax attributable to a qualifying business).

personal liability also is imposed on the personal representative under §2002.[6] Transferee liability imposed on any beneficiary or person in possession of includible property[7] thus is in addition to both the liability that normally attaches to the personal representative and the 10 year lien that attaches to estate property[8] and any proceeds from the sale of assets included in the estate.[9] In either case, personal liability is discharged once the tax is paid or payment is adequately secured.[10]

Extensions of Time to File or Make Payment

Extensions of time may defer liability for filing the federal estate tax return or for payment of the federal estate tax. A nearly automatic extension of a reasonable period to file the return, not to exceed six months (longer if the taxpayer is abroad), historically was granted with such regularity upon request that the government by regulation now has determined to grant it as a matter of course in most every case.[11] A similar extension of up to 12 months to pay the tax also is available upon a request that must show "reasonable cause."[12] In addition, an extension of up to 10 years to pay the tax may be granted in the discretion of the Secretary upon a showing of "undue hardship" and, if later, any installment payment under the tax deferral provisions of §6166 may be extended for up to 12 months after that installment is due.[13] Separate extensions to pay any assessed deficiency also are available upon a showing of undue hardship,[14] again in the discretion of the Secretary, but not to exceed four years.

The "reasonable cause" needed to justify an extension is illustrated under Treas. Reg. §20.6161-1(a)(1) Examples (1)-(4) as including an inability to marshal liquid assets because they are located in other jurisdictions or because litigation is required to collect them; an inability to borrow on better than disfavorable terms (in relation to returns otherwise available to the estate on its investments); and an insufficiency of funds to

---

6. Effected through a lien under §6321 (based on 31 U.S.C. §192, which imposes personal liability on anyone who distributes estate property prior to satisfaction of all indebtedness to the United States), and extending to any interest or penalties on the tax, which are treated as part of the tax liability for all these lien and liability purposes. See §§6601(e)(1) and 6665(a), respectively.

7. See §§6324(a)(2) (lien) and 6901(a)(1) and (h) (transferee liability).

8. See §6324(a)(1). Property used to pay allowable expenses of administration and charges against the estate is excepted from the lien.

9. See §6324(a)(2) and Treas. Reg. §301.6324-1(a)(2)(iii).

10. See §§2204(a) (discharge of personal representative), 2204(b) (discharge of fiduciary other than personal representative), and 6325(c) (discharge of transferee liability).

11. See §6081(a); Treas. Reg. §20.6081-1(b). The automatic extension is not available with respect to Forms 706-A, 706-D, 706-NA, or 706-QDT, but the discretionary extension remains available in those cases.

12. See §6161(a)(1).

13. See §6161(a)(2). Although it would appear that the same "reasonable cause" standard is applicable, Treas. Reg. §20.6161-1(a)(2) imposes the "undue hardship" standard for the longer extensions.

14. See §6161(b)(2). See Treas. Reg. §20.6161-2(b). However, §6161(b)(3) denies the extension for any deficiency attributable to negligence, intentional disregard of rules or regulations, or fraud with an intent to evade tax.

maintain the decedent's family, pay claims against the estate, and pay the estate tax, coupled with an inability to borrow at prevailing market rates. "Undue hardship" is a higher standard, illustrated by Treas. Reg. §20.6161-1(a)(2)(ii) Examples (1) and (2) as including a farm or closely held business that constitutes a significant portion of the estate (but not necessarily enough to qualify for deferral of the tax under §6166), sufficient other funds are not readily available, and an extension of time is needed to raise the capital without having to sell the farm or business; or the only available sale to generate liquidity would be at a sacrifice price or in a depressed market.

A second automatic extension of time for payment is granted under §6166 for that portion[15] of the tax attributable to inclusion of the value of a closely held business in a decedent's gross estate. Available only to the estate of a citizen or resident of the United States,[16] deferral allows payment of the estate tax in as many as 10 equal annual installments, with the first required no sooner than five years after the time otherwise specified for payment.[17] More than 35% of the value of the decedent's "adjusted gross estate"[18] must consist of an interest in a closely held business to qualify for this extension.[19]

The election to defer estate tax under §6166 must be made before the decedent's estate tax return is due, including any extensions otherwise allowed.[20] An election to defer any deficiency assessed with respect to an estate that includes an interest in a closely held business that otherwise qualifies may be made within 60 days after notice and demand for payment of the deficiency.[21] Finally, unlike other extensions available to defer the payment of tax, the §6166 deferral may be accelerated if certain events occur, such as accumulation of estate income, failure to timely pay an installment, or certain changes in or dispositions of the qualifying business interest.[22]

Problematic about all the automatic and discretionary deferrals is that each requires the taxpayer to pay interest on the taxes deferred. In addition, although the fiduciary's personal liability for payment of the deferred tax under §6321 may be supplanted by posting a bond under §§2204 and 6165,

---

15 Defined in §6166(a)(2), the portion is a pro rata amount based on a comparison of the §6166(b)(5) "closely held business amount" to the §6166(b)(6) "adjusted gross estate."

16. See §6166(a)(1).

17. See §6166(a)(3).

18. Defined for this purpose in §6166(b)(6) as the gross estate reduced by all amounts that are allowable as §2053 or §2054 deductions, even if not allowed (because, for example, a §642(g) election was made to claim those amounts as income tax deductions).

19. Defined in §6166(b)(1), substantial complexity surrounds this definition and the planning that is involved in making an estate qualify for deferral under it.

20. See §6166(d). Protective elections that are dependent upon final determination of the decedent's estate tax valuation are permitted under Treas. Reg. §20.6166-1(d).

21. See §6166(h). The election is not available, however, if the deficiency was attributable to negligence, intentional disregard of rules and regulations, or to fraud with intent to evade tax. Id. §6166(h)(1) (flush language).

22. See §6166(g).

often the requirements for the bond are so onerous[23] that this alternative seems unattractive. Thus, deferral may be costly, and the personal representative may have continuing liability if deferral is selected. All this makes the concept of deferred payment of tax a troubling prospect for many estates. One worrisome possibility is that the value of estate property available for payment of the tax will decline during the deferral period to a point at which it no longer is adequate. Another is that sufficient appreciation will occur to present a serious capital gain tax liability when the property ultimately is sold to produce liquidity for tax payment.

Apportionment Options

Congress determined in §2205 that the estate tax should be a burden on the estate as a whole, not on the individual beneficiaries of the estate as is the case with most state inheritance taxes. But Riggs v. Del Drago, 317 U.S. 95 (1942), held that state law or the terms of the decedent's estate plan may alter this apportionment of the federal estate tax. Thus, the estate plan may apportion the tax burden so that the impact of credits, deductions, and the inclusion of assets falls on those beneficiaries who receive includible assets, generate credits or deductions, and so forth. With this freedom to apportion, up to six major apportionment decisions must be made, several with additional subissues that may be addressed under state law or the estate plan.

Inside Apportionment

Inside apportionment deals with the question whether taxes ought to be borne by all classes of dispositions within (inside) a probate estate. Like §2205, the firmly established common law rule provides that taxes in the probate estate are a "burden on the residue." Thus, all taxes are paid out of the residuary estate before any taxes are allocated to or payable from other dispositions, such as general, demonstrative, or specific dispositions under a will. To the extent inside apportionment is dictated, such as by the modern statutes in most jurisdictions, every taker under a will bears a share of the taxes payable, regardless of the priority or class of disposition involved, and regardless of whether the subject property is realty or personalty. Usually the share is based on a proportionate determination.

At one time the common law distinguished between personalty and realty within any class of disposition, favoring the realty by specifying that the personalty should be used first to pay debts, expenses, and taxes. Thus, for example, even in a burden on the residue apportionment, the takers of residuary personalty would be disappointed prior to the takers of residuary realty. This antiquated system has been rejected by virtually every state,

---

23. See Treas. Reg. §§20.2204-1(b) and 20.6165-1(a), calling for bonds not in excess of twice the tax deferred, and §§2204(c) and 6324A, which provide for a lien with respect to taxes payable in installments under §6166. See §6324A(d)(6), which provides that the government may not require the §6165 bond if the taxpayer makes the appropriate §6324A lien election.

notwithstanding that this rule was consistent with the common law abatement rules that favored realty. In some estate plans it might be wise to embrace the concept by specifying certain assets for use first or to be protected until absolutely necessary in payment of estate expenses, debts, or taxes.

Outside Apportionment

Outside apportionment stands in juxtaposition to inside apportionment within testate and intestate estates alike. It involves the issue whether taxes ought to be apportioned among the takers of probate assets (either with or without inside apportionment) and the recipients of includible *nonprobate* (outside) assets. Thus, if nonprobate property is includible in the gross estate of a decedent under any of the estate tax inclusion provisions, then outside apportionment would dictate that the recipient of that property pay that portion of the taxes (state or federal) imposed on the total estate and attributable to that inclusion (computed in one of several methods discussed in more detail below).

This form of apportionment is particularly important because the interaction of state and federal law often creates confusion or gaps in the rules that govern the tax payment obligation. Moreover, the three most valuable assets includible in most decedents' estates all are nonprobate property: insurance, retirement benefits, and a personal residence held in joint tenancy with right of survivorship. As illustrated below, it is outside apportionment to which most state apportionment statutes apply and as to which the limited federal reimbursement rules exist. However, apportionment to some forms of nonprobate property is addressed far more clearly and appropriately than it is with respect to other forms.

Equitable Apportionment

Equitable apportionment involves the question whether dispositions that generate a tax deduction or other benefit should benefit exclusively from the tax advantage, rather than having it benefit all beneficiaries of the estate.

This arises most often when property passing to a surviving spouse qualifies for the marital deduction. The equitable apportionment question can apply in an intestate estate in which the spouse takes a statutory share of the estate, in a testate estate in which the spouse rejects the decedent's estate plan in favor of a statutory forced heir share, or in a testate estate (or will substitute) involving tax apportionment to the spouse's bequest (whether as a part of the residue or some other part of the total estate). It also could apply in any estate to the extent a premarital agreement or §2053 deductible property settlement agreement creates a claim against the estate (or a disposition under the will is in satisfaction of such a contractual claim against the estate). In that case the issue is whether deductible distributions in satisfaction of the claim are subject to apportionment of taxes.

Also a source of equitable apportionment is the §2055 charitable deduction and, although less obviously so, the §2032A reduction in tax attributable to special use valuation. There may be other benefits from time to time as well (witness the §2057 orphans' deduction, and then the §2057 ESOP sale proceeds deduction, and most recently the §2057 qualified family owned business interest deduction, all subsequently repealed).

Apportionment of Rate Differentials

Closely related to equitable apportionment is whether to apportion state estate or inheritance tax rate differentials based on each beneficiary's share of the estate. For example, some states impose a tax that favors more closely related beneficiaries over distant relatives or strangers. In such a state the issue is whether any apportionment should reflect these rate differentials.

Apportionment of Credits

Similarly related is the question whether to apportion the benefit of credits available to the estate that are connected with separate identifiable properties passing to designated individuals. For example, if some property incurs more state or foreign death tax than others, the apportionment issue is whether the beneficiaries thereof should receive the benefit of any credit attributable to the tax incurred on their entitlement.

To illustrate, consider the §2013 credit for previously taxed property, which may be apportioned and can be a source of real inequity if not considered properly. For example, assume that the decedent was the beneficiary of a trust created by a parent, with a §2041 general power of appointment that generates estate tax (to avoid generation-skipping transfer tax). A §2013 credit would be available to the decedent's estate if the parent and the decedent died within 10 years of each other. If §2207 liability for the estate tax attributable to the trust is imposed on the remainder beneficiaries of the trust (as discussed at page 17), it would seem that they also should receive the benefit of that credit, but they do not under most state laws.

The decedent could match the tax liability with the credit by waiving the §2207 reimbursement entitlement or by apportioning the credit. The issue is whether the decedent's estate can afford to pay the §2041 taxes on the trust. And in a more sophisticated plan in which the generation-skipping tax might be allowed to apply in some circumstances, it would be unwise to have the two tax liabilities payable by different sources, one by the decedent's estate and the other by the trust. If the plan were otherwise, differences in the source of payment might inform the decision of which tax to incur, rather than just weighing the amount of tax incurred under the respective systems.

Apportionment to Temporal Interests

A final apportionment alternative relates to the proper method for apportioning taxes attributable to property that is split into temporal interests, such as a life estate, a term of years, or an annuity given to one individual and the remainder or reversion belonging to another.

Apportionment Among Multiple Entities

If several estate planning documents (such as a will and a revocable inter vivos funded trust or an irrevocable insurance trust) are involved, apportionment issues are compounded by the need to decide how tax payment obligations should be imposed on the multiple entities. For example, the tax payment provisions in each document could:

- provide for payment of all taxes out of the probate estate (with or without inside apportionment);
- provide for payment of all taxes from the trust corpus (similarly with or without a form of inside apportionment among several shares created thereunder);
- provide for a ratable apportionment of taxes among the several entities (with or without apportionment under each as among the respective shares thereunder);
- provide that the trust shall contribute to the payment of taxes only to the extent the probate estate is insufficient to pay all the taxes imposed on the gross estate (or vice versa, and again with questions of apportionment under each disposition);
- provide that the trustee shall pay taxes only in the discretion of the trustee (under established guidelines, and with or without apportionment);
- provide that the trustee shall pay taxes to the extent the personal representative of the decedent's estate certifies the need therefor (again under guidelines and a specified apportionment regime);
- or simply permit the trustee to purchase assets from the estate to provide needed liquidity.

Not incidentally, these decisions must take into consideration the potential for conflicts of interest and the difficulty of exercising discretion if conflicting beneficial interests and different fiduciaries are involved.

Decedent's Choice

With respect to virtually all apportionment issues it is relatively clear (but not entirely without doubt) that a decedent may alter the customary burden under state or federal law. Thus, a testamentary disposition by clear provision may expressly specify the property and the takers who will bear the tax burden. By a clear provision in a testamentary disposition the decedent also may exonerate nonprobate property from any otherwise applicable state law directive requiring outside apportionment (and, although not nearly as clearly permissible, it is relatively well established that the decedent may impose the burden for tax payment on nonprobate assets through the use of a will provision).

In advising a client as to the best apportionment approach, a number of policies or considerations might be relevant and the client's wishes need to be ascertained. For example, with respect to inside apportionment, does the client favor the particular beneficiaries over the residuary takers? The common law abatement rules presume that this is the case, and failure to permit inside apportionment is consistent with it. In reality, often the particular beneficiaries fit into one of the following categories.

First is a marital deduction bequest that the client wants to maximize, in most cases resulting in no tax at the client's death, so apportionment is a moot issue. Even if the deduction does not totally eliminate taxes, however, protection of it is served by equitable apportionment. Second are those relatively minor dispositions that most individuals place in a separate article preceding the heart of the estate plan. For example, $100 to a despised sibling, or $10,000 to a favored employee. With respect to these, the common law abatement and apportionment rules are likely to be directly contrary to the intent of the client in the sense that, if anyone should suffer for insufficient assets in the estate, it should be these takers. But third are takers of special assets (think of the grand piano or special items of jewelry) who should not be asked to generate the liquidity to pay the tax attributable to their entitlement.

With respect to outside apportionment, does the client wish to have the probate estate pay taxes generated by property over which the client might have no control? This is particularly important with respect to §2044 qualified terminable interest property that is includible in the estate of a surviving spouse, especially in second marriage or related situations in which the trust property passes to beneficiaries for whom the surviving spouse may have no affinity.

With respect to the issue of equitable apportionment involving the marital deduction (and, to a certain extent, involving the charitable deduction as well), should the deductible share bear no tax because it generated no tax? Any estate tax imposed on the estate would be generated by property that did not qualify for the deduction. Most clients will embrace the notion that the marital deduction is designed for the benefit of the surviving spouse and, therefore, that the spouse ought to be the sole beneficiary of the deduction. A similar argument could be made in favor of charity. The most persuasive argument in favor of equitable apportionment is that the deduction itself will be reduced if the marital or charitable bequest bears a portion of the taxes imposed on a decedent's estate (if equitable apportionment does not apply). See §§2055(c) and 2056(b)(4)(A). Indeed, these deductions will be reduced by the full amount of tax that *could* be paid, even if for some reason it is not.

In some cases a reduction in the deduction correspondingly increases taxes that further serve to reduce the size of the bequest (because that share is a portion of the total estate available for distribution), which further increases taxes that again reduce the deduction, ad nauseam. For example, consider the following illustration of the comparative computations of a one-third forced heir share or intestate entitlement of a 2004 decedent's surviving spouse in an estate of $2.4 million:

1/3 of *Gross* Estate (i.e., *before* taxes)		1/3 of *Net* Estate (i.e., *after* taxes)
$2,400,000	Estate	$2,400,000
800,000	Marital	782,353
1,600,000	Taxable	1,617,647
45,000	Taxes	52,941
1,555,000	Residue	1,564,706

The final result is that a net estate division produces a marital share exactly half the size of the remaining residue, preserving the one-third entitlement dictated by the elective share provision, but the method of computation generates a smaller marital deduction (by $17,647) and more taxes (by $7,941). Curiously, the residue is actually better off (by $9,706) because of it. The issue whether the elective share should be a fraction of the net estate (after taxes) or the gross estate (before taxes) is simply the equitable apportionment issue working to protect the marital share from bearing a portion of the taxes in the gross estate division but not in the net estate computation.

Similar disputes can arise in applying the concept of equitable apportionment to the charitable deduction under §2055 and the question whether any fractional or percentage division ought to be before or after taxes.

Federal Rules Applicable to Tax Apportionment

In addition to the state law just discussed, there is federal law to consider in all of this. Notice how we have turned a full circle: federal law imposes the tax, state law or the document may alter apportionment of it and now we address a second layer of federal tax rules.

Estate Tax

The general rule that distinguishes the federal estate tax from an inheritance tax is §2205. It specifies that a nonprobate beneficiary who pays any federal estate tax is entitled to reimbursement from the personal representative out of probate property, "it being the purpose and intent of this chapter that . . . unless otherwise directed by the will of the decedent the tax shall be paid out of the estate before its distribution." This federal burden on the residue rule applies only to the extent neither state law nor the decedent's will provide otherwise. Nevertheless, it is subject in all events to four federal statutory rules that permit reimbursement for federal (but not any state) estate tax imposed on specific types of nonprobate property. That is, the residuary estate pays the tax and then may be entitled to *reimbursement* (as compared to apportionment in the first instance, which alters who pays the tax initially).

The oldest reimbursement provision is §2206. It provides a right of reimbursement for taxes paid by the estate with respect to §2042 inclusion of insurance proceeds payable to a third party. The personal representative is entitled to collect from every beneficiary of includible insurance proceeds the proportionate share of the total taxes paid by the estate that is attributable to that insurance.

Although waiver is authorized under the introductory clause of §2206, great care should be exercised to avoid inappropriate cancellation of this right. In this regard, consider *In re* Estate of Kapala, 402 N.W.2d 150 (Minn. Ct. App. 1987), in which the decedent's closely held corporation owned insurance on the life of the decedent, naming the decedent's partner as the beneficiary (it was intended to provide liquidity to perform under a buy-sell agreement when the decedent died). The insurance was includible under §2042(2) and the court found that §2206 reimbursement was not waived, notwithstanding that the buy-sell agreement provided that the surviving partner would receive all assets "free and clear of all claims of every kind." The court determined that waiver of §2206 must appear in an instrument with testamentary intent, which it found the buy-sell agreement to lack.

In some estates §2206 may be the only way to afford the taxes caused by unexpected inclusion. Care must be taken in drafting any contingent tax payment provision (for example, in an irrevocable life insurance trust) to preclude §2042(1) inclusion by virtue of that direction alone. But if for any reason the insurance is includible, either §2206 or a contingent tax clause may be essential for the estate to pay the estate tax attributable to that inclusion.

Added with the power of appointment provisions in 1942, §2207 employs virtually identical language to §2206 to grant an identical right of reimbursement for taxes attributable to property included in the gross estate under §2041. The personal representative may recover those taxes from "the person receiving such property by reason of the exercise, nonexercise or release of a power of appointment." Often this general power of appointment rule is critical because the decedent did not create the general power of appointment and the trust granting the power seldom includes a contingent tax payment provision.

Added in 1981, §2207A grants a significantly different right of reimbursement. Applying to §2044 includible qualified terminable interest property for which the §2056(b)(7) marital deduction was allowed, this right of reimbursement differs because it is an incremental rather than a proportionate entitlement. Effectively prorating all deductions and credits among all takers, §§2206 and 2207 apply to bottom line taxes imposed on a decedent's estate with respect to those portions causing inclusion under

§§2042 and 2041, respectively (and after considering the marital deduction). But §2207A permits recovery of the amount by which taxes were *increased* by inclusion of §2044 property, meaning the incremental taxes without benefit of deductions or credits available to the estate as a whole. In addition, interest and penalties attributable to §2044 property are subject to the incremental right of reimbursement. This also has no counterpart in §§2206 and 2207.

The difference between these reimbursement provisions is illustrated by Sarosdy v. Johnson, 894 S.W.2d 640 (Ky. Ct. App. 1994), in which a general power of appointment versus a qualified terminable interest property marital trust was involved. The estate was entitled to only pro rata reimbursement under §2207 rather than incremental reimbursement under §2207A, meaning that estate tax attributable to inclusion of the marital trust was payable in part from the decedent surviving spouse's own property. That estate would have passed totally free of tax (it was smaller than the applicable exclusion amount) had the marital trust not been includible, and arguably the estate should not have paid any of the estate tax that was attributable entirely to the marital trust.

To illustrate another significant issue under §2207A, assume spouses agreed that the surviving spouse would have the use of the decedent's wealth for the survivor's overlife, but that their respective shares would pass at the survivor's death to their respective beneficiaries. Incremental reimbursement under §2207A disrupts the intended equity of that plan by imposing a greater than pro rata share of the survivor's taxes on the decedent's qualified terminable interest property. Only if the survivor is willing to alter the incremental dictate of §2207A by a provision in the survivor's will would this be avoided, and the decedent cannot guarantee that the survivor will do so.

This inequity may be appropriate because otherwise the surviving spouse's unified credit would reduce the tax imposed on all the beneficiaries interested in the surviving spouse's estate tax computation, including those who take the qualified terminable interest property trust remainder (as well as the survivor's other beneficiaries). The first to die used his or her credit in most cases to shelter a nonmarital trust that favors that decedent's beneficiaries alone, so the §2207A rule may be a form of rough justice. Either way, this serious issue must be anticipated and may be addressed in drafting premarital agreements or coordinated estate plans that involve children by former marriages.

Finally, §2207B applies to taxes caused by inclusion of property under §2036. It calls for a pro rata right of reimbursement, like §§2206 and 2207, but includes interest and penalties attributable to the tax like only §2207A. Also like only §2207A, the entitlement created by §2207B may be waived by the decedent's revocable inter vivos trust as well as by a will, subject to a requirement that any waiver "specifically indicates an intent to waive" the reimbursement right. The tax simplification proposal that added this requirement to §2207A was accompanied by legislative history that almost surely will become a part of any regulations that are issued, providing that "a specific reference to QTIP, section 2044, or section 2207A" will suffice. Presumably a similar reference to §2036 or §2207B would suffice for §2207B specific intent purposes. Neither of §§2206 or 2207 includes any of these refinements.

For reasons that probably are more historical than substantive, there is no comparable federal provision for recovery of taxes attributable to nonprobate assets includible under §§2035 and 2037 through 2040, and none with respect to the estate tax aspects of §§2701 through 2704. There has been longstanding interest in a proposal to enact a provision similar to §§2207A and 2207B for the taxes caused by inclusion of §2039 retirement benefits in a decedent's gross estate. It is sensible to seek such an addition, because these benefits typically pass outside probate and often constitute a large share of the estate, risking bankruptcy of the probate estate in payment of estate taxes absent a right of reimbursement.

There has been some suggestion that the Treasury Department regards each of §§2206 through 2207B as matters properly left to state property law. Thus, it is suggested that, because these sections are not related to the imposition or collection of taxes in the first instance, the Treasury Department has no interest in adding a Code provision relating to §2039 or other nonprobate assets. This is particularly unfortunate, given the magnitude of some of these assets relative to a decedent's total estate and the assets otherwise available to pay taxes caused by their inclusion. But what it means to estate planners is that a well drafted tax payment provision must address the issues that federal law does not.

Generation-Skipping Transfer Tax Apportionment

Generation-skipping transfer tax §2603 contains its own reimbursement provision. It is an easily stated rule that, in essence, "the person with the generation-skipping property pays the tax out of that property." Like most simplifications, however, this statement is not entirely accurate.

To illustrate, assume that a decedent's will bequeaths $2 million to a grandchild. The issue is whether the decedent really meant to leave $2 million *after* the generation-skipping tax is paid from other property in the decedent's estate. Without more, the §2603 result is that $2 million is set aside and used to pay the tax as directed by §2603(b), with only the balance actually passing to the grandchild. In that case the tax (assuming no exemption or exclusion applies) would be computed (using 2004 figures) as

[rate] × [transfer (after tax)] = [tax]
.48 × $2 million / 1.48 = $648,649

The grandchild would actually receive $1,351,351, which is $2 million less $648,649 of tax.[24] If this is not the decedent's intent, then the document must clearly override §2603(b), causing a greater amount to be subject to the tax ($2 million rather than the $1,351,351 in this example) and causing the tax thereon to be greater ($960,000 in 2004 rather than $648,649). The difference in result is dramatic and should not be left to postmortem determination by litigation to determine the decedent's intent.

Summary of State Law: Silence Generates What Result?

The foregoing discussion reveals an amalgam of state and federal rules in this arena, and federal law that defers to the states in most respects (although it grants certain rights or imposes selected responsibilities that may trump state law). A number of legitimate choices might be made in determining the proper apportionment result, and conflicting results are dictated by the law in various jurisdictions in which the apportionment issues have been resolved. The following exegesis illustrates the state law results if an estate plan does not address the tax apportionment issue. If the documents are silent, in some states the issues are (partially) resolved by statute. In a declining number of states only judicial authority exists. But in a few states, on some issues, common law presumptions apply by default because statutory law is entirely silent. And from state to state (and occasionally within a given state), some of the results stated here are confused and inconsistent because the law is not uniform.

An established state dictate mandated under a state apportionment statute usually will apply unless the decedent clearly directs otherwise in an appropriate manner, whether by will, trust, or other document. The burden of proof normally is on those who challenge the state apportionment result when determining whether a decedent has provided otherwise with sufficient specificity and clarity. Thus, a direction to pay all taxes from the residue of a decedent's estate typically will cause taxes on nonprobate property to be paid from the residue in an apportionment state, although a nonspecific direction may cause litigation. For example, a general tax payment direction in a will may be read to negate apportionment, if any, only within the probate estate, leaving any state outside apportionment statute to apply with respect to nonprobate assets.

Because any effort to summarize the law in the 50 states is subject to unavoidable inaccuracies, and because the Uniform Estate Tax Apportionment Act is regarded by over 40% of the states as the best form of statutory apportionment, it is appropriate to consider its major provisions briefly here. The Act establishes rules of three major types:

---

24. As illustrated in the Form 706 Estate and Generation-Skipping Tax return, another formula to make this computation (in 2004) is

$$\frac{\text{Transfer (before tax)}}{3.08333}$$

The denominator is simply 1 plus the 48% tax rate, divided by the 48% tax rate.

Inside and Outside Apportionment. First, all taxes imposed on an estate (which would include an inheritance tax only if it were a charge against the estate as a whole, which is not normally the case with an inheritance tax as opposed to an estate tax) should be pro rated among all persons "interested in the decedent's gross estate for federal estate tax purposes." This is total inside and outside apportionment, applying a straight pro rata allocation based on the size of each interested individual's entitlement as compared to the size of the total estate for federal estate tax purposes.

As to apportionment, two special rules are designed to prevent unnecessary conflicts with federal law. One special rule, equitable apportionment, may be illustrated by a simple example. Assume that a decedent's estate passes to the decedent's surviving spouse in a fashion that qualifies for the federal estate tax marital deduction but not (entirely) for the state wealth transfer tax marital deduction. The state apportionment rule is not to apply if apportionment of a state tax to the marital share would have the effect of reducing the federal estate tax marital deduction. Thus the Act preserves the federal deduction without reduction.

The other special rule specifies that federal law will control if federal and state laws differ with respect to apportionment. It appears that the rationale for this provision was addition in 1981 of §2207A, calling for incremental rather than pro rata reimbursement of taxes. The Uniform Act is simply specifying that this difference between §2207A and state law will be resolved in favor of the incremental approach under federal law.

Alteration. The second major proposition established by the Act is how allocation under the Act may be altered. Two methods are authorized: in unusual circumstances a court may alter the proportionate allocation of taxes, and a decedent may waive or alter the dictates of the Act. Under existing law waiver may be accomplished only by a provision in the decedent's will. Under a newly promulgated revision of the Uniform Act, waiver may be by a provision in a revocable trust or other dispositive instrument, rather than just by a will. Unfortunately, a specific reference to the apportionment rule being waived or altered is not required by the existing Uniform Act, meaning that broad, nonspecific will provisions can raise important interpretative questions under the Act. Under the new revision waiver requires an "express" or "unambiguous" provision (the comments refer to "explicit" and "specific" references), which may reduce conflict or dispute.

Entitlements. Third, the Act establishes the proper treatment of certain entitlements that affect the tax burden. For example, federal credits generally inure to the proportionate benefit of all beneficiaries interested in the entire gross estate, rather than to the benefit of any particular recipient of property, such as the taker of property that was previously taxed or subjected to a foreign death tax. The new revision allocates the benefit of the §§2012 and 2014 gift tax and foreign death tax credits to the takers of the property that produced those benefits, but leaves unchanged the benefit of other credits.

Alternatively, however, individual takers of interests included in the gross estate benefit from exemptions, deductions, and credits that relate specifically to "the purposes of the gift," "the relationship of any person to the decedent," or the payment of any taxes attributable to the property. Thus, the charitable and marital deductions usually inure to the benefit of the recipient of the qualifying property, this being the rule of equitable apportionment.

This rule also provides that the recipient is entitled to an adjustment in the allocation of tax to reflect any reduced rate of tax for state or other tax purposes, based on the relation of the recipient to the decedent (for example, if a state inheritance tax is paid out of the estate and recognizes more closely related individuals with a reduced rate of tax).

Equitable Apportionment

If the estate plan is silent on the issue, state law determines whether equitable apportionment is available to any portion of the estate that qualifies for a deduction in the wealth transfer tax computation. The vast majority of states embrace equitable apportionment with respect to the computation of dispositions that qualify for the marital or charitable deductions. At least to a limited extent, however, a number of states do not embrace equitable apportionment.

In addition, in most states the treatment is not certain regarding distributions in satisfaction of a contractual entitlement, such as under a premarital agreement. These dispositions should be treated in the same fashion as a charitable or marital disposition if they are deductible under §2053 as a claim against the estate. In this respect, §2043 (an estate tax consideration rule) makes certain property settlements at death deductible under §2053 if incident to a divorce and otherwise meeting the requirements of §2516 (a gift tax consideration rule).

Moreover, an analogous result may apply in a limited number of cases if claims satisfied at death arising from a premarital agreement are treated as creditor claims against the estate. Notwithstanding that they are not §2053 deductible like most creditors' claims, the recipient of property under the premarital agreement is entitled to priority in payment, along with all other creditors. And because creditors are unaffected by the amount of taxes (except to the extent the estate is bankrupt, so that not all otherwise entitled claimants are satisfied) the claimant in these cases effectively is granted equitable apportionment. Otherwise, obligations incurred incident to divorce that are satisfied out of an estate at death but that are not deductible normally are ineligible for equitable apportionment.

Apportionment of State Inheritance and Foreign Taxes

Even in states that embrace full inside, outside, and equitable apportionment, state and foreign inheritance taxes imposed directly on individual recipients of a decedent's wealth usually are not subject to apportionment in a manner that equitably allocates or apportions the burden. Thus, the decedent's estate plan must direct the estate to pay those taxes and cause those taxes to become an item subject to apportionment by virtue of that direction.

Apportionment of Fees and Expenses

Outside apportionment of fees and expenses of administration has been dictated in several cases, but this sensible extension of the general apportionment theme is not common. See Roe v. Estate of Farrell, 372 N.E.2d 662 (Ill. 1978), cited in Estate of Fender v. Fender, 422 N.E.2d 107 (Ill. App. Ct. 1981); Cloutier v. Lavoie, 177 N.E.2d 584 (Mass. 1961); *In re* Estate of McKitrick, 172 N.E.2d 197 (Ohio Prob. Ct. 1960).

Apportionment of Interest and Penalties

Many state statutes (including the original and revised Uniform Act), dictate apportionment of interest and penalties assessed along with the underlying taxes imposed on an estate. In addition, §§2207A(d) and 2207B(d) specifically dictate this result for federal tax purposes. Unfortunately, this is not a universal rule and these added items are not chargeable in the same manner as the underlying tax in some states. As illustrated by Estate of Whittle v. Commissioner, 97 T.C. 362 (1991), aff'd, 994 F.2d 379 (7th Cir. 1993), interest on estate tax is not the same as the tax itself and may be chargeable in a different manner unless the document or applicable state or federal law specifically provides for it.

Computing Various Entitlements

An issue upon which estate planning documents must focus (because many state laws are silent) is the order in which shares, taxes, and allocations are to be determined. For example, the federal estate tax is computed after all deductions are reflected, but the discussion at page 16 about whether the marital share is computed before or after payment of those taxes illustrates that it is not always clear how computations interrelate for purposes of federal tax, state tax, marital and other "forced" shares, and division of the "residue."

Thus, for example, the question may arise whether state law provides that the federal estate tax (reflecting all credits) is to be paid from or charged against the available assets, followed by any division into shares (such as the elective or intestate share as illustrated at page 16), and finally computation and payment of state death taxes based on the various shares. Alternatively, state law may compute and subtract the federal and state taxes based on the same amount in the estate, and then divide the balance as provided in the estate plan. A third alternative mechanism would be to divide the estate according to the decedent's estate plan, then compute and subtract the federal and state taxes based on the size of those shares. Each alternative can produce different results and therefore must be made clear if state law is not.

Apportionment to Nonprobate Assets

It is not universally established that a decedent's will may apportion taxes to nonprobate assets in the absence of (or contrary to) state law. Clearly a decedent's will may negate a local law calling for apportionment of taxes, instead directing payment of all taxes out of the probate estate (assuming the decedent's intent is clear). Relieving a nonprobate beneficiary of a tax burden is essentially a bequest to that beneficiary, which the decedent's will may make. But if state law contains no apportionment authority, or if state law expressly directs against apportionment, the issue is whether a decedent's will may affirmatively direct that taxes will be allocated to nonprobate assets. This is a particularly acute issue if the nonprobate disposition is an irrevocable transfer as to which the decedent relinquished all rights of control and in which the decedent included no special tax payment directive.

A similar but perhaps less severe issue is whether a decedent may direct a different form of apportionment than that permitted or directed under state law, again in situations in which a will otherwise would be regarded as ineffective to alter or amend an irrevocable nonprobate transfer. Although the authorities in this respect are not uniform, the better supported position appears to be that a sufficient nexus to require inclusion for federal estate tax purposes is a sufficient nexus to permit the decedent to require apportionment or to direct a different form of apportionment than that specified under state law. See, e.g., United States v. Goodson, 253 F.2d 900 (8th Cir. 1958); and *In re* Will of King, 239 N.E.2d 875 (N.Y. 1968); but see Warfield v. Merchants Nat'l Bank, 147 N.E.2d 809 (Mass. 1958) (citing but refusing to follow *Goodson*).

Apportionment to Temporal Interests

The law is relatively clear regarding apportionment of taxes allocable to life estates and terms of years. The Uniform Act is representative of the law in most states, specifying that taxes attributable to either temporal interest are to be paid out of corpus, not charged against the temporal interest. Although this rule appears inequitable on its face, it actually is sensible, given the fact that a reduction of corpus for the payment of taxes correspondingly reduces income to be earned thereon and effectively amortizes the tax allocable to the income interest. The rule also is administratively attractive because the present interest income beneficiary need not contribute toward the payment of taxes that might exceed any income received at the time of payment.

A different situation is presented with respect to annuities, however, because the annuity may be a guaranteed amount, payable from corpus to the extent annual income is insufficient. Thus, a reduction of corpus in payment of taxes allocable to the annuity may not cause a reduction in the amount of the annuity. Another consideration is that many annuities precede a qualified charitable remainder in situations in which taxes attributable to the lead annuity are the only taxes attributable to the entire property (because the remainder qualifies for the charitable deduction). Payment from corpus is inequitable *and* it will reduce the charitable deduction under §2055(c).

Apportionment of the tax burden with respect to annuities could be addressed in drafting any estate plan, but the vast majority of plans do not mention it. The apportionment issue relating to annuities is extraordinarily important because of the high incidence of retirement benefit annuities. The issue can be avoided if the benefit qualifies for the estate tax marital deduction and state law recognizes equitable apportionment. Similarly, with respect to retirement benefit payments made in a lump sum, no serious issue is raised because the recipient has the funds to make immediate payment. Otherwise, because federal law does not grant a right of reimbursement with respect to §2039 includible benefits, this likely will be a significant issue because of the amount of wealth tied up in these plans. At a minimum, clients must be mindful of tax payment when selecting death benefit payout options, to ensure that liquidity will exist if needed to pay any taxes due.

Conflict of Laws and Enforcement Jurisdiction

Perhaps the most perplexing and least definite issues under the entire apportionment umbrella are whose law should govern apportionment questions in multiple state estates. Questions may arise as to how an apportionment rule in one state is to be enforced against property or beneficiaries in another state, especially if the law of that other state is at variance with the law of the state calling for apportionment.

Conflict of laws issues often are the most difficult and least predictable aspect of any controversy, and this certainly is true of apportionment. Based on how it sees the equities of the controversy, a court will want to decide an apportionment question a certain way on the merits. If so, the court may undertake to resolve the conflict of laws issue in a manner that allows the court to select the substantive law needed to render the decision it prefers. In the conflict of laws arena, looking for a state whose law supports the result a court may prefer frequently involves forum shopping that is not entirely copacetic under accepted conflict of laws principles. But it probably is fair to note that courts are prone to adopt their own state's law if possible, meaning that forum shopping to bring a case in a state whose law is favorable is a wily litigation tactic.

As a policy matter, probably the law should favor four essential conflict of laws objectives in this arena: (1) uniformity; (2) predictability;

(3) equal treatment of all parts of an estate, regardless of their physical or legal location for conflict of law purposes, with application of the same rules with respect to testate and intestate assets; and (4) equal treatment of various legal issues, applying the same conflict of laws rules for apportionment as, for example, for testing the validity of a will.

As an example of how confused this area may become, consider the following rules, all of which potentially apply in a particular situation. As to intestate property, the law of the actual situs of the asset with respect to immoveables (land) and the law of the state of the asset's situs (meaning the law of the decedent's domicile) with respect to moveables, may be applicable. Regarding testate property, classification of the apportionment issue for conflict of laws purposes will affect the choice of law rules applied. For example, in all likelihood the law of the decedent's domicile will govern the choice of law if the apportionment question is regarded as either a succession or a validity question. The law of the situs of the primary estate administration may be applicable, however, if apportionment is regarded merely as an administrative question. If inter vivos nonprobate transfers are involved, either the law of the donor's domicile at the time of the transfer or the law of the situs of the transferred property at the time the conflicts issue is resolved may apply for choice of law purposes (and these could differ).

Regarding apportionment and the use of trusts, the law of the situs of the trust for administration may govern for choice of law purposes. And, if appointive property is involved, the traditional conflict of laws rule applies the law of the state of the domicile of the person who created the power (its donor), on the fiction that appointment relates back to the donor's estate plan, with the powerholder merely acting as the donor's "agent" in exercising the power or otherwise with respect to the appointive assets. This conflict of laws rule (that the law of the donor's domicile shall govern, rather than that of the powerholder's domicile) is one of the most troublesome and least expected conflict rules applicable in the estate planning arena. Scoles, *Apportionment of Federal Estate Taxes and Conflict of Laws*, 55 COLUM. L. REV. 261, 285 (1955), suggests that §2207 was enacted in large part to minimize the difficult and unexpected effect of this conflict of laws rule.

Professor Scoles also argues that the proper resolution of a conflict of laws issue in the apportionment setting should follow a two step analysis. First, the law of the situs of property should apply to determine whose law will govern the choice of law question. Thus, if a trust is involved, the choice of law rules of the state of trust administration should govern the choice of law issue. With respect to transfers at death, situs law also should govern the choice of law, whether the assets are probate or nonprobate and regardless of whether administration is domiciliary or ancillary. Second, regardless of the state of situs, every state's choice of law rule should then dictate selection of the substantive apportionment rules of the decedent's domicile, on the simple theory that the decedent's intent should govern the apportionment issue and that the decedent most likely relied on domiciliary law.

This suggestion is not, however, necessarily what the courts of a given jurisdiction will adopt. As a consequence, probably the only way to ensure consistent apportionment results is either to designate the applicable law with respect to all assets (which cannot be done in some cases because there is no way to designate the governing law with respect to some assets) or to provide for tax payment and apportionment that does not rely in any manner on state law.

Planning Aspects of the Apportionment Rules

If state law shifts the tax payment liability to nonprobate takers under applicable apportionment rules, the interests of those takers must be considered during administration of the estate to avoid unintentionally affecting their rights without their knowledge or consent. Any failure to notify or join these beneficiaries may invalidate certain orders obtained or actions taken during administration of an estate if a state court might decide that they are entitled to representation regarding administrative decisions that affect them. One easy mechanism to avoid this concern (and the general lack of state law to dictate the requisite form of joinder or notice) is simply to direct that all taxes be paid out of the probate estate. If negation of apportionment under state law is not appropriate or desirable, however, state law might permit the decedent to indemnify the fiduciary from liability to nonprobate takers and direct that all decisions of the fiduciary in the ordinary course of probate administration shall be final, without notice or joinder. That is one of dozens of issues that inform the drafting of tax payment provisions.

Under §§2206, 2207, 2207A, and 2207B the estate initially pays its tax liability and then is entitled to reimbursement. As a consequence, liquidity may not be where it needs to be and collection problems may arise or may be exacerbated by the existence of multiple beneficiaries, all subject to these rights of reimbursement. In this respect, directing apportionment in the first instance rather than preserving these reimbursement rights may be more expeditious. In most cases, therefore, the better approach is to waive federal reimbursement rights but to preserve all state law apportionment rights, except with respect to specifically designated assets or beneficiaries (or classes of either). But this resolution only works properly to the extent state law calls for apportionment, and it exacerbates the potential of liability to nonprobate takers.

Retirement Benefits

Taxes attributable to retirement benefits includible in the estate under §2039 must be considered carefully in conjunction with beneficiary designations and the terms of the plan. The question is whether the beneficiary can afford to pay taxes imposed by apportionment if settlement of the plan is not in a lump sum. You may need to consider some other beneficiary designation or some other source for payment of the tax if the beneficiary does not have liquidity and if the plan does not permit apportionment against the plan itself. All other things being equal, it probably is wiser to impose tax on the beneficiary (because it is not likely permissible to impose it on the plan), and then attempt to provide the beneficiary with the funds to pay that tax, thereby avoiding the need to even study plan restrictions. You also must pay careful attention to whether the spousal annuity rules will prevent the type of payout otherwise desired. Finally, the income tax consequences of the payout option selected, and of the tax apportionment selected, also should be considered.

As a practical matter, the estate plan must consider whether the breadth of nonprobate assets is such that apportionment would be difficult (if not impossible) to administer and, if so, whether the tax clause should waive apportionment or reimbursement (at least with respect to certain assets or beneficiaries or classes of either). With all the various forms of nonprobate property and taxes that may be involved, however, it seems unlikely that blanket waiver of all apportionment or rights of reimbursement will be appropriate or even feasible.

Administrative Uncertainties

Finally, in some states it is uncertain how various computations and allocations are to be made and in what order, in which case the estate plan should establish the mechanism and dictate apportionment consistent with it. In addition, during (and in anticipation of) estate administration, a number of uncertainties or problems may affect the personal representative and ought to be considered at the time the estate plan is prepared.

One such uncertainty is the effect that an audit will have on the determination of estate and inheritance taxes and their apportionment and collection. Any previously determined allocation of taxes under an apportionment routine will be affected if values change, resulting in either a change in taxes payable or simply a readjustment in the relative size of various shares. This will be particularly problematic in a state that imposes different wealth transfer tax rates, based on degrees of consanguinity, if property subject to any audit changes passed to beneficiaries in different degrees and the rate differential is apportioned under state law. The issue is whether it is prudent to distribute the bulk of an estate prior to final determination and collection of taxes. You should consider whether needs of the beneficiaries are such that a mechanism must be established for early distributions with allocation of taxes secured by a lien, bond, repayment agreement, or other method, or whether apportionment should be waived entirely, or waived only with respect to certain beneficiaries or as to changes resulting from audit.

In addition, problems of collection and asserting jurisdiction over nonprobate takers should be considered before the death of a client, with measures taken premortem to alleviate potential problems either by waiving apportionment or by assuring an ancillary administration in the beneficiary's domiciliary state to obtain jurisdiction. Indeed, if multiple jurisdictions might be involved, conflict of laws issues should be anticipated, especially if a change of the client's domicile is likely or if a conflict of laws battle is anticipated because of the nature and location of nonprobate assets.

Conflict of laws issues probably are the easiest potential problems to address, with the estate plan adopting either or both of two defensive procedures. First, the estate plan may dictate the method of apportionment (if any) desired, thereby alleviating the vagaries of state law and uncertain application of any state's rules. Second, the estate plan may dictate the law that should apply. For the second procedure to succeed, there must be a substantial relation of the client's estate or estate plan to the jurisdiction whose law is selected and the policies of the governing law state must not violate any strong conflicting policy of any state that might be deemed to have the most significant relationship to the client's estate.

Spousal Planning Choices

A number of affirmative planning options or decisions are important with respect to apportionment and planning for a surviving spouse. For example, if only a partial QTIP marital deduction election is made, taxes generated by that decision usually should be paid out of the nonelected portion of the marital deduction trust. By proper accounting, assuring payment of taxes from the nonelected portion of the QTIP trust has the advantage of preventing an alteration of the decedent's estate planning equities if the QTIP and the nonmarital trusts benefit different remainder beneficiaries. Otherwise, payment from the nonmarital property of taxes incurred by virtue of a partial election would shift taxes from the death of S (under §2044) imposed on the QTIP trust (under §2207A) to the death of D, imposed on the nonmarital property (assuming that is how D's tax clause otherwise apportions all taxes).

A similar concern should apply if S disclaims part of the marital bequest, causing taxes to be incurred. These taxes should be payable from the disclaimed property.

In addition, some thought ought to be given to the proper sequence for payment of taxes in relation to division of an estate into shares under a fractional marital deduction entitlement or in conjunction with a partial QTIP election, again as illustrated at page 16 and in Chapter 7 at pages 123-124. As shown by the difference in the various beneficiaries' entitlements, a gross estate fraction is best if D's intent is to freeze S's estate to the extent possible, to minimize tax in S's estate. Most drafters probably call for a net estate division, however, either by inadvertence, for liquidity purposes, or because that result best protects S.

The issue is not determination of the size of the deduction, nor is it whether equitable apportionment should apply. The simple issue is whether taxes are paid first, followed by division, or whether division occurs first, followed by payment out of the nonmarital fund. And the same issue can be relevant in other planning contexts as well.

Simply put, the estate plan (and, for that matter, any premarital agreement that dictates such a bequest) ought to be clear whenever defining terms such as the "residue" available for division or distribution and whether it is being referred to as that amount before or after payment of taxes. See, for example, Barley v. Albertini, 694 So. 2d 843 (Fla. Ct. App. 1997), in which the tax payment provision preceded all other provisions in the document and directed payment from the "*residuary* estate," along with the proviso that "[I]n no event shall any portion of such taxes be apportioned or allocated to my spouse or any property passing to my spouse . . . which qualifies for the marital deduction." Two paragraphs below this the marital trust was described as "90% of the *remainder* of my estate . . . after the payment of . . . taxes . . . referred to above." The trial court held that taxes should be paid first and the marital trust created out of the remaining balance, meaning that 90% of the taxes effectively would be paid from the marital bequest. On appeal the court reversed and remanded because an ambiguity existed. This conclusion appears to be an understatement given the inconsistent statements in the two provisions (relating to nonapportionment to the spouse and division after payment) along with the different terms used in the two provisions. Do you think the drafter might have liability for the costs of resolving this mess?

A similar problem involving the charitable deduction is illustrated by two conflicting cases: Greene v. United States, 447 F. Supp. 885 (N.D. Ill. 1978), and *In re* Estate of Bell, 764 P.2d 689 (Wyo. 1988). In *Greene*, the decedent's placement of the tax burden on the residue of the estate created problems of interpretation of earlier provisions in the will giving 10% of the residuary estate to charity, half of "the rest, residue, and remainder" to the testator's surviving spouse, and "the entire remainder of my estate (hereinafter referred to as the 'Residuary Estate')" to a trust. In this context, payment of taxes from the residue was deemed to be after division into the charitable and marital shares, causing the tax payment to come from the "residue of the residue" and, not coincidentally, preserving a larger marital and charitable deduction.

In *Bell*, on the other hand, the court held that the Uniform Estate Tax Apportionment Act was superseded by a tax payment provision directing payment of all taxes from the residue of the decedent's estate. The residuary provision included two charitable bequests of a fraction of the residue. The charities argued that equitable apportionment should apply so that a gross residue division would be made and all taxes would be paid from the noncharitable portion of the residue. The court concluded that the tax payment direction overrode all portions of the Uniform Act, including equitable apportionment. Then it held that a net estate division was mandated by the chronological organization of the will, directing payment of taxes and then division of the balance of the residue. The court did not even mention the effect of this conclusion on the §2055 charitable deduction, nor did it discuss equitable apportionment as a matter of policy that might guide its decision.

Consistent about both cases is the courts' application of a chronological interpretation, by which division and payment of taxes were deemed to occur in the order in which the respective provisions were found in the documents. That approach is not always best, nor do courts always follow it, making proper anticipation of these issues essential in the initial drafting of the document and the order of each of its provisions.

A more subtle application of the same type of problem is illustrated by Technical Advice Memorandum 9126005, which involved a will that directed payment of all state and federal taxes from the residue of the decedent's estate. State law was the Uniform Estate Tax Apportionment Act, which would apportion taxes among all beneficiaries, subject to equitable apportionment, but only to the extent the decedent did not provide otherwise. The will made several preresiduary bequests and left the residue 25% to an individual and 75% to a charity. Faced with the question of how much the charitable bequest should be reduced under §2055(c) for taxes payable from the residue, the government concluded that equitable apportionment within the residue was not altered by the tax payment provision directing all taxes to be paid from the residue. But the effect was not to impose all taxes on the noncharitable portion of the residue. Instead, the tax on the preresiduary bequests was payable from the residue prior to its division, which effectively reduced the charitable bequest by 75% of the tax on the preresiduary bequests. Only taxes generated by the residue, all attributable to the noncharitable portion of the residue, were apportioned under state law entirely against that noncharitable portion.

The government stated that the question whether the tax payment provision was a direction against statutory apportionment of every dimension was very close, indicating the significance of careful consideration and drafting of tax payment provisions in general. The result reveals the need for careful thought in conjunction with charitable planning in particular. The tax payment provision did not waive all rights to apportionment or reimbursement, which distinguished it from many poorly considered tax payment provisions. It also seems unlikely that the decedent intended that the charitable beneficiary receive a portion of the residue before reduction for taxes attributable to the preresiduary bequests (that is, that the individual residuary beneficiary should pay all taxes), so the government probably reached the right result. But the decedent's intent was not as clear as it might have been and the Memorandum might have dictated an even greater diminution of the charitable deduction.

Benefit of Rates

The focus in so much of this Chapter on federal wealth transfer tax may seem incongruous given the focus in this course on planning for estates that are smaller than the applicable exclusion amount, but the federal tax cases are much more prevalent and often better highlight concerns that are applicable under state law as well. This will become more true in the future as more states restore their state taxes to replace revenue lost due to repeal of the revenue sharing aspects of the state death tax credit under federal tax law. In addition, a client also should consider whether the effect of any differentials in the rate of state wealth transfer tax imposed on the estate (based on degrees of consanguinity of the various takers) should be preserved to the benefit of the respective takers. A spouse typically enjoys this benefit, automatically through equitable apportionment (unless state law does not recognize that doctrine). The benefit of a lower rate for children or descendants as opposed to more distant relatives or strangers also is preserved under some states' laws, including under the Uniform Estate Tax Apportionment Act.

As an easy, common example of a situation in which this might be relevant, consider is the client with children and stepchildren whom the client wants to benefit equally. In some states the stepchildren would bear a larger share of any state wealth transfer tax burden if state law imposes a higher tax rate on stepchildren than it does on natural born or adopted children. The client may wish to alter the normal apportionment rule if the computation necessary to allocate rate differentials is not easy, or if the client does not wish to discriminate against the stepchildren. Indeed, even if preservation of this apportionment rule is the intent, it might be possible to do so in an easier and roughly comparable manner by adjusting the size of various shares or bequests (taking into consideration the effect of state taxes and the beneficiary's relation to the client) and override the state apportionment rule.

Generation-Skipping Transfer Taxes

Generation-skipping taxes are a major tax allocation concern but only in very large estates or those that will benefit multiple generations in trust. For that reason they are not a further subject here than already mentioned, except to the extent this caution reminds you to consider them if your practice takes you in that direction. For more assistance on the topic see Chapter 18 at page 33, or 1 Casner & Pennell, ESTATE PLANNING §3.3.11 (6th ed. 1995).

Principal and Income Rules

Finally, in considering apportionment of the tax or expense payment burden, an income and principal rule should be kept in mind. Typically estate income earned on assets that are expended for payment purposes remains income in the estate.[25] A will may, however, direct that this

---

25. See, e.g., Uniform Principal and Income Act (1997 Act) §201(2)(A), 7B U.L.A. 150 (2000), and Revised Uniform Principal and Income Act (1962 Act) §5(b), 7B U.L.A. 213 (2000). An extreme example that illustrates this rule is Union Planters Nat'l Bank v. Dedman, 1998 Tenn. App. LEXIS 9, in which the tax payment provision placed the burden on the residue of the probate estate without apportionment and taxes attributable to nonprobate property exceeded the value of the estate as determined at the date of death.

income be added to principal to help compensate for the diminution caused by the payment expenditures. Alternatively, or in addition, the will could provide that the income also be used to pay debts, expenses, and taxes, in either event shifting a part of the burden to the income beneficiaries.

Drafting Considerations

Equity favors equality. Thus, if the provisions of an estate plan are ambiguous the presumption favors apportionment of taxes to achieve equality, putting a heavy burden on drafting to alter that result. But the drafter also must make clear any intent to deviate from state law if, for example, the old burden on the residue rule is applicable.

The federal rights of reimbursement and whether to preserve or waive them is so important an issue that it ought to come first in thinking about drafting. Each of §§2206, 2207, 2207A, 2207B (and, in its special way, §2603(b)) create a right of reimbursement for taxes caused by an individual's death (or a generation-skipping taxable transfer). Inadvertent waiver of these rights could be calamitous, given all the other property that might generate taxes and the possibility that there will be insufficient assets otherwise available to pay taxes under a burden on the residue apportionment rule. In reflection of this fact, §§2207A, 2207B, and 2603(b) require a specific indication of intent to waive their rights of reimbursement for waiver to be effective.

Nevertheless, full apportionment is better than reimbursement for liquidity purposes, because apportionment forces the recipient of property to make the initial payment while reimbursement requires the estate to pay initially and then seek a recovery of the expended assets. Because of this format, there may be no right to receive interest even if the beneficiary who must contribute under a reimbursement provision delays in making payment.

Liquidity, and the apportionment versus reimbursement issue, is particularly important in a tax environment that includes state death taxes that could exceed the amount of a nonmarital trust, even in an otherwise nontaxable optimum marital deduction situation. Marital deduction property may be needed to pay taxes if this occurs, and use of that property will generate a loss of the marital deduction and a corresponding imposition of federal estate tax, with the need to further invade the marital property to pay those taxes, resulting in corresponding loss of more deduction and, ultimately, a whirlpool computation. Even equitable

---

There was sufficient postmortem income and capital appreciation, however, to satisfy the tax payment obligation, but the court held that postmortem income was payable to the residuary beneficiary under what it called the "Massachusetts" rule that the income beneficiaries enjoy the income from the entire residue and not just the income from whatever corpus remains after satisfaction of all payments from the residue. The result is counterintuitive in that it assumes there to be residuary income even though there is no residue. It does correctly reflect that, prior to payment of these estate charges, there is the possibility for investment returns to the estate that must be considered in drafting those provisions that dispose of the estate.

apportionment cannot protect against this result to the extent the marital bequest does not fully work to eliminate state taxes.

In addition, waiver of the §2207A reimbursement right should be considered carefully because Treas. Reg. §20.2207A-1(a)(2) provides that the simple failure to enforce the right of reimbursement is a gift (neither §2206, §2207, nor §2207B so provides). Often this liability will be unexpected and about which the beneficiaries deemed to have made the gift likely will be without knowledge. But liability can be avoided if the surviving spouse as beneficiary of qualified terminable interest property waives the §2207A right of reimbursement. It is particularly important that the surviving spouse have flexibility to decide whether to preserve or waive this right of reimbursement. Normally the QTIP trust should specify that taxes attributable to trust property will be paid from the trust before it is distributed, unless the surviving spouse's will overrides that direction by a provision making specific reference to the QTIP trust.

With respect to the indication of intent required under §2207A itself, consider *In re* Estate of Gordon, 510 N.Y.S.2d 815, 817 (Surr. Ct. 1986), in which the decedent's tax clause read, "I direct that all . . . taxes . . . imposed . . . by reason of my death with respect to any property includable in my estate . . . whether such property passes under or outside my will be paid out of my Residuary Estate . . . without apportionment." A charitable residuary bequest would have abated completely if the court had found that the §2207A reimbursement right had been waived by this provision. The court instead found that this provision was not adequate to work such a result, and a subsequent amendment to §2207A now will generate the same result nationwide.

For comparison purposes, the following language was adequate to waive §§2206 and 2207 rights of reimbursement in a case involving no "special" remainder beneficiary: "All estate taxes payable by reason of my death shall be chargeable against and payable out of my residuary estate without contribution by anyone." *In re* Estate of Bruce, 516 N.Y.S.2d 748 (App. Div. 1987). The court reached this result notwithstanding the drafter's testimony that the decedent and the drafter were unaware of nonprobate assets and that the purpose of the provision was to avoid inside apportionment only. The point is that you can't be too careful in specifying intent in the document.

Items to Consider

More specifically yet, a good tax clause will address the following topics clearly, even if state law is crystal on many of these concepts, because of the migratory nature of clients and the potential conflict of laws problems that could arise.

- Language should make clear which taxes are being apportioned (estate, generation-skipping, Chapter 14, state, income, alternative minimum income, and appreciation estate taxes).

- Both inside and outside apportionment, or the waiver thereof, clearly should be covered; often only outside apportionment is contemplated and statutory inside apportionment across the entire estate is forgotten.
- Equitable apportionment should be considered; it usually will be the client's intent to embrace it, even if no other form of apportionment is desired.
- Any intent to preserve the effect of state wealth transfer tax computation differentials (if any) should be stated clearly.
- Any desire to allocate credits to recipients of assets to which the credits relate should be covered.
- Alteration of the apportionment rule relative to temporal interests always should be considered, particularly in estates with annuity or installment payouts of retirement benefits.
- The provision should apportion or call for payment of interest and penalties in the same manner as the taxes to which they relate.
- If it is known that there will be deductible claims against the estate (such as pursuant to a premarital or separation agreement) and they are similar to or in lieu of bequests from the estate, the determination of the size of those dispositions and apportionment of taxes to them should be considered and specified in the tax clause, frequently applying the same considerations applicable to other bequests. Especially sensitive, however, is whether the agreement permits apportionment and whether various issues noted here were considered in the preparation of that agreement.
- It should be specified whether it is appropriate to look to particular assets first for tax payment. The desire to preserve certain assets should be noted rather than relying on the personal representative to ferret out the decedent's intent. However, stating a preference to protect certain assets probably should not be allowed to override other presumably more important apportionment principles. For example, the preference for preservation of farm property was alleged to cause marital deduction property to be tapped for tax payment in Estate of Reno v. Commissioner, 945 F.2d 733 (4th Cir. 1991), rev'g (en banc) 916 F.2d 955 (4th Cir. 1990), which aff'd 51 T.C.M. (CCH) 909 (1986). The tax payment provision would have negated the concept of equitable apportionment and generated a tax if this had been found to be correct, because the marital deduction would have been reduced.

As a checklist of other commonly overlooked apportionment issues that are discussed herein but don't always arise, remember to consider:

- fees and expenses;
- state taxes that don't conform to federal estate tax rules and that can produce disparities;

- special use valuation and recapture under §2032A;
- future interests that invoke tax that may be deferred under §6163;
- deferral of tax under §6166 and the question of who shall pay the deferred tax and interest on it;
- with respect to any apportionment that is preserved, how enforcement will be effected and whether to include a power of setoff in the client's will for any dispositions of probate property to takers of nonprobate property that will bear a share of the tax burden.

In any event, if apportionment is preserved, the order for computation of any bequest or share of the estate and for payment of taxes should be specified, even if it is clear under state law. It is surprising how seldom this is done, given the number of cases revealing that the proper method frequently is *un*clear. Thus, for example, the document should specify clearly whether a gross or a net estate division is desired in computing a marital deduction fractional share.

Often several tax clauses will (or should) be involved if a client has a funded living trust and perhaps an irrevocable insurance trust in addition to a will directing disposition of the probate estate. Most decisions indicate that the provision in the will controls to the extent those clauses differ or are contradictory. But some cases hold that the latter in time controls, which may be a trust. As among other documents, no clear order of priority exists.

Much more importantly, the Uniform Acts and §§2206 and 2207 all ostensibly require that waiver of apportionment or reimbursement be by a will provision. Only §§2207A and 2207B allow waiver by the decedent's revocable trust as well. Thus, although waiver of reimbursement by a provision in a trust or other document may not succeed if the will does not also waive the right, it probably can't hurt (unless there is an inconsistency) for each document to state the client's intent. But be consistent when doing so!

The significance of this is well illustrated by Estate of Roe, 426 N.W.2d 797, 798, 799 (Mich. Ct. App. 1988), in which the decedent's will provided that "I make no direction for the payment of . . . taxes assessed by reason of my death, as I have provided for their payment under a certain Agreement hereinafter mentioned." The trust called for tax payment and specified that "the Trustee shall not seek contribution from anyone for any portion of the taxes so paid." The court held that apportionment under state law would apply, notwithstanding this clear intent that the trust pay for all, because the will failed to waive application of the state apportionment statute.

The most notable aspect of *Roe* is that the tax clauses involved were verbatim from a major Chicago fiduciary's forms book. This problem exists in literally thousands of estate plans nationwide. With respect to the other end of the spectrum, if there is a tax payment obligation in more than one document, and taxes may be paid by more than one entity, the estate plan must coordinate these documents to specify how the burden is computed for each and how aggregated apportionment will work.

It also makes sense to include a safety valve tax clause in trusts (such as an irrevocable insurance trust or a grantor retained interest trust) that are intended to escape inclusion if everything goes as planned. Such a provision would specify that the fiduciary may purchase assets from the grantor's estate or loan money to it (to provide liquidity) and that taxes caused by inclusion of any part of the trust that is includible in the grantor's estate are payable from that portion. To succeed probably requires that the grantor's estate plan not waive apportionment with respect to the trust. Also, the trust document must clearly provide that this provision operates only if, quite independently, the trust is found to be includible, so as not to generate inclusion in the first instance.

Clearly Specify Intent

The case reporters are full of decisions involving the meaning of provisions relating to apportionment. It almost goes without stating that any intent to override any state apportionment rule must be stated clearly. The task requires more than just directing "payment of all debts and taxes from the residue of my estate" or "pay all taxes imposed on my estate by reason of my death" or "pay all taxes out of my residuary estate without apportionment." Among the questions raised by provisions like these would be whether these provisions actually waive apportionment or only direct payment of taxes that thereafter may be apportioned?[26] Could the

---

26. For example, in Estate of Fine v. Commissioner, 90 T.C. 1068 (1988), the decedent's will directed payment of taxes "without apportionment," which in all likelihood was meant to impose the tax burden on the residue without apportionment to or contribution from takers of includible nonprobate property. Unfortunately, the court determined that the effect was to override a state statute calling for equitable apportionment of all taxes to the nonmarital portion of the estate. As a result, the court held that the decedent's estate available for division between the surviving spouse and others was the residue left after payment of taxes rather than dividing the estate before such payment and charging the taxes to the nonmarital share. The net effect was to reduce the allowable marital deduction. Accord, Estate of Miller v. Commissioner, 76 T.C.M. (CCH) 892 (1998), aff'd per curiam, 2000-1 U.S. Tax Cas. ¶60,370 (5th Cir. 2000) (a tax payment provision directing the residuary estate to bear the entire burden was adequate to override state law equitable and outside apportionment, notwithstanding reduction of the marital deduction as a result); Estate of McKay v. Commissioner, 68 T.C.M. (CCH) 279 (1994) (notwithstanding that 75% of the residue passed to charities, the decedent's will directing payment of all taxes imposed on the probate estate from the residue without apportionment among the residuary beneficiaries was sufficient to require reduction of a charitable bequest and the corresponding charitable deduction). But in McKeon v. United States, 151 F.3d 1201 (9th Cir. 1998), and Estate of Brunetti v. Commissioner, 56 T.C.M. (CCH) 580 (1988), involving marital and charitable deductions, respectively, and similar tax payment provisions, the courts refused to accept the government's reduction of the deduction because the courts read the state law apportionment rules as applying unless clearly overruled, and found that sufficient ambiguity existed in each document to preclude a finding of a clear intent to abandon that otherwise favored result. The government itself reached the same result in Private Letter Ruling 200206024, finding that state law equitable apportionment applied to a pay from the residue direction such that residuary charitable and marital bequests were not obliged to contribute to the tax payment obligation.

To the same effect, after two different rounds of litigation with appeals, one through the federal courts and another through the state courts, is Estate of Swallen v. Commissioner, 98 F.3d 919 (6th Cir. 1996), rev'g 65 T.C.M. (CCH) 2332 (1993), and

provision be interpreted to include any additional estate tax imposed under §2032A upon a recapture event with respect to any special use property? Does the reference to "my estate" mean the gross estate, the taxable estate, the probate estate, or something else? Consider the sleight of hand performed in the following decision; do you agree that the court reached an appropriate result?

In re Estate of Ogburn
406 P.2d 655 (Wyo. 1965)

GRAY, J.

The will of Alice R. Ogburn, deceased, disposed of real and personal property . . . Out of that property a special devise was made to her foster son, . . . and a special bequest of certain stocks . . . was made to his children. A brother and five sisters of decedent were made the residuary devisees and legatees. In addition to the above-described property passing under the will, the foster son . . . acquired ownership of jointly held property . . . and proceeds of insurance policies . . . . [A]s executor, the foster son undertook to charge the residuary estate with the full amount paid for Federal estate tax and the full amount paid for Wyoming inheritance tax. Exceptions to the accounting treatment accorded such items were duly taken by the residuary legatees. . . .

The clause of the will that brought about this controversy states: "FIRST: I direct the payment of all my just debts, taxes, funeral expenses and expense of administration of my estate." Following this are articles "THIRD" and "FOURTH" making the specific devises and bequests to the foster son and his children, and article "FIFTH" granting the residuary estate to the brother and sisters of the testatrix. For our purposes that is the sum and substance of the will.

The Federal Taxes

As an initial approach to the matter of apportionment of Federal estate taxes we point out . . . that the public policy of this State, as declared by the legislature, is to apportion such taxes to the persons benefited. Section 2 of the Act succinctly lays down that proposition. It provides:

Matthews v. Swallen, 1995 Ohio App. LEXIS 4669 (Ct. App. 1995), in which the decedent's irrevocable inter vivos trust was includible in the gross estate and, although it provided for the decedent's surviving spouse, did not qualify for the marital deduction; the residue of the decedent's estate qualified for the marital deduction but only after payment of all taxes and subject to a direction "that no tax . . . shall be charged . . . against . . . any . . . trust beneficiary, so long as the funds or property in the hands of my Executor . . . are sufficient . . . ." Holding that this provision in the will was not adequate to override state law apportionment to the trust, and relying on an income tax provision in the will as stating the decedent's overall intent to minimize taxes, the court on appeal stretched to find the tax payment direction inadequate to impose on the residue the tax liability attributable to the trust and thereby salvaged the marital deduction for the residue.

Unless the will otherwise provides, the tax shall be apportioned among all persons interested in the estate. The apportionment shall be made in proportion that the value of the interest of each person interested in the estate bears to the total value of the interests of all persons interested in the estate. The values used in determining the tax shall be used for that purpose.

. . .

Practically all of the cases agree that a directive against apportionment should be expressed in clear and unambiguous language. Depending, of course, upon the complexity of the testamentary plan a few simple words may suffice to effectuate that purpose. It is essential, however, that the words, or combination of words, used in the will sufficiently indicate an intention against apportionment. In case of doubt the burden of the taxes must be left where the law places it. . . .

Turning now to article "FIRST" of the will, stripped of irrelevant language in order to reach the tax clause, it is provided "I direct payment of all my . . . taxes . . . of my estate. " We by no means commend this clause as a model directive against apportionment. It is a superficial, artless, and inept expression relating to this important and crucial element of a testamentary plan prepared by a nonresident attorney confessedly unfamiliar with the applicable laws of Wyoming.

As appellants point out, the tax clause fails by direct language clearly to specify the nature of the taxes embraced within the clause, the source from which the taxes affected were to be paid, and the persons interested in the estate who were to receive benefits freed of the burden of taxes. Such deficiencies, of course, prompted the present litigation. Furthermore, as we indicated above, there is some basis under the authorities for appellants' contention that such lack of clarity condemns the clause as an enforceable directive against apportionment or, at least, when related to the matter of the purpose intended, demonstrates that neither the testatrix nor the scrivener of the will had in mind the importance of fitting death taxes into the testamentary plan. . . .

Reminding that we are presently considering the relationship of the language used to the apportionment of the Federal estate taxes, an important consideration is the nature of the tax. Unlike our inheritance tax, the tax is not imposed upon the privilege of the devisees, legatees, and heirs to take and receive an interest in property from a decedent. Rather it is a tax imposed upon the interest of a decedent which ceased by reason of death thus causing the transfer of such interest to the recipients thereof. In other words, the tax might be described as a tax on the privilege of transferring an interest in the property upon death, which generally is understood as an obligation imposed upon the transferor.

When the nature of the tax is taken into consideration, together with the fact that testatrix, over the years, was a successful and experienced businesswoman, we think it must be assumed that she had some familiarity with the impact of death taxes and that by the language "all my taxes of my estate" she did intend to embrace at least a portion of such taxes. Further, by inclusion of the tax clause in the usual ritualistic and introductory portion of the will directing payment of debts, expenses, et cetera, which when possible are ordinarily satisfied from the residuary estate, it seems clear that testatrix also intended that the death taxes embraced within the language were to be paid from the same source.

That leaves for consideration the portion of the taxes affected. As stated above, we think that question cannot be precisely answered without relating the tax clause to each segment of the testatrix's property transferred as a result of death and upon which the tax was levied, i.e., testamentary gifts, nontestamentary gifts, and proceeds of insurance policies.

In fact the necessity for so doing seems inherent in the distinction made under the laws of Wyoming between what we shall term the "taxable" estate defined as being "the gross estate of a decedent as determined for the purpose of federal estate tax" and the "probate" estate, which as commonly understood consists of the property owned by a decedent at the time of death which is transferred in accordance with the provisions of the will or statute relating to intestacy through the processes of the probate court. While both estates have some interrelation, there is a substantial difference. The "probate" estate, as indicated, is concerned with the devolution of a decedent's interest in property at the time of death which does not occur otherwise than by the will or the intestacy statute. A property interest such as an unsevered interest in a joint tenancy forms no part of the "probate" estate. On the other hand, Federal law for purposes of determining the "taxable" estate, while including all of the assets of the "probate" estate, is not concerned with the manner in which property interests of a decedent are otherwise transferred, and interests such as the joint tenancy mentioned are treated as integral parts of a decedent's estate for purposes of the Federal estate tax. That such a distinction has special significance in considering the question before us can readily be seen. A somewhat ambiguous tax clause may contain language sufficient to disclose an intent on the part of the testator or testatrix to shift the burden of the Federal estate tax levied upon decedent's property passing under the will and yet be insufficient to shift the tax levied upon the transfer of a decedent's interest in property which is not controlled by the will. Such a possibility is much too important to be overlooked and we find nothing in the apportionment statute that would cause us to reject such an approach.

Relating the tax clause to the testamentary gifts, we are inclined to the view — based on the foregoing general discussion — that testatrix must be understood as having this portion of the taxes in mind when she referred to "my taxes of my estate" and that such language, although not entirely clear, sufficiently expressed the intention of testatrix to direct against statutory apportionment of the taxes imposed on such gifts. It is only by such an interpretation that force and effect can be given to such language, and as stated above we have concluded that this must be done. We are not disposed, however, to go further than that.

Just as testatrix must be assumed to have been familiar with the tax imposed upon the transfer of the property in her estate in accordance with the will, it must likewise be assumed she was familiar with the fact that a tax would be imposed upon the nontestamentary gift of the joint property to her foster son. As stated, such property formed no part of her probate estate, and that testatrix so understood can also be assumed. Yet no mention is made of an interest in property passing other than by the will, as a result of the death. Nor do we find language in the will from which a purpose to shift the burden of such tax to appellants can be inferred, a purpose which is required clearly to appear. The dominant words are "my estate." That such phrase fails to establish a basis for nonapportionment of the tax here being discussed seems well established by the authorities. In Union Trust Co. v. Watson, 68 A.2d 916, 919 (R.I. 1949), the court had this to say:

> We think that the testator's expression "my estate" in his later will has a very definite and explicit meaning. Such expression, it has been said, "has a fixed and a limited meaning; it is positive, clear-cut and free from doubt. It conveys an inference of existing title or ownership in the maker of the phrase and leads to the single conclusion that he had in mind the payment only of such taxes which might be levied upon his testamentary gifts or devises."

. . .

In view of the foregoing we think the only reasonable interpretation of the will which can be reached is that by the language testatrix could have intended nothing more than a shifting of taxes imposed upon the property passing under the will.

. . .

State Inheritance Taxes

Of this, we think little need be said. The statutes imposing such taxes clearly and specifically place the burden thereof upon the recipients of the testatrix's bounty. That such was to continue as the public policy of this State was clearly demonstrated when the legislature in adopting the Uniform Estate Tax Apportionment Act in 1959 deleted from the prescribed form any reference to inheritance taxes payable to the State. True, the inheritance tax statute does not take from a testator or testatrix the right to shift the statutory burden to a particular fund, but to accomplish such purpose the directive must clearly appear from the will. That the language here could not possibly constitute such a directive is self-evident. The testatrix refers only to "my taxes of my estate. " These were not her taxes, nor were the taxes levied upon her estate. To hold such language to constitute a sufficient directive would be to reach a most inequitable result in clear contravention of the statute that is designed to prevent such a happening. The State taxes paid were attributable entirely to the gifts made to appellees. The amounts received by the appellants were entirely exempt. The executor was clearly wrong in attempting to charge appellants' accounts with such taxes. . . .

See also Landmark Trust Co. v. Aitken, 587 N.E.2d 1076 (Ill. App. Ct. 1992), in which litigation was needed to ascertain the decedent's intent because the will simply directed payment of all taxes from the residue, which was insufficient, and it was not clear whether state common law equitable apportionment should apply with respect to the balance. The court determined that state law apportionment was negated entirely by the tax clause and that common law abatement principles were applicable to determine how the excess taxes were to be paid. The result was that general bequests abated while specific bequests were protected from paying their proportionate share of the excess taxes.

About a shockingly similar provision in the will of one Elmer Cohen, deceased, ("I direct my Personal Representatives to pay, without reimbursement or contribution, all estate [sic], inheritance taxes, and succession duties assessed by reason of my death by the United States or any State thereof"), the Probate Division of the Circuit Court of St. Louis County, Missouri, No. 113549 (April 22, 1996), ruled that the will was "not ambiguous. Ambiguous means reasonably susceptible of more than one meaning. [This provision] is not susceptible of any meaning and cannot be construed." This portion of the holding was overruled on appeal, Estate of Cohen v. Crown, 954 S.W.2d 409 (Mo. Ct. App. 1997), the court refusing to conclude that there was no meaning in the provision but still concluding that it did not effectively waive the §2206 right of reimbursement with respect to includible insurance proceeds and thereby protecting a charitable bequest that otherwise would have been reduced.

You do *not* want to be the drafting attorney about whose work such a controversy swirls!

As a practical matter, most estate plans probably still waive all apportionment, the effect being that taxes are a burden on the residue as provided under common law. Apportionment rules create a more equitable method for payment of taxes and may represent the average decedent's intent when thought is given to the issue. But they are not a panacea either, because they may create problems of their own, particularly of an administrative and enforcement nature. And even in states with well drafted apportionment statutes (such as either Uniform Act, in most respects), the estate plan always must address issues relating to the payment of taxes.

Sample Tax Clause

Because of the complexity of this matter, the following sample tax clause is offered for discussion purposes only. It is designed for use in a will and reflects far more complexity than the typical user would want to incorporate, on the theory that it is both easier to delete provisions that are not needed and better to be comprehensive if the user may not want to tailor the provision for every situation. It also may apportion taxes to recipients the client would want to spare. The presumption is in favor of apportionment except to the extent a recipient is absolved. By way of example, many users are likely to delete paragraph 1.2.1.2, requiring apportionment with respect to donees who received gifts during life, because the amounts involved are too small to be concerned with and the hassle of apportionment is too great.

1. *Debts, Expenses, and Taxes:* **My personal representative shall pay from the residue of my estate all proper obligations of my estate, including expenses of my last illness and funeral, costs of administration (including ancillary), other proper charges and enforceable claims[a/] against my estate, and (subject to apportionment as provided below) death taxes as defined next below. Payments may be charged to estate income or principal[b/] in the discretion of my personal representative to the extent no deduction otherwise allowable is reduced thereby.**

1.1. *Death Taxes Defined:* **Death taxes means all estate, inheritance, succession, or transfer taxes and any income or similar**

[a/] The term "proper" charges and "enforceable" claims is meant to preclude acceleration of charges that are not yet due and owing. Exoneration or premature payment of debts is *not* the intent of this provision.

[b/] Reference to using income is meant to authorize the flexibility authorized by the so-called *Hubert* regulations in Treas. Reg. §20.2056(b)-4(d)(5), and the restriction relating to reduction of any deduction refers to the government's position in Treas. Reg. §20.2056(b)-4(d).

taxes on appreciation (including interest, penalties, and any excise or supplemental taxes) imposed by the laws of any domestic or foreign taxing authority at the time of or by reason of my death, but shall not include:[c]

    1.1.1. Any additional estate tax incurred under §2032A(c) of the Internal Revenue Code or any similar or corresponding state tax law or any successor provision to any such law, all as amended prior to my death (hereafter collectively referred to as the Code) because of the disposition of or failure to use qualified real property or family-owned business interests; and

    1.1.2. Generation-skipping transfer taxes imposed by Chapter 13 of the Code [, except to the extent attributable to a direct skip of which I am the transferor and that is not caused by a qualified disclaimer by a nonskip person (as those terms are defined in the Code), which shall be paid from the residue of my estate without apportionment or reimbursement, notwithstanding the provisions of §§2603(a)(3) and (b) of the Code or any other provision of this will].[d]

    1.2. *Apportionment:* Except as otherwise provided herein, it is my intent that each recipient of property that is includible in my estate for death tax purposes (whether passing under this will or otherwise) pay the death taxes attributable to the property (s)he receives,[e] determined as follows:

---

[c] The exceptions here are designed to avoid imposition on the decedent's estate of certain taxes that ought to be left on particular beneficiaries, as further identified in the payment provision itself. By way of example, the first exclusion from payment is any recapture tax that might ought to burden the recipient of qualifying property because it would be their failure to comply with material participation rules that would cause this tax to be incurred. To make this fair, however, the benefit of the tax reduction attributable to that property ought to be allocated in their direction. Some clients will prefer to give the tax saving to all beneficiaries equally notwithstanding that the recapture liability is imposed on the recipient of the particular property, feeling that the property itself is their "crown jewel" asset and receipt of it alone is benefit enough. However, imposition of the recapture tax on beneficiaries other than the recipient of the qualifying property could create untenable administrative, enforcement, and equity concerns.

[d] The sense of this provision is that generation-skipping transfer taxes caused by a child's disclaimer of property should not be a burden on other children, because the tax on one child's share of an estate normally would reduce that one share, typically when the child dies. Acceleration of the tax by virtue of the disclaimer should not alter the source for its payment. This concern does not have the same merit if a generation-skipping tax was going to be incurred anyway (for example, because the bequest is to a grandchild who is disclaiming in favor of a great grandchild), in which case the optional provision appropriately might be included.

[e] The overarching principle of this provision is stated here: the default is full apportionment (everyone pays their own way) except to the extent the recipient or a particular asset is identified and exempted from carrying a portion of the total tax load. This approach avoids surprises because a

1.2.1. The death tax attributable to:

1.2.1.1. Appreciation is the full amount of income or similar taxes incurred by reason of my death.

1.2.1.2. Adjusted taxable gifts as defined by §2001(b)(1)(B) of the Code, any gift taxes includible in my gross estate by §2035(b) of the Code, any recaptured inter vivos transfer subject to §529(c)(4)(C) of the Code, or any comparable inclusion (hereafter collectively referred to as completed lifetime gifts) is the difference between (a) the total death taxes incurred by my estate, less those death taxes described in paragraph 1.2.1.1 and (b) the death taxes that would have been incurred if there were no completed lifetime gifts.[f] For apportionment purposes, the recipient of property that produced gift tax includible by §2035(b) of the Code shall be treated as having received the amount of that gift tax, and the recipients of completed lifetime gifts will pay the tax attributable thereto.

1.2.1.3. The death tax attributable to all other property is the difference between (a) the total death taxes paid by my estate and (b) those death taxes described in paragraphs 1.2.1.1 and 1.2.1.2 that actually are collected by my personal representative.

1.2.2. *Multiple Recipients:* If there is more than one recipient of property separately described in paragraphs 1.2.1.1 through 1.2.1.3, each recipient shall pay a proportionate share of the death tax attributable to all of the property described in that separate paragraph based on the value of the property received by the recipient as finally determined in the death tax computation as compared to the same value of all property described in that separate paragraph that is not excluded from apportionment under paragraph 1.2.6.

1.2.3. *Tax Benefits:* Credits, deductions, exclusions, exemptions, and similar benefits shall be reflected as follows:

1.2.3.1. In computing the death tax paid by my estate for purposes of paragraph 1.2.1.2 and determining the proportionate share of such tax to be paid by any individual recipient, any gift tax allowed as a credit by §2001(b)(2) that was paid by the recipient shall inure to the benefit of that recipient.

1.2.3.2. In computing the death tax paid by my estate for purposes of paragraph 1.2.1.3 and determining the proportionate share of such tax to be paid by any individual recipient, the credit granted by §2001(b)(2) for gift taxes that were not paid by any individual recipient, the unified credit granted by §2010 of the Code, the credit for gift taxes granted by §2012 of the Code, the credit for

---

particular tax or asset that was unknown to the planner would not be identified and the default full apportionment rule would apply.

[f] The logic behind this assignment of tax to lifetime gifts is that the beneficiary already received the benefit of early receipt of the gifted property and incremental tax versus pro rata liability is a form of rough justice.

property previously taxed granted by §2013 of the Code (but only to the extent attributable to property that cannot be identified specifically as includible in my estate at death), and any other tax benefit that is not allocated by paragraph 1.2.3.3 because it is not possible to identify the property passing to a recipient that produced the tax benefit shall inure to all recipients of property described in paragraph 1.2.1.3.

1.2.3.3. The benefit of any other tax benefit shall inure to the recipient of property that produced the tax benefit (e.g., the recipient of property that generates a state death tax shall enjoy the benefit of the deduction granted by §2058 with respect to payment of that tax, the recipient of property subject to foreign death tax shall enjoy the benefit of the credit granted by §2014 with respect to the taxation of that property, and the recipient of specifically identifiable property that is includible in my estate and that previously was taxed shall enjoy the benefit of any credit granted by §2013 with respect to that property).

1.2.3.4. The benefit of any reduction in tax attributable to an election under §2032A of the Code shall inure to the qualified heir who receives the property that is the subject of the election.

1.2.3.5. The benefit of any reduction in tax attributable to property qualifying for the marital or charitable deduction shall inure to the recipient of that property. Any increase in death taxes attributable to a disclaimer of such property or a failure to elect to qualify any part of a bequest that otherwise could constitute qualified terminable interest property under §2056(b)(7) of the Code shall be charged to the disclaimed or nonelected property without the benefit of any marital deduction otherwise available to my estate.

1.2.3.6. The benefit of any tax rate differential in computing state death taxes attributable to the relation of the recipient to me shall inure to that beneficiary.

1.2.3.7. The benefit of any other entitlement directly attributable to identifiable property shall inure to the beneficiary who receives that property.

1.2.4. *Temporal Interests:* Death tax attributable to property held in temporal interests (e.g., a life estate, annuity, or term of years, followed by a remainder or a reversion) shall be paid from corpus to the extent the effect thereof is to amortize the cost over the respective interests but otherwise shall be apportioned between the respective interests based on their respective values. Apportionment to a lead interest may entail a loan from principal or recomputation of an annuity or other guaranteed payment, but neither this paragraph nor any provision of state law shall apply to the extent the effect is to reduce a deduction otherwise allowable for any part of the property.

1.2.5. *Qualified Terminable Interest Property:* Notwithstanding paragraph 1.2.3.5, with respect to property includible in my estate under §2044 of the Code, all taxes attributable to all §2044 property shall be apportioned to the §2044 property with the highest inclusion ratio to the extent doing so will not constitute a constructive addition with respect to any §2044 property with a lower inclusion ratio.[g]

1.2.6. *Exoneration:* Notwithstanding any other provision of this will, the recipient of property described in this paragraph shall not be subject to apportionment and the taxes attributable to this property shall be paid by the remaining recipients of property includible in my estate according to the computation of attributable tax described in paragraphs 1.2.1 and 1.2.2:

1.2.6.1. To the extent apportionment of the attributable tax would violate federal law relating to retirement benefits and deferred compensation.

1.2.6.2. To the extent apportionment of the attributable tax would cause an acceleration of income taxation or to the extent the property otherwise would be eligible for exclusion from my estate by §§2039(c) or (e) of the Code pursuant to the transition rules in §§525(b)(2) through (b)(4) of the Tax Reform Act of 1984 as amended.

1.2.6.3. Proceeds of life insurance that are exempt from inheritance or similar state death taxes to the extent not subject to apportionment because paid to a beneficiary other than my personal representative.

1.2.6.4. Property not passing under this will to the extent the total tax attributable thereto is less than *% of the total death taxes described in paragraph 1.1.[h]

1.2.6.5. Personal effects passing under this will to the extent the total tax attributable thereto is less than *% of the total death taxes described in paragraph 1.1.[i]

1.3. *Reimbursement:* Because I intend to apportion death taxes as described above, it is unnecessary to assert the rights to reimbursement provided by §§2206, 2207, 2207A, 2207B, and 2603 of the Code (and any similar provisions hereafter adopted) and, except to the extent inconsistent with the foregoing, I hereby waive those entitlements.

1.4. *Interest and Setoffs:* In the discretion of my personal representative, death taxes attributable to property not passing under

---

[g] This mumbo jumbo is designed to avoid using GST exempt assets in payment of tax in the estate of the surviving spouse.

[h] This provision merely absolves the need to track down the recipients of nonprobate property if the tax attributable to that property is insignificant.

[i] This provision serves the same nonapportionment function as the prior provision, if the personalty disposed of in the identified provision of the will also is insignificant, avoiding the need for any recipient of this typically nonmarketable or illiquid property to generate cash with which to pay tax attributable to it.

this will may be paid out of the residue of my estate before recovering the attributable tax from the recipient of that property.

1.4.1. Attributable tax that has not been paid by the recipient before my personal representative pays death taxes or that is not yet due because my personal representative made a valid deferral election under §6161, §6163, or §6166 or any similar provision of the Code shall bear interest equal to that imposed by the Code on my personal representative.

1.4.2. In the discretion of either my personal representative or a beneficiary under this will, as a form of payment by that beneficiary to my personal representative, any entitlement of that beneficiary under this will may be applied in payment of that beneficiary's share of the taxes and interest attributable to other property received by that beneficiary.

1.4.3. In its discretion my personal representative may distribute my estate in whole or in part before final audit and settlement of the tax liability of my estate, notwithstanding that attributable taxes may be altered thereafter.

1.4.4. My personal representative shall not be personally liable for withholding an insufficient amount as a setoff against the liability of a recipient or for failing to recover attributable taxes or interest following reasonable efforts, and shall not be required to litigate to enforce apportionment unless indemnified against the costs thereof.

1.5. *Adjustments:* My personal representative's selection of assets to be sold to pay death taxes, and the tax effects thereof, shall not be subject to question by any beneficiary. My personal representative is hereby indemnified against any liability it may incur to any recipient of property not passing under this will for the effect of any action taken in the computation or payment of death taxes that directly or indirectly affects any recipient's liability under this provision. Elections or allocations authorized under the Code may be made by my personal representative in its discretion without regard to or liability for the effect thereof on any beneficiary. No adjustment shall be made between income and principal, in the relative interests of the recipients, or in the amount or selection of assets allocated to any beneficiary under this will, to compensate for the effect of any such action or for the effect on the amount of any tax attributable to any recipient of property includible in my estate for death tax purposes.[j]

---

[j] This provision largely is about compensatory or equitable adjustments that otherwise might be required, notwithstanding that the proper adjustment might be quite uncertain both in terms of the legal need for it and the proper action. Often these adjustments are asserted as the fiduciary's duty to treat all beneficiaries fairly, following an income or wealth transfer tax election that saved taxes but produced an inequity. See, e.g., Chapter 7 at pages 38-39 and 66-67.

Chapter 12

INTER VIVOS TRANSFERS

Most estate planning involves transfers made (or that become irrevocable) at death. Revocable inter vivos trusts serve important lifetime purposes, such as to provide asset management and protection against incapacity, but they generate no demonstrable income *or* wealth transfer tax benefits. Thus, in this Chapter we consider *irrevocable* inter vivos transfers that, in addition to family and business planning objectives, often represent tax minimization opportunities by shifting future income or reducing wealth transfer tax, usually by incurring gift tax instead of a more expensive estate tax.

The most immediate costs of irrevocable inter vivos transfers are acceleration of wealth transfer tax and loss of the income tax §1014 new-basis-at-death adjustment. We will see that gift tax can be cheaper than estate tax and that deferral will not alter that economy of inter vivos transfer. The loss of new basis is a detriment to the extent §1014 would eliminate unrealized appreciation and thereby avoid capital gain income tax on appreciated assets. On balance, we will learn that acceleration is not detrimental because deferral of the wealth transfer tax is almost never economically preferable, and new basis at death does not outweigh the economic advantages of inter vivos transfers. Nevertheless, many clients simply will not embrace the following concepts, even if the transfer would incur no immediate gift tax, particularly as we await the promised repeal of the estate tax (effective in 2010, for just that one year, and with it loss of §1014 new basis at death). Thus, this Chapter may have little value until the law "settles down" and a better view of the future materializes.

Basis

We begin with the income tax concept of basis, which measures appreciation or depreciation in the value of an asset. The difference between any amount realized on a taxable transfer and the basis of the transferred asset measures the gain or loss that may be subject to §1001 recognition for income purposes (in the year of the transfer). Basis essentially is the taxpayer's investment in the asset, usually the cost or amount paid for it. Basis "carries over" in property transferred by gift inter vivos. That is, gifted property retains its basis in the hands of the donee, meaning that any appreciation generated in the hands of the donor is preserved and may be realized by the donee and subjected to the capital gains income tax in the future.[1]

---

1. See §1015(a). Closely related to this "carryover of basis" rule is "tacking" of holding periods following a gift, meaning that the donor's long term ownership will produce long term gain or loss when the donee engages in a taxable transaction. See §1223(2),

On the other hand, under §1014(a) most property includible in a decedent's gross estate for federal estate tax[2] purposes receives a new basis at death equal to the includible fair market value of the asset. Sometimes inaccurately known as the "step-*up* in basis" rule (because it eliminates any unrealized capital gain in appreciated assets held at death), this rule also can have a step-*down* in basis consequence (if the fair market value of includible property is less than the owner's premortem basis).[3]

Even assuming appreciation is the case, however, this new-basis-at-death rule does not inform a strategy of holding property until death to avoid capital gain income tax on the appreciation. This counterintuitive notion reflects the reality that the advantages of making gifts that incur no gift tax, or of actually paying gift tax inter vivos, both outweigh the new-basis-at-death opportunity to eliminate capital gain by holding appreciated property until death. We explore that notion next below. Moreover, if the estate tax is repealed in 2010, the new-basis-at-death rule also will be repealed (it is replaced with §1022 carryover of basis), making new basis an even less informed reason to retain property until death.

The Economics Of Prepaying Wealth Transfer Tax

Everything (purportedly) changes in 2010, so the following discussion must be tempered with a clear eyed assessment of political realities. Will those changes ever take effect and will they be made permanent? Because that crystal ball gazing is too difficult, the following illustrations are premised on the law in 2004 and do not reflect the promise of estate tax repeal in 2010 (for just that one year). They also do not reflect the phased reduction of the highest marginal wealth transfer tax rate or increase in the applicable exclusion amount. All of these are moving targets that Congress may alter at any time.

As a result, this Chapter is more useful as a learning tool than as a way to model predictable results for particular situations. And it is presented with the caution that current uncertainty about the stability of wealth transfer tax changes will prevent most clients from making taxable inter

---

applicable if the basis in the hands of the taxpayer is the same "in whole or in part" as that of the taxpayer's transferor. As a result of both rules the donee effectively steps into the shoes of the donor, with one limitation. Under §1015(a) basis for property transferred inter vivos is the lesser of the donor's basis or the asset's fair market value for gift tax purposes, meaning that losses cannot be shifted from donor to donee.

2. Two important variations from the general rule are §1014(b)(6), which grants both halves of community property a new basis on the death of the first spouse to die, notwithstanding that only the decedent's half of the community property is includible in the gross estate, and §1014(c), which denies the new-basis-at-death rule with respect to §691 income in respect of a decedent. See Chapter 17 at pages 11-12 for a summary of common forms of income in respect of a decedent.

3. As explained in note 1, that loss of basis cannot be precluded by a premortem transfer because carryover basis for property transferred inter vivos is the lesser of the donor's basis or the asset's fair market value for gift tax purposes, meaning that losses cannot be shifted from donor to donee. The way to avoid loss of the loss therefore is to sell the asset before death. By the way, we all would prefer not to have economic losses, but if you have income tax losses you don't want to lose them. Losses are *good* for income tax purposes because they offset taxable gains.

vivos transfers, at least if the client expects to outlive the estate tax. Still, please don't stop reading! This will be valuable for you to know.

Even if doubt about the future were not our reality, most taxpayers with wealth will attest that there are lots of *other* reasons to resist making gifts during life. Leading the list for most people are loss of control over the transferred funds, lack of liquidity to pay any resulting gift tax, and a fear that the remaining wealth will be inadequate to finance the balance of the donor's life. These concerns are undeniable and frequently paralyze wealthy and less wealthy clients alike.

In addition, another reason commonly is given for not incurring wealth transfer tax earlier than necessary (for example, by making a completed taxable gift), but it is wrong minded, as the following discussion illustrates. That inappropriate justification is the "time-value of money" notion. It assumes that wealth transfer tax is deferred during the interim and that the taxpayer will invest the tax dollars that ultimately will be paid to the government. The hope is that the taxpayer will earn more on those deferred tax dollars over a sufficient period of deferral than any increase in tax attributable to deferral and differences in the estate and gift tax systems. This time-value notion not accurate. Even if just for educational purposes, it is good to understand why this "urban myth" is wrong. But first, let's illustrate why gifting itself is tax favored.

The Tax Exclusive Gift Tax Computation Outweighs New Basis at Death

One disparity between the gift and estate taxes (it also exists as among the three different forms of generation-skipping taxable transfer) is the tax base against which each tax is computed. The gift tax (and the generation-skipping direct skip tax) is computed "tax exclusive," which means that the tax is computed only on the value received by the donee. The dollars used by the donor to pay the gift tax (or the direct skip generation-skipping transfer tax) are not themselves subject to the tax.[4] On the other hand, the estate tax (and the generation-skipping taxable distribution and termination taxes) are computed "tax inclusive," meaning that the dollars used to pay the tax are subject to the tax.

Stated another way, under the estate tax the decedent's taxable estate includes some wealth that passes to the government in the form of taxes paid on the entire estate. The estate tax is computed on the entire taxable estate, not just on the residue that passes to beneficiaries after payment of the estate tax. (The generation-skipping taxable distribution and taxable termination rules work in the same manner.) The gift tax (and generation-skipping direct skip tax) is incurred only on what the donee receives. The

---

4. Only if the donor dies within three years after a gift are the gift tax dollars subject to wealth transfer tax, under the "gross up rule" of §2035(b). The wealth transfer tax incurred is an estate tax, not an additional gift tax. There is no counterpart to §2035(b) for generation-skipping transfer tax purposes, although §2515 provides that a donor's payment of the generation-skipping transfer tax is an additional gift for gift tax purposes.

dollars used to pay that tax are not themselves subject to the tax. This means that gifts (and direct skips) always are less expensive than taxing the same wealth at death (or under the generation-skipping taxable distribution or termination rules), because of the different method of computing the amount taxable.

To illustrate, assume a taxpayer is willing to part with $1 million during life rather than holding it until death. That is, between the gift tax incurred and the actual gift made, the taxpayer is willing to suffer a diminution in net worth of $1 million. The gift tax in this case is computed on that portion of the $1 million that passes to the donee after reserving the dollars needed to pay the tax on that gift. Although this creates a circular computation (the amount of the gift is not known until the amount of the tax is computed, and the tax cannot be determined until the amount of the gift is known), an algebraic formula is available to solve the math, in our hypothetical being:

$$\text{taxable transfer} = \frac{\$1,000,000}{1+\text{rate of tax}}$$

In this case, if the tax rate is (let's assume) 48%, the taxable transfer would be $675,676, the gift tax at 48% on that amount would be $324,324 (computed without subtracting any available credits), and the total of the tax paid and the amount given to the donee would equal the $1 million the taxpayer is willing to relinquish.

As a percentage of the $1 million that would have existed in the donor's estate at death if no gift were made, the $324,324 gift tax is an effective 32.43%. This compares to the 48% effective rate that would apply for estate tax purposes on the same wealth at death: the $1 million would have incurred an estate tax of $480,000 if held until death. Notwithstanding that the nominal tax rate (48%) is the same in both cases, the difference in tax is $155,676, attributable purely to the different base against which the tax is applied (and this differential is the same regardless of the amount of any available credits).

To honestly compare gifts to transfers taxable at death, this inter vivos gift tax saving should be discounted by any income tax that might be incurred on appreciation that would escape the income tax if the property were held until death and qualified for the §1014(b)(9) new-basis-at-death adjustment (if it still is the law).[5] Notice that the current 15% long-term *capital gains* income tax would not exceed the wealth transfer tax saving attributable to the tax exclusive computation of the gift tax. This would be true even if the income tax adjusted basis in the full $1 million of transferred property was zero and even in the unlikely circumstance in

---

5. It also would be offset by any income tax that the donor would incur in generating liquidity to pay any gift tax incurred, versus waiting until death and using new basis assets to provide cash with which to pay estate tax at little or no income tax cost. The liquidity equation is virtually impossible to quantify from one case to another, so the focus here is on only the income taxation of the gifted property itself.

which all the transferred property was subjected to a realization event (such as a sale, which is unlikely in many cases because the gifted assets are stock in the family business, the family farm, or other property the family intends to retain).

Put another way, retaining property until death to obtain the new-basis-at-death adjustment is no reason to forego the benefits of the tax exclusive gift tax computation. Deferring wealth transfer tax is not favored because of new basis at death. Instead, deferral would make sense only if the income tax capital gain rate is higher than the percentage saving attributable to the difference in the effective wealth transfer tax rates under the two different systems of computation. That *can* occur, but only if the wealth transfer tax marginal rate is sufficiently low[6] and the income tax will be computed at a higher than 15% long-term capital gain rate.[7]

The Time-Value-of-Money Myth

Now let's analyze the time-value-of-money notion. We considered this in Chapter 7 at page 23 in the context of marital deduction planning, and the same concept is relevant here as well. This is the wrong-minded assumption that deferral of wealth transfer tax is beneficial because, during the interim, the taxpayer may invest and enjoy the use of money destined to go to the government in the form of taxes.

Assume for illustration purposes that the estate and gift taxes are computed in the same manner, so that the tax exclusive advantage of gifting does not skew the example. Thus, assume again that the taxpayer has $1 million that will be relinquished (by transfer and the tax payment thereon) inter vivos or at death. Also assume that whatever amount that exists during life (that is, after payment of any gift tax incurred inter vivos, or before a taxable transfer at death) will earn income or produce capital appreciation over a sufficient period of time that the wealth doubles prior to the donor's death.[8]

If the time-value-of-money notion is correct, any favorable difference in wealth transfer tax attributable to gifting would be offset by the benefits of investing the dollars (that eventually will be paid to the government) during the period of any deferral in tax payment. Given long enough the time-value notion expects the investment return to exceed any tax saving from accelerating payment of the tax. So, assume the taxpayer could transfer the

---

6. A discussion such as this is not very meaningful if the wealth transfer tax rate is low because the client has very little wealth, because the taxpayer is not likely to consider gifts in any event: there simply is not enough wealth to afford taxable inter vivos transfers subject to the gift tax.

7. A little number crunching quickly will reveal whether the gift tax advantage will outweigh the potential income tax detriment if the donee ultimately realizes the appreciation on the asset. You just need to push a pencil and compare results.

8. Rather than engage in speculation whether the taxpayer will live x years and earn income after income tax at y% and generate capital appreciation after capital gains tax at z%, this assumption merely eliminates guess work and avoids suspect illustrations by assuming that the combination of relevant factors is adequate to produce the stated result of doubling the available wealth.

$1 million inter vivos by gift, or make no gift and instead hold it until death:

Gift		*Death*
$2,000,000	initial wealth	$2,000,000
1,500,000	gift	0
555,800	gift tax (before credits)	0
(345,800)	unified credit[9]	
210,000	gift tax paid	0
290,000	wealth remaining to invest	2,000,000
× 2	growth	× 2
580,000	wealth taxable at death	4,000,000
1,500,000	adjusted taxable gift in tax base	0
(263,400)	estate tax after all credits	(1,185,000)
316,600	estate remaining after estate tax	2,815,000
3,000,000	gifted property (plus its growth)	0
$3,316,600	family wealth remaining	$2,815,000

If the time-value notion were correct, the deferral result in the Death column should exceed the result in the Gift column, but that does not happen.

Assume that the gifted asset has zero basis and the full $3 million value of it is realized for income tax purposes in a taxable sale or exchange (which growth escapes tax in the Death column because it is eliminated by estate tax inclusion and the new-basis-at-death adjustment). A *capital gain* income tax of 15% ($450,000 on $3 million of gain) would not offset the $501,600 saving attributable to the gift and prepayment of wealth transfer tax. Thus, even if that gifted property had zero basis before the gift and would enjoy a full basis increase at death if retained, the capital gain income tax on realization of the full $3 million of gifted value would not consume the full saving until the tax rate on the gain exceeds 16.72%. And these are "worst case" illustrations (zero basis, full realization), which may be far from realistic.

A different illustration might be more relevant during the period prior to the promised repeal of the estate tax, this time illustrating a gift that does not require payment of gift tax (instead relying just on the unified credit).

---

9. Notice that each tax has been computed on the basis of the unified credits in effect in 2004, which shelters only $1 million for gift tax purposes (even through it shelters $1.5 million for estate tax purposes). Rather than predict the added phase-in of the unified credit to the amount that would shelter more than $1.5 million at death in a later year, this example uses the year 2004 figures for each tax, and they differ. The principle being illustrated will not change, even as the dollar amounts change over time, except that the illustration will no longer be revealing if the gift or the estate ever becomes entirely tax-free, because the unified credit will shelter the full transfer. New conclusions will need to be drawn in that case. For example, if the inter vivos transfer imposes no gift tax cost, then *any* delay in making the transfer — if appreciation is assumed — must produce a worse result if an estate tax *would* apply. This is because, if no inter vivos transfer were made, estate tax would be incurred at death that would not be fully sheltered by the available credit. Which is to say, any wealth transfer tax on appreciation generated during the deferral period would be a net loss to the taxpayer. The point is that during these changing times static assumptions need to be reconsidered and tested periodically against the then current tax environment.

Assuming the same situation, now with a nontaxable gift, the results are dramatic and still favor the taxpayer who makes the inter vivos transfer:

Gift		Death
$2,000,000	initial wealth	$2,000,000
1,000,000	gift	0
345,800	gift tax (before credits)	0
(345,800)	unified credit	
0	gift tax paid	0
1,000,000	wealth remaining to invest	2,000,000
× 2	growth	× 2
2,000,000	wealth taxable at death	4,000,000
1,000,000	adjusted taxable gift in tax base	0
(705,000)	estate tax after all credits	(1,185,000)
1,295,000	estate remaining after estate tax	2,815,000
2,000,000	gifted property (plus its growth)	0
$3,295,000	family wealth remaining	$2,815,000

Again, the $480,000 difference in remaining wealth is not consumed even if $300,000 of capital gain tax is incurred on sale of the $2 million of gifted property (assuming a worst case basis of $0). Indeed, if capital gain is a fair element, this gift is more favorable than the last, because more savings remain after the capital gain tax is paid.

To the question whether there simply was not enough growth in these illustrations to offset the gift tax advantage, the answer is that the greater the growth, the greater the advantage to an inter vivos transfer. To illustrate, do your own calculation by assuming that all the wealth triples (rather than just doubles, as first illustrated) and recompute the respective tax savings. Counter to the time-value-of-money notion that the wealth transfer tax savings will be recovered and that deferral will be preferable the longer the deferral period or the more the taxpayer can earn during it, the disparity in net worth *increases* rather than shrinks during a more profitable deferral. This is simply because the time-value-of-money notion is exactly wrong in the wealth transfer tax context. Put another way, in an appreciating environment, the sooner the tax is paid, the better the result.

The only exception to this conclusion applies if the capital gain income tax rate on growth (as opposed to the tax on income earned, which will be taxable to someone in all events) is sufficiently large and the wealth transfer tax saving is sufficiently small. In that case a failure to generate a new basis on the growth element by subjecting the transferred asset to the estate tax in these illustrations could result in an income tax that consumes some (or all) of the wealth transfer tax saving in the gift illustration. This will occur if appreciation subject to income tax is not eliminated by the §1014(b)(9) new-basis-at-death rule, but only if there is a realization event (such as a sale) and then only if the income tax rate is sufficiently higher than the wealth transfer tax effective rate (which is not often the case).

Otherwise, even after subtracting an income tax on the full appreciation, what we see is that the time-value-of-money explanation for favoring deferral of wealth transfer tax simply is not correct. As a consequence, unless there are other (nontax) reasons to favor deferral, inter vivos transfers that trigger the gift tax and avoid a subsequent estate tax (prepayment as it were) are preferable to the estate tax at death.[10]

Other Reasons to Favor Inter Vivos Transfers

Were it not for the promise of estate tax repeal (and retention of the gift tax) the tax exclusive method of computing the gift tax would be only one of several demonstrable reasons to favor an early and complete taxable transfer of wealth that will incur a transfer tax. Another reason to favor inter vivos transfers is the §2503(b) gift tax annual exclusion or the §2503(e) education and medical expense (ed/med) exclusion, which make it possible to transfer some wealth during life entirely tax free. A corollary is split annual exclusion gifts and gifts to use or to shelter a spouse's unified credit. Yet another is the ability to shift future income and appreciation from the transferred property to the new owner for income tax purposes (and in the process to avoid a future wealth transfer tax to the transferor on that income or the appreciation).

Income tax savings are a function of the spread between the marginal brackets applicable to the transferor and the transferee. In many cases this is not significant. And the opportunity to shift appreciation should be weighed against the different potential for consumption by the transferor or the transferee (in ways that, unlike investments, show *no* value for subsequent wealth transfer tax purposes). A consumption analysis should consider the transferor's ability to consume other retained wealth and even further reduce the amount subject to wealth transfer tax at death.

Notice also that shifting appreciation does *not* reduce wealth transfer tax when the tax is a flat rate excise (i.e., after 2005, when the maximum rate is no more than 46% and the applicable exclusion amount is at least $2.0 million). In a flat tax environment no saving is available from an inter vivos gift that shifts appreciation (other than the dollars saved by the tax exclusive feature of the gift tax). To illustrate, compare owning an asset worth $100x that is expected to double in value. If a 45% tax rate is imposed, leaving $55x that will double to $110x, the taxpayer is in no better position than if the $100x were held, it doubles to $200x, and 45% of that is paid in tax, leaving the same $110x. So, depending on whether Congress allows various phase-in changes to operate as adopted in 2001, shifting appreciation may be a tax neutral gambit in the future.

A related but slightly different opportunity *will* remain, however, even after the wealth transfer tax has become flat. That opportunity is to pay tax

---

10. For a more detailed discussion see Pennell & Williamson, *The Economics of Prepaying Wealth Transfer Tax*, 136 TRUSTS & ESTATES 49-60 (June 1997), 40-51 (July 1997), and 52-56 (Aug. 1997), the July issue being the most relevant to the gifting illustration.

early with assets that will not themselves grow in value. The "Half Hot Example" in Chapter 7 at page 27 illustrates this notion, and it is most likely available to a taxpayer who is using a frozen value asset (such as cash or the unified credit) to pay any gift tax. The concept is that the unified credit will shelter all of the gift tax on $1 million of value transferred inter vivos, but the same amount of credit would not offset all of the tax on the includible value if the property doubled in value before a deferred estate taxable event. This concept is not about freezing the value of the transferred property for wealth transfer tax purposes; it is about paying the tax with dollars that are frozen in value. This opportunity is the same even after the law imposes a flat tax.

A further example of the benefits of inter vivos transfers is to prepare for valuation discounts at death. A good illustration is conversion of joint tenancy between spouses into tenancy-in-common ownership that will generate a fractional interest discount in the estate of each spouse (which requires only that the two halves of that property not be aggregated in the estate of the surviving spouse, in the manner unsuccessfully sought by the government in the *Bonner* line of cases, as discussed in 3 Casner & Pennell, ESTATE PLANNING §13.7.3.1.1 n.25 and accompanying text (6th ed. 2001).

A final advantage relates to a major and apparently intentional distinction in the law between the method for valuing gifts and for valuing property at death. Consider Rev. Rul. 93-12, which involved a donor who transferred 100% of the stock in a corporation in five equal inter vivos gifts during one year. The Ruling stated that a minority interest valuation adjustment would not be denied to any of those five separate gifts, even though the donees were related family members. The Ruling did not even mention the fact that the estate tax would be imposed on the one undivided control block if the 100% were held at death and it passed to the same five donees then.

As explained by the government in Technical Advice Memorandum 9449001:

> Although the estate tax and the gift tax are generally construed in pari materia, there are some material differences in the administration of the two taxes. . . .
>
> Unlike the estate tax where the tax is imposed on an aggregation of all the decedent's assets, the gift tax is imposed on the property passing from the donor to each donee and it is the value of that property passing from the donor to the donee that is the basis for measuring the tax. Thus, where a donor makes simultaneous gifts of property to multiple donees, the gift tax is imposed on the value of each separate gift. Accordingly, the value of property that is the subject of multiple simultaneous gifts may be different from the value of that same property if that property were included in the donor's gross estate at his death. . . .

Significant about the government's conclusion that value is determined for gift tax purposes by the property each donee receives is that this concept fundamentally is unlike the estate tax (which does not consider whether a decedent disposes of property in a single bequest or divides the property between numerous legatees). Furthermore, Congress is aware of this disparity, which is just one of several subtle and not so subtle ways by which Congress preserves a system that provides benefits exploitable only by taxpayers with enough wealth to make inter vivos transfers.

To illustrate, consider a hypothetical: C owns the world's largest diamond and provides in C's will that C's personal representative shall hire a diamond cutter who will split the stone into several smaller diamonds of equal value, to be distributed to C's children. For estate tax purposes the value of the single undivided stone would be includible in C's gross estate, because that is what C could transfer to a single donee. If instead C called the diamond cutter to C's deathbed and directed that the stone be split and the niblets delivered before C's death, those gifts each would be valued separately for gift tax purposes and only the aggregate of the values of the smaller stones would be subject to gift tax. Together they would not equal the value of the undivided stone. The same opportunity exists with stock in a family corporation or any other asset with minority or fractional interest discount potential.

As thus revealed, the gift tax considers each gift separately, producing a different valuation result for transfers made before death as opposed to transfers made testamentarily, notwithstanding that the ultimate destination of the property and the property itself are the same in either event. Gifts are the way to go if valuation opportunities like this would apply (for example, by dividing the stock in a family corporation among multiple beneficiaries). The gift tax and estate tax differ, and that difference significantly favors the gift tax in cases in which fractional or minority interest discounts could be available.

Transfers That Avoid Gift Tax

So far our discussion has illustrated advantages of inter vivos taxable transfers. The following discussion addresses various consequences of making lifetime gifts, particularly those made without immediate wealth transfer taxation.

The purported repeal of the estate and generation-skipping transfer taxes (but not the gift tax) requires no more than passing comment here because it will not be effective until 2010, and then only for one year. It may be much later in this decade before it becomes clear whether repeal actually will become effective as promised. Until that is more certain, lifetime planning that incurs a gift tax likely will be curtailed significantly, and readers and their clients naturally will exercise caution in that regard. After all, why pay a gift tax inter vivos if you expect to live long enough to die with no estate tax? This just exacerbates the interest in inter vivos transfers that do *not* incur gift tax.

Among a slew of changes that do not become effective until 2010 is adoption of a definition in §2511(c) that ties completed gift treatment to the income tax grantor trust rules. Congress figured that the gift tax should be retained to preclude tax free income shifting and, as a backstop to the income tax, that the gift tax ought to define completion according to the same rules that apply for income tax purposes. That new definition will apply only for gift tax purposes, only for purposes of the completed gift provision (and not for such things as annual exclusion qualification), and in any event it is not yet (and may never be) the law.

The change in §2511(c) does, however, spotlight the current reality that the gift tax definition of a gift is difficult to cobble together. There is no single articulation of it in the Code or Regulations. By collecting requirements from a number of sources, however, the present definition of a gift for wealth transfer tax purposes[11] can be stated as "a voluntary and complete transfer of property by an individual for less than full and adequate consideration in money or money's worth."[12] For this discussion the gift tax definition is our premier focus because the only inter vivos transfer that is subject to immediate generation-skipping transfer taxation is a direct skip and the §2612(c)(1) definition of a direct skip requires that the transfer be "subject to" the gift tax. Furthermore, there is no need for a definition of a gift for estate tax purposes separate from that for gift tax purposes.

Considered in this exploration of pre-2010 law are transfers that are "subject to" the gift tax but that may not incur a tax payment obligation. This may occur for a wide variety of reasons, such as the transfer is not yet complete and therefore not yet ripe for taxation or because the transfer qualifies for an exclusion from the tax or a deduction. Also considered are gifts that are subject to taxation presently, along with valuation aspects that

---

11. The familiar income tax definition of a gift, found in Commissioner v. Duberstein, 363 U.S. 278 (1960) ("a gift proceeds from a 'detached and disinterested generosity' . . . 'out of affection, respect, admiration, charity or like impulses'") is *not* the proper definition for wealth transfer tax purposes. Indeed, there are cases in which a gift for gift tax purposes was a sale or income for income tax purposes, showing the inconsistent treatment attributable to the two different definitions. See, e.g., Technical Advice Memorandum 7921017:

The definition of a gift for gift tax purposes is not dependent upon donative intent or the common law concept of a gift. The definition is based upon whether consideration in money's worth is received by the transferor when the property is transferred. This definition is substantially different from the one applied to the income tax concept of a gift, namely, whether the transfer is primarily motivated by the donative intent of the transferor.

Fared-Es-Sultaneh v. Commissioner, 160 F.2d 812 (2d Cir. 1947) (a sale to a transferee for income tax basis determination purposes was a gift for the transferor's gift tax purposes); Getty v. Commissioner, 91 T.C. 160 (1988), rev'd, 913 F.2d 1486 (9th Cir. 1990) (a lump sum settlement paid to a child of the decedent by the residuary beneficiary of the decedent's estate, against whom the child had brought suit, was taxable income under §102(b) because it replaced taxable income the child would have received from the decedent; reversal was based on a determination that the Tax Court's factual determination about the nature of the payment was in error).

12. See §2512(b) and Treas. Reg. §§25.0-1(b); 25.2501-1(a)(1); 25.2511-2(b). The full and adequate consideration element is really a subset of the valuation rules.

often are the most significant issues and that may present the most attractive reasons to engage in inter vivos planning.

Before undertaking this journey, however, consider one additional introductory notion. The prospect of making inter vivos transfers based on known and reliable tax consequences to accomplish desirable long-term results is troubled by the fact that change is the only constant in this area of the tax law. If a taxpayer engages in a transaction based on the current state of the law, one persistent consideration must be whether Congress will change the rules in such a manner as to negate the taxpayer's reliance.

There also is the possibility that Congress may freeze the phase in to repeal in 2010, or even accelerate that change, and then there is concern about whether sunset of the repeal in 2011 will occur. Few observers believe that repeal and restoration of the estate and gift taxes both will occur, but it is pure speculation whether Congress is more likely to repeal the repeal, or eliminate the repeal of the repeal. Thus, those who can delay making taxable transfers might be well advised to avoid incurring these taxes entirely. The latter is a notion about which anyone foolish enough can speculate.[13]

Note that a gift tax may not be payable even if a transfer meets the definition of a taxable gift for federal gift tax purposes. Transfers that do not require a tax payment are discussed first because frequently they are the most appealing forms of inter vivos planning, and likely will be more so if repeal of the estate tax seems likely — because there is little value in paying gift tax if there is no estate tax to be avoided by early payment.

Exclusions and Exceptions

One form of transfer is excepted from gift taxation notwithstanding that it meets the technical definition of a gift (it was a voluntary transfer for less than full and adequate consideration). The "business transaction" exception protects such transfers from taxation if they are not meant to be gratuitous; instead, they merely represent bad business bargains. Thus, a transfer that is "a sale, exchange, or other transfer of property made in the ordinary course of business (a transaction which is bona fide, at arm's length, and free from any donative intent), [is] considered as made for an adequate and full consideration in money or money's worth" and therefore does not constitute a taxable gift. Treas. Reg. §25.2512-8.

By way of example, a purchaser of a used car who pays too much does not make a gift of the amount paid in excess of the fair market value of the automobile, unless the seller is a natural object of the buyer's bounty and the excess payment is motivated by donative intent in a less than arm's length transaction. This subjective test is the only place in the gift tax in which motive or intent is relevant to the evaluation of whether a gift was made. Otherwise any shortfall from full and adequate consideration is a gift.

---

13. This topic is much talked about, sometimes with prescience but usually just with a political agenda or prejudice. The prospect of repeal is tortured even now that Congress has spoken. For one fool's crystal ball gazing, see Pennell, Repeal? The Wealth Transfer Taxes?, 138 Trusts & Estates 52 (Jan. 1999).

The existence of a family relation between the parties normally is an indication that the exception cannot apply, although that relation will not necessarily defeat qualification for the business transaction exception.

Certain additional inter vivos transfers are excluded entirely from the gift tax calculation. These transfers constitute otherwise taxable gifts but they qualify for either the §2503(b) annual exclusion or the §2503(e) education or medical expense (ed/med) exclusion. As such, they do not exhaust any of the donor's unified credit and do not increase the tax base upon which the tax is determined for subsequent taxable transfers.

Annual Exclusion

If a transfer constitutes a "present interest" in property, the transferor may exclude gifts of up to $11,000 (plus an inflation index amount) per donee, per year, made to as many separate individual donees as the transferor chooses. These annual exclusion gifts are entirely gift tax free under §2503(b)(2). They don't eat into the gift tax applicable exclusion amount, they are not included in the adjusted taxable gifts base to compute future gift tax or estate tax at death, they don't even need to be reported on a gift tax return. This is not a deduction; it is an exclusion. These transfers just don't "count," they are not recorded, they slip totally below the radar. But not without some qualification requirements.

For example, the regulations reflect the §2503(b) parenthetical denial of the annual exclusion for gifts of "future interests in property" and refer to a qualifying present interest as "[a]n unrestricted right to the immediate use, possession, or enjoyment of property or the income from property (such as a life estate or term certain)." Treas. Reg. §2503-3(b). Only present interests qualify. A future interest is a legal concept that includes "reversions, remainders, and other interests or estates, whether vested or contingent, . . . limited to commence in use, possession, or enjoyment at some future date or time." Treas. Reg. §25.2503-3(a). But for annual exclusion purposes this disqualification is broader than the legal terminology might suggest.

Examples of interests that appear to qualify as present interests but that may not be excluded from the gift tax under §2503(b) are interests that do not guarantee to any particular beneficiary any specific entitlement or enjoyment, typically due to trustee discretion. For instance, Treas. Reg. §25.2503-3(c) Example (3) posits a trustee that must distribute all trust income annually but has discretion to distribute that income among a class of beneficiaries, no one of whom is entitled to receive any distribution during any given year. The regulation concludes that no beneficiary of that trust has an interest that can be presently ascertained. Therefore, no annual exclusions are available with respect to transfers to that trust.

With respect to partial qualification for the annual exclusion, if income from a trust (or other transfer) is payable to a designated beneficiary and that income entitlement can be valued, the income interest alone may constitute a present interest and the value of that entitlement alone may qualify for the annual exclusion. This is true even if other elements of the trust (or other transfer) do not qualify. Such an income interest may qualify notwithstanding a spendthrift provision prohibiting the beneficiary from alienating, assigning, or otherwise anticipating the income, and even if the trustee has the power to distribute principal to the income beneficiary. Treas. Reg. §25.2503-3(b). But a trustee's power to divert income producing principal to a third party will preclude qualification of an income interest. Further, interests that entitle the beneficiary to present enjoyment of an identifiable portion of the income of a trust (or other transfer) will not qualify if the underlying assets are such that there is no guarantee that any present income will be generated.

Hackl v. Commissioner, 118 T.C. 279 (2002), aff'd, 335 F.3d 664 (7th Cir. 2003), is a fine illustration of the present enjoyment requisite not involving a trust, holding that transferred interests in a limited liability company did not afford a substantial current economic benefit. Indeed, because the asset involved (a newly reforested timber plantation) was not likely to produce any income for quite some time, it was critically important that the court also found that the operating agreement foreclosed the donees' ability to presently access any substantial economic or financial benefit. This was because the agreement also precluded any transfer of the gifted units to third parties and therefore barred alienation as a means of reaching any present economic value. Therefore, the court disallowed annual exclusions for transfers of these interests.

A further example of transfers that cannot qualify for the annual exclusion because they are not present interests would be a transfer for less than full and adequate consideration in money or money's worth to an entity, such as a corporation. These transfers may fail to qualify as gifts of present interests if the real parties in interest are individuals (such as shareholders in the corporation) who cannot immediately benefit from the transfer. As articulated by Rev. Rul. 71-443, the logic for denial of the annual exclusion in such cases is that:

Shareholders of [a] corporation do not have any present or immediate right to use, possess, or enjoy the donated property or the income from the property. This they can do only upon liquidation of the corporation or declaration of dividends, the first of which usually requires approval by the owners of a majority of the stock, and both of which usually require approval by a majority of the corporation's directors.

Crummey Withdrawal Power

Often the present interest requirement is satisfied by granting a beneficiary an immediate, albeit limited, power to obtain possession of transferred property, typically through exercise of a withdrawal power (referred to as a Crummey power after the decision in Crummey v. Commissioner, 397 F.2d 82 (9th Cir. 1968), which concluded that the power of withdrawal constituted a transfer as immediately available to the powerholder and therefore qualified as a present interest for annual exclusion purposes).

A spate of rulings and a series of cases reveal the government's antipathy to this planning, and periodic proposals for law reform would negate this planning opportunity, all of which *confirms* that the Crummey power can be a very useful device. Thus, notwithstanding the government's dislike for its use, and the potential for its repeal or alteration in the future, the Crummey power is one of the most used and useful planning devices in the current arsenal of most estate planners.

A Crummey power of withdrawal authorizes beneficiaries to withdraw property transferred to a trust that otherwise would not satisfy the annual exclusion present interest requirement. See Chapter 19 at page 40 for an illustration. The donor's contributions to the trust constitute gifts of a present interest to the powerholder to the extent of this power of withdrawal. As a result, those contributions are not precluded from qualifying for the annual exclusion by the present interest requirement or the future interest prohibition.

Most often the power of withdrawal lapses if it is not exercised within a certain time period. Because the lapse is a potentially taxable event to the powerholder under §2514, the most common form of this planning limits the power itself (or the amount as to which the lapse occurs) to the greater of 5% of the value of the trust or $5,000, so as to fit within the exceptions and avoid gift tax liability to the donee under §§2514(e) and 2041(b)(2). If no withdrawal is made, these rules specify that lapse of the power is not treated as a gift by the powerholder and, when the powerholder dies, the lapsed property is not includible in the powerholder's gross estate for federal estate tax purposes. Only any amount subject to a nonlapsed power of withdrawal still available at the date of death would be subject to estate tax, under §2041(a)(2).

In almost all cases it is expected that the powerholder will not exercise the power. Thus, it is expected that the full contribution will remain subject to trust terms that do not otherwise satisfy the present interest requirement. Nevertheless, the ability to withdraw, even for only a limited term and even if not exercised, is regarded as adequate to qualify for the annual exclusion. This is true even if the powerholder with the withdrawal right is a minor, unable under local law to exercise the power, provided that there is no impediment to appointment of a legal guardian who could exercise the power of withdrawal on the minor's behalf. This is such a well accepted estate planning principle that the government in no way challenges the initial proposition any longer.

Notice and Timing

Until the government promulgated Rev. Rul. 81-7, there was little assurance that a powerholder would either know about the Crummey power to withdraw or have a sufficient opportunity to exercise the power with respect to contributions made late in the year in which withdrawal was permitted. The subject trust in the Ruling gave an adult beneficiary a noncumulative power of withdrawal that lapsed at year end, which was two days after the trust was established. Moreover, the beneficiary was not informed of the withdrawal right with regard to the initial contribution to the trust before that right lapsed. Not unexpectedly, the Ruling concluded that the beneficiary's power to withdraw did not create a present interest with respect to the initial contribution to the trust, because the timing and lack of notice made it illusory.

Subsequently, Rev. Rul. 83-108 announced that the annual exclusion *will* be available if an adequate notice and time for withdrawal exist. Subsequent pronouncements reveal that 30 days is an ample window within which to exercise a withdrawal right before its lapse and at least one notable case has allowed the exclusion with a 15 day withdrawal window.[14]

Caution must be exercised to ensure that several years' withdrawal rights do not inadvertently lapse in a single calendar year, in amounts causing unexpected §2514(e) consequences to the powerholder. For planning purposes like this, and to guarantee that the annual exclusion opportunity is not lost for any year, normally it is preferable to take advantage of annual exclusion giving early in a new year rather than waiting until the final moment.

Another interesting question is whether notice of each year's withdrawal right must be given. Many donors and trustees fail to actually notify the Crummey powerholders of their entitlement as transfers to a trust are made (or, at a minimum, they are unable to prove that the notice was given or that the beneficiary otherwise knew of the entitlement). All sorts of practices are employed to minimize the administrative hassle of giving notice on a periodic basis. One approach is to give one notice to the powerholder that recurring contributions will be made and that withdrawal powers will be available with respect to each of those transfers, with the notion being that the notice is an ongoing information until the powerholder is informed otherwise. Another is waiver by the powerholder of the right to receive future notices. In Technical Advice Memorandum 9532001 the government opined that:

Without the current notice that a gift is being transferred, it is not possible for a donee to have the real and immediate benefit of the gift. The immediate use, possession, or enjoyment of property is clearly restricted if the donee does not know of its existence. Accordingly, a donee must have current notice of any gift in order for that gift to be a transfer of a present interest.

---

14. Estate of Cristofani v. Commissioner, 97 T.C. 74 (1991), acq. in result only, a reviewed opinion with no dissent. The time period issue was not central to the government's challenge to the exclusion, and the timing aspect of *Cristofani* is not relied upon by careful planners.

Without present interest status, the contribution will not qualify for the annual exclusion, resulting in gift tax and frustrating the donor's most fundamental purpose.

On the other hand, a number of authorities hold that the annual exclusion is available if actual knowledge existed, even if no formal notice was sent to the powerholder. For example, notice would be assumed if the powerholder also was a trustee of a trust granting the right of withdrawal, or if the donor also was the legal guardian of the powerholder.[15] Nevertheless, the better practice probably leaves nothing to chance in this important planning arena and seeks to have written confirmation from each powerholder that actual notice was timely given as to each withdrawal power that the powerholder allows to lapse (the exercised powers being rare but also obvious and not an abuse in the government's eyes).

In this respect it also is critical to remember that §2514(e) is a safe harbor only if a power lapses by its own terms and *not* if the powerholder *releases* the power. Thus, it is not wise for the powerholder to acknowledge receipt of the notice and state an affirmative intent to not exercise the withdrawal power. Instead, the powerholder should let the power lapse on its own terms due to a failure to exercise the power.

Contingent Beneficiaries

The last comment reveals a reality that makes the government crazy. No one expects the powerholder to exercise the withdrawal right, and seldom is that expectation defeated — and certainly not more than once! Indeed, often the desire is to make a transfer that exceeds the amount of a single gift tax annual exclusion but nevertheless avoids gift tax to the donor and to beneficiaries to whom withdrawal rights are given (which requires that the lapse of these Crummey rights not exceed the §2514(e) five or five limitation in any given year). To accomplish this, donors sometimes grant withdrawal rights to many more individuals than the primary beneficiaries of an intended transfer.

For example, it is not uncommon to grant powers to withdraw the greater of $5,000 or 5% of the value of the trust to every descendant of the donor, and their spouses, all with the expectation that none of these beneficiaries (primary or much more remote) will exercise their rights of

---

15. Estate of Holland v. Commissioner, 73 T.C.M. (CCH) 3236 (1997) (the court refused to disallow the annual exclusion notwithstanding that notice of withdrawal powers never was given, because testimony indicated that adult beneficiaries knew of the powers on their own behalf and that the trustees also were guardians of the minor beneficiaries); Private Letter Ruling 8022048 ("in your dual capacity as donor and natural guardian, you possess actual knowledge of the legal right to withdraw trust property you have contributed"); Private Letter Ruling 9030005 (no actual notice need be given to a minor powerholder if the minor's parent is trustee of the trust granting the power, is another beneficiary of the trust, and is the child's natural guardian; as beneficiary the parent would receive notice both personally and on behalf of the minor and, although the Ruling did not so hold, it ought to be the case that being a trustee *or* a beneficiary as well as the guardian should suffice if in either capacity the parent is aware of the minor's withdrawal right with respect to any contribution made to the trust).

withdrawal. In the pejorative, these rights in nonprimary beneficiaries are regarded as "dummy Crummey" rights because neither the powerholders nor the donor really regard them as a legitimate entitlement; they are a device to shelter a large transfer with annual exclusions.

The government understands this use of Crummey powers and regards the dummy Crummey technique as an abuse. Thus, it has attempted through a series of Technical Advice Memoranda and a string of cases to deny the effect of Crummey powers of withdrawal in certain individuals whom it regards as not having legitimate interests in the subject property.

The government is correct in noting that drafters of trusts such as these assume that the withdrawal rights will not be exercised (especially in irrevocable life insurance trusts in which the annual contributions being sheltered by the annual exclusion through the Crummey withdrawal rights technique will be used by the trustee to pay insurance policy premiums). Nevertheless, intent is not a relevant factor in qualifying for the §2503(b) annual exclusion. And notwithstanding that most attorneys who draft Crummey withdrawal rights concede that they create a fictional present interest (because the likelihood of an actual withdrawal is slight), the Tax Court has not embraced the government's objection.

Thus, for example, *Cristofani* held that the government's challenge was meritless because *Crummey* did not require trust beneficiaries to receive vested present or remainder interests in either trust corpus or income to qualify for the annual exclusion:

> As discussed in *Crummey*, the likelihood that the beneficiary will actually receive present enjoyment of the property is not the test for determining whether a present interest was received. Rather, we must examine the ability of the beneficiaries, in a legal sense, to exercise their right to withdraw trust corpus, and the trustee's right to legally resist a beneficiary's demand for payment. . . . Based upon the language of the trust instrument and stipulations of the parties, we believe that each grandchild possessed the legal right to withdraw trust corpus and that the trustees would be unable to legally resist a grandchild's withdrawal demand. We note that there was no agreement or understanding between decedent, the trustees, and the beneficiaries that the grandchildren would not exercise their withdrawal rights following a contribution to the . . . trust.

97 T.C. at 83. The court could not have more directly rejected the government's notion that intent should be relevant for §2503(b) annual exclusion purposes.

Nevertheless, the government announced in Action on Decision 1996-010 that it "will deny the exclusions for *Crummey* powers, regardless of the power holder's other interests in the trust, where the . . . facts indicate that the substance of the transfers was merely to obtain annual exclusions and that no bona fide gift of a present interest was intended." Almost simultaneously Technical Advice Memorandum 9628004 became public, dealing with the same issue and announcing that:

> where nominal beneficiaries enjoy only discretionary income interests, remote contingent rights to the remainder, or no rights whatsoever in the income or remainder, their nonexercise [of withdrawal rights] indicates that there was some kind of prearranged understanding with the donor that these rights were not meant to be exercised or that their exercise would result in undesirable consequences, or both.

Based on the reality that "[n]one of the rights were ever exercised, even by those who had no other interests in the trusts," the government denied annual exclusions for those withdrawal rights, stating that:

> we conclude that as part of a prearranged understanding, all of the beneficiaries knew that their rights were paper rights only, or that exercising them would result in unfavorable consequences. There is no other logical reason why these individuals would choose not to withdraw $10,000 [the then annual exclusion amount] a year as a gift which would not be includible in their income or subject the Donor to the gift tax.

At the same time, however, the Memorandum stated that:

> The Service generally does not contest annual gift tax exclusions for Crummey powers held by current income beneficiaries and persons with vested remainder interests. These individuals have current or long term economic interests in the trust and in the value of the corpus. It is understandable that in weighing these interests, they decide not to exercise their withdrawal rights.

The logical expectation, therefore, is that the government will challenge the annual exclusion on a selective basis in only the most egregious cases that it hopes even the Tax Court can agree are over the edge.

Other Forms of Artifice

On occasion taxpayers have engaged in other thinly disguised artifices designed to increase the number of annual exclusions available in any given year. One recurring theme involves family members, business partners, or other close and reliable associates who employ reciprocal transfers. To illustrate, siblings A and B might each make annual exclusion gifts to their own children and to their nieces and nephews. Thus, sibling A would give the annual exclusion amount to each of A's two children and to each of B's three children, and B would give the same annual exclusion amount to each of sibling B's three children and to each of A's two children. A and B each claim five annual exclusions for gifts to the five children of A and B. Predictably, the government's conclusion is that the "reciprocal trust doctrine" properly applies to regard each sibling as making gifts of twice the annual exclusion amount to each of their own children (which exceed the annual exclusion limits for the year) and none to the sibling's children. In the overall picture, the substance of the reciprocal trust doctrine and its application clearly is correct.

A variation on this theme might entail business partners A, B, and C, who each create a trust for the benefit of their respective children, with each giving the beneficiary a Crummey power of withdrawal and each giving the other two partners a withdrawal power as well. The government would allow the annual exclusion with respect to each partner's own children, but not with respect to each partner's withdrawal powers. As a result, the respective transfers among the partners would net out because the reciprocal withdrawal rights represent gifts to each other partner, matched by the same gifts from those other partners. The effect is that no partner would be deemed to make a gift to any other partner and the amounts not subject to withdrawal by a child would be taxable gifts to the trusts that do not otherwise qualify as present interests for annual exclusion purposes.

A final obvious artifice involved a donor who attempted to manufacture additional gifting opportunities for annual exclusion purposes by giving stock to 29 individuals (many subordinates or employees of the donor), all in amounts sheltered by the annual exclusion. All but two of these donees immediately endorsed the stock they received in blank; those shares subsequently were reissued in the names of various members of the donor's family. According to Heyen v. United States, 945 F.2d 359 (10th Cir. 1991), the 27 purported donees ignorantly believed they were merely participating in stock transfers or they intentionally agreed before receiving the stock that they would endorse the certificates in furtherance of the donor's scheme. Either way, the court agreed with the government's characterization of the transaction as tax fraud and upheld the imposition of a fraud penalty. Obviously, then, as powerful as the annual exclusion is, a more legitimate mechanism than this is needed to take maximum legitimate advantage of the exclusion.

Hanging Powers

Unlike the foregoing approaches, the "hanging" power illustrated with a numerical example in Chapter 9 at pages 53-54 is regarded as an effective method of maximizing the annual exclusion opportunity presented by the use of Crummey withdrawal powers while not exceeding the §2514(e) safe harbor for tax free lapse of these powers. With a proper formulation, contributions may be made excludible in whole by a properly engineered collection of withdrawal rights, without resorting to techniques that are likely to be challenged by the government.

The problem facing many planners is that the per donee annual exclusion is greater than the amount as to which any donee may have a withdrawal power that lapses with no gift tax or subsequent estate tax liability. This is because lapse of a withdrawal power is harmless to the powerholder only to the extent protected by the $5,000 or 5% exception of

§2514(e). Thus, to take maximum advantage of the $11,000 (plus inflation index amount) annual exclusion without causing any gift tax exposure to the beneficiary if the power of withdrawal lapses (which is expected), many planners permit contributions in excess of the five or five exception and rely on a nonlapsing power of withdrawal to preclude immediate wealth transfer taxation to the powerholder.

As an alternative, the power could lapse with respect to the entire contribution amount, but the beneficiary would retain a testamentary power to appoint the amount that exceeds the five or five limitation. That testamentary power would make the lapse an incomplete transfer that avoids gift taxation, but instead there would be estate taxation at the powerholder's death. In whatever format it is used, this hanging power can lapse in subsequent years to the extent those subsequent lapses are tax free under §2514(e). The hope is that all of the hanging power can lapse out before the beneficiary dies. Notwithstanding use of such hanging powers for many years, there appears to be no authority testing the underlying premises or effect of this planning.

Multiple Powers

Also notable in designing a beneficiary's hanging power of withdrawal for Crummey power purposes is Rev. Rul. 85-88, which considered application of the five or five exception in the context of withdrawal rights in multiple trusts, or multiple withdrawal rights in a single trust. For example, a person might possess two separate $5,000 or 5% withdrawal powers created by the same donor in two separate trusts, or two such powers created by contributions to the same trust by two separate donors.

In each case a taxable gift will result if the beneficiary allows the multiple withdrawal rights to lapse in a single year unless an appropriate hanging power or testamentary power applies. The taxable gift results because the Ruling appropriately limits to one the number of $5,000 withdrawal rights that can be made available to any one beneficiary. The Ruling did not need to restrict application of the 5% lapse rule under §2514(e) because the 5% test properly is based on the value of total trust assets subject to the withdrawal right at the time of lapse. Thus, if the donee has multiple withdrawal rights in a single trust, the 5% test is based on "the maximum amount subject to the donee's withdrawal power *on the date of lapse of any such power* during the calendar year." As regards multiple withdrawal rights in separate trusts (regardless of their settlor(s)), the 5% test is applied by *aggregating* the amount subject to the power in each trust, determined in the same manner.

As an example that informs the need to know how many trusts (created by the same or different donors) grant the same beneficiary five or five withdrawal rights, the Ruling assumed withdrawal rights in each of two trusts, one of $300,000 and one of $400,000, and determined that the 5% test would be applied against the aggregate value of $700,000. Thus, the 5% exception under §2514(e) would be an aggregate $35,000 for the year.

Generation-Skipping Transfer Tax

Additional tax consequences to the powerholder relate to the generation-skipping transfer tax, and to income taxes. Giving skip persons Crummey withdrawal rights constitutes a direct skip for generation-skipping transfer tax purposes. These contributions are harmless (they qualify for inclusion-ratio-of-zero treatment under §2642(c)) if separate shares are created for each beneficiary. Otherwise they can incur generation-skipping transfer tax even though they qualify for the gift tax annual exclusion. See Chapter 18 at pages 34-35.

The other generation-skipping transfer tax consequence of the lapsing power is that the powerholder becomes the transferor of the trust for subsequent generation-skipping transfer tax purposes to the extent any lapse is gift taxable. New transferor treatment is important because of exemption allocation and generation assignment issues, but it is avoided to the extent lapse is tax free under the five or five provisions of §2514(e). See Treas. Reg. §§26.2601-1(b)(1)(v)(A) (penultimate sentence) and 26.2652-1(a)(5) Example 5.

Pseudo Grantor Trust Status

This new transferor treatment is mirrored and enlarged upon for §678 income tax purposes, which provides that a beneficiary who allows a Crummey power of withdrawal to lapse becomes a grantor of the full lapsed amount in the trust for future income tax purposes. This treatment applies to the entire lapse amount, not just the amount in excess of the §2514(e) five or five exception, and is avoided only to the extent the trust's original settlor retains an interest or power that causes overriding grantor trust income tax liability.

The powerholder is treated as the owner of a portion of the trust in the year the power is exercisable, and lapse of the withdrawal power is tantamount to a release for purposes of §678(a)(2). If the powerholder is entitled to trust income in future years, this release generates grantor trust exposure for the duration of the trust. This means that a portion of trust income is taxable to the powerholder every subsequent year. That often upsets individuals who do not receive the dollars on which they must pay income tax, and this exposure increases every time a withdrawal power lapses. Thus, the government will not treat a new lapse as occurring with respect to the same five or five portion every year. Instead, the increase in the portion subject to grantor trust treatment attributable to a new lapse is computed according to a formula:

$$\text{Increase} = \text{withdrawable amount} \times \frac{\underline{\text{trust portion not yet owned}}}{\text{total trust corpus}}$$

Subsequent distributions to the powerholder from the trust are deemed to come proportionately from the owned portion and from the balance of the trust.

To illustrate the computation, assume the powerholder may withdraw 5% of the trust corpus every year. In year 1 the owned portion would be 5% × 100% ÷ 100% = 5%. The year 2 increase would be 5% × 95% ÷ 100% = 4.75%, and a total of 9.75% would be deemed owned by the powerholder. The year 3 increase would be 5% × 90.25% ÷ 100% = 4.5125%, and a total of 14.2625% would be deemed owned by the powerholder. The year 4 increase would be 4.286875%, and the owned portion would increase to 18.549375%, and so on. Under this approach, the trust never would become totally owned, no matter how long the withdrawal power existed and lapsed, although the owned portion eventually would approach 100%. The government's computation is equitable but complicated, and underscores the notion that the lapse of a five or five withdrawal power is not harmless for income tax purposes the way it appears to be under §2514(e) for most wealth transfer tax purposes.

Qualified Minor's Trusts

Some transfers, typically in trust, that otherwise would not meet the annual exclusion present interest requirement nevertheless qualify for the annual exclusion because of a special exception for "qualified minor's trusts" in §2503(c). This tool is important because gifts to minors that take advantage of the gift tax annual exclusion may be a significant component of any comprehensive estate plan. And the dollar amounts involved may exceed the amount the donor (or the donee's parents) would want the minor to control at a tender age.

The subject matter of an annual exclusion gift may be transferred directly to a minor and qualify for the annual exclusion notwithstanding that the minor does not have legal capacity to deal with the transferred property and even if no legal guardian has been appointed. Legal incapacity has certain implicit protections against loss or mismanagement by the minor, but Congress recognized that the inherent disadvantages of transferring property outright to a minor make this an undesirable mechanism to take advantage of the annual exclusion. So Congress enacted §2503(c), which deems that a transfer creates a present interest in a minor beneficiary if the principal and income[16] of the gifted property may be expended by or for the benefit of a beneficiary who has not attained 21 years of age.

In addition, any unexpended principal and accumulated income must be subject to the beneficiary's control when the beneficiary attains age 21, or it must be distributed to the beneficiary's estate or be subject to the beneficiary's general power of appointment if the beneficiary dies before reaching that age. In many cases the power of appointment is the preferable alternative. This will be true especially if the donor is a potential heir of the beneficiary. In such a case, trust property that is payable to the beneficiary's estate if the beneficiary dies before reaching 21 years of age

---

16. Unlike the annual exclusion present interest requirement, there is no §2503(c) requirement that the trust property be income producing.

may pass back to the donor, who typically does not want to receive by inheritance any of the property the donor was seeking to remove from the donor's estate through annual exclusion gifts.

Because the beneficiary cannot make a will in most states until reaching a certain age, this possible inheritance is not avoidable if the trust provides for payment to the beneficiary's estate and the beneficiary dies before reaching that age. For this reason, it typically is preferable to provide that the trust property will pass as the beneficiary appoints pursuant to a general inter vivos or testamentary power of appointment.[17] This trust will qualify under §2503(c) notwithstanding that the beneficiary also may be unable due to age to exercise the power of appointment (and, thus, that the property will pass to designated default beneficiaries other than the donor).[18]

An income interest or other less than fee simple interest in such a trust also may qualify for the §2503(c) annual exclusion. For example, imagine a trust to pay income to a minor beneficiary for life, perhaps granting the trustee discretion to distribute trust corpus to the beneficiary, but reserving the remainder after the minor's death for other designated beneficiaries. Just the value of the life estate in such a trust standing alone qualifies for the annual exclusion. As another alternative, it is permissible to provide the beneficiary with a limited window of opportunity to withdraw the trust corpus upon reaching the age of 21 and, to the extent the power of withdrawal is not exercised, to provide after the time window has closed that the trust will continue until a later date.[19] As with a lapsed Crummey power of withdrawal, the trust will be regarded as the beneficiary's property for income and wealth transfer tax purposes following the lapse of such a power, and it too will qualify for the annual exclusion.

In lieu of drafting and administering separate trusts for minor beneficiaries (or a single trust with separate shares), a donor may wish to take advantage of the fact that every American jurisdiction has enacted custodianship legislation, usually modeled after the Uniform Gifts to

---

17. Under Treas. Reg. §25.2503-4(b) the general power may be exercisable by deed or by will or by either. It may be advisable to require its execution with all the formalities of a will to limit the possibility of inadvertent exercise by inter vivos document.

18. Treas. Reg. §25.2503-4(b) requires that there be no substantial restrictions on exercise of the power by the beneficiary but provides that restrictions under controlling local law that preclude the beneficiary from exercising the power do not prevent the power from satisfying this requirement.

19. See Rev. Rul. 74-43:

a gift to a minor in trust, with provision that the beneficiary has, upon reaching age 21, either (1) a continuing right to compel immediate distribution of the trust corpus by giving written notice to the trustee, or to permit the trust to continue by its own terms, or (2) a right during a limited period to compel immediate distribution of the trust corpus by giving written notice to the trustee which if not exercised will permit the trust to continue by its own terms, will not be considered to be the gift of a future interest as the gift satisfies the requirements of section 2503(c) of the Code, and the exclusion provided for in section 2503(b) is allowable.

Parameters such as those informing the validity of Crummey withdrawal powers probably are adequate.

Minors Act or its more recent replacement, the Uniform Transfers to Minors Act. These custodial arrangements qualify under §2503(c) and permit a donor to transfer property to a custodian for the benefit of a minor. That account usually is retained until the custodianship must terminate, typically at the beneficiary's age of 18 or 21 years (or the minor's death), at which time the property is distributable to the minor (or to the minor's estate).

Custodianships offer a convenient and inexpensive mechanism for making gifts to minors that qualify under §2503(c) and, until termination, protect against the hazards of an outright transfer. Nevertheless, certain cautions must be exercised. For example, the statutory provisions governing the account cannot be changed. Thus, a distribution to the beneficiary's estate and potential distribution back to the donor cannot be prevented.

More importantly, the government asserts that the value of custodianship property is includible in a donor's gross estate under §2038 if the donor dies while serving as the custodian, because the donor's powers are deemed to be retained powers over the gifted property.[20] Unfortunately, this estate tax exposure cannot easily be avoided by a donor who wants to maintain control over the gift. For example, the reciprocal transfers doctrine prevents avoidance of this exposure by merely employing reciprocal transfers by which one parent acts as fiduciary of accounts created by the other and vice versa.[21]

Similarly, the government has asserted §2036(a)(1) indirect retained beneficial ownership and §2041(a)(2) general power of appointment inclusion with respect to any donor or any third party acting as trustee or custodian over assets held for their own dependents. In each case the government's theory is that the donor or the fiduciary is the indirect beneficiary of funds that may be used to support or maintain a person the donor or the fiduciary is legally obligated to support or maintain.[22] As discussed in Chapter 5 at page 26, this discharge of obligation of support theory is significantly misunderstood and not supportable under the law of most states, but it never has been challenged.

---

20. Treas. Reg. §20.2038-1(a); Rev. Rul. 59-357, and Rev. Rul. 57-366, based on Lober v. United States, 346 U.S. 335 (1953).

21. See Exchange Bank & Trust Co. v. United States, 82-1 U.S. Tax Cas. (CCH) ¶13,444 (Ct. Cl. 1981), aff'd, 694 F.2d 1261, 1269 (Fed. Cir. 1982), in which spouses each transferred assets under custodianships for their children. To the extent the husband was the donor the wife was named as custodian, and to the extent the wife was the donor the husband was named as custodian. The husband died while several of the children were under 21 years of age, and the court held that assets held by the husband as custodian, which were transferred by his wife, were includible in the husband's gross estate as they would have been if he had been the transferor, under an application of the reciprocal trust doctrine: "The fact that the focus in this case is upon crossed custodianships rather than crossed trusts offers no basis for denying the application of the reciprocal trust doctrine." The court on appeal concluded "that the reciprocal trust doctrine should be applied to uncross the custodianships because the transfers were interrelated, and because the arrangements left the donors in the same economic positions as they would have been in had they retained the property as custodians under the Florida Gifts to Minors Act."

22. See Treas. Reg. §§20.2036-1(b)(2), 20.2041-1(c)(1).

Although the theory upon which the government's discharge theory rests is wrong, and trust or custodianship assets should not be included in the parent's gross estate, naming a parent as fiduciary in these cases may be begging for a controversy that it would be better to avoid. Alternatively, a provision precluding the use of assets in a way that may discharge a support obligation is wise drafting to guard against either §2036 or §2041 exposure (but note that Uniform Act accounts cannot be amended to make such a change).

The addition of language to a §2503(c) trust prohibiting distributions that might be deemed to discharge or satisfy any person's legal obligation to support or maintain a minor beneficiary will not cause the trust to fail the Treas. Reg. §25.2503-4(b)(1) requirement that there be no substantial restriction on the provision of benefits in a §2503(c) account for the minor beneficiary. Such a prohibition, sometimes referred to as an "Upjohn" clause,[23] "does not in any way impair but, rather, insulates the minor beneficiaries' present interest in the trust contributions. The trustee is empowered to distribute all or any part of these funds for any purpose and toward any end not already provided by law."

The government suggested that the restriction might be substantial if the settlors were not financially able to fulfill their legal obligations to the beneficiary. The *Upjohn* court rejected this notion because the settlors' financial condition made this possibility remote. In addition, under state law, the settlors' legal obligation would decline with any diminution in their financial resources, which would release the trustee from the restriction against expending funds for the beneficiary.

Although not articulated by the court, no distribution made by the trust would run afoul of the prohibition if state law provides that a parent's legal obligation is not discharged or satisfied by trust distributions. In that respect, the proscription on the trustee is meaningful only in that it blocks the government's improper discharge of obligation argument and does not impair the fiduciary or violate the substantial restriction prohibition.

Ed/Med Exclusion

In addition to the §2503(b) annual exclusion and §2503(c) qualified minor's trust version of it, §2503(e) allows an unlimited exclusion for amounts properly paid for the education or medical expenses of any person.[24] Qualified transfers include amounts paid for tuition of full or part time students (but not for ancillary expenses such as room and board, books, and fees. Treas. Reg. §25.2503-6(a)(2)). Medical expenses are more

---

23. So named after Upjohn v. United States, 72-2 U.S. Tax Cas. (CCH) ¶12,888 at 86,077-86,078 (W.D. Mich. 1972) (provision that "no income or principal shall be paid, distributed or applied for support or maintenance which the settlors or either of them are legally obligated to provide a beneficiary, nor to defray any legal obligation of the settlors or either of them" did not preclude §2503(c) qualification).

24. As with §2503(b), payments meeting the §2503(e) requirements may be shielded from generation-skipping transfer taxation by §2642(c)(3)(B) if its requirements are met.

broadly defined to include costs for "diagnosis, cure, mitigation, treatment or prevention of disease, or for the purpose of affecting any structure or function of the body or for transportation primarily for and essential to medical care." Treas. Reg. §25.2503-6(a)(3). Not covered, however, are amounts paid for expenses that are reimbursed by insurance or amounts paid for medical insurance for any individual.

Both the education and medical expense payments must be made directly to the education or medical service provider. Payments that reimburse the donee do *not* qualify. §2503(e)(2); Treas. Reg. §25.2503-6(c) Examples (2) and (4). For example, a deposit in a student's checking account to cover a check from the student to the university for tuition will not qualify; the donor must pay that amount directly to the university bursar. Similarly regarding medical expenses, any items paid by the donee for which the donor provided reimbursement also would be subject to gift tax. Further, a transfer to a trust for the ultimate payment of tuition charged by an educational institution is not a qualified tuition payment that would be excluded from the gift tax under §2503(e), because the qualifying transfer must be directly to a qualifying educational organization. Treas. Reg. §25.2503-6(c) Example (2).

Donors who do not want to transfer funds directly to an educational institution but who are considering a gift designed to further the education of a donee may wish to consult §529, which provides an income tax exemption for qualified state tuition programs. For gift tax purposes, §§529(c)(2), 529(c)(4), and 529(c)(5) provide that contributions to these programs are completed gifts for gift tax purposes, with present interest §2503(b) gift tax and §2642(c) generation-skipping transfer tax annual exclusion (but not §2503(e) ed/med exclusion) qualification. There is even a special five year ratable carry forward provision if the contribution exceeds the donor's annual exclusion limitation for the year of contribution.[25] Most importantly, distributions from the plan may be used for §529(e)(3)(A) qualified higher education expenses, which are more than just tuition and fees (such as for room, board, books, and other required expenses), and they are not gifts to the beneficiary (nor is a change of beneficiary usually taxable). These trusts provide a convenient form of transfer, with no income tax to the designated beneficiary and automatic qualification for the §2503(b) gift tax annual exclusion.

Other options include gift to minors act accounts and prepaid tuition plans.[26] The list of available options is rapidly changing and advisors can only help to evaluate various criteria that may be useful or important to a

---

25. With estate tax inclusion to the donor under §529(c)(4)(C) to "recapture" any outstanding carry forward amount if death occurs within the five year carry forward period.

26. Another potential income tax opportunity is §135, which permits the payment of qualified higher education expenses with United States savings bonds without recognition of any unrealized income in the bond. Unlike §529, there is a graduated reduction in the amount of income that may be excluded under §135, based on the taxpayer's adjusted gross income.

family, including questions of age limitations for contributions and withdrawals, contribution maximums, qualified expenditures, client control over account investments and distributions, spendthrift protections, and both state and federal income, estate, gift, and generation-skipping taxation.

Unified Credit

Any gift tax incurred on a taxable gift exceeding the allowable annual exclusion or the ed/med exclusion may be offset by the unified credit and therefore may not actually be payable. The unified credit is not elective and cannot be reserved for future use. Instead, it is automatic and offsets the tax on the first taxable transfers made by citizens and residents of the United States,[27] up to the gift tax applicable exclusion amount. To the extent it is not used during life, the unified credit remains available at death. There is no need to use it to avoid losing it. Nevertheless, as illustrated at page 8, because the unified credit is a fixed entitlement, the most benefit is garnered the sooner the unified credit is used to transfer property that is expected to appreciate in value in the future.

Gift Splitting

Married United States citizen or resident taxpayers may double the benefit of the unified credit, generation-skipping transfer exemption, or gift tax exclusions available to either of them alone. Authorized by §2513 are gifts made by one spouse that are treated as split equally and made half by each, just by executing the §2513(b) consent. Thus, for example, if a donor has substantial wealth but the donor's spouse has little, one way to take advantage of the spouse's tax benefits would be for the donor to make a taxable gift to third parties and for the spouse to consent to it for gift-splitting purposes. In this manner the donor can transfer double the amount of the transfers either could make alone and can generate effectively the same result as if the donor made a gift to the spouse tax free under the §2523 marital deduction and then each spouse made their own transfers to take advantage of their own benefits.

The advantage of gift splitting is that it does not give control to the donor's spouse or subject the gifted property to creditors of the donor's spouse. In many cases, however, an outright gift to the spouse followed by separate gifts by each may be preferable because gift splitting is an all-or-nothing endeavor. The spouses must make the §2513 election with respect to all gifts made by either of them during any part of the taxable period; spouses cannot elect split gift treatment for only selected gifts during the taxable period. §2513(a)(2); Treas. Reg. §25.2513-1(b)(5). Indeed, gift splitting is effective even with respect to inadvertent or unintended gifts made by either spouse during the election period.

---

27. Unlike §2101(c), which simply limits the unified credit at death with respect to nonresidents who are not citizens, §2505(a) does not allow the credit at all with respect to United States taxable inter vivos gifts made by nonresidents who are not citizens.

In addition, gift splitting is available only for gifts to donees other than the consenting spouse. Thus, a different approach is required if any portion of a gift benefits the consenting spouse and the value of that interest is not ascertainable (and therefore cannot be evaluated separately or severed). For example, if a donor wishes to establish an inter vivos trust to provide income and principal in the discretion of a disinterested trustee among a group consisting of the consenting spouse and the donor's descendants, no part of that gift could be split by the spouses unless the portion for the donor's spouse could be valued separately from the other interests given. In such a case a separate marital deduction trust for the donor's spouse and another separate trust for the descendants (as to which the spouse could make the gift-splitting election) might be a more appropriate technique. A similar separation might be required if the donor spouse wanted the consenting spouse to have control over the gifted property in the form of a power of appointment.[28]

Finally, you should consider conflict of interest and adequate representation issues when advising the consenting spouse regarding gift splitting. It may be that the §2513 consent is harmless or desirable in a given situation, but consider whether you would give the same advice to consent to split gifts if the donor was represented by someone else. For example, imagine that the marriage was not the first for either and the consenting spouse had natural objects of the bounty who differ from those of the donor spouse. Would you advise the consenting spouse that the donor spouse should compensate the consenting spouse for the use of the consenting spouse's unified credit or generation-skipping transfer exemption (which both are one-time benefits that cannot be replaced after they are used)? Annual exclusion gifts to objects of just the donor's bounty would be different, because the consenting spouse loses nothing by agreeing to split gifts that the consenting spouse otherwise would not make to those individuals. These are renewable and unlimited opportunities. But use of the consenting spouse's unified credit or generation-skipping transfer exemption to shelter gifts to the donor's beneficiaries denies the opportunity to use those benefits for transfers to the consenting spouse's own beneficiaries.

Those tax benefits may not be worth much to a consenting spouse who has little wealth currently, but people inherit, win the lottery, accumulate earnings, and find other ways to acquire wealth. Against that possibility, a separate advisor for the consenting spouse might suggest that the donor should compensate the consenting spouse for the use of the consenting spouse's nonrenewable entitlements. The challenging issue is: What are they worth? For example, should the unified credit be measured in terms of the actual tax offset by a gift taxed at the bottom estate or gift tax brackets, or

---

28. The express language of §2513(a)(1) denies gift splitting if the consenting spouse has a general power to appoint the gifted property. Apparently a nongeneral power in either spouse will not preclude gift splitting, although the power might cause the gift attributable to the powerholder to be incomplete.

should the cost to the consenting spouse of splitting a gift be measured by the tax that might be incurred at the top marginal brackets that could apply to wealth transfers by the consenting spouse during life or at death? How should the likelihood of acquiring sufficient wealth to take advantage of these tax benefits be factored into the equation? And would a demand for compensation cause such a rift between the donor and consenting spouses that the possibility should not be broached?

These ethical and practical concerns are in addition to several technical flaws in the operation of the gift splitting provision in the context of transfers that are brought back into the donor's gross estate at death. Together they ought to give pause to any advisor who is planning with spouses who make inter vivos transfers. Annual exclusion split gifts are relatively easy and potentially harmless; others gifts raise more significant concerns. Unfortunately, it is not yet known whether a separate marital deduction transfer to the spouse, followed by separate gifts by both spouses, will be respected by the government as a viable alternative to gift splitting. As a consequence, if the latter alternative is considered safer or more desirable, it should be pursued with some caution, the dollar amounts should not be identical to a split gift alternative, and some time might be inserted between the marital deduction transfer and the spouse's separate gift. Independence should be guaranteed, and even the appearance of an implied understanding or coerced planning should be avoided.

Inter Vivos Marital Deduction

The unlimited inter vivos marital deduction provides an opportunity for spouses to engage in asset reallocations for tax minimization or any other purpose. Planners should be cautious regarding planning in lieu of gift splitting, however, to avoid a marital deduction gift made by a donor spouse to what otherwise would be a consenting spouse, who the government then alleges by prearrangement thereafter made a gift to objects of the donor spouse's bounty. The concern is that the government will treat the gift as a transfer of all the property by the donor spouse to those objects directly, as to which neither the marital deduction nor gift splitting would apply (the latter because it was not elected and the former because of the agreement to pass the property along to the ultimate donees).

In addition, planning close to the end of a donee spouse's life should beware of inadvertent application of §1014(e), which would deny a new basis at death to any appreciated property transferred to a dying spouse who directly or indirectly transfers the property back to the donor spouse. Otherwise, by virtue of the unlimited lifetime marital deduction in §2523 and the nearly unlimited lifetime income tax free interspousal transfer rule in §1041, inter vivos interspousal property transfers are virtually ignored for income and wealth transfer tax purposes, as if the spouses were a single economic unit for all tax purposes.

One notable exception to this treatment applies if the donee spouse is not a citizen or resident of the United States, in which case the special rules in §§1041(d) and 2523(i) may deny tax free status for either income or wealth transfer tax purposes. A useful gift tax alternative in §2523(i)(2), however, authorizes a $114,000 (in 2004, plus an inflation index amount in later years) annual exclusion for transfers to the noncitizen, nonresident spouse.

One form of inter vivos planning may be particularly attractive to spouses with significant but disparate wealth. Assume, for example, that spouses D and S seek estate planning and that the initial interview discloses that S (whom you expect to be the surviving spouse, based on age, lifestyle, and physical characteristics) has more wealth than the maximum amount that can pass free of tax under the applicable exclusion amount of the unified credit. More importantly, assume that D has little independent wealth. In such a case one very obvious planning suggestion would be to encourage S to give D enough wealth to shelter D's tax benefits if D does die first. This might include an amount equal to D's unused estate tax applicable exclusion amount and generation-skipping exemption, and perhaps even enough wealth to run through the less than maximum estate tax brackets in D's gross estate.

In a typical situation S might balk at this advice until it is made clear that an inter vivos qualified terminable interest property trust may be employed to protect the wealth against predators who might attempt to reach those assets in D's hands. For example, a not unlikely scenario would entail D as the less wealthy spouse because of a failed business venture, with creditor problems that linger. The spendthrift nature of the inter vivos qualified terminable interest property trust for D's benefit, created by S, can provide protection against claims that might be respected if the property were transferred to D outright. Other reasons (such as denial of control) also might recommend use of the inter vivos qualified terminable interest property trust for D. With sufficient protection, S might be willing to engage in this form of inter vivos planning designed to shelter D's tax benefits. But a stumbling block might be S's desire to continue to enjoy the income from the trust property after D's death, if events turn out as this planning anticipates.

The planning issue is whether S may retain a secondary life estate following the qualified terminable interest property income interest in D for the balance of D's life. Under §2523(f)(5)(A) a donor spouse *may* retain such a secondary life estate and the trust property will not be includible in the donor's gross estate (under §2036(a)(1) or any other estate tax inclusion section). Nor will a subsequent transfer of the retained secondary life estate by the donor spouse generate any gift tax consequences. According to Treas. Reg. §25.2523(f)-1(f) Example 11, §2044 inclusion to D effectively cleanses the trust, meaning that S's secondary income interest is treated as if D created the trust.

As a result, it is relatively easy for a donor spouse to shift wealth to a donee spouse by inter vivos transfer with the only potential risk being that, if they divorce, the income interest for the balance of the donee spouse's life will be lost to the donor spouse. In addition, under §§672(e) and 677(a), that income will be taxed to the donor spouse even after the divorce. Depending on state law, that income interest may count in the divorce property settlement action and offset any obligation that otherwise might be imposed on the donor spouse anyway. And the income tax obligation similarly might be factored into any ongoing alimony, support, or property settlement negotiation.

Inter Vivos Charitable Deduction

Like the §2523 unlimited lifetime marital deduction, §2522 offers an unlimited gift tax charitable deduction for qualifying transfers made inter vivos. In addition, §2501(a)(5) allows a gift tax political contribution exclusion for transfers to a §527(e)(1) political organization.

Like gifts in general, a §2522 deductible inter vivos charitable gift can be more valuable than one made at death, for many of the same reasons. Most obvious are those that apply if the transfer has both taxable and deductible components: in that case shifting income and growth out of the donor's estate, paying any gift tax attributable to the transfer to avoid paying estate tax on the gift tax dollars themselves, and generating valuation opportunities all can be important. And the exclusion under §2501(a)(5) for inter vivos transfers to a political organization is preferable to a testamentary transfer to the same organization because there is no estate tax exclusion or deduction available for political contributions.

There is an additional reason to favor accelerating charitable transfers into lifetime planning, even in cases involving a 100% deductible charitable gift (as to which a charitable deduction at death is as effective as a charitable deduction inter vivos, regardless of the size of the transferred property). This advantage, unique to inter vivos charitable planning, is the §170 income tax charitable deduction, which has no counterpart for other gift planning and is not available at death. This deduction generates an income tax saving attributable to the inter vivos charitable gift, which can finance other planning that also may be attractive.

For example, a donor may choose to transfer the income tax dollars saved with an inter vivos charitable contribution to a donee who will use the money to help finance life insurance on the donor's life (or other investments) to compensate for the dollars contributed to charity. The transaction has many of the advantages of inter vivos giving in general, to the extent this replacement wealth is excluded from the donor's gross estate at death (in this case financed in part by the tax savings produced by the income tax deduction).

Just as gifts made inter vivos are more attractive for wealth transfer tax purposes than those at death, this income tax advantage makes the inter vivos charitable gift a better plan *if* the donor was going to make the charitable transfer in all events. The income tax deduction also recommends planning that relies on the estate tax marital deduction. If the decedent failed to provide for charity inter vivos, a desirable alternative is to leave property to a surviving spouse who then will make inter vivos charitable transfers. If the decedent otherwise would have made similar charitable gifts under a will a gift by the surviving spouse inter vivos clearly is preferable because of the §170 income tax deduction to the surviving spouse.

Besides the benefit of the §170 deduction, inter vivos charitable giving provides psychic benefits to the donor that are not available at death. To take the extreme example, a donor who contributes enough wealth to name a building (and who can afford to do so currently) may take immeasurable pleasure from *living* to see the day.

Notwithstanding occasional claims to the contrary, however, no charitable planning technique is likely to fully replace the wealth contributed to charity, and an inter vivos or testamentary plan cannot be undertaken without cost to the donor or the donor's family. Be especially wary of claims that charitable planning techniques can *increase* a client's net worth that will remain available to the client's ultimate beneficiaries. Inter vivos charitable giving may generate a smaller *reduction* in net worth, but it is not likely to prove beneficial in pure economic terms in comparison to no charitable giving whatsoever. Nevertheless, if charitable giving is a part of the donor's estate planning objectives, inter vivos execution of that portion of the plan can produce more favorable results than testamentary charitable transfers. So one lesson to learn is to compare inter vivos versus testamentary charitable planning for clients who are charitably inclined.

To illustrate the degree of caution required, however, let's use the insurance plan noted at page 32. A frequent flaw in the proposal is that the §170 income tax deduction is available only for a limited number of years but the premium payment obligation extends for the donor's entire lifetime. Or the plan is dependent upon techniques that the donor could employ without the charitable component, such as using inter vivos annual exclusion gifts to fund an irrevocable life insurance trust. Therefore the plan's success is not really a function of the charitable element at all. Further, in some cases the savings illustrated is a function of the donor dying prematurely, which *often* produces a tax savings when life insurance is involved. But betting on a premature death is not likely to be a successful strategy unless the taxpayer is better at predicting death than the insurer's actuary and medical examiner. Finally, planners also should be wary of unrealistic investment projections (which are just as dangerous as unrealistic life expectancy predictions).[29]

Conservation Easements

One notable exception to the suggestion that it is not common to benefit economically by charitable planning is the charitable conservation easement illustrated in Chapter 8 at pages 31-32. This benefit applies to the extent a

---

29. Hoisington, *The Truth About Charitable Remainder Trusts* (How to Separate the Help from the Hype), 45 TAX LAW. 293 (1992), is a very useful article illustrating the economics and the method needed to analyze a proposed "asset replacement" plan involving charitable planning.

qualified conservation easement is donated to a §170(h)(3) qualified organization, irrevocably and perpetually restricting the ability of the property owner to develop it for commercial purposes. The underlying asset is includible in the gross estate at death because it still is owned, but the estate is entitled to an exclusion — a tax benefit like a deduction — that reduces the estate tax liability, in addition to any estate tax §2031 valuation reduction. Generating a §170(h) income tax deduction for the donor during life can, at maximum tax rates, produce aggregate tax savings that may exceed 100% of the value of the easement involved.

It may even be that the property is such that no one in the decedent's family would likely want to change its current use by development or sale at a capital gain. Indeed, the location of the property may inform a meaningful benefit to the family through qualification for the exclusion, because it ensures that the present use will not ever change (think, for example, about a family compound that the elder generation wants to ensure will never be developed for any other purpose). As with any kind of charitable planning, however, careful calculations and evaluation are required before reaching that conclusion.

Charitable Gift Annuities

A simple approach to inter vivos charitable giving involves buying an annuity from a charitable organization. This represents the charity's general, unsecured promise to pay the designated annuitant a guaranteed annual amount. Most charities base their annuity payments on tables employing uniform rates published by the nonprofit American Council on Gift Annuities, which discourages donors from "shopping" and charities from "competing" based on relative rates rather than the merits of the charitable purpose. Regardless of how they are set, however, charitable gift annuity rates are not meant to be commercially competitive, because the charity is receiving a benefit from the transaction (often from 40% to 60% of the value of the transferred property). That charitable benefit constitutes the gift and income tax deductible element in the transaction and is determined by subtracting the value of the annuity from the value of the property transferred to the charity.[30]

To the extent of the annuity itself, however, the transfer of property to the charity is a purchase and sale transaction with potential capital gain consequences to the transferor. These two elements — the charitable gift and the purchase — cause the transaction to be taxed as a part-sale, part-gift transaction that, in the charitable arena, is subject to the bargain sale to charity rules. Treas. Reg. §§1.170A-1(d); 1.170A-4(c)(2); 1.1011-2(a)(4); 1.1011-2(b). For income tax purposes, these rules may produce a gain on the sale portion measured by the difference between the value of the annuity

---

30. The value of the annuity is determined under Treas. Reg. §§25.2512-5 and 25.7520-2. See also Rev. Ruls. 72-438 and 84-162. The value of the deduction will be greater if the annuity is deferred so that payments begin at a later date, because the charity has the use of the transferor's money for a longer period before having to pay anything back.

received and the transferor's allocated basis in the sale portion.[31] The balance of the income tax consequences relate to the annuity payments themselves, which follow the §72 rules.[32]

A charitable gift annuity is a useful alternative that is easier to create and administer than a charitable remainder trust (discussed next). The documentation is simple, and the relative cost of the transaction should be lower. The annuity payments are fixed at inception, so there is no ongoing revaluation required. Installment reporting of gain as a portion of each annuity payment received may be preferable to selling an asset and reinvesting the proceeds for a higher income yield. And the annuity may increase cash flow to the annuitant, relative to the income flowing from the assets used to fund the annuity.

Inter Vivos Charitable Remainder Trusts

One of the primary reasons cited for creation of an inter vivos charitable remainder trust — other than to provide a benefit for the charity — is to provide an opportunity to liquidate investments without gain or loss, reinvest the proceeds (unreduced by income tax) and any income tax saved by generating the §170 deduction, and produce a subsequent cash flow that is sufficiently better than before the reinvestment to make up for the gift of the charitable remainder.

The fact that the trust is a qualified charitable remainder trust means that the capital gain realized on reinvestment is not taxable *at the trust level*. §664(c). It also will not be taxable to the transferor *if* creation of the trust, the transfer of property to it, and then the sale of trust corpus and reinvestment of the proceeds is not one integrated transaction *and* there is no binding obligation on the trust to make a sale that was prearranged by the transferor.[33] However, the gain *will* be taxable to the extent it is carried

---

31. §1011(b); Treas. Reg. §1.1011-2; Rev. Rul. 72-436. A number of steps are required in a gift annuity transaction involving the sale of appreciated property in exchange for the annuity. The first is simple pro ration of the donor's basis between the gift portion and the sale portion. Then, with respect to the sale portion only, that percentage of the donor's basis is subtracted from the discounted present value of the annuity (which is the amount realized) to determine gain on the transaction. Treas. Reg. §1.1011-2(c) Example (8). That gain then may be taxable in installments over the life of the annuity if the annuity is nonassignable and the donor (or the donor and any designated survivor annuitant(s)) are the only annuitants. Treas. Reg. §1.1011-2(a)(4). Gain not taxable because the annuity terminates on the transferor's premature death is not recognized. Treas. Reg. §1.1011-2(a)(4)(iii)(a). The theory is that the amount realized on the sale portion is reduced due to termination of the annuity before the life expectancy used in valuing the annuity.

32. The amount of the property transferred, reduced by the amount of the charitable deduction, is the amount deemed invested in the annuity and determines the portion of every payment over the expected life of the annuitant that is excluded (the exclusion portion) as a tax free recovery of basis in the annuity. Amounts received in excess of that basis recovery are fully taxable under §72(b)(2). Thus, if the annuitant lives longer than the life expectancy used to determine the recovery of basis, the full amount of any payments received after full recovery of that basis is taxable. The unrecovered balance is deductible on the annuitant's final income tax return, however, if the annuitant dies earlier than full recovery of the entire basis. See §72(b)(3). Within the exclusion portion may be some element that constitutes capital gain deferred and reportable in installments.

33. An express or implied obligation on the charity will prevent avoidance of the tax, however. See Ferguson v. Commissioner, 174 F.3d 997 (9th Cir. 1999); Jones v. United

out under the income tax tier rules and taxed in that fashion to the beneficiary as part of the lead interest. See §664(b) and Prop. Treas. Reg. §1.664-1(d).[34]

Because the tier rules look to income from prior years until it all has been exhausted or the lead interest terminates, these rules may serve only as a capital gain *deferral* device rather than as a capital gain *avoidance* opportunity. Thus, although it often is represented that the gain is eliminated altogether (because the trust is nontaxable), these characterizations of charitable remainder trust planning are exaggerated.

Moreover, even if taxation of any gain to the transferor is avoided, the transferor cannot be better off for the transaction unless the increase in cash flow, discounted to present value, exceeds the value of the charitable remainder, also discounted to present value. For that to be the case, in almost every situation the charitable deduction must produce a sizeable income tax savings that can be used to endow a portion of the new increased income flow, *and* one of three things also usually must be the case:

(1) The property contributed to the trust is so substantially appreciated that the transferor's own sale during life would produce a significant capital gain tax that would reduce the income generating capital by a huge amount;

(2) The transferor is so young that the increased cash flow will continue for a significant period of time; or

(3) The transferor could not afford to hold those appreciated assets until death to obtain a new basis equal to fair market value,

---

States, 531 F.2d 1343 (6th Cir. 1976); Kinsey v. Commissioner, 477 F.2d 1058 (2d Cir. 1973); Hudspeth v. United States, 471 F.2d 275 (8th Cir. 1972); and Palmer v. Commissioner, 62 T.C. 684 (1974), acq. A step transaction analysis may yield the same result. Blake v. Commissioner, 697 F.2d 473 (2d Cir. 1982). Also beware of prenegotiated sales to a third party, which similarly will fail to shift the gain to the trust. Cf. Martin v. Machiz, 251 F. Supp. 381 (D. Md. 1966). Teitell, *Charitable Giving Strategies: Windfalls and Pitfalls*, 27 U. MIAMI INST. EST. PLAN. ¶1100.7 (1993). The form of the transaction will be respected, however, if there is no evidence of any prior understanding, agreement, or obligation. See Grove v. Commissioner, 490 F.2d 241 (2d Cir. 1973); Carrington v. Commissioner, 476 F.2d 704 (5th Cir. 1973); Crosby v. United States, 73-1 U.S. Tax Cas. (CCH) ¶9399 (S.D. Miss. 1973); Wekesser v. Commissioner, 35 T.C.M. (CCH) 936 (1976).

34. In order of priority, annual distributions are deemed to constitute income to the beneficiary to the fullest possible extent under an oldest, most expensive "worst in, first out" regime that treats distributions as (1) ordinary income of the trust from the pool of undistributed prior years' net ordinary income and then from current year ordinary income, then (2) net short term capital gain (on a cumulative basis) from the pool of undistributed prior years' and then current year net short term capital gain, followed by (3) net long term capital gain (on a cumulative basis) from the pool of undistributed prior years' and then current year net long term capital gain, then (4) "other" income of the prior and current years and, finally, (5) a tax free distribution of corpus. See also Notice 99-17 and Notice 98-20 with respect to the three tier capital gain priority carryout rules.

presumably because the transferor could not live on the income flow from the current investments until death.[35]

These three circumstances are not so common as to make the exaggerated claims about this planning a true panacea for most clients.

In cases of charitable intent, greater all around benefits may be available under an alternative plan by which the transferor takes a portion of the available wealth to purchase a commercial annuity, and gives the balance outright to charity. And absent any freestanding charitable intent, it often will be economically preferable to simply incur the capital gains tax and reinvest the balance or hold the property until death (perhaps by borrowing against the equity if necessary to finance the transferor's lifestyle in the interim).

In each of these situations, the point is that you must perform a clear eyed present value analysis based on assumptions regarding income yield, life expectancy, and tax rates. An informed prediction is impossible without running the numbers and yielding a good deal of uncertainty. Nevertheless, it is a relatively safe prediction that none of these plans is likely to be economically attractive in the vast majority of cases, absent a legitimate charitable motivation on the client's part.[36]

Gifts of Insurance to Charity

An owner of insurance may transfer the policy to a charity or a charitable split interest trust in most jurisdictions[37] as an alternative to merely naming the charity as the beneficiary of a policy of life insurance. A gift of the policy may be preferable to naming the charity as beneficiary of the proceeds because, otherwise, income and gift tax deductions are available[38] only if the owner is not the insured and the policy matures while the owner is still alive (a gift occurs when the proceeds are payable to the charity as beneficiary instead of to the owner). Future gift and income tax deductions may be available for on-going premium payments if the charity or a charitable trust is the owner of the policy, although valuation

---

35. This factor may change with the potential loss of §1014 new basis at death if §1022 carryover basis becomes the law, which will occur if estate tax repeal in 2010 proves to be real and does not sunset in 2011. That is a real imponderable.

36. Also be aware that any effort to increase the lead private beneficial interest to better engineer the economics runs the risk of not qualifying as a §664(d) charitable remainder trust because the remainder interest is valued at less than 10% of the initial fair market value of the trust corpus. See §§664(d)(1)(D) and 664(d)(2)(D). It also could disqualify the gift tax charitable deduction under the Treas. Reg. §25.2522(c)-3(b) standard that the charitable remainder is "so remote as to be negligible," measured by a 5% probability of exhaustion test evaluated in terms of the remainder being at risk due to the inter vivos payout. Cf. Rev. Rul. 77-374; Rev. Rul. 70-452. The lower the applicable federal rate, the higher the probability of this occurring (because the trust is assumed to be earning a lower amount of income to finance the lead private beneficiary's interest). This problem is most likely to arise if the annuity percentage exceeds the applicable federal rate, particularly with a younger beneficiary.

37. The government will not recognize the gift of a policy unless local law provides that the charity has a valid insurable interest in the insured.

38. §170(f)(3).

difficulties and limitations on the deduction[39] may make it more palatable to make a direct contribution to the charity of cash that the charity then can use to pay the premium. Added cautions relate to the transfer of policies subject to outstanding policy loans, which will constitute a bargain sale to charity[40] and may trigger application of the undesirable transfer for value rules.[41]

Economics of Charitable Transfers

As this discussion suggests, it is nearly impossible in most cases to formulate a charitable giving plan that generates a net increase in a family's wealth. Notwithstanding claims made to the contrary by some individuals who market insurance and other plans that rely on a charitable component, charitable planning will not normally generate more economic value than if no charitable element was involved. Careful analysis of a proposal that suggests otherwise will *almost* without exception reveal that doing better by doing good is not realistic — particularly when aspects of the proposal that are not unique to charitable planning are divorced from the illustration. For example, anyone can make use of an irrevocable life insurance trust or annual exclusion gifts to reduce their taxable estate at death. Any charitable plan that makes use of either technique should be compared with a similar noncharitable plan that makes use of the same generic opportunities, to avoid comparing apples to giraffes.

Nevertheless, a charitable plan may entail little diminution in the wealth remaining for a client's family *and* in the process provide a significant benefit to an intended charity. In many cases, clients who have pre-existing charitable intentions may be pleased to engage in planning that does not affect their family's ultimate wealth by any significant amount while it satisfies their charitable inclinations. They can do well by doing good.

For example, when Jacqueline Kennedy Onassis died in 1994, the news media reported that her estate plan included a $100 million charitable lead trust with a 24 year term and a remainder that would pass to her grandchildren. Calculations (based on information and supposition) estimated a 96.8% charitable deduction, leaving a taxable estate of only 3.2% of the value of the fund. Projections of the wealth that would be available after the 24 year term ended and after all generation-skipping transfer tax was paid further estimated that $96 million would remain for Mrs. Onassis' ultimate beneficiaries.[42] An aggregate loss of just 4% of the

---

39. The deduction with respect to an insurance policy cannot exceed the transferor's basis in the policy. §170(e)(1)(A). See Treas. Reg. §25.2512-6(a) for rules relating to the valuation of insurance policies for gift tax purposes, with differing rules for policies as to which further premiums are due, for policies as to which no further premiums are due, and for policies on the life of an individual who has become uninsurable.

40. Treas. Reg. §1.1011-2(a)(3).

41. See §101(a)(2), which may not be a problem because the charity is tax exempt but may create ordinary income that will carry out to the lead interest beneficiaries under §664(b) if the trust is a split interest charitable trust.

42. Produced by the appropriately well regarded charitable planner Conrad Teitell. Using his rough numbers, the calculation was:

original fund might be regarded as a tiny price to pay for the charitable benefit bestowed by this plan.

But these results might be compared to the results that could have been obtained if the plan had not employed the charitable element at all. In that case the estate tax at Mrs. Onassis' death would have consumed roughly $55 million, leaving only $45 million, which makes the $96 million result generated look pretty attractive at first blush. But if that $45 million had been sequestered in an accumulation trust that made the grandchildren wait for the same 24 years, and that trust was able to generate an aggregate growth consisting of the same income and appreciation yield assumed over the same period, it would compound to approximately $443 million and incur a generation-skipping transfer tax at termination of roughly $243 million, netting $200 million for the remainder beneficiaries. That's a huge difference in result.

This illustration is not very accurate because it does not factor into the equation income tax on the income or capital gain generated in the noncharitable accumulation trust over the 24 year period, but we don't know how those taxes were reflected in the comparative calculations either. It would take a crystal ball to know for sure what capital gain rate to use and whether the income earned by the trust would be taxable or exempt.

Because the income and gain accumulated in the charitable lead trust would have been exempt during the deferral period, however, it would be appropriate to subtract a certain factor for income taxes, and even at a 40% assumed combined annual income tax rate (reducing the assumed accumulation rate to 6% annually instead of 10%), trust accumulations still would have yielded approximately $382 million after 24 years and, after a 55% generation-skipping transfer tax (the rate then in effect, which would have informed their projections), the net amount for the family still would have been $172 million. Somewhere between those two numbers is probably a good estimate of what the remainder beneficiaries would have received had charity not been involved but all other facts had been the same. Either way the numbers are estimated, the remainder beneficiaries would have been far better off had the charitable lead interest not been employed.

The difference, however, is that the estate plan generated $8 million per year for 24 years for charity, a total of $192 million before the benefits of compounding or any income and appreciation is calculated on that amount in the hands of the charity. Overall the plan generated at least a $192 million charitable benefit at a "cost" to the remainder beneficiaries of somewhere between $76 and $104 million (using very rough numbers). In

---

- $100 million charitable lead trust paying $8 million annually to charity for 24 years.
- $96.8 million charitable deduction based on a 6.4% applicable federal rate.
- $214 million value after 24 years, assuming an 8% income yield and 2% appreciation.
- $118 million generation-skipping tax on the taxable termination.
- $96 million remaining wealth for the grandchildren.

the final analysis the remainder beneficiaries would receive virtually the same amount that existed at Mrs. Onassis' death.

Depending on how all the involved parties view the situation, the charitable element in this plan "cost" the family between $4 million (the original $100 million less the remaining $96 million to the beneficiaries when all is said and done) and $104 million ($200 million that the remainder beneficiaries might have received, less the $96 million they will receive), or it produced a net benefit of between $88 million ($192 million to charity less a cost to the family of $104 million) and $188 million ($192 million to charity less a family loss of just $4 million).

Although this illustration draws on a well known testamentary plan rather than inter vivos charitable giving, the caution it produces is the same. A charitable giving component to any plan may yield a huge benefit or a substantial cost, depending on how a family defines its views. Historically, inter vivos planning almost always generated a better result than testamentary planning, regardless of how the final consequences were defined. That may continue to be true even if the estate and generation-skipping transfer taxes are repealed but the gift tax remains, as legislated in 2001.

Comparisons of Alternate Charitable Plans

It is nearly impossible to fairly and accurately compare alternative wealth distribution plans without making assumptions or begging certain unanswerable questions. In a vacuum it is even more difficult to develop hard and fast rules about which plans are preferable to others. Indeed, it is reasonably difficult just to marshal all the factors that might be relevant in any comparison. But among all the elements that might be implicated, a couple of lists can be generated that you might consider when creating your own spreadsheet analyses. One of these lists the various commonplace alternative types of planning that a client might consider. The other gives the various costs and benefits that may visit the client or the client's family in the process.

On that first list of alternative types of planning, the questions that you might ask include: whether to do anything during life or wait until death; whether to make a transfer outright or through a split interest trust (and which type of split interest trust — lead or remainder, annuity or unitrust — is preferable); and whether to sell assets and reinvest the proceeds to produce a better return, purchase a charitable annuity, or transfer the assets in kind and allow the recipient to make any investment conversions.

On the second list of costs and benefits the questions that may be relevant include:

1. Will any wealth transfer tax be incurred inter vivos?
2. Will generating the liquidity to pay that wealth transfer tax cause any capital gain tax?
3. How much will investment returns be diminished by these wealth transfer and capital gain tax costs?

4. Will an income tax charitable deduction be generated and, if so, subject to what limitations?
5. How much will after tax investment returns be improved by any tax savings attributable to an income tax charitable deduction?
6. Will there be an improvement in investment performance generated by the underlying property or its reinvestment?
7. Who will enjoy the investment return — both income and appreciation — generated by the underlying property after any inter vivos planning but before the client's death, and with what income and wealth transfer tax costs?
8. Will capital gain before or after any inter vivos planning be eliminated by a new basis at the client's death?

There may be other factors to consider as well, and some assumptions almost certainly will be required regarding income yield, life expectancy, and tax rates before concrete estimates can be modeled, based on these factors.

Disclaimers

A less obvious form of inter vivos rearrangement of property as to which no wealth transfer tax is incurred is a qualified disclaimer (or, as it may be known for state law purposes, a renunciation). If the technical requirements of §2518 are met, the effect for purposes of the entire wealth transfer tax Subtitle (which includes the estate tax, gift tax, generation-skipping transfer tax, and the special valuation rules of Chapter 14) is "as if the interest had never been transferred" to the disclaimant.

Fortunately, numerous opportunities may be capitalized upon by making a qualified disclaimer. Unfortunately, there are almost as many ways to fail to successfully accomplish a qualified disclaimer. So, although disclaimer opportunities should not be overlooked or squandered, affirmative advance planning seldom should depend on disclaimers. It may work out, and options often present themselves, but this should not be more than reactive planning.

The lack of reliability of disclaimer planning is a function of a number of factors. The most common is sometimes labeled greed but probably is more accurately described as fear. People who renounce property must feel comfortable with the notion that there will be enough other wealth to support them for the balance of their lives. This need not be a problem when the disclaimant is a surviving spouse of a transferor whose plan anticipated disclaimer and directs that the disclaimed property falls into a nonmarital trust that provides a continuing benefit to the surviving spouse as authorized under §2518(b)(4)(A).[43] But for anyone else the cost of a

---

43. Indeed, as authorized by Treas. Reg. §25.2518-2(e)(5) Example (7), some planners might include a $5,000 or 5% withdrawal power in the nonmarital trust just to make it more palatable and less frightful for the surviving spouse to disclaim from a marital bequest — outright or in trust.

qualified disclaimer is loss of any enjoyment of the disclaimed interest. See §§2518(b)(3) and (b)(4)(B).

A second and related factor is that a qualified disclaimer cannot be made after acceptance of the interest or any of its benefits, meaning that inadvertent or unintentional enjoyment can disqualify an otherwise intentional disclaimer. A third factor is timing. It already is too late in many cases in which disclaimers would be a wise and tax free method of inter vivos property transfer. See §2518(b)(2). For example, the potential disclaimant may be incompetent to renounce enjoyment or may already be deceased, or the nine month limitation on making a qualified disclaimer may have elapsed before the plan can be recommended and implemented.

Without delving into the technical requirements for a qualified disclaimer, it pays to simply consider the types of circumstances in which renunciation might be effective wealth transfer tax planning. The most common is the least strategic. The disclaimant simply has more wealth than necessary and would prefer that the alternate taker of a disposition receive the property instead. For example, if Parent died leaving property to Child, who has done very well (through employment, marriage, winning the lottery, or whatever) and would prefer that Grandchild receive the wealth instead, Child's qualified disclaimer could effect a transfer to Grandchild in lieu of Child accepting the property and then making a taxable gift (of Child's own wealth or of Parent's wealth that Child moved along but not in a qualified manner). Alternatively, Child may be terminally ill and, although not possessing a great deal of wealth, also aware that not much additional wealth will be required for the short balance of Child's life.

In either case the disclaimer by Child could trigger a generation-skipping transfer tax as a direct skip, and that might be a second good reason to consider a disclaimer. If Parent had not planned for the use of Parent's generation-skipping transfer exemption, Child might disclaim to take advantage of that benefit by causing a direct skip to Grandchild (which will utilize Parent's exemption and avoid generation-skipping transfer tax at the same time the disclaimer avoids any gift tax that would apply if Child received the property and waited too long to give it away, or estate tax if Child received the property and held it until death). For generation-skipping transfer tax planning of a more strategic variety, Child also might make a disclaimer that causes the wealth to pass into a trust that could be made generation-skipping transfer tax exempt and held for multiple generations, making even better use of that exemption. This opportunity would be available, however, only if Parent's own plan both established the trust and provided that property not passing to Child would pass into that trust.

Other forms of generation-skipping transfer tax planning also are available through the use of disclaimers. For example, property left in trust for a surviving spouse might be made to absorb the transferor's generation-skipping transfer exemption that otherwise would be wasted. If the mechanism used by the transferor was an outright disposition to the surviving spouse, or a trust with a general power of appointment, disclaimer of the bequest or of the power to appoint could result in a secondary disposition in a trust. If the surviving spouse had the right to all trust income annually and the trust otherwise was eligible for the §2056(b)(7) qualified terminable interest property election, the concomitant opportunity would exist to make the §2652(a)(3) reverse qualified terminable interest property election to use the decedent's generation-skipping exemption.

Generation-skipping transfer tax planning with disclaimers actually gets pretty far afield from traditional disclaimer planning that is employed for transfer tax minimization purposes, the more likely of which being planning in the context of the marital deduction. One likely use of disclaimers — indeed probably the most common single use — is to adjust the size of the deduction or to qualify a trust for the marital deduction by eliminating interests that otherwise would preclude marital deduction entitlement (such as a discretionary income or principal entitlement in someone other than the surviving spouse, or a prohibited nongeneral inter vivos power in the spouse to appoint from a qualified terminable interest property trust).

In some cases it may be wise for the surviving spouse to selectively disclaim certain high growth assets and thus shelter their future appreciation from inclusion in the estate of the surviving spouse. An even more viable alternative may be available if the spouse obtains those assets through exercise of an inter vivos power of appointment or by distributions by the trustee and then makes a gift of them instead, intentionally incurring gift tax in the spouse's brackets rather than additional estate tax in the decedent's brackets. Along these lines, a counterintuitive but similarly preferable alternative would be an intentionally *non*qualified disclaimer by the surviving spouse, generating gift tax the same as if the spouse had a more affirmative control over disposition of the property.

To illustrate several of these consequences, consider first that in some cases too little property passes to the surviving spouse to make optimum use of the marital deduction, with nonspousal takers disclaiming to cause more property to pass to the surviving spouse. This is "expensive" postmortem planning for those disclaimants because they must relinquish all interests in the property during the surviving spouse's overlife.

Alternatively, it is more likely that too much property passes to the surviving spouse or otherwise qualifies for the marital deduction, leaving some of the transferor's unified credit unconsumed. This failure to optimize a bequest may spawn a disclaimer by the surviving spouse that will subject more property to tax in the transferor's estate and shelter the transferor's unified credit, precluding taxation of that property when the spouse ultimately disposes of it. This form of postmortem planning is not nearly so difficult with the adoption of §2518(b)(4)(A), allowing the surviving spouse to remain a beneficiary of disclaimed property in a nonmarital trust. Nevertheless, because of the problems associated with making a qualified disclaimer in general,[44] even this form of postmortem engineering probably is not wise as affirmative planning (as opposed to a rear guard defense or safety net technique).

Better yet, the surviving spouse could delay making a disclaimer just long enough to avoid qualification under the nine month rule. This might be wise planning if the decedent's unified credit has been fully sheltered. If the surviving spouse can afford to incur gift taxes (and otherwise is likely to incur estate tax at death), the benefit is by reducing the spouse's estate through payment of gift tax, with transfers at the cheaper tax exclusive gift tax rates. The marital deduction will be allowed in the decedent's estate, and gift tax will be incurred by the surviving spouse, which often produces the most favorable tax results over both estates (again, assuming the spouse is likely to die when the estate tax is applicable).

A third form of transfer tax planning that is similar to qualification for the marital deduction is to generate a charitable deduction. By way of example, if the transferor created a split interest entitlement that does not satisfy the special requirements of §664, the noncharitable beneficiary might disclaim all rights, title, and interest in the disposition to allow the charitable portion to qualify for the deduction. In other cases a partial disclaimer may make it possible for the balance of the trust to qualify for reformation under §2055(e)(3) or simply to cause more property to pass to a qualified charity. And in some instances the plan may anticipate that property a private beneficiary does not care to receive should pass to charity in the alternative and generate a deduction for the original transferor as opposed to the transferee accepting the asset and making a deductible transfer.

Further tax planning may entail income tax minimization through the redirection of property transfers that carry income tax liability.[45] One simple example is the income in respect of a decedent aspects of qualified retirement plan distributions that may be less onerous in the hands of some lower income beneficiaries or deferrable in the hands of the participant's surviving spouse (by qualifying for a rollover to the spouse's own individual retirement account). Another example might be to prevent the return of property subject to §1014(e),[46] transferred to a decedent and bequeathed back to the original donor within the prohibited one year of the transfer, all with an eye to obtaining a new basis at the death of the transferee decedent. And disclaimers might be employed to fractionalize the

---

44. The list of problem areas potentially includes acceptance of benefits, the need to renounce certain powers in a nonmarital trust to which disclaimed property passes, timing issues, and the possibility that the surviving spouse may die before a disclaimer is made and state law may not permit postmortem disclaimer on behalf of the spouse.

45. The income tax aspects of qualified disclaimer planning are unclear because §2518 speaks only of the Subtitle in which the wealth transfer taxes appear. Proposals occasionally are made to amend the Code to extend to the income tax the same consequences of §2518 qualified disclaimer planning for wealth transfer tax purposes.

46. Or the §1022(d)(1)(C) carryover basis three year counterpart that is slated to be effective after 2009.

ownership of property to generate discounts that otherwise would not be available.

Two final aspects of disclaimer planning are considered on occasion, both raising more concern about legitimacy and efficacy. One is to preclude attachment of federal tax liens and the other is to defeat the disclaimant's creditors. For those in need of care, disclaimers generally are regarded as disqualifying dispositions for Medicaid planning purposes, so the opportunity to produce an affirmative benefit in that regard may be precluded, although a disclaimer of property that drops into a special needs trust may be viable planning.

Although defeating a federal tax lien is not likely to work,[47] dodging or delaying creditor claims in the private sector may be facilitated by some disclaimers. State law goes both ways on the issue, although the Supreme Court has stated that one "important consequence of treating a disclaimer as an *ab initio* defeasance is that the disclaimant's creditors are barred from reaching the disclaimed property."[48] Fortunately, regardless of the proper state law result on this issue, the tax law provides that a disclaimer still qualifies for wealth transfer tax purposes unless it is totally invalid or it is voided by creditors; being voidable is not an impediment to its wealth transfer tax efficacy otherwise. Treas. Reg. §25.2518-1(c)(2).

Incomplete Gifts

There is a final manner in which inter vivos transfers can avoid gift taxation, although almost without exception it is a deferral and not a true avoidance of tax. Because deferral of taxation typically is not advantageous from an economic perspective, this final mechanism is not normally recommended except under unusual circumstances. For example, financing the payment of gift tax may be problematic until liquidity needs have been resolved.

Deferral by making a gift incomplete and therefore not yet ripe for imposition of gift tax may be desirable if the value of the property involved is likely to decline in the future, making it more appropriate to subject the lower value to tax in the future than the current higher value to immediate taxation. Making a gift of property expected to go down in value is unusual, so perhaps less unusual would be a transfer — such as an engagement ring or property subject to a premarital agreement — that is regarded by state law or the terms of transfer as conditional. Because the gift is contingent upon future events (in these cases, marriage) and therefore not final until a later time, more attractive results may be available (for example, the gift tax marital deduction that flows from completion of the gift upon marriage).

---

47. See Drye v. United States, 528 U.S. 49 (1999), aff'g sub nom. Drye Family 1995 Trust v. United States, 152 F.3d 892 (8th Cir. 1998) (state law is of no consequence to the question whether the federal lien attaches when the decedent dies and cannot be defeated by a subsequent disclaimer, even if timely and effective for state and federal wealth transfer tax purposes).

48. See United States v. Irvine, 511 U.S. 224, 239-240 (1994).

A third situation might beg for deferral if there is an expectation of a higher basis being generated without adverse tax consequence — for example, if a principal personal residence might, upon an expected sale, generate less than the maximum capital gain that is excludible under §121, followed by a gift of the proceeds with no built in capital gain tax liability. Finally, with the promise of estate tax repeal in 2010, there are cases in which the subject of a transfer may not trigger estate tax at death and therefore ought to be insulated from imposition of gift tax inter vivos. This may seem *very* likely for younger clients, but it likely is a chimera unless you believe that Congress is done tinkering with the wealth transfer tax (and that the client will die during the one year the estate tax is repealed).

No matter what your unique facts or client hopes and expectations, it is important to underscore a notion that is counterintuitive but well known and accepted by initiates of the intersecting worlds of wealth transfer and income taxation. There is no pari materia among the estate, gift, and income tax rules that may apply. Which is to say that an inter vivos transfer may be regarded as complete and taxable for gift tax purposes and yet trigger estate tax inclusion at death. Much less likely is that it may be incomplete inter vivos and also avoid estate tax inclusion at death. And regardless of whether complete or incomplete for wealth transfer tax purposes, it may be regarded as effective to preclude taxation of future income to the transferor or it may be such that all future income will be imputed and taxed to the transferor.

Reality almost always is consistent with the logic that an inter vivos transfer will not avoid both gift and estate taxation. Still, there is no other seemingly logical and predictable interplay among these taxes. Transfers that incur gift tax because complete can easily be includible at death and (at least prior to the 2010 effective date of §2511(c)) the income from transferred property either can or will not be taxable to the transferor, without regard to the wealth transfer tax consequences. So it is imperative to analyze each element in the taxation of inter vivos transfers separately, without relying on the consequence known under another arm of the tax law and extrapolating to a predictable result. It usually is not that easy.

A transfer may be incomplete for gift tax purposes for a variety of reasons, most relating to retained powers over transferred property that are exercisable without the consent of an adverse party. See Treas. Reg. §§25.2511-2(b) through 25.2511-2(e) for illustrations of powers retained by a transferor that will cause a transfer to be incomplete. For example, a gift is not complete to the extent the transferor has a power to affect the beneficial interests under the trust, even if the power is exercisable only in conjunction with a trustee or other nonadverse party. Treas. Reg. §25.2511-2(e).

It also may be attributable to retained enjoyment of some but less than all of the transferred property. This may result in a transfer that is either entirely incomplete, or complete in part (such as a gift of the remainder following a retained life estate) and incomplete in part (such as the income interest that is shared by the transferor and other named beneficiaries, all entitled to receive income in the trustee's discretion). Usually retained powers are intentional and obvious—such as a transfer into a trust as to which the transferor has retained a power of revocation or appointment. Sometimes retained powers are less obvious — as with a gift causa mortis, which is incomplete for gift tax purposes because it automatically is revoked if the transferor survives the apprehended peril. As a middle ground, there may be transfers in which powers are implied — as, for example, if the transferor allegedly did not intend to make a legitimate transfer but only engaged in the transaction to deceive creditors or a spouse in a divorce action, or had an oral understanding that differed from the terms of the transfer. Other reasons may relate to a failure to comply with state law requirements for making an effective transfer of property or, often more important, questions of the timing of an effective gift.

A transferor also must be certain to perform an effective act of inter vivos transfer. The intent to make a transfer is not enough if it is not supported by timely inter vivos action. Usually a transferor's retention of interests in transferred property causes an inter vivos transfer to be incomplete for gift tax purposes.

Finally, some gifts made by individuals inter vivos are incomplete because the transferor was unaware that a gift was made. Those unanticipated gifts often occur by indirection but need not concern our affirmative planning education.

Taxation of Completed Gifts

Notwithstanding the facial attraction of nontaxable inter vivos transfers, the discussion beginning at page 2 regarding the economics of prepaying wealth transfer tax reveals that incurring gift tax on a completed, taxable, inter vivos transfer is preferable to holding wealth and incurring an estate tax instead. That truism applies only in the current environment in which both taxes exist, but it will not persuade even the few clients otherwise willing to incur tax inter vivos if they believe the estate tax really will be repealed in 2010 (and not be restored in 2011) as Congress legislated in 2001. A client who expects to die when there is no estate tax is not likely to embrace any of it.

But when a gift tax *is* incurred, just a few remaining helpful opportunities or observations are worthy of study. These are valuation concepts that may affect the gift taxation of inter vivos transfers in ways that are taxpayer favorable, albeit in some cases they are not distinct from the valuation that would apply for estate tax purposes. In that respect, then, this discussion does not necessarily inform inter vivos transfers instead of testamentary dispositions so much as it encourages inter vivos planning to benefit from valuation opportunities in general.

Blockage Discounts

A taxpayer may own and transfer such a large quantity of a particular asset that the market for that asset would be depressed by an immediate sale of the entire holding. This depressive effect in the willing-buyer, willing-seller valuation context leads to a "blockage" discount and is well illustrated by Calder v. Commissioner, 85 T.C. 713 (1985), a gift tax case involving artwork that previously was included in the estate of the donor's deceased husband, artist Alexander Calder. The donor made transfers of over 1,000 gouaches (opaque watercolor paintings) to four separate trusts. The donor used the value of the gouaches established for federal estate tax purposes in the decedent's estate in valuing the transfer for gift tax purposes, reflecting a 60% discount for blockage because the art market could not readily absorb a sale of the number of watercolors involved.[49]

The government, wishing to increase the gift tax value of these transfers, argued that the total number of gouaches transferred to the four trusts could not be aggregated for purposes of determining blockage, notwithstanding the fact that the total transfers collectively would depress the market if all the gouaches were sold at one time. The Tax Court agreed with this proposition, citing the government's position in Treas. Reg. §25.2512-2(e) that the value of each gift must be determined separately. However, the government attempted to ascertain the value of each gouache, and thereby the value of each of the gifts, using a figure that it estimated as the total number of sales that the market could absorb in a given year, without prorating that total sales figure across the separate gifts made. The Tax Court took exception to this, holding that the market could absorb only a certain number in a given year, whether from a single trust or from several, and that it was improper to value each of the gifts as if *each* trust could sell the *total* number received in a given year.

Similarly to *Calder*, the sole issue in Estate of O'Keeffe v. Commissioner, 63 T.C.M. (CCH) 2699 (1992), was the appropriate blockage discount for the approximately 400 works of art created and owned by the decedent at death (rather than for gift tax purposes, but the same principles inform both determinations).

Blockage discounts can be applied to other types of assets (most commonly collectibles, precious stones or metals, some types of real estate, or other assets for which there is a relatively thin market) but on occasion, they also can be relevant with respect to even a small percentage of the stock of a publicly traded corporation, if the evidence supports the notion that sale of that holding all at once would depress the market value.

---

49. Dribble-out sales of the remaining works left by a deceased artist is the preferred method to preserve the market value of the artist's entire portfolio, which all may increase in value upon the artist's death because (we should hope) there will be no more works created by that artist.

Fractional Interests

A simple and relatively noncontroversial method to reduce values for wealth transfer tax purposes is to create a fractional interest in property that is not easily severed. For example, splitting a 1000 share holding of IBM stock is easy and no fractional interest discount would be generated by a gift of 50% of that interest. But undivided tenancy in common ownership of Blackacre usually is far different. As a consequence, with select assets the amount a willing buyer would pay a willing seller for an undivided fractional interest is less (in many cases substantially less) than a pro rata portion of the fair market value of an undivided property interest. Thus, especially in anticipation of estate tax liability at death, a transfer inter vivos that bifurcates ownership title in certain assets can be a particularly effective gifting technique.

As an excellent illustration, consider Mooneyham v. Commissioner, 61 T.C.M. (CCH) 2445 (1991). The court granted a 15% fractional interest discount in establishing the proper gift tax valuation of a half interest in the taxpayer's ownership of development realty that was transferred to the taxpayer's sibling (and, presumably, a similar discount would apply for the retained half if still owned when the taxpayer died). The court sharply rejected the government's argument that a discount should depend on the relationship of the donor and donee, adopting instead a hypothetical unrelated willing-buyer, willing-seller approach.

Citing the gift tax valuation decision in *Mooneyham*, the Tax Court in Estate of Pillsbury v. Commissioner, 64 T.C.M. (CCH) 284 (1992), similarly concluded that a hypothetical willing-buyer, willing-seller analysis should apply to value fractional interests in real estate. The government resisted that discount because 100% of the value of the property was owned by two trusts with the same trustee and the taxable portion (flowing out of a marital deduction trust at the death of a surviving spouse) passed to a nonmarital trust that owned the other portion of the property, meaning that the property could be sold as an undivided entirety. The court specifically stated that ownership of the remainder interest and the ultimate disposition of the fractional interest was irrelevant, instead noting that the government's unity of ownership notion is inconsistent with a willing-buyer analysis of the amount that would be paid to purchase only the taxable portion of the property.

Subsequently, and presumably reflecting its losses in *Mooneyham* and *Pillsbury*, the government issued Technical Advice Memorandum 9336002, in which it took a new position that did not challenge the discount itself. Instead, the new position was that the discount should be *limited*, to "the petitioner's share of the estimated cost of a partition of the property," based on the theory that partition would be the most efficient means to generate the most economic benefit from property owned by multiple parties. But in Estate of Cervin v. Commissioner, 68 T.C.M. (CCH) 1115 (1994), the property involved was such that partition would destroy its value because of issues relating to access, presence of a creek dividing the property, the number of acres needed to run a profitable agricultural operation, soil conditions in various locations, and the like. In this setting, the Tax Court rejected the very similar position advocated by the government that the estate's fractional interest discount should be limited to 5% *plus* half the cost to partition the property. Instead, the court granted a 20% discount to an undivided 50% fractional interest that was includible in the decedent's gross estate, even though it passed to the owner of the other 50% interest.

Several cautions in this arena may be relevant. One is illustrated by Estate of Casey v. Commissioner, 71 T.C.M. (CCH) 2599 (1996), which denied a fractional interest adjustment to a beneficial interest in a liquidating trust. The fractional interest discount likely will not be available if the ownership interest (in this case the trust corpus) is not a fractional interest, nor is it likely to be applied to a beneficial interest (such as the interest of one of several trust beneficiaries). A second caution is highlighted by Technical Advice Memorandum 9146002, in which a taxpayer purported to sell a 5% fractional interest in a personal residence (at 66% of the pro rata fair market value of that interest) and then leased it back, reporting on the taxpayer's estate tax return the 95% interest remaining with a 43% discount that the government rejected on the grounds that the sale and leaseback was not legitimate.

Finally, Estate of Young v. Commissioner, 110 T.C. 297 (1998), followed by Estate of Fratini v. Commissioner, 76 T.C.M. (CCH) 342 (1998), concluded that, once death occurs (at least in the two person joint tenancy situation), the co-ownership aspect of joint tenancy disappears and, with it, any impediments to sale that might justify a discount for fractional interests. So the ticket is to convert survivorship concurrent ownership into tenancy in common (notwithstanding loss of probate avoidance or some forms of creditor protection).

Nonmarketability and Minority Interest Discounts

Valuation may differ for gift tax purposes than for estate tax purposes, almost without exception favoring inter vivos transfers that involve minority interests. This is best described by the fact that each gift made inter vivos is valued separately, not as the diminution in the donor's net worth nor as the increase in the donee's net worth either, but essentially as the gifted interest travels between the donor and the donee. For example, recall the illustration at page 10 of the world's largest diamond, being gifted in undivided fractional interests inter vivos. If that diamond were held until death and given in equal shares to the same donees, the value for estate tax purposes would be the undivided diamond owned at death, regardless of the destination of the shares and the number of beneficiaries. But if that diamond were transferred to multiple donees inter vivos (including by deeds of gift of undivided fractional interests as tenants in common), then the value of the gift would be the aggregate value of each separate niblet gift. And the product of that valuation would be lower than the value of the undivided whole.

These valuation issues can be of great significance. Assume, for example, that the taxpayer owned 51% of the stock in a closely held corporation and that two children owned equal amounts of the remaining stock. If the taxpayer gave 1% of the stock to each of those children, the issue would be whether the collective value of those gifts is (1) two times a prorated 1% of the total value of the corporation, (2) a discount from that amount because each child receives a minority interest, (3) an amount equal to $2/51$ of the value of the taxpayer's 51% controlling interest, or (4) an even greater premium amount because, by virtue of the gifts, the taxpayer relinquishes the control element represented by the 51% interest. It appears that the government recognizes that (2) is correct, notwithstanding that a gift tax that truly served to backstop the estate tax would impose a tax on the diminution in net worth represented in (4). The inter vivos transfer in this type of situation is vastly preferable due to the difference between the estate and gift tax valuation involved and therefore the tax they would generate.

Also consider the simplicity of a 100% owner of a family corporation merely making an inter vivos gift of 49% to the owner's spouse, qualifying for a gift tax marital deduction in the same discounted value as the gifted stock, followed by a deeply discounted sliver interest gift of just over 1% to a child or other object, leaving under 50% for inclusion as a minority interest at death. The available discounts generated in this manner can only be garnered through effective inter vivos planning.

Statute of Limitation for Revaluation

A final notation to consider is the reality that questionable valuation cases may be addressed better inter vivos with a gift tax liability versus estate tax exposure. By virtue of §§2001(f) and §2504(c), a gift that is disclosed in a gift tax return that is "adequate to apprise the Secretary of the nature" of the gift[50] is protected under §6501(c)(9), which provides that the

---

50. Treas. Reg. §301.6501(c)-1(f)(2) describes adequate disclosure "to apprise the Service of the nature of the gift and the basis for the value reported" by requiring a description of the relationship of the parties, and a "detailed" description of the method used to determine the fair market value, including any relevant financial data and any discounts claimed. In addition, disclosure must articulate any restrictions on the transferred property considered in the valuation and a "statement describing any position taken that is contrary to any proposed, temporary or final Treasury regulation or revenue rulings published at the time of the transfer."

When considering disclosure it probably pays to ponder whether information ultimately will be produced in litigation (should things come to that), meaning that it may be wise to produce any relevant documents now, in hopes of garnering statute of limitation protection. Congress altered the §7491 burden of proof rules in 1997, which effectively only shifted the burden of persuasion. The government must produce some reasonable determination upon which an asserted deficiency relies, which the taxpayer must rebut with evidence that is credible enough that a reasonable person *could* believe it (*not* the more rigorous "more likely true than not" standard), which then shifts the burden to produce evidence back to the government for rebuttal. The burden of persuasion is on the government, however, in the sense that a 50-50 equipoise of evidence results in a taxpayer victory. Thus, the taxpayer still carries the burden of production — most notably of documents and proof of valuation. But once the taxpayer has met its obligation to produce credible evidence to support its position, the government then must counter with evidence of its own or risk losing the case under the burden of persuasion. Reflecting the

value of the gift for both gift and estate tax calculation purposes is the value as finally determined[51] for gift tax purposes. Thus, the government is bound by the value of the asset and cannot revalue it for either tax calculation purpose if the time within which to assess gift tax expires under the §6501(c)(9) gift tax statute of limitation.

Notable is that this closure is applicable more than just with respect to valuation questions. The statute of limitation precludes investigation and litigation if the adequate disclosure standard is met, even if an issue involves qualification for the marital deduction, charitable deduction, or annual exclusion. Disclosure designed to trigger the running of the statute of limitation may be desirable to prevent later challenges that question whether a marital or charitable bequest was funded in the proper amount and that question turns on the value of assets allocated. Or if the question is whether creation of a family limited partnership was a gift because the value of interests transferred into the partnership was greater than the partnership interests received. Or whether the taxpayer made gifts of difficult to value assets that were worth more than the annual exclusion. You can think of other cases in which disclosure would be worthwhile to start the statute of limitation to ultimately garner closure.

The §6501(c)(9) statute of limitation *never* prevents a gift tax assessment based on a revaluation if the taxpayer failed to properly disclose the gift, although an amended return may be filed to begin the adequate disclosure statute of limitation running.[52] The resulting lack of §2504(c) or

---

modesty of this change is Tax Court Interim Rule 142, which describes the shift in the burden of going forward with proof once the taxpayer has provided credible evidence to support the taxpayer's position. However, with respect to §7477 Tax Court declaratory judgments regarding valuation, the position stated in Interim Rule 217 is that the taxpayer continues to bear the burden of production and of persuasion. It is well to remember than none of these changes is relevant unless the taxpayer has met the significant administrative proceeding requirement of producing all information reasonably requested by the government in discovery, the case has gone to court, and the taxpayer falls under a $7 million net worth threshold. Clarified by technical correction in 1998 was that this net worth threshold does not apply to estates *or* to revocable inter vivos trusts that make the §645 election (but only during the period of that election).

51. Changes made in 1998 further specified in §2001(f)(2) (and added a cross reference in §2504(c) to that specification) that "final determination" of value means any of (1) the taxpayer's uncontested value as stated on the return, (2) a court's determination if the value is litigated, (3) a negotiated value if the Secretary of the Treasury contests the value and the taxpayer settles with the government, or (4) the Secretary's determination of value, but only if the value is not reported on a return and the taxpayer does not timely contest the Secretary's determination.

52. See Rev. Proc. 2000-34, which addressed the situation in which a gift tax return was filed but did not satisfy the adequate disclosure requirements (either because the gift was not reported on that return or the information provided was not adequate). This pronouncement reasonably provides that an amendment may be filed to the original return and, if prominently labeled on the top of the first page to put the government on notice, the adequate disclosure protection will begin to run with the amended return as if the statute of limitation for the gift began to run with the amendment. *Not* covered by this Procedure is the situation in which *no* return was timely filed, the rationale being that no permission or special rules are required to file a late return that will start the statute with adequate disclosure at that time. Also excluded from the amended return Procedure is any gift tax return that was false or a willful evasion, for which no subsequent protection may be had through the filing of an amendment.

§2001(f) protection for gifts not properly reported (or for transfers made under prior law) permits the government to redetermine the value or taxability of a prior gift, the proper gift tax thereon, the amount of unified credit exhausted thereby, and the effect on the determination of the donor's subsequent gift and estate taxes, all at any time in the future, regardless of how old and cold the facts and basis for determination of these questions may have become in the interim.

On the other hand, proper disclosure and statute of limitation protection can preclude a multitude of government challenges at death, which is when the government has been most vigilant in the past. One important consequence of all this, however, is that taxpayers must be careful to maintain adequate records upon which they may rely in future challenges, especially for future gift tax purposes with respect to gifts they otherwise would not think they needed to disclose, due to the annual exclusion, the marital or charitable deductions, or the unified credit.

Income Shifting

There can be some merit in income shifting techniques employed inter vivos that are in addition to incurring gift tax rather than a more expensive estate tax, prepaying tax, generating valuation opportunities, and taking advantage of tax free inter vivos transfers. Income shifting to reduce income tax is not of major significance in a system with compressed income tax rates. But income shifting has an added bonus of avoiding wealth transfer tax on income that otherwise would inflate the donor's net worth and be subject to estate tax at death. So it may be worthwhile to consider inter vivos transfer opportunities that shift future income, beginning with the most expedient mechanism: an outright gift of income producing property.

All sorts of income tax factors must be considered in making this evaluation, and they likely are best computed by using the "what if" feature of most income tax return preparation software. Otherwise "hidden" factors are too difficult to consider, including the impact of more or less income on alternative minimum tax calculations, the phase out loss of deductions under §§67 and 68, the impact on personal exemptions and standard deductions, and a variety of other disguised tax hickeys. So this discussion is for illustration purposes, but more individualized modeling usually is required before concluding that any particular plan is appropriate.

An additional concern in this arena lurks in the so-called Kiddie Tax of §1(g). This regime is imposed on the "net unearned income" of a child who has at least one living parent and is under the age of 14 years at the end of the child's tax year. The child is required to pay income tax as if (broadly speaking) any unearned income of the child belonged to the child's parents. The Kiddie Tax is applicable to *all* unearned income that is includible in the child's income for a current tax year, regardless of source and regardless of when earned. Tax exempt income is not subject to the Kiddie Tax because it is not includible in gross income in the first instance, and income that is generated currently but that is properly deferred until a tax year that ends when the child is over the age of 13 also will escape the Kiddie Tax.

Planning suggestions for avoiding the Kiddie Tax include: using Series EE, deep discount, or zero coupon bonds that in each case can be structured to produce their income in any tax year that would end after the child became 14; investing in low income growth stock that can be held for sale at a gain after the child reaches that age; use of a §2503(c) qualified minor's trust that can accumulate income until after the child has attained that age; and employment of the child (for example, in a family business) so that the child's wages will be earned income that is not subject to the Kiddie Tax.

Evaluating Alternative Income Shifting Devices

With these overriding concerns in mind, successful income shifting challenges you to find devices that generate sufficient savings under the current rate regime to make the transactional and other costs worthwhile. Determining the value of income shifting is as difficult as planning how to do it, because it involves so many variables, including whether:

- the transaction costs, compliance costs, administration costs, and wealth transfer tax costs of the device used will consume any income shifting advantages;
- the maximum income tax savings at the current time justify the device, in terms of any lock-in effect through a period of change that may diminish or destroy the benefits sought; and
- ancillary benefits may be generated by the device used, such as to preclude wealth transfer taxation of any appreciation in the property.

The following discussion is not an exhaustive summary of all possible methods for shifting income. Instead, listed are only methods that come within the reasonable reach of clients with average amounts of wealth, requiring no large investment, and no particularly complex or convoluted transactions. Several have the redeeming grace of ancillary benefits in the form of wealth transfers that make the modest income shifting seem more attractive.

Employment

One easy technique is to employ dependents in hopes of shifting enough earned income to ease the financing of a child's education or the support of an active but needy parent. This is such a traditionally viable income shifting alternative that §73 specifically protects a child's personal services earned income from taxation at a parent's rates and the Kiddie Tax does not apply. Nevertheless, there are elusive limits to what may be paid as reasonable (deductible) compensation, and any social security tax payments under §3111 would increase the cost of such a program.

Leasebacks

Classic leaseback transactions have ongoing vitality. Often a trust holds property subject to a lease back to the taxpayer who originally owned it, such as a doctor or dentist who transfers a building and the equipment in it to such a trust. The watershed leaseback transaction case, Mathews v. Commissioner, 61 T.C. 12 (1973), rev'd, 520 F.2d 323 (5th Cir. 1975), established standards to determine whether payments to a trust under a lease to the former owner of the property (or a business owned by the former owner) are deductible business expenses under §162(a)(3) that shifts income from the business to the trust: (1) the transferor must not retain substantially the same control over the property that existed before the transfer (use of an independent trustee or cotrustee will meet this requirement), (2) the leaseback normally should be in writing and must require payment of a reasonable rent, and (3) the leaseback (as distinguished from the original transfer) must have a bona fide business purpose.

Qualified Minor's Trusts

Qualified §2503(c) minor's trusts that will accumulate income during minority are effective to avoid the Kiddie Tax and can be used to earn income, taxed at the trust's tax rates, assuming that distribution of corpus and accumulated income will be acceptable at the beneficiary's age 21. The most important hurdle is that no income be taxed to the trust's grantor under the support obligation provisions of §677(b). This is not so easy to accomplish, because §677(b) does *not* require that distributions be made that *satisfy* or *discharge* a grantor's obligation of support.[53] Instead, §677(b) taxes the grantor to the extent income is distributed for the support or maintenance of anyone the grantor is obliged to support or maintain, even if those distributions do not satisfy or discharge the obligation. Thus, an Upjohn clause prohibiting distributions that have the effect of discharging anyone's legal obligation of support or maintenance is not sufficient to prevent taxation of distributed income to the grantor under §677(b). To avoid this inclusion, distributions for the support or maintenance of the beneficiary must be forbidden.

Distributions for other purposes should avoid taxation to the grantor under §677(b) if trust income is not needed for the routine support or maintenance of the beneficiary. This should be acceptable if the grantor lives in a state in which items like the cost of higher education are not part of the legal obligation of support, or if the grantor is not a parent with a legal support obligation. Furthermore, even in states in which trust distributions might be part of a grantor's legal obligation, this planning may entail an understanding that investment will be structured to minimize the income yield or to produce tax exempt income in those years in which §677(b) distributions are likely to occur.

---

53. See Chapter 5 at page 26 regarding the discharge of obligation concept.

Support Trusts

Much traditional income shifting is designed to direct income to a minor, such as a child or grandchild. But many potential consumers of income shifting advice also want to reduce the cost to support an elderly dependent, such as a parent. One manner to accomplish this is to create a trust to pay income to the parent for life, with remainder to the transferor's children. Income from this trust would be regarded as the parent's income for income tax purposes, which may allow it to be taxed at a lower income tax rate than if the income was received by the transferor and transferred after tax to the parent. Beware again of §677(b), which is not limited to the obligation to support or maintain *children*. In some states a taxpayer may have an obligation to support an otherwise destitute parent and, therefore, §677(b) might apply.

Additional care is required if distributing income to the parent may create problems in qualification for certain governmental benefits or in determining the standard deduction and personal exemption of the taxpayer who may claim the parent as a dependent. It also is wise to consider how many standard deductions are available to the parent under §63(c)(3) (for aged or blind taxpayers) and whether they will be regained under §63(c)(5) if the parent no longer is a dependent of the transferor.

Transferors who wish to avoid the potential problems created by such a trust may find a form of defective grantor trust planning appropriate. For example, a transferor's child who has funds (perhaps representing gifts from the transferor) could place property in trust to pay income to the transferor's parent (grandparent of transferor's child), with a reversion to the child as grantor on the death of the transferor's parent. Under §673, this reversion would create grantor trust treatment to the child (if the reversion is valued in excess of 5% of the value of the trust, which is likely, given the ages involved), making trust income taxable to the child, not to the transferor or to the transferor's parent. In such a case, the transferor effectively would be providing (through the gift to the child) the means to support the transferor's parent (with funds that belong to the child for wealth transfer tax purposes), taxing the income therefrom at the child's rates rather than as either the transferor's income or, more important, as income of the transferor's parent.

Even if the income tax bracket of the child is no lower than the income tax bracket of the transferor (or the Kiddie Tax applies), this transaction would work wealth shifting objectives without giving the transferor's parent property that might cause the loss of governmental benefits that otherwise are available to the parent. It also may protect the transferor's ability to claim the parent as a dependent and avoid any wealth transfer taxation when the transferor's parent dies.

Crown *Loans*

Demand loans at below-market-rate interest (*"Crown"* loans)[54] may make sense for an asset-rich lender (such as a retired parent) whose income tax bracket is no higher than that of a cash-poor borrower (such as a highly compensated but financially strapped child with large monetary obligations) who the lender wishes to benefit. In such a transaction, the lender is deemed to make a gift to the borrower in the amount of market interest that is foregone (thereby potentially incurring a gift tax liability), and is deemed to receive imputed interest from the borrower that may result in a §7872 income tax liability to the lender. The planning attraction underlying the *Crown* loan approach is the notion that the lender's payment of this income tax liability is an additional "gift tax free" transfer of wealth to the borrower, as illustrated below.

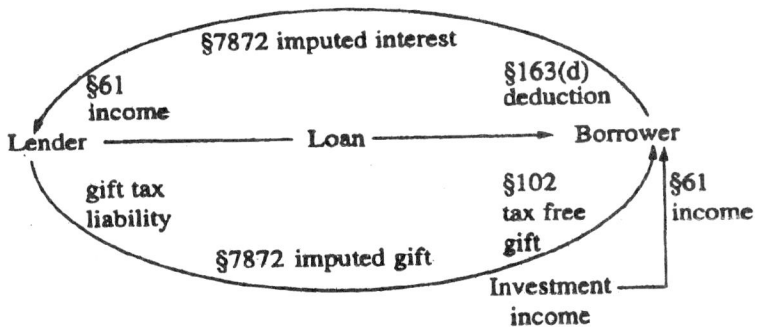

In a traditional *Crown* loan, the borrower should qualify under §163 to deduct the deemed payment of interest to the lender (to the extent the borrower has investment income attributable to the loan), allowing the borrower to shelter income earned by investment of the borrowed funds. The lender has income from the imputed interest payment, effectively resulting in the lender paying the tax incurred on income that was earned "tax-free" by the borrower.

This is not, however, as "unique" or appealing a result as some might suggest, nor is it abusive, because similar results are available if the lender simply invests the loan fund, earns the income therefrom, and gives that pre-tax income to the borrower, paying the income tax on that income from other assets. In this event, the borrower winds up with the same investment income, again without paying income tax on it. If income tax brackets of the lender and the borrower are unchanged, either transaction would be effective to give a benefit to the borrower, at an identical gift tax cost in each case.

---

54. So named after Crown v. Commissioner, 585 F.2d 234 (7th Cir. 1978), aff'g 67 T.C. 1060 (1977), which remained viable until the decision in Dickman v. Commissioner, 465 U.S. 330 (1984), and the eventual adoption of §7872.

The *Crown* loan transaction *can* be the better of the two alternatives *if* the borrower earns more on investment of the borrowed funds than could the lender (and more than the §7872 applicable federal rate). In such a case, a larger effective gift of the use of the money occurs than is taken into consideration under §7872. The *Crown* loan approach also has the advantage of allowing the borrower to invest the loaned amount, which may be wise for psychological reasons or because the lender is either unwilling or unable to invest as wisely as the borrower. And it allows any future appreciation in those investments to belong to the borrower.

Furthermore, a "safe harbor" provision permits de minimis interest free loans with no income tax consequences. By §7872(c)(2), a gift loan that does not exceed $10,000 on any given day is excepted from §7872 treatment, provided the borrowed funds are not used to acquire income producing property. This could be a modest means of assisting the borrower in acquiring a home or other property for personal use, or to fund educational, health, or other needs. This is, however, only an indirect method of shifting income, in the sense that the lender is foregoing investment income from the loan fund while the borrower is avoiding the need to borrow funds in a commercial transaction that would incur an interest expense.

Shifting Opportunities

Requiring less wealth in the form of property in the hands of a low bracket taxpayer is a form of "gifting" and income shifting effected by "shifting opportunities." For example, Parent informs Child of a certain-to-succeed business opportunity that Child pursues, earning a profit that Parent otherwise would have generated. This form of transaction is not subject to the gift tax (which applies only to transfers of "property," not to sharing knowledge or services) and effectively produces wealth that is income taxable to Child rather than to Parent.

The difficult problems that arise from such a deal are whether Parent may (or even should) make gifts or loans to Child to be used by Child to invest in the opportunity, or the tax consequences if Parent instead guarantees a third party loan taken by Child for these purposes. The direct Parent to Child gift or loan raises the possibility that the government would argue that a step or sham transaction has occurred, or that Parent acquired the opportunity and later gave it to Child. Furthermore, with respect to a loan guarantee, if Parent is never called upon to make good on the guarantee (which would generate significant gift or discharge of indebtedness income considerations), giving the guarantee alone should be treated only as a gift of the value of the guarantee (presumably what Child would pay an independent third party to obtain the guarantee). That could be quite expensive, but it is worth considering.

Similarly, a donor who owns an option that is transferable (for example, an incentive stock option that is transferable within a limited group of potential donees, such as lineal descendants) may transfer the option at its present gift tax value, effectively allowing the transferee to seize any future growth in the property that is the subject of the option. Income accrues to the transferor when the option is exercised by the transferee, in an amount equal to the difference between the fair market value of the stock acquired by exercise and the striking price. That is a traditional application of the income tax valuation and timing elements common to stock options. The gift is taxable, however, at the time and value when the option is assigned.

Tenancy at Will

Assume that Child has located the perfect residential property, but cannot afford to buy it because the debt service would be too great or the required down payment is too high. So Parent acquires the property and immediately transfers it to a §2702(a)(3)(A)(ii) Qualified Personal Residence Trust (or, using the Child's limited available capital, Child and Parent make a split purchase of the property, with Parent acquiring a term interest that meets the Qualified Personal Residence Trust requirements and Child acquiring the remainder). Then assume that Parent allows Child to enjoy Parent's term interest on a year-to-year tenancy-at-will. It appears that Parent is making a gift to Child to the extent the rent charged to Child is less than a fair market rental. This presumably occurs in each year that the tenancy is not terminated and ought to qualify as a present interest for gift tax annual exclusion purposes.[55] In many cases the annual exclusion should preclude the need to file a gift tax return to reveal the transaction.

More importantly, there appears to be no income tax concept similar to §7872 dealing with the rent-free (or rent-reduced) use of property, as opposed to the interest-free ("rent-free") or below-market-interest use of money, which is what a *Crown* loan is all about. Thus, this is an effective shift of "income" in the form of rents that Child has avoided paying or debt service that Child has not incurred. It is a transfer that need not be reported on an income tax return, and it is a transfer that is not dependent on Child's income tax brackets. Thus, there is no "limit" on the amount of this income that can be transferred before running through Child's brackets, making this a particularly attractive way of doing such a purchase with both wealth transfer and income shifting attributes.[56]

---

55. Indeed, the gift probably is being made to Child and Child's family, meaning that multiple annual exclusions may be available. If, however, Child is obligated under state law to provide housing for the family, it may be that the gift is entirely to Child (or perhaps to Child and Child's spouse, if any) due to the indirect benefit represented by this deemed transfer to the family.

56. Allowing Child to live rent-free in the home constitutes a §280A(d)(3) "use" by Parent for income tax purposes, meaning that the deductibility of items like amortization, depreciation, property taxes, and interest on a mortgage are the same as with any other residential property that Parent owns and personally uses. In that respect, the transaction is not all that a taxpayer may want. Amounts spent by the trustee on such personal-use residential realty would not qualify as §212 expenses incurred in connection with property held for the production of income, but most of those expenses would not be deductible even if the beneficiary had received the property outright.

Additional Income Tax Considerations

Some forms of transfer are more preferable for income tax purposes than others. Two that seem to raise the greatest income tax concerns are annuities (including the private or family annuity, and grantor retained annuity trusts or grantor retained unitrusts), and installment sales (including traditional sales and sales for death-terminating or self-canceling installment notes).

Private Annuities

An irrevocable inter vivos transfer of property can be an expensive form of planning for gift tax purposes if the property owner retains no interest and therefore incurs a gift tax on the full value of the transferred property. Incurring gift tax unnecessarily is never a good plan, and for many people incurring any gift tax is not likely desirable in the current environment in which estate tax repeal is promised for 2010.

An irrevocable inter vivos transfer can be even *more* expensive if the property owner must retain personal economic enjoyment of the transferred property for life to guarantee the transferor's future financial security. Retention poses potential estate tax inclusion of the transferred property at death under §2036(a)(1) or §2039. This might be savvy, however, if the estate tax has been repealed and gift tax was avoided by virtue of the retained interest. So there is some risk to evaluate.

These wealth transfer tax consequences may be reduced if the property owner *purchases* a lifetime annuity, rather than making a gratuitous irrevocable inter vivos transfer of the property with retained enjoyment. But a commercial annuity backed by the financial security of the issuer means that the property used to purchase the annuity is permanently removed from the taxpayer or the taxpayer's family (and it also may mean that a capital gain was incurred when the property was sold to provide the liquidity to purchase the annuity).

So the annuity of choice for many property owners is a noncommercial, nongratuitous irrevocable inter vivos transfer of the property to a trust or to a family member, subject to the transferee's agreement to pay the transferor an annuity. The annuity could be for life or for a defined term, in either case being a promise lacking financial security to the transferor if the transferee becomes insolvent. The absence of financial security is the hallmark of the private annuity and the linchpin of one of its prime advantages, because an exchange of appreciated property for a commercial annuity triggers immediate recognition of all appreciation realized on the exchange. Preferable to most transferors is deferred payment of the income tax on any realized gain through a private annuity transfer, which is treated differently if the annuity is not secured or otherwise collateralized.

The gain or loss and periodic income taxable to the transferor who exchanged property for the private annuity are reportable in a noncommercial annuity transaction under the annuity income rules of §72,[57] which determines the portion of each annual payment that is ordinary income, capital gain, and a tax-free recovery of basis. To ascertain the income taxation of each portion, it is necessary to determine the transferor's §72(c)(1) "investment in the contract" and the transferor's adjusted basis prior to the transfer.

Gain or loss on the transfer is measured by the difference between the transferor's amount realized and adjusted basis prior to the exchange. The amount realized is determined under the wealth transfer tax annuity valuation tables based on the life expectancy factor for a measuring life of the transferor's age multiplied by the amount of the annuity.[58] As explained in Dix v. Commissioner, 392 F.2d 313 (4th Cir. 1968), aff'g 46 T.C. 796 (1966), the §72 annuity valuation rules are reserved for the valuation of *commercial* annuities. *Private* annuities are valued differently because commercial annuities differ (and are more expensive) for at least three reasons: commercial annuity issuers are regulated, they price their products to make a profit, and they suffer from the self-selection of purchasers who expect to live *longer* than the mortality tables predict (meaning that the transferor receives the benefit of the annuity gamble). Private annuity transactions are most attractive to families in which death of the annuitant is expected *earlier* than the mortality tables predict (meaning that the transferee receives the benefit of the annuity gamble by making fewer annuity payments).

A loss may result if the amount realized as so determined is less than the transferor's basis[59] but a gain is realized to the extent the amount realized exceeds the transferor's basis. That gain is reportable in

---

57. *Not* under the installment reporting rules of §453, although they might appear to apply. See S. Rep. No. 1000, 96th Cong., 2d Sess. 12 n.12, and H.R. Rep. No. 1042, 96th Cong., 2d Sess. 10 n.12 (1980); 1980-2 C.B. 506 n.12. See generally the most comprehensive authority on the overall taxation of private annuities in General Counsel Memorandum 39503 (1986), issued in conjunction with Rev. Rul. 86-72. The Memorandum distinguishes annuities from installment obligations on the basis of duration. Annuity payments typically run until death of the annuitant; installment payments typically run until a designated amount is paid. A hybrid payment that runs until the earlier of the death of the transferor or payment of a stated monetary amount is regarded by the Memorandum as an installment obligation if the stated amount would be received before expiration of the transferor's life expectancy determined actuarially; otherwise it will be regarded as an annuity.

58. The reference in General Counsel Memorandum 39503 was to Treas. Reg. §20.2031-10 and Rev. Rul. 80-80, which have been superseded by Treas. Reg. §25.7520-3(b)(3), under which life expectancy must be determined using the standard mortality tables unless the transferor is terminally ill when the transaction is completed, applying a definition of terminal illness as "known to have an incurable illness or other deteriorating physical condition for which there is at least a 50% probability of death within one year" and a presumption against terminal illness if the measuring life survives for at least 18 months after the transfer.

59. Which loss may not be recognizable under the related party transfer rules of §267, in which case the loss could be recognized by the transferee on a future transfer of the property at a gain but otherwise the loss would be lost. The loss also may not be deductible if the property transferred in exchange for the annuity is a personal use asset as to which losses never are deductible, as opposed to an investment asset. See, e.g., Rev. Rul. 71-492 (involving a principal personal residence).

installments as the annuity payments are received. In addition, the transfer may constitute a part-sale, part-gift transaction if the amount realized is less than the fair market value of the asset transferred. In that case the income tax consequences are as just described and the transferor's gift tax liability is determined on the value of the transferred property in excess of the amount realized.

Each annuity payment received is deemed to consist of basis recovery and capital gain as determined under an exclusion ratio calculation that regards basis and capital gain to be received pro rata over the expected life of the annuitant. Any amount received in excess of those pro rata amounts (and all amounts received after recovery of the full amount of basis and capital gain) is ordinary income, essentially representing interest on the deferred payment of the annuity as the consideration for the original transfer (and, after full recovery of that interest element, as income representing the benefit of the transferor's annuity gamble, in this case attributable to being longer lived than the tables predicted).[60]

To illustrate, assume that the transferor's life expectancy is 20 years, basis in the transferred asset is $100,000, and the value of the annuity for amount realized purposes is $1 million. In each payment year the annuity amount received will consist of $5,000 of basis recovery ($100,000 basis divided by 20) and $45,000 of capital gain (gain equals amount realized ($1,000,000) over basis ($100,000) = $900,000, divided by 20). Any annual annuity payment in excess of the $50,000 per annum figure will constitute §72(a) ordinary income. If the annuity is paid for longer than 20 years (because the transferor lives longer than the predicted life expectancy), then the payments will become ordinary income in their entirety because, after 20 years, the full basis and capital gain portions will have been recovered.

If the transferor dies before receiving all 20 expected payments, however, the transferor's income tax return for the year of death will reflect a deduction for the amount of unrecovered basis[61] and the sale price will be regarded as adjusted downward, meaning that there will be no additional capital gain and the transferee will be regarded as having paid a smaller amount for the property, resulting in a downward basis adjustment for the transferee.[62] Although there appears to be no authority on the question, it is

---

60. See General Counsel Memorandum 39503, elaborating in detail on the deferred, ratable recognition of the various income taxable elements.

Although a portion of the annuity may be taxable to the annuitant as ordinary income as if it were interest paid on a loan, the transferee's payment of that amount is not regarded as interest and may not be deducted for income tax purposes, because the payor is regarded as making a capital investment and not as financing an installment purchase obligation. Bell v. Commissioner, 76 T.C. 232, 237 (1981), aff'd, 668 F.2d 448 (8th Cir. 1982); Dix v. Commissioner, 46 T.C. 796 (1966), aff'd, 392 F.2d 313, 318 (4th Cir. 1968); Garvey Inc. v. United States, 726 F.2d 1569 (Fed. Cir. 1984); General Counsel Memorandum 39503 (1986) (also stating that the imputed interest rules of §§483 and 1274 do not apply to private annuities).

61. §72(b)(3).

62. See Rev. Rul. 55-119 and Rev. Rul. 72-81. Basis to the transferee who is paying the

possible that the government might allege instead that there is a larger gift, particularly if the transaction was a part-sale, part-gift in its original iteration.

For gift tax purposes a gift is made to the extent the value of any transferred property exceeds the value of a private annuity received in exchange, and it is unlikely in the family context that the business transaction exception[63] would apply. Furthermore, a transferor who purchases a sole and survivor or a joint and survivor annuity makes a gift to the other annuitant measured by the value of the property transferred reduced only by the value of the transferor's annuity interest. If the other annuitant is the transferor's spouse, however, a gift tax marital deduction applies (unless the transferor opts out of automatic qualified terminable interest treatment).[64] And, for estate tax purposes, the value of any survivorship annuity attributable to any portion of the purchase price contributed by the transferor is includible in the transferor's gross estate at death under §2039. If the surviving annuitant is the decedent's spouse, however, the same value should qualify for the estate tax marital deduction if nothing passes to any other person upon termination of the spouse's survivorship interest.[65]

Death-Terminating Installment Notes

Also referred to as Self-Canceling Installment Notes, or simply as SCINs, an installment sale to a family member or other object of the transferor's bounty may be a viable alternative to a private annuity transaction. Under each, payments end at the transferor's death, with no estate tax inclusion in a proper case under the death-terminating note situation because the notes simply expire by their own terms when the transferor dies.[66] Thus, the difference between them may be analyzed on a purely economic and income tax basis.[67]

---

annuity is determined in three different ways, depending on when basis is being determined. While the annuitant is alive, basis is the present value of the prospective payments under the annuity agreement, which is equal to the amount realized to the transferor. If payments under the annuity exceed that amount because the annuitant outlives the life expectancy used to determine the amount realized, then basis increases with each additional payment, as made. Once the annuitant dies the transferee's basis becomes the total amount paid to the annuitant.

63. Treas. Reg. §25.2512-8 (a transfer made in the ordinary course of business that is bona fide, at arm's length, and free of donative intent is regarded as made for full and adequate consideration and therefore is not subject to gift tax).

64. See §2523(f)(6).

65. §2056(b)(7)(C).

66. See Estate of Moss v. Commissioner, 74 T.C. 1239 (1980), acq. in result only (decedent sold closely held stock at arm's length to individual employees who were not natural objects of the decedent's bounty, taking in exchange installment notes for a term less than the decedent's life expectancy; inclusion did not result notwithstanding the decedent's unexpected death within two years after the sale and the fact that the notes terminated by their own terms, because the parties stipulated that the sale was bona fide and for adequate and full consideration, and the cancellation provision was part of the negotiated agreement for which separate consideration was paid).

See also Estate of Musgrove v. United States, 95-2 U.S. Tax Cas. (CCH) ¶60,204

The death-terminating installment note approach may result in more wealth that is subject to inclusion in the estate of the transferor, particularly if death does not precede the term of the notes. This is because the death-termination or self-cancellation feature must be supported by added consideration, usually paid in the form of a premium added to the normal amortization of the installment note amount. Thus, a transferor may collect more under a death-terminating or self-canceling installment note approach than if the notes were not self-canceling, and potentially more even than if the transfer was for a private annuity. Nevertheless, a longer life than the actuarial tables predict will cause the holder of a lifetime annuity to receive more payments than anticipated and also cause an increase in the transferor's gross estate in ways that the installment notes will not, because the notes have a set duration that does not extend just because the transferor outlives the term of the notes.

The happy result in either case is that a larger estate is not a concern if repeal of the estate tax actually occurs in 2010, and both approaches avoid a taxable gift inter vivos (which would be subject to gift tax, which does not go away in 2010). In addition, the installment note approach will entail payment of interest by the recipient of the underlying property that may be deductible under §163, although the consequence to the transferor will not differ from that in a private annuity.

A third difference between annuities and installment notes that may arise if the transferee of the transferred property is a §453(f)(1) sufficiently related party who disposes of the property within two years. In the installment sale case there will be a §453(e) acceleration of the amount realized to the transferor who received the installment notes. This requires all unrecognized gain to be reported by the transferor in the year of the transferee's disposition. Moreover, cancellation of the note by the transferor's will, or its becoming unenforceable by its own terms, is treated

---

(Ct. Fed. Cl. 1995), which involved a transfer in exchange for an interest free, unsecured, self-canceling demand note made 18 days before the lender's death, which was held not effective to preclude estate tax inclusion of the principal amount of the debt. Although the loan amount was less than the repayment obligation, the court concluded as a matter of fact that this was not a negotiated premium for the forgiveness feature. Worse facts hardly could be involved, and the court correctly held that the mere designation of the transfer of funds as a debt could not preclude estate tax inclusion of the debt amount. That being the case, the significance of the decision is that it recognized *Moss* and distinguished it rather than refusing to follow it. According to the court, *Moss* was very different in that the loan was made at arm's length by a lender to parties who were not natural objects of the lender's bounty, the government stipulated that the sale price represented by the loan was full and adequate consideration for a bona fide sale of the lender's business and, perhaps most important, the parties also stipulated that the term of the loan did not exceed the lender's life expectancy. In *Musgrove* there was no term (and almost any term selected would have been in excess of the very seriously ill lender's life expectancy). Also different about *Moss* was that there was a clearly negotiated and denominated premium for the self-canceling feature, which also clearly was not the case in *Musgrove*.

67. See the comparison of death-terminating installment notes to private annuities in General Counsel Memorandum 39503.

as a disposition of the installment obligation for income tax purposes, resulting in gain or loss to the transferor.[68]

The favorable conclusion is that a death-terminating installment note is not includible in the transferor's gross estate for estate tax purposes. Thus, for estate tax purposes, both the private annuity and the death-terminating installment note cause the payments to cease at death and no part of the underlying annuity or note obligation to be includible. And, properly done, neither entails a taxable inter vivos gift subject to gift tax.

Selected Inter Vivos Transfer Approaches

Transfers in trust or other property management and protective, nonprobate vehicles predominate in sophisticated estate planning,[69] but in many circumstances outright transfers are appropriate.

In some circumstances the form or timing of a transfer is important because the transferor does not want to part with enjoyment or control of property prior to death. In these cases a transferor may want to make an inter vivos transfer of property that will be effective at death. This may prevent the property from passing through the transferor's probate estate but will not result in a loss of enjoyment or control over the property until death. Doing this may require the use of common probate avoidance devices, including trusts, annuities, joint ownership with survivorship rights, Totten trusts, payable on death accounts, and future interests, all depending on the circumstances, the nature of the property, and any ancillary objectives to be accomplished.

In each case, however, the transfer may not be complete for gift tax purposes and, even more important, the transferred property almost certainly will be includible in the transferor's gross estate at death. So, depending on the transferor's objectives with respect to taxation, intentional or unintentional retention may be problematic and should be analyzed carefully and fully, keeping in mind that any tax advantages explored in this Chapter on inter vivos transfers almost always require completed irrevocable gifts.

At least until repeal of the estate tax, in most cases both the nature of any transferred property and the income and wealth transfer tax objectives dictate that a no-strings-attached gift be made, and this may be wise for nontax reasons as well. For example, tangible personal property (even

---

68. The cancellation is regarded under §453B(f) as a transaction other than a sale or exchange for purposes of §453B(a)(2) and the fair market value of the obligation is treated as no less than the face amount of the notes, resulting in an acceleration of the unrecognized gain in those notes.

69. Many of the more sophisticated and tax sensitive planning techniques involving inter vivos property transfers are considered elsewhere in this material, as appropriate with respect to the particular wealth transfer tax objective and exposure they present. For an excellent practical summary comparison of various techniques, see Abbin, *[S]he Loves Me, [S]he Loves Me Not — Responding To Succession Planning Needs Through A Three Dimensional Analysis Of Considerations To Be Applied In Selecting From The Cafeteria Of Techniques*, 31 U. Miami Inst. Est. Plan. ¶1300 (1997).

income producing personal property) does not readily lend itself to trust ownership (nor to most other forms of bifurcated ownership designed to permit continued enjoyment or control until death). An exception might apply if it is contemplated that the property will be sold and the proceeds invested and administered in the trust.

Similarly, residential real estate (whether it will be occupied by the transferor or a different tenant) normally is not placed in trust because income tax benefits such as the exclusion from gain on the sale of a principal personal residence likely will be unavailable (unless the trust qualifies as a grantor trust for income tax purposes). On the other hand, land that will be managed to produce income may be just as adaptable to a trust as income producing personal property, although its management may entail a different form of expertise (such as farm, ranch, or timber management) than does the management of a securities portfolio. As an alternative to using a trust, however, land also lends itself more readily than does personal property to division into legal present and future interests (although historically bifurcation of title without the benefit of a trust has proven to be troublesome).

The point is that many varied tax and nontax considerations must be weighed when analyzing the time or form of inter vivos transfer to employ. Not the least of these should be the ability of the transferee to manage the property, particularly if expert management is necessary and especially if a trust is an appropriate vehicle to provide management that is separated from beneficial enjoyment.

Cancellation of Indebtedness

A taxpayer who wants to make a completed transfer of cash or other property to a transferee without incurring an immediate gift tax may attempt to leverage the gift tax annual exclusion. People do this by loaning the cash or selling the property in exchange for an installment note and then canceling a portion of the debt equal to the gift tax annual exclusion in each subsequent year until the notes have been extinguished. Without care, however, the gift and income tax consequences of this approach may be worse than if the taxpayer had conveyed a fractional portion of the property or a dollop of the cash in each year. Fractional periodic gifts forego the opportunity to freeze the value of transferred property and shift future income from it in an immediate transfer, but they are less prone to government attack.

For income tax purposes, a sale for an installment note generates gain or loss that is reportable in installments under §453, but the annual forgiveness constitutes a disposition under §453B that causes the deferred income tax liability to be recognized by the taxpayer. Furthermore, the forgiveness is a §61(a)(12) discharge of indebtedness that generates income to the transferee. The transferee's income tax liability is avoidable if forgiveness of the debt is deemed to be supported by the transferor's donative intent, making the discharge a gift that may qualify for the gift tax annual exclusion. The hazard with a gift characterization is that the government will successfully recharacterize the *initial* transfer as a gift rather than a loan or a sale, thereby accelerating into the initial year all of the taxpayer's gift tax liability, thereby defeating the objective of leveraging the annual exclusion.

Treatment as an immediate gift rather than as a loan may be based on the lack of any demonstrable intent to collect on the debt, as illustrated in Miller v. Commissioner, 71 T.C.M. (CCH) 1674 (1996),[70] in which most of the indicia of a bona fide loan were lacking. According to *Miller*, nine facts and circumstances may be considered in determining whether there is a real expectation of repayment and a bona fide intent to enforce a debt, as opposed to making a completed gift upon the original transfer of funds. These include: (1) a promissory note or other evidence of indebtedness, (2) interest charged, (3) security or collateral, (4) a fixed maturity date, (5) a demand for repayment, (6) actual repayment, (7) a transferee with the ability to repay, (8) records that reflect the transfer as a loan, and (9) federal tax reporting of the transfer that is consistent with a loan.

As applied to the *Miller* facts, there was a notation on each check constituting a transfer of funds that the transaction was a loan, and the transferees signed notes reflecting that the alleged loans were repayable in one balloon payment three years later or on any earlier demand. But the loans were unsecured, they were interest free, and only one payment ($15,000 out of $200,000 transferred) was made. The remaining amounts were forgiven in annual amounts that never exceeded the gift tax annual exclusion for split gifts by the transferor and the transferor's spouse (although no gift tax returns making the split gift election were filed for most of the years in question and, in those years in which returns *were* filed, the gifts reported did not match the forgiveness amounts stated in the transferor's letters of forgiveness).

Working from a presumption that transfers within a family are gifts in the year of the original transfer, the court found that the taxpayer failed to carry the burden of proving that they instead were loans, in this case meaning in the year of the original transfer, meaning that the annual exclusion did not shelter these transfers. Among the most damning factors were (1) inadequate and inconsistent documentation, (2) a lack of commercially reasonable terms (such as charging interest and obtaining adequate security or collateral), (3) a failure to establish the kinds of facts that a commercial lender would rely upon before making bona fide loans, such as evidence of the transferee's ability to repay, and (4) improper tax return documentation of the transaction reflecting the treatment asserted by the taxpayer.

---

70. See also Deal v. Commissioner, 29 T.C. 730 (1958), Estate of Reynolds v. Commissioner, 55 T.C. 172 (1970), and DeGoldschmidt-Rothschild v. Commissioner, 9 T.C. 325 (1947), aff'd, 168 F.2d 975 (2d Cir. 1948), accelerating the gift to the year of the initial transfer and denial of seriatim annual exclusions.

Regardless of the inter vivos tax results desired, the ultimate point to be carried away from this Chapter is that you must consider the variety of factors involved and the sometimes conflicting objectives that might be desired, such as to avoid paying gift tax in hopes of dying when there is no estate tax, reducing value in case the estate tax does exist at death, shifting income to pay a lower income tax, and such. In a world of such uncertainty as currently exists the number one criterion should be preservation of flexibility and, likely, payment of as little present tax as possible (notwithstanding the clear economic benefits of incurring the gift tax *if* any wealth transfer tax will be imposed). There is pain to the client in lifetime planning, in the form of tax liability, loss of control, and uncertainty. Be especially sensitive to the client's tolerance for these things.

Chapter 13
POSTMORTEM PLANNING AND ESTATE ADMINISTRATION

As immortal baseball legend Yogi Berra is quoted as saying: "It ain't over 'til it's over." Most elements of estate planning relate to premortem aspects of arranging a client's affairs to best maximize wealth and arrange for its disposition with a minimum of cost and disruption. But some elements of the process do not expire when the client does. These aspects of postmortem planning require some appreciation for estate and trust administration and various options and elections that are available or must be made after death. Estate administration is roughly the same whether the decedent died with a will or intestate, but a will can (and probably should) address significant postmortem administration requirements in estates of any size or complexity.

Personal Representative Defined

Administration of a decedent's estate is orchestrated by a personal representative, of which there are several varieties. An Executor is designated by the decedent's will. An Administrator is court appointed[1] if the decedent died intestate, or if the decedent's will did not make a valid designation, or the designated person or entity is not willing and able to act. An Administrator cum testamento annexo, or c.t.a. (with the will annexed), means the decedent died testate, and an Administrator de bonis non, or d.b.n. (of goods not administered), means the personal representative was appointed as a successor to complete the job begun by another. An Administrator both c.t.a. and d.b.n. is a successor acting under a will. Because there may be a delay in appointing a personal representative, particularly if a testate decedent's will is contested, a temporary or special administrator may be permitted to act. And in some jurisdictions a Public Administrator is appointed if no other suitable person or entity is willing and able to administer the decedent's estate.[2]

---

1. Statutes establish the order in which interested parties are entitled to be appointed as administrator. See, e.g., Uniform Probate Code §3-203.

2. The need for a public administrator can be illustrated by two cases. In Kurn v. Moran, 207 N.E.2d 688 (Mass. 1965), the decedent's heirs were overseas and unable to administer the estate, but they wanted to resist a claim being made against the estate. In United States v. Mize, 73-1 U.S. Tax Cas. (CCH) ¶12,923 (C.D. Cal. 1972), the public administrator was appointed at the request of the Internal Revenue Service, which wanted to file a claim to assert an outstanding 18-year-old estate tax liability.

Jurisdiction for Administration

A decedent's movables typically are subject to devolution and administration under the law of the state of the decedent's domicile at death. See RESTATEMENT (SECOND) OF CONFLICT OF LAWS §260 (1971). The decedent's immoveable assets (realty) must be administered where located. See id. §236. The existence of realty located in multiple jurisdictions may necessitate ancillary administration. A personal representative's authority to act is derived from the law of the state in which the personal representative is appointed. Thus, a domiciliary personal representative may have no authority to act elsewhere (such as to pursue claims of the decedent against debtors located in other states) unless by statute the other jurisdiction recognizes the domiciliary personal representative.[3]

An ancillary administration requires that the decedent's death be established and the decedent's will, if there is one, be admitted in the ancillary jurisdiction. This will entail cost and delay, and may allow a challenge to the validity of the will notwithstanding its admission to probate in the domiciliary state. For example, when a decedent's will is offered for probate to govern the disposition of ancillary movables, the ancillary court may allow an heir to challenge the domiciliary court's decision that the decedent's will is valid. It also may hold that the domiciliary court's determination was not binding, that the will must be proved in the ancillary state to dispose of the ancillary movables, and that full faith and credit of the domiciliary court's decree is subject to the ancillary court's determination of the domiciliary court's jurisdiction. This all would allow issues resolved by the domiciliary court to be relitigated in the ancillary court.[4] In addition, under Treas. Reg. §1.6012-3, the ancillary personal representative may be required to file income tax returns with respect to any income produced by those ancillary assets, notwithstanding that the domiciliary personal representative is filing returns for the balance of the decedent's estate. At a minimum, proper coordination of the respective administrations and allocation of tax payment obligations is a matter for real consideration.

Many states permit succession without formal administration of the decedent's estate, in some cases only if the estate is of a sufficiently small size, in some cases only if the decedent died with a will that authorized "independent" administration, and in most cases only if there is no objection by an heir, beneficiary, creditor, or other interested party.[5] In these and other

---

3. See, e.g., Uniform Probate Code §4-205.

4. See O'Brien v. Costello, 216 A.2d 694 (R.I. 1966), and Costello v. Conlon, 182 N.E.2d 532 (Mass. 1962).

5. See, e.g., Article 3 of the Uniform Probate Code, which provides several forms of administration of a decedent's estate, including small estate provisions in §§3-1201–3-1204, "informal" administration in §§3-301–3-311, "succession without administration" in §§3-312–3-322, "supervised" administration (which may be instituted by petition of any interested party or by the personal representative under §3-502) in Part 5, and "formal"

respects, administration of a decedent's estate is a uniquely localized process with significant variations in local law and procedure between states and even between counties or other subdivisions within a state.

As a consequence of all these factors, ancillary administration of property located in multiple locales becomes a matter of some significance. Frequently it is advisable to plan an estate for administration in a single jurisdiction and to avoid ancillary administrations by implementing nonprobate dispositions (such as inter vivos gifts, joint tenancy with the right of survivorship, or an inter vivos funded trust).

In light of these factors, normally it is preferable to nominate a personal representative by a testamentary provision. The will also should provide instructions regarding appointment of any successor that may be necessary and any special restrictions or grant of powers (such as authority to conduct independent administration if permitted by local law, waiving onerous bond or surety requirements, or directing that the personal representative not participate in managing the client's closely held business after death).

Together the client and the estate planner best know the nature of the estate and any peculiarities or problems that may arise in its administration. Effective estate planning includes the intelligent designation of a personal representative that considers personalities, talents, cost, jurisdictional prerequisites, and any potential tax consequences. In addition, postmortem administration involves many tax and related elections and decisions that are better informed and performed if adequate thought has been devoted to the process and appropriate powers and other provisions have been provided in the decedent's will.

Personal Representative's Primary Duties

The personal representative's primary functions are to marshal and preserve estate assets (including prosecution of any claims of the estate against others); to pay debts, expenses, taxes, and other proper claims against the estate; and to distribute the balance of the estate to the proper beneficiaries under the decedent's will or according to state law. Notice must be given to creditors to alert them to the decedent's death and the relatively short period within which to file a claim for payment or be barred. See, e.g., Uniform Probate Code §3-801. Tulsa Professional Collection Services, Inc. v. Pope, 485 U.S. 478 (1988), held that known or reasonably ascertainable creditors of an estate are entitled to actual notice of the decedent's death.[6] *Tulsa* also may require actual notice to known

---

testacy proceedings (meaning litigation to determine whether the decedent left a valid will and for appointment of a personal representative) in Part 4.

6. See Reutlinger, *State Action, Due Process, and the New Nonclaim Statutes: Can No Notice Be Good Notice If Some Notice Is Not?*, 24 REAL PROP., PROB. & TRUST J. 433 (1990), for a detailed discussion of *Tulsa*, and Kuether, *1988 Developments in Probate and Trust Law*, 25 REAL PROP., PROB. & TRUST J. 147, 192-199 (1990), for a summary of state nonclaim statutes that reflects amendments made since *Tulsa*. In re Estate of Van Praag, 684 N.E.2d 1080 (Ill. App. Ct. 1997), went so far as to find fiduciary duties to creditors in a

and reasonably ascertainable heirs, as well as to creditors, for purposes of the notice requirements to foreclose a will contest action.[7] Probate proceedings may be void if the court lacked in personam jurisdiction because proper notice was not given to known heirs.[8]

Besides notifying interested parties, the personal representative will prepare and file the decedent's final income tax return and all income tax returns for the estate during administration.[9] In addition, the primary obligation to file the estate tax return and pay the entire federal estate tax imposed on the decedent's gross estate rests on the personal representative under §§2002 and 6018(a)(1), respectively. These obligations exist even if assets included in the gross estate are not in the personal representative's possession or control. Treas. Reg. §20.2002-1.

An estate tax return must be filed only if the gross estate exceeds the amount as to which no tax is payable by virtue of the unified credit,[10] and payment of the tax is required nine months after the decedent's death. Under §6075(a) the estate tax return also is due nine months after the decedent's death, unless a six month extension to file is granted under §6081. Extensions of time to file the return do not extend the time to pay the tax; a separate extension of the time to pay must be secured. §6161(a)(2); Treas. Reg. §§20.6081-1(d); 20.6151-1(a).

A fiduciary must give notice to the government of its appointment and again after being discharged.[11] The personal representative remains liable for tax matters until the proper §6903 Notice of Fiduciary Relationship is filed with the government, (although personal liability for payment of tax may be discharged under §§2204 (estate tax) and 6905 (income and gift

---

case involving a personal representative that did not protect creditor rights as against the government's tax levy.

7. *In re* Estate of Weidman, 476 N.W.2d 357 (Iowa 1991), which held that the notice requirement would not apply retroactively because the period for filing a will contest action in that estate expired long before the decision in *Tulsa*. It also may have been relevant that the claimant was a child of the decedent who was well aware of the decedent's death and for whom formal notice was irrelevant. See Moore, *Fairness and Finality: Notice to Beneficiaries Under Prior Wills*, 29 REAL PROP., PROB. & TRUST J. 817 (1995), arguing for an extension of *Tulsa* to mandate notice to beneficiaries under prior wills who may have a will contest cause of action if they were excluded from the decedent's final will, and Wells, *Responding to the Call for Fairness and Finality: Would Notice to Beneficiaries under Prior Wills Produce Either?*, 29 REAL PROP., PROB. & TRUST J. 849 (1995) (responding to Moore).

8. *In re* Estate of Stanford, 581 N.E.2d 842 (Ill. App. Ct. 1991).

9. Although §644 requires trusts to report income on a calendar year basis, an estate may file its income tax return on either a calendar or a fiscal year basis (and §645 may permit the trust to be treated as part of the estate). In addition, §6654(l)(2) excepts estates (and certain trusts) from the estimated tax payment requirements for the first two tax years after the decedent's death.

10. For example, no return is required under §6018(a)(1) if the decedent was a citizen or resident of the United States whose gross estate was under the §2010(c) applicable exclusion amount. Notice that it is the *gross* estate, not the taxable estate, that is used as the filing threshold in §6018, even though the unified credit is equal to the tax on a *taxable* estate of the applicable exclusion amount.

11. Form 56 is the required submission, under §6903(a) and Treas. Reg. §301.6903-1(a).

tax) if proper applications are made). The government must notify the personal representative of the amount of tax within nine months after the later of making application or filing the return. Payment of that amount discharges the personal representative of personal liability for any subsequently determined deficiency (but it does not discharge the estate or its transferees).

The value of a closing letter is revealed by Singleton v. Commissioner, 71 T.C.M. (CCH) 3127 (1996), in which the court imposed personal liability on a personal representative who did not obtain a §2204(a) discharge and who distributed estate assets before obtaining a closing letter, ultimately to discover that all the estate tax had not been paid. Numerous cases hold that a closing letter will not preclude the government from assessing a timely filed deficiency. Thus, the result of the closing letter is to protect the personal representative from personal liability if estate assets have been distributed in reliance on the closing letter, forcing the government to assert transferee liability against the estate's distributees.

Note in all things that actions by one fiduciary may disadvantage the estate and all its beneficiaries. For example, in Eversole v. Commissioner, 46 T.C. 56 (1966), a personal representative who was discharged by the local probate court nevertheless consented to a government request, which bound the estate because no notice of termination of the fiduciary relationship had been given to the government.

More dramatically, Ewart v. Commissioner, 85 T.C. 544 (1985), aff'd, 814 F.2d 321 (6th Cir. 1987), involved a waiver of restrictions on assessment and collection under §6213(d), executed by only one of two personal representatives (two brothers, who also were the two estate beneficiaries). Only one signed returns and the nonsigner never complied with §6903(b) by filing a notice of fiduciary relation. Estate assets were distributed, and the brothers agreed that each would be liable for any taxes assessed with respect to any revaluation of assets that each received. The signatory brother received realty and sold it for an amount exceeding its reported federal estate tax value, which prompted the government correspondingly to revalue that property and assert a deficiency. Meanwhile, that brother declared bankruptcy and, when the government assessed the deficiency, that brother also executed a Form 890 waiver, upon which the government then proceeded in asserting liability against the nonsigning brother, in both his fiduciary and transferee capacities. The Tax Court rejected the nonsigning brother's argument that the signatory brother, acting alone, could not effectively execute the waiver and bind the estate. The court relied on the fact that federal law creates a joint action requirement only in Treas. Reg. §20.6018-2, which requires cofiduciaries to file a single return to prevent the filing of multiple returns by independently acting cofiduciaries. Otherwise, either fiduciary acting alone was capable of binding the estate and wreaking havoc. (This is just one of several reasons to disfavor cofiduciaries.)

Furthermore, the fiduciary could face personal liability for unpaid taxes. For example, in Garst Trust v. Commissioner, 53 T.C.M. (CCH) 506 (1987), the Tax Court prevented a beneficiary of a terminated trust from representing the trust because the trust had terminated and therefore could not be a proper party to the deficiency action. Instead, the proper party was the trustee who had failed to file the §6903 notice. That the beneficiary had signed an agreement with the trustee at the time of termination assuming all outstanding unresolved tax liabilities was deemed irrelevant. Presumably any judgment against the trustee might allow it to proceed against the distributee under that agreement, although the fiduciary may be left with no recourse if the beneficiary no longer is solvent.

In all its functions the personal representative must comply with basic fiduciary duties, such as the duty of impartiality. Severe conflicts may arise with estate beneficiaries in settling tax or other controversies in cases in which the personal representative is not disinterested.[12] Conflict should be anticipated and addressed by the decedent, who should select an appropriate personal representative.

Fees

Fees payable to a personal representative for administering the decedent's estate may be based on such factors as time spent, the difficulty of the administration, the amount involved, and whether any extraordinary tasks were assumed (such as liquidating a family business). Because the personal representative must consider and sometimes must deal with nonprobate assets (for example, to prepare the federal estate tax return or to coordinate the payment of taxes or other expenses), the fee should not be based solely on the size of the *probate* estate. Consideration also should be given to the proper allocation or proration of the fee to any nonprobate assets as to which tax and other services are performed.

Although some states specify the fees for personal representatives by statute, and a will (if one exists) may condition appointment of a personal representative on a fee agreement, it is more common to find that fees are subject to approval by the probate court subject only to a reasonableness standard. See, e.g., Uniform Probate Code §3-719. Fees paid to an attorney assisting in administration of an estate should be based on the same general criteria, and attorneys who also act as fiduciaries must consult state law to determine whether it is proper to charge two fees for acting in both capacities.[13]

---

12. See, e.g., Estate of Smith v. Commissioner, 77 T.C. 326 (1981) (the decedent's surviving spouse stood to benefit individually by a high estate tax valuation that would produce a high income tax basis that would minimize capital gain on a subsequent sale; because this value would negatively impact other beneficiaries, the spouse was removed as personal representative and a disinterested party was appointed to settle the estate's valuation dispute with the government).

13. See, e.g., Fla. Stat. §733.617(6). This assumes that acting in both capacities is permissible, or that an individual may hire his or her law firm to represent the entity, which may not be the law in some jurisdictions. See McGovern & Kurtz, WILLS, TRUSTS &

Attorney or personal representative fees based solely on the size of the estate may be too large in some cases and unfairly small in others, and therefore inappropriate unless agreed to in advance by the decedent or the estate beneficiaries. The amount involved may be a relevant factor in determining the amount of risk assumed and potentially the difficulty of the administration, however. And although minimum fee schedules relating to lawyers' fees in various matters are subject to the Sherman Act,[14] the use of fee schedules in some form still is relatively common as one factor among many in establishing a proper reasonable fee. Still, it seems fair to observe that special concerns with respect to fees arise in estate administration situations in which the fiduciary or the attorney charges a flat percentage fee: "Widespread public criticism of the cost of dying focuses in part on the belief that the estate lawyer receives an overly generous fee determined solely as a percentage of the estate's assets and far in excess of the value of the services performed."[15]

The fee issue is among the most disturbing to estates attorneys, who are being attacked on two relatively unexpected fronts. The first comes from the government because, like most administration expenses, fees paid to a personal representative and attorney for the estate are deductible for federal estate tax purposes. Treas. Reg. §20.2053-3(b)(1) limits the deduction to amounts paid or reasonably expected to be paid, and fees not fixed by a decree of the proper court will be allowed only if the government is satisfied that they will be paid and are allowable under controlling local law. More importantly, the government sometimes denies §2053(a)(2) deductibility of fees that are approved by local courts, thereby requiring a federal court to determine the deductibility of fees.

To illustrate, assume a personal representative petitions the local probate court for approval of its fees and the court consents, perhaps with the approval of the estate's beneficiaries. The issue is whether that approval determines the reasonableness of the fees for purposes of claiming a §2053 deduction. In Technical Advice Memorandum 8636100 the government opined that it is determinative under either of two

---

ESTATES 535 (3d ed. 2004). It is not necessarily unethical, however. See ABA Standing Committee on Ethics and Professional Responsibility Informal Opinion 1338 (1975) (involving the issue of appropriate fees for acting in both capacities). A written agreement addressing this issue would be wise, and at the same time the attorney should be mindful of the prohibition against solicitation in the designation of the attorney as fiduciary and the fact that in some jurisdictions the agreement itself also may be invalid.

14. As held in Goldfarb v. Virginia State Bar, 421 U.S. 773 (1975).

15. Johnston, *An Ethical Analysis of Common Estate Planning Practices—Is Good Business Bad Ethics*, 45 OHIO ST. L.J. 57, 102 (1984); Link et al., *Developments Regarding the Professional Responsibility of the Estate Administration Lawyer: The Effect of the Model Rules of Professional Conduct*, 26 REAL PROP., PROB. & TRUST J. 1 (1991). This issue has been of concern for decades, as illustrated by its being the subject of a portion of the *Statement of Principles Regarding Probate Practice and Expenses*, 8 REAL PROP., PROB. & TRUST J. 293, 294-296 (1973). Model Rule of Professional Conduct 1.5(a) requires a fee to be reasonable in relation to the work performed; only one of many listed factors is the custom in the community for charging fees, which along with the ambiguous factor referring to the "labor" involved usually are the only objective factors supporting the percentage fee approach.

circumstances: (1) the state court passed on all the facts and circumstances surrounding the fee request, and the determination was made in a genuinely adversarial proceeding involving those fees; or (2) the state court entered a consent decree that constitutes a bona fide settlement by the parties of a valid dispute or claim regarding fees. In other situations, the Memorandum said the court order will not necessarily bind the government, nor must the government accept a local court decree that is at variance with state law (for example, if the awarded fees exceed statutory fees, with no special justification for the excess).

In United States v. White, 853 F.2d 107, 113-114 (2d Cir. 1988), rev'g 650 F. Supp. 904 (W.D. N.Y. 1987), cert. granted, 489 U.S. 1051 (1989), and later retracted, 493 U.S. 5 (1989) (upholding the government's subpoena of attorney White's time records), the lower court determined that the government, under Treas. Reg. §20.2053-1(b)(2), is bound to accept the state court determination of fees unless there is prima facie evidence of fraud, overreaching, or some other reason to believe that the court did not pass on the factors upon which deductibility depends. In reversing, the Court of Appeals for the Second Circuit stated that

We do not read [§2053(a)(2)] as giving state *trial* court decrees preclusive effect with regard to IRS investigations. To be sure, the plain language of §2053(a)(2) indicates that the federal deductibility of estate administrative expenses is governed by state law. [But] . . . the deductibility of such expenses nonetheless remains a federal question.

According to the court, the government would be bound by state law factors that are to be applied in determining the allowability of fees, but would not be bound by a lower state court's application of those factors in a particular case.

Meanwhile, in Estate of DeWitt v. Commissioner, 54 T.C.M. (CCH) 759, 762 and n.4 (1987), the government challenged the deductibility of certain expenses of administration that were allowed for state law purposes. In allowing most of the deductions on motion for summary judgment, the Tax Court stated:

a court decree ordinarily controls the deductibility under the Federal estate tax [but] . . . the [taxpayer] . . . must show that all the facts necessary for deductibility under Federal estate tax were considered and found pursuant to the state court's inquiry.

In most instances the interest of the federal government in protecting its revenues will coalesce with the interest of the state in protecting its citizens, and state law may be relied upon as a guide to what deductions may reasonably be permitted for federal estate tax purposes.

Only deductions not proven by the taxpayer were denied.

The second unexpected challenge to fees in probate comes at the local level. Local courts on their own motion may challenge fees charged even though the beneficiaries are willing to pay without objection. A written fee agreement for the amount charged is no guarantee that it will not be an ethical violation or, it seems, that a court or the government will allow payment or deduction.

On the ethics front, Connecticut Informal Opinion 87-10 involved an attorney who was personal representative of an estate and acted as a broker for the sale of estate realty. In discussing fees, the opinion stated that no additional fee as personal representative was permissible in this added role. Furthermore, as an attorney, a reasonable fee request to the probate court must indicate the basis for the fee and the extent to which it was based on a sale of realty. The opinion indicated that a flat percentage fee for effecting a sale would be improper unless supported by other factors. Also included in the opinion was a strong caution, repeated twice, about potential conflicts of interest.[16]

White v. McBride, 937 S.W.2d 796 (Tenn. 1996), concluded that a contingent fee agreement with the decedent's surviving spouse for services to assist in recovery of a statutory elective share clearly was so excessive as to violate the state disciplinary rules and therefore was unenforceable. The court then reversed an award of quantum meruit because paying any compensation would fail to promote ethical behavior by providing a safety net of a reasonable fee if the endeavor to collect an exorbitant fee fails.

Even without answering the ethical question, it seems only prudent to suggest that attorneys be able to justify their fees with other factors, such as:

- the promptness, efficiency, and skill with which the administration was handled by the attorney,
- the responsibilities assumed by, and potential liabilities of, the attorney,
- the nature and value of the assets that are affected by the decedent's death,
- the benefits or detriments resulting to the estate or its beneficiaries from the attorney's services,
- the complexity or simplicity of the administration and the novelty of issues presented,
- the attorney's participation in tax planning for the estate and the estate's beneficiaries and tax return preparation or review and approval,

---

16. See also Conn. Inf. Op. 88-5 regarding real estate brokerage services by an attorney, stating that a flat 2% fee for brokering and closing a sale might be excessive. *In re* Lake, 702 N.E.2d 1145 (Mass. 1998), sanctioned an attorney for acting as real estate broker, for a separate commission, without disclosure of the conflict of interest or an informed written consent; it probably did not help that the broker was not a member of the multiple listing service where the property was located and attempted to retain the right to a commission even after associating with a local broker who *also* would charge a commission.

- the nature of the probate, nonprobate, and exempt assets, and the expenses of administration and liabilities of the decedent and the compensation paid to other professionals and fiduciaries,
- any delay in payment of the compensation after the services were furnished,

See Fla. Stat. §733.617(6). These factors are appropriate criteria to establish fees in any case, and attorneys might be well advised to consider this listing in justifying their fees as reasonable in all events, because allowable fees are likely to be scrutinized carefully.

If a personal representative or attorney intends to serve without compensation (for example, to avoid compensation income at the expense of the estate's deduction for estate or income tax purposes), this fact should be made known before the services are rendered. For example, Rev. Rul. 56-472 considered a personal representative's agreement to serve for an amount less than the statutory commission and held that the personal representative did not realize taxable income by the anticipatory waiver of a larger commission, nor did a gift occur for federal gift tax purposes. But Rev. Rul. 64-225 held that a waiver of statutory commissions after submitting intermediate accountings that contained a request for those commissions constituted a constructive receipt for income tax purposes and a taxable gift for gift tax purposes, distinguishing Rev. Rul. 56-472 because it involved a timely waiver.

Then Rev. Rul. 66-167 considered a taxpayer who served as sole personal representative of an estate in which the taxpayer and a child shared equally. Within a reasonable time after the decedent's death, the taxpayer decided to forgo compensation as personal representative and filed annual and final accounts consistent with that conclusion. The Ruling held that income was not constructively received and no gift was made, stating that the crucial test is whether the personal representative's actions evidence an intent to render a gratuitous service, based on whether the timing, purpose, and effect of the waiver make it serve any other important objective. The Ruling held that an adequate manifestation of intent to serve gratuitously would include a formal written waiver within six months after the initial fiduciary appointment and delivered to any principal legatee, devisee, or intestate taker, or by an "implied waiver" if the fiduciary never claims commissions when filing accountings and all other facts and circumstances are consistent with the intent to serve gratuitously. Claiming a commission as a deduction for income, estate, or inheritance tax purposes ordinarily would be considered inconsistent with an intention to serve gratuitously.

Postmortem Estate Planning

Often it is essential that a properly drafted estate plan exist to give the personal representative suitable powers and discretion to administer the estate, to apportion various tax and other burdens, to grant liberal powers of sale and reinvestment, to provide ample authority to liquidate or to conduct the decedent's business or other affairs, and ultimately to distribute the estate, all as the personal representative deems appropriate. As a further indication of the need for such authority, the following discussion notes elements of postmortem planning that may arise in a given estate and as to which the personal representative appropriately should be given special instructions, powers, and protections. Although it is possible to conduct an intestate administration and accomplish many of these tasks, they should be the subject of forethought and planning that is then reflected in a properly drafted estate plan.

For example, the personal representative should consult with the decedent's surviving spouse, if any, to determine whether to file a separate income tax return for the decedent or elect under §6013(a)(3) to file a joint return with the surviving spouse for the decedent's final tax year (and, if the decedent died before the prior year's return was filed, with respect to that outstanding return as well). Alternatively, the personal representative may elect under §6013(a)(3) to disaffirm a joint return previously filed with the surviving spouse. The personal representative and the spouse also should decide whether to consent under §2513(a) to split any gifts made while the decedent was alive, by either the decedent or the spouse, in years that have not yet been reported for gift tax purposes.

Although the personal representative has no duty to counsel the surviving spouse about postmortem elections available to the spouse,[17] in many cases these will be collaborative decisions made for the overall benefit of the decedent's entire surviving family. In some cases, the surviving spouse also may be deceased when these decisions are being made, meaning that the personal representative may be, or may be dealing with, the personal representative of the surviving spouse's estate. Examples of such decisions available to the surviving spouse are whether to claim a family allowance or the spouse's share in lieu of any entitlement under the decedent's estate plan, and whether to challenge any nonprobate transfers made by the decedent and as to which the spouse's entitlement otherwise may not apply.

---

17. Nor does the attorney engaged by the personal representative to assist in administration of the estate owe duties to the surviving spouse (or any other family members, as beneficiaries or heirs of the decedent). For an excellent illustration of the importance of an engagement letter making this clear, however, see Estate of Fitzgerald v. Linnus, 765 A.2d 251 (N.J. Super. 2001) (the decedent's surviving spouse and children unsuccessfully sued the attorney engaged by the surviving spouse as executor for failing to advise the spouse individually to disclaim insurance proceeds passing outside probate), in which the facts could not have been more helpful to the attorney, who was specifically engaged by the decedent (a CPA-attorney) and who was specifically limited to drafting documents rather than full fledged estate planning, because the decedent intended to undertake the necessary estate planning (which the decedent never did); the attorney also advised the spouse to obtain independent financial counsel, and made it clear that the attorney's undertaking was to assist the spouse in facilitating rapid distribution of estate benefits to the spouse, rather than to assess the wisdom of that course or to evaluate postmortem tax planning options such as disclaimer (to say nothing of the planning that would have been appropriate before the decedent died).

Additional collaborative planning may occur with respect to the marital deduction in the decedent's estate and whether a larger or smaller deduction would be desirable and can be generated by postmortem planning, such as disclaimers by descendants that would result in more property passing to the surviving spouse. Alternatively, the spouse (or the personal representative of a surviving spouse who died shortly after the decedent) may wish to disclaim any part of the decedent's estate passing to the spouse, thereby reducing the estate tax that will apply over both estates. Or it may be desirable for the personal representative to make only a partial qualified terminable interest property election under §2056(b)(7)(B)(v).

It also may be appropriate to make the §2056(b)(7)(C)(ii) election against automatic qualified terminable interest property marital deduction treatment afforded to a spousal annuity under a qualified retirement plan includible in the decedent's gross estate under §2039. And the surviving spouse should consider whether to roll any lump sum distribution from a qualified plan over to a spousal individual retirement account to defer the income tax liability until the spouse must begin receiving distributions from that account. Further, if the surviving spouse is not a citizen of the United States, postmortem planning and an election under §2056A(a)(3) will be required to comply with the Qualified Domestic Trust requirements to avoid loss of the marital deduction under §2056(d). And when the personal representative gets around to distributing any marital bequest or other entitlement from the decedent's estate, complex marital funding decisions must be made regarding such things as realization of capital gain or loss, distributable net income carryout, acceleration of income in respect of a decedent, whether to distribute frozen or split interests, and other consequences.

Numerous additional income tax issues confront the personal representative during estate administration. For example, the personal representative must decide: whether to deduct expenses for the decedent's medical care that are paid by the estate within one year after the decedent's death as an income tax deduction under §213(c) on the decedent's final income tax return or as a §2053(a)(3) estate tax deduction; whether to claim certain expenses of administration as an estate tax deduction under §2053(a)(2) or as an estate income tax deduction by making the §642(g) election; whether to use selling expenses to reduce the amount realized to determine gain or loss rather than as additional §2053(a)(2) administration expense deductions; whether to deduct uncompensated casualty losses as §165 income tax deductions rather than as either a §2054 estate tax deduction or a reduction in estate tax value under the §2032 alternate valuation rule; and whether to make the §454 election to accrue or recognize interest on any United States savings bonds owned by the decedent at death. Additional elections relate to the basis of partnership property under §754 and whether to revoke a §1362(a)(2) S Corporation election.

The personal representative also must select a §441 tax year for the estate's income tax purposes, which need not be the calendar year and, under §443, may be a short year in the first year after the decedent's death if that would fragment income received shortly after death and reduce the overall income tax burden. And when the estate is ready to terminate, the personal representative also must consider the §642(h) limitation regarding unused losses and deductions and select the most appropriate time for termination of the estate, all while considering the income tax consequences under §§661 and 662 of estate distributions, the amount of distributable net income carried out of the estate under the §643(e) limitation when property is distributed in kind, whether to make the §643(e)(3) election to treat distributions as a gain or loss realization event and correspondingly alter the distributable net income carryout amount and basis to the distributee, and the opportunity to make "trapping" distributions during interim years of estate administration. And if the estate is not terminated within two tax years after the decedent's death, §6654(*l*)(2) requires the personal representative to pay estimated income tax, which may be avoidable if a long first tax year is elected rather than a short year to fragment estate income.

Perhaps most relevant in most estates, the personal representative also must make various wealth transfer tax elections, beginning with the §2032 election to value estate assets on the alternate valuation date, which is six months after the decedent's death or the date of an earlier disposition, if any, all instead of valuation on the date of the decedent's death. Implicit in this election is the additional decision whether to dispose of any assets within the six month alternate valuation period, if §2032 might be elected and it is desirable to freeze the value of those assets by a disposition before the six month period elapses. Special use valuation under §2032A also may be available with respect to qualified real property used in a farm or ranch (or other agricultural property, under the §2032A(b)(2) definition) or in a closely held business.[18] And a reduction in estate value may be available if the decedent's personal representative is able to disclaim property received by the decedent within a short period prior to death. See Chapter 7 at pages 16-17.

The personal representative of an estate that holds closely held business property must consider whether a §303 redemption to pay estate or generation-skipping transfer taxes or a §6166 election to defer estate or generation-skipping transfer tax attributable to that property is available and would be desirable, along with the §6324A election to create a lien for §6166 deferred tax. And additional estate tax deferral requests may be available under §6161(a)(1) for up to six months or under §6161(a)(2) for up to 10 years for reasonable cause, or under §6163 with respect to the tax attributable to inclusion of future interests in the decedent's gross estate.

---

18. Similarly, the §2057 family-owned business interest deduction (which was repealed for decedents dying after 2003) may be restored by Congress and available with respect to a qualifying includible interest, also requiring an election under §2057(b)(1)(B).

An extension under §6081 to file the decedent's estate tax return also might become relevant.

With respect to allocation of the generation-skipping transfer tax exemption: the personal representative must decide whether to override the §2632 automatic allocation rules by making an affirmative allocation under §2631; whether to allocate exemption to transfers made during the decedent's life; and whether to make the §2652(a)(3) "reverse" qualified terminable interest property election.

All of this is sufficiently complex that you might ask yourself whether you want to serve as a fiduciary. Assuming you can figure it all out, there is an added bit of exposure, because the personal representative must decide whether to waive the right to receive compensation and must consider whether any of its actions during administration of the estate gives rise to the need to make "compensatory" or "equitable" adjustments to neutralize the consequences of elections made that, for example, reduce taxes at the inequitable expense of one or more beneficiaries. These various alternatives make the chore of administration infinitely more difficult than the average client anticipates, and they demand that special consideration be given to selection of the personal representative, making intestacy a particularly undesirable result in most substantial and even in many modest estates.

Chapter 14
PLANNING FOR INCAPACITY

Traditional estate planning generally is forward oriented planning for people anticipating their demise. Lifetime planning typically dovetails into the testamentary plan. This Chapter brings us up short to consider planning for people who are going to live, sometimes not very well in terms of mental or physical health, and potentially longer than they can afford.

The reality is that many estate planning clients actually worry more about the problems of living too long and becoming mentally or physically incapacitated or running out of money, or both. And the truth is that you either will know a great deal about such things as "entitlements" and "ElderLaw" and do very little traditional estate planning, or you will know a little about that constantly changing field, enough to be able to refer difficult cases to experts of that specialty. It is very hard and therefore quite uncommon for anyone to do both, and this Chapter opts for alerting you to issues to be aware of if your practice focus is traditional estate planning. There are entire treatises on planning for incapacity. And the subject is constantly being rewritten as the entitlements laws especially undergo continual change.

With respect to planning for mental incapacity, drafting several very simple documents in advance may avoid the need for a court to appoint a guardian or conservator[1] to manage property and make health care decisions for a client. A court appointed personal representative may not be the person the client would want to serve, and may not have the authority to do all things the client wants or needs. And, in all, events going to court initially and then periodically over the duration of such an appointment seldom is regarded as desirable.

In addition, a judicial determination of incapacity is time consuming, it is public and therefore potentially embarrassing, and it may require health care information or records that federal law (the Health Insurance Portability and Accountability Act, HIPAA) forbids the provider to release. Avoiding a court proceeding often is desirable because of the actual expense, missed opportunities, inadequate flexibility, and possible designation of the "wrong" representative that can result. Sidestepping a court's involvement is even more desirable if the personal representative is required to file reports with the court or to obtain prior approval for actions

---

1. In many states a court-appointed fiduciary to manage a ward's property is a *guardian of the estate* or a *conservator*, and a representative charged with care of the ward personally (including making health care decisions) is a *guardian of the person* or just a *guardian*. The same person may serve in both roles and all would fit under the definition of a "personal representative."

taken on behalf of the ward. A private arrangement created in advance of the need is preferable, to the extent there is no concern about mismanagement or neglect that might recommend court supervision.

Planning For Property Management

A poorly advised client might transfer assets to another person (such as a spouse, adult child, or other caregiver) in anticipation of incapacity, with an expectation that the transferee will continue to provide appropriately for the transferor. Alternatively, the client might create a convenience joint tenancy account with that person, to provide access to funds without a formal transfer. Either of those alternatives will trigger Medicaid prohibitions that address "spend-down planning" — efforts to diminish wealth so as to qualify for federal health care benefits. As discussed at page 5, without proper planning the result could be a period of Medicaid benefits ineligibility if the transfer occurs within three years (or five, if a trust is involved) before applying for benefits. In addition, the client may lose control of the assets with no real protection against mismanagement (or worse), the conveyances may be taxable as gifts, creditors of the transferee may gain access to the transferred assets, and inheritance rights will be affected. Consequently, more appropriate planning usually takes either of two alternative forms.

One approach is use of a funded, revocable, inter vivos trust. Frequently the settlor will serve as the sole initial trustee until the settlor becomes incapacitated. As discussed in Chapter 4 at pages 30-31, a court proceeding is not required to determine the settlor's incapacity if the trust instrument names the settlor as trustee and properly provides for a successor. Often a well planned trust provides for the settlor's incapacity to be determined by the settlor's physician(s), by a trusted family member or friend, or by a committee of several trusted persons (but not by the successor trustee, for fear that someone will allege that self interest informed a determination to take over). Because HIPAA concerns surround that determination, the plan may contain an appropriate release of medical information to inform the trustee succession procedure.

The other approach is a durable power of attorney for property management. This arrangement authorizes an *attorney-in-fact* to act on behalf of the client with respect to enumerated matters. Although common law agent authority terminated automatically if the principal became incapacitated, a *durable* power remains effective notwithstanding the principal's incapacity.

Like a self-trusteed revocable declaration of trust that provides for a successor trustee if the settlor is incapacitated, most durable power statutes authorize a power that "springs" into effect only if the principal becomes incapacitated. A springing power requires that the principal's incapacity be determined in a designated manner, again with implications under HIPAA. Usually springing powers make little sense, because a competent principal always can repudiate an errant agent's actions, and because an agent who is not trustworthy should not be selected to represent an incompetent principal. Nevertheless, springing powers are popular because principals often don't want to relinquish control until they absolutely must, or don't really trust the agent they have selected. It remains to be seen whether HIPAA issues will diminish their appeal.

Typical durable powers broadly authorize the attorney-in-fact to deal with the principal's property the same as could the principal (e.g., to buy, sell, exchange, lease, mortgage, etc.). In most states, however, durable powers do not automatically authorize the agent to make gifts of the principal's property, or to alter estate planning documents. Thus, a specific authorization in those areas may be appropriate, particularly if the principal has a taxable estate and wants to authorize the agent to make tax motivated transfers.

As between the two options, the revocable trust may be preferable because the trustee holds legal title to the client's assets, in trust. Generally, trustees deal with third parties with respect to trust assets more easily than do agents under durable powers of attorney. Banks, stock transfer agents, insurance companies, and other institutions tend to be concerned that the durable power may have been revoked (particularly if it was not executed recently), and they may ask to review the power of attorney to ascertain whether it authorizes the agent's action. A revocable trust also has the advantage of avoiding probate of trust assets. This advantage can be significant in jurisdictions in which estate administration is fully court supervised, or for clients who own real property in more than one state. Otherwise, as discussed in Chapter 4 at page 18, it is not likely to be a major consideration.

On the other side of the equation, durable powers of attorney are cheaper and easier because no inter vivos asset transfers are required. Transferring assets to a revocable trust can be time consuming and costly, and may raise questions that a durable power of attorney avoids, such as whether (1) a transfer of mortgaged real estate to a revocable trust triggers a due-on-sale clause, (2) the insurer of a car or home must be notified of the transfer and the trust added as an additional named insured under the policy, (3) the transfer of a home affects any available property tax exemptions (such as homestead), or (4) the transfer of a partnership interest or stock in a closely held business to a revocable trust is permitted by the governing partnership agreement or a shareholders' agreement for the corporation. In short, durable powers typically are plenty effective in smaller situations.

Planning For Health Care

Some competent clients use inter vivos trusts or property management powers of attorney because they don't want to manage their own property (for example, because they are going to travel for an extended period of time). But health care powers of attorney typically are used only if a client actually is (or expects to become) incapacitated. The plan of choice is a durable health care power (also is known as a health care proxy or a medical directive). A health care power may broadly or narrowly authorize the agent to make health care decisions for the principal. Some state statutes also permit a health care power to authorize the agent to decide whether life-sustaining treatment should be withheld or withdrawn. Otherwise, living wills are always permitted to address that issue.

A *living will*, also known as an *advance directive*, addresses questions involving life-sustaining treatment. Some states prescribe with some specificity the form that must be used and the circumstances under which living wills are respected. These parameters are extraordinarily important because the document may not accomplish its intended purpose if it does not meet statutory requirements. Most statutes authorize living will decisions only if the patient is in a terminal condition or a vegetative state from which there is no realistic hope of recovery.

In other states a living will is not effective unless the maker is comatose or brain dead. In those states someone who is in a terminal condition but awake (even if incompetent or severely handicapped) is not protected by an otherwise valid set of instructions under a living will. Some states also restrict when execution must occur — for example, only after the maker became terminally ill (the notion being that, until then, you may not really know what you want). A person who is competent until entering a permanent vegetative state (such as from an automobile or other accident) apparently cannot execute a binding living will in such a jurisdiction.

A person's right to enforce living will directions may be protected by a statutory requirement that an attending physician who is not willing to terminate or withhold treatment must refer the patient to another physician who will. Absent such a statute, however, enforceability of living wills also is a problem because some medical professionals simply will not respect them (often out of respect for human life or fear of litigation). As you can see, then, in some jurisdictions the living will simply is not reliable — there are just too many ways it can fail its intended purpose. Although a client who does not want to be kept alive in a terminal condition or a persistent vegetative state should *have* a living will, a health care durable power of attorney may be more reliable and effective to accomplish the desired objectives.

Further, living wills address only the issue whether life-sustaining treatment should be withheld or withdrawn. Durable health care powers of attorney can address all health care decisions that may arise if the principal becomes incapacitated from any cause, at any time, and with any level of debilitation, regardless of the expected duration of the incapacity. For example, if the principal is unconscious from an accident and needs surgery, an agent under a durable power can consent to the procedure from which, if successful, the principal will fully recover. Thus, a health care power of attorney and a living will together are the appropriate planning package.

Finally, in many jurisdictions an organ donation designation routinely is made on the client's driver's license, rather than on a document prepared by a lawyer. In view of the shortage of organs for transplantation and the ability to save lives by donating organs, many observers believe that estate planning lawyers should use their unique role in counseling with clients to discuss organ donation and to assist them in becoming organ donors if they so choose. Often this is done with a separate document that clarifies the client's intent, explains to family members the client's objectives, and gives directions that check-the-box driver's license designations do not provide.

Spend Down Planning[2]

This final segment may confirm to you that planning in anticipation of Medicaid qualification is not likely within the province of most traditional estate planners, because typical estate planning clients have too much wealth. Medicaid qualification limitations are very low, and the effort required to spend down to meet them normally is more than your clients are willing to embrace. This especially is true because major changes made in 1993 eviscerated trust planning that disguised assets of clients otherwise too wealthy to qualify for Medicaid benefits. Since then Medicaid Qualifying Trusts, Supplemental Needs Trusts, *Pollak* Trusts,[3] and other techniques have evolved, and prior techniques were made obsolete. Although a few trust formats survive that will not disqualify an applicant for Medicaid or Supplemental Security Income (SSI) benefits, generally they are unacceptable to clients who wish to preserve significant wealth for private beneficiaries to enjoy after the applicant no longer is in need.

This topic involves legal and procedural rules and practice that are a rapidly moving target, subject to substantial and potentially frequent change, and to possible criminal penalties.[4] As a result, you should pay

---

2. Liberal use has been made with the author's permission of the more comprehensive article on this subject: Henkel, Medicaid Changes and Effective Planning for Your Client, 134 Trusts & Estates 26 (Dec. 1995). An extremely useful resource (notwithstanding its date) is Dobris, Medicaid Asset Planning by the Elderly: A Policy View, 24 Real Prop., Prob. & Trust J. 1 (1989).

3. See Pollak v. Dep't of Health & Rehabilitative Services, 479 So. 2d 786 (Fla. Dist. Ct. App. 1991).

4. Legislation adopted in 1996 (and significantly amended in 1997) added 42 U.S.C. §1320a-7b(a)(6), providing that it was a criminal act to "knowingly and willfully dispose[ ] of assets . . . in order . . . to become eligible for medical assistance . . . if disposing of the assets results in the imposition of a period of ineligibility. . . ." Although a number of interpretations of this provision were possible, it was thought that Congress' intent was to prevent intentional asset transfers followed by a strategic application for benefits during an ineligibility period, hoping that the spend down transfers would not be discovered. This "Granny goes to jail" provision was amended to become a "Granny's advisor goes to jail" provision because it was limited to anyone who "*for a fee* knowingly and willfully *counsels or assists* an individual to dispose of assets . . . in order for the individual to become eligible . . ." (emphasis added).

No period of ineligibility is imposed if application is not made within a look-back period. Thus, legitimate planning appears to include asset transfers followed by a delay in making application for benefits until expiration of the appropriate three or five year (depending on the nature of the transfer) look-back period. In addition, by virtue of the 1997 amendments, it appears that no sanctions will apply unless the counseling or assistance was knowing and willing and for a fee, in addition to the previously imposed

careful attention to legislative and regulative developments. Moreover, because in the main these are state administered programs, there is no substitute for reviewing local variations as well as the underlying federal law. Indeed, the devil in much of this is that state-by-state enforcement is spotty and inconsistent. Techniques that allegedly work in some states are not regarded as effective in others, notwithstanding that each state purports to administer the same federal rules. This area is a quagmire.

An example of the quagmire is how Medicaid qualification operates. The applicable statute looks at the combined assets of a married couple. This renders asset transfers to a spouse ineffective to qualify one spouse for coverage while preserving their collective assets for the use of the other spouse (and ultimately for their intended beneficiaries). Wealth that exceeds established limits must be exhausted (spent down) before either spouse may apply for Medicaid, and unauthorized asset transfers made within a look-back period measured from a determination date may cause a period of benefits ineligibility.

The look-back determination date occurs when an individual both is institutionalized and has applied for Medicaid benefits. 42 U.S.C. §1396p(c)(1)(B). In most cases the look-back period is 36 months, but it is 60 months if an uncompensated asset transfer is made to a third party *from a trust* created by the Medicaid applicant or *to a trust* from which no income or principal may be distributed to the applicant. 42 U.S.C. §1396p(c)(1)(B)(i).[5] Thus, asset transfers involving trusts made within five years before a determination date will be considered in the ineligibility period computation.

Care is required here, because many observers misperceive that the *penalty period* is 60 months. It is the *look-back period* that is 60 months. The period of ineligibility could be many months more (or less) than that. The period of ineligibility is calculated by dividing (1) the aggregate uncompensated asset transfers made during the 60 month look-back period

---

requirement that it be with the purpose of becoming eligible for assistance, and a period of ineligibility actually is imposed.

Moreover, New York State Bar Ass'n v. Reno, 999 F. Supp. 710 (N.D. N.Y. 1998), granted a preliminary injunction against enforcement of this provision in the context of allegations that the statute constitutes an unconstitutional infringement of free speech and is invalid due to vagueness regarding the required intent (in the context of transfers with multiple purposes). A subsequent action challenging the rule was rejected as not presenting a cognizable case or controversy, absent objectively reasonable fear of prosecution, because the Attorney General had informed Congress of her unequivocal opinion that the statute was unconstitutional and had commanded U.S. attorneys not to investigate or prosecute alleged violations. See Magee v. United States, 93 F. Supp. 2d 161 (D. R.I. 2000). So, there may be less risk involved in advising clients in this arena today. Still, the last word on this issue may not have been written, and cautious advisors may continue to steer a wide berth around the provision by (at a minimum) advising clients to wait out the entire five year ineligibility period after making a potentially disqualifying transfer and before making any application for benefits.

5. If income or principal could be distributed *to the applicant* the trust would be a countable asset and it would preclude qualification for benefits. In 1999 somewhat parallel amendments were made to the Medicaid qualification rules that affect the even more limited entitlement to SSI. See 42 U.S.C. §1382b(c)(1)(A), which also uses a 36 month look-back period.

by (2) the average monthly cost of private nursing facility services in the applicant's community at the time of the Medicaid application.[6] 42 U.S.C. §1396p(c)(1)(E). The number produced by that division is the number of months of ineligibility, and a large transfer divided by the average cost could result in a period of ineligibility of many years.

The key to avoiding a substantial ineligibility period is to make unauthorized transfers involving trusts more than 60 months prior to the anticipated determination date, which requires some guess work as to how much wealth to retain on which to live during the 60 months following the last uncompensated transfer. There are exceptions to these rules for transfers to the recipient's spouse and minor or dependent children, transfers to certain family members under certain circumstances,[7] and transfers that were meant to be for full fair market value or that were not made with the intent to qualify for Medicaid.[8] None of these is likely to be of much use in the typical spend-down asset transfer context.

In determining need, revocable and irrevocable trusts created by or on behalf of a Medicaid applicant typically are regarded as countable assets to the extent distributions may be made to the applicant. 42 U.S.C. §1396p(d). There are, however, three exceptions to this rule, known as the (d)(4)(A), (d)(4)(B),[9] and (d)(4)(C) trusts, of which only the first and last are regarded as potentially useful. The generally accepted terminology for each is "special" or "supplemental" needs trusts (both abbreviated SNT and called a "snit") without distinction. Some commentators distinguish by name between these, based on who creates them. A 42 U.S.C. §1396p(d)(4)(A) trust may be created only for a disabled person who is under the age of 65 at the time of creation and funding, and only by that person's parents, grandparents, legal guardian, or a court. The (d)(4)(C) trust *also* allows trusts created or funded at any time by any of those parties *or* by the individual.[10] Often these trusts hold the proceeds from tort

---

6. The average cost of private nursing services varies from one jurisdiction and time period to another. The SSI penalty period calculation is similarly computed by dividing the prohibited transfer amount by, in this case, the transferor's combined monthly federal (and any state) SSI payment, but the penalty differs in that the period cannot exceed 36 months. 42 U.S.C. §1382b(c)(1)(A)(iv)(II).

7. 42 U.S.C. §1396p(c)(2). The similar, corresponding SSI exceptions are found in 42 U.S.C. §1382b(c)(1)(C).

8. 42 U.S.C. §1396p(c)(2)(C).

9. The (d)(4)(B) variety of trust often is referred to as a *Miller* trust after Miller v. Ibarra, 746 F. Supp. 19 (D. Colo. 1990), and is the subject of Issue Memorandum Concerning Miller Trusts After OBRA 1993, Elder Law Advisory No. 38 (May 1994), describing a government position not found in 42 U.S.C. §1396p(d). There is no corresponding *Miller* trust exception for SSI purposes. These trusts are used purely to avoid disqualification of a beneficiary in an "income cap" state that regards income in excess of specified amounts as a disqualification. These trusts may provide income that is not subject to the income cap calculation to the extent these court-created trusts pay income for nursing facility services or equivalent care. It is unlikely that this exception will provide much affirmative planning opportunity because of the manner in which these trusts are created, the limited use of the resource itself, and their modest function (to avoid the income cap limitation).

10. See also 42 U.S.C. §1382b(e) for the aligned SSI version of these rules.

litigation, but our concern is use for family wealth management and transfer.

A (d)(4)(A) trust differs from a (d)(4)(C) trust primarily in that the A trust remainder after a disabled person's lifetime enjoyment may provide for private beneficiaries. First, however, the trust must repay any Medicaid benefits provided to the disabled beneficiary during life, but any excess funds remaining after that repayment may be distributed to beneficiaries of the trust settlor's choice. A (d)(4)(C) trust is essentially a pooled fund managed by a nonprofit association that *either* reimburses the state *or* may retain the funds remaining after the disabled person's death for the nonprofit's own qualified programs.

Either trust permits safety net benefits for a disabled individual, without disqualification for Medicaid or SSI. To qualify, these trust distributions cannot be in lieu of *basic* governmental (or legally obligated family member) support. Instead, these trusts provide for items *in excess of* basic entitlements — hence the terminology "supplemental" needs: these are "luxury," quality of life, or added benefits. Trust drafters may hobble but not preclude distributions for food, clothing, or shelter that would reduce or supplant benefits otherwise available.

The primary problem with these trusts is that typically all or most of what remains after the recipient's death will not pass to private beneficiaries. Either it is distributed to the state in repayment or it is kept by the nonprofit that administered the (d)(4)(C) trust. To this extent the wealth is not preserved for other private parties, making these trusts of limited utility to many clients. They still may be desirable, however, because they provide a safety net for a disabled individual and because repayment by the trust to the state typically is a smaller amount than if the beneficiary had been totally under private care (because the state likely pays less for similar services) and is without interest (meaning that these essentially turn the state into an interest free lender of the cost of needed basic services).

For most estate planners these tools provide little opportunity for attractive results, and what little you now know about them should suffice to permit you to refer appropriate cases to Elderlaw specialists who traffic in this highly convoluted arena. (And you know they say the same thing about estate planning!)

Chapter 15

DEATH AND DYING

The emotional aspects of death and the process of dying typically are not addressed in estate planning materials, notwithstanding that both topics involve an unavoidable and highly charged experience for all involved parties. As an estate planner you will need to appreciate these emotions to better understand the immediate legal needs of your terminally ill clients and to help them and their survivors deal with the emotions that surround the estate planning process. This Chapter briefly examines death in contemporary American culture, including the so-called "stages" of dying. It also discusses bereavement and what you might expect when working with survivors.

Death

Estate planning anticipates death and what the client wants to happen thereafter, but death is an uncomfortable topic for many clients and their attorneys to confront. In part this is because death in America often is institutionalized and dehumanized. The majority of all Americans will die in a nursing home, hospital, or similar institution. By segregating the dying from the mainstream of society, we have made death more unfamiliar, frightening to discuss (let alone experience), and difficult to comprehend. The unfortunate reality is that, according to experts, many terminally ill individuals die feeling lonely and isolated. Some are shunned or even abandoned by family and friends, all because culturally we are not comfortable with death.

Moreover, all but unexpected deaths have been made into clinical experiences. People no longer simply die of old age. They die of heart disease, cancer, renal failure, pneumonia, staph infections, and other clinically defined conditions. For many people, death is not about the individual as much as it is about the individual's physical condition, with an emphasis on the medically defined causes of death rather than the emotional process of dying.

Worse, as medicine advances life expectancy, some people place blame if the dying individual did not embrace the gospel of proper health care (eating right, exercising, and doing what the doctor orders). The result can be the creation of a new breed of sinners: the smoker, the obese, the AIDS victim, and others who "could have been saved" from dying by advances of modern medicine or a change in lifestyle. Today it is not uncommon to blame the dying for not doing what they could to prevent their deaths. Compassion is reduced, and some terminal clients are made to feel guilty about their impending death.

Death also has changed for survivors. We no longer have a standard routine to cope with death. Public mourning is not common, and many of us have little experience with bereavement. Indeed, some studies suggest that the human unconscious cannot even conceive of an end to life and that many humans consciously reject the very concept of mortality. See DEATH AND DYING: A QUALITY OF LIFE 13 (Pegg & Metze, eds. 1981). As a result, it is natural (and maybe unavoidable) to focus on life and to reject death. In the process, we tend to isolate and abandon the terminally ill because they remind us of our own mortality. Consciously and unconsciously we are uncomfortable dealing with people who are dying and accepting the fact that we are unable to prevent death (theirs and, ultimately, our own).

To illustrate this, consider how modern customs deny or disguise mortality. Death is surrounded by euphemisms. People do not die; they "pass away" or the doctor "lost" a patient. The "dearly departed" are cared for by a "funeral director," we view them in a "slumber room," and make-up is used to make the decedent appear at rest. Condolence cards rarely contain the word "death" or any permutation of it. Even estate planners frequently deny death by using expressions like "*if* you should die" (as if there were any doubt) or "when you can no longer provide for your family." We subtly seek to soften the reality of death by disguising it or pretending that it does not exist. Unfortunately, indulging in the use of euphemisms to make clients more comfortable may disregard the effect of fear and ignorance about death and may suppress intense and complicated emotions rather than dealing with them. See Shaffer, DEATH, PROPERTY AND LAWYERS 117 (1970).

Estate planners who can confront their own feelings about death are better able to help clients deal with the estate planning process. You could become as comfortable talking about death and dying as you are in discussing wills, trusts, taxes, and gimmicks designed to move wealth at the least cost. To help you recognize and confront your own emotions about death, please consider the following list of questions.

- How would you feel about working with a terminally ill client?
- If it were your responsibility, how would you tell a client that he or she was terminally ill, and how would that discussion make you feel? How would you want someone to tell you of your *own* terminal illness?
- How would you want people to interact with you if you were terminally ill?
- If you have experienced the death of someone close to you, what were the unexpected aspects of the dying process and your relationship with that person?
- How do you feel at funerals? Indeed, have you been to many?

- How do you want people to act and feel when you die? If one end of a continuum was perpetual mourning and the other was total disregard, where on the continuum would you want your survivors to be?
- Do you agree with the following statements and, if so, what do your reactions mean to you as an estate planner?
  - You expect to feel very uncomfortable when talking to or being around a dying client.
  - You don't know what to say to clients who know they are dying.
  - You doubt that you could make a client more comfortable with the fact of rapidly approaching death.
  - You worry about becoming too fond of a dying client and not being able to control your emotions.
  - You can't imagine anyone as free of the fear of dying.
  - You think people should not be told they are dying; there's no point in adding to their suffering.

With respect to this last issue, in the early 1900s physicians thought it best not to tell patients they were terminal. Some physicians no doubt still prefer not to tell their patients, although today most patients are well informed. Many terminally ill patients who are not told of their illness probably discover it anyway. Indeed, even terminally ill children often learn about their treatment and the prognosis of their illness, although parents, the medical community, and others may try to hide that information. See Backer, Hannon & Russell, DEATH AND DYING: INDIVIDUALS AND INSTITUTIONS 143 (1982). Any effort to hide the fact may only hinder the process of accepting death and may lead to distrust and feelings of isolation by the client.

With knowledge of the situation, a client can begin to deal with the emotional aspects of death, address estate planning needs, avoid beginning projects that cannot be completed before death, and pursue plans so often put off until it is too late. As a consequence, even though estate planners usually are not the appropriate person to tell a client about a terminal diagnosis, if disclosure has not been made you may need to encourage others to inform the client (although it would not be appropriate unilaterally to violate the family's or doctor's confidence by revealing that information yourself to the client).

Many people share the anxiety of having to talk to and interact with dying clients. With practice, many become more comfortable with terminally ill individuals, learning that saying the "right" things is not difficult if you are sensitive and honest, considering what you would want to hear if you were in the client's position. Becoming close to and showing emotions about a dying client may help the client feel more comfortable; it also might help you to accept death and become more comfortable with the dying process. See Epstein, NURSING THE DYING PATIENT: LEARNING

PROCESSES FOR INTERACTION 4-18 (1975). Until you become comfortable dealing with and discussing death, you may inadvertently silence your dying clients, which could make them feel unsupported, and you may discourage them from conveying relevant information to you.

Stages of Dying

The following material is only a primer about the process of dying. It alone cannot make you skillful in working with the terminally ill or bereaved, but introspection, experience, and observation of others who deal effectively with the process will improve your sensitivity and skills. Elisabeth Kübler-Ross, a psychiatrist with an expertise in working with the dying and the bereaved, first outlined the stages of dying in ON DEATH AND DYING (1969). Because dying is a unique process that drastically alters an individual's behavior, it helps to remember that no exact scientific formula applies. Thus, a terminally ill individual may not go through the stages in the same order as Kübler-Ross presented, may return to a stage, or may skip one. Nevertheless, a discussion of these stages is useful here because the typical terminally ill client will go through this process, and so will family and friends, albeit usually at a different time or pace.

Stage One: Denial

Kübler-Ross reported that most individuals who learn of a terminal illness respond first with denial. During this stage the individual refuses to acknowledge the terminal illness, displaying characteristics such as refusing to talk about the illness or talking about and planning for a future significantly beyond a realistic life expectancy, participating in strenuous activity, or consulting several physicians in hopes of finding one who will disagree with the terminal diagnosis. Notice that diagnosis shopping may actually demonstrate that, on some level, the patient knows the truth, because an individual who truly thought the first physician was wrong might not spend the time and money seeking another professional opinion.

You need to know how to interact with an individual who is in denial. One effective method may be to simply listen to them, sending a message that you will not shun or abandon the client. This may foster a greater desire in the client to cooperate in the planning process and may help the client move beyond denial (because reportedly one reason individuals deny death is that they fear abandonment). A second important technique is to avoid telling a terminally ill client to "stop denying reality" or making other comments with a judgmental tone that may make the client feel rejected. A fear of abandonment, exacerbated by judgmental and critical comments, may cause the client to withdraw, which then leaves you impotent to create an appropriate estate plan.

Stage Two: Anger

The anger that often follows denial acknowledges that death is approaching. Now the client asks "why me" (or, more accurately, because we all eventually will die, "why now"). Inability to answer these questions may produce anger, rage, envy, or resentment. Those around the terminally ill during the anger stage discover that most everything they do evokes a hostile reaction. Here again the individual's response may stem from a fear of abandonment, the anger being a ploy that is used because it is hard to ignore someone who is enraged. Paralleling the denial stage, many terminal clients cease to respond with hostility once they realize that they will not be shunned.

To interact effectively with an angry client, you may need to make the individual feel respected, understood, and important, to show that the client remains worthy of your time and attention. Thus, it is important not to rush the client. In addition, because anger is contagious, you must avoid becoming irritable while working with an angry dying client. You must possess enough self awareness to recognize this response and to control the situation, which is difficult because people often are less tolerant of a terminally ill individual.

For example, research demonstrates that healthy people tend to remain at a greater distance when talking with the dying than when talking with other healthy individuals, symbolizing their lack of acceptance, affection, and desire to associate with dying individuals. Epstein, NURSING THE DYING PATIENT: LEARNING PROCESSES FOR INTERACTION 5 (1975).

> *Hypothetical*: Assume that a terminally ill client is in the anger stage. The past few times the client came to your office, he or she complained about everything from treatment by relatives and physicians to the color of the couch in your waiting room. The client called you yesterday but you were unable to return the call until today, at which time the client launched into a tirade about your being incompetent and unresponsive and complaining that the plan should have been finished long ago. You feel frustrated and the client is angry. What can you do to diffuse the situation?

The first key is not to escalate the acrimony. Angry reactions may enable others to justify their outrageous behavior. It might help to explain why you were delayed if your timing in returning the phone call appears to have caused the client's outburst. In addition, you might remind the client about your early communications explaining the estate planning process and the communications and progress a client can expect. Although it may seem difficult, you may discover that discussing subjects other than illness or the estate plan will minimize outbursts. In addition, try to remember that people find it difficult to maintain anger when treated with interest, kindness, and respect.

Besides trying your patience during the anger stage, a terminally ill client may want to make rash or irrational changes to the estate plan. See Schlesinger, *Dealing with the Dying Client*, 9 U. MIAMI INST. ON EST. PLAN. ¶200 at 2-34 (1975). Imagine, for example, that a hospitalized, terminally ill client contacts you to draft a codicil excluding the client's spouse because "he [or she] doesn't care about me anymore" or "she [or he] never visits me during the day." You both know that the spouse works and cannot visit during the day, so you ask the client a number of questions to discover why he or she really is upset, and what the client actually desires.

Some questions you could use to start a revealing discussion might include obvious inquiries about the spouse's job and when he or she does visit, but also consider asking questions about what the client wants to become of their possessions after death, why the client wants certain people and not others to have those assets, and how the client really feels about the spouse. Questions like these may help the client realize that irrational requests flow from anger that is unrelated to the estate plan, all without your making judgments about how the client should feel or who should be the client's beneficiary.

If the client actually admits to being angry, then you may respond in a manner that reveals your understanding and sensitivity to the client's thoughts and feelings. Many people who feel anger in this situation come to accept that the time and cause of their death is illogical and arbitrary. Your role is to work with the client in reaching this acceptance.

Stage Three: Bargaining

In the bargaining stage, a terminally ill individual seeks to negotiate for more time to complete unfinished business by promising something in exchange for life until a specified time, often a special event like a graduation or wedding. The promise may relate to something about which the individual feels guilt, such as not honoring religious customs, or the bargain might be to contribute a certain sum of money to a particular cause.

Bargaining should concern you because most estate plans should not represent the client's irrational effort to bargain for time. Nevertheless, if the client reveals a bargain, you should not respond in a manner that makes the client feel silly, and you must avoid being judgmental.

The most important aspect of dealing with a bargaining client is to avoid making the client whose bargain stems from guilt feel even greater guilt. Frequently this occurs if no one takes the bargaining seriously, which sends the client a message that the subject is taboo or unacceptable and may compound the original guilt with anguish for trying to negotiate regarding death. If the client is unsure about the propriety of bargaining, your refusal to listen with sympathy may imply that the bargain was not a proper approach even though it is a normal response to terminal illness.

> *Hypothetical*: Assume your client feels guilt about not being religiously active. The client, who is in the later stages of terminal cancer, requests an amendment to the estate plan you prepared, diverting assets from the client's spouse or children to a religious organization. How would you advise this client?

First, you probably should avoid conveying a message that you think the change is inappropriate. Instead, try to offer alternatives, such as devoting some time now to a religious purpose, making a more modest donation, or perhaps creating a split interest trust for family members and passing only the remainder to charity. In these ways you might show the client other methods to alleviate feelings of guilt, remind the client that there still is time to be useful, and help the client prioritize obligations and the bargain.

In addition, you will remind the client that it is proper to provide for surviving family members and, if necessary, you may need to inform the client of the right of a spouse or pretermitted child to elect against the will. Avoiding these topics usually is preferable, however, because they deny the client's sense of control in what may be a desperate emotional period. The client probably will feel happier if he or she maintains the present plan without feeling coerced.

Stage Four: Depression

When bargaining passes, frequently the next stage is depression, with the dying often experiencing two different types of melancholy. The first is "reactive" depression, during which the individual becomes depressed about their loss of health, the inability to perform tasks, and the creation of financial burdens. During reactive depression the terminal client may respond to the environment and remain concerned about daily living. This may be the last time the client has an active interest in helping you because, during this stage, the client's primary concern often is the family and the burden the illness places on them. Individuals who before their illness provided for their families, either as the "breadwinner" or "homemaker," often are more susceptible to these feelings. Thus, such a terminal client may find it reassuring to know that their family is coping well and that there are enough assets to provide for their needs. You can play an important role here by reassuring the client that the family burden will be minimized through estate planning.

After coming to terms with reactive depression, the individual must confront "preparatory" depression, which comes from mourning the impending loss of family and friends. This resembles the form of depression that accompanies changing residences, although it can be much more severe because, with impending death, the loss of friends or family is permanent. Expressions of sorrow are natural and usually beneficial in working through this stage. Indeed, when working with a client during preparatory depression, you should refrain from using "look at the bright side" expressions because they send a message that the client should not think about death. This is nearly an impossible task when an individual is surrounded by reminders of death, and it would be unreasonable to discourage clients from talking about the most predominant aspect of their daily existence. In the end, an individual must think about death to accept it.

Stage Five: Acceptance

During the final stage, acceptance, terminally ill individuals may become somnambulant, taking brief naps several times a day, and may prefer to see only a few visitors. They also may show little interest in the details of daily living. The important point about this stage is that the individual cannot reach acceptance if family, friends, and professionals do not allow them enough space and quiet. Sometimes professionals and family members try to push an individual to stay interested in the outside world, but at this stage a terminally ill individual might prefer to just talk a little or pass the time quietly. By not allowing the individual a peaceful environment, a visitor may be perceived as refusing to let the individual die or pretending that the individual will get better. The visitor also may be revealing their own disquieting fear of death.

Terminally ill individuals often need "permission" to die in peace, free from guilt. Talking as though the patient will get better may be perceived as denying permission to die. More useful may be communication in which all parties accept the situation, with survivors demonstrating an ability to function after the individual's death. Someone who tells a terminal person that "I will never make it without you" may create feelings of guilt about dying, which blames the individual for something that cannot be helped.

Estate planning during the acceptance stage can be difficult because terminal individuals in this final stage often lack interest in the orderly transmission of wealth. Although the terminal client may want nothing more than to pass time peacefully, you may want to concentrate on the need to finish tasks. During this stage you properly might convince an individual to sign a previously planned will, but numerous ethical issues may need resolution if the client lacks a complete estate plan and the family calls you to do it. For example, does a terminally ill individual who has no interest in what will happen to his or her estate after death have the requisite capacity to sign a will and, if not, is planning for such a client ethical? See Chapter 3 at page 51 for a discussion of this type of question.

Some terminally ill individuals in the acceptance stage are willing to demonstrate their knowledge of their assets, the natural objects of their bounty, and how the two relate, but estate planners working with clients who reach the acceptance phase often face difficult decisions regarding capacity. Each situation will require that you use special discretion. Overreaching and duress are particular concerns as well, if the client is so intent on passing peacefully that he or she becomes susceptible to pressure to resolve unfinished business.

Fear

At work during all phases of dying are fears that most dying individuals experience. Many terminal individuals fear being viewed as hopeless and then becoming isolated. Anyone who has been close to a terminally ill individual before the illness should consciously act to avoid making the individual feel shunned. This may include you if the client and you were well acquainted prior to the illness.

Many dying individuals also fear what will happen after they die. You will offer a unique service that may allay some of this fear, in part by giving the client a degree of immortality through dead hand control. The estate plan ensures that the client's family will be provided for monetarily, and it can express feelings about various beneficiaries. A person the client felt particularly fond of may receive a large bequest, a person who shared something with a client may receive a bequest related to their mutual interest, and clients who cannot vocalize their love and gratitude to their family may use the estate plan to express their emotions when the will is read after death.

Grief and Bereavement

In addition to dealing with dying clients, estate planners also frequently deal with bereaved survivors, typically when assisting in the administration of an estate or in drafting a new estate plan for a survivor. Thus, it helps to understand grief and bereavement, especially because our death-denying culture makes it difficult to mourn and express grief.

Bereavement can take many forms and may vary depending on the survivor's relation to and perceptions of the decedent. For example, many survivors experience sorrow if the decedent was perceived as a good person but relief if the decedent was perceived poorly or became a burden during the dying process. Indeed, many survivors perceive elements of both good and bad in the decedent, resulting in a combination of sorrow and relief that can generate confusion and guilt, or conflict. In addition, if the survivor was dependent upon the decedent for emotional, monetary, domestic, or other kinds of support, feelings of helplessness and fear may affect their emotions, particularly if the decedent was the principal person in the survivor's life, such as a spouse of a lengthy marriage. Despair over replacing that relationship often produces anxiety and depression, even if the survivor has a good support system in the form of other family or friends. Finally, an individual's grief may be influenced by how the decedent died, especially if the death was sudden or violent and therefore unexpected, in which case bereavement may be prolonged and more intense.

Grieving survivors often also suffer physical reactions, including lack of appetite, insomnia, gastric irregularities, headaches, weakness, exhaustion, and general physical malaise. Bereavement may produce restlessness that is most readily observable in an inability to pay attention or maintain consistent activity, or in excessive activity that seems to lack a purpose or direction. For example, the survivor may not pay attention when concepts are explained, may fail to complete necessary tasks in the estate administration or planning process, and may seem irritable, withdrawn, or distant. This also may occur because the survivor is afraid to establish close relationships for fear of becoming vulnerable again to the same kind of loss. None of these symptoms should cause immediate alarm unless the survivor is totally adrift or does not seem to be improving.

Some survivors exhibit symptoms that reveal a serious problem in dealing with bereavement. It is not unusual for a grieving survivor to dream about the decedent or speak to or feel the presence of the decedent. Some even adopt the decedent's mannerisms or experience physical symptoms of the illness that caused the decedent's death. None of these behaviors necessarily is abnormal if experienced temporarily, but they may be reason for concern if they persist or become more extreme. Moreover, any mention of suicide should be taken seriously, as should incapacity flowing from grief or extreme behavior such as exhausting levels of activity, a total loss of interest in the outside world, or irrational anger regarding the cause of the decedent's death. Although it is a difficult judgment call when a survivor needs professional help, you should be sensitive to these types of distress signals.

Bereavement, like dying, is a different process for each individual and may last for different periods of time. Still, the mourning process can be divided into four distinct stages, similar to the stages of dying. The first requires acceptance of the very reality of the decedent's death. Usually this occurs quickly, most survivors realizing that the decedent is dead and gone. Few mourners continue "talking" to the decedent or feeling the presence of or dreaming about the decedent after accomplishing this task. The second stage is when the mourner experiences the pain of grief, including loneliness, melancholia, and despair. This stage may last much longer and only as it nears completion are many survivors able to talk about the decedent without great effort or distress. Third, the survivor must adjust to a new life without the decedent, learning to do those things the decedent did for the survivor and generally finding ways to cope. This process often takes place along with the fourth, which involves withdrawal of emotional energy from the grieving process and reinvesting it in other activities and relationships that are not just substitutes for the survivor's loss.

The most difficult aspect of your role in the probate setting may be advising and consoling the decedent's survivors. The ability to deal with clients who are in shock and suffering volatile emotions may prove more important than a mastery of postmortem techniques and procedures. The following advice is offered in Leimberg & Plotnick, *What a Probate Attorney Must Know about the Psychological Aspects of Death and Dying*, 32 PRAC. LAW. 33, 40-41 (Oct. 1986):

Remember that the depression, unhappiness, insecurity, loneliness, or even anger of the family members involved should not be taken personally;

Don't force survivors to behave according to your preconceptions. Start where they are and work at their rate of

receptivity. Don't rush major decisions; planning as far ahead as possible alleviates most problems;

Make the proper decisions financially, legally, and ethically, even if you think making these decisions might provoke angry confrontations at some time in the future. Emotionally distraught beneficiaries are often tempted to do things that they would not do in a more stable emotional state;

Explain what you are doing and why. Be particularly clear about how long things will take and why. The more information you can provide and the better informed you can keep the executor and family members, the less likely you are to have problems with them.

Do not be provoked into anger. There will be times when you will be met with unreasonable hostility. Other times you will not be able to convince the executor to make the rational decision, or even any decision until it is too late to avoid some type of legal penalty or problem. In those cases be sure to document your suggestions and keep copies of your correspondence;

Take the time to care and show you care. Often a letter to clients explaining, in lay terms, what their responsibilities, potential pitfalls, and solutions to those pitfalls are will go a long way toward establishing the lawyer's compassion credentials;

Serve as a neutral outsider. Listen to the family's concerns, wishes, and needs and remember your capacity as a counselor may be as important as, or even more important than, your role as an advocate;

Examine your own feelings about death and dying. Your goal should be not to become more brave, but rather to become more human . . . .

Skills

As this Chapter illustrates, complex human emotions often surface when clients meet with estate planners, which makes the ability to deal with those emotions an important part of the estate planning art. Most successful estate planners have learned to feel comfortable hearing personal problems and helping clients confront their emotions in ways that facilitate problem solving.

A number of useful suggestions about this process can be found in D'Andrea & Salovey, PEER COUNSELING: SKILLS AND PERSPECTIVES (1983). For example, because estate planning should be a nonjudgmental endeavor, it is important to avoid sending critical messages to clients who are not acting rationally during the dying or bereavement process. People find it difficult to be honest if they are being judged or their actions are being critiqued, even if they know they make little sense. Avoid asking "why" questions or otherwise putting the client on the defensive by implying that you are seeking an explanation or justification of emotions and decisions rather than merely an elaboration.

As in most areas of the law, but especially in estate planning, ultimately the client must make the fundamental decisions that affect the dispositive provisions or influence postmortem planning, and usually should be allowed to feel comfortable with those choices, even if you are not. Estate planners who are judgmental dissuade clients from doing what they want, in an effort to appease the estate planner or avoid criticism. With dying clients, for whom there may be no second chance to revise the plan, it would be a travesty to influence a client's adoption of a plan that is not what the client really wants.

Unfortunately, there is a very fine line between educating a client and exploring options (which is appropriate counseling and maybe even obligatory) and inappropriate lobbying for (or to avoid) a particular result. Although estate planners often believe they know the best solutions to common problems, clients must be allowed to reach their own conclusions. Figuring out what the client really wants is a slow process, but you must remain patient and let the client decide. This can be particularly difficult if the client is terminally ill, but it is no less important.

In a related vein, usually it is best to refrain from giving personal advice unless specifically asked. Even then, clients who ask "what would you do" or "what do most people decide" usually are looking for help in weighing various options rather than really soliciting votes. In these cases, it is most useful to help the client generate and evaluate alternatives from which to choose, rather than offering a solution that is "best" for the situation.

Second, although you will want to protect your ability to move forward with effective counseling by avoiding personal emotional involvement in a client's emotional dilemma, you need to make it clear that you empathize with the client's feelings and are anxious to help the client deal with them. Make sure the client knows these emotions are not improper topics and that it is normal to feel them and to have trouble wrestling with them. Persuade the client that feelings that are not identified and openly confronted keep re-emerging, which eventually prevents accomplishment of the tasks that need completion.

Some clients may need more help in their emotional battles than you can provide. Suggesting that a client seek professional counseling can be a delicate matter. Some people believe that seeing a therapist carries a stigma, that it implies they are weak, abnormal, or bad, and it may make them think that you are unwilling to work with them personally. Some may view a suggestion to consult a professional counselor as an insult rather than a genuine effort to provide assistance.

Nevertheless, estate planners who deal with death and dying, grief and bereavement, have occasion to recommend additional help. Be prepared for this by thinking about how you would make such a recommendation and by compiling a list of professionals in your community who specialize in helping people cope with death and grief. The list might include social workers, psychologists, psychiatrists, doctors who specialize in medical problems that are related to stress or emotional turmoil, and members of the religious community who regularly consult with troubled individuals. If you lack such a list, a client who is receptive to your suggestion to seek assistance might feel disserved and may question whether you really are sincere about trying to deal with these problems.

In all of these matters, it is essential that you convey genuine concern and avoid giving the impression that you are just trying to push the client's problems out the door. It may be helpful to offer to schedule the first appointment with another professional, and it is important to follow up on the visit, which would remind the client that these are not taboo subjects and that the ability to confront emotions about the dying or bereavement process is essential to the task you have undertaken together. Allowing the client to know that other clients have benefited from therapy, and that you are prepared to work with the client while he or she goes through the dying or grieving process, lets the client know that these emotions are normal and that the client is not alone. Making a therapy referral can be a difficult task, but some clients are best served by professional help and cannot effectively continue the estate planning or administration process without it.

Additional Sources

You may find additional reading in these areas difficult to acquire in the libraries you normally frequent, so here is a short list of some sources that should be easy to find and that may be useful to you.

Backer, Hannon, & Russell, DEATH AND DYING: INDIVIDUALS AND INSTITUTIONS (1982).

Buckman, "I DON'T KNOW WHAT TO SAY . . ." HOW TO HELP AND SUPPORT SOMEONE WHO IS DYING (1992).

Epstein, NURSING THE DYING PATIENT: LEARNING PROCESSES FOR INTERACTION (1975).

Hansen ed., Frantz volume ed., DEATH AND GRIEF IN THE FAMILY (1984).

Kastenbaum, DEATH, SOCIETY AND HUMAN EXPERIENCE (2d ed. 1981).

Kavanaugh, FACING DEATH (1972).

Kübler-Ross, ON DEATH AND DYING (1969).

Kübler-Ross, QUESTIONS AND ANSWERS ON DEATH AND DYING (1974).

Pegg & Metze, eds., DEATH AND DYING: A QUALITY OF LIFE (1981).

Schlesinger, *Dealing with the Dying Client*, 9 U. MIAMI INST. EST. PLAN. ¶ 200 (1975).

Schoenberg, Carr, Peretz & Kutscher, eds. PSYCHOSOCIAL ASPECTS OF TERMINAL CARE (1972).

Shaffer, DEATH, PROPERTY AND LAWYERS (1970).

Simpson, THE FACTS OF DEATH: A COMPLETE GUIDE FOR BEING PREPARED (1979).

Tallner, Prichard, Kutscher, DeBelis, Hale & Goldberg, eds., THE LIFE-THREATENED ELDERLY (1984).

Worden, GRIEF COUNSELING AND GRIEF THERAPY: A HANDBOOK FOR THE MENTAL HEALTH PRACTITIONER (1982).

Conclusion

You may have noticed many similarities between this Chapter and the first in this book. In a sense we have come full circle. Notwithstanding all the tax and other technical mumbo jumbo that affects and often drives estate planning, in the final equation estate planning is about people and their feelings: about wealth, about death and inheritance, and about families and other beneficiaries. I hope you come to feel as comfortable with the human equation as you do with the technical side of the profession, and that you are successful and find fulfillment in the process.

Chapter 16
THE BIG PICTURE

As a way of wrapping up our study it may be helpful to stand back and look at the big picture regarding estate planning. There are truths and some truisms, maxims and objectives that may come to you only after years of experience, but some may resonate with you now that you've had a chance to gaze at this endeavor.

Most of what we've focused upon in this book is the techniques of estate planning, but not entirely. And in the final analysis the art of estate planning is more significant to clients than the science of it. Many professionals are competent to cobble together the documents of transfer and to select from among various tools available in the estate planning arsenal. Ultimately what will distinguish you from someone who just peddles paper and procedures is the ability to see what your clients want, determine what they and their beneficiaries need, and then exercise good judgment in marrying those wants and needs in a palatable and effective manner. After all, most beneficiaries would prefer to just receive the wealth outright (thank you very much!), and their benefactors would like to avoid all taxes or other interference with or constraints on their desire to preserve the wealth and govern how it will be enjoyed (the golden rule of wealth: those who have the gold get to make the rules). We know that often those are not consistent nor even viable goals or approaches, which makes all this such a challenge.

Objectives

Through the dual prisms of conflict avoidance and goal achievement, we can see at least half a dozen negatives that good estate planning seeks to avoid, and as many affirmative planning goals that it seeks to accomplish. In addition, for the small slice of the population subject to the wealth transfer tax, there may be another half dozen tax related notions to keep in mind. Consider:

Negatives to Avoid

Probably first on any person's list of things they would abhor is the loss of personal freedom that attends incapacity. Clients with wealth worry about their own inability to attend to their affairs, and they worry also about the possibility that their beneficiaries will be unable to manage wealth or to care for themselves. The typical answer to these fears is to create a plan today in contemplation of incapacity, providing a safety net in case the need arises.

Often for a client with real wealth this means creation of a self-trusteed declaration of trust or, for those with more modest means, execution of a durable power of attorney for property management. All clients also likely will favor execution of a durable power of attorney for health care. A living will also is useful and, due to widespread publicity and misuse of terminology, clients often believe that this is the document they want or need, and you'll certainly provide it as well.

Related to incapacity is improvidence, imprudence, or just plain inexperience, usually of beneficiaries in the management of wealth. Just as clients want to protect against their own inability to deal with their estate as they age, they want to provide management and protection until their beneficiaries have reached a maturity and level of experience, and sometimes for their entire lives.

A second concept that dovetails into the first is that hardly anyone wants their affairs to be subject to court supervision. If a personal representative (guardian, conservator, or other fiduciary) is needed, the loss of autonomy implicit in their obligation to the court that appoints them usually is regarded with disfavor. But not always: on occasion the factions vying for control of a situation inform the use of a disinterested intermediary who has the full support and authority of the judicial system. But ordinarily that oversight causes delay and second guessing that does not benefit the family, it entails a public scrutiny that is difficult to restrain, and it may follow an embarrassment (in the public forum) of establishing to the court that someone is unable to manage for themselves. As little as most folks care to know about another family's troubles, those who are in the middle of such a situation routinely feel the glare of public illumination and seek to avoid any semblance of the publicity that can be generated by a court supervised administration.

That said, it may be necessary to engage the services of special advisors who can assist with investments, management, and determinations of appropriate invasion or distributions. This need not involve a court appointed representative or fiduciary, but a third objective is to avoid the disadvantages that may flow from an unsatisfied need for outside assistance.

Fourth, as appropriate as may be some supervision or assistance, hardly anyone wants (or even needs) overlapping fiduciaries. For example, there typically is no need for a trust settlor to have both a trustee and a guardian, or for an estate to undergo ancillary administration (a second probate, such as would be required in a state in which vacation or investment realty is located). So avoiding the inconvenience, the disruption, and the added cost of overlapping fiduciary administration typically is desirable.

Fifth (and without a doubt first on the list of many clients) is avoiding taxes to the fullest extent possible. Let's remember that tax minimization is not an ultimate good that can be attained without cost: the client's entire estate could be left to a qualified charity and all taxes could be avoided. So the trick here is to minimize taxes with an acceptable level of cost. While we're at it, let's also be sure to consider minimization of both federal *and* state transfer taxes. The latter often get overlooked, notwithstanding that frequently they are the easiest to address. And they are becoming more prevalent.

Finally, those clients with a family business seek to avoid interruption or ultimate failure of the enterprise on account of death. Succession planning is a critical element of any successful plan for the business owner.

Affirmatives

The former are things to avoid. They're not nearly as fun or gratifying as the positives that clients seek. On the affirmative side of the ledger are another series of goals that frequently apply.

For example, it is easy to predict that many clients want a more intuitive or sensitive disposition of their estate than intestacy. Selecting among natural objects, engineering an age for distribution or incentives for good behavior, all are easy to appreciate.

And so is preservation of wealth for natural objects of the client's bounty, several generations removed, without dissipation by predators (such as creditors, tax collectors, plaintiffs in tort cases, or new spouses who may be feared sometimes as the "gold digger" or "gigolo" in terms of how the client feels about the next spouse of their surviving spouse (or even of their children)).

Third is supporting dependents, whether they be a spouse, children, or aging dependent parents. Clients don't want to think of their loved ones engaged in spend down planning to qualify for meager public benefits if they have enough wealth and it can be settled in a manner to protect those who they are supporting during life.

At the same time, many clients want to target disposition of certain assets to or away from certain beneficiaries. Wanting equality of entitlement is not the same as wanting every beneficiary to have an equal share of every asset. Most folks know which property they want to go to which beneficiary, particularly if one or more is instrumental in the operation or preservation of certain particularly favored assets (such as the family business, or realty).

A fifth objective is to provide flexibility, to plan affirmatively for changes in needs and concerns. We know the technique of choice is the second look opportunity provided by well drafted powers to appoint. This too is easy and very desirable planning.

And finally (but potentially viewed as a negative to avoid rather than a positive to accomplish) is the desire to provide spendthrift protection and defer possession of inherited wealth until a beneficiary is situated for outright enjoyment. For example, can any sensible professional (such as you) who stares at the risk of malpractice liability dislike the opportunity for their inheritance to be placed in the gilded cage of a spendthrift trust, where it may be enjoyed and kept free of claims? It may not always be the right choice for the law to favor inherited wealth over the claims of meritorious litigants, but to parties involved in estate planning this is one of the most desirable aspects of common law trusts. If you personally receive an inheritance in trust, you likely will thank the thoughtful planner who insured it against your professional foibles, because we're all going to make mistakes and many of us are going to be sued for them.

Taxes

And then there is the other certainty in life! We haven't figured out how to avoid death, but good estate planning for the sliver of the population subject to taxation is literally worth its weight in the gold that is preserved. There is nothing wrong or distasteful about making certain that clients pay no more than their fair share, as defined by law. And sizeable opportunities are afforded without going out on the limb of aggressive planning or questionable techniques.

In this regard it is wise to remember in the current environment that both state and foreign death taxes should be considered, along with the more ubiquitous federal wealth transfer tax. Shifting appreciation with estate freezing techniques is essentially a thing of the past, but closely related planning remains viable, such as paying tax with frozen value assets or accelerating the payment of tax to benefit from reduced effective rates. Certainly the shelter of both spouses' unified credits or generation-skipping transfer exemptions, and taking maximum advantage of the annual exclusion, all make sense in any situation in which taxes otherwise might be a burden. Don't forget income tax savings, and most important: always keep an eye on liquidity needs, either by engineering deferral (such as with the marital deduction or §6166 installment payment) or by striving to convert illiquid investments over time to make it possible to pay tax with the least disruption or financial strain.

Maxims

Over the years four fundamental notions often impress themselves on experienced estate planners. They are of such global significance that they might rightly be regarded as guiding principles or maxims of estate planning.

One is a reality that you already have witnessed in your lives, probably in a college classmate or perhaps even in law school, to say nothing of reading the papers or watching the news. Witness highly paid stars of sports, entertainment, or industry who have been injured by success. "Nothing destroys like too much money." It may be the scourge of thwarted ambition, the destructive nature of the habits of excess, or the lure of money that invites the attention of predators. You need only document the countless disasters that have visited winners of the lottery to see that, particularly in one not well prepared for its demands, the sudden acquisition of wealth can be an especially destructive force. It can be moderated, and beneficiaries can be "groomed" for the demands that it can create, but without proper planning and consideration of its negatives wealth is one of the worst things that can happen to a person. Good estate planners understand both the very positive things and the very bad consequences that attend to wealth, and try to foster the former while minimizing the latter.

A second notion is that a good plan provides maximum flexibility. It should be an extension of the donor's pocketbook, in the sense that the wealth will be used in the same well reasoned ways that the client would personally employ if still alive. If circumstances change and needs must be met, the good plan should provide the means to satisfy those desirable goals in as close to the same manner as if the wealth owner still was alive and able to act.

Third is that tax planning should never overshadow the appropriate plan. "The tax tail should not wag the family planning dog" by causing undesirable dispositions or discouraging results that the client otherwise would want. A good question to always ask early in an estate planning engagement is what the client would want done with the wealth if there were no outside influences like taxes or other restrictions. Then see how close to that desired plan the situation can be brought with a minimum of dissipation (through unnecessary taxes or other "costs"). Jumping through hoops with devices that no one would select were it not for the desire to minimize taxes often proves to be a fool's errand.

Finally, something that a newly minted estate planner can hardly apply but that experience will teach you is critically important: the traditional KISS principle ("keep it simple, stupid"). Or, to put it more mildly, it seldom is desirable to employ fancy techniques and use all the sophisticated gimmicks at your disposal if a more straightforward or simple technique will do just as well. As you acquire the skills of the best of the trade you will itch to use them, but frequently the situation just does not call for the heavy artillery that you have acquired. Try always to employ the least invasive techniques and literally to put yourself in the place of the client, who typically is not as enamored of your skills and toys as you are. It is tough, to have acquired a wonderful tool that will accomplish so much, and not to break it out and use it at every possible opportunity. But that literally is what prudence often recommends: be careful about what you use, and when, so as not to overwhelm the client or the situation.

Estate Planning Top Ten List

A number of years ago a newspaper reporter asked what the average "client on the street" ought to consider doing (or not doing) in terms of preparing an estate plan. In no particular order this is the "top ten" list that resulted. Read it as if you were the potential estate planning client, and consider how it coincides with your own notions of what an estate planning advisor should recommend that a client consider.

First, *determine what you own*. It sounds silly, but do it like Santa: make a list, check it twice. Be sure to include assets that you don't currently enjoy but that will benefit your survivors (e.g., life insurance and retirement benefit death payments), and nonprobate assets like jointly held property or property transferred into a revocable inter vivos trust. Remember that most people are worth more dead than alive; don't *just* consider your walk around wealth.

Next, *verify title*. Don't take anyone's word for it. Instead, actually ascertain who owns what. Be sure the title is accurate and in the name you thought. You'd be surprised how many people think they alone own property and find that it is held in joint tenancy with someone else (like a spouse - or ex-spouse! - or parent). Or folks who created an inter vivos trust for probate avoidance purposes, only to discover that they never transferred any assets to the trust.

Also *ascertain beneficiary designations*. Again, don't assume you know who has been designated as beneficiary of your insurance, retirement benefits, or other nonprobate assets. Is there a trust in place and was it properly designated as the beneficiary? What does your current will provide? Don't guess! Get out the documents and read them. Don't be surprised if the plan makes no sense to you anymore, or if it is outdated, in terms of your current situation and desires.

Now *ascertain values*. Many people underestimate the value of their net worth because they low-ball the value of assets. Sometimes they don't know the value at death (for example, many life insurance policies will pay double or even triple indemnity for an accidental death; if you are young and don't expect to die, you might want to assume that the accidental death payout will be the one your beneficiary is likely to receive). Be conservative by considering what the government would say is the value (e.g., for a closely held business, don't take the maximum valuation discount you hope your estate might be able to justify). Plan for your worst case, not the most favorable.

Consider the dispositive plan you would want if there were no taxes to avoid or minimize. There is no sense letting the tax tail wag your estate planning dog if the result you get really isn't what you want. Approach your planning with the notion that you want to come as close as possible to the disposition you have in mind, with as few modifications as necessary to accomplish the tax objectives that are in the realm of reason in terms of the changes they impose on your desires.

Evaluate liquidity. If your estate were to mature tomorrow, how would your personal representative pay the taxes owed? Would it require a sale of assets you favor or want to preserve for a particular beneficiary? If so, consider whether you want to acquire more liquidity through the purchase of life insurance or by making some portion of your wealth more liquid.

Decide whether you want to (and when) begin to *maximize your wealth*. Not through employment or investment decisions (you probably do that every day) but through such things as exercising options to purchase stock or more life insurance without proof of insurability, or putting more money in tax deferred vehicles like an IRA. But before you opt for more tax deferral techniques, also run the numbers on what the taxes will be when that money ultimately is received, by you or your beneficiaries.

If you are married, *consider when you* and your spouse would *prefer to pay any tax* that will be due on your aggregate wealth. In this regard, don't assume that deferral of the tax is best. A common "time-value-of-money" justification for deferral is exactly wrong for wealth transfer tax purposes (although you get to use Uncle's money during the surviving spouse's overlife, you will not earn back enough to offset the difference in tax generated by the delay). You might decide to defer payment for lots of good reasons (e.g., because the survivor of you is concerned that there won't be enough wealth to live on, you think maybe Congress will repeal the tax before the survivor dies, or because the survivor will make gifts during his or her overlife, which is the cheapest way to move wealth for transfer tax purposes). But don't be suckered into using the marital deduction to defer tax on the theory that you'll come out ahead. In most cases you will not, unless it just happens that the marital plan works an equalization of the wealth you own so that both of your tax benefits (like exemptions or credits) are fully used.

Think about *fiduciaries*. Often the most difficult choice in the estate planning process is who should be guardian of your minor children, who is capable of being your personal representative, is anyone trustworthy to be the holder of a durable power of attorney for property transfers, and (if a trust is involved) who would be the right long-term selection for the role of trustee. You might decide not to use a trust because you can't identify anyone better than your beneficiaries to manage the property (or you may decide to name the beneficiaries as trustees — that's okay, although it requires careful drafting to accomplish the trust purposes).

Finally, consider with your estate planner the package of *documents* that you want drafted to accomplish your desires. Do you want or need a trust? You will need a will in all events, and perhaps an irrevocable life insurance trust would be appropriate. At the same time be sure to request a durable power of attorney for health care and perhaps another for property transfers. Would you like organ donor cards, a living will, or perhaps prepaid funeral arrangements?

Take note that almost everything you read about in the papers involving estate or trust litigation is a function of planning or devices that made no sense to someone. Don't chase after (or be badgered into) techniques that gratify the planner more than you or your beneficiaries, and remember that most things that seem too good to be true usually are. Unless you want to benefit your attorney or tax advisor with fees paid now (and again later when the controversy arises), think hard about whether to be a bit more conservative. And where family controversy is involved, keep in mind that greed brings out the worst in people, and inequality makes beneficiaries crazy. If you plan to play favorites, consider leaving a note that explains why you thought it was appropriate, and be sensitive to the feelings of your survivors.

There is plenty of prejudice and personal opinion in that list, some of which you may embrace and other things about which you may disagree. Here at the end of our study is a good time to confront your particular quirks and feelings about the recommendations we all make, especially to consider whether they flavor your vision of the undertaking and the advice you would give. Because, after all is said and done, what you are dispensing is guidance and advice, not just (and hopefully not primarily) documents and gimmicks. In that regard, the talent that separates routine advisors from those that clients clamor to engage is the judgment and wisdom they bring to the table. For most of us that is an acquired commodity, often taking a lifetime to accumulate. The following collection is intended to give you a head start.

Estate Planning "Judgment"

The collection below is not the sort of thing that a pinheaded academic sitting in the ivory tower could offer without the substantial assistance of seasoned and savvy practitioners. And so it is that this list has been expropriated without shame from wise advisors who have been willing to share. Not any of us could hope to accumulate this much knowledge in a lifetime of practice, but we all can benefit from the collective wisdom. Use it well and prosper in your practice.

- Saving taxes isn't that important in the overall scheme of things. It becomes even less important the closer your client gets to death.
    - Your clients are not going to pay the *estate* tax. Their beneficiaries will.
    - Married couples don't need an estate planner's help. Most estate planning is for the benefit of the second generation (not the client *or* the client's spouse).
- Assume that your client won't return for a new will/trust (or even for a check up) for a decade. But draft as if they will die tomorrow.
- Assume that your client won't read anything you send for review. Some will, many will not, and most of those who do will not read carefully.
- Don't take your client's word (or that of other advisors) for anything that you can verify with little investment in time or other costs.

- There is pain for everyone in practice economics. Balance cost against competence and adjust your bill (if necessary) rather than cut corners.
- Know how much complexity the client can tolerate.
  - One of the hardest things any estate planner must learn is: don't use the $10 plan when a $2 approach will work.
  - Write documents with simple terms, titles that make them easy to understand, flow charts that illustrate concepts, client memos in plain English. Make it easy for clients who don't read documents to appreciate what they are doing.
  - Learn to explain complex issues in a simple and concise manner. It isn't easy!
  - Don't push your client into a plan that requires more record keeping or administration than the client wants (or is able) to handle.
  - Many individuals will fail to keep fiduciary or partnership accounts properly and probably will commingle assets or otherwise defeat the plan. So, create a letter explaining what the client needs to do, use a tickler system, and perform due diligence follow ups.
  - An estate plan that doesn't work is worse than no estate plan at all.
- It is okay to be creative, but don't be the first kid on your block to try any new gimmick. Be willing to get out front if you're satisfied that a strategy works, but remember: "The second mouse gets the cheese."
- Care as much that other respected professionals respect your work as you do about what your clients think of it.
- Don't create an estate plan that doesn't make sense, even if that is what the client wants.
- Walk away from trouble, including any client who is not honest or open.
- Don't sell snake oil:
  - Don't sell product if it means you cannot maintain your independent judgment. After all, the only thing you really have for sale is your credibility and integrity.
  - Think hard about the advisors, marketers, and clients you align yourself with. You *are* known by the company you keep.
  - Don't "sell" anything (including services) if all you're doing is "churning." (An exception is doing needed documents early, even if you must redo them later when all elements of the total plan have congealed.)
- A good question to ask yourself about the planning you propose (or that the client requested) is whether it is something you would recommend to your own family.
  - Be realistic about what you're creating.
  - Be realistic about what your clients *say* they want.
  - Remember that clients can tolerate disappointment, but not surprises.

- Keep your eye on the ball: don't overlook the primary objectives of any engagement.
- Remember the easy stuff! It is so easy to overlook basic, safe planning like annual exclusion gifts, the ed/med exclusion, tax exclusive gifting, lifetime equalization, early and complete use of both unified credits, fractional interest discounts, etc.
- Pay attention to demographics:
  o The average American will have more spouses than children.
  o Half of all marriages will end before death.
  o Over one-third of all births in America are nonmarital.
  o A growing percentage of children will die *before* being orphaned.
  o Think about the time of greatest need for wealth: children at 30 with a young family and a new career are far more in need than those who become orphans at age 60 or 70 when their surviving parent dies.
- Pay attention to trends in the law, and in life:
  o The new biology and adoption: children on demand, at any age, to anyone. Consider their impact on the plan you draft.
  o Modern portfolio investing: there is a changing paradigm in the tension between income and remainder beneficiaries.
- Establish rapport with your clients and "get to know them" in terms of such things as how their family works, where the torpedoes are buried, what issues are divisive.
  o Don't put bickering children "in the same rowboat" and expect them to reach any destination by working in concert.
  o Visit a client's business. You will enhance your relationship and credibility, and learn more about subtle issues than you can ever learn sitting in your own office.
- Look for the discomfort and pay attention to the subtle clues. Practice with your senses: by *ear* and *sight* and sense of *"smell."* Trust your instincts and intuition.
- Run the numbers, but don't be driven by them.
  o Know ballpark figures. The client may need estimates to make informed decisions. But remember that the numbers usually are no better than just a guess.
  o Always determine how the client will pay the tax. Think liquidity first *and* last.
  o Beware of planning that works only in a rising market.
- It may work to adopt tactics/tricks developed by others, but it never works to mimic someone else's style. Do your own thing.
- Mistakes cannot be avoided by a "never apologize and never explain" approach.

- The better course is to be forthright in virtually everything. Be truthful when the mistake is obvious. How you handle the mistake will say the most about you.
- Nobody likes someone who is hiding something. And clients have less trouble suing advisors they don't like.
- "When you're already in a hole, stop digging!"

- Don't make your client's problem *your* problem. Be sure that you are not an advocate whose proposals carry a representation that will take you down with the client's ship.

- Malpractice and bad ethics go hand in hand, and usually neither is about knowledge or brainpower. Instead, good judgment (good business practices and a sensitivity to the situation) will protect you from both.

Chapter 17

A BRIEF INTRODUCTION TO THE INCOME TAXATION OF ESTATES, TRUSTS, GRANTORS, AND BENEFICIARIES

The estate, gift, and generation-skipping transfer taxes are the items Congress addressed in 2001 with the slated repeal of the estate and generation-skipping taxes in 2010 (returning in 2011 unless Congress changes that sunset, or the repeal itself). The gift tax remains in all events, as does the topic of this abbreviated overview of the other federal tax system that applies to trusts and estates and therefore to our study of estate planning: the income taxation of estates, trusts, grantors[1] and beneficiaries.

Fiduciary entities are subject to passthrough or conduit taxation (similar to S corporations and partnerships, essentially as if the entity did not exist), but only for some income tax purposes. But for most income tax purposes estates and trusts are treated as separate income tax paying entities. The income tax provisions that apply to estates and trusts, and to their grantors and beneficiaries, are found in Subchapter J of the Internal Revenue Code, and for that reason most experienced planners simply refer to "Subchapter J" as shorthand for the title of this Chapter.

In addition to the normal need to know about and to comply with the income tax, these rules present various options and considerations that largely constitute the postmortem estate planning done by many estate and trust attorneys. They likely were ancillary (or totally ignored) in your basic trusts and estates and income tax courses. So we need to undertake this brief foray because this tax influences a variety of basic estate planning decisions.

Estates and trusts file annual income tax returns (Form 1041) and may incur income tax on net earnings, capital gains, and other income that is not distributed currently to their beneficiaries. On the other hand, they are treated as conduits to the extent they pass "distributable net income" (DNI) to their beneficiaries. DNI is a term of art, created by the tax law to serve a limited but pivotal role in the income taxation of estates and trusts. It limits the entity's "distribution deduction" and it identifies both the amount and the character of current income attributable to the beneficiaries for taxation in the current year.

In most respects income that is distributed currently to beneficiaries has the same character (tax exempt, capital versus ordinary, preference items for alternative minimum tax purposes, and such) in the beneficiaries' hands

---

1. The income taxation of grantor trusts is a separate subject of this corner of the tax law that is addressed briefly in this chapter at page 14. Those rules are very complex, arcane, somewhat inconsistent, and generally relevant only to sophisticated planning for lifetime income tax purposes and not for more traditional estate planning goals.

as it would on the fiduciary's return if it was not distributed. But the character of items accumulated by the entity in one year and distributed in another is not preserved. So timing distributions and comparing relative tax brackets are not the only factors that influence fiduciary decisions about whether to accumulate income or the proper time for distribution.

Because estates and trusts are subject to their own unique set of income tax rules, any comparison to passthrough entities or pure conduit taxation is an inexact generalization, and the operation of Subchapter J can become complex and technical. Nevertheless, its basic operation is relatively simple, and this discussion will reveal it in that light.

Taxable Income

The taxable income of an estate or trust generally is the same as it is for an individual taxpayer. See §641(b). The principal difference is the income tax deduction allowed to the entity under §§651(a) and 661(a) for distributions made (or required to be made) to beneficiaries. With very few exceptions, distributions are treated as carrying out current DNI regardless of whether the distributed amount on the fiduciary accounting ledger actually is current or accumulated income, or principal.

In computing taxable income, estates and trusts are denied the §151 personal exemption afforded to individuals but are allowed the §642(b) deduction in lieu of the personal exemption, granted in various amounts, all much less than the amount granted to individuals. For example, the deduction in lieu of an estate's personal exemption is $600, and the amount allowed to a trust is either only $300 or $100. There is no standard deduction or zero-bracket amount for fiduciary entities because §63(c) also does not apply to an estate or trust. Thus, every dollar of an estate or trust's net taxable income is subject to tax at the rates found in §1(e), which by far are the most onerous applicable to any taxpayer under the Code. Otherwise, with few exceptions, an estate or trust is permitted the same deductions allowed to individuals.

Two variations that influence customary estate planning are §§642(c) and 642(g). The former is a deduction granted in lieu of the §170 income tax deduction for charitable contributions. It allows an estate or trust to deduct any amount of its gross income that is paid for a charitable purpose or use, without limitation based on the type of property transferred or the nature of the recipient charity. The latter limits expenses of administration that are allowable as estate tax deductions under §2053 but that also may qualify as income tax deductions under §§162, 163, 165, or 212 (or as a reduction of the sales price in determining gain on the disposition of assets). Sometimes known as the "swing item election," §642(g) requires the decedent's personal representative to elect whether to take an income tax or an estate tax deduction (or some of each) with respect to these items. The object of §642(g) is to preclude use of the same expenditures to work double duty, once under each of the estate and income taxes.

Distributable Net Income

The concept of distributable net income is unique to the income taxation of estates and trusts. Its primary purpose reflects something you learned in the basic income tax course. You remember that §102(a) provides an exclusion from gross income for gifts and bequests, but §102(b) specifies that any income produced by the tax free gift or bequest is taxable. Similarly, if income producing property is placed in a trust, neither the transfer into the trust nor any subsequent distribution of the trust corpus constitutes gross income, but income distributions *are* taxable. In that vein, the beneficiaries of a fiduciary entity are taxed on their distributive share of any *taxable* income of the entity. So we need to know whether a distribution is income (§102(b)) or corpus (§102(a)), and we also need to know the tax exempt character of any estate or trust income that is distributed.

DNI addresses the statutory challenge of determining the extent to which distributions to beneficiaries are tax free distributions of corpus (or of tax exempt income) and which are distributions of taxable income. This identification process is more complex if distributions are made to multiple beneficiaries, especially if the nature of their beneficial interests vary (for example, income and remainder beneficiaries). Distributable net income is the device that determines the extent to which distributions to various beneficiaries are taxable. This role is both limiting and limited. DNI limits the amount of distributions that may be treated as taxable income to the beneficiaries. §§652(a), 662(a). It limits the maximum income tax deduction allowed to an estate or trust under §§651(a) and 661(a) for distributions made to its beneficiaries. And it also provides the basis for allocating various classes of income among the beneficiaries. §§652(b), 661(b), 662(b), and Treas. Reg. §§1.652(b)-2, 1.662(b)-2.

Known as the character rules, this last aspect is important because a distribution treated as *income* to a beneficiary is not necessarily *taxable* to the beneficiary, depending on the tax character of the item distributed (for example, interest from a state or municipal bond that is exempt from tax under §103, as opposed to taxable corporate bond interest). This character rule has the effect of treating the entity as a conduit through which income flows from its original source to the beneficiaries. Various classes of income are allocated ratably among beneficiaries according to the amount of DNI received by each (unless the governing instrument specifically allocates different classes of income to different beneficiaries, which is quite uncommon because it requires that the allocation have an economic effect independent of the income tax consequences of the allocation). See Treas. Reg. §1.652(b)-2(b).

Determining DNI

DNI is defined in §643(a) as the taxable income of the estate or trust, with a number of adjustments. The first is the §643(a)(2) "add back" of the amount of the deduction in lieu of the personal exemption, allowed under

§642(b) in computing taxable income. By this increase, distributable net income is larger than taxable income, meaning that a larger distribution deduction is available to the entity for current income distributions. In addition, a larger amount is subject to inclusion in the taxable income of the beneficiaries who received distributions. In each case the result flows from the fact that distributable net income is a cap on the deduction and on the inclusion rules. The consequence of this add back is to deny any benefit to the beneficiaries of the §642(b) deduction; it benefits only the entity.

The second adjustment is an additional add back, with a similar effect on DNI, dictated under §643(a)(5) for §103 tax exempt income. This adjustment permits this form of tax favored income to pass through to the beneficiaries by increasing DNI, and thus increasing the amount subject to inclusion at the beneficiary level. If tax favored income is distributed currently, the character pass through rules in §§652(b) and 662(b) permit the beneficiaries to enjoy the special status of income items that trigger this adjustment. Preservation of the tax exempt character also allows §265 (disallowance of certain deductions attributable to tax exempt income) to operate at the beneficiary level.

In addition to both add backs, three items normally considered in the determination of taxable income are ignored in computing DNI. Thus, the §643(a)(1) adjustment ignores the distribution deduction allowed by §§651(a) and 661(a). Because that deduction is limited to the taxable portion of DNI, an unavoidable circularity would develop if DNI were equal to taxable income after allowing for the distribution deduction: the deduction would be limited by DNI and DNI would be dependent for computation on the amount of the deduction. This rule just breaks that circularity.

The fourth and fifth adjustments relate to items of taxable income that are allocated to principal and not currently distributed. Thus, for example, under §643(a)(3) and Treas. Reg. §1.643(a)-3, capital gains allocated to corpus (under the terms of the document or under local law) are ignored for purposes of computing DNI. The effect is to reduce DNI and, correspondingly, to reduce the maximum distribution deduction, thereby causing these gains to be taxed to the entity in years in which they are not distributed to the beneficiaries. Similarly, applicable only to select trusts under §643(a)(4), certain dividends that are allocated to principal also are excluded from DNI, again reducing the maximum distribution deduction and causing the tax thereon to fall on the entity.

There is more complexity, but all you need to know is this: because of all these adjustments, fiduciary accounting income, taxable income, and distributable net income each may differ during any given year. In a sense a fiduciary will have three sets of "books" as a consequence. Also be aware of the §663(c) separate share rule by which substantially independent and separately administered shares of a single estate or trust are treated as separate trusts in determining the amount of DNI allocable to its beneficiaries. Consequently, activity such as accumulations or distributions in one separate share will not affect the tax consequences of activity in other shares, regardless of how many beneficiaries there are or whether separate books of account actually are maintained for the separate shares. §663(c); Treas. Reg. §§1.663(c)-3. What this means is that three sets of books may be maintained for tax purposes with respect to multiple separate shares, all within one estate or trust.

A final rule is important only for estate administration purposes (because only estates may have a tax year that is not a calendar year). Under §662(c) income that must be reported by a beneficiary and the time of its inclusion in the beneficiary's gross income are based on (a) the entity's income (b) for the entity's tax year that ends during the beneficiary's tax year. For example, if the beneficiary is on a calendar year (most individuals are) and the estate is on a fiscal year that ends on January 31, income distributed by the estate to the beneficiary on February 1 of year 1 is treated as the beneficiary's income in year 2 (the beneficiary's tax year in which the estate's tax year 1 ends — January 31 of year 2). This means that it will not be returned or tax paid on it until April 15 of year 3 at the earliest (unless estimated tax is being reported by the beneficiary, on a quarterly basis). This deferral opportunity has a downside at the end of administration, in which case a "bunching" of two years' worth of income may occur in a single year of the beneficiary. For example, in this illustration the prior year's income would be reported in the year of estate termination, plus the income of the year beginning February 1 and ending when the administration terminates in the same calendar year.

Because fiscal years are allowed for estates, careful attention is required to coordinate selection of the tax year chosen. This is just one item of postmortem tax planning customarily considered by the personal representative, and administration of even a simple, no frills estate can entail time consuming and often difficult details of this type that many planners, some fiduciaries, and most beneficiaries do not recognize or appreciate. Similarly, for both estates and trusts, some discretion exists in selecting when the last year of the entity will end for tax purposes, and care is required at that time as well.

Simple Trusts

Trusts are divided into two groups for income tax purposes. The terms "simple trust" and "complex trust" are not used in the Code, but they are common in tax parlance because they are used in the Regulations. See, e.g., Treas. Reg. §§1.651(a)-1, -2, -3; 1.651(b)-1; 1.652(a)-1; 1.661(a)-1. Most tax lawyers who are familiar with this area of tax law routinely speak in terms of simple and complex trusts, but in reality the distinction between them is of little significance since repeal of the accumulation distribution and throwback rules. With no exceptions of real merit, a simple trust and its beneficiaries would be taxed in an identical manner if the tax rules applicable to complex trusts (§§661-664) were applied. But the statutory provisions for simple trusts (§§651 and 652) are more concise, because much of the legislation originally needed for complex trusts need not apply to simple trusts.

In essence, then, the simple trust rules are the Reader's Digest version of the complex trust rules, stripped down to the bare essentials needed to deal with the form of trust that meets the requirements of §651(a): the trust (1) must distribute all current income annually, (2) must make no distributions for the year in excess of the amount of current income, and (3) may make no charitable distributions (or what are known as set asides).

The trust must *require* distribution of all income currently, but not all income actually must *be* distributed to qualify. That is, even if income is not currently distributed, the fact that distribution is required will satisfy the all income requirement. Treas. Reg. §1.651(a)-1(b). A trust might require distribution of income but not actually distribute it in a variety of circumstances. For example, often a trust's income tax year ends with income on hand that is not distributable until the next periodic income distribution date (monthly, quarterly, semi-annually, or whatever). This is proper administration of a trust and the Code recognizes it. Occasionally the beneficiary requests or authorizes a delay in the current distribution of income. Or the trustee may be unsure of the identity of the proper beneficiary and seek instructions while withholding trust income pending a judicial determination.

To avoid any change in the status of a simple trust in any of these events, the tax rule intentionally does not require actual distribution of all income annually. It also does not require specification of any given beneficiary's entitlement. For example, a trust requiring distribution of all income annually among a group of beneficiaries, in whatever proportions the trustee selects, would be a simple trust even though no single beneficiary has a guaranteed entitlement.

As to the requirement that there be no distributions in excess of current income, the trustee need not be prohibited from distributing amounts in excess of current income. Rather, the trustee simply must ensure that only income is distributed in a given year, thus allowing the trust to be taxed as a simple trust for that year. This imposes a burden on the trustee to carefully monitor distributions, because expected tax consequences may be lost due to inadvertent excess distributions. "Inadvertent" might seem to be an inappropriate term; you might think that even the most inexperienced trustee ought be able to tell whether a distribution exceeds income. Here, however, the difference between trust accounting income and income in a tax sense becomes important.

For simple trust qualification purposes, distributions made by a trust are income under §643(b) to the extent they do not exceed the amount of the current year's fiduciary accounting income. That is, "income" *means* fiduciary accounting income, as determined by the fiduciary in good faith under the governing instrument and applicable local law. Thus, Treas. Reg. §1.651(a)-2(a) recognizes the validity of reserves to which income may be allocated without constituting a failure to distribute all current income annually. Moreover, the *amount* of current income, rather than the actual identity of items received as income, is determinative for simple trust qualification purposes, regardless of the source of that distribution for trust accounting purposes. See §651(a) (last sentence, referring to "amounts of income" described in §651(a)(1)).

Thus, distributions not in excess of the current year's fiduciary accounting income are "income" for purposes of applying the simple trust rules, and it is the amount of fiduciary accounting income, not the actual source of the distribution, that the trustee must monitor to ensure qualification as a simple trust. So, for example, assume that a trust has income of $1,000 for the current year and is required to distribute all income currently. A distribution of stock held in the trust that has a fair market value of $1,000 would be regarded as a distribution of income, even though the stock was held as a part of trust corpus on the trust accounting ledger. However, questions about the value of that stock could make actual operation of these rules difficult in practice.

A trust that qualifies as a simple trust is taxed as a conduit. Effected under §§651(a) and 651(b) through the distribution deduction, resulting in a tax wash to the trust, distributions of fiduciary accounting income from the trust "carry out" DNI to the recipients of it. Those recipients correspondingly acquire the liability to pay income tax on the distribution under §652(a) and Treas. Reg. §1.652(a)-1. And a qualifying simple trust may deduct the amount of income it was required to distribute in computing its income tax liability for the year.

That deduction is subject to one limitation. To prevent a deduction larger than the trust's taxable income, which could put the trust in a loss position for tax purposes, under §651(b) the distribution deduction may not exceed distributable net income, computed without inclusion of the net amount of tax exempt income. Thus, Treas. Reg. §1.651(b)-1 requires reduction of DNI by the amount of tax exempt interest income specified in §643(a)(5). The effect of this adjustment is to limit the distribution deduction to the taxable portion of DNI. The tax exempt quality of the income is not lost, however, because it carries over to the recipients by virtue of the character rule in §652(b).

To beneficiaries entitled to receive required distributions of income the tax consequence of qualification as a simple trust is §652(a) inclusion in income of the amount allowed as a deduction to the trust, whether the income actually was distributed or only was required to be distributed. If distributions exceed the allowable deduction (because fiduciary accounting income is greater than the taxable portion of DNI), then each recipient includes a pro rata portion of the amount of the deduction, based on the total distributions made by the trust. So complete is the pass through of tax liability to the beneficiaries that, under §652(b) and Treas. Reg. §1.652(b)-1, amounts originally received by the trust retain their tax character (tax exempt income, capital gains, tax preference items, and so forth) when distributed to the beneficiaries.

Moreover, the character of all amounts included in DNI, both income (including tax exempt income) and deductions, effectively is allocated pro rata to the recipients by §652(b) and Treas. Reg. §1.652(b)-2 (unless that character is specifically altered by a provision of the governing instrument mandating non pro rata distribution of various classes of income). Discretionary non pro rata distributions of various classes of income do not alter this allocation. Treas. Reg. §1.652(b)-2(b)(1). And remember that all this is done with attention to separate shares, which often means there is just one beneficiary with respect to each separate share (and these proration issues become irrelevant).

In short, the overall effect of both the distribution deduction and the inclusion rules is conduit taxation that treats the beneficiaries generally as if the trust did not exist as an intermediary. The exception to this conclusion is the treatment of capital gains that are not treated under the instrument or local law as fiduciary accounting income: they are retained as corpus and taxed to the simple trust.

Estates and Complex Trusts

All estates, any trust that is not a simple trust for the year (because it either may accumulate income, provides for charity, or actually made distributions exceeding current income), and all trusts in the year of termination (because principal necessarily is distributed), are governed by the complex trust rules of §§661-664. The tax consequences to the entity and beneficiary essentially are the same as the conduit tax treatment of a simple trust to the extent income of an estate or complex trust is currently distributed (or is required to be distributed). The entity is entitled to a distribution deduction under §661(a), the beneficiaries include the deducted amounts under §662(a), and the character of each item in DNI carries through to the beneficiaries pro rata under §§661(b) and 662(b) (unless the governing instrument specifically dictates otherwise).

There is one difference between the distribution deduction for a complex trust and that for a simple trust. Neither deduction may exceed the amount of DNI (see §651(b) and the last sentence of §661(a)) as reduced by tax exempt income (see the last sentence of §§651(b) and 661(c)). But the amount of DNI will differ by virtue of application *only* to simple trusts of the §643(a)(4) exclusion from DNI of certain taxable dividends allocable to principal. This isn't very common, and for learning purposes it can be ignored if you want to embrace the notion that (otherwise) the simple and complex trust rules will produce the same result.

What *really* distinguishes simple and complex trusts (including estates) is that the latter may accumulate income and may make distributions of amounts in excess of the dollar amount of fiduciary accounting income (whether the distributed asset comes from fiduciary accounting income or principal). These distributions are deemed to carry out income to the extent of current DNI that is not exhausted by distributions of fiduciary accounting income. They can generate additional distribution deductions for the estate or trust, and they can require inclusion by the recipients under §662(a)(2).

To illustrate several differences between simple and complex trusts, assume a trust has $33,000 of fiduciary accounting income for the year, consisting of $24,000 of ordinary income and $9,000 of tax exempt income. The trustee is required to distribute all the income annually to B. If the trustee actually distributes more than $33,000 for the year, the trust would be a complex trust for that year. The distribution would carry out the $33,000 of DNI, of which $9,000 would be tax exempt to B and the trust would be entitled to a $24,000 distribution deduction (the taxable portion of DNI). No additional distribution deduction would be available to the trust for any amount distributed in excess of $33,000 (because all the DNI already was carried out to B). By way of comparison, if the trustee properly had distributed only $22,000 for the year, in this example the amounts distributed would be 24/33 × $22,000 of taxable income items and 9/33 × $22,000 of tax exempt income, and the trust would be complex by virtue of accumulating the income that was not currently distributed. B would include taxable income of 24/33 × $22,000 ($16,000) and report tax exempt income of 9/33 × $22,000 ($6,000), and the trust would deduct the full 24/33 × $22,000 ($16,000) of taxable income that was distributed. Further, the trust would pay income tax on the $6,000 of ordinary income not carried out or offset by the distribution deduction.

In-Kind Distributions and Specific Bequests

Under §643(e) distributions in kind from a complex trust carry out DNI only to the extent of the lesser of the distributed assets' adjusted basis or fair market value.[2] In addition, by §663(a)(1), excepted entirely from the income carryout rules applicable to complex trusts are transfers in satisfaction of a specific bequest, devise, or legacy if they are payable in

---

2. If a trustee wants to distribute $70 to a beneficiary, it could do so by distributing (1) an asset with a fair market value of $70 and a basis of any amount, (2) cash of $70, or (3) any combination of the two. Under §643(e) distribution of the cash will carry out up to $70 of DNI but a distribution in-kind will carry out no more DNI than the basis of the distributed asset. The justification for this limited DNI carry out is a feeling that it is inequitable to saddle a distributee with income equal to fair market value *plus* any unrealized appreciation represented by a basis that is lower than fair market value. Gain or loss may be realized under Treas. Reg. §1.661(a)-2(f)(1) by distribution of an asset in-kind, with a concomitant adjustment to basis (to fair market value) if the distribution is in satisfaction of the distributee's right to receive some other asset or cash. The income tax treatment is as if the proper asset or cash were distributed and then used to purchase the actual asset distributed, with gain or loss generated on that sale.

Because of this, the §643(e) rule does not apply to distributions governed by §§661(a)(1) and 662(a)(1) and to distributions from simple trusts governed by §§651 and 652 because those in-kind distributions are gain or loss realization events. As a result, fair market value and adjusted basis will be equal in the beneficiary's hands and DNI carryout will be that same amount (at least to the extent DNI is available for carryout).

less than four installments[3] and they are not required to be satisfied only out of income. To constitute a "specific" disposition, the identity of the property conveyed, or the dollar amount of a pecuniary gift, must be ascertainable as of inception of the estate or trust. Thus, formula bequests (for example, a marital deduction distribution that is tied to a concept such as a decedent's gross estate for federal estate tax purposes) do not qualify as specific bequests that will not carry out DNI. This is because they are dependent on variables (such as valuation and tax elections) that make them unascertainable at death or inception of the trust. Treas. Reg. §1.663(a)-1(b).

The Tier Rules

The principal difference between the taxation of simple trusts and the taxation of estates or complex trusts is attributable to accumulations of income in the latter. Only capital gains or other income properly allocable to corpus are taxed to a simple trust. All other income is offset completely by the distribution deduction and is taxed through to the beneficiaries. In a an estate or complex trust, income that is accumulated rather than distributed will be taxed to the estate or trust because the distribution deduction is less than the total taxable income and, thus, does not wash out the full amount of income for the year. By virtue of this essential difference, the estate or complex trust as a separate taxpayer permits fragmentation of income between the beneficiaries and the entity. At one time this made it possible to reduce the tax paid by all. Now, however, the current rate schedule taxes estates and trusts with just modest amounts of taxable income at the maximum income tax rate, so only a very modest potential reduction in tax is available by taxing some income to the entity and some to the beneficiary. Nevertheless, when the tax rates were more favorable it was recognized that this income fragmentation opportunity necessitated several concepts that do not apply to simple trusts.

Those concepts remain in the law but now they apply to virtually no cases. For reasons we do not need to explore, Congress has made those so-called accumulation distribution and throwback rules apply only to foreign trusts and certain old "multiple trusts." We can avoid them entirely here.

A concept made necessary by throwback that *does* remain in operation, however, is the "tier" rules. These apply in complex trusts because of those trusts' ability to accumulate income for later distribution. The term "tier" is not used in the Code or Regulations but is the accepted term of art that refers to the distinction drawn in §§661(a)(1) and 661(a)(2) between amounts of income required to be distributed currently ("Tier 1" distributions) and other amounts properly paid, credited, or required to be distributed ("Tier 2" distributions).

---

3. The terms of the governing instrument, not actual administration, are determinative in establishing whether payment is to be made in less than four installments. Treas. Reg. §1.663(a)-1(c)(1).

To illustrate, assume that a complex trust has $50,000 of fiduciary accounting income for the year but DNI of only $40,000 (due to a $10,000 income tax deduction for expenses that were charged to principal for fiduciary accounting purposes). Also assume that the trustee must currently distribute all income in equal shares to beneficiaries A and B, and that the trustee also makes a discretionary distribution of $50,000 to B. Without the tier rules it would appear that the $40,000 of DNI ought to be pro rated between A and B in proportions of $10,000 and $30,000 respectively, because A has received $25,000 while B has received $75,000 for the year. However, by virtue of the terms of the trust, it is apparent that A received half the current income, not just one-fourth, and should be taxed on half the DNI. The tier rules provide the mechanism for distinguishing between the various distributions to A and B to effect this treatment.

The technical definitions under the tier rules relate to distributions made by the trust. Under §661(a)(1), Tier 1 distributions are required current distributions of income (not in excess of DNI). So pervasive is the "required" distribution notion that, under §662(a)(1), a Tier 1 distribution is *treated* as having been made as required, resulting in DNI inclusion to the beneficiary, even if the distribution is not made in fact. Remember a similar rule with respect to required distributions in simple trusts. Under §661(a)(2) and Treas. Reg. §1.661(a)-2(c), Tier 2 distributions are all other distributions, whether required or discretionary and whether made from current income, from accumulated income, or from corpus.

In the preceding example, A and B are equal Tier 1 beneficiaries because the trustee must make equal current distribution of all income to them. Consequently, the $40,000 of DNI is pro rated equally between them under §662(a)(1) and Treas. Reg. §1.662(a)-2(b). Any DNI remaining after satisfaction of all Tier 1 required current distributions of income similarly would be pro rated under §662(a)(2)(B) and Treas. Reg. §1.662(a)-3(c) among the Tier 2 beneficiaries on the basis of their Tier 2 distributions. In the prior example, the $50,000 distributed to B is a Tier 2 distribution. It comes out tax free because all the DNI was carried out by the Tier 1 distributions.

To summarize, on a share by share basis DNI in both simple and complex trusts is carried out to trust beneficiaries by required current income distributions. Any remaining DNI is carried out by any other distributions made. DNI is shared pro rata by the respective shares and, within each, by the recipients within, and each item of income in DNI is shared pro rata within each tier (unless the governing instrument provides otherwise). There, that's it. Naturally there is much more complexity in the Code, but the fundamental operation is just that straightforward.

Income and Deductions in Respect of a Decedent

Neither income in respect of a decedent (IRD) nor deductions in respect of a decedent (DRD) is a concept unique to the income taxation or administration of estates and trusts or the taxation of beneficiaries. Nevertheless, IRD and DRD are common to fiduciary administration and the income taxation of trusts, estates, and beneficiaries because each applies to any taxpayer receiving income to which a decedent was entitled, or paying specified deductible expenses on the decedent's behalf. The fundamental tax objective of both the IRD and DRD concepts is to maintain the same character of the income and deductions as if they were received or incurred by the decedent while alive. For fiduciary income tax purposes, any IRD received or DRD incurred by an entity enters into the computation of its taxable income, and thus into the amount of DNI.

Broadly speaking, IRD is income earned by a decedent before death but not recognized for income tax purposes until after the decedent's death. Similarly, DRD consists of expenses or obligations incurred by the decedent before death that would have been deductible by the decedent if they had been paid before death. Although there is no *statutory* definition of IRD, we know from Treas. Reg. §1.691(a)-2 that the government regards the following items as IRD:

- Compensation for the decedent's services, including a bonus voted after the decedent's death that the employer had no obligation to pay;
- Renewal commissions of a deceased life insurance agent;
- Accrued but unreported interest on Series EE United States Treasury Bonds;
- Dividends on stock owned by the decedent that were payable to shareholders of record on a date before the decedent's death;
- Alimony arrearages;
- Deferred compensation death payments made to beneficiaries under a qualified retirement plan;
- Capital gain on a sale made during the decedent's life and reported on an installment basis (the recipient of the right to receive those payments will continue to report them on the same basis as did the decedent);
- A distributive share of partnership income paid to a deceased partner for the partnership's taxable year in which death occurs, attributable to the period ending with the partner's death (even if the deceased partner made cash withdrawals from the partnership as an advance against that income); and
- a share of profits for periods after the partner's death.

Helpful guidelines for identifying IRD refer to income that would have been taxable to the decedent had death not occurred prior to its receipt. See Ferguson, Freeland & Ascher, FEDERAL INCOME TAXATION OF ESTATES, TRUSTS, AND BENEFICIARIES §3.3 at 3:10 (2d ed. 1993).

Some cases refer to there being a legally significant arrangement that elevates the income above a mere expectancy and there being no outstanding economically material contingencies at the decedent's death. To establish that the decedent would have received and included the income had death not intervened, it is necessary to establish that the decedent, not the ultimate recipient, performed the substantive acts that spawned the entitlement. Thus, the recipient's acquisition must be "passive," not due to efforts made to generate the right (as opposed to enforcing it) after the decedent's death.

There are three primary tax consequences of an item being regarded as IRD, not all of which are bad, depending on the circumstances. First, income represented by the right to receive IRD is taxable in the year it is received. Second, under §691(a)(3), the character of the income is the same as if it was received by the decedent. Third, rather than having a new basis at death, the item has a §1014(c) basis equal to what the decedent's basis would have been if the decedent were living. This treatment is necessary because otherwise, to the extent of a new basis, the IRD would not be taxable as income as received.

As a counterpart to the rules governing income in respect of a decedent, a taxpayer who makes certain payments that would have been deductible if paid by a decedent before death is entitled to a §691(b) deduction in respect of the decedent. Those expenditures specifically are limited to §162 business expenses, §212 expenses of producing income or managing or safeguarding income producing property, §163 interest, and §164 deductible taxes (or the §27 credit for foreign taxes). In addition, the recipient of depletable property is entitled to any §611 percentage depletion attributable to income received therefrom, under Treas. Reg. §1.691(b)-1(b). In each case, the deduction is available to the recipient of property to which the expenditure is attributable, and without limitation by the otherwise applicable §642(g) rule denying double duty for deductions that may be taken on either the estate tax or the estate's income tax return. These deductions in respect of a decedent specifically are excepted from the operation of §642(g) because, had they been incurred by the decedent during life, they would have reduced the decedent's estate for estate tax purposes and still would have been deductible for income tax purposes.

In addition to DRD, an income tax deduction is allowed under §691(c) for estate or generation-skipping transfer taxes attributable to IRD. This deduction is based on a theory that, had the income been received by the decedent during life, any income tax incurred would have been paid before imposition of the estate or generation-skipping transfer tax. Payment of that income tax would have resulted in a smaller estate subject to tax and, thus, less of those taxes being payable. To approximate that result without recomputing the estate or generation-skipping transfer tax after the income tax on the IRD has been computed, Congress substituted an income tax deduction for the estate or generation-skipping transfer taxes attributable to the IRD. The general objective is to obtain a result that is administratively easier than recomputing the wealth transfer tax and that gives some rough approximation of what would have happened if the IRD had been received during the decedent's life. In some cases an item will be subject to income tax no matter who receives it, so treatment as IRD carries no detriment and allows the §691(c) deduction that otherwise would not be available. In those cases it pays to argue in favor of IRD treatment.

Grantor Trust Rules

Subchapter J establishes a third category into which trusts may fall. Unlike estates, which always are taxed as a complex trust and, by virtue of §671, cannot be subject to the following rules, any trust (whether simple or complex) may be subject in whole or in part to this third category of rules, being Subpart E (§§671 through 679) of Part I of Subchapter J: the grantor trust rules. Trusts may be subject to Subpart E in some years or only to a limited extent but, to the extent the grantor trust rules apply, Subpart E overrides the balance of Subchapter J.

Fundamental to application of the grantor trust rules is possession of prohibited enjoyment or control of trust income or corpus by a grantor or, under the §678 pseudo grantor trust rule, someone treated as if they were the grantor. When Subpart E applies, the normal principles we just studied are supplanted by the grantor trust rules, and the applicable portion of the trust is said to be "ignored" for income tax purposes. To the extent this occurs, income, losses, deductions, and credits allocable to that portion of the trust are attributed to the grantor (actual or pseudo), rather than to the trust or its beneficiaries. These tax attributes retain their character in the grantor's hands, in most respects as if no trust had been created. Thus, for example, a trust loss would be the grantor's deduction, a distribution to charity would be treated as the grantor's contribution, capital gains in the trust would be aggregated with the grantor's capital gains and losses, and the statute of limitation for the trust may be that of the grantor.

The key to application of the grantor trust rules is whether the grantor enjoys any trust benefits, has retained so much control, or has left so many "strings" attached to the trust that the grantor should be regarded as the true owner of the trust property for income tax purposes. Accordingly, the grantor trust provisions read like a laundry list of prohibited powers and interests in the trust, any one of which is sufficient to invoke grantor trust treatment. The most common powers and interests that will trigger grantor trust treatment under Subpart E include:

- Certain §674 powers in the grantor or the grantor's spouse (exercisable without the consent of an adverse party) to control some other beneficiary's enjoyment (subject to numerous exceptions);
- §675 administrative powers permitting the grantor or the grantor's spouse to deal at less than arm's length with the trust property;
- A §676 power in the grantor or the grantor's spouse to amend or revoke the trust;

- A §677 interest in income that may be used "for the benefit of the grantor," including income that may be paid to the grantor or to the grantor's spouse and income that is actually distributed to a person either the grantor or the grantor's spouse is obliged to support or maintain; and
- A pseudo grantor trust, which is taxed by §678 as if someone other than the grantor was the grantor.[4] Classic forms of exposure stem from five or five and Crummey withdrawal rights, along with inter vivos general powers of appointment, most often found in §2056(b)(5) marital deduction trusts or trusts for mature family members that permit withdrawal by the beneficiary as an alternative to mandatory termination when the beneficiary reaches a certain age.

There are other rules and exceptions, but for our purposes these are the ones on which planners tend to rely when they seek to make a trust subject to Subpart E. To appreciate why you might *want* to do so (by creating an intentionally defective grantor trust), consider the following perceived advantages of grantor trust planning:

- To the extent provided under the portion rules, all income, losses, deductions, credits, and other tax qualities of the trust are attributed to the grantor. Sometimes losses, deductions, and credits generated by the entity are more useful in the grantor's hands. It may be that the grantor is in a lower income tax bracket than the trust, and sometimes the grantor needs the income generated by the trust to offset deductions, losses, or credits generated in the grantor's individual capacity that otherwise would be lost.
- The grantor wants to pay income tax on income distributed to someone else, which constitutes a gift tax free benefit to that distributee.
- Various transactions involving the trust are deemed to be conducted with the grantor rather than with the trust. So, for example, Rev. Rul. 85-45 held that a principal personal residence owned by a marital deduction trust that was treated under §678 as a pseudo grantor trust was eligible for the §121 exclusion of gain on the trust's sale of the residence. Because the government treated the trust as nonexistent, the tax result was the same as if the surviving spouse was the deemed owner of the property and personally made the sale. Because it was used as the spouse's principal personal residence, it qualified for the capital gain exclusion. A second very

---

4. Technically §678 is not a grantor trust provision because it applies only to someone other than the grantor who has (or, under proper circumstances, who has released or modified) certain powers. It is included in Subpart E and it is appropriate to consider it as part of the grantor trust rules, however, because it has the effect of treating that person as the owner of that portion of the trust as to which the power applies, just as if that person was a grantor who transferred property into the trust and retained certain powers or interests.

common application of the same principle is for avoidance of the §101(a)(2)(A) income taxation of insurance that was transferred for value, because the exception for transfers to the insured under §101(a)(2)(B) is available. See Swanson v. Commissioner, 518 F.2d 59 (8th Cir. 1975), discussed in Chapter 9 at pages 42-43.

In addition to the variety of interests or powers that must be considered for grantor trust purposes, you need to consider whether grantor trust treatment will apply to an entire trust or only a portion. The Code provides that the grantor (or a pseudo grantor) is treated as the owner of only that portion of a trust as to which a requisite power or interest exists. Several different portions may be involved. Treas. Reg. §1.671-3. For example, a grantor with a §673 reversion or a §676 power to revoke the trust in its entirety is treated as the owner of the entire trust: essentially every item of income, loss, deduction, and credit in the trust is attributed to that deemed owner. Similarly, if the grantor or any nonadverse party is the trustee with unrestricted powers over income and corpus, §674(a) exposure could apply to the entire trust.

On the other hand, a grantor may be treated as the owner of only those items allocable to the fiduciary accounting income portion. For example, the grantor is treated as the current income beneficiary of only the ordinary income portion if the grantor possessed only a §677(a)(1) income interest. Treas. Reg. §1.671-3(c). To illustrate, if taxable income allocable to the income account is $5,000, taxable income allocable to corpus is $2,000, and deductible expenses total $6,000, the current income beneficiary would be taxed on zero income and the excess deduction of $1,000 would reduce income allocable to corpus; that excess deduction would not pass through to the income beneficiary.[5] Thus, the grantor would not be entitled to deductions in excess of ordinary income, which shows that grantor trust treatment is not the same as if no trust had been created — a frequent but sometimes inaccurate assumption about the application of the grantor trust rules.

Other portions include the corpus (all items not reflected in the ordinary income portion, meaning income, losses, deductions, and credits allocable or attributable to corpus, and all income earned thereon after accumulation as a part of corpus) and fractional portions that reflect rights that would cause one of the grantor trust rules to apply to less than all of the trust (for example, a §677(a)(1) right to receive half the income from a trust). In unusual circumstances the portion also may be a particular asset, such as a §675(4)(A) power to vote closely held stock transferred to a trust, in which case the grantor must report the income, losses, deductions, and credits attributable to just that asset (along with a pro rata share of any deductions not specifically identifiable with respect to the asset but properly spread

---

5. As in a nongrantor trust, the excess deductions do not pass through to the beneficiaries except in the year of termination. §642(h). Essentially the calculation of the portion is based on a distributable net income analogue.

among all trust assets, such as an otherwise unallocated trustee's fee. Treas. Reg. §1.671-3(a)(2)).

Often the most challenging grantor trust planning issue is how to make a trust taxable to the grantor or a pseudo grantor without encountering unwanted wealth transfer tax consequences. In this respect by far the most popular defect is the §675(4)(C) power to swap assets. This provision essentially authorizes any person not acting in a fiduciary capacity and without the consent of a fiduciary to exchange trust assets for a full and adequate consideration — to purchase trust assets for full and adequate consideration — with no wealth transfer tax exposure to the powerholder. A second easy approach can work in almost any situation involving a married grantor who feels confident that the marriage will last (but requiring a fall-back approach if the spouse dies before grantor trust exposure should terminate in the planning context involved). It is relatively easy to trigger grantor trust liability with an interest or power in the grantor's spouse that is only deemed to be an interest or power in the grantor. See §672(e). Like the §675(4)(C) power to exchange assets, this form of intentional grantor trust exposure will generate no wealth transfer tax consequence to the grantor (although care must be taken to avoid exposing the spouse to unexpected wealth transfer tax).

Alternatively, giving the grantor's spouse the power to remove and replace trustees and allowing the spouse to be a successor trustee would cause the trustee's powers to be attributed to the spouse. These may generate grantor trust treatment. Another relatively easy way to trigger grantor trust exposure, without direct involvement of the grantor's spouse, involves granting a nonadverse party a nongeneral inter vivos power to create a §677(a)(1) income interest in the grantor. And a relatively unconventional method of creating grantor trust liability, in this case without the help of a spouse or any third party, is for the grantor to borrow the corpus of the trust for less than adequate interest or security, triggering §675(3). Alternatively, if the trustee is the grantor's spouse or any other related or subordinate party, a loan to the grantor or to the grantor's spouse even for *adequate* interest and security will trigger §675(3) treatment. Equally effective is giving a trusted nonadverse party the power to lend to the grantor's spouse for less than adequate interest or security, causing §675(2) to apply even if no loan is made. There is much more. For added guidance and self study regarding the grantor trust rules in particular, see 1 Casner & Pennell, ESTATE PLANNING §5.11 (6th ed. 1995), and Ferguson, Freeland, & Ascher, FEDERAL INCOME TAXATION OF ESTATES, TRUSTS AND BENEFICIARIES ch. 10 (3d ed. 1999).

Summary

The income tax rules have a number of obvious influences on vanilla estate planning. For example, they impact the decision whether to provide a spray of income that may allow accumulations, or to require mandatory distributions of income. They also may influence the decision whether to create actual separate shares for trust accounting purposes. The rule in §663(a)(1) explains why many wills contain a separate provision for distribution of tangible personal property that may occur in a year when no other distributions might carry out DNI (and therefore the intent is to protect beneficiaries who receive unmarketable mementos from having an income tax liability attached). Subchapter J also affects day-to-day decisions such as whether to allocate capital gain to the income account and other periodic trust accounting issues. And it affects a variety of postmortem planning decisions, such as selection of tax year, when to close an estate or trust, which assets to distribute periodically, and on which return to claim deductions for various administration expenses. Finally, the grantor trust rules encourage certain strategic planning with defective grantor trusts, all making it important that you be aware of the pervasive application of Subchapter J in your work.

Chapter 18
A Brief Introduction to Wealth Transfer Taxation

The Internal Revenue Code imposes a wealth transfer tax on the gratuitous disposition by United States citizens or residents of property located anywhere in the world *and* on the gratuitous disposition of the United States situs property of nonresident noncitizens. Like the federal estate tax, most states also levy a tax on the transfer of property at death,[1] either "estate" taxes (a single tax determined by the amount of the estate of the decedent) or "inheritance" taxes[2] (separate taxes imposed on each benefit conferred on a devisee, legatee, or heir, the amount of tax usually being determined by the size of the gift and the relationship to the decedent of the person who receives it).

Few states impose a gift tax,[3] notwithstanding that the tendency of taxpayers would be to make inter vivos gifts if there is a heavy tax on transfers at death but no tax on transfers during life. The low number of states with gift taxes probably reflects the fact that state wealth transfer tax rates are relatively low and probably do not often influence the transfer planning of individual citizens. In addition, the federal gift tax adequately deters most gifting that otherwise would be made solely for tax minimization purposes. The federal gift tax buttresses the estate tax, and most individuals are disinclined to make gifts regardless of clear tax advantages of transferring property during life rather than waiting until death. See Chapter 12.

---

1. All states impose a sponge or pick up tax that originally was meant to equal the §2011 state death tax credit that was repealed in 2001 effective after 2004. The label sponge or pick up tax reflects that the states were taking the full amount they could collect without costing their citizens added taxes. Every state imposed a state death tax that was keyed to the amount of this credit, which effectively shifted revenue from the federal government to the taxing state. In 2003 only Ohio and Oklahoma imposed estate taxes exceeding the amount of the §2011 state death tax credit. Following repeal of §2011 many states began to "decouple" their tax from the federal regime, such that now it is impossible to predict or easily summarize the impact of state death taxes. *See* Schoenblum, Multistate Guide to Estate Planning Table 10.02 (2001). *And see* §2058, which is a federal deduction for state estate taxes that are imposed after 2004. Because credits (§2011) and deductions (§2058) have very different effects, that change was not a mere relabelling or a sleight-of-hand, and it visited a huge revenue shift from the states back to the federal government.

2. Indiana, Iowa, Kansas, Kentucky, Louisiana, Maryland, Nebraska, New Hampshire, New Jersey, North Carolina, Pennsylvania, South Dakota (repealed in 2000 with respect to intangibles and nonresidents), and Tennessee still impose inheritance taxes. See Schoenblum, Multistate Guide to Estate Planning Table 10.01 (2001), which also lists Connecticut (which phased out on a schedule, complete after 2004) and Montana (the legislature voted in 2000 to repeal their tax).

3. Only Connecticut, Louisiana, North Carolina, and Tennessee impose a gift tax. See Schoenblum, Multistate Guide to Estate Planning Table 10.04 (2001), which also lists New York (the legislature voted in 2000 to repeal the gift tax).

Congress enacted the generation-skipping transfer tax (GST, as Chapter 13 of the Internal Revenue Code) to prevent individuals from planning their estates to avoid all wealth transfer tax in the estates of their children or more remote descendants through the use of trusts that bestow benefits but do not grant sufficient enjoyment or control to require estate tax inclusion. The GST had its own credit under §2604 for state generation-skipping taxes, and several states adopted their own sponge or pick up tax version of this impost.[4] That credit also was repealed, effective in 2005.

This Chapter is a brief overview of the three federal transfer taxes (gift, estate, and generation-skipping transfers) and state death taxation, in that order.

It may be useful to remember throughout that payment of federal estate or gift tax is avoided to the extent the §2010 *unified credit* is available. (The GST also has an exception but it operates in a different manner, as discussed at page 36.) A credit is like money in the bank: you owe the tax but Congress says you need not pay it because you have this credit on deposit. So you pay only when your tax exceeds that amount. The credit is equal to the tax on the first chunk of wealth transferred in a taxable manner (the applicable exclusion amount). For example, in 2005 when the applicable exclusion amount is $1.5 million, the estate tax unified credit is $555,800. That also is the tax on an estate of $1.5 million. (For reasons too complex to explain now, the applicable exclusion amount for gift tax purposes is just $1 million and the unified credit for gifts is $345,800.)

So, for example, an estate of $20 million would incur a lot more tax than $555,800 but that estate would not pay the first $555,800 of its tax liability. An estate of just $1.5 million would not pay any of the tax on that amount, making that smaller estate "nontaxable" in street lingo. Actually, *every* estate is taxable, but most estates don't generate a tax large enough to consume the entire credit, so most do not require an actual payment to the government. We just *say* that those smaller estates are exempt or nontaxable. Indeed, as an administrative convenience, a *gross* estate (note that this is *not* the smaller *taxable* estate) that is below the applicable exclusion amount need not even file a return. Over 99% of the decedent population in 2004 was nontaxable due to the unified credit. Yes, you got that right: The wealth transfer tax applies to less than 1% of the decedent population in America. So, why have your elected representatives made such a big deal over "repeal of the death tax"?

---

4. Like state death taxes that took advantage of the §2011 credit, these state taxes merely diverted a portion of the federal generation-skipping transfer tax to the state and therefore cost their citizens nothing. Schoenblum, MULTISTATE GUIDE TO ESTATE PLANNING Table 10.03 (2001), reported that over half the states adopted a GST pick up tax. It was expected that most states would follow suit, as they all had in imposing a death tax taking advantage of the §2011 credit. Like §2011, however, this §2604 credit also was repealed in 2001, although unlike §2011 repeal was effective in 2005 all at once — it was not phased out. It is not clear how states will respond post repeal.

The Federal Gift Tax

The Internal Revenue Code imposes a graduated tax on taxable gifts. Primary liability to pay the gift tax is imposed on the donor under §2502(c), but transferee liability is imposed on the donee under §6901(a) to the extent the donor fails to pay the tax. Under §6019 a gift tax return must be filed for any gift (1) not excluded under §2503(b) (the annual exclusion) or §2503(e) (the education and medical expense exclusion), or (2) any gift not qualifying entirely for the §2523 gift tax marital deduction or the §2522 gift tax charitable deduction. Note that taxable inter vivos gifts that do not in the aggregate exceed the applicable exclusion amount must be reported, notwithstanding that a similar amount left at death would not require a return at all. The due date under §6075(b) for filing the gift tax return is April 15 following the close of the calendar year in which the gift was made (with an automatic extension to file if the taxpayer is granted an extension of time to file the taxpayer's income tax return). If the donor dies during the calendar year in which the gift was made, the time for filing the gift tax return is delayed until the due date for the donor's estate tax return.

The federal gift tax helps to preserve the integrity of the income tax system. The owner of income producing property is burdened with the income tax on the income it produces, and the gift tax impedes gratuitous transfers of property designed to shift that income tax liability. There is relatively little incentive for income shifting in the form of gifts or otherwise under current law given the relatively low income tax rates and, more importantly, the compressed income tax brackets in which income is taxed. Nevertheless, the estate tax is slated for repeal in 2010 (under legislation adopted in 2001), but the gift tax will remain on the books after 2009 to continue this income tax deterrence.

Gift Defined

According to §2512(b), a gift is any voluntary and complete transfer of property to the extent fair market value of the property transferred exceeds the value of any consideration received in money or money's worth. An exception applies if that differential in value meets the business transaction exception established in Treas. Reg. §25.2512-8 (meaning that the transaction is bona fide, at arm's length, and free from donative intent). Other exclusions or exceptions also may apply, such as the annual exclusion. But transfers for full and adequate consideration need no exclusion because they are not gifts in the first instance.

Thus, for example, outright gratuitous transfers of money, realty, tangibles, or intangibles normally would be taxable gifts. Some taxable transfers are less obvious than these, some transfers that look like gifts are not, and others that do not appear to be gifts are taxable transfers. In general, the test is whether an economic benefit has been transferred gratuitously, but this is only a rough description. Consider the following illustrations:

(1) P transferred $100,000 to a trustee in trust to pay the income to child C for life, remainder to C's descendants. P reserved a power to revoke the trust and therefore did not make a completed transfer for gift tax purposes. However, income distributed from the trust to C constitutes a gift, and a completed gift would occur if P released the retained power of revocation. This gift would consist of a transfer to C of the then value of C's life estate and a transfer to C's descendants of the value of the remainder interest, both valued when the power is relinquished on the basis of C's actuarial life expectancy and an assumed rate of return on trust assets dictated by §7520.

(2) X sold a house and lot to Y for 40% of its fair market value. This is a gift to Y of 60% of the fair market value unless X can establish that the sale was made in the ordinary course of business, in a transaction that was bona fide, at arm's length, and free from donative intent. This would be difficult to prove if Y is a natural object of X's bounty.

(3) A and B, sole owners of a corporation, each transferred stock they owned in the corporation to key employees who they considered important to the continued success of the corporation. A and B are not related, nor is any employee related to them. For income tax purposes the employees must include in income the fair market value of the stock they received, and their income tax basis in the stock is the same amount. A and B are treated as having made a capital contribution to the corporation, and the corporation is entitled to a deduction for compensation paid to the employees to the extent allowed by §§162 and 83(h). No gift has been made for gift tax purposes because these transfers were made for full and adequate consideration in money or money's worth. See Rev. Rul. 80-196.

(4) Assume that in example (3) only A transferred stock to the unrelated key employees and B did not make a matching contribution. A's transfer still constitutes a capital contribution to the corporation that generates an increase in basis for A's stock in the corporation. Because A alone made a transfer, however, A is deemed to have made an indirect gift to B of half the value contributed to the corporation.[5]

(5) P gratuitously guaranteed loans made by Bank to P's children. According to Private Letter Ruling 9113009:

---

5. See Treas. Reg. §25.2511-1(h)(1); Heringer v. Commissioner, 235 F.2d 149 (9th Cir. 1956); Tilton v. Commissioner, 88 T.C. 590 (1987); Ketteman Trust v. Commissioner, 86 T.C. 91 (1986); Estate of Hitchon v. Commissioner, 45 T.C. 96 (1965); Private Letter Ruling 9114023. This gift does not qualify for the annual exclusion because B does not have an immediate right to possession or enjoyment of the capital increase represented by A's transfer. A would be in a better position if there were no other shareholder, or if B made a matching proportionate transfer that would net out the gifts made by each. Indeed, the results would be more favorable if A made gifts to the employees out of affection or other nonbusiness related motives because, presumably, the gift tax annual exclusion would be applicable. As accomplished, however, all A gained from this transfer was a basis increase for the value of the deemed capital contribution.

> The agreements ... to guarantee payment of debts are valuable economic benefits conferred upon [the children] .... Consequently, when [the taxpayer] guaranteed payment of the loans, [the taxpayer] transferred a valuable property interest to [the children]. The promisor of a legally enforceable promise for less than adequate and full consideration makes a completed gift on the date the promise is binding and determinable in value rather than when the promised payment is actually made.

According to the Ruling, this gift was taxable immediately, with the gift amount being "the economic benefit conferred" by the guarantee. The government gave no indication of the gift tax value of the economic benefit bestowed. It might consist of the value of any reduction in interest rate attributable to the added security provided by the guarantee, the amount the borrower did not pay a third party for the guarantee, or the diminution in value of the guarantor's collateral pledged to secure the guarantee. If the taxpayer subsequently is required to make good on the guarantee, an additional gift would be made to the extent the taxpayer could, but does not, seek reimbursement from the borrower.[6]

Annual Exclusion and Exclusion for Education and Medical Care Expenses

Every year a taxpayer may give up to $11,000 (indexed for inflation in $1,000 increments) to each of an unlimited number of different donees without incurring a gift tax or even being required to file a gift tax return. This §2503(b) "annual exclusion" does not apply to future interests, such as a gift in trust to pay principal to the beneficiary at some future date. However, certain gifts to minors that are future interests are treated by §2503(c) as gifts of a present interest that qualify for the annual exclusion if the gift property and the income therefrom may be expended for the benefit of the donee before the donee attains the age of 21 and, (1) to the extent not so expended, the gift property and the income therefrom will pass to the donee when the donee attains the age of 21 or, (2) if the donee dies before attaining the age of 21, the gift property will be payable to the donee's estate or as the donee appoints under a general power of appointment.

In addition, §2503(e) provides that amounts paid on behalf of an individual as tuition to an educational organization for "education or training" or to any "medical" care provider also are not taxable. These "ed/med exclusion" payments may be made without reducing the per donee annual exclusion.

---

6. It is notable that the benefit to the borrower from receiving a guarantee does not constitute an immediate cost to the taxpayer who provides the guarantee. The government previously took the position that the value of a gift is not what the donee receives but what the donor relinquishes. In this case the government took the opposite position, stating that value to the donee measured the gift, which is a more traditional holding. It may be that either valuation is correct in appropriate situations, although it is difficult to see what property transfer has occurred in the guarantee situation to which the gift tax should apply.

Charitable Deduction

Transfers to qualified charities are deductible under §2522(a) regardless of amount, and the same is true for estate tax purposes under §2055(a). Only the §170 *income* tax charitable deduction is limited to certain percentages of the donor's contribution base. See Chapter 8. Qualified charitable donees are described in §§2055 and 2522 and include organizations designed to promote good government or world peace or to attain other political, economic, or social ends (if no substantial part of the organization's activities is carrying on propaganda or otherwise attempting to influence legislation). But a particular family in need is not a qualified charity because a general distinction is drawn between public and private charity.

Organizations customarily submit their charters and bylaws to the Treasury Department for a ruling that they are qualified charities, gifts to which are deductible for federal income, estate, and gift tax purposes. An organization typically will make such a determination known in its solicitation of funds, and it always makes sense to verify this fact before making a sizable charitable gift.

Split interest charitable gifts benefit charities and individuals, with the charity benefiting exclusively for a term and the remainder then passing to individuals, or vice versa. Very technical rules must be observed to obtain a charitable deduction for split interest charitable gifts, also as discussed in Chapter 8.

Marital Deduction

The gift tax marital deduction was enacted in 1948 along with joint income tax returns and gift splitting to provide parity between the taxation of spouses in community property and noncommunity property states. Beginning in 1976 and culminating with a change in 1981, Congress expanded the deduction to now make interspousal transfers totally free of tax. See Chapter 7. Transfers between spouses qualify for the gift tax marital deduction only to the extent the donee spouse receives a qualifying interest and is a citizen of the United States.[7] Qualifying interests include property transferred outright or property placed in a trust that meets the technical requirements of §2523(e) or (f).

Gift Splitting by Spouses

Also adopted in 1948 was the gift splitting authority now found in §2513, which applies to gifts by a married donor to a third party. Because a gift by spouses of community property is a gift by each of half the value

---

7. Gifts to a noncitizen spouse cannot qualify for the gift tax marital deduction. See §2523(i). However, §2523(i)(2) increases the §2503(b) gift tax annual exclusion for gifts to a noncitizen spouse, provided the interest transferred otherwise would qualify for the marital deduction. Treas. Reg. §25.2523(i)-1(c).

of the property, §2513 grants spouses the ability to elect to treat a gift of noncommunity property to a third party as made half by each as well.

Concurrent Interests

Joint ownership of property with the right of survivorship is quite common, particularly between spouses. A completed gift results from creation of a joint ownership to the extent the respective owners' contributions are not equal. However, any gift represented by unequal contributions is not complete and therefore is not taxable to the extent the joint owners' respective contributions are withdrawable without consent of the other joint owners. This normally occurs with respect to joint bank accounts, brokerage accounts, and jointly owned United States Savings Bonds. In addition, between spouses, even if the contribution constitutes a completed gift, the unlimited gift tax marital deduction makes the transfer tax free if the donee spouse is a citizen of the United States.

Preventing Valuation Freezes

Certain transactions minimize the value of transferred property in ways that Congress regards as improper. Chapter 14 of the Internal Revenue Code precludes a number of these devices, principally through application of valuation rules that negate the opportunity to minimize or freeze value.

The Unified Estate and Gift Taxes

The tax on those transfers that are *not* deductible or excepted is computed under a unified rate system found in §2001 and incorporated by reference by §2502 for both estate and gift tax purposes. This approach reflects the progressive nature of the estate and gift taxes and the policy that similar amounts of wealth should incur similar tax liability regardless of whether the transferor conveys it during life, at death, or some of each. Thus, gifts made during life are added to gifts made previously during life to determine the appropriate graduated tax rate to impose on the latest transfer, and lifetime gifts are reflected when computing the estate tax at death.

For example, because the gift tax rate on a gift of $150,000 is less than the rate on a gift of $250,000, it is necessary to consider the progressive rate that must be imposed if a gift of $150,000 is made after a prior gift of $100,000. Similarly, all taxable transfers made during a transferor's life must be considered in determining the proper rate for taxing transfers at death. To illustrate, if Donor transferred $X in year 1 and another $Y in year 2 and died with $Z in year 3, the tax on the year 2 gift would be computed as the tax on $X plus $Y and, because the tax on $X already was incurred in year 1, only the increase in tax attributable to the year 2 gift of $Y would be imposed. Similarly, the estate tax would be computed as the tax on $X plus $Y plus $Z and, again reflecting that the tax on $X and $Y was incurred during life, only the increase in tax attributable to the $Z taxable at death would be imposed for estate tax purposes.

There is a quirk in this unified rate system, attributable to the fact that the estate and gift taxes were not unified until 1976 but this integrated gift tax computation regime existed beginning in 1932. Thus, taxable gifts made before 1977 must be reflected in determining the applicable tax for taxable gifts but not for determining the estate tax for any decedent.

To illustrate, assume that Donor made taxable gifts before 1977 totaling $150,000 and a taxable gift after 1976 of $100,000. The gift tax on the $100,000 gift would be computed by determining the gift tax under the unified rate schedule on a gift of $250,000 and then subtracting the gift tax under the same schedule on a gift of $150,000; the difference is the gift tax on the post 1976 taxable gift of $100,000. Donor's estate tax, however, would be determined without regard to the gift made before 1977. Thus, if Donor's taxable estate were $700,000 at death, it would be added to the taxable gift made after 1976 of $100,000 but not to the taxable gift made before 1977 of $150,000. The tax on only $800,000 would be computed, and the tax on that amount would be paid to the extent it exceeds the tax on the $100,000 taxable gift made after 1976.

The tax computed under the unified rate schedule need not be paid until the aggregate tax incurred during life and at death exceeds the unified credit granted by §§2010 and 2505. In this example the tax would be satisfied by applying the unified credit and no tax payment actually would be remitted.

The Federal Estate Tax

As noted in Chapter 11, the federal estate tax is an obligation of the residue of the decedent's probate estate and must be paid by the "executor" of the estate,[8] which distinguishes the tax from an inheritance tax like that imposed by some states on recipients of a decedent's property.

The federal estate tax is imposed on a decedent's taxable estate and requires answers to three basic questions:

(1) What property is includible in the decedent's "gross estate"?

(2) What amounts are deductible from the gross estate in determining the "taxable estate"?

(3) How much tax is imposed on the taxable estate?

The Gross Estate

A decedent's gross estate includes "the value of all property to the extent of the interest therein of the decedent at the time of . . . death." §2033. Property a person owns at death is includible in the decedent's

---

8. §§2002 and 2205. The term "executor" is defined in §2203 as the fiduciary charged with administration of the decedent's estate or, if there is none, then any person in possession of the decedent's property.

gross estate,[9] but many other types of property or entitlements are includible even though the decedent did not own them in a classic sense. Thus, although §2033 is a general inclusion authority with respect to probate property:

> The word "property" in the statute is not limited in its scope by concepts of property that existed when the estate tax was conceived. When property rights have come into existence since the statute's enactment, the generalized term must be expounded.... The economy and many of the elements of life today are different than they were even a generation or less ago. The Congress in its wisdom decided to use a general word like property rather than trying to envision what the ingenuity of man would evolve as something substantial. The tax gatherer is directed to seek out the esoterics of ownership....[10]

Moreover, because Congress intends to tax all transfers of economic benefit upon a decedent's death, regardless of the niceties of property law or the legal forms employed, some property transfers must be reached by special provisions, including some provisions that (in the interest of preventing tax avoidance) reach certain inter vivos transfers notwithstanding that any economic benefit transferred at death is nearly or entirely nonexistent.

(1) Transfers Made Within Three Years of Death In 1981 Congress enacted what now is §2035(a)(2), which requires gross estate inclusion of transfers made within three years of death of property interests that, if retained until death, would cause inclusion in the gross estate under any of §2036, §2037, §2038, or §2042 (all of which are discussed below). This inclusion rule does not apply, however, to the extent the transfer was not a gift because it was made for full and adequate consideration in money or money's worth. §2035(d). In addition, §2035(b) requires inclusion of the amount of any gift tax paid by the decedent (or the decedent's estate) on any gift made by the decedent (or by the decedent's spouse) within three years of death. This "gross up" inclusion rule subjects the dollars used to pay the gift tax to estate tax. This matches the estate tax result at death because the dollars used to pay the decedent's estate tax themselves are part of the estate that is subject to the estate tax. A different approach applies for gift tax purposes: the dollars used to pay gift tax are not themselves subject to the gift tax. See the discussion of this difference in Chapter 12 at page 3.

---

9. A few notable exceptions exist by virtue of legislative grace. See, e.g., §2103, which excludes property not situated in the United States that is owned at death by a nonresident noncitizen.

10. First Victoria Nat'l Bank v. United States, 620 F.2d 1096, 1104 (5th Cir. 1980) (holding that "rice history acreage" is "property" for estate tax purposes).

(2) Revocable Transfers The value of property transferred by a decedent during life but subject to a power to alter, amend, revoke or terminate enjoyment is includible in the decedent's gross estate (except to the extent the transfer was for a full and adequate consideration in money or money's worth). This §2038(a)(1) inclusion is consistent with the gift tax rule that a revocable transfer is not a completed gift and therefore is not taxable for gift tax purposes. Because death constitutes termination of the retained power, which completes the transfer for wealth transfer tax purposes, the estate tax is imposed if the power existed any time within three years of the decedent's death. Release of the power within three years of death causes the same result as if the power were retained until death. See §§2038(a)(1) (last clause) and 2035(a)(2), noted above.

(3) Retained Life Estates Even if a transfer is irrevocable and therefore was subject to gift taxation, the transferor may be exposed to §2036(a) estate tax inclusion of the value of the transferred property if the transferor retained enjoyment of the property for life, or retained a power to designate who will enjoy the property and did not relinquish that power more than three years prior to death. These interests and powers are treated for estate tax purposes as if no transfer was made; the transferor's retained enjoyment or control causes the transfer to be regarded as testamentary.

Under §2038 the typical transfer during life is not complete and the gift tax is not imposed. But the §2036 estate tax result may be inconsistent with the gift tax consequences of the transfer. For example, if the donor retained only the right to receive income for life, the gift tax would be imposed on the value of the remainder interest transferred irrevocably during life. Because it was retained, the value of the life estate was not subject to gift tax when the initial transfer was made and it is subject to estate tax in the form of the increase in the transferor's net worth attributable to income received (to the extent that income has not totally been consumed before death). There is nothing inconsistent with this result.

But inclusion of the full value of the transferred property in the transferor's gross estate at death *is* inconsistent with the prior gift taxation, because the remainder taxed during life is exactly the same interest that is subject to estate tax at the time of the transferor's death (the remainder now being the full value of the trust). Because the value of the remainder is being taxed a second time by virtue of the retained life estate, an adjustment is provided under the flush language of §2001(b) to preclude double taxation of the same interest, due to the inconsistent application of the estate and gift tax rules.

With only one deviation the same results apply if the power to alter enjoyment of the income interest triggers §2036(a)(2) inclusion at death. Because the income interest was not retained, it was subject to gift tax at the time the trust was created and that wealth was not received by the transferor. So it is not subject to taxation at death. Thus, in both cases the value of the income interest is taxed only once, the difference here being that it was taxed at the time the trust was created and it was taxed at death in the prior case of retained enjoyment of that interest. In both cases, however, the value of the remainder interest is subjected to tax twice, and again the §2001(b) flush language adjustment is necessary.

For purposes of these rules, §2036(b) regards the transfer of stock in a controlled corporation as a §2036(a)(1) transfer with retained enjoyment if the transferor retains the right to vote the stock. A more appropriate rule would be to treat this as a §2036(a)(2) transfer with retained power to govern the enjoyment, but the result is the same either way: the transfer during life is ignored for estate tax purposes and treated as if it were a testamentary disposition.

(4) Transfers That Take Effect at Death Unquestionably the strangest estate tax inclusion provision is §2037. It applies only if (1) some beneficiary must survive the decedent as a condition to obtaining possession or enjoyment of property the decedent transferred during life, and (2) the decedent retained a reversion in the corpus of that property that was worth at death more than 5% of the value of the property that would revert. To illustrate, a transferor would have to make a transfer such as "to A for life, then reversion to the transferor if living and, if not, to B if living," and even then the value subject to §2037 would be only the value of the transferred property reduced by the value of the life estate in A (because it is not subject to the reversion). A reversionary interest that does not meet these requirements still may be includible in the decedent's gross estate under §2033, although only the value of the reversion would be subject to inclusion in that event rather than the full value of the property subject to the reversion. Notwithstanding that §2037 has been in the estate tax law since its inception, for decades it has been a veritable backwater, and all significant litigation involving its provisions is antiquated. This provision largely is irrelevant given that modern estate planning seldom would call for retention of anything closely resembling the reversion that would trigger §2037.

(5) Annuities The value of an annuity at a decedent's death is includible in the decedent's gross estate under §2039(a) if the decedent was entitled to receive annuity payments for life (including if the decedent had not yet begun to receive such payments but, once they began, they were payable for life). The most common illustrations of this are under a retirement benefit plan if some other beneficiary is entitled to enjoyment of an annuity after the decedent's death, such as under a joint and survivor payout option. Because most retirement benefit annuity payments also constitute income in respect of a decedent for purposes of §691(a), these entitlements that survive a participant's death constitute one of the most heavily taxed forms of wealth and require special attention in the planning process.

(6) Concurrent Interests Property held in joint tenancy with the right of survivorship or as tenants by the entireties (i.e., concurrent

interests with the right of survivorship) are subject to special inclusion rules under §2040, applicable with respect to the estate of all but the last concurrent owner to die. The general inclusion rule applies a consideration furnished test that requires inclusion in the gross estate of a portion of the value of the concurrently owned property that corresponds to the portion of the consideration furnished by the decedent to acquire the property. The presumption is that the decedent furnished the entire consideration, in which case the entire value is includible in the decedent's gross estate. However, any surviving concurrent owner may prove that the decedent did not provide all the consideration, in which case a lesser percentage will be includible. No part of the value will be includible in the decedent's gross estate if it can be proved that the decedent furnished none of the consideration. If, however, the concurrent owners acquired the property by gift from a third party, an equal portion of the value is includible (or such other portion specified by the donor if the gift specified that the owners would not share the property equally).

In 1976 Congress adopted the qualified joint interest rule in §2040(b), applicable only to property acquired after 1976 and held exclusively by spouses who are citizens of the United States. Only half the value of a qualified joint interest is includible in the gross estate of the first spouse to die, regardless of the source of the consideration furnished to acquire the joint interest.

Not subject to §2040 is concurrent ownership that lacks the right of survivorship, such as a tenancy in common or community property. Instead, only the decedent's undivided interest in the property (e.g., half the value of community property) is includible in the decedent's gross estate.

To illustrate the application of §2040(a) with respect to concurrent interests with the right of survivorship among persons who are not spouses, assume Donor devised Blackacre to A and B as joint tenants with the right of survivorship and not as tenants in common. Half the value of Blackacre will be included in the gross estate of the first of A and B to die, and the survivor will become the sole owner of Blackacre pursuant to the right of survivorship. When the survivor dies the full value of Blackacre will be subject to inclusion again, meaning that 150% of the value of Blackacre will be subject to federal estate tax over both estates.

Suppose instead that A had purchased Blackacre and placed the title in the names of A and B as joint tenants with the right of survivorship and not as tenants in common. A would make a taxable gift to B of half the value of Blackacre and still would suffer inclusion of 100% of the value of Blackacre in A's gross estate (because A furnished all the consideration for its acquisition). Any gift tax paid by A will be allowed under §2001(b)(2) as a credit against A's estate tax and, if the tenancy was created after 1976, the gift made upon creation will be purged from A's adjusted taxable gifts by the flush language of §2001(b). Still, the net result will be inclusion of 200% of the value of Blackacre over both estates. If, however, B were to die first, no part of the value of Blackacre would be includible in B's gross estate because A furnished all the consideration for its acquisition, and only 100% of the value of Blackacre will be subjected to federal estate tax over both estates (all in A's estate at the second death). Recall, however, that half the value of Blackacre was subject to gift tax when A created the joint tenancy, so in the aggregate 150% of the value of the property was subject to wealth transfer tax. All things considered, can you think of a worse form of property ownership for tax purposes?

(7) Powers of Appointment are important estate planning tools that provide flexibility in trust dispositions. Under §2041 the holder of the power is treated as the owner of any property that is subject to a general power, meaning that the powerholder may appoint the property to the powerholder, to the powerholder's estate, or to creditors of either. Any other power of appointment is a nongeneral power, which is harmless for estate tax purposes (unless the power is exercised in a manner that triggers the arcane provisions of the so called Delaware Tax Trap of §2041(a)(3), meaning that exercise is effective to extend the duration of a trust for Rule Against Perpetuities purposes). It generally makes no difference whether the power is exercised (unless the power predates 1942). Inclusion of the appointive property usually depends solely on whether the powerholder possesses a general power of appointment.

(8) Life Insurance proceeds are includible in the insured decedent's gross estate if at death the decedent possessed any "incidents of ownership" in the policies or if the proceeds are payable to the insured's estate. Recall Chapter 9.

(9) QTIP Property Property that qualifies for a marital deduction in a decedent's estate under §2056(b)(7) as "qualified terminable interest property" is subject to inclusion in the estate of that decedent's surviving spouse under §2044. This inclusion essentially is a payback for the grant of the marital deduction to the estate of the former decedent. Qualification for the marital deduction causes the property to be treated as if the surviving spouse had a sufficient ownership interest to cause estate tax inclusion, notwithstanding that the surviving spouse never owned the property and, in many cases, cannot govern its ultimate disposition.

The Taxable Estate

The §2051 taxable estate upon which the decedent's estate tax is computed under §2001 is determined by subtracting the total amounts of five deductions from the decedent's §2031 gross estate.

(1) Debts, Expenses, and Taxes. Ordinary and necessary expenses of administering the decedent's estate (including fees paid to the personal representative and to advisors such as an attorney or accountant), claims against the estate and recourse indebtedness for which the decedent was personally liable during life (in either case to the extent supported by full

and adequate consideration in money or money's worth), and taxes that were the decedent's liability during life (i.e., taxes other than wealth transfer taxes or any tax that accrues after death), are deductible under §2053.

(2) Casualty or Theft Losses. Losses incurred during administration of the estate that are not compensated by insurance are deductible under §2054.

(3) Charitable Deduction. The §2055 estate tax charitable deduction mirrors the gift tax charitable deduction.

(4) Marital Deduction. The §2056 estate tax marital deduction also mirrors the gift tax marital deduction, with only one difference of any significance. Although §2056(d) denies the estate tax marital deduction if the decedent's spouse is not a United States citizen, §2056A allows an estate tax marital deduction with respect to a noncitizen surviving spouse if certain "qualified domestic trust" requirements are met. No similar entitlement was granted for gift tax purposes, although §2523(i)(2) expanded the gift tax annual exclusion for gifts to a noncitizen spouse.

(5) State Death Tax Deduction. A §2058 state death tax deduction took the place of the §2011 state death tax credit beginning in 2005 and merely serves to reduce the financial impact of an estate incurring an estate or inheritance tax liability to a United States taxing jurisdiction other than the federal government.

Valuation

Among the most challenging tax issues are valuation questions, for both inclusion and deduction purposes and not just in taxable estates. These questions easily can arise in times of estate division or distribution, for annual exclusion lifetime giving, to qualify for federal entitlements, for federal income tax purposes, and for various state tax purposes (including property taxation). Most people focus on valuation in the federal estate tax arena, which can entail questions such as whether to determine the federal estate tax value as of the date of the decedent's death or on the alternate valuation date; and whether to determine the value of an asset under a willing-buyer, willing-seller hypothetical sale, as a going concern, using actual sales of comparable assets, by capitalizing future income, considering book value or asset liquidation,[11] or by some other unique or special evaluation. Setting up the appropriate estate tax valuation may

---

11. See Knott v. Commissioner, 55 T.C.M. (CCH) 424 (1988), in which a transferred partnership interest was deemed to have a value even though a partnership liability exceeded the net underlying asset value of the partnership, such that the donees would have received nothing if the partnership had been liquidated immediately after the transfer. Going concern value should exceed liquidation value because of the perceived benefits of continuing an existing business rather than taking the assets of that business and starting a new enterprise. One obvious benefit is avoiding costs associated with a start up endeavor. Liquidation value usually is a minimum value because of a perception that owners will liquidate a business that has a lower going concern value. See Estate of Leichter v. Commissioner, 85 T.C.M. (CCH) 991 (2003).

involve inter vivos transfers, and they may implicate gift tax valuation issues of the same or related varieties.

In addition, a slew of adjustments may affect value (such as a control premium or discounts for minority or fractional interests, for lack of marketability,[12] or for other more esoteric factors like blockage,[13] built in income tax liabilities, restrictions imposed by the securities laws, or the existence of only an illicit market for the asset). See Chapter 12 beginning at page 48 regarding these and other types of adjustments. With select assets another option may be to value property not at its highest and best use but instead at its actual use under a §2032A "special use" valuation regime applicable to realty used in farming, ranching, and other closely held businesses. See page 21. And there are other specialized valuation rules that may apply under Code Chapter 14 in the context of estate freezing techniques. See page 19.

Valuation is a particularly imprecise endeavor, referred to by one court as a "gross terminal logical inexactitude." Maris v. Commissioner, 41 T.C.M. (CCH) 127 (1980) (expropriating the words of Winston Churchill). Reliance principally on the willing-buyer, willing-seller hypothetical is especially trying because it begs reality. Reference to results reached in particular cases, to "average" discounts or premiums, or to other specific factors often is a fool's errand (reminiscent of using the manufacturer's statement of average miles per gallon fuel economy for a new car as indicating the performance of a particular used car, without specific regard to facts and circumstances such as the condition of the car or road, weather, speed, load, driver technique, and other variables). In addition, courts show a disturbing proclivity to do their own thing, sometimes differing diametrically in terms of such basic principles as whether to accept one litigant's theory of the case over the other or to strike a compromise between them. Thus, it pays to understand guidelines for valuation and the postmortem options that are available but not to embrace particular results in particular cases as if they were informative of *anything*.

Wrestling with valuation issues premortem usually cannot be very precise even on a case by case basis, because values are certain to fluctuate

---

12. Several cases deny the lack of marketability discount if using the book value of underlying assets is appropriate, because liquidation would yield the greatest return. See, e.g., Estate of Jephson v. Commissioner, 87 T.C. 297 (1986) (net asset value without discount was used because the decedent's willing buyer could liquidate the business and obtain its unleveraged portfolio of investments); Estate of Luton v. Commissioner, 68 T.C.M. (CCH) 1044 (1994) (there should be no lack of marketability discount in the case of a corporation consisting totally of cash and marketable securities that the corporation easily could liquidate); Estate of Jameson v. Commissioner, 77 T.C.M. (CCH) 1381 (1999), vac'd and rem'd on other grounds, 267 F.3d 366 (5th Cir. 2001) (a marketability discount to a 98% shareholder was severely limited because virtually all the assets in the corporation were marketable).

13. The fact that the market for a particular asset at a particular value is thin is not determinative unless less than all the asset could be sold at that price.

over time (usually in unpredictable and uncontrolled ways) and efforts to be accurate tend to be unnecessarily expensive in terms of appraisal and other costs. Although premortem planning may make certain valuation adjustments viable (such as engineering discounts that may apply later), most premortem valuations need to be no more accurate than appropriate to estimate liquidity needs or to judge the likely application of provisions that depend on includible assets meeting certain threshold value requirements. Usually marital and charitable deduction planning is accomplished with formula provisions that self-adjust to reflect valuation changes, and few dispositive or other provisions turn on precise valuation determinations. So, aside from periodic reviews that verify assumptions about operation of the plan, valuation is largely a postmortem estate administration function that requires individuated determinations and entails a great deal of uncertainty, guesswork, or compromise.

The one and only Code provision addressing the proper valuation of garden variety assets includible in the gross estate is §2031(b), and it essentially is worthless, which may explain why valuation is unquestionably the single most frequently litigated issue for all wealth transfer tax purposes. Curiously, more significant valuation guidance is found in §6662, which collars the valuation endeavor by placing overvaluation and undervaluation penalties on taxpayers who are too aggressive in establishing value for both income and wealth transfer tax purposes. Taxpayers are at a competitive disadvantage in this regard because there is no corresponding provision that imposes restrictions on the government when it challenges taxpayer valuations.

Willing-Buyer, Willing-Seller Valuation

Valuation largely is an application of standards established by regulation, ruling, and judicial guidance, the most classic formulation of which being the statement that "fair market value is the price at which the property would change hands between a willing buyer and a willing seller, neither being under any compulsion to buy or to sell and both having reasonable knowledge of relevant facts." Treas. Reg. §20.2031-1(b). The regulation goes on to provide:

The fair market value of a particular item of property includible in the decedent's gross estate is not to be determined by a forced sale price. Nor is the fair market value of an item of property to be determined by the sale price of the item in a market other than that in which such item is most commonly sold to the public, taking into account the location of the item wherever appropriate. Thus, in the case of an item of property includible in the decedent's gross estate, which is generally obtained by the public in the retail market, the fair market value of such an item of property is the price at which the item or a comparable item would be sold at retail. For example, the fair market value of an automobile (an article generally obtained by the public in the retail market) includible in the decedent's gross estate is the price for which an automobile of the same or approximately the same description, make, model, age, condition, etc., could be purchased by a member of the general public, and not the price for which the particular automobile of the decedent would be purchased by a dealer in used automobiles.

Actual sales of identical or, lacking that, comparable assets usually are the best evidence of the proper value, making valuation easy with respect to assets with a ready market. Only when there is no ready market does difficulty normally arise.

In this regard, for some assets there is reasonably good guidance on how to establish value. For instance, a huge percentage of valuation cases involve interests in land, both developed and investment grade or timber, or closely held businesses, in each case for which there may be no established or regular market. With respect to these less easily valued assets, courts sometimes take pains to stress that evidence of what a willing buyer would offer to pay is only half of the two-sided willing-buyer, willing-seller equation. The Tax Court has stated that fair market value requires a price at which both a willing buyer would purchase and a willing seller would sell. It is not established by satisfaction of half this equation.

Yet this message has been confused on occasion, the Tax Court itself once having said that "the highest price a willing buyer would pay is also the price that a willing seller wants,"[14] suggesting that a focus on the willing buyer is appropriate because it necessarily equates with a willing seller analysis. This, however, actually assumes an *un*willing seller — one who feels obliged to sell and therefore feels compelled to find a willing buyer and then take whatever is the highest amount that hypothetical party will offer. Indeed, if it were right, the converse of the statement also would be true: that a willing buyer will pay as much as the lowest price a willing seller would accept. If this were an accurate reformulation, it would posit that a willing buyer will not walk away from a sale even if the price is too high, which makes the buyer unwilling as well. As you can begin to sense, the willing-buyer, willing-seller hypothesis is not particularly realistic.

An additional factor illustrated by the regulation is that new assets should not be valued in the used asset market, or vice versa. Collectively, this differential in value sometimes is known as the difference between liquidation value and replacement cost, the higher replacement cost value being the controlling precept. This difference has been a topic of significant controversy, as illustrated by Estate of Scull v. Commissioner, 67 T.C.M. (CCH) 2953 (1994), which accepted the government's valuation of property sold at auction as the full amount paid by the buyer,

---

14. Estate of Newhouse v. Commissioner, 94 T.C. 193, 233 n.23 (1990), nonacq., 1991-1 C.B. 1 and 1991-2 C.B. 1 (does twice indicating disapproval mean the government was doubly offended?).

notwithstanding that the seller received only that amount less the auctioneer's commission (indeed, the auctioneer may receive another commission from the buyer, over and above the hammer price, and a commission from the seller out of the hammer price; the federal estate tax value is not the amount received by the seller, nor the hammer price unreduced by the seller's commission: it is the full amount paid by the buyer — basically including the two commissions, neither of which the seller will realize). This truly highlights the difference between replacement cost and liquidation value, the latter amount being what the seller received but the higher replacement cost being what the buyer paid. It should not be a surprise that the regulations view replacement cost as the proper measure of value for federal estate tax purposes.[15]

Finally, note that for estate tax purposes the destination of the includible property is irrelevant. Whether it passes all to one person or to many, or will be owned by a beneficiary who acquires with it control or some other valuable attribute, valuation looks to what the decedent owned and not how or to whom it is transferred.

Use of Postmortem Facts

Among the more controversial and least definite valuation issues is the effect on the valuation process of facts developed after the valuation date.[16] A fundamental wealth transfer tax notion is that the estate tax employs a snapshot principle: only facts about estate assets that appear in a snapshot taken on the valuation date are relevant, meaning (in theory) that facts developed thereafter should not be relevant. But the reality is that some courts have allowed evidence of value that includes facts that were neither known nor reasonably knowable on the valuation date.

Thus, for example, Estate of Keller v. Commissioner, 41 T.C.M. (CCH) 147, 148 (1980) (valuation of a farm and growing crop, sold and harvested, respectively, postmortem), stated that a "sale of property to an unrelated party shortly after date of death tends to establish such value at date of death." The difficulty with a paradigm allowing some postmortem facts as evidence of value is knowing the parameters of the rule. For example, in First National Bank of Kenosha v. United States, 763 F.2d 891 (7th Cir. 1985), a development company entered into an agreement to purchase includible property 21 months after the decedent's death. This was deemed relevant because no intervening events had drastically altered

---

15. If a sale meets the requirements of §2053(a)(2) and Treas. Reg. §20.2053-3(d)(2) (if it was necessary to pay the decedent's debts, expenses of administration, or taxes, to preserve the estate, or to effect distribution), then the commission paid to the auctioneer would be an allowable deduction that would subject only the net amount actually received by the estate to tax. But assets that are not sold, or sales that do not meet this necessity requirement, do not qualify for this reduction in the net effective amount subject to tax.

16. The issue may arise regardless of whether values are being determined as of the date of death or the alternate valuation date, and whether valuation is under traditional methods or a paradigm such as §2032A special use valuation.

the value of the property. Thus, the agreement was regarded as probative (albeit not necessarily conclusive) evidence of value. Notwithstanding that the buyer never completed the transaction! The court noted that a different result might apply if, for example, minerals were newly discovered or other unknown facts were revealed in the interim.

Even this "postmortem discovery" issue is uncertain, as illustrated by Rubenstein v. United States, 826 F. Supp. 448 (S.D. Fla. 1993), in which the existence of the includible asset was not even known at the valuation date, much less its value. The court held that a cause of action discovered only after the decedent's death was includible in the gross estate and that the best evidence of its value was the amount for which it was settled during the course of estate administration.

Given the result in these cases, Estate of Jung v. Commissioner, 58 T.C.M. (CCH) 1127 (1990), is not surprising. To help determine the estate tax value of the decedent' stock in a closely held corporation, the court honored the government's request for documents relating to a sale of the assets of that business 27 months after the valuation date. The court held that sale of those assets might help determine the earlier value of the stock. Similarly, in Estate of Scanlan v. Commissioner, 72 T.C.M. (CCH) 160 (1996), the court admitted as relevant to its valuation of a decedent's stock evidence of an offer to purchase and a redemption price between 18 and 28 months after the valuation date. These may be extraordinary results, and there are cases that go the other way. Still, it is well to remember that courts consider postmortem developments, and they may be relevant for deduction purposes as well as for inclusion or valuation purposes, with equally uncertain parameters.

Ignoring Options and Agreements that Affect Value

Assets includible in a decedent's gross estate may be subject to an agreement (such as a buy-sell, right of first refusal, put or call, or other option) that could (if respected) affect the value of assets subject to the agreement for federal estate tax purposes. These agreements may be desirable for a number of legitimate reasons (other than their effect on valuation), such as to provide a ready market for a decedent's otherwise illiquid investments, to keep the investment in a family unit, or to permit surviving business owners to avoid having to do business with a deceased partner's surviving spouse or other family members. But Congress was aware that these agreements also were used to freeze the value of subject property at the agreed upon striking price. To combat the possibility of abuse in such circumstances, §2703 addresses the valuation effect of options, rights to acquire or use property, and restrictions on the sale or use of property of any kind.

The primary thrust of §2703(a) is to restrict the ability of buy-sell agreements to establish the estate, gift, or GST value of property at a price that is less than fair market value for federal estate tax valuation purposes, determined without regard to the agreement. If applicable, §2703(a) also totally negates the effect of other restrictions on the sale or use of property in determining value for transfer tax purposes, and it may be deemed to apply with respect to limitations on liquidation of an entity, to leases with option provisions, and to certain easements.

An exception is provided if the option, agreement, right, or restriction meets three requirements: it is "a bona fide business arrangement," with terms that are comparable to those of "similar arrangements entered into by persons in an arm's length transaction," and it is "not a device to transfer . . . property to members of the decedent's family for less than full and adequate consideration." Moreover, all the pre-§2703 rules regarding the validity of agreements to peg values (such as the need to impose lifetime restrictions on transfer) are unaffected by §2703, meaning that even if the foregoing exception applies, the agreement still may fail on one or more of those additional traditional requirements.

Ignoring Rights and Restrictions that Affect Value

Also precluded is the use of voting, liquidation, and other rights or restrictions that have "the effect of reducing the value of the transferred interest [for wealth transfer tax purposes that do] not ultimately reduce the value of such interest to the transferee." §2704(b)(4). Applicable only to corporations and partnerships in which the transferor and family members hold 50% control before and after the transfer, §2704 essentially regards the lapse of a restriction as a taxable transfer of the difference in value measured before and after the lapse. Further, restrictions that are imposed but that do *not* lapse are disregarded for valuation purposes if they will lapse or can be removed by the transferor or by family members after the transfer. In effect, the higher value determined without regard to the right or restriction is the proper value for wealth transfer tax purposes.

Alternate Valuation

The alternate valuation date is six months after the decedent's death *or* any *earlier* date on which the asset is distributed, sold, exchanged, or otherwise disposed of. §2032(a)(1), Treas. Reg. §20.2032-1(c)(2), Rev. Rul. 78-378. Distribution occurs upon expiration of the executor's right to obtain possession of the property to satisfy creditor claims. Assets that are affected by the mere lapse of time — such as a temporal or split interest (life estate, term of years, or remainder), or an annuity — are valued without adjustment for any difference in value (as of the later date) that is due to the time element. §2032(a)(3). See Treas. Reg. §§20.2032-1(a)(3), 20.2032-1(f) (the concept does not, however, apply to obligations for the payment of money, with or without interest, as to which the value changes over time).

Alternate valuation is an all or nothing proposition: the election is made with respect to either every estate asset or none. The estate may not pick and choose assets to value under the normal date of death paradigm and others to value on the alternate valuation date. So postmortem planning requires the personal representative to accelerate the alternate valuation date for rapidly appreciating assets by forcing a distribution or other acceleration event that allows other assets to continue to benefit from the six month alternate valuation date, by drawing the curtain on only those assets that are becoming more valuable. If the entire estate is appreciating, however, alternate valuation will not be viable: among the qualification requirements is that the value of the estate as a whole must be less than if date of death valuation applies. §2032(c)(1).

A second qualification requirement for §2032 alternate valuation is that all taxes payable (*after* all credits are applied) under the estate and GST must be reduced. §2032(c)(2). As illustrated in Chapter 7, typical marital deduction planning reduces the estate tax incurred (after the unified credit) in any sized estate to zero, regardless of the valuation results, which makes qualification difficult and requires special planning to qualify for alternate valuation in such an estate.[17]

Finally, alternate valuation requires a timely election. §2032(d). This actually may be made on a late return filed no more than one year tardy. §2032(d)(2).

Special Use Valuation

The special use valuation election of §2032A provides an option to value certain includible realty at its actual use in farming or ranching or in a closely held trade or business, rather than at normal highest-and-best-use value. So, for example, Blackacre Farm sitting in the path of urban development might be worth $100x for tract housing but is worth only $25x in agricultural production. Special use valuation would allow use of the lower actual use value if the requirements for qualification are met. The actual use value of qualified special use real property is determined by a complex formula. Or the estate may elect to have the value of the qualified special use property determined under a special five factor alternative. This is a complex area, not well suited to any simplified summary description.

Administratively §2032A is cumbersome because it also requires the estate to determine the highest-and-best-use value under the traditional willing-buyer, willing-seller method. This is because the aggregate decrease in value resulting from special use valuation cannot exceed $750,000 (as adjusted for inflation; in 2004 this figure had risen to $850,000). Moreover, the estate must evaluate whether to determine this fair market value on the alternate valuation date; if it does, the special use value also will be determined on the alternate valuation date.

---

17. Because the estate will pay no estate tax in either event, the benefit of alternate valuation is to reduce the amount of marital deduction needed in the estate of the first spouse to die, which correspondingly reduces the wealth potentially includible in the subsequent estate of the surviving spouse.

As discussed next, the administrative hassles and added cost attributable to the valuation approach, along with recapture tax potential and other less obvious costs of qualification, may persuade the estate that §2032A is not worth pursuing, or that other alternatives for making the estate tax burden more palatable should be considered.

Qualification Requirements

Applicable only to the United States real property of a United States citizen or resident decedent passing to a "qualified heir," §2032A requires that the decedent or members of the decedent's family owned, and used in a qualified manner, property that constituted a significant portion of the decedent's total wealth. As you may well imagine, there are multiple definitional and sub-requirements lurking in all of this. So it probably makes sense to make a quick audit of the basic requirements to determine whether an estate is in the qualification ballpark, before spending substantial resources determining whether qualification would be viable or desirable and whether the respective valuation thresholds are met. In addition, it usually is relatively easy to determine whether the requisite activity requirements have been met, and whether allocation of the qualified use property under the terms of the estate plan (or in the fiduciary's discretion) will permit continued qualification.

This can be an important issue if some beneficiaries intend to be active material participants on the qualified use property and others not, such as children who remained active in the family farm or business and those who moved away. Premortem planning might sever assets or create ownership structures to segregate the qualified use property and allow its distribution to only those who will participate, while maintaining any intended equality with nonparticipants. For this purpose qualified use requires participation by the decedent or members of the decedent's family in activities that constitute farming or a trade or business (other than farming).

The availability of special use valuation in nonfarm trade or business activities is surprising to some. For example, §2032A special use valuation has been used in such diverse cases as a ski resort (in which highest-and-best-use was for condominiums but the actual use was as a slick slope for slip sliding), a vacant lot in a major urban downtown location (in which highest-and-best-use was for a skyscraper but the actual use was a parking lot), and an overland truck terminal located near the intersection of three major interstate highways (for which the highest-and-best-use was for light industrial development but the actual use was a trailer parking lot and a loading dock).

Qualified Use: Material Participation and Recapture

Material participation is required to qualify for special use valuation initially and then to avoid a §2032A(c) recapture of the tax benefit postmortem. It is defined in §2032A(e)(6) as qualified use for at least five years of any eight year period, by the decedent (or a family member of the decedent) during life and thereafter by a qualified heir (or a family member of the heir). This eight year material participation period spans the date of the decedent's death, and the recapture tax might be triggered quickly after death if neither the decedent nor any member of the decedent's family was active for almost a full three years during the eight years just before death. Because it may not be feasible for the qualified heir to make a rapid assumption of qualified use, relief is provided by a special hiatus that permits the qualified heir to delay assumption of material participation for up to two years, with a concomitant extension of the recapture period (which normally runs for a full decade after death). §2032A(c)(7). Other special accommodations are made for decedents who were retired (receiving old age benefits) or were disabled during the eight year period prior to death. §2032A(d)(4). And a relaxed "active management" standard is substituted by §2032A(e)(12) for the more demanding §2032A(c)(7)(B) material participation requisite if the qualified heir is the decedent's surviving spouse or other "eligible qualified heirs."

Ownership and qualified use are essential with respect to both the decedent before death and the qualified heir afterwards, the critical notion being that §2032A is not meant to benefit passive investors versus active participants. The qualified use aspect that most clearly illustrates this is cash leases of otherwise qualified property. Economic risk is the essential element in qualified use, which is negated by a fixed rent cash lease. A crop share lease qualifies, however, because both owner and tenant share the risk of a poor harvest.

A special rule in §2032A(e)(3) regarding residences on the qualified use property allows the home to meet the material participation requirement if it is occupied by the owner, a lessee, or an employee of either, if that occupancy permits the resident to operate or maintain the qualified use property. In some cases it may be wise to exclude such property from the qualified use election to permit a full §1014 basis adjustment with respect to the residence and occupancy by or rental to third parties that will not imperil material participation.

The amount of added recapture tax liability specified in §2032A(c) is the amount by which the decedent's estate tax was reduced. This amount is subject to a limitation that protects the taxpayer from owing more tax than the value of the property that avoided estate tax.

Computing the Estate Tax

The federal estate tax is computed under the §2001 unified rate schedule. The computation involves four basic steps:

(1) the §2051 taxable estate (gross estate minus deductions) is added to the decedent's adjusted taxable gifts made after 1976 (to the extent those gifts are not included in the decedent's gross estate);

(2) a tentative estate tax is computed on this amount under the unified rate schedule;

(3) the tentative tax is reduced by the aggregate gift taxes payable with respect to gifts made by the decedent after 1976; and

(4) the §§2010 through 2014 credits (e.g., the unified, the previously taxed property, and the foreign death tax credits) then are applied against this estate tax liability to reduce the amount of tax actually payable.

Under §2013 a previously taxed property credit is designed to protect against taxation of the same property in more than one estate within a short time. A 100% credit is allowed for the tax previously paid if the prior transferor and the current decedent died within two years of each other; the credit diminishes as the dates of death become more remote and several limitations may preclude the credit from being equal to the entire federal estate tax previously paid. Unfortunately, there is no credit against double taxation in rapid succession if a donor gives property inter vivos to a donee who dies shortly thereafter. There simply is no estate tax credit for gift tax previously paid. Nor is there a credit if the transferor incurs estate tax and the transferee incurs gift tax on an inter vivos transfer within 10 years after the transferor's death. And there is no previous GST credit either.

It may help to visualize the estate tax computation by reviewing the following truncated pro forma illustration.

- To determine the decedent's *gross estate*, add:
  1. §2033 Probate Estate
  2. §2035 Transfers and Gift Taxes Paid Within 3 Years of Death
  3. §§2036 through 2038 Property Transferred Inter Vivos
  4. §2039 Annuities
  5. §2040 Concurrently Owned Property
  6. §2041 General Power of Appointment Property
  7. §2042 Life Insurance Proceeds
  8. <u>§2044 Qualified Terminable Interest Property</u>
     Total Value of Gross Estate

- To determine the decedent's *taxable estate*, subtract:
  1. §2053 Expenses, Debts, Claims, and Taxes
  2. §2054 Losses
  3. §2055 Charitable Deduction
  4. §2056 Marital Deduction
  5. <u>§2058 State Death Tax Deduction</u>
     Total Value of Taxable Estate

- To determine the total tax base add adjusted taxable gifts after 1976 (excluding those included in the gross estate).
- Compute the tentative estate tax on the total tax base.
- Subtract gift tax payable on post 1976 adjusted taxable gifts.
- Subtract all allowable credits.
- The result is the total estate tax payable.

The Federal Generation-Skipping Transfer Tax

Before enactment of the generation-skipping transfer tax in Code Chapter 13, it was possible to avoid federal wealth transfer taxation of property enjoyed by successive generations of beneficiaries by placing the property in a properly drafted trust that created a succession of life estates. For example, a trust might "pay the income in equal shares to such of my children as are living from time to time, and after the death of my last child to die to such of my grandchildren as are living from time to time, and after the death of my last grandchild to die to such of my great grandchildren," and so on, until expiration of the permissible period of the Rule Against Perpetuities. Prior to 1976 such a trust would avoid the estate tax at each younger generation. So would a trust that permitted the trustee to distribute income or principal to descendants as the trustee deemed appropriate in its sole discretion, or any variety of similar trusts.

In addition to being granted income interests and the right to receive principal in the discretion of an independent trustee, beneficiaries in each generation could be given powers to withdraw up to $5,000 or 5% of the trust principal each year, powers to withdraw principal pursuant to an ascertainable standard, or both. Beneficiaries also could be given nongeneral testamentary powers to appoint the trust assets outright or in further trust, permitting redirection of the trust property within a designated class of appointees. Beneficiaries could even serve as trustee of the trust, if their powers were properly limited to avoid characterization as a general power of appointment. In sum, beneficiaries in multiple generations could be given the various rights and powers permissible in a bypass trust (see Chapter 5), all without corrupting the tax minimization or tax avoidance possibilities of the trust.

No part of the trust property would be includible in a beneficiary's estate for federal estate tax purposes as each beneficiary (child, grandchild, great grandchild and so forth) died, because no beneficiary possessed more than a life estate and nontaxable powers of appointment. Thus, after the transferor's[18] payment of gift or estate tax when the trust was created, no

---

18. The GST refers to a "transferor" who creates a generation-skipping trust. Although it is not the common lingo used by trust law or most planners, this Chapter uses that term also. It is synonymous with "grantor" or "settlor" in most cases, although on occasion the GST transferor will be deemed to change for purposes of applying these rules.

additional tax was imposed on the successive economic enjoyment of the trust property by one generation after another. Instead, the transfer tax was avoided or "skipped" by successive generations of beneficiaries who nevertheless enjoyed substantial benefits from the property.

Some states have modified their laws to permit various forms of perpetual generation-skipping trusts that may benefit successive generations and last literally forever. In every state, it usually is possible for a generation-skipping trust to continue for at least 90 or 100 years through the use of a carefully drafted perpetuities saving clause.[19] In effect then, before enactment of the GST, trust property that was taxed when a trust was established could be removed from the transfer tax rolls until it passed into the outright ownership of beneficiaries when the trust terminated, maybe a century (or more) later. By one estimate, through the use of dynastic trusts and other sophisticated planning arrangements, prior to 1976 the duPont family lost only 5% of its aggregate wealth to the transfer tax system since its inception. Cooper, A VOLUNTARY TAX? NEW PERSPECTIVES ON SOPHISTICATED ESTATE TAX AVOIDANCE 1 (1979). All of this finally prompted Harvard Professor A. James Casner to testify in 1976 regarding the proposed GST: "We haven't got an estate tax; what we have, you pay an estate tax if you want to; if you don't want to, you don't have to." Estate and Gift Taxes: Hearings Before the House Ways and Means Committee, 94th Cong., 2d Sess., part 2, 1335 (1976).

Congress was convinced in 1976 that significant abuse of the wealth transfer tax system was possible through the use of these generation-skipping trusts. It also concluded that these dispositions frustrated the policies and purposes of the wealth transfer tax system because the estate tax fell on most families every generation while wealthier families (who received proper advice and had enough property to employ the requisite devices) incurred wealth transfer taxes only after several generations of beneficiaries had enjoyed and controlled the family wealth. According to Congress, this perceived gap in the coverage of the transfer taxes had to be plugged to make the system work properly.

The GST was enacted to assess dispositions that provided economic benefits to several generations of beneficiaries. Thus, it applies only to trusts and "trust equivalents"[20] with beneficiaries assigned to more than one generation below the transferor. The classic example would be a trust for the benefit of the transferor's child for life, remainder to the child's descendants (or an equivalent life estate and remainder, not in trust). A "beneficiary" is any person with a present or future right to receive distributions from the trust, either absolutely or in the trustee's discretion.

---

19. See the sample saving clauses in Chapter 19 at page 30.
20. These are legal arrangements (other than estates) that have the same effect as a trust. §2652(b)(1). Examples include a legal life estate (that is, a life estate not in a trust) with a remainder or a life insurance policy settlement option or an annuity arrangement for successive beneficiaries.

The original rules governing who had an interest or a power and when it terminated in a taxable manner were so complicated that eventually everyone (the Treasury Department and Congress too) agreed that the 1976 version of the GST was a failure. In 1986 Congress corrected major deficiencies while simplifying the law through several fundamental changes. First and foremost, every taxpayer now is granted an exemption from the tax that can be applied to transfers during life or at death. It began at $1 million per taxpayer and many people still refer to it as such, but today it is tied to the applicable exclusion amount for estate tax purposes. With proper planning, a married couple may transfer double the amount of the applicable exclusion amount/GST exemption without ever incurring a GST. If it is properly employed this exemption insulates most estate plans from Chapter 13.

A caution is in order, however. At first blush the exemption might suggest that only the truly wealthy and their counselors must be concerned about the GST. Unfortunately even smaller estates, as to which the estate and gift taxes are not a problem and as to which the GST *should* be no problem, will require competent planning to properly allocate and use the exemption. You must ensure that generation-skipping transfers that could be protected by the exemption are protected under the not-always-simple exemption allocation rules. Moreover, generation-skipping has become more popular than before attention was drawn to the subject, now that the tax excepts smaller estates from its reach. Ironically, the exemption encourages the creation of more trusts designed to run for the full period of the Rule Against Perpetuities.

Skip Persons

The key to understanding the GST is to remember the abuses that the tax is meant to prevent: enjoyment of property followed by its movement down the generations without being subjected to estate or gift tax. All of Chapter 13 is related in some way to such planning. Thus, for example, to invoke the tax, there must be either a non-exempt "direct skip" transfer or a trust with a "skip person" as beneficiary. Under §2612(c), a direct skip essentially is any transfer made to or in trust for the benefit of a skip person. As defined in §2613(a)(1), a skip person is any one assigned to a generation more than one below the transferor (such as a grandchild).

Individuals are assigned to generations under §2651 in one of three ways, depending on the individual's relation to the transferor. First, all lineal descendants of the transferor's grandparents ("relatives" of the transferor) are assigned to generations on the basis of consanguinity, and relatives by adoption or by the half blood are treated as natural relatives by the whole blood. Thus, a child is in the first generation below the transferor, an adopted grandchild is in the second generation below the transferor, and a nephew or niece by the half blood (a half sibling's child) is in the first generation, all as illustrated in the diagram at page 28.

Second, any person who was at any time married to any lineal descendant of the transferor's grandparents (including the transferor's own spouse or former spouse) automatically is assigned to the lineal descendant's generation, regardless of the spouse's age. Moreover, the consanguinity rules apply to relatives of the transferor's spouse (or any former spouse) as if the transferor and the spouse were one person. Thus, for example, a child's spouse is assigned to the first generation below the transferor, even if young enough to be the transferor's grandchild, and even if subsequently divorced from the child. If the transferor's spouse had a child by a former marriage, the child would be in the first generation below the transferor even if the transferor never adopted that child, and the same treatment would equally apply to the spouse of the child.

All other non-relatives (beneficiaries who are not related by blood, adoption, or by marriage) are assigned on the basis of age, with spouses of non-relatives *not* automatically receiving the same generation assignment. Beware: many students assume that spouses always are assigned to the same generation, which is not true if neither spouse is a descendant of the transferor's grandparents.

In assigning generations on the basis of age, the fundamental assumption is that each generation is 25 years in length, and that the transferor is exactly in the middle of his or her generation. Thus, someone within 12.5 years above or below the transferor is deemed to be in the same generation as the transferor. Thereafter, every 25 years is a new generation. So, someone more than 12.5 years but not more than 37.5 years younger than the transferor is in the first generation below the transferor, while someone more than 37.5 years but not more than 62.5 years younger than the transferor is in the second generation below the transferor, and so on.

Same Generation	*Grantor and Spouse*	Sibling and Spouse	Cousin and Spouse	Non-Relatives within 12.5 years of age
First Level Below: Non-Skip Persons	Child and Spouse	Niece or Nephew and Spouse	Cousin Once Removed and Spouse	Non-Relatives 12.5 to 37.5 years younger
Second Level Below: Skip Persons	Grandchild and Spouse	Grandniece or Grandnephew and Spouse	Cousin Twice Removed and Spouse	Non-Relatives 37.5 to 62.5 years younger

If a person is assigned to two generations by virtue of these rules (for example, the transferor adopts a grandchild as a child), the general rule under §2651(e)(1) is that the younger generation assignment governs (making the adopted grandchild a skip person) and preventing efforts to move up a generation to avoid the tax.

Taxable Transfers

To incur a generation-skipping tax there must be a §2611(a) "generation-skipping transfer," of which there are three types: direct skips, taxable distributions, and taxable terminations.

Direct Skips

"Direct skips" are defined in §2612(c) as transfers that are subject to the estate or gift tax, made directly to or in trust for the benefit of a skip person. Applying a vision of property moving down the generations, the direct skip tax is imposed because no interest exists at the first level below the transferor. In essence, this is Congress' way of saying that it wants to tax property as it moves past every younger generation.[21] Thus, a tax should be paid if the property passes immediately to the second or a more remote generation. A direct skip will incur an estate or gift tax and then an immediate GST as well.

A transfer might be made to or in trust for the benefit of a grandchild whose parent was the child of the transferor (or of the transferor's spouse) but who is deceased. Because that direct transfer is not regarded as made for tax minimization reasons, a "predeceased child" exception in §2612(c)(2) precludes application of the direct skip tax in such a case. It provides that the grandchild is treated as a child (and all lineal descendants of the grandchild similarly are "moved up" a generation). For example, assume Transferor died leaving a will that bequeaths Transferor's residuary estate "to my descendants, per stirpes." Transferor is survived by two children, A and B, and grandchild X, the child of Transferor's deceased child C. One third of the residuary estate passes to grandchild X and is not taxed as a direct skip because C was not alive to be "skipped." If, instead, C had survived Transferor but disclaimed all interests under the will, the interest passing to X by reason of the disclaimer would be taxable as a direct skip transfer.

Taxable Distributions

A "taxable distribution" is any distribution from a trust (or trust equivalent) to a skip person. §2612(b). For example, in a trust for the transferor's descendants, a distribution to a child would not be a taxable distribution because the child is not a skip person. In the same trust, however, a distribution of either income or principal to a grandchild would be a taxable distribution because grandchildren normally are skip persons.

---

21. This analysis breaks down a bit because, if the property were left to the great grandchild level (skipping both the child and grandchild levels), a true once-per-generation tax would impose the direct skip tax twice, in addition to the estate or gift tax incurred on the initial transfer. Congress chose not to extend the direct skip treatment in this respect, probably because triple taxation would rarely be incurred and, if imposed, would virtually wipe out the subject wealth.

Taxable Terminations

A "taxable termination" is the termination (by death, passage of time, release or lapse of a power, or otherwise) of any present interest[22] in a generation-skipping trust. §2612(a). There are several exceptions to this definition. Under the first, a taxable termination occurs only if, after the termination, the remaining beneficiaries all are skip persons. This means that the GST is not meant to apply until all present interests at the first generation below the transferor have terminated, and then not again until all present interests at the next generation have terminated, and so on. Thus, no taxable termination occurs if "immediately after such termination, a non-skip person has an interest in such property." §2612(a)(1)(A).

This "postponed termination" exception serves to defer imposition of the GST until termination of the present interests of all beneficiaries in non-skip generations. To illustrate, assume Transferor creates a trust to pay income to children for life, remainder to grandchildren in equal shares. Transferor has two children, A and B. A dies, which constitutes the termination of A's present interest. Nevertheless, this is not a taxable termination because B is a non-skip person and has an interest in the trust. The taxable termination will occur on B's death (unless another non-skip person acquires an interest in the trust, such as by B's exercise of a power of appointment). Similarly, in this example if grandchild X were to die while either A or B were alive, X's death would not be a taxable termination for two reasons: (1) a non-skip person (A or B) still has an interest in the trust, and (2) X's interest was a future interest, not a present interest, making the definition of a taxable termination inapplicable.

Under a second exception, termination of a present interest is not taxable if "at no time after such termination may a distribution (including distributions on termination) be made from such trust to a skip person." §2612(a)(1)(B). This "no interest passing to a skip person" exception is consistent with the purpose of the statute, which is to impose a tax only if a generation-skipping transfer actually occurs. This will not happen if the property does not move down the generational ladder by passing to a more remote generation.

For example, assume in the prior illustration that the trust specifies that the trust property passes to the Red Cross if no grandchild is living when the last child dies. In this event, no taxable transfer occurs if the last surviving child outlives all the grandchildren, even though that child's death is the termination of a present interest. This result illustrates that the primary focus of the GST is not on the child's enjoyment but, instead, on

---

22. An interest is a present right to receive either income or principal, either in the trustee's discretion, as an absolute entitlement, or pursuant to a power of withdrawal. §2652(c)(1). It does not matter how limited an interest is. If the interest exists, the holder is a skip person (if assigned to an appropriate generation) as to the entire trust or that segregable portion from which the interest may be satisfied.

whether the trust property moved down a generation after the child's interest terminated.

Imagine in this last case that the last surviving child and grandchild die together under such circumstances that the order of their deaths cannot be proven. Under state law or the terms of the document, the grandchild might be deemed to have predeceased the child and the property would pass to the Red Cross. Thus, no taxable termination would occur. The GST would be imposed, however, by reason of the child's death if the child died and the grandchild died shortly thereafter. In that case the trust property would be taxed again under the estate tax in the grandchild's estate. For this reason, it would be appropriate to insert a provision requiring that remainder beneficiaries survive the prior income beneficiaries by a specified period (such as 60 days) as a condition to taking.[23]

A third exception involves terminations that also are direct skips. Without elaborating here on the complex ordering scheme, suffice it to say that the Code establishes a priority for treatment of transfers that meet more than one of the taxable event definitions: first direct skips, then taxable terminations, and finally taxable distributions. These ordering rules can have consequences relating to who pays the tax, deferral of the tax, and especially the method of computing the tax on direct skips as compared to taxable terminations and taxable distributions.

Amount and Payment of the Tax

The GST is a flat tax computed at the maximum stated estate tax rate. §2641(a)(1). The estate tax also is a flat tax (under phase-in changes enacted in 2001 and complete after 2005), so the historic disfavor for the GST no longer is a concern. Indeed, unlike prior times, today it may not be cheaper to expose property to estate or gift tax to take advantage of lower rates than the GST.[24] Moreover, some planning is available for GST purposes that is not possible under either the estate or gift taxes.

One example of such planning is the ability to defer the GST under the provisions of §2612(a)(1), as discussed at page 30. Thus, in a trust for child for life, remainder to grandchild, child could appoint the property to child's sibling for life, deferring the GST until the sibling's death. There is no comparable estate tax deferral opportunity.

Another illustration is the ability of a younger generation beneficiary to "layer" property to a more remote generation beneficiary through exercise of a nongeneral power of appointment. If the trust property were includible in the beneficiary's estate for estate tax purposes, such layering would be subject to the direct skip tax, yielding a double tax. But this form

---

23. This would not be a problem if Chapter 13 contained a counterpart to the §2013 estate tax credit for previously taxed property, but it does not.

24. As an aside, it may be worth considering whether sheltering a beneficiary's applicable exclusion amount and GST exemption would be appropriate, by causing estate tax inclusion to that beneficiary, instead of incurring the GST. Let's leave that topic for a later discussion.

of planning can escape the second tax if made within the GST system. So, for example, in a trust for child for life, remainder to child's descendants, child could appoint the trust property to child's grandchild (the transferor's great grandchild) without incurring an additional tax at the intervening generation, and avoiding the direct skip tax as well. Thus, only the GST at child's death would apply, rather than an estate tax and then an immediate direct skip tax. This layering opportunity also would not be available if the trust property were subject to estate or gift tax at the child level.

Finally, some property may escape both systems of taxation under proper circumstances. For example, in a trust for Child for life, remainder to Child's descendants (if any), otherwise to Child's siblings (if child dies without descendants), the property will pass to the siblings free of GST under §2612(a)(1)(B) if Child dies without descendants. In this situation it would be foolish to cause the trust property to incur estate or gift tax as Child's property, if instead all taxes could be avoided.

Thus, savvy estate plans are drafted to provide sufficient flexibility to determine which system of tax will be most favorable (if any must be imposed). We do this by providing an opportunity to subject trust property either to the GST or to the estate or gift tax, as appears best at the time of the appropriate taxing event.

Amount Subject to the Tax

Under §2621, the amount subject to tax in the case of a taxable distribution is the amount received by the distributee. Because the tax is imposed on the distributee, this system of tax is like the "tax-inclusive" estate tax system discussed in Chapter 12 at page 3. This is because dollars that the distributee uses to pay the tax are themselves subject to the tax. They are included in the tax base. Moreover, if the trust that made the distribution pays the tax on behalf of the distributee, that payment is regarded as an additional taxable distribution that also is subject to the GST, under §2621(b).

In a taxable termination, §2622 provides that the full amount subject to termination is the amount subject to tax. Because the tax is paid out of this fund, the result here also is a tax-inclusive system (like the estate tax), with the dollars used to pay the tax also being subject to the tax.

Direct skips receive a different treatment, under §2623. The amount subject to tax in a direct skip is the value of the property actually received by the beneficiary. Because the beneficiary does not pay the tax on a direct skip, these transfers are cheaper because no rule treats the tax payment (by the transferor in most cases) as an additional generation-skipping taxable transfer. Thus, the direct skip is like the "tax-exclusive" gift tax computation. For example, if a transferor left $1 million of property in a direct skipping transfer at death and directed that the direct skip tax be paid out of the residue of the transferor's estate, the direct skip subject to tax would be the $1 million actually received by the beneficiary. The dollars used to pay the tax would be subject to estate tax but not to the GST.

If the transferor had specified that the beneficiary should pay the tax on this direct skip bequest, then the taxable transfer first would be reduced under §2642(a)(2)(B)(ii) by any federal or state estate or other death tax that is paid out of the bequest. Then the GST would be determined on the fair market value of the bequest remaining after payment of the GST. To determine the tax on the amount left after the tax requires the use of the following algebraic formula:

$$\text{Generation-Skipping Tax} = \text{rate} \times \frac{\text{Fair Market Value}}{1 + \text{rate of tax}}$$

Thus, the amount of the direct skip transfer is the net amount passing to the beneficiary, after payment of all wealth transfer taxes.

An illustration of the relative costs of the various forms of generation-skipping transfer, both inter vivos and at death, would show that an inter vivos direct skip gift is roughly three times cheaper than a testamentary transfer to a trust that will spawn a taxable distribution or taxable termination at a later date.[25] Yet experience shows that the latter alternative is the most common, probably because most clients don't want to incur gift tax during life and cannot afford to cut children out of any portion of their wealth by using direct skip transfers to skip persons. Just as gifting alone is advantageous, so too is direct skipping, but neither is within the reach of less than extremely wealthy taxpayers. Both of these disguised benefits are intentional favors from Congress to the super wealthy.

Source of Payment of the Tax

Under §2603(a), the tax is paid by the distributee in the case of a taxable distribution, by the trustee in a taxable termination or a direct skip from a trust, and by the transferor in a direct skip not from a trust. Further, §2603(b) provides that, "unless otherwise directed pursuant to the governing instrument *by specific reference to the tax imposed by this chapter*," the GST tax is a charge against the property taxed. Collectively, these provisions establish an apparently easy rule that "the person with the generation-skipping property pays the tax, using that property."

Like most simplifications, however, this statement is not entirely accurate in cases involving direct skips. For example, because the transferor (or the transferor's estate) pays the tax in the case of most direct skips, and that tax is computed tax exclusive, the transferor effectively makes the direct skip transfer and then comes up with additional monies to pay the tax. So §2603(b) essentially is a fiction in the case of a direct skip

---

25. See 2 Casner & Pennell, Estate Planning §11.4.14.1 (6th ed. 1999), for an illustration comparing the inter vivos direct skip taxed under two tax exclusive systems (gift tax and a direct skip) to the testamentary trust subject to two tax inclusive systems (estate tax and either a taxable distribution or taxable termination).

because the tax is not actually paid from the taxable property that constituted the transfer. Otherwise §2603(b) states what should seem obvious: the trustee who holds the property following a taxable termination, or the distributee who just received a taxable distribution, should use the property to pay the tax imposed under §2603(a).

Exceptions to the Tax

Estate and Gift Tax Override

To prevent double taxation the GST effectively provides that Chapter 13 is superseded by Chapters 11 and 12 to the extent a taxable transfer (other than a direct skip) also is subject to either estate or gift taxation. Although nothing in the Internal Revenue Code establishes this priority (that the estate and gift taxes apply before the GST), this in fact is Congress' intent.[26]

Second-Time Around

There is a similar exception under §2611(b)(2) providing that, if property has been generation-skipping taxed once at a given generation (or at a lower generation), it will not be taxed at that level again. As an example, imagine a trust for Child for life (at death there being a taxable termination), then for Grandchild's education and, if Child's spouse is still alive after Grandchild's education is complete, then back up to the spouse for life, finally distributing on the spouse's death to Child's descendants. Having been taxed once at the child level, the trust is insured against being taxed at that level a second time at the death of Child's spouse. This provision also ensures that no taxable termination is deemed to occur when Grandchild's formal education is completed and the interest of Grandchild terminates (at least until death of the spouse), because the spouse's interest prevents the property from moving down a generation.

Nontaxable Gifts

In addition, §2611(b)(1) also grants an overall exemption under Chapter 13 for any transfer *from* a trust that would, if made by an individual, qualify as a gift tax free payment of education or medical expenses under §2503(e). This provision should not be confused with §2642(c), which provides an effective exemption for certain annual exclusion gifts. Like the §2503(b) annual exclusion and the §2503(e) ed/med exclusion, §§2611(b)(2) and 2642(c) are not duplicative. Section 2611(b)(2) gives a nontaxable result to any §2503(e) type transfer *from* a trust. Section 2642(c) deals only with §2503(b) type annual exclusion direct skip transfers made outright or by transfer *into* a trust.

---

26. See Private Letter Ruling 9123052. This occurs because application of the estate or gift tax will result in the existence of a new transferor (to the extent property is includible in that person's wealth transfer tax base). As such the GST posture of the trust is altered once either tax is incurred. See, e.g., Chapter 12 at page 22 regarding this effect with lapsing withdrawal rights.

Moreover, §2642(c)(2) does not guarantee that all annual exclusion additions to a qualifying trust will be exempt for GST purposes. It provides a zero tax result for direct skipping transfers only if the transfer is outright or into a trust in which a sole beneficiary has exclusive enjoyment of the trust *and* the trust will be includible in the estate of a beneficiary who dies before trust termination. The effect of this provision is most apparent in the context of direct skipping transfers that are made into trusts, as to which the transfer is nontaxable by virtue of a Crummey clause power of withdrawal (see Chapter 9 at pages 51-53). These direct skipping additions to the trust will not escape GST if more than one individual enjoys current benefits in the trust, or if estate tax inclusion of the trust in the beneficiary's estate is not guaranteed.

Stopped Moving Down

The exceptions under §2612(a)(1)(A) and (B) that were discussed at page 30 should be considered again here. They preclude taxable termination treatment if the property has stopped moving down the generations (either permanently or just temporarily) if "(A) immediately after such termination, a non-skip person has an interest in such property or (B) at no time after such termination may a distribution (including distributions on termination) be made from such trust to a skip person." To illustrate, consider a trust for Child and Grandchild, with present interests at both generations. If Grandchild dies, no GST will be incurred because Child, a non-skip person, has a continuing interest. §2612(a)(1)(A). When Child later dies §2612(a)(1)(B) would prevent application of the GST if the property does not move down the generational ladder (for example, if the trust goes to the Child's sibling in this event).

As a second example of these exceptions, consider a group trust for children for life, with distribution to grandchildren only on the death of the last child to die. Here the death of any but the last child is not a taxable event because every child is a non-skip person and the exception in §2612(a)(1)(A) will apply while any child remains as a beneficiary. If the trust were held after the last child's death as a group trust for grandchildren until the last grandchild reached a specified age, and a grandchild died before the trust were distributed, the existence of any other living grandchild as a beneficiary similarly would prevent termination of the dying grandchild's interest from being a taxable event.[27]

---

27. To fully understand how this operates at the grandchild level requires an understanding of the "move down a generation" rule in §2653(a). This provision specifies that, after a generation-skipping taxable transfer occurs in a trust, "the trust will be treated as if the transferor . . . were assigned to the first generation above the highest generation of any person who has an interest in such trust immediately after the transfer." In this example the transferor would be deemed to move down to the child level following the taxable transfer caused by the last child's death, making the grandchildren the first level below the transferor, meaning that they become non-skip persons. Once this occurs, the requirements of §2612(a)(1)(A) would be met when a grandchild later dies.

GST Exemption

The final (and most important) exception to the GST is the §2631(a) "GST exemption" available to all transferors. It is not as easy (or as direct) as it might be, because it is granted in the form of an "inclusion ratio" that is then tied, under §2642, to the rate of tax for computation purposes. The "inclusion ratio" approach specifies that, once determined, the exempt portion does not change with fluctuations in values or distributions that occur. The exemption is incorporated into the rate for computation of the tax with respect to that particular trust so that, once determined for the trust, it can be "retained" in a manner that allows it to be ignored for all other purposes.

As a simple example of the operation of the §2642 "inclusion ratio" approach, assume a trust of $3 million, of which the transferor wishes to exempt $1 million. One way to accomplish this would be to create two trusts, one of $1 million (to be totally exempt) and one of $2 million (to be totally taxable). If, however, the document did not divide the trust into two funds, the inclusion ratio would be determined by subtracting an "applicable fraction" from the number 1. The applicable fraction here would be 1/3, determined by taking the exemption amount as the numerator and the value of the trust as the denominator. The "inclusion ratio" would thus be 2/3, and this fraction then would be multiplied against the rate of tax to determine the applicable rate of tax on all taxable transfers with respect to the trust in the future.

Thus, in this example, if the maximum wealth transfer tax rate was 45%, the applicable rate for this 1/3 exempt trust would be 30% (2/3 times 45%). The result of this incorporation of the exemption into the tax rate is that no transfer from this trust would be totally tax free. Had the full amount of the trust been covered by the exemption, however, the applicable fraction would have been 1/1, producing an inclusion ratio of 0 for multiplication against the applicable rate, producing a 0 rate of tax. For a number of reasons, it is advisable to avoid creation of trusts that are partially exempt. Instead, it is better to create two trusts, one that is totally exempt and another that is totally taxable. To accomplish this requires actual division, accomplished under the authority of state law or specific terms of the trust instrument.

Division is preferable because the exemption will protect appreciation in value, meaning that a separate totally exempt trust could be invested to maximize growth under the umbrella of the exemption while a totally nonexempt trust could be invested to maximize income for non-skip beneficiaries or otherwise without special consideration of the generation-skipping taxability of the trust. Creating separate trusts also is preferable because doing so will permit the fiduciary to decide whether to make distributions from the exempt or from the taxable trust, based on the generation assignment of the beneficiary, the time of distribution, the applicable tax rate at the time, the possibility of further growth in the respective trusts, and so forth. This flexibility is lost if every distribution will be taxable, albeit at a reduced rate.

A great deal of complexity and some inequities may arise by virtue of allocating the exemption badly. Under §§2631 and 2632 the exemption is elective, in the sense that a transferor or the transferor's personal representative may decide how to allocate it (or whether to allocate it at all) among any generation-skipping trusts created. Unfortunately, allocating the exemption proved to be so fraught with error that §2632 now contains automatic allocation rules that apply unless an affirmative alternative allocation (or reservation of the exemption) is selected. Frequently this is the wise approach, because automatic allocation often is not the best use of the exemption.

The automatic allocation rules consume enough exemption to cause the inclusion ratio to be zero, if possible, with allocation first seriatim to lifetime direct skips, then pro rata to direct skips at the transferor's death, and finally pro rata among all other generation-skipping transfers. The important aspect of these rules is that exemption is "wasted" on inter vivos direct skip gifts, which are the cheapest transfers made. This may be appropriate in some cases, because lifetime direct skips, to which automatic allocation is first made, are the earliest transfers to incur the tax.

The balance must be made between deferral of tax (by allowing the exemption to be used on direct skips during life) and maximizing the exemption (by allocation against the more expensive forms of transfer or allocation to those dispositions that will extend the farthest into the future). In this respect, also consider that any allocation of the exemption against any outright transfer is the worst use of it, while allocation to trusts that will last for a long time, to prevent application of the GST on multiple taxable transfers in the future, is the most expeditious use of the exemption (all other factors being equal) in most cases.

There is much more complexity in exemption allocation, which would take us way beyond this introduction to the GST. Please note that failure to allocate exemption properly is fraught with such malpractice concerns that Congress enacted relief provisions in §§2632(d) and 2642 to protect taxpayer advisors who did it badly. You do not want to rely on those, so if you choose not to become expert in this endeavor, then you should refer this element to someone who is. And don't just rely on the return preparer to get it right. Scads of rulings granting relief are proof positive that many get it wrong (even some who purport to be well experienced in return preparation).

State Wealth Transfer Taxes

Every state imposes a tax on the transfer of property at death, although there is some variation in the nature of those taxes.

The oldest variety is the inheritance tax, also known as a legacy or succession tax. These are separate taxes imposed on each benefit conferred on a recipient of property passing from a decedent, the amount of each tax usually being determined by the size of the gift and the degree of consanguinity of the person who receives it. As of 2001 only a handful of states imposed inheritance taxes, and virtually none had their own estate tax any longer. With phase out repeal of the §2011 state death tax credit, some (perhaps most) states will enact or restore prior estate, inheritance, or other succession taxes.

Before repeal of §2011, every state imposed a tax that was a percentage of the federal estate tax as reported on the federal estate tax return (after application of the unified credit). Even those states that imposed their own taxes of the other two varieties collected this pick up or sponge tax to garner the benefit of the §2011 credit for state death taxes. Thus, every state imposed an estate tax that effectively shifted revenue from the federal government to the taxing state without increasing the tax burden on the estate. Indeed, failure to do so merely allowed money that could be diverted to the state to go to the federal government (without reducing the total death taxes payable by a decedent's estate or beneficiaries). Although this credit was repealed, some states continue to base their tax on the credit as it existed in a prior year, meaning that some pick up taxes will continue to apply after full repeal of §2011. See house.leg.state.mn.us/hrd/pubs/stesttax.pdf, prepared by the Minnesota House Research Department, or abanet.org/tax/groups/egt/egt_news.html, prepared by the Estate and Gift Tax Committee of the Tax Section of the American Bar Association, which reflect state death tax changes in response to the amended federal law. Before too long there likely will be even more Balkanization and difficulty in summarizing the various state death tax provisions.

Although most state death taxes follow the federal inclusion rules, not all estates with zero federal estate tax escape state wealth transfer tax. This largely is because not all state death tax laws grant a marital deduction in the same amount or for the same transfers as the federal law. As a result, state death tax may be incurred in some estates that are tax free for federal estate tax purposes.

Many states also adopted their own sponge or pick up tax version of the GST, in all cases equal to the §2604 state GST credit, but no state has yet imposed a GST in excess of that credit amount. This credit also was repealed in 2001, effective after 2004, and it simply is too early to know whether any state will impose a separate state GST in the wake of repeal.

A state may tax the personal estate of a decedent who was domiciled in the state at death and may tax real property and tangible personal property located in the state even if the owner was domiciled elsewhere. Because many wealthy decedents spent parts of the year in various states (snowbirds who went to the sunbelt during the winter or sunbelt residents who went north for the summer), several states may be entitled to tax. Each will determine for itself whether the decedent was domiciled in that state or otherwise was subject to that state's taxing jurisdiction. Occasionally multiple taxation of the same property results.

The most famous example of this may be the estate of John T. Dorrance, of Campbell's Soup fame, who died in 1930 with an estate of $115 million and residences in New Jersey and Pennsylvania. The New Jersey courts ruled that he was domiciled in New Jersey and owed New Jersey tax of $17 million. The Pennsylvania courts ruled that he was domiciled in Pennsylvania and owed Pennsylvania tax of the same amount. Both taxes were collected, as was a federal estate tax. See Worcester County Trust Co. v. Riley, 302 U.S. 292, 297 (1937), for a summary (a substantial part, but not all, of the state taxes was deductible from the federal estate tax as it existed at that time).

More extreme was the case of a Texas decedent whose estate was assessed by Texas, Florida, New York, and Massachusetts, all claiming the decedent as their domiciliary. Collectively they threatened to levy taxes in an amount exceeding the full value of the estate, which was so outrageous that it produced a good result in Texas v. Florida, 306 U.S. 398 (1939), which limited the state excise to only one tax. And the estate of eccentric billionaire Howard Hughes was involved in three United States Supreme Court cases before it was established that a forum even existed to resolve conflicting state tax claims. See California v. Texas, 457 U.S. 164 (1982) (allowing one state to sue another to establish their respective rights to tax the decedent's estate), and cases cited therein. Although the problem generally still exists, many state statutes provide a mechanism to resolve conflicting state claims regarding domicile.

In 2001 only four states still imposed gift taxes. The low number probably reflects the fact that state wealth transfer tax rates are de minimis and probably do not often on their own alter the transfer planning of individual citizens. It may be that a state gift tax will not correlate with the federal gift tax, which could result in imposition of a state gift tax when there is no federal gift tax. Nevertheless, there is no credit against the federal gift tax for gift taxes paid to a state, so there is no incentive for states to enact a gift tax merely to take advantage of the kind of revenue sharing made implicit by §2011 prior to its repeal.

Chapter 19
FORMS

As was the case in Chapter 5 dealing with Family Trust Planning, the sample Will and Irrevocable Life Insurance Trust forms below are courtesy of The Northern Trust Company, Chicago, and are reprinted with permission. Attorneys are specifically granted authority to reproduce these forms in their representation of clients. But that does not necessarily mean that you *should*.

Before we begin, let's be clear about a number of realities. Drafting is the devil. Estate planners dance with this devil because ultimately most planning culminates in some form of document for the client. Normally that is because whatever plan you craft for the client will not be self-executing. Something must put it into operation, and usually that something is orchestrated or represented by an agreement or other document, such as a deed, a will or a trust, a buy-sell agreement, a beneficiary designation, or such.

Lawyers always want *forms*, often because they understand that clients are paying for an estate plan and they expect some form of writing that provides tangible evidence that the lawyer created something of value. Sometimes lawyers also want forms because that writing is the most tangible evidence that they have a real expectation of how something is going to work (as opposed to merely having an idea about it). It is wise in this respect to remember that having a document is not the same as having a plan, but it also is true that some document usually is required to implement most plans. Still, you should not think of drafting documents as the be-all and end-all of estate planning. Indeed, sometimes you will find it useful to put together an interim document just to suffice until the full-fledged plan is complete, and you (as well as the client) will understand that the document is a stop-gap measure rather than the culmination of the engagement.

Obtaining forms from which to produce documents is not very difficult. You will discover plenty of resources available — so many that you'll find it somewhat overwhelming trying to determine which are reliable, and keeping track of what you've collected. Start collecting them now, including sample paragraphs you see here and there that address unusual needs or situations. Catalog them and store them in such a way that you can find them and use them to jog your creative juices when you need to draft something from scratch. Often the paragraph you snagged from another document will not solve your particular problem, but it will give you a place to start and make the next drafting chore easier.

As a practical matter, you probably ought to defer the search for full fledged forms until you settle in the community in which you intend to practice. Then you can seek guidance from experienced planners and drafters who can direct you to tried-and-true forms for that locale. A local fiduciary may make a book of forms available for a modest payment, or the bar association may have a Section or Committee devoted to estate planning, fiduciary law, wills and trusts, or elderlaw, and that body of volunteers may have produced a book of forms that is available to you. Because drafting varies a good bit from one locale to another, it is prudent to seek out recommendations from within the legal community where you intend to practice. State laws and local customs vary, approaches that are accepted or recommended in one place are disfavored elsewhere, fiduciary administration sometimes relies on notions of "the way we've always done it" (sometimes with good reason), and it pays to be circumspect in plowing new ground in a new community. Thus, you do not want to view the illustrative forms here as the backbone of a forms library that you will want to create for yourself. This is just for learning purposes.

The following items are truly meant just to illustrate how certain documents look, to give you an idea of how things fit together, and perhaps to persuade you that there is a lot going on in most well constructed documents. You will discover over time that typically there are a variety of ways that something can be done. Seldom is there a single "right" or even a "best" way to draft a provision.

You should, as efficiently and effectively as you can, become familiar with literally every sentence in the forms that you ultimately adopt. Then you will be in a better position to "tinker with" (alter and amend) the forms you obtain. Before you "personalize" the approach you have adopted, you really need to be certain that you're not making things worse, which is easy to do if you're not sure why particular provisions were drafted to read as they do. Indeed, one of the most dangerous things a rookie can do is "cut and paste" or "mix and match" forms. You like paragraph one from form one but you prefer paragraph two from form two so you cobble together a patchwork of provisions borrowed from each and, in the process, run the significant risk that mistakes of a somewhat subtle nature will be made. So, until you become comfortable with the documents that are available to you, the secret may be to accept 100% the approaches that are well regarded in your community and live with them until you have enough experience and background understanding to dismantle provisions and reconstruct them, adding to or deleting from them to suit your preferences and client needs.

In that regard, then, please use this material as a guide to how documents do the job, recognizing that there is nothing magical about these particular forms or the words used. They are *just* illustrations, and only to get you started up the learning curve. For example, the following will beginning at page 15 is a very good version of a "standardized" form, but it is not perfect, partly because it makes concessions that reflect "typical" practice in the industry. That makes it a good teaching tool, but not necessarily something you would adopt.

Reproduced below are a number of documents that allow you to get the look and feel of a variety of instruments to which reference is made in the text. Taken as a whole, they are typical of the document package that might be produced in a client representation (although *the* most typical combination — a pour over will and revocable unfunded insurance trust — is not used, because they don't provide the best exposure to as wide a variety of illustrations). These sample documents are not extensive, nor are they necessarily appropriate for you to adopt in any given client situation, practice setting, or jurisdiction. Your instructor (or employer) will be a much better source for information about form books and representative documents in your particular jurisdiction and for any situation or problem that you will consider in class or after you graduate.

In reality, these things vary a good bit by locale, size of the client's situation, and the particular needs being fulfilled. Every drafter has personal prejudices, and law firms especially want you to use their own forms so that they know what you're putting in commerce (because they worry about a variety of malpractice concerns, not the least of which being that you may have a better way of doing things and may make them look like they missed something!) So please, use these for the limited purpose for which they are provided, and don't even *consider* using them in the real world. Instead, badger those experts in your vicinity who have access to the best available forms suitable to your circumstance to give you a heads' up for where to obtain your "starter" forms.

As was the case in Chapter 5, annotations here (particularly in the will) are explanations and illustrations of options rather than the usual citation of authority, distractions, academic side trips, or ancillary information put in a note to signal their insignificance. These comments are critical to your becoming familiar with the task at hand so, please, read them! But remember that they don't belong in the document you ultimately draft for any client.

ENGAGEMENT LETTER

[LONG FORM]
Provided courtesy of the American
College of Trust and Estate Counsel

The purpose of this letter is to give both you and the firm a permanent, written record of the agreement we have reached to provide legal services. We have found from experience that a written record of the arrangements made between attorney and client serves both in good stead if questions later arise with respect to any of the services we have agreed to provide. Although we cannot answer all your questions here, this letter reflects the general terms of our engagement and serves as a point of reference. We encourage you to raise questions at any time relating to the cost or nature of our services.

Services We Will Perform

You have engaged us to provide the following legal services in connection with your estate plan, and we have agreed to provide these services in as cost effective and productive a manner as possible. Our services will include:

Compilation of pertinent data relating to your personal and family status, your income, expenses, assets and liabilities, and your estate planning needs and intentions;

Review and analysis of all documents and other information you provide relating to your estate plan, including your current wills, trusts, real property deeds, insurance policies, employee benefit plans, agreements incident to a prior divorce, and any other information you or your other professional advisors provide us;

Research and analysis of legal questions arising with respect to the proposed estate plan.

Analysis of the impact of state and federal gift and death taxes (including the generation-skipping transfer tax), debts and other expenses of estate or trust administration upon the desired disposition of your estate.

Preparation of all legal documents necessary to implement your estate plan, including one or more of the following: wills, living trusts, insurance trusts, durable powers of attorney (relating to property management and health care), real property deeds, stock and bond assignments, letters of instruction, "living wills", and any other documents you ask us to prepare and we agree to provide in connection with the foregoing.

Explanation of the material tax and other legal ramifications of each of the documents we have prepared for you.

Supervision of the execution of all original documents, conforming of copies, and the distribution and safekeeping of all documents, as well as the filing of real property deeds or other documents requiring filing in the public records.

Unless otherwise agreed, we will not be responsible for preparing or filing income tax or gift tax returns on your behalf but, at your request, we will be happy to work with your accountant or tax return preparer to assist in the preparation of such returns to the extent they relate to the estate planning services we will be doing for you.[a/]

Services Not Included

Estate planning is a dynamic process and your needs and desires may change as we proceed. However, except with your advance approval, we will not undertake any services outside the scope of the services discussed in this letter. We are not agreeing to undertake any such services nor are we agreeing to act as your general counsel. We will not be acting on your behalf with respect to any of your business interests or any other matter not covered by this letter unless you ask us and we agree to do so.

Charges for Legal Services and Out-of-Pocket Costs

Our charges for the estate planning services we have agreed to render for you generally are based on the amount of time spent by our attorneys and paraprofessional personnel.[b/] This means that we customarily charge at our basic hourly rates as determined and adjusted by the firm periodically. Presently, the hourly rates of the personnel who may be asked to assist with your estate plan range from $_____ per hour for senior partners' time to $_____ per hour for associates' time and $_____ per hour for legal assistants' time. As noted, these rates are subject to review and change by the firm on a periodic basis. However, you will be given 15 days' notice of any such changes. Following such notice you may ask us to terminate our work for you before the changes come into effect. We will be entitled to

---

[a/] Although there are places and firms in which this is not true at all, many lawyers eschew compliance to limit malpractice liability in an endeavor that is fraught with the possibility for error. You might question whether you want this kind of work, and the inevitable exposure that goes with it, perhaps because you have a special expertise and can capture a big chunk of the local practice.

[b/] Some estate planners charge a fixed fee for services, or a hybrid of fixed fee and time spent on extra matters. There even are some who purport to bill for some work on a "value added" basis.

assume that you concur in the rates as revised if we do not hear from you. We will handle our work for you to provide the most cost effective representation possible, consistent with our ethical and legal responsibilities to you as our clients.

At all times our services will be supervised by a partner in the firm, but matters that can be handled more efficiently by personnel who charge at lower hourly rates will be delegated to them. For example, we have found it very cost effective to have our legal assistants prepare many documents[c] involved in the estate planning process as well as compiling personal and financial data. All work product produced by the firm will be reviewed and approved by the partner ultimately responsible for your representation.

Although it is difficult at the outset of any matter to estimate accurately how much time will be required to perform the agreed upon services, we have discussed the fees we expect for your estate planning. We have therefore attached to this letter an exhibit setting forth the estimated fees for each detailed aspect of your estate plan to give you an idea of the approximate costs of your plan. The estimate of charges is merely that, an estimate, and it is possible the fees finally charged will exceed the estimate. However, we will keep you advised of the fees incurred on a monthly basis. If, during the course of our representation, you request us to provide services in addition to those checked on the attached form, we will charge for those services accordingly. At any stage of the work, however, we will be happy to give you an estimate of the fees you can expect to incur for additional work.

(Optional paragraph for use in special situations)

In accordance with and as permitted by the Rules of Professional Conduct of this state, we reserve the right to adjust our basic hourly rates (up or down) in accordance with the factors set forth in the Rules. These factors include the experience, ability, and reputation of the attorneys working on your planning; the nature of the employment (such as, for example, any specific time constraints imposed by the employment); the responsibilities assumed; the amounts at stake; the complexity of the matters addressed; and the results achieved. Thus, our fees may vary above or below the basic hourly rates noted above but will remain within the parameters of our fee estimate unless you are otherwise advised in advance.

---

[c] Yes, the scrivener function is *not* primary to many estate planning lawyers, who may draft the prototype documents but leave document assembly to paraprofessional staff on a day to day basis. Which may make your quest for forms even less immediately important.

It is our practice in connection with the opening of a new estate planning matter to request a fee deposit equal to half of the estimated fees. Our statement for that amount is enclosed. [Or, if appropriate: We acknowledge receipt of the requested deposit.] This fee deposit is placed in our clients' trust account, it remains your money, and it will not be drawn upon until services equal to the fees on deposit have been performed. The balance of the fees will be due upon completion of the final drafts of your documents. [Alternative: Fees over and above the deposit will be billed on a periodic (e.g., monthly) basis and payment is expected within 30 days after billing.]

We receive your fee deposit with the understanding that we are authorized to withdraw from our trust account sums necessary to pay for services and cost disbursements as they are incurred. You will always be notified in writing of the amounts applied or withdrawn from the trust account and will receive a statement explaining the services rendered and costs incurred. [Addition (for use in California, which has a statute on the subject): You may also at any time request us to provide a bill for you, which we must provide no later than 30 days after your request.] If amounts due remain outstanding for more than 30 days, we impose a late charge of 8% on the unpaid amounts. We must also reserve the right to terminate our services unless or until full payment on a delinquent account is received.

We are likely to incur out-of-pocket costs and other charges on your behalf, which the firm will advance subject to reimbursement. These costs include, but are not necessarily limited to, long distance telephone charges, postage, fax, telex and computer charges, printing and reproduction costs, filing fees, recording fees, delivery and messenger costs, document preparation charges, etc. We will not incur any major costs without discussing them in advance with you. We anticipate that the costs you will incur in connection with our representation will not exceed $_____.

Termination of Our Relationship

You may at any time terminate our relationship upon written notice and we will immediately cease performing services after receiving such notice. You will be obligated to pay the fees due for any services rendered and costs incurred before such termination. We will promptly return all of your papers upon termination but will retain our own files. If you wish copies of our files, we can make arrangements to copy them for you at your expense.

We may terminate our engagement for any reason permitted under the Rules of Professional Conduct of this state, which reasons include the failure to pay bills promptly or any other acts or circumstances that, in our judgment, impair or adversely affect the attorney and client relationship between us or conflict with our professional responsibilities.

Arbitration

We trust there will never be any disputes between us with respect to our services or our fees and costs, but if there is such a disagreement we will make every effort to resolve it without arbitration or litigation. If the dispute is not resolvable, you have the right to request arbitration by filing such a request with the [appropriate county bar association or other entity.] Arbitration generally provides a much quicker and more cost effective way of resolving disputes than litigation through the courts, although you retain that right as well.

Cooperation and Confidentiality

All matters you discuss with us are personal and confidential and will not be shared with any individuals outside the firm without your prior consent. Because we must have detailed information about your personal and financial affairs, we appreciate the importance of maintaining absolute confidentiality with respect to the information you provide.

At the same time, we are not in a position to fulfill our obligations to you and to do the best possible job on your estate plan unless you give us all of the relevant facts pertaining to your family and financial affairs. Therefore, we are relying upon and assume your complete candor and cooperation. In return, you may be assured of our complete cooperation and understanding that materials you give us are sensitive and confidential. With your permission, we will discuss matters pertaining to your family and financial affairs with your other advisors, agents, stockbrokers, etc., but only as appropriate and only as specifically authorized by you.

(Paragraph for inclusion when writing to a married couple)[d]

[Because both of you have retained us to prepare your estate plans, each of you is our client. Although we could agree otherwise, it is our agreement that matters one of you might otherwise tell us in confidence as regards all other persons are not protected by the attorney-client privilege from disclosure to the other of you. We encourage joint and mutual discussions of your objectives and interests. Nevertheless, there are times when a couple does not share the same objectives or when one spouse wishes to speak in confidence to his or her lawyer. We are willing to meet

---

[d] As discussed in Chapter 3 at page 33, this "show and tell" approach is not the only viable alternative to the mutual representation problem posed by representing a married couple. It is, however, the most common.

with you individually; however, because we represent both of you, we are not in a position to agree with either of you not to communicate freely with both of you. It is possible that conflicts may arise between you during the course of our estate planning work for both of you. For example, these might relate to the ownership of your property, its desired disposition, proposed gifts, beneficiary designations on life insurance and retirement plans, and other issues. If a present conflict of interest arises between you, we will advise you and recommend that you each retain independent counsel to avoid the possibility that our advice to one of you will be influenced by our representation of the other. At this time, however, with a full understanding of your respective rights and the advantages of retaining independent counsel, you have requested us to represent both of you in all of the above matters. You also have agreed that among the three of us there may be complete disclosure and exchange of all information and communications that we receive from either or both of you in the course of our representation (in other words, such information will not be keep confidential from your spouse, even if we receive it in private conferences with only one of you). We will withdraw from all further dual representation and advise you to obtain independent counsel if conflicts arise between you such that it is impossible in our judgment for the firm to perform its obligations to each of you in accordance with the terms of this letter.]

Conclusion

I apologize for the length and detail of this letter. However, clients and lawyers are better served by having these matters agreed upon and understood in advance. We trust you will not hesitate to call us at any time if you have questions or comments relating to our representation. It remains our aim to give you competent and cost effective representation. We appreciate the trust and confidence you have expressed in our firm, and we will do everything we can to warrant them.

Sincerely,

_____

For the Firm.

We have read the foregoing agreement and accept the arrangements as stated. [If applicable: We enclose our check in payment of your fee deposit statement.]

_____

_____

EXHIBIT A

The legal services we agree to perform and the documents we agree to prepare for your review and execution are those of the following that have a check mark beside them:

___ Review your estate planning needs and objectives

___ Analysis of existing life insurance program and make recommendations relating thereto

___ Analysis of your estate tax situation, including marital deduction, available exemption equivalent, and generation-skipping transfer tax issues

___ Preparation of revocable funded living trust

___ Preparation of no trust wills

___ Preparation of wills with trust provisions

___ Preparation of wills with tax related trust provisions

___ Preparation of pour over wills

___ Analysis and recommendations relating to gifting:

    ___ outright

    ___ in trust (together with preparation of trust) as follows: ___ life insurance trust, ___ charitable trust, ___ 2503(c) qualified minor's trust, ___ trust equivalent (e.g., custodianship)

___ Durable powers of attorney for financial matters

___ Durable powers of attorney for health care

___ "Living wills"

___ Preparation of appropriate transfer documents, consisting of ___ real property deeds, ___ stock and bond assignments, ___ other (specify) _____

___ Additional services as follows _____

The total estimated fees for the services to be rendered, as checked above, are $_____ to $_____.

We understand and agree to the above.

ENGAGEMENT LETTER

[SHORT FORM]
Provided courtesy of the American
College of Trust and Estate Counsel

This letter formalizes the agreement pursuant to which you have retained us to act as your estate planning counsel.

For a fixed fee of $____ [Alternative: for an estimated fee of $____ to $____] plus disbursements (not to exceed $____), we agree to review your present estate plan, make recommendations relating thereto and, following your instructions, prepare a new estate plan and the following documents implementing the plan:

___ No trust wills
___ Wills with trust provisions
___ Wills with tax related trust provisions
___ Revocable living trusts
___ Pour over wills
___ Durable powers of attorney for financial matters
___ Durable powers of attorney for health care
___ "Living wills"

In addition to our preparation of the foregoing documents and our supervision of their execution, we also will prepare appropriate deeds transferring real estate you may own into your trusts. You also will receive a memorandum explaining how to transfer additional assets into your trusts.

All of our attorneys and legal assistants are assigned hourly rates, which are reflected on our monthly time records. The hourly rates of the personnel who may be assigned to your planning vary from $____ per hour for legal assistants' time to $____ per hour for a senior partner's time. The fee estimate we have given above is based on our present analysis of the work required to complete your plan, and the total fees payable may vary from the estimate. However, we will advise you monthly of the time incurred on your planning as matters progress.

With respect to disbursements, we wish to serve you with the most effective support systems available while at the same time allocating the cost of such systems in accordance with the extent of usage by individual clients. Therefore, we charge separately for certain cost and expense disbursements, including telephone, fax, telex, messenger and other communication costs; reproduction; document retrieval; document preparation on our word processing facilities; computer research; and other expenses incurred on your behalf.

It is our policy to request a fee deposit equal to half of the estimated fees to be incurred. Our statement for this deposit is enclosed. [OR: We acknowledge receipt of your deposit of $_____.] **The balance of the fees will be due and payable upon completion of the final drafts of your documents** [OR: shall be charged and due and payable monthly]. **Our statements are due and payable upon receipt.**

It is our goal to provide legal services to you on the most cost efficient basis possible. I hope you will feel free to call me at any time with questions you may have with respect to any of our billing policies and procedures or any other matter. We appreciate the confidence and trust you have shown in us.

Sincerely,

_____

For the Firm.

We confirm the above agreement and request you to proceed with the work described. [If applicable: We enclose our check in payment of your fee deposit statement.]

_____

_____

ESTATE INVENTORY

List the assets you own and whether you own them alone or with someone else. Also list the debts your estate might owe. Married individuals may wish to use this document to identify assets that are in each spouse's estate.

ASSET REVIEW

Asset	My Sole Name	Spouse's Sole Name	Joint with Spouse	Joint With Other	Total Value
Checking Accounts					
Savings Accounts					
Marketable Stocks					
Nonmarketable Stocks					
Mutual Funds					
Bonds					
Partnership Interests					
Notes Receivable					
Residences					
Farm/Timber/Undeveloped					
Partial Interests in Land					
Investment Real Estate					
Life Insurance (Term)					
Life Insurance (Permanent)					
IRAs					
Retirement Benefits					
Tangible Personalty					
Royalties/Patents					
Trust Interests					
Expectancies					
Other Assets					
Total Values					

LIABILITIES AND DEBTS

Kind of Debt	My Sole Debt	Spouse's Sole Debt	Joint with Spouse	Joint w/ Other	Total Debt
First Mortgage(s)					
Second Mortgage(s)					
Credit Card Debt					
Notes (sole, co-, or gtd.)					
Other Debt					
Total Liabilities					

NET WORTH

Total Assets	
Total Liabilities	
Net Worth	

- Please record the designated beneficiaries for any life insurance, IRAs, and retirement benefits listed.
- Please provide copies of any trusts, details about any expectancies or powers of appointment, and note specifics regarding the "other assets."
- Please provide any existing will or trust and durable power of attorney documents, deeds to any land, and the summary plan description for any retirement benefits.
- Please note who you would like to select as fiduciaries (executor, trustee, guardian).
- Are you a citizen of the United States? Is your spouse? Have you been married before and are there any obligations from a prior marriage? Do you have a prenuptial or postnuptial agreement with your spouse? Please list states in which you and your spouse have lived while married.
- Please list the names and birthdates of all your children and grandchildren. Do any have special needs?
- Have you made any gifts that exceed the per donee annual exclusion ($3,000 before 1982; $10,000 until 2002; $11,000 since)?
- Please list your other advisors and give contact information: accountant, stockbroker, financial advisor, insurance agent, other attorneys
- Finally, please note the general disposition you would like to make of your estate.

WILL

I, *Testator*, of *City, State*,[e/] make this my will[f/] and revoke[g/] all prior wills and codicils.[h/]

FIRST: My executor shall pay all expenses of my last illness and funeral,[i/] costs of administration including ancillary,[j/] costs of

---

[e/] Normally it is wise to indicate the testator's domicile to help determine which law is applicable and otherwise resolve any questions that may turn on the issue. Some clients have ties to multiple jurisdictions. In cases in which domicile is not clear, a designation such as this could give weight to one state's assertion that the decedent was subject to state estate or inheritance tax in that jurisdiction. In some cases that could make matters worse, because sufficient facts might make it possible for a second state to claim the individual as their citizen, resulting in the potential for double taxation at the state level. See Chapter 18 at pages 38-39.

[f/] This declaration satisfies any state law publication requirement that may apply and establishes the requisite testamentary intent.

[g/] Unless there is a strategic reason to create a string of valid documents, revocation of any prior wills and codicils will avoid the state law presumption that these documents cumulate and must be construed consistently with each other (to the extent possible). In most cases there is no prior will or codicil. If there is, however, it makes sense to get a feel for the estate planning that was done previously and, with the number of recent tax law changes, it also pays to know whether any chronologically advantaged documents exist that should be left alone. If this was a codicil or a trust amendment it would be folly to draft the new document without first looking at the instrument being altered. That ought to be your approach even if you're charged with producing a total replacement.

[h/] Some exordium provisions contain recitations like "In the name of God, Amen, being of sound and disposing mind and memory and aware of the vicissitudes of life . . . " and stating things like "being free of fraud or duress" or "acting of my own free will." This is what you might expect from a drafter who sells documents by the word (or the pound) or, worse, if there was a question about such things and the statements are makeweight efforts to persuade. None of that is necessary, and it could be harmful (because it signals that there was a concern) if it is not the drafter's standard practice.

[i/] This provision is appropriate because state law in some jurisdictions makes the cost of a funeral an obligation of a surviving spouse or other family members.

[j/] This is needed because ancillary costs normally would be a charge against the ancillary assets, which often consist of land or other illiquid immoveables.

safeguarding and delivering[k] bequests, and other proper[l] charges against my estate (excluding debts secured by real property or life insurance). My executor shall also pay all estate and inheritance taxes assessed by reason of my death, except that the amount, if any, by which the estate and inheritance taxes shall be increased as a result of the inclusion of property in which I may have a qualifying income interest for life or over which I may have a power of appointment shall be paid by the person holding or receiving that property. Interest and penalties concerning any tax shall be paid and charged in the same manner as the tax. I waive for my estate all rights of apportionment or reimbursement for any payments made pursuant to this article.[m]

My executor's selection of assets to be sold to make the foregoing payments or to satisfy any pecuniary legacies, and the tax effects thereof, shall not be subject to question by any beneficiary.[n]

My executor shall make such elections[o] and allocations under the tax laws as my executor deems advisable, without regard to the relative interests of the beneficiaries and without liability to any person. No adjustment shall be made between principal and income or

---

[k] Without this provision a beneficiary might receive assets with no liquidity with which to pay those costs.

[l] The important note here is "proper" charges, which precludes acceleration of debts that otherwise are not due. Notice also the parenthetical following, which also speaks to the question whether to repay loans secured by life insurance, instead of allowing the insurer to reduce the policy payout by the amount of an outstanding policy loan.

[m] Recall Chapter 11 regarding payment of estate obligations. You now know that this abbreviated tax payment provision lacks many elements we studied. In a "chronological" will (such as this) it would be inappropriate to include a five page tax payment provision at this location, but this direction to pay taxes could be replaced with a simple sentence directing payment "as provided in Section * of Article ** below," and that provision could be as extensive as needed.

[n] This protection for the fiduciary is addressed first to any capital gain consequences of a liquidation, and also is designed to preclude a beneficiary from objecting to sale of a favored asset. Notice as you read how this document attempts to protect the fiduciary. It is wise to consider the liability visited on the fiduciary, and also to remember that these forms were produced *by* the fiduciary. It may be that you should eliminate some of those protections.

[o] This reference is directed at the kinds of elections we studied in Chapter 13, dealing with postmortem administration. Again the fiduciary is entitled to protection. Also notice the "no adjustment" provision, also as discussed in Chapter 13.

in the relative interests of the beneficiaries to compensate for the effect of elections or allocations under the tax laws made by my executor or by the trustee.

The balance of my estate that remains after the foregoing payments have been made or provided for shall be disposed of as hereinafter provided.

SECOND: My [husband's/wife's] name is *Spouse* and [he/she] is herein referred to as "my [husband/wife]." I have *number* children now living, namely:

    A, born *date, Year*

    B, born *date, Year*; and

    C, born *date, Year*[p/]

THIRD:[q/] I give all my personal[r/] and household effects,[s/] automobiles, boats and collections,[t/] and any insurance policies

---

[p/] Here is where you would insert a provision addressing issues such as whether nonmarital children not specifically mentioned are meant to be precluded from bringing a pretermitted heir claim, whether after born or (these days) after conceived children are meant to be treated the same as those mentioned, and whether adopteds are to be treated the same as natural born. Either here or elsewhere in the document you also may want to address these types of questions with respect to more remote beneficiaries, such as grandchildren who are nonmarital or adopted, the issue of adult adoptions, and such.

[q/] This separate disposition is appropriate even if the document leaves all tangible personalty to the same person who receives the residue of the estate. This seeming redundancy is justified because distribution of these items normally occurs early in the estate administration, to avoid the need to safeguard these items for the entire duration of a normal administration. Early distribution presents an income tax problem under §663(a), however, because those items are deemed to carry out distributable net income to the beneficiary. See Chapter 17. This means that the recipient of things like clothing, furniture, or personal mementos would incur an income tax liability. Imagine how you would provide the liquidity to pay the income tax on distribution of the baby grand piano — sell the black keys? An exception in §663(a)(1) to this DNI carryout regime applies if distribution is pursuant to a specific bequest, such as this preresiduary disposition. So to avoid the income tax hickey, two paragraphs properly are used (this and residuary disposition) to transfer all the decedent's property, even if it all goes to a single estate beneficiary.

[r/] "Personal" effects can have a wide variety of meanings, and you will find that various drafters use different terminology to describe what in essence is the decedent's tangible "stuff," as compared to intangibles (investments) or, in some cases, personal property of singularly high value

thereon,[u] to my [husband/wife] if [s]he survives me by 30 days,[v] otherwise to my children who so survive me to be divided equally

---

(imagine a farmer, for example, who has very valuable farm implements that constitute personal property, as opposed to the realty used in the farm business). The challenge in this provision is to describe things like clothing, jewelry (if not too valuable), books and papers (if not too extensive), tools, kitchen appliances (but not fixtures that should stay with the house), and so on. It isn't easy to be appropriately vague, so as to put your arms around the full panoply of "stuff" that people own that isn't very valuable but may have great practical or sentimental value, and yet avoid sweeping into this disposition items of real value that should be retained as part of a dwelling or an investment portfolio. You may recall that the Uniform Probate Code permits a testator to make a handwritten list of things to be disposed of under such a provision, because experience shows that testators tinker with this disposition more than any other provision in the will. Who gets the cut glass vase on the mantle, or the clock on the sideboard, or the divan, the painting over it, and the rug in front? And will the list change if someone falls from grace, or makes a particularly ugly (or gracious) comment about an item?

[s] Add here the words "**not otherwise effectively disposed of**" if there is a provision prior to this that makes more specific gifts to identified takers. These could be in a separate paragraph or could be structured such as: "**I give (a) my jewelry to my daughter Mary if she survives me by 30 days, (b) my tools to my son Arthur if he so survives me, and (c) all my personal and household effects not otherwise effectively disposed of . . . .**" Note also that household effects might not be an appropriate gift under this paragraph if a separate provision gives the "house and all the tangible household effects therein" to a named taker. This particularly is true if the home is a vacation property with its own unique and specially suited furniture. After all, should the Adirondack chair that sits on the lawn of the Newport beach house pass to the same beneficiary who gets the contents of the New York City co-op, or should it stay with the beach house?

[t] Care is required here if there are very valuable collections (such as art, guns, jewelry, rugs, coins, Barbie dolls, Pez dispensers, you name it — people collect the wildest things) that should be the subject of a separate special disposition. If collections are modest this provision appropriately sweeps them in with all the other tangible stuff, but not if they are worth coveting, especially if the collection should not be divided and more than one beneficiary is likely to want it.

[u] Certain tangibles are not easy to insure. If a policy already exists it is best to transfer the asset with the existing policy (assuming the insurer permits), rather than forcing the beneficiary to start from scratch to describe, appraise, photograph, and then find the right company to insure the item.

[v] This period should not be so long as to delay orderly distribution of these items, but the possibility of a common disaster should be considered so as to avoid the need to probate the same "stuff" in two estates. Notice

among them as they agree. My executor shall sell any property as to which there is no agreement[w/] within 60 days after admission of this will to probate and shall add the proceeds to the residue of my estate.[x/]

---

that this survivorship condition would preclude a state law antilapse statute from applying, meaning that the representatives of a deceased taker would not stand in the shoes of that designated beneficiary. Typically it is advisable to avoid passing these items to multiple generations of beneficiaries, but the client may desire that each blood line (for example) have its share of mementos.

[w/] You can't *imagine* how people will fight over the little stuff! So this provision must provide a mechanism to divide what the beneficiaries cannot agree to distribute. Some drafters establish elaborate procedures to divide assets among bickering beneficiaries. Round robin selection, oldest child to youngest and then youngest back to oldest, each choosing an asset. Or bidding on items in a "silent auction" system. Or some poor "arbitrator" chooses. The interesting thing is how squabbling ingrates will come to an agreement on the evening of the 59th day if everything is going to be sold the next morning! Or how they will not buy something at that 60th day sale for anything near the amount they claimed the item was worth when trying to prevent another beneficiary from receiving it. The point is: provide a mechanism to establish order among these takers because these fights are about emotions more than they are about value and that makes them *very* difficult to mediate or resolve.

[x/] Special attention may be appropriate if any of the beneficiaries may be a minor. Normally trust ownership of this type of property is not appropriate, because these items are not proper investments, don't produce income that could offset fiduciary fees, may require safekeeping or may drain resources to pay for insurance. A better approach may be to provide that: "**the guardian of or person in loco parentis to the child shall represent him or her in the division of the property, receipt for and hold his or her share or sell all or any part of it, and deliver the share or proceeds to the child when he or she reaches majority, or earlier if the guardian or person considers it to be for the child's best interests.**"

Other dispositions that also might appear in Third include bequests similar in form to the following:

$X to my [husband/wife] if [s]he survives me by 30 days[, in lieu of a surviving spouse's award].

$X to *sibling* **of** *City, State,* **if [s]he survives me by 30 days.**

$X to *charity/institution* **of** *City, State* **(or any successor organization), if still in existence at my death.**

$X to each of [a class, such as "*my grandchildren***"] who survives me by 30 days. If a [class member] is a minor, payment may be made for the benefit of the [class member] to a custodian under a Uniform Transfers or Gifts to Minors Act.**

If *Devisee* **survives me by 30 days I give to** *Devisee* **all of my**

FOURTH: All the residue of my estate, wherever situated, including lapsed legacies,[y/] but expressly excluding any property over which I may have power of appointment at my death,[z/] I give to [THE NORTHERN TRUST COMPANY, an Illinois corporation, of Chicago, Illinois],[aa/] as trustee, upon the trusts hereinafter provided.

---

interests in my residences, including seasonal and vacation homes, and any insurance policies thereon, along with all household goods located therein, [subject to any mortgage indebtedness and unpaid taxes and assessments on the properties] or [free of any mortgage indebtedness, which I direct shall be paid as an expense of administration of my estate].

Note that in the final paragraph, reference to a home in which the testator is living at death (or similar language) may be problematic if the client may not reside there at death (when the will speaks) due to end of life health care requirements that caused the testator to be moved to an extended care facility before death.

Other issues to consider in these types of specific bequests are the order of abatement if insufficient assets may exist, directions regarding accessions (stock-on-stock dividends or stock splits on shares given, or rent paid on realty), changes in form or a gift of the proceeds if there is a possibility for ademption if an asset is destroyed or sold, and payment of interest on a pecuniary bequest if payment is delayed for any reason.

y/ This merely confirms that state antilapse rules are not to apply, which requires that an alternative disposition be made of those items. In some circumstances the lapsed items *ought* to pass to representatives of the predeceased taker and this provision would dovetail into a gift that also failed in the alternative. For example: "**$X to Y if [s]he survives me by 30 days, otherwise to Y's surviving spouse if [s]he so survives me, and if not then in equal shares to Y's children who so survive me, and if none then this bequest shall lapse.**"

z/ As discussed in Chapter 5 at page 32 it generally is wise to avoid inadvertent or "silent" exercise of powers of appointment. The drafter of the power can prevent that with a specific reference requirement, and this residuary provision also protects against unwitting exercise by expressly disavowing any intent to exercise powers that are not identified. If a blending exercise of a known power was intended, this provision would say: "**. . . including lapsed legacies and any property subject to the power of appointment granted to me under the trust established by X dated** *Month, Day, Year,* **I give . . . .**"

aa/ The provider of the form book obviously wants you to name *it* as fiduciary! Be certain to verify that the fiduciary you name is willing to accept the business. Better to learn in the planning stage that the fiduciary has minimums or other policies that would cause it to decline to serve, and otherwise to verify that the document is to its liking and that it is prepared to accept appointment when or if that becomes relevant.

FIFTH:[bb] If my [husband/wife] survives me, the trustee as of my death shall set aside out of the trust estate as a separate trust for [his/her] benefit (undiminished to the extent possible by any estate or inheritance taxes or other charges) a fraction of the trust property of which (i) the numerator is the smallest amount that, if allowed as a federal estate tax marital deduction, would result in the least possible federal estate tax payable by reason of my death, and (ii) the denominator is the federal estate tax value of the assets included in my gross estate that became (or the proceeds, investments or reinvestments of which became) trust property. In determining the amount of the numerator the trustee shall consider the credit or the deduction for state death taxes only to the extent those taxes are not thereby incurred or increased and shall assume that none of the Family Trust hereinafter established qualifies for a federal estate tax deduction.[cc]

For purposes of the preceding paragraph, the trust property is all property in the trust estate that would qualify for the federal estate tax marital deduction if it were distributed outright to my [husband/wife].[dd] For purposes of this will, my [husband/wife] shall be deemed to have survived me if the order of our deaths cannot be proved.[ee]

[bb] Specific items included in this marital deduction bequest and trust that were addressed in Chapter 7 are not reiterated here. This is a fractional, optimum marital bequest with a residuary nonmarital disposition. If this were a pecuniary marital, the items in (i) and (ii) would be replaced with the pecuniary formula and the order of provisions might be changed to represent funding of the credit shelter bequest off the top, with the marital constituting the residue if that reversal of the traditional order employed here was appropriate.

[cc] This provision merely reflects the reality that some nonmarital trusts could qualify for the marital deduction if a QTIP election were made.

[dd] This provision reflects the "unidentified asset" rule in §2056(b)(2) and constitutes the "purge the pot" required in a fractional marital to ensure that nonqualifying assets (which D's estate could not deduct) are not deemed to pass as part of the marital bequest for inclusion in S's estate.

An addition to this sentence may direct that certain property (such as stock in a family business) not be included in the marital share. To wit: ", **except that any shares of [Family Corporation] shall be included only to the extent required to obtain a denominator in an amount equal to the numerator.**"

[ee] Here is where a survivorship provision (not to exceed 180 days) would be substituted if appropriate: "**For purposes of this article, my [spouse] shall be deemed not to have survived me if [s]he is not living on the 180th day after my death.**"

My [husband/wife] shall have the right by written notice to require the trustee to convert unproductive property in the trust to productive property within a reasonable time.

The trust shall be designated the "Marital Trust" and shall be held and disposed of as follows:[ff/]

SECTION 1: Commencing with my death the trustee shall pay the income from the Marital Trust in convenient installments, at least quarterly, to my [husband/wife] during [his/her] lifetime.

The trustee may also pay to my [husband/wife] such sums from principal as the trustee deems necessary or advisable from time to time for [his/her] health and maintenance in reasonable comfort, considering [his/her] income from all sources known to the trustee.[gg/]

SECTION 2: My executor may elect to have a specific portion or all of the Marital Trust, herein referred to as the "marital portion," treated as qualified terminable interest property for federal estate tax purposes. If an election is made as to less than all of the Marital Trust, the specific portion shall be expressed as a fraction or percentage of the Marital Trust and may be defined by means of a formula. I intend that the marital portion shall qualify for the federal estate tax marital deduction in my estate.

If the marital portion is less than all of the Marital Trust, at any time during the lifetime of my [husband/wife] the trustee in its discretion may divide the Marital Trust into two separate trusts representing the marital and nonmarital portions of the Marital Trust. The two separate trusts shall be held and disposed of on the same terms and conditions as the Marital Trust, except that the trustee shall make no invasion of the principal of the nonmarital

---

ff/ A marital trust is not required. If an outright marital was appropriate, the first paragraph of FIFTH would be altered to direct the trustee to distribute to the spouse the amount established by the formula fractional bequest.

gg/ This is where you would add a power to withdraw a percentage, a dollar amount, or any other portion of the marital trust to the extent denial of control over the marital trust is not the decedent's intent. "**In addition, my [spouse] may withdraw any part or all of the principal at any time or times. The trustee shall make payment without question upon [his/her] written request. The right of withdrawal shall be a privilege that may be exercised only voluntarily and shall not include an involuntary exercise.**" As noted in Chapter 5 note aaa, at page 31, the final sentence is an effort to provide a measure of spendthrift protection to the withdrawal power.

portion trust so long as any readily marketable assets remain in the marital portion trust.[hh/]

SECTION 3: Upon the death of my [husband/wife] the principal of the Marital Trust shall be held in trust hereunder or distributed to or in trust for such one or more of my descendants and their respective spouses and charitable, scientific or educational purposes, with such powers and in such manner and proportions as my [husband/wife] may appoint by [his/her] will making specific reference to this power of appointment.[ii/]

Upon the death of my [husband/wife] any part of the principal of the Marital Trust not effectively appointed shall be added to or used to fund the Family Trust,[jj/] except that, unless my [husband/wife] directs otherwise by [his/her] will or revocable trust, the trustee shall first pay from the principal of the marital portion, directly or to the legal representative of my [husband's/wife's] estate as the trustee deems advisable, the amount by which the estate and inheritance taxes assessed by reason of the death of my [husband/wife] shall be increased as a result of the inclusion of the marital portion in [his/her] estate for such tax purposes.[kk/] The trustee's selection of assets to be sold to pay that amount, and the tax effects thereof, shall not be subject to question by any beneficiary.[ll/]

---

hh/ This provision is designed to minimize the amount includible in the estate of S by cannibalizing the portion that will be subject to estate tax inclusion in S's estate. It could go farther by removing the "marketable asset" restriction on the operation of this limitation.

ii/ Apropos the notation in note z regarding silent or inadvertent exercise of powers of appointment, this is the type of specific reference requirement that savvy drafters include to preclude the powerholder's unwitting or blanket exercise of unidentified powers. This is not the broadest form of nongeneral power that could be granted to S, nor is it as limited. A general power could be used but there is little to recommend it, and doing so could confuse the issue whether a QTIP marital (with its postmortem planning options) was created instead of an all income, general power of appointment marital trust. Remember that no inter vivos power of appointment could be used in this QTIP trust.

jj/ Remember from our discussion in Chapter 5 that, if the nonmarital trust will have been divided or distributed prior to the death of S, an additional provision would be added here to direct addition or distribution as if the nonmarital trust were then being created or distributed.

kk/ This incremental tax payment provision mirrors the reimbursement right in §2207A. It could be altered to provide for pro rata apportionment instead.

ll/ Again, protection for the fiduciary.

SIXTH: The trustee as of my death shall set aside the balance of the trust estate, or all thereof if my [husband/wife] does not survive me, as a separate trust. The trust shall be designated the "Family Trust" and shall be held and disposed of as follows: [mm/] . . .

SEVENTH: The following provisions shall apply to the trust estate and to each trust under this will:

SECTION 1: If income or discretionary amounts of principal become payable to a minor or to a person under legal disability or to a person not adjudicated disabled but who, by reason of illness or mental or physical disability, is in the opinion of the trustee unable properly to manage his or her affairs, then that income or principal shall be paid or expended only in such of the following ways as the trustee deems best: (a) directly to the beneficiary or his or her attorney in fact; (b) to the legally appointed guardian of the beneficiary; (c) to a custodian for the beneficiary under a Uniform Transfers or Gifts to Minors Act; (d) by the trustee directly for the benefit of the beneficiary; (e) to an adult relative or friend in reimbursement for amounts properly advanced for the benefit of the beneficiary.

SECTION 2:[nn/] The interests of beneficiaries in principal or income shall not be subject to the claims of any creditor, any spouse for alimony or support, or others, or to legal process, and may not be voluntarily or involuntarily alienated or encumbered. This provision shall not limit the exercise of any power of appointment.

The rights of beneficiaries to withdraw trust property are personal and may not be exercised by a legal representative, attorney in fact, or others.

SECTION 3:[oo/] Income received after the last income payment date and undistributed at the termination of any estate or interest

---

mm/ Here is where the extensive discussion of nonmarital or family trust provisions found in Chapter 5 begins. No further discussion of those dispositive provisions and alternatives is needed here, and the family trust is omitted from this reproduction.

nn/ This is a classic spendthrift provision that most drafters include as if it was boilerplate. We could conduct a long discussion about whether spendthrift provisions prevent desirable planning more than they prevent undesirable invasions by creditors. There are predictable circumstances in which the provision absolutely ought to be used, and a few in which it clearly should not. Please simply be aware of the need to consider whether this is a beneficial provision in each separate document you draft.

oo/ This accrued but undistributed income (sometimes known as stub income) provision avoids the potential need to open a probate estate to

shall, together with any accrued income, be paid by the trustee as income to the persons entitled to the next successive interest in the proportions in which they take that interest.

SECTION 4: For convenience of administration or investment, the trustee may hold separate trusts as a common fund,[pp] dividing the income proportionately among them, assign undivided interests to the separate trusts, and make joint investments of the funds belonging to them. The trustee may consolidate any separate trust with any other trust with similar provisions for the same beneficiary or beneficiaries.[qq]

SECTION 5: The trustee shall hold, manage, care for and protect the trust property and shall have the following powers and, except to the extent inconsistent herewith, those now or hereafter conferred by law:

(a) To retain any property (including stock of any corporate trustee hereunder or a parent or affiliate company) originally constituting the trust or subsequently added thereto,[rr] and to invest and reinvest the trust property in bonds, stocks, mortgages, notes, bank deposits, options, futures, limited partnership interests, shares of registered investment companies and real estate investment trusts, or other property of any kind, real or personal, domestic or foreign;[ss] the trustee may retain or make any investment without liability, even

---

receive income otherwise payable to an income beneficiary who dies in the middle of an income distribution period.

pp/ A common fund is a private mutual fund operated by the fiduciary to provide economies of scale by permitting the fiduciary to hold and manage investments in larger blocks.

qq/ Consolidation of multiple accounts for the same beneficiaries can eliminate the separate base fee charged to multiple trusts and thereby reduce costs. A major impediment to consolidation of trusts created by different documents for the same beneficiary can be different perpetuity periods for each (lives in being plus 21 years from the date each document became irrevocable).

rr/ Retention of a decedent's portfolio often is desirable (particularly if there are unique assets or stock in favored investments), but authority may be required if the portfolio otherwise is not properly diversified or if the investment is not on the fiduciary's approved list of investments. Also note the otherwise improper self dealing element in this authorization.

ss/ Notice the breadth of the investments permitted. An added degree of discretion appropriately might permit the fiduciary also to invest in temporal interests (such as a life estate per autre vie or a term of years, or the remainder following either).

though it is not of a type, quality, marketability or diversification considered proper for trust investments;

(b) To cause any property, real or personal, belonging to the trust to be held or registered in the trustee's name or in the name of a nominee or in such other form as the trustee deems best without disclosing the trust relationship;[tt/]

(c) To vote in person or by general or limited proxy, or refrain from voting, any corporate securities for any purpose, except that any security as to which the trustee's possession of voting discretion would subject the issuing company or the trustee to any law, rule or regulation adversely affecting either the company or the trustee's ability to retain or vote company securities,[uu/] shall be voted as directed by the beneficiaries then entitled to receive or have the benefit of the income from the trust; to exercise or sell any subscription or conversion rights; to consent to and join in or oppose any voting trusts, reorganizations, consolidations, mergers, foreclosures and liquidations and in connection therewith to deposit securities and accept and hold other property received therefor;

(d) To lease trust property for any period of time though commencing in the future or extending beyond the term of the trust;[vv/]

(e) To borrow money from any lender, extend or renew any existing indebtedness and mortgage or pledge any property in the trust;[ww/]

---

tt/ Many settlors value the ability of a trust to insulate their wealth from public scrutiny, and nominee registration provides that plus a means to facilitate title transfers by permitting nominee execution of trades. Careful study of a publicly traded company list of major investors will reveal names of partnerships or other entities that you never have heard of, which often represent nominees of corporate fiduciaries that own a significant block of stock that is parceled among a multitude of trusts under their administration. Often this is the case if a single family once dominated that corporation and through inheritance in trust the holding has become fragmented, but voting control and ownership for the world to see is consolidated in the nominee registration.

uu/ Federal securities laws impose restrictions on owners of greater than certain percentages of a company's stock, sometimes requiring disclosures that are undesirable and potentially requiring divestment. This provision is designed to circumvent those issues if, for example, the aggregate of shares held in multiple trusts pushes the fiduciary over the relevant limit.

vv/ The issue with a lease is whether the fiduciary may encumber property for longer than the expected duration of the trust. This clarifies that power.

(f) To sell at public or private sale, contract to sell, convey, exchange, transfer and otherwise deal with the trust property and any reinvestments thereof, and to sell covered call options, from time to time for such price and upon such terms as the trustee sees fit;

(g) To employ agents, attorneys and proxies and to delegate to them such powers as the trustee considers desirable;[xx/]

(h) To compromise, contest, prosecute or abandon claims in favor of or against the trust;

(i) To distribute income and principal in cash or in kind, or partly in each, and to allocate or distribute undivided interests or different assets or disproportionate interests in assets,[yy/] and no adjustment shall be made to compensate for a disproportionate allocation of unrealized gain for federal income tax purposes; to value the trust property and to sell any part or all thereof in order to make allocation or distribution; no action taken by the trustee pursuant to this paragraph shall be subject to question by any beneficiary;[zz/]

(j) To deal with, purchase assets from, or make loans to, the fiduciary of any trust made by me or a trust or estate in which any beneficiary under this will has an interest, though a trustee hereunder is the fiduciary, and to retain any assets or loans so acquired, although not of a type, quality, marketability or diversification considered proper for trust investments; to deal with a corporate trustee hereunder individually or a parent or affiliate company;[aaa/]

(k) To determine in cases not covered by statute the allocation of receipts and disbursements between income and principal, except that (i) if the trust is beneficiary or owner of an individual account in any employee benefit plan or individual retirement plan, income earned after death in the account shall be income of the trust, and if the trustee is required to pay all trust income to a beneficiary, the trustee shall collect and pay the income of the account to the beneficiary at

---

ww/ This provision permits self dealing, most commonly if the corporate fiduciary also is a commercial lender.

xx/ Delegation by the fiduciary would be a breach of fiduciary duty without this authority (or a state law counterpart).

yy/ This authority to distribute in cash or in kind is critical to the marital funding endeavor that we studied in Chapter 7. It also could be made more useful if it authorized distribution of temporal interests. See note ss.

zz/ Note again protection of the fiduciary. A corporate fiduciary might not agree to serve without it, but it may not be appropriate for the beneficiaries.

aaa/ This too is authorized self dealing, most particularly appropriate among various funds created as part of an extended family representation.

least quarterly (and to the extent that all income cannot be collected from the account, the deficiency shall be paid from the principal of the trust), and (ii) reserves for depreciation shall be established out of income only to the extent that the trustee determines that readily marketable assets in the principal of the trust will be insufficient for any renovation, major repair, improvement or replacement of trust property that the trustee deems advisable;[bbb/]

(l) To elect, pursuant to the terms of any employee benefit plan, individual retirement plan or insurance contract, the mode of distribution of the proceeds thereof, and no adjustment shall be made in the interests of the beneficiaries to compensate for the effect of the election;[ccc/]

(m) To take such action in collecting the proceeds of any life insurance policy payable to the trustee (after deducting all charges by way of advances, loans or otherwise, for which the trustee shall not seek reimbursement) as the trustee deems best, paying the expense thereof from the trust property, but the trustee need not enter into or maintain litigation to enforce payment on a policy until indemnified to its satisfaction against all expenses and liabilities that might result therefrom; the insurance company shall not take notice of the provisions of this will or see to the application of the proceeds, and the

---

[bbb/] Fiduciary accounting is a subspecialty with its own quirks and sophistication, not always wisely addressed by generic state law principal and income acts. A revised Uniform Principal and Income Act was promulgated since these forms were drafted and many states have adopted unitrust entitlements, all of which likely requires some modification in this provision *if* the trust document authorizes or requires reliance on those modernizations. Notice the final sentence that essentially removes the duty to maintain a reserve for depreciation, which is driven largely by a federal income tax rule that denies the depreciation deduction to the beneficiaries to the extent of the reserve. Notwithstanding the bookkeeping issues involved, a fiduciary always must concern itself with maintaining hard assets in income producing repair lest depreciation degrade the asset to a point that it becomes a liability or robs the remainder beneficiaries of any value.

[ccc/] Both insurance (paragraph (m)) and retirement benefits present the designated beneficiary with a host of options and elections (not all of which being tax related) that the fiduciary must consider. Among the more difficult is balancing income taxation, fiduciary accounting, and marital deduction all-income-annually mandates in the benefits arena, and whether to litigate to collect on insurance unless indemnified against the cost of what may prove to be a losing battle. In addition, the final clauses in (m) are needed to maintain privacy as against inquiry by the insurer.

trustee's receipt to the insurance company shall be a complete release for any payment made;

(n) To inspect and monitor businesses and real property (whether held directly or through a partnership, corporation, trust or other entity) for environmental conditions or possible violations of environmental laws; to remediate environmentally-damaged property or to take steps to prevent environmental damage in the future, even if no action by public or private parties is currently pending or threatened; to abandon or refuse to accept property that may have environmental damage; the trustee may expend trust property to do the foregoing, and no action or failure to act by the trustee pursuant to this paragraph shall be subject to question by any beneficiary; and[ddd]

(o) To perform other acts necessary or appropriate for the proper administration of the trust, execute and deliver necessary instruments and give full receipts and discharges. [eee]

SECTION 6:[fff] The trustee shall render an account of trust receipts and disbursements and a statement of assets at least annually to each adult beneficiary then entitled to receive or have the benefit of

---

[ddd] CERCLA brings toxic tort due diligence and liability exposure. This is a legitimate concern to fiduciaries, which expect protection and likely will perform at least a phase one inspection of realty before agreeing to accept a trust that holds realty.

[eee] Somewhere in the powers provision a drafter may add instructions addressing a family business, land, difficult to manage assets (imagine a racehorse), or other important or unique assets that the fiduciary is not to manage. The document must exonerate the trustee from all liability relative to that asset if the trustee is expected to be willing to relinquish responsibility and continue to serve. Typically the fiduciary is relieved of any supervision or oversight with respect to the asset or the party to whom it is entrusted. The provision found at page 37 detailing special trustee and advisor provisions is typical.

[fff] A major sore subject among fiduciaries and beneficiaries is the level of accounting and disclosure, liability and foreclosure, compensation and reimbursement that is required, authorized, or avoided in the trust. Some settlors do not want beneficiaries (particularly young ones) to know how much wealth is involved, and some fiduciaries do not want beneficiaries constantly second guessing their performance. On the other hand, a trust cannot exist without enforcement of the fiduciary's duties, so there is a constant tension that this provision seeks to address. Consider whether this provision is too onerous or lax as you study and compare the Uniform Trust Code or the law of your state regarding issues of notice and accounting, the statute of limitation for objections, the requisite action required by beneficiaries to modify or terminate the trust, change trustees, and the like.

the income from the trust. An account is binding on each beneficiary who receives it and on all persons claiming by or through the beneficiary, and the trustee is released, as to all matters stated in the account or shown by it, unless the beneficiary commences a judicial proceeding to assert a claim within five years after the mailing or other delivery of the account. The trustee shall be reimbursed for all reasonable expenses incurred in the management and protection of the trust and shall receive compensation for its services in accordance with its schedule of fees in effect from time to time. The trustee's regular compensation shall be charged half against income and half against principal, except that the trustee shall have full discretion at any time or times to charge a larger portion or all against income.

SECTION 7: A corporate trustee in its discretion may terminate and distribute any trust hereunder if the corporate trustee determines that the costs of continuance thereof will substantially impair accomplishment of the purposes of the trust. The trustee shall terminate and forthwith distribute any trust created hereby, or by exercise of a power of appointment hereunder, and still held 21 years after the death of the last to die of myself and the beneficiaries in being at my death. Distribution under this section shall be made to the persons then entitled to receive or have the benefit of the income from the trust in the proportions in which they are entitled thereto, or if their interests are indefinite, then in equal shares.[ggg]

SECTION 8: Any trustee may resign at any time by written notice to each beneficiary then entitled to receive or have the benefit of the income from the trust. In case of the resignation, refusal or inability to act of any trustee acting or appointed to act hereunder, the beneficiary or a majority in interest of the beneficiaries then entitled to receive or have the benefit of the income from the trust shall appoint a successor

---

[ggg] This combination of the small trust termination and perpetuities savings provisions is sensible because in each case distribution would be to the same beneficiaries. The standard used for termination of an uneconomically small trust could constitute a taxable power of appointment if, unlike this form, the trustee might be a beneficiary to whom distribution might be made when that determination occurs. An alternative savings clause that would not cut short a trust that could last longer than the traditional perpetuities period would substitute for the second clause of the second sentence the following: "**one day prior to expiration of the permissible period under the relevant application of the Rule Against Perpetuities, if any, determined using as measuring lives in being only persons who are beneficiaries of any trust created by or pursuant to this instrument.**"

trustee, but no beneficiary or person legally obligated to a beneficiary shall be a successor trustee.[hhh]

Every successor trustee shall have all the powers given the originally named trustee. No successor trustee shall be personally liable for any act or omission of any predecessor.[iii] With the approval of the beneficiary or a majority in interest of the beneficiaries then entitled to receive or have the benefit of the income from the trust, a successor trustee may accept the account rendered and the property received as a full and complete discharge to the predecessor trustee without incurring any liability for so doing.

The parent or legal representative of a beneficiary under disability shall receive notice and have authority to act for the beneficiary under this section.

No trustee wherever acting shall be required to give bond or surety or be appointed by or account for the administration of any trust to any court.

SECTION 9: In disposing of any trust property subject to a power to appoint by will, the trustee may rely upon an instrument admitted to probate in any jurisdiction as the will of the donee or may assume that the power was not exercised if, within 3 months after the death of the donee, the trustee has no actual notice of a will that exercises the power. The trustee may rely on any document or other evidence in making payment under this will and shall not be liable for any payment made in good faith before it receives actual notice of a changed situation.[jjj]

SECTION 10: If for any reason the trustee is unwilling or unable to act as to any property, such person or qualified corporation as the trustee shall from time to time designate in writing shall act as special

---

[hhh] Without authority a trustee may not resign under most state laws. Not included here is the authority discussed in Chapter 6 for the beneficiaries to remove and replace trustees, which is a valuable check-and-balance that may ease tensions between beneficiaries and fiduciaries. Not surprisingly, this form (created by the fiduciary) does not grant that revolving door power. Also note that exclusion of a beneficiary or someone legally obligated to a beneficiary from serving is not required, but careful attention to changes in the dispositive provisions would be needed to insulate against unintended tax liability.

[iii] Fiduciary law would say that a successor is liable for any errors of the predecessor that the successor did not identify and sue to correct. Except in unusual situations, a knowledgeable fiduciary will not agree to serve as successor unless relieved of that exposure.

[jjj] This "donee's will" provision merely protects the fiduciary from liability flowing from an unknown exercise.

trustee as to that property. Any person or corporation acting as special trustee may resign at any time by written notice to the trustee. Each special trustee shall have the powers granted to the trustee by this will, to be exercised only with the approval of the trustee, to which the net income and the proceeds from sale of any part or all of the property shall be remitted to be administered under this will.[kkk]

SECTION 11: To enable trusts to be either completely exempt or nonexempt from generation-skipping tax, or for any other reason, the trustee may divide a trust into two or more separate trusts and may hold an addition to a trust as a separate trust. The rights of beneficiaries shall be determined as if the trusts were aggregated, but the trustee may pay principal to beneficiaries and taxing authorities disproportionately from the trusts. The trustee shall not be liable for deciding in its discretion to exercise or not exercise these powers.

Upon division or distribution of an exempt trust and a nonexempt trust held hereunder, the trustee in its discretion may allocate property from the exempt trust first to a share from which a generation-skipping transfer is more likely to occur.

If the trustee considers that any distribution from a trust hereunder other than pursuant to a power to withdraw or appoint is a taxable distribution subject to a generation-skipping tax payable by the distributee, the trustee shall augment the distribution by an amount that the trustee estimates to be sufficient to pay the tax and shall charge the same against the trust to which the tax relates.

If the trustee considers that any termination of an interest in trust property hereunder is a taxable termination subject to a generation-skipping tax, the trustee shall pay the tax from the portion of the trust property to which the tax relates, without adjustment of the relative interests of the beneficiaries.[lll]

---

kkk/ Traditionally known as an out-of-state property provision, notice that this paragraph allows the trustee to appoint a special trustee for *any* property, no matter where it is located. This too is a form of delegation that would not be permitted lacking this provision.

lll/ If we were to study the generation-skipping transfer tax in detail, you would be exposed to the rationale for authority to sever or consolidate trusts, and the need for exoneration from liability and directions regarding exercise of discretion in allocation of the GST exemption, payment of the tax, and the like. Those all are fit subjects for another day. Notice in the second line of the first paragraph of this Section "or for any other purpose." In this case another important purpose is to sever a trust that receives retirement benefits under the minimum distribution requirements. And a third use might be to sever separate shares for income tax purposes. These uses were not anticipated when this form originally was produced, but today they are very important. It pays to make provisions like this as

EIGHTH: If my [husband/wife] does not survive me or dies after my death without providing for the custody of a minor child of mine, I name *Guardian* as guardian of the person of that child. If a guardian of the estate of a minor child is necessary, I name *Custodian* to serve in that capacity. No bond or security shall be required of any guardian.[mmm]

NINTH: I appoint [THE NORTHERN TRUST COMPANY] as executor of this will. If for any reason [THE NORTHERN TRUST COMPANY] is unwilling or unable to act as executor as to any property,[nnn] I appoint as executor as to that property such person or qualified corporation as [THE NORTHERN TRUST COMPANY] shall designate in writing. The compensation of any corporate executor shall be in accordance with its schedule of fees in effect from time to time.

I give my executor the same powers as to the administration and investment of my estate that I have granted the trustee with respect to the trust property, to be exercised without authorization by any court and, as to property subject to administration outside the state of my domicile, only with the approval of my domiciliary executor. No bond or security shall be required of any executor wherever acting. If permitted by law and if not inconsistent with the best interests of the beneficiaries as determined by my executor, the administration of my estate shall be independent of the supervision of any court.[ooo]

---

generic as possible because useful authority germinated by one need often proves to be useful to satisfy a totally different calling in the future.

mmm/ Fiduciary appointments in general and guardians in particular are the most difficult decisions most clients make. Your clients predictably will have as much (or more) trouble with this provision as they will with any in the entire document, including fiduciary appointment in general or the dispositive provisions. Among the tough questions to ask them to consider is whether a married couple designated as guardian would relinquish the child in favor of another married couple if the former got a divorce (or if one died), whether special provisions should be added to authorize renovation of the guardians' home to accommodate added children, whether the trustee may make distribution to permit the guardian to purchase a larger home, and so on.

nnn/ This provision is an ancillary or out-of-state executor provision that is broad enough to permit delegation with respect to any undesirable or special asset, wherever located.

ooo/ Absence of bond and independent administration both are important elements of this provision.

If at my death any trust under this will has become executed, my executor shall make distribution to the beneficiary without the intervention of the trustee.^ppp/

IN WITNESS WHEREOF I have signed this will, consisting of [*] pages, [this/the following] page included, and for the purpose of identification have placed my initials at the foot of each preceding page, this *Day* day of *Month*, *Year*.

_____
Testator

We certify that the above instrument was on the date thereof signed and declared by *Testator* as [his/her] will in our presence and that we, at [his/her] request and in [his/her] presence and in the presence of each other, have signed our names as witnesses thereto, believing *Testator* to be of sound mind and memory at the time of signing.

_____ Residing at _____

_____ Residing at _____

_____ Residing at _____

STATE OF _____
COUNTY OF _____

We, the undersigned, being the testator and the witnesses, respectively, whose names are signed to the foregoing instrument, and being first duly sworn, do hereby declare to the undersigned authority that the testator, in the presence of witnesses, signed the instrument as [his/her] last will and that [s]he signed willingly; and that each of the witnesses, in the presence of the testator and in the presence of each other, signed the will as a witness and that to the best of his or her knowledge the testator was at that time of legal age, of sound mind and under no constraint or undue influence.

_____
TESTATOR

_____
WITNESS

---

ppp/ This "executed trust" provision simply makes administration easy if distribution straight to the beneficiary is appropriate, without the need to create and then terminate a trust. Many fiduciaries charge a termination fee, which this also would avoid.

_____
WITNESS

_____
WITNESS

Signed and sworn to before me by *Testator*, the testator, and by each of the above witnesses, this *Day* day of *Month*, *Year*.

_____
NOTARY PUBLIC
My commission expires _____

SPECIAL TRUSTEE AND ADVISOR PROVISIONS

General Saving Clause

ARTICLE X: Notwithstanding anything herein to the contrary, no distributions shall be made under this trust that would have the effect of discharging any person's legal obligation to support any beneficiary hereunder, and no individual fiduciary shall exercise any tax election that affects his or her interests or the interests of any person he or she is legally obliged to support or maintain, vote any securities, or possess any incidents of ownership with respect to any policy of insurance on his or her life, to the extent exercise of that tax election, that voting control, or possession of those incidents of ownership would subject that individual to any tax liability to which he or she otherwise is not exposed.

Distribution Advisor Provision

SECTION X: Notwithstanding the foregoing, while *Advisor* is living and not unable to manage [his/her] affairs, the trustee shall consult with and, to the extent not imprudent, shall follow the recommendations of *Advisor* with regard to the exercise of any discretion to determine the propriety and amount of payments of income or principal of the trust estate.

Distribution Director Provision

SECTION X: The trustee shall distribute so much or all of the principal of the trust estate to *Beneficiary* as *Advisor* while living and not unable to manage [his/her] affairs, shall direct as necessary or advisable for the health, maintenance in reasonable comfort, and education (including postgraduate) of *Beneficiary*, considering [his/her] income from all sources known to the trustee.

Investment Advisor Provision

SECTION X: While *Advisor* is living and not unable to manage [his/her] affairs: (a) No sale or investment shall be made without the written approval of *Advisor*, unless he or she fails to indicate approval or disapproval of any proposed sale or investment within ten days after being requested to do so in writing; and (b) *Advisor* shall have the power to direct the retention or sale of any trust assets and the purchase of any property with any principal cash in the trust. *Advisor* may at any time or times, with or without right of revocation, by a writing delivered to the trustee, delegate to any other person or to the trustee or relinquish any or all of [his/her] powers hereunder. The statement of the trustee that the trustee is acting according to this section shall fully protect all persons dealing with the trustee. The trustee shall have no responsibility for any loss that may result from acting in accordance with this section.

Voting Control

Any security as to which the trustee's possession of voting discretion would subject the issuing company or the trustee to any law, rule, or regulation adversely affecting either the company or the trustee's ability to retain or vote company securities shall be voted as directed by the beneficiaries then entitled to receive or have the benefit of the income from the trust.

Special Asset Provision

SECTION X: If any stock interest in [FamilyCo] or any successor organization, herein referred to as "special assets," are included among the trust assets, then notwithstanding any provision to the contrary:

(a) While the settlor is living and not unable to manage [his/her] affairs and has not relinquished the powers reserved to [him/her] hereunder, the trustee shall entrust to the settlor the management of the special assets insofar as the trustee takes part in or controls the management, and also the handling and decision of any questions that may arise by reason of ownership of special assets, and shall sell the special assets only as and when the settlor shall direct and shall follow the settlor's direction as to price and other terms and conditions of sale.

(b) After the death of the settlor, and during any period in which the settlor is unable to manage [his/her] affairs or has relinquished the powers reserved to [him/her] hereunder, *Advisor*, while (s)he is living and under no legal disability and has not relinquished the powers granted to [him/her] hereunder, shall have all the powers set forth in (a).

(c) While either the settlor or *Advisor* is acting hereunder, the trustee shall assume no responsibility in connection with the retention or sale of special assets and shall not be obliged to inquire into the affairs or condition of the special assets.

The foregoing powers shall be deemed to be and exercised as fiduciary powers.[qqq] They shall not disqualify the possessor from holding office in or acting in any other capacity with respect to the special assets. The statement of the trustee that the trustee is acting according to this section shall fully protect all persons dealing with the trustee. The

---

[qqq] Note that an exoneration provision that relieved the fiduciary of traditional fiduciary responsibility might cause a loss of any protection afforded by restrictions such as an ascertainable standard or powers exercisable only in an administrative or ministerial capacity, under Treas. Reg. §§1.674(b)-1(b)(5)(i), 20.2041-1(b)(1), 25.2511-1(g)(2), and 25.2514-1(b)(1).

trustee shall have no responsibility for any loss that may result from acting in accordance with this section.

In addition to this provision a similar statement should be included in the executor powers provision later in the will that mirrors this:

The restrictions on the powers of the trustee as to any stock interest in FAMILYCO or any successor organization, shall apply to the executor during probate of my estate.

[Trustee/Advisor/Director] Removal and Replacement

SECTION X: Any [trustee/advisor/director] may resign at any time by written notice to [, and may be removed at any time by written notice from,] the settlor if living, otherwise to [and from] each beneficiary then entitled to receive or have the benefit of the income from the trust. If any trustee/advisor/director dies, resigns, [is removed,] or refuses or is unable to act hereunder, the settlor if living, otherwise a majority in interest of the beneficiaries then entitled to receive or have the benefit of the income from the trust shall appoint a successor [trustee/advisor/director] [, but no beneficiary or person legally obligated to support a beneficiary shall be a successor [trustee/advisor/director]].

Designation of Successor Advisor

At any time and from time to time by instrument in writing delivered to the trustee, a majority in interest of the [adult] beneficiaries who are, or in the discretion of the trustee may be, then entitled to the income from the trust may designate an advisor who may be a person participating in the appointment of such advisor and any such designation may, in like manner, at any time and from time to time be revoked. Such advisor shall have all the rights, duties, powers, and responsibilities of *Advisor* set forth in SECTION X above during any period in which such [advisor] is acting hereunder.

Trust Agreement

I, *Settlor*, of *City*, *State*, as settlor, make this agreement with *Trustee*, of *City*, *State*, as trustee, this *Day* day of *Month, Year*.

I hereby transfer to the trustee the property listed in the attached schedule.[rrr/] That property and all investments and reinvestments thereof and additions thereto are herein collectively referred to as the "trust estate" and shall be held upon the following trusts:

FIRST:[sss/] . . . .

SECOND: During my lifetime the trust estate shall be held and disposed of as follows:

SECTION 1:[ttt/] I or any other person may make contributions to the trust at any time or times. For purposes of this agreement, the term "contribution" means any transfer of property to the trust for federal gift tax purposes, including property initially transferred to the trust or subsequently added thereto and payments of premiums on any insurance policy owned by the trustee that are paid otherwise than by the trustee. The amount of a contribution shall be its value for federal gift tax purposes.

---

rrr/ This is an unfunded irrevocable life insurance trust form. Frequently it is expected that the only asset scheduled will be $25, which is the cost of a United States Series EE savings bond. That corpus will validate the existence of the trust and it will not require the current trustee to perform any functions, which should prevent the need to pay any trustee fees while the trust otherwise is unfunded. At some point after creation of the trust, the trustee will apply for and acquire insurance on the life of the settlor, avoiding any ownership or transfer of that policy by the settlor and in that manner avoiding any §2042 inclusion of the proceeds of that insurance in the estate of the settlor.

sss/ This normally would be the same as the family definition provision in a will. Because this trust is irrevocable during the life of the settlor, it is more important that this provision anticipate and address changes in family, including the birth or adoption of more children, or a change in spouse. Some drafters define "spouse" to mean the person to whom the settlor is married from time to time or to whom the settlor was married at the time of the settlor's death.

ttt/ This provision is needed because it is anticipated that periodic contributions will be made to this trust that will be held by the trustee only long enough for the Crummey power of withdrawal in this Section to lapse. Those contributions then will be used to pay current premiums for insurance that is owned by the trust and payable to the trust on maturity.

My [husband/wife] and children who are living at the time of a contribution to the trust shall have the following rights to withdraw principal from the trust estate:[uuu]

(a) My [husband/wife] may withdraw property with a value equal to the first $5,000 of contributions made to the trust during any calendar year; and

(b) Each child of mine may withdraw from trust property an equal share of the value of the contribution which is not subject to withdrawal by my [husband/wife], except that a child may not withdraw more than the amount of the gift tax annual exclusion (or double the annual exclusion amount if I am married and my [husband/wife] and I split gifts for the year) in the aggregate during any calendar year.

By granting these withdrawal rights I intend that contributions to the trust shall qualify for the federal gift tax annual exclusion as gifts of present interests.

With respect to each contribution made to the trust during a calendar year:

(i) The trustee shall notify each beneficiary of his or her withdrawal right with respect to the contribution. The trustee may give notice after each contribution, once annually for all contributions made during the calendar year, or otherwise as the trustee deems advisable, but in no event later than December 31 of the calendar year.[vvv]

(ii) A beneficiary's withdrawal rights with respect to contributions to the trust shall continue from year to year until exercised, except that on December 31 of each year the beneficiary's aggregate withdrawal rights shall lapse as to the greater of $5,000 and 5% of the value of the trust estate, and except further that those withdrawal rights shall lapse upon the death of the beneficiary.[www]

A beneficiary may exercise a withdrawal right only by written request delivered to the trustee. The trustee shall make payment

---

[uuu] This entire provision constitutes the Crummey power of withdrawal that is discussed in Chapter 9.

[vvv] Recall from reading in Chapter 9 that it is not entirely clear what notice requirements apply for annual exclusion present interest purposes. This provision may be more severe than the law requires, or it might be altered to require notice at a minimum of 30 days before year end.

[www] This is the §2514(e) five or five tax free lapse provision that nibbles away at the taxable portion of the withdrawal rights given to the beneficiary. To the extent the power does not lapse under this clause, it remains for availability (and further lapse) in future years. This provision frequently is referred to as a hanging power.

pursuant to a written request in cash to the extent practicable, otherwise from other trust property selected by the trustee, including policies of life insurance.[xxx]

Each payment to a child under this section shall be treated as an advancement and charged without interest against the share hereinafter provided for the child or his or her descendants.[yyy]

The succeeding provisions of this agreement shall be subject to the terms of this section.

SECTION 2: The trustee may pay from the income and principal of the trust estate any premiums or assessments on any policy of life insurance owned by the trustee. The trustee may also pay so much or all of the income of the trust estate to any one or more of my [husband/wife] and children from time to time living, in equal or unequal proportions and at such times as the trustee deems necessary or advisable for their health and maintenance in reasonable comfort, except that no payment shall be made to satisfy any legal obligation of any person to a beneficiary. Any income not so paid shall be added to principal.

THIRD: If any portion of the trust estate shall be included in my gross estate for federal estate tax purposes,[zzz] then upon my death that portion shall be subject to the following:

(a) If my [husband/wife] survives me, the trustee shall forthwith distribute the portion to my [husband/wife], except that if there are one or more trusts that qualify in full for the federal estate tax marital deduction in my estate and that are not treated for federal generation-skipping tax purposes as if the qualified terminable interest property election had not been made, the portion shall be added in equal shares to those trusts.[aaaa] For purposes of this article, my [husband/wife]

[xxx] The notion that trust property could be used to satisfy a withdrawal right is merely a reflection that cash contributed to the trust might be used to pay premiums even before the Crummey power lapses, in which case exercise might be problematic. Here the only other asset in the trust is likely to be the policy itself, and the assumption is that this provision makes the withdrawal power qualify for the annual exclusion.

[yyy] This merely serves to further discourage exercise of the withdrawal power.

[zzz] Some drafters will add the express caveat that this provision applies only if the trust property is includible for reasons independent of the existence of this provision, in hopes of establishing that this provision itself cannot cause that inclusion.

[aaaa] If inclusion occurs for unexpected reasons the first line of defense to make that inclusion "harmless" for tax purposes would be to qualify the amount includible for the estate tax marital deduction. Notice that the

shall be deemed to have survived me if the order of our deaths cannot be proved. This distribution shall carry with it a proportionate part of the income of the trust estate from the date of my death to the date of distribution.

(b) If my [husband/wife] does not survive me, then notwithstanding any contrary provision in my will or revocable trust, the trustee shall pay from the principal of the portion the amount, if any, by which the estate and inheritance taxes assessed by reason of my death shall be increased as a result of the inclusion of the portion in my estate for such tax purposes. The trustee may make payment directly or to the legal representative of my estate, as the trustee deems advisable. I waive for the trust all rights of apportionment or reimbursement for any payment made pursuant to this paragraph.[bbbb/]

In making distribution or payment, the trustee shall accept without inquiry the statement of the fiduciary responsible for filing the federal estate tax return or paying the estate and inheritance taxes, as the case may be, of the amounts required to satisfy the provisions of this article.

The balance of the trust estate which remains after the foregoing distribution or payment has been made or provided for shall be held and disposed of as hereinafter provided.

FOURTH: After my death the trust estate shall be held and disposed of as follows:[cccc/] . . .

---

survivorship provision and payment of income during the interim period both are designed to guarantee that qualification.

bbbb/ This tax apportionment provision is an incremental payment of the taxes caused by inclusion and could conflict with a §2207A incremental right of reimbursement attributable to a QTIP marital trust includible in the settlor's gross estate at death. It also could conflict with a tax payment provision in the settlor's will or revocable trust, all of which should inform careful coordination among these various documents. Note the waiver of any right of reimbursement for payments made under this provision. That may envision a state law right but not §2206, which could not be waived by the provision in this trust. (Waiver is only permitted by will. The drafter probably assumes that there is no harm in trying and recognizes that the law could change after this trust becomes irrevocable.)

cccc/ The omitted provisions are standard nonmarital trust entitlements for the surviving spouse and descendants. It would be desirable in many cases if this trust and any created for those same beneficiaries under the settlor's other estate planning documents could be identical, such that they could be consolidated for administration. Remember that the permissible period under the Rule Against Perpetuities likely will differ because the period begins to run when this trust becomes irrevocable, which is upon

FIFTH: The following provisions shall apply to the trust estate and to each trust under this agreement:^dddd/

. . .

SECTION 2: . . . Except with respect to SECOND, the rights of beneficiaries to withdraw trust property are personal and may not be exercised by a legal representative, attorney in fact or others.^eeee/

. . .

SECTION 8: . . . Upon my death the then acting trustee shall cease to be trustee and [THE NORTHERN TRUST COMPANY, an Illinois corporation, of Chicago, Illinois,] shall be successor trustee.^ffff/

. . .

SECTION 10: If my marriage to my [husband/wife] is terminated by court order, then after the date of that order [s]he shall be deemed to be deceased for all purposes of this agreement.^gggg/

SECTION 11: The trustee may acquire, maintain and terminate policies of insurance on my life and may invest the trust solely in such policies. With respect to any policy of life insurance owned by or under which the death benefits are made payable to the trustee:^hhhh/

---

execution rather than death of the settlor (as would apply to either a revocable inter vivos or a testamentary trust).

dddd/ These also are identical to the trustee power and administration provisions in a standard trust. Reproduced are only those that are not common, needed because the trust is irrevocable and because it entails ownership of life insurance.

eeee/ This exception to the standard spendthrift provision is designed to guarantee annual exclusion qualification with a Crummey power of withdrawal that is meant to be exercisable by a next friend or guardian if the powerholder is a minor or is incompetent.

ffff/ Not until death of the settlor and maturation of the life insurance policies is there expected to be any real wealth involved that would require active management, so the typical plan would be for a family member or other individual to serve as trustee during the premium payment phase, to provide Crummey notices to beneficiaries and perform any modest due diligence regarding ownership of the insurance policy, but otherwise to charge no fees. The real work of fiduciary administration would begin once the proceeds are collected, and incurring fees at that time would be appropriate.

gggg/ This document is relatively conservative regarding the existence and inclusion of the spouse as a beneficiary. Other documents would follow the more aggressive approach mentioned in note sss.

hhhh/ Aside from those provisions that operate during the settlor's life, these paragraphs are typical of insurance clauses found in a standard trust. The primary object is to prevent the settlor as insured from having any

(a) The trustee or any other person, as owner of the policy, shall have all available benefits, privileges, payments, dividends, surrender values, options and elections, including the right at any time or times to change the beneficiary and to pledge or assign the policy or its proceeds as collateral security for any loan which the owner may obtain from any lender, including a trustee hereunder individually or a parent or affiliate company, except that the trustee's right to change the beneficiary shall be limited to naming the trustee or a successor trustee as beneficiary. I, as insured or otherwise, shall not have any incident of ownership in the policy if owned by the trustee and issued on my life.

(b) The trustee shall pay or see to the payment of premiums and assessments on the policy if owned by the trustee, except that if a person has advised the trustee that he or she will make a payment, the trustee may rely on that statement. If the trustee does not have sufficient assets to make a payment and the premium or assessment is not paid when due, the trustee in [his/her/its] discretion may solicit contributions to the trust, borrow money to make the payment, exercise any conversion privileges or terminate the policy. The trustee need not pay or see to the payment of premiums or assessments on the policy if not owned by the trustee.

(c) Upon the death of the insured thereunder the trustee shall take such action as the trustee deems best to collect the policy proceeds, paying the expense thereof from the trust estate, but the trustee need not enter into or maintain any litigation to enforce payment on the policy until indemnified to the trustee's satisfaction against all expenses and liabilities to which the trustee might thereby be subjected. The trustee may release the insurance company from its liability under the policy and make any compromise that the trustee deems proper.

(d) The insurance company shall not take notice of the provisions of this agreement or see to the application of the policy proceeds, and the trustee's receipt to the insurance company shall be a complete release for any payment made and shall bind every beneficiary under this agreement.

(e) The trust shall be operative with respect to the proceeds of the policy at the death of the insured thereunder, after deducting all charges by way of advances, loans or otherwise in favor of the owner

---

incidents of ownership that might cause inclusion in the settlor's gross estate under §2042 and to invest the trustee with the authority to provide for payment of premiums under any options provided by the policy or otherwise available to the trustee.

or owners or any other person, for which the trustee shall not seek reimbursement.

. . .

SECTION 13: The parent or legal representative of a beneficiary under disability shall receive notice and have authority to act for the beneficiary under this agreement, except that in no event shall I so act.[iiii/]

. . .

SEVENTH: I or any other person may transfer or bequeath property acceptable to the trustee, or make the proceeds under policies of life insurance payable to the trustee, to be held under this agreement and may designate the trust to which the property or proceeds shall be added. If the addition is made by will, the trustee shall accept the statement of the legal representative that the assets delivered to the trustee constitute all of the property to which the trustee is entitled, without inquiring into the representative's administration or accounting.[jjjj/]

EIGHTH: I may not amend or revoke this agreement in any respect.[kkkk/]

My [sibling/friend/advisor], if living and able to act and has not relinquished the powers granted to [him/her] hereunder, otherwise *Substitute*, at any time or times during my lifetime by instrument in writing delivered to the trustee may amend this agreement or terminate it and direct distribution of the trust estate in such manner as [s]he deems advisable, except that no distributee, or beneficiary of the agreement as amended, shall be a person other than a beneficiary under the agreement as originally executed, the person to whom I shall then be married, or a descendant or a spouse of a descendant of mine, and except further that [s]he shall not exercise the powers to

---

iiii/ This again is a provision designed to guarantee the annual exclusion, and to prevent inadvertent inclusion of insurance on the settlor's life in the settlor's gross estate.

jjjj/ It probably is unnecessary to specify that additions can be made to the trust, but this provision makes it clear that premium contributions and perhaps a pour over from the settlor's will or other estate planning trusts may be appropriate and are permissible.

kkkk/ In most jurisdictions this trust would be irrevocable even absent an express provision retaining the power to revoke, but for several reasons it is wise to specify the settlor's intent, most especially to be certain the settlor knows that he or she is not able to change this trust. The next paragraph is designed to provide flexibility notwithstanding, but not by the settlor.

amend and terminate to benefit [him/her]self or [his/her] spouse or descendants.

IN WITNESS WHEREOF I, *Settlor*, as settlor, and *Trustee*, as trustee, have signed this agreement the day and year first above written.

_____
Settlor

_____
Trustee

DURABLE POWERS

Three more forms are worth viewing, all powers of attorney. The first comes from The Northern Trust and is a durable power for transferring assets into a self-trusteed declaration of trust that the principal created inter vivos and did not transfer assets into. Instead, the client expects to wait for the agent under the power to do so when incapacity has occurred, the successor trustee has taken over administration of the trust, and assets need to be transferred into the trust for active administration. The second is a general all purpose durable power of attorney for asset management. And the third is a durable power for health care, sometimes known as a health care proxy. This last document is not predictably a good illustration anywhere, because state law often has very specific requirements for a valid health care durable power. Be certain to consult your local law rather than relying on this or any other form that just happens to be available to you.

POWER OF ATTORNEY

I, *Principal*, Social Security No. 000-00-0000, of *City*, *State*, executed a trust agreement on *Date*, *Year*, with myself, as trustee, and under which [THE NORTHERN TRUST COMPANY, an Illinois corporation, of Chicago, Illinois] (herein referred to as the "trustee"), is named as successor trustee. To facilitate transferring my assets to the trustee at any time or times, I appoint *Agent*, of *City*, *State*, as attorney-in-fact for me and in my name:

1. To have access to any safe deposit box rented by me or by me with others (including authority to have it drilled), to remove the contents therefrom and to terminate the lease of the box.

2. To assign, transfer and deliver all cash, bonds, stocks, securities, annuities and other property of any kind, real or personal, owned by me to the trustee or its nominee.

3. To withdraw any funds standing to my credit or to my credit jointly with others in any bank, savings and loan association or other financial institution and to pay the sums withdrawn to the trustee.

4. To endorse and deliver to the trustee any checks, drafts, certificates of deposit, notes or other instruments for the payment of money payable or belonging to me.

5. To convey any real estate, interest in real estate or beneficial interest in a trust holding real estate, which I may own or possess to the trustee or as the trustee directs.

6. To execute and deliver any assignment, stock power, deed or other instrument which my attorney-in-fact deems necessary or appropriate to carry out and effectuate this power of attorney, to sign my name to any instrument pertaining to or required in connection

with the transfer of my property to the trustee, and to give full receipts and discharges.

Every bank or other financial institution, insurance company, transfer agent, issuer, obligor, safe deposit box company, title insurance company or other person, firm or corporation to which this power of attorney or a photocopy hereof is presented is authorized to receive, honor and give effect to all instruments signed pursuant to the foregoing authority without inquiring as to the circumstances of their issuance or the disposition of the property delivered pursuant thereto. If permitted by law, this power of attorney shall not be affected by my disability. All acts done hereunder by my attorney-in-fact after revocation of this power of attorney or after my death shall be valid and enforceable in favor of anyone who relies on this power of attorney and has not received prior actual written notice of the revocation or death. All acts done by my attorney-in-fact pursuant to this power shall be binding upon me and my heirs, legatees and legal representatives.

The following is a specimen of the signature of my attorney-in-fact:

_____
Agent

IN WITNESS WHEREOF I have signed this power of attorney this *Day* day of *Month*, *Year*.

_____
Principal

STATE OF _____
COUNTY OF _____

I , _____, Notary Public, hereby certify that *Principal*, personally known to me to be the same person whose name is signed to the foregoing instrument, appeared before me this day in person and acknowledged that [s]he signed the instrument as [his/her] free and voluntary act, for the uses and purposes therein set forth.

Given under my hand and official seal this *Day* day of *Month*, *Year*.

_____
NOTARY PUBLIC
My Commission expires _____

UNLIMITED POWER OF ATTORNEY[1111]

This unlimited power is intended to be the broadest possible power of attorney, permitting the agent to act on behalf of the principal to do virtually anything the principal could do personally. It does not attempt to list specific powers granted because the very enumeration may imply that some power not specifically included in the list was not granted to the agent. By not having a specific list of powers, this durable power of attorney is expected to be broader than any other that might be prepared and, because of this breadth, it may be important for the attorney to impress on the client that it authorizes the agent to do *anything* the law allows. The drafter recommends that the client be asked to sign a copy of a memorandum confirming the fact that the client understood the extremely broad and powerful authority that this grants.

PART 1 — APPOINTMENT

By signing this document in the presence of two disinterested witnesses and acknowledging the same before a notary public, I, *Principal*, **of** *City, State*, **appoint** *Agent* **as my initial "authorized agent."**

PART 2 — SUCCESSOR AGENT(S)

If at any time Agent is unwilling or unable to act as my initial "authorized agent" I appoint *Successor Agent*, **to serve as the successor authorized agent and if at any time (s)he is unwilling or unable to act I appoint** *Alternative Successor Agent,* **as alternative successor authorized agent.**

PART 3 — AGENT MUST ACCEPT

Although this document is intended to be effective as of the date of execution, my appointment of each authorized agent shall be effective only after such agent signs the authorized agent acceptance set forth below. Except as I (or an authorized agent acting in my behalf with respect to any other agent acting hereunder) may have otherwise separately agreed in writing, no agent acting hereunder shall receive

---

[1111] This "unlimited power" is a durable general power that gives the agent all powers permitted by law — even the power to make gifts from the property of the principal. Especially important is the agent's power to execute other power of attorney documents (for example, on institutional forms) appointing the agent (or others) to act in the principal's behalf. This unlimited power was prepared in accordance with the Uniform Durable Power of Attorney Act and is adapted from a form copyrighted (1992) by Frederick R. Keydel of Joslyn, Keydel, Wallace & Carney in Detroit, who specifically grants free use in the practice of law by attorneys. This power of attorney is intended to be given effect on a full faith and credit, comity basis to the greatest extent possible in all states and countries.

compensation for (but each shall be entitled to reimbursement for actual and necessary expenses reasonably incurred in) the performance of such agent's responsibilities.

PART 4 — PART OF MY RECORDS

If a photo or faxed copy of (a) this document (as signed by me and any authorized agent), (b) any power of attorney executed in my behalf by any agent of mine (in the manner provided in part 5 below), or (c) a representation regarding my agent's authority as described in part 9 below is presented to any person (as broadly defined in part 12 below) with whom I have financial, business, or other dealings of any kind, such document(s) shall thereupon be made a part of my records with such person.

PART 5 — UNLIMITED POWERS TO ACT

Each authorized agent of mine is hereby granted the power to represent me and perform any and all acts in my behalf in all matters and affairs (except those relating to my health care),[mmmm/] without limitation of any kind (other than as provided in part 7 below), including the power to make every decision and take every action, even making gifts or disclaiming any or all benefits of any kind, for me that I could in my own behalf — excluding only those rare things (if any) which applicable law does not at the time of exercise permit any agent or attorney in fact to do for or in behalf of his principal, no matter how all encompassing nor how specific his authorization.

To allow my authorized agent to satisfy third parties who require more specific enumeration of an agent's powers in a power of attorney document before they will recognize the agent's authority, I expressly grant to each authorized agent the power to execute in my behalf, as I could myself, any and all kinds of power of attorney documents that name as my attorney in fact (a) my authorized agent or (b) any other person to whom my authorized agent deems it appropriate to delegate any powers set forth in such document. Any specific listing of powers in such document not expressly excluded by this document, including the power to make gifts, is hereby expressly authorized. Aside from that one express power, I list no examples of the powers hereby granted to my authorized agent because their very listing might appear to limit those powers. I intend the powers hereby granted to each of my authorized agents to be absolutely as broad as applicable law will allow — in other words, an unlimited power.

---

mmmm/ This document anticipates that a living will or a separate health care power of attorney will be prepared if it is appropriate.

PART 6 — RATIFICATION

I hereby ratify and confirm all that is done or caused to be done by virtue of this document in my behalf by any authorized agent, by each attorney in fact appointed by my authorized agent to act in my behalf in the manner provided in part 5 above, and by any third party dealing with any agent acting hereunder (hereafter collectively referred to as "persons relying on this power of attorney"). All documents of any kind (without limitation) executed or delivered in my behalf by any agent acting hereunder shall bind me and my estate, heirs, successors, and assigns.

PART 7 — PERMITTED SELF-DEALING

Transactions, both direct and indirect, between me and any agent acting hereunder carried into effect by the action of any agent acting hereunder are hereby expressly authorized, notwithstanding any rule of law relating to self-dealing, if such agent believes such actions to be in the best interest of me, my estate, or those who, in such agent's judgment, I would likely intend to be benefited by my estate. However, each agent acting hereunder shall assure that I receive in all financial transactions adequate and full consideration in money or money's worth and, in all other transactions, shall not appropriate property to himself, herself, or itself (within the meaning of §2041 of the Internal Revenue Code). This proviso shall not prohibit any action insofar as it reduces such agent's taxes nor any gifts or disclaimers in my behalf that benefit such agent if such gifts or disclaimers (a) do not exceed $11,000 (plus the inflation index amount) per donee in any calendar year (or whatever is the annual exclusion amount under §2503(b) of the Internal Revenue Code or double that amount if the split gift provisions of §2513 of that Code are meant to apply), (b) are in direct payment of tuition or medical expenses, or (c) are made by any other independent person to whom my authorized agent may, in my behalf, have delegated such gift or disclaimer powers hereunder in the manner provided in part 5 above, acting alone on the basis of that person's sole judgment. No agent acting hereunder shall have or exercise any incident of ownership in or control over any insurance on such agent's life or any property I have (or any trust as to which I am a trustee or beneficiary has) received from such agent by gift.

PART 8 — REVOCATION AND RESIGNATION

I may at any time revoke the powers of any authorized agent hereunder by a communication of any kind, direct or indirect, to such agent. My right to revoke any power of attorney document executed in my behalf by any authorized agent of mine (as provided in part 5 above), and thus terminate the powers of any other agent acting for me thereunder, shall be as set forth in that document. If this or any other power of attorney for me is recorded in any county records office, it shall not be deemed revoked until an instrument revoking such power of attorney also is recorded in that same office. If this power is recorded, the county name (or names) shall be listed as provided below. Any agent acting hereunder may resign by a writing received by me, a trustee of my revocable trust, if any, or my conservator.

PART 9 — INDUCEMENT

Each person relying on this power of attorney who also relies on representations made by any agent acting hereunder to the effect that:

1. this document and any power of attorney executed pursuant to it on which such agent relies have not been revoked,

2. such agent's powers hereunder are then in effect and such agent continues to serve as my attorney in fact,

3. such agent's authority under this document is as all inclusive as the law permits,

4. I was competent at the time this document was executed,

5. based on the opinion of counsel who prepared this power, it is valid under the laws of the state in which it was executed (or the state of my residence), and

6. such agent believes that I am then living

is hereby released by me from all liability to me and my estate, heirs, successors, and assigns for permitting such agent to exercise any particular power that the law would permit an agent to exercise if such agent were specifically and duly authorized to exercise that particular power. No person who deals with any agent hereunder shall be responsible to see to the proper application of any funds or property transferred to such agent. In behalf of myself and my estate, heirs, successors, and assigns, I agree to and do hereby indemnify and hold harmless each person who relies upon all six of the foregoing representations from any loss suffered or liability incurred by such party in acting in accordance with this power of attorney prior to such party's receipt of written notice of its termination.

Furthermore, I ask that:

A. My authorized agent, in the exercise of such agent's discretion, sue for and

B. the courts impose

the maximum penalties, damages, and punitive awards provided for by law against any person who, notwithstanding the above release and indemnity, wrongfully refuses to (a) honor this power of attorney, regardless of the lapse of time since its execution, or (b) implement the decisions and actions in my behalf of any agent acting hereunder.

PART 10 — EXCULPATION

Although I expect each of my agents to be guided by any directions I may communicate to such agent, no agent acting hereunder shall incur any liability to me or my estate, heirs, successors, and assigns for acting or refraining from acting, except for willful misconduct or clear negligence. Each agent acting hereunder may rely on reasonably selected and supervised agents and counsel. No agent acting hereunder, unless specifically appointed as an investment manager, shall have responsibility to make my assets income producing, to increase the value of my estate, or to diversify my investments (other than would be required of a prudent person under like circumstances in dealing with his or her own property).

PART 11 — DURABILITY

This power of attorney shall not be terminated or otherwise affected by any disability, incompetence, or incapacity that I may suffer at any future time, even if adjudicated by a court, it being my intent that the powers granted in this document shall remain exercisable notwithstanding any such occurrence.

PART 12 — GOVERNING LAW

This power of attorney shall be governed in all respects by the laws of the state in which executed by me, including its validity, construction, interpretation, and termination. However, I intend that this power of attorney and appointment of my authorized agent(s) be honored and given effect to the fullest extent possible wherever I or my authorized agent(s) may be. The term "person" shall have the broadest possible meaning, but in the context of who may be appointed to be an agent acting hereunder, shall mean only an individual who is sui juris or a bank or trust company which has trust powers, regardless of where located. Should any provision of this document be held invalid, such invalidity shall not affect the other provisions, which shall remain in full force and effect. Photo and faxed copies of this document (whether executed as a single original or in multiple counterparts) shall be relied upon as though they were signed originals.

PART 13 — NOMINATION OF GUARDIAN/CONSERVATOR

If protective proceedings for my person or estate are at any time commenced, I nominate as my guardian and conservator whoever is then my authorized agent under this document.

I am of sound mind and at least 18 years old. I understand the virtually unlimited extent of the powers granted to my authorized agent. I am fully confident of the integrity of such person. Should there arise a need for action under this document (as determined in the sole discretion of my authorized agent), I entrust to the judgment of such authorized agent the management of my financial affairs, including the possible gift or other disposition (in the broadest sense) of my properties. I sign this document of my own free will.

My address (and telephone number):
_____
_____

My social security number:
_____-_____-_____

At *City, State*, on the date last above written, and in our sight and presence, *Principal* (hereafter "the principal"), (a) signed this document and at the same time (b) declared that:

> This document is my power of attorney. I understand the virtually unlimited extent of the powers it gives to my authorized agent to act in my behalf (except as to medical care decisions) and I am fully confident of the integrity of the person I have appointed to act for me whenever any such person believes there is need for such action.

As attesting witnesses, we do now, at the principal's request and in the principal's sight and presence and in the sight and presence of each other, sign our names below. Each of us also declares that he or she (a) has attained at least 18 years of age, (b) is not the principal's authorized agent or successor authorized agent hereunder, and (c) is acquainted with the principal who, according to each of the undersigned's best knowledge and belief, at this time appeared to be (i) of sound mind, memory, and understanding and (ii) not acting under menace, constraint, duress, fraud, misrepresentation, or the undue influence of any person. Each of the undersigned does hereby further declare under penalty of perjury (under the laws of the state in which this document is executed) that the foregoing is true and correct.

_____ Residing at _____
_____ Residing at _____
_____ Residing at _____

State of _____
County of _____

The foregoing document was acknowledged before me this *Day* day of *Month, Year*.

_____
Notary Public

The principal's signature above should be guaranteed by a commercial bank or trust company or by a stock exchange member firm whose signature is known to transfer agents generally.

As the lawyer who prepared this unlimited power of attorney document, it is my opinion that such document is a valid durable power of attorney under the laws of the state in which executed once signed by (a) the principal in the manner provided above and (b) an authorized agent as indicated below.

_____
Attorney at Law

ACCEPTANCE

The undersigned hereby acknowledges the above appointment of herself, himself, or itself as authorized agent for *Principal* (hereafter "the principal"), and (a) accepts the same, (b) acknowledges that she or he is at least 18 years of age, (c) acknowledges receipt of a photocopy of this power of attorney and appointment of authorized agent, and (d) agrees to be bound by the same, to act in good faith in the best interests of the principal and the principal's estate and those interested in the principal's estate, and to follow the desires, instructions, guidelines, and preferences of the principal as from time to time expressed by the principal (in writing, orally, or as otherwise communicated to the undersigned by the principal). With respect to any period she, he, or it for any reason is unavailable (including being unwilling) to act (after reasonable effort has been made to contact her, him, or it), each of the undersigned hereby delegates her, his, or its authority hereunder to the next available person, if any, the principal has appointed as successor authorized agent (in the order appointed). Such next appointed successor authorized agent who is available is authorized to act until the initial authorized agent (or next preceding successor) becomes available. Absent any contrary communication from any predecessor, each successor's determination that such delegation to such successor is in effect shall be conclusively binding on all concerned.

Initial Authorized Agent: _____

Substitute Authorized Agent:_____

List on an attached sheet the name of each county in which recorded (if recorded) with date, liber/volume, and page.

Keep your signed original with your personal papers at home (or leave it for safekeeping with your attorney). Keep extra photocopies at home and give photocopies to your authorized agent(s).

REPRESENTATIONS

To whom it may concern:

As authorized agent under the attached unlimited power of attorney executed by *Principal* (the "principal") on *Date, Year* (the "attached document"), I hereby represent to you that, as of the date by my signature below:

    1. The attached document and the power of attorney that it represents have not been revoked (nor has any power of attorney executed pursuant to the attached document been revoked),

    2. my powers under the attached document are in effect and I continue to serve as the principal's authorized agent and attorney in fact under the attached document (and under any attached power of attorney executed pursuant to the attached document),

    3. the scope of my authority under the attached document includes everything the principal could do [him/her]self (even the power to make gifts),

        a. expressly including the power to execute in the principal's behalf any and all kinds of power of attorney documents that themselves name as the principal's attorney in fact (i) me or (ii) any other person whom I deem it appropriate to have any powers set forth in such document (any and all specific listings of powers therein not expressly excluded by the attached document being authorized) and

        b. excluding only (i) those rare things (if any) which applicable law does not at this time permit any agent or attorney in fact to do for or in behalf of such agent's principal, no matter how all encompassing or specific such agent's authorization, and (ii) the making of any gift (other than the direct payment of tuition or medical expenses) or disclaimer in the principal's behalf as a result of which I receive any direct or indirect financial benefit in excess of $11,000 (plus the inflation index amount) in any calendar year (doubled if the gift is expected to be split with the principal's spouse),

    4. the principal was fully competent to execute the attached document at the time it was executed,

    5. based on the opinion of the counsel who prepared the attached document, it is a valid durable general power of attorney under the laws of the state in which it was executed (or the state of the principal's residence), and

    6. I believe that the principal is living.

Part 9 of the attached document provides that each person relying on said unlimited power of attorney who also relies on representations any agent acting thereunder may make as set forth above shall be and is released from all liability to the principal and the principal's estate, heirs, successors, and assigns for permitting such agent to exercise any particular power that the law would permit an agent to exercise if such agent were specifically and duly authorized to exercise that particular power. Furthermore in said part 9, in behalf of the principal and the principal's estate, heirs, successors, and assigns, the principal not only releases such person but also agrees to and does indemnify and hold harmless each person who relies upon the foregoing six representations from any loss suffered or liability incurred by such party in acting in accordance with said power of attorney prior to such party's receipt of written notice of its termination.

                                                              Authorized Agent

DURABLE POWER OF ATTORNEY FOR HEALTH CARE[nnnn]

I, *Principal*, hereby appoint *Agent* to serve as my Agent and, to the extent she is unable or unwilling to act, I appoint *Alternate Agent* as my Alternate Agent, in each case to exercise the powers and discretions hereafter described.

ARTICLE ONE

My Agent is authorized in my Agent's discretion from time to time and at any time to exercise the authority described hereafter relating to matters involving my health care. In exercising the authority granted to my Agent, I first direct my Agent to try to discuss with me the specifics of any proposed decision regarding my health care and treatment if I am able to communicate in any manner, however rudimentary. If I am unable to consent, or refuse to consent, to my healthcare, and my Agent cannot determine the choice I would want made under the circumstances, my Agent shall give, withhold, modify, or withdraw such consent for me based on any health care choices that I may previously have expressed on the subject while competent, whether under this instrument or otherwise. If my Agent cannot determine the treatment choice I would want made under the circumstances, then my Agent shall make such choice for me based on what my Agent believes to be in my best interests. Accordingly, my Agent is authorized as follows:

1.01 Powers Relating to Medical Records and Other Personal Information

My Agent is authorized to request, receive, and review any information, verbal or written, regarding my personal affairs or my physical or mental health, including medical and hospital records, and to execute any releases or other documents that may be required to obtain such information, and to disclose or deny such information to such persons, organizations, firms, or corporations as my Agent shall deem appropriate.

1.02 Power to Employ and Discharge Health Care Personnel

My Agent is authorized to employ and discharge health care personnel including physicians, psychiatrists, dentists, nurses, and therapists as my Agent shall deem necessary for my physical, mental

---

[nnnn] This form is derived from Collin, Lombard, Moses, & Spitler, DURABLE POWERS OF ATTORNEY AND HEALTH CARE DIRECTIVES (3d ed. 2003).

and emotional well-being, and to pay them, or cause them to be paid, reasonable compensation.

1.03 Power to Give, Withhold, Withdraw, or Modify Consent to Health Care Treatment

My Agent is authorized to give, withhold, withdraw, or modify consent to any health care procedures, tests, or treatments, including surgery; to arrange for my hospitalization, convalescent care, hospice, or home care; to summon paramedics or other emergency medical personnel and seek emergency treatment for me, as my Agent shall deem appropriate; to give, withhold, withdraw, or modify consent to such procedures, tests, and treatments, as well as hospitalization, convalescent care, hospice, or home care that I or my Agent may have previously allowed or consented to or that may have been implied due to emergency conditions. My Agent's decisions should be guided by taking into account: (1) the provisions of this instrument, (2) any reliable evidence of preferences that I may have expressed on the subject whether before or after execution of this document, (3) what my Agent believes I would want done in the circumstances if I were able to express myself, and (4) any information given to my Agent by the physicians treating me as to my health care diagnosis and prognosis and the intrusiveness, pain, risks, and side effects of the treatment.

1.04 Power to Give or Withhold Consent to Psychiatric Treatment

My Agent is authorized to arrange, on the execution of a certificate by two independent psychiatrists who have examined me and in whose opinions I am in immediate need of hospitalization because of mental disorder, alcoholism, or drug abuse, for my voluntary admission to an appropriate hospital or institution for treatment of the diagnosed problem or disorder; to arrange for private psychiatric and psychological treatment for me; and to revoke, modify, withdraw, or change consent to such hospitalization, institutionalization, or private treatment that I or my Agent previously may have given. The consent of my Agent to my hospitalization for psychiatric help, alcoholism, or drug abuse shall have the same legal effect, subject to applicable local law, as a voluntary admission made by me.

1.05 Power to Maintain Me in My Residence

My Agent is authorized to take whatever steps are necessary or advisable to enable me to remain in my personal residence as long as it is reasonable under the circumstances. I realize that my health may deteriorate so that it becomes necessary to have round-the-clock nursing care if I am to remain in my personal residence, and I direct my Agent to obtain such care, including any equipment that might assist in such care, as is reasonable under the circumstances. Specifically, I do not want to be hospitalized or put in a convalescent or similar home as long as it is reasonable to maintain me in my personal residence.

1.06 Power to Exercise My Health Care Right of Privacy

My Agent is authorized to exercise all state and federal rights that I may have, including but not limited to my right of privacy to make decisions regarding my health care even though the exercise of those rights might hasten my death or be contrary to conventional health care advice.

1.07 Power to Authorize Relief from Pain

My Agent is authorized to consent to and arrange for the administration of pain-relieving drugs of any kind, or other surgical or health care procedures calculated to relieve my pain, including unconventional pain-relief therapies that my Agent believes may be helpful to me, even though such drugs or procedures may lead to permanent physical damage or addiction, or even hasten the moment of, but not intentionally cause, my death.

1.08 Power to Grant Releases

In conjunction with any instructions given under this Article, my Agent is authorized to grant releases to hospital staff, physicians, nurses, and other health care providers who act in reliance on instructions given by my Agent or who render written opinions to my Agent in connection with any matter described in this Article from all liability for damages suffered or to be suffered by me; and to sign documents titled or purporting to be a "Refusal to Permit Treatment" and "Leaving Hospital Against Medical Advice," as well as any necessary waivers of or releases from liability required by any hospital or physician to implement my wishes regarding medical treatment or non-treatment.

ARTICLE TWO

I wish to live and enjoy life as long as possible. However, I do not wish to receive health care treatment that will only postpone the moment of my death from an incurable and terminal condition or prolong an irreversible coma. For purposes of this instrument, (1) "terminal condition" refers to a condition that is reasonably expected to result in my death within twelve months regardless of the treatment I may receive, and (2) "irreversible coma refers to a permanent loss of consciousness from which there is no reasonable possibility that I will return to a cognitive and sapient life and includes but is not limited to that condition known as a *persistent vegetative state.*

Therefore, if two licensed, qualified physicians who are familiar with my condition have diagnosed and noted in my medical records that: (1) I am unable to give informed consent to health care treatment that is proposed or available for my condition and that my condition is terminal as defined above, or (2) I have been in a coma for at least sixty days and that the coma is irreversible as defined above, then my Agent is authorized to:

(a) direct that health care that will only postpone the moment of my death or prolong my irreversible coma be withheld or, if previously begun, to direct that such treatment be withdrawn, regardless of whether such treatment is related to my terminal condition or irreversible coma; and

(b) request, require, or consent to the writing of a "No-Code" or "Do Not Resuscitate" order by any of my attending physicians; and

(c) sign on my behalf any documents necessary to carry out the authorizations described in this instrument, including waivers or releases of liability required by any health care provider; and

(d) order whatever is appropriate to keep me as comfortable and free of pain as is reasonably possible, including the administration of pain-relieving drugs of any kind or other surgical or medical procedures calculated to relieve my pain, including unconventional pain-relief therapies that my Agent believes may be helpful, even though such drugs or procedures may lead to permanent physical damage or addiction, or even hasten the moment of, but not intentionally cause, my death.

I desire that my wishes be carried out through the authority given to my Agent by this instrument despite any contrary feelings, beliefs, or opinions of members of my family, relatives, friends, conservator, or guardian.

In exercising the authority granted to my Agent herein, my Agent shall first follow the instructions in this document and any other subsequent instructions, oral or written, that I may give my Agent while I am competent. Notwithstanding such instructions, if my Agent cannot determine the treatment choice I would want made under the circumstances, then my Agent shall make such choice for me based on what my Agent believes to be in my best interest.

If no Agent designated in this instrument is available or able or willing to serve as my Agent or to exercise the powers granted in this

Article, then I request that this document be given the same force and effect as any other written expression of intent under applicable law.

It is my intention that this instrument, both as a self-executing document and as a delegation of power to my Agent, be deemed an exercise of all rights and interests that I may have under the United States Constitution, the constitution of the state of my domicile, state and federal laws, rules, regulations, and decisions, judicial and administrative, to refuse health care treatment, including but not limited to artificial nutrition and artificial hydration.

I authorize my Agent to establish a new residency or domicile for me, from time to time and at any time, within or without the state, and within or without the United States, for the purpose of exercising effectively the powers granted to my Agent in this Article.

If I have been in an irreversible coma, as defined above, for at least sixty consecutive days, or if because of my terminal condition as defined above it is no longer possible to nourish me without severe discomfort, and the two physicians described above also conclude that the nourishment will not improve my physical condition and I will not experience pain as a result of the withdrawal of nutrition or hydration, then my Agent may require that procedures used to provide me with nutrition and hydration, including (by way of example only) all forms of intravenous and parenteral feeding, all forms of tube feeding, and misting, be withheld or, if previously instituted, may require that they be withdrawn.

My Agent is authorized to receive and retain custody of any instrument signed by me that is effective under law to require the withdrawal or withholding of life-sustaining treatment or procedures, including but not limited to a "Living Will," "Directive to Physician," and a "Declaration of a Desire for Natural Death" (hereafter referred to in the aggregate as "Advance Directives") and, if the circumstances described above authorizing my Agent to require that life-sustaining treatment be withheld or withdrawn have occurred, then as an alternative or supplemental act I authorize my Agent to deliver to my physicians, health care providers, and other appropriate recipients, this instrument and any other writings and Advance Directives signed by me that express my desire under the circumstances to require the withholding or withdrawal of futile health care treatment, and to instruct such physicians, health care providers, and other appropriate recipients to act immediately in accordance with my desires.

I authorize and request my Agent to (1) solicit the assistance of a licensed physician to provide whatever lawful means may be available and appropriate to hasten the moment of my death, and (2) to do all that is lawful to assure that the means used to hasten the moment of my death are appropriately administered to me, either by my Agent or others.

ARTICLE THREE

In connection with the exercise of the powers and discretions herein described, my Agent is fully authorized and empowered to perform any acts and things and to execute and deliver any documents, instruments, affidavits, certificates, and papers necessary or appropriate to such exercise or exercises, including without limitation the following:

3.01 Resort to Courts

My Agent is authorized to seek on my behalf and at my expense any or all of: (1) a declaratory judgment from any court of competent jurisdiction interpreting the validity of this instrument and any of the acts authorized by this instrument, but such declaratory judgment shall not be necessary for my Agent to perform any act authorized by this instrument; (2) a mandatory injunction requiring compliance with my Agent's instructions by any person, organization, corporation or other entity obligated to comply with instructions given by me; (3) actual and punitive damages, and the recoverable costs, fees, and expenses of such litigation, against any person, organization, corporation, or other entity obligated to comply with instructions given by me who negligently or willfully fails or refuses to follow such instructions.

3.02 Hire and Fire Generally

My Agent is authorized to employ, compensate, and discharge such domestic, health care, and professional personnel including lawyers, accountants, doctors, nurses, brokers, financial consultants, advisors, consultants, companions, servants, and employees as my Agent deems appropriate.

3.03 Sign Documents and Incur Costs in Implementing the Agent's Instructions

My Agent is authorized to sign, execute, endorse, seal, acknowledge, deliver, and file or record instruments and documents, including but not limited to contracts, agreements, and conveyances of real and personal property, instruments granting and perfecting security instruments and obligations, orders for the payment of money, receipts, releases, waivers, elections, vouchers, consents, satisfactions, and certificates. In addition, any Agent of mine who has the authority to incur costs on my behalf may render the bills for such costs to any Agent of mine who has been granted the authority to pay such costs or to any trustee of any revocable living trust of mine, or guardian, committee, or conservator who has authority to pay such costs, and I request that such costs be paid promptly. Any recipient thereof (i.e., my Agent with authority to pay or my trustee) shall promptly pay such costs.

3.04 Payment of Medical Expenses

My Agent is directed to pay, or cause to be paid, all bills incurred and presented by any agent representing me under a Durable Power of Attorney for Health Care.

3.05 Borrow, Spend, Liquidate, Secure

My Agent is authorized to expend my funds and to liquidate my property or to borrow money to produce such funds and to secure any such borrowings with security interests in any property, real, personal, or intangible that I may now or hereafter own.

3.06 Power to Do Miscellaneous Acts

My Agent is authorized to open, read, respond to, and redirect my mail; to represent me before the United States Postal Service in all matters relating to mail service; to establish, cancel, continue, or initiate my membership in organizations and associations of all kinds, to take and give or deny custody of all of my important documents, including but not limited to my will, codicils, trust agreements, deeds, leases, life insurance policies, contracts, and securities and, bearing in mind the confidential nature of such documents, to disclose or refuse to disclose such documents; to obtain and release or withhold information or records of all kinds relating to me, to any interest of mine or to any person for whom I am responsible; to house or provide for housing, support, and maintenance of any animals or other living creatures that I may own and to contract for and pay the expenses of their proper veterinary care and treatment; and if the care and maintenance of such animals or other living creatures shall become unreasonably expensive or burdensome in my Agent's opinion, to irrevocably transfer such animals to some person or persons willing to care for and maintain them.

ARTICLE FOUR

For the purpose of inducing all persons, organizations, corporations, and entities, including but not limited to any physician, hospital, nursing home, health care provider, bank, broker, custodian, insurer, lender, transfer agent, taxing authority, governmental agency, or other party, all of whom are referred to in this article as a "Person," to act in accordance with the instructions of my Agent as authorized in this instrument, I hereby represent, warrant and agree that:

4.01 Third Party Liability for Revocation and Amendments

If this instrument is revoked or amended for any reason, I, my estate, and my personal representative will hold any Person harmless from any loss suffered, or liability incurred by such Person in acting in accordance with the instructions of my Agent acting under this instrument before such Person receives actual written notice of any such revocation or amendment.

4.02 Agent Has Power to Act Alone

The powers conferred on my Agent by this instrument may be exercised by my Agent alone, and my Agent's signature or act under the authority granted in this instrument may be accepted by Persons as fully authorized by me and with the same force and effect as if I were personally present, competent, and acting on my own behalf. Consequently, all acts lawfully done by my Agent hereunder are done with my consent and shall have the same validity and effect as if I were personally present and personally exercised the powers myself, and shall inure to the benefit of and bind me, my estate and my personal representative.

4.03 No Liability to Third Parties for Reliance on Agent

No person who relies in good faith on the authority of my Agent under this instrument shall incur any liability to me, my estate, or my personal representative. In addition, no person who acts in reliance on any representations my Agent may make as to (1) the fact that my Agent's powers are then in effect, (2) the scope of my Agent's authority granted under this instrument, (3) my competency at the time this instrument is executed, (4) the fact that this instrument has not been revoked or amended, or (5) the fact that my Agent continues to serve as my Agent shall incur any liability to me, my estate, or my personal representative for permitting my Agent to exercise any such authority. Any Person who deals with my Agent shall not be responsible to determine or ensure the proper application of funds or property by my Agent. Any party dealing with any person named as Agent (including any person named as an Alternate Agent hereunder) may rely upon as conclusively correct an affidavit or certificate of such Agent that (a) my Agent's powers are then in effect, (b) the action my Agent desires to take is within the scope of my Agent's authority granted under this instrument, (c) I was competent at the time this instrument was executed, (d) this instrument has not been revoked, and (e) my Agent continues to serve as my Agent.

4.04 Alternate Agent May Give Affidavit or Certificate That He or She Currently Serves

Any party dealing with any person named as Alternate Agent hereunder may rely on as conclusively correct an affidavit or certificate under penalties of perjury of such Alternate Agent that those persons named as prior Agents are no longer serving.

4.05 Affidavits or Certificates Given By Agent Bind Principal

No person who relies on any affidavit or certificate under penalties of perjury that this instrument specifically authorizes my Agent to execute and deliver to such person shall incur any liability to me, my estate, or my personal representative for permitting my Agent to exercise any such authority, nor shall any Person who deals with my Agent be responsible to determine or ensure the proper application of funds or property by my Agent.

4.06 Authorization to Release Information to Agent

All Persons from whom my Agent may request information regarding me, my personal or financial affairs, or any information that I am entitled to receive are hereby authorized to provide such information to my Agent without limitation and are released from any legal liability whatsoever to me, my estate, or my personal representative for complying with my Agent's requests.

4.07 Authorization to Release Medical Information

I hereby authorize all physicians and psychiatrists who have treated me, and all other providers of my health care, including hospitals, to release to my Agent all information or photocopies of any records that my Agent may request. If I am incapacitated at the time my Agent shall request such information, all Persons are authorized to treat any such request for information by my Agent as the request of my legal representative and to honor such requests on that basis. I hereby waive all privileges that may apply to such information and records and to any communication pertaining to me and made in the course of any confidential relationship recognized by law. My Agent may also disclose such information to such Persons as my Agent shall deem appropriate.

ARTICLE FIVE

This power of attorney shall not be affected by my subsequent disability or incapacity, or lapse of time.

This instrument may be amended or revoked by me at any time by the execution by me of a written instrument of revocation or amendment, delivered to my Agent and to all Alternate Agents. If this instrument has been filed or recorded in the public records, then the instrument of revocation or amendment also shall be filed or recorded in the same public records.

My Agent and any Alternate Agent may resign by the execution of a written resignation delivered to me or, if I am mentally incapacitated, by delivery to any person with whom I am residing or who has the care and custody of me or, in the case of an Agent's resignation, by delivery to the Alternate Agent.

If my Agent desires to resign as my Agent and there is no Alternate Agent named in this instrument who is willing and able to serve as my Agent, and if I am incapacitated at the time of such resignation, then my Agent is authorized and empowered to appoint a substitute Agent to act and serve as my Agent, such appointment to be made in a written instrument that shall be signed by my Agent, delivered to my substitute Agent, and attached to this instrument.

ARTICLE SIX

My agent shall be entitled to reimbursement for all reasonable costs and expenses, including reasonable attorney fees, actually incurred and paid by my Agent on my behalf at any time under any provision of this instrument.

ARTICLE SEVEN

No part of this power of attorney shall be revoked or become inoperative on the appointment of a conservator or a guardian. I intend that the decisions of my Agent shall prevail over any contrary decisions of any guardian or conservator appointed for me.

If any part or any provision of this instrument shall be invalid or unenforceable under applicable law, such part shall be ineffective to the extent of such invalidity only, without in any way affecting the remaining parts of such provision or the remaining provisions of this instrument.

This instrument shall be governed by the law of the state in which I am domiciled at the time, with respect to all questions involving the validity, construction, interpretation, and termination of this instrument. I intend for this power of attorney to be honored in any jurisdiction in which it may be presented and given the most liberal interpretation available for purposes of granting my Agent the fullest amount of discretion in making health care decisions on my behalf. I also intend that any such jurisdiction refer to the laws of the state of my domicile to interpret and determine the validity of this instrument and any of the powers granted hereunder. Should any physician or health care provider fail to honor this power of attorney, then my Agent is authorized to terminate the services of such persons and to transfer my care to another physician or health care provider that will honor the instructions of my Agent.

If this instrument has been executed in multiple counterpart originals, each such counterpart original shall have equal force and effect. In addition, my Agent is authorized to make photocopies of this instrument as frequently and in such quantity as my Agent deems appropriate. Each photocopy shall have the same force and effect as any original.

ARTICLE EIGHT

My Agent shall have no responsibility to monitor on any regular basis the state of my physical health or mental capacity to determine whether any actions need to be taken under this instrument.

To induce my Agent to serve under this instrument I have directed my attorney at law to include in this instrument a provision exculpating my Agent from liability in certain instances. My attorney has explained to me the purposes of this instrument and, in general, both the applicable law and the consequences of signing it. After being so advised I have executed this instrument. It is my desire that the authorizations granted herein be given the broadest possible construction permitted by law. I understand and have had explained to me certain judicial rules of construction that would tend to require that the broad grants made in this power of attorney be given a narrow construction or disregarded altogether. I declare that such rules should have no application to this power of attorney and further declare that any court that shall interpret or construe the grants of authority made in this power of attorney in any restrictive manner shall do so in clear and complete violation of my express intent and in disregard of my wishes. I have been advised by counsel of the breadth of the delegations I have made in this power of attorney and I understand it and desire it. I also understand that there is always the possibility of abuse of such a broad delegation of power and I accept that risk.

I declare also that I have read the provisions of this power of attorney authorizing or directing my Agent to withhold or withdraw health care treatment and life support for me under the circumstances specified in this power of attorney, that such provisions have been explained to me to my satisfaction, that I understand those provisions, and that those provisions state my wishes and desires under the circumstances described.

IN WITNESS WHEREOF I have executed this durable power of attorney this *Day* day of *Month*, *Year*.

_____	_____
Witness	Signature of Principal
_____	_____
Witness	Name of Principal
	_____
	Social Security Number of Principal
	_____
	Sample Signature of Agent

The Undersigned acknowledges and accepts appointment as Agent and agrees to serve as Agent under the terms of this instrument.

_____	_____
Witness	Signature of Agent
_____	_____
Witness	Name of Agent
	_____
	Address of Agent
	_____
	Phone Number of Agent

State of _____
County of _____

The foregoing instrument was acknowledged before me this *Day* day of *Month, Year* by the individuals whose signatures appear as Principal, Agent, and Witness.

_____

LIVING WILL

Living wills are a creature of statute, for which state law is critical and widely varied. Rather than illustrate any one state's version here, it is recommended that you identify a particular state whose law is familiar or accessible to you and find the form provided by that state's legislature, along with the execution procedures established by that statute. Alternatively, consult Collin, Lombard, Moses, & Spitler, DURABLE POWERS OF ATTORNEY AND HEALTH CARE DIRECTIVES (3d ed. 2003).

Table of Cases

A v. B. v. Hill Wallack, 3-34 n.21
Ablamis v. Roper, 10-6 n.6
Advisory Opinion, In re, 4-31 at 31
Aetna Life Ins. Co. v. Boober, 9-30 n.31
Aetna Life Ins. Co. v. Bunt, 9-30 n.31
Aetna Life Ins. Co. v. Schilling, 9-34 n.40
Aetna Life Ins. Co. v. Wadsworth, 9-30 n.31
Allard v. Frech, 10-6 n.6
Allen, Estate of, v. Commissioner, 7-53 n.52
Anderson v. Idaho Mut. Benefit Ass'n, 9-30 n.31
Arlitt, Estate of, v. Paterson, 1-9 n.2
Atkinson, Estate of, v. Commissioner, 8-20 n.55, 8-26 n.60
Auric v. Continental Casualty Co., 1-10 n.3
Austin v. Sears, 9-33 n.39

Barley v. Albertini, 11-30
Beattie v. Firnschild, 3-58 n.45
Belcher, Estate of, v. Commissioner, 8-4
Bell, In re Estate of, 11-30
Bell v. Commissioner, 12-62 n.60
Benjamin v. Commissioner, 7-89 n.78
Bennett v. United States, 9-28 n.28
Bergeron v. Commissioner, 7-107
Berry v. Metropolitan Life Ins. Co., 9-30 n.32
Biakanja v. Irving, 1-9
Biltoft v. Wooten, 9-29 n.29
Bintliff v. United States, 9-38 n.47, 9-50 n.59
Blake v. Commissioner, 12-35 n.33
Blood v. Poindexter, 4-18
Boggs v. Boggs, 7-74, 10-6 n.6
Boivin, In re, 3-19
Boulger, In re, 3-23
Boyls, People v., 3-27 n.16
Brady v. Ceaty, 8-1 n.1
Brinley v. Commissioner, 8-16
Brooks, In re, 4-11 n.10

Brown v. Lee, 9-30 n.32
Bruce, In re Estate of, 11-34
Brunetti, Estate of, v. Commissioner, 11-37 n.26
Budd, Estate of, v. Commissioner, 6-9 n.6
Bunney v. Commissioner, 10-6 n.6
Burchell, Estate of, v. United States, 8-19 n.53
Burnett's Will, In re, 7-125 n.99
Burr v. Brooks, 8-1 n.1
Burris, Estate of, v. Commissioner, 9-29 n.30
Byrum, United States v., 6-9 n.5

Calder v. Commissioner, 12-48
California v. Texas, 18-39
Callahan v. Hutsell, Callahan & Buchino Revised Profit Sharing Plan, 10-22 n.19
Campbell v. Prothro, 8-5 n.10
Carmichael, In re, 10-9 n.8
Carrington v. Commissioner, 12-35 n.33
Casey, Estate of, v. Commissioner, 12-50
Catalano v. United States, 9-29 n.30
Cavenaugh, Estate of, v. Commissioner, 9-31 n.35
Cervin v. Commissioner (5th Cir. 1997), 9-31 n.35
Cervin v. Commissioner (T.C.M. 1994), 12-49
Chamberlain, Estate of, v. Commissioner, 7-18 n.18
Chenoweth, Estate of, v. Commissioner, 7-104
Christie v. Dold, 3-24 n.12
Cincinnati Bar Ass'n v. Kathman, 3-27 n.16, 4-31 n.31
Clark's Estate, In re, 3-25 n.14
Cloutier v. LaVoie, 11-23
Clymer v. Mayo, 4-20, 9-34
Cohen, In re, 4-10 n.9
Cohen v. Commissioner, 9-19 n.19
Cohen, Estate of, v. Crown, 11-42

TABLE OF CASES

Coker, In re, 4-14
Commissioner v. _____. See name of defendant
Committee on Professional Ethics and Conduct of the Iowa State Bar Ass'n v. Baker, 3-27 n.16
Connecticut General Life Ins. Co. v. Peterson, 9-33 n.39
Connelly v. United States, 9-45 n.52
Connor, In re, 10-9 n.8
Contella v. Contella, 4-28 n.30
Copenhauer v. Rogers, 1-9 n.2
Costello v. Conlon, 13-2 n.4
Crane v. Commissioner, 9-37 n.46, 9-41
Cristofani v. Commissioner, 12-16 n.14, 12-18
Crosby v. United States, 12-35 n.33
Crown v. Commissioner, 12-57 n.54
Crummey v. Commissioner, 9-52 n.61, 12-14

Davis v. Hunter, 4-15
Davis v. United States (U.S. 1992), 8-16
Davis, United States v. (U.S. 1962), 9-36
Deal v. Commissioner, 12-67 n.70
De Bonchamps, United States v., 6-6 n.4
Deeb v. Johnson, 1-9 n.2
DeGoldschmidt-Rothschild v. Commissioner, 12-67 n.70
DeWitt, Estate of, v. Commissioner, 13-8
Dickey v. Jansen, 1-9 n.2
Dickinson v. Maurer, 7-34 n.34
Dickman v. Commissioner, 12-57 n.56
Dix v. Commissioner, 12-62, 12-62 n.60
Dobert, In re Estate of, 9-34 n.40
Doland v. Doland, 9-30 n.32
Drye Family 1995 Trust v. United States, 12-45 n.46
Duberstein, Commissioner v., 12-11 n.11

Eversole v. Commissioner, 13-5
Everson v. Everson, 9-30 n.32
Exchange Bank & Trust Co. v. United States, 12-25 n.21
Ewart v. Commissioner, 13-5

Fared-Es-Sultaneh v. Commissioner, 12-11 n.11
Farkas v. Williams, 4-28 n.30
Federal Trade Commission v. Affordable Media, 4-14
Fender, Estate of, v. Fender, 11-23
Ferguson v. Commissioner, 12-35 n.33
Fidelity-Philadelphia Trust Co. v. Smith, 10-4 n.4
Fine, Estate of, v. Commissioner, 11-37 n.26
First Nat'l Bank v. Commissioner, 8-28 n.28
First Nat'l Bank of Kenosha v. United States, 18-18
First Victoria Nat'l Bank v. United States, 18-9 n.10
Fitzgerald, Estate of, v. Linnus, 3-48 n.32, 13-11 n.17
Florida Bar re: Advisory Opinion, 3-27 n.16
Florida Bar v. White, 3-22
Fogelman, In re Estate of, 3-46
Ford, Estate of, v. Commissioner, 6-9 n.6
Fratini, Estate of, v. Commissioner, 12-50
Freedman v. United States, 9-30 n.32
Fruehauf, Estate of, v. Commissioner, 9-45 n.52
Fuchs, Estate of, v. Commissioner, 9-45 n.52, 9-49 n.56
Funk v. Commissioner, 6-6 n.4

Gaethje v. Gaethje, 9-30 n.31
Garst Trust v. Commissioner, 13-6
Garvey Inc. v. United States, 12-62 n.60
Getty v. Commissioner, 12-11 n.11
Gillespie, In re Estate of, 3-19
Goldfarb v. Virginia State Bar, 13-7 n.14
Goodson, United States v., 11-24
Gordon, In re Estate of, 11-34
Gordon, Estate of, v. Commissioner, 7-42
Grace, Estate of, United States v., 6-14, 6-16 n.9
Green, Estate of, v. United States, 6-15
Greene v. Commissioner, 9-43

TABLE OF CASES

Greene v. United States, 11-30
Grove v. Commissioner, 12-35 n.33
Gulbankian, State v., 3-56 n.43
Guy v. Liederbach, 1-10 n.3

Hackl v. Commissioner, 12-14
Halas, In re Estate of, 3-14
Hansen, Jones & Leta v. Segal, 3-48 n.31
Harrison, Estate of, 3-25 n.14
Helvering v. _____. See name of defendant
Heringer v. Commissioner, 18-4 n.5
Heyen v. United States, 12-20
Heyer v. Flaig, 1-10, 1-10 n.3
Hillerman, In re, 9-30 n.34
Hisquierdo v. Hisquierdo, 9-30 n.34, 10-6 n.6
Hitchon, Estate of, v. Commissioner, 18-4 n.5
Holland, Estate of, v. Commissioner, 12-17 n.15
Hooper v. Commissioner, 9-38 n.47
Hotz v. Minyard, 3-13
Hubert, Estate of, v. Commissioner, 7-39 n.38, 8-16
Hudspeth v. United States, 12-35 n.33
Hunter v. United States (8th Cir. 1980), 9-45 n.52
Hunter v. United States (W.D. Pa. 1984), 6-11 n.7
Hurwitz v. Sher, 10-22 n.19
Huston, Estate of, v. Commissioner, 9-30 n.34
Hyde v. United States, 10-6 n.6

In re _____. See name of party
Inzinna v. Inzinna, 9-30 n.32
Irvine, United States v., 12-45 n.48

Jackson, Succession of, 9-30 n.32
Jameson, Estate of, v. Commissioner, 18-15 n.12
Jenkins v. Wheeler, 3-58 n.45
Jephson, Estate of, v. Commissioner, 18-15 n.12
Jones v. United States, 12-35 n.33

Jung, Estate of, v. Commissioner, 18-18

Kantner, In re Estate of, 7-125 n.99
Kapala, In re Estate of, 11-17
Kasch, Estate of, v. Commissioner, 6-9 n.6
Keller, Estate of, v. Commissioner, 18-18
Kenan v. Commissioner, 7-106 n.90
Ketteman Trust v. Commissioner, 18-4 n.5
King, In re Will of, 11-24
Kinsey v. Commissioner, 12-35 n.33
Knott v. Commissioner, 18-14 n.11
Krause v. Commissioner, 6-16 n.9
Kuralt, In re Estate of, 11-6
Kurn v. Moran, 13-1 n.2

Lacks, In re Estate of, 7-34 n.34
Lake, In re, 13-9 n.16
Lake Shore Nat'l Bank v. Coyle, 7-43
Landmark Trust Co. v. Aitken, 11-42
Lawrence, In re, 4-14
Le Gierse, Helvering v., 9-25
Leicher, Estate of, v. Commissioner, 18-14 n.11
Levin, Estate of, v. Commissioner, 10-4 n.4
Levy, Estate of, v. Commissioner, 6-16
Lewis, Succession of, 9-30 n.32
Licata v. Spector, 1-10 n.3
Lilyhorn v. Dier, 1-9 n.2
Lipton v. Boesky, 3-58 n.45
Lober v. United States, 12-25 n.20
Lock v. Lock, 9-30 n.31
Lockett, Estate of, v. Commissioner, 8-11 n.29
Looney v. United States, 10-4 n.4
Lucas v. Hamm, 1-8
Luton, Estate of, v. Commissioner, 18-15 n.12

Mackie, Estate of, v. Commissioner, 7-84
MacLean v. Ford Motor Co., 10-21

TABLE OF CASES

Macy, People v., 3-27 n.16
Magee v. United States, 14-6 n.4
Maierhofer, In re Estate of, 11-5
Margrave, Estate of, v. Commissioner, 9-45 n.52
Maris v. Commissioner, 18-15
Martin v. Machiz, 12-35 n.33
Martin v. United States, 6-11 n.7
Mathews v. Commissioner, 12-55
Mathias v. Fantine, 4-28 n.30
Matthews v. Swallen, 11-37 n.26
Matthews, Estate of, v. Commissioner, 9-38 n.47, 11-37 n.26
McCarty v. McCarty, 9-30 n.34
McCurdy v. McCurdy, 9-30 n.32
McKay, Estate of, v. Commissioner, 11-37 n.26
McKeon v. United States, 11-37 n.26
McKitrick, In re Estate of, 11-23
McStowe v. Borenstein, 1-10
Meyer, In re Estate of, 11-4
Mid-America Living Trust Assoc., Inc., In re, 3-27 n.16, 4-31 n.31
Miller v. Commissioner, 12-67
Miller v. Ibarra, 14-7 n.9
Miller v. United States, 7-89
Miller, Estate of, v. Commissioner, 11-37 n.26
Mize, United States v., 13-1 n.2
Modern Woodmen of America v. Gray, 9-29 n.29
Mooneyham v. Commissioner, 12-49
Morin, In re, 3-27 n.16
Moss, Estate of, v. Commissioner, 12-63 n.66
Musgrove, Estate of, v. United States, 12-63 n.66

Needham v. Hamilton, 1-10 n.3
Nesbitt v. Commissioner, 9-19 n.19
Nevin v. Union Trust Co., 1-9 n.2
Newell, In re Will of, 7-101 n.87
Newhouse, Estate of, v. Commissioner, 18-17 n.14
New York State Bar Ass'n v. Reno, 14-6 n.4
Nicolai, In re Estate of, 7-101 n.87
Noble v. Bruce, 1-9 n.2

Noel, Estate of, Commissioner v., 9-51

O'Brien v. Costello, 13-2 n.4
Ogburn, In re Estate of, 11-38
O'Keeffe, Estate of, v. Commissioner, 12-48
Old Colony Trust Co. v. Commissioner, 9-38 n.47
Old Colony Trust v. United States, 6-9 n.5

Palmer v. Commissioner, 12-35 n.33
Pardee, Estate of, v. Commissioner, 6-9 n.6
Parson v. United States, 9-30 n.32
Patterson v. Shumate, 10-9 n.8
Pearce, In re, 3-27 n.16
People v. _____. See name of defendant
Perry v. Perry, 9-30 n.32
Peters v. Peters, 9-29 n.29
Petty v. Commissioner, 8-4
Pierce, Commissioner v., 9-39
Pillsbury, Estate of, v. Commissioner, 12-49
Pollak v. Department of Health & Rehabilitative Services, 14-5 n.3
Porter v. Porter, 9-29 n.29
Portnoy, In re, 4-11 n.10
Powell, United States v., 6-9 n.6
Pritchard, Estate of, v. Commissioner, 9-50 n.58

Randall, In re, 3-23 n.10
Reeves, Estate of, v. Commissioner, 7-47
Regester, Estate of, v. Commissioner, 5-29, 6-5
Reinhold, Estate of, v. Commissioner, 9-38 n.47
Reno, Estate of, v. Commissioner, 11-35
Reynolds v. Commissioner, 12-67 n.70
Rhode Island Hosp. Trust Co., United States v., 9-49 n.56
Riethmann Trust v. Director of Revenue, 7-34 n.34
Rifkind v. United States, 8-3 n.4

TABLE OF CASES

Riggs v. Del Drago, 11-11
Robinson v. Benton, 1-9 n.2
Roe, Estate of, 11-36
Roe v. Estate of Farrell, 11-23
Rohnert, Estate of, v. Commissioner, 9-38 n.47
Rose v. United States, 9-45 n.53
Roselli v. Rio Communities Serv. Station, Inc., 9-30 n.32
Rothman v. Rumbeck, 9-30 n.32
Rubenstein v. United States, 18-18
Rueter, In re, 10-9 n.8
Ryerson, United States v., 9-50 n.58

Sachler, Will of, 4-28 n.30
Sarosdy v. Johnson, 11-18
Scanlan, Estate of, v. Commissioner, 18-18
Scott v. Commissioner, 9-31 n.35
Scull, Estate of, v. Commissioner, 18-17
Second Bank-State Street Trust Co. v. Pinion, 4-20
Securities and Exchange Comm'n v. Bilzerian, 4-14
Self v. United States, 5-29
Siegel, Estate of, v. Commissioner, 10-4 n.4
Silverman, Estate of, v. Commissioner, 9-47
Simon v. Zipperstein, 1-9 n.2
Singleton v. Commissioner, 13-4
Skifter v. United States, 9-45 n.52
Smith, Estate of, v. Commissioner (7th Cir. 1977), 7-119
Smith, Estate of, v. Commissioner (T.C. 1981), 13-6 n.12
Smither v. United States, 6-6 n.4
Sowell, Estate of, v. Commissioner, 6-11 n.7
Spear, In re Estate of, 6-15
Stanford, In re Estate of, 13-4 n.8
Stanland v. Brock, 3-41 n.29
State Street Bank & Trust Co. v. United States, 8-11
Stewart, United States v., 9-31 n.35
Stowe v. Smith, 1-10 n.3
Succession of _____. See name of Decedent

Suisman v. Eaton, 7-106 n.90
Sullivan v. Birmingham, 3-58 n.45
Swanson v. Commissioner, 9-43, 17-16

Taylor, In re, 3-58 n.45
Terriberry v. United States, 9-45 n.53
Texas v. Florida, 18-39
Thron, In re Estate of, 3-56
Tilton v. Commissioner, 18-4 n.5
Tingley, Estate of, v. Commissioner, 7-90 n.79
Tracy, Estate of, v. Commissioner, 9-50 n.59
Travelers Ins. Co. v. Johnson, 9-30 n.31
Treganowan, Commissioner v., 9-25
Tully, Estate of, v. United States, 10-4 n.4
Tulsa Professional Collection Serv., Inc. v. Pope, 13-3
Turner, Estate of, v. Washington State Dep't of Revenue, 7-34 n.34

Union Planters Nat'l Bank v. Dedman, 11-32 n.25
Union Trust Co. v. Watson, 11-41
United States v. _____. See name of defendant
Upjohn v. United States, 12-26 n.23

Van Praag, In re Estate of, 13-3 n.6
Verneuille, Succession of, 9-30 n.32
Virginia Nat'l Bank v. United States, 7-89 n.78
Volk, People v., 3-27 n.16

Wade, Estate of, v. Commissioner, 9-38 n.47
Wahlfeld v. United States, 6-11 n.7
Wall, Estate of, v. Commissioner, 75-26
Wallace v. United States, 15.3 n.8
Walsh, Estate of, v. Commissioner, 7-90
Walston, Commissioner v., 5-29
Warfield v. Merchants Nat'l Bank, 11-24
Weidman, In re Estate of, 13-4 n.7
Weingarten v. Warren, 1-9 n.2

TABLE OF CASES

Weinstock, In re Estate of, 3-56
Weir, Estate of, v. Commissioner, 6-9 n.6
Wekesser v. Commissioner, 12-35 n.33
Wells Fargo Bank v. Superior Court, 3-45
Whirlpool Corp. v. Ritter, 9-34 n.40
White v. McBride, 13-8
White v. United States, 8-16
White, United States v., 13-7
White's Estate, In re, 9-30 n.32
Whittle, Estate of, v. Commissioner, 11-23
Wilson v. Flowers, 8-1 n.1
Wilson v. Wilson, 9-29 n.29
Wilson v. United States, 7-89 n.78
Wissner v. Wissner, 9-30 n.34
Witco Corp. v. Beekhuis, 4-9 n.5, 4-23 n.28
Withers v. Commissioner, 8-6 n.16
Woodruff v. Tomlin, 3-58 n.45
Worcester County Trust Co. v. Riley, 18-39

Young, Estate of, v. Commissioner, 12-50

Zinn v. Donaldson Co. Salaried Employees Retirement Savings Plan, 10-22 n.19

Table of Internal Revenue Code Sections

§1(e)   17-2
§1(g)   12-53
§27   17-13
§56(g)(4)(B)(i)   9-40
§61   9-15
§61(a)(12)   9-36, 12-66
§62   8-4 n.6
§63(c)   17-2
§63(c)(3)   12-56
§63(c)(5)   12-56
§67   12-53
§67(e)   7-39 n.37
§68   8-43, 12-53
§72   9-3, 9-39, 10-17, 10-20 12-35, 12-61
§72(a)   12-64
§72(b)   9-41, 10-17
§72(b)(2)   12-35 n.32
§72(b)(3)   9-41, 10-17 n.16, 12-35 n.32, 12-62 n.61
§72(b)(3)(A)   10-17 n.16
§72(c)(1)   12-61
§72(e)   9-5 n.1, 9-26
§72(e)(4)(C)(i)   10-3
§72(e)(4)(C)(ii)   10-3
§72(e)(5)(E)   9-17 n.17
§72(h)   9-40
§72(s)   9-44
§72(s)(1)(A)   10-14
§72(s)(2)   10-14
§72(s)(3)   10-16
§72(t)   10-10, 10-12
§72(u)(1)   10-17
§72(u)(1)(B)   10-17
§73   12-54
§79   9-6
§83   10-9, 10-10
§83(a)(1)   10-10
§83(c)(1)   10-10
§83(e)(2)   10-9
§83(h)   18-4
§101   9-4, 9-25, 9-39, 9-40, 9-46
§101(a)   9-40
§101(a)(1)   9-18, 9-39, 9-41, 9-42
§101(a)(2)   9-9, 9-12 n.10, 9-18, 9-41, 12-38 n.41
§101(a)(2)(A)   9-41, 9-42, 17-16
§101(a)(2)(B)   9-9 n.7, 9-42, 17-16
§101(c)   9-39
§101(d)   9-39
§101(d)(2)(B)(ii)   9-39

§101(g)   9-18
§102   9-39, 9-46
§102(a)   9-37, 17-3
§102(b)   12-12 n.11, 17-3
§103   17-3, 17-4
§121   7-142, 12-46, 17-15
§135   12-27 n.26
§151   17-2
§162   7-38 n.35, 17-2, 17-13, 18-4
§162(a)(3)   12-55
§163   7-38 n.35, 12-58, 12-64, 17-2, 17-13
§163(h)   9-11
§164   17-13
§165   8-6 n.16, 13-12, 17-2
§166   9-37
§170   7-76, 8-3, 8-21, 8-35, 8-42, 8-45, 12-32, 17-2, 18-6
§170(a)(1)   8-4
§170(a)(3)   8-18 n.50
§170(b)(1)(A)   8-4, 8-4 n.6, 8-5 n.7, 8-6 n.14, 8-7 n.17, 8-8 n.18, 8-23 n.58, 8-28
§§170(b)(1)(A)(i) – 170(b)(1)(A)(vi)   8-13 n.30, 8-29
§170(b)(1)(A)(viii)   8-7 n.17
§170(b)(1)(B)   8-5, 8-8 nn.18, 19, 23
§170(b)(1)(B)(ii)   8-10 n.26
§170(b)(1)(C)   8-6 n.14
§170(b)(1)(C)(i)   8-5 nn.9, 12
§170(b)(1)(C)(ii)   8-5 n.11
§170(b)(1)(C)(iii)   8-5 n.13, 8-9
§170(b)(1)(C)(iv)   8-6 n.14
§170(b)(1)(D)   8-5 n.12
§170(b)(1)(D)(i)   8-8 n.20, 8-10 n.26
§170(b)(1)(D)(ii)   8-8 n.22
§170(b)(1)(E)   8-5 n.7, 8-7 n.17, 8-13 n.30
§170(b)(1)(F)   8-4 n.6, 8-7 n.18
§170(c)   8-7 n.17, 8-16 n.46, 8-19 n.52, 8-23 n.58, 8-27, 8-28, 8-28 n.64
§170(d)(1)(A)   8-4, 8-4 n.6, 8-6 n.15, 8-10 n.27
§170(e)(1)   8-5 n.13, 8-8, 8-9
§170(e)(1)(A)   8-6 n.14, 8-8 n.21, 12-38 n.39
§170(e)(1)(B)   8-5 n.13
§170(e)(1)(B)(i)   8-5 n.9, 8-8
§170(e)(1)(B)(ii)   8-8 n.21
§170(e)(5)   8-8, 8-8 n.21

7

§170(f)(2)(A) 8-19, 8-30 n.72
§170(f)(2)(B) 8-34 n. 97, 8-35 n.98
§170(f)(3) 12-37 n.38
§170(f)(3)(A) 8-19 n.51
§170(f)(3)(B) 8-31 n.77
§170(f)(3)(B)(ii) 8-17 n.49
§170(f)(3)(B)(iii) 8-32 n.79
§170(f)(4) 8-31 n.78
§170(h) 8-32 n.79, 12-34
§170(h)(1) 8-32 n.81
§170(h)(3) 8-32, 12-34
§170(h)(4) 8-32 n.82
§170(h)(4)(A) 8-32 n.83
§170(h)(4)(A)(iv) 8-32 n.82
§172 8-4 n.6, 8-7 n.18
§212 7-38 n.35, 12-61 n.56, 17-2
§213 7-38 n.35, 7-39 n.37
§213(c) 13-12
§264 9-12 n.11, 9-54 n.62
§264(a)(3) 9-11, 9-44 n.50
§264(a)(4) 9-12
§264(c)(1) 9-12
§264(e) 9-12
§265 17-4
§267 7-80 n.72, 7-141, 12-61 n.59
§280A(d) 8-30 n.75
§280A(d)(3) 12-59 n.56
§303 13-13
§401(a) 10-1, 10-7
§401(a)(9) 10-10, 10-11, 10-14, 10-14 n.14, 10-15
§401(a)(9)(A)(ii) 10-12, 10-13
§401(a)(9)(B) 10-13
§401(a)(9)(B)(i) 10-14
§401(a)(9)(B)(ii) 10-14, 10-16
§401(a)(9)(B)(iii) 10-14, 10-16
§401(a)(9)(B)(iii)(I) 10-16
§401(a)(9)(B)(iv) 10-16
§401(a)(9)(C) 10-11 n.10
§401(a)(9)(E) 10-14, 10-18
§401(a)(11) 7-71, 7-73, 7-75 n.65, 10-3, 10-6, 10-20, 11-7
§401(a)(11)(B)(iii) 10-21
§401(a)(13) 10-3, 10-6 n.6, 10-9 n.8
§401(a)(14) 10-12
§401(c) 10-1
§401(k) 10-8
§402 10-19
§402(a) 10-9, 10-17, 10-24 n.22
§402(b) 10-10
§402(c) 10-18
§402(c)(1) 10-18
§402(c)(5) 10-18
§402(c)(9) 10-18, 10-19, 10-20

§402(d)(4)(A) 10-18, 10-23
§402(d)(4)(B) 10-18
§402(d)(4)(F) 10-18
§403(b) 10-21
§403(c) 10-1, 10-10
§404(a) 10-9
§408 10-1, 10-6 n.6
§408(a)(1) 10-9
§408(a)(6) 10-11
§408(b)(13) 10-11
§408(d)(1) 10-17, 10-24 n.22
§408(d)(3) 10-18, 10-19, 10-20
§408(d)(3)(C)(ii)(II) 10-20
§408A 10-8 n.7
§408A(c)(3) 10-8 n.7
§410 10-7
§411 10-7
§412 10-7
§415 10-7
§417 10-3
§417(a) 7-73
§417(a)(1)(A) 10-22
§417(a)(2) 10-3
§417(a)(2)(A)(ii) 10-22
§417(a)(6) 10-21
§417(a)(6)(A) 10-22
§417(b) 10-20
§417(c) 10-21
§417(c)(1)(A) 10-21
§441 13-13
§443 13-13
§453 12-61 n.57, 12-66
§453(e) 12-64
§453(f)(1) 12-64
§453B 12-66
§453B(a)(2) 12-65 n.68
§453B(f) 12-65 n.68
§454 13-12
§483 12-62 n.60
§501(c)(3) 8-5 n.7, 8-13 n.30
§507(c) 8-14 n.42
§509 8-5 n.7
§509(a) 8-13 n.30
§509(a)(1) 8-13 n.30
§509(a)(3) 8-13 n.30, 8-14 n.43
§527(e)(1) 12-33
§529 9-4, 11-7, 12-27, 12-27 n.26
§529(c)(2) 12-27
§529(c)(4) 12-27
§529(c)(4)(C) 11-7, 11-45, 12-27 n.25
§529(c)(5) 12-27
§529(e)(3)(A) 12-27
§581 7-80
§611 17-13

TABLE OF INTERNAL REVENUE CODE SECTIONS

§641(b)   17-2
§642(b)   17-2, 17-4
§642(c)   8-35, 17-2
§642(c)(1)   8-35
§642(c)(5)   8-29 n.67, 8-30 n.72
§642(c)(5)(A)   8-29
§642(c)(5)(C)   8-30
§642(c)(5)(F)   8-30 n.69
§642(g)   7-12 n.12, 7-35, 7-38 7-39 n.36, 7-66, 13-12, 17-2, 17-13
§642(h)   13-13, 17-16 n.5
§643(a)   17-3
§643(a)(1)   17-4
§643(a)(2)   17-3
§643(a)(3)   17-4
§643(a)(4)   17-4, 17-8
§643(a)(5)   17-4, 17-7
§643(b)   10-25, 17-6
§643(e)   7-112, 7-126, 13-13, 17-9, 17-9 n.2
§643(e)(3)   7-126, 13-13
§643(f)   4-5, 7-137
§644 (formerly §645)   4-24, 13-4 n.9
§645 (formerly §646)   9-37 n. 45, 10-14, 13-4 n.9
§645(a)   4-24
§651   17-6, 17-9 n.2
§651(a)   17-2, 17-3, 17-4, 17-6, 17-7
§651(a)(1)   17-7
§651(b)   17-7, 17-8
§652   17-6, 17-9 n.2
§652(a)   17-3, 17-7
§652(b)   17-4, 17-7, 17-8
§§661-664   17-5, 17-8
§661   13-13
§661(a)   17-3, 17-2, 17-4, 17-8
§661(a)(1)   17-9 n.2, 17-10, 17-11
§661(a)(2)   17-10, 17-11
§661(b)   17-3, 17-8
§661(c)   17-8
§662   13-13
§662(a)   17-3
§662(a)(1)   17-9 n.2, 17-11
§662(a)(2)   17-9
§662(a)(2)(B)   17-11
§662(b)   17-3, 17-4, 17-9
§662(c)   17-5
§663   7-141
§663(a)   19-17 n.q
§663(a)(1)   5-2 n.a, 17-9, 17-18
§663(c)   7-137, 17-4, 17-5
§664   7-75, 8-17, 8-20, 8-23, 8-27 n.61, 12-44
§664(b)   8-45, 12-37, 12-38 n.41

§664(c)   12-35
§664(d)   12-37 n.36
§664(d)(1)   8-24
§664(d)(1)(A)   8-19 n.52, 8-20, 8-34 n.91
§664(d)(1)(D)   8-17 n.47, 8-21, 8-34 n.90 12-37 n.36
§664(d)(2)(A)   8-19 n.52, 8-20, 8-34 n.91, 12-37 n.36
§664(d)(2)(D)   8-17 n.47, 8-21, 8-34 n.90
§664(d)(3)(A)   8-21
§664(d)(3)(B)   8-21
§664(f)   7-76
§664(f)(2)   7-76 n.68
§667(c)   7-137
§§671-677   6-6
§§671-679   17-14
§671   17-14
§672(c)   5-26, 6-12, 6-14
§672(e)   17-17
§673   12-56, 17-16
§674   17-14
§674(a)   17-16
§674(b)(5)(A)   6-6
§674(d)   6-6
§675   17-14
§675(2)   17-17
§675(3)   17-17
§675(4)(A)   17-16
§675(4)(C)   17-17
§676   4-24, 4-26, 17-14, 17-16
§677   4-26, 17-15
§677(a)(1)   17-16, 17-17
§677(a)(3)   9-28 n.28
§677(b)   12-56, 12-55, 12-56
§678   5-21, 5-24, 6-4, 6-6, 6-14, 7-52 n.51, 7-92, 9-52, 10-20, 12-22, 17-14, 17-15, 17-15 n.4
§678(a)(2)   6-17, 12-22
§678(b)   6-6
§678(c)   6-6, 6-8
§691   7-110, 7-114, 10-23 n.20, 10-24 n.22, 12-2 n.2
§691(a)   18-11
§691(a)(2)   7-110, 7-132, 7-134, 7-135, 7-140, 10-25
§691(a)(3)   17-13
§691(b)   7-38, 17-13
§691(c)   17-13, 17-14
§754   13-12
§1001   12-1
§1011   2-5 n.1
§1011(b)   12-35 n.31

§1014   7-22, 7-27 n.25, 7-32, 7-32 n.20, 7-98, 7-128, 7-141, 9-35, 12-1, 12-37 n.35, 18-23
§1014(a)   7-111, 7-137, 12-2
§1014(b)(6)   4-19, 4-26, 12-2 n.2
§1014(b)(9)   12-4, 12-8
§1014(b)(9)(A)   9-44 n.50
§1014(c)   7-110, 10-22, 12-2 n.2, 17-13
§1014(e)   12-30, 12-44
§1015(a)   12-1 n.1
§1022   7-22, 7-32 n.30, 7-98 n.84, 10-22, 12-2, 12-37 n.35
§1022(c)   7-41
§1022(c)(3)   7-93, 7-98 n.84, 7-108 n.91
§1022(c)(3)(B)   7-81 n.74, 7-82
§1022(d)(1)(C)   12-44 n.46
§1031   7-128
§1031(b)   9-44
§1035   9-41, 9-43, 9-43 n.49, 9-44 n.50
§1040   7-112, 7-115, 7-122, 7-128 n.101, 7-140, 7-141
§1041   7-3 n.2, 9-42
§1041(a)   10-3
§1041(d)   12-31
§1223(2)   12-2 n.1
§1274   12-62 n.60
§1361(c)(2)(A)(i)   4-25
§1361(c)(2)(A)(ii)   4-25
§1361(d)(3)   4-26
§1361(e)   4-26
§1362(a)(2)   13-12
§2001   18-7, 18-13
§2001(b)   7-79, 7-86, 7-108, 18-10, 18-12
§2001(b)(1)(B)   11-45
§2001(b)(2)   11-45, 18-12
§2001(f)   12-51, 12-53
§2001(f)(2)   12-52 n.51
§2002   11-1, 11-9, 13-4, 18-8 n.8
§§2010-2014   18-24
§2010   7-10 n.12, 11-45, 18-2, 18-8, 18-23
§2010(a)   7-4
§2010(c)   7-4, 7-9 n.10, 13-4 n.10
§2011   4-18, 7-2, 7-5 n.4, 7-9 n.11, 7-34 n.34, 18-1 n.1, 18-2 n.4, 18-23, 18-38
§2012   11-21, 11-45, 18-23
§2013   5-4 n.d, 7-7, 7-9 n.11, 7-23, 7-25 n.23, 7-32, 7-32 n.31, 7-34 n.34, 7-48, 7-64, 7-80, 7-100, 9-20, 11-13, 11-46, 18-24, 18-31 n.23
§2013(a)   7-80
§2014   7-9 n.11, 7-127 n.100, 11-21, 11-46, 18-23
§2031   18-13

§2031(b)   18-16
§2031(c)   8-32, 8-33
§2031(c)(1)(A)   8-32
§2031(c)(2)   8-33 n.87
§2031(c)(6)   8-32 n.84
§2031(c)(8)(A)(ii)   8-32 n.86
§2031(c)(8)(B)   8-32 n.80
§2032   7-35, 13-12, 13-13, 18-21
§2032(a)(1)   18-20
§2032(a)(3)   18-20
§2032(b)(2)   7-35
§2032(c)(1)   18-21
§2032(c)(2)   18-21
§2032(d)   18-21
§2032(d)(2)   18-21
§2032A   7-35, 11-13, 11-36, 11-38, 13-13, 18-15, 18-18 n.16, 18-21, 18-22, 18-23
§2032A(b)(2)   13-13
§2032A(c)   11-44, 11-46, 18-22, 18-23
§2032A(c)(2)(A)(ii)   18-23
§2032A(c)(7)   18-23
§2032A(c)(7)(B)   18-23
§2032A(d)(4)   18-23
§2032A(e)(2)   8-32 n.85
§2032A(e)(3)   8-30 n.76, 18-23
§2032A(e)(4)   8-30 n.76
§2032A(e)(5)   8-30 n.76
§2032A(e)(6)   18-22
§2032A(e)(12)   18-23
§2033   7-8 n.7, 7-74, 7-74 n.64, 9-27, 9-47, 10-1 n.2, 10-4, 10-6, 11-3, 11-4, 18-9, 18-11, 18-24
§2035   8-3 n.4, 10-5, 11-19 18-24
§2035(a)   9-35 n.43, 9-47, 9-48, 9-49 n.56, 9-55, 10-1 n.2
§2035(a)(2)   11-43 18-9, 18-10
§2035(b)   11-45, 12-3 n.4, 18-9
§2035(d)   18-9
§§2036-2038   6-17, 18-24
§2036   6-11, 11-3, 11-4, 11-5, 11-18, 11-19, 12-26, 18-9, 18-10, 18-24
§2036(a)   18-10
§2036(a)(1)   6-9, 7-69, 7-73 n.63, 7-79, 7-86, 7-108, 7-143, 8-3 n.4, 8-31, 8-39, 9-28 n.28, 10-4 n.4, 10-5, 11-4, 12-25, 12-31, 12-61, 18-11
§2036(a)(2)   6-15, 8-29, 18-11
§2036(b)   6-9, 18-10
§§2037-2040   11-19
§2037   18-9, 18-11, 18-24
§2038   7-69, 11-3, 11-4, 11-5, 12-25, 18-9, 18-10, 18-24

§2038(a)(1)   4-21, 6-15, 8-29, 8-31, 10-4, 10-4 n.4, 11-4, 18-10
§2039   7-72, 7-74, 8-3 n.4, 8-27 n.62, 8-43, 10-4, 10-5, 10-5 n.5, 10-6, 10-25, 11-7, 11-19, 11-25, 11-27, 12-61, 12-63, 13-12, 18-24
§2039(a)   10-1 n.2, 10-4 n.4, 10-5, 10-6, 18-11
§2039(b)   10-5
§2039(c)   10-4, 11-47
§2039(e)   10-4, 11-47
§2040   7-143, 18-11, 18-12, 18-24
§2040(a)   7-77, 18-12
§2040(b)   7-77, 18-12
§2041   5-2, 5-4 n.e, 5-13 n.aa, 5-22, 5-25, 5-27, 6-3, 6-4, 6-5, 6-6, 6-9, 6-11, 6-14, 6-15, 7-52, 7-60 n.57, 7-69, 9-52, 9-54, 11-13, 11-17, 11-18, 13-26, 18-12, 18-24, 19-51
§2041(a)(2)   5-28, 5-30 n.yy, 6-3 n.3, 6-17, 12-15, 12-25
§2041(a)(3)   5-13 n.bb, 18-13
§2041(b)(1)(A)   5-22
§2041(b)(2)   12-15
§2042   6-7, 9-35 n.43, 10-5, 11-17, 11-18, 18-9, 18-24, 19-44 n.hhhh
§2042(1)   9-33, 9-35, 9-37, 9-38, 9-44, 9-50, 9-51, 11-17
§2042(2)   9-11, 9-33, 9-44, 9-49 n.56, 11-17
§2043   11-22
§2044   7-60, 7-60 n.57, 7-61, 7-64, 7-68, 7-70, 7-72, 7-73 n.63, 7-74, 7-74 n.64, 7-76, 7-86, 11-15, 11-17, 11-18, 11-19, 11-29, 11-47, 18-13, 18-24
§2051   18-23
§2053   7-10 n.12, 7-35, 7-38, 7-39 n.37, 7-105, 11-10 n.18, 11-12, 11-22, 13-7, 17-2, 18-14, 18-24
§2053(a)(2)   13-7, 13-8, 13-12, 18-18 n.15
§2053(a)(3)   13-12
§2054   7-35, 11-10 n.18, 13-12, 18-14, 18-24
§2055   7-9 n.11, 7-35, 7-75, 8-2, 8-12, 18-6, 8-28 n.64, 11-13, 11-16, 11-30, 18-14, 18-24
§2055(a)   18-6, 8-12, 8-13, 8-16 n.46
§2055(c)   11-15, 11-25
§2055(e)(2)   8-17 n.49, 8-18, 8-19, 8-31 n.77, 8-37
§2055(e)(2)(A)   8-30 n.72
§2055(e)(2)(B)   8-34 n.96

§2055(e)(3)   8-17, 8-23, 8-37, 8-38, 12-44
§2055(e)(3)(J)   8-21
§2055(f)   8-32
§2056   7-3, 7-41, 7-59, 7-69, 18-14, 18-24
§2056(a)   7-77
§2056(b)   7-41, 7-59
§2056(b)(1)   7-44, 7-45, 7-48, 7-59, 7-76 n.66, 7-101
§2056(b)(1)(A)   7-46
§2056(b)(1)(C)   7-46
§2056(b)(2)   7-47, 7-103, 7-127 n.100, 7-137, 19-21 n.dd
§2056(b)(3)   7-15, 7-25, 7-28, 7-48
§2056(b)(3)(A)   7-42
§2056(b)(4)(A)   11-15
§2056(b)(4)(B)   7-120
§2056(b)(5)   5-23, 5-31 n.bbb, 7-23, 7-40, 7-41, 7-50, 7-50 n. 49, 7-51, 7-52, 7-53, 7-56, 7-57, 7-58, 7-60, 7-60 n.57, 7-61, 7-63, 7-72, 7-76 n.66, 7-79, 7-81, 7-82, 7-83, 7-84, 7-85, 7-87, 7-89, 7-90, 7-90 n.79, 7-91, 7-93, 7-93 n.81, 7-96, 7-103, 7-103 n.89, 7-135, 10-19, 10-25, 17-15
§2056(b)(6)   7-40, 7-50 n.49, 7-81
§2056(b)(7)   4-6, 5-23, 7-37, 7-41, 7-50, 7-51, 7-56, 7-60, 7-63, 7-75, 7-76 n.66, 7-79, 7-81, 7-82, 7-85, 7-87, 7-96, 7-124, 11-17, 12-43, 18-13
§2056(b)(7)(B)(i)(II)   7-23, 10-25
§2056(b)(7)(B)(ii)   7-61 n.58, 7-62, 7-63, 7-69, 7-70, 7-76
§2056(b)(7)(B)(ii)(II)   7-61 n.59, 7-63, 7-76, 7-85, 7-93, 7-135
§2056(b)(7)(B)(iii)   7-65
§2056(b)(7)(B)(iv)   7-65
§2056(b)(7)(B)(v)   13-12
§2056(b)(7)(C)   7-46, 7-71, 7-74, 10-6, 10-25, 11-8 n.3, 12-63 n.65
§2056(b)(7)(C)(ii)   13-12
§2056(b)(8)   7-49, 7-75, 7-76 n.66, 7-79, 7-81, 8-21
§2056(b)(10)   7-58
§2056(c)   7-43, 7-49
§2056(d)   7-77, 7-78, 7-121, 9-27, 11-7, 13-12, 18-14
§2056(d)(1)   7-77
§2056(d)(1)(B)   7-77
§2056(d)(2)   7-78
§2056(d)(3)   7-80
§2056A   7-77, 7-78, 9-27, 18-14
§2056A(a)   7-79

§2056A(a)(1) 7-79
§2056A(a)(2) 7-79
§2056A(a)(3) 13-12
§2056A(b) 7-79, 7-80
§2056A(b)(2)(A) 7-80
§2056A(b)(3)(B) 7-81 n.73
§2056A(b)(7) 7-80
§2056A(b)(12) 7-81
§2056A(c)(3) 7-79 n.71
§2056A(d) 7-78 n.70
§2057 7-35, 11-13, 13-13 n.18
§2057(b)(1)(B) 13-13 n.18
§2058 7-35, 7-100, 11-46, 18-1 n.1, 18-14, 18-24
§2101(c) 12-28 n.27
§2103 9-44 n.51, 18-9 n.9
§2105(a) 9-44 n.51
§2106(a)(2) 8-13
§2203 11-1 n.1, 11-2, 18-8 n.8
§2204 11-10, 13-4
§2204(a) 11-9 n.10, 13-5
§2204(b) 11-9 n.10
§2204(c) 11-11 n.23
§2205 11-2, 11-11, 18-8 n.8, 11-16
§§2206-2207B 11-19, 11-27, 11-33, 11-36, 11-47
§2206 9-32, 9-35 n.43, 9-50, 11-17, 11-18, 11-19, 11-34, 11-42, 19-42 n.bbbb
§2207 5-32 n.ddd, 11-13, 11-17, 11-18, 11-19, 11-26, 11-34
§2207A 5-32 n.ddd, 7-70, 7-86, 11-17, 11-18, 11-19, 11-21, 11-29, 11-33, 11-34, 19-23 n.kk, 19-42 n.bbbb
§2207A(a)(1) 7-70
§2207A(d) 11-23
§2207B 11-4, 11-18, 11-19, 11-33, 11-34
§2207B(d) 11-23
§2501(a)(1) 7-4
§2501(a)(5) 12-32
§2502 18-7
§2502(c) 18-3
§2503 7-22, 19-51
§2503(b) 4-17 n.19, 7-78, 7-86, 7-108, 12-8, 12-13, 12-18, 12-24 n.19, 12-26, 12-26 n.24, 12-27, 12-28, 18-3, 18-5, 18-34
§2503(b)(2) 12-13
§2503(c) 5-23, 9-50, 12-14, 12-23, 12-23 n.16, 12-24, 12-24 n.19, 12-25, 12-26, 12-54, 12-55, 18-5
§2503(e) 12-8, 12-13, 12-26 n.24, 12-27, 12-28, 18-3, 18-5, 18-34
§2503(e)(2) 12-26, 12-27
§2503(f) 7-75 n.65, 10-3

§2504(c) 12-51, 12-52, 12-52 n.51
§2505 18-8
§2505(a) 12-28 n.27
§2511 7-71, 7-86, 7-86 n.76, 7-87
§2511(c) 12-11, 12-46
§2512(b) 12-11 n.12, 18-3
§2513 7-7 n.6, 7-68, 12-28, 12-29, 12-30, 18-7, 19-51
§2513(a) 13-11
§2513(a)(1) 12-29 n.28
§2513(a)(2) 12-28
§2513(b) 12-28
§2514 5-27, 6-3, 6-4, 6-11, 7-52, 7-60 n.57, 9-52, 12-15
§2514(e) 5-24, 5-30 n.yy, 6-3 n.3, 9-52, 9-53, 9-55, 12-15, 12-16, 12-17, 12-20, 12-21, 12-22, 12-23, 19-40 n.www
§2514(e)(1) 9-52
§2515 7-78 n.69, 12-3 n.4
§2515A 7-78 n.69
§2516 7-141, 11-22
§2518 7-14, 8-37, 10-24 n.22, 12-41, 12-44 n.45
§2518(b)(2) 12-42
§2518(b)(3) 12-42
§2518(b)(4)(A) 5-8 n.1, 7-18, 7-19, 12-42, 12-43
§2518(b)(4)(B) 12-42
§2519 7-60, 7-60 n.57, 7-68, 7-71, 7-72, 7-75, 7-86, 7-86 n.76
§2519(a) 7-87, 7-89
§2522 8-2, 8-28, 8-28 n.64, 12-32, 18-3, 18-6
§2522(a) 8-13, 8-16 n.46, 18-4
§2522(b) 8-13
§2522(c)(2) 8-17 n.49, 8-19, 8-31 n.77
§2522(c)(2)(A) 8-30 n.72
§2522(c)(2)(B) 8-34 n.96
§2523 7-3, 12-22, 12-28, 12-30, 18-3
§2523(b) 7-41, 7-43 n.42
§2523(e) 5-23, 7-40, 7-41, 18-6
§2523(f) 5-23, 7-41, 7-69, 18-6
§2523(f)(3) 7-69
§2523(f)(4) 7-63, 7-69
§2523(f)(5)(A) 12-31
§2523(f)(6) 7-71, 7-73, 12-63 n.64
§2523(g) 7-75, 7-76, 8-21
§2523(i) 7-78, 12-31, 18-6 n.7, 18-14
§2523(i)(2) 12-31, 18-6 n.7
§2523(i)(3) 7-78 n.69
§2603 11-19, 11-47
§2603(a) 18-34
§2603(a)(3) 11-44

TABLE OF INTERNAL REVENUE CODE SECTIONS

§2603(b) 11-19, 11-20, 11-33, 11-44, 18-34
§2604 18-2, 18-2 n.4, 18-38
§2611(a) 18-29
§2611(b)(1) 18-34
§2611(b)(2) 18-34
§2612(a) 18-30
§2612(a)(1) 18-31
§2612(a)(1)(A) 18-30, 18-35, 18-35 n.27
§2612(a)(1)(B) 18-30, 18-32, 18-35
§2612(b) 18-29
§2612(c) 18-28, 18-29
§2612(c)(1) 12-11
§2612(c)(2) 18-29
§2613(a)(1) 18-28
§2621 18-32
§2621(b) 18-32
§2622 18-32
§2623 18-32
§2631 7-36, 7-138, 13-14, 18-37
§2631(a) 7-100, 18-37
§2632 13-14, 18-36
§2632(d) 18-37
§2641(a)(1) 18-31
§2642 18-36, 18-37
§2642(a)(2)(B)(ii) 18-33
§2642(b)(2)(A) 7-138
§2642(c) 9-55, 12-22, 12-27, 18-34
§2642(c)(2) 18-35
§2642(c)(3)(B) 12-26 n.24
§2642(g) 11-10 n.18
§2651 18-28
§2651(e)(1) 18-28
§2652(a)(1)(A) 7-37
§2652(a)(3) 7-37, 7-61, 7-79, 7-81, 7-83, 7-93, 7-138, 12-43, 13-14
§2652(b)(1) 18-26 n.20
§2652(c)(1) 18-30 n.22
§2653(a) 18-35 n.27
§§2701-2704 11-19
§2702 4-22, 7-73 n.63, 7-86, 7-87, 7-108, 7-143
§2702(a)(3)(A)(ii) 12-59
§2702(e) 7-87
§2703 18-19, 18-20
§2703(a) 18-19
§2704 18-20
§2704(b)(4) 18-20
§2704(c)(2) 7-87
§3111 12-54
§4940 8-13 n.32
§4941 8-13 n.33
§4942 8-13 n.34, 8-20 n.55
§4943 8-13 n.35

§4943(c) 8-36 n.102
§4944 8-13 n.36, 8-36 n.102
§4945 8-13 n.37
§4946 8-14 n.40
§4946(a) 8-13 nn. 33, 35, 8-14 n.44, 8-15 n.45
§4947(b)(3)(A) 8-36 n.102
§4947(b)(3)(B) 8-36 n.102
§4958 8-14 n.38
§4958(c)(1) 8-14 n.39
§4958(f)(1) 8-14 n.40
§4974 10-10
§4974(a) 10-11
§4980A 10-5
§6013(a)(3) 13-11
§6018 13-4 n.10
§6018(a)(1) 13-4, 13-4 n.10
§6019 18-3
§6019(1) 4-17 n.19
§6075(a) 11-8 n.4, 13-4
§6075(b) 18-3
§6081 13-4, 13-13
§6081(a) 11-9 n.11
§6151(a) 11-8
§6161 10-4, 11-8 n.5, 11-48
§6161(a)(1) 11-9 n.12, 13-13
§6161(a)(2) 11-9 n.13, 13-4, 13-13
§6161(b)(2) 11-9 n.14
§6161(b)(3) 11-9 n.14
§6163 10-4 n.4, 11-8 n.5, 11-36, 11-48, 13-13
§6165 11-10, 11-11 n.23
§6166 2-8, 11-8 n.5, 11-9, 11-10, 11-11 n.23, 11-36, 11-48, 13-13
§6166(a)(1) 11-10 n.16
§6166(a)(2) 11-10 n.15
§6166(a)(3) 11-10 n.17
§6166(b)(1) 11-10 n.19
§6166(b)(5) 11-10 n.15
§6166(b)(6) 11-10 n.18
§6166(d) 11-10 n.20
§6166(g) 11-10 n.22
§6166(h) 11-10 n.21
§6166(h)(1) 1-10 n.121
§6213(d) 13-5
§6321 11-9 n.6, 11-10
§6324(a) 11-2
§6324(a)(1) 11-9 n.8
§6324(a)(2) 11-9 nn.7, 9
§6324A 11-11 n.23, 13-13
§6324A(d)(6) 11-11 n.23
§6325(c) 11-9 n.10
§6331 10-6 n.6
§6501(c)(4) 7-108

§6501(c)(9)　12-51, 12-52
§6601(e)(1)　11-9 n.6
§6654(*l*)　4-24
§6654(*l*)(2)　13-4 n.9, 13-13
§6662　3-52 n.36, 18-16
§6662(d)(2)(B)(i)　3-52 n.36
§6665　11-9 n.6
§6694　3-52 n.36, 3-53 n.38
§6694(a)(1)　3-52 n.36
§6694(a)(2)　3-52 n.36
§6701　3-53
§6901(a)　11-2, 18-3
§6901(a)(1)　11-9 n.7
§6901(h)　11-9 n.6
§6903　13-6
§6903(a)　13-4 n.11, 13-5
§6903(b)　13-5
§6905　13-4
§7477　12-51 n.50
§7491　12-51 n.50
§7517　15.3 n.14
§7520　7-33, 7-34 n.34, 18-4, 8-19
§7520(a)(2)　8-30 n.72
§7702　9-25
§7702(a)　9-26
§7702(a)(1)　9-26
§7702(a)(2)(A)　9-26
§7702(a)(2)(B)　9-26
§7702(g)(1)　9-25
§7702A　9-7 n.4, 9-10, 9-11 n.9, 9-26
§7702B(c)(2)　9-18
§7872　9-15, 9-36, 12-57 n.54, 12-58, 12-59
§7872(c)(2)　12-58

Table of Treasury Regulations

§1.61-22(d)   9-14
§1.72-6(a)(1)(i)   9-40
§1.72-9 Table VI   10-12 nn.11, 12
§1.79-3(d)(2)   9-6, 9-51
§1.101-1(b)(3)(ii)   9-42
§1.101-1(b)(5)   9-41 n.48
§1.101-1(b)(5) Example (5)   9-42
§1.101-1(b)(5) Example (7)   9-42
§1.101-4(c)   9-39, 9-40
§1.101-4(d)(3)   9-40
§1.101-4(e)   9-40
§1.101-4(g) Example (7)   9-40
§1.101-4(h)   9-10
§1.166-2   9-37
§1.170A-1(d)   12-34
§1.170A-1(e)   8-31
§1.170A-1(g)   8-5
§1.170A-4(a)   8-6 n.14
§1.170A-4(c)(2)   12-34
§1.170A-6(c)(2)(i)   8-36 n.103
§1.170A-6(c)(2)(i)(A)   8-34 nn.93, 95
§1.170A-6(c)(2)(i)(E)   8-33 n.88
§1.170A-6(c)(2)(ii)(A)   8-34 n.95
§1.170A-6(c)(2)(ii)(D)   8-33 n.88
§1.170A-6(c)(4)   8-35 n.98
§1.170A-6(c)(5) Example (3)   8-35 n.98
§1.170A-7(a)(2)(i)   8-19 n.51, 8-31
§1.170A-7(b)(1)   14.3.1 n.18
§1.170A-7(b)(1)(i)   8-17 n.49
§1.170A-7(b)(3)   8-30 n.75
§1.170A-7(b)(4)   8-30 n.76
§1.170A-8(a)(2)   8-5 n.8
§1.170A-8(b)   8-4 n.6, 8-5 n.8
§1.170A-8(d)(1)   8-5 n.9
§1.170A-8(d)(2)   8-5 n.13, 8-9 n.25
§1.170A-8(f)   8-10 n.26
§1.170A-10   8-4, 8-6 n.15, 8-10 n.27
§1.170A-10(a)(2)   8-10 n.28
§1.170A-12(a)   8-31 n.78
§1.170A-14(d)(4)(iv)(A)   8-32 n.83
§1.264-4(c)(1)(i)   9-11 n.9
§1.312-6(b)   9-40
§1.401(a)-11(c)   10-21
§1.401(a)-13(b)(1)   10-9 n.8
§1.401(a)-13(b)(2)(i)   10-6 n.6
§1.401(a)-20 Q&A 28   10-22, 10-22 n.19
§1.401(a)-20 Q&A 30 et seq.   10-22
§1.401(a)(9)-1   10-11
§1.401(a)(9)-2 A-1   10-12
§1.401(a)(9)-2 A-2   10-11 n.10
§1.401(a)(9)-2 A-5   10-15

§1.401(a)(9)-3 A-1(a)   10-16
§1.401(a)(9)-3 A-3(b)(2)   10-176
§1.401(a)(9)-3 A-4(a)(2)   10-16
§1.401(a)(9)-3 A-5   10-16
§1.401(a)(9)-4 A-3   10-14, 10-16
§1.401(a)(9)-4 A-4(a)   10-13 n.12
§1.401(a)(9)-4 A-5   10-16
§1.401(a)(9)-4 A-5(b)   10-15
§1.401(a)(9)-4 A-6(b)   10-15
§1.401(a)(9)-5 A-1(b)   10-12
§1.401(a)(9)-5 A-4   10-12, 10-13 n.12
§1.401(a)(9)-5 A-4(b)   10-12 n.11
§1.401(a)(9)-5 A-5   10-15
§1.401(a)(9)-5 A-5(a)(2)   10-15
§1.401(a)(9)-5 A-5(c)(2)   10-15
§1.401(a)(9)-5 A-7(a)   10-15
§1.401(a)(9)-5 A-7(d)   10-14 n.15
§1.401(a)(9)-8 A-2(a)(2)   10-15
§1.401(a)(9)-8 A-11   10-16
§1.401(a)(9)-9 A-2   10-13 n.12
Temp. §1.401(a)(31)-1 Q&A 14   10-21 n.18
§1.401(k)-1(d)(2)(i)   7-81 n.73
§1.408-8 A-1   10-11
§1.408-8 A-3   10-11 n.10
§1.408-8 A-5   10-18
§1.408-8 A-9   10-14 n.14
§1.451-2   9-19 n.19
§1.507-2(a)(8)   8-14 n.42
§1.509(a)-4(i)   8-15 n.45
§1.509(a)-4(i)(2)   8-15 n.45
§1.509(a)-4(i)(3)   8-15 n.45
§1.509(a)-4(j)   8-15 n.45
§1.642(c)-5(a)(3)   8-30 n.73
§1.642(c)-5(a)(4)   8-30 n.72
§1.642(c)-5(b)(1)   8-30 n.70
§1.642(c)-5(b)(2)   8-29, 8-30 nn.70, 71
§1.642(c)-5(b)(6)   8-29
§1.642(c)-5(b)(7)   8-30 n.70
§1.642(c)-6(e)(3)   8-30 n.72
§1.643(a)-3   17-4
§1.643(b)-1   7-88
§1.651(a)-1   17-5
§1.651(a)-1(b)   17-6
§1.651(a)-2   17-5
§1.651(a)-2(a)   17-6
§1.651(a)-3   17-5
§1.651(b)-1   17-5, 17-7
§1.652(a)-1   17-5, 17-7
§1.652(b)-1   17-7
§1.652(b)-2   17-3, 17-8

§1.652(b)-2(b) 17-3
§1.652(b)-2(b)(1) 17-8
§1.661(a)-1 17-5
§1.661(a)-2(b) 17-11
§1.661(a)-2(f)(1) 17.10 n.2
§1.662(a)-2(c) 17-11
§1.662(a)-3(c) 17-11
§1.662(a)-4 6-7
§1.662(b)-2 17-4
§1.663(a)-1(b) 17-10
§1.663(a)-1(b)(2)(iii) 7-126
§1.663(a)-1(b)(3) Example 2 7-126
§1.663(a)-1(c)(1) 17-10 n.3
§1.663(c)-3 17-5
§1.663(c)-4 7-129
§1.663(c)-5 Example 4 7-126
§1.664-1(a)(4) 8-20 n.55, 8-26, 8-27
§1.664-1(a)(5)(i) 8-26
§1.664-1(b) 8-36 n.102
Prop. §1.664-1(d) 12-37
§1.664-2(a)(1)(i) 8-28 n.66
§1.664-2(a)(1)(iii) 8-25
§1.664-2(a)(3)(i) 8-28, 8-29
§1.664-2(a)(3)(ii) 8-28 n.66
§1.664-2(a)(4) 8-23 n.58, 8-28
§1.664-2(a)(5)(i) 8-26
§1.664-2(a)(6)(i) 8-27
§1.664-2(a)(6)(iv) 8-28
§1.664-2(b) 8-25
§1.664-3(a)(1)(i) 8-28 n.66
§1.664-3(a)(1)(i)(b) 8-36 n.100
§1.664-3(a)(1)(i)(c) 8-21
§1.664-3(a)(1)(i)(d) 8-21
§1.664-3(a)(1)(iv) 8-25
§1.664-3(a)(1)(v)(b) 8-26
§1.664-3(a)(3)(i) 8-28, 8-29
§1.664-3(a)(3)(ii) 8-28 n.66
§1.664-3(a)(4) 8-23 n.58, 8-28
§1.664-3(a)(6)(i) 8-27
§1.664-3(a)(6)(iv) 8-28
§1.664-3(b) 8-25
§1.671-3 17-16
§1.671-3(a)(2) 17-17
§1.671-3(c) 17-16
§1.674(b)-1(b)(5)(i) 19-37 n.qqq
§1.677(a)-1(d) 8-27
§1.677(b)-1 5-27
§1.678(c)-1 5-27
§1.691(a)-2 17-12
§1.691(b)-1(b) 17-13
§1.1011-2 12-35 n.31
§1.1011-2(a)(3) 8-31, 12-38 n.40
§1.1011-2(a)(4) 12-34, 12-35 n.31
§1.1011-2(a)(4)(iii)(a) 12-35 n.31

§1.1011-2(b) 12-34
§1.1011-2(c) Example (8) 12-35 n.31
§1.1014-4(a)(3) 7-106 n.90, 7-126
§1.1015-4 9-42
§1.1031(d)-2 9-44
§1.1035-1(a) 9-43 n.49
§1.1035-1(c) 9-43 n.49
§1.6662-4(d)(3)(iii) 3-52 n.36
§1.6694-1(e) 3-52 n.36
§1.6694-2(b)(1) 3-52 n.36
§1.6694-2(c)(2) 3-52 n.36
§1.7520-3(b)(3) 8-34 n.95
§1.7872-15 9-14
§20.2001-1 7-109
§20.2002-1 13-4
§20.2031-1(a)(2) 11-4
§20.2031-1(b) 18-16
§20.2031-2(f) 9-46
§20.2031-8(a) 9-47
§20.2031-10 12-61 n.58
§20.2032-1(a)(3) 18-20
§20.2032-1(c)(2) 18-20
§20.2032-1(f) 18-20
20.2036-1(b)(2) 5-26, 5-27, 5-28, 6-9, 12-25 n.22
§20.2036-1(b)(3) 6-12
§20.2038-1(a) 12-25 n.20
§20.2038-1(a)(3) 6-12
§20.2041-1(b)(1) 5-25, 6-5, 6-12, 6-14, 19-37 n.qqq
§20.2041-1(c)(1) 5-27, 12-25 n.22
§20.2041-1(c)(2) 5-24, 5-27, 6-5, 6-11, 7-62
§20.2041-3(c)(2) Example (1) 6-4
§20.2042-1(c)(2) 9-44
§20.2042-1(c)(5) 9-31 n.35, 9-45
§20.2042-1(c)(6) 9-13, 9-46, 9-47
§20.2044-1(c) 7-64
§20.2044-1(d)(2) 7-61, 7-91
§20.2044-1(d)(3) 7-67, 7-92 n.80, 7-136 n.105
§20.2044-1(e) 7-136 n.105
§20.2044-1(e) Example 4 7-67
§20.2044-1(e) Example 5 7-86
§20.2053-1(b)(2) 13-8
§20.2053-3(b)(1) 13-7
§20.2053-3(d)(2) 18-18 n.15
§20.2055-2(b) 7-117
§20.2055-2(b)(1) 8-11
§20.2055-2(e)(2)(i) 8-17 n.49, 8-19
§20.2055-2(e)(2)(ii) 8-30 nn.74, 75
§20.2055-2(e)(2)(iii) 8-30 nn.74, 76
§20.2055-2(e)(2)(v) 8-29

TABLE OF TREASURY REGULATIONS

§20.2055-2(e)(2)(vi)(a) 8-34 nn.93, 95, 8-36 n.103
§20.2055-2(e)(2)(vi)(f) 8-33 n.88
§20.2055-2(e)(2)(vii)(a) 8-34 nn.93, 95
§20.2055-2(e)(2)(vii)(b) 8-36 n.100
§20.2055-2(e)(2)(vii)(f) 8-33 n.88
§20.2055-2(f)(2)(iv) Example (1) 8-34 n.94
§20.2056(a)-2(b) 7-43
§20.2056(a)-2(b)(1) 7-43
§20.2056(b)-1(d) 7-44
§20.2056(b)-1(e)(2) 7-45
§20.2056(b)-1(e)(3) 7-45
§20.2056(b)-1(g) Example (1) 7-44
§20.2056(b)-1(g) Example (3) 7-46
§20.2056(b)-2(d) 7-47
§20.2056(b)-4(a) 7-49 n.45
§20.2056(b)-4(d) 11-43 n.b
§20.2056(b)-4(d)(5) 7-39 n.38, 11-43 n.b
§20.2056(b)-5(a) 7-58
§20.2056(b)-5(c) 7-58
§20.2056(b)-5(c)(1) 7-136 n.105
§20.2056(b)-5(c)(5) Example 2 7-58
§20.2056(b)-5(e) 7-51, 7-57 n.55
§20.2056(b)-5(f) 7-53 n.53, 7-55
§20.2056(b)-5(f)(1) 7-53 n.53, 7-88
§20.2056(b)-5(f)(3) 7-54
§20.2056(b)-5(f)(4) 7-56, 7-88, 7-90, 7-103 n.89
§20.2056(b)-5(f)(5) 7-55, 7-88
§20.2056(b)-5(f)(6) 7-72
§20.2056(b)-5(f)(7) 7-89
§20.2056(b)-5(f)(8) 7-56, 7-91
§20.2056(b)-5(f)(9) 7-56, 7-90
§20.2056(b)-5(g)(3) 7-52
§20.2056(b)-5(g)(4) 7-52
§20.2056(b)-7(b)(2) 7-65
§20.2056(b)-7(d)(2) 7-72
§20.2056(b)-7(d)(3) 7-44
§20.2056(b)-7(d)(4) 7-61, 7-91
§20.2056(b)-7(d)(5) 8-30 n.70
§20.2056(b)-7(e)(2) 10-25
§20.2056(b)-7(f) 7-75
§20.2056(b)-7(g) 7-57 n.55
§20.2056(b)-7(h) 7-136 n.105
§20.2056(b)-7(h) Example 1 7-56
§20.2056(b)-7(h) Example 4 7-50 n.50
§20.2056(b)-7(h) Example 10 7-71, 10-25
§20.2056(c)-2(b)(1)(iii) 7-59
§20.2056(c)-2(c) 7-50 n.48, 7-84
§20.2056(c)-2(d)(2) 8-38
§20.2056(c)-2(e) 7-13 n.16, 7-42
§20.2056(d)-2(a) 9-28

§20.2056A-1(c) 7-78
§20.2056A-2(b)(1) 7-79
§20.2056A-2(b)(2) 7-78, 7-78 n.70
§20.2056A-2(d)(1)(ii)(B) 7-80 n.72
§20.2056A-2(d)(1)(ii)(C) 7-80 n.72
§20.2056A-2(d)(2) 7-79
§20.2056A-3(a) 7-78 n.70, 7-79
§20.2056A-3(b) 7-79
§20.2056A-4(b)(1) 7-78, 7-78 n.70
§20.2056A-4(b)(5) 7-78
§20.2056A-4(d) Example 1 7-79
§20.2056A-4(d) Example 5 7-78
§20.2056A-5(b)(1) 7-81
§20.2056A-5(c)(1) 7-81 n.73
§20.2056A-8(a)(3) 7-78
§20.2204-1(b) 11-11 n.23
§20.2207A-1(a) 7-71
§20.2207A-1(a)(1) 7-70
§20.2207A-1(a)(2) 7-70, 11-34
§20.2207A-1(a)(3) 7-70
§20.2207A-1(b) 7-70
§20.2207A-1(e) 7-71
§20.2207A-1(f) 7-71
§20.6018-2 13-5
§20.6081-1(b) 11-8 n.4, 11-9 n.11
§20.6081-1(d) 11-8, 13-4
§20.6151-1(a) 11-8, 13-4
§20.6161-1(a)(1) Example (1) 11-9
§20.6161-1(a)(1) Example (2) 11-9
§20.6161-1(a)(1) Example (3) 11-9
§20.6161-1(a)(1) Example (4) 11-9
§20.6161-1(a)(2) 11-9 n.13
§20.6161-1(a)(2)(ii) Example (1) 11-10
§20.6161-1(a)(2)(ii) Example (2) 11-10
§20.6161-2(b) 11-9 n.14
§20.6165-1(a) 11-11 n.23
§20.6166-1(d) 11-11 n.20
§20.7520-3(b)(3) 7-33 n.33
§20.7520-3(b)(3)(i) 8-34 n.95
§25.0-1(b), 12-11 n.12
§25.2501-1(a)(1) 12-11 n.12
§25.2503-3 9-51
§25.2503-3(a) 12-13
§25.2503-3(b) 12-13, 12-14
§25.2503-3(c) Example (2) 9-50 n.60
§25.2503-3(c) Example (3) 12-13
§25.2503-3(c) Example (6) 9-50 n.60
§25.2503-4(b) 12-24 n.17, 12-24 n.18
§25.2503-4(b)(1) 12-26
§25.2503-6(a)(2) 12-26
§25.2503-6(a)(3) 12-27
§25.2503-6(c) Example (2) 12-27, 12-28
§25.2503-6(c) Example (4) 12-27
§25.2504-2 7-109

§25.2511-1(b)(2) 6-5
§25.2511-1(g)(2) 5-29, 6-11, 19-37 n.qqq
§25.2511-1(h)(1) 18-4 n.5
§25.2511-1(h)(8) 9-51
§25.2511-1(h)(9) 8-31 n.36, 9-50
§25.2511-2(b) 12-11 n.12, 12-46
§25.2511-2(c) 8-23 n.58
§25.2511-2(e) 12-46
§25.2512-2(e) 12-48
§25.2512-5 12-34 n.30
§25.2512-6(a) 9-49 n.57, 12-38 n.39
§25.2512-8 12-12, 12-63 n.63, 18-3
§25.2513-1(b)(5) 12-28
§25.2514-1(b)(1) 19-37 n.qqq
§25.2514-1(b)(2) 5-29, 6-5
§25.2514-1(c)(2) 5-27
§25.2518-1(c)(2) 12-45
§25.2518-2(e)(5) Example (7) 7-20, 12-41 n.43
§25.2518-3(a)(1)(iii) 7-19 n.19
§25.2518-3(a)(2) 7-20
§25.2518-3(b) 7-17
§25.2518-3(c) 7-17, 7-20
§25.2519-1 7-86
§25.2519-1(a) 7-86
§25.2519-1(b) 7-64
§25.2519-1(c) 7-71
§25.2519-1(c)(3) 7-67
§25.2519-1(g) Example 4 7-86, 7-86 n.77

§25.2522(c)-3(b) 12-37 n.36
§25.2522(c)-3(c)(2)(i) 8-17 n.49, 8-19
§25.2522(c)-3(c)(2)(ii) 8-30 nn.74, 75
§25.2522(c)-3(c)(2)(iii) 8-30 nn.74, 76
§25.2522(c)-3(c)(2)(vi)(a) 8-34 nn.93, 95, 8-36 n.103
§25.2522(c)-3(c)(2)(vi)(f) 8-33 n.88
§25.2522(c)-3(c)(2)(vii)(a) 8-34 nn.93, 95
§25.2522(c)-3(c)(2)(vii)(b) 8-36 n.100
§25.2522(c)-3(c)(2)(vii)(f) 8-33 n.88
§25.2522(c)-3(d)(2)(iv) Example (1) 8-34 n.94
§25.2523(f)-1(c)(1)(iii) 8-30 n.70
§25.2523(f)-1(c)(4) 7-75
§25.2523(f)-1(f) Example 11 7-70, 12-31
§25.2523(i)-1(c) 18-6 n.7
§25.2523(i)-2(b) 7-78 n.69
§25.2702-6 7-87
§25.7520-2 12-34 n.30
§25.7520-3(b)(3) 8-34 n.95, 12-61 n.58
§26.2601-1(b)(1)(v)(A) 12-22
§26.2652-1(a)(5) Example 5 12-22
§301.6324-1(a)(2)(iii) 11-9 n.9
§301.6501(c)-1(f)(2) 7-109 n.92, 12-51 n.50
§301.6903-1(a) 13-4 n.11

Table of Revenue Rulings

54-19	10-1 n.2	75-127	10-1 n.2
55-87	10-1 n.2	75-145	10-1 n.2
55-119	12-62 n.62	75-414	8-18
55-138	8-5 n.10	75-440	7-94
55-275	8-5 n.10	75-553	11-3
55-408	9-50 n.60	76-7	8-27 n.63
55-531	8-5 n.10	76-8	8-27 n.63
56-472	13-10	76-102	10-1 n.2
56-603	9-30 n.34	77-357	7-39 n.37
56-637	10-1 n.2	77-374	8-11 n.29, 12-37 n.36
57-366	12-25 n.20	77-385	8-28 n.64
59-357	5-28, 6-17, 12-25 n.20	79-327	5-29
64-225	13-10	79-353	5-26, 6-12, 9-46
64-328	9-12 n.11	79-368	8-28 n.65
65-199	9-18 n.18	79-397	10-1 n.2
66-120	9-18 n.18	79-428	8-26
66-167	13-10	80-38	8-28 n.65
66-234	10-1 n.2	80-80	12-61 n.58
67-277	10-1 n.2	81-7	9-52, 12-15
68-80	4-18	81-20	7-121
68-88	10-1 n.2	81-110	8-4
68-174	8-4	81-182	10-1 n.2
69-56	7-54, 7-55	82-5	10-1 n.2
69-285	8-12	82-38	8-29 n.67
69-486	7-128 n.101	82-105	8-3 n.4, 8-27 n.62
69-505	6-16 n.9	82-141	9-47
70-400	7-48 n.44	82-184	7-84
70-452	8-11 n.29, 12-37 n.36	83-20	8-18
71-79	9-40	83-45	8-18
71-200	8-12	83-107	12-16
71-443	12-14	84-105	7-107
71-492	12-61 n.59	84-162	12-34 n.30
71-497	9-48	84-179	5-28, 6-7, 9-45
72-81	12-62 n.62	85-35	7-62, 7-90
72-154	7-51	85-45	17-15
72-241	10-13 n.13	85-49	8-34 n.92
72-283	7-56	85-57	8-29 n.67
72-395	8-24 n.59	86-72	12-61 n.57
72-419	8-19 n.51	88-27	8-36 n.103
72-436	12-35 n.31	88-82	8-36 n.101
72-438	12-35 n. 30	88-85	10-5 n.5
72-552	8-3 n.4	90-3	7-120
73-311	10-4	90-21	9-47
73-405	9-52	90-103	8-29 n.67
74-39	8-29	90-109	9-43 n.49
74-43	12-24 n.19	92-22	10-5 n.5
74-312	9-30 n.34	93-12	12-9
74-325	10-13 n.13	94-49	9-50
74-359	10-13 n.13	95-53	9-11 n.9
75-100	9-31 n.35	95-58	5-26, 6-12, 9-46 n.54
75-126	10-1 n.2	2000-2	7-71, 10-16, 10-25

2002-39	10-1 n.2	2003-91	9-5 n.1
2003-40	9-45	2003-92	9-5 n.1

Table of Revenue Procedures

64-19   7-98, 7-111, 7-113, 7-115 n.94, 7-116, 7-120, 7-121, 7-122, 7-126, 7-132, 7-139, 7-140
82-39   8-12
88-53   8-29 n.67
88-54   8-29 n.68
89-20   8-22 n.56
90-30   8-22 n.56, 8-24
90-31   8-22 n.56
90-32   8-22 n.57
90-33   8-22 n.57
2000-34   12-53 n.52
2003-53   8-22 n.56, 8-24
2003-54   8-22 n.56
2003-55   8-22 n.56
2003-56   8-22 n.56
2003-57   8-22 n.56
2003-58   8-22 n.56
2003-59   8-22 n.56
2003-60   8-22 n.56
2004-3   9-43

Table of Private Letter Rulings and Technical Advice Memoranda

TAM	7921017	12-11 n.11	PLR	9303031	10-19 n.17
TAM	8010011	8-11 n.29	TAM	9318002	7-62
PLR	8022048	12-17 n.15	PLR	9319029	10-24 n.22
TAM	8029001	6-14	PLR	9322025	8-12
TAM	8042006	10-1 n.2	TAM	9325002	7-95
TAM	8339004	6-11 n.7	PLR	9328015	6-12
TAM	8346008	6-11 n.7	TAM	9336002	12-49
PLR	8431007	8-30 n.75	TAM	9346002	9-43, 9-44 n.50
TAM	8446006	10-25	PLR	9416037	10-14 n.14
TAM	8447003	7-134	PLR	9419021	8-23
TAM	8503009	7-62	PLR	9426049	10-19 n.17
TAM	8508002	7-50 n.50	TAM	9443001	8-11 n.29
TAM	8512004	7-33	TAM	9443004	8-11 n.29
PLR	8535020	5-29	PLR	9445029	10-20
PLR	8604033	9-44	TAM	9449001	12-9
PLR	8610068	9-49 n.56	PLR	9450041	10-19
TAM	8636100	13-7	PLR	9450042	10-19
TAM	8706008	7-62, 7-90	PLR	9451059	10-19
PLR	8724014	9-48	PLR	9452026	8-28 n.65
TAM	8901008	7-90 n.79	PLR	9509028	10-19
TAM	8915004	7-92	TAM	9514002	7-90
PLR	8916032	5-26	PLR	9524020	10-20
TAM	8922003	9-46	TAM	9532001	12-16
PLR	8940003	11-3	PLR	9547004	8-23
TAM	8943006	11-8 n.3	PLR	9607008	5-26
TAM	9005001	8-12	TAM	9628004	12-19
PLR	9007016	7-122	PLR	9630034	10-24 n.22
PLR	9012053	6-11 n.7	TAM	9651004	9-49 n.56
TAM	9015001	11-3	PLR	9721014	8-19 n.51
PLR	9015049	8-27	PLR	9813018	10-19 n.17
PLR	9030005	12-17 n.15	PLR	9820020	10-19 n.17
PLR	9037048	10-24 n.22	TAM	199918060	9-15 n.16
PLR	9043052	5-26, 6-14	PLR	199925033	10-19 n.17
TAM	9044081	6-11 n.7	PLR	200011062	10-19 n.17
PLR	9113009	18-4	PLR	200035014	8-20 n.54
PLR	9113026	5-26	FSA	200036012	8-3 n.4, 8-27 n.62
PLR	9114023	18-4 n.5	PLR	200045038	8-20 n.54
PLR	9123052	18-34 n.26	PLR	200101021	7-69
TAM	9126005	11-31	PLR	200108032	8-3 n.4
TAM	9139001	7-50 n.50	PLR	200109006	8-20 n.54
TAM	9146002	12-50	PLR	200120016	8-20 n.54
TAM	9147065	7-50 n.50	PLR	200122055	9-32 n.38
PLR	9151022	8-22 n.57	PLR	200127023	8-19 n.51
PLR	9235025	6-15	PLR	200140027	8-19 n.51
TAM	9236003	8-11 n.29	PLR	200152018	8-19 n.51
PLR	9252023	8-28 n.65	PLR	200206024	11-37 n.26
PLR	9303018	6-12	PLR	200208030	10-19 n.17
PLR	9303027	10-24 n.22	PLR	200210009	8-3 n.4, 8-27 n.62

Table of Miscellaneous Statutes and Reports

Federal Statutes

11 U.S.C. §522(d)(10)(E)   10-9 n.8
11 U.S.C. §548   4-11 n.10
15 U.S.C. §80b-2(a)(11)(B)   1-15 n.5
15 U.S.C. §80b-3(b)(3)   1-15 n.5
31 U.S.C. §192   11-9 n.6
   §1320a-7b(a)(6)   14-5 n.4
   §1320d   14-1, 19-66
   §1382b(c)(1)(A)   14-6 n.5
   §1382b(c)(1)(A)(iv)(II)   14-7 n.6
   §1382b(c)(1)(C)   14-7 n.7
   §1382b(e)   14-7 n.10
   §1396p(c)(1)(B)   14-6
   §1396p(c)(1)(B)(i)   14-6
   §1396p(c)(1)(E)   14-7
   §1396p(c)(2)   14-7 n.7
   §1396p(c)(2)(C)   14-7 n.8
   §1396p(d)   14-7
   §1396p(d)(4)(A)   14-7, 14-8
   §1396p(d)(4)(B)   14-7, 14-7 n.9
   §1396p(d)(4)(C)   14-7, 14-8
   §§9601-9657   4-8, 19-29 n.ddd
   §9607(n)   4-8 n.5
   §9613(g)(3)   4-23 n.28

English Statute of 13 Elizabeth ch. 5   4-11 n.10

Tax Reform Act of 1984

§525(b)(2)   11-47
§525(b)(3)   11-47
§525(b)(4)   11-47

House of Representatives Reports

201, 97th Cong., 1st Sess. (1981)
   160   7-40
   162 n.4   7-76 n.66
220, 105th Cong., 1st Sess 719 (1997)   7-79 n.71
1042, 96th Cong., 2d Sess. 10 n.12 (1980)   12-61 n.57

Senate Report 1000, 96th Cong., 2d Sess. 12 n.12 (1980)   12-61 n.57

Hearings Before the Committee on Ways & Means, 94th Cong., 2d Sess. (1976)   18-26

Table of Actions on Decision, Code of Federal Regulations, Forms, General Counsel Memoranda, Publications, Notices, and Tax Court Rules

Action on Decision 1996-010   12-18

Code of Federal Regulations

31 C.F.R. §10.0 – 10.93   3-52 n.36, 3-54
31 C.F.R. §10.33   3-54 n.41
31 C.F.R. §10.34   3-52 n.36

Forms

56   13-4 n.11
706   7-18 n.18, 7-105, 7-125, 11-20 n.24
706 Schedule M   7-76
706-A   11-9 n.11
706-D   11-9 n.11
706-NA   11-9 n.11
706-QDT   11-9 n.11
890   13-5
938   9-49 n.57
1041   7-105, 17-1

General Counsel Memoranda

39503   12-62 nn.57, 58, 12-62 n.60, 12-64 n.67
39728   9-44 n.50

Notices

88-38   10-14 n.14
89-60   8-30 n.72
98-20   12-37 n.34
99-17   12-37 n.34
2001-10   9-15
2002-8   9-15

Publications

526   8-10 n.26
Cumulative List of Organizations Described in §170(c)   8-12

Tax Court Rules

Interim Rule 142   12-51 n.50
Interim Rule 217   12-51 n.50

Table of State Statutes

Alaska Stat. §34.40.110   4-10 n.9

California Prob. Code
§641   5-32
§15209   4-28 n.30

Colorado Rev. Stat. §38-10-111   4-10 n.9

Delaware Code Ann. tit. 12, §§3570-3576
   4-10 n.9

Florida Stat. §733.617(6)   13-6 n.13, 13-10

Missouri Rev. Stat. §456.080   4-10 n.9

Nevada Rev. Stat. §166.040   4-10 n.9

New York Est., Powers & Trusts L.
§2-1.9(b)(2)   7-113
§5-1.1-A(a)(4)(A)   7-84
§5-1.1-A(b)   7-84
§10-6.1(a)(4)   5-32
§10-10.1   6-15

Ohio Constitution Art. II, §28   9-34 n.40

Ohio Rev. Code Ann.
§1335.01(C)   4-28 n.30
§1339.63   9-34 n.40

Oklahoma Stat. tit. 60, §299.10   5-32

Rhode Island Gen. Laws §18-9.2   4-10 n.9

Utah Code Ann. §25-6-14   4-10 n.9

Wisconsin Stat. §766.61(3)   8-30 n.33

Table of Uniform Acts and Restatements

Uniform Estate Tax Apportionment Act

See Uniform Probate Code §3-916   11-20, 11-31, 11-32

Uniform Fraudulent Transfers Act

§4(a)(1)   4-11 n.10
§4(a)(2)   4-11 n.10

Uniform Gifts to Minors Act   4-8, 5-15, 12-25

Uniform Marital Property Act   9-30

Uniform Premarital Agreement Act §3   10-22 n.19

Uniform Principal and Income Act (1997 Act)

generally   19-28 n.bbb
§201(2)(A)   11-32 n.25
§202   7-126
§409(c)   10-23 n.20
§409(d)   10-23 n.20
§502(a)(6)   10-23 n.20
§505   10-23 n.20

Revised Uniform Principal and Income Act (1962 Act)

§4   10-23 n.20
§5(b)   11-32 n.25
§5(b)(2)   7-49 n.45, 7-126
§11   10-23 n.20
§13(a)(6)   10-23 n.20
§13(c)(4)   10-23 n.20

Uniform Probate Code

Most Uniform Probate Code provisions are substantively the same in the 1969 original version and the 1990 version. If a relevant change has been made, the respective version is noted.

§2-104   7-42 n.41
§2-511   4-20, 4-20 n.22, 9-34 n.41
§2-511(b)   4-17
§2-601 (1969)   7-42 n.41
§2-702 (1990)   7-42 n.41
§2-801(a) (1969)   7-18
§2-801(c) (1969)   7-17
§2-801(d)(1) (1990)   7-17, 7-18 n.17
§2-804 (1990)   9-34
§2-902   3-57
§3-203   13-1 n.1
§§3-301–3-311   13-2 n.5
§§3-312–3-322   13-2 n.5
§3-406(b)   3-51 n.35
§3-502   13-2 n.5
§3-719   13-6
§3-801   13-3
§§3-1201–3-1204   13-2 n.5
§4-205   13-2 n.3

Uniform Simultaneous Death Act   7-13, 7-42, 7-42 n.41

Uniform Testamentary Additions to Trusts Act   4-20, 4-20 n.22, 9-34

Uniform Transfers to Minors Act   4-8, 5-15, 5-26, 12-25

Uniform Trust Code

generally   4-5 n.4, 19-29 n.fff
§411   4-4 n.1

Restatement (Second) of Agency

§387   3-62
§388   3-26, 3-62
§389   3-62
§390   3-63
§391   3-63
§392   3-64
§394   3-64
§395   3-64

Restatement (Second) of Conflict of Laws

§236   13-2
§260   13-2

Restatement (Third) of the Law Governing Lawyers

generally 3-2
§4 3-27 n.16
§5(2) 3-27 n.16
§30 3-34 n.20, 3-60
§35(2) 3-38
§35(3) 3-38
§35(4) 3-38
§73(4) comment h 3-47
§74(2) 1-11 n.4
§76 3-60
§111 3-30
§111 comment b 3-30
§111 comment d 3-30
§112 comment c(i) 3-29
§112(1) 3-29
§134A 3-48 n.33
§163 3-46
§201 3-7
§201 comment c(iii) 3-7
§202(1) 3-19
§202 comment c(ii) 3-19
§206 comment c Illustration 3 3-25 n.15
§207 3-22
§207 comment b 3-24
§207 comment c 3-24
§208 3-23
§208 comment d 3-25 n.15
209 3-4 n.3
§211 3-4 n.3, 3-7, 3-16
§211 comment c 3-7
§212 3-50, 12-59 n.56
§213 3-5 n.4
§215(1) 3-19 n.9

Restatement of Property ch. 25, Introductory Note 5-22

Restatement (Second) of Property

§327 5-33
§329 5-33
§330 5-33
§331 5-33

Restatement (Second) of Property— Donative Transfers

§§5.1–10.2 4-3
§13.4 5-33

Restatement (Third) of Property—Wills and Other Donative Transfers §12.2 4-5 n.4

Restatement (Second) of Trusts

§17 4-28 n.29
§57 4-28 n.29
§57 comment c 9-34
§84 comment b 9-34
§151 4-9 n.6
§156 4-10 n.7, 4-19 n.20
§157 comment (a) 4-9 n.6
§330 4-9 n.8

Restatement (Third) of Trusts

§10 4-28 n.29
§25 4-28 n.29
§58(2) 4-10 n.7, 4-19 n.20
§59 4-9 n.6
§60 4-10 n.7, 4-19 n.20
§63 4-9 n.8

Table of Ethics Authorities

ABA Standing Committee on Ethics & Professional Responsibility

Formal Op. 94-380   3-49
Formal Op. 96-404   3-37 n.23
Formal Op. 122   3-27 n.16
Formal Op. 210   3-41 n.29
Formal Op. 314   3-53 n.37
Formal Op. 372   3-35
Inf. Dec. 564   3-14
Inf. Dec. C-682   3-25 n.14
Inf. Dec. C-709   3-25 n.14
Inf. Dec. C-778   5-19
Inf. Op. 89-1530   3-37 n.23
Inf. Op. 98   3-43
Inf. Op. 98-411   3-41 n.27
Inf. Op. 602   3-28 n.17, 3-55, 3-56 n.43
Inf. Op. 970   3-44 n.30
Inf. Op. 981   3-56
Inf. Op. 1254   3-44 n.30
Inf. Op. 1288   3-44 n.30
Inf. Op. 1293   3-29
Inf. Op. 1338   13-6 n.13
Inf. Op. 1356   3-41 n.29
Inf. Op. 1500   3-39
Inf. Op. 1517   3-44
Inf. Op. 1530   3-39

California State Bar Standing Committee on Professional Responsibility and Conduct Formal Op. 1989-112   3-37 n.24

Chicago Bar Ass'n Committee on Professional Responsibilty Op. 82-3   3-44 n.30

Colorado Ethics Opinion 96/97-7   3-37 n.23

Connecticut Bar Ass'n Informal Opinions

86-11   3-38 n.24
87-10   13-9
88-5   13-9 n.16

Florida Bar Ethics Department

Advisory Op. 95-4   3-31, 3-33
Ethics Op. 85-4   3-37 n.23

Illinois State Bar Ass'n Professional Ethics Opinion

89-12   3-38 n.24
89-14   3-24 n.13
90-2   3-27
90-13   3-27 n.16
99-06   3-25 n.14

Illinois State Bar Ass'n Ethics Advisory Opinion

98-07   3-47
00-01   3-17

Indiana Ethics Opinion No. 2 (2001)   3-19

Kansas Bar Ass'n Ethics Opinion 99-06   3-46

Kentucky Bar Ass'n Ethics Opinion E-391   3-44 n.30

Maine Bar Board of Overseers Professional Ethics Committee Opinion 84   3-37 n.23

State Bar of Michigan

Op. CI-889   3-37 n.23
Op. RI-146   3-25 n.14
Op. RI-191   3-27 n.16

Model Code of Professional Responsibility

generally   3-2
EC 2-22   3-41 n.28
EC 4-2   3-41 n.28
EC 5-5   3-23
EC 5-6   3-28
EC 7-12   3-38 n.24

Model Rules of Professional Conduct

generally   3-2
1.0   3-36
1.0(e)   3-4

TABLE OF ETHICS AUTHORITIES

1.1   3-40
1.2(d)   3-54
1.3   3-3, 3-41
1.4   3-3, 3-32, 3-41
1.5   3-42
1.5(a)   3-43, 13-7 n.15
1.5(b)   3-44
1.5(e)   3-41 n.28
1.6   3-39, 3-49, 3-53
1.6(a)   3-29, 3-30
1.6(a) comment 3   3-29
1.7   2-9, 3-4 n.4, 3-5, 3-9, 3-17, 3-27, 3-50
1.7(a)(1)   3-4, 3-4 n.3
1.7(a)(2)   3-4, 3-4 n.3
1.7(b)   3-18
1.7 comment 8,   3-16
1.7 comment 18   3-4
1.7 comment 20   3-5
1.7 comment 22   3-35
1.7 comment 27   3-46
1.7 comment 29   3-11
1.7 comment 31   3-11, 3-32, 3-33
1.8(a)   2-9 3-22, 3-25
1.8(c)   3-23
1.8(f)   3-13, 3-19
1.8(h)   3-24, 3-55
1.8 comment 8   3-24
1.9   3-5, 3-18, 3-35
1.11   3-36
1.11(d)   3-36
1.13   3-50
1.14   3-39
1.14(a)   3-37
1.14(b)   3-21, 3-37
1.14 comment 2   3-37
1.14 comment 4   3-21
1.14 comment 5   3-21, 3-39
1.14 comment 6   3-39
1.14 comment 7   3-39
1.14 comment 8   3.34
1.16(b)   3-53
2.2   3-6 n.5
3.3   3-47, 3-51
3.3(a)(1)   3-52
4.1(a)   3-53
5.3   3-40
5.4(a)   3-43
5.4(c)   3-27
5.6   3-17
5.7   3-24, 3-26
7.2(c)   3-43
7.3   3-56 n.44
8.4(c)   3-54 n.42

Scope Comment [6],   1-10
Scope Comment 20   3-57

Nassau County N.Y. Bar Opinion 90-17
   3-38 n.24

Nebraska State Bar Ass'n

Advisory Committee Op. 81-10   3-44 n.30
Advisory Committee Op. 81-12   3-44 n.30
Formal Op. 81-10   3-27 n.16
Formal Op. 81-11   3-27 n.16

New Jersey Advisory Committee on Professional Ethics Op. 625   3-37 n.23

New York City Bar Ass'n Committee on Professional Ethics Formal Op. 1987-7
   3-37 n.23

New York State Bar Ass'n Committee on Professional Ethics Opinions

481   3-55
555   3-31 n.19
610   3-55
667   3.23 n.14

Oregon Legal Ethics Opinion 457   3-28

Oregon State Bar Ass'n Board of Governors

Formal Op. 1991-41   3-37 n.23
Formal Op. 1994-119   3-48 n.33

Pennsylvania Bar Ass'n Committee on Legal Ethics and Professional Responsibility Formal Opinions

87-214   3-37 n.23
2000-100   3-25 n.14
2001-300   3-56

Texas Professional Ethics Committee Opinion

498   3-44 n.30
280   3-56

Utah State Bar Ethics Advisory Committee

Op. 146A   3-25 n.14, 3-27 n.16
Op. 97-09 3-27 n.16

Virginia Legal Ethics Opinion

570   3-37 n.23
1515 3-55

Table of Secondary Authorities

Abbin, [S]he Loves Me, [S]he Loves Me Not — Responding To Succession Planning Needs Through A Three Dimensional Analysis Of Considerations To Be Applied In Selecting From The Cafeteria Of Techniques, 31 U. Miami Inst. Est. Plan. ¶1300 (1997), 12-65 n.69

Abrams, A Reevaluation of the Terminable Interest Rule, 39 Tax L. Rev. 1 (1983), 7-47 n.43

Alces, The Law of Fraudulent Transactions ¶1.02[1][b] and ch. 5 (1989), 4-11 n.10

American Bar Association Real Property, Probate & Trust Law Section, Law Office Without Walls, A Handbook for the Correspondent Relationship Among Attorneys (1987), 1-14

American College of Trust and Estate Counsel Professional Standards Committee, Engagement Letters: A Guid for Practitioners, 3-9

American Council on Gift Annuities Model Standards of Practice for the Charitable Gift Planner, 8-2

American Law of Property §23.18 (Casner ed. 1952)   4-17 n.17

Annot., Attorney at law: disciplinary proceedings based upon attorney's naming of himself or associate as executor or attorney for executor in will drafted by him, 57 A.L.R.3d 703 (1974),   3-24 n.12

Annot., Attorneys at law: disciplinary proceedings for drafting instrument such as will or trust under which attorney-drafter or member of attorney's family or law firm is beneficiary, grantee, legatee, or devisee, 80 A.L.R.5th 597 (2000), 3-23 n.10

Annot., Conduct of attorney in capacity of executor or administrator of decedent's estate as grounds for disciplinary action, 3-24 n.11

Ascher, The Quandary of Executors Who Are Asked to Plan the Estates of the Dead: The Qualified Terminable Interest Election, 63 N.C. L. Rev. 1, 48 (1984), 7-65, 7-65 n.60

Backer, Hannon, & Russell, Death and Dying: Individuals and Institutions (1982), 15-3, 15-13

Ballsun, Summary Chart of Responses to Trust Mills, 21 Prob. Notes 330 (1996), 4-31 n.31

Beckwith, Estate & Gift Tax Charitable Deductions, 261-3d Tax Mgmt. (BNA) Estates, Gifts, & Trusts Port. (1991), 8-2 n.3

Beglieter, First Let's Sue All the Lawyers—What Will We Get: Damages for Estate Planning Malpractice, 51 Hastings L.J. 325 (2000), 1-9 n.2

Black & Skipper, Life Insurance (12th ed. 1994), 9-5 n.2

Blattmachr & Pennell, Using "Delaware Tax Trap" to Avoid Generation-Skipping Taxes, 68 J. Tax'n 242 (1988), or the expanded version in Adventures in Generation-Skipping, or How We Learned to Love the "Delaware Tax Trap," 24 Real Prop., Prob. & Trust J. 75 (1989), 5-13 n.bb

Boxx, Gray's Ghost — A Conversation About the Onshore Trust, 85 Iowa L. Rev. 1195 (2000), 4-11 n.10

Brody, Putting a Premium on Generation-Skipping Transfer Tax Planning — The Use of Life Insurance, 23 U. Miami Inst. On Est. Plan. Ch. 10 (1989), 4-34 n.35

Brody, The Irrevocable Life Insurance Trust: Forms with Drafting Notes (1995), 9-24 n.25

Brody & Weinberg, The Insured Stock Purchase Agreement with Sample Forms (1997), 9-24 n.25

Bromberg & Fortson, Selection of a Trustee: Tax and Other Considerations, 19 Sw. L.J. 523 (1965), 6-2

Bruce, Gray, & Luria, Exploring the Protection of Assets Trusts, 130 Trusts & Estates 32, 39 (Nov. & Dec. 1991), 4-11 n.10

TABLE OF SECONDARY AUTHORITIES

Buckman, "I Don't Know What To Say . . . " How to Help and Support Someone Who Is Dying (1992), 15-13
Burgess, Taxation: Special Powers of Appointment and Transfer Taxation — It Is the Courts' Move, 34 Okla. L. Rev. 907 (1981), 5-29

Cantrill, Fractional or Percentage Residuary Bequests: Allocation of Postmortem Income, Gain and Unrealized Appreciation, 10 Prob. Notes 322 (1985), 7-136 n.104
Cantwell, The Probate and Trust Lawyer in 2000 A.D., 10 Real Prop., Prob. & Trust J. 233 (1975), 1-5
Casner, Estate Planning §12.0 (5th ed. 1986), 5-26
Casner, Legal Life Estates and Powers of Appointment Coupled with Life Estates and Trusts, 45 Neb. L. Rev. 342 (1966), 7-58
Casner & Pennell, Estate Planning
    §3.3.11   11-32
    §5.11   17-17
    §7.1.1.10.1   5-27
    §7.1.6.6   7-18 n.18
    §11.4   4-23 n.27
    §11.4.14.1   18-33 n.25
    §12.3.2.4   6-11
    §12.4.2   5-27
    §13.3.6   7-39 n.38
    §13.7.3.1.1 n.25   12-9
Cesare, Private Foundations and Public Charities — Definition and Classification, 876 Tax Mgmt. (BNA) Estates, Gifts, & Trusts Port. (1999), 8-13 n.30
Choate, Life and Death Planning for Retirement Benefits (5th Rev. ed. 2003), 10-1 n.1, 10-18
Choate, When a "Trust For The Spouse" Is Treated The Same As "The Spouse," 140 Trusts & Estates 36 (Sept. 2001), 10-18
Christensen, Life Insurance: The Under-appreciated Tax Shelter, 135 Trusts & Estates 57 (Nov. 1996), 9-5 n.1
Collin, Lombard, Moses & Spitler, Durable Powers of Attorney and Health Care Directives (3d ed. 1994) 19-58 n.nnnn, 19-70
Comm. Rep., Current Tax Problems of Decedents' Estates, 3 Real Prop., Prob. & Tr. J. 361, 365, 367-368 (1968), 7-125 n.99
Comm. Rep., State and Local Action Against Trust Mills: The Unauthorized Practice of Law, 27 ACTEC Notes 162 (2001), 4-31 n.31
Cooper, A Voluntary Tax? New Perspectives on Sophisticated Estate Tax Avoidance 1 (1979), 18-26
Covey, Marital Deduction and Credit Shelter Dispositions and the Use of Formula Provisions, Appendix C (United States Trust Co. 3d ed. 1984 and Supp. 1994), 7-101 n.87
Covey, The Marital Deduction and Credit Shelter Dispositions and the Use of Formula Provisions (1984)
    57-60   7-102 n.88
    80   7-136 n.104
    95   7-125 n.99
Covey, The Marital Deduction and the Use of Formula Provisions at 22 (United States Trust Co. 2d ed. 1978), 7-101 n.87

Dacey, How to Avoid Probate — Updated! (Crown 1980), 4-17 n.15
Dahlquist, The Code of Professional Responsibility and Civil Damage Actions Against Attorneys, 9 Ohio N.U. L. Rev. 1 (1983), 3-58 n.45
D'Andrea & Salovey, Peer Counseling: Skills and Perspectives (1983), 15-11

TABLE OF SECONDARY AUTHORITIES

deFuria, Testamentary Gifts From Client to the Attorney-Draftsman: From Probate Presumption to Ethical Prohibition, 66 Neb. L. Rev. 695 (1987), 3-23 n.10

Devine, The Ethics of Representing the Disabled Client: Does Model Rule 1.14 Adequately Resolve the Best Interests/Advocacy Dilemma, 3-38 n.24

Dobris, Changes in the Role and the Form of the Trust at the New Millennium, or, We don't Have to Think of England Anymore, 62 Albany L. Rev. 543, 565 (1998), 4-4 n.2

Dobris, Medicaid Asset Planning by the Elderly: A Policy View, 24 Real Prop., Prob. & Trust J. 1 (1989), 14-5 n.2

Drennan, Swirnoff & Goldstein, Taxation and Funding of Nonqualified Deferred Compensation (1998), 9-24 n.25

Early, The Irrevocable Trust That Can Be Amended, 18 U. Miami Inst. On Est. Plan. Ch. 17 (1984), 4-36 n.37

Eason, Home From the Islands: Domestic Asset Protection Trust Alternatives Impact Traditional Estate and Gift Tax Planning Considerations, 52 Fla. L. Rev. 41 (2000), 4-11 n.10

Eastland, The Use of Partnerships in Lieu of Irrevocable Insurance Trusts, 16 Tax Mgmt. (BNA) Estates, Gifts, Trusts J. 123 (1991), 9-28

Engle, Using Foreign Situs Trusts for Asset Protection Planning, 20 Est. Plan. 212 (1993), 4-11 n.10, 4-12

Epstein, Nursing the Dying Patient: Learning Processes for Interaction (1975), 15-3, 15-5, 15-13

Esperti & Peterson, The Living Trust Revolution: Why America Is Abandoning Wills and Probate (Viking 1992), 4-17 n.15

Esperti & Peterson, The Loving Trust: The Right Way To Provide For Yourself and Guarantee the Future of Your Loved Ones (Viking 1988), 4-17 n.15

Ethics 2000 Commission Report with Recommendation to the House of Delegates (August 2001), 3-2,

Eubank, The Future for Estate Lawyers, 10 Real Prop., Prob. & Trust J. 223 (1975), 1-5, 1-14

Evans, Wills, Trusts and Technology: An Estate Lawyer's Guide to Automation (2d ed. 2004), 7-40 n.39

Federal Income Taxation of Life Insurance (1989), 9-24 n.25

Ferguson, Freeland & Ascher, Federal Income Taxation of Estates, Trusts, and Beneficiaries (2d ed. 1993) §3.3   17-12

Ferguson, Freeland, & Ascher, Federal Income Taxation of Estates, Trusts and Beneficiaries (3d ed. 1998)
§7.06[A] n.2,   9-40
Chapter 10   17-17

Gibbs, The Marketing of Living Trusts by Non-Attorney Promoters, 20 ACTEC Notes 193 (1994), 3-27 n.16

Gingiss, Putting a Stop to "Asset Protection" Trusts, 51 Baylor L. Rev. 987 (1999), 4-11 n.10

Gislason, Split-Dollar Life Insurance: Updated Planning Techniques, 20 Est. Plan. 201 (1993), 9-13 n.13

Haight, Policy Facts and Incidents of Ownership Under Estate Tax Section 2042(2): The Legacy of *Rhode Island Hospital Trust*, 28 Duquesne L. Rev. 109 (1989), 9-49 n.56

Halbach, Tax-Sensitive Trusteeships, 63 Or. L. Rev. 381 (1984), 4-23 n.26

Hansen ed., Frantz volume ed., Death and Grief in the Family (1984), 15-13

Hazard & Hodes, 1 The Law of Lawyering: A Handbook on the Model Rules of Professional Conduct §1.3:108 (2d ed. 1990), 3-47

Henkel, K. & Turner, Asset Preservation Aspects of Domestic Estate Planning, 29 U. Miami Inst. Est. Plan. ¶602 (1995), 4-11 n.10

Henkel, M., Medicaid Changes and Effective Planning for Your Client, 134 Trusts & Estates 26 (Dec. 1995), 14-5 n.2

Hodgman, Designing Private Foundations — Avoid the Cookie-Cutter Approach, 25 Est. Plan. 481 (1998), 8-5 n.7

Hoisington, The Truth About Charitable Remainder Trusts (*How to Separate the Help from the Hype*), 45 Tax Law. 293, 315 (1992), 12-33 n.29

Horn, Using Insurance Proceeds Not Included in Insured's Gross Estate to Provide Liquidity, 13 C.L.U.J. 44, 49-50 (1979), 9-38 n.42

Horn, Whom Do You Trust: Planning, Drafting and Adminstering Self and Beneficiary-Trusteed Trusts, 20 U. Miami. Inst. Est. Plan. ¶500 (1986), 4-23 n.26

Hoyt, The Family Wins When IRD Is Used for Charitable Bequests — How To Do It, 36 Univ. Miami Inst. Est. Plan. ¶400 (2002), 8-43 n.108

Hoyt, Transfers from Retirement Plans to Charities and Charitable Remainder Trusts: Laws, Issues and Opportunities, 13 Virginia Tax Rev. 641 (1994), 8-43 n.108

Huff, Use of Trusts in Estate Planning 238 (1977), 9-38 n.47

Ice, What Are Creditors' Rights in Retirement Plan Benefits, 21 Est. Plan. 30 (1994), 10-9 n.8

Issue Memorandum Concerning Miller Trusts After OBRA 1993, Elder Law Advisory No. 38 (May 1994), 14-7 n.9

Jaworski, The Will Contest, 10 Baylor L. Rev. 87 (1958), 4-14

Johanson, The Use of Tax Saving Clauses in Drafting Wills and Trusts, 15 U. Miami Inst. Est. Plan. ¶2100 (1981), 7-65 n.61, 7-94

Johnston, An Ethical Analysis of Common Estate Planning Practices — Is Good Business Bad Ethics, 45 Ohio St. L.J. 57 (1984), 3-23 n.10, 3-24 n.12, 13-7 n.15

Johnston, Estate Planners' Accountability in the Representation of Agricultural Clients, 34 U. Kan. L. Rev. 611 (1986), 3-43

Kastenbaum, Death, Society and Human Experience (2d ed. 1981), 15-13

Katzenstein, Running the Numbers: An Economic Analysis of GRATs and QPRTs, 32 U. Miami Inst. Est. Plan. ¶1407 (1998), 8-40 n.105

Kavanaugh, Facing Death (1972), 15-13

Keydel & Wallace, The Revocable Trust — Disclaimer Method for Integrating Qualified Plan & IRA Benefits into an Estate Plan, 13 Prob. Notes 158 (1987), 10-24 n.22

Kirschten & Freitag, Charitable Contributions: Income Tax Aspects, 863 Tax Mgmt. (BNA) Estates, Gifts, & Trusts Port. (1999), 8-2 n.3

Klein & Bahls, S Corporations and Life Insurance (1992), 9-24 n.25

Knecht, The Human Equation in Estate Planning, 114 Trusts & Estates 854 (1975), 1-20

Kübler-Ross, On Death and Dying (1969), 15-4, 15-13

Kübler-Ross, Questions and Answers on Death and Dying (1974), 15-13

Kuether, 1988 Developments in Probate and Trust Law, 25 Real Prop., Prob. & Trust J. 147 (1990), 13-3 n.6

Langbein, The Twentieth-Century Revolution in Family Wealth Transmission, 86 Mich. L. Rev. 722 (1988), 1-5, 1-6, 1-16

Leach, Powers of Appointment, 24 A.B.A.J. 807 (1938), 5-21

Leimberg & Plotnick, What a Probate Attorney Must Know about the Psychological Aspects of Death and Dying, 32 Prac. Law. 33, 40-41 (Oct. 1986), 15-10

TABLE OF SECONDARY AUTHORITIES

Link et al., Developments Regarding the Professional Responsibility of the Estate Administration Lawyer: The Effect of the Model Rules of Professional Conduct, 26 Real Prop., Prob. & Trust J. 1 (1991), 3-4 13-7 n.15

Longan, Middle-Class Lawyering in the Age of Alzheimer's: The Lawyer's Duties in Representing a Fiduciary, 70 Fordham L. Rev. 902 (2001), 3-45

Lopata, Can States Juggle the Unauthorized and Multidisciplinary Practices of Law?: A Look at the States' Current Grapple with the Problems in the Context of Living Trusts, 50 Catholic U.L. Rev. 467 (2001), 4-31 n.31

Lowndes, Kramer, & McCord, Federal Estate and Gift Taxes (3d ed. 1974)
  §8.9, 6-9 n.5
  §9.20, 6-9 n.5

McBryde & Keydel, Back to the Future for the Estate Planner: Building Flexibility in Estate Planning Documents, 30 U. Miami Inst. Est. Plan. ¶1200 (1996), abridged and reprinted as Building Flexibility in Estate Planning Documents, 135 Trusts & Estates 56 (Jan. 1996), 4-5 n.3

McCue, Planning and Drafting to Influence Behavior, 34 U. Miami Inst. Est. Plan. ¶600 (2000), 4-7 n.4

McGovern & Kurtz, Wills, Trusts & Estates (3d ed. 2004) 535   13-6 n.13

Mezzullo, An Estate Planner's Guide to Qualified Retirement Plan Benefits (American Bar Ass'n 2d ed. 1998), 10-1 n.1

Millard, Brody & Lane, Federal Gift, Estate, and Generation Skipping Transfer Taxation of Life Insurance (2d ed. 1998), 9-24 n.25

Mittelman & Balter, Using Life Insurance to Fund Buy-Sell Agreements for LLCs, 29 Est. Plan. 460 (2002), 9-40

Moore, Fairness and Finality: Notice to Beneficiaries Under Prior Wills, 29 Real Prop., Prob. & Trust J. 817 (1995), 13-4 n.7

Moore & Pennell, Practicing What We Preach: Esoteric or Essential?, 27 U. Miami Inst. Est. Plan. ¶1211 (1993), 3-2, 7-49 n.49, 7-99 n.86, 7-102 n.88, 7-111 n.93, 7-117 n.95, 7-120 n.96, 7-122 n.97, 7-131 n.102, 7-135 n.103

Moore & Pennell, Survey of the Profession II, 30 U. Miami Inst. Est. Plan. ¶1502 (1996), 1-21, 3-2

Munch, Financial and Estate Planning with Life Insurance Products ¶15.2 (1990), 9-51

National Society of Fund Raising Executives Code of Ethical Principles and Standards of Professional Practice, 8-2

Osborne, Asset Protection: Domestic and International Law and Tactics (1995), 4-11 n.10

Oshins, Megatrusts: Representation Without Taxation, 48 N.Y.U. Inst. On Fed. Tax'n (1990), 4-32

Pegg & Metze, eds., Death and Dying: A Quality of Life 13 (1981), 15-2, 15-13

Pennell, Estate Planning: Drafting and Tax Considerations in Employing Individual Trustees, 60 N.C. L. Rev. 799 (1982), abridged and reprinted in 9 Est. Plan. 264 (1982), 4-23 n.26, 6-10

Pennell, Marital Deduction Funding After ERTA '81, 7 Notre Dame Est. Plan. Inst. 289 (1983), 7-136 n.104

Pennell, Minimizing the Surviving Spouse's Elective Share, 32 U. Miami Inst. Est. Plan. ¶900 (1998), 3-7 n.6, 4-19, 7-83 n.75

Pennell, Professional Responsibility: Reforms Are Needed to Accommodate Estate Planning and Family Counselling, 25 U. Miami Inst. Est. Plan. Ch. 18 (1991), 3-16 n.8

Pennell, Repeal? The Wealth Transfer Taxes?, 138 Trusts & Estates 52 (Jan. 1999),   12-12 n.13

Pennell, Representations Involving Fiduciary Entities: Who Is the Client?, 62 Fordham L. Rev. 1219 (1994), 3-45

Pennell & Williamson, The Economics of Prepaying Wealth Transfer Tax, 136 Trusts & Estates 49-60 (June 1997), 40-51 (July 1997), and 52-56 (Aug. 1997), 7-26 n.24, 12-8 n.10

Pike, Reflections on the Meaning of Life: An Analysis of Section 7702 and the Taxation of Cash Value Life Insurance, 43 Tax L. Rev. 491 (1988), 9-26

Plaine & Siegler, The Federal Gift and Estate Tax Marital Deduction for Non-United States Citizen Recipient Spouses, 25 Real Prop., Prob. & Trust J. 385, 436-443 (1991), 7-78 n.69

Polasky, Marital Deduction Formula Clauses in Estate Planning — Estate and Income Tax Considerations, 63 Mich. L. Rev. 869 (1965), 7-125 n.99

Quilliam, How Leading Texas Probate Lawyers Are Handling Marital Deduction Problems (An Empirical Study), Advanced Estate Planning & Probate Course (State Bar of Texas) 1987, 7-49 n.46, 7-99 n.86

Report of the Special Study Committee on Professional Responsibility, Comments and Recommendations on the Lawyer's Duties in Representing Husband and Wife, 28 Real Prop., Prob. & Trust J. 765 (1994), 3-10, 3-15, 3-32

Report of the Special Study Committee on Professional Responsibility, Counseling the Fiduciary, 28 Real Prop., Prob. & Trust J. 825 (1994), 3-45

Report of the Special Study Committee on Professional Responsibility, Preparation of Wills and Trusts that Name Drafting Lawyer as Fiduciary, 28 Real Prop., Prob. & Trust J. 803 (1994), 3-55

Reutlinger, State Action, Due Process, and the New Nonclaim Statutes: Can No Notice Be Good Notice If Some Notice Is Not?, 24 Real Prop., Prob. & Trust J. 433 (1990), 13-3 n.6

Rothschild, Establishing and Drafting Offshore Trusts, 23 Est. Plan. 65 (1996), 4-11 n.10

Rothschild & Rubin, Asset Protection After *Anderson*: Much Ado About Nothing?, 26 Est. Plan. 466, 474 n.32 (1999), 4-14

Schiltz, Counseling Professionals on Disability Insurance with Sample Agreements and Drafting Notes (1997), 9-24 n.25

Schlesinger, Dealing with the Dying Client, 9 U. Miami Inst. Est. Plan. ¶200 (1975), 15-5, 15-13

Schoenberg, Carr, Peretz & Kutscher, eds. Psychosocial Aspects of Terminal Care (1972), 15-13

Schoenblum, Multistate Guide to Estate Planning
    Table 10.01 (2001)   18-1 n.2
    Table 10.02 (2001)   18-1 n.1
    Table 10.03 (2001)   18-2 n.4
    Table 10.04 (2001)   18-1 n.3

Schuyler, Drafting Provisions for Legal Life Estates and the Marital Deduction, 44 Ill. B.J. 452 (1956), 7-58

Schwartz & Turner, Life Insurance Due Care: Carriers, Products, and Illustrations ch. 3 (2d ed. 1994), 9-24 n.25

Scoles, Apportionment of Federal Estate Taxes and Conflict of Laws, 55 Colum. L. Rev. 261 (1955), 11-26

Scott & Fratcher, The Law of Trusts (4th ed.)
    §1   4-1
    §17.1   4-28 n.29
    §18   4-15 n.12
    §19   4-15 n.13

§54.1   4-20 n.21
§54.2   4-20 n.22
§54.3   4-17 n.16, 4-21 n.24
§54.4   4-21 n.23
§57.2   4-28 n.29
§57.6   4-28 n.29
§99   4-28 n.30
§100   4-28 n.30
§151   4-9 n.6
§156.3   4-10 n.7
§157.5   4-9 n.6
§172   4-18 n.18
§182   7-57
§220.1   4-15 n.14
§222.3   3-24 n.12
§260   4-18 n.18
§330.12   4-9 n.8, 4-11 n.10, 4-17 n.17
§333   4-15 n.12
§347   7-97
§642   5-34

Shaffer, Death, Property and Lawyers 117 (1970), 15-2, 15-13

Shaffer, Some Thoughts on the Psychology of Estate Planning, 113 Trusts & Estates 568 (1974), 1-18

Simpson, The Facts of Death: A Complete Guide for Being Prepared (1979), 15-13

Springs & Bruce, Marital Agreements: Uses, Techniques, and Tax Ramifications in the Estate Planning Context, 21 U. Miami Inst. Est. Plan. ¶700 (1987), 3-20

State and Local Action Against Trust Mills: The Unauthorized Practice of Law, 27 ACTEC J. 162 (2001), 3-27 n.16

Statement of Principles Regarding Probate Practice and Expenses, 8 Real Prop., Prob. & Trust J. 293 (1973), 13-7 n.15

Stein, Use of Insurance Proceeds in Irrevocable Trust for Payment of Death Costs, 3 Notre Dame Est. Plan. Inst. 71, 107 (1979), 9-36 n.44

Sterk, Asset Protection Trusts: Trust Law's Race to the Bottom?, 85 Cornell L. Rev. 1035 (2000), 4-11 n.10

St. Laurent, Estate Planning with Tax-Deferred Annuities — Special Problems Under Section 72, 21 Tax Mgmt. (BNA) Estates, Gifts & Trusts J. 234, 236 (1996), 10-17 n.16

Tallner, Prichard, Kutscher, DeBelis, Hale & Goldberg, eds., The Life-Threatened Elderly (1984), 15-13

Teitell, Charitable Giving Tax Strategies: Windfalls and Pitfalls, 27 U. Miami Inst. Est. Plan. ¶1100.3D (1993), 12-35 n.33

Teitell, Philanthropy & Taxation, Outright Charitable Gifts
    §1.02   8-4
    §1.03[2]   8-4
    §1.04   8-9 n.24
    §1.05   8-5 n.9

Thomason, How estate planners can cope with the increasing risk of malpractice claims, 12 Est. Plan. 130 (1985), 3-58 n.45

Trapp, Drafting and Funding Marital and Nonmarital Formula Bequests, 17 U. Miami Inst. Est. Plan. ¶¶301.2, 301.4 (1983), 7-125 n.99

Treacy, Supporting Organizations, 871 Tax Mgmt. (BNA) Estates, Gifts, & Trusts Port. (1999), 8-15 n.45

TABLE OF SECONDARY AUTHORITIES

Tremblay, On Persuasion and Paternalism: Lawyer Decisionmaking and the Questionably Competent Client, 3-38 n.24

Webel, The Supporting Organization, 15 Prob. & Prop. 55 (March/April 2001), 8-15 n.45
Weber, Understanding Life Insurance Illustrations, 133 Trusts & Estates 45, 47 (Feb. 1994), 9-25
Weiss, The Fiduciary: Guidelines for Selection, Powers and Succession, 33 N.Y.U. Inst. Fed. Tax'n 273, 274 (1975), 6-2 n.1
Wells, Responding to the Call for Fairness and Finality: Would Notice to Beneficiaries under Prior Wills Produce Either?, 29 Real Prop., Prob. & Trust J. 849 (1995), 13-4 n.7
Worden, Grief Counseling and Grief Therapy: A Handbook for the Mental Health Practitioner (1982), 15-13
Wynn, Split-Dollar Life Insurance (1991), 9-24 n.25

Index

Abatement, 7-49 n.45, 7-103, 11-15, 11-42, 19-19 n.x
Accelerated death benefit. See Life insurance: contract provisions
Accessions. See also Fiduciary accounting income
Accidental death. See Life insurance: contract provisions
Accounts receivable. See Income tax: income in respect of a decedent
Accrued/Accumulated income, 5-1, 5-4 n.d, 5-31 n.aaa, 19-24 n.oo. See also Marital deduction: accrued but undistributed income
Actuarial tables, 7-33, 8-34 n.95, 10-12 n.11, 10-13 n.12
Add to shares provision, 5-14 n.ee
Ademption, 19-19 n.x. See also Lapse
Adequate and full consideration in money or money's worth, 7-44, 7-143, 9-47, 10-3, 12-11, 12-12, 17-17, 18-3, 18-4, 18-10, 18-13, 18-20
Adjusted taxable gifts. See Estate tax
Administration. See Estate administration
Adoption, 2-4, 2-9, 19-17 n.p
    trusts, effect on, 4-24
    will provision regarding effect of, 5-2 n.a
Advance medical directive. See Durable powers of attorney: health care
Advancements, 4-24, 5-7 n.j, 19-41
Adverse party. See Grantor trusts
Agency, law of, 3-1 n.1, 3-62
Aided conception. See Children: of the new biology
Alien land laws, 6-2 n.1
Amendment. See Trusts
Anatomical gifts. See Organ donation
Ancillary administration. See Estate administration
Annual exclusion. See Gift tax
Annuities, 7-71, 12-60. See also Charitable deduction: gift annuities; trusts: split interest trusts; Estate tax: inclusion rules; Grantor retained annuity trust; Income tax: annuity income rules; deductions; Life Insurance: annuities; Marital deduction; Private annuity; Survivor/spousal annuity; Tax payment provisions: temporal interests, taxes attributable to
Antenuptial agreements. See Prenuptial agreements
Antialienation rule, 10-3, 10-6 n.6. See also Survivor/spousal annuity
Antilapse statutes. See Lapse
Applicable credit amount. See Credits: unified
Applicable exclusion amount. See Credits: unified
Applicable federal rate. See Loans: below market interest
Apportionment of tax liability. See Tax payment provisions
Artificial insemination. See Children: of the new biology
Ascertainable standard. See Estate tax: inclusion rules: powers to control enjoyment, retained; Gift tax: annual exclusion: present interest requirement; May versus shall; Powers of appointment: general powers of appointment, ascertainable standard exception
Asset management. See Trusts: uses of trusts
Asset protection. See Trusts: uses of trusts: creditor protection
Assignment. See Spendthrift trusts
Attorneys
    beneficiary under document drafted by, 3-22
    fees, estate administration, 13-6. See also Estate administration: expenses of
    fiduciary or attorney for fiduciary, employment as, designation drafted by, 3-28, 3-55
Audit lottery, 3-2, 3-54

INDEX

Balloon value interests. See Estate tax: inclusion rules: three years of death
Bank or bond requirements. See Marital deduction: forms of disposition: qualified domestic trusts
Bargain sale to charity, 8-31, 12-34, 12-38
Bar to inheritance. See Misconduct
Basis. See Income tax
Bastards. See Nonmarital children
Beneficiary designation. See Gifts: retirement benefits, irrevocable beneficiary designation of
Bequests,
   abatement of. See Abatement
   accessions. See Accessions
   exclusion from income, 17-3
   formula. See Marital deduction: size of deduction: formula clauses
   funding. See Marital deduction: funding marital bequests
   personal effects, 5-2 n.a, 19-17 nn.q, r, 19-18 n.t
   specific bequest, 5-1
Bereavement, 15-9
Blanket exercise provisions. See Powers of appointment: exercise: testamentary
Blended family, 5-2 n.a, 7-2
Boutique law firms, 1-12
Business transaction exception. See Gift tax
Buy-sell agreement, 2-8, 3-13, 3-14, 18-19. See also Life insurance: buy-sell agreement; Tax payment provisions
Bypass trust. See Nonmarital trusts

Capacity. See Crummey clauses/powers: capacity to exercise; Incapacity
Capital gains and losses. See Income tax
Care, direction to provide maximum. See Durable powers of attorney: health care
Carryout. See Income tax: trusts and estates income taxation: distributable net income: carryout rule
Carryover basis. See Income tax: basis
CERCLA, 4-8, 19-29 n.ddd
Change, adaptation to it, 4-4
Charitable deduction, 8-1, 12-38
   alternative strategies, 8-38, 12-40
   conservation easements, 8-31, 12-33
   dependents, support of, 8-16, 8-20
   disclaimer to produce, 8-37, 12-41
   donor advised funds, 8-7 n.17, 8-14, 8-14 n.42
   encumbered property, 8-27, 8-31. See also Bargain sale to charity
   equitable apportionment. See Tax payment provisions
   estate tax, 8-2
   farm. See Charitable deduction: remainder interest in personal residence or farm
   five year carry forward, 8-4, 8-8, 8-10
   foundations, 8-3 n.4
      community, 8-14
      private, 8-5, 8-7, 8-7 n.17, 8-13, 8-14, 8-20 n.55
      termination, 8-14 n.42
   gift annuities, 8-3 n.4, 8-43, 12-34
   gift tax, 8-2, 12-32, 18-3, 18-6

gifts inter vivos to charity, 8-1, 8-3
income in respect of a decedent, 8-43, 12-44
income tax, 8-1, 8-3, 8-8, 8-35, 8-42, 12-32. See also Income tax: trusts and estates income taxation
    contribution base percentage limitation, 8-3, 8-4, 8-7, 8-8, 8-9, 8-13, 8-30, 8-31
life insurance, 12-33, 12-37
missionary support, 8-16
personal residence. See Charitable deduction: remainder interest in personal residence or farm
pledge, 8-4
pooled income fund, 8-3 n.4, 8-29
power to select charitable beneficiaries, 8-27
public charity, 8-5, 8-7, 8-7 n.18, 8-14
qualification, time for, 8-37
qualified charity, 8-4, 8-11, 8-12, 8-27, 18-6
reduction for obligations imposed on charitable bequest, 7-119
remainder interest in personal residence or farm, 8-3 n.4, 8-30
remainders. See Charitable deduction: trusts: split interest trusts: charitable remainder trusts
residence, personal. See Charitable deduction: remainder interest in personal residence or farm
temporal interests. See Charitable deduction: trusts: split interest trusts
transfer "to" versus "for the use of" public charity, 8-5
trusts
    model forms, 8-22, 8-22 n.56, 8-36 n.99
    split interest trusts, 8-7, 8-11, 8-17, 12-37, 12-44, 15-7, 18-6
        charitable lead trusts, 7-143, 8-33
        charitable remainder trusts, 8-3 n.4, 8-19, 12-35
            additions to, 8-25
            annuity payout, maximum/minimum, 8-20 n.55, 8-25
            annuity trusts (CRATs), 8-20
            deficiency make up, 8-21
            income only CRUT, 8-21
            mandatory provisions, incorporation by reference of, 8-24
            minimum remainder value, 8-17, 8-21, 8-25
            permissible donor, 8-23
            qualified terminable interest property trust/charitable remainder trust, 7-75, 8-21
            remainder beneficiary, power to change, 8-27
            unitrusts (CRUTs), 5-11 n.s, 7-54, 8-20
        nonqualifying, reformation of, 8-17, 8-21, 8-23, 8-37
        taxes attributable to. See Tax payment provisions: equitable apportionment
    undivided portion of entire interest, 8-17
    unrelated use, 8-5 n.9, 8-8
Charitable lead trusts. See Charitable deduction: trusts: split interest trusts
Charitable remainder trusts. See Charitable deduction: trusts: split interest trusts
Children, 5-2 n.a, 5-6 n.g
    disabled, 2-9
    of the new biology, 2-4, 4-24, 5-2 n.a
Chronically ill defined. See Life insurance: contract provisions: accelerated death benefit
Citizenship, 2-4
    marital deduction for noncitizen surviving spouse. See Marital deduction; noncitizen spouse
Class gifts, 8-28

Clifford trusts. See Grantor trusts
Closely held business, 5-7 n.k, 11-10, 19-37
Collections, 2-5
Common disaster provision. See Life insurance: contract provisions; Survivorship
Community property, 2-4, 4-18, 4-26, 7-7, 7-74, 10-6
    life insurance, 2-6, 9-29, 9-45, 9-51
    transmutation, 9-31 n.37
Community standard defense, 3-2
Compensatory adjustments. See Equitable adjustments
Complex trusts. See Income tax: trusts and estates income taxation
Concurrent interests, 1-1
    convenience, joint tenancy for, 14-2
    estate tax inclusion rules. See Estate tax: inclusion rules
    gift taxation of, 18-6
    joint settlor trusts. See Joint settlor trusts
    joint tenancy with right of survivorship, 1-1
    marital deduction. See Marital deduction
    partition, 4-26, 12-49
    slayer statutes, effect of. See Misconduct
    valuation opportunities. See Valuation: fractional interests
Confidentiality. See Ethics
Conflicts of interest, 2-4, 2-9. See also Ethics
Conflict of laws
    governing law, 19-53
    powers of appointment, 5-34
    tax payment and apportionment, 11-25, 11-29
Consent, informed. See Ethics: consent
Consent, spousal. See Survivor/spousal annuity
Consenting spouse. See Gift tax: split gifts
Conservation easement. See Charitable deduction: conservation easements
Consultants, 2-7
Contemplation of death. See Estate tax: inclusion rules: three years of death
Contingent distribution provision, 5-14
Countable assets. See Medicaid qualification
Court trusts. See Estate administration: avoiding probate
CRAT. See Charitable deduction: trusts: split interest trusts: charitable remainder trusts: annuity trusts
Credit consuming marital deduction bequest. See Marital deduction: funding marital bequests: reverse pecuniary funding
Creditors
    nonclaim protection, 4-9, 4-17, 4-11, 13-3 n.6
    protection against, 4-34, 4-37, 7-83, 10-9 n.8. See also Spendthrift trusts; Trusts: uses of trusts
Credits
    apportionment of benefit of. See Tax payment provisions
    generation-skipping transfers, credit for state taxation of, 18-2
    previously taxed property, 5-4 n.d, 7-7, 7-48, 7-64, 9-20, 18-24
    state death tax, 18-14, 18-37
    unified, 1-1, 1-6, 2-7, 2-8, 7-4, 7-37, 7-70, 7-100, 12-28, 16-4, 18-2, 18-23
Credit shelter planning. See Marital deduction: size of deduction: formula clauses: optimum marital deduction
Credit shelter trust. See Nonmarital trusts
Crown loan. See Loans: below market interest; demand
Crummey clauses/powers, 5-23, 5-30 n.yy, 9-31, 12-14, 19-39, 19-40, 19-43 n.eeee

INDEX

    dummy Crummey powers, 12-18
    generation-skipping transfer tax consequences, 9-31, 9-55, 18-35
    grantor trust consequences. See Grantor trusts
    hanging powers, 9-53, 12-20, 19-40 n.www
    lapse of. See Powers of appointment: lapse
    multiple powers. See Powers of appointment: lapse
    notice requirements, 12-15, 19-40
CRUT. See Charitable deduction: trusts: split interest trusts: charitable remainder trusts: unitrusts
Custodianships. See Income tax: trusts and estates income taxation; Uniform Gifts/Transfers to Minors Act

Date of distribution pecuniary. See Marital deduction: funding marital bequests: true worth pecuniary
Dead hand control. See Trusts: restraints
Death
    stages of dying, 15-1, 15-4
Death-terminating installment note. See Self-canceling installment note
Declaration of trust, self-trusteed. See Trustees: settlor as
Default beneficiaries/takers in default. See Powers of appointment: definitions
Deferral of tax payment, marital deduction and, 7-1, 7-8, 7-23. See also Time-value of money
Deferred compensation. See Income tax: retirement benefits; income in respect of a decedent; Tax payment provisions
Delaware tax trap. See Generation-skipping transfer tax: powers of appointment
Demographics, 1-4, 1-7
Disability insurance, 2-6, 9-21 n.20
Discharge of legal obligation of support. See Obligations: discharge of legal
Disclaimer,
    benefit to surviving spouse permitted, 5-8, 5-8 n.m, 7-19, 12-43
    fiduciary authority, 7-18, 7-65
    nonqualified, 12-43
    postmortem estate planning, 5-22, 7-7, 7-29, 7-64, 8-37, 13-12, 13-14
    retirement benefit beneficiary planning, 10-24 n.22
    specific portion, 7-20
    taxes attributable to, 11-29, 11-44 n.d
Disclosure, adequate. See Valuation of gifts
Discounts. See Valuation
Disqualifying distributions. See Medicaid qualification
Distributable net income (DNI). See Income tax: trusts and estates income taxation
Distribution director, 5-22, 6-4, 19-36
Distributions deduction. See Income tax: trusts and estates income taxation
Divorce, 2-4, 4-24, 7-1, 7-141, 9-34, 10-2
Domicile, 2-4, 19-15 n.e
Dummy Crummey power. See Crummey clauses/powers: dummy Crummey powers
Durable powers of attorney, 4-8, 4-28, 6-1, 19-49
    health care, 2-8, 14-4, 16-2, 19-58
    property management, 2-8, 3-16, 4-1, 14-2, 16-2, 19-47
Dynasty trust, 2-6
Ed/med exclusion. See Gift tax
Education as inheritance, 1-6
Educational expenses, gift tax exclusion for. See Gift tax: ed/med exclusion
Elderlaw, 1-4, 14-1

Electing small business trusts. See Income tax: corporate income tax: S Corporations
Elective share. See Forced heir share: spouse, surviving
Emergency trustee. See Trusts: uses of trusts: creditor protection
Employee benefits. See Income tax: retirement benefits
Engagement letter. See Ethics
Entitlements. See Governmental benefits
Equalizer. See Marital deduction: size of deduction: formula clauses
Equitable adjustments, 7-39 n.36, 7-66, 11-48, 13-14, 19-16
Equitable apportionment. See Tax payment provisions
Estate administration, 1-7, 4-15, 11-1, 13-1
    ancillary administration, 2-5, 4-18, 4-28, 13-2, 16-2, 19-32 n.kkk, 19-33 n.nnn
    avoiding probate, 1-2, 4-2, 4-16, 4-23
    benefits of, 4-23
    delay in funding marital bequest. See Marital deduction: funding marital bequests;
        nondeductible terminable interests: all-income-annually requirement
    expenses of, 7-38, 11-1, 11-23, 13-6, 17-2
    independent administration, 4-17, 4-27, 13-2
    simplification, 1-6
Estate planning
    as a profession, 1-3
    future of, 1-5
    nontax considerations, 1-1
    postmortem. See Postmortem estate planning
    reasons for, 2-1
Estate stacking. See Marital deduction
Estate tax
    applicable exclusion amount. See Credits, unified
    charitable deduction. See Charitable deduction
    credits. See Credits
    deductions
        charitable. See Charitable Deduction
        double deductions. See Postmortem estate planning: swing item election
        expenses of administration, 13-7, 18-13, 18-18 n.15
        marital. See Marital deduction
        state death tax, 18-14
    Delaware tax trap. See Generation-skipping transfer tax: powers of appointment
    disclaimer. See Disclaimer
    gross up rule. See Estate tax: inclusion rules: gift tax on transfers made within three
        years of death (gross up rule); Tax exclusive tax computations; Tax payment
        provisions
    inclusion rules,
        annuities, 7-8 nn.7, 8, 10-3, 10-5, 18-11, 18-20
        concurrent interests, 18-11
        death-terminating installment note. See Self-canceling installment note
        employee benefits. See Estate tax: retirement benefits
        general powers of appointment. See Powers of appointment
        gift tax on transfers made within three years of death (gross up rule), 12-3 n.4, 18-9
        life estate
            retained, 12-26, 18-10
            secondary, 7-69
        life insurance. See Estate Tax
        powers of appointment. See Powers of appointment: general powers to appoint,
            estate tax inclusion of property subject to
        powers to control enjoyment, retained, 5-25, 6-9, 8-3 n.4, 12-25, 18-10

qualified terminable interest property, 7-64. See also Marital deduction
string provisions, 6-9
three years of death, 9-47, 18-9
voting control, retained, 6-9, 18-11
life insurance
annuities under life insurance policy, 10-5
controlled corporation as policy owner, 9-46, 9-47
estate settlement costs, discretion to pay. See Estate tax: life insurance: payable to decedent's estate
incidents of ownership, 6-7, 9-11, 9-44, 18-13
fiduciary capacity, 9-45. See also Estate tax: inclusion rules: power to control enjoyment, retained
three years of death, transfers within, 9-47
partnership as policy owner, 9-28
payable to decedent's estate, 9-33, 9-44
limited powers of appointment. See Powers of appointment: nongeneral powers of appointment
marital deduction. See Marital deduction
nongeneral powers of appointment. See Powers of appointment
obligation of support. See Obligations: discharge of legal
powers of appointment. See Powers of appointment: general powers of appointment, estate tax inclusion of property subject to
qualified terminable interest property. See Marital deduction: forms of disposition; Tax payment provisions; reimbursement rights; Valuation: family aggregation
reciprocal trusts. See Reciprocal trust doctrine
repeal, 1-3, 12-1, 12-10, 12-65
retained life estate. See Estate tax: inclusion rules: life estate
retained powers. See Estate tax: inclusion rules: powers to control enjoyment, retained
retirement benefits, 10-4, 18-11
special powers of appointment. See Powers of appointment: nongeneral powers of appointment
state death taxes, 18-1
string provisions. See Estate tax: inclusion rules
tax on prior transfers, credit for. See Credits: previously taxed property
time for payment, 11-8
transfers made within three years of death. See Estate tax: inclusion rules: three years of death
unified credit. See Credits
Estate trusts. See Marital deduction: forms of disposition
Ethics
advertising, 3-54
ancillary activities, 3-24, 3-44
assistance in unauthorized practice of law, 3-18, 3-27 n.16, 3-28, 3-44 n.30
bequests. See Attorneys: beneficiary under document drafted by
community property, 3-6
confidentiality, 2-7, 2-9, 3-8, 3-9, 3-17, 3-29, 3-33, 3-37, 3-45, 3-48, 3-64, 19-8
conflicts of interest, 1-13, 1-15, 2-9, 3-3, 3-14, 3-27, 3-45, 3-63, 3-64, 4-12, 8-2, 13-9
consent, 2-9, 3-4, 3-14, 3-16
corporation, 3-12
derivative clients, 3-47
diligence, 3-41
duty to disclose, 3-52
duty to the system, 3-50
dynastic family planning, 3-12, 3-14 n.7, 3-20, 3-37

engagement letter, 2-7, 3-34, 19-4, 19-11
exit letter, 3-41
fee agreement, 2-2, 3-42, 19-5, 19-11
fee paid by third party, 3-19, 8-2
fiduciary representation, 3-17, 3-19, 3-28, 3-44
former client consent, 3-18, 3-35
gifts, 3-22
incapacity, 3-19, 3-37, 3-39, 3-51
intermediation, 3-6 n.5, 3-13
joint representation letter, 3-9
lack of independent judgment, 1-14, 3-22, 3-24 n.13, 3-25
limitation on liability, 3-24, 3-60
malpractice distinguished, 1-11, 3-2, 3-40, 3-57
marital planning, 3-6
multidisciplinary practice, 1-15, 3-44
multiple representations, 3-3, 3-18, 3-32
overreaching, 1-15
power of attorney, 3-16
retention of executed will, 3-56
self-dealing, 1-15, 2-9, 3-22, 3-25
solicitation, 3-28, 3-54, 8-2, 13-6 n.13. See also Attorneys: fiduciary or attorney for fiduciary, employment as, designation drafted by
unauthorized practice of law, 3-18, 4-31 n.31, 8-2
will contest, 3-17
withdrawal, 2-9, 3-11, 3-31, 3-49, 3-53
Exclusions
  annual exclusion. See Gift tax
  conservation easement. See Charitable deduction
  educational expenses. See Gift tax: ed/med exclusion
  medical expenses. See Gift tax: ed/med exclusion
Exculpation, 3-55, 19-53
Exoneration, 3-24, 11-47, 19-37 n.qqq

Facility of payment provision. 5-15, 7-89, 19-19 n.x. See also Marital deduction: drafting considerations
Family law, 1-4
Family policy. See Life insurance
Family trust. See Nonmarital trust
Family, will provision designation of, 5-2 n.a. See also Adoption
Federal estate tax (FET) pecuniary. See Marital deduction: funding marital bequests: fairly representative pecuniary
Fiduciary accounting, 5-6 n.f
Fiduciary accounting income, 7-49 n.45, 7-51, 7-54, 7-55, 7-61, 7-88, 10-23, 11-32, 17-4, 17-6, 17-7, 17-16, 19-28 n.bbb
Fiduciary services, 1-15
Financial planning, 1-5, 1-13
Five or five exception. See Generation-skipping transfer tax: powers of appointment: lapse; Grantor trusts; Powers of appointment: lapse
Flexibility. See Powers of appointment
Forced heir share
  ethics issues, 3-6
  pretermitted heir, 1-10, 19-17 n.p

spouse, surviving, 9-33, 10-20, 11-12, 11-16, 11-23, 13-12
    planning to minimize elective share, 4-19, 4-37, 7-2
    qualified terminable interest property trust income interest, 7-7, 7-84

Formula clauses. See Marital deduction: size of deduction

Front end credit shelter. See Marital deduction: funding marital bequests: reverse pecuniary

Full and adequate consideration. See Adequate and full consideration

Funding. See Marital deduction: funding marital bequests

Future interests,
    annual exclusion denied for. See Gift tax

Gender neutrality, 1-20, 5-3 n.c

General powers of appointment. See Powers of appointment

Generation-skipping transfer tax
    allocation of exemption. See Generation-skipping transfer tax: exemption
    annual exclusion gifts. See Generation-skipping transfer tax: direct skips: exception for nontaxable gifts; inclusion ratio
    applicable fraction. See Generation-skipping transfer tax: inclusion ratio
    apportionment of tax, 11-13, 11-19, 11-44
    automatic allocation. See Generation-skipping transfer tax: exemption
    chronological exemption. See Generation-skipping transfer tax: effective dates
    constructive additions. See Generation-skipping transfer tax: effective dates, irrevocable trusts: additions to
    Crummey clauses/powers. See Crummey clauses/powers: generation-skipping transfer tax consequences
    Delaware tax trap. See Generation-skipping transfer tax: powers of appointment
    direct skips, 12-42, 18-27, 18-29
        defined, 12-11
        exception for nontaxable gifts, 9-55, 12-22, 18-34
        tax exclusive computation. See Generation-skipping transfer tax: direct skips: taxable amount
    division of trusts. See Generation-skipping transfer tax: severance of trusts
    ed/med exclusion. See Generation-skipping transfer tax: direct skips: exception for nontaxable gifts; inclusion ratio
    effective dates, irrevocable trusts
        additions to, 9-55
        merger of, 4-5
    exceptions for
        nontaxable gifts. See Generation-skipping transfer tax: direct skips: exception for nontaxable gifts; inclusion ratio
        previously taxed trusts. See Generation-skipping transfer tax: taxable terminations: exceptions: second time around exception
    exemption, 2-7, 7-36, 16-4, 18-2, 18-27
        allocation, 4-5, 7-66, 7-138, 8-36, 13-14, 19-32, 19-32 n.111
        automatic allocation of, 13-14, 18-37
        lapse of withdrawal rights, effect of. See Crummey clauses/powers: generation-skipping transfer tax consequences
        leveraging the exemption, 7-100, 7-138
        qualified terminable interest property trust, 7-83

reverse qualified terminable interest property allocation. See Generation-skipping transfer tax: reverse qualified terminable interest property election
separate shares, 19-32 n.111
severance for allocation, 19-32 n.111
generation assignment, 18-27
adoption, 18-27
multiple generations, assignment to, 18-28
relatives, 18-27
spouses and former spouses, 18-28
strangers, 18-28
grandfathered trusts. See Generation-skipping transfer tax: effective dates
group trusts, 18-35
inclusion ratio, 9-55, 12-22, 18-36
medical expense exception. See Generation-skipping transfer tax: direct skips: exception for nontaxable gifts; inclusion ratio
million dollar exemption. See Generation-skipping transfer tax: exemption
move-up-a-generation rule. See Generation-skipping transfer tax: predeceased ancestor exception
new transferor rule, 12-22, 18-35 n.27. See also Crummey clauses/powers: generation-skipping transfer tax consequences
powers of appointment
Delaware tax trap, 5-13 n.aa, 5-23, 18-13
general powers, 18-25
new transferor rule. See Generation-skipping transfer tax: new transferor rule
powers of withdrawal. See Crummey clauses/powers: generation-skipping transfer tax consequences
predeceased ancestor exception, 18-29
qualified terminable interest property trusts, 4-5
reimbursement provision. See Tax payment provisions: reimbursement rights
reverse qualified terminable interest property election, 4-5, 7-37, 7-61, 7-83, 7-138, 12-43, 13-14
same generation exception. See Generation-skipping transfer tax: taxable terminations
severance of trusts, 4-5, 18-36, 18-37. See also Generation-skipping transfer tax: exemption: severance for allocation
skip person defined, 18-27
taxable distributions, 18-29
exceptions. See Generation-skipping transfer tax: predeceased ancestor exception
taxable terminations, 18-30
deferral, 4-6
exceptions
estate and gift tax override, 18-34
predeceased ancestor exception. See Generation-skipping transfer tax: predeceased ancestor exception
same generation exception, 18-30
second time around exception, 18-34
stopped moving down exception, 18-30, 18-35
taxable transfers 18-29
relative costs, 18-33
transferor, 18-25 n.18
change following estate or gift tax inclusion. See Generation-skipping transfer tax: new transferor rule
new generation assignment. See Generation-skipping transfer tax: new transferor rule
trust equivalents, 18-26

Gifts and gift taxation, 1-2
- annual exclusion, 2-8, 7-22, 8-29, 9-50, 10-3, 12-8, 12-13, 12-59, 12-66, 18-3, 18-5, 18-34, 19-45 n.iiii
  - future interests, exclusion denied for, 7-86, 12-15
  - hanging powers. See Crummey clauses/powers: hanging powers
  - noncitizen spouse, 7-77, 12-30. See also Marital deduction: noncitizen spouse
  - present interest requirement, 5-23, 12-13, 18-5
- business transaction exception, 12-12, 18-3
- charitable deduction. See Charitable deduction
- completed gifts, 12-11
  - retained enjoyment or control, 12-46
- defined for wealth transfer tax purposes, 12-11, 18-3
- ed/med exclusion, 12-8, 12-13, 12-26, 18-3, 18-5, 18-34
- educational expense exclusion. See Gift tax: ed/med exclusion
- entities, gifts to, 12-14, 18-4
- exclusions. See Gift tax: annual exclusion; ed/med exclusion
- failure to [do something] as a gift, 7-71
- fractional interest, 12-9, 12-49, 12-66
- future interests. See Gift tax: annual exclusion
- gift loan. See Loans: below market interest
- incomplete, 6-9, 12-45. See also Estate tax: inclusion rules: powers to control enjoyment, retained
- insurance proceeds, owner not the beneficiary of, 9-32, 9-50
- lapse of power of appointment. See Powers of appointment: lapse
- medical expense exclusion. See Gift tax: ed/med exclusion
- net gift, 3-13
- part-sale, part-gift transaction. See Income tax: capital gains and losses
- present interest requirement. See Gift tax: annual exclusion
- qualified terminable interest property, assignment of income interest in, 7-71, 7-85
- retirement benefits, irrevocable beneficiary designation of, 2-3, 10-3
- split gifts, 3-6, 3-10, 7-7 n.6, 7-68, 12-8, 12-28, 12-30, 13-11, 18-6
- statute of limitation, 12-51
- tax exclusive computation. See Tax exclusive tax computations
- transfers made within three years of death. See Estate tax: inclusion rules: gift tax on transfers made within three years of death (gross up rule)
- tuition. See Gift tax: ed/med exclusion
- unified credit. See Credits
- zero tax gifts, 12-11, 12-58

Governmental benefits, 1-4, 4-37, 10-1 n.2, 12-45, 12-56, 14-1
Grace period. See Life insurance: contract provisions
Grantor retained annuity trust (GRAT), 4-22, 7-143
Grantor retained unitrust (GRUT), 4-22
Grantor trusts, 4-3, 12-11, 17-14
- accumulated income for future payment, 17-17
- adequate interest or security. See Grantor trusts: less than adequate interest or security
- administrative powers, 6-7, 17-14
- adverse party, 6-6, 17-17
- benefit of grantor or spouse, income for, 9-28 n.28, 17-15, 17-17
- Crummey clause powers of withdrawal, lapse of, 17-15
- defective grantor trusts, intentionally, 4-22, 6-9, 12-56
- demand trusts, 5-21, 6-6, 12-22, 17-14, 17-15
- five or five exception, 12-22, 17-15
- insurance premiums for insurance on grantor's life. See Grantor trusts: benefit of grantor or spouse, income for

joint powers, 6-6
less than adequate interest or security, 17-17
loans to grantor or spouse, 17-17
Mallinckrodt trusts. See Grantor trusts: demand trusts
portion rules, 17-15, 17-16
powers over beneficial enjoyment, 17-14
power to amend trust, 17-14
power to exchange assets, 17-17
power to remove/replace trustee, 17-17
pseudo grantor trusts. See Grantor trusts: demand trusts
reasonably definite (external) standard, 6-6, 6-10
spousal unity rule, 6-10
standards. See Grantor trusts: reasonably definite (external) standard
support or maintenance of dependent, 6-6, 6-14, 17-15
transfer for value rule, exception for. See Income tax
Grief counseling, 15-9
Gross up rule. See Estate tax: inclusion rules: gift tax on transfers made within three years of death (gross up rule); Tax exclusive tax computations; Tax payment provisions
Group trusts, 4-6, 5-16. See also Generation-skipping transfer tax; Peel-off provision
GRUT. See Grantor retained unitrust
Guardians, 19-33, 19-53
Guardianship, 2-8, 4-8, 6-1, 14-1, 16-2

Hanging powers. See Crummey clauses/powers: hanging powers
Health care, 1-6, 14-1, 14-3
Health care directives. See Durable powers of attorney: health care
Health Insurance Portability and Accountability Act (HIPAA), 14-1, 14-2, 19-66
Heirs, 4-15, 7-59
    are spouses included?, 5-14 n.ff
    determined when and how, 5-14 n.ff
HEMS standard. See Powers of appointment: general powers of appointment: ascertainable standard exception
Hold harmless agreement, 1-13
Homestead, 2-6. See also Trusts: uses of trusts: creditor protection

Illegitimates. See Nonmarital children
Incapacity, 1-4, 2-8, 4-27, 4-30, 7-59, 12-1, 12-23, 14-1, 14-2, 16-1. See also Life insurance: contract provisions: disability waiver of premiums
Incidents of ownership. See Life insurance
Income. See Fiduciary accounting income
Income in respect of a decedent. See Income tax
Income shifting, 2-8, 12-8, 12-53
    alternative devices, 12-54
Income tax, 1-3, 11-1
    annuity income rules, 9-41, 10-17, 12-61
    basis, 2-5, 7-1, 7-98 n.84, 7-102
        gifted property, 12-1
        new-basis-at-death rule, 7-32, 7-41, 12-2, 12-37 n.35, 12-44
    cancellation of indebtedness, 9-36, 12-58, 12-66

capital gains and losses, 7-106, 7-112, 7-115, 7-120, 7-126, 7-128 n.101, 7-135, 7-142, 8-6
   debts exceeding basis in transferred property, 9-41
   election to realize, nonrealization trust or estate distribution, 13-13
   part-sale, part-gift transactions, 3-13, 12-34
   personal residence, gain from sale of, 2-8
   transfers between spouses, 10-3
charitable deduction. See Charitable deduction; Income tax: trusts and estates income taxation: charitable set aside deduction
corporate income tax, in general,
   S Corporations, 4-5, 4-26, 13-12
     electing small business trusts, 4-24
     qualified Subchapter S trust, 4-24
     S Corporation qualified shareholders, 4-26
debt, income from discharge of. See Income tax: cancellation of indebtedness
deductions
   charitable. See Charitable deduction
   deductions in respect of a decedent. See Income tax: income in respect of a decedent
   distributions deduction. See Income tax: trusts and estates income taxation
   income in respect of a decedent. See Income tax: income in respect of a decedent: deduction for wealth transfer tax attributable to
   interest, 9-12, 9-39, 9-44 n.50, 12-64
   swing items. See Postmortem estate planning: swing item election
   wealth transfer tax attributable to income in respect of a decedent. See Income tax: income in respect of a decedent: deduction for wealth transfer tax attributable to
employee benefits. See Income tax: retirement benefits
estates, income tax advantages of, over trusts, 4-23
exclusion for life insurance proceeds, 9-25, 9-39
exclusion for gifts and bequests, 17-3, 17-9
grantor trusts. See Grantor trusts
income in respect of a decedent, , 7-109, 7-114, 7-118, 7-126, 7-132, 7-134, 7-135, 10-2, 10-22, 12-2 n.2, 17-11, 17-13
   deduction for wealth transfer tax attributable to, 17-13
   deductions in respect of a decedent, 7-38, 17-11, 17-13
   definition of, 17-12
interest free loans. See Loans: below market interest
part-sale, part-gift. See Income tax: capital gains and losses
retirement benefits, 10-6, 10-17, 18-11
   designated beneficiary requirement, 10-14, 10-18, 10-23
     contingent/successor beneficiaries, 10-15
     separate shares, 10-15
     trust as beneficiary, 10-16
   individual retirement account (IRA), 7-71, 7-72, 10-8
   life expectancy, redetermination of, 10-12, 10-15
   lump sum distributions, 10-18
   minimum required distribution, 7-72, 10-10, 10-11, 10-16
   nonqualified plan, 10-10
   participants, 10-1
   qualified plan, 10-7
   rollover individual retirement account, 10-9, 10-17
   spousal individual retirement account, 10-8, 12-44, 13-12
separate share rule. See Income tax: trusts and estates income taxation
swing item election. See Postmortem estate planning: swing item election
tax year. See Tax year

transfer for value rule, 9-9, 9-12 n.10, 9-18, 9-41, 12-38, 17-16
   exception for certain transfers, 9-42
trusts and estates income taxation
   beneficiary inclusion rule, 17-7
   character of income rule, 17-3, 17-4, 17-8, 17-12, 17-13
   charitable set aside deduction, 17-2, 17-6. See also Income tax; trusts and estates income taxation: complex trusts: distributions
   charitable trusts, income taxation of, 12-36
   complex trusts, 17-8
      distributions
         charitable distribution (intermediate tier), 17-2
         exemption from income carryout rules, 17-9
         in kind, 17-2
         mandatory income (first tier), 17-11
   conduit taxation, 17-1, 17-7
   differences between trusts and estates, 4-23
   distributable net income, 17-1, 17-3, 17-4
      adjustments to determine, 17-3, 17-4
      carryout rule, 7-106, 7-109, 7-112, 7-128, 7-132, 7-134, 7-135, 13-13, 17-7, 17-11
      capital gain includible in, 17-4
      taxable portion of, 17-7
      tax exempt income, 17-4, 17-7, 17-8
   distributions
      election to realize gain or loss on distribution. See Income tax: capital gains and losses
   distributions deduction, 17-1, 17-2, 17-3, 17-4, 17-8, 7-10
   estates. See Income tax: trusts and estates income taxation: complex trusts
   fiduciary accounting income. See Fiduciary accounting income
   grantor trusts. See Grantor trusts
   multiple trust rule, 4-5, 7-137, 17-10
   separate share rule, 17-4, 17-8, 17-18. See also Marital deduction
   simple trusts, 17-5
   taxable income, 17-2
   tax exempt income. See Income tax: trusts and estates income taxation: distributable net income
   tax year. See Tax year
   tier rules. See Income tax: trusts and estates income taxation: complex trusts: distributions
   trapping distributions, 13-13
Incorporation by reference, 4-20
Independent legal significance, doctrine of, 4-20
Inheritance, 1-5
Insurance. See Life Insurance
International taxation, 1-4
Interview, client, 1-17, 2-2, 19-13
Inter vivos transfers, 1-1. See also Life insurance: irrevocable life insurance trusts
Intestate succession, 1-1, 7-50
  adoption, effect of. See Adoption
  illegitimates. See Nonmarital children
  nonmarital children. See Nonmarital children
  out of wedlock, children born. See Nonmarital children
  paternity, proof of. See Nonmarital children
  representation, 1-19

INDEX

Investment counseling, 1-4, 1-15 n.5, 4-25, 19-36

Joint settlor trusts, 4-26, 7-7 n.6, 7-68
Joint tenancy. See Concurrent interests
Joint wills. See Wills: contractual

Kiersey Temperament Sorter, 1-21

Lapse, 4-24, 19-20 n.y
Lead trust. See Charitable deduction: trusts: split interest trusts: charitable lead trusts
Legitime. See Forced heir share: pretermitted heir
Life estates, 4-6, 4-7. See also Estate tax: inclusion rules: life estate; Tax payment provisions: reimbursement rights
Life expectancy, 7-33
Life insurance, 1-3, 2-6
    accelerated death benefit. See Life insurance: contract provisions
    additional purchase. See Life insurance: contract provisions
    advisor, insurance, 5-28, 6-8
    annuities, 9-2, 9-3, 9-39. See also Annuities; Life insurance: contract provisions: settlement options
    automatically renewable term insurance. See Life insurance: term insurance: renewable term
    beneficiary designation. See Life insurance: contract provisions
    buy-sell agreement, , 9-8, 9-26, 9-34, 9-42
    cash surrender value, 9-12, 9-50
    common disaster. See Life insurance: contract provisions
    comparing policies, 9-22
    composite life, 9-11
    contract provisions
        accelerated death benefit, 9-17
        accidental death, 9-20
        additional purchase, 9-6, 9-20
        assignment, 9-21
        beneficiary designation, 1-8, 9-16, 9-32
        common disaster, 9-20
        conversion, 9-6, 9-20
        disability waiver of premium, 9-21
        dividends, 2-6, 9-13, 9-18, 9-19
        fraud, 9-21
        grace period, 9-21
        nonforfeitability, 9-22
        policy loans, 9-11, 9-17, 9-50
        settlement options, 1-3, 9-17, 9-32, 9-39
        unnatural death, 9-22
        waiver of premium, 9-21
    convertible term insurance. See Life insurance: contract provisions: conversion
    credit life, 9-11
    decreasing term insurance. See Life insurance: term insurance: decreasing
    deferred life, 9-8
    dividend options. See Life insurance: contract provisions
    double indemnity. See Life insurance: contract provisions: accidental death

employer funded, 9-6
endowments, 9-3
equity split dollar. See Life insurance: split dollar
estate tax inclusion. See Estate tax: life insurance
exchange of policies, income tax free, 9-41, 9-43
exclusion from income. See Income tax: exclusion for life insurance proceeds; transfer for value rule
family income policy, 9-10
family maintenance policy, 9-10
family policy, 9-11
fifth option. See Life insurance: contract provisions: dividends
financing party. See Life insurance: split dollar
first to die coverage, 9-9
four-of-seven rule, 9-12, 9-54 n.62
incidents of ownership, 2-6, 5-28, 6-7, 6-9, 9-11, 9-44, 9-45, 9-46. See also Estate tax: life insurance: incidents of ownership
insurability, evidence of. See Life insurance: contract provisions: additional purchase
insurable interest, 9-27
insurance companies, comparison of, 9-23 n.25
"insurance" defined, 9-25
interpolated terminal reserve, 9-27, 9-49
irrevocable life insurance trusts, 2-8, 4-33, 9-27, 9-48
juvenile, 9-11
key man/person coverage, 9-11
lapse rates, 9-19
limited pay. See Life insurance: premiums
loan, transfer of policy subject to. See Income tax: transfer for value rule
mortgage insurance, 9-11
multiple protection, 9-11
next death coverage, 9-8
nonforfeitability. See Life insurance: contract provisions
order of death. See Life insurance: contract provisions: common disaster
ordinary insurance. See Life insurance: permanent insurance
owner, third party, 9-27, 9-28. See also Gifts: insurance proceeds
permanent insurance, 9-6, 9-12
persistency, 9-19
policy facts, 9-49
policy loans. See Life insurance: contract provisions
policy withdrawals, 9-5 n.1
premiums, 9-11, 9-29
   continuous pay, 9-7, 9-12
   for insurance on grantor's life. See Grantor trusts: benefit of grantor or spouse, income for
   graded/modified, 9-8
   limited pay 9-7
   single premium life, 9-7, 9-26, 9-49
   sixty-five pay life, 9-7
   split dollar. See Life insurance: split dollar
   twenty-year life, 9-7
   vanishing, 9-7, 9-21. See also Life insurance: contract provisions: disability waiver of premium
P.S. 58 cost. See Life insurance: split dollar
rated, 9-6 n.3
re-entry insurance. See Life insurance: term insurance

INDEX

second to die coverage, 9-7, 9-8, 9-12
settlement options. See Life insurance: contract provisions
seven-pay test, 9-26
Silverman rule, 9-47
sixty-five life insurance. See Life insurance: premiums
specialty products, 9-10
split dollar insurance, 9-6, 9-12, 9-14, 9-15, 9-19
spouse owned. See Life insurance: owner, third party
suicide. See Life insurance: contract provisions: unnatural death
survivor's insurability rider. See Life insurance: second to die coverage
survivor life. See Life insurance: second to die coverage
taxes attributable to. See Tax payment provisions: reimbursement rights
term insurance, 9-4
   decreasing, 9-6
   increasing, 9-13
   re-entry, 9-6
   renewable term, 9-5
   straight term, 9-5
   universal, 9-10, 9-12
   variable, 9-10, 9-12
transfer for value rule. See Income tax
trust as beneficiary, 9-16, 19-39
twenty-year life. See Life insurance: premiums
underwriting standards, 9-23 n.22
universal life. See Life insurance: term insurance
value, gift tax. See Life insurance: interpolated terminal reserve; premiums: single premium life
vanishing premium. See Life insurance: premiums
variable life. See Life insurance: term insurance
viatical settlement. See Life insurance: contract provisions: accelerated death benefit
whole life. See Life insurance: permanent insurance

Limited powers of appointment. See Powers of appointment: nongeneral powers of appointment
Litigation, 1-8
   standing. See Privity
Living trusts. See Trusts, inter vivos
Living wills, 2-8, 14-4, 16-2, 19-62, 19-70
Loans
   below market interest, 12-57. See also Grantor trusts: less than adequate interest or security
   demand, 12-57
   forgiveness, 9-36, 12-58. See also Income tax: cancellation of indebtedness
   to beneficiaries, 4-33
Look back period. See Medicaid qualification
Lump sum distributions. Income tax: retirement benefits

Mallinckrodt trusts. See Grantor trusts: demand trusts
Malpractice, 1-8, 1-14, 1-15, 3-2, 3-57
Marital deduction, 5-1, 7-1
   accrued but undistributed income, 7-57, 7-60, 7-91
   all-income-annually requirement. See Marital deduction: nondeductible terminable interests

annuities, 7-71
    joint and survivor annuity, 7-71
    survivor/spousal annuity, automatic qualification, 7-71, 7-73, 10-6, 12-63
charitable remainder trust. See Charitable deduction: trusts: qualified terminable interest property/charitable remainder trust
citizenship and residency requirements. See Marital deduction: noncitizen spouse
community property, 7-10, 7-16, 7-49 n.47
disclaimer planning, 7-14, 7-16, 11-5, 12-43
drafting considerations
    corpus, powers over, 7-91
    facility of payment clause, 5-16 n.jj, 7-62, 7-89. See also Facility of payment provision
    nongeneral testamentary power of appointment in, qualified terminable interest trusts, 7-93
    power to withdraw, 7-91
    savings clauses, 7-66 n.61, 7-94
    unproductive property provisions. See Marital deduction: nondeductible terminable interests: all-income-annually requirement
estate stacking, 7-25, 7-48
forced heir share of surviving spouse. See forced heir share: spouse, surviving
forms of disposition, 7-40, 7-49, 7-81, 7-87
    estate trusts, 7-59
    general power of appointment trusts, 7-50, 7-52, 7-58
        general power, 7-81
        QTIP trust compared, 7-82
    one-lung marital, 7-135
    outright, 7-11, 7-49, 7-59, 19-22 n.ff
    qualified domestic trusts (QDOTs), 7-43, 7-77, 7-78, 13-12, 18-14
    qualified terminable interest property (QTIP) trusts, 4-6, 7-2, 7-58, 7-60, 10-25, 18-13
        advantages of, 7-41, 7-82
        charitable remainder trusts. See Charitable deduction: trusts: split interest trusts: charitable remainder trusts: qualified terminable interest property trust/charitable remainder trust
        election, 7-60, 7-63, 19-21 n.cc
            partial election, 7-7, 7-29, 7-64, 7-66, 7-92, 10-25, 13-12, 19-22
                creation of rolling fraction, 7-67, 7-92 n.80
                gross v. net residue denominator, 11-16, 11-29, 11-30
                nonelected portion, paying taxes from. See Tax payment provisions: qualified terminable interest property
                previously taxed property credit. See Credits
            reverse. See Marital deduction: forms of disposition: qualified terminable interest property trusts: reverse qualified terminable interest property election
        individual retirement accounts, 7-71, 7-72, 10-16
        inter vivos trust, 7-7 n.6, 7-68, 12-32
        nongeneral testamentary power of appointment, 7-60, 7-93
        power to appoint, 7-93, 19-23 n.ii
        power to withdraw, 7-52, 7-61, 7-72, 7-93, 10-19, 17-15, 19-22 n.gg
        qualified plan spousal annuities. See Survivor/spousal annuity
        reverse qualified terminable interest property election, 7-61, 7-92, 7-93. See also Generation-skipping transfer tax: reverse qualified terminable interest property election
        stub income. See Marital deduction: accrued but undistributed income

INDEX

taxes attributable to. *See* Tax payment provisions: qualified terminable interest property; reimbursement rights
  undistributed income. *See* Marital deduction: accrued but undistributed income
  unproductive property. *See* Marital deduction: nondeductible terminable interests: all-income-annually requirement
fractional marital deduction bequest. *See* Marital deduction: funding marital bequests
front end credit shelter. *See* Marital deduction: funding marital bequests: residuary marital
funding marital bequests, 7-3, 7-90, 7-95
  comparison chart, 7-141
  date of distribution pecuniary. *See* Marital deduction: funding marital bequests: true worth pecuniary
  factors affecting choice, 7-101, 7-139
  fairly representative pecuniary, 7-98, 7-111
  federal estate tax (FET) pecuniary. *See* Marital deduction: funding marital bequests: fairly representative pecuniary
  minimum worth pecuniary, 7-98, 7-114
  pick-and-choose fractional, 7-99, 7-127, 7-131
  pro rata fractional, 7-99, 7-125
  purge the pot provision, 7-127, 7-137, 19-21 n.dd. *See also* Marital deduction: unidentified asset rule
  residuary marital, 5-2 n.a, 7-9 n.9
  residue: pre/gross versus true/net residuary fractional, 7-123
  reverse pecuniary, 7-98, 7-117, 7-121
  single fund marital, 7-57, 7-99, 7-135
  true worth pecuniary, 7-98, 7-102
gift tax marital deduction, 2-8, 12-30, 18-3, 18-6
income payable annually requirement. *See* Marital deduction: nondeductible terminable interests: all-income-annually requirement
noncitizen spouse, 7-43, 7-77, 9-27 n.27, 11-7, 12-30, 13-12, 18-6 n.7, 18-14. *See also* Marital deduction: forms of disposition: qualified domestic trusts
nondeductible terminable interests, 7-41, 7-43, 7-84
  all-income-annually requirement, 7-53, 7-56, 7-59, 7-72, 7-88, 7-94, 7-103 n.89, 10-23, 10-25
  exceptions, 7-41, 7-76
nonmarital trusts. *See* Nonmarital trusts
nonprobate property, 4-23
optimum marital deduction bequest. *See* Marital deduction: size of deduction: formula clauses
qualification requirements, 7-40, 7-51
  specific portion requirement, 7-57
qualified domestic trust. *See* Marital deduction: forms of disposition
qualified terminable interest property (QTIP). *See* Marital deduction: forms of disposition
residuary marital. *See* Marital deduction: funding marital bequests
savings clauses. *See* Marital deduction: drafting considerations
separate share rule, 7-90, 7-109, 7-112, 7-116, 7-126, 7-129, 7-132, 7-137
size of deduction, 7-20
  formula clauses, 7-34, 7-97, 19-21 n.bb
    bracket equalizer, 7-29
    credit shelter planning, 7-5, 7-9, 7-10, 7-35, 7-68
    equalizer, 7-6 n.5, 7-24, 7-64, 7-119
    optimum marital deduction, 7-9, 7-24
    six month equalizer plan, 7-28, 7-48 n.44

swing item election, 7-10 n.12. See also Postmortem estate planning: swing item election

survey of preferences, 7-48 n.46, 7-99

survivorship provisions, 5-16 n.ll, 7-7, 7-12, 7-13, 7-13 n.16, 7-41, 7-48, 19-21 n.ee

survivor/spousal annuity, automatic qualification for. See Marital deduction: annuities; Survivor/spousal annuity

unidentified asset rule, 7-47, 19-21 n.dd

Maxims, 16-1, 16-4

Medicaid qualification, 4-19, 12-45, 14-2, 14-5, 14-6, 16-3

Military service, 2-4

Minimum distribution rules. See Income tax: retirement benefits

Misconduct, 4-24

Mistake, 1-10

Modification
 charitable deduction. See Charitable deduction: trusts: split interest trusts: nonqualifying, reformation of
 Claflin doctrine, 4-4 n.2
 powers of appointment, exercise of. See Powers of appointment
 trusts. See Trusts: reformation

Mortality tables. See Actuarial tables

Mourning, 15-2

Multidisciplinary practice. See Ethics

Multiple trust rule. See Income tax: trusts and estates income taxation

Murder, as bar to inheritance. See Misconduct

Mutual wills. See Wills: contractual

Myers-Briggs, 1-21

Net gift. See Gift tax; Grantor trusts: benefit of grantor or spouse, income for

Networking, 1-13, 3-41, 3-58

NIMCRUT. See Charitable deduction: trusts: split interest trusts: charitable remainder: unitrusts

Noncitizen spouse. See Marital deduction

Nonclaim protection. See Creditors

Noncourt trust. See Estate administration: avoiding probate

Nondeductible charges, 7-10, 7-10 n.12, 7-37, 7-48 n.50, 7-100, 7-105

Nondeductible terminable interests. See Marital deduction: nondeductible terminable interests

Nongeneral powers of appointment. See Powers of appointment

Nonmarital children, 2-4, 2-9, 5-2 n.a, 19-17 n.p

Nonmarital trusts, 5-1, 7-9, 19-23 n.jj, 19-24

Nonprobate property, 1-6, 2-3, 10-2, 12-65

Objectives, 16-1

Obligations. See also Grantor trusts: support or maintenance of dependent
 discharge of legal, 5-26, 5-29, 6-5, 6-6, 6-7, 6-9, 6-14, 12-25, 12-55, 19-36
 Upjohn clause, 5-27, 5-29, 6-5, 6-7, 6-9, 6-14, 12-26, 12-55

Office atmosphere, 1-18

One-stop-shopping, 1-14

Optimum marital deduction. See Marital deduction: size of deduction: formula clauses

Organ donation, 14-5

Out of wedlock children. See Nonmarital children

Partial QTIP election. See Marital deduction: forms of disposition: qualified terminable interest property trusts: election: partial election
Participant. See Income tax: retirement benefits
Part-sale, part-gift transactions. See Income tax: capital gains and losses
Passing requirement, marital deduction transfers, 7-43
Peel-off provision, group trust, 5-18
Period of ineligibility. See Medicaid qualification
Permissible appointees. See Powers of appointment: definitions
Personal counseling, 1-11
Personal effects provision. See Bequests
Personality profile, 1-21
Personal representative, 4-8
Personal residence, 7-56, 12-46, 17-15
    gain from sale of. See Income tax: capital gains and losses
Pick up tax. See State taxation
Possession, postponement of, 5-14
Postmortem estate planning, 5-8 n.1, 7-34, 7-39, 7-51, 13-1, 13-10, 17-1
    estate tax aspects, 7-66, 11-5
    final return, decedent's. See Tax returns: decedent's final income tax return
    fiscal year selection. See Tax year
    generation-skipping transfer tax. See Generation-skipping transfer tax: exemption: allocation
    gift tax aspects, 7-21
    joint return. See Tax returns
    qualified terminable interest property election. See Marital deduction: forms of disposition: qualified terminable interest property trusts: election
    split gifts, election for year of death. See Gift tax: split gifts
    swing item election, 7-9 n.12, 7-38, 7-66, 13-12, 17-2
    valuation. See Valuation
Powers of appointment, 1-3, 4-5, 4-27, 5-8 n.m, 5-21
    definitions, default takers, and permissible appointees, 5-14
    Delaware tax trap. See Generation-skipping transfer tax: powers of appointment
    donee's will provision, 19-31
    exclusive v. nonexclusive, 5-30 n.xx
    exercise
        blanket, 5-31 n.ccc, 5-32 n.ddd, 19-23 n.ii
        creditor's rights, 5-33
        inadvertent, 5-31 nn.aaa, ccc, 5-32, 12-24 n.17, 19-20 n.z
        silent residuary clause, 5-32, 19-20 n.z
        specific reference requirement, 5-31, 19-20 n.z, 19-23 n.ii
    flexibility, 4-4
    invalid exercise, 5-33
    general powers of appointment, estate tax inclusion of property subject to, 2-3, 5-2, 6-4, 18-13
        ascertainable standard exception, 5-4 n.e, 5-22, 5-24, 5-27, 6-4, 6-6, 6-10, 6-14
        inadvertent/unexpected general powers of appointment, 5-25, 5-29
        legal obligation of support, discharge of. See Obligations: discharge of legal
        reasons to create general powers of appointment, 5-22
    hanging powers. See Crummey clauses/powers
    lapse, 9-52, 12-16, 12-22
        five or five exception, 5-22, 6-3 n.3, 9-52, 12-15, 12-20, 19-40 n.www
    limited powers of appointment. See Powers of appointment: nongeneral powers of appointment

marital deduction general power of appointment trust. See Marital deduction: forms of disposition: general power of appointment trusts

nongeneral powers of appointment, 5-1, 5-24, 7-60, 7-85, 7-93. See also Disclaimer: specific portion

special powers of appointment. See Powers of appointment: nongeneral powers of appointment

tax consequences of. See Powers of appointment: general powers of appointment: estate tax inclusion of property subject to

trustee powers, 7-19

Powers of attorney. See Durable powers of attorney

Powers of withdrawal, 4-27, 7-52, 7-61, 7-87. See Crummey clauses/powers; Generation-skipping transfer tax; Grantor trusts: demand trusts

Practice of law, 1-4

Prejudice, 1-19, 16-8

Prenuptial agreements, 2-3, 3-10, 3-13, 3-18, 7-142, 10-22, 11-22, 11-30. See also Tax payment provisions: equitable apportionment

Present interest. See Gift tax: annual exclusion

Presumptions of survivorship. See Marital deduction: survivorship provisions

Pretermitted heir. See Forced heir share

Previously taxed property. See Credits: previously taxed property

Principal and income accounting. See Fiduciary accounting income

Private annuity, 12-61

Privilege, 3-46

Privity, 1-9, 1-10, 3-46, 4-4 n.2

Professional skills, 1-21

Property settlement, 2-4. See also Divorce

Property taxation, 1-4

Prudent investor rule, 7-34, 7-88

Pseudo grantor trusts. See Grantor trusts: demand trusts

Psychic benefits, 1-5, 1-15

QDOT. See Marital deduction: forms of disposition: qualified domestic trusts

QTIP. See Generation-skipping transfer tax; Marital deduction: forms of disposition: qualified terminable interest property trusts

Qualified domestic trust. See Marital deduction: forms of disposition

Qualified joint and survivor annuity. See Survivor/spousal annuity

Qualified minors' trusts, 5-23, 12-23, 12-25, 12-55

Qualified pension plan. See Income tax: retirement benefits

Qualified personal residence trust. 4-22, 12-59

Qualified preretirement survivor annuity. See Survivor/spousal annuity

Qualified Subchapter S trust. See Income tax: corporate income tax: S Corporations

Qualified terminable interest property (QTIP). See Marital deduction: forms of disposition

Questionnaires. See Interview, client

Reciprocal trust doctrine, 6-5, 6-14, 12-19

Reciprocal wills. See Wills: contractual

Reformation. See Charitable deduction: split interest trusts: nonqualified, reformation of; Trusts

Reimbursement rights. See Tax payment provisions

Related or subordinate party. See Trustee

Remarriage, 7-52, 7-82, 7-93, 8-21

Renunciation. See Disclaimer

Residuary marital bequest. See Marital deduction: funding marital bequests: reverse pecuniary

Retained life estate. See Estate tax: inclusion rules

Retained powers. See Estate tax: inclusion rules: powers to control enjoyment, retained

Retained voting control. See Estate tax: inclusion rules: voting control, retained

Retirement, 1-6

Retirement benefits, 2-6, 3-10, 10-1. See also Income tax: retirement benefits

Revolving door power. See Estate tax: inclusion rules: powers to control enjoyment, retained; Grantor trusts: power to remove/replace trustee; Trustee: removal

Rev. Proc. 64-19 pecuniary. See Marital deduction: funding marital bequests: fairly representative pecuniary

Rolling fraction, 7-136. See also Income tax: trusts and estates income taxation: separate share rule; Marital deduction: forms of disposition: qualified terminable interest property trusts: election: partial election: creation of rolling fraction; funding marital bequests: single fund marital; separate share rule

Rule Against Perpetuities, 1-8, 4-3, 4-5, 5-10 n.r, 5-15 n.gg, 5-33, 8-34 n.93, 18-13, 18-25, 18-27, 19-30, 19-42 n.cccc
powers of appointment, 7-52 n.51, 18-13

Same sex couples. See Unmarried cohabitants

SCIN. See Self-canceling installment note

S Corporations. See Income tax: corporate income tax

Self-canceling installment note (SCIN), 12-63

Self-trusteed declaration of trust. See Trustees: settlor as

Separate property. See Community property

Separate share rule. See Generation-skipping transfer tax: exemption: separate shares; severance of trusts; transferor; Income tax: trusts and estates income taxation; Marital deduction: forms of disposition: qualified terminable interest property: election: partial election

Sexism, 1-19

Silverman rule. See Life insurance

Simple trusts. See Income tax: trusts and estates income taxation: simple trusts

Simultaneous death. See Survivorship

Slayer statutes. See Life insurance: contract provisions: unnatural death; Misconduct

Small trusts. See Trusts: small trust termination

Software, 7-39 n.38

Special powers of appointment. See Powers of appointment: nongeneral powers of appointment

Specific reference requirement. See Powers of appointment: exercise; Tax payment provisions: reimbursement rights

Spend down planning. See Medicaid qualification

Spendthrift trusts, 4-3, 4-9, 5-13 n.z, 7-59, 7-88, 8-19 n.51, 16-3, 19-22 n.gg, 19-24, 19-43 n.eeee. See also Gift tax: annual exclusion: present interest requirement

Split dollar. See Life insurance

Split gifts. See Gift tax

Split interest charitable trusts. See Charitable deduction: trusts

Split purchase, 4-7, 12-59

Sponge tax. See State taxation: pick up tax

Spousal annuity, 10-6, 10-20, 12-63. See also Survivor/spousal annuity

Spousal rollover, 10-18. See also Income tax: retirement benefits: individual retirement account

Spousal unity rule. See Grantor trusts: spouses and former spouses; Income tax: trusts and estates income taxation: spousal unity rule

Springing powers. See Durable powers of attorney: property management
Stages of dying: See Death
Standards. See Grantor trusts: reasonably definite (external) standard; Estate tax: inclusion rules: powers to control enjoyment, retained; Powers of appointment: general powers of appointment: ascertainable standard exception
State taxation, 7-5 n.4, 11-1
    inheritance tax, 4-18, 18-37
    pick up tax, 4-18, 18-38. See also Credits; Estate tax: deductions
    sponge tax. See State taxation: pick up tax
    tax payment and apportionment rules. See Tax payment provisions
    wealth transfer taxes, in general, 1-3, 4-25, 9-35 n.42, 16-4, 18-37
Statutory election. See Forced heir share: spouse, surviving
Statutory power. See Powers of appointment: nongeneral powers of appointment
Stub income. See Marital deduction: accrued but undistributed income
Subchapter S. See Income tax: corporate income tax: S Corporations
Substantial risk of conflict of interest, 3-7
Substituted judgment, 4-8
Survivorship, 5-9 n.p, 19-18 n.v. See also Lapse; Life insurance: contract provisions: common disaster; Marital deduction: survivorship provisions
Survivor/spousal annuity, 3-6, 3-10, 7-71, 7-73, 10-3, 10-6, 10-7, 10-11, 10-20, 11-7, 13-12. See also Marital deduction: annuities
Swing items. See Marital deduction: size of deduction; Postmortem estate planning: swing item election

Tax exclusive tax computations, 12-3, 12-8, 12-44, 18-32
Tax inclusive tax computations, 12-3, 18-32
Tax on prior transfers. See Credits: previously taxed property
Tax payment provisions, 5-2 n.a, 11-1, 19-16
    burden on residue rule, 11-1, 11-11, 11-33
    buy-sell agreement, taxes attributable to failure to set value, 11-17
    conflict of laws. See Conflict of laws
    credits, apportionment of benefit of, 11-13, 11-21, 11-45
    deductions, apportionment of benefit of. See Tax payment provisions: equitable apportionment
    drafting, 11-33, 11-34
    equitable apportionment, 7-70, 7-124, 11-5, 11-12, 11-15, 11-16, 11-21, 11-22, 11-25, 11-30, 11-33, 11-37 n.26, 11-46
    generation-skipping transfer tax, 18-33
    inside apportionment, 11-11, 11-21
    insufficiency tax clause, 9-35
    insurance proceeds. See Tax payment provisions: reimbursement rights
    multiple documents, coordination of, 11-14
    outside apportionment, 11-2, 11-12, 11-21, 11-24
    partial qualified terminable interest property election, 7-70, 11-29
    qualified terminable interest property, 1-5, 11-15, 11-46, 19-23 n.kk, 19-42 n.bbbb
    rate differentials, apportionment of benefit of state inheritance tax, 11-13, 11-31, 11-46
    recapture tax, 11-7, 11-44 n.c
    reimbursement rights, 5-32 n.ddd, 7-70, 9-32, 9-50, 10-4, 11-2, 11-16, 11-17, 11-18, 11-33, 11-42
        specific reference requirement, 11-19, 11-21, 11-28, 11-31, 11-34, 11-37, 11-47, 18-33
    retirement benefits, taxes attributable to, 11-27
    sample tax payment provision, 11-43

INDEX

state law, 11-20, 11-23. See also Conflict of laws
temporal interests, taxes attributable to, 11-24, 11-46
Tax returns
    decedent's final income tax return, 4-24, 13-4. See also Tax year
    estate tax return, 13-4
    fiduciary income tax return, 17-1
    gift tax return, 18-3
    joint returns, 13-11
Tax year, 4-24, 13-4 n.9, 13-13, 17-5
Temporal interests, 11-14, 18-4, 18-20, 19-25 n.ss. See also Charitable deduction; Gift tax: annual exclusion
Terminally ill, 7-33, 12-61 n.58, 15-1. See also Life insurance: contract provisions: accelerated death benefit
Tier rules. See Income tax: trusts and estates income taxation: complex trusts: distributions
Time-value of money, 7-23, 12-2, 12-5, 12-9
Transferee liability, 11-2, 11-3, 11-8, 18-3
Transfer for value rule. See Income tax
Transfers made within three years of death. See Estate tax: inclusion rules: gift tax on transfers made within three years of death (gross up rule); three years of death
Transfers proximate to death. See Transfers made within three years of death
Trapping distributions. See Income tax: trusts and estates income taxation
Trustee
    beneficiary as, 4-23, 6-3, 6-6, 18-25
    cotrustees, 4-28, 13-5
    deemed, 6-12
    discretion, 4-36, 5-3 n.d, 6-5, 6-14, 7-19
    factors for selection, 6-1
    fees, 1-2, 4-25, 5-6 n.f, 5-20, 13-6
    powers, 19-25
    power to terminate, 4-5
    related or subordinate, 5-26, 6-12, 17-17
    removal, 6-12, 9-46 n.54, 19-38. See also Estate tax: inclusion rules: powers to control enjoyment, retained; Grantor trusts: power to remove/replace trustee
    resignation, 6-17, 19-30
    settlor as, 4-27, 4-30, 6-8, 16-1, 16-2, 19-47
    special, 19-32, 19-36
    successor, 4-28, 4-29, 4-31, 6-1, 9-31
Trusts
    amendment, powers of, 4-5, 7-95
    complex trusts. See Income tax: trusts and estates income taxation
    court trusts. See Estate administration: avoiding probate
    electing small business trusts. See Income tax: corporate income tax: S Corporations
    foreign situs trusts, 4-3
    incentive, 5-4 n.e
    inter vivos, 2-8, 4-1, 4-7, 4-16, 12-1, 14-2
    insurance trust. See Life insurance: trust as beneficiary
    living trust mills, 4-4 n.2, 4-31 n.31
    living trust. See Trusts: inter vivos
    Medicaid qualifying trusts. See Medicaid qualification
    Pollack trusts. See Medicaid qualification
    qualified Subchapter S trust. See Income tax: corporate income tax: S Corporations
    receptacle or pour over, 4-21
    reformation, 4-4, 9-37 n.38. See also Modification

restraints, 4-2, 4-3
settlement trusts, 4-2, 4-21. See also Grantor trusts
simple trusts. See Income tax: trusts and estates income taxation
small trust termination, 4-3, 5-20, 6-8, 19-30
special needs trusts. See Medicaid qualification
spray. See Trustee: discretion
sprinkle. See Trustee: discretion
supplemental needs. See Medicaid qualification
support trusts, 12-56
testamentary trusts, 4-1
transportability, 4-2, 4-36
trust protectors, 4-13, 4-36, 9-29, 9-37 n.38
uses of trusts, 4-1
    asset management, 4-2, 4-6, 12-1, 14-2
    benefits of using, 4-1, 12-1
    creditor protection, 4-3, 4-9, 4-37
    generation-skipping transfer tax minimization, 4-23
    testamentary freedom, 4-2
    will contest avoidance, 4-14, 4-37
Tuition. See Gift tax: ed/med exclusion

Unauthorized practice of law. See Ethics
Understatement of tax liability, penalty for, 3-53 n.38
Unfulfilled purpose, bar to modification of estate plan. See Modification: Claflin doctrine
Unidentified asset rule. See Marital deduction
Unified credit. See Credits
Uniform Gifts/Transfers to Minors Act, 4-8, 7-63, 7-90, 19-24
Unitrust. See Charitable deduction: trusts: split interest trusts: charitable remainder trusts
Unmarried cohabitants, 7-1, 7-142
Unsupervised administration. See Estate administration: independent
Unusual assets, 2-6
Upjohn clause. See Gift tax: annual exclusion: present interest requirement; Obligations

Valuation, 18-7, 18-14
    adequate disclosure, 12-51
    alternate valuation, 13-12, 13-13, 18-18 n.16, 18-20, 18-21
    blockage, 12-48, 18-15
    control premium, 7-104, 18-15
    family aggregation, 7-61, 12-9
    fractional interests, 7-41, 7-138, 12-9, 12-44, 12-49
    gift tax, 12-9
    liquidation valuation, 18-14 n.11, 18-17
    marketability discount, lack of, 12-50, 18-15 n.12
    minority interest discount, 12-9, 12-50. See also Valuation: fractional interests
    mortality tables. See Actuarial tables
    partition, cost of, 12-49
    postmortem facts, use of, 18-18
    replacement cost, 9-49, 18-17
    restricted securities, 18-15
    restrictions on sale or use, 18-20
    special use valuation, 13-13, 18-15, 18-18 n.16, 18-21

    tax liability, valuation affected by, 18-15
    willing-buyer, willing-seller, 12-48, 18-14, 18-15, 18-16, 18-21
Viatical settlement. See Life insurance: contract provisions: accelerated death benefit
WIFO rule. See Income tax: trust and estate income taxation: worst in, first out rule
Wills, 19-15
    ambulatory, 1-1
    contest, 8-37, 13-4 n.7
        anticipation of, 7-143. See also Trusts: uses of trusts: will contest avoidance
        in terrorem provisions, 4-14
    contractual, 3-59, 7-46, 7-143
    duplicate originals, 3-56
    execution, 4-14
    in terrorem clause. See Wills: contest
    joint. See Wills: contractual
    mutual. See Wills: contractual
    pour over, 4-17, 4-19, 4-36
    production of, for probate, 3-56
    reciprocal. See Wills: contractual
    self-proving, 3-51
Withdrawal power. See Powers of withdrawal

ISBN 0-314-22671-0